BUREAU OF INTERNATIONAL RESEARCH
HARVARD UNIVERSITY AND RADCLIFFE COLLEGE

HARVARD STUDIES IN INTERNATIONAL LAW
MANLEY O. HUDSON, *Editor*

No. 2. THE INTERNATIONAL PROTECTION OF INDUSTRIAL PROPERTY

BY STEPHEN P. LADAS, S.J.D.

LONDON : HUMPHREY MILFORD
OXFORD UNIVERSITY PRESS

MAP OF THE INTERNATIONAL UNION FOR THE PROTECTION OF INDUSTRIAL PROPERTY

Key plate of Hammond's 10 x 14 Map of the World
Copyright by C. S. Hammond & Co.

The International Protection of Industrial Property

BY

STEPHEN P. LADAS

BUREAU OF INTERNATIONAL RESEARCH
OF HARVARD UNIVERSITY AND RADCLIFFE COLLEGE

CAMBRIDGE
HARVARD UNIVERSITY PRESS
1930

The Bureau of International Research of Harvard University and Radcliffe College has aided the author in carrying on research and in publishing the results. The Bureau assumes no responsibility for any statements or views expressed.

PRINTED AT THE HARVARD UNIVERSITY PRESS
CAMBRIDGE, MASS., U.S.A.

TO

MY FATHER AND MOTHER

PREFACE

THIS book was written in the attempt to satisfy a double purpose: to suggest a rational construction of, and to supply information as complete as possible on, a subject which is acquiring every day a greater importance. The author was struck by the fact that he was unable to discover any book in the English language on the subject of industrial property and its international protection. There are available in this country only a number of collections of foreign trade-mark and patent law information furnishing data on certain important points of foreign law. These form no counterpart to the abundant literature in Europe of treatises, studies, and monographs on the international protection of industrial property rights.

This lack of systematic exposition of foreign and international law reflects a similar situation in the domestic law. There is a complete absence in this country of creative juristic activity in this field of law, the legal profession being limited to analyzing and systematizing the decisions of the Courts. Any legislative activity that exists is disconnected, unsystematic, and empiric, without a general view of the interests to be taken into account and protected by the law. Moreover, Acts of Congress on patents and trade marks are samples of bad and obscure draftsmanship.

Different is the situation in Europe, where general systematic treatises and constructive monographs on industrial property rights are very numerous. Legislation in these countries is only a part of the law governing this subject. Juristic writing is an important element, and added thereto is a third element, decisions of the Courts, whose significance in shaping the law is ever increasing. Incidentally, this may show how inadequate is the picture of foreign law given in certain collections, which is based only on the text of legislative enactments.

Creative activity in this field in civil law countries received a great impulse by the creation of the International Union for the Protection of Industrial Property in 1883. The Convention creating this Union, to which the United States acceded in 1887, remained well-nigh ignored by the legal profession in this country. As a result, civil law countries have been more able to meet the demands of a growing and complex commercial and industrial society in the interior, and to protect more adequately the interests of their nationals abroad. The United States has been deprived of leadership in the development achieved in the field and has been unable to avoid losses to American interests in foreign countries. American views and desiderata on the international protection of industrial property have taken the form of proposals only at the Conferences of the International Union and at the Pan-American Conferences. There has never been a continuous and scholarly effort to study the problems and difficulties of international protection and to maintain a constant exchange of views with foreign jurists and institutions for the paving of the way to the solution of these problems. There are some indications of a growing dissatisfaction with respect to this state of things, and a change is deemed desirable. It is hoped that the publication of this study may contribute to a larger interest in the field.

The author is indebted to the Bureau of International Research of Harvard University and Radcliffe College for its assistance in the preparation and publication of this volume. He wishes to acknowledge his gratefulness to Professor George Grafton Wilson of Harvard University and Professor Manley O. Hudson of the Harvard Law School for their helpful advice throughout, and to Mr. Lawrence Langner, of New York City, for reading a part of the manuscript. In the preparation of his manuscript the author has received invaluable assistance from his wife, to whom he wishes to express his indebtedness.

To Professor Eldon R. James, Librarian, and to the Staff of the Harvard Law Library the author wishes to express his thanks for their generous coöperation in supplying him with necessary material.

An article on the Pan-American Conventions on Industrial Property, published in the *American Journal of International Law* (October, 1928), summarizes the exposition contained in Section VIII of this book. The substance of chapter XXXVII, on "Scientific Property," appeared in an article entitled "The Efforts for International Protection of Scientific Property," in the same journal (July, 1929).

STEPHEN P. LADAS

CAMBRIDGE, MASSACHUSETTS
October, 1929

CONTENTS

ABBREVIATIONS

As a rule, abbreviations have been avoided in this study. The complete title of books cited very often may be found in the bibliography appended here. Reports of court decisions are abbreviated in the customary way. As it is hoped that this book may serve to practitioners of various countries who may not be familiar with such abbreviations, these are explained below:

Annuaire, Annuaire de l'Association Internationale pour la Protection de la Propriété Industrielle.

App. D. C., Reports of cases adjudged in the Court of Appeals of the District of Columbia.

Arrêts Tr. Fed., Arrêts du Tribunal Fédéral Suisse.

Clunet, Journal du droit International privé de Clunet.

Dalloz, Jurisprudence Générale. Recueil Dalloz.

Darras, Revue de droit International privé, founded by Darras.

Entsch. Reichsg. Zivil., Entscheidungen des Reichsgerichts in Zivilsachen.

Entsch. Reichsg. Straf., Entscheidungen des Reichsgerichts in Strafsachen.

Fed., The Federal Reporter.

F. (2d), The Federal Reporter, Second series.

O. G., Official Gazette of the United States Patent Office.

Pasicrisie, Recueil général de la Jurisprudence des Cours et Tribunaux de Belgique.

Propriété Industrielle, Revue Mensuelle du Bureau International pour la Protection de la Propriété Industrielle.

R. P. C., Reports of Patent, Design, Trade Mark and other cases (London).

U. S., Reports of the United States Supreme Court.

PART I

THE PROTECTION OF FOREIGNERS' INDUSTRIAL PROPERTY BEFORE THE CREATION OF THE INTERNATIONAL UNION OF 1883

CHAPTER I

INTRODUCTION

§ 1. What is "industrial property"? It is a truism to-day to say that commerce is essentially international; that, as a result of the striking growth of industry and the great multiplication and development of means of communication in the last two or three generations, the unity of the world is real; and that no country in the modern world can expect to satisfy and protect adequately the interests of its own people without securing for them the protection of the other countries. This is even more true in regard to the multiple aspects of industrial and commercial activity which are known under the name of industrial property.

The French term "*propriété industrielle*" has given origin to the English term "industrial property" and to similar terms in all the other tongues.[1] It is not an altogether adequate term. First, the word "industrial" is ambiguous: it is derived from the word "industry," which may be taken in a strict sense, as opposed to trade, agriculture, and extractive work, or in a broad sense, embracing all sorts of human labor.[2] Second, the word "property" not only does not apply here to tangible things with which it is commonly associated but is made to include very dissimilar kinds of interests and rights.

1. The Spanish term is "*propiedad industrial*"; the Italian, "*proprietà industriale*"; the Portuguese, "*propiedade industrial*"; the Rumanian, "*proprietăţii industriale*"; the Dutch, "*industrieel Eigendom*"; the Norwegian, "*industrielle Retsvern*"; the Swedish, "*industrielt rättsskydd.*" In Germany the term "*industrielles Eigentum*" is sometimes used, although more general is the use of the terms "*gewerbliches Eigentum*" or "*gewerblicher Rechtsschutz.*"

2. Renouard, *Droit Industriel* (Paris, 1860), p. 5.

It is doubtful, too, whether the term is proper as serving to distinguish the rights in question from those of literary and artistic property. For a difference of substance would seem to be lacking in certain cases between the two categories of rights, and the classification of certain intellectual creations in the one or other category is sometimes difficult. But the division of intellectual property into literary or artistic and industrial property is very generally admitted.

Literary and artistic property is the right recognized by the law in authors of all forms of literary and artistic creations. Industrial property is only a collective name for an aggregate of rights referring to the industrial or commercial activity of a person. With the purpose of furthering his economic interest, a man invents, creates, devises or uses different things. He invents a new product or a new process of manufacture. He creates a new design or model. He adopts a distinctive mark for his goods, or uses a trade name or the name of the place where his business is established, and so forth. It is to all these aspects of a man's activity that the name "industrial property" is applied.[1]

The nature of the rights included in the term "industrial property," and their classification in the whole scheme of legal rights, are great questions of juristic speculation on which an agreement has not yet been reached. Following, however, Kohler's and Picard's studies and doctrinal speculation, it is very generally admitted today in the civil law countries that these rights, together with the authors' rights in literary and artistic works, form a distinct category, besides the classical Roman law categories of personal and real rights. These new rights are variously termed as "incorporeal rights," or "incorporeal property," "intellectual rights" or "intellectual property."[2]

In the common law countries there has never been, to the writer's knowledge, any thorough study or juristic search into the nature of

1. Moreau, *Traité de la Concurrence Illicite* (Bruxelles-Paris, 1904), p. 5; cf. Zoll, "À Propos de la Loi Polonaise du 2 Août, 1926" in *Propriété Industrielle* (1927), p. 64.

2. Kohler, *Deutsches Patentrecht* (Mannheim, 1878), Einleitung; *Forschungen aus dem Patentrecht* (Mannheim 1888), and *Handbuch des Deutschen Patentrechts* (Mannheim, 1900), Einleitung; Picard, *Des Droits Intellectuels* (Bruxelles, 1879); Braun, *Traité des Marques de Fabrique* (Bruxelles, 1880), p. 88; Moreau, *Traité de la Concurrence Illicite* (Bruxelles, 1904), pp. 27 ff.; Breuer Moreno, *Derecho Intelectual Comparado* (Buenos Aires, 1921), pp. 6, 67; Weiss, *Traité de Droit International Privé*, II, 2d ed. (Paris, 1908), 253 ff.

industrial property rights. They are considered interests of substance,[1] and the word "property," as applied to them, is not conceived in the common law idea of property, but, as Justice Holmes said, speaking of copyright, "has reached a more abstract expression. The right to exclude is not directed to an object in possession or owned, but is *in vacuo*, so to speak. It restrains the spontaneity of men when but for it there would be nothing of any kind to hinder their doing as they saw fit. It is a prohibition of conduct remote from the persons or tangibles of the party having the right." [2]

Leaving aside the questions of definition and classification, we shall find that no disagreement exists on the general scope of industrial property rights. In this respect they may be divided into two classes.[3]

Patents of invention, working models, and industrial designs and models are legal monopolies. The law recognizes in their authors the privilege of exclusive use or exploitation of their respective creations for a limited time. This is due to a policy of encouraging improvements of industry by which the community profits. At the lapse of the period for which the privilege is granted, the public becomes possessed of the invention, design or model.[4]

Trade marks, trade names, statements of place of origin, and other distinctive signs connected with the commercial or industrial organization of a manufacturer or merchant are vehicles of advantageous business relations. They are devices used by the latter to protect, maintain, and extend their activities and their association with the public. They cannot be conceived of apart from the business or goods to which, or in connection with which, they are applied. They are not creations in the same sense that in-

1. Dean Pound includes in the individual interests of substance: (*a*) property; (*b*) freedom of industry and contract; (*c*) promised advantages; and (*d*) advantageous relations with others. See his *Outline of Lectures on Jurisprudence*, 3rd ed. (Cambridge, 1920), pp. 80–82.

2. White-Smith Music Publishing Co. *v.* Apollo Co. (1908), 209 U. S. 1, 19.

3. This classification is adapted from Chafee's distinction of injuries to business, in his case book on *Equitable Relief Against Torts* (Cambridge, 1924), pp. 67, 81.

4. Allart, *Traité des Brevets d'Invention*, 3rd ed. (1911), p. 1, and Breuer Moreno, *Derecho Intelectual Comparado* (Buenos Aires, 1921), p. 5, distinguish the various rights of industrial property by three categories, making of industrial designs and models an additional category. In another part of this study the present writer points out the fact that industrial designs and models are more closely identified with artistic works than with inventions and describes the movement for extending to them the protection of the copyright law (*infra*, chap. XV). In regard to the general scope, however, of the right, industrial designs may properly be classified with inventions and working models.

ventions or designs and models are. They are understood only with the business in connection with which they are used, and their protection may last as long as the business continues.

However inappropriate the word "property" may be for all these interests and rights for the purposes of municipal law, it is not objectionable in view of their international protection. It is a convenient common denominator for various interests springing out of the commercial and industrial activity of men, which are considered today equally important and valuable with those in tangible objects.

It is not disputed that the genesis and development of all these rights, with the exception of patents, does not date back farther than the nineteenth century. For some of them, such as those referring to the indications of place of origin and the protection against acts of unfair competition, it may be said that recognition by the law is yet to come in some countries. Under these conditions it is apparent that the international protection of rights of industrial property could not possibly begin before the last century. And it will be seen that the maturity of the law of industrial property has often coincided with its international protection.

A branch of industrial property for which ancient origin is claimed is that of trade marks. Historical jurists have sought in marks of ancient Greece, of the Roman epoch, and of the Middle Ages, the embryo and the antecedents of the trade mark law and trade marks of to-day.

§ 2. Alleged trade marks of ancient Greece and Rome. The archaeological discoveries of ancient Greek inscriptions on sculptural works, paintings, vases, precious stones, lamps, glass works, bricks, and the like, reveal some features which might be thought, at first sight, to be trade marks or trade names.[1] The hypothesis that these inscriptions were intended, like the trade marks of today, to maintain or extend the trade reputation of the maker, or to guard against deceit to the public,[2] is disproved by the conditions of craftsmanship, work, and trade in ancient Greece. Neither industrial work, nor competition, in the commercial sense, in getting clients, existed. What was really wanting was craftsmen. There was rivalry only between them.[3] Whenever, therefore, these inscriptions did

1. See Salomon Reinach, *Traité d'Epigraphio Grecque* (Paris, 1885), pp. 434 ff.; Henri Francotte, *L'Industrie dans la Grèce Ancienne*, II, 136 ff.

2. See Dunant, *Traité des Marques de Fabrique et de Commerce* (Genève, 1898), p. 3.

3. Alfred Zimmern, *The Greek Commonwealth*, 4th ed. (1924), chap. VII; Guiraud, *La Main d'Œuvre Industrielle dans la Grèce Ancienne* (1900), p. 198.

not serve to attest ownership of the articles or to satisfy the sentiment of personal pride and announce the maker or creator of the goods,[1] they were, as Francotte points out, either official marks affixed by public authorities for the payment of a tax, or a means of disclosing the existence of a state monopoly,[2] or devices for the settlement of accounts between an entrepreneur and his workmen.

Supposing, however, that there was some kind of protection of industrial property, for which not the slightest evidence exists, it is almost certain that foreigners as well as citizen craftsmen would get the same protection. With the exception of Sparta, the Greek city-states, following the example of Athens, had admitted into the craft all foreigners, and even slaves, who were working on the same terms as citizens.[3] The commercial treaties deal only with questions of exports, imports, and duties.[4]

Inscriptions looking like trade marks, trade names, and statements of place of origin, appear more abundantly on objects which the archaeologists connect with the Roman epoch. The pottery, marble, gold and other medals, lamps, and even loaves of bread, found in Pompeii, bear stamps impressed on them, and symbols or names which seem to fulfill the different purposes of the Greek inscriptions.[5] Kohler, although he holds that the Roman world in the time of the Empire was moved by the same general impulses of trade as today, and that the above marks are connected with the same system of marking that is known in modern trade, is inclined to think that the institution of marks had no legal basis, but rested upon commercial honesty and integrity.

§ 3. Trade marks of the Middle Ages. During the Middle Ages trade marks present a new development. While their use and their character for identification or advertising purposes becomes more and more pronounced, in the beginning, the moving cause is not the individual interested in them, but the public authority. They are

1. See Jaton, *La Répression des Fausses Indications de Provenance* (Paris, 1926), pp. 1, 3, 4.

2. The existence of state monopolies of a strictly fiscal character is affirmed by Aristotle (*Politics*, I, 1259 a 20).

3. Francotte, *L'Industrie dans la Grèce Ancienne*, I, 214, and II, 119; Philipson, *The International Law and Custom of Ancient Greece and Rome*, vol. I, chaps. IV and VII.

4. *Ibid.*, vol. II, chap. XVII.

5. Salomon Reinach, *Manuel de Philologie Classique*, vol. II, book II, p. 46. Kohler, *Das Recht des Markenschutzes* (1884), pp. 33 ff.

mostly obligatory and rarely voluntary.[1] They are imposed by the sovereign for the purpose of protecting the public against frauds.[2] For any imitation of such obligatory marks, most severe and, indeed, horrible punishments were imposed.

The trade marks and names of this epoch are connected with the system of gilds and companies. Every gild had its own mark, and every master belonging to it had a special mark of his own. The organization of the gilds was in its origin a police measure. It aimed at putting an end to the frauds committed against the public. Every profession and its work was regulated in great detail. Since goods and persons not belonging to the gild were excluded, *a fortiori* foreigners were not admitted. This condition of things was hardly instrumental in developing international protection of industrial property. The markets, or fairs, held from time to time in different parts of Europe were only temporary armistices during which people from different countries forgot their national hatreds, and foreigners enjoyed a real, though momentary, protection.[3]

Neither did the Hanseatic League enlarge the rights of foreigners. In its statutes the prohibitions and disadvantages of foreigners are numerous. To be admitted to its privileges, it was not enough to be resident in a city joining the League. It was necessary to be a citizen of that city. Sales could not take place in the Hanseatic cities except between Hanseatic citizens. The private legislation of the League does not refer to trade marks or other rights of industrial property. It is almost exclusively maritime law, although certain provisions concern the accuracy of weights and measures, the fineness of currency, and the performance of obligations.[4]

§ 4. Beginnings of patent legislation. From about this time dates the beginning of the regime of monopolies and exclusive privileges, not only of articles of luxury and manufactured goods, but even

1. See, especially, Homeher, *Die Haus- und Hofmarken* (Berlin, 1870); and Schechter, *The Historical Foundations of the Law Relating to Trade Marks* (New York, 1925). See also, Braun, *Nouveau Traité des Marques de Fabrique ou de Commerce* (Bruxelles, 1880), chap. 1; Kohler, *Das Recht des Markenschutzes*, pp. 44 ff.

2. See an illustration in August Thierry, *Recueil des Monuments Inédits de l'Histoire du Tiers État*, 1ere sér. (1850), I, 675 (decree imposing the affixing of marks on iron products coming out of the workshop of the blacksmiths of Amiens, or brought into the city by foreign merchants).

3. See *The Mirror of Justices*, ed. by Selden Society (London, 1895), p. 14; Pardessus, *Collections des Lois Maritimes*, II, introduction, p. cv.

4. Worms, *Histoire Commerciale de la Ligue Anséatique*, pp. 264 ff., 280 ff.; Pardessus, *Collections des Lois Maritimes*, II, 455 ff.; Pradier-Fodéré, *Droit International Public*, IV, § 1919.

of the necessities of life. The Hanseatic cities were first granted such exclusive privileges and monopolies, in exchange for stipulated sums or annual tributes paid to the kings. And the practice was continued by granting them to individuals.

In England this was stopped by an early statute which constitutes a landmark for our subject. At the beginning of the seventeenth century the number and importance of commodities assigned over to patentees under patents of exclusive privilege was astonishing.[1] The "Case of Monopolies," or Darcy *v.* Allein,[2] which came before the King's Bench in the first year of the reign of James I, and in which it was held that the grant sued on was a restriction of trade and industry and therefore void, was followed by a Declaration of the King in 1610, and the famous Statute of Monopolies, 21 Jam. I, c. 3, enacted in 1623. This statute declared all monopolies void, with the exception of inventions. It constitutes the foundation of modern patent law and the first real legislative act of protection of rights of industrial property.

The terms of the sixth section, which deals with patents to be granted in the future, are as follows:

> Provided also and be it declared and enacted, that any declaration before mentioned shall not extend to any letters patent and grants of privilege, for the term of fourteen years, or under, hereafter to be made, of the sole working or making of any manner of new manufactures within this realm, to the true and first inventor and inventors of such manufactures, which others at the time of making such letters patents and grants shall not use. So as also this be not contrary to the law, nor mischievous to the State, by raising prices of commodities at home, or hurt of trade, or generally inconvenient; the said fourteen years to be accounted from the date of the first letters patent or grants of such privileges hereafter to be made, but that the same shall be of such force as they should be if this Act had never been made and of none other.

This statute is, as Kohler calls it,[3] the Magna Charta of the rights of the inventor as well as of the freedom of trade. It establishes for

1. Currants, salt, iron, powder, cards, calf skins, fells, potashes . . . vinegar, steel, aqua vitae . . . brushes, pots, bottles, oil, glasses, paper, starch, tin, etc., etc., were so monopolized. A speech of Queen Elizabeth's Secretary Cecil, at that time, accompanying a message sent by the Queen to the House and importing that the monopolies be revoked, is very characteristic. See Lord John Russell, *An Essay on the History of the English Government* (1823), pp. 475–477. See also John Coryton, *A Treatise on the Law of Letters-Patent*, introductory chapter.

2. Noy. 178; Web. P. R. 7. The case expresses the common law on the subject and is a great authority in determining the legality of patents.

3. J. Kohler, *Handbuch des Deutschen Patentrechts* (1900), p. 19.

the first time in history the requirements for the grant of a patent, and the limitation in time of the privilege, and it does away forever with arbitrary administrative action.

In relation to international law two things may be noticed in the act: the grant may be made to any person, "*the true and first inventor*," therefore to a foreigner also; but only for "*new manufactures within the realm*," and "*which others at the time of making such letters patent and grant shall not use.*" No patent, therefore, may be granted for an invention of manufacture which has been used abroad or is to be worked abroad. These restrictions have been adopted by all later legislation, as will be seen.

The other countries continued for a long time under the regime of the Middle Ages without legal regulation on the subject of patents.

In the United States, the Constitution, article I, section 8, provided that

> the Congress shall have power . . . to promote the progress of Science and useful Arts, by securing for limited times to Authors and Inventors the exclusive right to their respective writings and discoveries.

A statute was passed in accordance with this provision in 1790,[1] adopting the principles of the English act.

In France, the revolution of 1789 making *tabula rasa* of all the existing regulations of the gilds and restoring freedom of commerce and industry, relieved the independent inventors from the former restrictions, but at the same time did not give any protection to them. The two laws of January 17, 1791, and May 25, 1791,[2] transplanted to France the principles of the English act of 1623. The principles of this legislation were adopted little by little all over the world.[3]

§ 5. First legislation in industrial designs or models. In England also we find the first legislation on the subject of designs in the Act

1. Act of April 10, 1790: "An Act to promote the progress of useful arts." *Acts of the First Congress*, c. 34 (7).

2. *Lois et Actes du Gouvernement*, II, 314, and III, 203.

3. In Prussia, *Publicandum vom 14. Oktober, 1815* (Kohler, *Deutsches Patentrecht*, p. 22) which did not become really effective till the *Gewerbe-Ordnung* of January 17, 1845 (*Gesetz-sammlung*, 1845, p. 41). In Bavaria, *Gewerbegesetz vom 11. September, 1825*, and *Verordnung vom 15. August, 1834* (Kohler, *Patentrecht*, p. 23 and *Regierungs-Blatt für Bayern*, 1834, p. 989). The general principles were laid down for the whole of Germany by the Convention of the *Zollverein* of September 21, 1842 (*Gesetz-sammlung für die Preussischen Staaten*, 1843, p. 265). The first law of the Empire is the *Patentgesetz* of May 25, 1877 (*Reichsgesetzblatt*, 1877, p. 501).

of 1787 (27 Geo. III, c. 38), entitled "An Act for the encouragement of the arts of designing and printing linens, cottons, calicoes and muslins, by vesting the properties thereof in the designers, printers, and proprietors for a limited time." It provided that a designer should have the sole right of reprinting his design for two months, beginning from the day of the first publishing thereof. The term was extended to three months in 1794. France followed by a law passed in 1806,[1] which purported to protect only the designs of the industries of Lyon, but which was extended by the courts to all of France. In the United States, the Act of Congress of 1842 [2] protected the designs for the first time. In some Germanic states there existed decrees prohibiting the copying of designs, but the real protection of this right does not begin till the publication of the law of the Empire on January 11, 1876.[3]

§ 6. **Beginnings of legislation on trade marks.** The law of trade marks has been developed in England and the United States as part of the law regulating unfair trade, during the last two centuries. Prior to 1850 the cases are rare, and protection was not always afforded.[4] To obtain relief the trade mark should have been used for a long time by the claimant, so that it was an element of goodwill in his business and also the infringement must have been done fraudulently. The Act of August 7, 1862,[5] is the first legislative act in England, and reflects the rapidly changing conditions of life. Commerce, with the aid of the new and developed means of communication, is extending to new markets. The personal contact of the business man with his customers can no longer be preserved, and the old restrictions of trade-mark law are uncongenial to the

---

In Spain, a decree of 1826 (*Colleccion de Decretos*, 1826, p. 86) regulated the granting of patents very incompletely until the law of July 30, 1878 (*Colleccion Legislativa*, 1879, II, 210). See historical evolution in Spain, in José Pella y Forgas, *Patentes de Invencion y Derechos del Inventor* (Barcelona, 1892), pp. 31 ff.

In South America, legislation begins in Brazil by the Act of August 28, 1830 (*Leis do Brazil*, 1830, p. 20), in Chili by the Decree of September 9, 1840 (*Boletin de las Leyes*, 1840–1841, p. 29), and in Argentine by the Law of October 11, 1864 (*Registro Nacional*, 1864, p. 78).

1. Law of March 18, 1806 (*Bulletin des Lois*, 4e sér., t. 4e, pp. 352, 354).

2. Acts of 27th Congress (2d Sess.), c. 263, sec. 3.

3. *Reichsgesetzblatt* (1876), p. 13.

4. As is shown by the case of Blanchard *v.* Hill, 2 Atk. 484, in 1742, when an injunction against an infringement of a trade mark was refused, there existing no fraudulent design.

5. 25 & 26 Vict. c. 88.

new marketing conditions. Competition becomes rife and commerce needs a broader protection against the business parasites.

Under the same necessities and the same impulse legislation was enacted in the United States in 1870 and 1876.[1] The Supreme Court, in a narrow interpretation of the Constitution, held unconstitutional these acts in so far as they dealt with commerce generally and were not a regulation of commerce with foreign nations, or among the several states, or with the Indian tribes.[2] The Act of March 3, 1881, was then passed limiting the scope of the previous acts.[3]

In France after the abolition of the gilds in 1789, a decree of the Consulate enacted criminal penalties against infringement of trade marks. These provisions were incorporated in the Criminal Code, articles 142 and 143. Various special laws were passed until 1857, when the Law of June 13 coördinated and systematized the law of trade marks.[4]

In Germany also a systematic protection of trade marks began in the different states in the nineteenth century.[5]

§ 7. Origin and development of the law of trade names, unfair competition, etc. The law of trade names, indications of place of origin, and unfair competition has been developed in the last fifty years. In most countries its rise and maturity was brought about by judicial decision rather than by direct legislation. The great development of modern industrial and commercial society, and the consecutive new needs and demands compelled the courts to take cognizance of new interests, and to give them protection by the working-over of general principles and legal materials at hand. Necessary as the work of the courts had been, it was not up to the needs of the times, and a legislative activity in this direction begins when the International Convention of 1883 is entered into for the protection of industrial property.

General legislation dealing with all kinds of industrial property starts only after the conclusion of this convention.

1. Act of July 8, 1870 (XVI *U. S. Stat. at Large*, p. 580) and Act of August 14, 1876 (XIX *U. S. Stat.. at Large*, p. 141).

2. Trade Mark Cases, 100 U. S. 82.

3. XXI *U. S. Stat. at Large*, p. 502.

4. *Bulletin des Lois*, XIe Série, t. 4e, p. 1331.

5. The first law of the Empire dates from November 30, 1874 (*Reichsgesetzblatt*, 1874, p. 143). For a complete chronological table of legislation on industrial property in the various countries see *La Propriété Industrielle* (1900), p. 49.

§ 8. General observations on the municipal law of the various countries. As legislation on the various rights of industrial property was enacted in the various countries mostly in the second half of the last century, one might expect that identical principles would be enacted everywhere. The development of machinery, commerce, and communication created new relations and new interests in the world at large, very much alike in all countries, requiring a similar juridical sanction. Thus the law had only to be put into harmony with life. The same policy of encouraging the progress and, at the same time, avoiding an excessive restriction of the freedom of commerce and industry would seem to be imposed on the legislator everywhere.

However, the same conditions of industrial and commercial life were not found always and everywhere. The pressure of interests was not alike in all countries. Their dissimilar recognition and delimitation produced a differentiation of law. Besides, the traditional technique in handling legal materials and analogous legal principles, and the administrative practice are largely responsible for divergences between the laws.

Yet many countries felt the need of making use of experience and knowledge acquired in other countries which possessed before they did legislation on industrial property rights. They were led to adopt the general principles of protection and the regulation of those countries, the general law and legal phraseology of which were more akin to theirs. Thus, there resulted three general groups among the laws of the various countries in regard to underlying ideas, as well as to their general principles and administrative regulation — the English-speaking countries, the Latin countries (France, Italy, Spain, Latin American countries, and so forth), and the Germanic or Northern European countries (Germany, Austria, Hungary, the Netherlands, Norway, Sweden, and the rest).

All this legislative activity was far from being a complete edifice of law of industrial property at the time the Industrial Property Union was constituted, and is far from being perfect even today. It has been based on practical utility and determined by the needs of each time. A general view of the interests, claims, and demands to be satisfied, and a systematic process of seeking to adjust, harmonize, and secure them have often been lacking. It is only in recent years that in a few countries the whole matter of industrial property has formed the subject of systematic juristic [1] and legislative [2] ordering. Since the World War especially, there has been a legislative readjustment and a new legislative activity in almost all the countries, particularly with reference to the rights of industrial property, which were inadequately regulated and protected. In many countries also there has been an overhauling of legislation on industrial property. It would seem, therefore, that now is the time to take stock of what there is.

§ 9. General principles of international protection of industrial property. The divergences and defects of the municipal law of the various countries affected especially foreigners, the protection of whose rights forms the subject of this study. How far these diversities in themselves affected foreigners will be considered in the next chapter. But, besides this, foreigners did not enjoy the same pro-

1. See especially, Allfeld, *Grundriss des Gewerblichen Rechtsschutzes* (Leipzig, 1910), and *Urheber- und Erfinderrecht* (Berlin, 1923); Breuer Moreno, *Derecho Intelectual Comparado* (Buenos Aires, 1921); Bry, *La Propriété Industrielle, Littéraire et Artistique*, 3rd ed. (Paris, 1914); Cairo, *Moderni Regolamenti Giuridici della Proprietà Industriale* (Milano, 1926); Elster, *Gewerblicher Rechtsschutz* (Berlin, 1921); Huard, *Traité de la Propriété Intellectuelle*, 2 vols. (Paris, 1903–1906); Kohler's books on various rights of industrial property and his *Studien zur Förderung des Gewerblichen Rechtsschutzes* (Berlin, 1908); Osterrieth, *Lehrbuch des Gewerblichen Rechtsschutzes* (Leipzig, 1908); Pillet, *Le Régime International de la Propriété Industrielle* (Paris, 1911).

2. Portugal, Law of May 21, 1896, on Industrial Property (*Collecção Oficial*, 1896, p. 402).

Costa Rica, Decree No. 40 of June 27, 1896, on Intellectual Property (*Colleccion de Leyes y Decretos*,1896, p. 201).

Spain, Law of May 16, 1902, on Industrial Property (*Legislacion*, 1902, II, 88).

Brazil, Decree No. 16264 of December 19, 1923, for the creation of a General Direction of Industrial Property and annexed *Regulamento* under same date (*Collecção das Leis da Republica des Estados Unitos do Brazil, 1923*, III, 330).

Morocco, Act of June 23, 1916, on Industrial Property (*Propriété Industrielle*, 1917, pp. 3, 18, 37, 60).

Serb-Croat-Slovene State, Royal Decree of November 15, 1920, and Law of February 17, 1922, on Industrial Property (*Propriété Industrielle*, 1921, p. 34, and 1922, p. 61).

Syria and Lebanon, Decree No. 2385 of January 17, 1924, organizing the protection of Commercial, Industrial, Literary, and Artistic Property (*Bulletin Official du Haut Commissariat, 3e année*, February, 1924).

Poland, Law of February 5, 1924, on Patents, Designs and Trade Marks, and Law of August 2, 1926 on Unfair Competition (*Propriété Industrielle*, 1924, pp. 198, 221, 245, and 1927, p. 8).

Colombia, Law No. 31 of February 28, 1925, on Industrial Property (*República de Colombia, Leyes* 1925, p. 81).

Irish Free State, Industrial and Commercial Property (Protection) Act, 1927 (*Saorstát Eireann*, No. 16 of 1927).

A recasting of the separate laws on patents, designs, trade marks, etc., into an organic law embracing all industrial property rights, is under preparation in Italy. See *Propriété Industrielle* (1926), pp. 154, 173.

tection and the same rights everywhere. In some countries they were assimilated to citizens in all respects, while in others the protection of their rights was made conditional upon the existence of reciprocity, formal or factual; and in still others, foreigners were either definitely deprived of some rights which citizens enjoyed, or were subject to special obligations.

The attempts, from the middle of the last century, to secure international protection through provisions to this effect inserted in treaties of commerce or special agreements, did not prove satisfactory. The previous disparity and uncertainty was in no way diminished, since the municipal law was hardly derogated from by these international engagements, and the latter followed the instability inherent in treaties of commerce.

The whole situation, leading often to unreasonable denials of justice and to spoliation of foreigners' rights, was due to antiquated provisions of law, specious technical objections, and, in general, to lack of an adequate theory of private international law, applicable to rights of industrial property. The faith in the efficacy of effort, to use Dean Pound's admirable phrase, was lacking in jurists who were impeded by the tyranny of traditional conceptions and were satisfied to rationalize from the existing state of law. Thus, when by a stroke of pen the Convention of Industrial Property Union was concluded, several countries were unable to join it for a long time, and even in the countries which had acceded to it, practitioners and jurists long kept attacking it.

Following the conclusion of the Convention of Union, a theory of international protection of industrial property may now be outlined. For this purpose it is important to recall the division above made of the various rights of industrial property into legal monopolies (patents, working models, and industrial designs or models) and vehicles of advantageous business relations connected with a business organization.

In respect to the international protection of both classes of industrial property rights, two questions are involved: that of acquisition of a right of industrial property by foreigners, and that of the recognition and enforcement of a right acquired abroad. No theoretical or practical difficulty arises in respect to the matter of acquisition of rights of industrial property by foreigners. It is a pure question of legislative policy. A state may refuse to grant a patent to a foreigner or may make such grant conditional upon the compliance with special conditions and formalities. Likewise, it may refuse to admit for registration trade marks of foreigners, as it may refuse to allow them to carry on a business or enter a profession within its territory. But if the law does not expressly exclude foreigners from the acquisition of industrial property rights, it should be concluded that they have the power to acquire them, by applying for a patent, for instance, or for the deposit of designs, or for the registration of their trade marks.[1] Without entering into the quarrels of writers concerning the nature of these rights, this conclusion may be reached on a consideration of the interests to be taken into account. Whether a legal monopoly (patent, design, model) or a protection of a vehicle of advantageous business relations (trade mark, trade name, and so forth) is sought by a foreigner, his private interest is supported by the social interest in the progress of industry or trade that his invention or design and model advances, or in the furthering of fair dealing and the protection against deceit of the public that the protection of trade marks, trade names, and so forth, involves.

In the legislation of the various countries before the constitution of the Industrial Property Union, and even later, general or specific discriminations against foreigners in this respect are seldom found, although their capacity to acquire rights of industrial property is made conditional upon reciprocity. That is to say, the nationals of country A are able to acquire such rights in country B, if the nationals of the latter may acquire the same rights in the former. The reciprocity required is either formal or factual — that is, it should be proved either by the existence of a convention or treaty between the two countries in question securing to the citizens of each the same rights and protection, or by the fact that by the law of the country to which the foreigner belongs, a similar protection is granted to nationals of the country where protection is claimed.

As will be seen, one of the fundamental principles of the Industrial Property Union is that all such discriminations against foreigners are done away with. This is in consonance with the modern conception of economic unity of the world.

Whenever no discrimination against foreigners exists, or the requirement of reciprocity is satisfied, the further question arises whether and how far rights of industrial property acquired abroad

1. Weiss, *Traité de Droit International Privé*, 2 ed. (Paris, 1908), II, 302.

will be recognized and enforced. It is in respect to this question that many difficulties arise and that the need of a general theory is keenly felt.

In the Anglo-American world the territorial conception of law and rights includes the industrial property, namely, these legalized private interests in incorporeal things (inventions, creations, advantages connected with a business organization). But the same principle of territoriality is also admitted in the other countries in regard to rights of industrial property.[1] That is, when the law turns a private interest in an invention or a goodwill into property, this property is a mere creature of that law, and it can therefore exist only so far as the law that creates it extends. Consequently, a patent granted in country A cannot extend outside the territory of that country. And similarly, a trade-mark right acquired in one country is effective only in the country where it was acquired.

While this is true, the law of the various countries may allow foreigners, on the fulfillment of certain conditions, to seek the recognition and enforcement of their rights acquired abroad. Thus, the law may provide that a foreign patentee may apply for a patent for the same invention, and a trade-mark owner may register his trade mark, which is legally protected in his own country, in order to have it protected in the new country. When this is done, the question arises, what is the relation between the two patents, the domestic and the foreign, and between the two trade-mark rights? Is the new right an extension of the right acquired abroad, or is it an independent right? Very important and opposing results follow from the adoption of the first or second solution.

It is submitted that the distinction between the two classes of industrial property rights becomes important here. Those described above as legal monopolies, namely, patents, working models and industrial models, and designs, should be distinguished from other civil rights. They are privileges and rights at the same time; or, to speak in continental legal phraseology, they are extraordinary rights (*droits extraordinaires*), and may well be included within the excep-

1. Weiss, *Traité de Droit International Privé*, 2d ed. (Paris, 1908), II, 300; Von Bar, *Theorie und Praxis*, II, 263 ff.; Breuer Moreno, *Patentes de invención* (Buenos Aires, 1921), pp. 21 ff.; Ostertag, "International Unions for the Protection of Industrial, Literary and Artistic Property," *Michigan Law Review* (1926), XXV, 107, 109; Beale, *A Treatise on the Conflict of Laws*, § 153.

tion of public order. When, therefore, a foreign patentee applies for a patent in another country, and his invention satisfies all the conditions imposed by that second country, it is really a new privilege, a new patent that he gets, although for the same invention.[1] The opposite view, extending the doctrine of vested rights to such legal monopolies, and refusing the independent character of the new privileges,[2] while it does not take sufficient account of the exceptional nature of these legal monopolies, reaches unjust results. If the new patent be an extension of the foreign patent and, consequently, dependent on the latter, the annulment, cancellation, or forfeiture of the same will cause that of the national patent. It is not seen why the failure to comply with a condition in the first state should have any effect in the second. The foreign patentee may neglect to pay an annuity or a fee on the foreign patent, or may fail to work his patent in the foreign country, and thus forfeit it in that country; he may also transfer his foreign patent to another person who has been the cause of its forfeiture. In all these cases it is unjust to consider the destiny of the domestic patent as bound up with that of the foreign. It is usually argued in support of this view, that the industry of a country should not be restrained by a legal monopoly which has ceased in the foreign country. But it is difficult to see why there should be any difference in the results in state B from the accidental reason that a person applied first in state A and then in state B, instead of applying in the opposite way. In both cases a privilege is sought in a country, extending to the whole of its territory and no more. In both cases the same conditions must be fulfilled in state B, the same rights are granted and the same obligations imposed. The inventor, therefore, who has obtained many patents for the same invention has not a single right, more or less modified according to the different territories, but as many independent rights as the number of his patents.

In the case of vehicles of advantageous business relations connected with a business organization there is no element of monopoly. A trade mark, trade name, statement of place of origin, or any other

1. Bozérian, "Des Brevets d'Invention pris simultanément à l'Étranger et en France," *Journal de Droit International Privé* (1877), p. 217; E. Thaller, "Dépendance ou Indépendance des Brevets, pris pour une même invention des plusieurs États," 1909, *Revue de Droit International Privé* (1908), p. 5; Weiss, *Traité de Droit International Privé*, 2d ed. (Paris, 1908), II, 323; Kohler, *Handbuch des Deutschen Patentrechts*, p. 65.

2. Pillet, *Régime International de la Propriété Industrielle*, chap. 1, especially pp. 12 ff. Cf. Allart, *Traité des Brevets*, p. 266.

distinctive device used by business men to create, maintain, and extend the goodwill of their business, in no way curtails the liberty of honest commerce and industry. They presuppose competition. By their protection the free access to the purchasing market is protected. The prohibition of their infringement and imitation by third persons is in no way different from the prohibition of stealing another's property. It is in the interest of the business men as well as of the purchasing public that these advantageous business relations are protected; the latter is protected against deceit by fraudulent imitators. It is the social interest of preventing dishonest and unfair competition and of furthering fair dealing which is at stake and which it is the policy of every state to secure. Consequently, foreign rights in trade marks, trade names, and the like, should be recognized and enforced in each country, provided no undue injury to the interests of nationals is caused thereby, and the foreigner complies with the conditions and formalities imposed by the municipal law concerning the giving of a notice to the public of the claim in a trade mark, trade name, and so forth. Under these conditions the rights granted in the new country are not new independent rights, but only a validation of, and a giving effect to, the rights acquired abroad. Consequently, the cessation, for any reason, of the protection of the right abroad should terminate the domestic right.

§ 10. The Union for the protection of industrial property. The Industrial Property Union Convention of 1883 has helped the development of the law and theory of industrial property as it has made possible its rational international regulation and protection. But in the common law countries it has not formed the subject of study on the part of writers, and has not exercised any direct influence on legislation. The authors of books on various rights of industrial property are contented with brief and superficial references to the Convention. In the United States and in Great Britain, as will be seen, the domestic legislation has, at various times and for long periods, been kept in opposition to the Convention.

This state of things illustrates the important difference of approach to international law between the continental countries and the part of the world which has been under their influence (for instance, Latin America), and the English-speaking countries. The International Convention of 1883 is understood in the United States and the British Commonwealth of Nations in a different way from that in which it is understood on the Continent. Continental lawyers believe in the actual existence of the Industrial Property Union, and consider the Convention as an international common legislation superposed on the national legislation; they hold that the regime of industrial property is actually regulated by these two kinds of legislation.[1] The conception of the Convention by common law lawyers is only one of contract or bargain between the different countries on certain questions of industrial property protection. It is sufficient to read the minutes of the successive conferences of revision of the Convention to be convinced of this difference. It is the contrast between the analytical common law point of view and the synthetic continental method. An abstract formula, by its character of generality and its fecundity, attracts continental lawyers and is instinctively opposed by the others. Perhaps the English point of view is less disinclined to the continental way of approaching international legal problems than the American, and Englishmen are not under the handicap of a slow-moving and cumbersome legislative law-making, as is the case in the United States.

The writer believes that this difference of approach to international law in the United States is slowly disappearing under the more general interest and study of international law and international relations, and because of the vast expansion of American economic, commercial, and financial activities in foreign countries. A technique and a tradition in handling the legal problems involved in these activities is being built up. The writer has attempted in this study to present to the English-speaking legal profession a synthetic picture of the international regime of industrial property, by a method in which he has tried to combine the common law and civil law technique.

It is proposed to consider, in the first part, the international regime of industrial property before the constitution of the Industrial Property Union in 1883, as it was governed by the municipal law of the various countries and bipartite agreements. In the second, and main part, the protection and regulation of industrial property at the present time in the Industrial Property Union will be considered.

1. See Plaisant et Fernand-Jacq, *Nouveau Régime International de la Propriété Industrielle* (Paris, 1927), p. 5.

In a separate section of this part, the Inter-American regime of industrial property under the Pan-American conventions will be also described. In the last part, the future development of industrial property and the efforts for the protection of scientific property will be dealt with.

CHAPTER II

THE MUNICIPAL LAW OF THE VARIOUS COUNTRIES

§ 11. In general.

I. PATENTS

§ 12. Divergences of patent laws.
§ 13. Subject-matter of patents.
§ 14. Conditions and formalities for the grant of a patent.
§ 15. Administrative procedure.
§ 16. Terms of patents, and fees or taxes.
§ 17. Obligations of the patentee.
§ 18. How far the diversities of patent law affected foreigners indirectly.
§ 19. Provisions of patent laws concerning foreigners.

II. INDUSTRIAL DESIGNS AND MODELS

§ 20. Diversities of laws.
§ 21. Registration of designs or models of foreigners.

III. TRADE MARKS

§ 22. General remarks.
§ 23. What may be registered as a trade mark.
§ 24. Formalities, conditions, and procedure of registration.
§ 25. Legal effects of registration and their duration.
§ 26. How far diversities of trade-mark law affected foreigners.
§ 27. Registration of trade marks by foreigners.
§ 28. Protection of non-registered foreign trade marks.

IV. TRADE NAMES, INDICATIONS OF PLACE OF ORIGIN, AND UNFAIR COMPETITION

§ 29. Protection of trade names in the various countries.
§ 30. Foreigners' trade names.
§ 31. Protection of indications of place of origin.
§ 32. Protection of foreign indications of origin.
§ 33. Repression of unfair competition.
§ 34. Protection of foreigners against acts of unfair competition.

§ 11. In general. In order to realize the importance of the changes brought about in the international regime of industrial property by the constitution of the Industrial Property Union in 1883, it is necessary to consider the situation existing prior to this date. This is not only of historical interest. It is the regime still prevailing in the countries which have not joined the Union. Moreover, many remnants of that situation continue up to now since the Union does not purport to do away with the protection and regulation of industrial property through municipal law, but tends only to remove the difficulties and risks in the way of protection of foreigners' rights, and to superpose an international regulation on the national regulation of industrial property in each state.

Foreigners' rights of industrial property were affected in two ways by the provisions of municipal law: first, indirectly, by the divergences existing between the laws of the various countries which rendered their protection either difficult or impossible; and second, directly, by the provisions of the law of each country concerning the protection and rights enjoyed by foreigners. It is to the consideration of both these questions in regard to each separate branch of industrial property that this chapter is devoted.

I. Patents

§ **12. Divergences of patent laws.** All patent laws are very technical in character. The inventor is granted the exclusive privilege, called the patent, under the conditions, and with the limitations, which the law prescribes, with a view of protecting the freedom of commerce and industry and avoiding the danger of monopolies harmful to the public. The law of all countries, in the attempt to secure both ends — the encouragement of inventions and discoveries for the progress of industry and the minimum of restraint to the freedom of the public — defines the subject-matter of patents. It also prescribes the formalities and conditions which inventors must comply with, and the administrative procedure leading to the delivery of the patent, fixes the duration of the privilege for a limited time, and imposes certain obligations on the patentee.

The diversities of the law in all these respects affect foreigners, and it is necessary, therefore, to consider the following questions on the subject of patents: (1) what is a patentable invention; (2) conditions and formalities necessary for the granting of a patent; (3) administrative procedure of grant; (4) term of patents and taxes; and (5) obligations of the patentee.[1]

1. The laws of the different countries which are considered here are those in effect before the constitution of the Industrial Property Union, namely:

Argentina, Law of October 11, 1864, arts. 3, 4, 5, 20, 32, 33–38, 46, 47. (*Registro Nacional*, 1864, p. 78.)

Austria-Hungary, *Kaiserliches Patent* of August 15, 1852, §§ 1, 5, 9, 11, 13–17. 25, 29. (*Reichsgesetzblatt*, 1852, p. 817.)

Belgium, Law of May 24, 1854, arts. 1, 2, 3, 23, 24. (*Pasinomie*, 1854, p. 174.)

Bolivia, Decree of May 8, 1858, arts. 1, 4, 5, 8, 9, 10, 38, and Decree of September 11, 1877. (*Recueil Général de Législation, Bureau International de la Propriété Industrielle*, Berne, 1896, III, 176.)

Brazil, Law of October 14, 1882, arts. 1, 2, 3, 5. (*Collecção das Leis*, 1882, I, 82.)

§ 13. Subject-matter of patents. The English Statute of Monopolies provided for the granting of letters patent " of the sole working or making of any manner of new manufactures." The invention to be patentable should be a manufacture. As to this, it was left to the courts to decide. The statute, however, added the limitations: " so as they be not contrary to law, nor mischievous to the State, by raising prices of commodities at home or hurt of trade or generally inconvenient." The subsequent acts in England did not attempt to define a patentable invention. The same is true of the British colonies and possessions. In all these countries,

> if the invention is a manufacture (having a very close relation to something tangible), if it is new, if it is useful, if it is one which would not have been obvious to a person skilled in the art and acquainted with the common knowledge in that art at the date of the patent, then, it is a subject-matter for a grant.[1]

This was not different from the specific enumeration of " any new useful art, machine, manufacture or composition of matter or any new and useful improvement thereof," of the United States statute. Substantially similar were the provisions of Belgium, Germany, Sweden, Chile, and Bolivia.

In other countries, on the contrary, such as France, Turkey, Austria-Hungary, Spain, Italy, Argentina, and Brazil, the law enu-

---

Chile, Law of September 9, 1840, arts. 1, 2, 3, 5, 9, 11, 13, 15, 16; and Decrees of August 1, 1851, and January 20, 1883. (*Boletin de Las Leyes*, 1840–1841, p. 29; 1851, p. 279; *Recueil Général de Législation, Bureau International de la Propriété Industrielle*, Berne, 1896, II, 286.)

France, Law of July 5, 1844, arts. 2, 4, 11, 15, 19, 31, 32, and Law of May 23, 1868. (*Bulletin des Lois*, 1844, II, p. 18; 1868, I, p. 405.)

Germany, Law of May 25, 1877, §§ 1, 2, 5, 7, 9, 10, 11, 20–24, 29. (*Reichsgesetzblatt*, 1877, p. 501.)

Great Britain, Act of 1883, §§ 5, 6, 7, 8, 17, 22, 25, 26, 27. (46 & 47 Vict. c. 57.)

Italy, Law of October 30, 1859, arts. 2, 3, 4, 6, 7, 9, 10, 12, 37, 58. (*Raccolta Stati Sardi*, 1859, I, 1287.)

Spain, Law of July 30, 1878, arts. 5, 11, 12, 29, 38, 39–46. (*Colleccion Legislativa*, 1879, II, 210.)

Sweden, Royal Order of May 16, 1884, arts. 1, 2, 3, 10, 11, 15, 16, 17. (*Svensk Författningssamling*, 1884, No. 25, p. 1.)

Turkey, Law of February 18, 1879, arts. 2, 4, 6, 11, 12, 23, 25, 37, 38. (*Recueil Général de Législation, Bureau International de la Propriété Industrielle*, Berne, 1896, II, 607.)

The United States, Act of July 8, 1870, in *Revised Statutes of the United States*, 1878, §§ 4884, 4886, 4887, 4890, 4893, 4898, 4902, 4934.

The specific articles of the law of each country enumerated above contain the provisions which are especially considered in this chapter.

1. See Terrell, *The Law and Practice Relating to Letters Patent for Inventions*, 6th ed. (1921), p. 39.

merated more or less elaborately the inventions for which a patent might be granted. Moreover, in some countries certain inventions were expressly excluded from protection.

Some of the exceptions enumerated in different legislations may no doubt be read into the statutes of the United States and England; for instance, inventions contrary to the public order or *boni mores*,[1] or combinations of credit or finance,[2] which are not industrial inventions. In some countries scientific discoveries were expressly excluded, so far as they remain in the field of speculation and do not give immediate results; [3] this exception seemed to be well recognized everywhere.

However, there were also exceptions which presented great variations between the different countries. Thus, Spain and Bolivia did not grant patents for the invention of new industrial products or results, unless by their working a new branch of industry would be established in the country. Spain also refused patents for the use of natural products. Germany did not grant a patent for inventions regarding luxuries or for chemical products. Bolivia excluded inventions which concerned only a modification of dimensions, or purely ornamental objects. But the most important differences concerned inventions, the subjects of which were articles of food and medicines. With the exception of the United States, England, Chile, and Brazil, all the countries excepted inventions regarding medicines generally. Sweden, however, refused a grant for the product itself, but not for the special process of its manufacture. On the other hand, France, Spain, Turkey, and Argentina excepted pharmaceutical compositions, besides medicines.

As to articles of food, they were excepted by Germany, Austria, and Sweden; but again Sweden gave a patent for the process of manufacture merely. Austria-Hungary also excepted beverages.

§ **14. Conditions and formalities for the grant of a patent.** The granting of a patent was conditional upon compliance with certain formalities and the satisfaction of certain conditions calculated to define accurately the monopoly granted to the inventor, and to protect the interests of the public. There was extreme diversity between

1. They were expressly excepted in Italy, Sweden, Austria-Hungary, Germany, Brazil, and Argentina.

2. They were expressly excepted in France, Turkey, Spain, and Argentina. We may also put here the exception in Turkey of combinations of sales.

3. They were so in Italy, Austria-Hungary, Spain, Germany, Argentina, and Brazil.

the laws of the various countries as to what documents should be submitted with an application for a patent, and how these documents should be drawn and prepared. The formalities were determined by the peculiarities of language, habits, and administrative or judicial practice in each country. The conditions called for appointment of resident agents by the non-resident applicant, for submission of the various documents and taking the different steps of procedure within fixed periods, and so forth.

There is one condition for the grant of a patent, especially, which goes to the substance of the right. The condition itself and the diversities of the law of the various countries in respect to it constituted one of the most important obstacles to the protection of foreigners' inventions. This was the condition of novelty of the invention. Unless this condition was complied with, the patent was either refused or invalidated. The invention should be new within the meaning of the law of each country. Generally speaking, an invention was not considered new if it had been known or used by other people before the deposit of the patent application, or if its novelty had been destroyed by publication by the inventor. Publication means making known to the public. Printing is a means of publication, but not the sole means. Exhibiting the invention, or depositing it at a place where persons may get a copy or take notes, so that they may reproduce it, is also publication. Now, the use or knowledge of the invention or the different facts of publication may take place in the country where one applies for a patent or abroad. Does the use, knowledge, or publication abroad, as well as in the country, prevent the inventor from applying for a patent? The legislations of the different countries did not treat this question the same way. The following countries may be grouped together, although the law was not entirely identical in all of them. In France, Turkey, Argentina, Brazil, Spain, Sweden, and Italy all facts of publication, use, or knowledge in the country or abroad were fatal to the application or to the patent.[1] In the rest of the countries a distinction was made between publication by printing and other facts of publication or use and knowledge. Thus, in the United States, Germany, Austria-Hungary, Belgium, and Bolivia only the

1. In the countries where the invention was submitted to previous investigation, the non-novelty of it was fatal to the application. In the countries where no previous investigation was made, the previous publication or use of the invention caused the annulment or revocation of the patent.

publication abroad by printing destroyed the novelty of the invention; the other means of publication, or the use or knowledge abroad of the invention, did not. Moreover, in Great Britain and Chile anything done abroad was not considered, and the only facts destroying the novelty of the invention were public manufacture, use, or sale in England, and establishment or knowledge of the invention in the same manner in Chile. In Belgium, even the publication by printing abroad was not fatal, if it were made in performance of a legal obligation. Under the Italian law, if the publication abroad was a legal consequence of a foreign patent, the inventor might nevertheless apply for a patent in Italy, if he did so within the duration of the foreign patent and before anybody introduced the patented articles in Italy. By a special law passed in 1868, France gave a temporary protection of three months to inventions exhibited at international exhibitions.[1]

§ 15. **Administrative procedure.** The various countries have developed different systems of granting patents which will be considered more thoroughly in the second part of this study, but which for our purposes here may be said to be two: the system of preliminary examination and search, and the system of mere registration of the invention. In the first system, the invention sought to be patented was investigated by the administration as to its novelty and patentability; and it also was advertised before the grant of the patent, so that opposition to the grant might be filed by the interested parties. In the second system, the administration merely saw whether the application and the accompanying documents were in proper form, then registered the invention claimed therein without any examination into its patentability, and granted the patent. The difference between the two systems was merely procedural and did not affect the substantive rights.

The patent law of the United States might be taken as the type of the first system. Indeed, it was an extreme type because the examination and search was the most severe and minute of all countries. The examination of the invention extended to the question whether it was sufficiently useful and important. The act provided even for experiments to be made by the administration. The law of Chile and

1. The Brazilian Law of 1882, the British Act of 1883, and the Swedish Law of 1884 (cited above on pp. 23-24) granted rights of priority of seven months to foreign patentees, but these laws were passed after the Industrial Property Conferences of 1880 and 1883 which drafted the Industrial Property Union Convention.

Bolivia also provided for an extensive examination of the invention. In Great Britain there was no preliminary examination as to novelty. The application should comply with the formal requirements first. But after acceptance of the complete specification and advertisement thereof, any person might give notice of opposition to the grant, on the grounds specified in the act. In Germany, both an examination by the Patent Office, as in the United States, and an advertisement for opposition, as in Great Britain, constituted the system of grant. Austria-Hungary and Sweden followed the same system.

France, on the other hand, and the other countries had adopted the system of mere registration of inventions for which a patent was applied for. Provided the application was in good form, a patent was issued, whether or not the invention claimed was new and patentable. Sometimes the only ground on which a patent might be refused was that the invention was expressly excluded by the law, for instance, an invention concerning a medicine. In Italy, however, if the invention was of articles of food or beverages, the Board of Health (*Consiglio Superiore de Sanità*) gave its opinion whether such a patent might be granted, but only on the question whether the invention was harmful or not to the health. Similar investigation was made in Brazil as to inventions regarding articles of food and chemical or pharmaceutical products. In Turkey the army and navy authorities gave their opinion as to the usefulness of inventions of instruments and munitions of war.

Special mention should be made here of the *caveat* in the United States and Argentina. In these countries, an inventor desiring further time to mature his invention, and at the same time to secure his priority, might file a *caveat* setting forth his invention. It was kept in secrecy in the confidential archives for one year. If another applied for a patent for a similar invention within the year, then notice was given to the person who had filed the *caveat* to file specifications and drawings of the invention. In Argentina renewal of the *caveat* was possible.

§ 16. Terms of patents, and fees or taxes. The right of exclusive use of the patent was everywhere granted for a limited term of years only. This term in some countries was identical and fixed for all kinds of inventions, although by no means for the same number of years. Thus, in Belgium, for every invention, the privilege of exclusive use was granted for twenty years; in the United States, for seventeen; in Germany, Sweden, and Brazil, for fifteen; in Great Britain, for fourteen years. In other countries, on the contrary, the length of the term depended on the importance of the invention. Thus, in Spain, for original inventions the term was twenty years, for non-original only five years. In Bolivia, it was not less than ten or more than fifteen years. In Austria-Hungary, the maximum of fifteen years might be exceeded if a request by the proper authorities was made to the Kaiser for cases of particular importance. In the rest of the countries, the law simply either fixed the maximum of the term, and the applicant might ask for any term within that maximum; or it fixed two or three terms, and the inventor might apply for any of them. Thus, in Italy the law fixed a minimum of one year and a maximum of fifteen; in Austria-Hungary, maximum, fifteen; in Chile, maximum, ten. On the other hand, in France, Turkey, and Argentina the applicant might ask, at his election, a term of five, ten, or fifteen years.

As to the inventions which had been patented already in a foreign country, it will be seen later that the patent could not extend in time beyond the term of the original patent, and in some countries even the maximum term was shorter than that for domestic inventions.

Another question to be considered here is as to the extension of the term. That was always possible in Italy, if the originally granted term was under five years, but the whole term could not be extended beyond fifteen years. In Chile, renewal of the patent was possible in exceptional cases by the proper authorities. Also in Great Britain, the term might be extended for seven or fourteen years more by the Judicial Committee of the Privy Council. In France and Turkey, this was possible only by a special law. In the other countries, no extension was possible.

In regard to taxes payable for a patent, which varied in different countries not only as to the amount but also as to the mode of payment, the most important question for our purposes is the penalty for non-payment of a tax. Usually, forfeiture of the patent was provided for the non-payment of a tax, which generally had to be paid in advance. But in only a few countries notice for payment and warning of forfeiture was sent to the patentee. In others, the forfeiture was automatic in case of non-payment in due time. In Belgium, notice was sent, and if the tax was not paid six months after date, the patent was forfeited. In France, Turkey, Spain, and Great Britain the patent was forfeited for non-payment within the prescribed times. In Great Britain, however, Germany, Italy, and Sweden, the patent was forfeited only three months after the tax became due. In the United States, Austria-Hungary, Chile, and Bolivia all taxes and fees were paid in full on the grant of the patent.

§ 17. **Obligations of the patentee.** The granting of a patent consisting in a right of exclusive use of the invention for a limited time involves a curtailment of the freedom of industry and commerce. During the term for which the patent is granted, no one except the patentee is allowed to manufacture, use, or sell the new article or the new machine. It was deemed necessary then in most of the countries that there should be imposed upon the patentee the obligation to work his invention or to let other people work it. For the same reason the patentee should not be allowed to work his patent for a while and then stop.

Both these obligations were generally imposed on the patentee by the different legislations, but the period within which he should begin to work his invention, or during which he should not cease working, was not identical in the different countries. Both periods were fixed at two years in France, Turkey, and Argentina; also in Italy, unless the patent was for a term of five years, in such case the periods being one year. In Spain, the period to begin the working was fixed at two years and might be extended, by law, only for six months; the period during which the working of the invention should not cease was one year and one day. In Austria-Hungary, the first period was one year, and the second, two; in Brazil, the first, three years, and the second, one. In Belgium, both periods were one year but failure to work the invention caused the forfeiture only if the invention was worked abroad and not in Belgium. In Chile, when the invention was investigated by the experts, the latter expressed their opinion as to the difficulties and expense of establishing the invention in the country, and as to the time when the working of the invention should start. If, then, the work did not start at the proper time, the patent was deemed null. It was also forfeited if the work was stopped for one year, or if the articles produced were defective, or inferior to the samples or models deposited with the application.

In Sweden and Bolivia, there was only obligation to begin working the invention, and only in case of failure to do so was the patent forfeited. But while in Bolivia the period was one year, in Sweden it was three and might be extended to four. In Germany, also, there was only the obligation to begin working the invention within three years; but the patent might be revoked, not only for complete failure to work the invention, but also if the patentee failed to work it to a proper extent or to secure all that was necessary for such working within the fixed time. It might also be revoked after three years, if it appeared to be in the public interest to allow other people to work it, and if the patentee refused to do so on receiving proper indemnity and sufficient security. In the latter case, notice was given in proper time to the patentee. This amounted to compulsory license. The same was also possible in exceptional cases in Sweden.

In Great Britain, neither of the above-mentioned obligations existed, and the system of compulsory licenses was instituted instead. The Board of Trade had power to order the patentee to grant licenses on terms that the Board might deem just in cases where the patent was not being worked in the United Kingdom, or where the reasonable requirements of the public with respect to the invention could not be supplied. It will be seen that, in regard to foreigners, the best method of safeguarding their interests was the system of the English Law.

In France and Turkey another kind of obligation was imposed which did not exist in any other country. The patentee should not import articles manufactured abroad and similar to those guaranteed by his patent. By exception, and after special permission, he might import only models of machines or articles destined for public exhibition or experiments made with the consent of the government.

In the United States there was no obligation imposed on the patentee whatsoever.

§ 18. How far the diversities of patent law affected foreigners indirectly. In view of the above exposition, it is not difficult to conclude that foreign inventors met with great and sometimes insurmountable obstacles to the protection of their inventions. First of all, an invention patentable under the law of their country might be non-patentable in other countries. Then, it might not be new any longer, if it received a certain publication in any country. Even the filing of the application describing the invention, or the advertisement of the invention by the administration, was considered publication destroying the novelty of the invention in many countries.[1] And in cases where such official publication abroad was not a ground of refusal of a patent or of its invalidation, there was always the danger of a third person's obtaining knowledge of the invention through such publication, and applying for a patent in advance of the foreign inventor. Only a contemporaneous application in all the countries where protection was desired could secure the rights of the inventor. Next, there was the trouble of satisfying the extremely minute rules of each country concerning the drafting of applications and documents, and of discussing the patentability or novelty of the invention with the administration and defending against objections to the grant filed by third persons. When all this is recalled, and also that all these formalities and procedural steps were limited by fixed periods, it becomes apparent that foreigners were compelled to retain patent experts and agents in each country to represent their interests. This was a source of heavy expense and charges. To these should be added the fees and taxes payable in each country in which a patent was obtained.

When a foreign inventor was successful enough to obtain a patent at great sacrifice, he still was not secure in his right. A failure to pay a tax at the appointed time would cause the forfeiture of the patent. In a few countries a period of grace was allowed, but in no country was restoration of the patent, forfeited for non-payment of a tax in due time, possible. Lastly, the obligation to work the patent within a fixed, and often short, period, and not to interrupt its working, rendered the protection of foreigners very precarious, since it was almost impossible for a foreigner to take steps for the working of his invention in all countries. In some countries, even granting a license to other persons to work the invention was not held to be performance of the obligation to work the patent unless the licensee started working the invention within the fixed period.[2] And

1. So in France, the acceptance of a complete specification of the invention by the Patent Office in England and the printing of it was considered publication of the invention. See Liebert *c.* Pierre Petit, Cassation, December 20, 1886, (*Dalloz*, 1887, I, 352). Similarly, the deposit of specification in Germany with opportunity for the public to inspect it was deemed publication. See Seltsam *c.* Couillard, Cassation, March 9, 1883 (*Dalloz*, 1884, I, 143) and Banque Nationale d'Allemagne *c.* La Raffinerie Parisienne, Tribunal Civil de la Seine, June 14, 1893 (*Clunet*, 1894, p. 103).

2. See Power *v.* Griffin (1902), 33 Canada Supreme Court Reports, 39; and a decision of the Tribunal de Paris, July 12, 1901 (*Propriété Industrielle*, 1904, p. 8).

in France and Turkey, even the importation of a single article manufactured abroad with the patented invention caused the loss of the patent.

§ 19. **Provisions of patent laws concerning foreigners.** Concerning the original acquisition of patent rights by foreigners, the laws of the different countries were, in principle, uniform. Everywhere foreigners were allowed to apply for a patent under the same conditions and formalities, and were entitled to the same rights and subject to the same obligations, as nationals. The only obligation usually imposed on non-resident foreigners was to appoint a resident agent or attorney, on whom all service could be made in the different stages of administrative procedure and in the judicial proceedings arising out of the patent. However, in the United States a foreigner could not apply for a *caveat*, unless he had resided in the United States one year preceding the filing of the *caveat*, and had made oath of his intention to become a citizen.

As regards the recognition and enforcement of the rights acquired abroad, that is, the protection of foreign patentees, the laws of the various countries provided that an application for a new patent should be filed. These new patents were sometimes called patents of importation, because they imported a new industry into the country. It has already been pointed out [1] that in theory these new patents should not be considered as extending the original patent in the new countries, but as new grants of privilege of independent character, although for the same invention. It follows that the duration and validity of the new national patents should be independent of the duration and validity of the foreign original patent.

This independence of patents for the same invention was admitted partly only by the laws of the various countries, with the exception of the British law, under which patents granted to foreign patentees were like original patents. The normal duration of a patent granted to a foreign patentee could not exceed, in all the other countries, the term of the foreign patent, so that at the expiry of the term of the latter the national patent was terminated.[2] Only

1. See *supra*, § 9.

2. In Argentina and Spain, a shorter term was fixed for inventions already patented abroad. This could not exceed ten years and, of course, might come to an end even before the expiry of the ten-year period, in case the original foreign patent terminated. In Bolivia, the duration of the patent of importation was determined by the cost of establishing the new industry in the country.

in Argentina and Brazil was the new patent in all respects dependent on the validity and existence of the foreign patent; so that, if the latter was forfeited or cancelled for any reason, the former followed its destiny.

One might think that this was a liberal regime for foreign inventors. But it should be recalled that foreigners were subject to the same conditions and obligations as nationals, which means that they were affected by all the exigencies and diversities of municipal law described in the preceding section.

II. Industrial Designs and Models

§ 20. Diversities of the law on industrial designs and models. Industrial designs and models are distinguished from patents, inasmuch as they do not concern the production of an industrial product itself, an art, a manufacture, or a machine, but only the pattern, shape, configuration, or ornamentation of an industrial article or substance. It is immaterial whether any advantages will result to industry from a new design or model. It satisfies the fashion more than it tends to the progress of industry.

The United States, Great Britain, Germany, Austria-Hungary, France, Italy, and Belgium were the only states protecting this kind of property by special legislation before 1883.[1] The first law on the subject, the British Act of 1787, provided that every person who should design or cause to be designed any new and original pattern for printing linens, cottons, calicoes, or muslins should have the sole right of reprinting the same for the term of two months beginning

1. United States, Act of July 8, 1870 (*United States Revised Statutes*, 1878, §§ 4929–4933).

Great Britain, Act of August 25, 1883, Part III, §§ 47, 48, 50, 51, 52, 53, 54, 57, 103 (46 & 47 Vict. c. 57).

Germany, Law of January 11, 1876, §§ 1, 7, 8, 9, 10, 11, 13, 16 (*Reichsgesetzblatt*, 1876, p. 13).

Austria-Hungary, Law of December 7, 1858, §§ 1, 4, 5, 8, 9, 10, 11 (*Reichsgesetzblatt*, 1858, p. 707).

France, Law of March 18, 1806, Titre II, section III, and Decrees of June 5, 1861 and November 26, 1875 (*Bulletin des Lois*. 4e sér. IV, 352, 354; 1861, I, 803; and 1873, II, 733).

Belgium, the French Law of March 18, 1806.

Italy, Law of August 30, 1868, arts. 1, 2, 4, and Decree of February 7, 1869 (*Raccolta Ufficiale*, 1868, p. 1336; 1869, p. 135).

In some countries industrial designs and models were protected either by the copyright law, whenever they might be considered artistic designs or sculptural works, or, on application of general provisions of the civil or criminal law against fraud. It is hardly necessary to say that this protection was altogether inadequate.

with the day of the first publishing thereof. The creator of the design had the exclusive right to apply the design to any article of manufacture, and to prevent anyone else from copying or reproducing it. This act did not provide for any system of registering designs. This was done later by the Act of 1839 (2 Vict. c. 17). In the meantime, France had introduced it by the Law of March 18, 1806. This law concerned generally the industries of Lyon; section 3 of Title II, entitled "the preservation of ownership of designs," in articles 14 to 19 dealt with the protection of designs of the factories of Lyon through deposit and registration in the archives of the trade councils of each industry. The French law, however, in opposition to the system of temporary privilege of exclusive use of the design provided by the English act, gave to the creator of the design the option to reserve for himself the exclusive ownership of the design for all time. In this regard, the French law has not been followed. Only in Belgium the law was the same before 1883, because the French law of 1806 was extended to Belgium at its annexation to France by Napoleon, and it has been in force in Belgium ever since. In all other countries, the privilege of exclusive use of designs and models was much shorter than that of patents. This is easy to explain. The service performed by the creator of a design or model for the progress of industry is small, and the state therefore declines to curtail the freedom of industry to a great extent. On the other hand, designs and models are concerned with the form or shape of things, and the latter change very often with the fashion.

The conception of design or model was not the same everywhere. In the United States, designs were assimilated to inventions in many respects, while in other countries they were considered creations similar to artistic works. This differentiation was reflected in the whole regime of national regulation and protection, especially in the conditions and formalities of deposit or registration of designs, the term of protection, and the obligations of the registrant or depositor.[1]

In all the countries referred to above, the design or model, protection for which was sought, was to be filed with the administration. In France and Belgium the sample of the design or model was deposited under envelope, sealed and signed. In Austria-Hungary

1. See the specific articles indicated with the legislative act of each country, in the previous footnote.

and Germany it might be deposited sealed or unsealed. In Italy, Great Britain, and the United States the drawings, photographs, tracings, or copies of the design were deposited unsealed.

In the last two countries the same system of previous examination of the design prevailed as in the case of patents.

The condition of novelty of the design also caused difficulties here. The facts of publication in all the countries were fatal, irrespective of the country where they took place. In Great Britain alone these facts were taken into account only if they took place within the country.

In France and Belgium, in case of a dispute as to the ownership of a design, the parcels deposited by the parties were opened, and a certificate was given to the manufacturer who had priority. The same procedure was followed in Germany and Austria-Hungary as to designs deposited under seal, whereas with unsealed designs, inspection by the public was always possible. In Great Britain, inspection was not open to the public during the existence of the privilege of exclusive use of the design. Anyone might, however, on producing a registered design, inquire whether the privilege still existed and, if so, as from what date. In the United States and Italy, the provisions as to patents were applicable, inspection being always possible.

No two states provided uniformly on the question of term of protection. In England, it was five years. In Italy, two years. In the United States, three years and a half, or seven, or fourteen, at the election of the applicant. In Austria-Hungary, any term up to three years, and in Germany, one to three years, or up to fifteen years if the applicant applied for an extension. As has already been said, in France and Belgium, on depositing the sample, the applicant had the option to declare whether he reserved the exclusive ownership during one, two, or three years, or for all time.

In Great Britain, the applicant was required to state in his application the class or classes of goods in which he desired his design to be registered; he was protected only against the copying or reproducing of his design in the specified class or classes of goods. Moreover, the fact that the design was copyrighted had to be marked on goods sold. Upon failure to do so, the copyright ceased. Neither the former limitation nor the latter obligation existed in any other country.

Italy and Austria-Hungary imposed the obligation that the design or model should be used in the country within one year after its registration. No other country imposed such obligation. In Great Britain, however, the copyright in the design ceased if it was not used in the country within six months of its registration, while it was used in manufacture in any foreign country.

In Austria-Hungary there was the further obligation not to import articles with the design or model manufactured in a foreign country; otherwise the privilege of exclusive use was forfeited.

§ **21. Registration of designs or models of foreigners.** Foreigners as well as nationals might register their designs in Great Britain, the United States, Italy, and Austria-Hungary. In Germany, a distinction was made between foreigners having their industrial establishments in Germany and all others. The former were protected as nationals for their goods manufactured in Germany. The other foreigners were protected only if there was a treaty to that effect with their country. In France, by a decree of 1861, foreigners might register their designs and models in the registry of the respective trade-councils at Paris if diplomatic conventions had established reciprocal treatment for the protection of designs and models with their own country. A decree of 1873 allowed the same privilege to foreigners if the legislation of their country secured to Frenchmen the same protection. In Belgium, no foreigner could acquire ownership in a design by deposit.

The situation, therefore, before the Convention of 1883, as to the international protection of designs and models was very inadequate. Most of the countries afforded no protection at all to this kind of industrial property. Three out of the seven countries possessing legislation as to designs did not protect foreigners. Germany required an international agreement to that effect, and France made it conditional on the existence of legislation protecting Frenchmen. The requirement of non-publication of the design before the filing of the application for registration or deposit might prevent registration by foreigners, even in the countries where this was possible theoretically. The obligation in Austria-Hungary not to import any articles manufactured in a foreign country with the design, and the obligation in the same country and in Italy to use the design in manufacture in the country within one year, and in Great Britain within six months, might cause a forfeiture of the privilege of foreigners in these countries. It has already been seen that both these obligations were important, especially to foreigners. They constituted a greater handicap in the case of designs, than in that of patents, because of the short term of the exclusive privilege in a design.

III. Trade Marks

§ **22. General remarks.** The protection of trade marks does not involve any element of monopoly. It is the individual interest of advantageous business relations, and the social interest in furthering fair dealing and protecting the public against fraud, which are secured by the protection of the distinctive devices to which the name trade mark has been applied. Already, before the Industrial Property Union Convention of 1883 was entered into, it had come to be generally understood that the protection of trade marks is nothing less than the protection of business. Thus, in practically all the countries trade marks were protected. Even where there was no special trade-mark legislation, fraudulent infringements and, generally, fraudulent acts in respect to them were prohibited and punished. In most of the countries the system of registration of trade marks was introduced by the middle of the last century. It purports to give notice to the public of the registrant's adoption and ownership of a mark when, because of the extension of market possibilities in modern times, a notice by the mere use of the mark is no longer always possible.

As in the case of patents and designs, the trade-mark laws of the various countries presented many divergences. Those affecting foreigners particularly referred to the subject-matter of trade marks, conditions and formalities of registration, administrative procedure, and the legal effects of registration and their duration.

§ **23. What may be registered as a trade mark.** A trade mark is primarily a mark, a symbol or device which marks out and distinguishes the merchandise of one producer from that of another. In order that it may perform the function of identifying and distinguishing, it must be affixed or attached to the merchandise itself or to its container, and it must be obtrusive enough to thrust itself upon the attention of the buyer. Especially, it must be uncommon, odd, that is, distinctive. The law everywhere agreed on this, but when it came to specify what mark is distinctive and what is not, the agreement disappeared.[1] In some countries the law simply provided that the mark, in order to be admitted for registration, should be capable of distinguishing the goods of one producer from those of another. These countries were Belgium, Chile, Denmark, Germany, Portugal, the Netherlands, Spain, Switzerland, the United States, and Venezuela. In these countries, however, with the exception of Chile and Venezuela, the law expressly excluded certain things that could not constitute trade marks. In other countries an enumeration of things which might constitute a trade mark was added to that definition by way of illustration. These countries were: France, Great Britain, Italy, Austria-Hungary, Argentina, Uruguay, Brazil, and Rumania. But these again, with the exception of France, Great Britain, and Italy, expressly excluded certain things from being registered as trade marks.

These negative or affirmative definitions of what might be registered and protected as a trade mark resulted in great differences between the laws of the various countries.

1. The legislative acts and their specific provisions which are considered here are:

Argentina, Law of August 14, 1876, arts. 1, 3, 4, 11, 42 (*Registro Nacional*, 1876, p. 406).

Austria-Hungary, Law of December 7, 1858, §§ 1, 2, 3, 5, 9, 27, 30 (*Reichsgesetzblatt*, 1858, p. 688).

Belgium, Law of April 1, 1879, arts. 1, 3, 6 (*Pasinomie*, 1879, p. 66).

Chile, Law of November 12, 1874, arts. 1, 2, 3, 5, 7 (*Boletìn de las Leyes*, 1874, II, 414).

Brazil, Decree of October 23, 1875, arts. 1, 5, 13, 15, 16, 17 (*Collecção das Leis*, 1875, I, 179).

Denmark, Law of July 2, 1880, arts. 1, 6, 7, 12, 19 (*Lovtidende for Danmark*, 1880, p. 515).

France, Law of June 23, 1857, arts. 1, 2, 3, 9 (*Bulletin des Lois*, 1857, I, 1331).

Germany, Law of November 30, 1874, §§ 1, 4, 5, 8, 20 (*Reichsgesetzblatt*, 1874, p. 143).

Great Britain, Act of August 25, 1883, part IV, §§ 62, 64, 68, 69, 72, 73, 74, 75, 76, 79, 86, 103 (46 & 47 Vict. c. 57).

Italy, Law of August 30, 1868, arts. 1, 4, 9, and Decree of February 7, 1869, art. 19 (*Raccolta Ufficiale*, 1868, p. 1336; 1869, p. 125).

The Netherlands, Law of May 25, 1880, arts. 1, 2, 3, 8, 9 (*Staatsblad*, 1880, No. 85).

Portugal, Law of June 4, 1883, arts. 1, 4, 5, 6, 28, 29 (*Collecção Official*, 1883, p. 138).

Rumania, Law of April 15–27, 1879, arts. 1, 2, 7, 8, 10, 11 (*Recueil Général de Législation, Bureau International de la Propriété Industrielle*, Berne, 1898, II, 334).

Spain, Royal Decrees of November 20, 1850, arts. 5, 7, 8, 9, and August 14, 1873 (*Colección Legislativa*, 1850, III, 319; 1873, II, 204).

Switzerland, Law of December 19, 1879, arts. 2, 4, 5, 7, 8, 12, 35 (*Recueil Officiel*, N. S., V, 35).

United States, Act of March 3, 1881, §§ 1, 2, 3, 5, 7 (21 *Stat. at Large*, 502).

Uruguay, Law of March 1, 1877, arts. 2, 4, 5, 12, 43 (*Colección Legislativa*, 1873–1878, p. 524).

Venezuela, Law of May 24, 1877, arts. 1, 4, 7, 9, 16 (*Recopilatión de Leyes y Decretos*, VII, 534).

A very general exception concerned the personal name of a producer. This could not constitute a trade mark anywhere. But in the United States and Venezuela, the name of the applicant, in general—namely, of an individual, firm, or corporation—was not admitted to registration. In Great Britain, the name of an individual or firm might be a trade mark, if printed, impressed, or woven in some particular and distinctive manner. In Italy and Great Britain, a written signature (or a copy thereof) of the firm or individual applying for registration was a good trade mark.

Another general exception was that of marks, terms, or descriptive names of general use, and of marks containing scandalous or immoral representations.

In Germany, Austria, Denmark, the Netherlands, Rumania, Spain, and Switzerland, marks containing public armorial bearings were not admitted to registration. In Argentina and Uruguay all letters, words, names, or distinctive signs used in the service of the State were excluded.

An important exception in many countries concerned marks consisting exclusively of figures, letters, or a single word, such as the marks "4711" or "AAA." Such marks were excluded in Germany, Austria-Hungary, Denmark, Portugal, the Netherlands, Brazil, and Switzerland. In Rumania, marks consisting only of letters or monograms were excluded. In Great Britain and Italy, figures, letters, and single words were not admitted; but in the former, a word if it were a fancy one and not common, might constitute a trade mark by itself. In France, the United States, Spain, and Belgium, marks consisting of figures or letters were admitted to registration. In Portugal, one could not make the products of his industry or articles of his trade appear in his trade mark.

Another important exception was that of the use of a deceptive name in a mark. In Portugal, Denmark, and Austria-Hungary, the law provided that no mark might contain the personal or firm name of any other person than the applicant unless the former had authorized such use. But in Austria-Hungary, the restriction concerned only the unauthorized use of the name of a citizen, so that one might use a personal or firm name of a foreigner. In Denmark and Portugal also, the mark could not contain the name of a place which was not the one where the goods were manufactured. But in Portugal this might be done if it were used by tradition for the products of a certain region, and if they were known generally by the name of a locality. In such case, however, the Portuguese law provided that the personal or firm name of the producer should be included in the trade mark, and besides, in case of wine, the name of the place where the wine was first prepared and of the country where this place was situated. In England also, the Comptroller of the Patent Office did not register as a part of a mark any words the exclusive use of which would be disentitled to protection by reason of their being calculated to deceive.

Very special was the situation of trade marks in Italy, where it was required that every mark should show the place of origin, the factory, and the trade, so that there might be ascertained the name of the person, the firm, and the establishment where the goods were coming from. Only in case of cattle or small articles, a special abbreviation (*sigla*), or any other equivalent sign, was admitted as a trade mark.

§ 24. Formalities, conditions, and procedure of registration. A producer or merchant who wished to have his trade mark protected should apply for its registration. The application should be prepared in accordance with the legal regulations of each country, and be accompanied by samples or copies of the mark, and so forth. There was no condition of novelty of the mark similar to that required in the case of inventions. Its use by the applicant prior to the application for registration did not render the mark inadmissible to registration. But the mark should be new in the sense that it should not infringe on another's mark. Also it should be registrable according to the law of each country. On the question whether a mark filed for registration satisfied these two conditions, the law of the various countries followed three different systems.

In most countries the system of registration without previous examination prevailed. The mark, unless it was expressly excepted by the law, was registered at once and published by the administration a short time afterwards. If it infringed on a mark already registered, or if it was not a valid mark, it might be cancelled by the courts on application by the interested party.

In the United States, Great Britain, the Netherlands, and Spain, on the contrary, the system of previous examination of the mark prevailed. But, whereas in Spain the Director of the Conservatory of Arts reported on each application merely whether the mark had been registered before for articles of the same kind, in the other three countries the procedure was more elaborate. In the United States, on an application for registration of a trade mark the Commissioner of Patents decided on the lawfulness of the claim to the alleged mark, and he refused to register a mark which infringed, directly or indirectly, not only a registered, but also a known trade mark owned by another. In the Netherlands, a description of the trade mark was published by the applicant and by the tribunal of his place of domicile; any person might oppose the registration within six months. In Great Britain, the Comptroller of the Patent Office advertised the application, and oppositions might be filed within two months. The Comptroller might, however, *ex officio*, refuse to register a mark identical or very nearly resembling a mark already on the register, or one containing deceptive words.

In Switzerland, a third system was provided for by the law. If the Federal Office noticed that the mark was not new in its essential elements and infringed another mark, it sent a confidential notice to the applicant, and he might, at his election, insist on the application or withdraw it.

In regard to the United States, it should be recalled that the Act of March 3, 1881, dealt only with registration of trade marks used in commerce with foreign nations and with the Indian tribes. No trade mark could be registered, therefore, unless the same appeared to have been lawfully used by the applicant in foreign commerce or in commerce with the Indian tribes.

§ 25. Legal effects of registration and their duration. In most countries the registration was merely a means of giving notice to the public of the adoption and use of the mark by a manufacturer or merchant. This did not settle the question of ownership of the mark, which continued to depend on priority of use and not on priority of registration. To this effect was the law of the United States, France, Belgium, Italy, Switzerland, Denmark, Rumania, Brazil, and Venezuela.

In a number of countries registration amounted to acquisition of ownership in the mark. A producer or merchant who adopted and used a trade mark in these countries, but did not register it, could not prevail against another who registered it later. This was so in Austria-Hungary, Germany, the Netherlands, Spain, Chile, Argentina, and Uruguay.

But in Great Britain and Portugal, another system prevailed. The registration for some time was only *prima facie* evidence of ownership in the trade mark; but after a certain period of time it became conclusive evidence. In Great Britain, this period was five years after the registration, and in Portugal six months. But in the latter country, even within six months after registration, the person who had used it previously could not ask cancellation of the registered mark if he had been using it for more than six months without applying for registration.

In all the countries, with the exception of Austria-Hungary, Belgium, Italy, Spain, and Portugal, a trade mark was removed from the register unless the registered owner renewed the registration after a number of years. In the United States and Venezuela the legal effects of registration lasted thirty years. In France, Switzerland, the Netherlands, Rumania, and Brazil, fifteen years. In Great Britain, fourteen and in Germany, Denmark, Chile, Argentina, and Uruguay, ten years.

Only in Great Britain and Denmark, however, a notice that the mark would be removed from the register unless the registration was renewed was sent to the registered owner before the expiration of the fixed period. In Great Britain, restoration of the trade mark in the register was possible.

§ 26. How far diversities of trade-mark law affected foreigners. Assuming that foreigners could register their trade marks under the same conditions as nationals, the above described diversities of law would offer many obstacles to their protection. Particularly important were the differences of law as to the constitutive elements of a valid mark. A person might adopt and use a mark which could be registered and protected according to the law of his own country but not of the other countries in which he desired to be protected. Thus, in these other countries his trade mark might be freely imitated and the goodwill of his business be taken away. In fact, such cases were very usual, and the so-called "piracy" of trade marks was one of the serious dangers successful business had to face. Whenever no difficulty as to the form of the mark existed, foreigners needed to apply for registration of their marks in every country in which they desired to be protected, and in such case satisfy the requirements and formalities of each law, and pay various charges to agents representing them, and many fees and taxes.

Next, there was the divergence of the laws concerning the effects of registration. Whenever registration was the basis of ownership, foreigners could not prevail against persons who had registered the same marks in their own names, although such registration was wrongful. And in countries in which priority of use of the mark was the basis of ownership, foreigners either could not prevail against a prior registration or would have to show a prior use within the country. Lastly, in case a person had registered a mark in more than one country, he had to see that a timely renewal of registration was made in each country at the various periods when the effects of registration terminated.

§ 27. Registration of trade marks by foreigners. The assumption made in the previous section that foreigners could register their trade marks in the same way as nationals is true in part only. Original acquisition of trade-mark rights by foreigners was in no way different from that by nationals. Indeed, in many countries a distinction was made between nationals and foreigners having industrial or commercial establishments in the country and nationals and foreigners having such establishments abroad. Trade marks of the first two groups, applied on goods produced in the country, enjoyed an identical protection. The protection of such marks of foreigners as well as nationals was imposed by the social interest in the protection of national industry and trade.

The question of recognition and enforcement of trade-mark rights acquired abroad arose in respect of trade marks on goods produced by nationals or foreigners in a foreign country. These trade marks were not protected in most countries unless there existed reciprocity between the country where protection was claimed and the country in which the marks originated. In France, Germany, Switzerland, Denmark, and Portugal, legal or factual reciprocity sufficed, while in the United States, Belgium, Rumania, Brazil, and Venezuela, a convention or arrangement stipulating reciprocal protection of trade marks was required. In Austria-Hungary the legislation on trade marks protected only industrial or commercial establishments situated in the country.

Only in Great Britain, Italy, the Netherlands, Spain, Chile, Argentina, and Uruguay, was no distinction made between persons established in the country and those established abroad; and trade marks originating abroad were admitted to registration without condition of reciprocity. The same was true for Venezuela as to trade marks of foreign merchandise, the usefulness of which for the country was recognized by the government.

In all cases when foreign marks were admitted for registration, it had to be proved that they were protected in the country in which they originated, and the provisions of the domestic law had to be satisfied. This involved the difficulties of divergences of trade-mark law at to the form of a mark, its distinctiveness, and the rest, which were considered in the previous sections. In Italy alone, the law provided that marks legally used abroad could be registered although they did not satisfy the requirements of the law for an Italian mark. The only limitation was that the foreign trade mark should not imitate a mark already registered in Italy.[1] In Switzerland, the law granted protection for two years to marks exhibited at expositions in the country by persons established in countries with which Switzerland had no convention.

§ **28. Protection of non-registered foreign trade marks.** While trade marks of foreigners, or nationals established in a foreign country, were not admitted for registration in the countries in which legal or conventional reciprocity was required as a condition to such admission, they were not always bereft of any protection. This depended on the effects of registration according to the law of the country concerned. If registration conferred ownership, foreigners enjoyed no protection whatsoever against infringement of their trade marks.

But if registration was simply a means of giving notice of ownership of the trade mark, foreigners might be protected by the law against unfair competition in the countries in which such protection existed and was available to them.[2] They were deprived in such case of the benefits of registration, and should prove prior use of the trade mark, and fraud on the part of the defendant.[3]

1. A provision to the same effect, and one for a right of priority, were contained in the British Act of 1883, sec. 103 [1], [3]; but this act was passed after the signing of the Industrial Property Convention of 1883.

2. See on this, *infra*, § 34. In France, protection of non-registered foreign trade marks was denied in case of lack of reciprocity, although no ownership was acquired by registration in the country. See Spencer *c.* Peigney, Cassation, January 20, 1864 (*Dalloz*, 1864, I, 451); Stubs *c.* Astier et al., Cassation, February 4, 1865 (*Dalloz*, 1865, I, 197); Veuve Etienne Beissel et fils *c.* Selkinghaus, Cassation, January 13, 1880 (*Dalloz*, 1880, I, 225).

3. See, for the law of the United States, Taylor *v.* Carpenter (1844), 3 Story 458, 463; Story J. said: "It is suggested that the plaintiffs are aliens. Be it so. But in the

IV. Trade Names, Indications of Place of Origin and Unfair Competition

§ 29. Protection of trade names in the various countries. Trade marks are only a means of distinguishing the goods of one producer from those of another and, generally, of protecting advantageous business relations. This end may also be served by the trade name of a producer, by the indication of the locality of origin of his products, or by any other distinctive badge, such as get-up of goods, form of wrapping or container, and so forth. Conceivably, a general law on unfair competition might cover all cases of infringement of another's distinctive signs or badges. Any act contrary to honest practices of commerce and infringing the business organization of another person would be forbidden. But as it is difficult always to find whether or not an act is against the honest practices of commerce, the law might provide in respect of certain of these distinctive badges that certain conduct will be prohibited.

In the common law countries, before the creation of the Industrial Property Union, no legislation had been passed for the protection of trade names and indications of place of origin, or for the repression of acts of unfair competition. But protection was afforded by the equity courts, which went a long way toward protecting fair dealing in the relations of modern commercial life. The remedy of injunction especially afforded adequate protection in such cases.

In the other countries special legislative acts concerning the protection of trade names and indications of place of origin were not unknown.

In regard to trade names, Germany, Austria-Hungary, and Switzerland [1] required their registration at the commercial tribunal of the place where the business was established. This was not a condition of the acquisition or preservation of the right in a trade name in Germany and Austria-Hungary; it constituted notice to the public of the adoption and use of a name, which prevented anyone from adopting the same one. In Switzerland, by registration, a right of exclu-

courts of the United States, they are entitled, being alien friends, to the same protection of their rights as citizens." See also Collins Co. *v.* Brown (1857), 3 Kay and J. 423.

1. Germany, *Allgemeines Deutsches Handelsgesetzbuch*, §§ 15–27; Austria-Hungary, *Gewerbeordnung* of March 15, 1883, §§ 44–50 (*Reichsgesettblatt*, 1883, p. 113), and *Handelsgesetzbuch* of 1862, §§ 16–27; Switzerland, Federal Code of Obligations of 1881, arts. 868, 876.

sive use in the trade name was acquired, as well as a right to protection.

Registered trade names were protected, in these three countries, against adoption by another by an action for damages. In cases of fraudulent use on products or on their containers, the criminal and civil remedies against infringement of trade marks were applied. In Austria-Hungary the same liabilities were incurred in case of unauthorized use of the trade name as an external sign of another's establishment or on circulars, advertisements, price lists, and the like.

In Argentina and Uruguay, the law for the protection of trade marks contained provisions on trade names.[1] No registration of trade names was required, but the name of a trader or of a business house was declared to be an industrial property. The adoption of the trade name of another was prohibited, unless by a modification the name was distinguished. A right of action for damages was given to the person injured by any use of his trade name by another contrary to the provisions of the law.

In Italy and Denmark, the criminal and civil liabilities provided by law for the protection of trade marks were also imposed, by express provisions of that law, for infringements of trade names.[2] Such infringement was constituted, in Denmark, by the act of affixing, on merchandise destined to be put into circulation or on their container, the name of another or of his business house, or the name of the location where another's goods were produced. In Italy, the law prohibited the fraudulent use of the name, sign, firm, emblem, or title of an individual or company, and the act of affixing them on the business house or on an article of industry or commerce.

France and Belgium had two laws on the matter; one enacting civil liability and another criminal liability. Article 1382 of the Civil Code of both countries provided that: "Every act of man of what nature soever, which occasions damage to another, obliges him through whose fault it has happened to repair it." The courts in both countries worked out from this text a protection of trade names which always left much to be desired.

1. Argentina, Act of August 14, 1876, part III (*Registro Nacional*, 1876, p. 406). Uruguay, Act of March 1, 1877, part III (*Colección Legislativa*, 1873–1878, p. 524).
2. Italy, Law of 1868 on Trade Marks, art. 5 (*Raccolta Ufficiale*, 1868, p. 1336). Denmark, Law of July 2, 1880, on Trade Marks, arts. 1, 17 (*Lovtidende for Danmark*, 1880, p. 515).

The criminal liability was provided for in France by the law of 1824,[1] and in Belgium by article 191 of the Criminal Code of 1867, which transplanted the provisions of that law into Belgium. These laws imposed penalties of the criminal law for the act of affixing on manufactured articles the name of a manufacturer who was not the maker of the goods. Similar punishment was imposed on a merchant who knowingly exhibited for sale, or put in circulation, articles marked with fictitious or altered trade names.

Thus, the laws of these countries did not punish the fraudulent use of the name of a manufacturer or merchant generally, but only its application on manufactured articles. The fraudulent affixing of the name on establishments, on advertisements, and the like, was not covered by the law. Nor did the law provide against the fraudulent affixing of the trade name of a merchant on articles of trade. It protected names of manufacturers alone, and only in case they were affixed to manufactured articles.

In the Netherlands the protection of trade names could be based only on a provision in the Civil Code, article 1401, which reproduced article 1382 of the Code Napoléon, with the addition of the word "unjust" (every unjust act).

§ 30. Foreigners' trade names. The protection of foreigners' trade names presented the same situation as that of trade marks. Persons established in a country could acquire rights in trade names and have them protected in the same way, whether they were nationals or foreigners. The enforcement of rights in trade names of persons established abroad was unconditional in the United States, Great Britain, Italy, Belgium, Argentina, and Uruguay.[2] On the other hand, in France, Germany, Austria-Hungary, Denmark, and the Netherlands, foreigners' trade names were protected, like trade marks, on condition of reciprocity. In all these countries a legal reciprocity was required and not a formal one through a convention or arrangement. Only on such conditions could foreigners claim in

1. Law of July 28, 1824 (*Bulletin des Lois*, 7e sér., XIX, 65).

2. In the United States and Great Britain the protection of trade names was a part of the common law of unfair competition, the protection of which was enjoyed by foreigners. See Hanover Milling Co. *v.* Metcalf (1915), 240 U. S. 403, 415–416. In the other countries mentioned above, trade names of foreigners were protected as trade marks, as to which no distinction was made between persons established in the country and abroad. See also as to Italy, Grezier *v.* Freund, Supreme Court of Turin, March 3, 1880 (*Giurisprudenza Italiana*, 4th ser., XXXIII, I, p. 690). As to Belgium, see case Ephelin, Cassation, June 5, 1876 (*Pasicrisie*, 1876, p. 302) and Blasco *c.* Spier, Cassation, November 9, 1876 (*Pasicrisie*, 1877, p. 7).

France even the protection of article 1382 of the Civil Code, unless they were foreigners authorized to reside in France, according to articles 11 and 13 of the Civil Code.[1] In Germany and Austria-Hungary the law prohibited expressly only the fraudulent use of the trade name of a national manufacturer or producer.[2] A foreigner's name was protected in these countries if, in his country of origin, German or Austro-Hungarian names were protected. But this protection concerned only the fraudulent affixing of the foreign trade name on products or merchandise. Foreigners were without remedy against registration in these countries — as well as in Switzerland, where registration of trade names was required — of a trade name identical with or similar to theirs, unless they possessed commercial or industrial establishments in the territory of these countries.

§ **31. Protection of indications of place of origin.** Legislative provisions for the protection of indications of origin or the repression of false indications were scarce before 1883. The French Law of 1824 and the corresponding provisions of the Belgian Criminal Code repressed false indications of origin in the same way as false trade names. In Argentina and Uruguay, the trade-mark acts contained provisions for criminal and civil liability against the affixing on merchandise of a false indication relative to the locality or country where the merchandise was manufactured, or whence it was exported. Damages for injuries suffered by false indications of origin could be recovered by virtue of article 1382 of the Belgian and French Civil Codes, article 1151 of the Italian, and article 1401 of the Dutch Code. Fraudulent representations on sales, as to the substance, and sometimes as to the origin, of merchandise were reached in France, Belgium, Greece, Germany, and Brazil by provisions of the criminal codes.[3]

1. See Pouillet, *Traité des Marques de Fabrique et de la Concurrence Déloyale, 6e éd., par Taillefer et Claro* (Paris, 1912), pp. 702 ff. and cases cited therein.

2. Germany, arts. 14 and 70 of the law on trade marks of 1874 (*Reichsgesetzblatt*, 1874, p. 143). Austria-Hungary, *Gewerbeordnung* of 1883, §§ 46 and 48 (*Reichsgesetzblatt*, 1883, p. 113).

3. France, Law of July 28, 1924 (*Bulletin des Lois*, 7e sér., XIX, 65) and Criminal Code, art. 423.
Argentina, Law of 1876 art. 28 (5) and (6) (*Registro Nacional*, 1876, p. 406).
Uruguay, Law of 1877, art. 29 (5) (*Colección Legislativa*, 1873–1878, p. 524).
Belgium, Criminal Code, art. 498, § 3.
Greece, Criminal Code, art. 396.
Brazil, Criminal Code, art. 355.
For Germany, see Kohler, *Der Unlautere Wettbewerb*, pp. 178 ff.

In the common law countries the common law of unfair competition protected reputations existing or created by the use of names of places. If such names had acquired an especial trade significance of value, they could not be lawfully used except by the producers at the place in question.[1]

The peculiarity about this kind of industrial property is that it is not an individual right of a person to the exclusive use of the name of a place, but a class or community right. Any producer of a city, region, or country may use its name in case it possesses an especial trade significance, and he may exclude all other persons who are not established in the city, region, or country in question from using the same name in designating their business or their products. It was this fact that prevented the early recognition and delimitation of the interests concerned. As will be seen in the next chapter, the legislative and juristic effort to adjust the conflicting interests has not yet achieved entirely satisfactory results.

§ 32. Protection of foreign indications of origin. As in the case of the protection of trade marks and trade names, many countries distinguished between persons established in the country and those established abroad, and protected the latter only on condition of reciprocity, so in the case of indications of place of origin, the same countries were reluctant to protect foreign indications of place of origin by enforcing foreign rights in respect to them. The interests of the national industry and trade carried more weight than the interests of the buying public, which was being deceived by false indications of origin. The use of foreign reputed indications of origin by nationals was thought to secure benefits in favor of the national industry and trade, especially in the international market. This also satisfied the bias and prejudice of the buying public in favor of foreign goods. Even when reciprocity existed, no adequate remedy was available in the civil law countries. In the latter, the law provided only for damages to the plaintiff in case of injury, which was difficult to prove in such cases of infringement of a community right.

In the common law countries no discrimination was made between foreigners and nationals. And the same was true in Argentina and Uruguay.

1. See California Fruit Canners' Ass'n *v.* Meyer (1899), 104 Fed. 82; Nims, *The Law of Unfair Competition and Trade Marks*, 2d ed. (New York, 1917), §§ 105–111; Hopkins, *Trade Marks, Trade Name and Unfair Competition*, 4th ed. (Cincinnati, 1924), sec. 68.

§ 33. Repression of unfair competition. Unfair competition, in the general sense of all inequitable acts of competition to the injury of a competitor and of fair dealing, includes all sorts of infringement of rights of industrial property. In the previous sections the special laws dealing with the various rights of industrial property were considered. The repression of all other acts contrary to honest practices in trade and outside the scope of the above laws constitutes the law of unfair competition in a restricted sense. In this sense the acts of unfair competition are legion. Such are especially all acts calculated to encroach upon the goodwill of another's business (in particular by producing a confusion in the public's mind between the goods of one producer and those of another), and acts injuring the goodwill without constituting an encroachment upon it (for instance, slander or disparagement of another's goods). Since the legislative regulation of the rights in trade names and indications of place of origin was very defective before the Convention of 1883, persons had to fall back on the law of unfair competition for their protection against acts infringing these rights, as against any other acts of unfair competition.

But at that time the law of unfair competition was still nebulous. No country possessed special legislation reaching acts of unfair competition. The courts everywhere tried to satisfy the needs of a new commercial and industrial life by applying old legal materials.

In the common law countries a general principle applicable to acts of unfair competition was worked out by the courts: that no man should be allowed to palm off his goods as the goods of another. But this principle was not sufficient to cover all cases of unfair competition. Indeed, the courts under the doctrine of *stare decisis*, and mistaking the applications of a principle for the principle itself, denied every new application of the principle which was not discovered in earlier cases. Thus they found unfair competition only when there was intent on the part of the defendant to palm off his goods as the goods of another. For all old cases happened to be cases of passing off. Similarly, they excluded from the law of unfair competition those acts the object of which was to throw a discredit upon a rival business.[1]

1. See McLean *v.* Fleming (1877) 96 U. S. 245, 251. On the Anglo-American Law see Nims, *Unfair Competition and Trade Marks*, 2d ed., secs. 5–9 and chaps. IX, X, XVII, and XIX; Hopkins, *Trade Marks, Trade Name and Unfair Competition*, 3d ed., secs. 19–23.

In the civil law countries the law of unfair competition was worked out from a general principle of the civil codes. In France, the courts with a great power of adaptability reached all acts of unfair competition by application of the principles of articles 1382 and 1383 of the Civil Code. The same may be said of Belgium, and in a lesser degree of Italy, Switzerland, and the Netherlands. In Austria, the similar principle of article 1295 of the Civil Code was restricted by the courts to cases of violation of a contract, a law, or a decree. Thus, only acts of unfair competition involving such a violation could be reached.[1]

In Germany there was no provision of the civil law similar to that of the French Code, or any other special provision against unfair competition. Certain decisions of the Reichsgericht show that acts of unfair competition were repressed in Germany only in case a provision of the Criminal Code was violated, or a money damage was done. German states on the Rhine had provisions similar to article 1382 of the French Code, but the Reichsgericht held that they were without effect in cases which were dealt with by a law of the Empire. Thus, in all cases of unfair competition involving in any way a patent, design, trade mark, or trade name, the provisions in question were held inapplicable. Professor J. Kohler criticized in this respect the German decisions, revealing their tedious formalism and awkwardness in handling legal materials.[2]

Fraudulent acts of unfair competition could be reached in many countries by provisions of the criminal codes.

§ 34. Protection of foreigners against acts of unfair competition. In the common law countries, foreigners as well as citizens were protected against acts of unfair competition, because of the territorial idea of the common law applying to all persons within the territory. On the contrary, the civil law of the continental countries, being a personal law, applied primarily to citizens and to those foreigners who were allowed to acquire a domicile in the country. Thus, in

1. On the French law, see: Pouillet, *Traité des Marques de Fabrique et de la Concurrence Déloyale*, part III; and Pichot, *De la Concurrence Déloyale*, pp. 299 ff. On the Belgian law, see decisions of courts in Jamar, *Répertoire Général de la Jurisprudence Belge, 1814–1880*, III, 45 ff. On the Italian law, Giannini, *La Concorrenza Steale*, (Napoli, 1898); also in *Recueil Général de Législation, Bureau International de la Propriété Industrielle*, II, 113. On the Dutch law, see *Recueil Général, etc.*, II, 206. On the Swiss law, see Schüler, *Die Concurrence Déloyale und ihre Beziehungen zu Name, Firma, Marke, Fabrik und Geschäftsgeheimnis* (Zürich, 1895), pp. 33, 90 ff. On the Austrian law, see *Recueil Général de Législation, Bureau International de la Propriété Industrielle*, IV, 49.

2. Kohler, *Der Unlautere Wettbewerb*, pp. 35, 57.

France, a foreigner could not bring action for an act of unfair competition under article 1382, unless, in accordance with articles 11 and 13 of the Civil Code, he was admitted to enjoy civil rights in France.

In Belgium, however, by virtue of the Constitution, Article 128, foreigners residing in Belgium were treated like citizens as to acts of unfair competition, and had a right of action for damages.

The provisions of the criminal codes, of course, were applicable in all the countries in favor of foreigners as well as of citizens.

CHAPTER III

BIPARTITE CONVENTIONS, TREATIES, AGREEMENTS, ETC.

§ 35. General observations on bipartite conventions. The protection of foreigners' rights in industrial property was sought, before the creation of the Union for the Protection of Industrial Property in 1883, by various bipartite international acts. There were in 1883 no less than sixty-nine such acts, divided very unequally between the different countries.[1] These bipartite acts deserve a number of observations.

1. These bipartite treaties and conventions and their specific provisions, which are considered here, were the following, arranged in chronological order:

Russia and Great Britain, Treaty of Commerce, art. 20, December 31–January 12, 1859 (XLIX *Br. & For. State Papers*, 49).

Belgium and France, Convention, art. 16, May 1, 1861 (*De Martens, N. R.*, XVII, part I, 379).

France and the Zollverein, Treaty of Commerce, art. 28, August 2, 1862 (LV *Br. & For. State Papers*, 298).

France and Italy, Convention, art. 13, June 29, 1862 (LVII *Br. & For. State Papers*, 766).

Russia and Italy, Treaty of Commerce, art. 11, September 16–28, 1863 (LIII *Br. & For. State Papers*, 731).

Great Britain and Columbia, Treaty of Commerce, art. 13, February 16, 1866 (LVI *Br. & For. State Papers*, 13).

Belgium and Portugal, Convention, art. 16, October 11, 1866 (*Recueil des Traités, Bureau International de la Propriété Industrielle*, Berne, 1904, p. 154).

Italy and Switzerland, Protocol annexed to the Convention on Literary and Artistic Property, § 3, July 22, 1868 (LVIII *Br. & For. State Papers*, 724).

United States and France, April 16, 1869, (LIX *Br. & For. State Papers*, 256).

United States and Germany, Consular Convention, art. 17, December 11, 1871 (LXI *Br. & For. State Papers*, 76).

United States and Austria-Hungary, November 25, 1871 (LXI *Br. & For. State Papers*, 100).

Great Britain and Russia, Declaration, June 29–July 11, 1871 (LXI *Br. & For. State Papers*, 32).

Germany and Norway and Sweden, Declaration, June 19, 1872 (*Recueil des Traités, Bureau International de la Propriété Industrielle*, Berne, 1904, p. 106).

First, the international protection of industrial property, like other matters of international relations (for instance, extradition,

---

Germany and Russia, Declaration, July 11–23, 1873 (LXIII *Br. & For. State Papers*, 58).

United States and Russia, Declaration, March 16–28, 1874 (*De Martens, N. R.*, 2d ser., I, 43).

Russia and France, Treaty of Commerce, art. 19, March 20–April 1, 1874 (LXV *Br. & For. State Papers*, 255).

Austria-Hungary and Russia, Declaration, January 24–February 5, 1874 (*De Martens, N. R.*, 2d ser., I, 505).

Belgium and France, Additional Article to the Convention of 1861, February 7, 1874 (*De Martens, N. R.*, 2d ser., I, 139).

France and Italy, Declaration, June 10, 1874, (LXV *Br. & For. State Papers*, 932).

United States and Belgium, Treaty of Commerce, art. 15, March 8, 1875 (LXVI *Br. & For. State Papers*, 116).

Germany and Belgium, Declaration, September 10, 1875 (*De Martens, N. R.*, 2d ser., II, 216).

Austria-Hungary and Lichtenstein, Customs Convention, December 3, 1876 (LXIX *Br. & For. State Papers*, 1260).

France and Spain, Declaration, June 30, 1876 (*De Martens, N. R.*, 2d ser., II, 189).

Germany and Luxembourg, Arrangement, March 11, 1876 (*Recueil des Traités, Bureau International de la Propriété Industrielle*, Berne, 1904, p. 104).

Belgium and Brazil, Declaration, September 2, 1876 (*De Martens, N. R.*, 2d ser., II, 152).

France and Brazil, Declaration, April 12, 1876 (*De Martens, N. R.*, 2d ser., II, 190).

Great Britain and Austria-Hungary, Treaty of Commerce, art. 4, December 5, 1876 (LXVII *Br. & For. State Papers*, 31).

United States and Great Britain, Declaration, October 24, 1877 (LXVIII *Br. & For. State Papers*, 12).

Germany and Brazil, Arrangement, September 13, 1877 (*Recueil des Traités, Bureau International de la Propriété Industrielle*, Berne, 1904, p. 94).

Italy and Brazil, Declaration, July 21, 1877 (*De Martens, N. R.*, 2d ser., IV, 271).

United States and Brazil, September 24, 1878 (*De Martens, N. R.*, 2d ser., IX, 248).

The Netherlands and Brazil, Arrangement, July 26, 1878 (*De Martens, N. R.*, 2d ser., VIII, 192).

Belgium and Denmark, Declaration, November 15–16, 1879 (*De Martens, N. R.*) 2d ser., VI, 677).

Denmark and Venezuela, Declaration, June 21, 1879 (*Recueil des Traités, Bureau International de la Propriété Industrielle*, Berne, 1904, p. 169).

Denmark and Germany, Arrangement, March 17, 1879 (*Recueil des Traités, Bureau International de la Propriété Industrielle*, Berne, 1904, p. 96).

Denmark and Great Britain, Declaration, November 28, 1879 (LXX *Br. & For. State Papers*, 12).

France and Venezuela, Declaration, May 3, 1879 (*De Martens N. R.*, 2d ser., VI, 505).

Portugal and Brazil, Declaration, October 29, 1879 (*De Martens, N. R.*, 2d ser., XII, 541).

Great Britain and Ecuador, Treaty of Commerce, art. 13, October 18, 1880 (LXXII *Br. & For. State Papers*, 144).

Austria-Hungary and Belgium, Arrangement, January 12, 1880 (*De Martens, N. R.*, 2d ser., VI, 683).

Denmark and France, Declaration, April 7, 1880 (*De Martens, N. R.*, 2d ser., VI, 491).

France and Luxembourg, Declaration, March 27, 1880 (*De Martens, N. R.*, 2d ser., VI, 490).

consuls, etc.), had a certain evolution. Originally the agreement to this effect was inserted in a treaty of commerce or treaty of

Belgium and the Netherlands, October 22, 1880 (*De Martens, N. R.*, 2d ser., VI, 674).

Belgium and Portugal, Additional Article to the Convention of 1866, January 7, 1880 (*De Martens, N. R.*, 2d ser., VI, 676).

Great Britain and Portugal, Declaration, January 6, 1880 (LXXI *Br. & For. State Papers*, 8).

Great Britain and Switzerland, Declaration, November 6, 1880 (LXXI *Br. & For. State Papers*, 47).

United States and Serbia, Treaty of Commerce, art. 12, October 24, 1881 (*De Martens, N. R.*, 2d ser., XI, 744).

Belgium and Russia, Declaration, January 29, 1881 (*De Martens, N. R.*, 2d ser., VIII, 454).

France and Portugal, Treaty of Commerce, art. 7, December 19, 1881 (LXXIII *Br. & For. State Papers*, 237).

Denmark and the Netherlands, Declaration, January 14, 1881 (*De Martens, N. R.*, 2d ser., VIII, 167).

Germany and Austria-Hungary, Treaty of Commerce, art. 20, May 23, 1881 (LXXV *Br. & For. State Papers*, 859).

Germany and the Netherlands, Arrangement, December 28, 1881 (*Recueil des Traités, Bureau International de la Propriété Industrielle*, Berne, 1904, p. 106).

Germany and Switzerland, Treaty of Commerce, art. 11, May 23, 1881 (LXXII *Br. & For. State Papers*, 1003).

Belgium and Rumania, Convention, February 24–March 8, 1881 (*De Martens, N. R.*, 2d ser., VIII, 472).

Belgium and Switzerland, Convention, February 11, 1881 (*De Martens, N. R.*, 2d ser., VIII, 449).

Denmark and Brazil, Declaration, April 25, 1881 (*De Martens, N. R.*, 2d ser., XII, 548).

France and Norway and Sweden, Treaty of Commerce, art. 13, December 30, 1881 (LXXII *Br. & For. State Papers*, 325).

The Netherlands and Russia, Declaration, March 26–April 7, 1881 (*De Martens, N. R.*, 2d ser., VIII, 150).

The Netherlands and Switzerland, Convention, May 27, 1881 (*De Martens, N. R.*, 2d ser., VIII, 172).

France and Great Britain, Convention, art. 10, February 28, 1882 (LXXIII *Br. & For. State Papers*, 22).

Germany and Rumania, Declaration, January 7–19, 1882 (*Recueil des Traités, Bureau International de la Propriété Industrielle*, Berne, 1904, p. 107).

Spain and Venezuela, Treaty of Commerce, art. 7, May 20, 1882 (LXXIII *Br. & For. State Papers*, 592).

Belgium and Venezuela, Arrangement, May 25, 1882 (*De Martens, N. R.*, 2d ser., VIII, 506).

France and Switzerland, Convention, February 23, 1882 (*De Martens, N. R.*, 2d ser., IX, 100).

Great Britain and Montenegro, Treaty of Commerce, art. 9, January 21, 1882 (LXXIII *Br. & For. State Papers*, 5).

Italy and the United States, Declaration, June 1, 1882 (*De Martens, N. R.*, 2d ser., VIII, 641).

Belgium and Italy, Treaty of Commerce, art. 17, December 12, 1882 (LXXIII *Br. & For. State Papers*, 597).

Italy and Montenegro, Treaty of Commerce, art. 9, March 16–28, 1883 (LXXIV *Br. & For. State Papers*, 685).

Denmark and Argentina, Declaration, January 9, 1883 (*De Martens, N. B.*, 2d ser., XII, 494).

amity. Such was generally the case before 1865. Later, a special declaration, arrangement, or agreement was entered into by two countries: and lastly, a special convention for the protection of industrial property was concluded. Thus, in 1883, the various agreements for the protection of industrial property rights were constituted by provisions inserted in twenty-two treaties or conventions of commerce, one consular convention, thirty-eight declarations, arrangements, and the like, and eight special conventions.

Again, all of these international agreements dealt with the protection of trade marks. One third of them protected also industrial designs or models. But there were only two conventions containing stipulations for the protection of patents, two for trade names, and two for indications of place of origin. The Treaty of Commerce of 1881 between Germany and Austria-Hungary, and the Customs Convention of 1876 between Austria-Hungary and Lichtenstein, were the only international agreements providing for the reciprocal protection of patent rights. The first was of a very late date; it was concluded after the International Conference of 1880 had adopted the draft convention for the protection of industrial property. The international importance of the second is minor, in view of the very close political relation of those two countries. The indications of place of origin were protected only by the convention concerning the commercial and maritime relations between France and Great Britain, of February 28, 1882, and by the Treaty of Commerce between Italy and Montenegro, of March 16–28, 1883. Trade names were protected by the above Convention between France and Great Britain, and by the Convention for the Protection of Trade Marks, Trade Names and Designs, between France and Switzerland, of February 23, 1882.

So it may be said that the only rights of industrial property which were protected before the Convention of 1883 were trade marks and designs or models. It is an open question whether trade names, also, were protected together with trade marks by the agreements dealing with the latter. It has been so contended on a reasoning by analogy, and on the consideration that trade names should be supposed to be impliedly protected. The French courts held to this effect,[1] but the

1. Case of Marchand, Cassation, May 27, 1870 (*Dalloz*, 1871, I, 180), and Howe Machine Co. *c.* Onfray et autres, Cassation, November 18, 1876 (*Dalloz*, 1878, I, 492), both involving Franco-British treaties protecting only trade marks. Also, Singer *c.* Dufayel, Tribunal Commercial de la Seine, June 23, 1893 (*Clunet*, 1894, p. 871), involv-

Belgian and German courts decided the other way.[1] The position of the French courts was sound, for both trade marks and trade names are vehicles of advantageous business relations, and it was at the protection of these relations that these agreements aimed. But then, it should also have been held in regard to indications of place of origin and acts of unfair competition, that foreigners were to be protected, at least in all cases when an agreement was made for the protection of trade marks. The French courts, however, held the other way,[2] although they declared that the reason for protecting trade names of nationals of a country with which a treaty for the protection of trade marks existed, was that "the treaty aimed at maintaining good faith in the commercial relations between the citizens of the two countries." [3]

A third general remark to be made in regard to the bipartite conventions in question is that, limited as they were to trade marks and designs or models, they present a progressive completeness as they approach the year 1883. The earlier arrangements merely guarantee reciprocal protection of trade marks and designs. Later, provision is made as to the conditions or formalities which the nationals of the contracting countries should comply with. Lastly, specific provisions are made on questions of validity, forfeiture, and duration of protection.

§ **36. Persons protected.** With the exception of a few bipartite conventions, all used a standard form for the reciprocal protection of trade marks and designs. They provided that "the subjects of each of the contracting states shall enjoy respectively in the other state the same protection as nationals." This provision involves two questions which should be dealt with before any other examination

---

ing the Convention of 1869 between France and the United States; Barracco *c.* Carenon et Tur, Cour d'Appel de Nîmes, June 10, 1905 (*Darras*, 1906, p. 142), involving the Convention of 1862 between France and Italy.

1. Germany, *Reichsgericht*, First Criminal Chamber, January 15, 1885 (XI *Entsh. Reichsger. Strafs.*, 398), involving the Franco-German Convention of 1865; the German Supreme Court protected a French trade name in this case, only because article 28 of the Treaty of 1862 between France and the Zollverein protected not only trade marks, but also the designation and label of merchandise.

Belgium, Kiss *c.* Le Ministère Public et al., Cour d'Appel de Bruxelles, July 8, 1876 (*Pasicrisie*, 1876, II, 267).

2. Sedlmayr *v.* Winkler, Cour de Lyon, December 9, 1904, involving Germans and the Treaty of 1862 (cited by Pillet, *Régime International de la Propriété Industrielle*, p. 153 n.); see also Pelletier et Vidal Naquet, *Convention d'Union*, pp. 262–263.

3. In Singer *v.* Dufayel, Tribunal Commercial de la Seine, June 23, 1893 (*Clunet*, 1894, p. 871).

of these conventions. First, who were the persons protected; second, what is the meaning of this clause which secures to these persons the same protection as to nationals?

Most conventions protected, generally, the "subjects" of the contracting countries, sometimes the "nationals," and in other cases the "citizens" of each country. The term "subject" is more general than the others, and it may include non-nationals. On the other hand, "nationals" and "citizens" are not interchangeable terms.[1] It was a question, then, whether persons who could not strictly be included in the term used in the treaty might claim its protection.[2] In cases of trade-mark protection, every country was interested in the protection of the advantageous business relations of all manufacturers and traders established in its territory, and not only of nationals or citizens.

In some conventions entered into by the United States with other countries,[3] expressions were used making it clear that what was protected was the national industry and trade of each country. Yet, in the treaty between the United States and Belgium, of 1875, it was expressly provided that it purported to protect "the manufacturing industry of their respective citizens."

Whenever the treaty purported to protect only the nationals or citizens of the contracting countries, the further question arose whether nationals of these countries, established in a foreign country and denied protection in their own countries under their laws, could claim protection under the convention. For instance, might a Belgian citizen, established in Argentina, whose trade mark was not protected in Belgium unless there existed reciprocity with Argentina, claim protection in the United States by virtue of a convention between the latter country and Belgium for the reciprocal protection of trade marks of the citizens of each country? It was argued that it would be strange that Belgium, while she did not protect this citizen under her law, should seek his protection in another country. The treaty, therefore, should be understood as extending only to citizens of the contracting countries protected by their own legislation.[4]

1. A Filipino, for instance, is an American national, but not an American citizen.

2. It would seem that Pillet (*Régime International de la Propriété Industrielle*, p. 147) is wrong in the opinion that all these terms should be taken as meaning nationals.

3. For instance, with Austria-Hungary, France, and Serbia (see note 1 on p. 54.)

4. Weiss, *Traité de Droit International Privé*, II, 354; Mesnil, *Marques de Fabrique*, pp. 212 ff.

§ 37. **Principle of national treatment.** The standard clause of the bipartite conventions considered here secured to the persons protected in each contracting country the enjoyment of "the same rights as nationals" or "the same protection as nationals."

Such rights were, especially, the admission to registration of trade marks of the contracting countries respectively, and the enjoyment of remedies against any infringement or fraudulent use of marks. No discrimination against the nationals of the other party should be made. This was so understood generally.

But the United States presented a peculiar situation in this respect. In this country the Act of Congress of 1881 provided for the registration of trade marks used in foreign commerce or in commerce with the Indian tribes. On the other hand, the common law protected foreign as well as national trade marks if they were lawfully acquired. A foreigner was protected by a Federal or a state court in a state, as to a non-registered trade mark, if he proved use of the mark in that particular state. A Federal court, however, protected a foreign trade mark if registered, even though it had not been used in a particular state. But the Federal court applied in such case the Act of Congress, and could not impose any criminal liability, because none was provided for by that act. A state, however, in the United States, might punish as a crime the fraudulent infringement of trade marks of its citizens. Thus, a citizen of one of the states, who is also an American citizen, might eventually enjoy a greater protection than a citizen of a country with which the United States had a treaty providing for national treatment.

A further exceptional state of things was produced in the United States by the decision of the United States Supreme Court in 1879, declaring unconstitutional the Trade Mark Acts of 1870 and 1876.[1]

Undoubtedly, the international engagement of a country to grant to the nationals of another country the same protection and rights as to its own nationals, does not affect the power of that country to change its municipal law by enlarging or relaxing the legal protection existing at the time the international engagement was undertaken. But is it possible for a country to abolish entirely all such protection by the law, thus depriving also of protection the nationals of the other country with which it entered into an agreement?

1. The Trade Mark Cases (1879), 100 U. S. 82.

The decision of the Supreme Court of the United States in the Trade Mark Cases amounted to an abrogation of the acts of 1870 and 1876. Questions arose as to the effect of this decision on treaties of the United States with other countries for the reciprocal protection of trade marks,[1] and on the status of about 8000 foreign trade marks registered at Washington, and of many hundreds pending at the Patent Office.

Notwithstanding the emotion produced in foreign countries by the above decision of the Supreme Court, foreign trade marks continued to be protected because the common law already protected foreigners as it did nationals against infringement of trade marks whether or not registered. The only change brought about by the decision of the Supreme Court was that thereafter the proof of prior use would be made by the foreign claimant, whereas by the registration the burden of proof rested with the defendant. Besides, all treaties made under the authority of the United States are the supreme law of the land, and the judges in every state are bound thereby. The decision declared the law unconstitutional, but it did not touch the treaties.[2] The latter, in conjunction with the common law, protected foreigners.[3]

The case would be different if, by the abrogation of the legislation on trade marks in a country, a total lack of protection of domestic trade marks would result. Would it then be possible for foreigners to be protected against infringement of their trade marks by virtue of a treaty alone? It is submitted that no difficulty, in principle, exists in according to foreigners greater rights than to nationals. Such was the case in 1879, in Switzerland, where national marks were not protected by law at all, and yet infringements of trade marks of French nationals were prohibited and punished by virtue of a convention entered into between Switzerland and France.[4]

1. The United States had at that time treaties with France (1869), Germany (1871), Austria-Hungary (1871), Russia (1874), Belgium (1875), Great Britain (1877), and Brazil (1878). See references in note 1, p. 54.

2. How far the treaty-making power of the United States may conclude treaties concerning trade marks is considered below, generally, in chap. VII, and especially in § 96.

3. See articles by Edouard Clunet, Edmond Kelly, A. Huard, Eugène Pouillet and Professor Ch. Lyon-Caen, discussing the effect of the above decision of the Supreme Court on the Franco-American Convention of 1869 and on French marks in the United States in *Journal de Droit International Privé* (1879), pp. 442–465.

4. The Convention of June 30, 1864, for reciprocal protection of literary, artistic, and industrial property, between France and Switzerland contained very detailed pro-

But it is difficult to see how any protection could be claimed under the mere national-treatment clause.

§ 38. Conventions containing a clause other than the national-treatment. In a number of bipartite agreements the reciprocal protection of trade marks was secured on a different basis from the mere national treatment. One party in these conventions was, with one exception, either the United States or Russia.[1] In the conventions to which the United States was a party it was agreed that

> every reproduction in one of the two countries of trade marks affixed in the other to certain merchandises to prove their origin and quality shall be forbidden, and shall be a ground for an action for damages in favor of the injured party, to be prosecuted in the courts of the country in which the counterfeit shall be proved, just as if the plaintiff were a subject or citizen of that country.

These conventions, then, prohibited only the reproduction of trade marks in use in either country, and provided for an injunction and right of action similar to those granted by the municipal law to nationals. They left out the importation, circulation, sale, or exhibition for sale of merchandise bearing counterfeited trade marks, and several other kinds of infringement of a trade mark.

The treaty between France and Russia, and the Declaration between France and Spain, went a little further. They prohibited also the expedition or circulation of articles bearing counterfeited trade marks, regardless of the country where the counterfeiting took place.

The treaties between Russia and Italy, and Russia and Great Britain, prohibited the counterfeiting or fraudulent imitation of marks alone. But the Declaration between Russia and Great Britain of 1871 extended the protection, by forbidding the exhibition for sale or the circulation of products bearing counterfeited trade marks of either country.

This special enumeration of acts of infringement of trade marks, and the express provision that they should be prohibited by the contracting states, was not without reason. Some of these countries had not yet enacted legislation protecting trade marks of their na-

---

visions for the protection of French marks. One might say that the whole French law on trade marks of 1857 was inserted in the Convention, especially in arts. 15, 17, 19, and 29–40.

1. These treaties were entered into by the United States with Austria-Hungary (1871), Belgium (1875), France (1869), and Serbia (1881); by Russia, with France (1874), Italy (1863), and Great Britain (1859 and 1871); and between France and Spain (1876). See references in note 1, p. 54.

tionals, and the others could not, therefore, be satisfied with the national-treatment clause, which was without substance. The latter sought an agreement by which the countries in question engaged themselves expressly to protect trade marks of their subjects. At least, they obtained a protection by executive justice, when no judicial protection was at hand. Thus, the pressure was greater on these countries to enact legislation affording to their own nationals a protection enjoyed by foreigners. In the conventions with Italy and Great Britain, Russia expressly engaged "to adopt such measures as will enable it to execute in the most complete manner the stipulations of the Treaty."

§ 39. **Effects of the national-treatment clause of conventions on trade marks.** By the national-treatment clause of the bipartite conventions, treaties, and so forth, foreigners were granted the same rights and protection as nationals. The legal and factual implications of this assimilation to nationals should be more specifically considered. Many of these treaties contained no provisions concerning these implications; other treaties stipulated that the subjects of each country should comply with the conditions and formalities of the law of that country; and still others contained specific provisions dealing with the questions involved in the protection of foreign trade marks.

The first class of treaties should be assimilated to the second class. It is implied that foreigners were assimilated to nationals on condition that they comply with the formalities and requirements prescribed by the municipal law to nationals. They could not be discriminated against, but neither could they escape the requirements of the law. Consequently, the citizens of each of the contracting countries had to apply for registration of their trade marks in the other country whenever registration of trade marks by nationals was necessary for their protection, or for the enjoyment of the specific rights granted to registered trade-mark owners. A prior examination of the marks could be made in the countries in which the examination system prevailed. The usual fees and taxes had to be paid.

A mark could be refused registration in case it infringed a mark previously registered, or, in the United States, a known mark even though non-registered. In this respect the system of the law of each country as to the effects of registration was of material significance.

The foreigner might or might not apply for cancellation of the registered mark and registration of his own. This depended on whether registration was declaratory of ownership of the mark or the basis of acquisition of property.

A mark also could be refused registration if, by reason of its form or its constitutive elements, it was not registrable according to the law of the country in question.

Certain conventions of the third class attempted to relieve foreigners from the unfavorable legal and factual implications of the mere assimilation to nationals. Thus, a small number of bipartite agreements purported to make the lawfulness of the form of the mark governed by the law of the country of origin alone. But the provisions to this effect varied with each treaty, were often inadequately drawn, and gave rise to divergent interpretations.[1]

All the bipartite treaties sought to secure the acquisition of trade-mark rights by foreigners, and the recognition and enforcement of trade-mark rights acquired in a foreign country. The latter implied that a trade mark should be owned in one of the contracting countries before it could be protected in the other as a foreign mark. But this did not mean that this mark should be registered in the other country if ownership in a mark in that country could be acquired without registration.

An interpretation to the opposite effect was given by the French courts of a provision of the Treaty of Commerce of 1862 between France and the Zollverein.[2] This provision purported to relieve

1. For instance, the Declaration between France and Luxemburg of 1880 provided that it should apply to trade marks which were lawfully acquired in conformity to the legislation of the country of origin. In the treaties of France with Belgium (Additional Article of 1874), Italy (Declaration of 1874), Norway and Sweden (Treaty of Commerce of 1881), Russia (Treaty of Commerce of 1874), and Switzerland (Convention of 1882), to the above stipulation the explanatory provision was added that the "character" of a French mark should be appreciated according to the French law and vice-versa. See references in note 1, p. 54.

These provisions, of course, did not have the effect of making registrable, marks or terms of general use, or marks devoid of distinctive character. On this see The Magnolia Antifriction Metal Co. *c.* Régnac Frères, Cassation, May 25, 1906 (*Pasicrisie*, 1906, I, 268), involving the treaty of 1884 between Belgium and the United States; and Vautier *c.* Naze, Tribunal de la Seine, January 27, 1886 (*Clunet*, 1886, p. 449), involving the Convention of 1882 between France and Switzerland.

2. Article 28 provided:

"Il n'y aura lieu à aucune poursuite à raison de l'emploi dans l'un des deux pays des marques de fabrique de l'autre, lorsque la création de ces marques dans le pays de provenance des produits remontera à une époque antérieure à l'appropriation de ces marques, par dépôt ou autrement, dans le pays d'importation." LV *Br. & For. State Papers*, 298.

from prosecution subjects of each country using a trade mark the right to which was acquired in the country of origin before its registration in the name of another in the other country.[1] French courts required as a condition to such exemption from prosecution that the mark, used by Germans, should have been registered in Germany and not only acquired by adoption and use before its registration in France. However, when the treaty with the Zollverein was entered into, Germany had no law for the registration of trade marks. The act of the Empire requiring registration of trade marks as a condition of acquiring ownership thereof, was passed in 1874.

The duration of the effects of registration was governed by the municipal law of the country where registration was effected. A number of treaties provided for the case when a mark was abandoned in the country of origin, or its protection by the registration had ceased. As is seen in another place,[2] whenever a foreign trade mark is admitted to registration and protected, no new right is acquired but only a right acquired abroad is validated or enforced. Consequently, the termination for any reason of the right in the country of origin terminates it in the other countries as well. But the removal of a trade mark from the register alone might not destroy the right in the trade mark. This was always so in countries in which registration was not a condition of ownership in the mark. Marks removed from the register in these countries were still possessed by their owners (although the latter did not enjoy the special protection granted to registrants), unless they were abandoned. In such cases it would seem that the removal from the register in the country of origin [3] should not affect the protection of the mark in the other contracting country. A number of treaties contained provisions to the effect that the abandonment of a trade mark in the country of origin terminated the exclusive right to the use of the mark in the other contracting country.[4] They should be interpreted in the above sense.

1. Pillet, *Régime International*, p. 164; Mesnil, *Des Marques de Fabrique*, p. 230; Brégeault, "De la Protection des Raisons de Commerce et Marques de Fabrique Allemandes en France," in *Journal de Droit International Privé* (1879), p. 358.
2. See *supra*, § 10.
3. This might be caused by failure to renew the registration, or by failure to pay a tax.
4. Such provisions were included in the treaties of Austria-Hungary with France (1869), and the United States (1871); of Belgium with France (1861), Italy (1882), and Portugal (1866); of France with Italy (1862), and Norway and Sweden (1881); and of Germany with Austria-Hungary (1881), and Switzerland (1881). See references in note 1, p. 54.

§ **40. Conventions on industrial designs and models.** All the bipartite international agreements dealing with the protection of designs and models were at the same time dealing with trade marks. The national-treatment clause in respect to them raises similar questions to those considered in the previous section. Their different solution here in some cases results from the different nature of the right in a design or model. The latter is a legal monopoly more than an interest in advantageous business relations. Whenever a right in a design originating in one country was to be protected in the other contracting country, it was not a case of enforcement of a vested right, but a new right, a new privilege, independent of the original one. Consequently, each of the two privileges was independent of the other and the destiny of the one could not affect the other.

However, a number of treaties provided that the exclusive privilege to use an industrial design or model in the contracting countries ceased at the termination of the similar privilege in the country of origin.[1]

A number of treaties relieved the subjects of the contracting countries reciprocally from the obligation to work the design or model in the country in which protection by the treaties was secured.[2]

By their assimilation to nationals of the country where protection was claimed, the subjects of the contracting countries could not deposit validly their designs or models unless their novelty had not been destroyed before the application for deposit. No provision was made in any treaty protecting the priority of foreigners against the invalidation of their rights by reason of facts taking place between the time of the first application in the country of origin and the new application in a contracting country.

The Convention of February 23, 1882, between France and Switzerland [3] was very peculiar. The latter country had no legislation protecting designs or models prior to 1888.[4] This convention, in articles 7 to 23, contained a number of provisions in regard to the protection of designs or models of Frenchmen in Switzerland,

1. Such provisions were contained in the treaties of Belgium with France (1861), Italy (1882), and Portugal (1866); and of France with Italy (1862), and Sweden and Norway (1881). See references in note 1, p. 54.

2. See treaties enumerated in the previous note.

3. *De Martens, N. R.*, 2d ser., IX, 100.

4. The first Law of Designs was passed in Switzerland on December 21, 1888. *Recueil Officiel des Lois*, N. S., XI, 71.

and practically laid down a complete system of legislation for the protection of designs or models, applicable, however, only on designs or models of Frenchmen deposited in Switzerland.

§ **41. Conventions on patents, indications of place of origin, and trade names.** The Convention between Austria-Hungary and Lichtenstein provided, in respect to patents for inventions, that the exclusive privileges granted in either country should be considered as valid also in the other country, and that the nationals of either country were to be assimilated to nationals of the other in respect to the acquisition of these privileges. The Treaty of 1881 between Germany and Austria, secured to the nationals of the two countries the national treatment in respect to patents, subject to compliance with the obligations and conditions prescribed by the laws and regulations. However, by a provision of the final protocol annexed to the treaty, it was agreed that, " The publication of the patent in Germany shall be no legal impediment to the legality of the Austrian-Hungarian privilege, if application be made within three months from the day of the above publication." This was the only case of a right of priority given by a convention before 1883. But it is to be noted that this convention was entered into after the International Conference of 1880 had adopted the Draft Convention for the creation of the Union.

The indications of place of origin and trade names were protected by the Conventions of 1882 between France and Great Britain and France and Switzerland by the national-treatment clause. Indications of origin were also protected by the Treaty of Commerce of 1883 between Italy and Montenegro on the same basis. There was no condition or formality required for this protection by the municipal law of either country. The Convention of 1882 between France and Switzerland protected French trade names without obligation of deposit and registration, which was required by the Swiss law.

§ **42. Other conventions.** A small number of treaties contained, besides the national-treatment clause, the most-favored-nation clause.[1] An agreement between Italy and Switzerland provided that the subjects of either country should be granted the protection enjoyed by the subjects of the most favored nation in respect to

1. Such provisions were contained in the Declarations of the United States with Great Britain (1877), and Italy, (1882); of Great Britain with Denmark (1879), and Switzerland (1880); and of Italy with Montenegro (1883).

trade marks.[1] It was not always easy to say which nation's citizens were most favored in the case of industrial property rights.

The most-favored-nation clause was found also in other conventions and treaties of commerce, but not in connection with provisions dealing with the protection of industrial property. In such case it could not entail protection of the latter, as it is generally connected with, and applied to, specific matters (for instance, custom duties, navigation, transit, and the like).

A similar question was involved in the general provisions of treaties of commerce, granting to the citizens of the one country complete commercial liberty, or national treatment, in all matters connected with commercial activities in the territory of the other. The protection of trade marks, trade names, and indications of place of origin, and generally the protection against unfair competition, inasmuch as it is the protection of individual interests in advantageous business relations, would seem to be included in such general provisions of commercial liberty and protection.

However, the international practice and the municipal legislation was to the contrary. For different reasons, the laws of many countries did not protect foreigners except by special agreements entered into with the country to which they belonged. And such special bipartite agreements were often concluded, as the previous exposition has disclosed. Under these conditions, no country could expect or claim to have the trade marks or trade names, and so forth, of its manufacturers and traders protected by the mere general provisions in treaties of commerce in regard to commercial liberty and national treatment in commercial activities.

§ 43. **Conclusions on bipartite conventions.** The net outcome of the bipartite conventions entered into by the various countries before 1883 for the protection of industrial property rights was not important. Trade marks and designs were the only branches of industrial property protected by treaties. Under these, the discriminations of municipal law against foreigners were abolished, and the requirement of reciprocity for their protection was satisfied. But foreigners were very seriously, although indirectly, affected by the divergences of municipal law, as was shown in the preceding chapter. Very few conventions on trade marks and industrial designs or

1. Paragraph III of the Protocol of July 22, 1868, made part of the convention on literary and artistic property between Italy and Switzerland. LVIII *Br. & For. State Papers*, 724.

models attempted to relieve foreigners from the obstacles to their protection caused by such diversities of municipal law.[1]

Besides, the provisions for the protection of trade marks or designs, and the rest, were often contained in treaties of commerce, and they followed the uncertainty and unstableness of these treaties. Even the separate agreements or conventions were usually entered into with the provision that they should last until denunciation by either party. Thus private rights were exposed to sudden changes. Only a small number of agreements provided that they were to remain in effect until one year after denunciation by either party.

1. See treaties enumerated in note 1 on p. 64 and 1 on p. 66.

PART II

THE INTERNATIONAL REGIME OF INDUSTRIAL PROPERTY AFTER THE CREATION OF THE UNION OF 1883

SECTION I

THE UNION FOR THE PROTECTION OF INDUSTRIAL PROPERTY

CHAPTER IV

ORIGIN AND HISTORY OF THE UNION

§ 44. The International Exposition at Vienna in 1873.
§ 45. The Congress of Vienna for Patent Reform in 1873.
§ 46. The International Congress on Industrial Property at Paris in 1878.
§ 47. The International Conference of 1880 at Paris.
§ 48. The International Conference of 1883 at Paris.
§ 49. Accession of other countries.
§ 50. First Conference of Revision at Rome in 1886.
§ 51. Second Conference of Revision at Madrid in 1890–1891.
§ 52. Third Conference of Revision at Brussels in 1897–1900.
§ 53. Fourth Conference of Revision at Washington in 1911.
§ 54. The World War and the Union.
§ 55. Fifth Conference of Revision at The Hague in 1925.

§ **44. The International Exposition at Vienna in 1873.** The uncertainty, incompleteness, and inadequacy of the protection of foreigners' rights of industrial property afforded by the municipal law of the various countries, and the bipartite conventions entered into before 1883, have been described in the two preceding chapters. The lack of adequate protection of foreign patents and inventions became especially apparent when the government of Austria-Hungary invited the different countries to an international exposition to be opened at Vienna in 1873. In various countries doubts were expressed as to the willingness of foreign inventors to exhibit their inventions at the Exposition, in view of the inadequate protection afforded them. Even if the inventors were to get a patent from the Austrian government before exhibiting their inventions, it would not help them very much. Because, as it was said in an article in the *Scientific American* dated December 23, 1871, "It was almost equivalent to prohibition to require that the locomotive engines of Great Britain, the telegraph instruments of the United States, and the printed muslins of France shall be manufactured on Austrian soil within a year from securing the patent."

The same article accused the Austrian legal administration of not protecting the rights of foreigners. It intimated a suspicion that "the value of Austrian patents issued to Americans and other foreigners can be easily escheated to the benefit of the Austrian public," and an opinion that the Austrian invitation would be met by a contumelious refusal. This article and the complaints of Americans were brought to the attention of the Austrian Foreign Office by the American Minister at Vienna, John Jay, who, at the request of the Foreign Minister, sent an informal note, on the basis of which a special law was passed tending to protect temporarily, up to December 31, 1873, foreigners exhibiting at the Exposition, from infringements of their inventions, trade marks, and patterns or models.[1]

It was then thought that advantage should be taken of this international gathering at the Exposition, and arrangements were consequently made for a congress to deliberate on the reform of patent laws of the various countries, in order that adequate protection might be afforded to inventors everywhere. Accordingly, a congress of specialists met at Vienna in 1873. This constituted the first step leading to the formation of the Union of 1883.

§ 45. The Congress of Vienna for Patent Reform in 1873. The Congress for Patent Reform met at Vienna from August 4 to 9, 1873. Its discussions were limited to patents. The problems arising from the diversity of the laws of the various countries were not dealt with, even indirectly. The Congress was very keen, however, in discussing the nature of the rights of inventors, and in laying down the rules which would afford them complete protection. Its aim was to achieve uniform patent legislation in all the countries.

To this effect it voted four resolutions. The first affirmed the natural right of the inventor, which "should be protected by the laws of all civilized nations," and assigned seven reasons therefor. The second resolution laid down an equal number of "principles on which an effective and useful patent law should be based."[2]

1. See the article in the *Scientific American*, also notes of the American Minister at Vienna, special law, etc., in *Papers Relating to Foreign Relations of the United States* (1872), pp. 46–60.

2. It is interesting to note, in this regard, that the system of preliminary examination, and the abolition of forfeiture of the patent for the non-working of the invention in the country granting the patent, were adopted by the Congress (principles *a* and *g*). At the second Congress, in 1878, the opposite propositions were adopted on both these questions. This is explained by the fact that no French delegates took part in the first Congress, whereas they predominated in the second.

International law was touched upon slightly, and only by the third resolution, noting that "the necessity of reform is evident, and it is of pressing moment that Governments should endeavor to bring about an international understanding upon patent protection as soon as possible."

The last resolution converted the preparatory committee of the Congress into a permanent executive committee, and it empowered them to continue the work commenced, "to use all their influence that the principles adopted be made known as widely as possible and carried into practice . . . and to call from time to time meetings and conferences." [1]

§ 46. The International Congress on Industrial Property at Paris in 1878. On the occasion of the International Exposition at Paris in 1878, an International Congress on Industrial Property was organized by an order of the French Minister of Commerce. It met September 5 to 17, 1878. About five hundred persons attended its meetings, either in a private capacity from all countries, or as official representatives of the following states: Germany, Spain, the United States of America, Hungary, Italy, Luxembourg, Russia, Sweden and Norway, and Switzerland. At the opening session the ministers of commerce of France and Austria-Hungary presided over the Congress. Senator Bozérian of France, who was at the head of the organizing committee, was elected Chairman of the Congress.

This Congress took up all matters relating to patents, trade marks, designs and models, photographic work, trade name, and industrial rewards. It divided its work into three sections, and gave a great deal of its time to doctrinal discussion. This feature of its work was blamed,[2] but no adequate system of international protection of the rights of industrial property could be arrived at, unless the questions of doctrine and theory were first well understood and agreed upon.

Several modes of approach to the problems which caused the meeting of the Congress, were possible. It might, first, adopt the method of the Universal Postal Union, and lay down the principles of uniform legislation on industrial property, which by a multipar-

1. See resolutions, in *Foreign Relations of the United States* (1873), pp. 73, 75. Also Osterrieth und Axster, *Die Internationale Übereinkunft zum Schutze des gewerblichen Eigenthums, Pariser Konvention* (Berlin, 1903), pp. ix–x.

2. Pelletier et Vidal-Naquet, *La Convention d'Union pour la Protection de la Propriété Industrielle*, p. 9; *Propriété Industrielle* (1885), p. 10.

tite convention would constitute a law common to the parties to it. This unification of legislation seemed to many impossible. Lyon-Caen expressed forcibly his opinion at the Congress:

Il ne faut pas espérer, dans l'état actuel des choses, arriver à avoir dans tous les pays des lois sur la propriété industrielle qui soient communes sur tous les points; c'est une utopie. . . . Ce qui rend impossible la confection de lois unifiées absolument, dans tous les pays, sur ces matières, c'est qu'elles se rattachent étroitement au droit civil, à la procédure civile, au droit commercial, au droit pénal et à la procédure criminelle. Il faudrait que toutes les branches de la législation fussent uniformisées, pour qu'on pût unifier complètement les lois relatives à la propriété industrielle, et ce n'est pas possible.[1]

It is doubtful whether such a sweeping unification was as necessary as Lyon-Caen seemed to think. However, a unification of the law on industrial property was difficult for other reasons. The Postal Union involved administrative questions rather than private rights. The industry and commerce of a country and its economic conditions did not introduce any difficulty in the matter of posts and telegraphs, as they did in the case of industrial property. The interdependence between the various countries was not as close, and the unity of the world not as real, as to-day. It could not, therefore, be expected that the various countries would consent to changes of the municipal law and to concessions of a large scope which a unification of legislation would involve.

It was in 1874 that representatives of twenty-two states met at Berne and formed the General Postal Union which, in 1878, became the Universal Postal Union. The Latin Monetary Union was already accomplished. Conferences and congresses for the formation of unions for other purposes — as, for example, against the Trade in Slaves, for the Unification of Coins, for the Red Cross, on Sanitation, Literary and Artistic Property, Telegraphs, Weights and Measures, and so on — had already been held in various countries. Such congresses were also meeting in that year at Paris, and in the same building, the Trocadéro. The word "Union" was somehow in the air at that time. The Minister of Commerce of France thought, perhaps, of such a union, when in his opening speech he declared that

la propriété industrielle ne sera vraiment protégée que quand elle trouvera partout des règles simples, uniformes, précises, formant entre

1. *Compte Rendu du Congrès* (Imprimerie Nationale, Paris, 1879), p. 139.

les États une sorte d'assurance mutuelle contre le plagiat et la contrefaçon.

But this was not to be. Lyon-Caen's opinion was, in fact, justified. When the discussion on the nature of the rights of the inventor was concluded, and the Congress took up the existing diversities of the laws in the different countries, it became apparent that the dream of union would remain a dream. The French members of the Congress, more numerous than those of other nations, wished that the uniform universal rules should be taken from the French law, while foreign delegates stood by their own laws.

Thus, while the Congress applauded a Belgian delegate who remarked that the word " foreigner " should not be pronounced in an international congress, while a French orator believed that the Congress should lay down the principles of a universal system of legislation, and a Swiss saw in the Congress the prelude to a universal understanding and the formulation of the basis of the peace and welfare of the world, it became apparent, by the 11th of September, that the only important question upon which an agreement could be reached was the principle of national treatment of foreigners. Such important questions as previous examination of the invention, conditions of patentability, effects of registration of trade marks, were not to obtain a unanimous solution at the Congress.

The Congress might, then, fall back on another mode of approach to the problems before it: it might draft an international convention dealing exclusively with international law questions, in order to achieve, at least, a uniform treaty system.

The forces for unification, however, were strong in the Congress, and something more was desired. A minimum of unification, at least, should be achieved. The legislation of each state should be forced to meet the *desiderata* of the Congress. Thus an agreement was sought and reached on some points. They concern, first, general questions; second, patents; third, designs and models; fourth, trade marks; fifth, trade names; sixth, industrial rewards.[1]

Thus, the Congress affirmed that " the right of the inventor is a right of property that the civil law does not create, but simply regu-

1. See resolutions, in *Compte Rendu du Congrès* (Paris, 1879), and in *Journal de Droit International Privé* (1878), p. 412.

lates." It enumerated the exceptions in which no patent is granted. It declared itself against the system of examination of the invention, and for a system of previous notification by the administration to the applicant of the invalidity of the patent. It defined a design, and declared that a trade name should be protected everywhere, regardless of nationality or deposit.

Moreover, there were men in the Congress who stood for action and results. On the proposition of the Italian delegate, Romanelli, and the French delegates Clunet and Rendu, on September 11 a resolution was adopted creating a Permanent International Commission.

The Commission met promptly on September 18 and 19, 1878. The resolution creating it read:

> Un des buts de la commission permanente sera d'obtenir de l'un des gouvernements la réunion d'une conférence internationale officielle à l'effet de déterminer les bases d'une législation uniforme.

So the talk was still about uniform legislation. The French section of the Commission was appointed its executive committee. It drafted an *avant-projet* containing what was considered to be the minimum of unification. In fact, it was a very long and detailed draft of a complete universal law. Everything that had been talked of in the Congress, even though objected to, was incorporated in this draft. In this form it was presented, together with the resolutions of the Congress, to the French Minister of Commerce, with the request that the French government take the initiative in bringing about the assembling of an international official conference for the adoption of this draft. The French Minister remarked that such a draft, with so many details, encroaching in many respects on the municipal law of each country, and without elasticity, had no chance of being adopted, and advised the drafting of a more modest project.

The French section, then, drafted the *Projet d'une Union Internationale pour la Protection de la Propriété Industrielle*, which was sent by the French government to the other states, with an invitation to an official conference. It was this project which formed the basis of the discussions of the International Conference of 1880. Its author was the French delegate, Jagerschmidt.[1]

1. See *Journal de Droit International Privé* (1880), p. 628; Osterrieth und Axster, *Pariser Konvention*, pp. x–xi; Esperson, *La Proprietà Industriale* (Torino, 1899), p. 42.

§ 47. The International Conference of 1880 at Paris. The Conference met at Paris on November 4 to 20, 1880. Eighteen states were represented, namely: Austria-Hungary, Argentina, Belgium, Brazil, the United States of America, France, Great Britain and Ireland, Guatemala, Italy, the Netherlands, Portugal, Russia, Sweden and Norway, Salvador, Switzerland, Turkey, Uruguay, and Venezuela. The invitation of the French government defined the work of the Conference, stating that

> in case the labors of the Conference should result in the adoption of a number of provisions suitable for incorporation in an international convention, the draft prepared by the special delegates might subsequently be invested with the signatures of the representatives of all the adhering governments, being clothed with the necessary powers for that purpose.[1]

Thus, the objective now was not uniform legislation, but "a number of provisions suitable for incorporation in an international convention." However, at the opening session of the Conference, the French Minister of Commerce and Minister of Foreign Affairs broadened the scope of the Conference. The aim would be the creation of a union which, without encroaching on the municipal law of the contracting countries, would lay down a number of general principles securing the interests of industrial property in the interior of a country as well as abroad. The Chairman of the Conference, Senator Bozérian of France, described accurately the objective of the Conference when he said that "it is the preface of a book which is to be opened, and is not to be closed, perhaps, until after long years."[2]

When the chairman invited the delegates to declare whether they were prepared to coöperate with France in laying down the bases of an international union, most of the delegates answered affirmatively. But the delegates of four states — the United States, Great Britain, Russia, and Uruguay — declared that they had no instructions to this effect, and the delegates of Switzerland and the Netherlands declared that they did not wish to make any engagement. The delegates of the United States shortly afterwards received instructions, but to the effect that

> the internal regulation of those matters by the legislation of this country is so much a matter for domestic consideration and control, especially

1. *Foreign Relations of the United States* (1880), p. 383.

2. *Conférence Internationale pour la Protection de la Propriété Industrielle* (Imprimerie Nationale, Paris, 1880), pp. 13, 16, 17, 20.

with reference to the question of trade marks and their Federal protection under existing treaties, that this Department cannot agree to submit such questions to the proposed congress . . . without the reservation that the conclusions of the conference on the subject must be considered as absolutely subordinate to such legislative provisions as may hereafter be made by this country.[1]

At the same session the French delegate, Jagerschmidt, deposited the preliminary draft prepared by the French section of the Permanent Commission. This was distributed to the delegates and formed the basis of the deliberations of the Conference.[2]

In the second session, on November 6, the Conference started the discussion of the Draft Convention. The discussion began on article 2, which concerned the national treatment of citizens and subjects of the contracting states as to all kinds of industrial property. Two of the countries represented at the conference, the Netherlands and Switzerland, had no legislation for the protection of inventions and the grant of patents. A question then arose whether these countries would be bound by the Convention to protect citizens of the contracting states, when they did not protect their own citizens. The author of the draft answered negatively,[3] and the Conference expressed the same opinion by striking out the word *réciproquement*, contained in article 2 after the word *jouiront*. Thus, for the enjoyment of the protection granted to nationals in the contracting countries, no reciprocity was to be required.

National treatment was to be accorded under article 2 to subjects and citizens of the contracting states. The Conference, however, at the second reading of the draft, added a new article 3 which assimilated citizens or subjects of the contracting states and subjects of non-contracting states who were domiciled, or had industrial or commercial establishments, within the territory of any of the states of the Union. This article was added, at the proposal of the Swedish delegate, as a middle solution between two opposing views. The delegates of Belgium and Salvador expressed the opinion that the Union should be open, and that all foreigners should enjoy, in the territory of the Union, all the advantages accorded to subjects of the Union. On the contrary, the French delegation remarked that the Convention should concern only the contracting states, and the Swiss

1. *Foreign Relations of the United States* (1880), pp. 378–379.
2. *Conférence Internationale de Paris* (1880), pp. 23, 26.
3. *Ibid.*, p. 33.

delegation thought that, by denying the advantages of the Union to subjects of other states, these states would be forced to accede to the Convention.[1]

As the Italian delegate, Indelli, remarked at the third session, article 3 of the draft, which became article 4 of the Convention, was its most important provision. This article concerned the rights of priority. The true significance and effect of the article was not entirely understood by the Conference. This is clearly shown by the fact that it adopted, on the proposition of the Dutch delegate, an amendment which has caused a great deal of trouble. The right of priority was granted by this article to persons applying for a patent, for the deposit of a design, or for the registration of a trade mark. It purported to eliminate the danger of invalidation of patents, designs, or trade marks by reason of their publication or use, or of a previous application by another before application by the true owner. The amendment of the Dutch delegate as originally proposed read: "sauf les droits qui seraient déjà acquis légitimement par les tiers." [2] Had the amendment been adopted, as proposed at first, it would have been harmless. But after successive recastings, it came to read "sous réserve des droits des tiers." The difficulties that this reservation caused will be seen in another place.

It should be noticed that the provision as to the rights of priority was encroaching on the legislation of all the states. No state at the time accorded any such right to foreign applicants. On the contrary, the law of many countries refused or invalidated patents for inventions which received the necessary publication upon application for a patent abroad.

The draft had left blank the periods of priority. The Swiss delegate proposed one year for patents and six months for designs and trade marks. He thought that the period for inventions should be sufficiently long, because of the system of previous examination of inventions in some countries causing the lapse of a long time before the grant of the patent. He mentioned particularly the United States, where the examination lasted for more than a year. However, the objection was made that a long delay would keep the industry of other countries in suspense, and do injustice to persons making the same discoveries at about the same time. In conse-

1. *Conférence Internationale de Paris* (1880), pp. 129–132, 137–138.
2. *Ibid.*, pp. 47–50.

quence, the periods proposed by the Swiss delegation were reduced by one half.

The next provision of the draft, stipulating that the importation by the patentee of articles manufactured with the invention in another country, should not entail forfeiture, constituted a second derogation from the municipal legislation of many states, among them France. In the discussion some confusion prevailed in regard to this provision, due to the diversity of legislation of the different states. Certain delegates confused the forfeiture for importation, which was automatic whenever a single article manufactured abroad with the patented invention was imported, and the forfeiture for the non-working of the patent in the country, which became effective only after a period of one, two, or three years from the grant of the patent, according to the law of each country.

The Chairman of the Conference, Senator Bozérian, did not hesitate to declare that the provision of the French law forfeiting a patent for importation of articles manufactured abroad was barbarous, absolutely useless, and also harmful to trade. However, the proposition of the Belgian delegate that the forfeiture for the non-working of a patent in the country be also abolished, although supported by the British, Russian and Turkish delegates, was objected to by the Austrian, Swiss, Hungarian, Italian, and French delegates, the last two acting thus against their own personal view, from the desire to conform to their municipal law and the consideration that more could not be expected at the time.[1]

The draft next stipulated that trade marks and industrial designs and models, valid by the law of the country of origin, were to be validated throughout the Union. The Austrian delegate immediately voiced objection to the article as a whole. He remarked that a trade mark consisting of figures, valid by the law of France, could not be admitted in Austria. On the contrary, the Brazilian delegate, though recognizing that the provision was a derogation from the Brazilian law, expressed the opinion that it might be adopted by the Brazilian government. On the observation of the chairman that the Convention would necessarily derogate in some points from the municipal law of the contracting states, the Austrian delegate withdrew his objection in principle, but renewed it at the second reading of the draft. Moreover, the Swiss delegate now insisted that de-

1. *Conférence Internationale de Paris* (1880), pp. 56–70.

signs and models be excluded from such validation. This exclusion was admitted; but, against the opinion of the Austrian delegate, the majority of the Conference adopted the validation of trade marks throughout the Union.[1]

These are the most important of the provisions of the Draft Convention adopted by the Conference of 1880.

A Final Protocol explaining different provisions of the Convention was also adopted. The delegates of all the countries represented at the Conference signed the *procès-verbal* containing the text of the Convention and the Final Protocol.

Various criticisms were made of the work of the Conference. In France, the French delegates were violently attacked on the ground that they had sacrificed the interests of their country.[2] The frankness of the eminent French delegate, Senator Bozérian, in denouncing the provision of the French law prescribing the forfeiture of a patent for importation of articles manufactured abroad with the patented invention as barbarous and useless, was interpreted as a desire to make all possible concessions to foreigners for the sake of the Union, which was considered to be a utopia.[3]

Other writers blamed the Conference for having undertaken a work of domestic legislation on many points, when the attempt for uniform legislation had been shown to be unsuccessful, instead of restricting itself to the drafting of an international agreement for the recognition and protection of rights of industrial property acquired abroad.[4]

It undoubtedly is true that the Conference surpassed the limits fixed by the invitation of the French government, but it did not go as far as the Congress of 1878 wished to go. That Congress was too ambitious in its desire for unification, and it was a spirit of precaution that prompted the French government to limit the scope of the Conference. To-day it is unnecessary to deal with the criticism that the Conference was wrong in attempting to force a modification of the existing domestic legislations, in order to secure a more complete

1. *Conférence Internationale de Paris* (1880), pp. 70, 138 ff.

2. See *Petit Journal* of August 13, 1885 (cited by Pelletier et Vidal-Naquet, *La Convention d'Union*, p. 12), where it was proposed that the delegates should be brought before the High Court of Justice for a crime of high treason.

3. Louis Donzel, *Commentaire de la Convention de 1883*, p. 138 n. Such an eminent writer as André Weiss (in the preface to this book, p. xvii) agreed with this view. He thought that the benefits of the Union were too often illusory.

4. Pillet, *Régime International*, p. 187.

protection of industrial property rights of foreigners; but it should be remembered that the Convention was perhaps in advance of its time. The Conference wished to attain a minimum of unification, a uniform solution of some important difficulties standing in the way of the protection of foreigners, and so far it succeeded.[1] It made the first difficult step in the direction of effective international protection of business interests and business organizations, on which modern international economic life is founded.

§ 48. The International Conference of 1883 at Paris. The Draft Convention adopted by the Conference of 1880 was transmitted by the French government to the other governments. A new conference was called together on March 6, 1883, for the final approval of the text of the Convention and for its signature. The same countries represented at the Conference of 1880 were represented at this conference, with the exception of Austria-Hungary, Turkey, and Venezuela, and with the addition of Luxembourg, Rumania, Serbia, and Spain. A committee was appointed to examine the various proposals or reservations by some governments. Certain reservations and explanations were adopted and inserted in the Final Protocol. On March 20, eleven of the countries represented — Belgium, Brazil, France, Guatemala, Italy, the Netherlands, Portugal, Salvador, Serbia, Spain, and Switzerland — signed the Convention for the creation of the Union for the protection of industrial property, and its Final Protocol.[2]

The last step for the creation of the Union was the exchange of ratifications, provided for in article 19 of the Convention. The representatives of the eleven states that signed the Convention of March 20, 1883, met for this purpose in Paris, at the Ministry of Foreign Affairs, on June 6, 1884. At the same meeting were deposited the acts of accession to the Convention of Great Britain and Ireland, Tunis, and Ecuador, which already had been transmitted to, and accepted by, the French government.

In conformity with article 18, the Convention went into effect one month after the exchange of the ratifications, that is, on July 7, 1884.[3]

1. Pradier-Fodéré, *Traité*, IV, 1192, *accord.* On the work of the Conference of 1880, see also Lyon-Caen, in *Revue de Droit International et de Législation Comparée* (1882), pp. 191 ff., and Devaux, *Protection Internationale des Inventions* (1892), pp. 137 ff.

2. See *Conférence Internationale pour la Protection de la Propriété Industrielle* (Imprimerie Nationale, Paris, 1883).

3. The text of the original Convention and of the Final Protocol is found in

§ **49. Accession of other countries.** According to article 16, the Convention was open to the accession of all other states by a notification to the Swiss government and, through it, to all the other contracting states. Thus, to the fourteen original member countries of the Union, twenty-four more were added on the following dates: Sweden and Norway, July 1, 1885; the United States of America, May 30, 1887; Dominican Republic, July 11, 1890; Denmark and Faeroe Islands, October 1, 1894; Japan, July 15, 1899; Germany, May 1, 1903; Mexico, September 7, 1903; Cuba, November 17, 1904; Austria-Hungary, January 1, 1909; Morocco, July 30, 1917; Czecho-slovakia, October 5, 1919; Poland, November 10, 1919; Rumania, October 6, 1920; Bulgaria, June 13, 1921; Finland, September 20, 1921; Free City of Danzig, November 21, 1921; Luxembourg, June 30, 1922; Canada, September 1, 1923; Esthonia, February 12, 1924; Syria and Lebanon, September 1, 1924; Greece, October 2, 1924; Latvia, August 20, 1925; Turkey, October 10, 1925; Irish Free State, December 4, 1925.[1]

Moreover, the Netherlands acceded to the Union for their colony of the Dutch East Indies on October 1, 1888, and for that of Surinam and Curaçao on July 1, 1890. Likewise, Great Britain acceded for New Zealand, September 7, 1891, Ceylon, June 10, 1905, Australia, August 5, 1907, and Trinidad and Tobago, May 14, 1908. New Zealand and Australia are now member countries of the Union.

On the other hand, Ecuador, Salvador, and Guatemala denounced the Convention and withdrew from the Union on December 26, 1885, August 17, 1886, and November 8, 1894, respectively.[2] The Dominican Republic had originally acceded on October 20, 1884, but it denounced the Convention March 15, 1888, and acceded anew July 11, 1890.[3]

§ **50. First Conference of Revision at Rome in 1886.** The Convention, in article 14, provided for periodical conferences of revision for the purpose of amending the Convention in the light of the experience of its practical application. Five such conferences have been held up to the present time, and very important im-

---

Propriété Industrielle (1885), official part, p. 1. Also in De Clercq, *Recueil des Traités de la France*, XIV, 203; in LXXIV *Br. & For. State Papers*, 44; and in XXV *U. S. Stat. at Large*, 1372.

1. *Propriété Industrielle* (1928), official part, pp. 1–2.
2. *Ibid.* (1886), p. 24; (1886), p. 73; (1894), p. 145.
3. *Ibid.* (1889), p. 57; (1890), p. 89.

provements of the Convention were made. A brief account of each of them is given here.

The First Conference of Revision was held at Rome from April 29 to May 11, 1886. The Italian government, in coöperation with the International Bureau of the Union, prepared a *Règlement d'exécution* of the Convention for the interpretation and development of some of its principles. They were of the opinion that the text of the Convention should not be touched for the time being. The Convention had been in force only two years, and in such a short time its defects or its merits could not be definitely established.[1]

The Swiss government, on the other hand, submitted a Draft International Arrangement, apart from the Convention, for the international registration of trade marks, to substitute national registration in each of the countries of the Union.

However, the French and Belgian governments wished to change the text of the Convention itself. They both attacked article 5, but in opposite senses. France wished to strike out its first paragraph which provided that importation of articles manufactured abroad with the patent should not entail the forfeiture of the patent, and also to make more strict the obligation of working the patent in the country, maintained in the second paragraph of the same article, by adding to it the words, "en y fabriquant les objets auxquels il s'applique." This seemed to France necessary because the Chairman of the Conference of 1880, Senator Bozérian, had stated that the term "exploiter" of article 5 meant "vendre," and that therefore the obligation to work the patent meant that the patentee should sell patented articles in the country in which the patent was granted.[2] Belgium not only desired to maintain the provision of the first paragraph of article 5, but proposed also to strike out the second paragraph of that article, thus abolishing the obligation to work the patent. France proposed also an amendment to article 10 of the Convention, concerning the protection of indications of place of origin, with a view to making such protection more stringent.[3]

1. The *Règlement*, composed of ten sections, contained explanatory provisions, provisions for the accession of colonies and possessions of the contracting countries; for uniform forms of evidence of legal protection of trade marks in the country of origin; for publications of the Bureau; for statistics; and for uniform classification of patents, designs, and trade marks. See *Conférence de l'Union pour la Protection de la Propriété Industrielle* (Rome, 1886), pp. 15 ff.

2. *Conférence Internationale de Paris* (1880), p. 56.

3. In France, at that time, there was a strong opposition to the Convention led by the French writer Donzel. Various chambers of commerce had petitioned the govern-

When the Conference met on April 29, all the member countries of the Union were represented, with the exception of Guatemala, Salvador, and Ecuador. The last country had already denounced the Convention, on December 26, 1885. The Italian government had also invited other countries, not members of the Union. Germany, the United States of America, Luxembourg, Mexico, Paraguay, Rumania, and Uruguay were represented and took part in the discussions.

On the proposal of the delegate of the Netherlands, the Convention decided that the text of the Convention should not be touched, but that additional articles might be adopted.[1] The crucial question concerned article 5. France did not insist on revising the first paragraph. The law of no other country of the Union contained this prohibition of importation, and the acceptance by France of this provision of the Convention was not an important concession on its part, as Pouillet points out.[2]

In regard to the second paragraph of article 5, the Belgian delegation proposed that, if the patentee should work his invention in any of the countries of the Union, he would not forfeit his patent in the other countries for failure to work it in their territory. On the other hand, France insisted on adding the words "en y fabriquant les objets auxquels il s'applique," thus making compulsory the manufacture of the invention in any country in which a patent is taken. In this form, the second paragraph of article 5 would not only have tended to preserve the obligation imposed already by municipal law, but would have compelled countries which imposed no such obligation (for instance, Great Britain) to do so in the future.

After long discussion the Conference adopted a proposition of the delegate of Tunis to the effect that each country should determine the sense in which the term "exploiter" should be interpreted. This was to constitute an amendment to article 5 of the Convention. It was an unfortunate stipulation. It gave rise to as many interpretations of a word of the Convention as there were countries in the Union.[3]

---

ment for a revision of the Convention on these points. See Pelletier et Vidal-Naquet, *Convention d'Union*, p. 12.

1. *Conférence de l'Union* (Rome, 1886), p. 87.

2. *Tratié Théorique et Pratique des Brevets d'Invention*, 6ᵉ ed., par Taillefer et Claro (Paris, 1915), p. 657.

3. *Conférence de l'Union* (Rome, 1886), pp. 91, 99–108, 113–114.

The Conference adopted also two amendments to article 10 of the Convention. This article provided for the seizure of goods bearing a false indication of place of origin, but only in case such indication was joined to a fictitious trade name, or was applied with fraudulent intent. On the proposition of France and Great Britain, and against Italy's opposition, two additional articles were adopted. The condition that the indication should be joined to a fictitious trade name, in order that the goods bearing it might be siezed, was eliminated. And it was made clear that the seizure might be made in the country in which the false indication was applied, as well as in the country into which the goods were imported. On the Belgian delegate's proposition, an interpretation of "fraudulent intent" was also added to article 10.[1]

The *Règlement d'exécution* was adopted by the Conference, following many amendments. The majority of the Conference consistently refused to adopt anything which would compel any change in municipal legislation. Thus, it refused to adopt a uniform form of evidence of legal protection of trade marks in the country of origin, and to establish a uniform classification of patents, designs, and trade marks.[2]

§ 51. The Second Conference of Revision at Madrid in 1890-1891. The second Conference of Revision met at Madrid on April 1, 1890. The acts signed at the Conference of Rome had not been ratified by any country. A part of the provisions adopted at that conference was dropped, and another part was taken up again at this conference in a new form. In the meantime a great industrial country had acceded to the Union: the United States of America. An American delegate had attended the Conference of Rome *ad referendum*, and had reported its work to Washington. A few months later the United States announced its accession.[3] The *voeu* of the Conference of Rome, that all members of the Union complete

1. *Conférence de l'Union* (Rome, 1886), pp. 112, 115–122.

2. *Ibid.*, pp. 126 ff. On the work of the Conference of Rome, see two articles by N. Droz, Director *pro tempore* of the International Bureau, in *Journal de Droit International Privé* (1886), pp. 17 ff. and 257 ff.; also *La Propriété Industrielle* (1886), pp. 43–44, 51–53. For the Protocol of the Conference, containing the Additional Articles and the *Règlement*, see *Conférence de l'Union* (Rome, 1886), p. 179; *Propriété Industrielle* (1889), official part, pp. 44–46; and *Foreign Relations the United States*(1886), p. 553.

3. Accession announced by the Minister Resident of the United States at Berne to the Federal Council of Switzerland, May 30, 1887; ratifications exchanged at Washington, June 27, 1887, proclaimed June 28, 1887. See XXV *U. S. Stat. at Large*, 1372, 1383, 1384.

their legislation on industrial property,[1] had been complied with by Switzerland, which meanwhile had passed for the first time a law on patents and a law on industrial designs and models.[2]

In the meantime an unofficial international congress on industrial property had been held at Paris, August 5 to 10, 1889, on the occasion of the International Exposition of the same year. It discussed various questions of industrial property, with the object of arriving at uniform legislation throughout the Union. In this congress, for the first time, the question of the protection of scientific property came up, and was remitted to the Permanent Commission. The world was not yet ripe for it.[3]

All the members of the Union, with the exception of Serbia, were represented at the Conference of Madrid. Germany, although not a member, was represented, *ad audiendum*, by the Director of the German *Patentamt*.

Four texts were submitted to the Conference, all prepared by the Spanish government and the International Bureau. The first was a protocol of interpretation and execution of the Convention. It was made up mostly of different provisions of the *Règlement* adopted by the previous conference. The second was a protocol concerning the administration of the International Bureau. The two last texts were two arrangements, providing, one for the international registration of trade marks, and the other for the repression of false indications of origin.[4]

The arrangements will not be taken up here, as they are considered in detail below.[5] It suffices to say at present that, as it was clear that it would not be possible to have all the members of the Union consent to certain improvements of the international regime of industrial property, it was thought wise to create restricted unions between those members of the general Union that agreed on such improvements.

The Protocol of Interpretation and Execution of the Convention caused the most serious difficulties. All the questions so much debated in the previous Conference, came up again. The Protocol re-

1. *Conférence de l'Union* (Rome, 1886), p. 184.
2. Loi Fédérale du 29 Juin, 1888, sur les brevets d'invention (*Recueil Officiel des Lois*, N. S., X, 658); and Loi Fédérale du 21 Décembre, 1888, sur les dessins et modèles industriels (*Recueil Officiel des Lois*, N. S., XI, 71).
3. Resolutions passed at the Congress are found in *Clunet* (1890), p. 171.
4. *Procès-Verbaux de la Conférence de Madrid de 1890*, pp. 11 ff.
5. See chaps. XXVIII and XXX.

peated the interpretation of the word "exploiter" of article 5; and it proposed that the various patents obtained by a patentee for the same invention in different countries of the Union stand as independent patents.

The United States, also, proposed two amendments to the Convention. By one, the period of the right of priority for patent applications provided for in article 4 would have started from the publication of the invention, and not from the deposit of the application; by the other, the sanction of seizure of goods bearing a false trade mark, trade name, or indication of origin, of articles 9 and 10 of the Convention, would have been replaced by that of prohibition of importation.[1]

The arrangement concerning the repression of false indications of origin was adopted at Madrid by ten countries — Brazil, France, Great Britain, Guatemala, Norway, Portugal, Spain, Sweden, Switzerland, and Tunis. The arrangement concerning the international registration of trade marks was adopted by nine countries — Belgium, Guatemala, Italy, Norway, the Netherlands, Portugal, Spain, Sweden, and Switzerland.

The Conference adopted unanimously the proposition of the Protocol establishing the independent status of patents taken out by the patentee for the same invention in several countries.[2]

The struggle on article 5 began once more. The United States, supported by Norway and Sweden, Italy, and Great Britain, took up again the Belgian proposition at the previous Conference to the effect that, if the patentee work his patent in any of the countries of the Union, his rights should not be forfeited in the other countries of the Union for failure to work the patent within their borders. France, however, again objected. Article 5 remained unchanged, while the Conference adopted the proposition of the Protocol that the word "exploiter" is to be interpreted in each country according to its law.[3]

Of the remaining provisions of the Protocol, the most important was the one introducing the protection of municipal or association trade marks. It was adopted by the Conference against the objections of Great Britain, Italy, and Switzerland.[4] A proposition of the Belgian delegation, as an amendment to article 6, to the effect that

1. *Conférence de Madrid*, pp. 51–53.
2. *Ibid.*, p. 135.
3. *Ibid.*, pp. 135–139.
4. *Ibid.*, pp. 114 ff., 125, 127.

a trade mark should never be considered as in the possession of the public in any country of the Union so long as it was in the ownership of a person in the country of origin, was objected to by Great Britain, Norway and Sweden, and Brazil.[1]

The proposition of the United States, tending to an amendment of article 9, was not adopted by the Conference. It was explained by other delegates that articles 9 and 10 of the Convention did not impose the seizure unless the legislation of a country contained provisions therefor. Consequently, the American delegation did not insist on its amendment to article 9. The other American proposition for an amendment of article 4 was objected to by the British and Belgian delegations.[2]

On April 14, 1891, the delegates of the countries of the Union met again in Madrid and signed the texts adopted the preceding year. All of these, with the exception of the Protocol for the Interpretation and Application of the Convention, were ratified and the ratifications exchanged on June 12, 1892, at Madrid.[3]

§ 52. Third Conference of Revision at Brussels in 1897–1900. The Third Conference of Revision met at Brussels, December 1, 1897. Meanwhile several events had taken place. Three new countries had acceded to the Union — the Dominican Republic, Denmark, and New Zealand.

A conference for the protection of industrial property had been held at Berlin, October 12 and 13, 1896, in which only Germany Austria-Hungary took part, by representatives of their patent offices, chambers of commerce, and business organizations. The conference discussed the question of accession of these two countries to the Union. The German as well as the Austro-Hungarian report was in favor of the Union, and the conference came to the conclusion that accession to the Convention was necessary, but only after the Convention should be amended in some respects. This conference also adopted a number of resolutions concerning the improvement of the legislation on industrial property.[4]

1. *Conférence de Madrid*, pp. 123 ff.

2. *Ibid.*, pp. 51, 52 ff., 103 ff., 116 ff., 127 ff.

3. On the work of this conference see: *Propriété Industrielle* (1890), pp. 45, 55, 63, 77, 87, 97, 109, 121, 133. The texts adopted at the Conference, and the *procès-verbal* of ratification, are contained in *Procès-Verbaux de la Conférence de Madrid*, pp. 189 ff.

4. See Osterrieth und Wechsler, *Berichte und Verhandlungen des Deutschen-Osterreichischen Gewerbeschutz Konferenz* (Berlin 1898); also *Propriété Industrielle* (1897), pp. 4, 21, 51, 73, 87.

Lastly, on May 8 and 9, 1897, a meeting of engineers, manufacturers, business men, and jurists had been held at Brussels, and founded the International Association for the Protection of Industrial Property, a sort of society of research and propaganda for the development of the law of industrial property. The International Literary and Artistic Association, founded many years earlier, had been an inspiration to the new association, which superseded, by a permanent institution with regular and frequent meetings, the irregular congresses on industrial property, which had been held only on the occasion of an international exposition and lacked the spirit of continuity and unity. The ultimate goal was to achieve, by progressive steps, a uniformity of law on industrial property in all countries. The first Congress of the Association had been held at Vienna in October of the same year, 1897. A long general report was presented by the well-known French jurist Georges Maillard, and special reports by associates from all countries.[1]

The Third Conference of Revision met under conditions assuredly better than ever before. The idea of the Union and of its influence for progress was now implanted in the minds of interested persons in all countries. Thus, besides the official delegates of all the members of the Union (with the exception of the Dominican Republic), delegates from other countries — Austria-Hungary, Chile, Ecuador, Germany, Japan, Mexico, and Turkey — took an active part in the work of the Conference.

The Conference adopted two protocols. The first, entitled "Additional Act to the Convention of March 20, 1883," contained amendments to articles 3, 4, 9, 10, 11, 14, and 16 of the Convention, and an article 4*b*, declaring the independent status of the different patents obtained by the patentee for the same invention in several countries. The second protocol, entitled "Additional Act to the Arrangement of April 14, 1891, concerning the international registration of trade marks," modified articles 2, 3, 5, and 8 of that Arrangement, and introduced three new articles therein.

Many questions arose during the Conference. As many a delegation could not commit itself without consulting its government and obtaining the opinion of interested circles in its country, the

1. See, on the creation of the Association, *Annuaire de l'Association Internationale* (1897), pp. 20 ff. General and special reports at the first Congress, *ibid.*, pp. 104 ff.

Conference adjourned, with the intent of meeting again within the next year for the resumption of deliberations. Instead of 1898, the second session of the Conference of Brussels met on December 11, 1900. It redrafted the additional acts adopted at the first session. It increased the periods of rights of priority from six to twelve months for patents and from three to four months for designs and trade marks. It added section *3b* to the Final Protocol, to the effect that the patentee should not forfeit his patent for non-working of the invention in a country of the Union unless a period of three years has elapsed and only in case he did not give sufficient grounds for his failure to work it. Lastly, it added article *10b*, by which, for the first time in the Union, the contracting countries undertook to afford protection against acts of unfair competition.[1]

The additional acts were to be ratified within eighteen months. This was done by all the countries with the exception of Serbia and the Dominican Republic, which unduly postponed ratification for several years.[2]

In between the two sessions of the Conference, Japan acceded to the Union (1899). Germany, Mexico, Cuba, Ceylon, Australia, Trinidad and Tobago, and Austria-Hungary also became members of the Union before the next Conference was called together.

§ **53. Fourth Conference of Revision at Washington in 1911.** The Fourth Conference of Revision met at Washington on May 15, 1911. The Union now included twenty-two countries; all were represented at the Conference with the exception of Serbia. The Conference interested also a great number of countries not members of the Union. Thus, the work of the Conference was attended by delegates of nineteen other countries — Bolivia, Canada, Chile, Colombia, Costa Rica, Ecuador, Greece, Haiti, Honduras, Liberia, Nicaragua, Panama, Paraguay, Peru, Persia, Russia, Salvador, Siam, and Turkey.

In contrast to the previous conferences, no additional texts distinct from the Convention and Arrangements were presented at

1. See *Actes de la Conférence de Bruxelles* (1897–1900, Berne), 1901, On the work of the Conference see Pelletier et Vidal-Naquet, *La Convention d'Union*, pp. 415 ff., and *Propriété Industrielle* (1897), p. 189; (1898), pp. 2, 6; (1900), p. 201. See texts in Malloy, *United States Treaties*, II, 1945, and XXXII *U. S. Stat. at Large*, 1936.

2. These two countries acceded to the Additional Acts of Brussels on August 4 and October 10, 1909, respectively. See *Actes de la Conférence de Washington* (1911), pp. 14–15.

Washington. The new propositions and amendments, as well as the Additional Acts to the Convention and to the Arrangement of Madrid, were incorporated in the original texts. In this way, the original numbering of the articles was preserved, for the sake of continuity of interpretation and application, and the new provisions, whenever they could not be inserted in the old articles, were incorporated as separate articles with the addition of *bis* or *ter*. The Final Protocol of the Convention also disappeared in the same way; but a new one was created, explaining some of the provisions adopted at this Conference.

No new principle was adopted, but many important amendments were made. It may be noted here that the national-treatment clause of article 2 was extended to indications of place of origin and models of utility, and to protection against acts of unfair competition. New provisions were added to article 4, specifying the requirements and formalities which should be complied with in the contracting countries whenever a right of priority is claimed.

The Conference made clearer the principle of independent status of patents in article 4*b* by declaring that this provision should be understood in an absolute manner — namely, the patents were to be independent in respect to the grounds for refusal and for revocation, as well as in respect to their normal duration. Unanimity was not obtained for extending the period of the rights of priority for designs and trade marks to twelve months, and that of four months was maintained. The majority in the Conference also pronounced itself against the suppression of the obligation of the patentee to work the patent in the country, and the substitution of compulsory license therefor.

The Arrangements of Madrid were also amended on secondary points.

Four questions were left over, as no agreement could be reached. The International Bureau was directed to make a study of them and prepare propositions for the next conference, which was to be held at The Hague. These questions were: the simplification of formalities relating to applications for patents; an agreement for the international deposit and registration of designs and models; a system of uniform classification of trade marks to be adopted by all countries of the Union; and the creation in countries of extraterritorial jurisdiction, especially in China, of a register for the registration of trade marks and their protection in consular courts, without the necessity of registration in the countries to which these courts belonged.[1]

The Conference lasted until June 2, 1911, when the revised and recast texts were signed. The deposit of ratifications took place at Washington on April 1, 1913, as provided by article 18 of the Convention and by the Arrangements. However, New Zealand, Ceylon, Trinidad and Tobago, Australia, Belgium, Brazil, Cuba, Denmark, Serbia, and Sweden delayed ratification, and had to accede to the revised texts at a later time.[2]

§ **54. The World War and the Union.** The World War affected among other relations and situations, the general and special unions for the protection of industrial property. Of the twenty-two states, members of the general Union, eight only — Denmark, the Dominican Republic, Mexico, the Netherlands, Norway, Spain, Sweden, and Switzerland — did not take part in the war. Two members of the special union for the repression of false indications of origin — Spain and Switzerland, — and four members of the union for the international registration of trade marks, — Mexico, the Netherlands, Spain, and Switzerland, — remained neutral.

The advantage, however, of having a multipartite International Convention of Union, instead of bipartite agreements, was clearly proved by the events of this war. Not one country denounced the Convention and Arrangements, expressly or impliedly. It is true that these acts did not retain all their effects during the war. But in almost all the countries of the Union, belligerent as well as neutral, several measures were taken to preserve rights of industrial property protected by the Convention. The war was a case of *vis major*, and was treated as such. The measures taken purported to preserve vested rights from forfeiture by the lapse of periods fixed by the law for the performance of formalities or payment of taxes;

1. See *Actes de la Conférence Réunie à Washington* (Bureau International, Berne, 1911); on the work of the Conference, see *Propriété Industrielle* (1911), pp. 91, 103, 114, 137; Osterrieth, *Die Washingtoner Konferenz* (Berlin, 1912), pp. 1–8 ff. See texts in *Actes de la Conférence de Washington*, pp. 327 ff.; *Propriété Industrielle* (1911), official part, pp. 93 ff.; CIV *Br. & For. State Papers*, 116; Malloy, *United States Treaties*, III, 2953; and XXXVIII *U. S. Stat. at Large*, 1645.

2. New Zealand, Ceylon, and Trinidad and Tobago acceded to the revised texts June 20, 1913; Belgium, August 8, 1914; Denmark, August 30, 1914; Brazil, December 17, 1914; Sweden, January 11, 1917; Serbia (Serb-Croat-Slovene State) February 26, 1921; Cuba, January 3, 1921; and Australia, October 10, 1925. See *Actes de la Conférence de La Haye*, p. 15. See also for ratifications and accessions to the Arrangements, *ibid.*, pp. 18 and 22.

to revest rights forfeited for failure to comply with legal requirements by reason of the war; and to extend periods of rights of priority during the existence of war. These measures benefited, generally, all foreigners.[1]

The treaties of peace undertook to reëstablish the rights of industrial property affected by the war. The task was difficult and the attempt not very successful, as is seen below in chapter XXXIII.

These treaties concerned the relations between Germany (or Austria-Hungary, Bulgaria, or Turkey) on the one part, and the Allied and Associated Powers on the other part. The relations of the latter between themselves and between the neutral members of the Union also needed regulation. The International Bureau took the initiative of an arrangement transferring and extending the provisions of the treaties of peace into the other relations just mentioned. This Arrangement was entered into at Berne on June 30, 1920.[2] It was transitory in its nature, destined to disappear by the mere lapse of the period for which it was created. The periods extended by this Arrangement expired, at the latest, on September 30, 1922. After that date the Arrangement had practically no force, unless rights created under it were involved. The original contracting parties were France, Germany, the Netherlands, Poland, Portugal, Sweden, Switzerland, Czechoslovakia, and Tunis. Several other countries acceded later — Austria, Belgium, Brazil, Denmark, Free City of Danzig, Great Britain (also Ceylon, New Zealand, and Trinidad and Tobago), Hungary, Japan, Morocco, Norway, Rumania, Serb-Croat-Slovene State, and Spain.[3]

§ 55. Fifth Conference of Revision at The Hague in 1925. The membership of the general Union increased from twenty-two to thirty-four between the previous Conference and the year 1925. New states were created by the treaties of peace, and old states felt the need of effective international protection of industrial property. Moreover, new international organizations, such as the League of Nations (through its Economic and Financial Committee and Committee on Intellectual Coöperation) and the International Chamber of Commerce (through its Standing Committee for the Protection

1. The situation created by the World War is considered in section VII of this book.
2. For text of the Arrangement, see *League of Nations Treaty Series* (1920), I, 60.
3. The situation created by the treaties of peace and the Arrangement of June 30, 1920, is discussed by Chabaud, *La Propriété Industrielle et les Traités de Paix* (Paris, 1921).

of Industrial Property) extended their attention and activity to the improvement and extension of the Union. The International Association for the Protection of Industrial Property, which had interrupted its work and meetings, resumed its activity in 1925. In view of the coming Conference at The Hague, all these organizations adopted various resolutions for amending and revising the Convention and Arrangements.

The International Bureau, in coöperation with the Dutch government, having in view the *voeux* adopted by the Conference at Washington and the aforesaid resolutions,[1] prepared the work for the Fifth Conference of Revision which met at The Hague on October 8, 1925. Following the example of the Conference of Washington, no separate acts amending the Convention were prepared, but the new amendments and provisions, as well as the Protocol adopted at the Washington Conference, were incorporated in the old text. Only one separate text was prepared: that of the new Arrangement concerning the international deposit of designs and models, which is destined to create a new restricted union. All the members of the Union were represented, with the exception of Greece, Latvia, Luxembourg, and Rumania. Delegates of the Economic Committee of the League of Nations and the Director of the International Bureau took part in the discussions; representatives of the International Chamber of Commerce were also present *ad audiendum*. Many other countries not belonging to the Union were represented at the Conference by delegates, namely: Argentina, Colombia, Egypt, Guatemala, Hedjaz, Haiti, Liberia, Panama, Peru, Salvador, San Marino, Siam, the Union of South Africa, and Venezuela.

The general principles of the Convention were not touched upon by this Conference. An attempt was made, however, by the American delegation to modify one of the main principles of the Convention. It proposed an amendment to article 2, to the effect that every country of the Union should have the right to impose upon nationals of the other contracting countries the fulfilment of some or all of the conditions imposed on its nationals by those countries. This was sailing direct into the troubled waters of the old "reciprocity system," generally prevailing before the Convention of 1883. The attempt was abandoned by the American delegation itself, which withdrew its proposition.

1. All these are collected by the International Bureau in its publication, *Documents Préliminaires de la Conférence de La Haye*, part II.

One of the most important rights granted by the Convention is the right of priority. An attempt to make this right more secure by striking out the phrase "sous réserve des droits de tiers" failed by reason of the opposition of three countries. The period of rights of priority for designs and trade marks was extended from four to six months.

With the extension of the Union so as to include almost all important industrial and commercial countries, the obligation to work the patent in every country in which one is taken out, maintained through all the revisions of the Convention, became now almost impossible. The Conference, after long discussion, adopted a proposition of the American and English delegations, to the effect that the patentee is permitted for three years not to work his patent, and at the end of that period may be compelled to grant a license to allow others to use his invention. Only, in case such license does not prevent the abuse of the exclusive right granted to the patentee, his patent may be forfeited.

Many important improvements were also made in the regime of trade marks and designs. The repression of acts of unfair competition was put on a sound basis. These matters are considered in following chapters.

The Convention was signed on November 6, 1925, by all the states represented, with the exception of Turkey and Bulgaria. The new Arrangement of The Hague for the international deposit of designs and models was signed by the following countries — Belgium, France, the Free City of Danzig, Germany, Morocco, Portugal, Spain, Switzerland, Syria and Lebanon, and Tunis.[1]

The Convention, by express provision of article 18, and the Arrangements, by virtue of similar provisions, were to come into effect one month after the deposit of ratifications, which should take place, at the latest, on May 1, 1928. At this date, delegates of the Governments of Italy, Germany, Great Britain and Northern Ireland, Austria, Canada, Spain, and the Netherlands deposited ratifications of the revised Convention at the Foreign Office of the Netherlands.[2]

1. See *Actes de la Conférence de La Haye* (Berne, 1926). See revised texts of the Convention and Arrangements, in *ibid.*, pp. 599 ff.; *Propriété Industrielle* (1925), pp. 221 ff. On the work of the Conference see *ibid.* (1925), pp. 237, 252; Osterrieth, *Die Haager Konferenz, 1925, zur Revision der Pariser Übereinkunft* (Leipzig-Berlin, 1926); Plaisant et Fernand Jacq, *La Conférence de La Haye* (Paris, 1927).

2. On the same day ratifications were deposited for the Arrangement concerning the repression of false indications of origin, by Switzerland, Germany, Great Britain and

Before adjourning, the Conference accepted an invitation of the British Government to hold its next meeting at London, and decided to meet in 1933, the year of the fiftieth anniversary of the creation of the Union.[1]

Northern Ireland, and Spain; for the Arrangement concerning the international registration of trade marks, by Switzerland, Italy, Germany, Austria, Spain, and the Netherlands; for the Arrangement concerning the international deposit of designs and models by Switzerland, Germany, Spain, and the Netherlands. See *procès-verbaux* of ratification, in *Propriété Industrielle* (1928), pp. 97–98.

1. See *Actes de la Conférence de La Haye*, p. 595.

CHAPTER V

ORGANIZATION OF THE UNION

§ 56. The Union as an international organization. The Union for the Protection of Industrial Property constitutes one aspect of the organized community of international society of to-day. The Convention of Paris and the Arrangements of Madrid and of The Hague are not only international engagements between the contracting countries for the regulation and protection of industrial property; they are also texts of international legislation, and create between the members an international organization. The study, therefore, of the international regime of industrial property under the Convention and Arrangements should be preceded by an exposition of the organization of this Union. In this respect, the following matters will be considered: the territory and membership of the Union; its executive or administrative organ — the International Bureau; and its legislative power — the Conferences of Revision.

I. Territory and Membership

§ **57. Territorial extent of the Union.** Article I of the original text of the Convention of 1883 read as follows: "Les *Gouvernements* de . . . sont constitués à l'état d'Union." On the other hand, the preamble of the Convention proclaimed that the aim of the Union was to secure a complete and effective protection to the industry and commerce of the nationals of the respective states ("des nationaux de leurs États respectifs"). And the Convention used the term "États" in all its articles.

These contradictory expressions and loose terminology were eliminated in the revision of the Convention at the Washington Conference. The original preamble was left out. The first article was worded as follows: "Les pays contractants sont constitués a l'état d'Union pour la protection de la propriété industrielle." Thus it omitted the enumeration of members of the Union, which rendered the text inaccurate since the membership of the Union was subject to change. In all the other articles of the Convention the word "pays" was substituted for the word "État." This was preferred in view of the diversity in the internal constitution of many of the contracting parties and in view of the example of other multipartite conventions.[1]

Questions arose especially as to the extension of the Convention and Arrangements to the colonies, possessions and other dependencies of various states. A distinction was made between the French colonies on one hand, and British and Dutch colonies on the other, on the ground that the legislation of the first on industrial property was applicable to the mother country as well as to its colonies, whereas the opposite was true of Great Britain and the Netherlands. But the distinction was not admitted, as treaties and laws are different matters, and because in practice, before the creation of the Union, a treaty of commerce with France did not extend to her colonies unless it expressly so provided.[2]

1. See *Actes de la Conférence de Washington*, p. 41 n.

2. See Pelletier und Vidal-Naquet, *Convention d'Union*, pp. 25–27; Pouillet et Plé, *Convention d'Union*, p. 21; Pillet, *Régime International*, pp. 204 ff.

The Rome Conference of Revision attempted to solve these difficulties by adopting article 3 of the *Règlement* for the execution of the Convention. This provided that the different administrations should communicate to the International Bureau the list of those territories, colonies, or possessions to which the Union was to be considered as extending by the mere fact of accession of the mother country. The Rome *Règlement* has not been ratified. However, in accordance therewith, France, Portugal, and Spain declared that their accession to the Convention includes that of the following colonies and possessions respectively:[1]

France: Martinique, Guadeloupe and dependencies, Réunion and dependency (St. Mary of Madagascar), Cochin-China, St. Pierre, Miquelon, Guiana, Sénegal and dependencies (Rivières du Sud, Grand Bassam, Assimie, Porto Novo, and Kotonou), the Congo and the Gaboon, Mayotte, Nossi-Bé, the French establishments in India (Pondicherry, Chandernagore, Karikal, Mahé, Yanaon), New Caledonia, the French establishments in Océanica (Tahiti and dependencies), Obock, and Diego Suarez.
Portugal: the Azores and Madeira.
Spain: Cuba, Porto Rico, and the Philippines.

Subsequently the Dutch Administration notified the Bureau that the Convention should be considered as extending to the Dutch East Indies as from October 1, 1888, and to Surinam and Curaçao as from July 1, 1890.[2]

At the Madrid Conference the matter was taken up again. In the Protocol of Interpretation and Application of the Convention, a provision, number 8, was adopted, to the effect that, whenever one of the contracting parties should wish that any of its possessions or colonies be considered as included in the Union, it should notify the Swiss government. This protocol also was not ratified. However, the British government notified the Swiss Federal Council that the Convention should be considered as applicable to New Zealand and Queensland, Ceylon, Australia, and Trinidad and Tobago, as from September 7, 1891, June 10, 1905, August 7, 1907, and May 14, 1908, respectively.[3]

At the Brussels Conference of Revision the Spanish delegation declared that neither the Spanish colonies nor the Spanish zone of Morocco should be considered as included in the territory of

1. (1887–1888) XXV *U. S. Stat. at Large*, 1383.
2. *Propriété Industrielle* (1888), p. 93; (1890), p. 36.
3. *Ibid.* (1891), p. 124; (1905), p. 73; (1907), p. 157; (1908), p. 49.

the Union.[1] It would seem, however, that the Convention should be deemed to extend to the Balearic Islands, the Canaries, and Melilla, inasmuch as they are considered as maritime provinces of Spain.[2]

At the Washington Conference article 16*b* was adopted, which now regulates the application of the Convention in the colonies, possessions, and other subject territories:

Les pays contractants ont le droit d'accéder en tout temps à la présente Convention pour leurs colonies, possessions, dépendances, et protectorats, ou pour certains d'entre eux. Ils peuvent à cet effet soit faire une déclaration générale par laquelle toutes leurs colonies, possessions, dépendances, et protectorats sont compris dans l'accession, soit nommer exclusivement ceux qui y sont compris, soit se borner à indiquer ceux qui en sont exclus.

Cette déclaration sera notifiée par écrit au Gouvernement de la Confédération suisse, et par celui-ci à tous les autres.

Les pays contractants pourront dans les mêmes conditions dénoncer la Convention pour leurs colonies, possessions, dépendances, et protectorats, ou pour certains d'entre eux.

By the substitution of the word "pays" for "États" and the adoption of article 16*b*, it is now made clear that the territory of the Union comprises only the territories of the specific parts of the world to which the names of the contracting countries properly apply, and only those colonies, possessions, and the rest which, before the Washington Conference, had been declared, by their mother countries, to be included in the Union, or which, after the Washington Conference, acceded in accordance with article 16*b*. Under this article, a mother country may make a general declaration of accession of all its subject territories, or may name specifically those that are to be deemed as included in the territory of the Union or as excluded therefrom. This declaration should be communicated to the Swiss government and by the latter to the other contracting countries.

In accordance with article 16*b*, Great Britain has acceded in behalf of Canada, September 1, 1923, and of the Irish Free State, December 4, 1925; France acceded for the mandated territories of Syria and Lebanon, September 1, 1924; and Spain declared that

1. See *Actes de la Conférence de Bruxelles*, pp. 94, 203, 333.

2. See Statement of the International Bureau, in *Actes de la Conférence de La Haye*, p. 181 n.

the Spanish zone of Morocco is to be included in the Union as from July 27, 1928.[1]

Thus to-day (June 1929) the Union for the Protection of Industrial Property extends to the territory of the following countries: Australia (including the territory of Papua and the mandated territory of New Guinea), Austria, Belgium, Brazil, Bulgaria, Canada, Cuba, Czechoslovakia, Denmark (and the Faeroe Islands), Danzig (Free City), Dominican Republic, Esthonia, Finland, France (including Algeria and the colonies), Germany, Great Britain (including Ceylon, New Zealand, and Trinidad and Tobago), Greece, Hungary, Irish Free State, Italy, Japan, Latvia, Luxemburg, Morocco (French zone), Mexico, Norway, the Netherlands (including the Dutch East Indies, Surinam, and Curaçao), Poland, Portugal (including the Azores and Madeira), Rumania, Serb-Croat-Slovene State, Spain (including the Spanish zone of Morocco), Sweden, Switzerland, Syria and Lebanon, Tunis, Turkey, and the United States of America.[2]

The restricted unions constituted by the Arrangements of Madrid and of The Hague should be understood as extending territorially in the same way as the general Union. They use the term "pays" in all their provisions. Article 16*b* is expressly referred to by these Arrangements in their provisions concerning accession.[3]

Thus, the restricted Union created by the Madrid Arrangement for the repression of false indications of origin extends to the territory of the following countries: Brazil, Cuba, Czechoslovakia, Danzig (Free City), France (including Algeria and the colonies), Germany, Great Britain (including New Zealand), Irish Free State, Morocco (French zone), Portugal (including the Azores and Madeira), Spain, Switzerland, Syria and Lebanon, and Tunis.

The restricted Union created by the Madrid Arrangement for the

1. See *Propriété Industrielle* (1923), p. 125; (1925), p. 237; (1924), p. 149; and (1928), p. 145.

2. *Ibid.* (1928), pp. 1–2.

3. Article 11 of the Trade Mark Arrangement, article 22 of the Arrangement of The Hague, and article 5 of the Madrid Arrangement for the repression of false indications of origin. The latter was amended to this effect at the Conference of The Hague. But even without this amendment, the application of article 16*b* to the accession of colonies to this Arrangement should be impliedly admitted, inasmuch as accession of other countries was allowed and article 16 of the Convention was expressly referred to.

See as to the international registration of marks of colonies, possessions, and other dependencies, Statement of the International Bureau, in *Actes de la Conférence de La Haye*, p. 181 n.

international registration of trade marks includes in its territory the following countries: Austria, Belgium, Brazil, Cuba, Czechoslovakia, Danzig (Free City), France (including Algeria and the colonies), Germany, Hungary, Italy, Luxemburg, Morocco (French zone), Mexico, the Netherlands (including the Dutch East Indies, Surinam and Curaçao), Portugal (including the Azores and Madeira), Rumania, Serb-Croat-Slovene State, Spain, Switzerland, Tunis, and Turkey.[1]

The recent Arrangement of The Hague for the international deposit of industrial designs and models has been ratified up to this time only by Germany, Spain, Switzerland, and the Netherlands.[2]

§ 58. **Position of colonies, possessions, and other dependencies in the Union.** Colonies, possessions, and dominions present, besides the question of their inclusion in the territory of the Union, that of their position therein. Are they members of the Union in the same way that their mother countries or the other contracting countries are? Are they entitled to the rights and subject to the obligations of members of the Union? The rights of membership are, especially, to vote at the conferences of revision, and to receive gratis the publications of the International Bureau. The obligations are to contribute to the expense for maintaining the International Bureau, to establish a special government department of industrial property, and so forth. According to article 1 of the Convention, the Union is created between the contracting countries ("les pays contractants"), and the question is whether colonies and possessions are "contracting countries." The preamble of the Convention, as revised at the Conference of The Hague, enumerates specially, with the other contracting countries, only the British Dominions of Canada and Australia, the French Protectorates of Morocco and Tunis, and the mandated territories of Syria and Lebanon. Thus, the French colonies and possessions, the Dutch East Indies, Surinam and Curaçao, Ceylon, Trinidad and Tobago, and the rest, do not appear as contracting countries.

Moreover, article 16*b*, which concerns the mode of accession of colonies, possessions, dominions, and protectorates, provides that "the contracting countries have the right to accede for their colonies. . . ." This would seem to exclude the title of "contracting

1. *Propriété Industrielle* (1928), p. 2.
2. *Ibid.* (1928), p. 98.

country" from all those territorial entities for which accession is made in accordance with article 16*b*. Should this also exclude, however, dominions, protectorates, and mandated territories, which are enumerated with colonies and possessions in article 16*b*, from being contracting countries?

It does not seem that such an interpretation of article 16*b* would be warranted. Its main purpose was to settle the question of territorial extent of the Union. After the adoption of this article, there could not be any question of *ipso facto* application of the Convention to the colonies, possessions, and other subject territories of some countries, unless a declaration to this effect was made by the latter. At the Washington Conference, the British delegation called attention to the fact that the British Dominions were "countries" in the meaning given by the Convention to this word, and that they should have the right to vote at the Conference. The Chairman, Ambassador Tower of the United States, seemed to agree with this view, and he recalled the precedent of the Rome Conference of Revision, where the right to vote of Tunis was recognized at the suggestion of the French delegation. However, the Dutch delegation remarked that other countries also have colonies with a greater or less amount of autonomy, and no one knew where the limit was to be. In fact, the only British Dominions included in the Union at the time were Australia and New Zealand, and neither was represented at the Conference. Thus the question remained open.[1]

At the Conference at The Hague, Australia and Canada exercised the right to vote,[2] as Morocco and Tunis have always done since their original accession. They also signed the acts adopted by the Conference.

The right to vote is correlative with the obligation to contribute to the expense of maintaining the International Bureau. The practice in this respect is instructive. The Netherlands did not claim a

1. It is to be noted that the term "dépendances," as a French translation of the term "dominions," was inserted in article 16*b* on the proposal of the British delegation itself. Thus Great Britain, which claimed a right to vote for the Dominions, included them in article 16*b*, which requires a declaration of a "pays contractant" for the accession of its "dependances." See *Actes de la Conférence de Washington*, pp. 181, 221, 257.

2. See, for instance, the discussion on article 4*b*, when a French proposition was defeated by the combined vote of Great Britain and Australia, in *Actes de la Conférence de La Haye*, p. 431.

right of membership for its colonies, for which it acceded in 1888 and 1890. The latter are not contributing to the above expense. Tunis and Morocco are contributing since their original accession.[1] No right of membership was claimed by Great Britain in 1891, 1905, and 1908, for New Zealand and Queensland, Ceylon, and Trinidad and Tobago. In the case of accession of Canada, however, the first declaration of accession by the British Government, August 21, 1923, was followed by a second declaration, dated April 22, 1925, by which Great Britain notified the Swiss government that Canada, according to article 16 of the Convention, should be considered as a contracting country in regard to its accession to the Convention. By a circular of May 12, 1925, the Swiss government notified all the members of the Union to this effect.[2] Likewise, Great Britain, by a note of August 21, 1925,[3] to the Swiss government, declared that the Commonwealth of Australia, which had already acceded on August 5, 1907, desired to be considered as a "contracting country" of the Union.[4] Spain, in acceding recently for the Spanish zone of Mo-

1. Tunis deposited its own ratification of the Convention on June 4, 1886, *Propriété Industrielle* (1885), p. 5. For Morocco's contribution see *ibid.* (1917), p. 81.

2. *Ibid.* (1923), p. 125; (1925), p. 85.

3. *Ibid.* (1925), p. 174. By a further note (February 25, 1926) the British government notified the Swiss government that the Commonwealth of Australia desired that the members of the Union be notified of the "adhesion" to the Convention of the territory of Papua and of the mandated territory of New Guinea, *ibid.* (1926), p. 49. The Irish Free State acceded, also, as a contracting country, by declaration of the British government, dated October 22, 1925, *ibid.* (1925), p. 237.

4. The evolution in two other unions of the position of the British colonies is interesting. Great Britain acceded to the Convention for the Protection of Literary and Artistic Works in 1886, in behalf of the United Kingdom and all the colonies. (*Procès-verbal* of signature of the Convention of September 9, 1886; LXVII *Br. & For. State Papers*, 22, 33). At the revision of this Convention in Berlin in 1908, however, article 26 was adopted, which is identical with article 16*b* of the Convention of 1883. In pursuance thereof, Great Britain, at the deposit of ratifications on June 14, 1912, declared that she acceded for all British colonies and possessions with the exception of India, Canada, Australia, New Zealand, Newfoundland, Union of South Africa, Channel Islands, Papua, and Norfolk Island. *League of Nations Treaty Series* (1920), I, 218, 240–241.

In the case of the Universal Postal Union, being especially a Union of postal administrations, only Malta was taken in as a part of the British administration in 1874. (Rules, art. XXIX, *Ressort de l'Union*, sec. 4, in LXV *Br. & For. State Papers*, 13.) At the revision of that Convention in Rome in 1906, India, Australia, Canada, New Zealand, and the colonies of South Africa were represented and signed as separate parties. Besides, by article 27 of the Convention, they are considered as contracting countries for the application of articles 22, 25, and 26, relating to the International Bureau, conferences and propositions to be made in the interval between conferences. For the same purpose, all the other British Colonies are treated as one country. XCIX *Br. & For. State Papers*, 254, 270, 272.

rocco, declared that such accession is made in conformity with article 16*b*. No demand was made for its admission as a contracting country.[1]

Territories under mandate would seem to raise the same questions as dominions. The French government, in acceding for the mandated territories of Syria and Lebanon on June 18, 1924, asked that they should be classified in category VI in respect to their contribution for the expense of maintaining the International Bureau, and announced that a special government department of industrial property was organized in these territories. The Swiss government, in notifying the contracting countries of such accession of Syria and Lebanon, called attention to the fact that the position of the mandated territories in the Union, in respect to their representation at the conferences, as well as in respect to their obligation to contribute to the expenses of the Bureau, should be determined at the next conference of revision.[2] At The Hague Conference the British government proposed the insertion of the words "ou territoires administrés en vertue d'un mandat de la Société des Nations " in article 16*b*, after the words "colonies, possessions, dépendances et protectorats." This amendment was adopted by the Conference. Thus the accession of territories placed under a mandate of the League of Nations is to be effected in the same way as that of colonies, dominions, and other subject territories.

On the adoption of this amendment, however, the Director of the International Bureau, Professor Röthlisberger, expressed the view that countries placed under a mandate of the League of Nations are not bound to contribute to the expenses of the Bureau, as members of the Union, and have not the right to vote at the conferences. No objection was raised in the sub-committee.[3] However, Syria and Lebanon appear as a distinct contracting country in the preamble of the revised text of the Convention, and they signed the same at the closing meeting of the Conference. It should be assumed, therefore, that the view expressed by Professor Röthlisberger was not the view of the Conference. Moreover, the International Bureau now holds a contrary view.[4]

1. See *Propriété Industrielle* (1928), p. 145.
2. See *ibid.* (1924), p. 149.
3. See *Actes de la Conférence de La Haye*, pp. 353, 420, 549.
4. See *Propriété Industrielle* (1926), p. 122. Syria and Lebanon are now listed as a member of the Union, by the International Bureau, in its list of member countries. See *ibid.* (1928), pp. 1–2.

The opinion was expressed that, if these autonomous entities (dominions, protectorates, mandated territories) be admitted as "contracting countries," it would be possible for the "ressortissants" of the mother country to claim in those countries, and vice versa, the rights granted by the Union, in case they are broader than those granted by the municipal law.[1] This would seem hardly possible. A dominion or mandated territory has not a complete international personality. It may become a party to a treaty or a convention with third countries only through the mother country. The latter acts on its behalf. There cannot be a treaty between the mother country and its dependency in international law.[2] But this question is not raised if it be admitted that the nationals of a country of the Union may claim the rights and advantages granted by the Convention and Arrangements, even in their own country.[3]

§ 59. **Changes in political structure or territory of members of the Union.** The effect of changes in the political constitution of members of the Union, or in their territory, on their position in the Union, is a general question of public international law. There are a number of such cases in the history of the Union. Sweden and Norway acceded to the Convention by a note of the Foreign Office of Sweden and Norway, dated May 29, 1885. From the date that their accession became effective, July 1, 1885, they were dealt with separately for their contribution to the expenses of the International Bureau.[4] They were thus deemed two separate countries for the purpose of the Convention; nothing was necessary, therefore, to confirm their changed situation in the Union since their separation in 1905. No new act of accession was made by them. Indeed, this was a Convention acceded to by Norway and Sweden in common, and each government declared its willingness to perform the obligations arising from such a convention.[5] The same is true of Austria and Hungary.[6]

1. See article in *Propriété Industrielle* (1926), pp. 122, 124.

2. The International Bureau has no direct relations with the administration of the colonies and possessions which are not "contracting countries." It receives their deposits, notifications, etc., through the medium of the administration of the mother country. See Statement of the Bureau, in *Actes de la Conférence de La Haye*, p. 181 n.

3. See *infra*, chap. VIII, § 120.

4. See *Propriété Industrielle* (1885), pp. 62, 75.

5. See Bonfils, *Manuel*, 7th ed., p. 143.

6. Austria-Hungary acceded to the Convention by a declaration of the Austro-Hungarian government, dated November 30, 1908. The accession was deemed as of two distinct countries, *Propriété Industrielle* (1908), p. 173. After the World War these

Yet, although Serbia was a member of the Union from its origin, the new Serb-Croat-Slovene State, which was formed by the annexation of territories of other countries to Serbia, acceded again, February 26, 1921. But the accession was necessary for another reason. Serbia had not ratified the texts revised at Washington in 1911 in time, and, according to the practice observed in similar cases, it must accede to the revised texts.[1]

New states springing up from the dismemberment of another state need, of course, to accede to the Union. Thus Czechoslovakia (1919), Poland (1919), Danzig (1921), Finland (1921), Esthonia (1924), and Latvia (1925) acceded after the war. The question of new accession, of course, is raised only in regard to the first three states; the Union extended over their territories until the treaties of peace came into effect. These states became parties to the Arrangement of 1920 for the reëstablishment of rights of industrial property affected by the war, so that the effects of the Convention on their territories have never been interrupted.[2]

§ 60. Accession of new countries to the Union. The membership of the general Union is constituted to-day (January, 1929) by thirty-eight countries. That of the restricted union for the repression of false indications of origin by fourteen; of the union for the international registration of trade marks by twenty-two. The Ar-

two countries became distinct states, yet no new declaration of accession was necessary. It is true, however, that by article 237 of the treaty of peace with Austria and article 220 of that with Hungary, the Convention of 1883 came again into effect between the Allied and Associated Powers and each of these countries; also both became parties to the Arrangement of September 30, 1920, for the reëstablishment of industrial property rights affected by the war, which is based on the theory that the Convention is still in force. In fact, Austria, on September 25, 1920, declared, by a communication to the Swiss government, that "it is a contracting party to the Convention of 1883 and to the Arrangement for the international registration of trade marks, and that this recognition was retroactive to January 1, 1909, the date of accession of Austria-Hungary." The Swiss government in its circular of notification to the members of the Union, interpreted this note as constituting not a new accession, but a declaration of continuity of membership, *Propriété Industrielle* (1920), p. 113. See also Bonfils, *Manuel*, 7th ed., p. 578.

1. See *Propriété Industrielle* (1921), p. 27.

2. Czechoslovakia by a note of January 29, 1920, addressed to the International Bureau, declared that although it acceded on October 5, 1919, to the Convention, it would assume the obligations of the Convention as of October 28, 1918, the date of the constitution of the State of Czechoslovakia, *Propriété Industrielle* (1920), pp. 37, 46 ff. By this declaration, the territory of Czechoslovakia is divided for the purpose of the protection of industrial property into two parts, corresponding to the former Austrian and Hungarian territories. The rights of industrial property existing in each of these parts of the territory are to be protected in that part alone, and not in the whole of Czechoslovakia.

rangement of The Hague for the international deposit of designs and models was signed by ten countries; four of them had ratified it on May 1, 1928.

Thus, while the original signatory countries to the Convention numbered only eleven, twenty-seven more have acceded to it successively up to this time. They took advantage of article 16 of the Convention, which reads as follows:

Les pays qui n'ont point pris part à la présente Convention seront admis à y adhérer sur leur demande.

Cette adhésion sera notifiée par la voie diplomatique au Gouvernement de la Confédération suisse, et par celui-ci à tous les autres.

Elle emportera, de plein droit, accession à toutes les clauses et admission à tous les avantages stipulés par la présente Convention, et produira ses effets un mois après l'envoi de la notification faite par le Gouvernement de la Confédération suisse aux autres pays unionistes, à moins qu'une date postérieure n'ait été indiquée par le pays adhérent.[1]

Article 16 uses an inaccurate term. It provides for "adhesion" to the Convention, instead of accession thereto; for the act contemplated is not a mere declaration of acceptance of the obligations and principles of the Convention, but an act by which a country joins itself to other countries that have entered into the Convention in order to become a party thereto.[2]

The facility given to any country to accede to the Convention is an important feature of the provision in question. It is possible for any country to become a member of the Union by merely communicating a declaration of accession to the Swiss Government. The latter shall give notice thereof to members of the Union. And, unless a later date is indicated in the communication of the acceding country, it becomes a member of the Union automatically one month after the Swiss government's notification to the contracting countries.

Accession of new countries is always provided for in treaties or conventions of general import, and the formalities necessary thereto have become more and more simple. That they have the ambition

1. The second part of the last paragraph ("et produira . . .") was added by the Additional Act of Brussels of December 14, 1900.

2. Bonfils, *Manuel*, 7th ed., p. 569. Dupuis, "Les Relations Internationales," in *Académie de Droit International, Recueil des Cours* (1924), I, 329. Wilson, *International Law*, 8th ed., p. 212. The Agreement of September 30, 1920, for the reëstablishment of rights of industrial property affected by the war speaks, rightly, in art. 5, sec. 3, of the "accession" of other countries.

to become universal unions is a main characteristic of almost all the unions constituted since the last quarter of the past century. They are "open conventions." [1]

This provision of the "open door" of the Union provoked severe criticism at an earlier period.[2] Nevertheless it has proved sound. The fears that certain countries would attempt, by accession, to obtain the benefits of the Union without enacting adequate legislation protecting foreigners, have not been justified. In fact, there was a genuine desire on all sides to protect industrial property, and the Union and accession thereto exercised great influence in the countries which did not possess adequate legislation. Switzerland amended its Constitution in order to protect inventors, and passed two Federal laws for the protection of inventions and industrial designs and models, in 1888.[3]

Article 16 was a natural consequence of the principle of article 2, which secured national treatment to the subjects of all the contracting parties without the condition of the existence of similar protection in the country of origin of the claimant.

The last paragraph of article 16 provides that the acceding country may declare that its accession shall become effective at a date later than a month after the Swiss government's notification of such accession to the members of the Union.[4] This, *ex contrario*, would

1. K. Neumeyer, "Les Unions Internationales" in *Revue de Droit International*, Genève (1924), II, 345.

It is of the essence of a treaty, of course, that there should be consent of the contracting parties to another country's becoming a party to it. Such consent is given in advance by the adoption of article 16.

2. Donzel, *Commentaire de la Convention de 1883*, p. 343, is a good illustration of the spirit of suspicion and nationalism: "L'article 16," he writes, "constitue un traité de commerce en blanc et au porteur. . . . On ne pouvait fouler aux pieds plus imprudemment le principe élémentaire de défense industrielle, qui veut que chaque traité soit pesé et délibéré, en contemplation de l'intérêt que la nation peut avoir à obtenir, de tel ou tel État particulier, telle ou telle concession spéciale, qui peut être achetée au prix d'une concession réciproque."

It should be recalled that this author was writing in 1890.

3. *Recueil Officiel des Lois de Suisse*, VI, N. S., 190, 530; X, N. S., 684; and vol. XI, 71. But in the Netherlands, where the patent legislation introduced in 1817 was repealed in 1869, it was not possible to reënact a new patent law until 1910, notwithstanding the engagement entered into by the Dutch administration at the Madrid Conference. The various bills introduced in the Legislature in the interval had been opposed too vigorously by enemies of the protection of inventions. See *Propriété Industrielle* (1888), p. 86; (1889), p. 64; (1893), p. 130; (1905), p. 92; (1908), p. 108; (1910), pp. 52, 102, 165; (1911), p. 101.

4. Germany, in acceding to the Madrid Arrangement for the international registration of trade marks, declared that its accession should become effective on December 1, 1922, which was more than a month after the Swiss government's notification of October 24, 1922. See *Propriété Industrielle* (1922), p. 137.

imply that an earlier date could not be chosen. In case, however, that this is done, no rights under the Convention may accrue to the acceding country, although, possibly, obligations under it may be incurred by that country. Such an accession was that of Canada in 1923.[1]

Accession to the Convention implies accession to Additional Acts, Protocols, or *Règlements*, if any exist, which constitute parts of, or are annexed to, the main text of the Convention. Furthermore, no accession to the text in effect before its revision is possible. The old text is no longer the Convention to which accession may be made according to article 16. This provides that the declaration of accession "emportera, de plein droit, accession à toutes les clauses et admission à tous les avantages stipulés par la présente Convention." "La présente Convention" after the revised text becomes effective, is the revised Convention. This is so, even though one or more of the contracting countries have not yet ratified the revised Convention. The second paragraph of article 18 provides that the old text shall remain in effect as to the relations between the countries that have not "ratified" the new text. Only the signatory countries can "ratify" a treaty.

Accession to the Convention does not imply accession to the two Madrid Arrangements and to the Arrangement of The Hague. These are distinct international acts, although entered into by members of the general Union. A distinct accession to each of them is necessary. But any country cannot accede to these Arrangements, as it can to the Convention. By express provisions of these acts, accession is possible only to members of the general Union.[2] But a country may accede simultaneously to the Convention and to any of the Arrangements.

§ 61. Accession of colonies. Colonies, possessions, dominions, protectorates, and territories under mandate of the League of Nations may accede to the Convention and Arrangements by a declaration of their mother country, according to article 16*b*. This

1. The British government, in acceding on behalf of Canada, on August 21, 1923, declared that such accession was to become effective September 1, 1923. The Swiss government notified the members of the Union of this accession on the same day, September 1, 1923. See *Propriété Industrielle* (1923), p. 125; also *League of Nations Treaty Series*, XXXV, 331.

2. Art. 11, sec. 1, of the Arrangement for the international registration of trade marks; art. 5 of the Arrangement for the repression on false indications of origin; art. 22 of the Arrangement of The Hague.

article does not contain any provision as to the time when the accession becomes effective. The provisions of article 16, as to the date the accession becomes effective and the effects of such accession, are here applicable. Article 16*b* purports to determine only the form of accession of colonies, and the rest, and refers, impliedly, in all other respects, to article 16. This has been always so understood in practice.[1]

§ 62. **Denunciation of the Convention and Arrangements.** No period is provided for, during which the Convention and Arrangements will remain in effect. Their duration is indefinite, so long as they are not denounced. Any country of the Union may denounce the Convention, which remains in effect between the other countries. This is expressly provided by article 17*b*. Three countries have withdrawn from the Union: Ecuador, Guatemala, and Salvador; the Dominican Republic denounced the Convention in 1888, but it acceded anew in 1890.

Denunciation is made by a declaration addressed to the Swiss government, and becomes effective at the expiration of one year from the date it is made.

Colonies, possessions, dominions, protectorates, and territories under mandate may denounce the Convention or Arrangements without the mother countries' doing so. But in such case, the declaration of denunciation must be made by the mother country, in the same form as the accession, by express provision of the last paragraph of article 16*b*. This article does not determine when the denunciation becomes effective. But the general provision of article 17*b* applies also to colonies, article 16*b* concerning only the form of denunciation.

The Arrangements have no provision similar to that of article 17*b* of the Convention. Each of them, however, provides that it "aura la même force et durée que la Convention générale." [2] Thus, by implication, the provisions of article 17*b* of the Convention are applicable to the Arrangements.[3] However, the relation between the

1. See, for instance, circulars of the Swiss Government in the case of accession of Morocco, Irish Free State, and Syria and Lebanon, *Propriété Industrielle* (1917), p. 81; (1925), p. 237; (1924), p. 149.

2. Arrangement for the repression of false indications of origin, art. 6; Arrangement for the international registration of trade marks, art. 12; Arrangement of The Hague, art. 23.

3. See denunciation by Latvia of the two Madrid Arrangements, *Propriété Industrielle* (1926), p. 2.

general Convention and the Arrangements gives rise to some matters in regard to denunciation. First, a member of the general Union and of the restricted unions constituted by the Arrangements may, undoubtedly, denounce any of the Arrangements, although it continues to be a member of the general Union.[1] By its accession to an Arrangement, it does not incorporate the same in the Convention. It still remains a distinct international act. In the case of Latvia's denunciation of the Madrid Arrangements, it was understood that that country remained a member of the general Union.[2]

On the other hand, a country may not denounce the Convention and yet claim to remain a party to the Arrangements. In case the Convention is denounced, it must be implied that the Arrangements to which the country in question is a party are also denounced. This is clear from the provision of the Arrangements: "Les pays de l'Union pour la protection de la propriété industrielle qui n'ont pris part au présent Arrangement seront admis à y adhérer." [3] Only those countries may become parties to the Arrangements which are countries of the Union for the Protection of Industrial Property. It would seem, then, that when a country by denouncing the general Convention ceases to be a "country of the Union," it can no longer be a party to the Arrangements. Besides, the Madrid Trade-Mark Arrangement and the Arrangement of The Hague are dependent for their execution on the International Bureau, which is constituted and provided for by the Convention, and all the Arrangements refer constantly to the latter act.

§ **63. Effects of denunciation.** By denunciation, the obligations and rights of the denouncing country under the Convention or Arrangements cease for the future. The rights, however, acquired before the denunciation are preserved. Thus a trade mark admitted to registration under article 6 of the Convention, or registered at the International Bureau under the Madrid Arrangement, will remain on the register as long as the legal effects of registration last, according to the municipal law of each country. The denunciation cannot have retroactive effects.

In the case of the recent denunciation by Latvia of the two Arrangements of Madrid this principle has not been followed. Indeed,

1. Pillet, *Régime International*, p. 213, *accord*.
2. *Propriété Industrielle* (1926), p. 2.
3. Art. 6 of the Arrangement for the repression of false indications of origin; art. 12 of the Trade-Mark Arrangement; art. 23 of the Arrangement of The Hague.

this country declared that the international registration of trade marks of the contracting countries at the International Bureau, which took place during the time it was a party to the Madrid Arrangement, would cease to have any effects in Latvia after the date on which its denunciation of the Arrangement became effective. In exchange, Latvia granted a right of priority of four months for the renewal of registration of the trade marks in question in the country through an attorney domiciled therein. Thus, the denunciation becoming effective on December 21, 1926, the trade marks registered with the International Bureau during the time Latvia was a party to the Madrid Arrangement might be registered anew in Latvia until April 21, 1927. Trade marks, registration of which should not be renewed by that time, could claim no protection. The correctness and international legality of this action of the country in question are subject to serious doubts.[1]

II. The International Bureau

§ 64. Need of the Bureau. The Union needed a common organ; an institution belonging, not to the individual member countries, but to the Union itself; a link between the members; something to make the Union a living organism. Such an institution was established by article 13 of the Convention:

> L'office international institué à Berne sous le nom de Bureau International pour la protection de la propriété industrielle est placé sous la haute autorité du Gouvernement de la Confédération suisse, qui en règle l'organization et en surveille le fonctionnement.[2]

There was some divergence of opinion at the Paris Conference of 1880 as to the advisability and practicability of maintaining an international bureau. Six countries out of nineteen were opposed to it in principle. It was insisted, however, that a union could not be understood without a common organ; or, as the Portuguese delegate put it, the Union without such an office would be like a body without a head.[3]

1. *Propriété Industrielle* (1926), p. 215; (1927), p. 11.
2. Article 13 speaks of an office "institué," as something existing before the Convention which already "est placé" under the authority of the Swiss government. This was, in fact, true in 1913 and 1928, when the texts of the Convention revised at Washington and at The Hague went into effect. The old article 13 of 1883 read differently: ". . . un office international sera organizé . . . sera placé sous la haute autorité, etc."
3. *Conférence Internationale* (Paris, 1880), p. 115.

§ 65. Functions of the Bureau. It may be that the Bureau is not the head of the Union; but it is perhaps its soul. It is sufficient for this purpose to consider its functions, as provided for by article 13:

Le Bureau International centralisera les renseignements de toute nature relatifs à la protection de la propriété industrielle, et les réunira en une statistique générale, qui sera distribuée à toutes les Administrations. Il procédera aux études d'utilité commune intéressant l'Union et rédigera à l'aide des documents qui seront mis à sa disposition par les diverses Administrations, une feuille périodique, en langue française sur les questions concernant l'objet de l'Union.

Le Bureau devra se tenir en tout temps à la disposition des membres de l'Union, pour leur fournir, sur les questions relatives au service international de la propriété industrielle, les renseignements spéciaux dont ils pourraient avoir besoin.[1]

The Union did not achieve uniformity in the laws of its members. A great number of the provisions of the Convention and Arrangements referred to the provisions of the municipal law of each country and made it applicable. One of the basic principles of the Convention is that of assimilation of persons entitled to its benefits to the nationals of each country. The protection, therefore, and rights afforded in each country should be brought to the knowledge of the members of the Union. It was the business of the International Bureau to gather these numerous and scattered data, whether legislative provisions, judicial decisions, or administrative practices, and communicate them to all the members of the Union. It was its business also to study these different data from the standpoint of international law and of the purpose of the Convention, and communicate the results of such investigation to the members of the Union; also to keep an eye on the execution of the Convention, see how it worked in practice, and propose ameliorations of the Convention, should it appear necessary.

The Bureau was most successful in fulfilling its mission. Its activity extended more and more in a very beneficial way. In fact, while remaining within the sphere attributed to it by the Convention, it covered a much broader field. It collected and published in its monthly magazine, and in separate collections, data concerning the protection of industrial property within the Union, as well as in countries outside it — bilateral conventions, legislative acts, and judicial decisions. It held itself at all times at the disposal, not only

1. Article 13 incorporated the provisions of sec. 6 of the original Final Protocol.

of members of the Union, as provided by article 13, but also of any private person, and furnished information concerning questions of industrial property. Its publication is not a dry official organ. Besides the excellent handling of the materials, its general studies on questions of industrial property, and its opinions on questions of interpretation of the Convention, in the form of *avis*, which constitute the unofficial part of the periodical are always of great value. There have also been cases in which the Bureau intervened and brought its influence to bear upon individual member countries, with the view of securing the proper application and execution of the Convention.[1]

Moreover, the International Bureau prepares the work of the conferences of revision in coöperation with the Administration of the countries in which these conferences are held. Its Director has the power to attend the sessions of the conference and take part in the discussion, without a right to vote.

Finally, by the Arrangements of Madrid and The Hague, for the international registration of trade marks and the international deposit of designs and models, a further function was attributed to the Bureau, which distinguishes it from all other similar bureaus. It is a function analogous to that of a state administrative or judicial organ. Under the Madrid Arrangement, trade marks deposited in the country of origin may be registered at the International Bureau, instead of being registered in all the contracting countries. Under the Arrangement of The Hague, industrial designs and models may be deposited direct at the International Bureau by interested parties, without the condition of a previous deposit in the country of origin.[2]

§ 66. Juridical nature of the Bureau. The International Bureau of Berne is an international administrative organ belonging to the Union and not to the individual members. It is not under the control of any of the members. At the same time, as its functions make clear, it is not an organ with power to control the actions of the members; such, for instance, as the Permanent Sugar Commission,

1. See, for instance, the erroneous application of article 7 of the Convention in the Serb-Croat-Slovene State and the successful intervention of the Bureau, *Propriété Industrielle* (1922), p. 95.

2. As a result of this function, the Bureau has published a second periodical since 1892, — *Les Marques Internationales*, — in which all trade marks registered with the Bureau are advertised; and a third periodical is to be issued in the near future for the publication of designs and models deposited at the Bureau.

which possesses the unusual power of adjusting the sugar tariffs of the member states, even without their consent, of determining whether or not bounties exist in non-signatory states, and of passing on requests for admission to the Union.[1] Its functions are of an informational and ministerial character.[2] It cannot control in any way the free exercise of sovereignty by any state. If a member of the Union contravenes the Convention in any respect, the Bureau's only power is to bring this to the knowledge of the members of the Union, as any other member of the Union might do. It is questionable whether it could call to the attention of the transgressing member that the measure taken by it was contrary to the Convention.[3] Nor may it advise a member to simplify or modify a procedural formality for the sake of more adequate protection of the persons under the aegis of the Union.[4]

And yet the Bureau might be given such power. Its constitution does not prevent its taking over such larger powers of control. It is detached from the influence of the member countries. Article 13 places it under the high authority of the Swiss government. The latter "regulates its organization and supervises its operation." Although at first hand this superintendence by the government of the state where the Bureau is situated gives the impression of an organ dependent on that government, it secures, in fact, its absolute freedom. The regulation by the Swiss government consists practically in the appointment of its personnel, and the supervision of its finances. In all other respects, and in all the activities of the Bureau concerning the Union, the Swiss government carefully avoids any interference whatsoever. Nor have the other members of the Union, separately or in Conferences, any powers of control or supervision. Thus the Bureau enjoys complete liberty in all its activities.[5]

1. International Sugar Convention of March 5, 1902, art. 7, and Final Protocol as regards art. 3. XCV *Br. & For. State Papers*, 6.

2. Francis B. Sayre, *Experiments in International Administration* (1919), p. 13.

3. Yet, the Bureau, by an exchange of letters with the administration of the Serb-Croat-Slovene State, lasting from December 5, 1920, to June 22, 1922, submitted to that member the grounds of the Bureau's view against the interpretation of article 7 by its administration, and succeeded in having its view adopted. *Propriété Industrielle* (1922), p. 95.

4. Under the Madrid Arrangement for the international registration of trade marks and that of The Hague for the international deposit of designs and models, the Bureau possesses discretionary and quasi-judicial powers. See chap. XIX, § 291, and chap. XXVIII, § 436.

5. Karl Neumeyer, "Unions Internationales," in *Revue de Droit International* (Geneva, 1924), p. 349.

§ 67. **Organization of the Bureau.** The Bureau, originally an organ only of the Union of Industrial Property, became in 1888, when the Copyright Union came into effect, a common central organ for both unions.[1]

The Swiss government thought it advisable to place both bureaus under one direction. The functions of each are of the same nature and thus there is a complete fusion. The Director and Secretary General are doing work for both unions. The results of their work are transmitted, however, to the members of either union by two separate magazines: *La Propriété Industrielle* and *Le Droit d'Auteur*.

The official language of the Bureau, as well as of its magazines and other publications, is French, by express provision of article 13. At the time of the constitution of the Union, French was the only general diplomatic language. Besides, the persons who read these publications are mostly lawyers, or are concerned with international questions, and as a general rule know French.

At the recent Conference of The Hague, the American delegation proposed that the English language should be an official language of the Bureau as well as the French. Several countries, however, suggested that, if a language other than French were made official, their languages also should be used. In these circumstances the American proposal was not adopted. Instead, to meet the desire of the American delegation, a resolution was adopted to have the International Bureau supply translations of the Convention and other acts in effect in the Union, as well as of the propositions at the conferences of revision and of the articles and essays published in the *Propriété Industrielle*.[2]

§ 68. **The League of Nations and the Bureau.** The Covenant of the League of Nations in article 24 provides: "There shall be placed under the direction of the League all International Bureaus already

1. The supervision of the Bureau by the Swiss Federal Council is exercised through the latter's political department. The personnel of the Bureau is appointed by the Federal Council itself, which also fixes their salaries according to a special scale comprising six classes. Each of the member countries may ask the appointment of one of its own nationals. The Swiss Federal Council, however, makes its decisions in the interest of the service. Nineteen officials are appointed now in the united Bureaus. The division of work between them is made according to the needs of the service. The international registration of trade marks constitutes an important part of the service. *Les Bureaux Internationaux pour la Protection de la Propriété Industrielle, Littéraire et Artistique, Communiqué par la Direction des Bureaux* (Berne, September, 1923), p. 4; and Letter of the Director, no. 528, November 9, 1926.

2. These translations will be supplied on the demand and at the expense of any country of the Union. See *Actes de la Conférence de La Haye*, pp. 353, 416, 527, 548, 568.

established by general treaties, if the parties to such treaties consent." The League might exercise its authority over the Bureau if the members of the Union consented. It prepared itself for that task, by constituting a section of International Bureaus; by publishing, since October, 1923, a quarterly bulletin of information on the work of international organizations; and by composing a Repertory of International Organizations. M. Hanotaux, the French delegate to the Council of the League, presented to the Council on June 27, 1921, a report on the general principles to be followed in gradually placing international bureaus under the authority of the League.[1]

No action was taken toward placing the International Bureau of Berne under the direction of the League, in accordance with the above provision of the Covenant. Regardless of the fact that there are some members of the Union which are not members of the League, it is not clear how the International Bureau and the League could usefully coöperate. M. Hanotaux's report is very carefully drawn. It stresses especially the moral support which the League would give to the international bureaus, interfering only in case of abuses or inactivity on the part of a bureau. Neither the seat of a bureau, nor its organization and its sphere of activity would have to be modified. Such a loose connection with the League does not seem to have been the intention of the founders of the League.[2]

§ **69. Finances of the Bureau.** It remains to be seen how the expenditure for the maintenance of the Bureau and for its publications is covered. Article 13 provides as follows:

. . . Les dépenses du Bureau international seront supportées en commun par les pays contractants. Elles ne pourront, en aucun cas, dépasser la somme de soixante mille francs par année.

Pour déterminer la part contributive de chacun des pays dans cette somme totale des frais, les pays contractants et ceux qui adhéreraient ultérieurement à l'Union seront divisées en six classes, contribuant chacune dans la proportion d'un certain nombre d'unités savoir:

1e *classe*	25 *unités*
2e "	20 "
3e "	15 "
4e "	10 "
5e "	5 "
6e "	3 "

1. *Minutes of the 13th Session of the Council of the League*, pp. 54, 249–251.

2. Karl Neumeyer, "Unions Internationales," in *Revue de Droit International* (Geneva, 1924), pp. 142 ff.

Les coëfficients seront multipliés par le nombre des pays de chaque classe, et la somme des produits ainsi obtenue fournira le nombre d'unités par lequel la dépense totale doit être divisée. Le quotient donnera le montant de l'unité de dépense.

These provisions in article 13 were taken from the original Final Protocol on the revision of the Convention at Washington. The following paragraph was then added: "Chacun des pays contractants désignera, au moment de son accession, la classe dans laquelle il désire être rangé."

Already before 1911 the practice was in accordance with this provision. Every country on its accession to the Convention indicated the class in which it desired to be ranked. It could hardly be otherwise. Even in the unions in which the contribution of each member is to be determined by its economic capacity or commercial importance, in practice the class in which a member is to be ranked is chosen by the member itself. Each country is too jealous of its sovereignty and independence, and could not allow other countries to judge of its capacity or importance.[1]

Originally the Final Protocol of the Convention provided that the yearly expenditure of the Bureau could not exceed a total sum representing an average of 2,000 francs for each contracting country. It was hoped, at that time, that all the countries would accede to the Convention in a short time and that thus a sufficient sum for the needs of the Bureau would be constituted. But the membership did not increase fast enough, and the average of 2,000 francs for each country proved to be a very meagre amount on the whole. In the Madrid Protocol of April 5, 1891, the present provision was adopted, which considers the needs of the Bureau and not the number of

1. The method of division of expenditure between the members may be seen in the hypothetical account annexed to the *procès-verbal* of the 10th session of the Paris Conference of 1880 (p. 154). It is supposed that the total expenditure amounts to 40,000 francs, and that an equal number of countries belong to each class. The quotient of 128.21 results from the division of the total amount of expenditure (40,000 francs) by the total number of units of each class (312).

ORDER OF CLASSES	*Units of contribution of each country*		*No. of states of each class*		*No. of Units of each class*		*Value of the units of contribution of each country*		*Amount of contribution of the countries of each class*	*Amount of contribution of each country of each class*
1st.	25	×	4	=	100	×	128.21	=	12,820	3,205
2d.	20	×	4	=	80	×	128.21	=	10,257	2,564
3d.	15	×	4	=	60	×	128.21	=	7,693	1,923
4th.	10	×	4	=	40	×	128.21	=	5,128	1,282
5th.	5	×	4	=	20	×	128.21	=	2,564	641
6th.	3	×	4	=	12	×	128.21	=	1,538	385
	78		24		312				40,000	

members. This very provision had already been adopted in the Copyright Union of 1886.

The contribution of each member is toward the expenditure for the maintenance of the Bureau. In return, the Bureau sends to the administration of each member copies of its magazines and all other documents published by it, in the proportion of the number of units contributed by each member. Any copy or document applied for by any administration in excess of the number due it, or by private persons, is to be paid for.

By the last paragraph of article 13 it is provided that: "Le Gouvernement de la Confédération suisse surveillera les dépenses du Bureau International, fera les avances nécessaires et établira le compte annuel, qui sera communiqué à toutes les autres Administrations."

Thus the expenses are advanced by the Swiss government, which, later, collects them from the members, on communicating to them the annual account. No case of a failure of a country to pay its contribution seems to have arisen in the Union. Such a case in the Union of Weights and Measures found a practical solution. The general Conference directed the Bureau to refuse its services to the countries which should fail to pay their contributions for a period of three years.[1]

At the Conference of The Hague in 1925 the sixth paragraph of article 13 was amended to read as follows:

> Les dépenses du Bureau International seront supportées en commun par les pays contractants. Jusqu'à nouvel ordre, elles ne pourront pas dépasser la somme de cent vingt mille francs suisses par année. Cette somme pourra être augmentée, au besoin, par décision unanime d'une des Conférences prévues à l'article 14.

Thus the original sum of 60,000 francs was doubled. This became necessary as a result of the war and the increase of membership of the Union. In fact, prior to the Conference of The Hague, at the request of the Bureau, the Swiss government in 1921, by a circular to all the members of the Union, had obtained their consent to an increase of the credit to the Bureau to the sum of 120,000 francs.[2]

1. Karl Neumeyer, "Unions Internationales," in *Revue de Droit International* (Geneva, 1924), p. 347.

2. *Conférence de La Haye, Documents Préliminaires, 3e fascicule*, pp. 51–52. At Brussels (December, 1900) the Conference, following the example of the Postal Union, decided to organize a pension fund for the employees of the Bureau. The reserve of the Bureau was turned into this fund.

§ 70. Special government departments for industrial property. The International Bureau could not, perhaps, accomplish much if the Convention of 1883 had not compelled the member countries to create national institutions with which the Bureau might coöperate in an effective way. It would seem useful, therefore, to deal at this place with the government departments, or offices of industrial property of the member countries.

The Congress of 1878, in one of its *voeux*,[1] had pointed out the need of a special government department, and a central office of industrial property, in each of the contracting countries. The Convention, in article 12, gives satisfaction to this *voeu*. It provides:

> Chacune des Hautes Parties contractantes s'engage à établir un service spécial de la Propriété Industrielle et un dépôt central pour la communication au public des brevets d'invention, des dessins ou modèles industriels et des marques de fabrique ou de commerce. Ce service publiera une feuille périodique officielle.

The members of the Union are bound by article 12 of the Convention to establish a special government department for all matters relating to patents, designs, and trade marks, and a central office for the communication to the public of all information. It was intended to do away with the previous practice of having separate and numerous departments or offices for patents, designs, and trade marks, and to join them together, in order to afford the public the necessary facilities of information and procedure.[2]

The provision for publication of an official periodical by the government department for industrial property of every country was originally but a *voeu*: "autant que possible." However, at the Conference of The Hague in 1925 the words " autant que possible " were struck out; and thus it was made an obligation for each country to publish an official periodical. As to the contents of the periodical, the Austrian delegation proposed an amendment to article 12 and the British delegation a *voeu*, which were eventually merged into a *voeu* adopted by the Conference of The Hague. It is declared desir-

1. *Tableau des Voeux 1873–1909* (International Bureau, Berne, 1911), p. 21.

2. For instance, in France, there were four government departments for patents: the Préfecture de la Seine, for application for a patent; the Recette Centrale de la Seine, for payment of the annual tax; the Ministère de Commerce for information on patents in existence; and the Conservatoire des Arts et Métiers for expired patents. On the other hand, designs were deposited in the trade councils of each city, and trade marks were registered at the clerk's office of the commercial tribunals all over France. The situation in many other countries was similar.

able that the periodical should contain a reproduction of all registered trade marks; that the drawings and descriptions of patented inventions should be printed and made available at a reasonable price; and that a register should be kept in each country in which notices of transfer and the facts concerning the validity and ownership of patents, designs and models, and trade marks should be recorded.[1]

However, the provisions for the establishment of a special government department and a central office were also practically treated as *voeux*.[2] Few members of the Union executed the Convention in this respect at an early date. These are Belgium, Italy, Switzerland, the Netherlands, and Portugal.[3] Patent Offices for patents, designs, and trade marks existed in the United States, Great Britain, and Germany before their accession to the Union. The International Association for the Protection of Industrial Property, in its successive congresses, adopted *voeux* calling upon the members of the Union to fulfill the obligation assumed by article 12.[4] France did so only in 1901, by constituting the Office National de la Propriété Industrielle.[5] To-day practically all the countries have centralized departments and offices of industrial property, which publish often more than one official periodical.[6]

III. The Conferences of Revision

§ 71. **Necessity of revising the Convention.** Municipal legislation can at any time be altered by the sovereign law-maker. There is no such sovereign in conventional International Law. A way out, then, is to make conventional law limited in duration, or to allow revisions from time to time. The latter is by far the better way, because it secures unity and continuity. Revision of the Convention for the Protection of Industrial Property was particularly necessary, in view of the fact that several of its provisions constituted an inno-

1. *Actes de la Conférence de La Haye*, pp. 354, 415–416, 547–548, 568.

2. Pelletier and Vidal-Naquet, *Convention d'Union*, p. 33, interpreted these provisions of article 12 as *voeux*. But the terms are too clear to permit such interpretation, since each country "s'engage" to establish such offices.

3. Belgium, Italy, Portugal, and Switzerland in 1884; the Netherlands in 1885. See *Propriété Industrielle* (1885), pp. 5, 6, 7, 19, 40.

4. See official collections of the International Bureau, *Tableau des Voeux 1873–1909*, p. 21, and *Tableau des Voeux 1910–1924*, p. 25.

5. *Propriété Industrielle* (1901), p. 102. Pillet, *Régime International*, p. 261.

6. A complete list of these government offices and of their publications, with addresses, prices, etc., is given in *Propriété Industrielle* (1923), pp. 6, 24, 34, 53, 136, 152.

vation in International Law and their practical working might raise the need of amendments. On the other hand, the Convention did not satisfy the aspirations of complete uniformity of law, and it was hoped that a progressive uniformity might result from successive revisions. The Chairman of the Conference of 1880 expressed epigrammatically this hope: "This Convention constitutes only the preface of a book which has still to be written in the years to come." [1]

Provision for conferences of revision is made in article 14 of the Convention, which reads as follows:

La présente Convention sera soumise à des révisions périodiques, en vue d'y introduire les améliorations de nature à perfectionner le système de l'Union.

À cet effet, des Conférences auront lieu, successivement dans l'un des pays contractants entre les Délégués des dits pays.

L'Administration du pays où doit siéger la Conférence préparera, avec le concours du Bureau International, les travaux de cette Conférence.

Le Directeur du Bureau International assistera aux séances des Conférences et prendra part aux discussions sans voix délibérative.

The successive conferences of revision at Rome, Madrid, Brussels, Washington, and The Hague have been considered in the previous chapter. It is necessary now to describe the preparation of the work of the conferences, the proceedings thereof, and the coming into effect of the revised texts.

§ 72. Preparation of the work of the Conferences. Contrary to the practice of other international conventions, in which the time of each successive revision is expressly provided for,[2] there is no set time here. Thus the conferences of revision were very frequent in the first decade of the existence of the Union, but not in later years. There was a lapse of ten years between the Conference of Brussels and that of Washington, and of fourteen between the latter and that of The Hague.

In the first Conferences, adequate time was not given to the different administrations to study the various proposals. The result was that all the acts adopted at Rome and one adopted at Madrid have never been ratified, and a period of three years has separated the two sessions of the Brussels Conference. On the motion of the

1. *Conférence Internationale de Propriété Industrielle* (Paris, 1880), p. 20.

2. Article 25 of the Postal Convention provides for a congress of revision every five years, unless called at an earlier date on the demand of two thirds of the members. XCIX *Br. & For. State Papers*, 254; *De Martens*, 3d ser., I, 355.

American delegation, the Conferences at Madrid and Brussels voted a *voeu* to the effect that all proposals should be presented to the International Bureau six months before the meeting of the conference of revision, and all amendments and counter-proposals within three months. These should be communicated immediately to the contracting countries by the International Bureau.[1] With rare exceptions, this *voeu* was followed in later conferences.[2]

The International Bureau prepares the work of the conferences and obtains the approval of the administration of the country in which the Conference is to be held.[3] The Bureau takes into consideration, in preparing the work of the Conference, the various *voeux* and proposals adopted by the previous conferences or by unofficial organizations, such as the International Association for the Protection of Industrial Property. After the World War two more international institutions were concerned with improvements of the Convention: the International Chamber of Commerce and the various committees of the League of Nations, especially the Economic and Financial Committees.[4]

§ 73. Proceedings at Conferences. At its preliminary meeting, the Conference elects its chairman, vice-chairman, secretary-general, and a number of secretaries. The chairman, according to the practice, is a national of the country in which the Conference meets, and the vice-chairman a national of the country in which the previous Conference was held. The Conference then adopts its rules of procedure. At the opening session, after the usual formal speeches, the Conference is constituted into a Committee of the Whole, which is divided into a number of sub-committees for the separate consideration of the various proposals.[5] The sub-commit-

1. *Actes de Madrid*, p. 172; *Actes de Bruxelles*, p. 328.

2. At the Conference of Washington late proposals were submitted by Austria, France, Great Britain, Italy, Japan, Russia, and Switzerland (*Actes de Washington*, p. 220). At the Conference of The Hague, Austria sent in late its proposals, which were admitted by exception. See *Actes de la Conférence de La Haye*, p. 383.

3. The invitations for the Washington Conference, to be held on May 15, 1911, were sent out by the government of the United States on June 30, 1910. The International Bureau, however, began preparing the work of the Conference in January, 1910, and, by twelve consecutive circulars, it sent to the administrations of the members of the Union the preliminary documents. (*Actes de la Conférence de Washington*, pp. 33 ff.) Similarly, in the case of the Conference of The Hague, see *Actes de la Conférence de La Haye*, pp. 33 ff., 215, 331, 383.

4. See as to the Conference of The Hague the preliminary remarks of the International Bureau, *Conférence de La Haye, Documents Préliminaires, 3e fascicule*, p. 3.

5. See as to the last two Conferences, *Actes de Washington*, p. 264, and *Actes de La Haye*, pp. 404 ff.

tees prepare separate reports, which are submitted to the Conference assembling again in plenary session. In all the conferences of revision the only language used was French. At the recent Conference of The Hague, the American delegation proposed that the English language, as well as the French, should be used as official. This proposition was not adopted, but the right to speak in a language other than French in the discussions of the Conference was recognized, provided that any delegation desiring to avail themselves of this privilege supplied their own interpreter.[1]

In the first conferences of revision amendments to the Convention were adopted in the form of separate documents, called Protocols or Additional Acts. In the last two conferences the amendments and new proposals were incorporated in the old text, with the insertion sometimes of additional articles. The recent practice avoids the confusion arising from the multiplication of texts, and secures continuity of interpretation and application of the various articles of the Convention.[2]

§ **74. Unanimity rule.** There is a feature of the proceedings of conferences of revision, the importance of which transcends all other questions. This is the unanimity rule, according to which no amendment to the Convention or Arrangements may be adopted unless there is a unanimous vote in its favor. Thus any country which is loath to subordinate national interests or national regulation to international interests or international regulation, may defeat any proposals supported even by all the other members.

This becomes extremely serious when it is recalled that the Union is constituted to-day by thirty-eight countries, the interests and municipal laws of which differ, and that it is practically impossible to hope that any improvement of the international regime of industrial property in the Union can be obtained without compromise between the various countries. The last two conferences of revision, at Washington and at The Hague, have shown that such compromise is not always forthcoming, and that desirable improvements of the

1. The American, British, Canadian, Australian, and Danish delegations did in fact make some of their speeches in English. See *Actes de la Conférence de La Haye*, pp. 353, 386, 390 ff. Also, *Papers and Correspondence Relative to the Conference of The Hague* (H. M. Stationery Office, London, 1926), p. 102.

2. The revised texts, like the original Convention and Arrangements, are made in a single copy in the French language, and are signed and filed in the archives of the government of the country in which the Conference takes place. A certified copy is issued by this government to each of the other governments. See art. 19 of the Convention.

Convention have failed through the opposition of one, two, or three countries.

Mr. Alingh Prins, President of the Board of Patents of the Netherlands, concludes from his experience that it will be practically impossible in the future to revise anything. He also remarks that conferences of revision are called after long intervals, and that the fact that the delegations of the various countries change at each conference makes impossible a spirit of continuity in the legislative activity of the Union similar to that existing in the legislature of a country.[1]

The question, then, arises of the possible safeguards against the consequences of the unanimity rule. A first solution is to permit the country or countries opposing an amendment adopted by the great majority of the members of the Union (for instance, three fourths thereof) to make reservations on this amendment on depositing their ratification of the revised text. This is the practice in the International Copyright Union. It has been adopted very reluctantly, and is a cause of much dissatisfaction.

Another solution is to resort to restricted unions between the countries that agree on an amendment of the Convention which other countries are not prepared to accept. This was done by the adoption of the two Madrid Arrangements and the recent Arrangement of The Hague. It is a sound solution so long as it concerns important amendments and is resorted to rarely. If a special Arrangement should be adopted for every amendment of the Convention which is opposed by some members of the Union, a great multiplication of international acts would result, and only the name of the Union would remain.

Both these solutions have the defect of defeating the main idea and the fundamental aim of the Union, which is to achieve progressively a uniform international regime of industrial property, and a harmonizing of the laws of the various countries through the disappearance of those peculiarities of municipal law and practice which do not respond to actual national necessities and interests. It is submitted that it is time that it should be frankly considered whether the unanimity rule can coexist with the idea of a union of thirty-

1. See his article "La Conférence de La Haye de L'Union Internationale pour la Protection de la Propriété Industrielle," in *Grotius Annuaire* (1927), p. 27. M. Prins was Chairman of the Conference of The Hague in 1925. See also Plaisant et Fernand-Jacq, *Le Nouveau Régime International de la Propriété Industrielle* (Paris, 1927), p. 13.

eight countries. But this question is taken up in the last part of this study.[1]

§ **75. The coming into effect of revised texts.** The revised texts go into effect, according to article 18 of the Convention and the final articles of the Arrangements, after, first, ratification; second, the deposit of ratifications; and third, one month following the expiration of the period of time fixed for the deposit of ratifications.

In the text adopted at the first conferences of revision, the period within which ratifications should be deposited was too short, and article 18 was not complied with in that respect. The later conferences extended this period. Thus, while the text adopted at the Paris Conference of 1883 stipulated that the deposit of ratifications should take place within one year, and that adopted at the Madrid Conference provided for a six-months period, at Brussels the period was enlarged to eighteen months, at Washington to twenty-two, and at The Hague to almost thirty months. This long period makes it possible for all countries to take steps for the ratification of the revised texts and deposit their ratification, in order that the revised text may go into effect at the same time for all of them. But it has also the effect of postponing for a long time the coming into effect of improvements of the international regime.

However, the provision of article 18 concerning the period within which ratifications should be deposited is not peremptory. The revised texts do not become null and void nor, in case of failure to comply with its terms, are the contracting countries precluded from depositing ratifications at a later time. The period fixed in the Convention purports only to supply a common date from which it begins to develop its effects as to the countries that have ratified it on various dates in the interval. The ratifications of the acts of the Conferences of Paris and Madrid were deposited after the period for deposit had lapsed.[2] The deposit of ratifications of the Additional Acts of Brussels was made within the fixed period of eighteen months.[3] The texts revised at Washington were signed on June 2,

1. See *infra*, chap. XXXVI, § 571.

2. The exchange of ratifications of the original Convention signed at Paris on March 20, 1883, which should have taken place one year later, did in fact occur on June 6, 1884. See *Propriété Industrielle* (1885), p. 5. The deposit of ratifications of the Acts of Madrid took place on June 15, 1892, instead of October 15, 1891. *Procès-Verbaux de la Conférence de Madrid*, p. 223; XXVII *U. S. Stat. at Large*, 959.

3. The *procès-verbal* was opened on May 3, 1901, and was closed on June 14, when the period came to an end. *Actes de Washington*, p. 13; XXXII *U. S. Stat. at Large*, part II, p. 1943.

1911. They provided that the ratifications should be exchanged at Washington not later than the first of April, 1913. This was complied with.[1]

At the Conference of The Hague article 18 of the Convention was amended so as to provide that ratifications should be deposited at The Hague not later than the first of May, 1928, but that, nevertheless, if before that date it had been ratified by at least six countries, it should come into force, between these countries, one month after the deposit of the sixth ratification had been notified to them by the Swiss Government.[2] This possibility has not occurred. The ratification of the Acts revised at The Hague as well as of the new Arrangement of The Hague were deposited at The Hague on May 1, 1928.[3]

Countries not depositing their ratifications within the period provided for in article 18 should be able to deposit them at a later time. These acts are not closed treaties, in which time may be essential. Members of the Union participating in the revision of the texts, and signing them should be able to deposit their ratifications after the lapse of the period of article 18. However, article 18 contains no provision for such late deposits, and the practice has been to have these countries accede to the revised texts.[4]

The question is not altogether one of form. There exists a difference as to the time when the revised texts will go into effect. In the case of a deposit of ratification, the new texts go into effect as to the country in question one month after the deposit (article 18), while the accession produces its effects one month after the notification of accession by the Swiss government is sent to the members of the Union (article 16).

§ 76. Texts applicable in countries failing to ratify revised texts. The long period for the deposit of ratifications, undesirable though it may be, has been preferred to the evil resulting from the non-

1. See *Actes de la Conférence de La Haye*, pp. 15, 18, 22; XXXVIII *U. S. Stat. at Large*, part II, *p*. 1658; *Propriété Industrielle*, (1913), pp. 65, 66.

2. Similar provision is made by the Madrid Arrangement for the repression of false indications of origin, article 6.

3. See *Propriété Industrielle* (1928), pp. 97–98. See also *supra*, p. 98.

4. In the case of the Additional Acts of Brussels, Spain and Brazil deposited their ratifications a few months after the lapse of the period of eighteen months, and after the *procès-verbal* of ratifications had been closed. Serbia and the Dominican Republic, which did not ratify the Acts until seven years later, were advised by the Swiss government to accede to these Acts. See *Actes de Washington*, p. 14, and *Propriété Industrielle* (1921), p. 27.

ratification in due time by all the members of the Union. Indeed, many countries have been unable to deposit their ratifications before the lapse of the period fixed in article 18 of the Convention and the final articles of the Arrangements. On May 1, 1928, only seven out of the thirty-eight members of the Union deposited their ratifications of the Convention revised at The Hague: Italy, Germany, Great Britain and Northern Ireland, Austria, Canada, Spain, and the Netherlands. Only in the relations between these countries is the revised text applicable from the above date. In their relations with the other countries, the texts in force prior to the revision at The Hague will continue to be in effect, according to the second paragraph of article 18 of the Convention and of similar provisions of the Arrangements. Thus, in effect, there is a duality of regimes, or two superposed Unions, one governed by the new text and the other by the old.

However, this temporary coexistence of two texts is preferable to the system of reservations of the International Copyright Union, which is the cause of confusion and lack of uniformity in that Union.[1] In the Copyright Union, by the facility of reservations, there arises a tendency toward differentiation whereas in the Industrial Property Union a country may either ratify the whole of the new Convention or remain bound by the old text. Thus pressure is brought to bear upon a country to ratify the new Convention. Practice has unmistakably proved this. All the members of the Union have at an earlier or later date ratified the new texts.[2]

§ **77. Adoption of Règlements.** The Arrangement of Madrid for the international registration of trade marks, and the recent Arrangement of The Hague, which make of the International Bureau a real executive organ, necessitated a number of administrative regulations between the parties to these Arrangements. These *Règlements* are prepared by the Bureau and the Conference. Their scope is limited. They carry out the principles established by the Arrangements. They are prepared, adopted, and revised without

1. Articles 25 and 27 of this Convention allow countries acceding for the first time to the Union, or members thereof ratifying the new Convention, to elect to remain bound by the old text. *Actes de Conférence de Berlin* (International Bureau, Berne, 1908), pp. 321, 322. *League of Nations Treaty Series*, I, 218.

2. When Germany acceded in 1903 to the Convention of 1883 and to the Additional Act of Brussels, it declared that it would not enter into any legal relations, on the basis of the Convention, with members of the Union that had not yet ratified the Additional Act of Brussels. *Propriété Industrielle* (1903), p. 37.

the formalities attending the adoption and revision of the Arrangements.

The first *Règlement* for the execution of the Arrangement concerning the international registration of trade marks was prepared by the International Bureau, according to a decision of the Conference of 1890 directing the Bureau to this effect. It was then submitted to the Swiss government, and by it communicated to all the members of the Union through diplomatic channels. The *Règlement* did not need to be ratified. The final article (11) provided as follows:

Le présent Règlement entrera en vigueur en même temps que l'Arrangement auquel il se rapporte et il aura la même durée.

Les Administrations contractantes pourront toujours y apporter, d'un commun accord, conformément aux dispositions de l'Article 10 du dit Arrangement, les modifications qui leur paraîtront nécessaires.

Article 10 of the Arrangement to which reference is made reads as follows: "Les Administrations règleront d'un commun accord les détails relatifs à l'exécution du présent Arrangement." Thus article 10 of the Arrangement provided only for "un commun accord." Such *accord* was expressed by a declaration of all the countries signing the Arrangement on April 14, 1891, that their administrations had approved of the *Règlement*.[1]

At the Conferences of Brussels, Washington, and The Hague, the Bureau proposed some amendments of the *Règlement*. The sub-committee on trade marks of the Conference considered these amendments and rejected some of them, and the Conference simply approved those approved by the sub-committee. The new *Règlement* went into effect without being either signed or ratified.[2]

The *Règlement* for the execution of the Arrangement of The Hague was prepared by the International Bureau, and, following its consideration and slight modification by the sub-committee and the committee of the whole, was adopted by the Conference of The Hague. It is not included among the texts signed by the delegates.[3]

§ 78. Urgent measures during intervals between Conferences. Following a proposal by the International Bureau, the Conference of The Hague adopted a resolution to the effect that, in case, in the interval between two conferences, the International Bureau should

1. See *procès-verbal*, in *Propriété Industrielle* (1892), p. 91.
2. See *Actes de Washington* (1911), pp. 261, 295, 315; *Propriété Industrielle* (1913), pp. 65, 66; *Actes de la Conférence de La Haye*, pp. 15, 18, 22.
3. *Ibid.*, pp. 323, 512, 532, 585.

consider it useful to cause the application of an urgent measure in the interest of the general Union or of any of the restricted Unions, it may request the Swiss Federal Council to submit to the contracting countries the adoption of this measure. Recourse will thus be had to the procedure followed by the Bureau in 1921, when the need of an increase of credits at its disposal was presented. The modifications which would be brought in this way to the regime of the Unions will be of a provisional character until definite decisions are taken by the following Conference.[1]

This resolution is important as showing the accentuation of the character of executive authority with which the International Bureau has been clothed since 1890. It is a question to what extent the Bureau may use the power granted by this resolution. It would seem also that the approval of a majority of the countries of the adoption of the measure in question should be sufficient for its application. But countries disapproving of the measure should not be bound by its application.

1. See *Actes de la Conférence de La Haye*, pp. 330, 527, 569, 586.

CHAPTER VI

RELATION OF THE CONVENTION CREATING THE UNION FOR THE PROTECTION OF INDUSTRIAL PROPERTY TO BIPARTITE TREATIES

§ 79. Two questions for consideration. The Union for the Protection of Industrial Property was created between countries that had already entered into bipartite treaties [1] between themselves for the protection of trade marks, industrial designs or models, and so forth.[2] Most of these treaties which were dated before 1883 have perhaps ceased to exist. However, many countries have acceded at recent times to the general Union, and the restricted Unions constituted by the Madrid Arrangements. Before such accession, these countries had entered into bipartite treaties with members of the Union, which had not expired at the time their accession was effected.

The question, then, arises whether or not these bipartite treaties should he deemed to be abrogated by the fact that the contracting countries have become members of the general or restricted Unions. If it should be concluded that they are not abrogated the persons protected by them may continue to claim their protection in addition to the protection granted by the Convention of 1883–1925 and the Arrangements. In this respect it should be noted that, while the bipartite treaties concluded before 1883 afforded, in general, a less adequate protection than that of the Union, those concluded after that date not only adopted many of the principles of the Conven-

1. The term "treaty" is used in this chapter as including all treaties of commerce, conventions, arrangements, declarations, exchanges of notes, etc., relating to, or containing provisions for, the protection of industrial property rights.
2. See *supra*, chap. III.

tion, but sometimes went further in protecting industrial property rights. Consequently, there may be cases in which a person would desire to claim the protection of a bipartite treaty in addition to that of the Industrial Property Convention. A further consequence of the coexistence of this Convention and the bipartite treaties would be that, in case of withdrawal of a country from the Union, its relations with members of the Union would continue to be governed by the bipartite conventions concluded before its accession to the Union.

Besides the relation of the acts creating the Union to the bipartite treaties entered into by countries before their accession to the Union, the question also arises as to the relation of the same acts to bipartite treaties entered into by members of the Union between themselves after their accession to the Union.[1]

§ 80. Theory of abrogation of bipartite treaties entered into before accession to the Convention of 1883. In respect to the first question, namely, the effect of the accession to the Union on bipartite treaties entered into before accession, two views may be supported. First: that these treaties, in so far as they refer to matters not provided for in the Union, or contain stipulations more favorable to the persons protected than those of the Industrial Property Convention remain in force after the accession of the contracting parties to that Convention; in all other cases and as to all other provisions, these treaties should be considered as abrogated. Second: that no bipartite treaty is to be deemed to be abrogated by the sole fact that the contracting countries have become members of the Union. The protection of such treaty may be claimed concurrently with that of the acts creating the Union.

The first view is formed from the consideration that a multipartite convention is, in fact, a number of bipartite conventions concluded together. A treaty, in other words, between A, B, C, D, and others is an aggregate of treaties between A and B, A and C, A and D, B and C, B and D, C and D, and so forth, of the same content. A prior bipartite agreement, then, between A and B alone may be superseded by the new agreement between the same parties, implied and contained in the multipartite convention. When the provisions of the former are similar to those of the latter, or less favorable to the citizens of each country, the former convention

1. See compilation in *Propriété Industrielle* (1919), pp. 87 ff.

should be held to be impliedly abrogated by the latter. On the contrary, when some of the provisions of the former are more favorable to the citizens of each country, they should be deemed as remaining in force and should be given effect over and above the provisions of the multipartite Convention.[1]

It is submitted that this view is theoretically unsound and arbitrary, and that it cannot be supported, particularly in respect to the Convention under consideration.

The theory that a multipartite convention is really an aggregate of bilateral agreements cannot go too far. It is true in so far as it means that it is an aggregate of mutual obligations between one and another of the contracting countries as well as between each and all the others. But it is very questionable, when it implies that a bipartite treaty will be abrogated implicitly by the multipartite convention. There is no mutual intent to discontinue a prior bipartite treaty, manifested in the fact that the two countries enter with the other countries into a general convention dealing with the same matter. The general convention has advantages of its own for the parties thereto, namely, a uniform solution of some problems involved in all bipartite conventions; a more permanent international situation; an international organization and administration of interests of international character. It does not necessarily involve an intent of the parties to do away with separate agreements with each other.

This is shown by the fact that, even after the adoption of the Convention of 1883 or accession thereto, the member countries of the Union continued to include, in bipartite agreements among themselves, the old provision of national treatment in respect to rights of industrial property, and other provisions now contained in the Convention of 1883. Two of these treaties were entered into in 1884[2] and 1892,[3] while the others are very recent.[4] Moreover, four recent

1. So Pillet, *Régime International*, pp. 212, 245 ff.; Pelletier et Vidal-Naquet, *Convention d'Union*, p. 29; Donzel, *Commentaire de la Convention de 1883*, p. 345; Osterrieth und Axster, *Pariser Konvention*, p. 240.

2. Treaty of Commerce, art. 3 (June 2, 1884), between Italy and Spain (*Recueil des Traités*, Bureau International de la Propriété Industrielle, p. 173).

3. Treaty of Commerce, art. 11 (June 27, 1892), between Spain and Norway and Sweden (LXXXIV *Br. & For. State Papers*, 113).

4. Commercial Convention, art. 21 (December 15, 1922), between France and Canada (*League of Nations Treaty Series*, XXI, 38).

Treaty of Commerce, art. 22 (June 22, 1923), between Great Britain and Latvia (*Propriété Industrielle*, 1928, p. 107).

treaties contain an express engagement to give effective application to the Convention of 1883.[1] All this shows clearly the desire of members of the Union to have individual engagements, so to speak, besides the general agreement of the International Convention of 1883.

Nor is there any impossibility of execution of such bipartite treaties by countries becoming members of the Union. The citizens of each state may claim the protection of these treaties as well as of the Union. The courts of each state may apply either.[2]

Moreover, article 15 of the Convention seems to be against the view discussed here. This article reads as follows:

> Il est entendu que les pays contractants se réservent respectivement le droit de prendre séparément, entre eux, des arrangements particuliers pour la protection de la propriété industrielle, en tant que ces arrangements ne contreviendraient point aux dispositions de la présente Convention.

This reservation of the right of each member of the Union to enter into separate arrangements does not seem to concern the future only.[3] The preparatory work of the Conference of 1880, which adopted article 15 in its present form, shows that, in the *arrangements particuliers* in article 15, both the bipartite agreements already entered into and those to be concluded in the future were included.[4]

Treaty of Commerce, art. 20 (May 22, 1924), between Austria and Great Britain (*League of Nations Treaty Series*, XXXV, 176).

Treaty of Commerce, May 12, 1927, between Great Britain and Serb-Croat-Slovene State (*Propriété Industrielle*, 1928, p. 197).

Treaty of Commerce, art. 7 (July 26, 1927), between Austria and Latvia (*Propriété Industrielle*, 1927, p. 194).

1. Between: France and Latvia, October 30, 1924 (*Propriété Industrielle*, 1925, p. 93); France and Portugal, March 4, 1925, art. 8 (*Propriété Industrielle*, 1925, p. 138); Finland and Hungary, May 29, 1925, art. 29 (*Propriété Industrielle*, 1926, p. 121); and France and Germany, Commercial Agreement, August 17, 1927, art. 27 (*Propriété Industrielle*, 1927, p. 176).

2. Thus the Court of Appeals of Nîmes (France) applied in 1905 the Treaty of 1862 between France and Italy in a case involving the protection of trade name and trade mark of an Italian. (Baracco Frères *c.* Carenon et Tur, January 10, 1905, in *Darras*, 1906, p. 122). The criticism of the case by this Revue and Pillet (*Régime International*, p. 248 n.) does not seem justified.

3. So held in A. Weiss and Co. *c.* Randon, Cour d'Appel de Genève, May 14, 1888 (*La Semaine Judiciaire*, Geneva, 1888, p. 673), affirmed by the Federal Tribunal, September 29, 1888 (*Journal des Tribunaux*, 1888, p. 705).

4. *Conférence de 1880* (Paris), p. 121. The Italian Delegate in explaining the article and supporting it stated: "Il est évident que les États auront le droit de maintenir ou de modifier les arrangements qu'ils ont signés avec d'autres États."

Nor can the view that the Convention of 1883 abrogated all bipartite treaties which covered the same ground with it be supported, because the consequences to which it would lead are not accepted by its supporters themselves. Indeed, while maintaining that the bipartite agreements are abrogated by the Convention of 1883, these authors hold: (*a*) that the provisions of these agreements which are more favorable to the subjects of each country than the provisions of the Convention of 1883 will remain in effect; and (*b*) that eventually, the provisions of these agreements that are deemed to be abrogated would revive in case the Convention of 1883 should be denounced.

There is some inconsequence between these results and the view these authors are taking in respect to the relation of bipartite treaties to the multipartite Convention of 1883. If the latter should be deemed to include a bipartite agreement between countries that are parties to both, it is not seen why it should not be held that the last expression of will of the two countries, implied in the multipartite Convention, should always prevail over the will manifested in the prior bipartite agreement, whether this is more or less favorable to the subjects of each country. Besides, it is not easy to say when a provision of a bipartite treaty is more or less favorable than the equivalent provision of the Convention of 1883. Such a provision may be more favorable to the one country and less so to the other. Or it may favor one class of nationals of the one country and be harmful to another. What, then, is the test to be used in arriving at the conclusion that a provision of a bipartite treaty is or is not superseded by the Convention of 1883?

On the other hand, the result that a bipartite treaty may revive at the denunciation of the Convention of 1883 is founded on the theory that the former is not altogether abrogated, but only suspended. The theory of suspension, in so far as it is not based on an express understanding of the parties, is a mere subterfuge to avoid the impossible results to which a wrong theory leads. No principle or basis for this theory may be discovered. Pillet can do no better in this respect than appeal to the *sentiment général* as its foundation.[1]

§ 81. Theory of concurrent application. It is submitted then, that, according to the above second view,[2] no bipartite treaty is

1. Pillet, *Régime International*, p. 250.
2. Neuberg, *Der internationale gewerbliche Rechtsschutz*, 2d ed. (1923), p. 49, intimates an opinion in accordance with the one suggested here.

abrogated by the sole fact that the parties thereof have become members of the Union for the Protection of Industrial Property. The parties, as well as the purposes of each, are different.

No intent to put an end to the engagement contained in the bipartite convention may be implied in the act of acceding to the Convention of 1883. The latter may be done at different times. Whenever there is intent to terminate the bipartite treaty, it may not be renewed. Article 15 of the Convention in connection with the preparatory work of the Conference of 1880 shows the independence of the two sorts of agreements.

Since the bipartite treaties and the Convention of 1883 are concurrently in effect, the provisions of either will be applicable in a case involving the protection of a right of industrial property. When a state transforms a bipartite and a multipartite convention into municipal law by an act of its own, the following situation is created. On the one part, there are two sets of dispositions of law, and the courts will do with them what they always do in the case of two ordinary laws dealing with the same matter. They will apply the provisions of the latest text in all cases where there is diversity between the two.

On the other hand, the multipartite and bipartite conventions are to each other in the relation of general and special laws; that is, a law concerning all or many classes of persons, and a law concerning only a special class of persons. In such case, the bipartite treaty will always apply over the general Convention, unless there is express provision to the contrary. Article 15 of the Convention of 1883 provides that only separate arrangements contravening the stipulations of the Convention are to be excluded.

Thus Swiss courts have applied the Convention of 1882 between France and Switzerland rather than the International Convention of 1883, in the protection of a French trade mark, when it appeared that both acts were to the same effect, but that the former was clearer in stipulating that a trade mark valid under the French law should be validated in Switzerland.[1]

Whenever the intention was that the bipartite treaties concluded before accession to the Union should be abrogated, the contracting

1. A. Weiss and Co. *c.* Randon, Cour d'Appel de Genève, May 14, 1888 (*La Semaine Judiciaire*, Geneva, 1888, p. 673; also *Propriété Industrielle*, 1888, p. 107); affirmed by the Federal Tribunal, September 29, 1888 (*Journal des Tribunaux*, 1888, p. 705).

countries have taken affirmative action to this effect. Thus, Germany, before acceding to the Union, in 1903, entered into new agreements with Switzerland [1] and Italy,[2] by which the provisions of bipartite treaties which were identical with the stipulations of the Convention were abrogated, and those which granted to the nationals of each party a broader protection were maintained. The same took place in 1908 at the accession of Austria and Hungary to the Convention.[3]

On the other hand, according to the view advanced here, no question of revival of bipartite conventions arises. These are always in force, in so far as they are not terminated by any of the generally admitted grounds of termination of treaties, such as lapse of the period for which they were entered into, denunciation, and so forth.

§ **82. Bipartite treaties between members of the Union after their accession to the Union.** The relation to the Convention of 1883 of bipartite treaties entered into by two members of the Union between themselves after their accession to the Union is governed by article 15, already cited. This article expressly permits any separate arrangements between members of the Union, "in so far as these arrangements do not contravene the stipulations of the Convention."

The meaning of this qualification is not very clear. The clause seems to be one of style, borrowed from the Postal Union and Telegraphic Union conventions. It should be interpreted with reference to the purpose of each particular provision of the Convention and to the whole purpose of the Convention, which is to secure, to persons entitled to the benefits of the Union, the most complete and effective protection of industrial property. Thus, no bipartite treaty relaxing this general protection of industrial property between two member countries is permitted under article 15. But agreements enlarging the protection afforded by the Convention may well be entered into.[4] For instance, a bipartite treaty may be concluded between two members of the Union for extending the period of rights of priority beyond the time provided for by the Convention of 1883, but not for limiting this period. Also an agreement may be made abolishing the

1. Arrangement of May 26, 1902 (*De Martens N. R.*, 2d ser., XXXI, 348).
2. Arrangement of June 4, 1902 (*De Martens N. R.*, 2d ser., XXXI, 352).
3. Conventions with Germany of November 17, 1908 (CI *Br. & For. State Papers*, 666).
4. Osterrieth und Axster, *Pariser Konvention*, p. 241.

forfeiture of a patent for failure of the patentee to work his invention in the country granting the patent, but not one declaring the forfeiture of a patent for importation of goods manufactured abroad with the patent.[1]

§ 83. The Arrangements of Madrid and of The Hague. The Arrangements of Madrid and the recent Arrangement of The Hague were entered into under the same power reserved to the members of the Union by article 15 of the Convention. The Arrangements of Madrid concerning the repression of false indications of origin was entered into with the express purpose of doing away with the limitations of article 10 of the Convention. The latter provided for the seizure of articles bearing a false indication of origin only in case such indication was joined to a fictitious trade name, or borrowed with a fraudulent intention. The Arrangement does away with these limitations.

On the other hand, the Arrangement of Madrid and the Arrangement of The Hague, concerning the international registration of trade marks and the international deposit of industrial designs or models respectively, purport to relieve the persons entitled to their benefits from the obligation of registering or depositing in each of the contracting countries their trade marks or industrial designs and models, which obligation was maintained by the Convention.

§ 84. Contents of bipartite treaties between members of the Union. In the first years of the existence of the Union few bipartite treaties were entered into by member countries. They became more numerous after 1900, when the Convention did not entirely satisfy certain countries which desired a more effective protection of the industrial property of their nationals. A number of arrangements were also entered into by members of the Union for the mutual protection of rights of industrial property of their nationals in countries of extraterritorial jurisdiction.[2]

Some bipartite treaties do away with the obligation of working a patent, which was maintained by article 5 of the Convention;[3]

1. A bipartite convention between two members of the Union contravening the Convention of 1883, although in violation of article 15, would not be for this reason void.

2. This whole regime is rapidly reaching the point when it will go out of existence. See *Propriété Industrielle* (1925), p. 75.

3. United States and Denmark, Agreement, June 22–26, 1906 (XCIX *Br. & For. State Papers*, 1039).

United States and Switzerland, Declaration, February 2, 1908 (*Recueil Général des Traités et de Législation*, Bureau International de la Propriété Industrielle, VII, 542).

or with the obligation to work in a country an industrial design or model deposited in that country but originating in the other contracting country and being worked therein; or with the forfeiture for importation of articles manufactured with the design or model.[1]

Denmark and Sweden and Norway made a declaration, to go into effect on the date of Denmark's accession to the Union (October 1, 1894), according to which the validity of trade marks of their respective nationals was to be governed by the law of the country of origin.[2] France, in accordance with article 289 of the Treaty of Versailles, notified Germany on February 9, 1922, that it desired to revive article 11 of the Convention of October 12, 1871, which had revived, after the war of 1870, article 28 of the Treaty of Commerce of August 2, 1862, between France and the Zollverein, dealing with the protection of trade marks.[3] France and Italy, by a Declaration of March 16, 1887, agreed to protect rights of industrial property of associations of the two countries.[4]

A great number of bipartite treaties undertake to protect indications of place of origin without the limitations of the Convention of 1883 or of the Madrid Arrangement for the repression of false indications of origin. The provisions of the treaties of commerce between Great Britain and Serbia, of June 28–July 11, 1893 (article 5),[5] and between Norway and Portugal, of December 31, 1895 (article

---

United States and Germany, Arrangement, February 23, 1909 (CII *Br. & For. State Papers*, 443).

Germany and Switzerland, Arrangement, May 26, 1902 (*De Martens N. R.*, 2d ser., XXXI, 348).

Germany and Italy, Arrangement, June 4, 1902 (*De Martens N. R.*, 2d ser., XXXI, 352).

1. Spain and Sweden and Norway, Treaty of Commerce, art. 10, June 27, 1892 (LXXXIV *Br. & For. State Papers*, 113).

Denmark and Belgium, April 22, 1906 (C *Br. & For. State Papers*, 707).

Denmark and Italy, March 3, 1907 (CI *Br. & For. State Papers*, 282).

Denmark and Sweden, June 19, 1908 (CI *Br. & For. State Papers*, 962).

The treaty of commerce of October 20, 1906, between France and Switzerland, in article 23, provided that, in order that protection of designs and models should be enjoyed mutually by the nationals of the contracting countries, it was not necessary that an industrial establishment was possessed by them in either country (C *Br. & For. State Papers*, 935).

2. See *Recueil des Traités*, Bureau International de la Propriété Industrielle, p. 168.

3. See on this, *supra*, p. 64.

4. LXXVIII *Br. & For. State Papers*, 722.

5. LXXXV *Br. & For. State Papers*, 77. It protects special marks indicating origin and quality of merchandise.

13),[1] hardly add anything, perhaps, to the stipulations of the Convention and the Madrid Arrangement. But Portugal entered into separate arrangements with Germany,[2] Austria-Hungary,[3] Norway,[4] and Czechoslovakia,[5] to the effect that false indications of origin should be prohibited, and that the designations "Porto" and "Madeira" should be considered as strictly appellations of origin and not generic terms. On the other hand, the provisions of the treaties of peace concerning the protection of indications of origin,[6] have been transferred to bipartite conventions entered into by France with Finland,[7] Norway,[8] Czechoslovakia,[9] Poland,[10] Latvia,[11] Austria,[12] and Belgium-Luxembourg,[13] and in an Arrangement between Austria and Czechoslovakia.[14] Thus, in all these arrangements, in addition to the engagement of executing the Madrid Arrangement, it is provided that each country shall follow the other's administrative regulations or judicial decisions on the question whether a designation of wine products is an indication of origin or a generic term. A recent Arrangement between France and Switzerland provides that the use of the indications "Cognac"

1. LXXXVII *Br. & For. State Papers*, 534. It prohibits the sale and importation of agricultural and industrial products bearing a false indication of origin.

2. Final Protocol to Treaty of Commerce of November 30, 1908 (CI *Br. & For. State Papers*, 932); and Commercial Arrangement, art. 6*b*, March 20, 1926 (*Propriété Industrielle*, 1926, p. 194).

3. Exchange of Notes, July 8, 1911 (CIV *Br. & For. State Papers*, 736); see also Exchange of Notes, December 18, 1925, with Austria (*Propriété Industrielle*, 1926, p. 90).

4. Arrangement, art. 6, April 11, 1923 (*League of Nations Treaty Series*, XVI, 380).

5. Arrangement, art. 3, December 11, 1922 (*Propriété Industrielle*, 1922, p. 61).

6. Treaty of Versailles, arts. 274, 275; Treaty of St. Germain, arts. 226, 227; Treaty of Trianon, art. 210; Treaty of Neuilly, arts. 154, 155; Commercial Convention annexed to the Treaty of Peace of Lausanne with Turkey, arts. 12, 13. See on these provisions *infra*, chap. XXX, § 474.

7. Treaty of Commerce, arts. 15, 16, 17, July 13, 1921 (*League of Nations Treaty Series*, XXIV, 446).

8. Convention, art. 4, April 23, 1921 (*League of Nations Treaty Series*, XIV, 376), and Convention of April 12, 1927 (*Propriété Industrielle*, 1927, p. 97).

9. Convention, arts. 24, 25, 26, November 4, 1920 (*Propriété Industrielle*, 1924, p. 43).

10. Convention, arts. 12, 13, 14, February 6, 1922, (*Propriété Industrielle*, 1922, p. 165).

11. Commercial Convention, art. 13, October 30, 1924 (*Propriété Industrielle*, 1925, p. 93). This provision concerns not only wine appellations of origin, but all regional appellations for products deriving their qualities from the soil or climate of a region.

12. Convention, arts. 14, 15, 16, June 22, 1923 (*Propriété Industrielle*, 1924, p. 9).

13. Convention, art. 9, May 12, 1923 (*Propriété Industrielle*, 1924, p. 28); see also, Commercial Agreement, art. 21, February 23, 1928 (*Ibid.*, 1928, p. 161).

14. Arrangement, art. 5, May 4, 1921 (*League of Nations Treaty Series*, XV, 14).

and "Armagnac" shall not be permitted in Swiss territory, except for the products for which the French law recognizes the right of using this appellation of origin.[1]

These last bipartite treaties of France and the other countries,[2] following the treaties of peace, contain also mutual engagements of the contracting countries to take all necessary measures for securing effective protection to the products of each country against acts of unfair competition. The provisions in this respect enumerate the various acts to be repressed; they were, at least before the revision of the Convention of The Hague, broader and more complete than the stipulations of article 10*b* of the Convention.[3]

Some treaties, as was pointed out earlier in this chapter, contain only provisions repeating the stipulations of the Convention of 1883.[4] The treaty of 1893 between Great Britain and Serbia (article 5)[5] accorded to the nationals of each country, besides the national treatment, the benefit of the most-favored-nation clause. The same clause is contained in the Treaty of Commerce (article 1) of June 28, 1926, between Germany and Latvia.[6]

§ **85. Treaties between members of the Union and other countries.** The question of bipartite treaties between members of the Union and other countries does not present any difficulty. Article 15 concerns only arrangements of the members of the Union " between themselves." A member of the Union may enter into any kind of agreement concerning the protection of industrial property with countries not belonging to the Union. Consequently it may give them the privileges and benefits of the most-favored-nation clause in respect to the protection of industrial property rights. This may have the result of granting to the nationals of that country on the territory of the member of the Union, all the rights enjoyed by members of the Union.

The Convention of 1883 has exercised an indirect influence on bipartite treaties entered into by countries not belonging to the

1. *Avenant à l'Arrangement Commercial Franco-Suisse,* signed March 11, 1928 (*Propriété Industrielle,* 1928, p. 79).
2. With the exception of the treaties with Norway, and Belgium-Luxembourg.
3. The same provisions are contained in the Commercial Convention of May 29, 1925 (art. 6) between Finland and Hungary (*Propriété Industrielle,* 1926, p. 121); and in the Commercial Agreement, August 17, 1927, art. 28, between France and Germany (*Propriété Industrielle,* 1927, p. 176).
4. These treaties are cited *supra,* in notes 2, 3, and 4 (p. 137), and 1 (p. 138).
5. LXXXV *Br. & For. State Papers,* 77.
6. *Propriété Industrielle* (1927), p. 29.

Union, whether with members of the Union or with other countries. Not only the principle of national treatment of the Union for all rights of industrial property has been adopted, generally, in such treaties, but also the specific advantages granted by the Convention such as the right of priority and the validation of trade marks, are met with in a number of bipartite treaties and agreements. The most outstanding examples of such influence are the Pan-American conventions on industrial property.[1] Equally interesting is the Convention between Germany and the Union of Socialist Soviet Republics of October 12, 1925,[2] which contains, among others, provisions identical with articles 2 and 4 of the Convention of 1883–1925.

1. See *infra*, section VIII.
2. See text in *Propriété Industrielle* (1926), p. 14, and a study, in *ibid.*, p. 194.

CHAPTER VII

RELATION OF THE CONVENTION AND ARRANGEMENTS OF THE UNION TO THE MUNICIPAL LAW OF THE MEMBER COUNTRIES

§ 86. Place of the Convention of 1883 and the Arrangements in the municipal legal order. The most important aspect of the acts creating the general and the restricted Unions is that of their place in the municipal legal order of the member countries. Indeed, this aspect is important in regard to all treaties or conventions. To use a forceful simile from Triepel,[1] conventional international law is like a field marshal who gives his orders only to the chiefs of armies, and who can achieve his aims only if he is sure that his generals, follow-

1. Triepel, *Les Rapports entre le Droit Interne et le Droit International* (Académie de Droit International, Recueil des Cours, 1923), p. 106.

ing his orders, will give further orders to those under them. If the generals fail to do so, the field marshal loses his battle. If the contracting states fail to transfer the stipulations of a convention into the municipal legal order, their object fails.

The object of the Convention of 1883 is to create a situation in which foreigners' rights of industrial property will be most completely and effectively protected. The Convention attempts to accomplish this object by various provisions, all of which are obligatory on the state. The important question, however, is, how and when do they become obligatory on the citizens and subjects of each country and its courts.

The Convention, like any international treaty, does not by itself make municipal law, the making of the latter being always an act of the state, distinct from its participation in the development of the international legal order.[1] This is affirmed by the Convention of 1883 itself, in article 17, which subordinates execution of the engagements contained in the Convention to compliance with the formalities and regulations established by the constitutional law of each country.

The place of a treaty in the legal order of each country is, of course, determined by its public law. On this point, clear and explicit constitutional provisions exist but rarely. The solution often depends on the general theories concerning the relation of international and municipal law. These theories, however, differ widely.[2]

§ 87. Nature of general international conventions. Whatever the general theory of bipartite treaties may be in the various countries, it is impossible not to realize the difference between such treaties and international multipartite conventions, such as the Convention of 1883 for the creation of the Union for the Protection of Industrial Property. These have nothing of the character of favors or concessions between states of the usual bipartite treaties. They are more than simply contractual obligations between countries. They deal with private interests of an international character.

1. Triepel, *Droit International et Droit Interne* (Washington, 1920), pp. 20 ff., 118 ff.

2. Compare, especially, J. Kohler, "Völkerrecht als Privatrechtstitel," in *Zeitschrift für Völkerrecht und Bundesstaatsrecht* (1908), p. 209; Diena, "L'Individu devant l'Autorité Judiciaire et le Droit International," *Revue Générale de Droit International Public* (1909), XVI, 57, 67; Kaufmann, *Die Rechtskraft des Internationalen Rechtes* (Stuttgart, 1899), pp. 41 ff.; Triepel, *Droit International*, pp. 118 ff.; Anzilotti, *Il diritto internationale nei gudizi interni* (Bologna, 1905), pp. 109, 115; Reinsch, *Public International Unions* (1911), chap. v.

They embody common action on the part of the contracting countries for the recognition and protection of world-wide economic relations and interests which call for regulation and ordering. They attempt to establish an international legal order needed for the full protection of national economic interests, and the economic life of each country whose prosperity is dependent on international co-operation. They constitute a legal ordering and regulating of claims, demands, and interests which hundreds of international associations try to promote by constant and arduous efforts.[1]

It would seem, therefore, that such international multipartite conventions as the Convention of 1883 should be considered as international legislation by the community of countries, parties thereto.[2] Their application and interpretation should be the immediate affairs of courts.[3] As soon as the international and national validity of such a convention is accomplished, its provisions should be applied if they are self-executing.

This conception of the Convention of 1883, as of other general international agreements, is confirmed by the terms in which it is couched. It does not read, as the strict contractual conception should imply: "Chacun des pays contractants s'engage à faire jouir les sujets de l'autre." On the contrary it provides that "Les sujets de chacun des pays contractants jouiront dans tous les autres pays de l'Union . . ." Thus what is bargained for principally is the enjoyment by the citizens of all the contracting countries of the rights protected by the Convention, and not the international engagement of the states.[4]

§ 88. Distinction of three classes of provisions in the Convention. In respect to the Convention of 1883, the problem might be much simplified by distinguishing three classes of provisions contained therein.

1. "It [the legislation enacted by such general international agreements] represents the result of persistent attempts to meet specific problems of international society in a very practical way, and it has frequently been the work of the experts in various governments who were in closest touch with the international actualities which made legislation desirable." Hudson, "The Prospect for International Law in the Twentieth Century," *Cornell Law Quarterly* (1925), X, 446.

2. Hudson, "The Development of International Law since the War," in *American Journal of International Law* (1928), XXII, 330, 339.

3. Quincy Wright, "The Legal Nature of Treaties," in *American Journal of International Law* (1916), X, 706, 734.

4. Diena, "L'Individu . . . et le Droit International," in *Revue Générale de Droit International Public* (1909), p. 68.

1. Provisions referring merely to the municipal law of each country and making it applicable. (For instance, the national-treatment clause of article 2.)

2. Provisions obligating the contracting countries to create and maintain certain provisions of municipal law. (For instance, the stipulation in article 11 for a temporary protection of industrial property at international expositions.)

3. Provisions establishing common legislation for all members of the Union. (For instance, the right of priority in article 4, the validation of trade marks in article 6, the protection of trade names in article 8.)[1]

It will not be disputed that the provisions of the second class are wholly inoperative in the municipal legal order, unless legislative action is taken by the contracting countries to carry out the principles laid down by these provisions. The operation of the two other classes of provisions in the municipal legal order of a country depends upon whether in that country a treaty is immediately effective or not.

§ 89. Introduction of the Convention in the municipal legal order of various countries. In many of the countries of the Union a treaty is introduced into the municipal legal order by the sole fact of its publication in the official journal, after its approval and ratification by the organs of the state which have this power by the constitutional law. Often, the fact that the legislative body itself must approve a treaty before its ratification by the head of the state gives to the provisions of the treaty an immediate effect in the municipal law. Thus, the Convention of 1883 became immediately effective in continental Europe; for instance, in Belgium,[2] France,[3] Germany,[4]

1. A somewhat similar distinction is made by Mr. Ostertag, Director of the International Bureau of the Union, in 25 *Mich. L. R.* (1926), 107.

2. See Law of July 5, 1884, art. 3, approving the Convention of 1883 (*Pasinomie*, 1884, p. 294). The Convention was applied directly in the case of Criem et Heintz *c.* Trinchant et État Français, Cassation, May 8, 1911 (*Pasicrisie*, 1911, I, 247).

3. Fauchille, *Traité*, 8th ed., I, part III, 346; Esmein, *Eléments de Droit Constitutionel*, 7th ed., II, 188. The Convention of 1883 formed the basis of decision in the cases of Pratt *c.* Lycett, Cour de Paris, April 11, 1892 (*Dalloz*, 1892, II, 592), and Diez Hermanos *c.* Blandy Frères, Cour de Rouen (*Dalloz*, 1902, I, 65).

4. Osterrieth und Axster, *Pariser Konvention*, pp. 4, 10 ff. The Reichsgericht, September 22, 1885 (12 *Entsch. Reichsg. Strafs.*, 381, 384), held that the contents of a treaty constitutionally concluded with the consent of the Bundesrath and the Reichstag and published, becomes a legal norm, binding on the courts. The same Court, on November 23, 1891 (22 *Entsch. Reichsg. Strafs.*, 259, 261), held that the copyright treaty with France of 1883 superseded a German statute of 1870, and of its own force deprived a German subject of his right, valid under the German law, to publish a French musical

Austria,[1] Greece,[2] the Netherlands,[3] Portugal,[4] Serb-Croat-Slovene State,[5] Switzerland,[6] and Italy.[7]

§ 90. **Situation in Great Britain, Norway and Sweden.** In Great Britain the situation is different. English courts do not apply treaties immediately, even though they have been approved by

---

work. The Convention of 1883 was directly applied by the courts. See Eagle Oil Co. of New York *v.* Vacuum Oil Co. (10 *Entsch. Reichsg. Zivils.*, N. E. 217). The Reichsgericht, in its decision of October 26, 1914 (85 *Entsch. Reichsg. Zivils.*, 374), held that the Convention of 1883, after its approval by the legislature and its publication in the *Reichsgesetzblatt*, became an integral part of the German law on industrial property. It went even so far as to say that the application of the Convention in the municipal legal order could not depend on its continuing obligatory force in international law during the war. This conception in Germany of treaties as having force and effect of municipal law is accentuated by the provision of article 4 of the new Constitution of August 14, 1919, declaring international-law rules an integral part of the law of the German Reich and binding as such.

1. See decision of the Supreme Court of Austria of December 4, 1916, voicing agreement with the German decision of October 26, 1914, referred to in the previous note. Article 9 of the Constitution of the Republic of Austria, of October 1, 1920, is to the same effect as article 4 of the German Constitution.

2. A bill is submitted to Parliament, purporting to give its consent to the ratification of the treaty and the latter is published with the law after ratification and exchange of ratifications. No further legislation is necessary. Saripolos, *Σύστημα Δημοσίου Δικαίου* II, § 8.

3. The Convention of 1883 was approved by the Law of April 23, 1884 (1884 *Staatsblad*, No. 53) before the deposit of ratifications on June 6, 1884. No further legislation was necessary. See information given by the Dutch administration to the International Bureau, in *Propriété Industrielle* (1889), p. 145.

4. According to the Portuguese Law of June 4, 1883, article 32 (*Collecção Oficial de legislação Portugueza*, 1883, p. 140), the provisions of the law cannot contravene the stipulations of treaties or conventions concluded or to be concluded by Portugal. See, also, information given by the Portuguese administration to the International Bureau, in *Propriété Industrielle* (1889), p. 145.

5. The Convention of 1883, having received the approval of the Legislature, became a law of the country. See information given by the Serbian administration to the International Bureau, in *Propriété Industrielle* (1889), p. 146.

6. Blumer-Morel, *Schweizeriches Bundesstaatsrecht*, II, part II, 349 ff. The Bundesgericht, on April 21, 1882 (8 *Entsch. Schw. Bundesgerichtes*, 259, 275), held that a treaty supersedes a prior statute by its own effect. The provisions of the Convention of 1883, duly ratified, are applicable as law of the country in all cases when the municipal law contains no provisions or is to the contrary. See explanations given by the Swiss administration to the International Bureau, in *Propriété Industrielle* (1889), p. 146.

7. In Italy the Act No. 2473, of July 7, 1884 (72 *Raccolta Ufficiale*, 2097), was passed after the ratification of the Convention, giving full execution to the provisions of the latter. According to article 5 of the preliminary dispositions of the Italian Civil Code, all provisions which might be in conflict with the Convention are abrogated. See also explanations given by the Italian administration to the International Bureau in *Propriété Industrielle* (1889), pp. 127, 135.

The Act No. 169, of January 10, 1928, gives "full and entire execution" to the Convention of 1883 and the Madrid Arrangement for the international registration of trade marks as revised at The Hague, and accords to Italian nationals all the rights and advantages that foreigners may claim under the revised Convention and Arrangement in Italy. See *Propriété Industrielle* (1928), p. 146.

Parliament before their ratification by the king. A treaty affecting the rights of citizens, or existing statutes, is not completed with regard to the municipal legal order, until an act of Parliament is passed to render its provisions effective.[1]

For matters subject to international regulation provision is usually made by a general law for giving effect to treaties to be concluded thereafter. Thus the Act of 1883 on Patents, Designs, and Trade Marks (46 & 47 Vict. c. 57), in article 103, gives such a power to the Crown, but only for a certain object. The Convention could not transcend the provisions of the Act of 1883 or go beyond the object provided for in article 103. This is shown by a case which came up in 1888 before the Courts. Judge Sterling said: [2]

> By that article [art. 6 of the Convention of 1883] Her Majesty is now bound. Certainly according to my construction of the Act (Act of Patents of August 25, 1883, 46 & 47 Vict. ch. 57, sec. 103), the Act does not afford the means of carrying out that article and it will be for Her Majesty's Government to consider, and seeing the Attorney General here, I have no doubt that they will consider, what legislative steps ought to be taken to give effect to that article, if necessary.

In Norway and Sweden the situation is similar to that of Great Britain. These countries acceded to the Convention on May 29, 1885, their accession becoming effective on July 1, 1885. A royal decree, dated June 26, 1885, pronounced the Convention applicable in Norway and Sweden, but, in fact, it has not been applied as to the provisions which are in conflict with the existing legislation.[3]

§ 91. Completion of a treaty with regard to municipal legal order in the United States. In the United States the situation is controlled by the Constitution, article VI, section 2.[4] Treaties are

1. Walker *v.* Baird (*Appeal Cases*, 1892, p. 491); T. E. Holland, *Studies in International Law* (Oxford, 1898), pp. 190–191, citing legislation which has been necessary to carry into practical effect numerous conventions; Piccioto, *The Relation of International Law to the Law of England and of the United States of America* (London, 1915), p. 71; Crandall, *Treaties, Making and Enforcement*, pp. 280, 282, 286; Esmein, *Droit Constitutionel*, 7th ed., II, 181.

2. *In re* Californian Fig Syrup Co.'s Trade Mark (1888), 40 Chancery Div., 620, 627.

3. A law of June 16, 1885, and the decree promulgating the Convention sought to conform the municipal law to it. *Norsk Lovtidende* (1885), pp. 201 ff. See also information given by the Swedish administration to the International Bureau, *Propriété Industrielle* (1889), p. 146.

4. "This Constitution, and the Laws of the United States, which shall be made in pursuance thereof; and all treaties made, or which shall be made, under the authority of the United States, shall be the supreme Law of the land; and the Judges in every State shall be bound thereby, anything in the Constitution or laws of any State to the contrary notwithstanding."

the supreme law of the land. After they become effective in international law, the President proclaims them with the command: " . . . to the end that the same and every article and clause thereof may be observed and fulfilled with good faith by the United States and the citizens thereof." It has been repeatedly held that a treaty is an immediate source of municipal law. By the mere proclamation by the President, after ratification with the advice and consent of the Senate, the treaty becomes obligatory on the citizens and the courts. The latter have applied the stipulations of a treaty as against the provisions of an earlier Act of Congress.[1]

The only distinction made is that between treaties that are self-executing and those that are not. The distinction was first laid down by Chief Justice Marshall, as early as 1829, as follows:

> Our Constitution declares a treaty to be the law of the land. It is, consequently, to be regarded in Courts of Justice as equivalent to an act of the legislature, whenever it operates of itself, without the aid of any legislative provision. But when either of the parties engages to perform a particular act, the treaty addresses itself to the political, not to the judicial department; and the legislature must execute the contract, before it can become a rule for the Court.[2]

This distinction has been adhered to since.[3]

Treaties requiring payment of money or containing penal provisions have been followed by acts of Congress appropriating the amount, in the former case, and enacting penal legislation, in the latter. The latest development appears in the cases involving the so-called " rum-treaties." Two cases stand out in this respect: United States *v.* The Pictonian (1924), 3 F. (2d) 145 and The Over the Top (1925), 5 F. (2d) 838. The treaty involved in both cases is the American-British Treaty of May 22, 1924, waiving objection to seizure, outside the limits of the territorial waters of the United States, of any British ship attempting to commit an offence against the prohibition law of the United States. The first of the above cases held the treaty self-executing, and, therefore, the seizure of a vessel under it, valid. The second case, on the contrary, held the same treaty not self-executing, because it does not define the acts

1. United States *v.* Schooner Peggy (U. S. 1801), 1 Cranch 103; and other authorities collected in United States *v.* Lee Yen Tai (1902), 185 U. S. 213, 221. See also Piccioto, *International Law and the Law of England and the United States*, pp. 111, 113; Crandall, *Treaties*, pp. 160 ff.

2. Foster and Elam *v.* Neilson (1829), 2 Peters 253, 314.

3. See a good note in *Columbia Law Review* (1926), XXVI, 859.

constituting an offense against the laws of the United States. It is believed that the latter decision is the right one, because by the treaty the British Government simply waives its objections to the seizure of British vessels within certain limits. The United States never authorized its officers to seize beyond the limits of the territorial waters.[1] The Over the Top decision has since been followed in two more cases.[2]

However, in The Over the Top, the Court made it clear that its decision is based exclusively on the nature of the legislation and the drafting of the treaty involved. The Court said:

> Whether the Senate and the Executive may constitutionally enact criminal legislation by the device of a mere treaty is a question which fortunately we need not discuss. It is sufficient to conclude that the American-British Treaty did not in fact enact new criminal legislation.[3]

§ 92. Pronouncements of the executive on the Convention of 1883. In relation to the Convention of Union of 1883, there are, first, two pronouncements of the executive. The first is contained in a letter addressed by Secretary of State Bayard to the British Chargé Herbert on January 18, 1889, in reply to a note of the British Foreign Office inquiring as to the manner in which effect is given in the United States to the stipulations contained in the Convention of 1883. The British government wished to know "whether the Convention has immediately force of law in the United States, or whether it only becomes of effect, as in England, by virtue of separate legislative enactments."

The Secretary of State expressed the opinion that the general provisions of the Convention, so far as they were effective at all, took effect at once. The general provisions are contained in article 2 of the Convention concerning the national treatment of the citizens of all members of the Union in each country. But some provisions, the Secretary said, would seem to need further legislation to carry them into effect. Such provisions are contained in articles 9 and 10 relative to the seizure, upon importation, of merchandise bearing a trade mark or trade name unlawfully. "No machinery exists for

1. The government, in its effort to seize vessels attempting to smuggle liquor into the United States, relied in most cases upon the Tariff Act of 1922 (42 Stat. 980–982, *U. S. Comp. Stat.*, Suppl. 1923, §§ 5841 *h*, 3, 4, 5, 11).

2. The Sagatind (1926) 11 Fed. (2d) 673, and Hennings *v.* United States (1926) 13 Fed. (2d) 74.

3. The Over the Top (1925) 5 Fed. (2d) 838, 845.

such seizure in the United States and it may be doubted whether these provisions can be carried out without legislation by Congress."[1]

A contrary position, however, was taken by Attorney General Miller in an opinion addressed to the Secretary of the Interior for the Commissioner of Patents, and dated April 5, 1889, a few months after the Secretary of State expressed the above view. The opinion of the Attorney General was sought in consequence of an application by a Swiss for a *caveat*, provision for which was made in section 4902 of the Revised Statutes. This section, however, provided that a *caveat* may be filed by a citizen of the United States, or an alien who has resided for one year in the United States and has made oath of his intention to become a citizen. The Swiss claimed his right to file a *caveat* by virtue of article 2 of the Convention of 1883. The Attorney General's opinion was that

> the treaty is a reciprocal one — each party to it covenants to grant in the future to the subjects and citizens of the other parties certain special rights in consideration of the granting of like special rights to its subjects or citizens. It is a contract operative in the future infraterritorially. It is, therefore, not self-executing but requires legislation to render it effective for the modification of existing laws.[2]

The opinion of Attorney General Miller has been followed since that time by the Patent Office as the correct construction.[3] The Convention has thus been overlooked by the Patent Office in all cases where it was in conflict with the existing legislation of Congress. The latter was brought into harmony with the Convention only in 1897.[4]

§ 93. Critique of Attorney General Miller's opinion. Attorney General Miller was referring to the distinction made by Chief Justice Marshall in the extract quoted above (§ 91). It is submitted that the opinion cannot find support therein. It is not true that the Convention was a reciprocal treaty, any more than any treaty of this nature is a reciprocal treaty. No reciprocity in the true sense

1. Moore, *Digest of International Law*, II, 42–44.
2. *Off. Gaz. of U. S. Patent Office* (1889), XLVII, 397.
3. *Ex parte* Zwack & Co. (1896), 76 O. G. 1855; Butterworth *v.* Boral (1901), 97 O. G. 1896. It has been accepted by the Court of Appeals of the District of Columbia, in interference proceedings, carried up from the Commissioner of Patents: Rousseau *v.* Brown (1903), 21 D. C. App. 73, 76. The judgment rendered in the latter case is not a final judgment, subject to an appeal or writ of error to the Supreme Court of the United States. The decision of the Court is returned to the Commissioner only to be made of record in the Patent Office, to govern further proceedings in the case.
4. Act of March 3, 1897, c. 391, 29 Stat. 693 (*U. S. Comp. Stat.*, 1901, p. 3882).

was provided for or intended by the Convention of 1883.[1] At the time this Convention came into force, and for a number of years thereafter, two countries of the Union, the Netherlands and Switzerland, had no legislation on patents, and afforded no protection to foreign patentees while their own citizens were protected in the other countries of the Union.

Judge Archibald, in 1909, thought that the above opinion of Attorney General Miller could not be supported and that the Convention and the Additional Protocol of Brussels were self-executing:

> Having respect to their terms it cannot be said that either the treaty of 1883 or the additional act of 1900 required legislation to make it effective. They both undertake in the most direct and positive way to say what shall and what shall not be as to matters with which they deal, and, being ratified in that form, nothing further, by our laws, was necessary to put them into operation. They cannot be treated as mere agreements by the high contracting parties to bring the domestic laws of each into conformity with them by subsequent action. That resulted by virtue of their own force and origin.
>
> A treaty is a law of the land, as an act of Congress is, whenever its provisions prescribe a rule by which the rights of the private subject or citizen may be determined.[2]

The Convention " was not a contract operative in the future." It was not so generally. Some of its provisions — for instance, the right of priority, the national treatment clause of article 2 — were self-sufficient. On the contrary, the provision for an adequate protection at international exhibitions, or for the seizure, upon importation, of merchandise bearing unlawfully a trade mark or trade name (articles 9, 10, 11 of the Convention), required the enactment of municipal law for their fulfillment.[3]

The claim to file a *caveat* was a claim for national treatment according to article 2 of the Convention, and no further legislation was necessary. If in any case, when a claim is made under a Convention in derogation of the existing legislation, the Convention is not self-executing, then in all cases of conflict between a treaty and an earlier act of Congress, the treaty would not be given effect. This certainly, is not the meaning of the Constitution and it has never been sanctioned by the Supreme Court.

1. See *supra*, p. 80.
2. Hennebique Co. *v.* Meyers (1909), 172 Fed. 869, 887.
3. See letter of Secretary of State Bayard, *supra*, p. 154.

The opinion is based also on the consideration that, by the eighth clause of the eighth section of the first article of the Constitution, the whole legislative power over the subject of patents is committed to Congress. This was not considered a serious objection by a Federal Court in 1907, in the United States Shoe Mach. Co. *v.* Duplessis Shoe Mach. Co.:

So far as the conventions pertinent here (Convention of 1883 and Additional Act of Brussels) are concerned, the fact that the Constitution commits the power "to promote the progress of Science and Useful Arts by securing for limited times to authors and inventors the exclusive right to their respective writings and discoveries," is of no consequence, because all the powers of Congress are especially vested, either directly or indirectly, by the Constitution in similar manner; and to hold that a treaty could not abrogate a prior statute regarding patents, because this particular legislative power is committed to Congress, could not be permitted so long as the general rule as to statutes superseding treaties, and *vice versa*, declared by the Supreme Court, in the way we have pointed out, exists.[1]

§ 94. The Convention of 1883 before the lower Federal Courts of the United States. The first case which came before the courts of the United States was La République Française et al. *v.* Schultz, in 1893. It is the only case ever decided where the Convention of Union was really material. The case came up on a demurrer to a suit to enjoin the use of the French trade name "Vichy." The Court held that it must be protected in view of article 8 of the Convention, which provides that a trade name must be protected in the countries of the Union without obligation of deposit, whether or not it forms part of a trade mark. It is true that the defendant in this case claimed through the Convention, so that the latter was not put in issue; but the Court had not the least doubt of the immediate application of the Convention, without any reference to the existing prior law.[2] The case has been followed in Kerry *v.* Toupin,[3] decided in 1894, which protected a trade name of a Canadian by applying articles 3 and 8 of the Convention of 1883.

A number of later cases involved the Additional Act of Brussels and article 4*b*, which this Act added to the Convention of 1883. Article 4*b* declares, in its first paragraph, that patents obtained by

1. (1907), 155 Fed. 842, 845. The Court cited the case United States *v.* Lee Yen Tai (1902), 185 U. S. 213, 220, where all the cases are collected.
2. (1893), 57 Fed. 27, 40–42.
3. (1894), 60 Fed. 272, 273.

persons entitled to the benefits of the Convention in any country of the Union are independent of patents obtained for the same invention in other countries, members of the Union or not. The independence concerns the duration, as well as the facts which might cause the invalidation or forfeiture, of the patent. By the second (now third) paragraph of the same article, the previous dispositions were made applicable to patents existing at the moment this article went into effect.

In the United States, even before the adoption of article *4b* by the Conference of Brussels, the Act of March 3, 1897,[1] had been passed, which took effect January 1, 1898, and which did away with the provision of section 4887, Revised Statutes, limiting the term of the United States patent by that of a foreign patent. But the Act of March 3, 1897, did not apply to applications filed prior to January 1, 1898, the old section 4887, as it stood prior to that act, being still in force as to these applications and patents granted thereon.

At the Conference of Brussels, the American delegate, Mr. Forbes, declared that patents granted to foreign patentees before January 1, 1898, could not extend beyond the term originally affixed to them under old section 4887. He asserted that the opposite was possible in the United States only by special law, and was against the spirit of non-retroactivity which inspires all American legislation. All the other delegates who took part in the discussion, the Director of the International Bureau himself included, seemed to agree with the American view. Another delegate of the United States proposed the addition to the second paragraph of article *4b* of the words: "néanmoins, la durée fixée par la loi intérieure de chaque pays reste intacte." On the motion of its Chairman, the Conference finally adopted the text of article *4b*, with the interpretation given to it by the American delegation. However, the British delegation urged that it could take the indicated act of interpretation only as a declaration of the American delegation, and not as a decision of the Conference.[2]

Later, the United States Congress passed the Act of March 3, 1903,[3] purporting to give effect to the Additional Act of Brussels, revising section 4887, but omitting the paragraph of article *4b* referring to patents existing at the time it went into effect.

1. 29 Stat. 693 (*U. S. Comp. Stat.* 1901, p. 3882).
2. *Actes de la Conférence de Bruxelles*, pp. 311 ff.
3. 32 Stat. 1225, c. 1019 (*U. S. Comp. Stat.*, Suppl. 1905, p. 663).

Under these conditions a case came before a Federal Court, as follows: British patentees had obtained an American patent for the same invention in 1889. The British patent expired in 1902. The question was whether the American patent also expired at that time, in accordance with old section 4887, in force when the patent was taken out, or whether it was still in effect, in conformity with the general terms of the second paragraph of article 4*b* of the Convention.

The Court after reviewing the authorities and stating that treaties become immediately effective, continued: [1]

> But the respondent maintains that article 4*b* of the Convention (added by the Act of Brussels) was not effectual until enacted into a statute by Congress. An examination of the decisions of the Supreme Court on this topic will show there is no practical distinction whatever as between a statute and a treaty with regard to its becoming presently effective without further legislation. . . . Both statutes and treaties become effective when their purposes are expressed as presently effective; and on its face, article 4*b* of the Convention in question is so expressed.

This discussion, however, as to the self-execution of the Act of Brussels, is *obiter dictum*. The Court held that the American patent came to an end at the expiration of the British patent, on the ground that article 4*b* of the Convention, as controlled and construed by the Act of March 3, 1903, did not have the effect of changing the term of an existing United States patent, as fixed by statute at the time of its issuance.

The same view as to the immediate effectiveness of the Convention and Additional Protocol was held by another Federal Court in 1909, already referred to above in relation to Attorney General Miller's opinion. Judge Archibald considered specifically articles 2, 3, 4, and 5 of the Convention and concluded:

> It is idle to suggest, in the face of these provisions and others of like character, that could be quoted, that the treaty, as well as the additional act by which it was supplemented, was inoperative and lay fallow until Congress, by statute, was moved to give life to it.[2]

1. United Shoe Mach. Co. *v.* Duplessis Shoe Mach. Co. (1907), 155 Fed. 842, 845. Followed by Malignani et al. *v.* Hill-Wright Electric Co. (1910), 177 Fed. 430, 435; Malignani *v.* Jasper Marsh Const. Electric Lamp Co. (1910), 188 Fed. 442, 444; Commercial Acct. Co. *v.* Searchlight Gas Co. (1912), 197 Fed. 908, 918.

2. Hennebique Co. *v.* Meyers (1909), 172 Fed. 869, 888.

§ 95. The Convention of 1883 before the Supreme Court of the United States. The Convention of 1883 came before the Supreme Court of the United States in the case of The French Republic *v.* Saratoga Vichy Spring Co.[1] The plaintiffs claimed that their trade name "Vichy" was unlawfully used by the defendant. The Supreme Court inquired whether the position of the plaintiffs was affected or strengthened by article 8 of the Convention. Although the case may be disputed as to the result, the Court arrived thereat after holding that the rights of the plaintiffs were no greater under the Convention than under the municipal law.

The above question as to article 4*b* of the Convention came before the Supreme Court of the United States in 1913.[2] This was the first case in the Supreme Court to deal with the effect of the Convention on prior acts of Congress. The decision might well rest on the same ground as the United Shoe Machinery Co. *v.* Duplessis Machine Co. Its language, however, is unnecessarily broad. It holds not only that the Act of Brussels should be construed in accordance with the declarations of the American delegation at the Conference at which it was framed and adopted, but also that it was the sense of the Congress of the United States that the Additional Act was not self-executing, because of the fact that the Act of 1903 was passed for its execution, and that some other countries of the Union did not consider it self-executing.

The first ground seems strong enough to support the decision. The reasoning of the Court on the second ground is very unfortunate. No consideration is paid either to the Constitution or to authority. It is based mainly on the fact that "in explaining the object of the bill, the member in charge of it in the House of Representatives said that it was to carry into effect the Additional Act of the Convention held at Brussels." In fact, the Act of 1903 omitted two parts of the Additional Act which referred to patents existing at the time it went into effect, and to newly acceding states. The Act of 1903, therefore, by no means carried into effect the Act of Brussels.

The Supreme Court was influenced by the fact that the International Bureau of Berne, through the Swiss chargé d'affaires at Washington, declared its embarrassment on account of the uncer-

1. (1903), 191 U. S. 427, 438–439.
2. Cameron Septic Tank Co. *v.* City of Knoxville, Iowa (1913), 227 U. S. 39.

tainty of the action of the United States in regard to the Additional Act of Brussels. The Bureau referred to the Convention of 1883, to its approval by the Senate in 1887, and to the fact that " Congress had not brought into the Federal law the changes required to make it consonant with the Convention," and that, " according to the opinion rendered by Attorney General Miller in 1889, American courts have consistently decided that the Convention of 1883 could not be enforced in the United States except so far as it accorded with the law of the country." [1] Now, as a matter of fact, the courts had never decided that the Convention could not be enforced in the United States without appropriate legislation. The International Bureau referred to the practice in the Patent Office, which followed Miller's opinion. On the contrary, in La Rėpublique Française *v.* Schultz and Kerry *v.* Toupin, above cited, the courts applied the Convention of 1883 immediately. Furthermore, the Circuit Courts of the United States both in United Shoe Machinery Co. *v.* Duplessis Machine Co. and in Hennebique Const. Co. *v.* Meyers used very strong dicta to the effect that the Convention and Act of Brussels were self-executing.

The opinion of Attorney General Miller is no authority for the courts. It is simply a construction given to the Convention by the legal counsel, so to speak, of the executive, and as Judge Archibald put it:

> If the contemporaneous construction given to the treaty by the executive branch of the government, following the opinion of the Attorney General, is insisted on, what is to be said of the contrary view taken by the French and the Italian governments, which is entitled to equal respect — this being a treaty? [2]

The Cameron case was followed by the District Court of Columbia in In Re Stoffregen,[3] on an appeal from decisions of the Patent Office rejecting an application for right of priority by a German patentee, basing his right on provisions of the Treaty of Berlin of 1921 restoring friendly relations with Germany.[4] This treaty incorporated certain provisions of the Treaty of Versailles, among which the stipulation of article 308, giving an extension to rights of priority, terminated, according to the applicant's claim, on May 11,

1. 227 U. S. 39, 48–49.
2. (1909), 172 Fed. 869, 888. The claimant patentee in this case was a French citizen.
3. (1925), Fed. 56 App. D. C. 23; 6 Fed. (2d) 943.
4. XLII *U. S. Stat. at Large*, 1939.

1922, while under the Act of Congress of March 3, 1921, the Nolan Act, the extension of rights of priority terminated September 3, 1921. The District Court of Appeals relied in its decision on the non-self-executing character of the Treaty of Berlin and, especially, on the alleged fact that the German Patent Office had refused a similar extension to American citizens.

Subsequently, the General Electric Co., assignee of Stoffregen's title, brought a bill of complaint in equity against the Commissioner of Patents, in the District Court of Maryland, claiming that Stoffregen's patent should be issued to the corporation. The motion by the United States to dismiss the bill was overruled, and recently the Court held that the plaintiffs are entitled to register their patent.[1] The Court was not influenced by the position of the German Patent Office, and pointed out that this was due mainly to a prior announcement of the United States Patent Office that it would not regard the treaty provisions as applicable for the registration of German patents.

The Court passed in review all the cases concerning the self-executing character of the treaties concerning patents. It found that a study of the cases holding that a treaty which purports to modify the patent laws of the United States needs an act of Congress to effectuate it, showed that this view originated in the opinion of Attorney General Miller, which has been accepted without an independent examination of the authorities. It concluded that the language of the International Convention of 1883 does not import a promise to be effectuated by subsequent legislation, but a grant of privileges immediately effective, and that "the weight of authority in the intermediate Courts of appeal favors the proposition that international conventions, relating to patents, may be self-executing." As to the Cameron case, this Court pointed out that it did not purport to lay down the rule that the Additional Act of Brussels was not self-executing.[2]

The Convention of 1883 is, indeed, of the same character as treaties which regulate the mutual rights of citizens and subjects of the contracting countries in regard to the descent or inheritance of property when the individuals concerned are aliens. With refer-

1. General Electric Co. *v.* Robertson, Commissioner of Patents (1927), 21 Fed. (2d) 214, and (1928), 25 Fed. (2d) 146.
2. (1927), 21 Fed. (2d) 214, at p. 220.

ence to the latter treaties, the Supreme Court of the United States, as early as 1884, declared:

> A treaty, then, is a law of the land as an act of Congress is, whenever its provisions prescribe a rule by which the rights of the private citizen or subject may be determined. And when such rights are of a nature to be enforced in a Court of Justice, that Court resorts to the treaty for a rule of decision for the case before it, as it would to a statute.[1]

The Convention of 1883 is clearly a treaty which regulates rights of private persons, partakes of the nature of municipal law, and is capable of enforcement as between private parties in the courts of the country.

§ 96. Power of the United States to enter into treaties for protection of trade marks and repression of unfair competition. A further question to be considered is whether or not the fact that Congress has no power to legislate in respect to trade marks, trade names, indications of place of origin, and unfair competition, except when incidental to the regulation of interstate and foreign commerce, prevents the treaty-making power of the United States from entering into international agreements concerning their protection.

The Supreme Court decided in 1879[2] that a trade mark was neither a discovery nor writing within the meaning of the provisions of the Constitution (Article 1, section 8, clause 8), which confers upon Congress the power to secure to authors and inventors the exclusive rights in their writings and inventions; that, if acts of Congress relative to trade marks could be upheld as regulations of commerce, they could be upheld only so far as the use of trade marks in commerce with foreign nations, or among the several states and with the Indian tribes, is concerned; that as the Acts of Congress of 1871 and 1876[3] did not come within these limits, they were void for want of constitutional authority. The Court expressly avoided an opinion as to regulation of trade marks by treaties. It said:

> In what we have said, we wish to be understood as leaving untouched the whole of the question of the treaty-making power over trade marks, and of the duty of Congress to pass any laws necessary to carry treaties into effect.[4]

1. Head Money Cases (1884), 112 U. S. 580, 598–599.
2. The Trade Mark Cases (1879), 100 U. S. 82.
3. Act of March 3, 1871 (XVI *U. S. Stat. at Large,* 580), prohibiting as fraudulent, trade marks similar to those of foreign manufacturers; Act of August 14, 1876 (XIX *U. S. Stat. at Large,* 141), imposing criminal punishment as a sanction of such prohibition.
4. (1879), 100 U. S. 82, 99.

At the adoption of the Convention of 1883 by the Paris Conference of 1880, the American delegate, Mr. Putnam, called attention to the fact that in the United States the power to legislate on trade marks belonged in certain measure to the states of the Union, and proposed an amendment making the enjoyment of the rights secured by the Convention subject to the constitutional limitations. The Conference later adopted a provision in the Final Protocol giving satisfaction to the American point of view and reading as follows:

Le plénipotentiaire des États-Unis d'Amérique ayant déclaré qu'aux termes de la Constitution fédérale, le droit de légiférer, en ce qui concerne les marques de fabrique, ou de commerce, est, dans une certaine mesure, réservé à chacun des États de l'Union Américaine, il est convenu que les dispositions de la Convention ne seront applicables que dans les limites des pouvoirs constitutionels des hautes parties contractantes.

The Conference refused, however, to add after the words "des pouvoirs constitutionels" the phrase "et les conditions qui doivent être imposées par la législation," as was asked by the American delegate, who in a letter addressed to the Chairman of the Conference stated that his government did not consent to submit to the Convention questions of trade marks except under the reservation that the conclusions of the Conference should be subject to all future legislation of the United States.[1]

At the Paris Conference of 1883, when it appeared that the United States would not sign the Convention, although it was expected that it would accede to it at a later time, the above provision was struck out from the Final Protocol, but, instead, the following insertion was made in the *procès-verbal* of the Conference at the suggestion of the Swiss delegate and with the assent of the American delegate, Mr. Morton:

La Conférence est d'avis que le Gouvernement fédéral suisse est autorisé à accepter l'accession des États-Unis d'Amérique sous la réserve formulée au quatrième paragraphe du protocole de clôture de 1880.[2]

However, no such reservation or qualification whatsoever was made by the United States when it acceded to the Convention on March 29, 1887.[3]

1. *Conférence de Paris* (1880), pp. 51, 52, 64, 126, 127, 150.
2. *Conférence de Paris*, (1883), pp. 25–26.
3. XXVIII *U. S. Stat. at Large*, 1372, 1384. See also *Foreign Relations of the United States* (1887), p. 1067.

A number of cases protected trade marks of foreigners on application of treaty stipulations.[1] The Convention of 1883 came up in relation to trade names in the two cases before the Federal courts, which have already been referred to.[2] The constitutionality of the treaties, or even their immediate effectiveness, was in no way questioned.

It would seem, indeed, that the United States has power to enter into treaties concerning trade marks, although Congress has no power to legislate generally on trade marks except in respect to commerce with foreign nations. In the case of Missouri *v.* Holland, decided in 1920 and involving the Migratory Birds Treaty with Great Britain, a similar question had arisen. Mr. Justice Holmes, delivering the opinion of the Court, stated the principle quite clearly:

> Whether the two cases cited [3] were decided rightly or not they cannot be accepted as a test of the treaty power. Acts of Congress are the supreme law of the land only when made in pursuance of the Constitution, while treaties are declared to be so when made under the authority of the United States. It is open to question whether the authority of the United States means more than the formal acts prescribed to make the convention.

And a little later, speaking of the rights of the States, Mr. Justice Holmes asserts, on the basis of authorities: "No doubt the great body of private relations usually fall within the control of the State, but a treaty may override its powers." [4]

§ 97. Conclusions as to relation of the Convention to municipal law in the United States. It must be concluded, then, that in the United States the relation of the Convention of 1883 to the municipal law is not like that in Great Britain, but similar to that in many other countries, such as France, Germany, and Switzerland. The great weight of authority is in favor of the self-execution of those provisions of the Convention of 1883 which are not merely contractual engagements of the United States. Analytically, and

1. Richter *v.* Reynolds (1893), 17 U. S. App. 427, 434; J. & P. Raltz Brewing Co. *v.* Kaiser Brauerei Beck & Co. (1896), 39 U. S. App. 229, 232.

2. La République Française et al. *v.* Schultz (1893), 57 Fed. 37; Kerry *v.* Toupin (1894), 60 Fed. 271.

3. An Act of Congress regulating the killing of migratory birds had been held bad by a district court. United States *v.* Shauver (1914), 214 Fed. 154; United States *v.* McCullagh (1915), 221 Fed. 288.

4. Missouri *v.* Holland (1920), 252 U. S. 416, 433–434.

historically also, this relation should be admitted, in view of the constitutional provision and its interpretation by the courts. Finally, for the theoretical and practical reasons referred to above,[1] the stipulations of the Convention should not be looked upon as concessions between the states, but as regulations of world-wide interests, and should thus be given effect immediately by government officials and the courts. The practice of the Patent Office, in reliance on Attorney Miller's opinion, in denying protection to foreigners in violation of the Convention, is, it is submitted, wrong.[2]

§ **98. Conflict between provisions of the Convention and prior municipal law.** The above exposition shows that in most of the member countries of the Union, the Convention may give the rule for decision in a judicial tribunal, whenever its stipulations are not mere promises by the signatory states to act affirmatively in the future, but are capable of being applied immediately in private litigation. Of this latter type are the first and third classes of provisions of the Convention of 1883, as they have been distinguished above;[3] namely, provisions merely referring to the municipal law of each country and making it applicable, and provisions enacting common legislation for all the members of the Union. Whenever, then, there is a conflict between the earlier provisions of the municipal law and the stipulations of the Convention, the latter will be applied by the courts.

§ **99. Conflict between the Convention and later municipal law.** The conflict might arise, however, between the Convention of 1883 and a later legislative act of a member country of the Union, containing provisions in opposition to the stipulations of the Convention. This unilateral violation, or pretended legislative repeal, of the Convention, has, of course, no effect upon its binding force on the country in question in international law, unless the Convention is denounced in the prescribed form. Nor does it affect the execution of the Convention in the other contracting countries, even in regard to nationals of the country in question.[4] But what is the effect on

1. See *supra*, § 87.

2. The protests voiced at the Congress of the International Association for the Protection of Industrial Property, at Turin, in September, 1902, against such violation of the Convention by the United States, were, therefore, justified. See *Annuaire de l'Association Internationale pour la Protection de la Propriété Industrielle* (1902), pp. 21 ff.

3. See *supra*, § 88.

4. See Pratt *c.* Lycett, Cour de Paris, April 11, 1892 (*Dalloz*, 1892, II, 592); Diez Hernanos *c.* Blandy Frères, Cour de Rouen, 1900 (*Dalloz*, 1902, I, 65); Charlton *v.* Kelly (1913), 229 U. S. 447, 473–476.

the municipal legal order of such a legislative act? Does the Convention or the later legislative act give the rule for decision in the judicial tribunals of the country in question?

In the countries where a treaty may constitute an immediate rule for decision, it is generally admitted that a change in the general legislation does not vary the effect of the treaty in the municipal legal order. For this result it is not necessary to accept the view which makes international law a super-national law.[1] The legal precepts, or "norms," introduced by the treaty in the municipal legal order constitute special law, which will prevail over the subsequent general legislation.[2]

In Great Britain this question could not arise, because a treaty or convention is not, by itself, a rule of decision for the courts, in so far as it affects private rights. The latter will always look exclusively to the municipal law.[3]

In the United States it is a well-established rule that a posterior Act of Congress abrogates a prior treaty with which it is in conflict, so far as its effects on the municipal legal order are concerned.[4] But a clear intent of Congress to "abrogate" the treaty is required. A mere implication is held insufficient. This is made clear in the cases involving the Convention of 1883 or its Additional Acts, where the courts held their stipulations superseded by a later Act of Congress. In the United Shoe Machinery Co. *v.* Duplessis Machine Co.,[5] the Court arrived at this conclusion from the consideration that the Act of 1903 [6] was entitled, "An Act to effectuate the provisions of the additional act of the international convention for the protection of industrial property," and by application of the rule of construc-

1. Kohler in *Zeitschrift für Völkerrecht und Bundesstaatsrecht* (1908), II, 210. However, see an article by Mr. Van Eysinga, calling attention to the prevailing authority which Resolutions, International Conventions, etc., of the League of Nations possess over the municipal law of states which is in conflict with them. *Revue de Droit International et de Legislation Comparée*, 3d ser., I, 143 ff.

2. Fauchille, *Traité*, I, part I, 50; Pillet, *Régime International*, pp. 231, 237, 242; Donzel, *Commentaire*, pp. 227 ff.; Blumer-Morel, *Schweizeriches Bundesstaatsrecht*, II, part II, 355–356. The following decisions of the Swiss Bundesgericht hold that a Federal statute cannot derogate from a prior treaty with Germany: In Sachen Stübler (1892), 18 *Ent. Schweiz. Bundesg.*, 189, 193; In Sachen Köster (1893), 19 *Ent. Schweiz. Bundesg.*, 122, 129; In Sachen Lux (1895), 21 *Ent. Schweiz. Bundesg.*, 76, 79.

3. See *supra*, § 90.

4. Taylor *v.* Morton (1855), 2 Curtis 454; Cherokee Tobacco Case (1870), 11 Wall, 616, 621; Head Money Cases (1884), 112 U. S. 581, 599; Whitney *v.* Robertson (1880), 124 U. S. 190; Hijo *v.* United States (1904), 194 U. S. 315, 324.

5. (1907), 155 Fed. 842, 846–848.

6. 32 Stat. 1225 c. 1019 (*U. S. Comp. Stat.*, Suppl., 1905, p. 663).

tion announced by the Supreme Court in Dallemagne *v.* Moisan,[1] that

> the statute having been passed by the United States for the purpose of executing the treaties it had entered into with foreign governments, must be regarded as the only means proper to be adopted for that purpose.

The Act of 1903 omitted two provisions of the Additional Protocol of Brussels, and the Court concluded that this was done purposely, in view of the declaration to that effect made at the Conference of Brussels by the American Commissioners.

In Hennebique Const. Co. *v.* Meyers,[2] on the other hand, the Court held the argument drawn from the title of the Act of 1903 wholly unwarranted, because only one tenth of that Act had anything to do with the title, the rest of it being entirely unrelated, except as it dealt with the general subject of patents. This case supported the view that a treaty cannot be set aside in any such indirect and inconclusive manner.

The Supreme Court, however, in Cameron Septic Tank Co. *v.* City of Knoxville, refused to be drawn into this discussion by adopting an alternative solution. Either the Additional Act of Brussels was ambiguous and should be interpreted against the contentions of the patentee, on the basis of the proceedings at the Conference of Brussels, or the said Additional Act was not self-executing and the Court should apply only the provisions of the legislative enactment. Thus, the question of derogation from the treaty by the Act of 1903 has not been considered by the Court.

Oppenheim's opinion [3] that there is a presumption against the existence of a conflict between provisions of municipal law and stipulations of a treaty will be readily accepted in the United States.

In case the courts will not afford redress, because of a pretended legislative repeal of the Convention, the state, of course, is liable to the persons who have been damaged by the application of the municipal law by its courts.[4]

§ 100. Relation to the municipal law of the provisions of the Convention which merely refer to the former. Following these general

1. (1905), 197 U. S. 169, 175.
2. (1909), 172 Fed. 869, 889–890.
3. *International Law*, 3d ed. (1920), § 23.
4. Fauchille, *Traité*, I, 52–53. Wharton, *A Digest of the International Law of the United States*, 2d ed. (1887), I, 35–36. Arbitration between Great Britain and Costa Rica, Opinion and Award of William H. Taft, Sole Arbitrator, *American Journal of International Law* (1924), XVIII, 147, 160.

considerations of the relation of the Convention of 1883 to the municipal law of the members of the Union, we shall now take up each of the three classes of provisions of the Convention distinguished above (§ **88**).

The most important of the provisions referring merely to the municipal law of the member countries of the Union, and making it applicable, is that of article 2. It prescribes that the *ressortissants* of each of the contracting countries shall enjoy in all the countries of the Union the advantages which the respective laws now grant, or may hereafter grant, to the nationals of each country with regard to patents, working models, industrial designs or models, trade marks, trade names, indications of place of origin, and repression of unfair competition. Article 2 does not purport to give to the persons protected by the Convention any further protection than the nationals of each country enjoy. The international obligation of the contracting countries is merely to place the citizens or subjects of the other countries in the same position as their own nationals. The municipal law of each country is left free to decide what is to be that position, common for the nationals of all the contracting countries. So a country that does not, for instance, grant patents to its own nationals is not bound to grant or protect patents of the nationals of the other countries. Or a country may abolish all legislation on patents, and will not commit an international delinquency thereby. In the same manner, it may shorten the term of patents or apply its own conception of what should be comprised under the name patent.

The same reference to the municipal law is made explicitly or impliedly in almost all the articles of the Convention, although at the same time provisions are inserted restricting the province of the municipal law (for instance, articles 5, 6, 7*b*, 9, 10, 10*b*).

§ 101. Relation to municipal law of the provisions of the Convention ordering creation and maintenance of law. The second class of provisions in the Convention contain an obligation for affirmative action by the contracting countries. This obligation is either to create and maintain municipal law, or to maintain in existence municipal law already created before entering into the Convention. In fact, what is desired by the stipulation is not merely the existence of the law itself, but rather a situation in which some rights will be effectively protected. These provisions restrain the freedom of the municipal legislation; at the same time, they do not contain a complete rule of law which might be received in the municipal legal order and be given immediate effect. These stipulations are not self-executing. They need legislation in each country to carry them out. A typical illustration of this kind of provisions is the stipulation of article 11 to the effect that the contracting countries shall grant a temporary protection to patentable inventions, working models, designs, and trade marks exhibited at international expositions. The international obligation of each member of the Union is to maintain any legislation that it passed to that effect before the Convention, or, in the absence of such legislation, to create and maintain it. Indeed, a country may change its legislation in any way, but there should always be a situation in the municipal law where "a temporary protection" shall be had, as provided by article 11. The stipulation of article 11, of itself, could not afford this protection, and the courts would be unable on the basis thereof to give any relief.

Similar are the stipulations of article 12 for the establishment of a special government department and central office of industrial property; of article 10*b* for an effective protection against unfair competition; of articles 9 and 10 for the seizure on importation of products bearing illegally a trade mark or trade name or an indication of place of origin, and so forth.

A country which does not create and maintain, or does not maintain, the legislation necessary for bringing about the situation intended by the Convention, violates an international obligation, commits what is known in German terminology as *Dauerdelict* (permanent international crime).[1]

§ 102. Relation to municipal law of the stipulations of the Convention establishing common legislation. Provisions of the Convention of 1883 creating common legislation for all the member countries of the Union differ essentially from the two previous classes. They differ from the first, as they do not refer to the municipal law but contain new rules of law, regardless of whether they are in accordance with, or in derogation of, the municipal law. They differ from the second also, in that they constitute, not simply international obligations of the contracting countries, or statements of principles which need the creation or maintenance of municipal law to carry them out, but, rather, rules of law which are by themselves

1. Triepel, *Droit International et Droit Interne* (Washington, 1920), p. 287.

sufficient to carry out the ends desired, and which may and should be given effect immediately in the municipal legal order of each country.

These stipulations, then, may well be deemed common legislation of the Union, because they, like the municipal law of each country, establish legal rules and precepts for certain relations between persons.[1] By the mere publication or proclamation of the Convention, after its ratification according to the public law of each state, with the order for its execution, these provisions may be applied directly by the judicial tribunals and the officials of each country. In other words, according to American terminology, these provisions of the Convention are self-executing.

The greater part of the provisions of the Convention of 1883 are of this class. It may also be noticed that the successive revisions of the Convention attempted, in many respects, to increase this set of provisions by diminishing those of the other two classes, so as to make the stipulations of the Convention generally and immediately applicable, independently of any legislative action on the part of the contracting countries.

Stipulations establishing common legislation by the Union are, especially, the following: article 4, concerning the rights of priority; article 4*b*, declaring the independent character of patents obtained by the same inventor for the same invention in various coutries; article 5, section 1, providing that the importation of articles manufactured abroad by the patentee will not entail forfeiture; article 5, sections 2, 3, and 4, restricting the obligation to work a patent; article 5, sections 5 and 6, declaring that the protection of a design cannot be forfeited by importation of articles manufactured with the design in another country, and that no sign of registration of the design shall be required on the product for the recognition of the right; articles 6, 6*b*, 6*c*, and 7, concerning the validation of trade marks; article 8, concerning the protection of trade names. The stipulation of article 2 is also connected with this class of provisions. It is of the first class, in so far as it refers to the municipal law and is dependent upon it for its contents. It is of the third class, in so far as it may derogate from any provision of the municipal law which discriminates between foreigners and citizens, and should be given effect immediately.

1. Diena, "L'Individu devant l'Autorité Judicaire et le Droit International," in *Revue Générale de Droit International Public* (1909), XVI, 57, 67.

§ 103. Utility of the distinction of three classes of provisions. The distinction suggested here is indispensable for a clear understanding of the international obligation assumed by the member countries of the Union, and a due application of its stipulations by the courts and officials in each country. It is especially important in questions involving the interpretation of the provisions of the Convention and of the municipal legislation which purports to give effect thereto.

Thus it is clear that in case of provisions referring to the municipal law of each country — for instance, in respect to the protection granted in each country to patents, designs, models, and so forth (article 2 of the Convention) — the rules of interpretation and the meaning given to these juridical conceptions by the law of each country will be applicable. In case of provisions of the second class, the previous rule in its exclusiveness cannot be applied. The extent, of course, to which the courts and officials of each country will give effect to the legislative act enacted to effectuate the international engagement, will depend entirely on the intent of the municipal legislator. In case, however, this intent is not clear, the intent of the Convention and all the parties thereto may be resorted to. For instance, the municipal legislation may provide for the repression of acts of unfair competition, in accordance with article 10*b* of the Convention. In case this legislation does not define the acts of unfair competition, the common intent of the parties, when they adopted article 10*b*, may and should be taken into consideration.[1]

Provisions constituting common legislation by the Union should be interpreted differently from the other two classes. Even in cases when a country passes legislation purporting to effectuate such provisions of the Convention, or merely "receiving" them into the general municipal law, the common intention of all parties to the Convention, as manifested in the proceedings of the Conferences or otherwise, should be taken into consideration in the interpretation of such provisions.[2]

§ 104. Difficulties of interpretation of the provisions establishing common legislation. It is in respect to the interpretation of these

1. This is especially so since the revision of the Convention at The Hague. Indeed, at this Conference a definition of acts of unfair competition and an especial enumeration of certain acts were added to article 10*b*.

2. Diena, "L'Individu devant l'Autorité Judicaire et le Droit International," in *Revue Générale de Droit International Public* (1909), XVI, 68.

provisions that very serious difficulties arise. The common intention that should be sought is not always easy to find. Also, the weight that should be given to different manifestations of that intention, before and after the final adoption of the Convention, is not always agreed upon.

Oppenheim was already observing in 1911 [1] that

> no generally received rule of the law of nations exists for the interpretation of international treaties, [and that] whilst in Germany and France the judge avails himself more or less liberally of the Materialien of a Statute in order to arrive at its meaning, the English judge limits himself to the strict wording of the text, and utterly refuses to listen to an argument based on the historical origin of the Statute.

Now, this difficulty with regard to the Convention of 1883 does not exist in England. The Convention is not immediately applied there and, therefore, no question of interpretation of the Convention by the English courts arises. As to the American courts, they are more liberal and not much different from the continental courts in this respect. They have often availed themselves of the preparatory work of treaties for the interpretation of their stipulations.[2] Concerning the Convention of 1883 and the Additional Act of Brussels, the proceedings at the Conferences were used freely by the courts of the United States.[3]

Special attention should be called to the Final Protocol, which was adopted and ratified at some Conferences at the same time with the Convention, and in which the common intention of all parties in regard to some provisions of the Convention was expressed. On these particular points of the Convention the Final Protocol is the only expression of the common intention, and the discussions at the Conference should not be resorted to unless the Protocol itself is not clear. At the Conference of The Hague no such Protocol was adopted. The meaning and interpretation of certain provisions of the Convention were inserted in the *procès-verbaux* of the Conference.

For the rest, the usual rules of interpretation should be used, with the purpose always to give a reasonable construction to the Conven-

1. *Die Zukunft des Völkerrechts* (Leipzig, 1911); published also in London, *The Future of International Law* (1921), pp. 35, 37.

2. Kinkead *v.* United States (1893), 150 U. S. 483; United States *v.* Texas (1896), 162 U. S. 1, 23–27.

3. United Shoe Mach. Co. *v.* Duplessis Mach. Co. (1907), 155 Fed. 842, 846; Hennebique Const. Co. *v.* Meyers (1909), 172 Fed. 869, 881–884; Cameron Septic Tank Co. *v.* City of Knoxville (1913), 227 U. S. 39, 45–47.

tion, instead of taking the literal sense; to make the meaning adequate to the whole purpose of the Convention; to avoid a construction which makes a stipulation meaningless or ineffective; and to hesitate to adopt a construction that would tend to defeat the object which the Convention had in view.

Whether the fact that the Convention is drawn in French, and that all the discussions at the Conferences are conducted in French, has any effect upon the interpretation of the Convention, is not certain. No such express agreement was ever made at any Conference, and it is difficult to imply a reception of a particular municipal law by the Convention, to fill its gaps or define its meaning.

However, in a case in the United States, La République Française et al. *v.* Schultz, the Court thought that as the terms "marque de commerce" and "nom commercial," used in the Convention, are terms used in the civil law of France, it became necessary to examine their meaning in the French law, in order to understand the distinction between them.[1] In this particular case, it would seem, the Court did not err in looking into the French Law. However, as a general rule, this sort of interpretation should not be adopted.

§ **105. Proposal for an international jurisdiction for interpretation of the Convention.** At the Conference of The Hague an attempt was made to establish an international jurisdiction for questions of interpretation of the Convention. The origin of this attempt was a resolution adopted by the Economic Committee of the League of Nations. This resolution formed one of the proposals of the British delegation at the Conference of The Hague as an amendment to article 17 and read as follows:

> Les États contractants conviennent de soumettre au jugement de la Cour internationale permanente de justice à La Haye tout différent qui pourrait surgir entre eux au sujet de l'interprétation ou de l'exécution de la présente Convention et qui n'aurait pas pu être aplani par accord mutuel ou d'une manière prévue par la Convention ou par transaction entre les deux États intéressés.

Unanimity, however, has not been obtained on this amendment, notwithstanding its support by the Economic Committee of the

1. (1893) 57 Fed. 37, 41. Article 8 of the Convention, protecting the trade name, was involved in that case. The treatise of the French author Pouillet, and his definition of trade name, were taken into consideration and followed by the Court.

League of Nations and the French delegation. The American and Turkish delegations were unprepared to vote for it, in view of the fact that their respective countries had not adhered to the Protocol establishing the Permanent Court. The Canadian delegation also did not agree with the British proposal.[1]

§ 106. Theory of minimum protection. The provisions establishing legal rules applicable immediately and generally in all the countries of the Union give rise to a further question, relating to the interpretation of the Convention. A country of the Union may pass legislation, either before or after the adoption of the Convention covering the matters dealt with by such provisions of the Convention. It is clear, in accordance with the previous exposition and with the limitations stated therein, that in so far as this legislation is less favorable to the persons protected by the Convention it will not be given effect. The matter to be considered here is the application of provisions of municipal law more favorable to foreigners than provisions of the Convention. For instance, instead of the periods of rights of priority provided in article 4, the municipal legislation of a country may accord longer periods. Or the indications of place of origin may be protected by municipal legislation to a greater extent than by article 10 of the Convention, and without the latter's limitations. In such cases, may the persons protected by the Convention claim this more favorable protection, or are they to be restricted solely to the protection accorded by the Convention?

At an earlier date, this question was more acute than it is now. Senator Bozérian of France, Chairman of the Paris Conferences of 1880 and 1883, gave origin to what has been called the theory of minimum protection.[2] According to this theory, the provisions contained in the Convention of 1883 are to be considered as a minimum of protection, which is secured to the persons protected, and which may be extended by the municipal legislation of each country of the Union. This larger protection may be claimed by the persons protected by the Convention.[3]

1. *Actes de la Conférence de La Haye*, pp. 353, 420–424. This question of international jurisdiction is considered at length, *infra*, chap. XXXVI, §§ 574 ff.

2. *Convention Internationale du 20 Mars, 1883, pour la Protection de la Propriété Industrielle*, Paris (1886).

3. Against this theory, Pillet, *Régime International*, pp. 236 ff.; Donzel, *Commentaire de la Convention de 1883*, pp. 278 ff.; Despagnet, *Précis*, 5th ed., p. 256. In accord with Bozérian, Pelletier et Vidal-Naquet, *La Convention d'Union*, pp. 30–32; Weiss, *Traité*, II, 381.

The argument for such an interpretation is twofold. First, it has been urged that the intention of the Conference which adopted the Convention of 1883 was that the Convention should be regarded as a minimum protection. This is not substantiated by the discussions at the Conferences of 1880 and 1883. Also, it has been argued that article 15 of the Convention, which allows the countries of the Union to enter between themselves into separate agreements more favorable than the Convention, manifests this idea of considering the Convention as a minimum protection. This article undoubtedly permits the members of the Union to afford to their respective nationals a larger protection, but this is to be done only through a separate arrangement.

It is submitted that there is no need of such a theory in order to arrive at the conclusion that the persons protected by the Convention may claim the more favorable treatment of general municipal law. The country enacting such legislation may expressly exclude from its operation or its benefits the persons protected by the Convention of Union, or may restrict them to the protection accorded thereby. In so doing, such country would not violate any international obligation. If, however, it chooses not to exclude these persons, they may enjoy the protection of the general municipal law, in accordance with the national-treatment clause of article 2. The general principle of this article is not limited, but enlarged, by the special advantages and rights granted by the other articles of the Convention.[1]

The view suggested here seems to be supported now by the sentence added to article 2 at the Conference of Revision at The Hague. According to this sentence, the persons protected by the Convention enjoy the advantages that the respective laws grant now, or shall grant in the future, to nationals, without prejudice to the rights provided for specifically by the Convention — "le tout sans préjudice des droits spécialement prévus par la présente Convention."[2]

1. Thus, in the United States, until the revision of section 4887 of the Revised Statutes by the Act of March 3, 1897 (29 Stat. 692), foreigners were accorded the greater advantages of that section, instead of the six months' right of priority under the Convention. Similarly in Italy, "an importation patent" is granted to foreign patentees at any time so long as the term of the foreign patent has not expired and the invention has not been introduced and worked in Italy; such a patent may be granted to persons entitled to the benefits of the Convention, even though it is applied for after the lapse of the period of priority. See Decision of the Court of Appeals of Milan, March 23, 1917, in *Propriété Industrielle* (1917), p. 55.

2. See *Actes de la Conférence de La Haye*, pp. 222, 224, 413, 517, 536, 572.

CHAPTER VIII

THE "RESSORTISSANTS" OF THE UNION

§ 107. Persons constituting the "ressortissants" of the Union. The Union for the Protection of Industrial Property has its own "ressortissants," that is to say, the persons who are entitled to its benefits. The juristic concept of "ressortissant" of the Union is not easy to define, but this is not a reason to deny its existence. The term has been adopted by the latest conferences of revision in new amendments to the Convention of 1883.[1] It is the scope of this chapter to explain this term and accurately define the various classes of persons who come under it and may, therefore, claim the advantages of the Union.

Articles 2 and 3 of the Convention of 1883 undertake to enumerate these classes of persons. The original draft Convention contained

1. See, for instance, art. 2 (§ 2), 4*b*, 10*b*.

only article 2, and the persons enumerated therein were to be the only ones entitled to its benefits. These were the subjects or citizens of the contracting countries. In this the Convention would have in no way differed from the bipartite conventions entered into before 1883. At the second reading of the draft, when the whole scope and purpose of the Convention became clear, article 3 was added, assimilating to nationals of the contracting countries persons belonging to non-contracting countries, but domiciled or possessing business establishments in the Union.[1]

I. Nationals of Contracting Countries

§ 108. "Ressortissants" of each country of the Union. Article 2 of the Convention of 1883 provides that the persons who shall enjoy in all the countries of the Union the rights and protection granted to nationals in each country, and the special advantages provided for by the Convention, are the "ressortissants de chacun des pays contractants." The term "ressortissants" was substituted at the Conference of The Hague for the words "sujets ou citoyens" of the previous text, as being, in its brevity, more comprehensive. It is a term used generally in treaties and conventions entered into after the World War. It may sometimes include more than nationals of a country. However, in this Convention, it was substituted for the previous terms as a matter of form,[2] and, in view of article 3, which enumerates certain classes of foreigners domiciled or established in countries of the Union, it would seem that its equivalent English term is "nationals."

Thus the nationals of each of the contracting countries constitute the first class of persons who are entitled to the benefits of the Convention of 1883 and to whom the term "ressortissants" of the Union may be applied. The matter whether a person is a national of a country of the Union raises several questions:

First, by what law is it to be determined whether a person is a national of a country of the Union? Whether a person is a national of a country is determined by the municipal law of that country. The only government which can bestow nationality upon a person

1. This article was added at the insistence, especially, of the Belgian delegate, who thought that all persons, in general, living in the Union should be entitled to the benefits of the Convention. See *Conférence de Paris* (1880), pp. 129 ff.

2. *Actes de la Conférence de La Haye*, p. 536.

is the government of the country of which that person claims to be a national. Each government bestows it according to its own law.

Whenever, therefore, the question of nationality of a person comes up in another country, his nationality is a fact to be determined objectively; in other words, the question always will be whether the country of the Union of which a person claims to be a national has bestowed nationality on this person.[1] The same is true as to the loss of nationality, which also will be determined objectively.

§ 109. Persons possessing double nationality. Another question may arise, as to persons having a double nationality. This may have three aspects. A person may be a national (*a*) of two countries of the Union; (*b*) of a member country of the Union and one not a member; (*c*) of two countries in one of which he claims protection.

(*a*) In the first case there is no difficulty; he may claim nationality in either country. The Convention protects the nationals of each country regardless of reciprocity. The fact, then, that one of the countries of which the person in question is a national affords protection to the nationals of the country where protection is sought, while the other does not, is immaterial.

(*b*) In the second case, the question is more difficult. Suppose a Chilean, domiciled and established in Chile, at the same time a national of Germany, claims protection of a right of industrial property in Austria, under article 2 of the Convention. May he claim before the Austrian court his German nationality and be protected as a German national, or is the Austrian court at liberty to consider him a Chilean national and deny protection? On the other hand, should the fact that he is domiciled or established in Chile affect the decision of the Austrian court?

Mr. Weiss [2] is inclined to think that the fact that the person in question is domiciled in one of the two countries shows his election to be treated as a national of that country. It is difficult to infer such an election, since the double nationality may be acquired voluntarily, and the domicile may be a creation of the law irrespective of the intent of a person.

1. Osterrieth und Axster, *Pariser Konvention*, p. 12; Marck, *Internationale Rechtsschutz der Patente*, p. 25; Stoek *v.* Public Trustee (1921), 2 Ch. 67, 37 T. L. R. 666; *in re* Chamberlain's Settlement (1921), 2 Ch. 533, 37 T. L. R. 966; Fasbender *v.* Attorney General (1922), 1 Ch. 232, 38 T. L. R. 144; Kramer's Case (1922), 2 Ch. 850, affirmed in 1923, A. C. 528.

2. Weiss, *Manuel de Droit International Privé*, 7th ed. (1914), pp. 80–81.

In case the person in question is not domiciled in either of the countries of which he claims to be a national, Mr. Weiss would have the court decide according to the principle of nationality similar to that of its country. Thus, if the law of the country of the court accepts, in the matter of nationality, the principle of *jus soli*, and the two countries in question recognize respectively the rule of *jus sanguinis* and *jus soli*, the court should decide as to nationality according to the second. The author himself admits that such a solution would not be possible before an international court. It is not seen why the court should apply its own law, when its business is to find a fact objectively, according to the law of the countries that have bestowed nationality.

It is submitted that the court should apply the Convention, and protect any person who may prove to be a national of one of the contracting countries. The fact that this person is also a national of a country not a member of the Union should not change the situation.[1]

(c) A third case of double nationality may be presented if one of the two countries is the one in which protection is claimed. In such case, whether or not the second country is a member of the Union, the court will apply its own law.[2] If, then, under this law, the person in question is a national of the country where protection is sought, he will be treated as a national of this country, regardless of the fact that he may also be a national of another country.

The question whether nationals may claim the advantages of the Convention in their own country is considered later in this chapter.

§ **110. Effect of changes of nationality on protection by the Convention.** Persons entitled to the advantages of the Convention of 1883, by reason of their being nationals of member countries of the Union, may cease to be entitled thereto by losing their nationality and acquiring that of a country not belonging to the Union.[3] However, rights acquired before such loss of nationality continue to be protected. The application of this general rule in certain cases is not free from difficulties.

Such a case is presented when a person loses his nationality in a member country of the Union before the period of the rights of priority of article 4 of the Convention has expired. Is such person

1. *Propriété Industrielle* (1922), p. 143, *accord*. 2. Weiss, *Manuel*, p. 76.
3. Unless, of course, they may come under the provisions of article 3.

entitled to enjoy the right of priority for the purpose of filing applications in the other countries of the Union, during the remaining period? The answer is not free from doubt. The question really is, does a person who files an application in a country of the Union for the grant of a patent, or for the deposit or registration of a design or trade mark, acquire, under article 4, a right which will not be divested by his loss of nationality in such country? Or is the so-called right of priority merely a defense *a posteriori* against, for instance, the loss of the character of novelty of the invention by reason of acts occurring in the interval? In the latter case, the person in question, being no longer a national of a country of the Union, cannot have the advantage of this defense. The question of the nature of the "right of priority" is considered below.[1] It is concluded there that the right of priority is not an independent right acquired by the mere fact of filing an application in a country of the Union, but only a legal defense, operative in the future when a second application is made in other countries of the Union. Consequently, a person losing his nationality in the country in which he filed the first application during the period of article 4 of the Convention cannot claim the right of priority.

There may also be cases in which a national of a country not belonging to the Union, acquires nationality in a country of the Union. The benefits of the Convention will accrue to him at the moment he becomes a national of the latter country. No difficulty is presented in this case in respect to the right of priority. If the person in question filed a patent application in a country not a member of the Union, he cannot claim a right of priority under the Convention, because he did not file his prior application in a "country of the Union," as article 4 provides. If the first application was filed in a country of the Union, it was not filed by a "ressortissant" of the Union, and, therefore, no right of priority may be claimed on filing the second application.

A change of nationality may also occur by reason of cession or annexation of territory or dismemberment of a country. As a rule, vested rights should be respected. But this rule could not be applied in all cases. Thus a patent privilege might not be recognized and enforced in the new country if, by its law, no patent is granted for inventions or for certain kinds of inventions. In general, no pro-

1. See *infra*, § 165.

tection may be claimed in cases in which none is provided for by the municipal law, unless it is specifically granted by the Convention of 1883.

Most important changes of this kind have taken place as a result of the World War. The treaties of peace took care to preserve the rights of industrial property of the persons changing nationality. These rights were preserved in the countries of which these persons were nationals before the War, and in those of which they became nationals as a result of the treaties.[1] As to the other countries of the Union which were belligerents and parties to the treaties of peace, the same rights were restored and preserved by special provisions.[2] The neutral member countries of the Union were not affected by the treaties of peace, and did not undertake any obligation to restore or preserve such rights, unless by the Arrangement of Berne, of 1920, "for the reëstablishment of rights of Industrial Property affected by the War."

A stateless person, *heimatlos*, cannot, of course, claim any protection under article 2. He may only claim under article 3, if he comes under its provisions.

§ 111. Citizens and inhabitants of colonies, dominions, mandated territories, etc. As seen above,[3] colonies, possessions, protectorates, dominions, and the like, are not deemed to be included in the Union by the mere fact of accession of the mother country. There must be a declaration to this effect by the latter, or a distinct act of accession for the dominion, colony, and so forth which is to be considered as forming part of the territory of the Union. Since the Convention of 1883 is not applicable in such territorial entities excluded from the Union, it follows that their inhabitants are not "ressortissants" of the contracting countries and cannot claim the advantages of the Convention.

This is true particularly in respect to citizens of British dominions and colonies. They are British nationals,[4] but not "ressortissants" of Great Britain. All British possessions have a local government,

1. Article 311 of the Versailles Treaty; art. 274 of the Treaty of Saint-Germain; art. 257 of the Treaty of Trianon.

2. Articles 306 ff. of the Treaty of Versailles; arts. 258 ff. of the Treaty of Saint-Germain; arts. 241 ff. of the Treaty of Trianon.

3. See *supra*, § 57.

4. That they are British nationals is clear from the acts relating to British nationality (1914), 4 and 5 Geo. V, c. 17, part I, and part II, 8; amended in 1918, 8 and 9 Geo. V, c. 38.

which may bestow citizenship upon persons belonging to the particular parts of the Empire.[1] There is a British nationality and a citizenship in each of the British possessions. The citizens of the dominions are British nationals only in the sense that they owe allegiance to the supreme sovereignty of the Crown, and are protected and treated as British nationals everywhere. But they are not "ressortissants" of Great Britain in the stipulation of a treaty that she makes for herself to the exclusion of her colonies, possessions, and so forth.[2]

The status of the inhabitants of mandated territories is no longer in dispute. These people are not "nationals" or "subjects" of the mandatory power. In accordance with the suggestions of the Permanent Mandates Commission, the Council of the League decided on April 23, 1923, that the status of the inhabitants of the mandated territories of classes B and C is distinct from that of the nationals of the mandatory.[3] The latter cannot, therefore, claim the advantages of the Convention as "ressortissants" of the mandatory country.[4] *A fortiori*, citizens of territories under mandate of class A are not nationals of the mandatory. These territories are described by article XXII, section 4, of the Covenant of the League as "independent nations."[5]

§ 112. Nationals need not be domiciled in country in which they claim protection. Nationals of the contracting countries may be domiciled or resident in the country of which they are nationals, in another member country of the Union, or in a country not belonging to the Union. Their claim to protection may arise in the country of which they are nationals, or in another country of the Union.

1. See Act of 4 and 5 Geo. V, c. 17, part III, § 26. In fact even nationality, as distinct from citizenship, may be bestowed to-day upon citizens of certain dominions. Thus the Canadian Act of 1921, 11 and 12 Geo. V (Canada), c. 4 (*Statutes of Canada*, 1921).

2. Thus, a Canadian was held not entitled to the benefits of the Convention by a decision of the German Patent Office of June 8, 1914 (*Blatt für Patent-, Muster- und Warenzeichenwesen*, XX, 221). Canada did not accede to the Union until 1923.

3. See Permanent Mandates Commission Minutes, 2d session, 3d meeting, August 2, 1922, pp. 16, 19, and 13th meeting, August 8, 1922, pp. 66, 68; also a resolution of the Council of the League on April 23, 1923. *League of Nations Official Journal* (1923), p. 604.

4. The mandates contain provisions making it an obligation of the mandatory to extend to the mandated territories the benefit of general international conventions such as the Convention of 1883.

5. See British Mandate for Palestine, article 7, providing that "the Administration of Palestine shall be responsible for enacting a nationality law." *League of Nations Official Journal* (1922), p. 1007.

The first case is considered below. In the latter case, when a claim under the Convention is presented, it is to be considered whether the persons in question should be domiciled or established therein or in the Union in general. For instance, when a French national claims the benefit of the Convention in Germany, the latter might conceivably require that he be domiciled or established in Germany, or in the Union and not outside the Union.

The condition of domicile, or establishment, in the particular country of the Union in which an advantage under the Convention is sought, is excluded by the second paragraph of article 2, which provides explicitly:

> Toutefois, aucune condition de domicile ou d'établissement dans le pays où la protection est reclamée ne peut être exigée des ressortissants de l'Union, pour la protection d'aucun des droits de propriété industrielle.

This paragraph was added at the Washington Conference, for the purpose of doing away with the erroneous interpretation of article 2 by the courts of certain countries, which held that, since under the Convention of 1883 nationals of the contracting countries were to be protected as nationals of each country, and since nationals were not protected by the municipal legislation unless they were established in the country, the above persons also could be protected only on this condition.[1] Under such an interpretation the Convention would be useless; for even before the Convention foreigners established in a country were assimilated by the municipal legislation to nationals of this country.[2]

§ 113. Nationals need not be domiciled or established in the Union. The question whether the "ressortissants" of the contracting countries must be domiciled or resident in the territory of the Union, as a condition for claiming its advantages, should not be difficult to solve. The International Bureau, at an earlier time, finding the question very difficult, declared itself unable to give an

1. France, Cassation, February 5, 1904, in Grauer Frey *c.* Daltroff (*Dalloz*, 1905, I, 149). Belgium, Cassation, May 8, 1911, in Creim et Heintz *c.* Tinchant et État Français (*Pasicrisie*, 1911, I, 247); and June 20, 1912, in Société Française des Cotons *c.* Société Hebebrand (*Pasicrisie*, 1912, I, 354). In Germany, on the other hand, the opposite was held by the Reichsgericht on March 3, 1905, in Eagle Oil Co. of New York *v.* Vacuum Oil Co. (10 *Entsch. Reichsg. Zivils*, N. F., 217, 218). This was also the view of Osterrieth und Axster, *Pariser Konvention*, p. 26.

2. Under a reservation of the third paragraph of article 2, the law of each country may prescribe that foreigners must elect a domicile, or appoint an attorney, in the country in which they claim protection.

opinion.[1] The difficulty arose because of the attempt to discover the intent of the founders of the Union. Indeed, before 1883, in most countries trade marks and trade names of citizens and foreigners established in the country were equally protected, while those of citizens as well as of foreigners established abroad were protected only on condition of reciprocity. Thus the legislation on trade marks and trade names aimed at protecting national industry and trade, and not nationals wherever they may be established. Did the founders of the Union intend to continue this territorial regime, or did they undertake to protect their nationals wherever established or domiciled? The bipartite treaties entered into before the creation of the Union, concerning nationals of the contracting countries, were interpreted [2] as protecting only those nationals of each country who were protected by its municipal legislation. If the Convention of 1883 were merely an international engagement, like the bipartite treaties entered into before 1883, the same interpretation should be given to article 2.

However, the Union was created not only for the protection of the national industry and trade of each country, but for giving an effective and complete protection to industrial property rights of the nationals of each country. The Convention of 1883 is the result of private efforts of inventors, business men, and jurists tending to the securing of individual interests of industrial property. It embodies international legislation purporting to harmonize the various legislations, and to establish uniform rules for the protection of industrial property. Under these conditions, it is impossible to read into article 2 a condition that nationals of the contracting countries will be protected only if they are protected by the municipal law of their own countries.

Besides, the preamble of the Convention, in its original text, stated clearly that the purpose was to secure a complete and effective protection to the industry and commerce of "nationals of the contracting countries," and to contribute to the guaranty "of the rights of inventors and of loyalty in commercial transactions."

Furthermore, the third paragraph of article 6 and its history strengthen this opinion considerably. Indeed, this paragraph provides that "country of origin," for the purpose of the application of

1. *Propriété Industrielle* (1895), pp. 76–77. Pillet (*Régime International*, p. 217) considers it beyond doubt that no such condition is to be read into article 2.

2. See *supra*, p. 59.

article 6, will be considered as meaning the country to which the applicant belongs in case he does not possess a business establishment in the territory of any member of the Union. This provision was added at the Paris Conference of 1880, to avoid the danger indicated by the Swiss delegate that the proposed draft, by defining as country of origin the country where the applicant has his main establishment, would exclude a national of a country of the Union who might be domiciled, or have his main establishment, in a country not belonging to the Union.[1] The Conference, by adopting this paragraph, manifested its intention to protect in all cases nationals of the contracting countries, even though they were not domiciled, or did not possess an establishment, in a country of the Union.[2]

The adoption of the revised paragraph of article 2, at the Conference of Washington, to the effect that no obligation of domicile or establishment in the country in which protection is claimed may be imposed on nationals of the contracting countries, cannot be taken as implying that these must be domiciled or established in one of the countries of the Union.[3] As shown by the proposals and discussion at the adoption of this paragraph by the Conference of Washington, its purpose is to override the requirement of the municipal law of certain countries of the Union that foreigners not domiciled or established in their territory cannot claim protection unless there exists reciprocity.[4]

II. Foreigners Domiciled in the Union or Possessing Business Establishments Therein

§ 114. Meaning of term "domiciliés." Article 3 of the Convention of 1883/1925 provides as follows:

> Sont assimilés aux ressortissants des pays contractants les ressortissants des pays ne faisant pas partie de l'Union, qui sont domiciliés ou ont des établissements industriels ou commerciaux effectifs et sérieux sur le territoire de l'un des pays de l'Union.

Thus two classes of foreigners are entitled to the same advantages

1. The Swiss delegate said in part: "Il importe de prévoir ce cas, afin que chaque État assure à ses nationaux établis en dehors de l'Union les avantages attachés à celle-ci." See *Conférence de 1880*, pp. 133-134.
2. The text of this paragraph of article 6 as revised at the Conference of The Hague makes this much clearer.
3. This opinion was supported by Laborde, *Traité des Marques* (Paris, 1914), pp. 243-244.
4. *Actes de la Conférence de Washington* (1911), pp. 94, 245, 270. See also *Propriété Industrielle* (1922), p. 143 n.

as nationals of the contracting countries, and constitute also "ressortissants" of the Union. These foreigners are those who are domiciled in the territory of a country of the Union, or who possess business establishments therein.

In respect to the former, the element which connects them with the Union is the domicile in a member country. The important question then is the meaning to be given to the term "domiciliés." A Chilean, for instance, domiciled in the United States may claim the advantages of the Convention in France, although Chile is not a member of the Union. What is the meaning of the word "domiciled" (*domiciliés*) in this connection? Domicile, as a concept of law, is the relation which the law creates between an individual and a particular locality or country; but sometimes it is used indiscriminately as equivalent to residence. In the first sense, domicile governs the civil status of persons (Anglo-American law), or determines the enjoyment of civil rights (French law). In the common law countries the law ascribes automatically a domicile to a person under certain conditions of fact: namely, to a person residing in a place with the intent to remain there indefinitely. In Germany the concept of domicile is also based on residence, but it is less strict, it being possible for a person to have more than one domicile.[1] But in France domicile until recently was acquired by permission from the government (French Civil Code, article 13). One might reside for a great number of years in France with the intent of making this country, or a particular place therein, his permanent abode; but so long as he had not been authorized by a decree to fix his domicile in France, he was not "domiciled" there within the meaning of the French law.[2]

Pillet thinks that the Convention did not use the word domicile in the legal sense, varying as this does in the different countries, and that it was inserted in article 3 because patentees may not be merchants or manufacturers, and therefore would be excluded under the other requirement of article 3, that foreigners should possess a com-

1. *Bürgerliches Gesetzbuch*, § 7: "Wer sich an einem Orte ständing niederlässt, begründet an diesem Orte seinen Wohnsitz. Der Wohnsitz kann gleichzeitig an mehreren Orten bestehen."

2. Weiss, *Manuel*, p. 304. As a result of the abolition of articles 10, 12, and 13 of the Civil Code by the Law of August 10, 1927, art. 13 (*Bulletin des Lois*, 1927, pp. 2769, 2774) the special authorization for acquiring a domicile in France is no longer required. Domicile is now acquired in France at the place of the "principal establishment" of a person.

mercial or industrial establishment in a country of the Union.[1] This opinion seems right. It should be taken that a factual rather than a legal situation is implied by the word "domiciled."[2] From the discussions at the Paris Conference of 1880 it appears that the purpose was to admit to the benefits of the Convention foreigners merely residing in a country of the Union.[3]

The domicile or residence must be real and not fictitious. This is always a question of fact for the courts. A temporary residence or sojourn, of course, would not fulfill the requirement of article 3. There must be a more or less permanent situation.[4]

In case of change of domicile, the rule laid down for the case of change of nationality will be applied. As soon as the national of a country not belonging to the Union abandons his domicile in the territory of a country of the Union and makes his home outside the Union, he ceases to be protected. The question when a domicile in the sense of the Convention is abandoned, is again a question of fact.[5]

On the other hand, it is clear that no obligation of domicile or establishment in the country in which protection is claimed may be imposed on this category of persons. Article 3 demands only a domicile in any country of the Union. Besides, this article, in admitting these persons to the same benefits of the Convention as the persons described in article 2, impliedly refers to the last paragraph of the latter article which provides that no such obligation may be imposed. The municipal legislation of each country, however, may impose on these persons, as well as on those of article 2, the election of a domicile, or appointment of an attorney, in the country in which protection is claimed.

§ 115. Meaning of term "établissements effectifs et sérieux." The second class of foreigners entitled to the same advantages

1. Pillet, *Régime International*, p. 218.

2. It is interesting to note that the word "domicile" was struck out from the original draft of article 6, concerning the place of origin of the applicant for the registration of a trade mark, on account of a remark made by the Belgian delegate that the word "domicile" refers to civil and political rights. *Conférence de 1880*, pp. 134, 139.

3. *Conférence de Paris* (1880), pp. 129–131. The opposite view is held by Pelletier and Vidal-Naquet, *La Convention d'Union*, p. 42, who, however, produce no reasons for its support.

4. Weiss, *Manuel*, p. 307, taking into consideration the fact that for many purposes the French courts hold that a foreigner is domiciled in France, even though not authorized, extends to him article 103 of the Civil Code, which lays down the elements of domicile, viz., a real home in a place, and an intention to be established therein.

5. *Propriété Industrielle* (1922), p. 146.

as nationals of the contracting countries are those who possess "effective and *bona fide* industrial or commercial establishments in the territory of any of the countries of the Union." The element, then, which connects these persons with the Union is the possession of such establishments in the Union.

Originally the Convention did not contain the qualifications that the establishment should be effective and *bona fide*. To some, this has seemed to leave too wide a gap in the Convention, through which many foreigners might pass.[1] At the Rome Conference of 1886, an attempt was made to make the provision more precise. The Rome *Règlement*, which has never come into effect, provided that persons possessing industrial or commercial establishments in the Union "may claim its advantages if they are exclusive owners of these establishments, are represented there by a general agent, and prove, in case of dispute, that they exercise there in a real and continuous way their industry or their commerce." [2] On the other hand, the Protocol for the interpretation of the Convention adopted at the Madrid Conference of Revision required the persons in question to possess "their main industrial or commercial establishments in the territory of the Union." [3]

The qualification "effectifs et sérieux" was added at the Brussels Conference. It was adopted in a desire to eliminate frauds, but at the same time to break away from the spirit of restriction which prevailed at the Conferences of Rome and Madrid.[4] It was thought that the term "sérieux" was sufficient to exclude fraudulent and fictitious establishments, while the term "effectifs" made it possible to claim the advantages of the Convention for a person possessing an establishment in the Union which, even though it was not a main or *the* main one, was, however, of real and sufficient importance.

Thus, under this provision of article 3, a national of a country not belonging to the Union may claim the advantages of the Convention if he has a branch establishment in the territory of the Union.[5] But a mere office or storehouse in the territory of the Union, and a representative of an industrial or commercial establishment situated out-

1. Donzel, *Commentaire de la Convention de 1883*, pp. 181 ff.
2. *Conférence de Rome* (1886), p. 165.
3. *Conférence de Madrid*, pp. 129–131, 215.
4. *Actes de la Conférence de Bruxelles*, p. 200.
5. Pillet, *Régime International*, p. 218; Pelletier and Vidal-Naquet, *La Convention d'Union*, pp. 44–45; Osterrieth und Axster, *Pariser Konvention*, p. 57.

side the Union, would not satisfy the requirements of article 3.[1] However, it is not necessary that a manufacturing establishment be possessed in the Union. An establishment for selling goods is sufficient. Article 3 requires, in the alternative, an industrial or a commercial establishment.[2]

The last paragraph of article 2 applies to this class of persons, so that no obligation of domicile or establishment in the country in which protection is claimed may be imposed on them. It is sufficient if they own an establishment in any country of the Union. Thus a citizen of Venezuela having an industrial or commercial establishment in Mexico may claim the advantages of the Convention in France.

§ 116. Establishment or domicile alone in a country of the Union does not entitle one to benefits of the Convention in that same country. The phrase "in the territory of any of the countries of the Union," of article 3, raises the question whether a foreigner may claim the advantages of the Convention in a member country by being domiciled or possessing an industrial or commercial establishment in that country and not in any other of the Union. For instance, a national of Venezuela, established in Mexico, obtains a patent in France, and claims the right of priority of article 4 of the Convention in an application for a patent for the same invention in Mexico. If he should apply first in Mexico and then in France, he would be clearly entitled to this right under article 3. The sole fact of having obtained a patent in a country of the Union does not entitle a person, not a national of a country of the Union, to the right of priority.[3] The only ground, then, on which this national of Venezuela may claim the right of priority in Mexico is that he owns an establishment therein.

The argument in favor of such protection in Mexico may proceed from a liberal interpretation of article 3, which requires an establishment "in the territory of *any* country of the Union," and on the ground that the person in question, who may successfully claim the advantages in the Convention in all the other countries of the Union, should be able to do so in the country in which he possesses his estab-

1. Cf. Marck, *Internationale Rechtsschutz der Patente*, p. 31; Neuberg, *Internationale Gewerbliche Rechtsschutz*, pp. 16–17.

2. The decision to the contrary of the Civil Tribunal of Brussels in the case of Thonet Frères *v.* Cambier Frères, in 1890 (*Pasicrisie*, 1891, III, 56), seems wrong.

3. *Propriété Industrielle* (1910), p. 102.

lishment. However, under the Convention of 1883, a national of a member country of the Union may claim protection in all the other countries of the Union, even though he is not protected by the municipal law of his own country.

On the other hand, article 3 was adopted in order to protect the commerce and industry of foreigners established in a country of the Union. How far a country of the Union would protect foreigners established in its own territory is outside the scope of the Convention. Mexico has an interest in having protected in France a national of Venezuela possessing a commercial or industrial establishment in Mexico. Venezuela cannot claim any such protection of her nationals in Mexico, because she is not a party to the Convention. A Belgian court held, in accordance with this view, that article 3 does not modify the situation of foreigners who possess establishments in Belgium but do not belong to member countries of the Union.[1]

§ 117. Concurrent application of the Convention of 1883 and bipartite treaties. Persons of the classes described in article 3 may be nationals of a country that has entered into a bipartite treaty with the country of the Union in which they claim the advantages of the Convention. In such case, whenever it shall be found that the bipartite treaty protects nationals of the contracting countries, wherever established, the persons in question may claim concurrently the protection of the Convention of 1883 and of the bipartite treaty.

III. Juristic Persons

§ 118. Juristic persons entitled to benefits of the Convention. Articles 2 and 3 speak of "ressortissants" of a country. Under this term the different sorts of legal entities, or juristic persons, are included. If any doubt existed before the Brussels Conference, there should not be any at present. Indeed, an official interpretation of the term was given by that Conference. The Belgian delegate demanded that it be expressly provided that legal entities may claim the advantages of the Convention. It was pointed out that this was obvious, and that no provision to this effect was necessary. The Chairman of the Conference asserted that this was the unanimous opinion of the Conference, and ordered, on the demand of

1. Thonet Frères *c.* Cambier Frères, Court of Appeals of Brussels, February 21, 1892 (*Pasicrisie*, 1892, p. 242).

the Belgian delegate, that these statements be taken down in the *procès-verbal*.[1]

Any legal entity, therefore, which proves to have the nationality of a country of the Union, or is domiciled, or owns an effective and *bona fide* industrial or commercial establishment in the territory of any such country, may claim the advantages and rights given by the Convention. The laws of the various countries are not in agreement as to what groups of persons are endowed with a legal personality. In Anglo-American law only corporations are generally recognized as being juristic persons. There has been no thorough-going and consistent recognition of partnerships, business trusts, and other associations, as juristic persons, though many decisions may be found which for one purpose or another appear to treat these organizations as legal entities.[2] In the civil law countries, persons may choose different forms of grouping ("société en nom collectif, société en commandite, société anonyme,") all of which are considered as legal units.

The question then may arise whether an American partnership firm, or business trust may claim any advantage under the Convention, for instance, in France. If the partners are nationals of the United States or of any other country of the Union, or if they are domiciled or established therein, there should be no difficulty. But in the case of two Chileans, who form a partnership in New York and claim a right under the Convention in France, the lack of entity of the partnership formed in the United States might be a good defense against them. A "société," on the other hand, formed in France by the same persons might enter claim as a legal entity under the Convention in the United States.

§ 119. Application of conditions of nationality, domicile, and establishment in regard to legal entities. The basis of business establishment on which a juristic person may claim protection under the Convention is similar in all aspects to that of a physical person.

1. *Actes de la Conférence de Bruxelles*, pp. 196–197.

2. Empire Co. *v.* Neumond (1912), 199 Fed. 800; Rally *v.* Clyne (1925), 234 Pac. 35; State *v.* Paine (1926), 243 Pac. 2. Professor Magruder believes that "the tendency of the courts in shaping the substantive law of Partnership has been a half-hearted, often unconscious, but none the less definite, approach toward the mercantile conception of the firm as an entity distinct from the partners who compose it." *Harvard Law Review*, XXXVII, 795. See also Cowles, "The Firm as a Legal Person," *Century Law Journal*, LVII, 343; Crane, "The Uniform Partnership Act—a Criticism," *Harvard Law Review*, XXVIII, 762, 766–768.

On the contrary, domicile and nationality of juristic persons present themselves under a new aspect. It may be said, generally, that domicile and nationality are connected here, in the sense that one springs from the other. In other words, the domicile of a legal entity is determined by its nationality, or its nationality by its domicile. The Anglo-American law treats both as necessarily and absolutely connected with the state under the laws of which the corporation is created.[1] The application of this rule in the conflict of laws, however, leads to undesirable results. This is due to the fact that in the civil law countries the question is more complicated; the place of creation of a juristic person, of its principal establishment, or of its seat, may be, and actually is, taken into consideration in deciding the question of domicile or nationality.[2] Thus, an American court will decide that a company formed in France, under the French laws, is a French company; while the French courts may decide as to the same company that it is Chilean, if its seat or its principal establishment is in Chile.

Be this as it may, the existence of the three various bases on which a legal entity may claim protection under the Convention makes the above diversities of law of small importance. A juristic person created in one state, having its seat in another, and its main business establishment in a third state, even if it be not considered as having the nationality of the first country, may claim to be domiciled in the second, or established in the third. Besides, the extent of the Union at the present time makes rarer and rarer the cases where real difficulties of decision on this question may arise.

IV. Nationals in Their Own Country

§ 120. Applicability of the Convention to nationals in their own country. Article 2 provides that the nationals of member countries of the Union shall enjoy the rights and protection that the law of

1. Clark, *Corporations*, Hornbrook Series, 2d ed. (1907), §§ 36, 37; Taylor, *Private Corporations*, 5th ed. (1902), § 410; Bank of Augusta *v.* Earle (1839), 13 Pet. 519; Continental Tyre & Rubber Co. *v.* Daimler Co. (1915), 1 K. B. 893, 903; Fairbanks Steam Shovel Co. *v.* Wills (1916), 240 U. S. 642; Lepaulle, *De la Condition des Sociétés Étrangères aux États Unis* (1923), pp. 62 ff.

2. Thaller, "Sur la Nationalité des Sociétés par Action," in *Annales de Droit Commercial* (1890), p. 257; Weiss, *Manuel*, pp. 321 ff.; *Propriété Industrielle* (1922), p. 144; Reynal, *Nationalité des Sociétés Commerciales* (Paris, 1923), pp. 38 ff., 81 ff.; Gain, *La Nationalité des Sociétés* (Paris, 1924), pp. 45 ff.; Cuq, *La Nationalité des Sociétés* (Paris, 1921), pp. 81 ff.; Isay, *Staatsangehörigkeit der Juristischen Personen* (Tübingen, 1907), pp. 51 ff.; Pépy, *Nationalité des Sociétés* (Paris, 1920), pp. 49, 94.

each country grants now, or shall grant in the future, to its nationals, without prejudice to the rights and advantages granted specifically by the Convention. The question arises whether in the words "nationals of the member countries of the Union" are included the nationals of the country in which protection is claimed. In other words, may the nationals of a country claim the protection of the Convention of 1883 in their own country? The cases in which this question may arise are only those in which a specific advantage granted by the Convention might be claimed, for in all other respects the municipal law of a country is applicable.

Thus article 4 of the Convention grants a right of priority to a person who has filed an application for a patent or for registration or deposit of a trade mark or design in a country of the Union, and files a similar application within a certain period in another country of the Union. Also article 5 prohibits the forfeiture of patents for importation of articles manufactured with the invention in another country of the Union. The municipal law of a member country may not grant a right of priority to nationals, and may maintain the forfeiture for importation of articles manufactured abroad with the invention. The nationals of this country have an interest in claiming the protection of the Convention.

In countries in which the Convention of 1883 is not immediately effective, the question could not arise. In the other countries, the applicability of the Convention in favor of nationals in their own country may be supported by the character of the Convention as international legislation of the Union.[1] However, the argument that the contrary opinion would result in placing foreigners in a more favorable situation than nationals of a country [2] is not convincing, since a country may always grant to foreigners a broader protection than to its own nationals. Besides, it is difficult to maintain that the Convention constitutes international legislation regulating any other relations except international relations. This is the reason French

1. Dalloz, *Répertoire, Suppl.; Brevets d'Invention*, No. 69.

2. Allart, "Application en France à l'Egard des Français des Conventions sur la Propriété Industrielle," in *Revue de Droit International Privé* (1908), pp. 121, 123–124. See also, Pouillet et Plé, *La Convention de 1883*, pp. 14 ff.; Michon, *Traités Internationaux devant les Chambres*, p. 224; Mesnil, *Marques de Fabrique*, p. 251; Devaux, *Protection Internationale des Inventions*, p. 91; also German writers: Damme, *Das Deutsche Patentrecht*, p. 219; Rhenius, *Warenzeichenrecht*, p. 164; Kent, *Patentgesetz*, II, 259.

and German writers opposed the inclusion of nationals in their own country in the "ressortissants" of the Union.[1]

Nevertheless, French, Belgian and German courts have decided in many cases that nationals may claim in their own country the advantages of the Convention.[2] In France, the Law of July 1, 1906,[3] settled the theoretical controversy in favor of the view adopted by the courts. It provided that French nationals may claim application in their favor, in France and its colonies, of the stipulations of the International Convention for the protection of industrial property, as well as of the Arrangements, in all the cases in which these stipulations are more favorable to them than the French law. An amendment of the municipal law so as to bring it into conformity with the Convention would seem to be a better method.[4]

However, the French way has been followed in Belgium and Italy. The Belgian law of June 10, 1914,[5] which approved the new text of the Convention after its revision at Washington in 1911, contains in article 3, a provision to the same effect as the French law of 1906. Of similar effect is article 3 of the Italian law no. 169, of January 10, 1928, concerning the carrying out of the Acts of The Hague.[6]

§ 121. Persons entitled to benefit of article 6 of the Convention. Article 6 of the Convention of 1883, before its recent revision at The Hague, raised certain doubts as to the persons who were en-

1. Weiss, *Traité*, II, 331 n; Lyon-Caen, "De la Non-Applicabilité en France à l'Egard des Français des Conventions," in *Revue de Droit International Privé* (1906), p. 482; Pillet, *Régime International*, p. 226; see also Pelletier et Vidal-Naquet, *La Convention d'Union*, p. 69; Osterrieth und Axster, *Pariser Konvention* (1903), p. 15; Marck, *Internationale Rechtsschutz der Patente*, p. 26.

2. France: Chapin *c.* Syndicat, Cour de Paris, November 18, 1892 (*Dalloz*, 1893, II, 147, 148); Société des Raffineries *c.* Ben Simon, Tribunal de Commerce de Marseilles, February 4, 1896 (*Clunet*, 1898, p. 1907); Martell *c.* Levé Diéval, Cour de Douai, May 18, 1900 (*Jurisprudence de la Cour de Douai*, 1900, p. 224); Picon *c.* Aurie, Cour de Montpellier, March 14, 1903 (*Propriété Industrielle*, 1903, p. 197); Société des Carbures et Sullier *c.* Garnault et Hyvert, Tribunal Civil de la Seine, December 23, 1905 (*Darras*, 1906, p. 500).

Belgium, Tribunal de Commerce de Mons, February 2, 1887 (*Propriété Industrielle*, 1887, p. 54).

Germany: Opinion of the Director of the German *Patentamt*, April 19, 1905 (*Propriété Industrielle*, 1905, pp. 182–183); Decision of the *Patentamt*, July 3, 1909 (*Ibid.*, 1910, p. 131).

3. *Bulletin des Lois* (1906), II, 2438; amended in 1922, *Ibid.* (1922), II, 2110.

4. As to the curious consequences of the Law of July 1, 1906, in France, see: Lyon-Caen, "De la Non-Applicabilité en France à l'Egard des Français des Conventions," in *Revue de Droit International Privé*, (1906), pp. 482, 489; Lallier, "Conséquences Pratiques de la Loi du 1er Juillet, 1906," *Ibid.* (1907), p. 114.

5. *Pasinomie* (1914), p. 373.

6. *Propriété Industrielle* (1928), p. 146.

titled to claim its advantages. This article concerns the validation of trade marks registered in the country of origin. In defining the country of origin, the last paragraphs of article 6 provided that this should be primarily the country in which the applicant possesses his main business establishment, and, in the second place, "the country to which the applicant belonged." If the latter country is that of which the person in question is a national,[1] there were two bases for claiming the special advantage of article 6: nationality of a country of the Union, and principal establishment therein. Thus domicile, or effective and *bona fide* establishment, which are bases for claiming all benefits of the Convention under articles 2 and 3, would not be sufficient in the case of article 6.

An opinion was expressed that the word "appartient" of the last paragraph of article 6 should be taken as meaning "appartient par sa nationalité, son domicile ou par un établissement sécondaire."[2] By this interpretation, the conformity of article 6*b* with articles 2 and 3 would be established. But it was not warranted. The divergence of these articles was very probably unintentional and is explained by the circumstances under which articles 3 and 6 were adopted by the Conference of 1880, on account of which the attention of the Conference was not drawn to the discrepancy between them.[3]

At the Conference of The Hague of 1925, the two paragraphs in question of article 6 were omitted, and a new paragraph was adopted which brings article 6 into agreement with articles 2 and 3.[4] Thus all the classes of persons included in the latter articles may claim the special advantage of article 6. Yet, as is seen below, an order of priority is established in this article among the three bases, business establishment, domicile, and nationality, on which a person may claim its advantages.[5]

V. Persons Entitled to Benefits of the Arrangements

§ 122. The Madrid Trade Mark Arrangement and the Arrangement of The Hague. The Arrangements for the international registration of trade marks and the international deposit of industrial

1. *Propriété Industrielle* (1922), p. 152; Pelletier et Vidal-Naquet, *La Convention d'Union*, p. 230.
2. Osterrieth und Axster, *Pariser Konvention*, p. 159.
3. See *Conférence de Paris* (1880), pp. 78, 132 ff., 138–139.
4. *Actes de la Conférence de La Haye*, pp. 239, 341, 450, 522, 542, 577.
5. See *infra*, § 364.

designs and models contain provisions similar to those of articles 2 and 3 of the Convention. The first of these Arrangements in articles 1 and 2, and the latter in article 1, provide that the persons who may enjoy the advantages accorded by them are, first, the "ressortissants" of the contracting countries, and, second, the "ressortissants" of the countries not parties to the Arrangement which satisfy the conditions provided for by article 3 of the Convention in the territory to which the Arrangement extends. In other words, the persons domiciled or having effective and *bona fide* commercial or industrial establishments in the territory of any of the countries parties to the Arrangements, are admitted to the same benefits as the nationals of the member countries of the restricted Unions.

The above interpretation of the three bases for the application of the Convention — nationality, domicile, or business establishment — applies to these two Arrangements.

§ 123. The Madrid Arrangement for repression of false indications of origin. The situation in the Arrangement for the repression of false indications of origin is different. This Arrangement is devoid of the independent character of the other two. It is, in a certain way, a different form of article 10, section 1, of the Convention. Those countries that are not satisfied with article 10, section 1, have adopted, or acceded to, this Arrangement. There is no provision describing the persons entitled to the benefits of the Arrangement. However, article 1 defines the cases in which goods bearing false indications of origin may be seized, and article 2 provides that "the seizure shall be made on application . . . of the interested party, an individual, or an association."

The definition of "the interested party" is given in article 10, section 2, of the Convention of 1883, and resort should be had thereto for discovering the persons who may claim the protection of this Arrangement.[1] Article 10, section 2, of the Convention reads as follows:

> Est reputé partie interessée tout producteur fabricant ou commerçant, engagé dans la production, la fabrication ou le commerce de ce produit, et établi soit dans la localité faussement indiquée comme lieu de provenance, soit dans la région ou cette localité est située.

1. Pillet (*Le Régime International*, p. 220) thinks that all the persons of article 3 of the General Convention may claim the advantages of this Arrangement. This opinion seems wholly unwarranted. *La Propriété Industrielle* (1922, p. 154) is of the opinion advanced in the text.

The "interested party," then, that may claim the application of the Madrid Arrangement should possess two qualifications: first, it should be engaged in the production or manufacture of, or commerce in, the product in question; and, secondly, it should be established in the region or place which is falsely indicated as place of origin. Only the second needs further explanation.

The region or place in question, according to article 1 of the Arrangement, should be one of the contracting countries or a place situated in one of them. Thus, the persons who may claim the advantages of this Arrangement should be established in the territory of one of the member countries of this restricted Union. Nationality and domicile, then, are not bases for the application of this Arrangement.

Nationals of the member countries of this restricted union, who are not properly established in the country which is falsely indicated cannot claim the protection of this Arrangement. But nationals of member countries of the general Union, as well as of countries not belonging to it, may claim the advantages of this Arrangement if they are established in the country, region, or place, the name of which is falsely indicated on the goods in question. The qualification of producers, manufacturers, or merchants, which is required of these persons, in connection with their being established in the countries in question, shows the nature of the establishment required. It should be an effective and *bona fide* industrial or commercial establishment.

CHAPTER IX

GENERAL ASPECTS OF THE REGIME OF INDUSTRIAL PROPERTY IN THE UNION

§ 124. Scope of the Convention. The relation of the Convention and Arrangements of the Union to the municipal law of the member countries, and the extent to which these acts may generally constitute a rule of decision, is considered in a previous chapter.[1] The international régime of each branch of industrial property in the Union is dealt with in detail in the next chapters. Here an attempt will be made to define more accurately the scope of the Convention, that is, its subject; to consider its main principles; and to show what is, in general, the position of industrial property rights in the Union.

The scope of the Convention is expressed in the first paragraph of article 1: "Les pays contractants sont constitués, à l'état d'Union pour la protection de la propriété industrielle."

The protection of industrial property is the object of the Union. A definition of industrial property is given in the two next paragraphs of article 1. The second paragraph defines it by enumerating the various rights which are included in the term "propriété industrielle." The third paragraph gives to the word "industrielle" a broad meaning, comprising not only industry proper, but also commerce, and agricultural and extractive industries. These paragraphs read as follows:

La protection de la propriété industrielle a pour objet les brevets d'invention, les modèles d'utilité, les dessins ou modèles industriels, les marques de fabrique ou de commerce, le nom commercial et les indications de provenance ou appellations d'origine, ainsi que la répression de la concurrence déloyale.

1. Chap. VII.

La propriété industrielle s'étend dans l'acception la plus large, et s'applique non seulement à l'industrie et au commerce proprement dits, mais également au domaine des industries agricoles (vins, grains, feuilles de tabac, fruits, bestiaux, etc.) et extractives (minéraux, eaux minérales, etc.).

The third paragraph was incorporated in article 1 from the Final Protocol adopted at the Conference of Washington. It originated at the Paris Conference of 1880 when the question arose whether agriculture should be excluded from the scope of the Convention.[1] In some countries protection by the municipal law was not extended to agricultural products.[2] The Conference adopted the above provision in the first paragraph of the Final Protocol, using, however, unfortunate language. It referred to "produits de l'agriculture" to which the term "propriété industrielle" must be applied. The term "industrial property" does not signify tangible things, but intangible rights. At the Washington Conference, the Dutch delegation remarked that the Convention of 1883 does not protect products or the ownership of products, but the rights included in the term industrial property, which may have no direct relation with any products, as, for instance, a trade name. At its suggestion the word "production" was substituted for the word "produits."[3]

At the Conference of The Hague a more accurate text was adopted. The term "industrial property" now applies to the rights enumerated in the second paragraph of article 1, and extends to industry and commerce as well as to certain fields of work which may not be included in the term "industry." These are agricultural and extractive industries. Specific illustrations inserted in parentheses explain these two terms. Thus, under agricultural industries are placed wines, grain, tobacco leaves, fruit, cattle, and so forth. These examples are not exhaustive. The tobacco leaves were added, at the Conference of The Hague, on the insistence of the Cuban delegation. The Brazilian delegation urged the specific enumeration of lumber industries. The Conference thought that they

1. *Conférence de 1880*, pp. 32, 33, 124.

2. For instance, in France, the law of July 28, 1824 (*Bulletin des Lois*, 7th Ser. 1824, XIX, 65) protected the trade name against infringement through fraudulent use on industrial products alone.

3. *Actes de la Conférence de Washington*, pp. 109, 268–269. The text adopted at this Conference was as follows: "les mots 'propriété industrielle' doivent être pris dans leur acception la plus large; ils s'étendent à toute production du domaine des industries agricoles (vins, grains, bestiaux, etc.) et extractives (minéraux, eaux minérales, etc.)."

were included in agricultural industries, and declined to lengthen any further an enumeration which could never be complete.[1]

Thus, a trade mark, a trade name, or an appellation of origin used in connection with a strictly industrial business, or with an agricultural or extractive business, is within the scope of the Convention of 1883.

The second paragraph of article 1, as amended at the Conference of The Hague, is a new provision in itself, but its contents are taken from article 2 of the Convention as this was in effect before its amendment at the Conference of The Hague. Indeed, article 2, in proclaiming the principle that nationals of the contracting countries were to enjoy the rights and protection granted by the law of each country to its nationals, specified that this principle applied "as regards patents of invention, working models, industrial designs or models, trade marks, trade names, indications of origin, and the repression of unfair competition."

At the suggestion of the French administration this enumeration of rights of industrial property was omitted from article 2, and the words "en ce qui concerne la propriété industrielle" were substituted. The words omitted from article 2 were then added to article 1, just after the provision of the first paragraph proclaiming the creation of the Union for the Protection of Industrial Property. Thus industrial property is defined by the enumeration of the rights which are grouped together under it. In the introduction to this book, it was suggested that these various rights are of two different categories.[2]

According to the second paragraph of article 1, the protection of industrial property is concerned, among other things, with the repression of unfair competition. Thus the right to be protected against acts of unfair competition is made a right of industrial property. The Polish delegation proposed a more logical enumeration, which would have established the bipartite division of rights of industrial property, as suggested above. According to its proposal, the paragraph would have provided that the protection of industrial property comprises patents, working models, industrial designs or models, and repression of unfair competition in the broadest sense, in particular as regards trade marks, trade names, and indi-

1. *Actes de la Conférence de La Haye*, pp. 221, 332, 410, 535.
2. See *supra*, § 1.

cations of origin. The Conference preferred to maintain the old enumeration, in order to avoid possible misconceptions by the courts.

The provision under consideration was declared by the Conference to be strictly one of definition and to impose no new obligation on the contracting countries. Especially, it contains no engagement by these countries to enact special legislation concerning all the kinds of industrial property rights enumerated. A proposition to make the protection of artistic works cumulative by the Convention of 1883, as well as by the Copyright Convention, did not meet with the approval of the Conference.[1]

The British delegation proposed that, in the enumeration, the words "appellations d'origine" be substituted for the words "indications de provenance," as corresponding more precisely to the definition of the rights which it is proposed to protect and as easier to translate accurately in English. Eventually, both terms were included in view of the fact that article 10 of the Convention and the Madrid Arrangement of 1891 referred to "indications de provenance."[2]

The last paragraph of article 1 of the Convention provides as follows:

> Parmi les brevets d'invention sont comprises les diverses espèces de brevets industriels admises par les législations des pays contractants, telles que brevets d'importation, brevets de perfectionnement, brevets et certificats d'addition, etc.

This provision was taken into article 1, at the Conference of The Hague, from the Final Protocol adopted at the Washington Conference of 1911. It serves to make clear that the patents of invention which are comprised in the protection of industrial property in the Union include the various forms of patents provided for by the laws of the various countries. The Conference of The Hague omitted the final words, "tant pour les procédés que les produits," of the provision of the Final Protocol, giving effect to a remark of the Spanish delegation that it gave rise to misconceptions.[3]

§ 125. Two fundamental principles of protection by the Convention. The nature and extent of the international protection of

1. See *infra*, § 248.
2. *Actes de la Conférence de La Haye*, pp. 332, 410, 534.
3. *Ibid.*, pp. 411, 536.

industrial property under the Convention of 1883 is determined by its several articles. Two fundamental principles may be deduced from these various provisions. On the one hand, the "ressortissants" of the Union enjoy, in each of the member countries of the Union, the rights and advantages granted by the municipal law to its own nationals. No discrimination may be made in this respect between them and nationals of a member country. This is the principle laid down in article 2 of the Convention. On the other hand, the "ressortissants" of the Union enjoy the special rights and advantages specifically recognized, defined, and delimited by the Convention. These rights and advantages are enjoyed over and above the rights and advantages which the nationals enjoy under the municipal law of each country. This second principle of the Convention is expressed in the provisions of articles 4, 4*b*, 5, 5*b*, 6, 6*b*, 6*c*, 7, 8, 10, and 10*b*.

§ **126. "National treatment."** The principle of article 2, commonly termed the "national treatment," is couched in these terms:

> Les ressortissants de chacun des pays contractants jouiront, dans tous les autres pays de l'Union, en ce qui concerne la protection de la propriété industrielle, des avantages que les lois respectives accordent actuellement ou accorderont par la suite aux nationaux, le tout sans préjudice des droits spécialement prévus par la présente Convention. En conséquence, ils auront la même protection que ceux-ci et le même recours légal contre toute atteinte portée à leurs droits, sous réserve de l'accomplissement des conditions et formalités imposées aux nationaux.

The second sentence of this article ("En conséquence . . .") is a commentary on and supplement to the first paragraph. It helps to define and delimit the scope of the national treatment of "ressortissants" of each of the contracting countries. It should be recalled that, by virtue of article 3, certain classes of foreigners are admitted to the same advantages as nationals of the contracting countries.[1] Thus the national-treatment principle of article 2 extends to all the "ressortissants" of the Union.

Before the last revision of the Convention at the Conference of The Hague, article 2 enumerated the various rights of industrial property in respect to which the national treatment of "ressortissants" of the Union was provided for. Now this enumeration appears in article 1. The national treatment extends to the protection

1. See *supra*, §§ 114–116.

of industrial property, as this term is defined in article 1 of the Convention. The scope of the advantages which are enjoyed by the "ressortissants" of the Union in each of the member countries as regards the protection of industrial property is defined by the second paragraph of article 2. From the combined provisions of the first and second paragraphs, it should be understood that the national treatment refers to: (1) the acquisition of all rights of industrial property; (2) the extent and duration of these rights, and the obligations, fees, and so forth, for the maintenance of the same; (3) the actions, and other legal means by which these rights are enforced, and the forms and rules pertaining thereto; (4) the penal sanctions afforded by municipal law for the protection of industrial property.[1]

The advantages granted by the municipal law of each member country are enjoyed by the "ressortissants" of the Union, "sous réserve de l'accomplissement des conditions et formalités imposées aux nationaux." The original draft of the Convention submitted to the Conference of 1880 required compliance only with the formalities imposed upon nationals. Upon the insistence of the Swiss delegate, the words "des conditions" also were added.[2] He was anxious that foreigners should not be placed in a more favorable position than nationals, and wished that foreign as well as national patentees should be subject to the obligations of working their patent in the country and of granting compulsory licenses. Such subjection, however, to the conditions and obligations of municipal law is implied in the principle of national treatment.

"Ressortissants" of the Union are placed on the same footing with nationals in all questions concerning the acquisition, recognition, and enforcement of rights of industrial property. All conditions or formalities pertaining to such acquisition, recognition, or enforcement should be complied with by the "ressortissants" of the Union, as they are to be complied with by nationals of each member country.

Since the "ressortissants" of the Union shall enjoy in each country of the Union the same advantages, protection and remedies as the nationals of that country, no discrimination against such persons is possible under the Convention. Whenever, therefore, the

1. Cf. Neuberg, *Der Internationale Gewerbliche Rechtsschutz*, p. 11; Osterrieth und Axster, *Pariser Konvention*, pp. 28–29.

2. *Conférence de 1880*, p. 46.

municipal legislation of a country of the Union makes the acquisition, preservation, or enforcement of rights of industrial property by foreigners subject to special conditions not imposed upon nationals, no compliance with these conditions may be required from the "ressortissants" of the Union. Similarly, whenever the municipal law discriminates against foreigners by granting to them lesser advantages than those granted to nationals,[1] it shall not apply as against the above persons.

§ 127. Procedural discrimination against foreigners. There is one kind of discrimination against foreigners by the municipal law of member countries of the Union which may prevail against the "ressortissants" of the Union. Provision to this effect is made by the last paragraph of article 2:

> Sont expressément réservées les dispositions de la législation de chacun des pays contractants relatives à la procédure judiciaire et administrative et à la compétence, ainsi qu'à l'élection de domicile ou à la constitution d'un mandataire, qui seraient requises par les lois sur la propriété industrielle.

The substance of this provision was contained, before the revision of the Convention at the Conference of The Hague, in the Final Protocol. It purports to preserve the procedural discriminations against "ressortissants" of the Union which might exist against foreigners. In continental Europe there are two such discriminations which may come up in matters of industrial property.

A foreigner bringing an action in civil law countries may have to deposit the *cautio judicatum solvi*, or *cautio pro expensis*. When the question arose at the Paris Conference of 1880 whether "ressortissants" of the Union would be bound to make such deposit, it was understood that this was a procedural formality with which the Convention had nothing to do.[2] On the other hand, in civil law countries a citizen may sue a foreigner in the national courts in certain cases, although the latter does not reside therein and no service with process is made on him. This exception to the rule *actor sequitur forum rei*, in favor of nationals of member countries of the Union, is also a procedural question, or a question of jurisdiction of the courts. It was the intent of the Conference of 1880

1. For instance, the duration of patents granted to foreign patentees is shorter than that of patents granted to nationals.
2. *Conférence de 1880*, p. 38.

that it should not be included in the national-treatment principle of article 2.[1]

The importance of the procedural formality of the *cautio judicatum solvi* is much minimized since the conclusion of the Convention signed at The Hague on July 17, 1905,[2] which, by its article 17, abolished the obligation of this *cautio* in favor of nationals of the contracting countries. This Convention was entered into by Austria-Hungary, Belgium, Denmark, France, Germany, Italy, Luxembourg, the Netherlands, Norway, Portugal, Rumania, Russia, Spain, Sweden, and Switzerland. Besides this multipartite Convention, several bipartite conventions abolish, as to nationals of the contracting parties, the obligation of the *cautio*.[3] At the Conference of The Hague the Italian delegation, giving effect to a *voeu* adopted by the International Chamber of Commerce at its Rome Congress of 1923,[4] proposed the insertion in the Convention of a provision to the effect that persons entitled to the benefits of the Convention need not deposit a *cautio* in filing their suits. This proposition did not meet with approval at the Conference and was not insisted upon.[5]

Of the same category of procedural questions is the obligation imposed by most of the member countries of the Union upon foreigners to elect a domicile, or appoint an agent or attorney domiciled, in the country, in order that service may be made in judicial or ad-

1. *Conférence de 1880*, p. 38. To confirm this interpretation as to both points, section 3 of the Final Protocol was adopted by this Conference. See *Conférence de 1880*, pp. 124–125.

The writers generally agree that the *cautio judicatum solvi* is a matter of procedure within the meaning of the provision of the Final Protocol. See Pelletier et Vidal-Naquet, *La Convention d'Union*, p. 37; Pouillet and Ple, *La Convention d'Union*, p. 31; Weiss, *Traité*, II, 379 n.; Osterrieth und Axster, *Pariser Konvention*, pp. 28–29. The decisions of the courts are to the same effect. See the Belgian case, Compagnie Belge *c.* Edison Gower Bell Tel. Co., Cassation, April 5, 1888 (*Pasicrisie*, 1888, I, 164); and decision of the Tribunal Civil de la Seine, France, February 4, 1888 (Sirey, 1888, II, 199).

That questions of the jurisdiction of the courts are also included in the proviso of the last paragraph of article 2, see Pillet, *Le Régime International*, p. 298. It was so held by the Supreme Court of Spain, January 13, 1905 (*Colección Legislativa de España, P. II, Jurisprudencia administrativa*, 1905, XVI, 199) and by the Court of Nancy France, November 14, 1894, in Didot *c.* Leturcq-Desrosiers (*Dalloz*, 1895, II, 349, 350).

2. This Convention was drafted by the Conference of International Private Law, and took the place of a similar convention of November 14, 1896. Ratifications were deposited on April 24, 1909. See XCIX *Br. & For. State Papers*, 990.

3. Weiss, *Manuel*, pp. 638–639.

4. *Chambre de Commerce Internationale, Brochure*, no. 31, p. 57; and *Actes de la Conférence de La Haye*, p. 80.

5. *Actes de la Conférence de La Haye*, pp. 354, 424.

ministrative proceedings in regard to rights of industrial property. This obligation, according to the last paragraph of article 2, may be imposed on "ressortissants" of the Union.[1]

§ 128. No reciprocity required. The national-treatment principle of article 2 is opposed to the principle of reciprocity. The "ressortissants" of the Union enjoy in each country of the Union the advantages granted to nationals by the municipal law as regards the protection of industrial property, to the full extent that these advantages are enjoyed by nationals, regardless of whether or not in their country of origin the municipal law affords the same advantages. The Paris Conference of 1880, in confirming this view, omitted from the original draft of the Convention the word "réciproquement," which appeared in article 2.[2]

The national-treatment principle of article 2 of the Convention may lead to inequalities between the advantages enjoyed by the nationals of each country. These are unavoidable so long as the industrial property law of the various countries of the Union is not uniform. Nationals of country A may enjoy greater advantages in country B, where the legislation is more liberal, — for instance, providing longer duration of patents, less taxes, no obligation to work the patent, and the like, — than the nationals of the latter country will enjoy in country A. These inequalities are to be preferred to the confusion arising from the regime of reciprocity.[3] Beside the difficulties of proof of reciprocity and of diversity of treatment of foreigners of different nationalities in the same country,[4] this regime is irreconcilable with the idea of the Union. In effect, it is a regime of bipartite agreements between the various countries. Moreover, it does not tend to harmonize and make uniform the various

1. The Final Protocol adopted at the Paris Conference of 1880 did not contain this provision. On the contrary, it was understood that such a provision of the municipal law derogated from the principle of article 2, and could not be applied to "ressortissants" of the Union. See *Conférence de Paris* (1880), pp. 35, 37–38, 40. The addition in question was made at the Washington Conference. See *Actes de la Conférence de Washington*, pp. 270, 246.

2. *Conférence de Paris* (1880), pp. 39–40. Switzerland and the Netherlands possessed no legislation for the protection of patents at the time the Convention of 1883 was entered into. It was agreed at the Conference, nevertheless, that their nationals would be entitled to enjoy protection for their inventions and to obtain patents in the other contracting countries. See also *supra*, p. 112, note 3.

3. See on this point, *supra*, § 9.

4. Indeed, under the regime of reciprocity, in the United States for instance, a different protection would be meted out to nationals of France, to those of Germany, to those of Italy, etc.

enactments, as the national-treatment principle necessarily tends to do.

After the World War, during which the regime of reciprocity had been adopted by legislation in the different countries in respect to the conservatory measures taken for the preservation and reëstablishment of industrial property rights of foreigners, there was a desire to reconsider the wisdom of the national-treatment principle of the Convention. Such a reconsideration in Europe led to the conclusion that the principle in question should be regarded as constituting the fundamental basis of the Union.[1]

However, at the Conference of The Hague, the American delegation proposed the following amendment to article 2:

> Toutefois il est entendu que chacun des pays contractants se réserve le droit d'imposer en matière de propriété industrielle, aux ressortissants de tout autre pays contractant l'accomplissement de certaines ou de toutes les conditions imposées en cette matière à ses ressortissants par cet autre pays.

The proposal amounted in effect to a substitution of the principle of legislative reciprocity for that of national treatment in the Union. The American delegation did not fail to realize the importance of the change proposed. It based its proposal on the fact that for forty years the United States accepted the national-treatment principle and granted to foreigners the advantages of the liberal protection of its legislation, receiving in exchange less liberal treatment for its nationals in the member countries of the Union. It referred specifically to the facts that the duration of patents in the United States is seventeen years, longer than in many countries of the Union, that no taxes are payable by the patentees as in all other countries, and that no obligation is imposed on them to work their patents in the United States.

True as the complaints of the American inventors might be, they could not be remedied in the way proposed by the American delegation. The adoption of its proposal would have brought back the situation existing before 1883. Of the Union would remain but the name. The work of progressive uniformity begun two scores of years earlier would come to an end. The harmonizing force exercised by the Convention of 1883 would cease. The American

1. See *Travaux de Groupe Français de l'Association Internationale* (1919–1922), no. 1 pp. 92 ff., 130 ff.; (1923–1925), no. 2 p. 25.

proposition was opposed by all the other delegations and was not insisted upon.[1]

§ **129. Insufficiency of national-treatment principle.** The "ressortissants" of the Union may claim national treatment in each member country, either for the acquisition of rights of industrial property, or for the recognition and enforcement of such rights acquired abroad. In other words, an inventor or a trade-mark owner will be protected in a country of the Union, under article 2 of the Convention of 1883, as a national of that country, whether he files there his first application for a patent or for the registration of a trade mark, or seeks to obtain a new patent for an invention patented abroad, or seeks to register a trade mark which he has already registered in another country of the Union.

The bipartite treaties entered into before 1883 sought to secure in both these cases national treatment. However, this is not sufficient in the latter case, that is, in the case of recognition and enforcement of rights of industrial property acquired in another country. It purports to establish a legal equality between foreigners and nationals in each country, but no equality in fact is created. This is so by reason of the diversities of the municipal law, which have been considered in chapter II. The national-treatment principle does away with all discriminations against foreigners existing under the law of the member countries of the Union. It does not remedy the unfavorable position in which foreigners are necessarily placed by the mere fact of the divergences existing between the laws of the various countries or by the territorial limitation of industrial property rights.

Thus a "ressortissant" of the Union who has registered his trade mark in country A of the Union is entitled, under article 2 of the Convention, to the same advantages as a national of country B of the Union, in applying for registration of his mark in the latter country. He may then be refused registration in case, under the law of country B, the mark in question is not admitted to registration or has been in the meantime registered by another. Similarly, a patent might be refused in country B to a patentee of country A of the Union, in case the invention was published in the meantime and the law of country B granted no patent to nationals for inventions made known to the public.

1. See *Actes de la Conférence de La Haye*, pp. 333, 413, 573.

§ **130. "Unionist treatment."** The insufficiency of the national-treatment principle for securing an effective and complete protection of foreigners' rights in industrial property is remedied in the Convention of 1883 by what has been felicitously called the principle of "unionist treatment." In this respect the Convention of 1883 constitutes the most important innovation in comparison with the previous bipartite treaties. It sought to achieve between foreigners and nationals both an equality in fact and an equality in law. By various provisions constituting a common legislation for all the members of the Union, it laid down a number of rules and principles purporting to furnish an equitable solution of the problems arising from the diversities of legislation and the need for protection of vested rights of industrial property having a really international character. These provisions grant to the "ressortissants" of the Union a number of special rights and advantages, which they may claim over and above the advantages granted to nationals by the municipal law of each country.

In order to bring out this duality of treatment under the Convention of 1883, the French delegtion at the Washington Conference of 1911 proposed that the words, "ainsi que des droits spécialement accordés par la présente Convention," be added at the end of the first paragraph of article 2, which then would have read thus:

> Les sujets ou citoyens . . . jouiront . . . des avantages que les lois respectives accordent actuellement ou accorderont par la suite aux nationaux, ainsi que des droits spécialement accordés par la présente Convention.

The British delegation, supported by the American, objected to this addition on the ground that it would be in derogation of its constitutional law, by which a private right cannot be claimed under a convention, but only under the law.[1]

At the Conference of The Hague, the International Bureau proposed the same addition in a different form, satisfying the British point of view. It substituted the word "prévus" for the term "accordés."[2] The following phrase was then added to the first paragraph of article 2: ". . . le tout sans préjudice des droits spécialement prévus par la présente Convention."

1. *Conférence de Washington*, pp. 94, 269.
2. *Actes de la Conférence de La Haye*, pp. 222, 333, 536.

§ 131. Special advantages and rights constituting "unionist treatment." The special advantages and rights accorded by the Convention are the following:

(*a*) *The right of priority* (article 4 of the Convention). A person who has filed an application for a patent, utility model, industrial design or model, or a trade mark in a country of the Union, enjoys, for the purpose of filing application in the other countries of the Union, a right of priority during specified periods: twelve months for patents and models of utility, and six months for industrial designs or models, as also for trade marks.[1] The importance of the right of priority is manifest. During the specified periods, the right of the foreign patentee or owner of trade mark, and the like, cannot be cut off or invalidated by acts performed in the interval, such as another application, publication of the invention, or the working of the same, or the use of the trade mark.

An inventor is not compelled to file contemporaneous applications in all the countries in which he wishes to have his rights protected. He is naturally prompted to apply first in the country in which he resides or carries on his business. During a year he may be able to apply in other countries without fear that his right may be invalidated in the interval by the publication and working of his patent or by the application of a third person. Within this year he will be in a position to ascertain the possibilities afforded by his invention, and to assign his rights to other persons in various countries. In the same way, a manufacturer or merchant, who adopts and registers a trade mark in a country of the Union, enjoys during six months the right to apply for the registration of his trade mark in the other countries of the Union, and is protected against adoption and registration of the same mark by third persons in the interval.

(*b*) *Independence of patents* (article 4*b* of the Convention). The patents applied for in the different countries of the Union, by persons admitted to the benefits of the Convention, are independent of the patents obtained for the same invention in other countries, whether or not members of the Union. The independence is as much from the point of view of the causes of nullity and forfeiture, as from the point of view of the normal duration of the patent. The fact, therefore, that a person forfeits his patent in a country for non-

1. The period of priority for designs and trade marks was increased from four to six months in the revision of the Convention at the Conference of The Hague in 1925.

payment of taxes, for instance, does not cause the forfeiture of the patent obtained in another country of the Union. Similarly, the expiry of the patent in one country does not terminate the privilege in other countries. The same is true as to other causes of forfeiture or nullity.[1]

(c) *Abolition of forfeiture for importation of patented articles* (article 5, section 1). By the law of some countries, the importation, by the patentee, into the country in which a patent was obtained, of articles manufactured in a foreign country entailed forfeiture of the patent. The Convention abolishes this ground of forfeiture, provided the articles are manufactured in any of the countries of the Union. This special advantage is related to the one immediately following.

(d) *Restriction of the obligation to work the patent* (article 5, sections 2, 3, and 4). In almost every country of the Union, the patentee is compelled to work his patent within such country. This requirement is particularly irksome to foreign inventors. The entire abolition of this obligation has not yet been accomplished, notwithstanding the attempts toward this end in conferences of revision of the Convention. Instead, an important restriction of the obligation has been achieved. Under the text of article 5, as amended at the Conference of The Hague, the countries of the Union may take measures only for the prevention of the abuses resulting from the exclusive right of the patentee. These measures cannot include the forfeiture of the patent unless the grant of compulsory licenses would not prevent such abuses. And in any case, no forfeiture is possible unless three years have elapsed since the grant of the patent, and the patentee is unable to justify himself by legitimate reasons.

(e) *Restriction of obligations of the proprietor of a design or model* (article 5, sections 5 and 6). At the Conference of The Hague two new paragraphs were added to article 5, constituting two specific advantages granted to proprietors of designs. According to the fifth paragraph, the protection of industrial designs and models shall not, under any circumstances, be liable to revocation by reason of the importation of articles corresponding to those which are protected. Under the sixth paragraph, no sign or mention of registration shall be required on the goods for the recognition of the right on an industrial design or model.

1. On the situation before the Convention of 1883, see *supra*, p. 33.

(*f*) *Restriction of the obligation to use a trade mark* (article 5, section 7). The last paragraph of article 5, added by the Conference of The Hague, grants a specific advantage to trade-mark owners. By the law of some countries, a registered mark should be used by the registrant if the right therein is to be maintained. Under this provision of the Convention, the registration of the mark cannot be cancelled for failure to use the same until after a reasonable period has elapsed, and then only if the person interested cannot justify the causes of his inaction.

(*g*) *Periods of grace and restoration of patents* (article 5*b*). At the Conference of The Hague a new special advantage was accorded by the Convention. Three months' grace for the payment of taxes required for the preservation of rights of industrial property shall be granted in all the countries of the Union. Furthermore, in the case of patents, the period of grace shall be six months, unless the law provides for the restoration of patents forfeited by reason of failure of payment of a tax.

(*h*) *Validation of trade marks* (articles 6, 6*b*, 6*c*, and 7). The laws of the various countries of the Union are not in agreement on the subject-matter of registrable trade marks and on the effects of registration, or on the basis of ownership of trade marks. As a result, trade marks regularly registered and owned in a country of the Union may not be admitted to registration and protected in another country. Thus the manufacturer or merchant who has adopted such a mark may find himself deprived of protection in the latter country. Article 6 of the Convention of 1883 remedied this situation by declaring that a trade mark regularly registered in the country of origin shall be admitted to registration and protected, in the form originally registered, in the other countries of the Union, except in certain specifically defined cases. Article 6*b* provides for the refusal or invalidation of marks infringing on well-known marks of foreigners, and article 6*c* contains provisions for the refusal or invalidation of trade marks containing public armorial bearings, official signs, hall marks, and the like.

Lastly, by virtue of article 7 of the Convention, the nature of the goods to which the trade mark is to be applied can, in no case, form an obstacle to the registration of the mark.

(*i*) *Protection of trade names* (article 8). Before the Convention of 1883, under the law of some countries a trade name was not protected unless it was registered. In others, if a trade name formed part of a trade mark and the latter was invalidated, the former was not protected any longer. Under the Convention both these disadvantages disappear. A trade name will be protected in all the countries of the Union without obligation of deposit or registration, whether or not it forms part of a trade mark.

(*j*) *Protection of indications of origin* (article 10). Special measures of repression of false indications of origin are provided for by the Convention in cases in which the false indication is joined to a fictitious or borrowed trade name, or is used with a fraudulent intention.

(*k*) *Protection against unfair competition* (article 10*b*). While the Convention refers to the municipal law of each country for the repression of acts of unfair competition, it contains, since its revision at the Conference of The Hague, a definition of unfair competition and enumerates two general categories of acts which shall be prohibited in the various countries.

§ 132. Advantages and rights accorded by the Arrangements. The two Madrid Arrangements of 1891 and the Arrangement of The Hague of 1925 contain no provision of national treatment similar to that of article 2 of the Convention. Their provisions constitute the "unionist treatment" in the restricted union created by each of these Arrangements. Thus persons entitled to the benefits of the Convention of 1883, as well as of these Arrangements, enjoy certain further advantages and rights.

Indeed, under the Convention, a person desiring to have his industrial design or model, or his trade mark, protected in the various countries of the Union must file an application and deposit his design or register his trade mark in all these countries. This is possible only through the medium of special agents and experts in each country, which is a source of expenses and charges. Besides, the compliance with formalities and technical regulation in each country is a course of much waste of time and money. Under the Madrid Trade-Mark Arrangement, trade-mark owners are relieved from all these difficulties. They may register their trade marks in the country of origin, and request the administration of that country to register their marks at the International Bureau of the Union at Berne. The latter immediately registers the mark and gives notice thereof to the administrations of the other contracting countries, which may refuse protection within one year, only in the cases provided for in article 6 of the general Convention. The registration by the International Bureau is tantamount to a separate registration in all the contracting countries.

The Arrangement of The Hague for the international deposit of designs and models went still further. It is not necessary for the proprietor to deposit an industrial design or model in his country of origin and request the administration of this country to deposit it at the International Bureau. He may apply for its international deposit directly. The International Bureau notifies the various administrations and publishes the design or model in a special magazine. The depositor is considered *prima facie* the proprietor of the design or model. From the time it is effected, the international deposit produces its effect in all the contracting countries as if it were directly deposited in each of them.

Lastly, under the Arrangement of Madrid for the repression of false indications of origin, the protection of indications of origin is secured without the limitations of article 10 of the Convention. Any product bearing a false indication of origin may be seized in all cases where the place falsely indicated, directly or indirectly, is one of the contracting countries, or a place situated in one of them.

These are the general aspects of the international regime of industrial property in the Union, which comprises to-day (January, 1929) thirty-eight countries with a total population of 717,000,000. The dream of uniformity of legislation on industrial property has not yet been realized. The difficulties which Lyon-Caen saw in the way of unification in 1878 still exist. At least, the practical disadvantages of differences of legislation have been and are fully appreciated, and a harmonizing of the municipal laws of the various countries on the most important questions of industrial property has been achieved. The agreement embodied in the Convention on some important topics, and the regulation of a number of questions, mark great progress in comparison to the chaos previously prevailing. It is a nucleus of a further development. This appears more clearly in the study made in the next chapters of the international regime of each branch of industrial property.

SECTION II

THE INTERNATIONAL REGIME OF PATENTS

CHAPTER X

NATIONAL TREATMENT OF PATENTS

§ 133. Lack of uniformity in patent laws of various countries. Under article 2 of the Convention of 1883, the nationals of the contracting countries enjoy in each of the member countries of the

Union, with regard to patents of invention, "the advantages which the respective laws now grant, or may hereafter grant, to the nationals of that country." The scope of this provision of national treatment, in general, is considered in a previous chapter.[1] Its special significance with regard to patents is to be considered here. It makes applicable the patent law of each country of the Union in respect to the protection of foreign inventors in their rights. Thus, with the exception of the special advantages and rights accorded to foreign patentees by articles 4, 4*b*, 5, and 5*b*, of the Convention, the municipal law of each country controls in all questions in the matter of patents.

In a previous chapter [2] an attempt has been made to depict the diversities of municipal legislation on patents prior to the Convention of 1883. Many of those diversities still persist. Economic reasons and motives are responsible for some of them. More often, however, they are due to deep-rooted habits and traditional routine. Each country, being overconscious and excessively jealous of its own independence, is not disposed to give up its own habits and administrative practice for the sake of uniformity. Of course, uniformity of legislation is not an end in itself. It is sought as a means of regulating and protecting most effectively and completely the interests of inventors and of the public. Indeed, it will not be disputed that everyone concerned in the matter of patents would be much better off if in all the countries of the world the formalities, conditions, and procedure for the granting of patents, as well as the patentability of inventions, the rights and obligations of the patentee, were identical. Such general uniformity might have been possible, perhaps, when the first International Congresses met at Vienna and at Paris in 1873 and 1878. At that time the patent law was still in its infancy. Many countries had not a complete body of law on the subject. In others, although patent legislation had begun some decades earlier, the increase of modern inventions had not yet begun to be reflected in the shaping and crystallizing of administrative procedure and practice and court decisions.

At the present time, it is too late to seek a general uniformity of patent law. Many questions in the matter of patents have become crystallized in every country. The content of patent law is now extremely technical in character. An administrative technique has

1. See *supra*, §§ 126–128.

2. Chap. II, 1.

developed, which is hard to break. The stupendous growth of business in some countries and the stagnant situation of industry in others have caused profound differentiation in the legal machinery. It was much easier, for example, to have the United States accept uniform legislation with the other countries in 1870, when only about 1000 patents were granted every year, than in 1925, when there were 100,000 patent applications received and the patents granted amounted to 50,000. In the meantime, the patent law in each country has become an inseparable part of the general system of law. This is the reason also that it is difficult to expect general uniformity of patent law to-day.

If, therefore, a general unification of patent law seems improbable, uniform solutions of some questions in the matter of patents are within the range of practicability, and may coexist with the independent character of the patent law of each country. Indeed, among the various questions considered in the study of the patent law before 1883, — patentability, formalities of application, administrative procedure, duration, taxes, rights and obligations of the patentee, — there are some which admit of little uniform solution, while others may easily be defined or regulated in the same way in all the countries. The questions of patentability, administrative procedure, duration of the patent, and taxes are apparently of the first class. What inventions alone may be patented, what the administration shall consider before granting a patent, how long the exclusive privilege of a patent shall last, and what fees or taxes must be paid for the grant of a patent — all these are matters which cannot be the same everywhere. In each country the conflicting claims as to all these questions which must be balanced vary widely; moreover, their different regulation by the various countries is not very prejudicial to inventors who wish to be protected in more than one country. On all other questions, however, there is room for uniform regulation.

This will be better shown in a separate consideration of each of the above questions. This consideration will take into account the thirty-eight countries of the Union, as well as many countries not members of the Union.[1]

1. The author is indebted for the data as to the patent law of each country in particular, to the *Tableau des Conditions et Formalités dans les Différents Pays* of the International Bureau of the Union, 4th ed. (Berne, 1925). Whenever these data are not sufficient — for instance, on the question of rights and obligations of the patentee — reference is made to other sources. Account also has been taken of all legislative changes in the

I. Patentable Inventions

§ **134. What is a patentable invention?** This question remains practically as it was before 1883. There are relatively few countries in which legislation attempts to define patentable inventions with precision, or to enumerate exhaustively what things may be patented. In recent legislative acts, the usual provision is that a patent may be granted for any new invention capable of being used or applied industrially. In some countries, in which old legislation is still in force, some kind of enumeration of patentable things, in general terms, is attempted. Usually, then, the task of finding what is a patentable invention and what is not is left to the administration, or to the courts applying the general principles laid down in the law. Thus patentability is often defined by exclusion rather than by positive assertion.[1] A patent is denied, or held invalid, because an invention is declared to be non-patentable. In the same way, legislation lays down negative criteria of patentability, or excludes expressly some kinds of inventions.

It is of especial importance from the point of view of rights of foreigners, to consider here the criterion of novelty of an invention, and the express exceptions of certain things, which are declared non-patentable in various countries.

§ **135. The question of novelty of invention in the laws of various countries.** An invention which may be the subject of a patent must be new; that is to say, it must be something which was not previously known or used by others. Moreover, its novelty must not have been destroyed by facts occurring prior to the application for a patent. Such facts may be a public use or sale by the inventor, an exhibition to the public, a description of the invention by printing or otherwise, made available to the public, or the like. In other words, an invention may have been known or used by others before it was "discovered" by the applicant for a patent; or it may have been abandoned, or published, by the inventor. The prior knowledge

different countries since 1925, when the above *Tableau* was prepared. On the patent rights of foreigners in Soviet Russia, see Heifetz, *Der Gewerbliche Rechtsschutz in der U. d. S. S. R. auf der Grundlage der deutsch-russischen Staatsverträbe* (Berlin, 1926), pp. 22 ff.

1. Kohler, in *Forschungen aus dem Patentrecht*, p. 3, gives a very helpful definition of invention in the sense of patent law illustrated by many examples: "Das Wesen der Erfindung besteht in einer technischen Combination der Naturkräfte; die Erfindung enthält daher stets einen technischen Gehalt: eine neue Anordnung ohne technische Eigenheit ist daher keine Erfindung, sollte sie auch wirthschaftliche Vorteile bieten."

or use may have existed, or the abandonment or publication of the invention may have taken place, either in the country in which the application for a patent is filed or in any other country. Novelty has different definitions in the various countries, according to the importance given to these various facts that affect the novelty of an invention.

In some countries, the law is that these various facts destroy the novelty of an invention wherever they take place; while in other countries, they do so only if they occur in the country in which the application for a patent is filed; and in still others, different distinctions are made between conditions that destroy the novelty of an invention.

The various countries may be divided, accordingly, into three classes, in each of which a general rule prevails, although the same is subject to exceptions and qualifications.

§ 136. **First system as to novelty.** In most of the countries an invention is not deemed new if, prior to the application for a patent, it has received sufficient publicity to enable its being put into operation, either in the country in which the application is filed or in any other country. The provision is sweeping. Any use, knowledge, or publication of the invention, anywhere, at any time prior to the application, takes away the element of novelty of the invention. Such is the law in France, the French Colonies, Morocco, Tunis, and the mandated territories of Syria and Lebanon. Similar is the situation in Bolivia, Brazil, Chile, Colombia, Costa Rica, Dominican Republic, Esthonia, Finland, Latvia, Luxembourg, the Netherlands, Salvador, Sweden, Turkey, Uruguay, and the U. S. S. R.

In Belgium and Mexico, only the description in a printed publication in their territory or in any foreign country destroys the novelty of the invention, while the use or working by the inventor prior to the application renders a patent invalid if the use or working was of a commercial character.

In Honduras and Guatemala, the mere description or exhibition is no bar to a patent. Only the proof of its knowledge or use in the country or abroad takes away the element of novelty.

In Cuba, a patent is invalid if its subject-matter has been known previously, in the same manner and in the same form, in the island, or if it is commonly used in a foreign country.

In Canada and Venezuela, the prior use, knowledge, or publication of the invention *in any country* destroys its novelty. But this provision does not extend to applications filed before the lapse of two years from the publication or the public use or sale.

In Hungary, the law is similar to that of France, with the exception that an invention is considered new if one hundred years have elapsed since its last publication or working.

In Italy, an invention is "new" if it has not been known before *in any country*, or if the particulars necessary for putting it into practice were unknown, though a general notion thereof existed. Publication abroad, however, by reason of the application for a patent, does not prevent the patentee from applying for an Italian patent, provided the application in Italy is filed before the expiration of the foreign patent, and before the invention has been freely imported and worked in Italy. Similarly, in Newfoundland, knowledge or use of the invention in the colony or in any other country is a bar to a patent unless it has been patented in another country, in which case the applicant must file his application before the invention is introduced into public or common use in Newfoundland.

In Belgium, Chile, and Salvador, as in Italy, if the publication abroad was in performance of a legal formality (by reason of the application for a patent), it does not destroy the novelty of the invention. But the application for a patent in Chile must be made before the invention is introduced into commercial use in the country. In Belgium there is no such limitation. Thus the foreign patent prevents the grant of a valid patent to anyone but the inventor to whom the foreign patent was granted.

§ 137. Second system. In the second class of countries, the facts of publication or prior use which will bar the grant or invalidate a patent are those only that take place in the country in which a patent is applied for. The law of Great Britain, Australia, India, New Zealand, Trinidad and Tobago, Bulgaria, Danzig, Denmark, Greece, Japan, Liberia, Rumania, Norway, Poland, and Switzerland is to this effect. In Bulgaria, Denmark, Greece, Japan, Norway, and Switzerland, the publication of the invention which destroys its novelty must be a printed publication, accessible to the public in the country. In Great Britain, publication by way of a foreign specification reaching the country before the date of the British application does detract from the novelty of the British case. On the other hand, a British specification more than fifty years old will not in itself invalidate a British patent, if it be the only publication of the alleged invention. Similarly, in the Commonwealth of Australia, an invention is new although a patent for it has been applied for or granted fifty years before, so long as it has never been in the possession of the public in the Commonwealth within those fifty years. In Norway and Japan, patent specifications laid open by the Patent Office to public inspection are not a bar.[1]

§ 138. **Third system.** Lastly, a third class is constituted by the countries which distinguish between publication by printing and other means of rendering an invention known to the public, such as the working of the invention, use, sale, exhibition, and the like. In these countries only the publication by printing of the invention *in any country* destroys its novelty, while the fact of its having been known, used, or worked in a foreign country, is not a bar. Such is the law in the United States, Germany, Austria, Argentina, Czechoslovakia, Haiti, Nicaragua, Paraguay, Portugal, Serb-Croat-Slovene State, and in the Union of South Africa.

In the United States, the following are bars to a valid patent: (1) the fact that an application for a patent has been filed in another country more than twelve months before the date of filing in the United States, by the same person, for the same invention, and that a patent has been granted for it; and (2) the fact that the invention has been patented or described in any printed publication *in any country*, or has been in public use or on sale in the United States before it was "invented" by the applicant, or for more than two years prior to the date of filing application in the United States. In Germany and Portugal, the description of the invention in a printed publication is no bar if one hundred years have elapsed since. On the other hand, in Germany, the official publication of an invention in a foreign country is not considered "publication" within the meaning of the law: (*a*) if the application in Germany is filed within three months after such publication; (*b*) if the person applying in Germany is the applicant in the foreign country or his legal representative; and (*c*) if there exists reciprocity between the two countries.

1. In Japan, publication which destroys novelty is real knowledge and public use in the territory of Japan. See case of Unosuke Kajima *v.* Tatsuko Sakamoto, Supreme Court of Japan, May, 1903, *Propriété Industrielle* (1904), p. 37.

In Haiti, a patent is invalid if the invention has been used or sold publicly in the country, or was registered or described *in any country* one year prior to the filing of the application in Haiti.

The importance of the diversity of legislation in respect to the novelty of an invention is reduced to a great extent by the right of priority accorded by article 4 of the Convention to persons who have duly applied for a patent in one of the countries of the Union, and who apply, within twelve months, for another patent in other countries of the Union. The right of priority is considered in the next chapter.

§ 139. Things, otherwise patentable, which cannot be patented because expressly excepted by the law. An invention may have all the general elements of patentability, yet be unpatentable because of express exceptions by the laws of various countries. Some of these exceptions are not really exceptions, because the subjects to which they refer are devoid of the generally accepted elements of a patentable invention. Such are: (*a*) purely theoretical inventions, or mere scientific theories or principles, which are incapable of being used immediately for industrial purposes; (*b*) inventions which are against the law, morals, or public security, or are harmful to health; the same may be said of (*c*) inventions concerning the mere use or employment of natural forces;[1] (*d*) inventions concerning articles which are monopolies of the state; [2] (*e*) inventions devoid of any real importance;[3] and (*f*) mere modifications in the shape or form of known articles.[4]

In Switzerland, inventions for obtaining products for the improvement of raw or manufactured textile fabrics of all kinds by the application of processes not purely mechanical, in so far as these inventions relate to the textile industry, cannot be the subject-matter of a patent. In Chile, systems of labor and secrets of factories are unpatentable. Schemes of finance and credit cannot be patented in Argentina, Bolivia, Brazil (also systems of ciphering), Chile, Dominican Republic, France, Morocco, Paraguay, Peru, Rumania (also methods of teaching and systems of ciphering), Spain, Syria and Lebanon, Turkey, and Uruguay.

1. Expressly excepted in Bolivia, Chile, and Mexico. In Spain, direct products of the soil and of breeding, and in Colombia, natural products, cannot be patented.
2. Expressly excepted in Austria, Hungary, and Rumania.
3. Expressly excepted in Denmark, Esthonia, and Latvia.
4. Expressly excepted in Brazil, Chile, Costa Rica, and Ecuador.

The most important exceptions concern articles of food, or objects of human and animal consumption, on the one hand, and pharmaceutical compositions, medicines, and substances obtained by chemical means upon the other. Each of them will be taken up separately.

Foodstuffs. In Bulgaria, Chile, Danzig (Free City), Denmark, Latvia, Rumania, and Switzerland, inventions concerning articles of food, as well as the processes for their production, are unpatentable. In Chile, Rumania, and Switzerland the exception extends to articles of food for animals. In Denmark and Switzerland, beverages as well as foodstuffs are excepted.

On the other hand, in Austria, Czechoslovakia, Esthonia, Finland, Germany, Hungary, Japan, Luxembourg, Norway, Poland, Sweden, and Soviet Russia, only inventions concerning articles of food as such cannot be patented, while the processes for the production of such articles are patentable. In Hungary, the exception extends to articles of food for animals, and in Japan, beverages and stimulants also are excepted.

In Italy, in the case of inventions relating to beverages or eatables, the Superior Board of Health gives its advice before a patent may be delivered.

Chemical products. Substances obtained by chemical means, cannot be patented in the following countries: Austria, Bolivia, Chile, Czechoslovakia, Danzig (Free City), Esthonia, Finland, Germany, Hungary, Japan, Latvia, Luxembourg, Mexico, Norway, Poland, Portugal, and Soviet Russia. The processes, however, for the production of such substances may be patented in all these countries, except Chile and Latvia. In Switzerland, neither substances produced by chemical means, nor the processes for such production, can be patented, if these substances are destined principally for food.

In Canada, in the case of inventions relating to substances prepared or produced by chemical processes *and* intended for food or medicine, the patent will not cover the substance itself, except when prepared or produced by the special methods or processes of manufacture described and claimed, or by their obvious chemical equivalents. The same is true in Great Britain as to substances prepared or produced by chemical processes, *or* intended for food or medicine.

Medicines, as well as the processes for their production, are nonpatentable in Chile, Danzig (Free City), Italy, Japan, Latvia, Paraguay, Rumania, Switzerland, and Turkey. On the contrary, processes for manufacturing medicines are patentable, although the medicines themselves are not patentable, in the following countries: Austria, Czechoslovakia, Denmark, Finland, Germany, Hungary, Norway, Poland, Soviet Russia, Spain, and Sweden. In Ecuador secret remedies only cannot be patented.

Pharmaceutical compounds. This is a wider exception than the last and extends to products as well as to processes, in Argentina, Bulgaria, Chile, Esthonia, France, Greece, Paraguay, Peru, Rumania, Syria and Lebanon, Turkey, and Uruguay. Only the processes for producing pharmaceutical compounds are patentable in Bolivia, Luxembourg, Morocco, Portugal, and Spain.

In the Dominican Republic pharmaceutical compounds, chemical products, and medicines are patentable on the condition that they be examined and approved by the Board of Health (*Juro Medico*) of the Republic.

§ 140. Patentability of processes and products. An invention may relate either to a thing made, — a machine, an engine, an instrument to be employed in the making of an article,— or to a new process, to be carried on by known implements, or elements, acting upon known substances, but producing something in a cheaper or more expeditious manner, or of a better and more useful kind.[1] In most countries, patents are granted for industrial products or engines, as well as for new processes.[2] In Cuba, however, industrial products cannot be patented. Only machines, machinery or apparatus, and mechanical or chemical processes or operations, may be the subject-matter of a patent. In Spain also, these things alone may be patented, while new industrial products, or results obtained by new or known means, may be the subject-matter of a patent only when by their working a branch of industry is established in the country for the first time within the last fifty years.

In the common law countries the patentability of new processes has been doubted for a long time. In Great Britain and its colonies and dominions, the subject-matter of a patent has not been defined by legislation since the Statute of Monopolies of 1623. The courts, in defining the words "new manner of manufacture" of that statute, were at first inclined to limit the subject-matter of patents to new

1. C. J. Abbott, in King *v.* Wheeler, (1819) 2 B. & Ald. 345, pp. 349–350. Cf. Pouillet, *Brevets d'Invention*, pp. 20, 25, 29; Allart, *Brevets d'Invention*, p. 27.

2. As to patents for processes in general, and in particular in the chemical industry, and their advantages, see article in *Propriété Industrielle* (1924), pp. 43, 46.

articles produced or to engines or instruments to be employed in the making of known or new articles. With the development, however, of arts and industrial inventions in the last century the courts extended the meaning of "manufacture" so as to include new processes.[1]

A case decided in 1842 [2] settled the law on this question. It held that "if the result produced by a new combination (of known means) is either a new article, or a better article, or a cheaper article to the public than that produced before by the old method, such combination may be the subject of a patent."

It has since been held that a new and alternative method of arriving at the same result, irrespective of whether this result is better or cheaper, may be patentable. "The process must merely lead to some result, and the result arrived at must be useful, though it need not be an article at all." [3]

In Canada this change of view has been confirmed by legislation. The Act of 1923 (13–14 George V c. 23, sec. 2 (1)) provides expressly that any new and useful art, process, machine, manufacture, or composition of matter may be patented.

In the United States the successive patent acts included an "art" as one of the subjects of a patent. A process which is a new and useful art, and has been invented or discovered, may be patented. When this is the case, has been one of the mootest questions of American patent law. This distinction is thus laid down by a leading case: [4]

> When the term process is used to represent the means or method of producing a result, it is patentable and includes all methods or means which are not effected by mechanism or mechanical combinations. . . . But when the term process is used in a more vague sense, as representing the function of a machine or the effect produced by it on the material subjected to the action of the machine, it cannot be the subject of a patent.

In other words, something concrete is patentable, not a "principle," or "a mode of operation," or an idea, or any other abstraction.[5] Thus processes involving chemical or other elemental action, in other words, chemical processes, are held patentable, while mechanical

1. Gibson and Campbell *v.* Brand (1841), 1 W. P. C. 631, 633. See also Terrell, *Patents*, 6th ed., p. 30; Frost, *Patents*, 4th ed., I, 60.
2. Crane *v.* Price, 4 M. & G. 580, 602–603.
3. In the matter of Alsop's Patent (1907), 24 R. P. C. 733, p. 752.
4. Corning et al. *v.* Burden (1853), 15 How. 252, 268.
5. Burr *v.* Duryee (1863), 1 Wall. 531, 570.

processes can be the subject of a patent if they are not simply the function or the operative effect of a machine;[1] or, as the Federal Court put it recently, the inventive process "must consist in the subjection of a specific object to the influence of a specific force through a specific mode of application."[2]

II. Formalities of Application

§ 141. The extreme technical character of regulation. The exclusive privileges accorded by a patent serve to encourage the development of arts and manufactures, while, on the other hand, they curtail the freedom of industry and commerce. For both these reasons, the patent is restricted to the specific discovery made by the inventor. The latter must, therefore, use the utmost diligence in describing precisely and with all details his invention or discovery. The law in all the countries seeks to achieve this end by detailed regulation, which often is of an extremely technical character. The form and precise content of the application, the preparation of drawings, models, and samples, their dimensions, and so on — all these must be made in conformity with legal provisions. They must therefore be made thoroughly accurate. No small detail or mechanical feature may be overlooked. This is necessary, not only for the acceptance of the application and specifications by the patent office, but also in order to avoid contingencies which may arise during the investigation of the application or in infringement proceedings.

If it be added that all the documents must be written, generally, in the national language of each country, it becomes apparent that a foreign inventor or his representative must seek the services of a local patent agent or attorney familiar with patent law, for the preparation of his documents and the prosecution of his application for a patent. Indeed, in a number of countries the profession of patent agents has been a subject of regulation by special legal provisions,[3] the effect of which is that patent applications cannot be prosecuted there except through these agents. The legal profession has generally abandoned patent law to a specialized group of lawyers, who must be equipped for patent business not only with this most technical legal

1. Westinghouse *v.* Boyden Power Brake Co. (1898), 170 U. S. 537, 555–557.

2. American Chemical Paint Co. *v.* C. R. Wilson Body Co. (1924), 298 Fed. 310, 311. See on the whole question of processes, an article in the *Journal of the Patent Office Society*, IV, 375.

3. See on this subject, "La Question des Agences de Brevets," *Propriété Industrielle* (1926), p. 57.

training and a knowledge of the intricate machinery of patent litigation, but also with understanding of the mechanical arts.[1]

Although the technicality and the need for accuracy and thoroughness make indispensable the preparation of the application and other documents by specially trained persons in each country, it is not clear why the formalities should vary in the different countries. Everywhere the end sought through detailed regulation on this matter is the same; namely, to describe with utmost precision the invention and the claims of the inventor. From the nature of things this regulation follows general lines identical in all the countries. The diversity of laws, often accidental, causes serious inconveniences to inventors. They have to prepare as many different applications, drawings, models, and so forth, as the countries in which they wish to have their invention patented. This causes them a great loss of money and time. An agreement between the countries of the Union for the purpose of making uniform the formalities of application would seem to be highly desirable. The inventor would then have to make only a single set of documents, copies of this to be presented to the various administrations after being multiplied by a technical process, and translated by local agents.

§ 142. Attempts to make uniform the formalities of application. The need of such general uniformity of formalities was first declared by the International Association for the Protection of Industrial Property at its first congress in Vienna in 1897.[2] The *voeu* of the Association was repeated by the Brussels Conference of Revision of the Convention of 1883, restricted, however, to uniformity only of drawings to be annexed to the application for a patent.[3] The Association took up the question again at its congress in Amsterdam in 1903. As a result of its efforts an informal invitation was sent out by the International Bureau for a special meeting of the directors of national patent offices, to be held at Berne in 1904, for the adoption of a plan of uniform formalities prepared by the International Association. Nineteen countries were represented, namely: Austria,

1. Felix Frankfurter, "The Business of the Supreme Court. A Study in the Federal Judicial System. IV. Federal Courts of Specialized Jurisdiction," *Harvard Law Review* (1926), XXXIX, 587, 616.

2. See the *voeu* of that congress in *Annuaire de l'Association* (1897), p. 187. Also similar *voeux* of later congresses in *Tableaux des Voeux* (International Bureau, 1911), p. 26.

3. *Conférence de Bruxelles* (1901), p. 351.

Belgium, Bulgaria, Denmark, France, Germany, Great Britain, Hungary, Italy, Japan, Luxembourg, Mexico, the Netherlands, Norway, Portugal, Sweden, Switzerland, Tunis, and the United States.[1] On August 5, 1904, the representatives signed a *procès-verbal* containing their resolutions and *voeux*. The first three resolutions concerning patents contained a number of regulations on the preparation of drawings and on the contents of specifications and copies of printed patents. These regulations were declared to be not obligatory on the various countries, but only a basis for national regulation, and a maximum of administrative exigencies. The meeting expressed the *voeu* that the national administrations should bring their regulations into harmony with the above resolutions before January 1, 1906. It would seem that the resolution as to the preparation of drawings which alone contained a complete regulation, was complied with by various administrations.[2]

The Washington Conference of Revision in 1911 manifested an intention of going further. It adopted a *voeu:* "Que le Bureau International mette à l'étude un projet d'arrangement ayant pour but d'assurer la simplification des formalités relatives aux demandes de brevets." [3] A new arrangement, then, was contemplated, analogous to those of Madrid, for establishing uniform regulation of formalities. The International Bureau, in a *Tableau* published in 1913 and in a supplement in 1922, collected the regulations concerning the formalities of application and other documents in the various countries. The Bureau also drew a model statement of rules according to which the specifications and drawings should be prepared. This model statement was prepared by taking into consideration the regulations of the various countries, and in such a way as to satisfy the most severe regulations. This, and a set of rules concerning the form of the application itself and the documents accompanying it, were submitted by the Bureau to the Conference of Revision which met at The Hague in October, 1925.

The Conference of Washington had contemplated a new arrangement; the Bureau and the Dutch government deemed it more advisable to propose the adoption of a *règlement*, annexed to a protocol by which the contracting countries should declare that they would accept applications for a patent drawn and prepared according to

1. *Propriété Industrielle* (1904), p. 131.
2. *Ibid*. (1926), p. 240.
3. *Conférence de Washington*, pp. 261 and 353.

the provisions of the *règlement*.[1] The Conference of The Hague, considering that this question was of administrative and technical character rather than juridical, decided to refer it to a conference of experts which had been proposed by a sub-committee for the purpose of making a uniform classification of trade marks and patents.[2]

§ 143. The Technical Conference of Berne, 1926. The proposed Technical Conference, analogous to that of 1904, met at Berne from October 18 to October 23, 1926, and adopted five resolutions concerning the formalities and rules for preparation of applications for patents, and the accompanying documents, specifications, and drawings.[3] These resolutions do not constitute an arrangement or a diplomatic act. They were submitted by the Bureau to the countries of the Union, to serve as a basis for harmonizing their respective rules of practice. It is not even a type of rules to be enacted by each country, and complete in itself. The national provisions are expressly reserved on some points.[4] On the other hand, they are not merely a "maximum" of formalities, but a set of "uniform rules, as simple as possible, for the deposit of applications for patents to which the national regulations must be harmonized." National regulations may contain more liberal or more favorable provisions with regard to applicants.

Having once been put into harmony with the resolutions, national regulations cannot be modified except after a new exchange of views between the different administrations.[5] The countries which took part in this Conference by representatives of their patent offices, and adopted the resolutions, were the following twenty: Austria, Belgium, Czechoslovakia, Denmark, France, Germany, Great Britain, Hungary, Italy, Japan, Mexico, Morocco, the Netherlands, Norway, Poland, Serb-Croat-Slovene State, Spain, Sweden, Switzerland, and Tunis.[6] The Conference expressed the *voeu* that the resolutions

1. *Conférence de La Haye, Documents Préliminaires*, 3me fascicule, pp. 113, 115; also *Actes de la Conférence de La Haye*, p. 325.

2. *Actes de la Conférence de La Haye*, pp. 437–438, 586.

3. See the resolutions in *Propriété Industrielle*, 1926 (Off. Part), p. 209.

4. See, for example, Resolution I, par. 1; Resolution II (1) *a*, par. 2, and (2); Resolution III (*e*); Resolution V (1, 7).

5. See *Procès-verbal* no. 1 of the Technical Conference of Berne, *Propriété Industrielle* (1926), p. 207.

6. Denmark made the reservation that the profession of the applicant must be indicated on his application. Resolution II, (1) *a* does not contain such requirement. Japan also made a reservation in regard to the shape of the paper on which the specification and drawing must be made, in view of the fact that in Japan the paper used and the manner of writing are quite different from that of other countries.

adopted should go into effect in all the countries of the Union, at the latest on January 1, 1928. The Resolutions appear in Appendix B, on page 919.

III. Administrative Procedure

§ 144. Two aspects in which the procedure must be regarded. Everywhere a compliance with the formalities prescribed by law is necessary before the delivery of a patent. The application may be rejected if the documents deposited with the administration are not found to be in due and proper form. In some countries nothing more than such compliance is necessary for the granting of a patent. In others, the administration proceeds to an investigation into the alleged invention, in respect to its patentability, its novelty, and, sometimes, its industrial usefulness. Thus the procedure for the delivery of a patent presents itself under various forms in the different countries, which are commonly distinguished under two general systems, that in which there is previous examination of the invention and that in which a patent is granted without any previous examination by the administration. On the other hand, in the various countries which are classified under either of these systems, several essential differences exist in the delimitation of the invention, and in its effect in subsequent infringement proceedings involving the validity and extent of a patent. It is therefore necessary to consider the administrative procedure of each country under two aspects: (*a*) the procedure leading to the delivery of a patent; (*b*) the delimitation of the invention and its ambit for novelty and infringement.

It will appear that a country must be classified differently according to whether its law is regarded from the first standpoint or from the second.

§ 145. Various types of procedure leading to grant of patent. The procedure leading to the grant of a patent in the various countries is presented in seven main types. The first three belong to the general system of delivery of a patent without previous examination, while the other four types are various forms of the general system of previous examination of the invention.

First type. This is the type of administrative procedure which might be called the mere registration of the invention. It is the system commonly known as the Latin or French system. It has been the method of the French law primarily, and is followed by the law of Belgium, Costa Rica, Cuba, Danzig, Dominican Republic, Greece, Haiti, Italy, Latvia, Luxembourg, Morocco, Paraguay, Poland, Rumania, Spain, Syria and Lebanon, and Turkey. In these countries the administration sees only that all the formalities of the law as to the preparation and presentation of the documents have been complied with; if they have been, the patent applied for is registered, unless it appears that the alleged invention is expressly declared by the law unpatentable. After registration, a patent title is delivered to the applicant and is advertised within a short time. Anyone whose rights are infringed by the grant of a patent may at any time procure its annulment by the courts.

Second type. Closely related to the former type is the method of administrative procedure in which the administration, while it does not submit the invention applied for to a previous examination, precedes the delivery of the patent by an advertisement of the invention, so that parties who are interested may oppose the grant, within a limited period from such advertisement. The administration or the courts decide the question raised. If the objections are not substantiated, the patent is granted to the applicant. Such is the law in Bolivia, British Guinea, British Honduras, Colombia, Esthonia, Finland, Panama, Portugal, Tunis, Uruguay, and Venezuela. The periods within which objections may be entered are: three months in Esthonia, Panama, and Portugal; two months in Finland and Tunis; thirty days in Bolivia and Colombia; thirty or fifty days (according to the nature of the invention) in Venezuela; and twenty days in Uruguay.

Third type. The administrative procedure of Mexico constitutes another type by itself. In this country the Patent Office makes no investigation as to the novelty or usefulness of the invention, or even as to the accuracy and sufficiency of the documents deposited. At the request, however, of the interested party, it examines the invention as to its novelty, at the expense of the applicant and without any guaranty.

Fourth type. This and the following three types are forms of the general system of previous examination of the invention by the administration. The larger group of these countries follow, in its essential lines, the mode of procedure of the German patent law, namely, the system of previous examination and search into the patentability and novelty of the invention, coupled with an appeal for opposition to the grant, by an advertisement of the invention in the official publication of the Patent Office. In other words, in these countries the administration does not grant a patent to the inventor unless, after searching into its records and after hearing the objections of opposing parties, it is satisfied that the invention applied for is new. This system, in its general features, prevails, besides in Germany, in Australia, Austria, Ceylon, Czechoslovakia, Denmark, Hungary, India, Japan, the Netherlands, Norway, Soviet Russia, Serb-Croat-Slovene State, Sweden. In Brazil and Salvador, an appeal for opposition is made by the administration. At the end of the period within which objections may be filed, the administration proceeds to an examination as to the novelty of the invention. In Guatemala, Honduras, Nicaragua, and Peru, the examination bears also on the usefulness and the advantages or disadvantages of the invention.

Fifth type. The law of the United States is an illustration of another type. The examination consists in a thorough investigation of the prior "art" with respect to the invention sought to be protected in the application. Every material device or process is disclosed in the records of the Patent Office. An application may be rejected for want of novelty with reference to prior domestic or foreign patents, to printed publications anywhere in the world, or even to facts within the personal knowledge of the examiner. It may also be rejected on the ground of public use or sale; or because the alleged invention is held to be inoperative, frivolous, or injurious to public health or morals. No objections are invited by the Patent Office. But if two or more parties claim substantially the same patentable invention, a proceeding is instituted for the purpose of determining the question of priority of invention. This proceeding is called an *interference.* Similar is the law in Argentina, Canada, and Ecuador.

Sixth type. An examination of a limited character by the administration, with an appeal for objections, constitutes another type of administrative procedure. It is the mode of procedure prevailing in Great Britain and in many of her colonies. The examination in the Patent Office is not as complete as in Germany or in the United States. The examiner's duty is not to examine into the validity of the specifications or the novelty of the invention, with reference to foreign specifications and books not available to the public in Great Britain. The investigation is only as to whether the invention claimed has been wholly or in part claimed or described in any specification left with an application for a patent made in the United Kingdom within the last fifty years. The acceptance of the complete specification is advertised and the grant may be opposed by interested parties.

Seventh type. The laws of Switzerland and Bulgaria enact the system of previous notification by the administration. In these countries, if the previous examination as to the novelty of the invention, made by the administration, discloses that the invention is not new, notice thereof is given to the applicant, who thereupon may amend, withdraw, or maintain his application. In the last case, the administration cannot refuse to grant him the patent applied for.

§ 146. Practical value of the differences between various types. From the preceding exposition it appears that the administrative procedures of France and of the United States are the two extreme types, the excesses of which the other types attempt to mitigate. In other words, in France the administration is not desirous of preventing a person from obtaining a patent for an invention which he claims to be new and patentable according to law; while in the United States the administration is reluctant to grant a patent to any person, before it is satisfied that it is a new and useful art or manufacture within the meaning of the law.

In the United States, however, as well as in the other countries in which the law subjects the application to a more or less severe examination, the legal or juridical validity of the patent is in no way enhanced by the examination into its patentability, novelty, or usefulness. Indeed, nowhere is the validity of the patent guaranteed by the government. A patent is everywhere, in France as well as in the United States or in other countries, subject to annulment by a court, before which its validity is brought in question.[1] The previous examination of an alleged invention is purely a question of administrative policy. It aims at giving a *prima facie* value, economically speaking, to the patent. In the United States, it is considered for the best interests of the inventors themselves and of the public that the administration should investigate the invention before granting a patent. In France, it is held that the same interests are better protected by the opposite course, because it is considered impossible

1. However, in Germany, after the expiration of five years from the publication of the grant, a patent cannot be annulled on the ground that the invention was not one which could be patented.

that a previous examination of the invention can ever be sufficiently complete and free of errors, while on the other hand it involves great delay and expense on the part of inventors.[1]

The tendency perhaps to-day is toward instituting a preliminary examination of inventions even in the countries where the opposite system has prevailed. It is characteristic that the Director of the French National Office of Industrial Property, in an address made by him in 1919 before Allied delegates and experts, admitted that the French system was obsolete and did not meet the requirements of the present day. He pointed out that it was relatively easy for inventors, at the time the patent law of 1844 was enacted, to search for themselves and find out whether their invention was new; but that this became impossible with the present enormous increase and multiplication of inventions. He also admitted that manufacturers and capitalists in general give a greater value to German and English patents than to French, because of the greater certainty attached to the former.[2] The introduction of the system of prior examination of inventions at the request of the applicant is now under consideration in France.[3]

In the countries in which a previous examination of the invention is made, foreigners applying for a patent will be confronted with the necessity of discussing with the administration the patentability of their invention. The most important element in this connection is the novelty of the invention. To avoid unnecessary expenses and delays, and to secure a previous investigation into the novelty of the invention by the inventor himself, before applying in any country, several schemes have been devised and proposed, to the end of preparing and maintaining an international index disclosing all material devices or processes invented, described, published, or patented in the various countries.[4]

The possibilities of such an index will be better realized if the second aspect of the administrative procedure of each country is first considered.

1. See on the advantages and disadvantages of both systems, an article by Lavoix in *Propriété Industrielle* (1924), p. 252.

2. *Travaux du Groupe Français*, No. 1 (1919–1922), pp. 68, 71–72.

3. See Marcel Plaisant, *Rapport sur le Projet de Loi sur les Brevets d'Invention*, No. 1690, Chambre des Députés, Session de 1925, pp. 30, 166.

4. See *Propriété Industrielle* (1925), p. 93 and (1926), p. 96; also address by Mr. Drouets, Director of the French National Office of Industrial Property, in *Travaux du Groupe Français*, No. 1 (1919–1923), p. 68.

§ 147. Procedure for delimitation of the invention. A patent should not only be valid otherwise, but it should also delimit with great precision the invention which is patented. The exclusive privilege granted by it should cover the whole of the new invention or inventions claimed by the applicant, but no more. It should secure the inventor against imitation of a part of his invention or of an idea implied in his invention, but it should not be so broad as to prevent improvements of, or additions to, the original invention by another person. Thus the procedure for the granting of a patent involves this further question: how will this double end be achieved? Must the inventor be allowed to describe in general terms the whole of his invention, or must every particle of the invention, every partial device, and every implication thereof, be described and claimed? [1]

The United States patent law demands of the inventor a final and conclusive enumeration of every claim, improvement, or combination which he regards as his own invention or discovery. The specification must be concluded with an enumeration of specific and distinct claims. All functions, operations, features, and advantages of the machine or device, and every new idea which is implied in every part of the invention or in the combination of different parts or details, must be described in detailed, or narrow, and in broad or generic, claims. In case the inventor forgets one of these claims, it is lost to him even if it is apparent on the face of the application. The courts will not protect a part of an invention or an idea implied therein which has not been specifically claimed in the accepted specification.[2] The laws of Switzerland, Sweden, and Norway follow the American system, although less strictly.

In France and Belgium, the system is just the opposite. No enumeration of claims by the inventor is required. It is enough if he describes the general operation or function of his invention, and concludes the description with a *résumé*. The further and specific

1. See, on the question of drafting claims, Potts, *Patents; Invention and Method* (London, 1924), chap. IV, "The logical problem of definition in patent law." The author considers the chief methods of logical classification: peripheral, central, and teleological; and examples of these methods as exemplified in German, American, English, and French law and practice.

2. "Valuable inventions are lost by too limited claims, by claims to the instrument, when the invention is a process, and *vice versa*, by functional and sweeping claims and by claims that define an incident to the invention instead of the real point thereof." *Library of Amer. Law* (Law of Patents), XII, 120–123.

delimitation of the invention belongs to the tribunals, which will decide in every specific case involving the validity or the effect of a patent, whether a special function, operation, feature, or idea is covered by the patent or not, taking into consideration the whole description of the invention, the drawings, and the like.[1] Similarly, in Germany and many of the countries which follow its system the tribunals decide when an idea or a function is covered by a patented invention. In these countries, although the inventor must make an enumeration of distinct claims, the courts have held that it is not possible to follow the American formalistic and mechanical method of division of an invention into its parts.[2]

In Great Britain, the law holds a middle position between the American and the French systems. The specification must contain claims. But they serve only to define the invention for which the monopoly is claimed. It is necessary for the applicant to ascertain and define particularly what his monopoly covers, so that any person may know of the invention claimed.

> The ambit of the claim for novelty and infringement depends on the nature of the object to be attained by the device described. . . . The claim is construed in the light of the common knowledge in the art at the date of the patent. It must be determined by the court whether the monopoly claimed is for the precise mechanism described or for the attainment of a result by any means substantially equivalent to the precise mechanism described.[3]

The French system of drafting is calculated to favor the inventor, and is the reasonable corollary of the system of granting patents without any administrative examination of the invention. The American system of drafting claims considers especially the interest of industry, by restricting the monopoly granted by the patent within very definite limits. The English and, in a way, the German systems attempt to satisfy the interests both of industry and of inventors.[4]

1. Article 6, sec. 3, of the French Law of 1844. See also Allart, *Brevets d'Invention*, 3d ed., p. 103, and case of Consorts Block *c.* Ferlié et Cie., Cour d'Appel de Douai, December 22, 1913 (*Recueil de la Gazette des Tribunaux*, 1914, IV, 12).

2. R. Wirth, "Les Différents Systèmes de Protection des Inventions" in *Propriété Industrielle* (1921), pp. 66, 67; and "Differences between German and American Claims" in *Journal of the Patent Office Society* (1924), vol. VII, p. 22.

3. See Terrell-Jaffé, *The Law of Patents*, pp. 99, 104, 126, and cases cited. See also, for Canada, Fisher and Smart, *Canadian Patent Law* (1914), pp. 169–170.

4. See an address by Mr. Armstrong on the drafting and interpretation of claims, in *Travaux de Groupe Français*, No. 2, p. 55.

§ **148. Importance of diversities of the law in this respect.** The diversities of the law on the presentation and phrasing of the claims are of great importance in two respects. On the one hand, the right of priority under article 4 of the Convention and the independence of patents under article 4*b*, are secured to the "same invention." It is then a question whether an invention claimed in one country in general terms, and in another by distinct and specific claims, is the same. This question is considered below.[1] On the other hand, the schemes for an international index must necessarily fail, or be deferred unless and until a uniform way of phrasing and examining claims is achieved. In the existing state of the law in the various countries there is an extreme variety in this respect, due to the different ambit of claims. In Germany, the claims protect "functions" of the mechanical parts of a machine. In the United States "functional claims" are not allowed. As Mr. Wirth said, "an index edited by taking into account the 'functions' has an altogether different aspect from one which would indicate the features or composition of parts of a machine or of their combination." [2]

IV. Term of Patents

§ **149. Three questions in respect to term of patents.** There are three questions in respect to the term of patents: the moment from which the term begins to run, the length of the term, and the possibility of its extension.

As to the first question, the various countries are divided into three classes. In Australia, Belgium, British Guiana, British Honduras, Bulgaria, Ceylon, Belgian Congo, Danzig, Esthonia, Finland, France, Germany, Great Britain, Greece, Hungary, India, Italy, Luxembourg, Mexico, Morocco, Norway, New Zealand, Paraguay, Rumania, Sweden, Switzerland, Syria and Lebanon, Tunis, and the Union of South Africa, the term begins to run from the deposit of the application. In Austria, Czechoslovakia, Japan, Soviet Russia, the Serb-Croat-Slovene State, the term starts from publication of the application. In all other countries, among them the United States, Spain, and almost all the countries of the American continent, the term begins from delivery of the patent.

1. See chap. XI, §§ 188 ff.
2. *Propriété Industrielle* (1926), pp. 95, 98.

The duration of the patent is as follows:[1]

In Uruguay, 3, 6, or 9 years;
Colombia and Peru, 1 to 10 years;
Esthonia and Portugal, 1 to 15 years;
Argentina, Chile, Dominican Republic, France, Salvador, Tunis, Turkey, and Venezuela, 5, 10, or 15 years;
Panama, 5, 10, 15 or 20 years;
Nicaragua, 5 to 10 years;
Guatemala, 5 to 15 years;
Ecuador, 10 to 15 years;
Honduras, 10, 15, or 20 years;
British Guiana, British Honduras, Newfoundland, Trinidad and Tobago, and Union of South Africa, 14 years;
Austria, Bolivia, Brazil, Bulgaria, Czechoslovakia, Denmark, Finland, Greece, Hungary, Italy, Japan, Latvia, Luxembourg, Morocco, the Netherlands, Paraguay, Poland, Rumania, Soviet Russia, Serb-Croat-Slovene State, Switzerland, Syria and Lebanon,[2] 15 years;
Australia, Ceylon, Great Britain, India, and New Zealand, 16 years;
Cuba, Danzig, Norway, Sweden, and the United States, 17 years;
Canada and Germany, 18 years;
Belgium, Belgian Congo, Costa Rica, Liberia, Mexico, and Spain, 20 years.

These terms, of course, concern principal and original patents. Patents granted to foreign patentees, or patents of importation, expire, by the law of many countries, upon the termination of the foreign patent. Furthermore, in Spain, patents of importation are granted for only five years, unless the articles are manufactured in Spain; in Argentina, they are not granted for a longer term than ten years; in Panama, for no longer than fifteen years; and in Ecuador, the term may be only from three to ten years, according to the capital invested in Ecuador. Additional patents, or certificates of addition, granted to patentees of the original invention, cease to be in effect at the expiration of the principal patent, unless they have been declared independent or principal patents.

An extension of the term of a patent is possible in the countries in which the term is not uniform for all patents and in which a patent

1. See *Tableau des Conditions et Formalités* (Bureau International, 1925), p. 2, for most of the data in this connection.

2. In Switzerland patents for chemical processes for manufacturing medicines are granted for a term of ten years only.

has been granted for a term below the maximum allowed. It is also possible in Great Britain and in the British dominions and colonies, on petition, at least six months before the expiration of the patent, after advertising the petition and hearing objections from any interested party. In Great Britain, the court, having regard to all the circumstances of the case, may extend the patent for a further term not exceeding five years and, in exceptional cases, ten years. In British Guiana, British Honduras, Australia, Ceylon, India, and the Union of South Africa, the corresponding terms are seven and fourteen years. In Newfoundland and in Trinidad and Tobago the extension can never exceed seven years.

In the United States, France, and Paraguay, an extension cannot be granted except by act of the legislature. In Chile, Mexico, Paraguay, Soviet Russia, and Salvador an extension of five years may be granted over the ordinary or maximum term. In Japan, the extension may be of three to ten years, while in Colombia two successive extensions of five years are allowed in exceptional cases.

A *caveat* for the protection of an unmatured invention is granted for one year in Argentina, Bolivia, Canada, Chile, Salvador, and the United States. But while it cannot be renewed in Canada and in the United States, it may be extended for one more year in Bolivia, Chile, and Salvador, and indefinitely from year to year in Argentina.

The deposit of a provisional specification in Great Britain and the provisional protection conferred upon the applicant has some elements of the American *caveat;* but it is not quite the same. The object of the provisional specification is to enable the inventor, during the period of the provisional protection, to improve and perfect his invention, but also to protect him against the consequences of publication. This "provisional protection" lasts for nine months. An extension of one month only may be granted.

Much of the importance of the diversity of the law in respect to the term of a patent is taken away by article 4*b* of the Convention, which provides that patents applied for, by persons admitted to the benefit of the Convention, in the different countries for the same invention shall be independent of each other. Thus, the normal duration of a patent in each country is independent of the duration of the patent for the same invention in another country. The import and precise significance of article 4*b* is considered below.[1]

1. See chap. XII.

V. Taxes

§ 150. Diversities of municipal law. The matter of taxes would seem hardly appropriate for uniform regulation. Especially, the amount of the tax or taxes to be paid for a patent and the mode of payment are usually said to be matters in which every country claims entire independence. However, there is no reason in the nature of things why there should not be uniformity in some questions relating to taxes. As early as 1905, Dr. Damme, Director of the German Patentamt, proposed that a uniform date for the payment of annual taxes be fixed, with a uniform period of grace, and showed the great advantage of such a measure for inventors and for the administration.[1] Article 5*b*, added at the Conference of The Hague, tends to accomplish uniformity in this respect. At the present time, the amount of taxes varies in the different countries. It is payable either in advance, by annuities, or at the end of some period in the life of a patent.

In whichever way the taxes are to be paid, the penalty for non-payment is everywhere the same, namely, forfeiture of the patent. In view of this serious consequence, a period of grace is accorded in most countries. In Belgium, Greece, and Japan, six months grace is allowed; in Bolivia, five months; in Austria, Bulgaria, Czechoslovakia, Danzig, Denmark, Esthonia, Finland, France, Italy, Latvia, Luxembourg, Morocco, the Netherlands, Norway, Paraguay, Poland Serb-Croat-Slovene State, Spain, Sweden, Switzerland, Tunis, and Turkey (at the discretion of the Administration), three months; in Germany, Hungary, and Portugal, two months; and in Rumania, thirty days. In Great Britain and in the British dominions and colonies, where the tax is payable at the end of two periods in the life of the patent (before the end of four years and of eight years from the date of the patent in Great Britain), the time for payment may be extended on application by the patentee. This extension cannot exceed one year in Australia, six months in Canada, Ceylon, and British Guiana, and three months in Great Britain, India, New Zealand, and the Union of South Africa. After a patent becomes void, owing to failure in payment of a tax, it may be restored in Great Britain, Australia, and Canada, on application, duly advertised, by the patentee, if it appears that the omission was uninten-

1. See *Propriété Industrielle* (1905), p. 42.

tional. In such cases the interests of third parties are saved. Germany, since 1920, provides for a similar restoration in case of war, or by reason of natural events, and in all other cases of *vis major*.[1] Austria also, since 1924,[2] allows restitution for *vis major*. Two more countries, Portugal[3] and Switzerland,[4] passed similar legislation recently, following the adoption of article 5*b* at the Conference of The Hague, by which the contracting countries undertake to allow such restoration.

In Denmark and Germany, if the tax is not paid in due time, the patent office notifies the patentee that his patent will be forfeited if the tax, increased by a surtax for penalty, is not paid within one month from such notice.

Article 4*b* of the Convention, making the patents granted to a person in several countries for the same invention independent of each other from the point of view of the causes of forfeiture, eliminates the risk, which existed prior to the Convention, that a patent granted in a country might cease to exist because of the forfeiture of the original patent, granted in another country, for non-payment of a tax.

§ 151. Article 5*b* of the Convention added by the Conference of The Hague. At the Conference of The Hague the first uniform regulation in respect to taxes was adopted. The American delegation proposed two amendments to article 5 of the Convention: (1) that no tax or annuity higher than those provided for in the country of origin could be imposed for a patent taken out in any country of the Union; (2) that a patent becoming void owing to failure in payment of a tax might be restored if the omission was unintentional or accidental.

The British delegation, on the other hand, submitted a *voeu* that a period of grace might be accorded in all countries for payment of taxes on patents. The first proposition of the United States has not been adopted; but the second proposition and the *voeu* of Great Britain formed the basis for the new article 5*b*, adopted by the Conference of The Hague, which reads as follows:[5]

1. Law of April 27, 1920, art. 2 (*Reichsgesetzblatt*, 1920, p. 675).
2. Law No. 56 of February 20, 1924 (*Bundesgesetzblatt*, 1924, p. 79).
3. Decree of November 19, 1926 (*Colecção de Legislação Portuguesa*, 1926, p. 683).
4. Loi Fédérale of October 9, 1926 (*Recueil des Lois*, 1927, No. 2, p. 9).
5. See *Actes de la Conférence de La Haye* (1926), pp. 338, 354, 431, 520, 576.

Un délai de grâce, qui devra être au minimum de trois mois, sera accordé pour le payement des taxes prévues pour le maintien des droits de propriété industrielle, moyennant le versement d'une surtaxe, si la législation nationale en impose une.

Pour les brevets d'inventions, les pays contractants s'engagent en outre, soit à porter le délai de grâce à six mois au moins, soit à prévoir la restauration du brevet tombé en déchéance par suite de non-payement de taxes, ces mésures restant soumises aux conditions prévues par la législation intérieure.

The first paragraph of this article concerns all rights of industrial property, while the second deals only with patents. Every country of the Union is obligated to accord to foreign patentees: (*a*) either three months grace for payment of taxes, *and* restoration of the patent which became void for non-payment of taxes under the conditions of the municipal law; or (*b*) if no such restoration is granted, six months grace for payment of the taxes.

Thus the legal situation in respect to payment of taxes prevailing in Great Britain and the British dominions and colonies is generalized as a result of article 5*b*, and the dangers of forfeiture of foreigners' patents are greatly reduced.

In the United States no taxes are due during the life of a patent. All fees are paid during the administrative procedure leading to the grant of a patent. The final fee is payable on the definite acceptance of the application and before the delivery of the patent. For the payment of this fee a delay of six months is provided for in the United States Patent Act. The American delegation at the Conference of The Hague declared that it interprets the provisions of article 5*b* as not applicable to this final fee required by the American law. This declaration was ordered to be taken down in the *procès-verbal*, by the Chairman of the Conference, without any objection.

IV. Rights of Patentee

§ 152. Extent of privilege of patentees. A patent granted to a foreigner confers the same rights that a national enjoys. The extent, therefore, of the protection of the patentee and of his privilege are matters left by the Convention to the province of the municipal law. The diversities in the laws of the various countries in this respect may be very great. The question of criminal or civil liability, of seizures of counterfeited articles, of injunction against further infringement, and, especially, of the probative force of the patent vary in the different countries.

The effects of a patent extend generally to the whole territory of a country. However, in Bolivia, Brazil, British Honduras, and Ecuador, the privileges conferred by a patent may be limited to a special part of the territory. In Brazil this is done *a posteriori*, if it is proved that the articles manufactured with the patented invention are supplied in an insufficient measure in proportion to the needs of the public. This limitation by act of the executive must be approved by the legislature. In British Honduras such limitation is inserted in the letters patent by the commissioners if it appears expedient or necessary. In Ecuador the patent granted to importers of machines or new methods of manufacture or industry, already known and used abroad, has no effect outside of the locality where the machine is operated, or of the area necessary to secure the remuneration of the inventor.

In a number of countries, for example, in Bulgaria, Czechoslovakia, Danzig, Denmark, Germany, Greece, Hungary, Japan, the Netherlands, and Poland, a patent granted for a process of manufacture extends also to the products manufactured by this process.

The most important questions from the standpoint of international protection are two limitations of the privilege of patentees which are recognized by the law of many countries.

§ **153. "Right of personal possession."** The first limitation is the so-called "right of personal possession" of the invention. It is recognized by the law of the following twenty-two countries: Austria, Belgium, Bulgaria, Canada, Czechoslovakia, Danzig, Denmark, Finland, France, Germany, Greece, Hungary, Japan, Luxembourg, Mexico, the Netherlands, Norway, Poland, Serb-Croat-Slovene State, Sweden, Switzerland, and the U. S. S. R.[1] This right is fully

1. Austria, Law No. 366, on Patents of September 23, 1925, sec. 18 (*Bundesgesetzblatt*, 1925, p. 1367).

Belgium, Law of October 11, 1919, art. 9 (*Pasinomie*, 1919, II, 29).

Bulgaria, Law of July 29, 1921, art. 7 (*Propriété Industrielle*, 1921, p. 130).

Canada, Act of June 13, 1923, sec. 50 (13–14 George V, c. 23, in *Stat. of Canada*, 1923 p. 145).

Czechoslovakia, Austrian Law of 1897, sec. 9, made applicable in the country by the Act of May 27, 1919, art. 2 (*Sammlung der Gesetze*, 1919, p. 473).

Danzig, Law of July 14, 1921, art. 6 (*Gesetzblatt für die freie Stadt Danzig*, 1921, No. 19).

Denmark, Law of April 13, 1894, art. 6 (*Lovtidende for Danmark*, 1894, p. 323).

Finland, Imperial Decree of January 21, 1898, art. 2 (*Finlands Författnings-Samling*, 1898, p. 1).

considered below in connection with the reservation of rights of third parties under article 4 of the Convention.[1] It is sufficient to say here that, by force of the right of personal possession of an invention recognized by the law of the above countries, a patentee cannot prevent the working of his invention by a person who, prior to the filing of his application for a patent, was already using the same invention or had taken the necessary steps and made preparations for its working. The third person's right is called a right of personal possession, because, while the patentee may grant licenses for the working of his invention, the person in question can work it only personally and cannot transfer it, except with the business in connection with which he uses the invention.

§ 154. Limitation as to vessels and other means of transportation. The second limitation of the patentee's privilege in many countries relates to permission to third parties to use a patented invention either for the purpose of navigation of a foreign vessel or in the construction and functioning of foreign means of transportation in general, provided that such vessels or other means of transportation are temporarily in the country in which the patent is granted. In Austria, Bulgaria, Czechoslovakia, Danzig, Denmark, Finland, Germany, Greece, Hungary, Japan, Luxembourg, the Netherlands, Norway, Serb-Croat-Slovene State, and Switzerland the limitation applies to all foreign means of transportation, while in Great Britain, the British dominions and colonies, Mexico, and Salvador it con-

---

France, see Pouillet, *Traité des Brevets*, 6th ed., pp. 38 ff.

Germany, Law of April 7, 1891, sec. 5 (*Reichsgesetzblatt*, 1891, p. 79).

Greece, Law No. 2527 of September 24, 1920, art. 6 (*'Εφημερὶς τῆς Κυβερνήσεως, Μέρος Α'*, p. 2315).

Hungary, Law of July 14, 1895, sec. 12 (*Recueil Général de Législation*, Bureau International, IV, 303).

Japan, Law of April 29, 1921, art. 37 (*Propriété Industrielle*, 1923, p. 128).

Luxembourg, Law of June 30, 1880, art. 5 (*Recueil Général de Législation*, Bureau International, II, 122).

Mexico, Law of August 25, 1903, art. 7, par. 2 (*Anales de la Legislación Federal*, 1902–1903, p. 286).

The Netherlands, Law of November 7, 1910, art. 32 (*Staatsblad*, 1910, No. 313).

Norway, Law of July 2, 1910, art. 7 (*Norsk Lovtidende*, 1910, p. 243).

Poland, Law of February 5, 1924, art. 9 (*Propriété Industrielle*, 1924, p. 198).

Serb-Croat-Slovene State, Law of November 15, 1920, art. 14 (*Propriété Industrielle*, 1921, p. 36).

Sweden, Law of May 16, 1884, art. 16 (*Svensk Författnings-Samling*, 1884, No. 25).

Switzerland, Federal Law of June 21, 1907, art. 8 (*Recueil Officiel des Lois*, N. S., XXIII, 631).

The U. S. S. R., Decree of September 12, 1924, art. 16 (*Propriété Industrielle*, 1924, p. 250).

1. See *infra*, § 202.

cerns only foreign vessels.[1] In the United States it was held by the Supreme Court in 1856 [2] that

the rights of property and exclusive use granted to a patentee do not extend to a vessel lawfully entering one of our ports; the use of such improvement, in the construction, fitting out or equipment of such vessel, while she is coming into or going out of a port of the United States, is not an infringement of the rights of an American patentee, provided it was placed upon her in a foreign port, and authorized by the laws of the country to which she belongs.

The right of the patentee to prevent the use of his invention in foreign vessels or other means of transportation coming temporarily into the jurisdiction of a state may cause much inconvenience to the freedom of communication. It is too rigid to require a foreigner, who may be altogether ignorant of the grant of a patent in a country, to secure a license from the patentee for the use of the invention at the risk of being subjected to seizure of the machine or engine employed in the construction, fitting out, or functioning of his vessel or other means of transportation. An English decision to this effect in 1851 was deemed so inconvenient that a statute was passed promptly in Great Britain, in consequence of that decision, declaring that a patent shall not prevent such use of the patented invention.[3]

§ 155. Attempts at international regulation in this respect. The first attempt at international regulation was made in 1919 by the Convention for the Regulation of Aërial Navigation, signed in Paris on October 13 of that year. Article 18 of this Convention provides:

Every aircraft passing through the territory of a contracting State, including landing and stoppages reasonably necessary for the purpose of such transit, shall be exempt from any seizure on the ground of infringement of patent, design or model, subject to the deposit of security the amount of which in default of amicable agreement shall be fixed with the least delay by the competent authority of the place of seizure.[4]

1. Cf. *Propriété Industrielle* (1926), pp. 21, 22.
2. C. J. Taney, in Brown *v.* Ducherne, 19 How. 183, 198–199, 15 L. Ed. 593.
3. Caldwell *v.* Van Vlissingen, Court of Chancery (1851), 9 Hare. 415. The statute is 15 & 16 Vict., c. 83.
4. *League of Nations Treaty Series*, XI, 174, 193. At the present time (November, 1928), the countries parties to this Convention are twenty-four: Australia, Belgium, Bulgaria, Canada, Chile, Czechoslovakia, Denmark, France, Great Britain and Northern Ireland, Greece, India, Irish Free State, Italy, Japan, New Zealand, Persia, Poland, Portugal, Rumania, Saar Basin, Serb-Croat-Slovene State, Siam, Union of South Africa, and Uruguay. Seventeen of these countries are members of the Industrial Property Union. See *Official Bulletin of Committee on Aërial Navigation*, No. 12 (June, 1927), p. 10. As to Denmark's accession, see *League of Nations Treaty Series*, LXIII, 389.

This timid attempt concerned only aircraft. Furthermore, it did not declare permissible the use of a patented invention in its construction, fitting out, or functioning. The Convention exempted aircraft from seizure only on condition of deposit of security.

In 1923 the Standing Committee on Industrial Property of the International Chamber of Commerce took up the question in its bearing on all means of transportation. It submitted to the National Committees of Industrial Property the question whether it is desirable to insert in the Convention of 1883 uniform provisions for the regulation of the use of an invention on board ships, or in the construction or functioning of trains, automobiles, or airships of a country, entering the territory of another country.[1]

Several national committees answered affirmatively, and the French Committee sent in a draft of an article to be adopted to this effect. This draft was later adopted by the International Chamber of Commerce at its third Congress (Brussels, June 21–27, 1925),[2] and submitted by the French administration to the Conference of The Hague as its own proposition.[3]

§ **156. New article 5*c* of the Convention.** This text, as proposed, was adopted by the Conference without much discussion, and now forms article 5*c* of the Convention.[4] It is divided into two paragraphs reading as follows:

> Dans chacun des pays contractants ne seront pas considérés comme portant atteinte aux droits du breveté:
>
> 1° l'emploi à bord des navires des autres pays de l'Union, des moyens faisant l'objet de son brevet dans le corps du navire, dans les machines, agrès, apparaux et autres accessoires, lorsque ces navires pénétreront temporairement ou accidentellement dans les eaux du pays, sous réserve que ces moyens y soient employés exclusivement pour les besoins du navire.
>
> 2° l'emploi des moyens faisant l'objet du brevet dans la construction ou le fonctionnement des engins de locomotion aérienne ou terrestre des autres pays de l'Union ou des accessoires de ces engins, lorsque ceux-ci pénétreront temporairement ou accidentellement dans ce pays.

The first paragraph deals with the use of an invention on board ships, the second with its use in engines of locomotion for air or land.

1. *Propriété Industrielle* (1926), p. 221.
2. *International Chamber of Commerce*, Brochure No. 36, p. 25. See also *Actes de la Conférence de La Haye* (1926), p. 108.
3. *Ibid.*, (1925), p. 339.
4. *Ibid.*, pp. 435, 577.

In both cases, the use of the invention will not be considered as infringing the rights of the patentee, if the ships or other engines of locomotion enter only temporarily or accidentally the waters or the territory of the country.

"Temporairement," it was admitted at the Conference of The Hague, on the suggestion of the Czechoslovakian delegation, comprises also the periodical entries of vessels into the territorial waters of another country. Its meaning, beside the term "accidentellement," is implied by the latter. Not only the accidental and unintentional entry, but also the intentional and regular going into a port is within the scope of article 5*c*, provided the vessel or the engine of locomotion does not remain permanently in the territorial waters or in the territory of the country.[1] When the entry ceases to be temporary and becomes permanent, is a question of fact.

In both cases also this use is permitted on board ships, or in engines of locomotion, of other countries of the Union ("d'autres pays de l'Union"). The expression "des autres" refers undoubtedly to the nationality of the ship or of the person to whom the engine belongs. The word "autres" also implies that national ships, or engines belonging to nationals of countries which are not members of the Union, are not within the purview of article 5*c*.

It should be noted that not everything which can be the subject of a patent may be used on board ships and in engines. The invention which may be so used must be a "moyen." The term "moyen" needs to be defined. The French Committee which drafted originally the proposition that became article 5*c* of the Convention used the term "moyen" of the French Patent Law of 1844. Indeed, article 2 of this law distinguishes between the invention of "nouveaux produits industriels" and that of "nouveaux moyens" for obtaining an industrial result or product. Pouillet defines "moyens" as: "les agents, les organes ou les procédés qui mènent à l'obtention soit d'un résultat, soit d'un produit."[2] "Agents," he says, are especially the chemical means; "organes," the mechanical means; "procédés" are the different methods, or processes, of working and combining either chemical or mechanical means. Those "moyens" are patentable which serve for obtaining an industrial product or

1. *Actes de la Conférence de La Haye*, 1925, p. 435; *Propriété Industrielle* (1926), p. 223.

2. Pouillet, *Traité des Brevets*, 6th ed., p. 42; Allart, *Brevets d'Invention*, (3d ed. 1911), p. 27.

an industrial result. Result differs from product in this: that it is not a tangible thing, but, as Pouillet says, the sum of the advantages obtained by a certain kind of manufacture.[1]

The extent of the permissible use of a patented invention, under article 5*c*, by the various means of transportation is not the same. It is far broader in respect to vessels than to other means. An invention may be used in the case of a ship without being considered an infringement: (*a*) in the body of the ship; (*b*) in the machinery, tackle, apparatus; or (*c*) in all other accessories of the ship.

When it is considered that modern big ships are like floating cities, it will be seen that these terms, especially "apparatus" and "accessories," cover an immense number of "moyens," the use of which may be permitted.

Still, these "moyens," by express provision of the first paragraph, may be so used "if they are employed exclusively for the needs of the vessel." The needs of the vessel must be understood in a broad sense, as including every apparatus or machine necessary for the navigation, fitting out, and good equipment of a vessel. Thus, they include machinery necessary for the lighting of the ship, its heating, and the like. Every vessel has different needs. A floating hospital, a cargo boat, a sailboat, and a steamer have not the same needs. In each case it must be considered whether a "moyen" is used in connection with the destination of the ship.

This wide exemption is justified by the nature of the modern vessel, by the fact that a ship enters only the territorial waters of a country, and by a desire to exempt vessels from all unnecessary inconveniences and impediments. The only restriction which the British delegation at the Conference of The Hague proposed to introduce was that it be prohibited to sell in the ports articles produced on board the vessel. But, as was pointed out by the French delegation, the last provision of the first paragraph clearly prohibited such a sale.[2]

In respect to engines of locomotion in the air or on land, the "moyens" which may be used without being considered an infringement of the rights of a patentee are those which are used in the con-

1. Pouillet, *Traité des Brevets*, 6th ed., p. 38.

2. *Actes de la Conférence de La Haye*, p. 435. The restriction proposed by the British delegation is provided for by sec. 48 of the British Act of 1907 in these terms: "provided that it is not used therein for or in connection with the manufacture or preparation of anything intended to be sold in or exported from the United Kingdom or Isle of Man."

struction or functioning of the engines or of the accessories of these engines. If an apparatus or machine contained in such an engine is not used in the construction or functioning of such engine it is not within the exemption of article 5*c*. This limitation rendered unnecessary the repetition in the second paragraph of the final provision of the first paragraph to the effect that the "moyen" must be employed exclusively for the needs of the engine.

The engines covered by the second paragraph of article 5*c* may be of any sort, and not only trains, automobiles, or aircraft, as the original proposal of the Committee of the International Chamber of Commerce had in view. The term "des engins de locomotion aérienne ou terrestre" is very wide. Engines of locomotion for land especially may range from a train to a bicycle.

Obligations of Patentee

The patent, being an exclusive privilege and involving a curtailment of the freedom of industry and commerce, is granted in almost all countries under various restrictions, and with certain obligations imposed on the patentee. In the United States only, no obligation whatsoever is imposed on the grantee of a patent. The most important of these obligations and restrictions are the following four:

§ 157. Obligation of patentee to work his patent. The patentee is obliged by the law of most countries to put his invention into commercial use within a fixed period from the grant of the patent. If he does not start working the invention within this period, the patent is revoked or forfeited. Besides in the United States, in Danzig, Haiti, and Salvador no such obligation is imposed by law on the patentee. In Greece and Switzerland, foreign patentees, on condition of reciprocity, do not forfeit their patent for non-working. Thus American citizens are not compelled to work their patents in these countries.[1] On the other hand, in Mexico, Norway, and Sweden,[2] on failure to work a patent for three years, a compulsory license may be granted to others for putting the invention into commercial

1. Greece, Law No. 2527 of September 20, 1920, art. 9 ("'Εφημερὶς τῆς Κυβερνήσεως," 1920, part I, p. 2315).

Switzerland, Law of 1907, art. 18 (*Recueil Officiel des Lois*, N. S., XXIII, 631).

2. Mexico, Law of August 25, 1903, arts. 19 ff. (*Anales de la Legislación Federal*, 1902–1903, p. 286).

Norway, Law of July 2, 1910, art. 9 (*Norsk Lovtidende*, 1910, p. 243).

Sweden, Law of May 9, 1902, revising art. 15 of the Royal Ordinance of May 16, 1884 (*Svensk Författnings-Samling*, 1902, No. 45).

use. In some of the countries in which the patent may be revoked for failure to work it, the administration may, in the alternative, grant compulsory licenses. The question of compulsory licenses is considered below.

The period within which the working of the patented invention should begin is not the same in all countries. It is one year in Belgium, Ecuador, Guatemala, Honduras, and Nicaragua; [1] two years in Argentina, Australia, Bolivia, Costa Rica, France, Italy, Newfoundland, Peru, Portugal, Syria and Lebanon, Tunis, Turkey, and Union of South Africa; [2] three years in Austria, Brazil, Bulgaria, Canada, Ceylon, Czechoslovakia, Denmark, Esthonia, Finland, Germany, Greece, Hungary, Japan, Luxembourg, Morocco, Poland, Serb-Croat-Slovene State, Spain, and Switzerland; [3] four years in

1. Belgium, Law of May 24, 1854, art. 23 (*Pasinomie*, 1854, p. 174). Ecuador, Law of Nov. 3, 1880, art. 38 (*Leyes y Decretos*, 1880, p. 53). Guatemala, Decree No. 550 of Dec. 17, 1897, art. 8 (*Recopilación de las Leyes*, 1897–98, p. 637). Honduras, Law No. 123 of April 15, 1919, art. 8 (*Propriété Industrielle*, 1921, p. 56). Nicaragua, Law of Oct. 11, 1899 (*Recueil Général de Législation*, Bureau International, IV, 904.

2. Argentina, Law of Oct. 11, 1864, art. 47 (*Registro Nacional*, 1864, p. 78). Australia, act of Oct. 22, 1903, sec. 87 (*Acts of the Commonwealth of Australia*, 1903, p. 132). Bolivia, Law of Nov. 16–Dec. 2, 1916, arts. 42, 45, 51, 52, 56 (*Anuario de Leyes*, 1916, p. 685). Costa Rica, Law of June 27, 1896, arts. 66, 67 (*Colección de las Leyes*, 1896, pp. 201, 212). France, Law of June 5, 1844, art. 47 (*Bulletin des Lois*, 1844, II, 18), and Law of April 7, 1902 (*Bulletin des Lois*, 1902, II, 263). Italy, Law No. 3731, of Oct. 30, 1859, art. 58 (*Raccolta Stati Sardi*, 1859, I, 1287). Newfoundland (*Consolidated Statutes of Newfoundland*, 3d series, 1919, II, chap. 152, 1499). Peru, Law of Jan. 28, 1869, art. 15 (*Leyes y Resoluciones*, 1868–1873, p. 507). Portugal, Law of May 21, 1896, art. 39 (*Collecção Oficial*, 1896, p. 402). Syria and Lebanon, Ordinance of Jan. 17, 1924, art. 46 (*Bulletin Officiel mensuel des actes du Haut-Commissariat*, février, 1924, p. 2; also *Propriété Industrielle*, 1924, p. 153. Tunis, Law of Dec. 26, 1888, art. 26 (*Officiel Tunisien* No. 53 of Dec. 27, 1888; also *Propriété Industrielle*, 1899, p. 105). Turkey, Law of Feb. 18, 1879, art. 38 (*Recueil Général de Législation*, Bureau International, II, 607, 616). Union of South Africa, Act 9 of 1916 (*Statutes of the Union of South Africa*, 1916, p. 24).

3. Austria, Law No. 366 of 1925 on patents, secs. 21, 27 (*Bundesgesetzblatt*, 1925, p. 1367). Brazil, Decree No. 16264 of Dec. 19, 1923, arts. 70, 71 (*Collecção das Leis*, 1923, III, 329, 340). Bulgaria, Law of July 29, 1921, arts. 11, 17 (*Propriété Industrielle*, 1921, p. 130). Canada, Act of June 13, 1923, secs. 40, 41 (13–14 George V, c. 23, *Stat. of Canada*, 1923, p. 145). Ceylon, Ordinance No. 15 of 1906, sec. 27 (*Legislative Enactments of Ceylon*, rev. ed. of 1923, II, 670). Czechoslovakia, Austrian Law of 1897, secs. 21, 27 (*Reichsgesetzblatt*, 1897, No. 30) made applicable by law of May 27, 1919 (*Sammlung der Gesetzedes Čechoslovakishen Staates*, 1919, p. 473). Denmark, Law of April 13, 1894, art. 23 (*Lovtidende for Danmark*, 1894, p. 323). Esthonia, Law of May 21, 1921, sec. 96 (*Propriété Industrielle*, 1922, pp. 65, 67). Germany, Law of April 7, 1891, sec. 11 (*Reichsgesetzblatt*, 1891, p. 79), as revised by the Law of June 6, 1911, sec. 1 (*Reichsgesetzblatt*, 1911, p. 243). Finland, Law of Feb. 11, 1921, revising sec. 18 of the Imperial Notification of 1898 (*Författnings-Samling*, 1921, p. 139). Hungary, Law of July 14, 1895, arts. 15, 27 (*Recueil Général de Législation*, Bureau International, IV, 303), as revised by the Law of April 13, 1913, art. 1 (*Ungarische Reichsgestzsammlung*, 1913, p. 257). Japan, Law of April 29, 1921, sec. 41 (*Propriété Indus-*

Great Britain, India, and Rumania;[1] five years in the Dominican Republic, the Netherlands, and Soviet Russia.[2] In Panama the period is one third of the term of the patent, which may be five, ten, fifteen, or twenty years. In Cuba, Venezuela, and Uruguay, the period within which the invention must be worked is determined by the administration on the issue of each patent; but it cannot exceed two years in Venezuela.[3]

Extension of the time is possible in Belgium (by royal decree), Bolivia (one or two years), Denmark (by the Commissioners of Patents), Poland, and Uruguay (not to exceed two years in all). In the other countries the forfeiture of the patent is either automatic on the lapse of the time fixed or is declared by the administration. Moreover, in some countries a patent may be revoked before the lapse of the specified period within which it should be put into commercial use, if in the meantime it is worked exclusively or primarily in a foreign country. These countries are Austria, Czechoslovakia, Esthonia, Great Britain, and certain British colonies.

In Germany and Finland,[4] if the working of the invention has not begun within three years from the delivery of the patent, the administration will grant compulsory licenses. The patent will be revoked only if the invention is being worked exclusively, or primarily, in a foreign country. In Nicaragua, it is sufficient that the patent is worked in the country of origin of the patentee within the specified period. In Venezuela, the working in a foreign country is sufficient,

---

trielle, 1923, pp. 109, 129). Luxembourg, Law of June 30, 1880, art. 18 (*Recueil Général de Législation*, Bureau International, II, 122). Morocco, Dahir of June 23, 1916, art. 54 (*Codes et Lois du Maroc*, édition officielle, I, supp. 1, 326). Poland, Law of Feb. 5, 1924, art. 13 (*Propriété Industrielle*, 1924, p. 198). Serb-Croat-Slovene State, Law of Nov. 15, 1920, art. 32 (*Propriété Industrielle*, 1924, p. 34). Spain, Law of May 16, 1902, arts. 98–102 (*Legislación*, 1902, II, 88). Switzerland, Law of June 21, 1907, art. 18 (*Recueil Officiel des Lois*, N. S., XXIII, 631).

1. Great Britain, Act of 1907 as amended by the Act of 1919, sec. 27 (7 Edw. VII, c. 29, and 9 & 10 George V, c. 80). India, Act of March 1, 1911, "The Indian Patents and Designs Act," secs. 22, 23, and 25 (*Acts of the Governor General in Council*, 1911, No. 2). Rumania, Law of Jan. 13–26, 1906, art. 9 (*Propriété Industrielle*, 1906, p. 38).

2. Dominican Republic, Law of April 26, 1911, art. 20 (*Gaceta Oficial*, No. 2194). The Netherlands, Law of Nov. 7, 1910, arts. 34, 50 (*Staatsblad*, 1910, No. 313). Soviet Russia, Decree of Sept. 12, 1924, art. 18 (*Propriété Industrielle*, 1924, p. 250).

3. Panama, Law of Nov. 14, 1908, art. 12 (*Leys de Panamá*, 1908–1909, p. 34). Cuba, Royal Ordinance of July 30, 1883, art. 23 (3) and (4) (*Propriété Industrielle*, 1909, p. 69). Uruguay, Law of Nov. 13, 1885, art. 36 (*Colección Legislativa*, 1885, p. 292); and Law of Nov. 28, 1916, arts. 1, 2 (*Registro Nacional*, 1916, p. 769). Venezuela, Law of May 31, 1913, arts. 4, 5 (*Recopilación de Leyes*, 1913, p. 105).

4. Finland, Imperial Decree of Jan. 21, 1898, sec. 4; Imperial Order of same date, sec. 4, and Decree of Feb. 11, 1921 (*Författnings-Samling*, 1898, pp. 1, 5; 1921, p. 139).

if the patentee meets the demand of the public in Venezuela. In Morocco, the commercial use of the invention in a country of the Union within the specified period frees the patentee from the obligation to work in Morocco. In Denmark, the Commissioners of Patents may exempt a patentee from the obligation to work his patent in the country, if it be proved that the expenses of production would not be in proportion to the consumption of the article in question in Denmark.

The extent of the working which will prevent forfeiture for non-working varies in the different countries. In certain ones it is required that the invention be worked fully, or exclusively, or primarily in their territory, while in other countries a "sufficient" (Austria), or "effective" (Brazil), or "substantial" (Hungary) working is a due compliance with the law. Forfeiture may be avoided in some countries if the patentee shows that the failure to work the invention was not voluntary (Italy); or that he did his best to secure such working (Japan); or that he offered, and did not refuse, to grant licenses (Syria and Lebanon). Also the meaning of the word "working" (exploitation) varies in the different countries. In some countries it is construed as meaning "manufacturing," or establishing an industry; in others, merely making available to the public the patented article or the products of a patented process.[1] It may be added here that in Guatemala and Honduras a patent will be forfeited if the products manufactured with the invention are inferior to the samples lodged with the application.

§ 158. Obligation not to interrupt the working of the patent. Closely connected with the last is the obligation not to interrupt the working of the patent for more than a specified period continuously. The countries in which this obligation is imposed are among those in which the previous obligation also is imposed on patentees. In Venezuela, the working of the invention must not cease for more than six months. In Belgium, Bolivia, Brazil, Cuba, Denmark, Guatemala, Honduras, Nicaragua, Spain, and Uruguay, it must not be interrupted for more than one year. In Argentina, France, Italy, Portugal, Rumania, Tunis, and Turkey, the interruption must not continue for more than two consecutive years. In Costa Rica, Japan, and Morocco, a three years' interruption of the

1. See on all this, and on court decisions, *Propriété Industrielle* (1924), pp. 86 ff., 97 ff.

commercial use of the invention causes forfeiture of the patent. In Denmark, the time may be extended by the Commissioners of Patents. In Nicaragua, interruption of the working is allowed, so long as the invention is being worked in the country of origin of the patentee. In Morocco, the working of the invention in a country of the Union frees one from this obligation. In Belgium, the interruption causes forfeiture of the patent if the working continues abroad and the patentee does not justify his inaction.

§ 159. **Prohibition of importation of patented articles.** In a few countries the patentee must not import into the country in which he is granted a patent articles manufactured in a foreign country and similar to those patented in the country. On a single importation of such articles the patent is forfeited. In Morocco alone, the importation of patented articles causes forfeiture of the patent after three years from the date of the patent, and in case the quantity imported exceeds the quantity manufactured in Morocco.

This restriction is provided for by the law of the Dominican Republic, France, Morocco, Syria and Lebanon, Tunis, and Turkey. The only articles which may be imported without risk of forfeiture are models of machinery and articles destined for public exhibition or for experiments to be made with the authorization of the government. For this exceptional importation a special authorization must be applied for.

§ 160. **Compulsory licenses.** There are relatively few countries, outside Great Britain and the British dominions and colonies, in which the obligation to grant licenses is provided by the patent law. In Danzig,[1] Mexico, Norway, and Sweden, the granting of compulsory licenses is the only obligation imposed on the patentee. In Danzig this may be ordered by the court at any time if it is in the public interest. In the other three countries, it is resorted to by the administration in case three years have elapsed from the date of the patent and the latter has not yet been worked; or, in Mexico, if the working of the patent has been interrupted for three years.

In Austria, Czechoslovakia, and Hungary, a license to work the invention may be granted to other persons three years after the

1. Law of July 14, 1921, sec. 9 (*Gesetzblatt für die freie Stadt Danzig*, 1921, p. 19). The law of the other countries is cited in note 2 on p. 250.

grant of the patent if the public interest so requires. In Bolivia and Japan, compulsory licenses are granted by the administration in the alternative, instead of revocation of the patent for failure to work the invention in the country. In the Netherlands, revocation of the patent is not possible before five years have elapsed from its date, while compulsory licenses may be granted three years after the grant, if this appears to be in the interest of the industry in the Netherlands or its colonies or possessions, or for any other reason of public interest. In Germany the regular course is to grant compulsory licenses on failure to work a patent within three years from its grant, forfeiture being resorted to in case the patent is worked exclusively or primarily in a foreign country. In Greece, compulsory licenses are granted if the invention is declared of public utility. A patentee, on the other hand, may declare at any time in Greece that his patent is subject to "licenses of right." Patents so indorsed are subject to one half of the usual taxes.

In Great Britain and the British dominions the system of compulsory licenses is regulated on a different basis and must be considered separately. The provisions of the law of Great Britain are adopted more or less by the British dominions and colonies. The British Act of 1907, as amended by the Act of 1919 (sections 24 and 27),[1] provides in effect that any person may complain to the comptroller that there has been an abuse of monopoly: (*a*) if, after the expiration of five years from the date of a patent, the invention has not been worked on a manufacturing scale in the United Kingdom; (*b*) if it is prevented from being so worked by importation of the patented articles by the patentee; (*c*) if the demand for the article is not met on reasonable terms, or the trade is prejudiced by the refusal of grant of licenses on fair terms.

In such case the Comptroller may (*a*) order the patent indorsed "licenses of right," and any person may then obtain a license on terms set by the Comptroller, (*b*) order the grant to the applicant of a license on such terms as the Comptroller may think expedient, (*c*) grant exclusive license to another, (*d*) order the patent to be revoked either forthwith or after a reasonable time, if he is satisfied that the objects of this section (section 27, the prevention of abuse of monopoly) cannot be attained by the exercise of any of the foregoing powers.

1. 9 & 10 George V, c. 80.

It may be said, therefore, that revocation of the patent will rarely be ordered in Great Britain and the British dominions, the ordinary course being to grant licenses or exclusive license. On the other hand, such licenses are granted, not only if the invention is not worked in the United Kingdom, but also if it is prevented from being so worked by importation of patented articles from abroad by the patentee; and moreover, if the demand for the article is not met on reasonable terms, or, as the law of some British dominions provides, if the reasonable expectations of the public are not satisfied.[1]

In the countries of the Union the persons entitled to the benefits of the Convention may claim protection under the provisions of article 5, which deals with restrictions of the obligations of the patentee. A study of this article is made in one of the following chapters. As will be seen, the principles of the British law on this matter were adopted at the recent Conference of The Hague.

VIII. Conclusions

§ 161. To sum up the above exposition, it appears that in the Union for the Protection of Industrial Property created by the Convention of 1883, although the independence of the patent law of each country is almost entirely preserved, the incursions of the Conventional law into what was formerly held to be the exclusive province of the different countries are many and important. The diversity of the laws on the subjects of patentability of inventions and duration of patents lose much of their effect on foreigners by the provisions of the Convention on the right of priority and on the independence of patents, as will be seen in the next chapters. A beginning of international regulation of formalities for patent applications may be seen in the work of the Technical Meeting of Berne of 1926. A similar tendency is exhibited in the efforts for the establishment of an international index of patents, concerning the administrative procedure for the grant of patents in the various countries. The new article 5*b* of the Convention eliminates the principal difficulty affecting foreigners in respect to fees and taxes for patents. The rights of the

1. In Canada sections 40 and 41 of the Act of 1923 were amended by an Act of March 29, 1928 to the effect of giving the power to the Commissioner to grant a compulsory license in case the patentee has failed to manufacture adequately the patented invention and of restricting his power to revoke the patent which is being worked outside Canada. The latter may take place only if a license in respect of the patent has previously been ordered.

patentee are limited in one respect by the new article 5*c* of the Convention, and it may be hoped that they will be better secured by the abolition of the reservation of the rights of third parties in article 4 of the Convention. Lastly, article 5 of the Convention restricts the obligations of the patentee.

Thus all the important questions of patent law are touched upon by the Convention in an attempt at harmonizing the laws of the various countries, and affording more adequate protection to interests that by their nature are world-wide.

IX. Statistics

§ **162.** In order to give a general idea of the extent and importance of patents at the present time, a number of statistical tables are appended to this chapter. The first of these tables gives the number of patents granted in the various countries during the fifty-two years from 1870 to 1922. The United States leads in this respect with 1,329,745 patents, and is followed by Great Britain with 557,985 and France with 526,528. Germany has delivered during the same period 376,603 patents, Belgium 280,965, Canada 220,155, Italy 165,378, and Austria 119,800.

Table II gives the number of patents granted in the countries of the Union in the years 1900, 1913, 1922, 1923, 1924, 1925, and 1926, and shows the progress between these years in the countries in question. Table III gives the number of applications for patents filed in certain countries of the Union, and the patents granted in the years 1922, 1923, 1924, and 1925. Thus the volume of work and, incidentally, the time taken in each country for the grant of a patent, may be seen. In the United States there were 80,443 applications filed in 1925, while the patents in this year numbered 46,716. The same proportion may be seen in Great Britain, Austria, Australia, Japan, and the Netherlands, and a smaller proportion of patents granted in comparison to applications filed in Germany. On the contrary, in Belgium, France, Spain, and Switzerland, this difference is not found.

Tables IV and V show the proportion between patents granted to nationals and those to foreigners, in a number of countries of the Union. The average of the five years 1895 to 1899, and the average of recent years has remained practically the same in the United States of America. Patents granted to foreigners in this country are a small proportion of the total number of patents. In the other countries there has been change. Thus, in Great Britain the average of patents granted to foreigners in the years 1895 to 1899 was 25 per cent of the total; it was increased to 46 per cent in the years 1921 and 1924. On the contrary, in Germany the earlier average of 36 per cent is reduced to 20 per cent in the years 1920 to 1923. A reduction is found also in Italy, Switzerland, and Austria. These tables also show the great number of foreign patents in many countries.

Table VI gives the number of patents granted in the various countries for each million inhabitants. The average of the five years 1895 to 1899 and that of the five years 1922 to 1926 may also be compared. Belgium and Switzerland stand quite high in this respect. These averages should be considered together with the averages of patents granted to foreigners in each of these countries, in order to appreciate the importance of each country in respect to the number of patented inventions.

TABLE I

NUMBER OF PATENTS GRANTED IN THE VARIOUS COUNTRIES FROM 1870 TO 1922

Argentina	18,993	Japan	42,389
Australia	73,991	Luxembourg	12,705
Austria	119,800	Morocco (French zone)	205
Belgium	280,965	The Netherlands	8,746
Bolivia	65	New Zealand	23,214
Brazil	13,727	Norway	37,267
Bulgaria	252	Paraguay	102
Canada	220,155	Peru	609
Ceylon	829	Portugal	11,737
Chile	4,552	Rumania	1,116
Colombia	1,406	Russia	30,844
Costa Rica	100	Serb-Croat-Slovene State	940
Cuba	4,444	Spain	69,681
Czechoslovakia	9,700	Sweden	55,034
Denmark	38,077	Switzerland	99,123
Ecuador	10	Trinidad	317
Finland	9,069	Tunis	1,214
France	526,528	Turkey	2,560
Germany	376,603	Union of South Africa	8,692
Great Britain	557,985	United States	1,329,745
Guatemala	57	Uruguay	1,331
Hungary	83,174	Venezuela	510
India	17,787		
Italy	165,378		

[See (1925) 331 Official Gazette of the U. S. 485]

TABLE II

NUMBER OF PATENTS GRANTED IN THE MEMBER COUNTRIES OF THE INDUSTRIAL PROPERTY UNION, FROM 1900 TO 1926 [1]

	1900	1913	1922	1923	1924	1925	1926	Average 1922-1926
Australia.......	...	1,495	3,207	2,464	2,313	2,474	3,493	2,790
Austria	2,577	5,900	4,450	4,000	3,300	3,300	3,000	3,610
Belgium	6,885	11,116	7,229	7,153	7,958	8,370	6,854	7,512
Brazil	274	668	1,027	749	432	616	...	706
Bulgaria	...	...	206	147	263	193	180	198
Canada	4,522	...	...	...	9,144	11,043	11,151	10,446
Cuba	...	272	398	548	494	...	595	509
Czechoslovakia	...	...	2,400	2,499	2,800	3,000	3,000	2,739
Danzig	...	...	317	193	231	206	169	223
Denmark	877	1,493	1,941	1,606	1,324	1,465	1,517	1,570
Domini. Republic	...	3	8	7	...	...	...	7
Esthonia	...	...	...	177	163	209	195	186
Finland	...	...	571	699	426	543	391	526
France.........	12,399	15,967	18,300	19,200	19,200	18,000	18,200	18,580
Germany [2]	27,004	61,070	52,315	47,326	49,989	56,477	56,100	52,441
Great Britain ..	13,170	16,599	17,366	17,073	16,839	17,199	17,333	17,162
Greece	...	...	...	171	250	302	292	254
Hungary	2,398	4,497	2,029	2,923	2,208	2,511	2,487	2,431
Italy [3]	3,124	10,560	3,978	6,377	23,850	13,964	6,468	10,927
Japan [2].........	577	5,753	7,797	6,607	5,320	16,789	11,139	9,530
Latvia	...	...	...	...	...	155	205	181
Luxembourg....	...	...	360	407	386	481	493	425
Mexico	...	...	1,153	...	1,111	996	1,110	1,092
Morocco	...	...	118	171	102	133	140	133
Netherlands ...	...	111	1,975	2,155	1,864	1,648	1,625	1,853
New Zealand ...	...	713	1,388	1,106	1,127	979	1,267	1,173
Norway........	1,180	1,196	2,711	2,256	1,997	1,611	1,218	1,958
Poland [2]	...	...	...	...	510	2,572	2,818	1,966
Portugal	328	415	404	376	637	621	280	463
Rumania.......	...	...	667	1,508	1,767	1,095	1,095	1,226
Serb-Croat-Slovene State	4	...	808	1,143	971	813	553	857
Spain	1,498	1,773	3,552	3,718	4,032	3,935	5,250	4,097
Sweden	1,317	1,915	2,749	2,715	2,266	1,929	2,176	2,367
Switzerland	1,889	5,916	4,513	5,533	5,388	4,819	5,175	5,085
Syria & Lebanon	...	...	...	...	...	15	15	15
Tunis..........	76	99	112	153	116	107	126	123
Turkey	...	...	...	...	...	129	130	129
United States...	25,322	35,624	38,670	38,860	42,829	46,716	45,025	42,420

[1] *Propriété Industrielle*, 1902, p. 15; 1912, p. 178; 1916, p. 111; 1924, pp. 166, 258; 1925, p. 266; 1926, p. 274.
[2] The numbers for Germany, Japan, and Poland include patents for inventions and models of utility.
[3] The number for Italy includes patents of extension.

TABLE III

NUMBER OF PATENTS APPLIED FOR AND PATENTS GRANTED IN SOME COUNTRIES OF THE UNION

Countries	1922		1923		1924		1925	
	Applied	Granted	Applied	Granted	Applied	Granted	Applied	Granted
Australia	5,432	3,207	5,306	2,464	5,432	2,313	5,307	2,474
Austria	5,980	4,450	5,937	4,000	6,885	3,300	6,980	3,300
Belgium	7,151	7,229	7,200	7,133	8,066	7,958	8,504	8,370
Canada	...	...	...	...	14,697	9,144	11,347	11,043
Denmark	2,467	1,941	2,314	1,606	2,696	1,324	2,735	1,465
France	17,719	18,300	17,491	19,200	18,960	19,200	19,896	18,000
Germany [1]	51,762	20,715	45,209	20,526	56,831	18,189	64,910	15,877
Great Britain	35,494	17,366	32,621	17,073	31,370	16,839	33,003	17,199
Hungary	3,143	2,029	2,952	2,923	2,804	2,208	2,730	2,511
Italy [2]	10,354	3,978	10,072	6,377	9,073	23,850	9,702	13,964
Japan [1]	10,056	2,936	7,969	2,131	9,894	1,928	12,680	5,088
Mexico	1,357	1,153	...	...	1,281	1,111	1,218	996
Netherlands	2,400	1,975	2,481	2,155	3,078	1,864	3,330	1,648
Norway	2,263	2,711	1,957	2,256	2,295	1,997	2,347	1,611
Poland [1]	1,786	...	1,576	...	1,930	315	2,035	2,572
Spain	3,558	3,552	3,873	3,718	4,236	4,032	4,350	3,935
Sweden	3,781	2,749	3,696	2,715	4,031	2,266	4,387	1,929
Switzerland	4,856	4,513	5,219	5,533	5,923	5,388	6,544	4,819
United States	84,167	38,670	76,972	38,860	77,121	42,829	80,443	46,716

[1] The numbers for Germany, Japan, and Poland include patents for inventions and models of utility.
[2] The number for Italy includes patents of extension.

TABLE IV

PATENTS GRANTED TO NATIONALS AND FOREIGNERS — AVERAGE OF THE FIVE YEARS 1895 TO 1899 [1]

	Nationals		Foreigners	
	Number	Per cent	Number	Per cent
Portugal	28	10	254	90
Turkey	12	15	68	85
Hungary	520	19	2,268	81
Norway	167	20	680	80
Denmark	103	21	390	79
Switzerland	601	30	1,378	70
Italy	755	32	1,587	68
Austria	1,876	37	3,152	63
Sweden	383	37	546	63
Brazil	142	58	104	42
Germany	3,785	64	2,129	36
Great Britain	10,040	75	3,400	25
United States	19,438	90	2,272	10

[1] See *Propriété Industrielle*, 1900, pp. 121, 127.

TABLE V

PATENTS GRANTED TO NATIONALS AND FOREIGNERS IN RECENT YEARS [1]

	Years	Nationals Number	Nationals Per cent	Foreigners Number	Foreigners Per cent
The Netherlands	1920–1923	335	21.5	1,249	78.5
Italy	1921–1924	4,883	42.3	6,690	57.7
Switzerland	1922–1925	2,294	45.0	2,769	55.0
Austria	1922, 1924, 1925	3,410	51.0	3,205	49.0
France	1921–1924	11,246	60.0	7,353	40.0
Great Britain	1921 and 1924	8,974 [2]	54.0	7,408	46.0
Germany	1920–1923	41,203	80.0	10,601	20.0
United States	1923–1925	37,625	89.0	4,734	11.0
Russia	1925–1926	854	89.0	94	11.0

[1] This table is made up of statistical data published in the *Propriété Industrielle,* 1923. pp. 108, 179; 1924, pp. 12, 215; 1925, pp. 82, 106, 130, 154, 171, 195; 1926, pp. 85, 176, 200, 251; 1927, pp. 55, 84, 127, 142.

[2] This number comprises patents granted to citizens of the United Kingdom (Great Britain, Scotland, Wales, Northern Ireland, Channel Islands and the Isle of Man), but not those granted to citizens of the dominions and colonies. The latter represent 7 per cent of the patents granted to "foreigners."

TABLE VI

NUMBER OF PATENTS GRANTED IN THE VARIOUS COUNTRIES FOR EACH MILLION INHABITANTS

Countries	Average of years 1895–1899	Countries	Average of years 1922–1926	Countries	Average of years 1922–1926
Belgium	1,028	Luxembourg	1,580	Spain	188
Switzerland	634	Switzerland	1,290	Esthonia	168
Norway	403	Canada	1,160	Japan	159
Great Britain	332	Belgium	931	Finland	149
France	306	Germany	841	Cuba	148
United States	290	New Zealand	833	Latvia	97
Denmark	214	Norway	738	Portugal	82
Austria	197	Danzig	575	Mexico	76
Sweden	186	Austria	568	Serb-Croat-Slovene State	71
Hungary	167	Australia	507	Rumania	70
Germany	110	Denmark	461	Poland	67
Spain	82	France	457	Tunis	56
Italy	74	Sweden	391	Greece	41
Portugal	56	Great Britain	388	Bulgaria	36
Brazil	14	United States	357	Morocco	31
Japan	5	Hungary	290	Brazil	18
		Italy	269	Turkey	17
		The Netherlands	249	Dominican Republic	6
		Czechoslovakia	201	Syria and Lebanon	4

CHAPTER XI

THE RIGHT OF PRIORITY FOR PATENT APPLICATIONS

§ 163. Questions to be considered. The most important of the specific advantages and rights granted by the Convention of 1883 to the "ressortissants" of the Union, as regards patents, is the right of priority. The provisions of the Convention in this respect are contained in article 4. For its extreme significance this article is cited here *in extenso*, as it is in effect to-day, following its revision at the Conference of The Hague in 1925.

(*a*) Celui qui aura régulièrement fait le dépôt d'une demande de brevet d'invention, d'un modèle d'utilité, d'un dessin ou modèle industriel, d'une marque de fabrique ou de commerce, dans l'un des pays contractants, ou son ayant cause, jouira, pour effectuer le dépôt dans les autres pays, et sous réserve des droits des tiers, d'un droit de priorité pendant les délais déterminés ci-après.

(*b*) En conséquence, le dépôt ultérieurement opéré dans l'un des autres pays de l'Union, avant l'expiration de ces délais, ne pourra être invalidé par des faits accomplis dans l'intervalle, soit, notamment, par un autre dépôt, par la publication de l'invention ou son exploitation, par la mise en vente d'exemplaires du dessin ou du modèle, par l'emploi de la marque.

(*c*) Les délais de priorité mentionnés ci-dessus seront de douze mois pour les brevets d'invention et les modèles d'utilité, et de six mois pour les dessins et modèles industriels et pour les marques de fabrique ou de commerce.

Ces délais commencent à courir de la date du dépôt de la première demande dans un pays de l'Union; le jour du dépôt n'est pas compris dans le délai.

Si le dernier jour du délai est un jour férié légal dans le pays où la protection est réclamée, le délai sera prorogé jusqu'au premier jour ouvrable qui suit.

(*d*) Quiconque voudra se prévaloir de la priorité d'un dépôt antérieur sera tenu de faire une déclaration indiquant la date et le pays de ce dépôt. Chaque pays déterminera à quel moment, au plus tard, cette declaration devra être effectuée.

Ces indications seront mentionnées dans les publications émanant de l'Administration compétente, notamment sur les brevets et les descriptions y relatives.

Les pays contractants pourront exiger de celui qui fait une déclaration de priorité la production d'une copie de la demande (description, dessins, etc.) déposée antérieurement. La copie, certifiée conforme par l'Administration qui aura recu cette demande, sera dispensée de toute légalisation, et elle pourra en tous cas être déposée à n'importe quel moment dans le délai de trois mois à dater du dépôt de la demande ultérieure. On pourra exiger qu'elle soit accompagnée d'un certificat de la date du dépôt émanant de cette Administration, et d'une traduction.

D'autres formalités ne pourront être requises pour la déclaration de priorité au moment du dépôt de la demande. Chaque pays contractant déterminera les conséquences de l'omission des formalités prévues par le présent article, sans que ces conséquences puissent excéder la perte du droit de priorité.

Ultérieurement d'autres justifications pourront être demandées.

(*e*) Lorsqu'un dessin ou modèle industriel aura été déposé dans un pays en vertu d'un droit de priorité basé sur le dépôt d'un modèle d'utilité, le délai de priorité ne sera que celui fixé pour les dessins ou modèles industriels.

En outre, il est permis de déposer dans un pays un modèle d'utilité en vertu d'un droit de priorité basé sur le dépôt d'une demande de brevet et inversement.

(*f*) Si une demande de brevet contient la revendication de priorités multiples, ou si l'examen révèle qu'une demande est complexe, l'Administration devra, tout au moins, autoriser, le demandeur à la diviser dans des conditions que déterminera la législation intérieure, en conservant comme date de chaque demande divisionnaire la date de la demande initiale et, s'il y a lieu, le bénéfice du droit de priorité.[1]

The construction of this article and the exposition of the special right accorded by it involves the following questions:

1. Nature of the right of priority.
2. Who may claim it.
3. Requirements of the prior deposit.
4. Period of the right of priority.
5. Conditions and formalities as to the new deposits.
6. Identity of the first and later applications.
7. Effects of the right of priority.

Each of these questions is considered below.

1. The second and third paragraphs of section (*c*), the second paragraph of section (*e*), and section (*f*) of this article, were added at the Conference of The Hague. No other amendment of article 4 was made at this Conference, with the exception of certain minor modifications in the third paragraph of section (*d*).

I. Nature of Right of Priority

§ **164. History of article 4 of the Convention.** The crucial question involved in the construction of article 4 is the exact nature of the right which it purports to grant to persons admitted to the benefit of the Convention. A great number of problems arising in connection with this article depend for their solution on the meaning and import of the right of priority. Much confusion has always reigned in this respect, causing divergences of application in the various countries of the Union.

It is necessary to keep in mind the history of article 4. When it was first proposed to the Conference of 1880 by the French delegate Jagerschmidt, it read as follows: [1]

> Tout dépôt d'une demande de brevet d'invention . . . régulièrement effectué dans l'un ou l'autre des États contractants, constituera pour le déposant un droit de priorité d'enregistrement dans tous les États de l'Union pendant un délai de . . . .

Thus deposit of an application in a country of the Union was to constitute a right of priority. This stipulation was preferred by the French Committee of the Permanent Commission, constituted by the Congress of 1878, to the *voeu* adopted by this Congress that applications for patents (as well as designs, models, and trade marks) should be deposited simultaneously with the local authorities in each country and with the consulates of the various foreign countries.[2] Why did the Congress of 1878 wish that an application for a patent should be so deposited "simultaneously"? Why did the Draft Convention propose that every deposit of an application for a patent was to constitute a right of priority of registration in the other countries?

The discussion at the Conference leaves no doubt on this point. The Chairman of the Conference of 1880, who had also presided over the Congress of 1878, explained the meaning of article 4. In France, he said, when an invention has received any kind of publicity, it cannot then be patented. Honesty requires that this provision of the French law should cease to exist. Inventors, in general, are not rich, and it is not easy for them to apply for a patent at the same time in several countries. But if they apply in France for a patent, after having applied in another country, their invention may not be

1. *Conférence de Paris* (1880), p. 47. 2. *Propriété Industrielle* (1886), p. 18.

"new" any longer under the French law. At the Congress of 1878 a practical means of remedying this state of things was suggested. The simultaneous deposit of the application with the local administration and the foreign consuls was deemed to be sufficient to save the rights of the inventors in all the countries. But it was objected that in certain places there are no consuls, and that this procedure would be too expensive. Then it was proposed to provide that the filing of the application in one of the contracting countries should be equivalent to a filing in all the other countries. The applicant would not be granted a patent by virtue of this understanding alone, but he would be able to obtain a patent within a specified period, without running the risk of forfeiting his rights for absence of novelty in his invention.[1] No objection to the principle, or to this import of the article, was made at the Conference.

Inventors are naturally prompted to apply first for a patent for their inventions in their own country. It is expensive, and in many cases inexpedient, to apply in several foreign countries. There is often uncertainty as to the completeness and immediate applicability of an invention, and ignorance as to the state of the specific art in other countries. Another difficulty is to get agents in foreign countries, or persons interested in the invention. For all these reasons, prior to 1883 it was practically impossible for inventors to apply simultaneously in several countries. As a consequence, their opportunities in foreign countries were lost by an intervening publication or working of the invention, or by filing on the part of a third person.

The *voeu* of the Congress of 1878 having been considered inexpedient, it was proposed that the filing of an application in one of the countries of the Union be considered as filing in the other countries of the Union as well. The Union was to be deemed for this purpose a single territory. But this did not mean, as the Chairman of the Conference made clear, that a patent would be granted in every country of the Union on the basis of that single filing of an application. A new application was to be filed in every other country of the Union in which the inventor desired to obtain a patent. Only on the basis of this latter filing might a patent be granted. The first filing would have only the effect of a warning to the other countries that an application might be deposited within a certain time, and in such case all steps taken in the interval, which ordinarily would de-

1. *Conférence de Paris* (1880), pp. 49–50.

stroy the novelty of the invention, were to be without effect. For the explicit warning to the consulates, which the Congress of 1878 had suggested, was now substituted a fictitious warning, implied in the mere fact of the filing of an application in one of the countries of the Union.[1]

The language used by the draft was not particularly apt to impart to the first filing the meaning of warning alone. It spoke of every deposit as constituting a right of priority. Thus it made of the first filing an independent right, while the question was about the protection of the rights of the inventor for a certain time, as the Belgian delegate Demeur observed.[2] On the latter's motion, and after the British delegate had asked that for the words "constituera pour le déposant un droit" be substituted the words "le déposant pourra réclamer la priorité," [3] a new wording of article 4 was adopted, which has remained since practically unmodified: [4]

> Celui qui aura régulièrement fait le dépôt d'une demande . . . jouira, pour effectuer le dépôt dans les autres États . . . d'un droit de priorité pendant les délais . . .

Thus the right of priority exists in respect to a filing made within a specified period from the date of the first filing. It exists "for the purpose of filing application in the other countries." It serves to prevent the invalidation of such filing by acts performed in the interval.

§ 165. Right of priority is not an independent right but a legal defense only. It would seem, then, that the so-called right of priority may by no means be considered as an independent right, created by the first filing of a patent application, existing by itself for the specified period, and ceasing at the expiration of this period. The first filing, on the contrary, operates only as notice to the whole Union that a certain invention is claimed by a certain person. But this warning ceases to operate and has no effect in case the inventor does not apply in other countries of the Union within the specified period. It is only on the basis of this latter application that any question of his priority will be considered. The right of priority

1. The same idea of warning is better realized in the Madrid Trade Mark Arrangement and the Arrangement of The Hague by the registration of a trade mark and the deposit of an industrial design or model at the International Bureau. Cf. Pouillet, "Du Sens de l'Article 4 de la Convention," in *Propriété Industrielle* (1894), p. 21.

2. *Conférence de Paris* (1880), p. 50.

3. *Ibid.*, p. 51.

4. *Ibid.*, pp. 60–64.

is, then, a legal defense, accorded by article 4 of the Convention, to the persons admitted to its benefits, against the grounds of invalidation which, under the provisions of the municipal legislation concerning the novelty of the invention, might be opposed to them, or against persons who might file in the meantime a patent application for the same invention.

It has been said that this legal defense is based on the fiction that the subsequent filing in country B of the Union is supposed to have been made at the time of the first filing in Country A.[1] Yet this fiction, if resorted to, should be restricted to the purpose only of this right — that is, in regard to actions taken in the interval, in consequence of which, by force of the municipal legislation, the subsequent filing would be invalidated. It would seem wrong, therefore, to state generally that an invention by force of article 4 is protected from the first application.[2] Such a view would imply that all acts of infringement of the patent granted on the first application would be actionable and punishable in all other countries, before the filing of a patent application in these countries. Yet the opposite conclusion has always been supported in this respect, as will be seen later in this chapter. Equally wrong is the application given in England to article 4 by antedating the patent applied for under the provisions of this article to the date of the first application in the foreign country. On the other hand, it is likewise erroneous to consider the right of priority as an independent right, transferable by itself, and apart from the first patent application.[3]

It is believed that the precise nature of the right of priority as advanced here is in accordance with the history of article 4, and should be kept in mind in the solution of several questions to be considered below.

II. Persons Who may claim this Right

§ 166. "Ressortissants" of the Union. Article 4 provides that the right of priority is enjoyed, generally, by any person, "celui

1. *Propriété Industrielle* (1886), p. 19; Kohler, "Lettre d'Allemagne," in *Propriété Industrielle* (1892), p. 96.

2. Cottancin *c.* Hennebique, Cour d'Appel de Paris, May 14, 1902 (*Propriété Industrielle*, 1903, p. 195).

Ateliers de Construction d'Oerlikon *c.* Mertz, Tribunal Civil de la Seine, April 3, 1908 (*Gazette du Palais*, 1908, I, 550).

3. Austrian Patentamt, Sept. 20, 1912, and Nov. 9, 1912 (*Propriété Industrielle*, 1913, pp. 184, 185); German Patent Office, Dec. 16, 1905 (*Propriété Industrielle*, 1906, p. 134). Pillet, *Régime International*, p. 285, is of the opinion advanced in the text.

qui. . . ." This expression however purports only to delimit the right of priority, and has no relation to the general question of the persons entitled to the benefit of article 4. The latter is determined by articles 2 and 3 and forms the subject of chapter VIII.[1]

The question whether nationals of a country of the Union may claim the benefits of the Convention, considered above, reappears here in relation to the right of priority. For instance, a French national files a patent application first in Germany, and then applies in France for a patent; may he claim the right of priority in the latter country by reason of his prior application in Germany? In France and Belgium this claim is allowed by court decisions and by legislation, and in Germany by decisions of the Patent Office.[2] Under the Austrian law,[3] nationals may claim the right of priority only in case they are domiciled, or possess effective and *bona fide* commercial or industrial establishments, in the territory of a country of the Union.[4] In Great Britain and the United States the municipal legislation which purports to give effect to article 4 of the Convention applies to all persons, nationals included.[5]

A person claiming right of priority under article 4 should be a national of one of the countries of the Union, or a person domiciled or possessing business establishments in the Union, at the time he first makes known his invention in the Union by filing a patent application in one of the member countries, as well as at the time he claims the right of priority at the subsequent filing.[6]

§ 167. Successors and assigns of first applicant. It was an open question until the revision of the Convention of 1883 at the Washington Conference of 1911, whether the assignee or legal representative of the person who first applied for a patent in a country of

1. See the preparatory work of the Paris Conference, *Conférence de 1880*, pp. 129 ff.; *Propriété Industrielle* (1910), p. 102; Weiss, *Traité*, II, 382 n. 1. Pelletier et Vidal-Naquet, *Convention d'Union*, p. 89, *accord.*

2. See *supra*, § 120.

3. Law of Dec. 29, 1908, sec. 2 (*Reichsgesetzblatt*, 1908, p. 933).

4. It has also been held that a national not domiciled or established in the territory of a contracting country may claim the right of priority if he claims it jointly with a person, not a national of Austria, admitted to the benefit of the Convention; see decision of the Austrian Patentamt, June 28, 1913 (*Propriété Industrielle*, 1913, p. 185).

5. British Act of 1907, as amended in 1919 (7 Edw. VII, c. 29, and 9 & 10 Geo. V, c. 80), sec. 91; United States Revised Statutes, sec. 4887.

6. See *supra*, § 110. A decision of the Austrian Patent Office of November 23, 1910 (*Propriété Industrielle*, 1911, p. 69) held that an inventor, not a national of a country of the Union, and not domiciled or possessing business establishments therein, who had filed a patent application in France and later acquired a domicil in France and filed a similar application in Austria, was not entitled to a right of priority.

the Union might claim the right of priority in the other countries. The affirmative was maintained by writers [1] and decided by the courts,[2] on the ground that the right of priority was impliedly assigned with the patent or patent application. This opinion found support in the preparatory work of the Paris Conference of 1880.[3]

In order to dissipate any doubt on this point [4] the Conference of Revision at Washington added the words "ou son ayant cause" in the first paragraph of article 4, thus making it clear that the first applicant, as well as his "ayant cause," may claim the right of priority. The term "ayant cause," as the British Delegate, Mr. Innes, declared at the Conference, is equivalent to the English expression: "heirs, executors, administrators and assigns." [5]

That the assignee should be a person admitted to the benefits of the Convention seems to have been the intention of the Washington Conference.[6] Already before this Conference the opinion granting to assignees of the first applicant the benefit of the right of priority maintained this limitation.[7] No doubt in this respect is possible, as no person may claim any benefit under the Convention unless he is a national of one of the contracting countries or a foreigner within the provisions of article 3.[8] On the other hand, it is not sufficient

1. Pelletier et Vidal-Naquet, *Convention d'Union*, pp. 89–90; Pillet, *Régime International*, p. 285; Osterrieth und Axster, *Pariser Konvention*, p. 74; Kohler, *Deutsches Patentrecht*, p. 294; *Propriété Industrielle* (1900), p. 65.

2. Allgemeine Elektrizitätsgesellschaft *v.* Compagnie des Lampes à Filament Métallique, Swiss Federal Tribunal, June 24, 1916 (*Arrêts du Tribunal Fédéral Suisse*, 1916, II, 400); Pratt *c.* Lycett, Cour de Paris, April 11, 1892 (*Dalloz*, 1892, II, 593).

3. The Belgian delegate Demeur, who proposed the text of article 4, stated that the applicant, as well as his assignees and successors, would enjoy the right of priority; see *Conférence de Paris* (1880), p. 61.

Allowing an assignee of the first applicant to claim the right of priority makes it possible for an inventor to transfer his rights to other persons in foreign countries, in which financial or other difficulties might prevent him from applying personally. See on this point Armengaud Jeune et Ed. Mack, Report in *Annuaire de l'Association Internationale* (1897), p. 426.

4. In Great Britain, where article 4 of the Convention was given effect, under the Patent Act of 1907, sec. 91, by antedating the British patent to the date of the foreign application, no such antedating could be claimed by the assignee of the first applicant or by his agent See Matter of Shallenberger's Application (1889), 6 R. P. C. 550; Matter of Carez's Application (1889), 6 R. P. C. 552. This was changed, in consequence of the revision of article 4 by the Washington Conference, by the act 4 & 5 Geo. V, c. 18.

5. *Actes de la Conférence de Washington*, p. 247.

6. See *Ibid.*, p. 275.

7. Pelletier et Vidal-Naquet, *Convention d'Union*, p. 89; Pillet, *Régime International*, p. 285; Osterrieth und Axster, *Pariser Konvention*, p. 74; Kohler, *Deutsches Patentrecht*, p. 296; *Propriété Industrielle* (1897), p. 167.

8. See decision of the Austrian Patent Office, Dec. 30, 1922 (*Propriété Industrielle*, 1924, p. 12), *semble*.

that the assignee of the first applicant be a "ressortissant" of the Union, if the assignor were not one. No right of priority exists based on an application not filed by a "ressortissant" of the Union.

The assignee who may claim the right of priority must have obtained the assignment after the first deposit of the patent application and before the subsequent filing in other countries. Indeed, there is no assignment of a patent application, or a patent, when no such application has yet been filed. And a person who files the subsequent patent application before obtaining an assignment by the first applicant is not the assignee of the latter at the moment the second filing is made; it is for the purpose of such filing that the right of priority is granted by the Convention.[1]

The form in which the assignment must be made is a general question of private international law. The law of the place where the assignment was made governs in such case (*locus regit actum*).[2]

The assignment need not be an out-and-out transfer of the rights of the inventor in all countries. It may be an assignment of such rights for a particular country. Nor is it implied that an assignment of a patent application or a patent in one country carries with it the right to claim the right of priority in the other countries of the Union.[3] Indeed, as is suggested above,[4] the patent granted to a foreign patentee is a new privilege, a new patent, though for the same invention; it is not a recognition of the privilege granted in the first country. The inventor may apply for and obtain as many patents as there are countries in which he desires to be protected. Consequently, he may assign his rights in the invention in one or several countries to other persons, although he retains his rights in other countries.[5]

1. Cf. German Patentamt, Dec. 16, 1905 (*Propriété Industrielle*, 1906, pp. 134–135).

2. In the above decision (see note 1) of the German Patent Office, there is a *dictum* to the contrary, in application of German municipal law.

3. So held by the Austrian Patentamt, Sept. 20, 1912, and Nov. 9, 1912 (*Propriété Industrielle*, 1913, pp. 184, 185) and by the German Patentamt, Dec. 16, 1905 (*Propriété Industrielle*, 1906, p. 134). The writer, however, disagrees with the ground of these decisions which state that, by the first application, as many rights of priority independent of each other are created as there are countries of the Union. See *supra*, § 165.

4. See *supra*, § 9.

5. Pillet (*Régime International*, p. 285) thinks that the right of priority cannot be claimed unless the first patent is assigned to the assignee. This is consistent with Pillet's theory of the grant of patents to foreign patentees as constituting a recognition and enforcement of vested rights.

III. Requirements of Prior Deposit

§ **168. Due filing of prior application.** The right of priority may be claimed by the person "qui aura régulièrement fait le dépôt d'une demande de brevet d'invention . . . dans l'un des pays contractants."

Three things, then, are required in respect to the prior deposit: (*a*) a due filing (*b*) of an application for a patent (*c*) in one of the countries of the Union..

(*a*) The word "régulièrement" refers to the formalities only of application, and not to substance, such as the right of the applicant in the invention. This point was discussed at the Conference of 1880 and it was agreed that the word applies only to the formalities.[1]

It is generally agreed that the question whether an application was duly filed or not is a question of fact, and is controlled by the law of the place where such filing was made.[2] An application, for example, is duly filed in France, if the formalities and conditions of the French law are complied with. An English court, passing on the question whether a prior application was duly filed in France, will decide it according to the French law. Thus if the administration of the country where the prior application was filed certifies that the application was filed in the prescribed manner, this cannot be put in issue in the country in which the right of priority is claimed.[3]

§ **169. No patent need be granted.** It is required that an application shall have been *filed* in one of the countries of the Union. It is not necessary then that a patent be granted on the application, and it is immaterial that the application has been abandoned or rejected before the filing of the new application at which the right of priority is claimed.[4] Were it otherwise, the right of priority would be of

1. *Conférence de Paris* (1880), pp. 61–62. See also Osterrieth und Axster, *Pariser Konvention*, pp. 69–70; Pelletier et Vidal-Naquet, *Convention d'Union*, pp. 102–103.

2. Pelletier et Vidal-Naquet, *Convention d'Union*, p. 102; Osterrieth und Axster, *Pariser Konvention*, p. 69; German Patentamt, Jan. 29, 1913 (*Propriété Industrielle*, 1913, p. 51); Austrian Patentamt, Nov. 19, 1921 (*Propriété Industrielle*, 1923, p. 87).

3. An applicant filed an application in Germany on Dec. 16, 1908, not in the prescribed manner. It was filed anew on March 24, 1909. The German Patent Office admitted Dec. 16, 1908 as the date of filing. The Austrian Patent Office, before which a right of priority was claimed, based on the German filing, considered that the "due filing" was made on December 16, 1908 and, consequently, that the right of priority began to run from that date. See decision of May 29, 1911, *Propriété Industrielle* (1912), p. 174.

4. Pillet, *Régime International*, p. 283; Bureau International, *Avis*, in *Propriété Industrielle* (1901), p. 96, and (1912), p. 76.

little use, especially to persons applying first in a country in which the system of previous examination of the invention prevails; for such examination often lasts for many months, and may extend beyond the period within which the right of priority may be claimed.

On the other hand, the supervening rejection of the application, or its abandonment by the inventor, in the first country is of no effect on subsequent applications. This is consistent with theories advanced here, that the patent granted later in another country is a new patent and a new privilege, though for the same invention, and that the first deposit of application is only a notice to the Union that a certain invention is claimed by the applicant. Furthermore the lack of effect on the right of priority of the rejection or abandonment of the first application saves the rights of assignees of the first applicant.

It should follow, also, that the fact of publication of the invention in the interval, in addition to the rejection or abandonment of the first application, has no effect on the right of priority.[1] The warning of the first filing still subsists.

§ 170. Prior application must be application for a patent. (*b*) The second requirement is that an application for a patent must have been filed. This implies that the documents accompanying an application, in particular the description or specification of the invention, must have been filed also. Indeed, this is clear from the nature of the right of priority constituting a notice or a disclosure of an invention to the Union. All applications, therefore, which are not accompanied by a disclosure of the invention, or which contain no request for the grant of a patent, are not applications for a patent in the meaning of article 4.

Thus the filing of a *caveat* in the United States or Canada is not a filing of a patent application. No grant of patent is requested by the *caveat*. The applicant thereby requests that his rights in the invention be reserved until he is able to make his invention more mature and then apply for a patent. It would seem, therefore, that a *caveat* cannot give rise to a right of priority.[2]

Nor does a reissue application in the United States constitute a patent application in the meaning of article 4. By such application

1. Pillet, *Régime International*, p. 284, *contra*. It would seem that this opinion is inconsistent with that of the same writer on page 283.

2. Osterrieth und Axster, *Pariser Konvention*, p. 73; *Propriété Industrielle* (1903), pp. 61–62, *accord*.

a reissue of a patent is asked when the original patent is inoperative or invalid by reason of a defective or insufficient specification, or by reason of the patentee's claiming as his invention or discovery more than he had a right to claim as new. This is not an independent application for a patent, but a granting of the same patent under a new form.[1]

On the contrary, the filing of an application in Switzerland or France, with a request for secrecy for a certain period,[2] is a patent application, and the period of the right of priority begins to run from such a filing.[3] The fact of non-publication by the administration of the description of the invention is immaterial. It is sufficient if a patent application has been filed. Indeed, the question of publication of the invention cannot be controlling, as it is altogether foreign to the application itself and subject to wide varieties in the different countries of the Union. Thus, in the United States pending applications are preserved in secrecy and are open to general inspection only after a patent has been issued.[4] On the contrary, in England, on the acceptance of the complete specification, the application and other documents are open to public inspection; even the provisional specification may be published.[5]

§ 171. Filing of provisional specification. The provisional protection enjoyed in Great Britain by the applicant filing a provisional specification is in one respect similar to the protection enjoyed by a person filing a *caveat* in the United States, inasmuch as it enables the inventor during the time of such provisional protection to improve and perfect his invention. However, the provisional specification accompanies an application, in which the applicant declares that he desires to obtain a patent; it may be required that suitable drawings

1. So held by the German Patentamt, Sept. 26, 1905 (*Propriété Industrielle*, 1906, p. 55).

2. Such application may be made in France by any person who asks a patent for an improvement of, or addition to, a patented invention. The application is preserved under seal for a year, at the end of which the seal is broken and the patent is delivered. Article 18 of the Law of 1844 (*Bulletin des Lois*, 1844, II, 18). In Switzerland, the applicant may request that the description of his invention be withheld from publication for a year. The patent is granted when the documents are ready for publication. Arts. 31 and 32 of the Law of 1907 (*Recueil Officiel des Lois*, N. S., XXIII, 631).

3. Bureau International, *Avis*, in *Propriété Industrielle* (1913), p. 30. A decision to the contrary, of the American Patent Office in the case Roschach *v.* Walker (1899), 88 O. G., 1333, is based on section 4887 of the Revised Statutes before its revision by the Act of March 3, 1897 (XXIX *Stat.*, 692).

4. *Rules of Practice* (U. S. Patent Office, 1925), Rules 15 and 16.

5. Patents and Designs Acts, 1907 and 1919, secs. 4 and 9 (7 Edw. VII, c. 29; 9 & 10 Geo. V, c. 80).

be supplied with it; it is referred to an examiner to report if it has been prepared in the prescribed manner; it must be followed by a complete specification, within nine months from the date of the application, at the risk of being considered as abandoned; lastly, the patent is dated from the filing of the application, whether the latter is accompanied by a provisional or a complete specification.[1] For all these reasons the filing of an application with a provisional specification is filing an application for a patent ("une demande de brevet") in the meaning of article 4 of the Covention.[2] It is another question, how far the disconformity between the provisional and the complete specification affects the extent of the right of priority. This is considered later in this chapter.[3]

§ 172. Only first filing of application entitles to the right of priority. Article 4 requires the filing of an application for a patent ("d'une demande de brevet)." It has been one of the most debatable questions until recently whether the words "le dépôt d'une demande" should be taken literally, or as meaning the filing of the *first* patent application. If these words be taken literally, then every application for a patent for the same invention, by the same inventor or his assigns, gives a new right of priority. Thus the inventor P might apply in his own country A for a patent, then, within a year, apply in country B, and within another year from such second application apply in country C, and so on. The inventor would have, in such case, not one right of priority, but several. Such was not the intention of the Conference of 1880, nor is it justified by the theory of the right of priority. The first application for a patent in one of the countries of the Union discloses the invention and affirms the priority of the inventor in question.

The writers were divided on this question, but the weight of au-

1. Patents and Designs Acts 1907 and 1919, secs. 1–5; Terrell, *Letters Patent*, p. 88.

2. *Propriété Industrielle*, Bureau International (1890), p. 135, and (1903), p. 198. Hardingham, "Lettre de Grande Bretagne," in *Propriété Industrielle* (1891), p. 7, and (1904), p. 44; Pouillet, "Du Sens de l'Article 4 de la Convention," in *Propriété Industrielle* (1894), p. 21; Pelletier et Vidal-Naquet, *Convention d'Union*, p. 103. The Civil Tribunal of Brussels, in Pneumatic Tyre Co. *c.* Ateliers de la Seine, Feb. 26, 1896 (*Propriété Industrielle*, 1896, p. 126), held that the period of priority begins to run from the filing of the provisional specification. Similarly, in England it is held that an opponent will not be allowed to rely on a prior application filed between the applicant's provisional and complete specifications under article 4 of the Convention. Thus, the filing of a provisional specification is deemed to determine the question of priority. See (1913) 30 R. P. C. Ruling A.

3. See *infra*, § 190.

thority was in favor of the restrictive interpretation of article 4.[1] The courts also held in accordance with this opinion.[2] The German Patent Office had changed the tenor of its prior decisions on this matter and admitted the opinion that a right of priority may be based on the first as well as on all intervening applications.[3] With the express purpose of affirming the unsoundness of this opinion, a provision was added in the second paragraph of section (*c*) of article 4, by the Conference of The Hague, on the proposal of the International Bureau, reading as follows:[4] "Ces délais [les délais de priorité] commencent à courir de la date du dépôt de la première demande dans un pays de l'Union."

The right of priority is based, therefore, on the first application in one of the countries of the Union. If, before the deposit of such an application, the inventor had already applied in a country not a member of the Union, it would seem that he still may claim a right of priority on the basis of his first application in the Union, provided his invention has received no publication, and no application by another person for the same invention has been filed.[5]

§ 173. Prior application must have been filed in a country of the Union. (*c*) The prior application must have been filed in one of the contracting countries ("dans l'un des pays contractants"). This is quite clear on the theory of the right of priority adopted here, that is, the theory of disclosure of the invention and notice by the inventor to the whole Union. No such disclosure to the Union exists when the country in which the application is filed is not a member. Whether or not the country in which the first application is deposited accedes to the Union before the subsequent deposit of a patent application in a country of the Union is immaterial. On the contrary, if the first filing is made in a country of the Union and the

1. For a restrictive interpretation, Osterrieth und Axster, *Pariser Konvention*, p. 73; Damme, *Patentrecht*, p. 243; Wirth und Ganz, in *Annuaire de l'Association Internationale* (1904), p. 43; Pelletier et Vidal-Naquet, *Convention d'Union*, p. 95, *semble*; *Propriété Industrielle*, Bureau International (1907), p. 172; (1914), p. 14; (1924), p. 210. In favor of the opposite opinion, Kent, *Patentgesetz*, p. 74; Seligsohn, *Patentgesetz*, 5th ed., p. 526; Ephraim, in *Annuaire de l'Association Internationale* (1903), p. 123.

2. Cour de Bruxelles, July 31, 1925 (*Propriété Industrielle*, 1926, p. 21); Dutch Patent Office, Oct. 21, 1918 (*Propriété Industrielle*, 1918, p. 140); Austrian Patentamt, Dec. 30, 1911, March 2, 1912, and July 4, 1914 (*Propriété Industrielle*, 1913, p. 45, and 1916, p. 38).

3. German Patentamt, June 27, 1913 (*Propriété Industrielle*, 1914, p. 11).

4. *Actes de la Conférence de La Haye*, pp. 226, 518.

5. Pillet, *Régime International*, p. 272; Bureau International, *Avis*, in *Propriété Industrielle*, 1900, p. 46.

new filing in a country which in the meantime has acceded to the Union, the right of priority may be claimed from the time the Convention became effective in the latter country. Article 4 does not require that the country in which the subsequent filing is made shall be a member of the Union at the time the first deposit is made. It is sufficient if it be so at the time the right of priority is claimed.[1]

It is not necessary that the country in which the first application is filed be the country of origin of the applicant. It may be any other country of the Union.[2] The opposite is true as to validation of trade marks under article 6 of the Convention, by express provision of that article.

IV. Period of Right of Priority

§ 174. Fixing period by weighing conflicting interests. The right of priority purports to secure the interests of an inventor against acts that might destroy the novelty of his invention until he is able to apply in the various countries for patents. The presumption, then, is that the inventor will seek to obtain patents in the other countries of the Union. This he should be compelled to do in a relatively short time. His notice to the Union keeps in suspense two classes of persons in all the countries of the Union: first, the manufacturers, who are attentive to every improvement and every new idea, and are ready to apply them to their production for the benefit of the general public; second, the experts and inventors in other countries, who may invent the same thing and should be allowed to claim the reward of their efforts.

The period, therefore, within which the right of priority may be claimed should not be too long. On the other hand, it should not be too short. It should be measured by the purpose and object of this right. A sufficient time should be given to the first applicant to overcome the difficulties at home and abroad, to ascertain the results and business possibilities of his invention, to solve the financial difficul-

1. The German and Austrian patent offices have held the opposite, in respect to claims of right of priority based on prior applications filed in countries of the Union before the accession of Germany or that of Austria. See *Propriété Industrielle* (1905), p. 23; (1906), p. 55; and (1909), p. 22. The German Reichsgericht decided in accordance with the opinion in the text, accepting the view taken by Kohler, Osterrieth, and Schanze, with the sound reservation that all rights vested before the Convention entered into effect (rights of another applicant or of the public through publication of the invention) are preserved. See decision of Nov. 9, 1912 (*Entsch. Reichsg., Zivilsachen*, N. F., XXX, 375).

2. Pelletier et Vidal-Naquet, *Convention d'Union*, p. 109; Decision of the Austrian Ministry of Public Works, February 1, 1910 (*Propriété Industrielle*, 1913, p. 43).

ties involved in applications in foreign countries, to secure agents or assignees in those countries, to communicate with them, and to satisfy the legal formalities and conditions in each country. All this is by no means an easy matter. It is much more difficult when the first application is filed in a country in which the system of previous examination of the invention prevails.

Indeed, in the countries in which a patent is granted without any search into the novelty or patentability of the invention, the applicant obtains his patent in a short time (generally in a few weeks). The patentee may easily sell his invention and, not being handicapped at home, he may give all his attention to securing patents in foreign countries. On the contrary, in countries in which every invention is examined as to its novelty, patentability, and so on, a very long time is often required before a patent may be granted to an applicant. It appears, for example, from statistical data of the American and German patent offices that in many cases more than a year, indeed, sometimes two, five, ten, and fifteen years elapse before the grant of a patent.[1] In such countries it is very difficult for an applicant to apply for a foreign patent, at least before the examination of his invention has well progressed.[2]

At the Conference of 1880, at the end of a long discussion on this point, the period of the right of priority for patent applications was fixed at six months.[3]

§ 175. Starting-point of period. The question of length of the period is closely connected with that of its starting-point. Article 4 did not specify the date from which the period of the right of priority begins. At the Conference of The Hague a provision was added to section (*c*) to the effect that the period begins to run from the date of the first filing. Already before this amendment it was generally admitted that the period starts from the first filing on which the claim for a right of priority is based.[4] It was soon found,

1. Wirth, "De la Protection des Inventions dans l'Union," in *Annuaire de l'Association Internationale* (1897), pp. 212, 224.

2. Max Georgii, "Report on the United States and the Convention of 1883" in *Annuaire de l'Association Internationale* (1897), pp. 391, 393–394.

3. The period for countries beyond the seas was longer by a month, that is to say, seven months, by express provision of article 4. Great Britain and the colonies and possessions of continental countries raised difficulties on the question whether or not they were to be deemed as beyond the seas. See on this, Pelletier et Vidal-Naquet, *Convention d'Union*, pp. 93–94.

4. Pillet, *Régime International*, pp. 273–274; Pelletier et Vidal-Naquet, *Convention d'Union*, pp. 92, 95; Osterrieth und Axster, *Pariser Konvention*, p. 73. See also the

after the creation of the Union, that a period of six months starting from the first filing was too short for an effective securing of the interests of inventors, especially those who deposited their first application in countries in which the system of previous examination of the invention prevailed. Various suggestions were then made with the purpose of making the period longer.

§ 176. American proposal for changing starting-point, and its advantages. Thus, it was proposed by the American delegation at the Madrid Conference of 1890 that the period of the right of priority should begin from the date of the official publication of the invention, instead of the date of filing the first application. This amendment was deemed necessary for the protection of the interests of American inventors, for two reasons. It was practically impossible for them to obtain an American patent before the lapse of the period of six months. If they decided to await the grant of the patent before applying in foreign countries, as in many cases they had to do for practical reasons, this benefit of the Convention was lost to them. On the other hand, if they chose to file patent applications in foreign countries before the grant of the patent in the United States, they might be granted a foreign patent before the issue of the American patent, or their invention might be published abroad, while it was preserved in secrecy by the Patent Office of the United States. Both cases were undesirable. For, under the law of the United States, the duration of a patent could not exceed the term of a foreign patent issued to the inventor for the same invention. In many countries the term of a patent is shorter than that of an American patent, so that the last would be cut down. On the other hand, the publicity given to the invention in foreign countries might be prejudicial to the American patentee in the United States Patent Office in the question of determination of priority in interference proceedings.[1]

As was also observed by the American delegate, Mr. Forbes, the real object of the right of priority was to prevent the loss of the novelty of the invention, especially by publication following the application for a patent. Such publication was made soon after the filing of the application in other countries, and therefore it was proper and convenient to have the period of the right of priority

Belgian case, Wauters et Loesser *c.* Ries et Cie., Cassation, Dec. 28, 1905 (*Pasicrisie*, 1906, I, 71).

1. See *Conférence de Madrid*, p. 52.

start from such filing. Such was not the case in the United States. In this country, the invention was preserved in secrecy pending the application and was published at the date of the grant of the patent. The date of filing of application in the United States was too remote and too unconnected with the real object of the right of priority, namely, the publication of the invention.[1] This is the reason why the American delegation proposed that the period of the right of priority should begin to run from the date of the official publication of the invention. The proposal was not assented to by the other delegations, especially on the ground that, by reason of the diversity of legislation in the various countries, it was very difficult to say when the first official publication of the invention took place.

The American delegation declared its readiness to accept either of two other proposals made by the Swiss and Belgian delegations. The first repeated the American proposal in a modified form. Every country would have the right to determine that, for all patent applications filed in its territory, the right of priority should begin to run from the official publication of the invention. This proposal, as well as that of the American delegation, did not tend to extend the length of the period. The period would still be six months. It would merely begin later. The disclosure of the invention to the Union would be deemed to have taken place at the date of its official publication in any country of the Union (or, according to the Swiss proposal, in the country of the Union which should choose to determine the period in this way). All acts which might destroy the novelty of an invention in the interval between the filing of the application and the official publication of the invention would not be covered by the right of priority.[2] This point, although stressed by the American delegation, does not seem to have been quite realized by the other delegations. Thus, the French delegates argued repeatedly against the American and Swiss proposals on the ground of the uncertainty which would reign in the industry because of the long period resulting between the filing of the application and the grant of the patent in the United States.[3]

The American and Swiss proposals had a further advantage, besides that of making the right of priority equally beneficial to inventors of all countries. In countries in which the system of previous

1. See *Conférence de Madrid*, pp. 93–94.
2. *Ibid.*, pp. 105, 120.
3. *Ibid.*, pp. 104–105 (Mr. Nicolas) and 122 (Mr. Pelletier).

examination of the invention prevails, it is often possible to amend and perfect the substance of the invention during the time of the examination. Some claims are abandoned and others are improved. Thus, the original description of the invention is sometimes modified at the end of the examination by the patent office. This is most conspicuously so in Great Britain, where the provisional specification is followed within nine months by the complete specification. Inventors would prefer that the description of their invention in its final shape should be the basis of their right of priority.[1] And this could have been provided for by making the period of the right of priority begin to run from the official publication of the invention. The Swiss proposal was defeated, the majority of the delegates be ing unwilling to accept any amendment which would require a change in their laws.

§ 177. **Wiping out of previous disadvantages by extension of period.** The Belgian proposal to the effect that the period be increased from six to twelve months was eventually withdrawn at the Madrid Conference. The Brussels Conference, giving effect to the *voeux* adopted by the successive congresses of the International Association for the Protection of Industrial Property (Vienna, 1897; London, 1898; Zurich 1899; Paris, 1900),[2] increased the period from six to twelve months. In the meantime the United States had revised (by the Act of March 3, 1897) section 4887 of the Revised Statutes, thus doing away with the provisions of this section limiting the term of the United States patent by that of a foreign patent. This state of the municipal law in the United States, coupled with the extension of the period to twelve months, wiped out many of the disadvantages previously existing for American inventors.

The extension of the period of the right of priority to twelve months made possible the accession of Germany to the Union. This country, having the system of previous examination of the invention, labored under the same difficulties as the United States. In its bipartite treaties with some countries (Austria-Hungary, Switzerland,

1. The difficulties arising in this respect are considered below, § 190. See also Wirth, "De la Protection des Inventions dans l'Union," in *Annuaire de l'Association* (1897), pp. 212, 226 ff.

2. See these *voeux* in *Tableau des Voeux* (Bureau International, 1883- 1909), pp. 10–11; and *Annuaire de l'Association* (1897), p. 65. The Swiss proposal was taken up again at the Congress of the Association in 1897, with much ability and vigor, by Mr. Wirth, a German representative, and Mr. Maillard, a French representative. See reports and discussion, *Annuaire de l'Association* (1897), pp. 62–65, 170 ff., 219 ff.

and Italy) Germany had adopted a different system as to the period of the right of priority. The period was three months only, beginning to run from the delivery of the patent to the first applicant; but the invention was also protected from the time of filing the first application. Thus, the period of three months was added to the period during which the invention was being examined in the Patent Office, however long the latter might happen to be.[1] Such a system would be inapplicable in the Union. The cases of injustice and inequality between the various countries would be too great, in view of the diversity of legislation among members of the Union. Germany, therefore, was satisfied with the extension of the period to twelve months.

At the Conference of The Hague, the Belgian delegation proposed that the period be extended to eighteen months. This proposal, although supported by the International Chamber of Commerce, was voted down by all the other delegations including the American.[2] A longer period does not seem necessary.

The extension of the period in 1900 from six to twelve months raised the question of its applicability to patent applications filed before the going into effect of the Additional Act of Brussels. The question, of course, concerned only applications in respect to which the period of six months had not expired at the moment of the going into effect of the above act. From the nature of the right of priority, it is clear that such applicability should be admitted. It was so understood by the Brussels Conference.[3] The United States Patent Office decided the same way, though applying immediately the Act of Congress giving effect to the Additional Act of Brussels.[4]

§ 178. Computation of period. Article 4 of the Convention contained until recently no provision for the computation of the

1. Articles 3 and 4 of the Convention of Dec. 6, 1891, between Germany and Austria-Hungary (*De Martens*, N. R., 2d ser., XVII, 930); articles 3 and 4 of the Convention of Jan. 18, 1892, between Germany and Italy (*Ibid.*, 637); arts. 3 and 4 of the Convention of April 13, 1892, between Germany and Switzerland (*Ibid.*, XXI, 514).

2. *Actes de la Conférence de La Haye*, p. 427.

3. The Italian delegation desired that this view be affirmed by the Conference. The Director of the International Bureau stated that this needed no affirmation, and deemed sufficient the insertion of these declarations in the *procès-verbaux* of the Conference. See *Conférence de Bruxelles*, pp. 388, 389.

4. *Ex parte* Klingelfuss (1903), 104 O. G. 2149. See also information to the International Bureau, in *Propriété Industrielle* (1903), p. 89; Stiff *v.* Galbraith (1903), 107 O. G. 2532, *semble.*

period of the right of priority. Consequently, this question was decided in every case according to the law of the country in which the right of priority was claimed. Thus:

(*a*) The date of filing was counted in the period, in Brazil, France, Great Britain, Italy, the Netherlands, Norway, Portugal, Serb-Croat-Slovene State, Spain, and Tunis. It was not counted in Austria, Belgium, Denmark, Japan, Sweden, and the United States.

(*b*) The period was from date to date inclusive in Belgium, Brazil, Denmark, France, Great Britain, Italy, the Netherlands, Norway, Portugal, Serb-Croat-Slovene State, Spain, and Tunis; that is to say, in these countries a period beginning on the tenth of July, 1920, would terminate on the tenth of July, 1921. In the United States, the months were computed according to the calendar, which is not different from the above system in case the period is twelve months. In Japan, the period was computed according to the civil year, while in Sweden the months were reckoned at thirty days each.[1]

(*c*) The question of holidays was another point of diversity. In Belgium, France, Italy, Japan, the Netherlands, Norway, Serb-Croat-Slovene State, Tunis, and the United States, if the last day of the period happened to fall on a Sunday or a holiday, it had no effect on the period; consequently, the filing of the patent application for which a right of priority was claimed should be made on the day before. In Brazil, Denmark, Great Britain, Portugal, Spain, and Sweden, if the last day of the period happened to be Sunday or a holiday, the termination of the period was postponed until the next day.[2]

To put an end to these diversities, the Conference of The Hague, at the proposal of the International Bureau, adopted an amendment to article 4, section (*c*), reading as follows:[3]

1. In Japan the period ends on the eve of the corresponding date of the last month of the period, unless it begins on the first day of a month, or the last month of the period has no corresponding date; in the latter case, the period ends on the last day of that month. In Sweden twelve months means 360 days.

2. See on all this an inquiry of the International Bureau, *Propriété Industrielle* (1897), pp. 155 ff.; (1898), p. 49; and (1901), p. 54. See also, as to the United States, the cases *ex parte* Ravelli (1907), 130 O. G. 982, and *ex parte* Meier (1908), 136 O. G. 657; as to Austria, Decision of the Patent Office, Oct. 22, 1910 (*Propriété Industrielle*, 1913, p. 44).

3. *Actes de la Conférence de La Haye*, pp. 227, 518, 538, 572. It was agreed at the Conference, on the suggestion of the delegation of the Serb-Croat-Slovene State, that holidays do not comprise the vacations of the administration. *Ibid.*, p. 427.

Ces délais commencent à courir de la date du dépôt de la première demande dans un pays de l'Union; le jour du dépôt n'est pas compris dans le délai.

Si le dernier jour du délai est un jour férié légal dans le pays où la protection est réclamée, le délai sera prorogé jusqu'au premier jour ouvrable qui suit.

The original proposal of the International Bureau provided that the period should begin from the date of the first filing, and include the anniversary ("le jour anniversaire") of that date. It would seem that the proposal of the Bureau should have been preferred. It would have solved all difficulties. There is no uncertainty as to the anniversary of a day. But it was objected that the expression could not be successfully translated into English, and did not apply to the periods of priority for designs, models, and trade marks, which are less than a year.

According to the provision adopted, it is now certain that the day of the filing is not taken into account in the computation of the period. But the previous uncertainty as to the end of the period has been allowed to continue.[1]

The question of holidays is now solved. If the last day happens to be a legal holiday in the country in which the right of priority is claimed, the period is extended until the next working day.[2]

The Belgian National Association on Industrial Property adopted a resolution, at its meeting of February 28, 1925, that it should be possible to extend the period of the right of priority, or to reinstate an applicant if the period lapsed without his fault. The *voeu* seems sound, with the qualification that rights of third parties should be preserved.[3]

1. See as to the municipal law of various countries, generally, Francis Deàk "The Computation of Time in International Law" (1926), *Am. Jour. Int. Law*, XX, 502, 509 ff.

2. Does filing within the period mean actual filing, or is it sufficient that the application has been mailed? The United States Patent Office required actual filing, on the ground that the postal authorities are not agents of the Government. *Ex parte* Meier (1908), 136 O. G. 657.

3. See above resolution in *Propriété Industrielle* (1925), p. 79. A decision of the Austrian Patent Office of Nov. 21, 1922, refused to extend the period for a single day, the application having reached the office one day late, because of a strike of the post office employees. *Propriété Industrielle* (1924), p. 12.

V. Conditions and Formalities for Claiming Right of Priority

§ 179. Situation prior to the Washington Conference. The original article 4 of the Convention did not provide when and how the right of priority might be claimed. Of course, it could be claimed in relation to all subsequent filings of applications made within the specified period from the first deposit of an application for a patent for an invention. Questions arose as to whether the applicant should claim his right of priority at the moment of filing his subsequent applications in other countries, or at a later time, when the priority or validity of the invention came in issue in the patent office or in the courts; also as to the form in which the right of priority could be claimed, and as to the consequences for any omission in this respect. All these questions were disputed by writers and decided differently by various countries of the Union.

It may be admitted that article 4 did not purport to prevent any country from requiring special formalities for the claim of a right of priority. This was generally so understood.[1] Before the Washington Conference of Revision, some countries of the Union required no declaration and no formality whatsoever. The applicant might claim the right of priority at any time after the grant of a patent. This was not quite fair to national inventors and the public in general. An inventor applying for a patent in his own country used his utmost diligence to discover any previous application for the same invention in his own country. Ordinarily, he waited for a year after his filing, in order to be certain that no application for the same invention was made by another person claiming a right of priority. For in such case this latter person prevailed. But, when the law did not require a declaration of a claim of a right of priority, it was not always of use for him to search into the applications filed during the twelve months following his filing. In the countries in which opposition or interference was possible before the grant of patents, the foreign applicant might have been forced to declare his claim of a right of priority. In the other countries this was not possible. For this reason the inventor, even if he discovered, during the year following his filing, another application for the same invention, had no means of knowing that this application was filed with the

1. *Propriété Industrielle* (1895), p. 135; Pelletier et Vidal-Naquet, *Convention d'Union*, p. 101.

protection of the right of priority. He then reasonably believed himself to be the first inventor. He made preparations for the working of his invention, incurred expenses for manufacturing goods, and sold his invention to third parties. Suddenly, he was told that his patent was not good, that another claimed a right of priority which was then for the first time made known. Thus, the innocent inventor and persons to whom he may have granted licenses to work his invention, or others selling the goods manufactured by the invention — all these people were in danger of serious losses and perhaps liable for infringement.[1]

Many countries of the Union required a mere declaration concerning the prior filing, either at the time of filing the new application or within a specified period. And, in still other countries, the declaration as to the prior filing had to be supported by various documents and information duly verified and authenticated.[2] In most of the latter countries, in case the formalities were not complied with within the periods specified by the law of each country, the right of priority was lost.[3]

§ **180. Addition of new provisions to article 4.** The Washington Conference, seeking to introduce a certain uniformity in respect to the formalities required for claiming a right of priority, added two new sections, (*d*) and (*e*), to article 4. The amendment, as originally proposed by the International Bureau, was much simpler; it aimed to require the necessary declaration in respect to the first filing, and to free the applicants from needless and excessive formalities. It gave effect to the *voeux* adopted by the successive congresses of the International Association for the Protection of Industrial Property.[4] The enjoyment of the right of priority would have been made subject to no other condition or formality except that of the deposit of a copy of the first application, verified by the administration to which it was submitted. However, the proposition did not pre-

1. Pilenco, "La Question des Formalités," in *Propriété Industrielle* (1897), pp. 171, 174.

2. See a compilation of these formalities in *Actes de la Conférence de Washington*, pp. 119–122.

3. Austrian Patentamt, Nov. 19, 1912 (*Propriété Industrielle*, 1914, p. 133); Great Britain, Acetylene Ill. Co. *v.* United Alkali Co. (1902), 19 R. P. C. 213, affirmed in (1902), 20 R. P. C. 161. See as to the other countries, *Propriété Industrielle* (1897), pp. 135, 136.

4. See proposal of the Bureau, in *Actes de la Conférence de Washington*, p. 46, and *voeux* of the congresses, in *Annuaire de l'Association* (1897), p. 98; (1898), p. 491; (1899), p. 147; (1900), p. 486; and *voeux*, in *Actes de la Conférence de Washington*, pp. 361–363.

scribe the time when, or the period within which, such copy should be deposited.

The text of paragraph (*d*) was taken, with one exception (concerning the time when the declaration as to the first deposit should be made), from a proposal submitted by the German administration.[1] There are five questions concerning the formalities for claiming a right of priority, which now are dealt with in article 4:

§ 181. Declaration concerning country and date of first filing. (*a*) According to the proposal of the German administration, on the filing of the new application, a declaration would be made concerning the country and date of the first filing. The Conference did not deem it proper to impose on all the countries this requirement. Instead, it adopted the provision that each country may determine for itself the latest time at which this declaration must be made. The information given by such declaration must be inserted in the publications issued by the competent administration, particularly in the patent and the specifications relative thereto. This last obligation, imposed on the administration of each country, limits necessarily the time within which the declaration as to the country and date of the first filing must be made. It must be made before delivery of the patent or publication of the specifications.

The provision for a declaration of priority is mandatory. Whoever wishes to avail himself of the priority of an anterior filing shall be bound ("sera tenu") to make the declaration. It would seem, therefore, that the making of the declaration is a condition for claiming the right of priority. The absence of such declaration might possibly constitute a ground for invalidation of the patent issued. This is especially interesting when one recalls that some countries, such as France, did not require such a declaration before the revision of the Convention at the Washington Conference. Thus the Convention undertakes to protect French inventors and the French public against foreign inventors claiming a right of priority, while the French municipal law does not afford such protection. This exhibits the character of the Convention as one of international legislation for the Union rather than one of mere international engagement.

The power given to each country to determine the time within which the declaration in question must be made might be explained

1. *Actes de la Conférence de Washington*, pp. 91–92, 276.

by the differences in the modes of administrative procedure in granting a patent. In the countries in which the invention is merely registered and the patent granted within a few weeks following application, the information as to the date and country of the first deposit may be required at the moment of filing the patent application, or shortly thereafter. On the other hand, in the countries in which the invention is subjected to previous examination and a patent granted only after a long time, the declaration showing the date and country of the first filing might be made long after filing the patent application.

Yet in practice the differences are not along this line. The requirement that the declaration in question be made at the time of filing the patent application exists in the following countries, which follow either of the two systems of administrative procedure: Austria, Belgium, Bulgaria, Czechoslovakia, Danzig, Germany, Great Britain, Greece, Hungary, Italy, Japan, Morocco, Norway, the Netherlands, Poland, Portugal, Rumania, Serb-Croat-Slovene State, and the United States. On the contrary, in France, Luxembourg, and Tunis the declaration must be made, at the latest, within sixty days from the filing of the patent application; in Denmark and Sweden, before the publication of the application; in Brazil, before examination of the invention; in Finland and Switzerland, before the delivery of the patent.[1] In Cuba, Dominican Republic, Esthonia, Mexico, and Spain the law does not provide the time within which the declaration in question should be made.

§ 182. Production of certificate of the date of first filing. (*b*) In the countries of the Union in which the application is not subject to previous examination in respect to the novelty of the invention, the mere declaration of the country and date of an anterior filing may be sufficient. Like all other allegations of the applicant, this also is merely registered by the administration for the information of all third parties. The truthfulness of the allegation of the anterior filing, as of all other allegations, remains to be proved in court proceedings involving the validity of the patent. On the other hand, in all countries in which all allegations of the applicant, in particular that of novelty of the invention, are subject to examination by the administration or to opposition by third parties, it might be expected

1. *Propriété Industrielle* (1924), pp. 208, 209. *Actes de la Conférence de La Haye*, pp. 129–133.

that the declaration showing the country and date of the anterior filing should be proved by the applicant.

This explains the further provision in article 4, that the contracting countries may require ("pourront exiger") any person making a declaration of prior filing to produce a certificate from the proper authority showing the date of the deposit, and also a translation. This provision is not mandatory. A country may or may not require such a certificate. It is rather intended to allow a country of the Union to impose such a requirement.

§ 183. Production of a copy of first application. (*c*) As will be seen, the right of priority is enjoyed when the prior and subsequent applications concern the same invention. Whether the invention is really the same will be looked into only in the countries in which the system of previous examination of the application prevails. In these countries, it might be expected that the administration would require the production not only of a certificate of the date of the first deposit, but also of the proof that the new application concerns the same invention as the prior one.

A provision of section (*d*) of article 4 allows the members of the Union to require such proof. In order, however, to avoid the possible diversity of municipal law on this matter, it specifies that the only thing that may be required is a copy of the application (with the specification, drawings, and so forth) of the anterior filing.[1] It expressly provides that no legalization of this copy may be required. It is sufficient if it is certified as correct by the authority which received the application. But a country may require a certificate of the date of filing such application and a translation.

No provision was made in article 4, before the revision of the Convention at the Conference of The Hague, in respect to the time when this copy of the first application should be produced. It might be inferred that a country may require such production at the time of the declaration of the right of priority. Thus, a country might require presentation of the copy of the specification, drawings, and so forth, at the time of filing the patent application. This might be too

1. If priority is claimed on the basis of an anterior filing in a country in which an application may be deposited with a provisional specification followed by a complete specification later, the copy to be filed in the second country is the provisional specification. The complete specification might be filed instead, if it were accompanied by certification of the patent office that it in no way differs from the provisional specification. It was so held by the Austrian Patentamt, Jan. 21, 1915 (*Propriété Industrielle*, 1917, p. 89).

stringent in certain cases. At the Conference of The Hague, on the proposal of the United States, a provision was added, to the effect that the copy of the application might be filed at any time within three months from the deposit of the subsequent application.[1]

§ **184. Production of further proof.** (*d*) The certificate concerning the date and country of the anterior filing, a copy of the application (with specification, drawings, and so forth) and a translation thereof, constitute the maximum of formalities which a country of the Union may require for claiming a right of priority at the time of depositing the application ("au moment du dépôt de la demande").[2] On the contrary, article 4 permits a country of the Union to require further proof of the right of priority at a later stage of the administrative procedure, and, of course, in court proceedings. The last paragraph of section (*d*) of article 4 provides expressly that "ultérieurement d'autres justifications pourront être demandées." Thus, the proof that the applicant is the successor or assignee of the person who filed the first application cannot be required at the time of depositing the subsequent application, although it may be required later. The expression "ultérieurement" is, of course, very uncertain, and may mean very shortly after the deposit of the application.

§ **185. Consequences following the omission of prescribed formalities.** (*e*) Article 4, fourth paragraph of section (*d*), permits each country of the Union to determine for itself what consequences shall follow the omission of the formalities prescribed above; such consequences, however, shall in no case be more serious than the loss of the right of priority ("sans que ces conséquences puissent excéder la perte du droit de priorité"). In many cases the loss of the right of priority entails loss of the right to a patent. This is the case when, before the filing of the second application, the invention received publicity destroying the novelty of the invention, according to the law of the country in question.

For foreign applicants compliance with the formalities required in each country is not always an easy matter. The preparing of documents requires much time, and errors are always likely to occur. It should be possible to correct mistakes and satisfy the administrative

1. See *Actes de la Conférence de La Haye*, pp. 336, 429, 518.

2. That they constitute the maximum is clear from the provision of the fourth paragraph of section (*d*) of article 4: "D'autres formalités ne pourront être requises"; also from the report of the Sub-Committee at the Washington Conference, *Actes de la Conference de Washington*, p. 276. *Propriété Industrielle* (1911), p. 115, *accord.*

rules within a short time after filing the various documents. Practice has shown many cases of real hardship,[1] especially in Germany and Austria, where formalism reaches its height in this matter. In particular, the obligation of producing the documents proving the priority should be more liberal.[2]

§ 186. Proposals for revision at the Conference of The Hague. The German and French groups of the International Association for the Protection of Industrial Property, meeting soon after the World War, adopted a number of resolutions calling for a liberalization of the formalities of the right of priority.[3] Both groups were desirous of granting to the person claiming a right of priority a period within which the declaration of priority should be made after the filing of the new application, and a longer period for the deposit of the documents proving such priority. The German group decided that a minimum period of one month should be accorded for the declaration, with the privilege of correcting within that time the information given originally. The French group wished that the minimum period should be three months. As to the period for producing the documents proving the priority, both groups wished a minimum of six months. The French group thought also that no

1. The German Patent Office held that the right of priority was lost in the following cases. (*a*) An Austrian applicant, on filing an application in Germany, declared the country of the prior filing, but not the date. The omission was corrected before any official communication to the applicant. (Decision of April 25, 1914; *Propriété Industrielle*, 1914, p. 118.) (*b*) An English applicant declared the number and year of his prior filing and added that the exact date of filing would be indicated later. (Decision of Sept. 24, 1917; *Propriété Industrielle*, 1918, p. 81.)

The Austrian Patent Office held that the right of priority was lost in the case of the declaration of a prior filing indicating erroneously as date of filing the 19th instead of the 27th Nov., 1919. The mistake was corrected fourteen days later. (Decision of Dec. 9, 1921; *Propriété Industrielle*, 1922, p. 157.)

In a similar case the German Patent Office allowed correction on the ground that the letter of the law had been complied with by indicating a date. (Decision of Feb. 3, 1924; *Propriété Industrielle*, 1924, p. 127.) But an earlier case of this office refused to allow correction of a fictitious date. (Decision of Dec. 19, 1914; *Propriété Industrielle*, 1915, p. 8.)

2. The Austrian Patent Office declared the right of priority lost: (*a*) because a due certification of the German translation of the documents was not submitted within the prescribed time (decisions of Feb. 16, 1923, and Dec. 17, 1924; *Propriété Industrielle*, 1924, p. 13, and, 1926, p. 102); and (*b*) because the German translation was not submitted with the application on Dec. 7, 1923, but a few days later, namely, Dec. 15, 1923, although it was admitted that all officials of the Austrian Patent Office knew English, and English specifications had been deposited in time. (Decision of April 1, 1925; *Propriété Industrielle*, 1926, p. 102.)

3. See *voeux*, in *Conférence de La Haye, Documents Préliminaires*, 2me fascicule, pp. 7–8 and 10–11.

penalty should be imposed for failure to comply with the above obligation, at least when the applicant showed that he did his best within the period to obtain the required documents.

At the Conference of The Hague the French administration proposed that the declaration of priority be made within a period following the new filing of application. This period should be no less than three months, provided that the patent is not delivered before the expiration of such period. On the other hand, the American delegation proposed the insertion of a provision to the effect that the copy of the application (with specification, and so forth) may be deposited at any time within six months following the date of filing the application, without penalty of fine for such delay. [1] The American proposal was supported by the International Chamber of Commerce. It was finally adopted for half the time proposed as seen above.[2] The French proposal did not meet with the agreement of the other delegations, so that each country of the Union is still free to require that the declaration of priority be made on the filing of a patent application.[3]

VI. Identity of the First and Subsequent Applications

§ 187. Identity of applicants in the two applications. The right of priority is granted by article 4 of the Convention for the purpose of filing application in the other countries ("pour effectuer le dépôt dans les autres pays"). Although it is not expressly said that the new application must be for the same invention, this is necessarily so. The object of the right of priority, as is explained at the beginning of this chapter, is to secure the rights of the first inventor in the whole Union from the time he files his first patent application in any of the countries of the Union. The first application is to be deemed a disclosure of the invention to the whole Union, and a warning that the rights in a certain invention are to be preserved in favor of the inventor, or his assigns and successors, during a specified period. It is for this invention alone that a right of priority may be claimed subsequently.[4]

Consequently, it is clear that, in order that a right of priority may

1. *Actes de la Conférence de La Haye*, p. 336. 2. See *supra*, § 183.
3. *Actes de la Conférence de La Haye*, pp. 429, 518, 538.
4. Pillet, *Régime International*, p. 276; Osterrieth und Axster, *Pariser Konvention*, p. 74. See also the Italian case of Thomas and Prevost *v.* Borghi, Court of Errors of Turin, Dec. 17, 1901 (*Annali della Guirisprudenza Italiana*, XXXVI, 68).

be claimed, two conditions must concur: (*a*) identity of applicants; (*b*) identity of invention in the first and second applications.

The first of these subjects has been dealt with earlier in this chapter,[1] in so far as the assignee or successor of the first applicant is concerned. Questions of identity may arise when the applicants at the anterior filing are more than one, some of them not participating in the later application, or when new applicants are added to those of the first filing.

For example, A and B apply first in England, and later A, B, and C file an application in Germany. The existence of identity of applicants in this case, for the purposes of article 4, should not be subject to any doubt. A and B might assign their rights in the invention. If they may transfer their invention in whole, they may also transfer it in part. By joining C as an applicant they manifest their intention to make such a transfer.[2] The opposite also should be possible in principle. If A and B file an application first in England, and then A alone applies in Germany, he should be allowed to claim the right of priority. A, the inventor, may well transfer part of his rights in a country and apply jointly with the transferee, and retain for himself the rights in his invention in other countries. Or if B, the co-owner of the invention in the first country, is unwilling to claim any right in his invention in other countries, there is no reason why A should be prevented from doing so. The new patent granted in another country is not an extension or recognition of the first patent, but a wholly new privilege, in no way dependent on the prior patent. The argument that the right of priority is acquired in common by A and B as a joint right and cannot be claimed separately by A, based on the theory that the right of priority is an independent right, is criticized in another place.[3]

1. See *supra*, § 167.

2. German Patentamt, July 3, 1909 (*Propriété Industrielle*, 1910, p. 131), *accord*. But, decision of Solicitor General in the matter of Lentz and Berner application (1913), 31 R. P. C. 71, *contra*. The English case is as follows: A files first application in Germany and takes B, by transfer of part of his rights, as joint patentee. German patent is delivered to both. Held, only A can claim right of priority in England, because he alone deposited the first application, the date of which the English patent will bear. The case is explained by the fact that the right of priority is given effect in England by antedating the application filed under article 4 of the Convention. But the application in England is not rejected unless applicant does not amend his application so as to show only A as applicant.

3. See *supra*, § 165. The argument in question is used by the Austrian Patent Office in deciding against the opinion advanced in the text. See decisions of June 13, 1912, and Dec. 20, 1912 (*Propriété Industrielle*, 1913, pp. 134 and 185).

§ 188. Invention must be the same in the two applications but need not be described in identical terms. The question of identity of the invention contained in the first and second applications presents a number of difficulties. The applications should concern the same invention. This does not mean, however, that the specifications accompanying the applications should be worded in identical terms. The applicant must satisfy the authorities receiving his subsequent application that the invention claimed therein is the same as in the first application.

Especially, the delimitation of the ambit of the invention is necessarily different in the various countries. In France and Belgium, the invention is claimed by a short *résumé*, often in a single long phrase. In Germany, an enumeration of claims in terms of functions must be made. In the United States, and in some degree in England, every detail and every part of the invention must be specifically claimed. The diversity of municipal law in this respect will necessarily cause differences between the first and later applications. The English Patent Office, in comparing the copy of a first application filed in France with the new application deposited in England, decides whether the invention is the same by examining the whole French specification and drawings annexed thereto.[1]

§ 189. Case of disconformity between the two applications. In case the subsequent application contains more than the original, in the sense that something is claimed in the former which was not claimed in the latter, the right of priority should be recognized in favor of the part of the invention disclosed in both applications and denied for the residue.[2]

§ 190. Case of disconformity between provisional and complete specifications. As is seen above,[3] the filing of an application accompanied with a provisional specification is a filing of an application for a patent within the meaning of section (*a*) of article 4. The period within which the right of priority may be claimed begins to run from the moment of such filing. It is clear, then, that the inven-

1. So decided by the Australian Patent Office, June 16, 1910 (*Propriété Industrielle*, 1913, p. 44); and the Cour d'Appel de Douai, Dec. 22, 1913, in Consorts Block *c.* Ferlié et Cie (*Recueil de la Gazette des Tribunaux*, 1914, IV, 12). Cf. *Propriété Industrielle* (1906), p. 43; Pillet, *Régime International*, p. 276.

2. So held by the Austrian Patentamt, March 30, 1911 (*Propriété Industrielle*, 1913, p. 44). See also Pillet, *Régime International*, p. 276; Stringham, "International Convention Filings: Inventions Embraced," *Journal of Patent Office Society* (1927), X, 69.

3. See *supra*, § 171.

tion claimed in a subsequent application in other countries of the Union will be protected by the right of priority in so far as it is identical with the invention disclosed in the provisional specification.

British inventors, however, use the right to file a provisional specification somewhat like a *caveat*, in the sense that they merely describe the nature of the invention without entering into all its details, employing the period of nine months allowed them for the deposit of the complete specification, in working out the invention more completely and improving it in some degree.[1] They may not amend substantially the invention, although a fair development is allowed. They may enumerate a number of sub-claims in addition to the claims enumerated in the provisional specification.[2]

The question, then, arises whether it is possible to protect by the right of priority the excess of the invention contained in the complete specification. This excess may often be the most important part of the invention, namely, the description of the methods for carrying it out.

In Great Britain this problem had been important also among English inventors themselves. The Act of 1907 section 42,[3] solved this problem in a most successful manner, saving all the interests concerned. It provides:

> A patent shall not be held to be invalid on the ground that the complete specification claims a further or different invention to that contained in the provisional, if the invention therein claimed, so far as it is not contained in the provisional, was novel at the date when the complete specification was put in, and the applicant was the first and true inventor thereof.

It is submitted that the same question under article 4 of the Convention of 1883 should be decided similarly. It is not necessary that a revision to this effect be made. The part of the invention contained in the provisional specification should enjoy a right of priority as of the time of filing that specification; while the further or different invention contained in excess in the complete specification should enjoy a right of priority as of the date of filing the latter. This would mean that, if the excess has received any publicity or been the subject of an application by another person before the date of filing the complete specification, it is outside the scope of article 4.

1. See Terrell, *Letters Patent*, pp. 86–88, and cases cited. Also article by Mr. Hardingham, in *Propriété Industrielle* (1891), p. 7.

2. Terrell, *Letters Patent*, p. 189.

3. 7 Edw. VII, c. 29.

The International Bureau expressed an opinion close to the one advanced here.[1] It thought that the applicant might choose to claim a right of priority on the basis of either the provisional or the complete specification. Such an option would not seem to be warranted under article 4, in view of the fact that, as to the part of the invention contained in the provisional specification, the application for a patent is made at the filing of the latter. In practice, the German and Austrian patent offices have held, in opposition to each other, to the effect that only the complete, or only the provisional, specification enjoys the right of priority.[2]

The only objection that might be made against the opinion suggested here is that article 4 speaks of *an* application for a patent and *a* right of priority, while it would be possible under the above view to claim two rights of priority based on one nominal application, although on two specifications. It might be sufficient to answer that the right of priority is claimed in favor of the later application, and it is immaterial whether it is based on one or several specifications or additional applications in the country in which the anterior filing was made. Furthermore, it is hardly possible to compare the case of additional patent applications with the case of disconformity between the provisional and complete specifications. Indeed, in the former case, a doubt might exist as to the possibility, under article 4, of their forming a basis for a right of priority in favor of an application in the other countries of the Union, containing all the additional elements of the invention.[3] In the latter case, there is only one patent application, the complete specification being a fair development of the provisional.

§ 191. Joining of several patent applications. At the Washington Conference an attempt was made to introduce a provision in article 4 permitting the joining together of several patent applications, or additional applications and certificates of addition referring to the same invention in a single filing in the other countries of the

1. *Propriété Industrielle* (1912), p. 86. Cf. Pillet, *Régime International*, pp. 276–277.

2. German Patentamt, Jan. 29, 1913 (*Propriété Industrielle*, 1913, p. 51); Austrian Patentamt, July 13, 1912, Feb. 11, 1913, and Nov. 19, 1921 (*Propriété Industrielle*, 1913, p. 137; and 1923, p. 87). Pelletier et Vidal-Naquet, *Convention d'Union*, p. 106; Pouillet et Plé, *Protection de la Propriété Industrielle*, p. 53, agree with the Austrian Patentamt.

3. See inquiry of the International Bureau to the various administrations on this point in *Propriété Industrielle* (1905), p. 117. See also decision of Czechoslovakian Patent Office, Feb. 24, 1922 (*Propriété Industrielle*, 1922, p. 89).

Union, for the purpose of claiming the right of priority. This attempt was unsuccessful on account of the single opposition of Great Britain.[1]

The attempt was repeated at the Conference of The Hague, meeting this time with partial success.[2] According to the original French proposal, supported by the International Chamber of Commerce and the delegations of Germany, Switzerland, and the United States, an application might be filed claiming a right of priority based on several anterior filings, on condition that the number of the latter be less than four and that there be unity of invention; also, that a patent application deemed complex might be divided, in order to preserve for each partial application the date of the original deposit and the right of priority. The British and Czechoslovakian delegations opposed the first part of the proposal. Finally, a middle solution was reached by the adoption of the following provision which forms section (*f*) of the new article 4 of the Convention:

> Si une demande de brevet contient la revendication de priorités multiples, ou si l'examen révèle qu'une demande est complexe, l'Administration devra, tout au moins, autoriser le demandeur à la diviser dans des conditions que déterminera la législation intérieure, en conservant comme date de chaque demande divisionnaire la date de la demande initiale, et s'il y a lieu, le bénéfice du droit de priorité.

The import of this provision is that, if an applicant claims in his application several priorities (rights of priority based on several anterior filings), his application will not be rejected, nor will he lose his rights of priority. The administration may allow him to join together his several anterior filings. But if this be not allowed, the applicant will, at least, be authorized to divide his application, according to the requirements of the municipal law. In such case, each of the partial applications will preserve the date of the application which is so divided and, consequently, the right of priority which might be claimed in favor of that application, if it were allowed to stand as filed. The same is true in the case of an application which the examination shows to be complex. There exists complexity in an application when several distinct matters are contained in the specification.[3]

1. *Actes de la Conférence de Washington*, pp. 45, 46, 247, 277.

2. The International Bureau did not propose this amendment, fearing that unanimity could not be obtained. The proposal this time came from the French government. See *Actes de la Conférence de La Haye*, pp. 218, 337, 430–431, 518–519, 539.

3. Allart, *Brevets d'Invention*, p. 117; Terrell, *Letters Patent*, p. 157.

§ 192. Non-substantial differences between the two applications. Another proposal of the French administration, the adoption of which would have been very desirable, failed because of a disagreement on a minor point between the delegations of Great Britain and the United States. In its final form the proposal read as follows: [1]

La priorité ne peut être refusée par le motif que certains éléments de l'invention pour lesquels on réclame la priorité ne figurent pas parmi les revendications formulées dans la demande originaire, pourvu que ces éléments soient nettement précisés dans la description et que cette description vaille revendication d'après la loi du pays où cette demande à été déposée. Mais la priorité ne pourra être acquise pour des modifications substantielles aux revendications de la demande originaire.

There was unanimity on the first part of this provision. It did not really contain anything new. It merely asserted what was already true, namely, that the application by which a right of priority is claimed need not be drawn in identical terms with the prior application. The diversity of municipal law on the delimitation of the invention necessarily causes dissimilarities in the preparation of applications and claims.[2]

The latter part of the proposal would seem to be implied in the former. The delegation of the United States insisted on its suppression. This was not assented to by the British delegation.[3] The demand of the former delegation is explained by the fact that the claims enumerated in an American application are subject to substantial changes during the procedure for the delivery of the patent, either at the initiative of the applicant, or as a result of the examination by the Patent Office or of the interference proceedings. It

1. *Actes de la Conférence de La Haye*, pp. 519, 539.

2. See on this point, *supra*, §§ 147, 148.

3. *Actes de la Conférence de La Haye*, p. 519. Osterrieth (*Die Haager Konferenz*, pp. 36–37), German delegate at the Conference of The Hague, states that the Committee of the whole declined to adopt the proposal, on the the ground that it concerned Great Britain exclusively, and that the declaration of the British delegation on the practice in Great Britain was deemed sufficient. This declaration was to the effect that, although in Great Britain the invention for which priority is claimed must correspond exactly to the claims of the original application, such correspondence would be assumed if the prior application was not in the form of special claims, this not being required by the law of the country of the prior filing and the description being equivalent to special claims.

In the United States, it would seem that, a Convention filing being considered a constructive reduction to practice (Philips *v.* Carlsson, 1925, 3 F. [2d], 1018; 335 O. G. 539), the priority extends to all inventions disclosed in the prior application and is not limited to the specific claims. See on this Stringham, "International Convention Filings; Inventions Embraced," *Journal of Patent Office Society* (1927), X, 69.

should be recalled that, from the date of filing the application until the delivery of the patent in the United States, all documents (specifications, drawings, and so forth) are preserved in secrecy. So there is no disclosure of the invention in the meantime, as there is in the other countries. This again shows that the wrong is with the starting-point of the right of priority, which is unequally beneficial to the various countries in view of the diversity of municipal law as to administrative procedure and publication of the application.[1]

VII. Effects of Right of Priority

§ 193. No valid patent may be granted in the interval to other persons. The foregoing exposition of the nature of the right of priority would seem to render unnecessary a discussion as to its effects. The first deposit of a patent application constituting, by virtue of the Convention, a disclosure of the invention to the whole Union and a notice that the applicant may apply for a patent in the other countries within the specified period, it follows, as article 4 in section (*b*) expressly provides, that:

> En conséquence, le dépôt ultérieurement opéré dans l'un des autres pays de l'Union, avant l'expiration de ces délais, ne pourra être invalidé par des faits accomplis dans l'intervalle, soit, notamment, par un autre dépôt, par la publication de l'invention ou son exploitation.

Thus the right of priority of article 4 furnishes to an applicant a legal defense against the invalidation of his patent by contingencies occurring within the period of the right of priority. Its effects are purely negative; it gives rise to no positive rights.

During the period of the right of priority, the following possibilities may take place in the country in which the right of priority is subsequently claimed.

(1) Another person may have applied for a patent for the same invention. Article 4 expressly provides that the subsequent filing will not be invalidated by another deposit ("par un autre dépôt"). While this is clear and has been generally admitted, the opinion has been advanced that a patent might validly be granted to the person applying in the interval. Thus this patent would coexist with the patent granted later, on the application claiming a right of priority.[2]

1. See on this point, *supra*, § 176.
2. Hardingham, "Lettre de Grande Bretagne," in *Propriété Industrielle* (1891), pp. 47–48. The Hungarian Patent Court held the same view in its decision No. 2973 of 1925 (*Propriété Industrielle*, 1926, p. 130).

This would be in opposition to the theory of the right of priority which aims at securing in the whole Union the rights of the inventor who first made known his invention by filing application in one of the countries of the Union.[1] When it is provided that an application enjoys a right of priority, this means, after all, that the application in question, although in fact subsequent, will be considered prior to any other within the specified period. This question is closely connected with the question of the reservation of rights of third parties, discussed below.[2]

§ **194. Extent of liability of intervening patentee.** Since no valid patent may be granted on such intervening application, the person claiming a right of priority may bring an action for annulment of the patent granted in the meantime. Any further use or working of the invention by the patentee in question may be ground for an action for infringement. Ordinarily, such an action may be brought after a patent is granted. In the countries in which the protection of an invention begins earlier than the date of the grant from the filing of the application or from its publication, for instance, action for infringement may be brought for acts of use or working of the invention since that time.

The intervening patentee, however, cannot be held liable for infringement for using or working the invention before the filing of the application claiming the right of priority. Article 4 of the Convention does not purport to grant a right of exclusive use of an invention in the whole Union from the time of the first application in a country of the Union. This is generally admitted [3] and is best explained by the theory of the right of priority advanced here, according to which the first application is a mere disclosure of the invention to the Union and a notice that the inventor may apply for a patent in the other countries within the specified period. The first deposit of an application gives no other right in the other countries than that of claiming a priority in case an application is filed in the other countries within a year. The preparatory work of the Conference of 1880 strengthens this view to some extent.[4]

1. Pillet, *Régime International*, p. 278; Pelletier et Vidal-Naquet, *Convention d'Union*, p. 116; Osterrieth und Axster, *Pariser Konvention*, p. 82; Pouillet et Plé, *Protection de la Propriété Industrielle*, p. 40, *accord*. 2. See *infra*, §§ 200 ff.

3. Pelletier et Vidal-Naquet, *Convention d'Union*, p. 118; Pillet, *Régime International*, p. 278; Pouillet et Plé, *Protection de la Propriété Industrielle*, p. 41.

4. The Belgian delegate, who proposed the text of article 4, explained that "pendant le délai dont parle l'article 4, l'exploitation à l'étranger sera licite, puisque les tiers

§ 195. Cases of excess of intervening patent. In case the intervening application concerns an invention which goes further than the invention for which a right of priority is claimed, the invalidity of the patent granted on the former does not extend beyond the limits of the latter. The practice of provisional specifications accompanying applications in Great Britain and the British dominions and colonies raises difficult questions, which have already been considered.[1]

§ 196. Cases of conflict of priorities. A question of conflicting priorities may arise either between two foreign applications which have been filed on the same date in two different countries by two different persons for the same invention, or between a foreign and a domestic application. It would seem that the question of priority in both cases is controlled by the municipal law, which may determine it by considering the exact hour of filing or by other methods.[2]

§ 197. Publication of invention by the inventor or third parties is no bar. (2) The invention may also have been published or worked in the interval. This may have been done either by a third party or by the first applicant himself. It was a matter of controversy, prior to the revision of the Convention at the Brussels Conference, whether the right of priority might be claimed in case the applicant himself published or worked his invention in the interval.[3] The trouble was caused by the phrase "par un tiers," which then terminated the phrase "par la publication de l'invention ou son exploitation." Yet this possibility of loss of the novelty of the invention and the filing of an application by another, were referred to as an illustration of contingencies. This was clear from the words preceding such enumeration,—"soit, notamment,"—which are equivalent to the expression "for example."[4] Moreover, the purpose of article 4 was in favor of giving to the applicant the

---

ne sauront pas si le déposant prendra oui ou non un brevet dans leur pays. *Conférence de Paris* (1880), pp. 51, 60.

1. See *supra*, §§ 190, 192.

2. It was so admitted at the Paris Conference of 1880 (*Conférence de Paris*, pp. 47, 63), and was so held by the Austrian Patentamt, March 20, 1917 (*Propriété Industrielle*, 1920, p. 22).

3. See the French case of Pratt *c.* Lycett, Tribunal Correct. de Paris, July 21, 1891 (*Propriété Industrielle*, 1891, p. 121), holding that an American applicant who had published the invention in the United States during the period of the right of priority lost this right. The decision was subsequently reversed by the Cour de Paris, April 11, 1892 (*Dalloz*, 1892, II, 594).

4. Pelletier et Vidal-Naquet, *Convention d'Union*, p. 113.

opportunity to publish and work his invention, in order to facilitate his plans and find in other countries persons interested in it. At the Brussels Conference the words "par un tiers" were struck out.

§ 198. Effects of right of priority in Great Britain and British colonies, etc. In Great Britain and the British dominions and colonies, a right of priority is granted to persons who have filed a patent application in another country, not by immediate application of article 4 of the Convention, but by virtue of specific provisions of the municipal legislation. It may be asked, then, whether the effects of the right of priority in these countries are in any way different. According to section 91 of the British Act of 1907 (7 Edward VII, c. 29), the patent applied for by virtue of article 4 of the Convention is antedated, so that it has the same date as the date of the application in the foreign country. This antedating has the following consequences:

(*a*) The duration of the patent granted in Great Britain to the person claiming the right of priority is shortened by the period of time lapsing between his first filing in a country of the Union and the filing in Great Britain.

(*b*) No question may arise concerning the validity of the intervening patent of another person. This patent will bear a later date, and in consequence it will be invalid.[1]

(*c*) But for the express provision of section 91, (1) (*b*) to the contrary,[2] an action might lie for infringements in Great Britain from the time the first application was filed in a foreign country.

At the Washington Conference of Revision a proposal was made by the French delegation to insert a provision in article 4 to the effect that the duration of a patent taken out by virtue of the right of priority should not be governed by the date of the filing on which the right of priority is based. The purpose of this provision would be to do away with the British practice.[3] However, on the opposition of

1. Thus an applicant may oppose the grant of a patent on an application lodged in the British Patent Office between the first application in the foreign country and the subsequent application in Great Britain. See Ruling C (1913), 30 R. P. C., and *in re* Halsey's Application (1913), 31 R. P. C. 101. The decisions to the contrary under the Act of 1883 are no longer applicable. See Terrell, *Letters Patent*, p. 188.

2. This paragraph reads as follows: "Nothing in this section shall entitle the patentee . . . to recover damages for infringements happening prior to the actual date on which his complete specification is accepted . . . in this country."

3. In Greece also the duration of patents granted to foreign patentees starts from the day following the first filing of a patent application abroad. Act No. 3092 of July 14, 1924, art. 2, § 5 (Ἐφημερὶς τῆς Κυβερνήσεως, 1924, I, No. 159).

Great Britain alone, the proposal was defeated.[1] Similar proposals, in the form of amendments to article 4*b*, made by the French and American delegations at the Conference of The Hague, were defeated on the opposition of the British and Australian delegations.[2] It should be noted that Great Britain in the meantime had increased the term of patents from fourteen to sixteen years.[3]

§ 199. **Effects of right of priority in the United States.** The risk of loss of novelty of an invention by publication did not exist in the United States at the time the Convention went into effect. In fact, foreign patentees enjoyed a provisional protection for two years for the purpose of filing application in the United States. However, they were not protected against a filing by another person during the period of the right of priority.[4] After the accession of the United States to the Union, the Convention was not immediately applied in this respect. The law was not amended until 1903.[5] Section 4887 of the Revised Statutes was revised so as to be put in harmony with the Convention. As will be seen, no complete harmony was achieved. This section reads now as follows:

No person otherwise entitled thereto shall be debarred from receiving a patent for his invention or discovery by reason of its having been first patented or caused to be patented by the inventor or his legal representatives or assigns in a foreign country, unless the application for said foreign patent was filed more than twelve months prior to the filing of the application in this country, in which case no patent shall be granted in this country.

An application for patent filed in this country by any person who has previously regularly filed an application for a patent for the same invention or discovery in a foreign country which by treaty, convention, or law, affords similar privileges to citizens of the United States shall have the same force and effect as the same application would have if filed in this country on the date on which the application for patent for the same invention or discovery was first filed in such foreign country, provided the application in this country is filed within twelve months from the earliest

1. *Conférence de Washington*, pp. 247-248, 277.

2. *Actes de la Conférence de La Haye*, pp. 519, 572. The British delegation, however, read a declaration promising to request the government to amend the act in this respect, in view of the unanimous opinion of the other delegations.

3. Sec. 17 of the Act of 1907, as amended by the Act of 1919 (9 & 10 George V, c. 80).

4. Rousseau *v.* Brown (1903), 104 O. G. 1120; (1903), C. D. 587; Boral & Kymer *v.* Butterworth *v.* Ecob (1901), 97 O. G. 1596; *Propriété Industrielle* (1897), p. 23.

5. By the Act of March 3, 1903 (32 Stat. 1225). Prior to this act, the Act of March 3, 1897 (29 Stat. 692), had reduced the period of two years during which foreign patent applications enjoyed a provisional protection, to seven months, in conformity with the provisions of article 4 of the Convention at the time.

date on which any such foreign application was filed; but no patent shall be granted upon such application if the invention or discovery has been patented or described in a printed publication in this or any foreign country or has been in public use or on sale in this country, for more than two years prior to the date of filing in this country.

The first paragraph of the section deals with the effect of having obtained a patent in a foreign country, before filing an application in the United States for the same invention, as a bar to a valid patent in this country. The second paragraph concerns the benefits to be derived from a prior application for the same invention in a foreign country.[1]

Thus, a valid patent in the United States cannot be had, according to the first paragraph of the section, if a patent has been granted (*a*) in another country,(*b*) to the inventor or his legal representatives or assigns, (*c*) on an application filed more than twelve months before the date of filing in this country, (*d*) for the same invention.

This paragraph, then, means that a patent will be refused, or, if granted, will be held invalid by the mere fact that an application for it has been filed in a foreign country more than twelve months before filing application in the United States, and if a patent has been granted on such application before one is granted in the United States.[2] It is immaterial that no publication of the invention may have been made meanwhile, and no filing by another person taken place. But the above four conditions must concur. In other words, if the prior application in a foreign country was filed more than twelve months before the application in the United States, it will constitute no bar, so long as no patent has been granted on such application before one is granted in the United States. In this respect the last clause of the second paragraph comes into play, providing that a description of the invention in a printed publication in this or a foreign country, or the public use or sale in this country for more than two years prior to the date of filing in this country, debars an applicant from receiving a patent.

Thus, the provisional protection in the United States of foreign inventions, the protection of which has been applied for in other countries, against the risk of loss of novelty by publication of the

1. See a very good interpretation of section 4887 by Tullar, Examiner of the U. S. Patent Office, in *Journal of Pat. Off. Society* (1918), I, 178, 186 ff. The writer is greatly indebted for information to the author of this article.

2. Müller *v.* Lauber (1903), 106 O. G. 2016.

invention by the inventor himself or by third parties, is secured by force of the first paragraph of section 4887 and of the last clause of the second paragraph. It is secured even better than by the Convention. It lasts for two years, unless a patent has been granted on the application, in which case the protection lasts for only twelve months.

On the other hand, the second paragraph of section 4887 purports to give the benefit of a prior application in a foreign country as against a filing by another person. It provides that the application in the United States "shall have the same force and effect as the same application would have if filed in this country on the date on which the application . . . was first filed in such foreign country." Therefore, when an application is involved in interference, and the applicant has made declaration of an application for the same invention in a foreign country, the examiner will grant the benefit of the foreign application, if the claim in issue is disclosed therein.[1] But no antedating of the patent is made as in Great Britain.[2] To effect this four conditions must concur:

(*a*) The foreign country in which the prior application is filed must be one which by treaty, convention, or law, affords similar privileges to citizens of the United States.

(*b*) The domestic and the foreign applications must have been filed by the same person.

(*c*) The application in the United States must have been filed within twelve months from the earliest date on which the foreign application is filed.

(*d*) The two applications must concern the same invention or discovery.

The third and fourth conditions do not present any differences from article 4 of the Convention. The words "earliest date" in the third condition would seem to mean that the application for an invention filed at the earliest date constitutes the starting-point of the period of right of priority. In other words, the original application (the provisional specification in Great Britain) is taken into consideration.[3]

1. Tullar, Rules 28 and 29, *Journal of Pat. Off. Society*, I, 178, 194–195.

2. *Ex parte* Pauling (1905), 115 O. G. 1848.

3. As to British provisional specifications, *in re* Swinburne (1902), 99 O. G. 1625; 19 App. D. C. 565; *in re* Bastian (1916), 225 O. G. 1106; 44 App. D. C.4 25, hold that it is immaterial that the provisional specification does not disclose the invention, unless

The second condition appears to differ from article 4 of the Convention, in that it accords the benefit of the prior filing only to the same person who filed the first application, and not to his successors and assigns also, as the Convention does. It must be recalled that article 4 was revised in this respect in 1911; prior to that time it was disputed whether the assigns of the first applicant enjoyed the right of priority. Section 4887 stands to-day as revised prior to 1911, namely in 1903.

The first condition is also different from article 4 of the Convention. The benefit of priority is enjoyed by any person who filed the prior application in a foreign country which affords similar privileges to citizens of the United States. The Convention of 1883 is a convention under which similar privileges are afforded to American citizens in the member countries of the Union.[1] Therefore, if the first application is filed in a country of the Union, the benefit of priority may be claimed under the second paragraph of section 4887. Thus, this benefit is not restricted to nationals of, or foreigners domiciled or established in, a country of the Union.

The new text of article 4 of the Convention as revised at the Conference of The Hague causes further discrepancy between it and section 4887. If it be admitted, as is urged in another place,[2] that the Convention of 1883 is immediately effective or self-executing in the United States, the persons admitted to the benefit of the Convention may enjoy the advantages of article 4 without regard to section 4887.

VIII. Reservation of Rights of Third Parties

§ 200. History of reservation of rights of third parties. When the Conference of 1880 began the discussion of the article of the original draft of the Convention concerning the right of priority, the Dutch delegate, Verniers van der Loeff, finding the article incomplete, proposed the following amendment: "sauf les droits qui se-

the provisional specification has been cancelled and the patent bears the date of the complete specification, *ex parte* Hayes (1914), 209 O. G. 1317.

1. When the Department of the Interior is duly advised that a foreign country has acceded to the International Convention of 1883, the Patent Office is warranted in assuming that similar privileges are afforded United States citizens. However, the presumption is not conclusive. Anyone may prove the contrary. National Metallurgy Co. *v.* Whitman *et al.* (1910), 156 O. G. 1068; 35 App. D. C. 420; Winter *et al. v.* Latour (1910), 157 O. G. 209; 35 App. D. C. 415. In a certain way, then, reciprocity is the basis of protection by the second paragraph of section 4887.

2. See *supra*, §§ 93, 97.

raient déjà acquis légitimement par des tiers." He explained his amendment thus:[1]

Suppose qu'un Hollandais se serve depuis de longues années d'une marque de fabrique, mais pour de produits qu'il n'exporte pas. Ce négociant n'aura donc déposer sa marque que dans son pays. Un fabriquant étranger s'avise d'adopter de bonne ou de mauvaise foi, cette même marque, et il la dépose dans son pays. On ne saurait admettre que ce dépôt, bien qu'effectué régulièrement, puisse lui donner, en Hollande, un droit de priorité d'enregistrement. It convient donc de compléter l'article.

By reading the amendment and its explanation by the Dutch delegate it is easy to conclude that it was proposed only because of the inadequate wording of the original draft article. Indeed, the latter provided that every deposit was to constitute a right of priority of registration regardless of existing rights. It did not contain the second paragraph of the present article 4, which limits the effects of the right of priority to acts taking place after the first application. The Dutch merchant, in the Dutch delegate's illustration, would be cut off by the registration enjoying the right of priority. By the proposed amendment *rights which would have been already validly acquired*, namely, acquired before the filing giving rise to a right of priority, were to be saved.

When, at the following meeting of the Conference, two new drafts of article 4 were proposed by the French and the Belgian delegations, the French preferred its original form with the Dutch delegate's amendment in a shorter form which greatly impaired its meaning: "sous réserve des droits acquis par des tiers." On the contrary, the text proposed by the Belgian delegation did not insert this phrase; instead, it contained a second paragraph defining and limiting the effects of the right of priority to acts occurring in the interval between the first and subsequent filings. The Conference adopted the latter text, but inserted in it the reservation demanded by the Dutch delegate, doubtless without realizing that the amendment was now unnecessary. Yet, the amendment was still shortened and now read: "sous réserve des droits des tiers."[2] Thus, step by step the words "qui seraient déjà acquis légitimement," meaning the rights of third parties which had been acquired before the first filing, were dropped. The initial amendment, which would

1. *Conférence de Paris* (1880), pp. 47, 48.
2. *Ibid.*, pp. 49, 60, 64.

have been simply useless and superfluous, became in its last form devoid of clearness and dangerous.

§ 201. Interpretation of reservation by subsequent conferences. Six different interpretations of the phrase "sous réserve des droits des tiers" were maintained before the Brussels Conference of Revision.[1] The attempt, at this Conference, to strike out these words, or at least to determine accurately their meaning, did not succeed. The Conference adopted without discussion the report of the special subcommittee, which advocated the maintenance of the *status quo*, and justified this course by observing that in certain countries the personal possession of an invention is granted in certain cases to persons acting in good faith; that in such cases the words in question are not useless; and that a precise determination of such cases is impossible in view of the diversity of the law.[2]

Thus the historical explanation of the phrase in question was abandoned and a new interpretation, so to speak, was given by the Brussels Conference itself.[3] This interpretation was maintained by the Washington Conference of Revision, which, while rejecting the proposal of the International Bureau tending to eliminate these words, attempted to define the limits of the right of "personal possession" of an invention.[4]

§ 202. Right of "personal possession." The so-called right of "personal possession," or "personal use" (*Vorbenutzungsrecht*), of an invention was considered in the previous chapter in connection with the rights of a patentee.[5] An inventor may neglect to apply for a patent and yet make all the necessary preparations for the working of his invention, and actually begin its working. Subsequently another person may invent the same thing and apply for a patent for the same invention. The right of exclusive use will be granted to the latter, who secured a patent for the invention. Should, however, the person who first invented the thing in question and incurred expenses in preparing to work or in actually working the invention be excluded from using his own invention? Should his failure to obtain

1. See these interpretations in Pelletier et Vidal-Naquet *Convention, d'Union*, pp. 120 ff. Cf. Pillet, *Régime International*, p. 279; Pilenco, "Les Droits des Tiers" in *Propriété Industrielle* (1897), p. 104; "La Réserve des Droits de Tiers," in *Propriété Industrielle* (1921), p. 63.

2. *Actes de la Conférence de Bruxelles*, p. 210.

3. Pillet, *Régime International*, p. 282; *Propriété Industrielle* (1921), pp. 76, 78–79.

4. *Actes de la Conférence de Washington*, pp. 44–45, 273–275.

5. See *supra*, § 153.

a patent cause him, besides the loss of the exclusive right in the use of the invention, also affirmative liability to the patentee? In many countries it was deemed proper to allow such a person the personal use of his invention, but he could not grant any licenses for the working of his invention, or transfer it, except with the business in connection with which he used his invention. This right is granted only to persons who in good faith have begun working the invention, or have taken the necessary steps for its working before the filing of application by the person to whom a patent is subsequently granted.

§ **203. This right may be recognized if originating before first filing of application.** A right of personal possession might undoubtedly be recognized under article 4 of the Convention of 1883, in the member countries of the Union, in case this right originates before the filing of the first application in a country of the Union. Article 4 accords a right of priority only for the purpose of filing a second application. All acts occurring in the interval between the two applications are within the purview of the right of priority, and no others. In respect to acts which occur prior to the first application, the principle of article 2, which treats foreigners as nationals, controls the situation. The Washington Conference had no difficulty in pronouncing itself unanimously to this effect on this point.

§ **204. Doubtful whether predominant over right of priority.** On the question whether a right of personal possession may also be recognized, under article 4, in case it originates in the interval between the two filings, unanimity was not reached at the Washington Conference. Eight delegations voted for the following proposal, while five voted against, and three declined to vote:

> Les faits accomplis dans l'intervalle écoulé entre la première demande et celle déposée dans le pays où la priorité est réclamée, ne font naître aucun droit dont l'effet puisse se prolonger au delà de cette seconde demande.

If this proposal were adopted, the right of personal possession would not prevail over the right of priority. The person who, under the municipal law of a country of the Union, could use personally the invention during the whole term of the patent would not be permitted to do so under the Convention beyond the date of filing of the subsequent application in that country.[1]

1. *Actes de la Conférence de Washington*, p. 274.

The Washington Conference, by refusing to adopt the above proposal has left this question to the determination of the municipal law. Under the latter, a right of personal possession may, under the Convention, originate after the first filing of a patent application in a country of the Union. This view was already held by German courts.[1] The writers were not in agreement.[2]

§ 205. Abuses to which right of personal possession may give rise. Proposed distinction. The interpretation of the "reservation of third parties," adopted by the Conferences of Brussels and Washington, was an unfortunate backward step. It is against the theory of the right of priority, which tends to make of the first filing of an application a disclosure of the invention to the whole Union, and to secure the rights of the inventor who first applied for a patent in the whole Union. The value and purpose of the right of priority are defeated when a right of personal possession may be allowed to be claimed for an invention originating in the interval.

Reasonable as the claim of the personal user of the invention may be under the municipal law, it may give rise to many abuses under article 4. Indeed, under the former, it may be claimed whenever the invention was used or worked in good faith *prior* to the filing of the patent application by the other inventor. Under article 4 of the Convention, as interpreted in some countries, it may be claimed if the invention was used or worked in good faith *after* the first filing of an application, although before the second filing. The invention, however, may be published in the interval, and another person may obtain knowledge thereof and work it or take the necessary steps for its working, before the second filing. He would then be entitled to claim a right of personal possession. The only obstacle to this would be that it must be proved that he acted in good faith.

The burden of proof is an important question in this respect. It will be very difficult for the foreign applicant to prove conclusively the lack of good faith of the other party, and very easy for the claim-

1. Berlines Landgericht, Feb. 12, 1918 (*Propriété Industrielle*, 1920, p. 106); Reichsgericht, June 4, 1920 in Deutsche vereinigte Schuhmaschinen *v.* Maschinenfabrik Moenus (*Entsch. Reichsg.*, *Zivilsachen*, N. F. 49, p. 145); Austrian Patentamt, Dec. 21, 1920 (*Propriété Industrielle*, 1922, p. 44).

2. In favor of this view: Damme, *Das deutsche Patentrecht*, p. 362; Richard-Alexander-Katz, *Der Anschlusz des deutschen Reiches an die internationale Union*, p. 82; Allfeld, *Patentgesetz*, p. 710; Seligsohn, *Patentgesetz*, 5th ed., p. 529.

Against this view: Kohler, *Lehrbuch des Patentrechts*, pp. 218, 224; Osterrieth und Axster, *Pariser Konvention*, p. 88; Pouillet et Plé, *Protection de la Propriété Industrielle*, pp. 42–43.

ant to prove the absence of bad faith. In this respect the Danish law adopted an arbitrary rule to the effect that everyone is presumed to know a published invention.[1] Thus a right of personal possession cannot be claimed after publication of the invention. A similar distinction was proposed under article 4 of the Convention, whereby such a possession was only to be claimed in case it originated between the first filing of a patent application in a country of the Union and the publication of the invention. The person who used or worked an invention after such publication would be presumed to have acted in bad faith.[2]

Following the Washington Conference, the laws of Switzerland and of Morocco were amended as follows: under the Swiss law no right of personal possession may be based on acts performed during the period of the right of priority; in Morocco such right cannot extend beyond the date of the subsequent filing of an application.[3]

At the Conference of The Hague the International Bureau, giving voice to various *voeux* and its own conviction that the right of priority is seriously impaired by the recognition of a right of personal possession coming into existence during the period of priority, proposed again, as in the previous two Conferences, an amendment of article 4, to the effect that no such right may be acquired in the interval between the two filings.[4] It may be regretted that unanimity was not obtained, four countries (Cuba, Hungary, Italy, and Japan) having voted against this proposal.[5]

1. Law of April 13, 1894, art. 6 (*Danmark Lovtidende*, 1894, p. 223).

2. *Annuaire de l'Association Internationale* (1903), p. 83; Wirth, "Lettre d'Allemagne," in *Propriété Industrielle* (1903), p. 10.

3. Swiss Federal Law of April 3, 1914, art. 5 (*Recueil Officiel des Lois*, 1914, pp. 317, 318–319); Morocco, Dahir of June 23, 1916, art. 18 (*Codes et Lois du Maroc*, Suppl. I, pp. 326, 331).

4. *Actes de la Conférence de La Haye*, pp. 82, 227, 233.

5. *Ibid.*, pp. 427–428. On a second vote on this point, the countries of the minority were reduced to three — Hungary, Italy, and Serb-Croat-Slovene State. See *ibid.*, p. 517.

CHAPTER XII

THE INDEPENDENCE OF PATENTS

§ 206. When question of dependence or independence of patents may arise. Patentees entitled to the benefit of the Convention of 1883 may apply for and obtain a patent in a country of the Union:

(1) Within the period of the right of priority, notwithstanding the acts occurring in the interval, in consequence of which the novelty of the invention is lost.

(2) After the lapse of the period of priority, if by the law of the country in question the invention is still new (by virtue of the national-treatment clause of article 2 of the Convention).

(3) After the lapse of the period of priority, if by the law of the country in question a special kind of patent is still granted under certain conditions, although the invention is no longer new. (Italian law — patents of importation.)

In all these cases the question arises whether the patent granted to the foreign patentee is dependent upon or independent of the original patent; in other words, whether the duration of the second patent is limited by the term of the first, and whether the invalidity, abandonment, revocation, or forfeiture of the first causes the second also to terminate.[1]

§ 207. Object of the Convention of 1883, and independence of patents. In the International Convention of 1883 the national treatment as regards patents of invention is provided for in ar-

1. On the general theory in this respect, see *supra*, § 9.

ticle 2. The whole spirit of the Convention,[1] as well as this general principle, would seem to contemplate the elimination of any kind of interdependence among patents granted in various countries of the Union to the same inventor. The principle of independence of patents had been adopted without discussion by the Congress of Paris of 1878 and in the project of union drawn by the permanent commission of that congress.[2] That the Convention meant to include the same principle in the national-treatment clause might be concluded from the discussions at the Conference of 1880.[3]

The object of the Convention would be defeated if the various patents for the same invention should be held to be dependent. An inventor may seldom realize from the beginning the possibilities of his invention. He may find the most profitable place for working his invention to be the last country in which he applies for a patent. He may prefer to discontinue paying fees and taxes on the previous patents in the other countries. If the patents obtained in the different countries should not be deemed independent, the termination or forfeiture of the patent in which the inventor is least interested might cause the invalidation of the most important patent. Moreover, in case the inventor granted licenses for the working of his later patents, the licensees would risk having their patent forfeited by the revocation, forfeiture, or invalidation of the other patents of the inventor.

The usual argument against the independence of patents is that a country should not continue maintaining a privilege in favor of a foreign patentee when that privilege has come to an end in other countries. This places that country in a disadvantageous position, by curtailing the freedom of its industry, while the industry of the other countries is free. This argument carries less weight than appears. The inventor might, indeed, obtain a patent for his invention in only one country and, it is true, thus curtail the freedom of its industry for the whole term of the patent, while in all other countries his invention might be used freely.[4] The fact that he may

1. Cf. Osterrieth und Axster, *Pariser Konvention*, p. 105.

2. *Comptes-rendus du Congrès*, pp. 418, 725.

3. To a question of the Turkish delegate, the author of the Draft Convention, Mr. Jagerschmidt, answered in effect that an Italian patentee would obtain in Austria a patent for fifteen years, although the Italian patent lasted ten years. *Conférence de Paris* (1880), p. 36.

4. Rapport par G. Maillard, *Annuaire de l'Association Internationale* (1897), p. 180; *Actes de la Conférence de Bruxelles*, p. 41; Weiss, *Traité*, II, 323 ff.

obtain patents in other countries and thus prevent free use of his invention in those countries also, for a certain time, does assuredly not tend to make the situation worse in the first country.

Pillet makes a theoretical argument against the independence of patents, based on his theory that, when a patent is obtained for an invention already patented in a foreign country, no new patent is really granted, the effects of the prior patent being only extended in the other countries.[1] The unsoundness of this theory has already been exposed.[2]

However, in the absence of a clear provision in the Convention proclaiming the independence of patents, there existed some doubts whether the situation prevailing prior to the Convention of 1883 had come to an end.[3] Indeed, by the law of some countries, the patents granted to foreign patentees, sometimes called patents of importation, were dependent for their duration on either the shortest (Brazil, France, the United States) or longest (Belgium, Italy) term of the foreign patent, while in other countries the term was always shorter than that of the original (Spain, for example).[4] Moreover, in some countries the patent granted to a foreign patentee terminated at the moment any of the foreign patents ceased, whatever might be the reason for the expiration.[5] This state of the law continued until article 4*b* of the Convention went into effect in 1902.[6]

1. Pillet, *Régime International*, pp. 299 ff. This theory leads the author to the absurd conclusion that an obligation to grant licenses to the patentee by the law of origin of the patent extends to foreign countries, although the law of these countries imposes no such obligation. See *ibid.*, p. 314.

2. See *supra*, § 9.

3. *Conférence de Rome*, p. 16; *Conférence de Madrid*, p. 15; Armengaud Jeune et Mack, in *Annuaire de l'Association Internationale* (1897), p. 430; Pelletier et Vidal-Naquet, *Convention d'Union*, pp. 127 ff.

4. Brazil, Law of Oct. 14, 1882, art. 6, § 2, No. 6 (*Colecção das Leis*, 1882, I, 82).
France, Law of July 5, 1844, art. 29 (*Bulletin des Lois*, 1844, II, 18).
The United States, Revised Statutes, sec. 4887.
Belgium, Law of May 24, 1854, art. 14 (*Pasinomie*, 1854, p. 174).
Italy, Law of Oct. 30, 1859, arts. 4, 11 (*Raccolta . . . Stati Sardi*, 1859, I, 1287).
Spain, Law of July 30, 1878, art. 12 (*Colección legislativa*, 1879, II, 210).

5. See French cases: Rebour *c.* du Bucheron, Cassation, Jan. 14, 1864 (*Dalloz*, 1864, I, 146); Sainte Marie Dupré *c.* Paterson et Betts, Cassation, June 28, 1881 (*Dalloz*, 1882, I, 252). Also Austrian decision of the Ministry of Commerce, Oct. 28, 1887 (*Propriété Industrielle*, 1892, p. 23).

In the United States, on the contrary, the patents were only dependent as to expiration by lapse of time, not as to expiration through a forfeiture by breach of a condition. See Pohl *v.* Anchor Brewing Co. (1890), 134 U. S. 381.

6. Compagnie Thomson Houston *c.* Société Westinghouse, Cassation, Nov. 5, 1912 (*Gazette du Palais*, 1912, II, 495) reversing a decision of the Cour de Douai and confirming one of the Cour de Paris. The case declares terminated a French patent, by

It would seem that at least the first of the above enumerated (§ 206) possibilities as to foreign patentees seeking patents in a country of the Union should be free of doubt. In France, the opinions were divided on this point, the weight of authority being against independence.[1]

§ **208. Adoption of article 4*b* at the Brussels Conference.** To eliminate any doubt on the question of independence of patents, attempts were made at the Conferences of Rome (1886) and Madrid (1890) to introduce a provision in the Convention to this effect. The provision as proposed at these conferences, besides being inadequately drawn,[2] concerned only patents applied for in the several countries of the Union within the period of priority of article 4. At the proposal of the French delegation, a provision was added at the Madrid Conference making the patents applied for in any country of the Union independent of the patents obtained for the same invention in countries not members of the Union.[3] As no period of priority existed in the latter case, the result was that the above limitation concerned only patents applied for in countries of the Union.

At the Brussels Conference a new text was adopted, which omitted the limitation to patents applied for during the period of priority, and declared all patents obtained by persons entitled to the benefits of the Convention independent of each other.[4] This text formed article 4*b* of the Convention and read as follows:[5]

Les brevets demandés dans les différents États contractants par des personnes admises au bénéfice de la Convention aux termes des articles 2 et 3, seront indépendants des brevets obtenus pour la même invention dans les autres États adhérents ou non de l'Union.

---

reason of the fact that a foreign patent for the same invention had been forfeited for non-payment of taxes before 1902.

1. Cassation, Nov. 5, 1912 (*Gazette du Palais*, 1912, II, 495) expressly rejects the theory of independence of patents applied for within the period of priority. Also, Pouillet and Plé, *Convention d'Union*, p. 47; and Barberot, *Propriété Industrielle*, pp. 200–201. Devaux, *Inventions Brevetées*, pp. 123, 125; and *Propriété Industrielle* (1886), pp. 27, 28, *contra*.

2. It provided that ". . . les droits résultant des brevets ainsi demandés seront indépendants les uns des autres." See *Conférence de Rome*, p. 128.

3. *Conférence de Madrid*, p. 135. The entire stipulation was adopted at this Conference as article 3 of the Protocol for the interpretation and application of the Convention. This Protocol was never ratified.

4. The same text had been adopted by the International Association at its first Congress in Vienna, on motion of Mr. Maillard. The latter saw no reason for the limitation when it is once admitted that the independence of patents is a just principle. *Annuaire de l'Association Internationale* (1897), pp. 98, 180.

5. *Actes de la Conférence de Bruxelles*, p. 311.

Cette disposition s'appliquera aux brevets existants au moment de sa mise en vigueur.

Il en sera de même, en cas d'accession de nouveaux États, pour les brevets existant de part et d'autre au moment de l'accession.

§ **209. Doubts remaining under original article 4*b*.** The above text did not solve all difficulties. There still remained two questions on which a doubt existed. First, whether the provisions of article 4*b* applied to all patents obtained by persons entitled to the benefits of the Convention, or only to those applied for within the period of priority. Second, whether independence should be understood in respect only to the causes of invalidation or forfeiture of patents, or also in respect to their duration.

This first point should hardly have been subject to any doubt, in view of the wording of article 4*b*, which did not contain the phrase appearing in the earlier drafts of the same: "lorsque, dans les délais fixés à l'article 4 de la Convention une personne aura déposé . . ."[1] Such a limitation, moreover, would be inapplicable when the previous patent has been obtained in a country not a member of the Union, for no period of right of priority exists in such case. This restrictive interpretation, however, was given in Italy, soon after the coming into effect of article 4*b*.[2] By reason of special provisions of the Italian law,[3] a patent of importation is granted to a foreign patentee, although his invention has been published or worked abroad, provided he applies for a patent in Italy before the expiry of the foreign patent and before the invention is freely worked by others in Italy. The patent so granted ceases on the expiry of the foreign patent of the longest term for the same invention. The argument of the Italian government was that, when a patent was applied for in Italy for an invention already patented and published or worked abroad, and the application was filed within the period of priority, the Italian patent was granted by virtue of article 4 of the Convention; when, however, the application was filed after the period of priority, the patent was granted by virtue of the Italian law only, which might then grant it under any limitations. This

1. Osterrieth und Axster, *Pariser Konvention*. pp. 107, 109.

2. Decision of the Italian Minister of Agriculture, Industry and Commerce, May 25, 1903 (*Propriété Industrielle*, Off. Part, 1903, p. 94).

3. Arts. 4 and 11 of the Law of Oct. 30, 1859. This kind of patents constitutes, as Kohler says, a reminiscence of old-time patent conception, being not properly patents of invention, but privileges of persons importing a new industry in the country. *Handbuch des Deutschen Patentrechts*, p. 15.

point of view prevailed at the Washington Conference, as will be seen.

On the question of absolute or limited independence of the several patents, the view holding for the former might be supported by the history of article 4; by the considerations following the proposal of the International Bureau; [1] by the declaration made at the Brussels Conference by the Swiss delegate, following which article 4*b* was adopted without any discussion; [2] lastly, by the interpretation given to the provisions of the article by various countries of the Union.[3] The opposite view, holding that the independence of patents provided for by article 4*b* should be understood only in respect to the causes of invalidation or forfeiture of the foreign patent, but not in respect to its duration, was maintained in Belgium. It was based on certain discussions at the Brussels Conference, and on a declaration of the Belgian delegate at the time of the signature of the Final Protocol.[4]

But this declaration, as well as the discussion in question, referred only to the second paragraph of article 4*b*, namely, the patents already existing in respect to which article 4*b* was declared to have a retroactive effect.[5] This point of view was confirmed at the Washington Conference, as will be seen presently.

§ **210. Absolute independence of patents confirmed at the Washington Conference.** At the Washington Conference of 1911 the International Bureau proposed that a new paragraph be added to article 4*b*, making the independence of patents absolute and doing away with patents of importation. But the Bureau repeated in its proposal the old restriction limiting the provisions of article 4*b* to patents applied for within the period of priority.[6] On the other hand,

1. *Propriété Industrielle* (1905), p. 234.

2. ". . . que la durée d'un brevet d'invention délivré à un ayant droit auquel la Convention est appliquable ne peut, dans aucun État de l'Union, dépendre de la durée du brevet accordé pour la même invention dans un autre pays." *Actes de la Conférence de Bruxelles*, pp. 182, 311.

3. Italy, Decision of the Minister of Agriculture, Industry and Commerce, May 25, 1903 (*Propriété Industrielle*, 1903, p. 94); France, "Exposé des motifs du projet de loi approuvant l'Acte Additionel de Bruxelles," in *Propriéte Industrielle* (1903), p. 99. See also opinion of the International Bureau, in *Propriété Industrielle* (1898), p. 8 and (1903), pp. 99–100.

4. *Actes de la Conférence de Bruxelles*, p. 331. See also *Propriété Industrielle* (1905), p. 234; Osterrieth, *Washingtoner Konferenz*, pp. 33–34.

5. *Propriété Industrielle* (1903), p. 99; Osterrieth und Axster, *Pariser Konvention*, pp. 110, 112.

6. *Actes de la Conférence de Washington*, p. 47.

the Italian government proposed that all patents, whether applied for during the period of priority or after its lapse, should be independent of foreign patents, but that the municipal law of each country should be applicable as to the duration of patents of importation.[1]

In the discussion of article 4*b* the Italian delegation made it clear that the limitation it proposed concerned patents of importation granted in Italy on applications filed after the lapse of the period of priority, and for inventions published or worked abroad, which consequently had no longer the element of novelty.[2] A text was suggested by the Plenary Committee that would take care of the special patents of importation granted in Italy, while it would declare the absolute independence of patents in all other respects. But this text was objected to as not being clear. Finally, the following second paragraph of article 4*b* was adopted: [3]

> Cette disposition doit s'entendre d'une façon absolue, notamment en ce sens que les brevets demandés pendant le délai de priorité sont indépendants, tant au point de vue des causes de nullité et de déchéance, qu'au point de vue de la durée normale.

By this provision an end was put to the doubts existing previously in Belgium as to whether or not the independence of patents should be also understood in respect to their normal duration.[4]

§ 211. Article 4*b* applicable only to patents applied for within period of priority. It would seem that, under this provision of the second paragraph of article 4*b*, the independence refers only to patents applied for within the period of priority.[5] This surpasses the limitation proposed by the Italian delegation and suggested by the Plenary Committee; in other words, patents applied for after the lapse of the period of priority are no longer covered by article 4*b*, while the Italian proposal concerned patents applied for after the lapse of that period and covering inventions which from lack of novelty could no longer be subjects of ordinary patents.[6]

1. *Actes de la Conférence de Washington*, p. 222.
2. *Ibid.*, pp. 249–250, 312.
3. *Ibid.*, p. 312 n. 2.
4. It must be said that the Belgian delegation itself joined with the Bureau in making clear this point. See *Actes de la Conférence de Washington*, pp. 250–251, 312.
5. So held by the Cour de Bruxelles, July 31, 1925 (*Propriété Industrielle*, 1926, p. 21).
6. Osterrieth, *Washingtoner Konferenz*, p. 36.

Moreover, the dependence of a patent of importation on the foreign patent in Italy is only in respect to the normal duration, not to its effective duration; that is, the nullity or forfeiture of the foreign patent does not affect the patent of importation. By the text adopted at Washington, all patents applied for after the lapse of the period of priority may be dependent on foreign patents in respect to the term as well as the causes of nullity or forfeiture. The municipal law of each country alone governs in such cases.

On the other hand, countries of the Union are placed in an inferior position in respect to countries not members of the Union. Indeed, by the first paragraph of article 4*b*, patents obtained in a country of the Union are made independent of previous patents applied for in countries not members of the Union. It is clear that, as to patents applied for or obtained in the latter countries, there is no period of priority within which other patents may be applied for. It would seem then that patents applied for in the countries of the Union are always and in all respects independent of patents obtained in countries not members of the Union, however long a time may have passed since filing in the latter.

§ 212. The independence applies only to patents obtained for "same invention." Patents are declared independent by article 4*b* if they are obtained for the "same invention." It is an important question, then, whether the inventions for which patents are obtained in several countries are the same. The same difficulties, as in the case of the claim of a right of priority, reappear here in respect to the identity of an invention, in view of the different modes of delimiting the ambit of the invention in the various countries. What has been said above concerning the right of priority is applicable here, especially in respect to disconformity between the two applications or between provisional and complete specifications, to the joining of several patent applications, and to non-essential differences.[1]

§ 213. Practice in some countries of antedating patents applied for by foreign patentees. By declaring the patents applied for in the different countries of the Union independent of the patents obtained in other countries, members of the Union or not, in respect to their normal duration article 4*b* would seem to require that the date of the patent should be independent of any previous foreign

1. See *supra*, §§ 188–192.

application. In particular, the practice in Great Britain and British dominions and colonies of antedating a patent applied for by a foreign patentee during the period of priority as from the time of filing the foreign application, from which the period of priority starts, is opposed to article 4*b*. The law of Greece reads to the same effect.[1] At the Conferences of Revision at Washington and at The Hague various proposals, with the aim of doing away with this practice, were made by the French, German, and American delegations. They were defeated by the opposition of the British delegation supported at The Hague by the Australian.[2] At this last Conference the British delegation declared that in view of the weight of opinion opposed to the English practice, it would recommend to the British government a change of the municipal law in accordance with the wishes of the Conference.[3]

§ **214. Retroactive effect of article 4*b*.** The third paragraph of article 4*b* provides that the previous disposition as to independence of patents "s'applique à tous les brevets existant au moment de sa mise en vigueur."

Article 4*b* went into effect on September 14, 1902.[4] All patents existing at that time in any country of the Union became independent of other patents for the same invention granted in other countries. "Existant" means patents that had not yet become invalid or had not ceased by reason of nullity, forfeiture, or expiry of a foreign patent for the same invention.[5]

In the United States the Act of March 3, 1903,[6] purporting to give effect to the Additional Act of Brussels, enacted section 4887 in a new form, but omitted the paragraphs of article 4*b* referring to patents existing at the time it went into effect and to newly acceding states. This needs explanation. In the United States, prior to the adoption of article 4*b* by the Brussels Conference, an act had been

1. The duration of patents granted to foreign patentees starts from the day following the first filing of the patent application in the foreign country. Act No. 3092 of July 14, 1924, art. 2, par. 5 (Ἐφημερὶς τῆς Κυβερνήσεως, 1924, I, No. 159.)

2. *Actes de la Conférence de Washington*, pp. 92, 95, 247–248, 276–277; *Actes de la Conférence de La Haye*, pp. 337, 431, 519, 539, 572.

3. *Actes de la Conférence de La Haye*, p. 572.

4. Article 3 of the Additional Act of Brussels of Dec. 14, 1900, and *procès-verbal* of Ratification of June 14, 1902 (*Actes de la Conférence de Washington*, p. 13).

5. Compagnie Thomson Houston *c.* Société Westinghouse, Cassation, Nov. 5, 1912 (*Gazette du Palais*, 1912, II, 495), declaring void a French patent, a foreign patent for the same invention having been forfeited for non-payment of taxes before 1902.

6. 32 Stat. 1225, c. 1019 (*U. S. Comp. Stat.* Suppl. 1905, p. 663).

passed abolishing the dependence of United States patents on the duration of foreign patents. The Act of March 3, 1897,[1] which took effect January 1, 1898, did away with the provisions of section 4887, Revised Statutes, limiting the term of the United States patent by that of a foreign patent. But the Act of March 3, 1897, did not apply to applications filed prior to January 1, 1898, old section 4887, as it stood prior to that act, being still in force as to those applications and patents granted thereon.

At the Conference of Brussels, the American delegate, Mr. Forbes, declared that the patents granted to foreign patentees before January 1, 1898, could not extend beyond the term originally affixed to them under old section 4887, the opposite being possible in the United States only by special law, and being against the spirit of non-retroactivity which inspires all American legislation. All the other delegates who took part in the discussion seemed to agree with the American view. Another delegate of the United States proposed the addition to the second paragraph of article 4*b* of the words: "néanmoins, la durée fixée par la loi intérieure de chaque pays reste intacte." This was not adopted. Moreover, the British delegate maintained that he could take the indicated act of interpretation only as a declaration of the American delegation and not as a decision of the Conference.[2]

All this took place at the first session of the Conference, in December, 1897. At its second session, in December, 1900, article 4*b* was not debated further. Although no limiting protocol was annexed to the Act of Brussels, and no qualification of article 4*b* was made at its ratification by the President of the United States, and notwithstanding the remark of the British delegate, it is difficult to see a violation of the Additional Act by the United States in legislating in accordance with the declaration of its delegates at the Conference and with what appeared to be the view of many other delegations.[3] The Supreme Court of the United States gave effect to the Act of March 3, 1897 (section 4887, Revised Statutes), limiting an American patent granted before 1900 to the duration of the patent previously granted by a foreign country (Great Britain), holding

1. 29 Stat. 693 (*U. S. Comp. Stat.* 1901, p. 3882).

2. *Actes de la Conférence de Bruxelles*, pp. 311 ff.

3. Osterrieth und Axster, *Pariser Konvention*, p. 112 and Pelletier et Vidal-Naquet, *Convention d'Union*, pp. 427–428, agree with the American interpretation.

that the above act of Congress had not been superseded by article 4*b* of the Convention, as revised at Brussels.[1]

§ 215. Its application to newly acceding countries. The last paragraph of article 4*b* provides that the dispositions of this article apply also "en cas d'accession de nouveaux pays pour les brevets existant de part et d'autre au moment de l'accession."

Thus, if a new country accedes to the Union, from the moment the accession becomes effective, the patents existing in that country and in the other countries of the Union for the same invention become independent. This provision is material only to citizens or persons domiciled or established in the acceding country who have obtained patents for the same invention in that country, as well as in those already members of the Union. The citizens or persons domiciled or established in these latter countries enjoy the independence of their patents taken out therein, and of those obtained in the acceding country before its accession, by virtue of the first paragraph of article 4*b*.

In respect to the patents to which this last paragraph of article 4*b* refers, the above limitation of the period of priority does not exist. Citizens of the newly acceding countries, who had obtained patents in their own country and in any other countries of the Union, did not enjoy the right of priority and consequently are not limited by its period.

1. Cameron Septic Tank Co. *v.* City of Knoxville (227 U. S. 39). It has been seen in another place (§ 95) that this decision may rest on such ground, and that its wording is bad in so far as it purports to deny the self-executing character of the Convention of Union.

CHAPTER XIII

THE RESTRICTION OF OBLIGATIONS OF THE PATENTEE

I. Importation of Patented Articles

§ 216. Abolition of forfeiture of patents by reason of importation of patented articles. In a previous chapter[1] the law of the various countries in regard to the obligations of patentees is considered. The Convention of 1883, in its article 5, contains specific provisions, constituting common legislation for the Union, by which the most important of these obligations are restricted with the purpose of securing a more complete protection of patent rights.

By the law of certain countries a patent is forfeited in case the patentee imports into the country articles manufactured with the invention in a foreign country. This cause of forfeiture is abolished by the first paragraph of article 5 of the Convention which provides as follows:

1. See *supra*, §§ 150, 157–160.

L'introduction par le breveté, dans le pays où le brevet a été délivré, d'objets fabriqués dans l'un ou l'autre des pays de l'Union, n'entraînera pas la déchéance.

This provision has remained unmodified as it was first adopted at the Paris Conference of 1880. The only attempt at revision was made by France at the first Conference of Revision, at Rome, in 1886. It was proposed to amend this paragraph by allowing the municipal law of a country to prohibit the importation of patented articles by the patentee.[1] At the time the original text of the Convention went into effect, France alone among the countries members of the Union prohibited such importation. To-day this restriction is provided for by the laws of the Dominican Republic, France, Morocco, Syria and Lebanon, Tunis, and Turkey.[2] The Convention derogates from the municipal law of these countries on this point, and as this provision constitutes a new rule of law, which needs not the creation of municipal law to carry it out, it must be given effect immediately in the municipal legal order of these states, whenever the benefits of the Convention are claimed.[3]

This restriction, indeed, was impossible in the Union. According to the French law, before the Convention of 1883 was entered into, on a single importation of such articles the patent was forfeited. Thus the patent taken out in France by a foreign patentee was not always of much use. It was often necessary for a patentee to see whether a market could be found in France, before working his invention there. This could be found only if he were allowed to import patented articles from the country where he was already working the invention. By the prohibition to import, such trial in another country was impossible.

Besides, the view which considers the importation of patented articles manufactured abroad prejudicial to the national industry is a narrow one. By the importation of new and superior products from outside, the industry of the country benefits in the long run through being stirred to emulation.[4]

1. *Conférence de Rome* (1886), pp. 11, 91, 110. See also *supra*, p. 86.

2. See *supra*, § 159.

3. See *supra*, § 102. A recent French case, in which it was so held is Wright *c.* Wahl Co., Tribunal Civil de la Seine, Nov. 23, 1925 (*Propriété Industrielle*, 1926, p. 248). See also Ducharge, Barière, Sommer et autres *c.* Société Auer, Cassation, June 5, 1897 (*Dalloz*, 1904, I, 433, 440).

4. Pelletier et Vidal-Naquet, *Convention d'Union*, p. 146.

§ **217. Importation of patented articles not to be prevented by other means.** The Convention of 1883 stipulates that importation shall not entail revocation of the patent. May a country, however, prevent that importation by other means; for instance, by some penalty or imposition of fine or by heavy customs duties? Although the literal sense of the provision does not exclude such measures, its reasonable construction is opposed thereto. The provision was taken from the Draft Convention prepared by the French delegate, M. Jagerschmidt,[1] who had in mind the only law containing the prohibition of importation, namely, the French law. Moreover, it is against the whole spirit of the Convention to allow a country by such circuitous methods to violate its provisions.[2] Of course, the provision of article 5 cannot be interpreted as meaning that importation of patented articles by the patentee shall be free of duties. These articles may be subject to the ordinary and general customs duties of the country concerned.[3]

§ **218. Application of the provision regarding importation.** Importation shall not entail forfeiture of the patent, according to the provision of article 5, only in case the articles are manufactured in any of the countries of the Union. It is immaterial from which country the articles are imported.[4] Thus the patented articles, after being manufactured in a country of the Union, may be imported from a country not a member of the Union. It is not always easy to detect the real place of manufacture.[5] Articles may be imported from a country of the Union, as manufactured therein, although they are manufactured outside the Union. Or a person entitled to the benefit of this article may have industrial establishments in a country of the Union and in another not a member of the Union, and may manufacture his articles in the latter.[6] Or some articles

1. *Conférence de Paris* (1880), p. 56.

2. Pillet, *Régime International,* p. 290; Pouillet et Plé, *Convention d'Union,* p. 68; Pelletier et Vidal-Naquet, *Convention d'Union,* p. 153.

3. The authors referred to in the previous note, however, hold that a country may, without violating the Convention, impose heavy taxes on patented articles imported by the patentee. This would seem against the spirit of the Convention.

4. Gestetner *c.* Eyquem, Tribunal Correctionel de la Seine, Dec. 5, 1894 (*Clunet,* 1895, p. 578); Pelletier et Vidal-Naquet, *Convention d'Union,* pp. 147–148; Osterrieth und Axster, *Pariser Konvention,* p. 119.

5. Pratt *c.* Lycett, Cour de Paris, April 11, 1892 (*Dalloz,* 1892, II, 594). The proof is to be made by the person petitioning for the forfeiture of the patent by reason of such importation, and such proof will often be difficult. See Moureaux et Weismann, *Brevets d'Invention,* p. 155.

6. Société Auer *c.* Guyot, Cour de Douai, June 22, 1896; and Société Auer *c.* Deselle, Tribunal de la Seine, June 19, 1896 (*Clunet,* 1897, p. 324).

may be produced in a country and taken in a raw state to be completely manufactured in another.

All these difficulties are for the greater part disappearing, in view of the fact that most of the industrial countries of the world are now members of the Union.

The manufacture of the articles should be performed in a country of the Union, but it is unnecessary that a patent be taken out in any of the other countries of the Union.[1] In other words, a Russian patentee may import into France articles manufactured in Germany, even though he has not obtained a patent in Germany or in any other country of the Union. Of course, the Russian patentee must be a "ressortissant" of the Union under articles 2 and 3 of the Convention.

§ **219. Persons benefiting by this provision.** The persons entitled to the benefits of the Convention in general, under articles 2 and 3, may claim this advantage of article 5. The importation entails no revocation of the patent if it is made "by the patentee." Questions may arise in case the importation of patented articles is made by another person who is not the patentee. For instance, a German patentee sells the articles manufactured by him to someone in Germany, and the latter imports them into France. The patent granted to the German patentee in France cannot be revoked, according to the French law, because the patentee himself does not import the articles.[2] But the importation is, of course, considered as made by the patentee if the third person who actually makes the importation is his representative.

On the other hand, does *breveté* mean the original patentee alone, or his grantee also? Indeed, two cases may arise. An original patentee who is not entitled to the benefits of the Convention, transfers his patent to a person entitled thereto; or, conversely, a person who may claim the advantages of the Convention assigns his patent to a person who cannot claim them. The second case should leave no doubt. The grantee cannot claim advantages and rights to which he is not entitled, it being immaterial that his grantor was entitled to them. It is not the patent which is protected by the Convention, but the patentee. In the first case, the answer should not be difficult. The material point is the situation at the moment

1. Osterrieth und Axster, *Pariser Konvention*, p. 120.

2. See the cases in note 6 on p. 325; also Osterrieth und Axster, *Pariser Konvention*, pp. 119–120. Allart, *Brevets d'Invention*, pp. 308–309.

of importation. If the person who obtained a patent in France imports articles manufactured in another country of the Union with a similar patent, his French patent cannot be revoked. The possibility that he obtained the patent abroad by assignment from a person not entitled to the benefits of the Convention is immaterial.[1]

The question whether nationals may claim the advantages of the Convention in their own country arises also under the provision of article 5. Will French patentees be governed by the municipal law of France and forfeit their patent in case they import articles manufactured in a country of the Union similar to those patented in France, or will they be protected by the Convention? French courts have held the latter view; [2] its theoretical value has been discussed elsewhere.[3]

II. Working of Invention

§ 220. Restriction of obligation to work invention. The second, third, and fourth paragraphs of article 5, as amended at the Conference of The Hague, concern the obligation to work the patent in the country in which it was granted. They read as follows:

> Toutefois chacun des pays contractants aura la faculté de prendre les mesures législatives nécessaires pour prévenir les abus qui pourraient résulter de l'exercice du droit exclusif conféré par le brevet, par exemple faute d'exploitation.
>
> Ces mesures ne pourront prévoir la déchéance du brevet que si la concession des licenses obligatoires ne suffisait pas pour prévenir ces abus.
>
> En tout cas le brevet ne pourra pas faire l'objet de telles mesures avant l'expiration d'au moins trois années à compter de la date où il a été accordé et si le breveté justifie d'excuses légitimes.

The history of this provision is in a sense the history of the Union. In all the conferences of the Union attempts were made for its revision, and the provision became more and more liberal with every new conference.[4] The original Draft Convention did not contain any

1. Pelletier et Vidal-Naquet, *Convention d'Union*, p. 150; Pouillet et Plé, *Convention d'Union*, pp. 65–66; Pillet, *Régime International*, pp. 289–290, Moureaux et Weismann, *Brevets d'Invention*, p. 154. It was so held by the Cour de Paris, Jan. 7, 1897, confirmed by the Cour de Cassation, June 5, 1897, in Ducharge, Barrière, Sommer et autres *c.* Société Française d'Incadescence, système Auer (*Dalloz*, 1904, I, 433, 440).

2. Société des carbures métalliques et Bullier *c.* Garnault et Hyvert, Tribunal de la Seine, Dec. 23, 1905 (*Darras*, 1906, p. 500). See also authorities cited in notes 2 on p. 194, and 1 and 2 on p. 195.

3. See *supra*, § 120.

4. See on this, *supra*, chap. IV, especially §§ 50–55. Also a comprehensive series of articles in the *Propriété Industrielle* (1924), pp. 65 ff., 86 ff., 118 ff., 213 ff.

provision against or in favor of maintaining the obligation to work a patent.[1] The discussion was somewhat confused, and this was likewise the case in the first Conference of Revision, at Rome. On the insistence of the Austrian and Swiss delegations at the Conference of Paris in 1880 the second paragraph of article 5 was added, reading in its original form thus: "Toutefois le breveté restera soumis à l'obligation d'exploiter son brevet conformément aux lois du pays où il introduit des objets brevetés."

Already at that Conference the delegations of Belgium, Great Britain, Russia, and Turkey [2] urged that this obligation be also abolished by the Convention as well as the one against importation of patented articles. The attempts at revision at Rome and at Madrid did not succeed in striking out the provision of the second paragraph of article 5. Meanwhile, the United States acceded to the Convention and threw all its weight in the liberal direction, inasmuch as the law of the United States subjected the patentee to no obligation whatsoever.

At the Brussels Conference the International Bureau proposed, originally, an arrangement for a restricted union of the countries which agreed that the non-working of the patent should not cause its forfeiture, provided the patentee is willing to grant licenses within a certain period.[3] But it was contended that the system of restricted unions should not be encouraged.[4] And the project of the Bureau did not go far enough to meet the *desiderata* of some delegations, while it went too far in the view of other delegations.[5] After long discussions in both sessions of that Conference, a provision was adopted in the Additional Act of Brussels, to the effect that a patent cannot be forfeited for non-working unless a period of three years has elapsed from the date of filing the patent application, and in case the patentee is unable to justify his failure. This provision was substantially inserted in the text of the general Convention, and added

1. *Conférence de Paris* (1880), p. 56.

2. *Ibid.*, pp. 66–68.

3. Article 1 of this draft arrangement read as follows: "Un brevet d'invention appartenant à un sujet ou citoyen (ou assimilé) de l'un des États contractants ne pourra être déclaré déchu pour cause de non-exploitation dans le pays, que si, après l'expiration d'une période de trois ans, comptés à partir de la délivrance du brevet, le breveté a repoussé une demande de license réposant sur des bases équitables. See *Actes de la Conférence de Bruxelles*, p. 87.

4. *Actes de la Conférence de Bruxelles*, p. 319 (French delegate, M. Pelletier).

5. *Ibid.*, p. 169.

to the second paragraph of article 5 at the Washington Conference, as follows:

. . . mais avec la restriction que le brevet ne pourra être frappé de déchéance pour cause de non-exploitation dans un des pays de l'Union qu'après un délai de trois ans, compté à partir du dépôt de la demande dans ce pays, et seulement dans le cas où le breveté ne justifierait pas des causes de son inaction.

It was only at the last Conference, at The Hague, that the obligation to work the invention was substituted in principle by the obligation to grant compulsory licenses.

§ 221. Reasons for obligation and their refutation. Although in most of the countries of the Union it is generally admitted that the obligation to work an invention serves no real interest, there is no desire to abolish it, so long as it is maintained by other countries. Moreover, Great Britain, which originally did not impose such obligation, resorted to it by its law in 1907, although she alleviated this obligation by the system of compulsory licenses in 1919. Even in the United States, in which no obligation was ever imposed on the patentee, voices began to be heard in favor of requiring foreigners to work their inventions in this country.[1] It was apparent that only through the International Convention of 1883 could this obligation be everywhere abolished. The attempts to revise article 5 to this effect have always failed through the opposition of a very few countries which strongly favored the obligation to work the invention, either from attachment to a juristic theory or from the view that in that way the interest of their national industry would be better served.

The juristic theory is commonly formulated as follows:[2] Society, by consenting to give up for a certain time, in favor of the inventor, the right to use freely a useful discovery, imposes on the latter the obligation to make available his invention by working it in the country thus favoring him.

1. Vaughan, *Economics of our Patent System* (New York, 1925), pp. 173 ff., 245, 246. In the United States, the attempt was made to apply the equitable principle of "clean hands," against patentees seeking injunction in infringement cases, whenever they did not work their patent. But the courts accepted the view that equitable principles are not applicable in patent law, which is statutory law.

2. See Wirth, "De la Protection des Inventions dans le Domaine de l'Union," in *Annuaire de l'Association Internationale* (1897), pp. 212, 234; and "Motives of the French Law," in *ibid.*, pp. 242–243, 245.

Kohler puts it better, in terms of his social-philosophical interpretation of law:

Die Einführungspflicht ist eine Pflicht gegen den Staat als soziale Einheit: sie entspricht den Anforderungen der Rechtsordnung, dass jedes Recht in vernünftiger, sozialgemässer Weise gebraucht, dass mindestens mit dem Recht kein schroffer Missbrauch getrieben werden soll. [And elsewhere:] . . . so darf der Einzelne dem Volke nicht durch Nichtausübung ein wesentliches Kulturgut entziehen.[1]

It is sufficient to say here that the creation and delimitation of the inventor's right is essentially a recognition and delimitation of the interests of inventors in a process in which account is taken of the whole scheme of interests which must be satisfied. When the law imposes the obligation of compulsory working of the invention on the patentee, it really takes into account and attempts to give satisfaction to the social interest of encouraging inventions, to the interests of the buying public, and to those of the national industry. This obligation, therefore, may be justified only if these various interests are thus satisfied with the least waste and sacrifice. It will not do to look at this matter in an abstract way.

Placed on this plan and viewed in this light, the obligation of compulsory working of the invention imposed on the patentee by the law of many countries, does not satisfy any of the interests concerned. This is true whether a national or a foreign invention is in question. The working clauses of the law (1) discourage inventors, (2) are prejudicial to the buying public, and (3) hinder the free development of industry.

(1) Many inventions cannot be worked on a business basis and brought into commercial use until after long experiments and many improvements, which may require much time and take up the whole period within which they must be worked according to the law of many countries. These experiments, moreover, are very costly and may not result in anything really worth while. The inventor cannot afford capital for such experiments, when he risks having his invention forfeited in case he is unable to put his invention on a commercial basis before the period is up.[2] Furthermore, the "art" is not

1. Kohler, *Deutsches Patentrecht*, pp. 613, 618.

2. See Frederick P. Fish, "Letters Patent in Relation to Industrial Conditions," *Reports of the American Bar Association* (1913), XXXVIII, 805, 816–817. Mr. Fish, a distinguished patent lawyer in the United States with a long and rich experience, cited to the writer (in a conference that he had with him on December 4 1927) several cases

always ready for an invention. Most of the inventions to-day are not new and special things which may be easily and independently produced. They are mostly inventions of details, technical improvements. Their immediate application and adoption by the industry is not always technically possible. A scrapping of machinery and a modification of manufacturing methods are often necessary. An inventor will work the patented invention as soon as it is possible for him, because it is in his own interest to do so.

(2), (3) With the interest of encouraging inventors, the interests of national industry and of the buying public concur. The best interests of the industry of a country require that all patents, whether domestic or foreign, be protected, because the monopolies secured by them, limited as they generally are to specific features or specific articles, are harmless in themselves, incite national inventors to new efforts, and tend to stimulate competition.[1]

The exclusive privilege is granted to an inventor in exchange, not for working his invention, but for disclosing it immediately and fully to the public. This disclosure is secured by the application for a patent, which involves a complete description of the invention. By the disclosure, as an expert puts it,[2]

> the scientific and technical public are at once enabled to utilize the invention in two ways: (1) research is stimulated to find an alternative solution of the problem which will not be tributary to the patent, so that the competitive spirit is fostered; and (2) the general fund of technical knowledge is increased, so that it is easier to evolve entirely different inventions.

Even assuming that there may be cases of suppression of patents by some big concerns, which invent and patent several new improvements of machinery or process, and adopt or use only the best among them, or which are not willing to scrap their machinery or stop their actual manufacture, as soon as they obtain a patent for a

---

in which the experiments for making commercially and industrially possible a patent have lasted for three, five, or more years and have cost millions of dollars. He believes that the non-existence of working provisions or compulsory license obligations in the American patent law has had two consequences: first it has made it possible to have the capital in this country ready to back and finance new inventive ideas through long and costly experiments, and thus bring about the development of industry and the production of new, cheaper and better commodities; second, it has made of the people of the United States an inventive people. He also pointed out to the writer that he always discourages his clients from taking out patents abroad, because it costs too much and they are almost never able to work the invention there.

1. Vaughan, *Economics of Our Patent System*, p. 26; "L'Obligation d'Exploiter" in *Propriété Industrielle* (1924), p. 120.

2. Potts, *Patents: Invention and Method* (London, 1924), pp. 134, 135.

new invention, such cases are very rare. The favorable operation of working clauses of the law in such cases is generally outweighed by their definitely destructive operation. A forfeited patent is a loss to the industry of any country, and it is a loss to society as a whole. By the forfeiture of the patent the public becomes possessed of the invention theoretically; but the advantages of the exclusive right now having disappeared, there is no inducement for the working of the invention. This is especially true, when, as is often the case, extensive and costly experiments are required to bring the invention into commercial use or when the public's interest in the invention must be aroused by expensive advertising. Besides, it is only rarely that the printed description of a patent conveys sufficient information to enable a new process to be commonly worked.[1]

§ **222. Obligation to work patent in regard to foreigners.** If nationals should not be compelled to work their inventions, foreigners, then, should likewise be free to work inventions whenever and wherever they please.

What has been said on the practical impediments to the immediate working of national inventions applies with greater force in case of foreign inventions. Inventors cannot be expected to be able to work their invention in many countries at the same time. The interests of the buying public are best served when the invention is worked in the country in which the cost of production is least.[2] Of this the inventor himself is the best judge, and he should be left free to work his invention wherever he prefers.

Such freedom is in the interests of national industry. The importance of an invention consists in its use in general, not in its place of working. The best use of an invention is obtained when the inventor is allowed to work it where the conditions are most favorable. Most inventions concern new means of production, which may be obtained by the industry of any country most profitably if they are effected with the least sacrifice and least waste by the inventor. Perhaps a temporary competition of the foreign industry with the national may exist in cases of inventions of new products. But this competition will appear also if, by reason of the obligation to work the invention within a certain country, the foreigner establishes his

1. Mond, "The Patents and Designs Bill," *Journal of the Society of Chemical Industry* (1919), XXXVIII, 323.
2. See *Actes de la Conférence de La Haye*, p. 235.

new industry in the territory of that country. Moreover, in such case, the country will lose the customs duties it would collect on the importation of the new products from foreign countries, and competition in the national industry will be more severe, as the products manufactured in the country will be free from transportation expenses and customs duties. Furthermore, the compulsory working provisions cause the installation of foreign industries in the country, movements of capital, and foreign investments, the effects of all of which may be far reaching.[1]

§ 223. Difficulties caused by obligation in the Union. In respect to the Union the following two further points may be made in favor of abolishing this obligation.

First, if in principle it is admitted that the inventors must be protected in all the countries of the Union, it is really a negation of this principle to ask them to work the invention in all those countries. With the expansion that the Union has taken on it is absolutely impossible for an inventor to work his invention in all the thirty-eight countries of the Union, not only within three or five years from the date he obtained his patent, but not even within the entire life of the patent.[2]

Indeed, a great number of inventions are inventions of details or of minor importance, which for technical reasons are not easily workable in all countries. No working of the invention is possible in countries where the industry which it concerns does not exist, or is not sufficiently developed. In such instance, the obligation to work, and the consequent forfeiture of the patent in case of failure, are merely a prize set up for persons who import articles manufactured fraudulently with the invention in other countries. As to countries in which the industry in question is sufficiently developed, minor inventions do not appeal at once to manufacturers. People are not always eager to change their technique and their method of production for minor improvements whose economic value is not, and can-

1. See the best exposition of the effects of the obligation to work an invention, in a conference by von Schütz published in *Annuaire de l'Association* (1897), pp. 241 ff. Mr. Vaughan, in his book *Economics of our Patent System*, p. 245, enumerates several American companies, such as the International Harvester Co., National Cash Register Co., Singer Sewing Machine Co., Gillette Razor Co., Cloumbia Phonograph Co., Remington and other typewriter companies, American Pencil Co., Diamond Match Co., which have established factories in foreign countries so as to save their patents. Other corporations and individuals have granted licenses in foreign countries.

2. Gariel, "Après la Conférence de La Haye, les Tâches du Lendemain." in *Propriété Industrielle* (1926), pp. 146, 149.

not be, proved at first hand. The presence of the inventor, long experiments, proper technical facilities, and various expenses are often necessary; this is not possible in several countries at the same time.

Many of these difficulties exist also in respect to more important inventions, or those concerning an independent industry. Moreover, the establishment of a new industry, its financing, its direction are not simple matters.[1]

A second point to be made in respect to the obligation of working in all the countries of the Union, is that article 5 merely provided that the patentee shall remain subject to the obligation to work his patent according to the law of the various countries of the Union ("restera soumis à l'obligation d'exploiter son brevet conformément aux lois du pays où il introduit les objets brevetés"). The Convention does not attempt to define what "exploiter" means.[2] Although the term is French and was suggested by the equivalent term in the French law,[3] its meaning varies in the various countries of the Union.[4] The Convention does not impose the obligation; no uniform meaning of the term, then, can be sought. Every country of the Union now may give any meaning to the term, so long as it does not violate any other provision of the Convention.

Strictly construed, the obligation to work a patent in a country would amount to a prohibition of importation of patented articles; in such case, a country would violate the first paragraph of article 5. Indeed, an inventor who has to manufacture the patented articles in the country in which such obligation is imposed upon him cannot be

1. It is not strange that even Kohler misses the point, for he is dealing with the subject too much in abstract, in *Lehrbuch des Patentrechts*, pp. 140–141.

2. It was attempted at the Rome Conference to define "exploiter" as meaning "manufacture." Instead, the Conference adopted a proposal of Tunis, that each country may determine for itself the meaning of the term "exploiter." *Conférence de Rome*, pp. 11, 93, 99. 164.

3. The meaning of the term given by the French courts does not accord with its meaning as given by the standard French dictionaries. Thus, Littré's Dictionary and that of the *Académie Française* give to *exploiter* the meaning of: "faire valoir une chose; en tirer le produit," The same meaning was given by the Cour de Paris in its decision dated March 5, 1867, in a case involving *exploitation* of a spring of mineral water. But, in general, the French courts, in applying art. 32, sec. 2 of the Patent Law of 1844, which imposes the obligation to "exploiter," interpret it as meaning "manufacture." See Ch. Constant, "De la Déchéance du Brevet pour Défaut d'Exploiter," in *Annuaire de l'Association* (1897), pp. 432, 438; Pelletier et Vidal-Naquet, *Convention d'Union*, pp. 155–156; H. A. Toulmin, *Patent Law for the Inventor and the Executive* (New York and London, 1928), p. 213.

4. See Pillet, *Régime International*, p. 291. See *supra*, § 157.

expected to be able to import with profit the same articles from other countries.[1]

Besides, it is not always possible to ascertain whether any particular invention has been "worked" sufficiently to satisfy the requirements of the law, no fixed rule or standard existing by which to decide.[2] This introduces an element of uncertainty into the life of a patent and the industries based thereon.[3]

It is submitted, then, that the obligation of working the invention in every country of the Union, on the one hand, is a result of a theoretical fear, rather than of experience and sound economics; and on the other hand, it is a great handicap, and particularly irksome, to foreign inventors, often resulting in a denial of the protection promised by other provisions of the Convention.

If there is any benefit at all in having the invention worked in any country in which a patent is granted to an inventor, it may well be found in the system of compulsory licenses in force in a number of countries; [4] that is, the patentee may be compelled to grant a license for the working of his invention in the country in which a patent was granted to him, provided he manifests no intention of working it himself in that country within a certain period.

This view has gained of late strong foothold even in the countries which stood for a long time in favor of the obligation in question,[5] with the result that at the last Conference of The Hague the obligation to work the patent was in principle replaced by that of compulsory license, as will be seen presently.

§ 224. Double restriction of obligation in the Union. Under the text of article 5, in force prior to its revision at the Conference of The Hague, a double restriction of the penalty of forfeiture of the patent for failure to work it, existed in the Union. The patent could not be subjected to forfeiture because of non-working in one of the

1. See *Conférence de Paris* (1880), p. 66; Constant, "De la Déchéance du Brevet pour Défaut d'Exploitation," in *Annuaire de l'Association* (1897), p. 434; Capuccio, "Comment Doit se Combiner avec l'Obligation d'Exploiter la Permission par le Breveté d'Introduire," in *Annuaire de l'Association* (1902), pp. 51, 52.

2. See *Annuaire de l'Association* (1902), pp. 57, 58.

3. See *ibid.* (1897), pp. 390, 397.

On the various ways that the municipal legislation and the courts of the member countries of the Union understand and impose the obligation to work a patent in the country, see *supra*, § 157, and *Propriété Industrielle* (1924), pp. 65, 86, 118, 213 ff.

4. Kohler, *Handbuch des Deutschen Patentrechts*, p. 615.

5. *Travaux du Groupe Français de l'Association Internationale pour la Protection de la Propriété Industrielle, 1919–1922*, (Paris, 1923), pp. 65–66, 101–102.

countries of the Union, until after a term of three years from the date of filing the application in that country, and only in case the patentee should fail to show sufficient cause for his inaction. Thus the restriction worked in two ways:

(1) A period of three years was accorded to the patentee within which he might comply with the legal obligation to work the invention. In case the municipal law required that the patentee should work his invention within one or two years, it would not be applicable in respect to persons entitled to the benefits of the Convention. The latter was in opposition to the municipal law on this point, and the provision being a complete self-executing legal precept it should be given effect irrespective of the provisions of the municipal law.[1]

The three-year period began from the date of filing the application in the country in question. The starting-point of the period was unwisely chosen. The moment on which the inventor may really be called the patentee, and is able to consider the possibilities of his invention, is the date of delivery of the patent. This should be the starting-point of the period. The nominal period might be very much shortened, as the previous examination of the invention by the patent office might last for a long time. For the same reason, the real period might be unequal in the different countries.

(2) The patent could not be forfeited even though the three-year period had elapsed and the patentee had not yet worked his invention, if he should show sufficient cause for his inaction ("justifierait . . . des causes de son inaction"). Whether the cause of failure to work is sufficient or not is left to the municipal law and the courts of each country to decide. The provision was so understood by the sub-committee of the Brussels Conference which proposed the text of the second paragraph of article 5.[2] The attempt to indicate a sufficient cause (namely, an offer to license) was defeated in the discussions of the sub-committee as well as in those of the Conference.[3] At the Washington Conference the *status quo* was maintained.[4]

This double restriction of the obligation might be claimed by all persons entitled to the benefits of the Convention in respect to all patents obtained by them in any of the countries of the Union. It

1. See on such provisions, *supra*, § 102.
2. *Actes de la Conférence de Bruxelles*, pp. 317–319.
3. *Ibid.*, p. 326.
4. *Actes de la Conférence de Washington*, pp. 282–283, 250.

was immaterial whether or not the patent was applied for within the period of priority.[1]

As seen above,[2] under the municipal law of some countries, the patentee is not only bound to start working his invention within a certain period after the date a patent is granted to him but must not cease to work it during the life of the patent for longer than a certain time. It is clear from the wording of the provision of article 5 that this obligation is not covered by it. Consequently, the municipal law alone controls in this respect.[3]

§ 225. Amendment adopted at the Conference of The Hague. At the last conference of The Hague the International Bureau resumed once more its efforts for the revision of article 5. It took into consideration various *voeux* of the International Association for the Protection of Industrial Property and its national groups, and of the International Chamber of Commerce.[4] It proposed to the Conference of The Hague an amendment of article 5 to the effect that the municipal legislation of the countries of the Union may impose on the patentee the grant of a compulsory license only after the lapse of three years from the date of the delivery of the patent.[5]

A great number of delegations at the Conference voiced their agreement with this proposal. The American delegation, recalling the liberality of the American legislation on patents and the unequal treatment to which American citizens were subjected in the other countries of the Union, proposed that:

Aucune obligation que celles imposées par la législation du pays d'origine ne pourra frapper, en ce qui concerne l'exploitation ou la concession de licenses obligatoires, les brevets pris dans l'un des pays de l'Union.

In other words, the American delegation proposed to insert in general terms in the Convention of Union the stipulation already inserted in some bipartite conventions of the United States with other countries.[6] The adoption of such a provision in the Convention of

1. See *Propriété Industrielle* (1903), p. 132.
2. See *supra*, § 158.
3. Pillet, *Régime International*, pp. 293–294.
4. See these *voeux* in *Actes de la Conference de La Haye*, p. 87. See also similar propositions and *voeux* of earlier congresses and at earlier conferences, *ibid.*, pp. 235–236.
5. *Actes de la Conférence de La Haye*, p. 237.
6. United States and Germany, Arrangement of Feb. 23, 1909 (CII *Br. & For. State Papers*, 443); United States and Denmark, Agreement of June 22/26, 1906 (XCIX *Br. & For. State Papers*, 1039); United States and Switzerland, Declaration of Feb. 3, 1908 (*Recueil Général*, Bureau International, VII, 542).

Union would upset its principle of national treatment. It was defeated by an almost unanimous vote.[1]

On the other hand, the delegations of Japan, Poland and Serb-Croat-Slovene State proposed the maintenance of the *status quo*. They argued that the undeveloped state of their industry did not permit the abolition of the obligation to work the patent in their countries; also, that the system of compulsory licenses did not present the same guaranties to national industry.

It becoming apparent that no unanimity could be obtained on the proposal of the International Bureau, a new text was proposed jointly by the delegations of Great Britain and the United States. This text consisting of the three paragraphs above quoted [2] was finally adopted by the Conference in place of the previous second paragraph of article 5.[3]

§ 226. Prevention of abuses of monopoly rights of patentee. For the penalty of forfeiture of the patent, which was maintained by the old provision of article 5, is now substituted the possibility of "the necessary legislative measures to prevent the abuses which might result from the exercise of the exclusive rights conferred by the patent." Each of the contracting countries "shall have the right to take" these measures.

Two improvements may be noticed in this stipulation, one in form and one in substance. While the old provision read: "le breveté restera soumis à l'obligation d'exploiter," the new stipulation is that each country "aura la faculté de prendre" some legislative measures. Thus the somewhat imperative character of the old stipulation disappears.

The improvement in substance is much more important. The provision lays stress, not on the obligation to work the invention, but on the abuses which might result from the exercise of the exclusive rights of the patentee. In any case, the important question will be, not whether the patentee has fulfilled his obligation to work the patent, but whether or not any abuses have resulted from the exercise of his patent right.

1. *Actes de la Conférence de La Haye*, p. 432. 2. See *supra*, p. 327.

3. *Actes de la Conférence de La Haye*, pp. 433, 434, 576. Both American Delegates, Mr. Lane and Mr. Robertson, made declarations at the Conference, inserted in the *procès-verbaux*, to the effect that they accepted the new text of article 5 as temporary and as a compromise, and that the member countries of the Union should consider for the future the absolute abolition of the obligation to work as well as of the obligation to grant compulsory licenses. See *ibid.*, pp. 573, 575.

The original joint proposition of the American and British Delegations read: "pour prévenir l'abus des droits de monopole." The chairman of the Conference, after reading to the assembly this proposition, explained that the term "abus des droits de monopole" is taken from the English law,[1] and that it comprises, especially, the non-working of the invention, the refusal of the patentee to grant licenses upon reasonable terms, and the limited working of the invention so that the demand for the patented article is not being met to an adequate extent and on reasonable terms. The chairman then expressed the opinion that the phrase "abus des droits de monopole" did not possess a clear meaning in French and suggested that the following words be inserted in its stead: "les abus résultant de l'exercice du privilège conféré par le brevet."[2] This expression was substantially adopted in the new text.

Later, in the discussion of article 5 in the Plenary Committee, the Canadian delegation proposed that it be made clear that failure to work the invention is such an abuse of the exercise of the patentee's exclusive rights. To satisfy this desire, the last words of the second paragraph of article 5 were inserted, viz., "par exemple, faute d'exploitation."[3]

An interesting question of interpretation arises in respect to the provision of the second paragraph of article 5, in view of the history of its adoption: namely, if and to what extent the British law on the abuses of monopoly may be resorted to in finding out the cases in which there exists an abuse of monopoly, and when a state may properly, under the Convention, take legislative measures to prevent it. In the existing state of things, only the law of Great Britain and the British dominions and colonies provides for various cases of abuse of monopoly, while in the other countries the only abuse taken into consideration is that of failure to work the invention. The latter is expressly indicated by the last sentence of the second paragraph of article 5. The law and the decisions of the courts in each country must be resorted to, in order to find out whether or not there has been a failure to work the invention.

1. Sec. 27 of the Patent and Designs Act of 1907, as revised by the Act of 1919 (9 & 10 Geo. V, c. 80), entitled: "Provisions for the prevention of abuse of monopoly rights."

2. *Actes de la Conférence de La Haye*, p. 434.

3. *Ibid.*, p. 519.

§ 227. Suppression, in principle, of forfeiture of patents. While the second paragraph of article 5 provides that each contracting country shall have the right to take the necessary measures to prevent abuses, the third paragraph singles out one of these measures, the forfeiture of the patent, and limits its application. A country may take that step, that is, order the forfeiture of the patent, only in case the grant of compulsory licenses is insufficient to prevent such abuses.

Thus, before any revocation of the patent, the grant of compulsory licenses must be considered. This provision is almost literally the original text proposed by the American and British delegations and is couched in terms of the English Patent and Designs Act. Indeed, that act provides that the Comptroller of the Patent Office, on being satisfied that a case of abuse of the monopoly rights under a patent has been established, may order the patent to be revoked, "if he is satisfied that the objects of this section [that is, the prevention of abuse] cannot be attained by the exercise of any of the foregoing powers [that is, different kinds of compulsory licenses]."[1]

In most of the countries of the Union the system of compulsory licenses was unknown when this provision was adopted at the Conference of The Hague.[2] In those countries the provision in question cannot be carried into effect of its own force. It is not self-executing. The municipal legislation must be modified for the purpose of effectuating the above stipulation of principle.

It may not be expected that the law will be identical in all the countries. It can hardly be said that the English law ought to be adopted because the provision is worded in terms of that law, or even because it was intended to apply the principles of the English law. The provision will be carried into effect in each country so as to fit with its whole administrative and judicial procedure on patents.[3]

The question whether the grant of compulsory license would or would not be sufficient to prevent abuse of the exercise of the patent

1. Sec. 27 of the Act of 1907 and 1919 (9 & 10 Geo. V, c. 80). See also Terrell, *Letters Patent*, p. 289. Generally, on the question of compulsory licenses in Great Britain, see Gordon, *Compulsory Licenses* (London, 1899). This book is old and treats of the subject under the Patent Act of 1883, but the analysis of decisions is very useful.

2. See as to countries in which the system of compulsory licenses exists, *supra*, § 160.

3. For instance, there is no officer, in France and in other countries adopting the system of no previous examination of the invention, who has the powers and jurisdiction of the Comptroller. Compare also as to conditions of compulsory license in Germany, and the effects of the new article 5, Osterrieth, *Die Haager Konferenz*, p. 42.

right is decided in Great Britain, on application of an interested person, by the Comptroller, who may deem such grant expedient in the circumstances.[1] Must the countries which make the necessary changes in their law in order to effectuate the provision of compulsory licenses of the Convention leave the above question to be decided according to the circumstances of each particular case, or may they determine beforehand the various sets of circumstances and apply to them definite remedies? In other words, is the English practice of discretion to be adopted — or one of hard-and-fast rules?

May a country declare by law that, in a certain set of circumstances, it is presumed that the measure of the grant of compulsory license would be insufficient to prevent abuse, and that therefore the patent may be ordered revoked forthwith? May this set of circumstances, which may cause the unconditional forfeiture of the patent, be merely the non-working of the invention in a country within a definite period?

No assured answers may be given to all these questions. It would seem, however, that the less liberal solution is not excluded. In respect to the last question, this would mean almost a continuation of the situation existing prior to the revision of the Convention at The Hague.[2] Undoubtedly, this would be hardly in accordance with the spirit and purpose of the amendment of article 5, but the terms are too general and too indefinite, and it must not be forgotten that some delegations insisted on maintaining the *status quo* of article 5.

It is submitted that the serious error in drafting this provision, the most important of article 5, is in putting it too much in terms of British law. Thus, while it has a definite meaning against the background of the British patent law, it has no such meaning in continental law, and is susceptible to any interpretation.

§ **228. Maintenance of old double restriction.** Article 5, in its new fourth paragraph, retains the former double restriction against forfeiture of the patent. This restriction concerns now not only the forfeiture of the patent, but all measures provided for in the second paragraph of article 5 for preventing abuses of the exercise of the

1. See Terrell, *Letters Patent*, pp. 285 ff.

2. Osterrieth is almost right, therefore, in contending that in a veiled way the obligation to work the patent, to its full extent, is recognized by the new article 5. See his book, *Die Haager Konferenz*, p. 41.

exclusive rights conferred by the patent. Such measures cannot be taken against the patentee in the following cases.

(1) Before the expiry of at least three years from the date of grant of the patent. Here is a substantial difference from the period provided for in old article 5. Although the latter also was three years, it began with the date of filing the patent application; thus the period was in fact much shorter, and was unequal in the different countries, as stated above.[1] Now the period begins with the date of grant of the patent, which eliminates the above objections.

(2) If the patentee is able to justify himself by legitimate reasons. There is no substantial change in this respect from the old text,[1] although for the phrase "causes de son inaction," the words "excuses légitimes" are substituted.

§ 229. Value of amendment of article 5. In conclusion, the value of the amendment of article 5 at the Conference of The Hague remains to be seen. In fact, it is recognized now in principle that abuse of the exercise of the exclusive rights conferred by the patent ought to be the only reason for taking any measures against, and imposing any obligations upon, the patentee; also, that the penalty of forfeiture of the patent should not be resorted to, if that of compulsory license would be sufficient for preventing such abuse. Yet, no definite engagement is taken by any country, and no greater security than before is afforded to foreign inventors.

In this state of things, it is to be regretted that the original suggestion of the International Bureau, for constituting a restricted union between the countries admitting definitely the system of compulsory license, has not been followed. Although the method of restricted unions should not be encouraged, it is perhaps much worse that all the rest of the countries of the Union should yield to the only three countries which are unwilling to take the liberal view and thus be compelled to maintain an undesirable provision.[2]

1. *Supra*, § 224.

2. The objection that the countries remaining outside the restricted union would constitute an asylum where the foreign patents would be freely worked by other people, is not serious, because those countries would be bound at any rate by the provisions of article 5 of the Convention, and otherwise the situation would not be worse than it is to-day. See objection in Gariel, "Après la Conférence de La Haye, les Tâches du Lendemain," in *Propriété Industrielle* (1926), pp. 146, 152.

At a meeting of the Standing Committee for the Protection of Industrial Property of the International Chamber of Commerce, on Feb. 12 and 13, 1926, an opinion in accordance with the one advanced in the text was expressed by the German delegation, and after discussion the Committee decided that, ". . . owing to the small number of

III. Payment of Fees

§ **230. Restriction of penalty for non-payment of fees.** An important obligation of the patentee in all the countries of the Union, with the exception of the United States, is the annual or periodical payment of fees during the life of the patent. The penalty for non-payment is everywhere the forfeiture of the patent. In view of this severe penalty, a period of grace is accorded in many countries. Moreover, in Great Britain and the British dominions, as well as in Austria. Germany, Portugal, and Switzerland a patent may be restored on application, if it appears that the omission to pay was unintentional.[1]

At the Conference of The Hague it was proposed by the American delegation that no fee or annuity greater than those provided by the law of the country of origin could be imposed for patents taken out in the Union, and that the restoration of patents forfeited for non-payment of fees should be made obligatory on all the countries of the Union by a specific provision of the Convention.[2] On the other hand, Great Britain proposed a *voeu,* to be adopted by the Conference, calling upon the members of the Union to grant a three months' period of grace for fees and the restoration of patents forfeited for non-payment.[3]

§ **231. Period of grace under article.** The first proposal of the United States, constituting a derogation from the principle of national treatment which is at the basis of the Convention, was defeated.[4] On the other hand, the second proposal was the subject of many discussions in the sub-committee, the Editing Committee, and the Committee of the Whole.[5] At last, an agreement was reached on a distinction between a provision for a period of grace and one for the restoration of patents. This agreement is embodied in the new article 5*b* of the Convention, reading as follows:

Un délai de grâce, qui devra être au minimum de trois mois, sera accordé pour le payement des taxes prévues pour le maintien des droits de la

countries opposing, . . . the question of the suppression of forfeiture of patents for non-working might in its opinion perhaps be solved by an exchange of declarations at the time of ratifications." See International Chamber of Commerce, *Supplement to Journal,* No. 9, April, 1926, pp. 5–6.

1. See *supra,* § 150.
2. *Artes de la Conférence de La Haye,* p. 338.
3. *Ibid.,* p. 354.
4. *Ibid.,* pp. 431–432.
5. *Ibid.,* pp. 434–435, 520, 541, 576, 577.

propriété industrielle, moyennant le versement d'une surtaxe, si la législation nationale en impose une.

Pour les brevets d'invention, les pays contractants s'engagent en outre, soit à porter le délai de grâce à six mois au moins, soit à prévoir la restoration du brevet tombé en déchéance par suite de non-payement de taxes, ces mesures restant soumises aux conditions prévues par la législation intérieure.

The first paragraph of article 5*b* deals with the period of grace. It concerns all rights of industrial property. If for the maintenance of such rights the municipal law of a country of the Union imposes the payment of a fee, a three months' period of grace shall be allowed for the payment of such fee. The municipal legislation may grant a longer period of grace, but if none, or a lesser period, is granted, the three months' grace shall be enjoyed by virtue of the above provision. In other words, the provision under consideration is one constituting common legislation of the members of the Union, like the provision of the right of priority. It is complete in itself, and needs no municipal law to carry it into effect. The only thing left to the municipal law is to dertermine whether a supplementary fee shall be paid for the payment within the period of grace.

This grace shall be allowed for the payment of fees for the maintenance of rights of industrial property. Fees payable for the filing of an application or for the delivery of the patent would not seem to be covered by the provision.[1] In the United States, no fees are payable during the life of a patent. All fees are paid during the procedure leading to the grant of a patent. The final fee is payable on the definite acceptance of the application and before the delivery of the patent. For the payment of this fee a delay of six months is provided for by the United States Patent Act.[2] The American delegation at the Conference of The Hague declared that it interprets the provision of article 5*b* as not applicable to this final fee payable in the United States. This declaration was taken down in the *procès-verbaux* by order of the chairman.[3]

The provision of article 5*b* concerning the period of grace is unqualified, in the sense that the three months' extension of time shall

1. As article 5*b* was first drafted, it spoke of fees provided for in the matter of industrial property (taxes prévues en matière de propriété industrielle), which raised objections on the part of some delegates, as is recorded in the *procès-verbaux*, *Actes de la Conférence de La Haye*, p. 520.

2. Sections 4885 and 4935 of the Revised Statutes.

3. *Actes de la Conférence de La Haye*, p. 576.

always be allowed, whatever the cause of the delay might be. This is confirmed by the *procès-verbaux* in the commentary on article 5*b*, where it is said that the period of grace shall be allowed "sans avoir à justifier d'aucune excuse." [1]

The computation of the three months' period should follow by analogy the rules established by article 4 in respect to the periods of the right of priority.[2] Thus the date on which payment is due, according to the municipal law, is not included in the three-months period, and if the last day of the period is a legal holiday in the country where payment is due, the period is extended until the first following working day.

§ **232. Restoration of patents.** The second paragraph of article 5*b* concerns patents alone. In respect to them, the contracting countries undertake either to increase the above-mentioned period of grace to not less than six months, or to provide for the restoration of a patent which has expired by reason of the non-payment of fees. This provision is not self-executing; it is not common legislation of the Union. It enacts only a principle, and the contracting countries undertake to carry it into effect by appropriate legislation. The last phrase of the paragraph adds: "ces mesures restant soumises aux conditions prévues par la législation intérieure."

In accordance with the above provision, every contracting country is bound to allow to patentees either a six months' grace or an application for the restoration of the patent. But each country may determine the conditions for the enjoyment of these advantages. It may make such enjoyment conditional on the payment of a penalty, and on the existence of accidental circumstances or of *vis major*. Indeed, this is expressly said in the commentary on article 5*b*, and in the report of the Editing Committee, and it was so understood by various delegations.[3]

The municipal law may determine also the time within which the application for restoration should be made after the expiration of a patent by reason of non-payment of fees.

As article 5 was originally drafted by the Editing Committee, it provided that the restoration of patents should be subject to the rights of personal possession of third parties who should work the invention before the restoration of the patent. This reservation was

1. *Actes de la Conférence de La Haye*, pp. 541, 577.
2. *Propriété Industrielle* (1927), p. 49.
3. *Actes de la Conférence de La Haye*, pp. 434–435, 541.

attacked by the Belgian delegation. It does not appear in the final text of article 5*b*. Should it be assumed that the Conference, by omitting this reservation, established the opposite? This can hardly be supported.[1] The Conference struck out this reservation as well as the condition of *vis major*, but it inserted the phrase, "ces mesures restant soumises aux conditions prévues par la législation intérieure," which leaves the municipal law free to lay down any conditions it pleases.[2]

Since the Conference of The Hague, two countries have passed laws allowing restoration of patents expired by reason of non-payment of fees, — Portugal [3] and Switzerland.[4] In the former, restoration may be applied for within a year from the expiration of the date of payment, on condition of paying three times the fee, the non-payment of which caused the forfeiture of the patent, and on condition of showing that the rights of third persons are not prejudiced by such restoration. In Switzerland, restoration may be obtained within a three months' period following a first three months' period of grace, on condition of paying a fee for restoration of not less than fifty francs.

1. However, an article in *Propriété Industrielle* (1927), pp. 48, 49, intimates such an opinion.

2. Doubtless, however, no reservation of rights of third parties may be made in respect to the three months' period of grace of the first paragraph of article 5*b*. This provision has the effect of withholding the forfeiture of the patent until the expiration of the three months' period. And since the patent is not forfeited before that time, the use of the invention by third parties not only does not create any rights for them, but it constitutes an infringement of the patent, for which they are liable.

3. Decree of Nov. 19, 1926 (1926 *Colecção de Legislação Portuguêsa*, p. 683).

4. *Loi Fédérale* of Oct. 9, 1926 (1927 *Recueil des Lois*, No. 2, p. 9).

CHAPTER XIV

PROTECTION OF INVENTIONS AT INTERNATIONAL EXHIBITIONS

§ 233. International exhibitions and need of general protection of patentable inventions. From the rudimentary markets or fairs of the Middle Ages sprang the national and international exhibitions for the encouragement of industry and commerce at the end of the eighteenth and the beginning of the nineteenth century. Whereas in the Middle Ages the markets and fairs were only temporary armistices and foreigners could enter a country on such occasions and find protection,[1] in modern times they are invited to international exhibitions with the bait of exceptional treatment, exemptions, and special privileges.[2] However, the international protection of industrial property at such exhibitions left much to be desired before the creation of the Union in 1883; and in another place in this study[3] it is told how the inadequacy of such protection at the Inter-

1. See *The Mirror of Justices*, ed. by Selden Society, London, 1895, p. 14. Also, Pardessus, *Collections des Lois Maritimes*, II (Introduction), cv.

2. See *Fairs and Exhibitions*, Digest No. 56, International Chamber of Commerce, June–Dec., 1927, listing and furnishing comprehensive data on all fairs and exhibitions organized for 1927 and 1928. As facilities and exceptional treatments, are inserted freight reduction on exhibits, reduction of railway fares, passport facilities, custom facilities, etc. It may be noted also that the general fairs and exhibitions held from May to Dec., 1927, in the various countries number 152, while the special fairs and exhibitions number 316.

3. See *supra*, § 44.

national Exhibition of Vienna in 1873 led to the first step toward the formation of the Union. Inventors, as well as authors of designs and owners of trade marks, could not be expected to exhibit their respective discoveries, creations, and distinctive marks. By the exhibition and the consequent or probable publication, description, or use by third persons of their inventions, and so forth, their novelty would be lost. Also they would risk having them copied, imitated, or counterfeited by other persons in the country in which the exhibition was held, or in any other country. It was not enough, indeed, to grant inventions a temporary protection in the country of the exhibition. There should also be assurance that they would be protected in all the other countries.

Thus, the protection of industrial property at international exhibitions is essentially a matter of international concern, and cannot be fully effected by a single country. In consideration of this fact, the Convention of 1883 attempted to secure the necessary protection of rights of industrial property exhibited at international exhibitions by its article 11, which originally read as follows:

> Les Hautes Parties contractantes s'engagent à accorder une protection temporaire aux inventions brevetables, aux dessins ou modèles industriels, ainsi qu'aux marques de fabrique ou de commerce, pour les produits qui figureront aux expositions internationales officielles ou officiellement reconnues.

This article was adopted by the Conference of 1880 in the form that was proposed in the Draft.[1] The Conference did not wish to go further than to lay down a general principle, and had no sympathy with the proposal of the Italian delegate Indelli for a different form of article 11, which, notwithstanding its defects, purported to create a uniform and actual temporary protection in all the countries of the Union.[2]

1. But a second paragraph of this article was rejected by the Conference. It read: "Les objets argués de contrefaçon pourront être saisis dans l'enceinte des expositions. See *Conférence de Paris* (1880), p. 105.

2. Indelli's proposal read thus: "Les auteurs des inventions brevetables, des dessins ou modèles industriels, ainsi que des marques de fabrique et de commerce, pour les produits qui figureront aux Expositions internationales officielles ou officiellement reconnues, auront, après une notification faite au Bureau Industriel, un délai de deux mois après la clôture de l'Exposition, pour faire le dépôt des demandes de brevet, des dessins ou modèles et des marques, conformément à l'article 3 [4]." See *Conférence de Paris* (1880), p. 105.

§ 234. Legal effect of the stipulation of article 11. Article 11 of the Convention contained, therefore, only an engagement of the contracting states to provide by their municipal legislation for the temporary protection of inventions, designs or models, and trade marks at international exhibitions. This is quite clear from the discussions at the Conference [1] and from the wording of the article, stipulating that the high contracting parties "s'engagent à accorder une protection." The provision of article 11 is, therefore, one of those which obligate the contracting parties to create and maintain certain provisions of municipal law, and which are distinguished above,[2] on the one hand from the provisions merely referring to the municipal law of each country and making it applicable, and on the other, from the provisions establishing common legislation for all countries of the Union.[3] The stipulation of article 11 does not define either the nature or the extent of the protection which must be accorded. It is impossible then to base on article 11 alone any protection whatsoever.[4]

All contracting countries, by virtue of article 11, must afford temporary protection for industrial property at exhibitions by creating and maintaining municipal law to that effect. A country which does not create and maintain, or does not maintain, the legislation necessary to bring about the situation intended by the Convention,

1. The French author of the Draft Convention, Mr. Jagerschmidt, said in opposing the Italian delegate's proposal: "Actuellement il n'y a pas de législation ayant trait aux expositions. On demande seulement aux Gouvernements de s'engager à donner une protection aux inventions admises a ces expositions; mais ils feront comme ils l'entendront." The Swiss delegate concurring in that view thought that: "il faut se borner à voter le principe, en laissant aux Gouvernements le soin de régler le mode d'application." See *Conférence de Paris* (1880), p. 107.

2. See *supra* , §§ 88, 101.

3. The following authorities agree in considering the stipulation of article 11 as merely an engagement of the contracting parties to legislate for the temporary protection of industrial property at expositions: Pouillet et Plé, *Convention d'Union*, p. 86; Pelletier et Vidal-Naquet, *Ibid.*, p. 169; Osterrieth und Axster, *Pariser Konvention*, p. 227; Dorff et Pholien, *Les Expositions et le Droit*, pp. 143, 144.— *Contra*, Pillet, *Régime International*, pp. 395 ff., 403 ff.; Donzel, *Commentaire de la Convention*, p. 340.

4. Pillet (*Régime International*, p. 396) thinks otherwise. His point that, in holding that article 11 contains only an engagement of the various countries, we deprive it of all usefulness, is certainly untenable, because it is better than no engagement at all. His other point, that the case is the same as that of article 4, is not very happy either, because this latter article contains a definite and certain provision which leaves no doubt of the nature and extent of the protection stipulated, and may constitute the rule of a decision without the need of further legislation. Pillet's argument fails to make the distinction among the three kinds of provisions in the Convention which is suggested above, § 88.

violates an international obligation, commits a *Dauerdelikt* (permanent international crime).[1]

§ 235. Shortcomings of article 11 and its amendments. Like all provisions of this kind, that of article 11 was not making for uniformity of legislation and for uniform solution of the problems arising in an effective protection of industrial property at exhibitions. While some countries had legislated on this matter before the creation of the Union,[2] and others took legislative measures in execution of their engagement,[3] a few failed to act and thus did not afford

1. Triepel, *Droit International et Droit Interne* (Washington, 1920), p. 287. Pelletier and Vidal-Naquet (*Convention d'Union*, p. 169) miss this point when they speak of the engagement of article 11 as merely *un voeu*, or even as *un engagement réciproque*. The stipulation is a formal international engagement, and no reciprocity is intended here as in all other provisions of the Convention.

2. France, Law of May 23, 1868 (*Bulletin des Lois*, 1868, I, 405). This law was abrogated in 1908 by the Law of April 13, which now governs the matter of expositions (*Bulletin des Lois*, 1908, I, 2163).

Brazil, Act of Oct. 14, 1882, art. 2 (*Collecção das Leis*, 1882, I, 82). The matter now is governed in Brazil by the *Decreto* of Dec. 19, 1923. art. 37 (*Collecção das Leis*, 1923, III, 329, 335).

3. Austria, Act of Jan. 11, 1897, sec. 3, superseded recently by Act No. 67 of Jan. 27, 1925 and Order No. 75 of Feb. 23, 1925 (*Bundesgesetzblatt*, 1925, pp. 250. 255).

Belgium passed no general law on the matter. It provides for each exposition by a special *Arrêté*. See Dorff et Pholien, *Les Expositions et le Droit*, pp. 152 ff.

Czechoslovakia, Acts of May 27, 1919 and June 30, 1922 (*Sammlung der Gesetze des Čechoslovakischen Staates*, 1919, p. 473, and 1922, p. 1241).

Ceylon, No. 15 of 1906, An Ordinance to amend the Law relating to Patents, sec. 46 (*Legislative Enactments*, 1900–1907, pp. 375, 389).

Danzig, The German Law on Exhibitions of 1904, cited below (in force in Danzig, as the writer is informed by letter from the Senate of the Free City of Danzig, No. J. 6342/27 dated Dec. 21, 1927).

Denmark, Act of April 13, 1894, art. 28 (*Lovtidende for Danmark*, 1894, p. 223).

Germany, Law of March 18, 1904 (*Reichsgesetzblatt*, 1904, p. 141).

Great Britain, originally Act of June 25, 1886, sec. 3 (49–50 Vict. c. 37), now superseded by sec. 45 of the Act of 1907, as amended by the Act of 1919 (7 Edw. VII, c. 29 and 9 & 10 Geo. V, c. 80).

Hungary, Act No. XI of 1911 and Decree of May 16, 1911 (*Ungarische Reichsgesetzsammlung*, 1911, p. 570).

Irish Free State, Industrial and Commercial Property Act, 1927, sec. 60 (*Saorstat Eireann*, No. 16 of 1927).

Italy, Act of July 16, 1905 and Decree of April 19, 1906 (*Raccolta di Leggi e Decreti*, 1905, IV, 3690, and 1906, II, 1226).

Japan, Act of April 2, 1909, art. 8 (*Propriété Industrielle*, 1909, p. 92), superseded by Act of April 29, 1921 (*Propriété Industrielle*, 1923, p. 109).

Latvia, Act of March 14, 1925 (*Propriété Industrielle*, 1925, pp. 186–187).

Mexico, Act of Aug. 25, 1903, art. 5 (1) (*Anales de la Legislación Federal*, 1902–1903, p. 286).

Morocco, Decree of June 23, 1916, title VIII, chap. 1 (*Codes et Lois du Maroc, édition officielle*, I, suppl. 1, 326).

The Netherlands, Act of Jan. 15, 1921, art. 8 (*Staatsblad*, 1921, No. 15).

the protection provided for by article 11.[1] On the other hand, on many essential points of that protection the law of the various countries differed.

Besides, a certain defect was disclosed in article 11 soon after the Convention went into effect. It was not certain whether the stipulation of this article bound the member countries of the Union to protect the industrial property of persons entitled to the benefits of the Convention at the exhibitions held on their own territory only, or at all exhibitions held on the territory of any country of the Union.[2] It is easy to see that protection granted only in the country on the territory of which the exhibition is organized is utterly insufficient. The purpose of article 11 was to secure to inventors a general protection, in all the countries of the Union, for their inventions exhibited in any official or officially recognized international exhibition.

In all the conferences of revision attempts have been made to amend and perfect article 11 by doing away with the above defect, and by defining the nature and extent of the protection stipulated. All these attempts have practically failed.[3] At the Brussels Conference two amendments were adopted and inserted in article 11, one of form only and the other of substance. The first words of the article were replaced by the following: "Les pays contractants accorderont, conformément à la législation de chaque pays." Thus, instead of ". . . s'engagent à accorder," article 11 provided now

---

Norway, Act of July 2, 1910, art. 46 (*Norsk Lovtidende*, 1910, p. 243).

Poland, Law of Feb. 5, 1924, art. 3 (*Propriété Industrielle*, 1924, p. 198).

Portugal, Decree of Feb. 11, 1911 (*Collecção oficial*, 1911, p. 123).

Serb-Croat-Slovene State, Orders of Nov. 15 1920, chap. VIII, § 160, and Nov. 17, 1920, chap. VI, §§ 94–99 (*Propriété Industrielle*, 1921, pp. 34, 87).

Spain, Act of May 16, 1902, art. 146 (*Legislación*, 1902, II, 88).

Sweden, Law of May 16, 1884, art. 3, modified by Law of March 26, 1897 (*Svensk Författnings-Samling*, 1884, No. 25 and 1897, No. 19).

Switzerland, Law of June 29, 1888, art. 33, now superseded by Law of April 3, 1914, title II, arts. 7–9, and *Règlement* of July 24, 1914 (*Recueil Officiel des Lois*, N. S., XXX, 317, 319–320, 323).

Tunis, Decree of June 11, 1906 (*Propriété Industrielle*, 1907, p. 127).

1. Cuba and Dominican Republic. See *Propriété Industrielle* (1923), p. 80; also letter of the Cuban Ministry of Agriculture, Commerce, and Labor to the writer, No. 8887, of May 30, 1928.

2. See Pelletier et Vidal-Naquet, *Convention d'Union*, pp. 171 ff.; Esperson, *Proprietà Industriale*, p. 61.

3. See a complete account in *Propriété Industrielle* (1923), pp. 49 ff., 61 ff., 79 ff., 95 ff.

"accorderont," which is not different substantially, if it does not make the engagement less imperative.[1]

The other amendment consisted in the addition of the phrase: "organisées sur le territoire de l'un d'eux" at the end of the article. This removed all doubts as to the protection intended by article 11. Every contracting country must provide for the protection of patents as well as of other rights of industrial property, whether the exhibition is organized on its own territory or on that of any other country of the Union.[2]

At the Washington Conference the words "aux modèles d'utilité" were added to article 11, thus including this kind of industrial property with the rest already enumerated in the article. Following these amendments, article 11 of the Convention, as in effect prior to the Conference of The Hague, read as follows:

> Les pays contractants accorderont, conformément à leur législation intérieure, une protection temporaire aux inventions brevetables, aux modèles d'utilité, aux dessins ou modèles industriels ainsi qu'aux marques de fabrique ou de commerce, pour les produits qui figureront aux Expositions internationales officielles ou officiellement reconnues, organisées sur le territoire de l'un d'eux.

§ 236. When is an Exposition international and official or officially recognized? The temporary protection of article 11 shall be granted to patentable inventions in respect of goods exhibited at official, or officially recognized, international exhibitions. First, the exhibition must be international. It would seem to be sufficient for an exhibition to be considered international if it admits products and exhibits from all countries and not only from the country in which it is organized.[3] It is not necessary that products from other countries be actually exhibited.

1. Compare *Propriété Industrielle* (1923), pp. 49, 53. Although the expression is weaker, the meaning should not be considered so. Indeed, the Committee, in adopting that expression, commented upon it as follows: "Cette disposition nouvelle implique, dans la pensée de la Commission, l'obligation pour chacun des États contractants de légiférer sur ce point, à l'example de la France, de la Grande Bretagne et d'autres nations." See *Actes de la Conférence de Bruxelles*, p. 186. One writer, (Mesnil, "De la Protection aux Expositions Internationales," in *Annuaire de l'Association Internationale*, 1899, pp. 61, 70) thinks that the new expression is more imperative.

2. Pillet, *Régime International*, p. 403; Pelletier et Vidal-Naquet, *Convention d'Union*, pp. 431–432; Dorff et Pholien, *Les Expositions et le Droit*, p. 143.

3. Dorff et Pholien, *Les Expositions et le Droit*, p. 24; Pillet, *Régime International*, p. 395; Pelletier et Vidal-Naquet, *Convention d'Union*, p. 166; Osterrieth und Axster, *Pariser Konvention*, p. 228.

The International Chamber of Commerce, in its *Fairs and Exhibitions* published

Second, the exhibition must be official or officially recognized. Exhibitions are organized by the government or public authorities, or by private persons with the coöperation or the financial and moral assistance of the government.[1] Whether or not an exhibition organized in the latter way is official depends on the law of the country in which the exhibition takes place.[2] It is of great importance for foreign inventors to know whether the exhibition is official or officially recognized, for in such case only they will be protected in accordance with article 11 of the Convention.

At the Washington Conference, Great Britain had argued for a restriction of the protection provided for in article 11 to serious exhibitions and that the term "expositions internationales" be interpreted as meaning important exhibitions in which a sufficient number of contracting countries participate by assisting in its organization financially, and by sending to it authorized delegates. Other delegates having remarked that the question of the seriousness and the international character of an exhibition should be left to each country, the Committee decided that a provision should be added to article 11, defining the exhibitions which would benefit by the temporary protection.[3]

This was not carried out. But on the initiative of the Dutch government, the International Bureau, by its circular of November 3, 1913, asked the offices of industrial property of the member countries of the Union to transmit to the Bureau, within the first three months of each year, a list of the officially recognized international exhibitions to be held in their territory within that year. The suggestion has been followed by several countries, although sometimes the notifications were made late. The Bureau published those lists in the *Propriété Industrielle*.[4]

At the last conference, at The Hague, the Bureau proposed to add to article 11 a provision making obligatory on all countries of the Union what had been done hitherto by some. This proposal, which was eventually rejected, read as follows:[5]

---

twice a year, indicates the exhibitions in which products from all countries are admitted. Thus, out of the 152 General Exhibitions listed in the issue of June–Dec., 1927, 85 were international.

1. Dorff et Pholien, *Expositions et le Droit*, p. 26.
2. Osterrieth und Axster, *Pariser Konvention*, p. 228.
3. *Actes de la Conférence de Washington*, pp. 279–280.
4. See *Propriété Industrielle* (1923), pp. 80–81.
5. *Actes de la Conférence de La Haye*, p. 259.

Chaque pays contractant devra communiquer d'avance et en temps utile au Bureau International de Berne les listes des expositions internationales qui se tiendront sur son territoire et qu'il considère comme officielles ou officiellement reconnues. Le Bureau International publiera ces listes dans sa Revue, *La Propriété Industrielle.*

§ 237. Is the period of priority of article 4 prolonged by the temporary protection of article 11? Article 11 of the Convention speaks of temporary protection which must be assured by the contracting countries to patentable inventions, and so forth, exhibited at industrial exhibitions. The purpose of this protection is to make it possible for inventors to exhibit their inventions without fear of having a subsequent filing of a patent application invalidated by acts occurring in the interval, such as the publication or use of the invention, an application by a third person, and the like. The protection, therefore, which should be assured to inventions exhibited at exhibitions is similar to the protection which is needed by the persons applying for a patent first in one country and subsequently in others.

The latter protection is afforded by article 4 of the Convention, in definite terms and under well-defined conditions. On the other hand, the extent and conditions of the temporary protection provided for in article 11 are determined exclusively by the municipal law, which is enacted in fulfillment of the international engagement. There is one aspect, however, of the temporary protection which cannot be left altogether to the determination of each country, namely, its relation to the rights of priority granted by article 4 of the Convention. Does the temporary protection which must be assured to patentable inventions under article 11 lengthen the period of right of priority of article 4, or does it coincide therewith?

The first would seem to be the proper answer, in principle, in view of the fact that the provision of article 11 is quite independent of the provision of article 4, and purports, on its face, to grant a new and distinct advantage besides that of article 4.[1] In practice, this would result in inequalities of treatment between the nationals of the various countries of the Union, and in unequal prolongations of the right of priority in case the temporary protection under article 11 should not be of the same duration in the different countries

1. Pillet, *Régime International,* p. 398; Dorff et Pholien, *Expositions et le Droit,* p. 149; Mesnil, in *Annuaire de l'Association Internationale* (1899), pp. 61, 72.

of the Union.[1] But this being a defect of article 11 it should not change what, from an analysis of articles 4 and 11, appears to be an unavoidable conclusion.

If the temporary protection under article 11 could be held not to prolong the period of right of priority, the latter period would be much shortened, while the practical interest of the former would disappear. The importance of the temporary protection of article 11 consists in making it possible for an inventor to exhibit his invention to the public, and to judge from the interest shown whether the invention is likely to be profitable to him if patented and worked. He will then apply for patents in the countries in which he desires to be protected. The purpose of article 11 is to have the inventor protected by the municipal law of all the countries of the Union from the time of the exhibition of his invention until the time he first applies for a patent in any country of the Union.

From this latter moment the period of his right of priority begins, and the inventor is protected in all the countries of the Union for the whole duration of that period. If it be held that there is no cumulation of the two protections, then the period of the right of priority will begin with the exhibition of his invention (or before it; for instance, from the commencement of the exhibition), and not from the moment he first applies for a patent in a country of the Union, as article 4 provides.

While, on the one hand, the interest of inventors and the clear purpose of articles 4 and 11 is in favor of the cumulation of the two periods of protection, on the other, the interests of third parties, inventors or manufacturers, are injured by too great a prolongation of the right of priority. Thus, while the right of priority must not be reduced, an unequal and immoderate prolongation thereof must be avoided.

At the Madrid Conference a provision was adopted to the effect that the two periods of protection should be added,[2] but the acts adopted at that Conference were not ratified. All attempts to amend article 11 to the same effect in the subsequent conferences of revision [3] have failed. At the last conference, at The Hague, however,

1. *Propriété Industrielle* (1923), p. 80.

2. Protocol, art. 6, § 3. See *Conférence de Madrid*, p. 217.

3. See *Actes de la Conférence de Bruxelles*, pp. 48, 147; *Actes de la Conférence de Washington*, pp. 53–54, 231–232; *Actes de la Conférence de La Haye*, pp. 255, 259 ff.

a provision was added to article 11 which gives a solution in opposition to the opinion advanced here.[1]

§ **238. Execution of article 11 of the Convention.** Consideration of the question of temporary protection of inventions in the member countries of the Union raises various questions. First, it may be inquired how far the various countries of the Union have fulfilled their obligation under article 11 by assuring to inventors a temporary protection at exhibitions. Out of thirty-eight countries which constitute the Union (January, 1929), the following countries seem to have failed to execute their engagement: Australia, Bulgaria, Cuba, Dominican Republic, Esthonia, Greece, Luxembourg, Rumania, and Turkey. It may be noted that, with the exception of Cuba and the Dominican Republic, which have been members of the Union for a long time, the countries enumerated above have but recently adhered to the Union, and may be expected to take measures to execute their engagement.[2]

Canada and the United States, although they have not passed special legislation for the protection of patentable inventions at exhibitions, do in fact afford such protection by their general patent law. Indeed, a patent may be applied for, in both these countries,[3] for any invention not patented or described in any printed publication in the country or abroad, and not in public use or on sale in the country for more than two years prior to the application. And if a patent has been obtained or applied for abroad, it may also be applied for in Canada or in the United States within one year from the earliest date on which an application was filed in any foreign country. Thus, the exhibition at expositions does not destroy the novelty of the invention in these countries if a patent is applied for within two years thereafter, or within one year from the first application abroad. In other words, patentable inventions exhibited at expositions practically enjoy temporary protection for a maximum of one year, if it be assumed that only at the end of a year the inventor who exhibited his invention applies for a patent in a foreign country.

Two countries of the Union, Italy and Norway, while they have

1. See *infra*, § 243.

2. Letters to the writer from the Greek and Luxembourgian administrations, under date of Nov. 28, and Dec. 23, 1927, respectively, affirm that legislation for the protection of industrial property at international exhibitions is being prepared, and will be passed in the near future.

3. Canada, Act of June 13, 1913, secs. 7 and 8 (13–14 Geo. V, c. 23; 1923, Stat. of Canada, p. 145). The United States, Rev. Stat., sect. 4886 and 4887.

passed special legislation for the temporary protection of inventions at exhibitions, afford such protection on condition of reciprocity.[1] Thus these two countries do not grant temporary protection for exhibitions in a foreign country, unless that country grants protection to inventions exhibited at exhibitions. It is submitted that these countries have not fully executed their engagement, because article 11, like all other stipulations of the Convention, is not subject to the condition of reciprocity.[2] Every member country of the Union is bound to grant temporary protection for exhibitions organized in any of the countries of the Union, regardless of the law of other countries.

Spain, on the other hand, grants temporary protection to inventions exhibited at expositions organized on its own territory and not on the territory of any other country of the Union.[3] So that that country has practically not executed her obligation under article 11 of the Convention.[4]

§ 239. **Exhibitions in which inventions are protected by the various countries of the Union.** The next question concerns the kind of exhibitions at which patentable inventions enjoy temporary protection by the laws of various countries. In some countries (Brazil, Finland, Hungary, Mexico, Morocco, the Netherlands, Portugal, Serb-Croat-Slovene State, Sweden, and Tunis), the law concerns generally international exhibitions, with the addition sometimes of the qualification "official" or "officially recognized," while national exhibitions are also included. In other countries (Austria, Belgium, Denmark, France, Germany, Great Britain, Italy, Japan, Latvia, Norway, Poland, and Switzerland), although the same general provision is often found in the law, a condition is added that a decree or an order of the government must certify as to every exhibition whether the provisions of the law for temporary protection for inventions exhibited will apply in that case.[5] It is in respect to these

1. Italy, Act of July 16, 1905, art. 3 (*Raccolta di Leggi e Decreti*, 1905, IV, 3690); Norway, Act of July 2, 1910, art. 46 (*Norsk Lovtidende*, 1910, p. 243).

2. See *Propriété Industrielle* (1923), p. 80.

3. Act of May 16, 1902 (*Legislación*, 1902, II, 88).

4. Austria was in the same situation until recently, but by Act No. 57 of Jan. 27, 1925, and Order No. 75 of Feb. 23, 1925 (*Bundesgesetzblatt*, 1925, pp. 250, 255), she executed fully article 11 of the Convention.

5. The writer is indebted for information on the law of each country of the Union on this question to the *Tableau Comparatif* prepared by the International Bureau and published in the *Actes de la Conférence de La Haye*, pp. 165 ff., and to the article of the Bureau in *Propriété Industrielle* (1923), pp. 80 ff.

countries that foreigners must be informed for each particular exhibition, whether they may expect to be protected. As seen above, the International Bureau proposed that an early notification to it, and publication in the *Propriété Industrielle* was necessary.[1]

§ 240. Duration of temporary protection in the countries of the Union. The question of the duration of the temporary protection in the various countries of the Union is bound up with the question of the starting-point of the period of protection. Some countries hold it necessary that the invention should be protected from the moment it is introduced in the locale of the exhibition, because from that time, and before the inauguration of the exhibition or the actual presentation to the public in general, while its exhibition is being prepared, third persons may obtain knowledge of the invention and counterfeit it. In other countries, on the contrary, the moment of such introduction of the invention being considered as subject to uncertainty, the protection starts only from the date of the official commencement of the exhibition. And in a number of countries, in order to avoid the uncertainty inherent in the question of introduction of the invention in the locale of the exhibition, the protection starts from a fixed moment before the commencement of the exhibition, or from the moment notice is given by the person who intends to exhibit his invention.

The duration may be fixed for a certain period, irrespective of the time during which the exhibition may last, or it may continue during the whole time the exhibition lasts and extend during a certain period thereafter. Each system is adopted by various countries, with all the varieties as to the starting-point which are pointed out above. The result is an extreme divergence among the laws of the various countries of the Union as to the period of the temporary protection.

Thus, in Brazil, France, Morocco, and Tunis the period is twelve months from the date of the commencement of the exhibition. In Italy, to this twelve-month period a further period of one month before the commencement of the exhibition is added, unless the exhibition takes place in a foreign country, in which case the period of protection is no longer than the one provided by the law of that country.

In Germany, Great Britain, Japan, and Norway the period is six months from the date of the commencement of the exhibition. The

1. See *supra*, § 236.

same is the case with Belgium in regard to exhibitions organized in a foreign country. In Denmark, Hungary, the Netherlands, Poland, Portugal, and Sweden the period is six months from the time the invention is exhibited to the public. In Finland, six months from the date notice is given of the intended exhibition, and in Spain, six months from the admission of the invention to the exhibition. In Switzerland, the period is six months from the moment the invention is introduced into the locale of the exhibition, but this moment cannot precede the commencement of the exhibition by more than three months. In Latvia the period lasts only three months from the commencement of the exhibition.

On the other hand, in Austria, Belgium (as to exhibitions organized in the country), and Czechoslovakia the period starts from the moment of the introduction of the invention into the locale of the exhibition and lasts until three months after its closing. In the Serb-Croat-Slovene State and Mexico, the period, while terminating three months after the closing of the exhibition, begins from the moment of exhibition in the former country and from the commencement of the exhibition in the latter.

It would seem, then, that most of the countries grant a six-month period, although with different starting-points. A six-month period has been adopted as the maximum period of the duration of all general or special exhibitions by a diplomatic conference which met at Berlin, October 8, 1912, and signed the Convention concerning international exhibitions on October 26, 1912. This Convention has been signed by fifteen countries of the Union.[1]

§ 241. Conditions and formalities for temporary protection. The divergences as to the starting-point of the period of temporary protection, on the one hand, and the differences of administrative procedure for granting patents, on the other, are responsible for the fact that the conditions and formalities required in each country for claiming this temporary protection vary greatly. As a rule, in coun-

1. See text of the Convention in *Feuille Fédérale Suissé* (1913), V, 245. Art. 13 of this Convention provides: "La durée des expositions universelles ou spéciales ne peut dépasser six mois." The Convention was signed by Austria-Hungary, Belgium, Denmark, France, Germany, Great Britain, Italy, Japan, the Netherlands, Norway, Portugal, Russia, Spain, Sweden, and Switzerland. Only Russia and Switzerland ratified this Convention. Bulgaria, Greece, and Turkey acceded to it. But the Convention has not gone into effect, because no *procès-verbal* cf deposits of ratifications was signed, article 33 of the Convention requiring that one half of the contracting parties should ratify it. See *Propriété Industrielle* (1923), p. 81 n. 2.

tries in which no previous investigation of the invention is made, and thus the question of the validity of the patent may arise long after its grant to the applicant, it is required that the fact of exhibition be certified officially. Thus an official descriptive certificate of the object exhibited and photographs or designs thereof must be obtained by the person exhibiting an invention, and later applying for a patent, in Austria, Czechoslovakia, France, Belgium, Hungary, Italy, Japan, Morocco, Mexico, Serb-Croat-Slovene State, Spain, and Tunis. This certificate must often be accompanied by documents or declarations of the date of entering the article in the exhibition, and of the date of commencement or of closing of the exhibition. In Brazil, Denmark, and the Netherlands, only an official certificate of the exhibition of the object is required, while in Switzerland the applicant must only make a declaration showing the date of exhibition of the object and the date of the commencement of the exhibition. In Finland, where the period of protection begins from the date of the notice to the Patent Office of the intended exhibition, nothing more is required than this notice. The same is true for Great Britain in regard to exhibitions organized in that country, while in regard to exhibitions organized in other countries, this formality may be dispensed with by an Order certifying that the exhibition is one for which the provisions of the law for temporary protection are applicable.[1]

In Germany, Norway, Poland, Portugal, and Sweden no formality or condition whatever is required for claiming temporary protection, so long as the patent application is filed within the time fixed by law as the period of temporary protection.

This diversity of formalities and requirements in the various countries renders the protection of inventions at exhibitions an exceedingly complicated and difficult question. Any inventor exhibiting his invention and wishing to be protected in several countries of the Union must comply with the conditions and formalities of each state.[2] He must obtain various certificates from the Committee organizing the exhibition, or from the authorities representing each state at the exhibition, according to the law of the country for which

1. Sec. 45 of the Act of 1907, as amended by the Act of 1919 (7 Edw. VII, c. 29, and 9 & 10 Geo. V, c. 80).

2. Pillet, *Régime International*, p. 406. See also Mario Ghiron, "Protection of Industrial Property at Exhibitions," in *Fairs and Exhibitions*, Jan.–June, 1926, International Chamber of Commerce, Digest No. 53.

it is destined. Sometimes these certificates must be obtained within a certain time from the commencement of the exhibition (Belgium, France, Hungary, Morocco, Serb-Croat-Slovene, State, and Tunis). This reduces greatly the importance of the protection.

§ 242. Special nature of protection provided for in article 11, and other privileges granted to persons exhibiting their inventions. The protection granted to persons exhibiting patentable inventions at expositions may be likened to the right of priority granted by article 4 of the Convention. Its purpose is the same as that of the period of priority of article 4; namely, to enable the inventor to retain his right to apply for a patent notwithstanding the exhibition, publication, or use of his invention during the period of temporary protection. The laws of all the countries agree on this point.

The question, however, may arise, whether the persons so protected at exhibitions may take legal steps against persons counterfeiting their inventions. The law of no country of the Union gives such right. On the contrary, the laws of Austria, Czechoslovakia, and France expressly provide that no such right exists before filing application for a patent. It would seem, however, that, after filing an application, or after the grant of a patent, according to the law of each country, persons who had infringed the inventors' rights during the temporary protection may be sued, if they have acted fraudulently.[1]

The law of some countries accords special exemptions and privileges to persons exhibiting their inventions at exhibitions organized in their own countries, such as the assimilation, by French and Italian law, of the exhibition of an invention to the working of the invention, the exemption from forfeiture for importation of patented articles, the exemption from seizure, and so on. All these are special favors aiming at encouraging inventors to participate in the exhibitions, and thereby assure their success.[2] They are independent of, and foreign to, the protection provided for in article 11 of the Convention.

§ 243. Amendments proposed at the Conference of The Hague, and actual additions to article 11. The International Bureau, resuming once more its efforts to amend article 11 with the view

1. Dorff et Pholien, *Expositions et le Droit*, p. 150.

2. See Mesnil, "De la Protection aux Expositions Internationales," in *Annuaire de l'Association Internationale* (1899), pp. 64–65.

of bringing about uniformity and simplicity in the matter of temporary protection of inventions in the member countries of the Union, proposed at the Conference of The Hague three different texts of amendments to article 11. The Conference might adopt any one of these texts; each would have the effect of making uniform the protection of inventions at exhibitions in all the countries of the Union.[1]

By both the first and second texts the period of temporary protection of article 11 would be added to the period of priority of article 4. But in the first, the priority of article 4 would begin from the date of filing a patent application in any of the countries of the Union, within six months of the commencement of the exhibition; in the second, the right of priority of article 4 would begin from the date of filing the patent application in the country in which the exhibition was organized within six months of the commencement of such exhibition.

On the other hand, by the third text of amendment, the period of temporary protection of article 11 would not prolong the period of priority of article 4. The latter would begin from the date when the invention was introduced at the exhibition.

All three texts provided that the special advantage of article 11 could be claimed if, at the time the patent application is filed or published, a declaration is made concerning the introduction of the invention at the exhibition, and a certificate of the management of the exhibition is produced testifying to the fact of the exhibition and accompanied by a photograph of the exhibited article.

In addition, all three texts would make it obligatory on every country of the Union to communicate to the International Bureau within the proper time a list of the official international exhibitions to be held in its territory, which should be published in the *Propriété Industrielle.*

In the discussions of article 11 and its amendments, by the Sub-Committee on Patents of the Conference of The Hague, it appeared that opinions were extremely divergent on many points. Moreover,

1. See *Actes de la Conférence de La Haye*, pp. 255 ff. The Bureau had in view, in preparing those amendments, its previous proposals at the preceding conferences of revision, the objections and discussions raised on those occasions, and the *voeux* of the congresses of the International Association of Industrial Property and of the International Chamber of Commerce. See *Propriété Industrielle* (1923), pp. 95 ff., and *Actes de la Conférence de La Haye*, pp. 102–103.

the American, British, and Australian delegations declared themselves opposed to any modification of article 11, holding that only the filing of the patent application prior to the exhibition, with provisional specification, may give a right to a period of priority, as no other means permits the identification of the exhibited article with the one deposited later. These delegations insisted that the legislation of each country should be left free to regulate the temporary protection as it saw fit.

The Dutch delegation, however, insisted that article 11 should at least be amended so as to afford a solution of the disputes existing as to the effect of its provisions, and it proposed the following addition to article 11:[1]

Cette protection temporaire ne prolongera pas les délais de l'article 4. Si plus tard la protection de l'article 4 est invoqué, les délais commencent à courir de la date de l'introduction dans l'exposition. Chaque pays peut demander comme preuves de l'introduction les pièces justificatives qu'il jugera nécessaires.

This proposal, in its first part, was substantially identical with the provision of the third text of amendment proposed by the International Bureau; and in its second part, it renounced the attempt to set up a uniform regulation of the requirements for claiming the temporary protection of article 11, and preserved the independence of each country's legislation in this regard.

Thus the inventor who exhibited his invention at an international exhibition would have the right, by virtue of article 11, to claim that the period of the right of priority, to which he is entitled in accordance with article 4, should begin with the date of the introduction of his invention at the exhibition. But each country would be free to require the most severe and convincing proof of identification of the invention exhibited at the exhibition. The objections of the British delegation would seem to have been met by the proposal of the Dutch delegation. However, the latter delegation was not entirely satisfied with this proposal. It asked for its modification in a way that destroys the whole importance of the amendment, and renders article 11 now more imperfect than before it was amended.[2] The two new paragraphs added to article 11 at the Conference of The Hague read as follows:

1. See *Actes de la Conférence de La Haye*, pp. 436–437.
2. See *ibid.*, pp. 526, 547.

Cette protection temporaire ne prolongera pas les délais de l'article 4. Si plus tard le droit de priorité est invoqué, l'Administration de chaque pays pourra faire partir le délai de la date de l'introduction du produit dans l'exposition.

Chaque pays pourra exiger comme preuve d'identité de l'objet exposé et de la date d'introduction, les pièces justificatives qu'il jugera nécessaires.

Thus, while by the Dutch proposal the periods of the right of priority would necessarily begin ("commencent à courir") with the date of the introduction of the article at the exhibition if the inventor should so demand, by the text adopted by the Conference each country may or may not, as it sees fit, allow the period of priority to begin with that moment. In other words, a country may deny the temporary protection established in principle by article 11 of the Convention, by refusing to accept as starting-point of the period of priority the moment of the introduction of the invention at the exhibition.

Thus the outcome of the amendment of article 11 at the Conference of The Hague is rather negative, if it be admitted that the provision against prolongation of the period of priority of article 4 by the temporary protection of article 11 is a distinct backward step.[1]

1. See Gariel, "Après la Conférence de La Haye," in *Propriété Industrielle* (1926), pp. 166, 167. Plaisant et Fernand-Jacq, *La Conférence de La Haye*, pp. 74–75.

The International Chamber of Commerce passed a resolution at the Stockholm Congress (June 27–July 2, 1927), approving the principle of the creation by the Chamber of an international committee "to consider without delay questions respecting International Fairs and Exhibitions and which shall endeavor to conciliate the interests at stake." On the other hand, it recommended (*a*) an early notice by each country to the Berne Bureau of Exhibitions, in connection with which it accords a temporary protection; (*b*) the adoption by all countries of a uniform system of proof of the introduction of an article at an exhibition; (*c*) an agreement with regard to the commencement and duration of the period of temporary protection, etc. See International Chamber of Commerce, Brochure No. 60, pp. 24–25, 30.

SECTION III

THE INTERNATIONAL REGIME OF INDUSTRIAL DESIGNS AND MODELS

CHAPTER XV

NATIONAL TREATMENT OF INDUSTRIAL DESIGNS AND MODELS

§ 244. Inadequate protection of designs and models under the Convention of 1883.
§ 245. Should designs and models form a separate branch of industrial property.
§ 246. Should designs and models be classified with literary and artistic property?
§ 247. Rational regulation of whole field of creations.
§ 248. Attempt to extend protection of the International Copyright Convention to industrial art.
§ 249. Present state of law of designs and models.

I. What may be Deposited or Registered
§ 250. What is a design or model in the various countries.
§ 251. Publication of design or model before depositing entails forfeiture in most countries.
§ 252. Who may deposit or register design or model.

II. Formalities of Deposit
§ 253. Lack of uniformity and simplicity of formalities.
§ 254. Open and secret deposits.
§ 255. Scarcity of foreign deposits.

III. Administrative Procedure
§ 256. The two systems of mere registration and of previous examination.
§ 257. Need of secrecy of deposit.
§ 258. Regulation of deposits under seal.

IV. Duration of Protection
§ 259. Need of long and elective terms.
§ 260. Term of duration in the various countries.
§ 261. Fees.

V. Legal Effects of Deposits or Registration
§ 262. Patent right or copyright?
§ 263. Consequences of copyright.
§ 264. Regime of designs and models in France.
§ 265. Deposit as regulation of public order.
§ 266. Designs are registered in respect to a special class or to classes of goods.

VI. Obligations of Depositor
§ 267. Should obligations of patentees be imposed on proprietors of designs?
§ 268. Obligation to work design and prohibition of importation.
§ 269. Obligation of marking the design.

VII. Conclusions. § 270.

VIII. Statistics. § 271.

§ 244. Inadequate protection of designs and models under the Convention of 1883. The Convention of 1883, in its second article, assures the national treatment to the persons entitled to the benefits of the Convention in respect to industrial designs and models, as in respect to other rights of industrial property. The precise scope of this assimilation to nationals is considered above.[1] It may be repeated here that, as a result of such assimilation, the persons claiming the advantages of the Convention, on the one hand, are entitled to all the rights and protection provided for by the municipal law of each country of the Union for its citizens; that no discrimination against them other than in matters of procedure is allowed; that their enjoyment of these rights and protection is subject to no condition of reciprocity. On the other hand, these persons remain subject to all conditions, formalities, and obligations precribed by the municipal law of each country for the acquisition, preservation, and enforcement of rights in an industrial design or model. In this last respect, as is also seen above, mere assimilation to nationals is most insufficient for an effective protection of foreigners, and may practically result in a complete lack of protection.

In the matter of patents, as well as of trade marks, the Convention contained provisions which remedied the insufficiency of the mere assimilation to nationals, by according special advantages and rights over and above, or in derogation of, the municipal law. The same was not true in respect to industrial designs and models. Outside the national-treatment provision, the only further protection which owners of designs and models might claim until recently was that of right of priority and of temporary protection at international exhibitions. The right of priority was not of great importance, because the period of priority was only four months up to the last conference of The Hague, when it was extended to six months. Thus the international protection of industrial designs and models was more theoretical than real, as has been repeatedly admitted in the congresses of the International Association for the Protection of Industrial Property.[2] The condition that a design or model should not have been published or worked prior to its deposit, the obligation to work it within a short period after its deposit, the prohibition against importation of articles bearing the design, and the shortness

1. See chap. IX, especially §§ 126–129.

2. *Annuaire de l'Association Internationale* (1899), p. 19; (1901), pp. 107, 108–109; (1902), p. 81.

of the duration of protection, made the international protection of designs and models in the Union almost impossible.[1]

§ **245. Should designs and models form a separate branch of industrial property?** When this state of things became apparent, the persons interested in the protection of designs and models, as well as jurists of different countries, began to inquire whether industrial designs and models should constitute a branch of industrial property at all, by being likened to inventions, or whether they should be classified with artistic works. In the latter case, indeed, the requirements for the protection of industrial designs and models would be the same as for the protection of artistic designs and sculptural works. For these, creation is the basis, and in some countries the only requirement, for protection, while in others, very simple formalities are prescribed for the establishment or protection of the right.

The formation of a special branch of industrial property to include designs and models was a historical accident. First of all, in Great Britain an act was passed "for the encouragement of the arts of designing and printing linens, cottons, calicoes and muslins by vesting the properties thereof in the designers, printers and proprietors for a limited time," granting the sole right of reprinting the design for two months, beginning with the day of the first publication.[2] This act did not provide for any system of registering or depositing designs. This was done later by the Act of 1839 (2 Vict., c. 17). Thus the regime of designs under the first English statute was similar to that of artistic property, although the duration of the right was very short. Industrial designs were made a branch of industrial prorty by the French Law of 1806, and it was this law which was copied or imitated all over the world. This law was an accident.

France during the Revolution had passed the law of July 19–24, 1793,[3] for the protection of literary and artistic property. The provisions of the law were broad enough to cover any kind of designs. But in 1806 Napoleon made a trip to Lyon. The manufacturers of that city made different complaints to him in respect to the inadequate regulation and protection of their industries; among other things, they complained that the law of 1793 concerning artistic

1. *Annuaire* (1897), p. 153; *Travaux de Groupe Français de l'Association Internationale* (1919–1922), pp. 33–34, 118, 172.
2. 27 Geo. III, c. 38.
3. *Lois et Actes de Gouvernement*, VII (*Avril, 1793 à Vendémiaire an II*), 203.

property did not protect them sufficiently. Napoleon promised to remedy the situation.[1] The law of 1806 [2] was a law concerning generally the industries of Lyon; section 3 of title II, entitled "the preservation of ownership of designs," dealt with the protection of designs of the factories of Lyon by deposit and registration in the archives of the trade councils of each industry.

These provisions of the law might be regarded as merely supplementing the law of 1793, and recognizing, by registration of a design, a proof of creation and ownership. But the law spoke of "dessins de fabricants," and the French courts exerted themselves to define an industrial design and distinguish it from an artistic design. With the subsequent extension of the provisions of the law of 1806 to all industries and to industrial models, the theoretical separation of industrial designs and models from artistic property was accomplished, though in fact the definite boundaries between the two fields have never been established. Moreover, the law of 1806, as construed by the French courts, required compliance with its formalities as a condition to the acquisition of ownership in a design or model. This, by analogy to the patent law. On the other hand, the provisions of the latter, compelling the patentee to work his patent in France and not to import articles manufactured with the invention, were also extended to designs and models. Thus the process of putting industrial designs and models, in many respects, on the same footing as inventions was completed.

The law of France influenced and inspired the legislation of all other countries. The result was, as is said above, that not only international protection of designs and models became impossible, but domestic protection itself suffered greatly. For the law, generally, provided that the acquisition of ownership in a design or model was subject to the condition of prior deposit of the design, and that, therefore, publication of the design or public use by the author before deposit destroyed its novelty, and no valid registration of it might be made. Also, in many countries industrial designs or models were protected only for a short time — two, three, four, or five years.

1. Ducreux, "Législation sur les Dessins et Modèles en France," *Annuaire* (1898), p. 350. See as to the history of special protection of the manufactories of Lyon, Philipon, *Des Dessins et Modèles de Fabrique en Droit Français* (*Thèse*); Paris (1880), pp. 13 ff., and on the history of the Law of 1806, *ibid.*, pp. 34 ff.

2. *Bulletin des Lois*, 4ᵉ sér., IV, 352, 354.

§ 246. Should designs and models be classified with literary and artistic property? The movement for classifying industrial designs and models with artistic works, while, on its practical side, instigated by the consideration that more adequate protection of industrial designs and models could be secured thereby, on its doctrinal side was caused by the great difficulty of finding any real distinction between industrial art and so-called "pure art." The attempts to base such a distinction on either merit, or importance, or use, or destination of the creation have fallen down.[1] It is urged that the whole field of creations can be divided into only two classes: that of usefulness and that of beauty; and that all useful creations should be considered as inventions and be taken care of by the patent law, while all artistic creations, whatever their merit or importance or object, should be protected as artistic works by the copyright law. The placing of a third class of creations between these two is arbitrary, and, besides, confusing.

Industrial art in recent years has made remarkable progress. Industry and commerce appeal at the present time more and more to the artistic taste and sense of the public. Many articles of luxury, and even industrial products of common use, constitute marvels of artistic production. It is a far cry from the crude and ugly aspect of the industrial products of the first half of the nineteenth century. "The divorce of artist and art from the life"[2] of the times is no longer true to-day. Design has become the soul of industry, and beauty is rapidly crowding out ugliness. That Hephaestus, the workshop God, was able to marry Aphrodite, the Goddess of Beauty, is no longer an ancient myth. The forms of artistic production are multiplied. Great works of "pure art" are adapted to and reproduced in industrial products. Original creations and beautiful designs ornament and beautify many articles of silver, bronze and glassware, silk manufacture, and so on. The old craft tradition is revived on a

1. Osterrieth, "L'art Appliqué à l'Industrie," in *Annuaire de l'Association Internationale* (1898), p. 347; Georges de Ro, "De l'Assimilation des Dessins et Modèles Industriels aux Dessins et Modèles d'Art," in *Annuaire* (1898), pp. 348–349; Soleau, "De la Propriété des Dessins et Modèles d'Art Appliqués à l'Industrie," in *Annuaire* (1898), pp. 357 ff., and "De la Protection Législative et Internationale des Arts Décoratifs," in *Annuaire* (1902), pp. 73 ff.; Lucien-Brun, "Amélioration des Rapports Internationaux, Dessins et Modèles," in *Annuaire* (1901), pp. 97 ff.; Coppieters, *Protection des Oeuvres d'Art Appliqué* (Bruxelles, 1919), p. 32; *Travaux du Groupe Français de l'Association Internationale* (1919–1922), p. 36.

2. See André Maurois, *Quatre Études Anglaises, de Ruskin à Wilde* (Paris, 1927), p. 123.

larger scale. Inspirations come from multiple sources. Art by being applied to industry is not depreciated. If a certain kind of industrial designs is of too low a quality to be classified with artistic works, that means only that it is not worth protecting as a creation at all, and it may constitute only a distinctive mark of the manufacturer and be protected as a trade mark. And if a certain industrial creation is more useful than ornamental, it may be protected as an invention. Thus, industrial designs or models may conveniently disappear as a separate branch of industrial property, and be absorbed either as inventions, or as artistic works, or as trade marks.

§ **247. Rational regulation of whole field of creations.** The division of the field of creations into two classes — usefulness (inventions), and aesthetic value (artistic works) — not only simplifies the whole matter but also permits a rational regulation of each class of creations. All inventions are on a different footing from all artistic works. The interests which must be taken into consideration in delimiting and regulating the interest of the inventor are not the same as in the case of the author of an artistic work.

An invention, although it implies an exertion of inventive genius, is something outside of the person making the discovery and is taken from the common stock of nature. The exclusive privilege granted to the inventor curtails the freedom of commerce and industry and prevents other people who might make the same discovery from using it. It is possible, indeed, to imagine that two or more persons may invent the same thing at the same time, or at almost the same time. All this explains why the patent laws of all countries require the filing of a patent application and other formalities for the grant of the exclusive right in an invention, limit its duration, and often impose various conditions and obligations on the patentee.

An artistic work is not the same. Nothing is taken by an artistic creation from the outside. It is eminently personal. No curtailment of the freedom of art is implied in the protection of an artistic work. The field of original artistic creation is unlimited. No interests of the public are at stake. The right of the author in the artistic work is not an exclusive privilege: it is only a right to prevent others from copying his work. It is extremely rare — one might say it is almost impossible — for two persons to create the same artistic work at the same time, or at almost the same time, unless there is piracy or imitation. If this should ever happen, either of the authors is entitled to prevent others from copying his work. This explains why in many countries no condition or formality whatsoever is imposed on authors for claiming their rights in their works, the only bases of their rights being the original creations; why the duration of the copyright is very long; and why no obligation whatsoever is imposed on authors for the preservation of their rights.

Industrial designs or models must clearly be put on the same footing with artistic works. The protection of a design in no way curtails the freedom of honest commerce and industry. A design is not an indispensable element in the progress of industry. The number of designs or models which may be created by the creative genius of man is unlimited. No monopoly is created by recognizing the right of the owner of a design to prevent others from copying it. It is practically impossible that two persons will create the same design, unless they imitate or copy each other. No interest of national industry is promoted by denying protection to original designs and models. On the contrary, their adequate protection causes a greater variety and richness of creation, which ultimately benefits industry. Why, then, should conditions and formalities be required for the establishment and protection of ownership in a design? Why should such ownership be conditioned on deposit and registration? Why should the publication or working of the design by the author cause the loss of his right? Why should the duration be extremely short, and various obligations be imposed on the author of the design? [1]

It is another question whether it should be possible for authors of industrial designs or models, and, in general, of works of art applied to industry, to deposit or register their creations, not as a condition of the establishment of their right, but as a convenient proof of priority of creation. By such deposit designers or manufacturers might obtain what have felicitously been called "birthday certificates" of their creations,[2] as in the case of artistic works in general in some countries. This certification is necessary in respect to such designs or models which have not a very pronounced personal element.[3]

§ 248. Attempt to extend protection of the International Copyright Convention to industrial art. An attempt was made at the

1. *Travaux du Groupe Français de l'Association Internationale* (1919–1922), Report by Mr. Maillard, p. 17. and conference by Mr. Claro, p. 35.

2. Soleau, Report, in *Annuaire de l'Association Internationale* (1902), p. 85; *Travaux du Groupe Français* (1919–1922), pp. 38, 120–121; *Propriété Industrielle* (1924), p. 184.

3. *Propriété Industrielle* (1909), p. 179.

Conference of Berlin, meeting for the revision of the International Convention of Berne for the protection of literary and artistic property, to extend to artistic works applied to industry, whatever their merit or object may be, the protection of artistic property which is secured by that Convention in the territory of all the contracting countries without any formality or condition. This did not succeed by reason of the opposition of Great Britain and Switzerland.[1] Instead, the following provision was added to article 2: "Les oeuvres d'art appliqué à l'industrie sont protégées autant que le permet de le faire la législation intérieure de chaque pays."

Thus national treatment is promised, and no more; that is, the stipulation is similar to that of the Convention of 1883 as to designs and models. It may be very difficult to draw any line between the latter and artistic works applied to industry. The notion of artistic works applied to industry applies usually, not only to works which originally constituted "pure art" and were later combined with industrial products or multiplied industrially, but also to creations which are admitted to be artistic and were meant originally for a practical or ornamental purpose.[2] It is in respect to the latter that their distinction from industrial designs and models is particularly difficult.[3] Be this as it may, the situation of industrial designs and models has been slightly altered by the adoption of the above provision in the Copyright Convention. By both Conventions foreigners enjoy mere national treatment. In the countries in which the notion of "art applied to industry" ("oeuvres d'art appliqué à l'industrie," "Kunstgewerbe," or "Kunstindustrie") has been so extended as to cover what before was considered an industrial design and model, foreigners claiming the benefits of the Copyright Convention of 1886 may claim the protection that the municipal legislation assures to nationals.[4]

At the Conference of The Hague in 1925, France proposed a new paragraph in the first article of the Industrial Property Convention,

1. *Actes de la Conférence de Berlin* (1909), pp. 41, 178, 179, 185, 186, 230, 233, 286, 315.

2. See *Propriété Industrielle* (1909), pp. 172, 177–178.

3. See Coppieters, *Protection des Oeuvres d'Art Appliqué*, p. 32.

4. See, on the protection of artistic works applied to industry, *Propriété Industrielle* (1909), pp. 155 and 172, and Coppieters, *Protection des Oeuvres d'Art Appliqué*, 3d and 4th parts. Pillet (*Régime International*, p. 336) maintains that foreigners cannot claim in France the advantages of the Law of 1902 extending the protection of artistic works of the Law of 1793 to artistic works applied to industry. Yet it is not seen why persons who may claim the benefit of both conventions could not claim the protection of either.

reading thus: "Les oeuvres artistiques restent protégées par la législation sur les œuvres artistiques même si elles ont un emploi ou une destination industrielle." As was rightly remarked by the President of the Sub-Committee, Sir Hubert Llewellyn Smith, the proposal was ambiguous; it might mean that the fact that a work of art is protected by the Copyright law does not preclude its protection by the Industrial Property law, or that the fact that a work of art is protected by the latter does not prevent its being protected by the copyright law. The latter interpretation placed the proposal outside of the competence of the Conference; the first interpretation made it devoid of practical importance. At any rate, the British and American delegations were unwilling to accept the principle of cumulative protection of works of art by the Copyright and Industrial Property laws. By reason of their opposition and the abstention of other delegations the French proposal was not insisted upon.[1]

§ 249. Present state of the law of designs and models. The movement for the absorption of industrial designs and models by the law of artistic property seems to have spent itself.[2] Some industries seem to favor the maintenance of special legislation on industrial designs and models with the obligation of deposit and registration. These are, especially, the textile and embroidery industries, which deposit and register a very great number of designs in some countries. The designs of these industries are often very simple, and their artistic character being not very apparent, the deposit is necessary for their protection.[3] Moreover, the law of artistic property has been more or less crystallized, in such a way that it does not cover some kinds of artistic creations, either because of their industrial purpose, or of their minor aesthetic character. Lastly, in some countries industrial designs and models are not merely

1. See *Actes de la Conférence de La Haye*, pp. 332, 412, 570–571.

2. The Standing Committee for the Protection of Industrial Property of the International Chamber of Commerce, at its meeting at Paris, in Nov., 1924, adopted by majority vote a proposal to the effect that designs and models should be assimilated to artistic works in general, and be protected by the law of literary and artistic property. However, this proposal was not adopted by the Congress of the Chamber at Brussels, in June, 1925. See *Propriété Industrielle* (1925), pp. 20 and 152. The International Association for the Protection of Industrial Property at its three congresses after the War, at Zürich (1925), Geneva (1927), and Rome (1928), did not touch the question. See *Propriété Industrielle* (1925), p. 127; (1927), pp. 104, 135; (1928), pp. 178, 201.

3. See discussions at Congress of International Association of Industrial Property, in *Annuaire* (1909), pp. 313, 316.

creations pleasing to the eye, but also creations for practical purposes.

Thus the attempts to lay down general principles for the protection of industrial designs and models involved a revision and modification of the law of artistic property and of inventions. It soon appeared that the same sort of difficulties which prevented the unification of the law of industrial property in general existed also in the case of designs and models.[1] It has been thought wiser and more practical to go step by step, and to attempt to harmonize the laws of the various countries on some points, concerning especially the international protection of designs and models. This could be achieved in two ways: first, by relieving foreigners from some conditions and obligations imposed by the municipal law of each country upon the protection of their rights in industrial designs and models; [2] and second, by the constitution of a special Union for the International Deposit of Designs and Models. As will be seen, the last conference of The Hague accomplished the latter, and achieved an amelioration as to the former.

The results accomplished will be better appreciated after an examination of the various questions involved in the protection of industrial designs and models, and of the legal situation in the different countries of the Union. In almost all the countries of the Union to-day there exist special laws for the protection of designs and models. Exceptions are Brazil, Bulgaria, Dominican Republic, Finland, Greece, Latvia, Luxembourg, the Netherlands, Rumania, and Turkey. However, in Bulgaria [3] and Greece [4] industrial designs and models are assimilated to trade marks. Indeed, in these countries the forms of products as well as of their containers constitute trade marks. For the regime, therefore, of designs and

1. See as to the impracticability of these efforts, Frey Godet, "De l'Amélioration des Rapports Internationaux," in *Annuaire de l'Association Internationale* (1901), p. 103; "Le Dépôt International des Dessins et Modèles Industriels," in *Propriété Industrielle* (1924), pp. 181 ff.; *Travaux du Groupe Français de l'Association Internationale* (1919–1922), pp. 36–37.

2. Those obligations and conditions are, especially: the requirement of compulsory registration; the condition that the design or model must not have been published or worked before registration; the obligation of compulsory working of the design or model; the obligation to indicate the fact of registration and the number of registration on the design or model; and the excessive shortness of the period of protection.

3. Article 1, No. 4 of the Law of Jan. 14–29, 1904 (*Propriété Industrielle*, 1904, p. 74).

4. Article 5 of the Decree of Nov. 12, 1927 (Ἐφημερὶς τῆς Κυβερνήσεως, 1927, p. 1819).

models in these two countries reference should be made to the regime of trade marks, described in the next section, chapter XXII. In Luxembourg and the Netherlands industrial designs and models are protected by the law on literary and artistic property in so far as they are artistic productions. Moreover, they are protected by the law of unfair competition whenever their infringement constitutes an act of unfair competition. In Finland, a law for the protection of industrial designs and models is in preparation.[1]

Important questions in the protection of designs and models are the following: what may be deposited or registered; who may deposit a design or model; formalities of deposit; administrative procedure; open or secret deposit; duration of protection; fees; legal effects of the deposit; and obligations of the depositor. Each of these questions will now be considered.

I. What may be Deposited or Registered

§ 250. What is a design or model in the various countries. One of the main obstacles to the adequate international protection of industrial designs and models comes from the fact that there is no general agreement as to what is a design or model which may be deposited and protected under the legislation on industrial designs and models. Designs are not, as they should be, always distinguished from inventions, — aiming at ornamentation and not at usefulness, — and from trade marks, — being creations of the intellect and not mere distinctive signs. Furthermore, as said above, the distinction between industrial designs and models and artistic designs and plastic or sculptural works is not well established. Classification of artistic works applied to industry with artistic works in general in most countries narrows further the field of industrial designs and models and renders the boundaries much more uncertain.

The literal meaning of the word design is the representation, in lines or in forms, constituting an ornament, a figure, or a plan. A model is a design in relief. In this sense designs and models are always artistic whenever there is an element of personal and original creation. If no such element exists, if they are but simple geometrical plans, which everybody may trace without personal or original effort, they may properly constitute industrial designs or

1. Letter to the writer from the Commissioner of Patents (Finland) under date of Jan. 14, 1928.

models in case they are pleasing to the eye and aim at ornamenting an article.

The laws of the various countries do not consider industrial designs or models in such a restricted sense. One thing may be deposited and protected in one country, as an industrial design, which in other countries is properly a trade mark or an invention. Furthermore, artistic creations are protected as industrial designs only if they are applied to industrial products or reproduced industrially.

The definitions of designs given by the laws of some countries are singularly valueless, as, for instance, that of the United States, which provides that a patent for a design is granted to any person who has invented any new, original, and ornamental design for an article of manufacture.[1] It has been said that no lawyer in the United States can advise a client as to the patentability of a design, and that "in no branch is there a more hazy and indefinite line of decisions from which to endeavor to extract principles and rules which should lead to the establishing of definite standards of what is, and what is not, patentable in the way of a design." [2] The word "invented" has led the courts to seek for an invention in a design.[3] The word "ornamental" has been stretched to cover the field of "pure art."[4] It is insisted that the objects be ornamental, artistic or pleasing.[5] Color would seem to constitute no element of a design patent.[6]

In Great Britain the definition of a design given by the Act of

1. Section 4929 of the Revised Statutes as revised by the Act of 1902. Before the amendment of this section, the word "useful" was used instead of the word "ornamental." The weight of authority, however, was to the effect that the word "useful" meant useful as a result of creating an ornament or a beautiful thing. See Symons, *The Law of Patents for Designs* (Washington, 1914), pp. 18 ff.; Simonds, *The Law of Design Patents*, New York (1874), p. 188.

2. Allen, *Design Patentability* (1927), *Jour. of the Pat. Off. Society*, IX, 298, 299.

3. See Knapp *v.* Will & Baumer Co. (1921), 272 Fed. 380. (Mere change of shape is not invention.) See also Symons, *Law of Patents for Designs*, pp. 41 ff. and cases cited.

4. Faris *v.* Patsy Frock & Romper Co. (1921), 272 Fed. 900. (No patent can be issued for a design, unless it possesses both originality and beauty.) See also Symons, *Law of Patents for Designs*, pp. 14 ff. and cases cited.

5. Symons (*op. cit.*, pp. 17–18) cites cases in which shade-rollers, jars, bottles, lamp brackets, etc., have been held not ornamental, artistic, or pleasing objects, and patents for these designs have been refused by the Patent Office, or invalidated by Federal courts.

6. Star Bucket Pump Co. *v.* Butler Manufacturing Co. (1912), 198 Fed. 857, 864. The adaptation of old devices or forms to new purposes, however convenient, beautiful or useful they may be in their new rôle, is not invention. And invention is just as essential to the validity of a design as to the validity of a patent for a mechanical device.

1919,[1] which substituted the earlier definition of the Act of 1907, comes nearest to clear expression. A "design" is declared to mean only the features of shape, configuration, pattern, or ornament applied to any article by any industrial process or means, whether manual, mechanical, or chemical, separate or combined, which in the finished article appeal to, and are judged solely by, the eye. It is added that "design" does not include any mode or principle of construction, or anything which is in substance a mere mechanical device. No element of utility is required, and no insistence on aesthetic quality of the design is made. Appeal to the sense of beauty is not necessary in a design. The difficulties presented in the United States are not likely to occur here. The eye is the judge of a design. If the appearance of an article to the eye is new and original, it may be registered and protected as a design. This was also held by the courts under the old Act of 1883.[2] The provision that a mere mechanical device cannot be registered as a design confirms prior decisions in Great Britain.[3] The insistence upon features and shape implies that a mere effect, for instance a color, is not a design.[4]

The law of the British dominions and colonies is similar to that of Great Britain in this respect.

In Germany, Japan, and Poland, besides inventions protected by the patent law, and industrial designs and models (*Geschmacksmuster*) protected by special law, there is allowed another class of industrial property: models of utility (*Gebrauchsmuster*). In those countries designs and models are those which satisfy the sense of beauty, while models of utility satisfy only a practical purpose, that is, are inventions concerning small practical improvements in articles or tools.

Although the German Law of 1876 defines as designs or models (*Muster oder Modelle*) the "new creations presenting an original character," [5] the courts have held that the law protects only designs

1. Patents and Designs Act, 1919 (9 & 10 Geo. V, c. 80), sec. 19 amending sec. 93 of the principal act.

2. Hecla Foundry Co. *v.* Walker, Hunter & Co., in the House of Lords (1889), 6 R. P. C. 554.

3. Moody *v.* Tree (1892), 9 R. P. C. 333; Cooper *v.* Symington (1893), 10 R. P. C. 264.

4. See Edmunds, *The Law of Copyright in Designs* (London, 1895), p. 15. Cf. Fulton, *Law and Practice Relating to Patents and Designs* (London, 1910), pp. 382 ff., 387–388.

5. "Als Muster oder Modelle im Sinne dieses Gesetzes werden nur neue und eigenthümliche Erzeugnisse angesehen." Sec. 1, par. 2, of the Act of Jan. 11, 1876 (*Reichsgesetzblatt*, 1876, p. 11).

or models possessing an artistic character, satisfying the artistic taste and sense of the public.[1] This would seem to be the case in Japan also, where special legislation takes care of models of utility, although the definition of an industrial design or model is quite broad.[2]

In Poland, the Law of February 5, 1924, expressly provides that, when the new form aims at facilitating the use of the article, this is called a "model of utility," and when it serves for ornamental purposes the article is called a design or model of ornament ("wzór zdobniczy").[3]

Thus, dispositions, combinations, or features which may be registered and protected in Great Britain as designs or models cannot be so protected in Germany, Japan, and Poland. On the other hand, artistic or ornamental effects admitted as designs or models in the latter countries, such as color effects, are not so admitted in Great Britain.

In France, the conception of a design or model is broader than in Germany or Great Britain or the United States: it includes any distinct configuration of an article, or any external effect giving to an article a distinctive appearance.[4] The same is true in Morocco, Tunis, and Syria and Lebanon.[5] The law of Mexico is similar.

Among the rest of the countries notions of design and model differ as much as among the previously named. Usually, every original creation relating to the form or aspect of an article, in general, is considered a design or model. Consequently, a mere color effect may be

1. Osterrieth, "L'art Appliqué à l'Industrie," in *Annuaire de l'Association Internationale* (1898), p. 345; and Decision of the Reichs-Oberlandsgericht of Sept. 3, 1878, cited *Ibid.;* Schmid, "Der Musterschutz und seine internationale Bedeutung," in *Annuaire* (1897), p. 297.

2. ". . . new applicable to an article and relating to its form, its design, its colour, or to the combination of these various elements." Act No. 98, of April 29, 1921, sec. 1 (*Propriété Industrielle*, 1924, p. 6).

3. *Propriété Industrielle* (1924), p. 221.

4. ". . . tout dessin nouveau, toute forme plastique nouvelle, tout objet industriel qui se différencie de ses similaires, soit par une configuration distincte et reconnaissable lui conférant un caractère de nouveauté, soit par un ou plusieurs effets extérieurs lui donnant une physionomie propre et nouvelle." Law of July 14, 1909, art. 2 (1909 *Bulletin des Lois*, I, 1231).

5. See data on the law of these countries in *Tableau Comparatif des Conditions et Formalités Requises pour le Dépôt des Dessins et Modèles Industriels dans les Divers Pays*, published by the International Bureau, 2d ed., Berne, 1925.

The writer is indebted to the International Bureau for most of his information as to the laws of the various countries on designs and models. He has obtained what is not given in the above *Tableau* by independent research. He refers to original sources in the latter case. When he does not do so, he takes his data from the above *Tableau.*

considered as such. In the Serb-Croat-Slovene State the law defines separately designs and models, but a design can be only a figure or illustration which may serve as a model form and be reproduced on an industrial product.

More sweeping restrictions of what may be registered and protected as a design occur in Sweden and Switzerland. In the latter, dispositions of lines or plastic forms, combined or not with colors, which may serve as model forms for the industrial production of an article, are considered as designs or models. A color, then, or a blending, arrangement, or combination of colors, cannot constitute a design. Moreover, designs that may be printed on cotton tissues, and designs for silk or half-silk tissues (with the exception of "Jacquard" tissues) are not admitted for deposit. In Sweden, the law protects only designs or models which may be used for the manufacture of products belonging to the metal industry.

§ 251. Publication of design or model before depositing entails forfeiture in most countries. The difficulties arising from the various meanings given to a design or model in the different countries are increased by the requirement that, in order that a design or model may be deposited, it must not have been published before.

Of course, by definition, there cannot be a right of property in a design unless there is a new and original creation. In order that the protection of the law may be claimed, there must have been a personal effort in producing something new. If a person copies or imitates or adopts a shape or plastic form known or used by others, or published by others, he cannot claim the protection of the law. There is no dispute on this point.

The question, however, is whether a person creating a new and original design or model forfeits his right and the protection of the law if he publishes the design or uses it on articles put on the market, and thus makes his design publicly known, before he applies for its registration. In other words, should novelty in a design be considered in relation to the state of knowledge at the date of the creation of the design or of its registration? Or, to put it in terms of Anglo-American law, is abandonment of a design to be conclusively presumed from the fact that its author publishes or applies it industrially, before he deposits it for registration? As said above,[1] the considerations compelling an inventor to file a patent application

1. See *supra*, § 247. See also *Annuaire de l'Association Internationale* (1897), p. 116.

before he uses publicly or makes known his invention have no bearing in the case of a creator or owner of a design. Yet, only in France, Morocco, Tunis, and Syria and Lebanon does the law provide that publication of a design, before its deposit, either by public sales or otherwise, entails no forfeiture either of ownership in the design or of the special protection granted by the law. In Belgium also the courts have held, under the Law of 1806, that publication of the design or model by its author before deposit does not entail forfeiture of the right *ipso facto*, but the courts will consider each case on its merits to find out whether an abandonment of the design or model was intended.[1]

In Great Britain and the British dominions and colonies, as well as in Japan and Poland, public knowledge, use, or publication in the country prevents a design or model from being validly deposited. In Russia, a design may be validly deposited only if it has not been publicly used before in the country, or has not been explicitly described in print in the last fifty years preceding the deposit. In Switzerland, the design or model must be deposited before it is known either to the public or to interested manufacturers and traders.

In Germany, Danzig, Esthonia, and Norway, no valid deposit of a design or model may be made if there has been, prior to the deposit, a public sale of articles manufactured according to the design or model.

In Austria, Czechoslovakia, Denmark, Hungary, Mexico, Serb-Croat-Slovene State, Spain, and Sweden the property right in a design is forfeited if, before its deposit, articles made according to the design are put on the market, or the design is published in print, or registered in the country in the name of a third party.

In Italy, the provisions of the law as to prior use or prior publication in the matter of patents are applicable also in the case of designs.[2] In the United States, a patent for a design cannot be obtained if (*a*) an application for a patent for the same design has been filed in another country by the same person more than four months before his application in the United States, and a patent has been granted thereon; or if (*b*) the design was known or used in the

1. Van Damme *c.* Lammens, Cassation, July 11, 1912, (*Pasicrisie*, 1912, I, 388). Société Américaine de Saint-Gobain et al *c.* Falleur et consorts, Tribunal de Charleroi, July 28, 1913 (cited *in extenso* in Coppieters, *Oeuvres d'Art Appliqué*, pp. 121 ff.).

2. See *supra*, p. 221.

United States, or patented or described in a printed publication in the United States or in any foreign country, more than two years prior to his application.

§ **252. Who may deposit or register design or model.** In the United States, Italy, Japan, Mexico, New Zealand, and Poland, only the inventor, author, or creator of a design or model may deposit it. On the contrary, in Portugal only manufacturers, in Cuba only manufacturers, traders, and agriculturists, and in Spain only these classes of persons and also craftsmen, trade unions, associations, municipal councils, and provincial deputations may deposit a design or model. This is explained by the fact that in the latter countries designs and models are likened to trade marks.

In the other countries of the Union, the author of a design, as well as his legal representatives or assigns, may deposit it. In Great Britain, a design may be deposited by anyone claiming to be the owner or his legal representative or assign, or by the person in whose behalf the design has been executed. Indeed, British manufacturers buy many of their designs from designers.[1] In some countries, also, it is expressly provided that owners of business establishments may deposit designs created by employees working in their pay.

In Germany, a design may be deposited by the creator or by the owner of a German business establishment. Foreign manufacturers are therefore excluded. Similarly, in Spain, only national manufacturers, traders, or agriculturists may deposit a design. Foreigners may apply, provided they have already registered their designs in their own country, and if there is legal and diplomatic reciprocity between the two countries. In Portugal, the manufacturers who may deposit a design must be nationals, or foreigners domiciled or established in Portugal, its colonies, or any of the countries of the Union. The same is true as to non-resident foreigners in Czechoslovakia, Danzig, and Japan. In Belgium, foreigners residing in the country may deposit their designs with the trade council of their place of establishment. Non-resident foreigners may deposit only if there is diplomatic reciprocity with their own country. Legal or diplomatic reciprocity is also required in the same case in Cuba, France, and Serb-Croat-Slovene State.

In many countries non-resident foreigners cannot claim registra-

1. See *Travaux du Groupe Français de l'Association Internationale* (1919–1922), p. 19.

tion of their designs or models unless they appoint an attorney or agent domiciled in the country.

Thus non-domiciled or non-resident foreigners are not purely assimilated to nationals, by the laws of many countries, as in the case of patents. Many countries did not protect designs and models up to recent times, and the other countries were reluctant to extend protection to non-resident foreigners. The Convention of 1883 raised itself to the level of a fecund and creative instrument by extending the protection afforded to nationals to all persons entitled to the benefit of the Convention.

II. Formalities of Deposits

§ 253. Lack of uniformity and simplicity of formalities. That designs and models should not be put on the same footing with inventions has been said here several times. In the case of inventions, it may be necessary to require compliance with many formalities in the different countries in which a patent application is filed. The need of accuracy and thoroughness in describing an invention, for the exact delimitation of the exclusive right granted by the patent, and the curtailment of the freedom of industry and commerce that this right involves, justify the detailed regulations in each country.

In the case of designs and models, the freedom of industry and commerce is in no way hampered by the prohibition to use, copy, or imitate a design created by another. The field of original creation is unlimited. Besides, there are several reasons which make very onerous the necessity of complying with the formalities and depositing a design or model in several countries. This may be better appreciated if the present status of the formalities of deposit in the different countries is taken into consideration.

Everywhere an application must be made for the admission of a design or model to deposit or registration. The application is filed in most of the countries in a central office, generally a branch of the patent office. In Germany, and Hungary, the design or model is deposited with the Tribunal of Commerce, in France and Belgium with the Trade Council, in Austria and Czechoslovakia with the Chamber of Commerce of the seat of the industrial establishment of the applicant. Foreigners, however, not domiciled or established in the above countries, may deposit with the Tribunal, Trade Council, or Chamber of Commerce of the capital (in Germany, at Leipzig).

In Great Britain, designs for tissues may be sent to the Patent Office or to the branch office at Manchester, at the choice of the applicant. In Australia, the application for registration may be sent to the Design Office at Melbourne, or to any of its branch offices. In Morocco, the deposit may be made with the *Office Marocain de la Propriété Industrielle* at Rabat, or with the secretariat of a tribunal of primary jurisdiction.

The application must be accompanied everywhere with documents, the number and kind of which are the same in no two countries. The kind of paper to be used, its dimensions, weight, and so forth, are specifically defined. In some countries, only a number of samples of the design or model are required; in others, a number of photographs or figurative reproductions; in others, three, four, ten, or twelve sketches, samples, or photographs; and in still others a description or specification, and even an enumeration of claims (for instance, in the United States [1] and Mexico [2]) must be deposited or filed. Several other documents, certificates, powers of attorney, and the like, must sometimes accompany the application.

Moreover, in most countries a separate application, accompanied by all the above array of documents, must be made for every design or model. In Austria and Czechoslovakia, several designs may be deposited together in packages. Also in Switzerland, provided the box containing the designs does not weigh more than ten kilograms, and all its dimensions do not exceed forty centimeters. In Danzig, Denmark, and Tunis, to the limitations of the Swiss law the further restriction is added that no more than fifty designs or models may be deposited with the same application. In Germany and Hungary, the only limitation is that no more than fifty designs may be deposited together; while in France, Morocco, and Syria and Lebanon, the limit is one hundred. In Poland, designs or models of ornament may be deposited together to the number of ten.

§ 254. **Open and secret deposits.** The deposit of designs or models may be made either open or under seal in Austria, Czechoslovakia,

1. In the United States a description of the design is not necessary if the design is complex and words would not explain, but rather confuse, when added to the disclosures of the drawing. Also, the practice of the Patent Office in late years has been to allow but one claim for a design. Yet the claim must contain a description of what an applicant has invented, that is, of the prominent and essential features of his design. This is often not easy to do. See Symons, *Patents for Designs*, pp. 79 ff. and cases cited.

2. The requirement that the depositor indicate the nature of the design or model claimed, that is, formulate a claim, was condemned by the International Association; see *Annuaire* (1900), pp. 327–329.

Cuba, Danzig, Denmark, Germany, Hungary, Japan, Norway, Serb-Croat-Slovene State, and Switzerland. The deposit is always open in Australia, Canada, Italy, Poland, Spain,[1] and the United States. On the other hand, in Belgium, Ceylon, France, Great Britain, Irish Free State, Morocco, Syria and Lebanon, Trinidad and Tobago, and Tunis, the deposit of designs is always made under seal or kept secret.[2] Thus, in most countries the deposit of designs or models may be kept secret. Whether this secrecy is terminated after a period and interrupted in some cases is considered a little later in this chapter. It is sufficient to say here that the secrecy of deposit of designs responds to a necessity inherent in their protection.

With respect to the question of formalities, it may be pointed out here that the secrecy of the deposit reduces the number of formalities which must be complied with at the time the application for registration is filed. Moreover, it protects national, and especially foreign, applicants from hazards and indiscretions to which they are exposed by disclosing their designs or models to agents or to officials.

§ **255. Scarcity of foreign deposits.** All these formalities are very expensive and onerous, especially to foreigners. They must retain counsel and agents in all the countries in which they wish to be protected. They must undergo great trouble and expense for the preservation of their rights in designs which have not yet been applied industrially, and are therefore of uncertain commercial value. These formalities are entirely prohibitory in respect to industries of articles of luxury and of fashion, which produce many sets of designs and models for every new season and are therefore very short-lived commercially.

It is no wonder, then, as has been repeatedly urged, that international protection of designs and models is not yet a reality,[3] be-

1. In Spain only the method of executing a design may be kept secret and deposited under seal. The law of Austria is the new Law No. 118 of May 26, 1928 (*Bundesgesetzblatt*, 1908, p. 739).

2. The law of Ceylon is the Ordinance for the Registration of Designs of 1904 (*The Legislative Enactments of Ceylon*, 1904, IV, 247). The law of Trinidad and Tobago is chapter 189 of the laws of the colony concerning patents, designs and trade marks, No. 76 (*Laws of Trinidad and Tobago*, rev. ed., 1925, III, 2186). The law of the Irish Free State is the Industrial and Commercial Property Act of 1927, sections 64–79 (*Saorstát Eireann*, No. 16 of 1927).

3. G. Maillard, Rapport Général, in *Annuaire de l'Association Internationale* (1897), pp. 162 ff., and statement of the Austrian delegate in footnote, p 163; Soleau, "Propriété des Dessins et Modèles," in *Annuaire* (1898), pp. 357, 364; Lucien-Brun, "Améli-

cause manufacturers do not deposit their designs or models in foreign countries at all.

The best solution would be to assure through the Convention the protection of designs and models throughout the Union, on condition only that the formalities of one country of the Union have been complied with. No injury would be caused thereby to innocent persons. No two persons may create the same design or model, unless they imitate or copy each other, as is the case with artistic and literary works. Besides, when the design or model is deposited under seal, it cannot be said that the public is warned of the existence of a right in a design. By the existence of such formalities no real interest is served, but only dishonesty and unfair competition are encouraged as against foreigners. The maintenance of complicated formalities of deposit and registration can be explained only by the undue assimilation of designs and models to inventions.

The international deposit of designs and models with the International Bureau, provided for by the Arrangement entered into at The Hague by some of the countries of the Union, is a very happy solution in this respect, as will be seen in a later chapter.

III. Administrative Procedure

§ 256. The two systems of mere registration and of previous examination. Patents for inventions are granted in the different countries according to two main systems of administrative procedure, namely, either after a previous examination of the invention with respect to its patentability, novelty, and usefulness, or without any previous examination. The deposit of designs and models is also made under one or the other of these systems. However, the system of previous examination would seem to be unpractical, and almost impossible in the case of designs and models.

True, it may be practical and possible to examine whether an invention is new, that is, whether it contains something that has not previously been discovered, — something not in the public's possession, — and that it does not infringe on a prior patented invention.[1] In every patent granted, the ambit of the invention is

oration des Rapports Internationaux," in *Annuaire* (1901), pp. 97, 102; *Travaux du Groupe Français de l'Association Internationale* (1919–1922), pp. 21, 35.

For statistics of designs and models registered by foreigners see the last section of this chapter and Table V annexed thereto.

1. See *supra*, § 146.

accurately delimited. It is often reduced to a number of claims, functions, principles, formulated details. On the other hand, designs and models are often but new forms of prior types. Like all art, industrial art is a development of prior elements. The combination of lines and colors from which designs and models are constituted cannot be reduced to principles, functions, or claims. It is not easy to decide whether a design or model is original or not in the abstract. With the most thorough aesthetic equipment a person cannot be aware of all the artistic movement and all new forms of industrial art. Only direct comparison between the design or model, the deposit of which is applied for, and a design or model owned or registered by another, or in the public's possession, may disclose the former's lack of originality.

Moreover, designs and models cannot conveniently be subjected to the expenses and delays caused by previous examination of inventions. Many manufacturers deposit a great number of designs at a time, and in the industries of articles of fashion designs are deposited each season. In the latter case, the delay involved in the previous examination proves harmful because of the nature and purpose of these designs. Unless their protection is assured within the shortest possible time, their value disappears.

In a great number of countries, designs and models are admitted to deposit without any examination whatever, provided the applicant has duly complied with the formalities of the law concerning the application and the other documents. These countries are Austria, Czechoslovakia, Belgium, Danzig, Esthonia, France, Germany, Hungary, Italy, Morocco, Serb-Croat-Slovene State, Syria and Lebanon, and Tunis. It may be noted that among these countries are Germany, Austria, Czechoslovakia, and Hungary, which subject inventions to a previous examination. In Denmark, Japan, Norway, and Switzerland, previous examination of the design or model is made by the Patent Office, but only as to the question whether the design or model is one that may be admitted to deposit according to the express provisions of the law. Thus, in Switzerland the admission for deposit will be refused if the design is not a disposition of lines, combined with colors or not: for instance, if it is a mere color or blending of colors, or if it is a design destined for tissues of silk or half-silk (unless for "Jacquard" tissues). In Mexico the administration, at the applicant's expense, may examine the novelty of the design or model without any guaranty.

On the contrary, in Great Britain, Canada, Ceylon, Australia, Irish Free State, New Zealand, and Trinidad and Tobago, and the United States, as well as in Poland, Portugal, and Sweden, designs and models, before being admitted to deposit, are subject to an examination by the administration.

In Great Britain, before the Act of 1907, the examination bore on the question only of identity of the design with another already registered. But by the Act of 1907, as slightly amended by the Act of 1919, the Comptroller, if he thinks fit, may, subject to appeal to the court, refuse to register any design presented to him for registration.[1] No specific grounds on which the Comptroller may base his refusal are given in the act. To be sure, section 75 provides that the Comptroller may refuse to register a design, the use of which would, in his opinion, be contrary to law and morality. But from this refusal an appeal lies to the law officer, as section 75, as amended by the Act of 1919, provides.[2] From this amendment, and from the insertion of the words "except where the refusal is given on a ground mentioned in section seventy-five of this Act," [3] in section 49 (3) of the Act of 1907, it appears that the refusal of registration in the two cases is not the same, and that the Comptroller may refuse to register a design even though its use would not, in his opinion, be contrary to law and morality. The refusal to register, therefore, would seem to be a matter of discretion of the Comptroller in Great Britain, although subject to appeal to the court. In fact, the Comptroller refuses to register a design if it is identical with a design already registered, as appears from section 56 (1), which provides that, when registration of a design is refused on the ground of identity with a design already registered, the applicant for registration is entitled to inspect the design so registered. The situation is the same in Ceylon, Irish Free State, and Trinidad and Tobago. In Australia and New Zealand, the Registrar examines the application, and if he thinks that the design should be registered according to the law (that is, if it is new and original and has not been published before in the country), and the applicant is the real owner, he registers it. In all these countries, in fact, an examination is made of the prior registrations in the Patent Office. Some manufacturers in these countries seem to

1. Sec. 49 (3) of the Act of 1907 (7 Edw. VII, c. 29).
2. Sec. 17 of the Act of 1919 (9 & 10 Geo. V, c. 80).
3. *Ibid.*, sec. 20, Schedule.

prefer this system because of an alleged guaranty of novelty of the design.[1]

In Canada registration of a design is refused if it is found that it is identical with, or resembles so closely, any other design already registered as to be confounded therewith.[2] In Poland, Portugal, and Sweden, the administration examines the novelty of the design or model and its conformity with the provisions of the law.

In the United States, the procedure prevailing in the case of patent applications for mechanical inventions applies also in the case of designs. A search is made by the Patent Office into the novelty of the design and its patentability. Designs are classified in a number of classes, and the search is made in the class to which the design belongs, or in other classes. Foreign designs, however, are rarely searched. In case the design for which a patent is applied for is identical with, or resembles closely, another design patented or pending before the Patent Office, an interference is declared, as in the case of patents for mechanical inventions.[3] Moreover, the Patent Office passes upon the artistic merit of designs and the inventive skill of the applicant. It has been seen that in this respect great difficulties and arbitrariness prevail.[4]

The expense and delay involved in the examination in the United States are almost prohibitive. Prompt protection of designs of a fugitive character, whose life from a business point of view terminates with the change of fashion, style, or taste of the public, is impossible under the present system of procedure of American patent law.[5] This state of things might have come to an end in the United States, with the adoption of the bill for the copyright registration of designs, which put ornamental designs in the class of literary and artistic works, and subjected them to the rules governing the latter.[6]

1. See as to the manufacturers of Manchester (Great Britain), who buy their designs from third persons and desire to be assured that what is sold to them is a really new design, Report of Mr. Maillard, *Travaux du Groupe Français de l'Association Internationale* (1919–1922), pp. 19–20.

2. Sec. 26 of The Trade Mark and Design Act, Rev. Stat., c. 63.

3. Symons, *Patents for Designs*, pp. 109 ff.

4. *Supra*, p. 376.

5. See protests and resolutions of the congresses of the International Association for the Protection of Industrial Property concerning the protection of designs in the United States, collected in *Actes de la Conférence de La Haye*, p. 122.

6. Bill (1925) H. R. 6249. See two articles in this connection in favor and against the bill in *Jour. of Pat. Off. Society* (1926), VII, 540, and VIII, 425.

In Cuba and Spain, the Patent Office does not subject to examination a design submitted for deposit, but publishes it and invites objections from interested parties within a certain period. In Cuba, this is the procedure only as to designs which are not deposited under seal.

§ **257. Need of secrecy of deposit.** It has been seen above, in connection with the formalities of deposit or registration of designs and models, that they may be submitted either open or under seal. In some countries in which the system of previous examination prevails, for instance in Great Britain, a design or model, if not refused, is kept secret by the administration.

The question whether a design should be kept secret after admission to registration or deposit has been much debated. In some industries it is very important that designs should not be disclosed for a certain time after deposit. Indeed, in the industries of style and fashion, new designs are created and deposited with every new season. These designs are often created and submitted for registration or deposit ahead of the season. Then the articles which they ornament, usually tissues and embroideries of all kinds, are manufactured and put on the market at the beginning of the season. If those designs should be published or inspected freely by the public as soon as they are deposited or registered, competitors would imitate and copy the designs deposited and take away the market of the original creators or owners of the designs, although they might be held liable to pay damages after long fights in the courts. Or the competing manufacturers might, without imitating or copying the designs themselves, imitate and follow the general mode or style of the deposited design, and thus again rob the creators of the originality, peculiarity, and distinctiveness of their designs and diminish the sale of their products.[1]

Of course, the creator of a design can claim an exclusive right in the use only of the design submitted, and not of the general style indicated by his design. But it is unjust that he be deprived of the fruits of his labor and originality. After he has put on the market his own products, others may and should be allowed to follow his

1. Edmunds, "Du Dépôt des Dessins et Modèles en Grande-Bretagne," in *Annuaire de l'Association Internationale* (1898), p. 369; Frey-Godet, "Dessins et Modèles Industrielles," *Ibid.* (1899), pp. 26–27, and discussions on this point, *Ibid.* (1900), pp. 330–335; articles in *Propriété Industrielle*, Bureau International (1897), pp. 73, 78; (1919), pp. 51, (452; (192, pp. 180, 185

path, imitating the general style of his design. The early publication of the deposited design can be justified only if without it interests of other persons are impaired. The only hypothetical case of conflict of interests is when third persons create a design identical with, or closely resembling the one deposited, and use it on their own products, unaware of the fact that the same design has been already deposited. This case is not possible in reality. No two persons can create the same design, if they do not imitate or copy each other. There is something personal in the creation of a design. There is a limitation of physical elements and forces which may cause two persons to invent the same article or the same process. But there is an infinity of forms and combinations which may constitute a design.

However, when the reasons for keeping a design secret cease to exist, the latter should be disclosed to the public. Indeed, new designs and models are often adaptations and developments of old ones. People should have the means of knowing whether or not a particular design or model in vogue at an earlier time is in the ownership of a person, and whether or not an adaptation or close resemblance to it would be permissible.

§ 258. Regulation of deposits under seal. The law of many countries at the present day takes a proper account of all the interests concerned and allows a secret deposit of designs and models for a certain period. In Austria, Czechoslovakia, and Norway, designs deposited under seal are opened, and the public may inspect them, a year after their registration. In Germany, Danzig, Denmark, and Japan, the period during which designs are kept in secret is three years.

In Switzerland, designs deposited may be kept secret for five years at most, unless they are designs of embroidery, which may not be disclosed during the whole fifteen-year period of protection. In Great Britain, designs registered are not open to inspection for two years from the date of registration; but the period is five years as regards designs in classes 13, 14, and 15, namely, printed or woven designs on textile piece goods, on handkerchiefs, and on shawls.[1] At the request, however, of any person, the Comptroller, being furnished with information enabling him to identify the design, in-

1. Sec. 69 and Third Schedule of the Designs Rules, 1908. (*Statutory Rules and Orders*, 1907, pp. 77, 78, 127.)

forms such person whether a design is registered, as of what time, and in respect to what classes of goods. The situation in the Irish Free State is similar.

In Hungary, Serb-Croat-Slovene State, and Tunis, while the deposit of the design may be open or under seal, no limitation is made as to the time during which the design may remain secret.

In France, Morocco, and Syria and Lebanon, the deposit of the design is always made under seal. It may be kept secret during the first two periods of protection, of five and twenty years. The design is open to inspection by the public only at the end of the second period, that is, twenty-five years following the original registration, and may be protected only as an open deposit during the third period of protection which is of twenty-five years more. The applicant, however, may ask that the design be opened to inspection by the public from the date of original registration or at any time thereafter.

In Belgium, designs deposited with the Trade Councils are opened by the Councils only in case of controversies. In Ceylon and Trinidad and Tobago, during the existence of copyright in a design, the design is not open to inspection except by the proprietor or a person authorized by him, by the Colonial Secretary or by a court. Information, however, may be given as to whether a design produced by any person is still protected, and as to what class or classes of goods. In the United States, Canada, Australia, Italy, Poland, Portugal, and Sweden, the design is published, or may be inspected by the public, as soon as it is duly registered. In Spain, only the means used for the execution of a design or model may be deposited under seal.

IV. Duration of Protection

§ 259. Need of long and elective terms. The public policy which calls for limitation of the duration of patent rights does not exist in respect to designs and models. The latter may be created in an unlimited number of new forms. No real curtailment of freedom of commerce and industry is involved in the exclusive right in a design or model, although unfair and dishonest copying and imitation is not permitted. However, too prolonged protection of designs and models is not necessary. Many designs are of a fugitive character, owing to changes of fashion, style, and public taste. There is no reason why a design should still be owned by a person when it has long been discontinued. Styles and fashions sometimes are copies of earlier forms. It should be possible for persons able to foresee the coming vogue to adopt and develop designs and models which have ceased to be in public use, more or less, for a long period. But designs and models which are not of short-lived popularity should continue in the ownership of the creator for a much longer time than patents, and as long as the copyright in a literary or artistic work. Whether a design or model should have a brief or a long commercial life the owner himself can best know, and should be left to decide. Thus the best determination of the question of duration of the exclusive right in a design or model would be to fix a maximum of duration of protection, and let the applicant elect a term of years, with possibility of renewal of that term up to the maximum of duration.

§ **260. Term of duration in the various countries.** In the various countries of the Union the term of duration of designs and models presents great variations. In Italy, it is only two years.[1] In Austria,[2] Czechoslovakia, and Hungary three years is the maximum. In Australia, Ceylon, Sweden, and Trinidad and Tobago, it is always five years. In Canada, Esthonia, Japan, Mexico, Poland, Serb-Croat-Slovene State, and Russia, it is ten years. But in Japan and Poland the term is always ten years, while in Esthonia and the Serb-Croat-Slovene State it may be from one to ten; in U. S. S. R. it is divided into three terms of three, three, and four years; in Mexico, a term of five or ten years may be applied for, and in Canada the term is five years, but may be renewed for a further period of five years or less.

In Cuba, Danzig, Denmark, Germany, Great Britain, Irish Free State, New Zealand, Norway, Switzerland, and Tunis, the duration of the exclusive right in a design or model is fifteen years. But in Cuba and Danzig, the term is always fifteen years, while in Germany, fifteen years is a maximum, and the same may be reached by consecutive terms of three years in Denmark and Norway, and of five years in Great Britain, Irish Free State, New Zealand, Switzerland, and Tunis.

1. This is the greatest defect of the Italian law, which accounts for the fact that people do not deposit designs in Italy. See Report by Feruccio Foa, in *Annuaire de l'Association Internationale* (1902), p. 89. See also statistical tables, *infra*, § 271.

2. On the inadequacy of the short term of protection of designs and models in Austria (the law dates from 1858), see "Lettre d'Autriche," in *Propriété Industrielle* (1925), p. 261.

In the United States, patents for designs are granted for the term of three and one-half years, or for seven years, or fourteen years, as the applicant may, in his application, elect. No renewal is possible, even though the term elected was three and one-half years or seven years. In Spain, the term is always twenty years.

In France, Morocco, and Syria and Lebanon, at the end of the first period of protection, which is five years, the sealed box containing the deposited designs is returned to the depositor, unless he applies for a renewal of deposit. The same takes place at the end of the second term, which is twenty years. At that time the depositor may ask for a third term of protection, which will be twenty-five years more.

In Belgium the protection continues to be as it was under the old French Law of 1806, namely, a design or model may be deposited for one, three, five years, or for all time. In Portugal, the first term of protection is five years, but it may be renewed indefinitely.

Although theoretically in these last two countries the protection may become perpetual, in fact, manufacturers are loath to pay big fees, and are satisfied with a short period. But the period of protection in Italy, Austria, Czechoslovakia, Hungary, and even in Australia and Sweden, is much too short. For one thing, in these countries the protection of foreign designs or models is rendered impossible. Furthermore, manufacturers deposit or register their designs or models ahead of the time that they are going to manufacture, and if the period is short, they not only get no benefit out of their creation, but cannot even be compensated for the expense they have gone into for making the designs, for complying with the formalities, and for the taxes and fees.

A maximum duration of fifteen years was advocated by the International Association for the Protection of Industrial Property,[1] and was adopted in the Arrangement for the International Deposit of Designs and Models, as will be seen below.

§ **261. Fees.** In most of the countries of the Union, fees for the deposited designs and models are payable on deposit or on registration. No annual tax during the period of protection of a design or model is paid in these countries, although a renewal fee is due on an application for a new period of protection. Only in Japan and Serb-Croat-Slovene State, an annual tax is payable besides the original

1. *Annuaire* (1899), pp. 22, 101–103, 119; *Ibid.* (1901), pp. 18, 19.

fee for registration; and in Danzig, Poland, and Spain, besides the latter, a periodical tax is due at certain periods during the duration of the protection.

The amount of the fee or tax differs, not only in the various countries, but sometimes in the same country, according to different classesof designs or models. This is true in Australia, Great Britain, New Zealand, and Portugal.

The tax or fee on designs and models deposited should not be too large. In some industries, especially textile and embroidery industries, a manufacturer may deposit hundreds and thousands of designs each year, and the amount of fees might be prohibitive. A large fee assuredly makes impossible the deposit and protection in many foreign countries. For designs of fashion and of brief commercial life it should be possible to pay a minimum amount of fee for every deposit of a package or box containing the number of designs allowed by each country. And in general the fee should be proportioned to the length of the period of protection elected by the applicant.

In most countries the fee is proportioned to the number of years of protection, or a new fee is paid in case of extension of protection or renewal of registration. In only a few countries, however, the fee is not paid for each separate design, but for each deposit of a number of designs. Thus in Switzerland, packages containing more than five designs or models are taxable at the fixed rate of five francs. In Germany, the same fee is paid for the deposit of one design, or a package containing fifty designs or models, for the first period of protection of three years. But if an extension of protection is asked, a fee is payable for each design deposited. This system of taxation is very commendable.

V. Legal Effects of Deposit or Registration

§ **262. Patent right or copyright?** What is the effect of the deposit or registration of an industrial design or model? Does the depositor acquire an exclusive right in the design or model itself, or only the right to prevent others from copying his design, that is, a copyright? Or, to put it in continental phraseology, is a right of property in the design granted, or only declared, by the deposit?

This question is the same that has been dealt with above from another angle.[1] All depends upon the way designs and models are

1. See *supra*, §§ 245, 246.

considered; that is, whether they are classified with inventions or with literary and artistic works. By the grant of a patent for a new discovery or invention it is undisputedly admitted that an exclusive right in the use and industrial application thereof is granted. This is so, although in some countries a right of personal use or personal possession is recognized in favor of third persons who have made the same discovery and have used it or made preparations for its use prior to the patentee's application. Indeed, there is a public interest in a new invention. Law encourages the inventive spirit by rewarding with exclusive privileges those who make contributions to the progress of science and the useful arts. There is no public interest in the design itself. Its ornamental or artistic qualities may satisfy the sense of beauty and the taste of the public, but no immediate material addition to the stock of the public's goods is effected by the creation of a design. Its utility is mediate, by inciting the creation of other designs or models, and enriching the variety of forms and types of products, and thus causing in the long run the progress and development of industry and commerce. In other words, the effect of designs and models is similar to the effect of writings and artistic works in general on the progress of science and art. That which is protected in artistic works is not the novelty or priority of creation, but the originality. That which is prohibited is the copying and pirating of one person's creation by another, and not the independent production of the same work by another person, so long as it is an original creation. Indeed, in the case of designs and models, as well as in the case of literary and artistic property, such independent production of more than one identical or substantially identical creations is extremely rare and, for all practical purposes, impossible.

§ **263. Consequences of copyright.** If then that which must be protected in designs and models is not the novelty or priority of creation, but the originality of creation, the deposit should not have the effect of granting property in a design or model, but only of establishing a proof of creation. The deposit would be a convenient method of proving that a design is owned by the depositor, and of determining the duration of the copyright. If that basic principle is admitted, these consequences will follow.

First, publication of the design or model by the author before deposit does not entail forfeiture of the right of property in a design.

As is seen above,[1] only the law of France, Belgium, Morocco, Tunis, and Syria and Lebanon, is to that effect.

Second, examination of the design or model, before admission to deposit, search into its novelty, and interference proceedings to determine priority, is rendered unneccessary.

Third, the objections against deposit of designs or models under seal will disappear, because what is prohibited is the copying, not of a deposited design, but of an original design, even though it is not deposited, or rendered public.

All three consequences are admitted in the French and Belgian law, and this gives to the regime of designs and models under the law of those countries a logical coherence. On the contrary, in many other countries only the second and third situations are admitted, but not the first, so that the system is somewhat illogical, and is explained by the fact that in these countries novelty and priority are the basis of ownership in a design, and not originality of creation. In the countries, however, in which none of the above situations is admitted, as for example in the United States, the system is logical, the identification of designs and models with inventions being complete.

Wherever an exclusive right in the use and application of a design or model is acquired by the deposit, the protection and rights of the depositor are similar to those of a patentee. The law of each country determines the probative force of a patent or certificate of registration granted for a design or model admitted to deposit. By the same law are governed the questions of criminal or civil liability, of seizures of articles on which the design or model is unlawfully applied, and the like.

§ **264. Regime of designs and models in France.** Assuming that originality of creation should be the only basis of ownership in a design, a question arises as to the legal effects of the deposit. In this respect the present regime of designs and models in France may be looked into. In this country, on the one hand, the Law of March 11, 1902,[2] extended the scope of the Law of 1793, concerning the protection of literary and artistic property, to industrial designs and models, thus protecting the latter without any formality what-

1. See *supra*, § 251.

2. Art. 2 "... le même droit appartiendra aux sculpteurs et dessinateurs d'ornament quels que soient le mérite et la destination de l'oeuvre." *Bulletin des Lois* (1902), I, 2227.

soever. On the other hand, by the Law of July 14, 1909,[1] authors of designs and models may, if they see fit, deposit their designs and models, as they had been doing under the Law of 1806, thus enjoying by such deposit some special advantages; authors of designs or models not so depositing their creations cannot claim the benefits of that law. Thus, in France, the system of optional deposit of designs and models exists. Even without depositing, authors of designs are protected, in the same way as authors of literary and artistic property, against piracy of their works. In such case they must prove that they created the design or acquired it from the creator, and that the defendant fraudulently copied or imitated it. If, on the other hand, authors of designs choose to deposit them, they enjoy the following advantages: (*a*) the first depositor of the design or model is presumed to be the author, until the contrary is proved: thus, by the deposit of the design a convenient proof may be had of creation and ownership of the design, which is not easy under the rules of the common law; (*b*) special protection against acts of infringement perpetrated after the deposit.

This French law has also solved the difficulties arising as to a deposit under seal, by providing that, so long as the deposit of the design is kept secret, the depositor in an action of infringement must prove the bad faith of the defendant; after the deposit of the design is made public, the defendant in an action of infringement must prove his good faith.

In France, deposit of the design is only a way of proving creation and ownership. The Decree of March 10, 1914, and the Ministerial Order of March 13, 1914,[2] in execution of article 4 of the law of 1909, determine the conditions on which, in some industries (textile, silk, embroidery, jewelry, bronze wares, and the like),[3] the creation of designs and models may be proved by private registers authorized by the administration and by a special double envelope, called "Soleau envelope" from the name of a French manufacturer, formerly President of the French Association for the Protection of Industrial Property, who invented it.[4] Thus, manufacturers who

1. *Bulletin des Lois* (1909), I, 1231.

2. *Ibid.* (1914), I, 597. See *Arrêté*, in *Propriété Industrielle* (1914), p. 82.

3. New industries were allowed to avail themselves of the provisions of the Decree of 1914 by the Decrees of August 2, 1922, May 9, 1923, and April 15, 1924. *Bulletin des Lois* (1923), II, 1344, and (1924), I, 954.

4. On the French law and the institution of the Soleau envelope, see *Propriété Industrielle* (1915), pp. 103 ff.; *Travaux du Groupe Français de l'Association Internationale* (1919–1922), pp. 22, 25 ff., 37 ff.

are not desirous of depositing their designs or models may still prove their creations, and identify them by registration in their own registers and by the Soleau envelope. The institution of the envelope consists in this: Two copies of the design whose creation must be proved are placed in the two compartments of the double envelope. This is sent to the Office National de la Propriété Industrielle, where the envelope is perforated with the date of arrival in a way that renders it inviolable. Then the two compartments are separated, the one being returned to the manufacturer and the other being kept in the archives of the Office.[1]

The attempts to institute the use of the Soleau envelopes in other countries through the International Bureau has not succeeded, because in other countries, by the deposit of designs and models, the right in the exclusive use thereof, or the copyright, is established and not merely declared.[2]

§ **265. Deposit of designs as regulation of public order.** The late French legislation on the deposit of designs is not only a step toward complete absorption of industrial designs and models by the law of artistic works in general: it is also a regulation of public order. The deposit is but the means of identifying and proving certain creations whose originality is not very pronounced. The law of 1909 concerns designs and models in general — not merely industrial. Thus even artistic designs or plastic works destined for no industrial application may be deposited.

For the countries which are not prepared to do away with industrial designs and models as a distinct class of industrial property, the French law of 1909 offers a good model of adequate and logical regulation of the interests concerned.

In Belgium also, the courts and the writers admit that the right in a design or model is acquired by creation alone; that the deposit is only a means of declaring the right, fixing the duration, and affording a convenient proof of creation. Even without deposit, the

1. The system of the Soleau envelope does not seem to be much in favor with manufacturers in France. In 1923, the number of envelopes presented for perforation to the Office National was only 364, while the number of designs and models deposited was 33,183. See Chabaud, *Notions Practiques sur les Dessins et Modèles* (Paris, 1925), p. 14. The use of the envelope has progressed very slowly. Thus, it passed from five in 1914 to 79 in 1919, 276 in 1922, 592 in 1924, and 671 in 1926. Letter to the writer from the *Direction de la Propriété Industrielle* (France), under date of Dec. 31, 1927.

2. *Travaux du Groupe Français de l'Association Internationale* (1919–1922), pp. 123 ff.

author of a design retains ownership in the design, unless he abandons it, for instance, by allowing it to be infringed upon by third persons.[1]

In Great Britain, by the registration of a design a copyright is acquired by the depositor. In fact, however, the right acquired is similar to a patent right. For no design is registered if it has been published by the creator before deposit, or if, in the examination in the Patent Office, it does not satisfy the administration as being new and admissible to registration. And there is no common law right in designs. Such right is acquired only by registration. Therefore, creation alone is not the source of ownership, but creation and registration together.[2]

In the United States the assimilation of patents for inventions to patents for designs is complete so far as the question under consideration here is concerned.[3]

In Spain, designs and models are assimilated to trade marks. They may be deposited only by agriculturists, manufacturers, craftsmen, and merchants who apply the designs on their products. Thus they are treated as distinctive marks of industry and commerce rather than as artistic creations or as inventions. The depositor is considered *juris tantum* owner of the design or model, and after three years from the date of the deposit he acquires complete ownership if he is of *bona fides*. A design or model is not protected unless it is registered and a certificate of registration is obtained.

1. Van Damme *c.* Lammens, Cassation, July 11, 1912 (*Pasicrisie*, 1912, I, 388); Société Américaine de Saint-Cobain et al. *c.* Falleur et consorts, Tribunal de Charleroi, July 28, 1913, (cited *in extenso* in Coppieters, *Oeuvres d'Art Appliqué*, pp. 121 ff.); Anpach et Coppieters, *Dessins et Modèles Industriels* (Bruxelles, 1905), p. 39; Coppieters *op. cit.*, pp. 39–40.

2. Secs. 49, 53, and 60 of the Act of 1907 (7 Edw. VII, c. 29). See also Fulton, *Patents and Designs*, pp. 403 ff., 412 ff.

3. See *Jour. of the Pat. Off. Society* (1925), VII, 540, and VIII, 425.

The bill H. R. 6249, introduced in Congress in 1925, for the Copyright Registration of Designs, subjected industrial designs and models to the rules of law concerning artistic and literary property. It proposed to shift the registration of designs from the Patent Office to the Copyright Office. However, the bill was framed too much in terms of patent law and involved many elements of patent theory inconsistent with copyright as understood in the United States. Preliminary examination of the designs was omitted by the bill, but instead there was an excess of formalities of application for registration. The bill gave a working definition of "design." Public use of the design by or with the consent of the author or proprietor for four months prior to the filing of application would not cause forfeiture of the copyright. On the contrary, the conception of copyright in the United States is that publication forfeits the copyright unless the statute is availed of. The filings would be open to inspection by the public, according to the bill. The rights secured by the registration would endure for a term of two years from registration. An extension might be applied for for a further period of eighteen years.

§ **266. Designs are registered in respect to a special class or to classes of goods.** In most of the countries of the Union it is required that the author of a design or model on depositing the same should indicate the class or classes of goods in which the design ought to be registered.[1] In these countries copying or imitating the design is prohibited only if it is applied to articles of the class or classes of goods in respect to which it is registered.[2] In some countries, on the contrary, the law prohibits the application of the design or a fraudulent imitation thereof as an ornament to any article of manufacture, or to any article to which an industrial design may be applied.[3]

The indication of the class of goods in which the design is to be registered is necessary in countries in which the administration examines the novelty of the design; the search is thus made easier. Even in the countries in which no previous examination of the invention is made, there is an advantage in classifying the designs. Indeed, in cases involving the originality of creation, priority of deposit may be a convenient proof, and can more easily be verified if the design is deposited with indication of the special class of goods.

The limitation, however, of the protection of designs and models only as against their application or use in the class of products for which they are registered, may be unjust to the author of the design or model, and to the manufacturer who acquires it from him. The author of the design ought to be protected in his property right against any unauthorized use or application of the design. If a manufacturer chooses to use a design in ornamenting his articles, it means that the design is profitable to him, and therefore he should not be allowed such use without paying for the same.

The manufacturer, also, who acquires the design from the author and uses it in one class of products may suffer damage by the use of the same design by another manufacturer without his authority. The latter may use the design on articles of competitive nature, though not of the same class. Or he may use it on goods of a much inferior quality, and thus vulgarize the design. In both cases, the manufacturer who deposited the design may suffer damage.[4]

1. Great Britain, Australia, New Zealand, United States, Germany, Japan, Portugal, Serb-Croat-Slovene State.

2. Read and Gresswell's Design (1889), 6 R. P. C. 471 (*dictum*).

3. For instance, Canada and France.

4. Frey-Godet, "Dessins et Modèles Industriels," in *Annuaire de l'Association Internationale* (1899), p. 25, and *Ibid.* (1900), pp. 328, 338–339.

Therefore, although the law might require of the applicant to indicate the class of goods for which his design ought to be registered, he should not be held as waiving his right to proceed against any person using or applying his design, or a copy thereof, without his authority, on other classes of goods, so long as such person acts fraudulently and knowingly, and damage is caused thereby to the owner of the design.[1]

VI. Obligations of Depositor

§ 267. Should the obligations of patentees be imposed on depositors of designs? Patents for inventions are granted almost everywhere, under various restrictions. Although, as has been maintained in a previous chapter,[2] those restrictions are due to a theoretical fear more than to practical experience, they may be explained by the social importance attached to inventions. Because of assimilation in many cases of designs and models to inventions, the same restrictions are imposed in many countries on the depositors of designs and models.

The latter are not in themselves of social importance. The freedom of industry is in no way curtailed by the prohibition involved in the copyright of a design. There may be cases when an industrial result can be accomplished only by a patented invention. There may be cases of suppression of patents by interested persons. Such cases are impossible in respect to designs and models. There is no element of usefulness in a design. The number of ornamental forms and configurations or shapes is unlimited. If a manufacturer deposits several forms of a kind, a *genus*, of designs, and uses only one of them, thus protecting his design by surrounding it with the protection of a whole *genus* of designs, other manufacturers are still free to create an original design of another kind. They do not need to follow the kind deposited by the first creator.

The restrictions imposed on depositors of designs and models are not justified by any consideration, and are merely the consequence of assimilation of designs and models to inventions. In the matter of international protection, these restrictions constitute one of the

1. The International Association for the Protection of Industrial Property adopted resolutions to this effect in the congresses of 1899 and 1900. See *Annuaire* (1899), pp. 103–104, and *Ibid.* (1900), p. 339.
2. Chap. XIII, especially § 221.

main obstacles to such protection, rendering it in many instances well-nigh impossible.[1]

The restrictions and obligations imposed on the depositor of a design or model follow:

§ 268. Obligation to work design and prohibition of importation. One obligation demands working the design or model within the country. This is imposed by the law of Czechoslovakia, Cuba, Denmark, Germany, Great Britain and the British dominions and colonies, Hungary, Italy, Mexico, Serb-Croat-Slovene State, Spain, and Switzerland. The meaning and extent of this obligation differ in the various countries.

In Mexico, the penalty for the non-working of the design or model for three years from the date of registration, or for interrupting its use for three months after the three-year period, is a compulsory license granted by the Patent Office.

In Great Britain and the Irish Free State, at any time after the registration of a design the Comptroller, on application, may cancel the registration if the design is applied by manufacture to any article in a foreign country, and is not so applied by manufacture in the United Kingdom or in the Irish Free State to a reasonable extent. If the time which has elapsed since registration is insufficient in the opinion of the Comptroller, he may adjourn the application. The Comptroller also may, in lieu of cancellation, order the grant of a compulsory license on such terms as he may consider just.

In Germany and Denmark, only those designs are protected which are applied on articles manufactured in these countries. Foreigners, moreover, must have an industrial establishment in the country. In Switzerland, the right to the exclusive use of the design is forfeited if the design is not worked in the country adequately, and if at the same time it is worked abroad and articles on which it is applied are imported into the country. In the Serb-Croat-Slovene State, the right in a design is forfeited if it is not worked sufficiently in the country.

In Ceylon and Trinidad and Tobago, the copyright in a registered design ceases if it is used in manufacture in any foreign country and is not used in the colony within six months from its registration. In

1. See on this point, reports and discussions at the congresses of the International Association of Industrial Property, *Annuaire* (1897), pp. 160, 415; (1898), p. 370; (1899), p. 21; (1900), p. 177; (1901), p. 107. Also *Travaux du Groupe Français* (1919–1922), pp. 35, 175; *Propriété Industrielle* (1924), p. 184.

Austria, Czechoslovakia, Hungary, Italy, and New Zealand, forfeiture is pronounced if the design is not worked in the country within one year from the deposit (from publication, in Italy). In Cuba, the period within which the depositor of a design must begin working it is two years, and also he must not stop working it for more than a year and a day. In Spain, he need not begin working a design for three years.

In Australia, a design must be applied by manufacture in the country within two years from registration. But if the design is applied by manufacture on any article in a foreign country, the period within which it must be worked in Australia is reduced to six months.

The prohibition of importation of articles manufactured with the deposited design or model exists in Czechoslovakia, Denmark, Hungary, Norway, and Serb-Croat-Slovene State. By a single importation of such articles the right in a design is forfeited in those countries.

§ 269. **Obligation of marking the design.** Besides the preceding, a further restriction is imposed by the law of some countries. In order to avoid infringement of a design through ignorance of its registration, and to give proper notice to the public, owners of designs are required to mark them in a way denoting the fact of registration. This requirement exists in Great Britain and the British dominions and colonies, in the United States, Japan, and Esthonia.

In the United States, the word "patented" and the day and year the patent was granted must be marked on the designs.[1]

In Great Britain, before selling and delivering any article to which a registered design has been applied, each such article must be marked with the word "Registered," or the abbreviation "Reg^{d}" or "R^{d}," and the number of registration. However, the Board of Trade, on representation on behalf of any trade or industry in the interest of the latter, may dispense with or modify any of the requirements as to marking in respect to any class or description of articles. Under the Design Rules of 1908, in case of designs registered in classes 9, 13, 14 and 15, — laces, printed or woven designs on textile goods, handkerchiefs, and shawls, — the number of registration need not be marked on the articles.[2] In Canada, the name of the manufacturer

1. Rev. Stat., Secs. 4900 and 4901.
2. Sec. 54 of the Act of 1907 (7 Edw. VII, c. 29), and sec. 68 of the Design Rules of 1908 (1907 *Statutory Rules and Orders*, 77, 87, and Schedule, p. 127).

must be marked with the abbreviation "R^{d}" on designs for woven fabrics, and the same, with the year of registration, on any other article. In Australia only the mark "Reg^{d}" must be applied on designs of textile wares, and the mark "R^{d}" on other articles.

In Esthonia, the sign of protection must indicate the period for which the exclusive right is granted. In Japan, no more than a sign of protection is needed.

Upon failure of the proprietor of a design to mark the articles, as required by law, in the United States, the burden of proof is on the plaintiff to show that the defendant had notice of the fact that the design is patented.[1] In Great Britain and the British dominions, the proprietor of the design is not entitled to recover any penalty or damages for any infringement of his design, unless he shows that he took all proper steps to ensure the marking of the article, or unless he shows that, before the infringement, the defendant had notice of the existence of the copyright in the design.[2] In Japan, on omission to mark the articles on which the design has been applied with a sign indicating the registration of the design, no damages may be collected from the infringer of the design, in case he had no notice of the existence of the plaintiff's right in the design.[3]

It is very doubtful whether the obligation to mark the articles on which a design has been applied serves any practical purpose. It may be repeated here once more, that no two original designs may be alike. Too close resemblance is always a result of imitating or copying. The nature of the designs, being ornamental, hardly admits of marks extraneous to the design itself. The aesthetic quality of the design or model would be impaired. Such marking becomes often impossible when the owner of the design must comply with the requirements of several countries in which he may deposit his design. It cannot be supposed, indeed, that three or four marks,

1. Schofield *v.* Dunlop (1890), 42 Fed. 323.

2. The obligation of marking was much more severe under the Act of 1883 (sec. 51), the copyright in the design ceasing on failure to mark before delivery on sale of any article to which a registered design has been applied (Wooley *v.* Broad [1892], 9 R. P. C. 429; L. R. 2 Q. B. 307), unless the registered proprietor could show that he took all proper steps to ensure the marking of the article. This is the law to-day in Ceylon, and Trinidad and Tobago.

3. Sec. 64 of the Patent Act of April 29, 1921, made applicable by sec. 25 of the Designs Act of same date; see *Propriété Industrielle* (1923), pp. 109, 144, and (1924), pp. 6, 8.

with numbers and dates of registration, may be made on many articles of industrial art.[1]

VII. Conclusions

§ 270. It may fairly be said, in conclusion of the preceding exposition, that the international protection of industrial designs and models must be very difficult in view of the many formalities, obstacles, and restrictions imposed by the municipal laws of the different countries and their great diversity. International protection will become much easier and more adequate when national protection shall be rid of unnecessary regulation, which has outgrown the present needs of industry and art. A great amelioration in this respect is being achieved in countries in which the scope of the law on literary and artistic property has been extended so as to cover many kinds of designs and models previously governed by the law on industrial designs and models. The French system of optional declarative deposit of designs and models, and the new French methods of establishing an official proof of creation, would seem to afford all the necessary regulation on the matter.

VIII. Statistics

§ 271. The following statistical tables are very eloquent in confirming many points made in the course of this chapter. The first table gives the number of industrial designs and models registered in certain countries in the years prior to 1900. Germany

TABLE I

Number of Industrial Designs and Models Registered in Certain Countries before 1900*

Country	Years	Total
Austria	1876–1899	53,150
Belgium	1885–1899	2,193
France	1813–1839	47,592
	1840–1897	1,431,758
Germany	1876–1899	1,834,565
Great Britain	1876–1899	450,987
Hungary	1882–1898	13,815
Italy	1874–1899	678
Japan	1889–1898	725
Portugal	1895–1899	825
Serbia	1888–1899	30
Switzerland	1889–1899	231,828
United States	1843–1899	32,054

* This table and table III are made up from data published in *Propriété Industrielle* (1900), pp. 141 ff.

1. See Frey-Godet, "Protection des Dessins et Modèles, in *Annuaire de l'Association Internationale* (1901), pp. 103, 108–110.

TABLE II

NUMBER OF INDUSTRIAL DESIGNS AND MODELS REGISTERED IN THE VARIOUS COUNTRIES OF THE UNION IN RECENT YEARS*

Countries	1900	1910	1913	1922	1923	1924	1925	1926
Australia	...	163	268	380	377	453	446	539
Austria	10,865	12,451	13,269	4,571	4,823	6,174	6,279	6,697
Belgium	167	340	394	573	640	831	1,308	1,665
Canada	129	...	...	...	...	417	522	347
Cuba	...	...	...	...	...	...	...	13
Czechoslovakia	...	...	...	3,675	3,737	5,141	5,353	7,129
Denmark	...	648	812	1,293	1,329	1,572	1,522	1,497
Esthonia	...	...	...	...	14	4	15	10
France	52,011	52,609	53,713	31,378	33,183	41,876	40,347	38,721
Germany	131,666	206,730	183,426	30,676	...	35,277	57,035	78,021
Great Britain	16,282	32,212	39,275	14,419	17,807	20,155	22,308	21,874
Hungary	...	1,287	13,158	354	268	404	516	647
Italy	60	97	210	170	124	600	800	370
Japan	130	637	1,173	1,522	...	1,874	3,049	3,774
Latvia	...	...	...	...	...	...	32	35
Mexico	...	69	...	149	...	69	71	65
Morocco	...	...	...	5	14	13	18	14
New Zealand	...	...	...	153	171	168	156	158
Norway	...	...	241	418	450	412	546	520
Poland	...	...	...	254	283	40	338	311
Portugal	61	17	38	31	37	81	...	71
Serb-Croat-Slovene State	...	...	...	40	48	25	28	36
Spain	...	170	144	123	173	248	385	493
Sweden	13	35	12	36	53	65	90	81
Switzerland†	66,380	307,984	483,545	183,933	221,290	194,756	234,778	202,142
Syria and Lebanon	...	...	...	...	...	...	7	85
Tunis	...	...	...	5	20	10	8	12
United States	886	639	144	1,627	1,927	2,671	2,824	2,602

* This statistical table is compiled from statistical data communicated by the various administrations to the International Bureau, and published by the latter in *Propriété Industrielle* (1902), p. 16; (1912), p. 179; (1916), p. 112; (1924), pp. 167 and 259; (1925), p. 267; (1926), p. 275; (1927), p. 231.

† In Switzerland, of the 202,142 designs and models for 1926, 192,681 are designs of embroidery. The same analogy more or less exists for the other years.

leads in this respect, and France comes next to her. In about the same period of the second half of the nineteenth century, 1,431,758 designs and models were registered in France, as against only 32,054 in the United States. It is interesting to compare this table with that of patented inventions.[1] In the second table, appear the number of designs and models registered in member countries of the Union in the years 1900, 1910, 1913 and 1922 to 1926. The effects of the war

1. See *supra*, § 258.

on many belligerent countries are apparent from the discrepancy existing between the numbers registered in 1913 and in post-war times. Switzerland is far ahead of all other countries, by reason, especially, of the very great number of designs of embroidery. Germany comes next, with a number of registrations that has steadily increased since the decline brought about by the war. In France, registrations of designs and models continue at a high point, notwithstanding the new regime of designs and models created in that country by the recent laws, under which registration is not necessary. Great Britain has also a great number of registrations. Only a small number of patents for designs are granted in the United States and Italy, where the whole regime of designs and models is very inadequate.

Tables III and IV bring out more prominently the data of the previous tables. The two five-year periods, 1895–1899 and 1922–1926, should be compared. The yearly average for Switzerland has risen from 38,008 registrations to 207,380. The same average for the United States has increased from 1,626 to only 2,330. But this nominal increase in the United States is not real, if we consider the average to a million inhabitants. For the latter was 22 in the five year period 1895–1899 and 20 in the five-year period 1922–1926. On the contrary, in Switzerland the increase in the number of registrations is a real increase, since the average number rose from 12,191 to 51,845 to a million inhabitants.

In France and Germany there was a marked decline of the average of registrations in the two periods under consideration. But this is to be explained by the fact that many designs and models in these countries are protected as artistic works, or as works of art applied to industry.

Most of the countries do not publish statistics of the number of designs or models registered or deposited by foreigners. Table V gives the numbers for four of the countries in respect to which data are available. It is clearly seen that the total number, as well as the proportion, of designs or models registered by foreigners is totally negligible.[1] Indeed, until the recent revision of the Convention at the Conference of The Hague and the adoption of the new Arrangement for the international deposit of designs and models, no real international protection of this right of industrial property existed.

1. Compare this table with table V of the chapter on patents, on p. 261.

TABLE III

Average Number of Industrial Designs and Models Registered in Certain Countries in the Years 1895–1899

Countries	Yearly average	Countries	Average to a million inhabitants
Austria (1898–1899)	10,246	Switzerland	12,191
Belgium	187	Germany	2,187
France (1893–1897)	57,679	France	1,488
Germany	118,121	Great Britain	486
Great Britain	19,699	Austria	400
Hungary (1894–1898)	945	Hungary	50
Italy	91	Portugal	37
Japan (1894–1898)	79	Belgium	29
Portugal	165	United States	22
Serbia	3	Japan	7
Switzerland	38,008	Italy	3
United States	1,626	Serbia	1

TABLE IV

Average Number of Industrial Designs and Models Registered in the Countries of the Union in the Years 1922–1926

Countries	Yearly average	Countries	Average to a million inhabitants
Australia	439	Switzerland	51,845
Austria	5,709	France	913
Belgium	1,003	Austria	874
Canada	428	Germany	806
Czechoslovakia	5,007	Great Britain	436
Denmark	1,443	Denmark	412
France	37,101	Czechoslovakia	368
Germany	50,252	Norway	176
Great Britain	19,312	Belgium	127
Hungary	438	New Zealand	115
Italy	413	Australia	79
Japan	2,555	Hungary	52
Mexico	88	Canada	47
Morocco	13	Japan	42
New Zealand	161	United States	20
Norway	469	Spain	13
Poland	245	Sweden	11
Portugal	55	Italy	10
Serb-Croat-Slovene State	35	Portugal	10
Spain	284	Poland	8
Sweden	65	Mexico	6
Switzerland	207,380	Tunis	5
Tunis	11	Morocco	3
United States	2,330	Serb-Croat-Slovene State	3

TABLE V

NUMBER OF INDUSTRIAL DESIGNS AND MODELS REGISTERED BY FOREIGNERS

Countries	Years	Average	Per cent
France	1893–1897	3,027	5.2
	1923–1927	385	1
Hungary	1894–1898	403	42
Italy	1895–1899	13	14
	1920–1924	47	11
Switzerland	1923–1927	1,063	0.5

CHAPTER XVI

THE RIGHT OF PRIORITY AND THE PROTECTION AT INTERNATIONAL EXHIBITIONS OF INDUSTRIAL DESIGNS AND MODELS

§ 272. Enjoyment of the right of priority. Article 4 of the Convention of 1883 provides that a right of priority is enjoyed by any person who has duly filed an application for registration of an industrial design or model in one of the contracting countries. The interpretation and study of this provision in respect to patent applications may also be applied, *mutatis mutandis*, to designs and models. This is so especially with reference to the nature of the right of priority,[1] the persons who may claim this advantage,[2] and the requirements as to the prior deposit.[3] The right of priority here also operates as a warning on the part of the person who first applies for the registration of his design or model in a country of the Union. The fact of the first filing of an application in a country of the Union is a legal defense operative at the later filings of applications for registration of the same design in other countries of the Union, if such filings are made within the period specified in article 4 of the Convention. The person who has filed the first application, as well as his successors or assigns, may claim the right of priority so long as they belong to the classes of persons provided for in articles 2 and 3.

§ 273. Period of the right of priority. The period of the right of priority in respect to designs and models was four months until the last conference at The Hague. At the Conference of Washington, Germany and France proposed that the period of the right of pri-

1. See *supra*, §§ 164, 165.
2. See *supra*, §§ 166, 167.
3. See *supra*, §§ 168–173.

ority for designs and models should be extended to twelve months, and it seemed that a general agreement could be reached on an extension to six months.[1] While the extension was finally defeated by the objection of a single country at Washington,[2] it was adopted without discussion at the Conference of The Hague, on the proposal of the International Bureau. The French and Spanish delegations had again urged the adoption of a uniform period of twelve months for all rights of industrial property, but there was a strong minority against such an extension.[3]

There are several reasons in favor of a further extension of the period of the right of priority in respect to designs and models. The system of previous examination of the design or model in some countries takes up a great part of the period. Besides, designs and models may be deposited under seal in some countries, and the risk of publication in such cases does not exist; at the same time, since these designs or models are not published, the industry is not under any uncertainty in regard to them. Furthermore, it very rarely happens, and is practically impossible, that two persons create the same design or model, unless they copy or imitate each other. Therefore, no prejudice to third parties is caused by an extension of the period of priority. Lastly, designs and models are often of ephemeral value, and their authors or owners cannot decide upon depositing them in foreign countries unless they are convinced of their commercial importance after using and working in the domestic market. For all these reasons, the extension of the period of priority for designs and models to twelve months, as for patents and utility models, would seem to be necessary.

The computation of the period in case of designs and models and the questions pertaining thereto are identical with those of the right of priority for patents.[4]

§ 274. Conditions for claiming this right. The same is true in respect to the conditions and formalities concerning new deposits,[5] and in respect to the identity of the first and later applications.[6] Especially the new paragraphs of article 4 added at the Conferences

1. *Actes de la Conférence de Washington*, pp. 91, 95, 275, 307.
2. *Ibid.*, p. 247.
3. *Actes de la Conférence de La Haye*, pp. 223–224, 334, 426–427.
4. See *supra*, § 178.
5. See *supra*, §§ 179–186.
6. See *supra*, §§ 187, 188.

of Washington and of The Hague will be applied in case of designs and models, as in case of patents. Thus, a declaration of priority must be made by the person claiming a right of priority for a design according to section (*d*) of article 4. In Austria, Czechoslovakia, Australia, Belgium, Denmark, Germany, Italy, Morocco, Poland, Serb-Croat-Slovene State, Sweden, and Switzerland, such declaration must be made on the deposit of the application for registration of a design or model. In the rest of the countries, the municipal law does not regulate the formalities for claiming the right of priority for designs. In such case the provisions of article 4 will be applicable. In the United States, the formalities are the same as in the case of patent applications. The difficulties in respect to the identity of two patent applications are not likely to arise in respect to industrial designs or models. Rarely are claims required, and the specifications are not as complicated as those concerning mechanical inventions.

§ 275. Relation of designs to utility models in respect to the right of priority. In Germany, Japan, and Poland, besides the designs and models, there is another branch of industrial property, the working models or utility models (*Gebrauchsmuster*). The international protection of the latter is studied in the next section of this book. It is necessary to note here that utility models are either small inventions or ornamental designs possessing a character of utility. It may happen that a person who has filed for registration a design or model in a country of the Union and files the same in Germany, Poland, or Japan, will have it registered in these countries as a utility model. Or the opposite may happen, namely, a utility model filed in Germany, Poland, or Japan, may be deposited in another country as a design or model. The period of the right of priority for utility models being twelve months, the question arises, what will be the period in these two cases.

At the Washington Conference a provision on this point was inserted in the Final Protocol, and the same was incorporated in article 4, section (*e*) at the Conference of The Hague. It reads as follows:

> Il est entendu que, lorsqu'un dessin ou modèle industriel aura été déposé dans un pays en vertu d'un droit de priorité basé sur le dépôt d'un modèle d'utilité, le délai de priorité ne sera que celui que l'article 4 a fixé pour les dessins et modèles industriels.

Thus, if the second application is for the registration of a design or model, the period of priority is always six months, although by the first application the registration of a utility model was applied for. In other words, the second application determines the right of priority and its duration. This is in entire harmony with the exposition on the nature of the right of priority made in an earlier part of this book.[1] In the opposite case, that is, when, in an application for the registration of a utility model, a right of priority is based on a prior application for the registration of a design or model, on the same reasoning, the period of priority will be twelve months.[2] Cases of the second kind would be rare, as in a model of utility an element of practical usefulness must exist, and that is not the case with ornamental designs and models.

§ **276. Effects of the right of priority.** The effects of the right of priority in the case of industrial designs and models are much the same as in the case of patents. Thus, no valid registration of a design or model by a third person may take place in the interval, and the publication, use, or working of the design or model during the period of the right of priority, either by the proprietor himself or by third persons, constitutes no bar. The precise scope of these effects and the question of liability of third parties, considered above in respect to patents, apply, *mutatis mutandis*, to designs and models.[3]

It has been said [4] that the importance of the right of priority is not so great in the case of designs and models as it is in the case of patents. Patentees risk having the novelty of their invention destroyed by the mere application for a patent, or the consequent publication or advertisement by the patent office. Proprietors of designs or models can avoid that danger by depositing their crea-

1. See *supra*, § 165.

2. The International Bureau, in order to make this free from any doubt, proposed at the Conference of The Hague to add in the provision under consideration the words, "ou inversement." But the Editing Committee thought it not amiss to strike out these words. Apparently they could not be inserted as it was proposed. A rephrasing of the whole provision would be necessary. See *Actes de la Conférence de La Haye*, pp. 231, 232, 495.

3. See *supra*, §§ 193 ff. In Great Britain and the British dominions and colonies the registration of the design for which priority is claimed under the Convention is antedated as of the date of filing the first application in the foreign country. The objections which are raised against this British practice under the Convention have been considered above (§ 198). They are more serious in the case of designs, in view of the short duration of the exclusive right in them.

4. Pillet, *Régime International*, pp. 326–327; Pelletier et Vidal-Naquet, *Convention d'Union*, p. 283.

tions under seal in most countries. Inventors may be assured on the lapse of twelve months after filing an application for a patent that their invention is good and their patent valid, if no other application for the same invention with a claim of right of priority is made within this period. This assurance cannot exist for authors or proprietors of designs or models. For during the period of the right of priority, industrial designs or models may be deposited under seal. However, the same uncertainty exists in respect to sealed deposits of designs or models in the same country. And it should not be forgotten that cases of independent creation of identical designs or models are extremely rare and almost impossible.

The protection of designs and models by the right of priority is necessary in the following cases. First, against the legal destruction of their novelty in some countries, by reason of their use and working after deposit and registration in one country. Second, against their imitation or copying by third persons who discover them on the market. And third, against registration in the name of a third person who obtains in like manner a knowledge of the design.

It has been seen above that article 4 of the Convention reserves rights of third parties as against a person claiming a right of priority in respect to a patent application. Is the reservation of the rights of third parties also operative in the case of designs and models?

The history of the phrase, "et sous réserve des droits des tiers," in article 4 is considered above; and it is seen how the interpretation of the "right of personal possession" was put behind this phrase by two conferences of revision.[1] But the right of personal possession is recognized only in respect to inventions, and the above conferences admitted it expressly only for inventions.[2] The discussions at the Conference of The Hague also limited the reservation in the same way.[3] It would seem then that the reservation of the rights of third parties is without effect in the case of industrial designs and models.[4]

§ 277. Need of temporary protection of designs and models at international exhibitions. Article 11 of the Convention provides for the temporary protection of industrial designs and models in respect to goods exhibited at official, or officially recognized, interna-

1. See *supra*, §§ 200, 201.
2. *Actes de la Conférence de Bruxelles*, p. 210; *Actes de la Conférence de Washington*, pp. 273-274.
3. *Actes de la Conférence de La Haye*, pp. 227, 427-428, 517.
4. Coppieters, *Œuvres d'Art Appliqué*, p. 182, *accord*.

tional exhibitions held in the territory of any of the countries of the Union. The need of such protection for designs and models is far more important than for patentable inventions. A much greater number of new designs and models than inventions are exhibited at modern international exhibitions. Besides, the former may be copied and imitated with far less difficulty than the latter. There is a greater risk that designs and models exhibited may be considered as having lost their character of novelty, or be misappropriated by others and deposited by them as their own property.

The subject Index of *Fairs and Exhibitions* listed by the International Chamber of Commerce [1] shows among the special fairs and exhibitions, that is, those in which special classes of goods only are admitted, a great number of goods in respect of which new designs and models are exhibited; for instance, decorative arts, jewelry, watchmaking, hairdressing, textiles, colors, foodstuffs, paper, perfumery, shoes, leather, furs, and furniture.

New designs and models may be exhibited only if their proprietors are certain that third persons will not infringe upon their rights by copying and imitating them, and that their creations will not be considered as abandoned or as having lost their novelty. Article 11 was intended to protect proprietors of designs and models against these risks. However, while stipulating in principle the temporary protection of designs and models exhibited at international exhibitions, it left the regulation of such protection and its extent to the municipal law of each country of the Union. The precise legal effect of the stipulation of article 11, its shortcomings and its amendments, are dealt with in the consideration of article 11 in relation to patentable inventions.[2] We have also seen when an exhibition is official or officially recognized, within the meaning of article 11.[3]

The controversy as to whether or not the period of temporary protection of article 11 is added to the period of priority of article 4 was settled in the negative at the last conference of The Hague.[4] This amendment is considered above as a distinct backward step. It is so, especially, with respect to industrial designs and models. The period of the right of priority is only six months in the case of designs and models; if this period must begin, as provided for by the new second paragraph of article 11, from the date of the introduction

1. See Digest No. 56, *Fairs and Exhibitions*, June–December, 1927.
2. See *supra*, §§ 234, 235.
3. See *supra*, § 236.
4. See *supra*, § 243.

of the goods into the locale of the exhibition, it is singularly useless. Exhibitions often last for several months, and it is only after they are over, or nearly so, that manufacturers usually apply for registration of their designs and models in the countries in which their goods may find a market.

§ **278. Duration and formalities of the temporary protection.** The duration of the temporary protection in the various countries of the Union is as follows. In Ceylon, Denmark, Germany, Great Britain, Irish Free State, Japan, and Norway, the period is six months, beginning with the official opening of the exhibition; while in Hungary, Portugal, and Sweden, the same period begins with the public exhibition of the design or model, and in Spain, with the date of admission of the same at the exhibition.

In Switzerland the period is six months from the moment the design or model is introduced in the exhibition, but this moment cannot precede the commencement of the exhibition by more than three months.

In France and Morocco, the period is twelve months from the commencement of the exhibition. In Italy the same period is increased by a month preceding the commencement; for foreign exhibitions, however, the period of temporary protection is only that which is fixed by the law of the country in which the Exhibition is held, if it is shorter. In Austria, Czechoslovakia, Mexico, and Serb-Croat-Slovene State, the period, while lasting for three months after the closing of the exhibition, begins from the moment of introduction of the design in the exhibition in the first two countries, and from the commencement of the exhibition in the two latter.

In Latvia, the period of temporary protection is only three months after the commencement of the exhibition. In Belgium, the duration of the temporary protection is fixed specifically for each exhibition by an order.[1]

In Denmark, Germany, Norway, Portugal, and Sweden, no formality whatsoever is required for claiming the temporary protection. In the other countries, various formalities and conditions must be fulfilled by persons intending to claim it. These conditions and formalities are considered and discussed above.[2]

1. See the legislative enactments of the various countries in footnotes 1 and 2 on p. 350. See also *Tableau*, in *Actes de la Conférence de La Haye*, pp. 168–171.
2. See *supra*, § 241.

Reference is also made above,[1] in respect to the countries which have not executed article 11 of the Convention, to the exhibitions at which protection is afforded by the municipal law of the various countries, and to the practical value of the amendments adopted at the last conference of The Hague.

1. See *supra*, §§ 238, 239, 243.

CHAPTER XVII

INDEPENDENCE OF RIGHTS IN DESIGNS AND MODELS

§ 279. Independence of rights in designs and models should be recognized. Article 4*b* of the Convention establishes the independence of patents applied for in the different countries of the Union for the same invention. This is understood as well from the point of view of nullity and forfeiture of the various patents, as from the point of view of their normal duration. The stipulation of article 4*b* concerns expressly patents obtained for an invention. It would seem therefore that designs and models are not covered by this provision. Nor is it possible to apply it by analogy to designs and models. The preparatory work for the adoption of article 4*b*, namely the texts proposed at the Conferences of Rome, Madrid, and Brussels, and the discussions thereon, concern only patents for invention.[1]

However, the Congress of Paris in 1878 had adopted the principle of independence of designs and models as well as of patents.[2] It is submitted above [3] that, even without the stipulation of article 4*b*, the independence of patents for inventions should be admitted under the Convention, on general principles and on an interpretation of the general spirit and scope of the Convention.[4] This applies with greater force to industrial designs and models.[5]

Indeed, in the countries where ownership in a design is acquired only by registration, the registrant's right should be independent of the right in the same design or model in the other countries. The registration of a design in foreign countries does not purport to extend in the territories of these countries the right acquired by the registration in the first country. It is a new right, although for the same design, that is granted by the new registration. The prior

1. See quotations and references, *supra*, § 208.
2. *Comptes-rendus du Congrès*, p. 418.
3. See *supra*, § 207.
4. Cf. Osterrieth und Axster, *Pariser Konvention*, p. 105; Maillard, Report to the International Association, *Annuaire* (1897), pp. 179–180.
5. Maillard, Report to the International Association, *Annuaire* (1897), p. 162.

registration in one country is not a condition of the acquisition of the right in another country. It should, then, follow that the duration in the latter cannot be affected by the termination or cancellation of the registration in the former country.

Besides, from a practical point of view, when the proprietor of a design has undergone all the expense and trouble, and complied with all formalities and conditions of each country, he should enjoy to the full extent the protection that the law of each country affords. A mere accident — the fact that he applied first in one country for the registration of the design, and later in another country instead of in reverse order, should be of no importance.

The usual argument that, if the design continues to be protected in a country while it has ceased to be protected abroad, the industry of that country is prevented from using a design which is in the possession of the public in other countries, and is prejudiced thereby, is hardly available in the case of designs and models. The latter do not restrain honest industry and commerce. No design or model limits freedom of production. The number of designs that may be created is unlimited. An invention may be the only way of reaching a certain result, or producing a certain product. There is any number of designs or models that have an ornamental character. Industry is always free to follow the general style, fashion, or kind of a design in vogue. The right in a design is the right in a very distinct and individualized configuration, shape, form, or aspect.

In the countries in which ownership in a design is based exclusively on creation, and the deposit is only a means of establishing an official proof of creation, — "a birthday certificate," — the recognition of independence of the rights and protection afforded in each country should be in no doubt. When the protection of a design ceases in a country because of revocation of the certificate of registration, or of annulment of the registration, or of termination of the duration of protection, all this affects the "birthday certificate" of the right, not the "birth" itself.

It follows then that, when a person entitled to the benefits of the Convention registers his design or model in several countries of the Union, his rights and protection in each country are independent of such protection or of its extent in the other countries.[1] Thus, the

1. Pillet (*Régime International*, pp. 331 ff.) holds otherwise, mainly on the basis of his theory of dependence of patents which has been discussed elsewhere (*supra*, § 9).

abandonment of a design in a country, or its forfeiture for non-working or for importation of articles on which the design has been applied, does not affect the protection of the design in the other countries.[1] Similarly the termination of the duration of protection in a country does not put an end to the protection in the other countries. This is very important in view of the fact that there is great discrepancy of protection in the various countries of the Union (for instance, two years in Italy and fifty years in France).[2]

It may be noted that in the congresses of the International Association for the Protection of Industrial Property, resolutions have been adopted for the independence of the protection of trade marks in the various countries of the Union,[3] but not of designs and models.[4] This is explained by the fact that hardly any designs or models were registered in more than one country, because of the many obstacles and difficulties of the national regulation and protection.[5]

Regarding the opinion maintained here as to the independence of the protection of designs and models in the various countries of the Union, an argument *in contrario* may be drawn from a number of bipartite conventions and treaties, entered into by member countries of the Union prior to the Convention of Union. Indeed, in those conventions and treaties the rights as to the same design or model in the two contracting countries were made dependent, by express stipulation.[6] This stipulation in these conventions followed the stipulation of national treatment. But no such provision exists in the Convention of Union. The spirit of the latter is different from the spirit of the bipartite conventions which constituted only reciprocal engagements and mere bargains between the contracting countries. The Convention of 1883 aims at harmonizing the law of the member countries of the Union on many questions affecting foreigners, and at securing an effective and complete protection of foreign-

1. A Belgian court held to this effect on an allegation of abandonment of a design in a foreign country. Société Américaine de Saint-Gobain et al. *c.* Falleur et consorts, Tribunal de Charleroi, July 28, 1913 (cited *in extenso* by Coppieters, *Œuvres d'Art Appliqué*, p. 121, at p. 124).

2. See *supra*, § 260.

3. See *voeux* in *Actes de la la Conférence de La Haye*, pp. 90–91.

4. At the Congress of Vienna in 1897, the independence of designs and models was not adopted, because something else was expressly preferred to it, namely, their identity with artistic works. See *Annuaire* (1897), pp. 97, 162. In the later congresses, attention was turned to the creation of a special union for the international deposit of designs and models.

5. See *supra*, § 244.

6. See *supra*, § 40.

ers' rights of industrial property. This end is achieved only by a liberal interpretation of the various stipulations of the Convention.

§ 280. Designs and models are not validated in the Union. Article 6 of the Convention provides that every trade mark duly registered in the country of origin shall be admitted for deposit and protected in its original form in the other countries of the Union. This provision secures the validation of trade marks in the Union.

The original text of article 6 (then article 5) proposed at the Paris Conference of 1880 concerned designs and models as well as trade marks.[1] In this form it was adopted by the Conference at the first reading.[2] But at the second reading the Swiss delegation, following instructions of the Swiss government, refused to accept the validation of designs and models registered in the country of origin, and asked that the stipulation of article 6 be restricted to trade marks alone. The reasons put forward by this delegation, as well as by that of Hungary which alone concurred in this view, were very specious and ill-founded. However, the Conference decided on the omission of the words "design and model" from article 6, without any discussion.[3] It was pressed by the difficulty of arriving at a formula of this article which would satisfy all countries, and the delegations were much more concerned with its importance for trade marks.

From this history of article 6, it must be concluded that its stipulation cannot be applied by analogy to designs or models.[4] Many designs and models may not be admitted to deposit and protected in other countries, — although they are deposited or registered in a country of the Union, — as not possessing the elements required by the law of these countries.[5]

1. *Conférence de Paris*, pp. 27, 70,
2. *Ibid.*, pp. 78–79.
3. *Ibid.*, pp. 132–133, 134.
4. Pouillet et Plé, *Convention d'Union*, p. 75; Pelletier et Vidal-Naquet, *Convention d'Union*, p. 289.
5. See on the divergences of municipal law in this respect, *supra*, § 250.

CHAPTER XVIII

RESTRICTION OF THE OBLIGATIONS OF DEPOSITORS OF DESIGNS AND MODELS

§ 281. New provisions of article 5 in respect to industrial designs and models. It has been seen above[1] that by the assimilation in many respects of designs and models to, and their classification with, patents for inventions, various obligations are imposed on depositors of designs and models for the preservation and enforcement of their rights. It has also been pointed out that by the existence of these obligations, the international protection of designs and models is rendered impossible. The Convention of 1883 contained until recently no provision abolishing or restricting any of these obligations, as it did in respect to patents for inventions in its article 5. The persons claiming its benefits were entitled only, by virtue of article 2, to the national treatment, and were therefore subject to these obligations, according to the municipal law of each country.

Some of the members of the Union entered into bipartite international engagements, abolishing in favor of their respective nationals the obligation to work the design or model, or the prohibition of importation of articles on which the design was applied.[2]

The congresses of the International Association have repeatedly adopted *voeux* for the abolition of the obligations of proprietors of designs and models.[3] At the Washington Conference, the French and German delegations proposed the abolition of both — the obligation to work a design, and the prohibition of importation of articles manufactured according to the design. But because of the opposition of many delegations, the proposals were defeated.[4] At the

1. See *supra*, §§ 267–269.
2. See on these bipartite treaties, *supra*, p. 143, n. 1.
3. See various *voeux*, in *Actes de la Conférence de Washington*, pp. 366–368, and *Actes de la Conférence de La Haye*, pp. 87, 121.
4. *Actes de la Conférence de Washington*, p. 283.

Conference of The Hague, as a result of similar proposals, the following provisions were adopted, which form the fifth and sixth paragraphs of the new article 5:[1]

La protection des dessins et modèles industriels ne peut être atteinte par une déchéance quelconque pour introduction d'objets conformes à ceux qui sont protégés.

Aucun signe ou mention d'enregistrement ne sera exigé sur le produit, pour la reconnaissance du droit.

Thus, the obligation to work the design in every country in which the design is registered (in case the law of that country requires such working) was not abolished or in any way restricted by the Convention. This unfortunate result was due to the opposition of two countries only — Italy and the Serb-Croat-Slovene State.[2]

§ **282. Abolition of the prohibition of importation.** The prohibition of importation of articles manufactured according to the registered design is now abolished by the Convention. The similar prohibition in respect to patents was abolished from the creation of the Union in 1883.

The above provision of the fifth paragraph of article 5 is substantially identical with the provision of the first paragraph of article 5. Consequently, the interpretation of the latter[3] applies here, *mutatis mutandis*, with the following qualification.

In case of patents, the importation of articles manufactured under the patent entails no revocation of the patent if the articles have been manufactured in any of the countries of the Union. This condition is not required in the case of designs and models, by the new fifth paragraph of article 5. Nor is it possible to supply it by analogy. The provision in this respect was taken from the proposals of Germany, Austria, France, and Switzerland, which were not qualified by any condition.[4] Therefore, the protection of designs and models cannot be forfeited in any of the countries of the Union, even if the articles imported and corresponding to those which are protected are manufactured outside of the Union.

1. *Actes de la Conférence de La Haye*, pp. 339, 495–498.

2. In the first discussion of the proposal for abolition of that obligation, the British delegation refused to take a position; but on receiving instructions from the British government, it declared itself in favor of the abolition. The two opposing delegations are referred to once in the *procès-verbaux* of the Conference as having agreed to the abolition (*Actes*, p. 498); later however the Serb-Croat-Slovenian delegation changed its position, and was followed by the Italian (*Actes*, pp. 506, 520, 540–541).

3. See *supra*, §§ 217–219.

4. *Actes de la Conférence de La Haye*, p. 339.

The stipulation of the fifth paragraph of article 5, like that of the first, is of the kind that constitutes common legislation for all the countries of the Union, and therefore is immediately effective in each of these countries without the need of special legislative action to carry it into effect.[1]

§ **283. Restriction of the obligation of marking.** The new sixth paragraph of article 5 provides that no sign or mention of registration shall be required on the product, for the recognition of the right ("pour la reconnaissance du droit"). It is not clear whether the last phrase of the provision means the right of ownership in the design, or the right given by the registration. In the first case, the meaning of the whole provision would be that the right in the design cannot be forfeited by the omission to mark the articles manufactured according to the design. But each country would be free to impose such marking as a condition of the recognition of the protection given by the registration. In other words, by the omission to mark the articles, the right in the design would not be forfeited, but the protection afforded by the registration might not be given; that is, in case of infringement of the design, its proprietor might be required to show that the infringer had notice of the existence of the copyright in the design.

As the meaning of the provision is dubious, it is necessary to go into the preparatory work of the Conference. The sixth paragraph of article 5 was taken from a proposal of the German delegation, which proposed to insert in the text of the Convention the provisions of article 5 of the draft arrangement for the international deposit of designs and models. This article read as follows: [2]

> Les États contractants conviennent de ne pas exiger que les dessins ou modèles déposés internationalement soient revêtus d'une marque ou mention obligatoire outre que celle prescrite, le cas échéant, par la loi du pays d'origine.

Thus Germany proposed that the only mark which could be required on articles manufactured according to a deposited design, was the mark, if any, imposed by the law of the country of origin. The proposal did not indicate the scope of this provision. It proposed only that the contracting countries agree not to require an obligatory mark or sign. The abolition of the obligation of marking was to be unqualified.

1. See on this kind of provision, *supra*, § 102.
2. *Actes de la Conférence de La Haye*, pp. 321, 339.

In the discussions on this proposal, on the one hand, the Spanish delegation proposed that not even the mark or mention of the country of origin be required for the protection of designs and models in the other countries of the Union. This view was eventually accepted and part of the original proposal was struck out.[1] And, on the other hand, the British and American delegations declared themselves ready to accept the German proposal, on condition, however, that the proprietor of an infringed design could not claim damages unless he could show that the infringer had notice that the design was registered.[2] Thereupon the Chairman of the Sub-Committee declared the discussion closed and the proposal was adopted unanimously. Later, the Editing Committee rephrased the provision, in order to place it as a new paragraph in article 5, and in that new form it was adopted:[3] "Aucun signe ou mention d'enregistrement ne sera exigé sur le produit pour la reconnaissance du droit."

On the final adoption of article 5 at the second Plenary Session of the Conference, declarations were made on the sixth paragraph of this article by the Japanese and American delegations.[4] The former declared that it accepted the above stipulation, because it would be excessive to require in all cases that a mention of registration be affixed on the product. But the delegation thought that it would be justifiable in cases in which mention of registration is easy. The effect of this declaration is that Japan retains the right to require the marking of articles manufactured according to a deposited design in all cases in which such marking is not difficult. This is in direct opposition to the stipulation in question, and its effect on the clear meaning of the stipulation is doubtful.

The American delegation's declaration was to the effect that it interpreted the provision of the sixth paragraph of article 5 as not derogating from the provisions of the municipal law of the United States, which were stated to the members of the Conference. Apparently the delegation referred to the position taken at the original discussion of the German proposal in the sixth Sub-Committee of the Conference, as mentioned above.

1. *Actes de la Conférence de La Haye*, pp. 496, 506, 540.
2. *Ibid.*, pp. 496–497. The American delegation pointed out that in the United States the proprietor of a design or model is not bound to mark his articles if he notifies the infringers, even by letter, of the existence of his deposit.
3. *Ibid.*, pp. 498, 520, 541.
4. *Ibid.*, pp. 575–576.

From the position taken by the American and British delegations at the first discussion of the German proposal, and the subsequent addition of the phrase "pour la reconnaissance du droit," as well as from this last declaration of the American delegation, it appears that the abolition of the obligation of marking concerns only the recognition of the right in a design, and that the existing provisions of the municipal law of some countries, the effect of which is to shift the burden of proof to the proprietor of the design in an infringement case, if he fails to mark his products, are not derogated from by the sixth paragraph of article 5.[1]

§ 284. Period of grace for payment of fees for designs or models. A further lightening of the obligations of the proprietor of a design is introduced in the regime of the Union by the new article 5*b* adopted at the Conference of The Hague. The first paragraph of this article, which only is material here, provides as follows:

> Un délai de grâce, qui devra être au minimum de trois mois, sera accordé pour le payement des taxes prévues pour le maintien des droits de propriété industrielle, moyennant le versement d'une surtaxe, si la législation nationale en impose une.[2]

Thus, an extension of time of not less than three months must be allowed in all the countries of the Union for the payment of the prescribed fees for the maintenance of the right in a design or model. This advantage is of importance in those countries of the Union in which an annual fee is payable besides the original fee of registration, or a periodical fee is due at certain periods of the duration of the protection. The countries of the former class are Japan and Serb-Croat-Slovene State and of the latter Danzig, Poland, and Spain. Already Danzig, Poland, Serb-Croat-Slovene State, and Spain accorded a three months' period of grace (Spain four months). Only in Japan the Convention derogates from the municipal law which grants no such grace.

1. In the British *Papers and Correspondence Relative to the Conference of The Hague*, of 1925 (London, His Majesty's Stationery Office, 1926), p. 120, the sixth paragraph of article 5 is translated as follows: "No sign or mention of registration shall be required on the goods *in order to maintain recognition of the rights given by such registration.*" It is submitted that the translation of the part italicized by the present writer is inaccurate, and that the meaning it conveys is unwarranted, as is seen by the discussion in the text.

2. See the interpretation of this provision in respect to patents, *supra*, §§ 230–231.

CHAPTER XIX

THE INTERNATIONAL DEPOSIT OF INDUSTRIAL DESIGNS AND MODELS

The Arrangement of the Hague of 1925

§ 285. Origin and history of the Arrangement of The Hague. The attempts to make uniform the law of industrial designs and models in all the countries of the Union, or to lay down some general principles to which the law of all countries should conform, have proved unsuccessful. So too has the movement for the absorption of industrial designs and models by the law of artistic property.[1] As early as 1901, Mr. Frey-Godet, Secretary of the International Bureau, urged the creation of a restricted union between countries parties to the International Convention, by an arrangement for the unification of the law on some essential questions as to the protection of industrial designs and models.[2] In 1904, at the Congress of the International Association for the Protection of Industrial Property at Berlin, Mr. Albert Osterrieth proposed that an organization for

1. See on this point, *supra*, p. 374.
2. *Annuaire de l'Association Internationale* (1901), p. 104.

the centralization of deposits of designs and models be created at the International Bureau at Berne, similar to that for the international registration of trade marks established by the Madrid Arrangement of 1891. In the following congresses of the International Association (Liège, 1905; Milan, 1906; Nancy, 1909; Brussels, 1910; Berne, 1911; London, 1912) the idea was debated and the original proposal grew into a draft arrangement, the various provisions of which were earnestly discussed.[1]

At the Washington Conference in 1911, the French delegation deposited a draft arrangement, accompanied by a statement of motives. But it seems that the proposal was made at a very late time, and the other delegations had not been able to study it; besides, it was incomplete, containing no provisions on some essential questions of international protection.[2] Instead, the Conference adopted a *voeu* to the effect that

> the International Bureau should get in touch with the administrations of the countries of the Union, with a view to preparing a project of international registration of designs and models, and to taking the necessary steps for the adoption of an international arrangement.

The Bureau, as early as 1912, prepared a draft arrangement, and communicated it to the administrations of the contracting countries in April, 1914.[3] No administration of a country of the Union sent to the Bureau any remarks or observations on the draft, and no concerted action was ever taken on the plan. But after the War, the International Association having not yet resumed its congresses, the French and German groups of the Association, each separately, and the International Chamber of Commerce took up again the plan of an arrangement and adopted resolutions to this effect.[4]

At the last conference of The Hague, the International Bureau proposed a new draft arrangement, so complete and admirably constructed that, with the exception of one basic amendment and a few changes in form, it was adopted in its entirety. The Arrangement was accompanied with a *règlement* of execution which was also adopted practically unmodified.

1. See *Annuaire* (1905), pp. 33, 283–293, 324–330; (1909), pp. 48–53, 154; (1910), pp. 168, 252–256; (1912), pp. 322–355, 527 ff.

2. *Actes de la Conférence de Washington*, pp. 100 ff., and 290–291.

3. This project is published as Annex VI *bis* in *Travaux du Groupe Français de l'Association Internationale* (1919–1922), pp. 177–182.

4. See *Propriété Industrielle* (1924), pp. 180 ff.

§ 286. Directive ideas in preparation of the Arrangement. The directive ideas in the preparation of the scheme of arrangement by the Bureau, and in the discussions at the congresses of the International Association have been set forth by the International Bureau in an article in *Propriété Industrielle* (1924, pp. 180, 183 ff.), and in a statement prefacing the draft arrangement.[1] They may be resumed here, before the discussion of the various provisions of the Arrangement.

First, a special arrangement for the international deposit of designs and models was necessary, because it was impossible to have all the countries of the Union agree on the insertion in the general Convention of provisions assuring a more adequate international protection of designs and models. Moreover, such an Arrangement would be the best way to compel the contracting countries to revise their municipal law, and to realize in the municipal legal order the progress achieved in the international legal order. Thus the uniformity of the law of designs and models on some essential points, which long efforts in the past had failed to realize, would be brought about by the provisions constituting common legislation of the countries parties to the Arrangement.

What should this Arrangement be like? An agreement on some essential points for the international protection of industrial designs and models, doing away with some obstacles and difficulties which remained under the general Convention — something like the Madrid Arrangement for the repression of false indications of origin? Or, in addition to that, an agreement for the centralization of deposits of designs and models, doing away with the necessity of applying in all the countries of the Union, similar to the Madrid Arrangement for the international registration of trade marks?

The latter was the point of view generally sponsored by the propounders of the idea, and it was adopted by the International Bureau.[2] The proposed arrangement should primarily be one for the international deposit of designs and models, and should contain provisions making uniform some essential conditions and obligations as regards the protection of designs and models. Of the above-enumerated[3] questions of the law of designs and models which affect

1. Published in the *Actes de la Conférence de La Haye*, pp. 313, 316–320.
2. See Osterrieth, *Die Haager Konferenz* (1925), p. 132.
3. See *supra*, p. 375.

foreigners by their diverse solutions in the various countries, there are some which would without difficulty admit of a uniform solution. For instance, it should be possible for the countries parties to the arrangement to agree on a uniform duration of protection of the designs and models deposited with the International Bureau. Indeed, this was almost an indispensable element of the international deposit. Again, it should be possible to agree on giving the author of a design the option to deposit under seal, and on the time during which the deposit of a design should be kept secret. Besides, the various obligations imposed on the depositor of a design, such as that of compulsory working of the design, the prohibition of importation of products on which the design has been applied, and the obligation of marking the design, could be dispensed with under the regime of international deposit. Lastly, the taxes or fees payable for the international deposit, and the formalities of deposit, should necessarily be established by the proposed arrangement.

There remain the questions, what may be deposited as a design, who may deposit it, the administrative procedure of each country, and the effects of deposit. The first three questions depend for their solution on the answer to be given to the last. What should be the effect of the deposit at the International Bureau? Should it be a means of establishing and creating ownership in a design, or only of declaring such ownership? The first should clearly be excluded. No one ever thought of subjecting the Bureau to the difficulties inherent in examining the design and searching into the right of the depositor. The international deposit of the design should be only convenient proof of creation of the design by the depositor. The latter, instead of being under the necessity of applying for registration or admission to deposit of his design or model in the various countries, and thus of obtaining an official proof of creation in all these countries, would reach the same result by a deposit at the International Bureau. Whether he has really created the design or model, or whether he is the owner thereof, should be decided in each country according to its law.

But should the deposit of the design or model at the International Bureau be subject to the following two conditions or to either of them: (*a*) to the prior deposit or registration of the design or model in one of the contracting countries; (*b*) to notification by the other contracting countries that they do not object to the international deposit of the design so far as each of them is concerned? Both these conditions exist in the case of the international registration of trade marks. Those trade marks only may be registered at the International Bureau which are admitted for deposit in the country of origin. The countries in which the system of previous examination of trade marks exists may declare to the International Bureau within a year that they refuse to protect the mark on their territory.

The impracticability of the application of the above second condition in the Arrangement under preparation was generally agreed upon. Designs and models do not offer themselves for a previous examination as readily as trade marks do. The latter may be examined through a publication or copy. The former have aesthetic qualities which can be judged only from a close examination of a reproduction and accurate description of the design. If the contracting countries should have the right to examine the design which has been deposited at the Bureau, it would be necessary to send to all of them reproductions and descriptions of the design. The need of doing away with various difficult formalities would not be satisfied thereby. Besides, such examination and procedure would lessen the possibility of secrecy of the international deposit. The equivalent procedure in the matter of international registration of trade marks is not free from delays and complications, and would not recommend itself for adoption in the case of designs and models, which are often of ephemeral value and brief commercial life.

The non-subjection of the international deposit of designs and models to such condition is a reasonable corollary to the principle that the deposit at the International Bureau should constitute only proof of creation of the design. The countries which subject applications for deposit or registration of a design to previous examination in respect to its novelty or its admissibility for registration would have to forego such examination as regards designs or models deposited at the International Bureau. Such examination would devolve upon the courts when, in an infringement case, the right to prevent others from copying the plaintiff's design should be brought into question.

§ 287. Should international deposit be based on deposit in country of origin? The question whether or not the design which is sent for deposit to the International Bureau should have been previously admitted for deposit in one of the contracting countries has been a subject of much controversy and discussion. Either solution presents advantages and disadvantages. The original proposals of a draft arrangement had advocated the system of direct and immediate deposit at the International Bureau, without previous deposit in a country of the Union. The sponsors were dominated by the idea that industrial designs and models are essentially artistic creations, and that deposit or registration should be required as, at most, an official means of proof of creation. Thus a single deposit of designs or models should be sufficient. If it were not possible to protect designs and models in all the countries of the Union after they have been deposited in one of those countries, it could assuredly be so after they have been deposited at the International Bureau.

If a national deposit should be the condition of the international deposit, as in the case of registration of trade marks, the dependence of the two deposits, and therefore of the protection in the country of origin and in the other countries, would be established. This would be a retrogression from the existing régime, where no such dependence would seem to exist. And if this dependence should be avoided by express provisions in the Arrangement, the situation would still remain such that no design or model could be deposited at the International Bureau, if by the law of the country of the original deposit such design could not be admitted for deposit. Thus, Swedish nationals or foreigners domiciled in Sweden would be able to deposit at the International Bureau only designs applied by manufacture on products of metal industries, because only those are admitted for registration in Sweden.

But if a national deposit should not be required as a condition to the deposit at the International Bureau (the latter being made directly and immediately by the proprietor of the design or model), it was argued that the International Bureau would find it difficult to decide whether an industrial creation, whose deposit is applied for, is a design or model which should be admitted for deposit at all. Such inquiry would be unnecessary for the Bureau if the design had been admitted first in the country of origin. The difficulty would disappear only if a definition of design or model could be agreed upon and inserted in the Arrangement. Otherwise the Bureau would have to admit for deposit as a design or model everything the deposit of which might be applied for.

Two more disadvantages of direct deposit at the International Bureau, and advantages of the opposite system, are urged. The persons who may deposit a design in the various countries are not always the same. In the United States only the author, and in Portugal only manufacturers and so forth, may apply, for a patent in the former and for a certificate of registration in the latter. It would complicate matters in the International Bureau if the latter should inquire whether the applicants from various countries had the qualifications to apply for admission to deposit of their designs or models. The answer to this is that the Bureau did not need to do so. It would register the designs in the name of the applicants, who subsequently should prove their rights in the courts. Besides, under the existing regime foreigners applying for admission to deposit of their designs and models need not show that they have the right to deposit in their own country, unless they claim the right of priority.

The last point urged is that, through the prior national deposit and the indirect deposit by the administration of the country of origin, any technical examination by the Bureau, of the application and the documents accompanying it, such as the copy, reproduction, or picture of the design or model, becomes unnecessary. This examination and the comparison of the copies and reproductions of the design would be made by the national administration. For any irregularity in this respect, the country making the deposit is alone responsible, not the International Bureau. It is difficult to see what this "responsibility" of the country amounts to. Besides, errors are more likely to occur if two deposits of identical documents, instead of a single deposit, are to be made. However, there is a distinct advantage in making the deposit at the International Bureau free of any technical examination of documents. Yet such examination may hardly be dispensed with entirely, so long as compliance with the provisions of the Arrangement and the *règlement* of execution must be looked into.

All in all, then, the direct and immediate deposit of designs and models at the International Bureau would seem to be preferable to the indirect deposit through the national administration, after a deposit with the latter.[1]

§ 288. The Arrangement adopts immediate international deposit. The International Bureau, in its draft arrangement, sub-

1. Cf. Osterrieth, *Die Haager Konferenz*, pp. 134–136.

mitted to the Conference of The Hague, had adopted the system of indirect international deposit of designs and models already admitted to deposit in the country of origin.[1] The Conference adopted the direct and immediate deposit, and this is the only important change made in the scheme of the Bureau. This solution was adopted as a result of two opposing proposals of Germany and Switzerland, both nevertheless inspired by the same desire for simplification. The German delegation argued for the independence of the protection of designs and models in the different countries, and maintained that in some countries, as in Germany, France, and Belgium, many authors of designs do not deposit them, because of the extension of the protection of artistic and literary property to artistic works applied to industry. This delegation proposed that the international deposit should be the only deposit, and should be made through a national office which would simply receive the deposit and transmit it to the International Bureau. The deposit should be made in as many copies of the design as there are contracting countries, and the Bureau would transmit a copy to each of those countries.[2]

The Swiss delegation preferred also a single deposit. It stressed the difficulties of obtaining identity between the two deposits, and the complications consequent thereon. The deposit in the country of origin should be sufficient, and there would be a mere notification of the national deposit to the International Bureau. The latter should inform the other contracting countries of such notification.[3]

The Belgian delegation proposed the direct and immediate deposit at the International Bureau by the interested persons, with a single copy of the design. It pointed out that this system is recommended by its simplicity; it takes account of the fact that in some countries no deposit may be required for the protection of a design, and, lastly, it establishes the independence of the protection of designs and models in each country. This principle was adopted without opposition by the Conference.[4]

The various provisions of the Arrangement and the entire matter

1. *Actes de la Conférence de La Haye*, pp. 317, 320, 500–501.
2. *Ibid.*, pp. 366, 500, 502.
3. *Ibid.*, pp. 366–367, 499.
4. *Ibid.*, pp. 502–503.

of the international deposit of designs and models are considered in the following sections.[1]

§ **289. Basis of right of international deposit.** The basis of the right to apply for admission to deposit at the International Bureau is contained in article 1 of the Arrangement, which reads as follows:

Les ressortissants de chacun des pays contractants ainsi que les personnes ayant satisfait sur le territoire de l'Union restreinte aux conditions établies par l'article 3 de la Convention générale, pourront s'assurer dans tous les autres pays contractants la protection de leurs dessins et modèles industriels, au moyen d'un dépôt international effectué au Bureau International de la propriété industrielle, à Berne.

The question, who are the persons who may claim the benefit of this Arrangement, is considered in an earlier chapter.[2] These persons may secure the protection of their industrial designs or models, through international deposit, in all the other contracting countries. "Contracting countries" are those only that are parties to this Arrangement. The word "other" ("les *autres* pays contractants") shows that the international deposit does not secure the protection of designs or models in the country of which the applicant is a national, or in which he is domiciled or possesses effective and *bona fide* industrial or commercial establishments.[3]

The reasons for this limitation are not apparent, nor are they disclosed by the discussions at the Conference. The word "autres" was contained in article 1, as proposed by the International Bureau, because protection in the country of origin would be assured through the prior deposit in that country, which would have been the basis of the international deposit. With the adoption by the Conference of the immediate deposit at the International Bureau, the word "autres" should have been struck out, and the protection in the country of origin, as well as in the other countries, should have been assured through the international deposit.

As things are now, nationals are put in a disadvantageous position

1. See on the Arrangement of The Hague, a note of information concerning the international deposit, in *Propriété Industrielle* (1928), p. 98; and a general study, *Ibid.*, p. 107.

2. See *supra*, § 122.

3. See explanations to this effect by the Director of the International Bureau and the French delegation in *Actes de la Conférence de La Haye*, pp. 505 and 584.

in comparison with foreigners, without any reason whatsoever.[1] Moreover, the position of persons possessing the qualifications of article 3 of the Convention is not clear. Suppose a person, national of a country party to the Arrangement and domiciled or established in another country party to the same Arrangement, deposits his design or model at the International Bureau. Which are the "other" countries as regards this person? It would seem that he would not be sure of his protection in either the country of which he is a national or the country in which he is domiciled or established, unless he deposits his design in both these countries, besides depositing it at the International Bureau.

For protection in the country of origin, there must be a compliance with the formalities and conditions of the municipal law of that country. Thus, if in that country a deposit or registration of the design or model is a necessary requirement for its protection, its admission to deposit or registration must be obtained. On the contrary, if the deposit is only a means of proving the creation of the design, as, for instance, in France, no such deposit is necessary so long as the international deposit affords such a proof. Likewise, in the countries in which legal protection of artistic and literary property has been extended to artistic works applied to industry, and certain designs or models may be protected, as belonging to the latter class, without deposit, the protection of the same will still be assured in those countries, as well as in the other contracting countries, through the international deposit at Berne.

Article 1 of the Arrangement merely substitutes for the deposit and compliance with the formalities of each contracting country the single international deposit at the Berne Bureau. Whether the design or model deposited is one which may be protected in any of the contracting countries, or whether it is new according to the law of that country, or whether the applicant may claim protection as owner of the design, and the extent of such protection — all these are matters which are governed by the municipal law of each country,[2] as will be seen later in considering article 4 of the Arrangement. The Bureau cannot refuse to register anything sent as a design or model for deposit. Possibly it may only advise the applicant that

1. See Ostertag, "Exposé sur la Conférence de La Haye," made at the Congress of the International Association at Geneva, 1927, in *Propriété Industrielle* (1927), p. 136.

2. See Osterrieth, *Die Haager Konferenz*, pp. 136–137.

the article has no chance of being protected in any contracting country as a design or model.[1]

§ **290. Formalities of application.** The formalities of application for deposit of designs or models at the International Bureau are provided for in articles 2 and 6 of the Arrangement, and 1, 2, and 3 of the *Règlement* of execution. The effect of these provisions is as follows: an application for the international deposit, in duplicate, written in French, should be sent to the International Bureau. Forms of such applications are supplied gratuitously by the International Bureau to interested persons, or to the administrations. The application should contain the following indications: (1) the name and address of the depositor; (2) a short designation of the title of the designs or models, and of the kind of products to which they may be applied; (3) the nature of the deposit (open or under seal); (4) the number of the designs or models, if several are deposited together; (5) the date of prior deposit in a country of the Union, whenever a right of priority is claimed in accordance with article 4 of the Arrangement. With the application, the designs or models whose admission for deposit is applied for are sent to the International Bureau. They are sent either in the form of the industrial product for which they are destined and to which they are applied,[2] or in the form of a design, a photograph, or any other graphic representation. The latter form is recommended by the *Règlement* for fragile models, although the deposit of samples of the same is not excluded.

The deposit may comprise either a single design or model, or several. In the latter case, the number should be indicated in the application. The deposit may be either open or under sealed cover. The Arrangement expressly provides (article 6, paragraph 2) that the Bureau will accept as a means of deposit under a sealed cover the double envelope with perforated control number of the Soleau system [3] or of any other system assuring identity. The sealed packages should bear the inscription: "Deposit under seal."

1. See Ostertag, "Exposé sur la Conférence de La Haye," made at the Congress of the International Association at Geneva, 1927, in *Propriété Industrielle* (1927), p. 136.

2. The *Règlement* (art. 1) mentions as illustrations of designs which may be deposited in form of samples, designs for tissues, papers, embroideries, etc.

3. See as to those envelopes *supra*, § 264. The original provision of article 6 of the Arrangement in respect to the Soleau envelopes was more restrictive. It read: "seront acceptées spécialement comme moyens de dépôt sous pli cacheté les enveloppes perforées d'après le système Soleau." The German delegation remarked in the discussion

The *Règlement* determines the maxima of dimensions and weight of the things which may be deposited. They should not exceed thirty centimeters on each dimension, nor weigh more than two kilograms.[1] The number of designs or models which may be deposited together, otherwise unlimited, is limited only by the above maxima of dimensions and weight.

The application must be accompanied by the fee for the international deposit, which should be addressed to the International Bureau by postal check or postal mandate, or by any other effects payable at Berne, with indication of the name and address of the depositor.

§ **291. Procedure at the International Bureau.** The procedure at the International Bureau for the deposit of designs and models is provided for in article 3 of the Arrangement and 4 and 5 of the *Règlement*. Upon receipt of the application for international deposit, the International Bureau does three things.

First, it registers the application in a special register, kept by the Bureau, and containing several data enumerated in article 4 of the *Règlement*. This the Bureau must do immediately (*aussitôt*) upon receipt of the application. When this is done, the international deposit is consummated. The Bureau must certify the fact that the deposit has taken place by affixing the signature of the Bureau and its stamp on the two copies of the application. One of the copies of the application is to be kept in the archives of the Bureau and the other sent to the interested person.

May the Bureau refuse to register the deposit? The only cases in which such power is given to the Bureau is when the package containing the designs or models does not fulfill the conditions of the first article of the *Règlement* — in other words, in the following three cases: (*a*) when the package exceeds the *maxima* of dimensions and weight (art. 1, par. 1 of the *Règlement*); (*b*) when the designs or models are sent neither in the form of products or samples, nor in the form of reproductions; (*c*) when the inscription "deposit under seal" does not appear on the sealed package. In these cases the

---

of article 6 that it would perhaps be sufficient to mention the Soleau envelopes in the text in parentheses. The new phrasing of the provision is more adequate, being more general. See *Actes de la Conférence de La Haye*, pp. 321, 506, 564.

1. The original draft of the Arrangement fixed the maxima as follows: dimensions twenty centimeters and weight one kilogram. They were increased on the suggestion of the German delegation. See *Actes de la Conférence de La Haye*, pp. 323, 512, 566.

package is returned to the sender, and he is advised of the reasons for the refusal.

Neither the Arrangement nor the *Règlement* provides for the cases in which the application accompanying the designs or models is not in the proper form. In case, however, the fee for the international deposit is not properly addressed, the deposit cannot be registered, according to article 15 of the Arrangement.

The second act of the International Bureau upon receipt of the application is to notify the contracting countries of the registration of the deposit. The notification is sent by the Bureau to the office or administration "which shall be indicated to the Bureau by each country." This expression was used instead of the original "diverses autres administrations" as a result of the change wrought by the Conference in the basic principle of the first article of the Arrangement.[1] The notification shall be sent to all the contracting countries, including the country of origin of the applicant. This is necessary in view of the fact that no indication as to the country of origin of the applicant is required in the application, and the Bureau has no means of knowing about it. The notification of the deposit shall contain all the indications which the application contains according to article 2 of the *Règlement*, and which have been enumerated above. For this reason, a summary designation of the title of the designs or models, and of the kind of goods to which they are applied, must be contained in the notification.

The third act which the International Bureau has to perform is the publication of the application which is registered. This publication is to be made in a periodical of the Bureau, to be distributed gratuitously to each administration. The latter may ask for any number of copies of the periodical that it desires. An annual subject-index of the periodical shall also be published by the Bureau, which shall be distributed in like manner. In the publication, all the matters contained in the notification to each administration, and the fact of the notification itself, shall appear.

Thus, the design itself, or its reproduction, is not published, because the deposit may be under seal for the first period of protection. But the archives of the Bureau are open to inspection by the public in the case of deposits which are not under seal. Any person may in

1. See the proposals for this change in *Actes de la Conférence de La Haye*, pp. 321, 504, 531.

such case inspect them in the presence of an employee of the Bureau, or may obtain information in writing or a reproduction of the design. The whole question of deposits under seal is considered below.

§ 292. **Effects of deposit.** Article 4 of the Arrangement deals with the effects of the international deposit. For its importance, this article is cited here *in extenso:*

Celui qui effectue le dépôt international d'un dessin ou modèle industriel est considéré jusqu'à preuve du contraire comme propriétaire de l'oeuvre.

Le dépôt international est purement déclaratif. En tant que dépôt, il produira dans chacun des pays contractants les mêmes effets que si les dessins ou modèles y avaient été directement déposés à la date du dépôt international, sous bénéfice toutefois des règles spéciales établies par le présent Arrangement.

La publicité mentionnée dans l'article précédent sera considérée dans tous les pays contractants comme pleinement suffisante et aucune autre ne pourra être exigée du déposant, sous réserve des formalités à remplir pour l'exercice du droit, conformément à la loi intérieure.

Le droit de priorité établi par l'article 4 de la convention générale sera garanti à tout dessin ou modèle qui a fait l'objet d'un dépôt international, sans l'obligation d'aucune des formalités prévues par ce même article.

The deposit at the International Bureau is merely declarative. This is the main proposition of article 4. It means that the deposit is only, as the Bureau put it in its statement preceding the draft arrangement at the Conference of The Hague,[1] the means of establishing a definite date of creation of the design or model deposited. It is an "international authentication" of the creation. In an infringement case in any of the contracting countries, the person who has deposited his design or model at the International Bureau may base his right in the design, and to protection against copying by other persons, on the international deposit. Moreover, he shall be considered *prima facie* owner of the design. The other party has the burden of proof of the contrary. In this respect the Arrangement stipulates as between the contracting countries the principle of the French Law of 1909.[2]

No ownership, therefore, in his design, or right to prevent others from copying it in the other contracting countries, is acquired by the depositor by virtue of the international deposit alone. That question is governed exclusively by the municipal law of each country,

1. *Actes de la Conférence de La Haye*, p. 319.
2. See on this point, *supra*, § 264.

in so far as this law is not derogated from by other provisions of the Arrangement. The deposit at the International Bureau is only a substitute for the several national deposits. The effects of the international deposit in the other countries are the same as if the deposit was applied for in those countries at the time the international deposit took place.

Thus, if at that time the applicant was not the owner, or could not apply for admission to deposit or registration of his design in one of the contracting countries; or if the design deposited at the International Bureau was not one which could be protected according to the law of that country; or if the design was not new in the eye of the same law — in all these cases the international deposit is without effect in the country in question, and no protection is afforded to the applicant.[1]

The above questions are matters examined either by the administration, in some countries, as part of the procedure upon receipt of the application for registration, or by the courts, in other countries, when the questions come up in infringement or annulment proceedings. The Arrangement subjects the international deposit to no previous admission to protection by the administration of any country. A country cannot notify the Bureau that it refuses protection to a design or model which was deposited at the Bureau and was communicated and published by the latter. In other words, the system of previous examination of the design by the administration is of no avail and is practically abolished in the countries practising it, in respect to the designs or models which are deposited at the International Bureau. In those countries the inadmissibility of the design to deposit, and therefore its non-protection by the law, may be decided, as regards the internationally deposited designs or models, only by the courts, whenever the depositor's right is disputed.

§ 293. Publication by the Bureau sufficient for protection. The third and fourth paragraphs of article 4 tend to restrict the domain of the municipal law. The former provides that the publicity given to the international deposit by the Bureau, that is, the publication in its periodical, shall be considered in all the contracting countries as fully sufficient, and no other publication shall be required from the depositor. Thus, the advertisement or publication of the application

1. See *Actes de la Conférence de La Haye*, pp. 317, 318, 504–505.

or of the design required in some countries is not necessary as regards the designs or models deposited at the International Bureau.

A reservation to this provision was introduced at the discussion of article 4 at the suggestion of the French delegation. This delegation drew a distinction between the formalities required by the municipal law for the acquisition of the right and those for the exercise or enforcement of the right. It proposed that the provisions of the municipal law as to the latter should be complied with by the depositor. The sub-committee wished to expound this reservation so as to make it clear that it referred to the legal formalities which must be fulfilled in some countries for the publicity of the designs and models in case of judicial proceedings. For the sake of simplification, however, it left the provision as proposed by the French delegation, "des formalités à remplir pour l'exercice du droit." But the sub-committee made it clear that this reservation referred only to the publicity, and for this purpose it separated the third paragraph from the second, with which it formed previously one paragraph.[1] This caution is very commendable when one recalls the difficulties that the reservation of the right of third parties in article 4 of the Convention has caused.

Article 6 of the *Règlement* supplies what the sub-committee would have wished to insert in article 4 of the Arrangement. It provides that, when the interested party shall request a reproduction of the article for the publicity required in a contracting country, it will be granted by the Bureau of Berne under conditions which shall be determined by agreement with the administration of the country in question.

Thus, according to the French Law of 1909 no action for infringement can be brought before the design is published. A party wishing to start proceedings in France should, under the Arrangement and the *Règlement*, request of the International Bureau to send a reproduction of the design or model to the Office National de la Propriété Industrielle of France. This reproduction will be open for inspection by the public, and the proprietor of the design may subsequently start infringement proceedings.

§ 294. Right of priority for international deposit. The last paragraph of article 4 concerns the right of priority which may be

1. See *Actes de la Conférence de La Haye*, pp. 505, 531; also Osterrieth, *Die Haager Konferenz*, p. 140.

claimed on the international deposit of a design or model. A national deposit may form the basis of a right of priority to be claimed on a new deposit within the period fixed by article 4 of the Convention. This new deposit must be made, according to that article, in a country of the Union. It may now be made at the International Bureau. Thus the right of priority acquires a real significance in the matter of designs and models. Previously it was very difficult for the author or the proprietor of a design or model to deposit it in all the countries of the Union within four months (or six, as amended by the Conference of The Hague). For the persons entitled to the benefits of the Arrangement of The Hague, the enjoyment of the right of priority is made much easier, since it is sufficient for them to deposit their designs or models at the International Bureau within the period of the right of priority. The period is the same as that fixed in article 4 of the Convention. It begins from the filing of an application for registration or deposit in a country which is a party to the Arrangement. The computation of the period follows the rules of article 4 of the Convention.[1]

Furthermore, by express provision of the last paragraph of article 4 of the Arrangement, the right of priority may be claimed on an international deposit of designs or models, without compliance with any of the formalities provided for by article 4 of the Convention ("sans l'obligation d'aucune des formalités prévues par le même article"). In other words, no declaration indicating the date and the country of the first deposit is required at the international deposit, and consequently no other documents in support of such declaration. To be sure, the *Règlement*, article 2, in enumerating the indications which the application for deposit at the Bureau must contain, provides for the date of the prior deposit, in case a right of priority is claimed. But this indication is only optional and the applicant may omit or withhold it. It is often to his own interest to declare it. The omission of such indication of the prior deposit, which forms the basis of a right of priority, is without sanction in all the countries parties to the Arrangement of The Hague. The Plenary Committee at the Conference declared expressly that the observance of that provision of the *Règlement* is "abandonnée à la bonne volonté du requérant." To make this clear, the words "s'il y a lieu" were put at the beginning of the provision.[2]

1. See *supra*, § 178. 2. See *Actes de la Conférence de La Haye*, p. 532.

The provision of the Arrangement under consideration secures the right of priority for any design or model which has been deposited at the International Bureau. In all the contracting countries therefore no facts occurring in the interval, that is, between the national and the international deposit, can invalidate the right of the depositor. Is the opposite also true, however? That is, may the international deposit form the basis of a right of priority to be claimed on a subsequent national deposit within the period fixed in article 4 of the Convention? Such an occurrence is perfectly possible. A depositor may desire to secure the larger protection that a national deposit in one of the contracting countries grants (such as a longer duration than that of the international protection).

The question of right of priority cannot arise in such case. The international deposit is equivalent to national deposits in all other contracting countries except the depositor's own country. As to these countries, the deposit at the International Bureau is as a deposit in each of them. The design or model deposited at the Bureau is protected, if at all, in each of these countries from the date of the international deposit. There is no scope, then, for the application of the right of priority. The larger protection granted by the national deposit in those countries may be secured by such a deposit at any time before the expiry of the international protection.[1]

The question can arise only in respect to the country of origin of the applicant. The international deposit produces no effects in the country of origin of the depositor, as is seen above.[2] The international deposit is a foreign deposit so far as that country is concerned. Foreigners domiciled or established in that country may undoubtedly claim a right of priority on a subsequent deposit in that country based on the international deposit. Whether nationals of that country may also claim such right has been considered above in another connection.[3]

§ **295. Duration of protection.** Article 7 of the Arrangement fixes the duration of the international protection at fifteen years, to begin with the date of the deposit at the International Bureau at Berne.[4] It also provides that this period is divided into two — one of five years and another of ten years. As is explained in the programme of

1. See *Actes de la Conférence de La Haye*, p. 318.

2. See *supra*, § 289.

3. See *supra*, § 120.

4. The computation of this period should follow, by analogy, the rules of article 4 of the Convention.

the Conference,[1] and as article 21 of the Arrangement affirms, the fifteen years is a minimum of duration of protection assured to persons depositing designs or models at the International Bureau. In all the contracting countries, the designs and models deposited at the Bureau must necessarily be protected for fifteen years, if at all. In case, however, in any of those countries (for instance, in France) the duration of the protection is longer, it may be claimed by the proprietors of those designs or models on compliance with the conditions and formalities of the municipal law of that country. A fifteen-year period is quite sufficient for the protection of designs and models.

Within the first six months of the fifth year of the first period of protection, the International Bureau shall give notice to the depositor of the design or model of the expiration of the period. If the depositor should wish to obtain an extension of the protection during the second period, he shall remit to the Bureau an application to this effect, at least three months before the expiry of the first period (articles 10 and 11 of the Arrangement). The form of the application is analogous to that of the original deposit. The fee for the extension of the period should be joined to the application and addressed as in the case of the original application.[2] The application is registered and notice of the extension is sent to the various administrations and published in the Bureau's periodical.[3]

The depositor may at any time renounce his deposit, either entirely or partially, by a declaration addressed to the International Bureau, which is published according to article 3 of the Arrangement. The package of the deposit is returned to the depositor at his expense (article 13 of the Arrangement).

§ 296. Open and secret deposit. The Arrangement provides for an open or a secret deposit. The formalities as regards deposits under seal have been described above.[4] A deposit under seal is admitted, according to article 8 of the Arrangement, only for the first period of protection of five years. During the second period the deposits are open to inspection. This is in accordance with sound principles, as explained above.[5]

1. See *Actes de la Conférence de La Haye*, pp. 318, 507.
2. Articles 2 and 3 of the *Règlement*. See *supra*, p. 438.
3. Article 11, No. 2, of the Arrangement, and article 5 of the *Règlement*.
4. See *supra*, § 290.
5. See *supra*, § 257. The Italian delegation declared in the discussion of the Arrangement that the admission of deposits under seal would constitute the most serious

A deposit under seal may be opened by the Bureau during the first period only on application by the depositor or by a competent court. When a court or any other competent authority shall order that a secret design or model be communicated to it, the International Bureau, properly requested, shall open the deposited package, take out the design or model in question, and send it to the authority asking for it. If other designs or models are found in the package, they shall continue to be kept secret. The court or authority to which the design or model in question has been communicated shall return it within the shortest possible period, and it shall be returned to the package or envelope.[1]

It may not be necessary always, in cases involving the right of the depositor in the deposited design or model, to have the design or model itself sent out by the Bureau. The latter has the power, by virtue of article 18 of the Arrangement, to deliver, on application, to any person a copy or a reproduction of the design or model, if such has been supplied to the Bureau by the applicant; or, if not, by causing a copy to be made at the expense of the applicant, and to certify it as conforming to the one deposited. Such certified copies or reproductions are delivered to any person by the Bureau only if the deposit is not under seal. It is not clear why the Bureau could not do the same in case of deposits under seal on the application of the depositor or of a court. The sending out of the design or model deposited at the Bureau may not be free from risk. It might be recommended that, in case of deposit under seal, several samples or reproductions be deposited with each design or model.

At the end of the first period of protection, if no extension is applied for, or at the expiry of the second period, the designs or models deposited are returned to their proprietors, on their application and at their expense. If the protection has ceased at the end of the first period, and the deposit was under seal, it shall be returned in its

obstacle to the adhesion of Italy to the Arrangement. However, articles 8 and 9 of the Arrangement were adopted by the Conference as proposed by the Bureau. See *Actes de la Conférence de La Haye*, p. 507.

1. Articles 9 and 14 of the Arrangement. These provisions are somewhat indefinite and their working remains to be seen. What is a competent authority who may ask a deposited design to be communicated to it? When will the Bureau consider that it is being properly requested? How will the return of the design to the Bureau be assured? The consent of the depositor will often facilitate the solution of the first two questions. The administrations of the contracting countries will probably take care of the third. See Osterrieth, *Die Haager Konferenz*, pp. 146–147.

sealed cover or envelope to the depositor. If no application is made for its return it is destroyed at the end of two years.[1]

If a proper application is made for a second period of protection, the sealed packages or envelopes of the deposits under seal are opened by the Bureau at the expiry of the first period, and the deposit is open to inspection during the second period.

§ **297. Changes in ownership of design or model.** All changes affecting the ownership of designs or models may be communicated to the Bureau by the interested parties. It is not required that such communication be made. The Bureau shall register all such changes, and shall notify the administrations of the contracting countries and publish the same in its periodical. Article 17 of the Arrangement provides that for these acts the Bureau may collect a fee, the amount to be fixed by the *Règlement*. However, the amount of such fee was not fixed by the *Règlement*. Unless the *Règlement* is amended in this respect, no fee is payable on this account.[2]

The usefulness of the provision of article 17 is doubtful. As proposed by the Bureau, it contained a first paragraph reading as follows:

> L'administration du pays d'origine notifiera au Bureau International les annulations, radiations, renonciations, transmissions et autres changements qui se produiront dans la propriété du dessin ou modèle.

After this paragraph followed two others. The latter remained in article 17 only and their effect is described above. The first paragraph was struck out as a result of the modification of the basic principle of article 1 of the Arrangement by the Conference. The designs or models are not deposited at the International Bureau by the administrations of the contracting countries, nor is the international protection dependent on the protection in the country of origin.

What are the "changes" of which article 17 in its adopted form speaks, and which are registered by the Bureau on proper application? And who are the "interested parties" who may notify the Bureau thereof? Article 4 of the *Règlement* provides that in the register kept by the Bureau the following entries shall be made:

1. Article 12 of the Arrangement.
2. Article 7 of the *Règlement* provides specifically the cases in which a fee is payable. The case under consideration in the text is not provided for.

3° la mention relative aux modifications du dépôt, telles que . . . transmissions, radiations, renonciations, etc.;

6° la cessation de la protection dans un des pays contractants à la suite de décisions judiciaires, etc., lorsque ces communications sont notifiées au Bureau International.

These provisions were adopted as proposed by the Bureau. They were proposed as a necessary regulation of the stipulation of article 17 in its original form. With the striking out of the first paragraph of article 17, this regulation should also have been modified. May the words "changes affecting the ownership of a design or model" be taken as including all the acts enumerated in the original first paragraph of article 17, or in the above data of article 4 of the *Règlement*?

Furthermore, who are the "interested parties" who may notify the Bureau of these changes? The depositor will usually have no interest to do so. Is the Bureau to decide, or find out, whether or not a third party is an "interested party"? How will the Bureau proceed? And if the Bureau must always register any change notified to it, how can these notifications be trusted, or by what law will their validity be tested?

After the basic amendment of the Arrangement by the Conference, and the independence of protection of designs and models in each contracting country following thereon, all these provisions are without practical purpose.[1] The only end they could serve would be to permit the keeping of what might be called "the civil status" of a design or model by the Bureau. This is of small interest in view of the independence of protection in each country, and besides it is not always possible to ensure the truthfulness of the entries, since the source of information may be unofficial.

§ **298. Fees.** The fees payable to the International Bureau are fixed by articles 15 of the Arrangement and 7 of the *Règlement*. Unless they are paid, no registration is made by the Bureau. The fee for a single design and for the first period of five years is five francs;

1. Plaisant and Fernand-Jacq in their work (*La Conférence de La Haye, Le Nouveau Régime de la Propriété Industrielle*, Paris, 1927, p. 135) interpret the words "tous les changements affectant la propriété des dessins et modèles" as meaning all acts entailing in any degree "un démembrement de la propriété." This restrictive interpretation does not seem to be warranted. Osterrieth (*Die Haager Konferenz*, pp. 147–148) agrees that the entries provided for in article 17 have no effect on the right ("rechtsbekundete Wirkung"). Likewise Mr. Ostertag, in his *Exposé* at the Congress of the International Association, Geneva, 1927, published in *Propriété Industrielle*, pp. 136–137.

for the second period of ten years, ten francs. The fee for a joint deposit of several designs is ten francs for the first period and fifty for the second period of protection. A fee of five francs is payable for any extract from the register, for any certificate or search, and for any written or oral information concerning any deposit. The same fee is due for the opening of a sealed cover or a perforated envelope, as well as for the resealing of the same. All fees must be paid in Swiss money, by express provision of article 7 of the *Règlement.*

All these fees would seem to be quite high,[1] and they are so fixed because of the many original expenses that the service of international deposit will impose upon the International Bureau.[2]

§ 299. Abolition of obligations of the depositor. Article 5 of the Arrangement provides as follows:

> Les pays contractants conviennent de ne pas exiger que les dessins ou modèles ayant fait l'objet d'un dépôt international soient revêtus d'une mention obligatoire. Ils ne les frapperont de déchéance ni pour défaut d'exploitation, ni pour introduction d'objets conformes à ceux protégés.

In accordance with this article, the protection of designs and models deposited at the International Bureau is not subject to any of the above conditions, which may exist by the municipal law of any of the contracting countries. The designs or the articles to which they have been applied need not be marked with memoranda of the fact of the deposit or registration of the design. Likewise the protection of designs or models cannot be forfeited for failure to work them, or for importation of articles similar to those which are protected.

As to the obligation of marking, the original text of article 5, as proposed by the Bureau, provided that no other mention or mark may be required except the one which may possibly be imposed by the law of the country of origin. This last phrase was struck out at the suggestion of the Spanish delegation.[3] This provision of the Arrangement is broader and more sweeping than the corresponding provision of article 5 of the Convention. In the latter it is stipulated

1. The amounts of the fees, as proposed by the Bureau originally, were two, five, and twenty francs, respectively. They were quite low, because the depositor was bound to deposit his designs or models in his own country before the international deposit. The fees were increased by the Conference. See *Actes de la Conférence de La Haye*, pp. 322, 509, 565.

2. See Plaisant and Fernand-Jacq, *La Conférence de La Haye*, p. 134.

3. *Actes de la Conférence de La Haye*, pp. 321, 497.

that "no sign or mention of registration shall be required on the product *for the recognition of the right.*" The italicized words of that provision do not occur in article 5 of the Arrangement, and the limitations which those words introduce into the regime of designs and models under the Convention [1] are not to be admitted under the Arrangement.

The abolition of the prohibition of importation is identical with the respective provision of article 5 of the Convention and its interpretation above [2] applies here.

Because of the opposition of two countries it has been impossible to abolish the compulsory working of designs or models by the Convention. This has been achieved by the Arrangement. The delegation of the Serb-Croat-Slovene State declared itself against such abolition in the discussion of the Arrangement, as it did also in the case of the Convention. But article 5 was adopted over that delegation's objection. The Serb-Croat-Slovene State did not sign the Arrangement. The other countries succeeded in abolishing, so far as their nationals and the persons assimilated to them are concerned, this obligation, which is a great obstacle to the international protection of designs and models.

Article 5 of the Arrangement provides that the protection of a design or model shall not be forfeited in case of non-working and of importation. Thus, only the penalty of forfeiture is really abolished. Conceivably, the obligation of compulsory license might be imposed in such cases.

§ 300. The Hague Arrangement affords minimum of protection. The Arrangement of The Hague provides only a minimum of protection for the persons entitled to its benefits. Article 21 of the Arrangement provides in this respect as follows:

> Les dispositions du présent Arrangement ne comportent qu'un minimum de protection; elles n'empêchent pas de revendiquer l'application des prescriptions plus larges qui seraient édictées par la législation intérieure d'un pays contractant; elles laissent également subsister l'application des dispositions de la Convention de Berne revisée de 1908 relatives à la protection des oeuvres artistiques et des oeuvres d'art appliquées à l'industrie.

It is important to make clear what this minimum of protection means. The formula is taken from the International Arrangement

1. See on this point, *supra*, § 283.

2. See *supra*, § 282.

of 1920 for the preservation and reëstablishment of rights of industrial property affected by the World War.[1] It means here that the persons entitled to the benefits of the Arrangement of The Hague are not excluded from the rights which they might claim if this Arrangement had not been entered into. The Arrangement purports only to grant an additional protection. Article 21 specifies two headings of protection which may be claimed by those persons — the larger protection that may be provided for by the municipal law of a contracting country, and the protection afforded by the Convention of Berne.

The first is evident, since the countries parties to the Arrangement are necessarily parties to the general Convention, whose second article assures national treatment in each country to all the persons entitled to its benefits under articles 2 and 3. The persons claiming the advantages of the Arrangement are also entitled to the benefits of the Convention, and therefore may claim the rights and protection which the municipal law of each country assures to nationals in respect to industrial designs and models. But such larger protection may only be claimed, — *revendiqué*, — not enjoyed. The conditions and formalities of the municipal law must be complied with in order that such larger protection may be enjoyed. Thus, if the municipal law of a country party to the Arrangement protects designs and models for a longer period than the fifteen-year period of the Arrangement, such longer duration of protection cannot be enjoyed by the person who deposited his design or model at the International Bureau, unless he complies with the conditions and formalities of the municipal law of that country (for instance, deposits his design there).[2]

The provisions of the Berne Convention concerning the protection of artistic works and works of art applied to industry continue to be applied ("laissant subsister l'application"), notwithstanding the Arrangement of The Hague. This means that the regime of the literary and artistic union is in no way disturbed by this Arrangement.[3] If a design or model may be protected in a country of that union, as an artistic work applied to industry, without any formality, it will continue to be protected. If that country is also a party to this Arrangement, this does not render necessary the international

1. See *Actes de la Conférence de La Haye*, pp. 318, 511.
2. See *ibid.*, p. 318.
3. See *ibid.*, p. 511.

deposit of the same design as a condition for its protection in that country.

§ **301. The "Règlement."** For the details of application of the Arrangement a *Règlement d'exécution* was proposed by the Bureau and adopted by the Conference at the same time with the Arrangement. According to article 20 of the Arrangement, the provisions of the *Règlement* may be modified, at any time, by agreement of the administrations of the contracting countries. Thus it will not be necessary to wait for a new conference of revision in order to amend the *Règlement* if, from the experience acquired through its application, a modification of its provisions is to be desired. The *Règlement* is not signed by the delegates, but only approved by the Conference.[1] Consequently it needs no ratification.

If a modification of the *Règlement* is desired, the procedure is to be the following, according to article 10 of the *Règlement*. The proposals for modification shall be transmitted to the International Bureau, which will communicate them with its own proposals to the administrations of the contracting countries. The latter shall send to the Bureau their opinions on the proposals within six months. If, at the expiration of this period, a proposal is agreed upon by the majority of the administrations, and no opposing view has been expressed thereon, the amendment embodied in the proposal will go into effect on the notification of the International Bureau.

§ **302. Financial regime of the international deposit.** The international deposit will cause various expenses for the International Bureau (new employees, registers, publications, postal fees, and the like) and will bring in receipts from fees. It is expected that the receipts will exceed the expenses. The Arrangement and *Règlement* provide only for the division of the balance remaining after the deduction of the expenses from the total amount of fees collected by the Bureau.

At the beginning of every year the International Bureau shall establish the total sum of expenses incurred during the preceding year for the service of the international deposit. This sum will be deducted from the total of the receipts, and the balance will be distributed among the contracting countries in equal parts, or according to a mode of distribution to be approved later.[2] The mode of

1. See *Actes de la Conférence de La Haye*, p. 585.
2. Article 16 of the Arrangement and 8 of the *Règlement*.

distribution caused some disagreement at the Conference. The Bureau proposed to insert in article 16 of the Arrangement a provision that the distribution be made in equal parts. But the Brazilian delegation opposed this, claiming that the various countries should profit variously by this Arrangement, as in the case of the Madrid Arrangement for the international registration of trade marks. This delegation proposed a mode of distribution, by which those countries that profit least by the Arrangement would receive the greatest part of the receipts.[1] The Conference, however, adopted the division in equal parts in the *Règlement*. The provision "or according to a mode of distribution to be approved later" means only that a proposition for modification of the *Règlement* in this respect may be made according to the procedure of article 10 of the *Règlement*.[2]

During the discussion of the Arrangement by the sub-committee, a wish was expressed to have the designs and models sent from foreign countries to the International Bureau of Berne made free of Swiss custom duties. In the discussion in the Plenary Committee, the Director of the International Bureau and the Swiss delegation promised to make the necessary requests to the Swiss government to make this concession. The committee then desisted from the adoption of a *voeu* on such a delicate question.[3]

§ 303. Importance of the Arrangement of The Hague. The Arrangement for the international deposit of industrial designs and models was signed by the following ten countries: Belgium, Danzig (Free City), France, Germany, Morocco, Portugal, Spain, Switzerland, Syria and Lebanon, and Tunis. The Austrian and Czechoslovakian delegations made declarations at the Conference, justifying the belief that those countries will accede to the Arrangement in the near future.[4] Other countries parties to the Madrid Arrangement for the international registration of trade marks may also be expected to accede.

The Arrangement hardly derogates in any respect from the municipal law of the countries which signed it. The provisions constituting common legislation for all the contracting countries, such as the abolition of the obligations of the depositor, the duration of in-

1. See *Actes de la Conférence de La Haye*, p. 509.
2. See *supra*, § 301.
3. See *Actes de la Conférence de La Haye*, p. 532.
4. See *ibid.*, p. 583.

ternational protection, the possibility of deposits under seal, the lack of previous examination of the design by the administration, are in accord with the municipal law of those countries. Moreover, in some of the countries the municipal law affords a broader protection than the Arrangement.[1] The real controversial questions on which there is no uniformity or agreement in the laws of the various countries, such as the questions, what may be deposited as a design, and when a design is new, and the question of the effects of the deposit, are not touched upon by the Arrangement. Even as to the limited field of the provisions of common legislation contained in the Arrangement, whether this will help make the law of the various countries uniform will appear when the countries, whose municipal law is not in agreement with these provisions, shall accede to the Arrangement. For instance, Italy protects designs and models for only two years and Austria and Czechoslovakia for three years. The same countries impose on the proprietor of the deposited design the obligation to work it within a year from such deposit, and in the two latter countries the protection of the design is forfeited in case of importation of articles to which the design has been applied. The Arrangement derogates from the municipal law of these countries on the above questions. It remains to be seen whether they will accede to this Arrangement, as they have to the Madrid Arrangement for the international registration of trade marks.

The United States and Great Britain and the British dominions and colonies, are not expected to become parties to this Arrangement, as they have not acceded to the Madrid Arrangement concerning trade marks.

The actual value of the Arrangement to the countries that are parties to it lies especially in the international deposit itself. Until now designs and models were rarely deposited in foreign countries. The formalities to be fulfilled in each country, the fees to be paid, and the expenses for retaining agents were prohibitive. Foreign designs and models were, therefore, freely copied in the other countries.[2]

1. For instance, in France the duration of protection may reach fifty years, and in Belgium may be perpetual. Also in some countries the deposit is always under seal. And in France, Belgium, and Germany designs and models may often be protected, as works of art applied to industry, without deposit.

2. See complaints of the French delegation against the fraudulent imitation of French designs of curtains and laces by American manufacturers, in *Actes de la Conférence de Washington*, p. 291. See also statements by the German delegation in *Actes de la Conférence de La Haye*, pp. 495–496, 502. See also *supra*, § 244.

The international deposit does not guarantee to the depositor always protection in all the contracting countries. He may need to fight for his right in the courts of those countries. But the international deposit will operate, as the Bureau put it in a felicitous simile,[1] like the sword of Damocles. Counterfeiters and manufacturers will not dare to copy and apply on their own products a foreign design or model found in the market, fearing that it may be deposited at the International Bureau, and that its owner may start infringement proceedings against them. Such fear did not exist before the Arrangement of The Hague, because practically no foreign design or model was deposited in any country.

1. See *Actes de la Conférence de La Haye*, p. 320.

SECTION IV

THE INTERNATIONAL REGIME OF UTILITY MODELS

CHAPTER XX

NATIONAL TREATMENT OF UTILITY MODELS

§ 304. Nature of utility models. In three countries, Germany, Japan, and Poland, a special kind of industrial property is recognized and protected — the so-called utility models, or working models ("Gebrauchsmuster"). They are distinguished from patents, on the one hand, and industrial designs and models, on the other. Indeed, they have in common with the latter but the name "models" ("Muster"), and the fact that in both the procedure for registration follows similar lines. The subject-matter, however, of a utility model, as well as the nature of the right granted to an inventor of such a model, is similar to the subject-matter and the nature of a patent right.

In this respect the history of this branch of industrial property is illuminating. The German patent laws of 1877 and 1891 [1] provided that patents might be granted for new inventions capable of an industrial application. The patent office and the courts in Germany interpreted a patentable invention as a technical improvement or discovery which constitutes a considerable technical progress.[2] This

1. *Reichsgesetzblatt* (1877), p. 501; (1891), p. 79. Sec. 1. "Patente werden ertheilt für neue Erfindungen, welche eine gewerbliche Verwerthung gestatten."

2. See Osterrieth, "L'Art appliqué à l'industrie," in *Annuaire de l'Association Internationale* (1898), pp. 344, 345. See also Allfeld, *Grundrisz des gewerblichen Rechtsschutzes* (Leipzig, 1910), p. 80.

left without protection small inventions of instruments or objects of practical use which were protected in other countries as patentable inventions. Germany then passed the Law of June, 1 1891,[1] which affords the necessary protection to those inventions. Japan followed Germany with the Laws of March 15, 1905 and April 2, 1909,[2] which are now replaced by the Law of April 29, 1921.[3] Recently, Poland, by the Law of February 5, 1924,[4] distinguished and regulated at the same time utility models and designs or models of ornament. Japan imitated Germany on that point, as she did in many other branches of law. Poland adopted this branch of property, because this kind of industrial property existed in the Polish territory which was under German sovereignty before the War.

In substance, therefore, utility models are inventions. Instead of a patent, however, a certificate of registration is granted to the inventor of such a model. On the contrary, in all other countries but the above three these same inventions are considered patentable inventions, and a patent is granted to the inventor thereof.

§ 305. National treatment in respect to utility models. Article 2 of the Convention secures national treatment to the persons entitled to its benefits in respect to patents for inventions and to utility models. The latter were not enumerated in article 2 before the revision of the Convention at Washington in 1911. They were added, on the proposal of the International Bureau, as being a branch of industrial property.[5] As between Germany, Japan, and Poland the persons entitled to the benefits of the Convention may claim the rights and protection enjoyed by the nationals of those countries in respect to utility models. As between those three countries and the other countries of the Union the same persons are in the following situation.

If they are nationals of, or domiciled or established in, Germany, Japan, or Poland, and wish to have a utility model protected in the other countries of the Union, they must apply for a patent in those countries, so long as the latter do not register utility models as a

1. *Reichsgesetzblatt* (1891), p. 290. Sec. 1. "Modelle von Arbeitsgeräthschaften oder Gebrauchsgegenständen oder von Theilen derselben werden, insoweit sie dem Arbeits- oder Gebrauchszweck durch eine neue Gestaltung, Anordnung oder Vorrichtung dienen sollen, als Gebrauchsmuster nach Massgabe dieses Gesetzes geschützt."

2. See *Propriété Industrielle* (1909), p. 122.

3. See *ibid.* (1923), p. 188.

4. See *ibid.* (1924), p. 221.

5. See *Actes de la Conférence de Washington*, p. 42.

distinct kind of industrial property. In case their utility model is not an invention that can be patented in those countries, the persons in question may register their utility model as an industrial model. In either case they must comply with the conditions and formalities of the municipal law of each country on patents or on designs and models. In this respect reference is made to the preceding chapters X and XV.

On the other hand, nationals of, or persons domiciled or established in, the other countries of the Union who desire to have their inventions protected in Germany, Japan, or Poland, may claim no more than the rights and protection afforded by the municipal law of these three countries to their own nationals; that is, if by the law of these countries the invention in question is admitted only as a utility model, they should apply for its registration as such.

The regime of utility models in the three countries mentioned is, according to the above exposition, of general interest to all the countries of the Union. It is considered here in the same way that the national regime of patents and industrial designs or models is considered above.

§ **306. Who may register a utility model.** In Japan and Poland, the inventor of a utility model, or his legal representative, whether national or foreigner, may register it. In Germany, only persons domiciled or established in the country may register utility models. Persons domiciled or established in another country are admitted to the benefits of the law only if there exists legal reciprocity with the other country, and such reciprocity is affirmed by an official proclamation of the government.

The persons admitted to the benefits of the Convention of 1883 may apply for the registration of a utility model in Germany, regardless of the above provisions.[1]

§ **307. What may be registered.** As utility models, may be registered in Germany implements, tools, or articles of practical use, or parts thereof, in so far as by a new configuration, a new arrangement, or a new mechanism, they serve a practical purpose. In Japan, any new industrial form relating to the configuration, construction, or combination of articles, may be registered as a utility model. The utility model is for the form of the article, but this form

1. The Convention of 1883 does away with all conditions of reciprocity of municipal law. See *supra*, § 128.

need not be ornamental, but may concern the shape of an article, or the manner of its construction, or the combination of materials making up the article. The idea in the Japanese law is not different from the German. The Polish law, while it protects any new form manifested by a model or design, distinguishes those new forms which aim at facilitating the use of an article — called utility models — and those which serve for ornamentation — called models of ornament.

Utility models are, therefore, distinguished from patentable inventions in those countries, primarily because they always refer to tangible things, to products, and to their form, and never to means of production, or to industrial results or processes. Utility models are always concrete articles. A machine may be the subject-matter of a utility model, but only for its external form, not for the idea that it embodies or the technical improvement that it achieves.[1] The second element of utility models, by which they are distinguished from ornamental designs and models, is that they serve a practical purpose. There should be an element of practical usefulness in the article in order that it may be deemed a utility model. If an article satisfies at the same time an ornamental purpose and a practical one, it may be registered both as a utility model and as an industrial design or model.[2] The new Japanese law does not stress the point of usefulness, like the old Law of 1909.[3]

A utility model should also be new. The novelty should exist at the time of application for registration. A model is not considered new, therefore, if before that time it had been used publicly in the country, or had been described in a printed publication. It is immaterial whether it had been published by third persons or by the inventor himself. The publication in a foreign country is prejudicial if it were accessible to the public of the country in which application is filed.

§ **308. Formalities of application.** In Germany an application for registration of a utility model should be addressed to the patent office, containing the usual formalities and, especially, the title of the model under which it should be registered and published, and an

1. Allfeld, *Grundrisz des gewerblichen Rechtsschutzes*, p. 82.
2. Allfeld, *ibid.*, p. 83.
3. The Law of April 2, 1909 (*Propriété Industrielle*, 1909, p. 122), required "a new *useful* industrial design relating to the configuration, construction or combination of articles" (writer's italics). The new Law of April 29, 1921 (*ibid.*, 1923, p. 188) requires only "a new industrial form relating," etc.

indication of the configuration or of the arrangement of the article to be protected. At the option of the applicant a description of the model may be inserted in, or annexed to, the application. The application should be accompanied by a graphic or plastic reproduction of the model, in two copies in the former case, and one in the latter. The form and dimensions of the documents are specifically determined by the law.

In Poland, the formalities are substantially the same, with the exception that a complete description of the utility model, in two copies, should always accompany the application, unless it may be replaced totally or partially by drawings or samples (in two copies) which set off sufficiently the subject of the deposit. In all cases where a description is necessary, it should contain an enumeration of claims, in which the applicant should state all that he considers as new elements in his invention.

In Japan, also, two drawings of the model, a description, and an enumeration of claims are required. In case the utility model concerns an invention for which a patent has been refused, an authenticated copy of that decision should be joined to the application.

§ 309. Administrative procedure. In Japan, the application for registration of a utility model is submitted to an examiner of the patent office, who may render a decision refusing the registration in case the utility model does not satisfy the provisions of the law. An appeal from this decision may be taken. Similarly, in Poland, an examination of the application is made by the patent office. If the conclusion is reached that the model deposited is not new, its registration is refused, with possibility of appeal. In both countries, if the result of the examination is favorable to the applicant, the model is registered and published, and a certificate of registration is delivered to the applicant.

In Germany, the only examination made is as to whether the application and other documents comply with the formalities prescribed by the law. If there is such compliance, the model is registered without any examination, and a certificate of registration is delivered to the applicant.

§ 310. Duration of protection, and fees. In Germany,the duration of protection of the registered utility model is three years, beginning with the day following the date of deposit. An extension of three years may be granted on application. In Japan and Poland, the period of protection is ten years, beginning with the date of registration. No extension is allowed.

The fee for registration is quite low in Germany for the first period of three years, amounting to ten Reichsmarks. But for the second period of three years, the fee is one hundred Reichsmarks, payable before the expiry of the first period. In Japan and Poland, besides a fee for registration, a tax is payable on each registered utility model. This tax is due annually in Japan, and at three periods in Poland during the continuance of protection.

§ 311. Effects of registration, and restrictions of the privilege. Although the source of right in a utility model is invention or creation, the recognition and enforcement of such right depends on registration at the patent office. By the registration an exclusive privilege in the use, manufacture, and sale of the model is acquired by the depositor, if he is the owner of the model.[1] The first depositor is deemed *prima facie* owner of the utility model. This is true in Germany, where no previous examination of the utility model is undertaken by the administration, as well as in Japan and Poland, where the administration examines the novelty of the model.

A right of personal possession of a utility model is recognized in Japan and Poland in favor of the person who, at the time of the filing of an application for registration of a model, uses in good faith the same model in the country.

Special provisions exist in the law of all three countries governing the cases in which a utility model infringes on a prior patent or industrial design or model.

In Poland, by analogy to patents, the proprietor of a utility model is under obligation to work it in the country within three years from the date of delivery of the certificate of registration. The sanctions of this obligation are like those in the case of patents; namely, the owner of the model may cause at any time an investigation to be made into the reasons of his inaction, or into the measure of his working of the model; but if he does not prove either to the satisfaction of the administration, the certificate is revoked.

§ 312. Conclusions. It results from the above exposition that utility models are very much like patents. The fundamental difference is that the latter concern an idea which may be applied industrially, whereas the former refer only to the special form of an article.

1. Allfeld, *Grundrisz des gewerblichen Rechtsschutzes*, p. 89.

The other differences lie in the less complicated character of formalities, the shorter duration of the privilege, and the smaller fees. In Germany, there are still other differences from patents, such as the lack of previous examination, the non-recognition of a right of personal possession in a utility model, and the lack of obligation to work it in the country.

The Polish law went into effect on April 10, 1924.[1] The statistical data sent by the Polish administration to the International Bureau show that during 1924 the applications for registration of utility models numbered 267, and the certificates of registration delivered in the same year reached the number of 195. As to Germany and Japan, the following statistical table shows the number of certificates of registration of utility models delivered in 1910, 1913, 1922, 1923, 1924, and 1925.[2]

Countries	1910	1913	1922	1923	1924	1925
Germany	42,470	47,550	31,600	26,800	31,800	40,600
Japan	3,341	3,757	4,861	4,476	3,392	11,701

It is interesting to compare these numbers with the respective numbers of patents granted by these countries, which are as follows:

Countries	1910	1913	1922	1923	1924	1925
Germany	12,100	13,520	20,715	20,526	18,189	15,877
Japan	1,616	1,996	2,936	2,131	1,928	5,088

The comparison shows that the number of utility models registered is far greater than the number of patents granted.

From the statistical data communicated to the International Bureau by the German administration, it is shown that in the above years nationals of the following countries have deposited the following numbers of utility models in Germany:[3]

1. See art. 162 of the Law of February 5, 1924 (*Propriété Industrielle*, 1924, p. 249 and final note).

2. This and the following table are made from statistical data published in *ibid.* (1912), p. 178; (1916), p. 111; (1924), pp. 165 and 258; (1925), p. 266; (1926), p. 274.

3. This and the following table are compiled from statistical data published in *ibid.*

Countries	1910	1913	1922	1923	1924	1925
Austria	693	1,085	350	404	304	286
France.	276	343	185	101	82	116
Great Britain and Ireland	362	575	353	345	421	397
Switzerland	730	969	689	558	527	627
United States.	249	686	265	211	204	219

The numbers of patents granted in Germany in the years 1922, 1923, 1924, and 1925, to nationals of the above countries, are as follows:

Countries	1922	1923	1924	1925
Austria	390	361	326	247
France.	743	807	872	764
Great Britain	785	777	738	523
Switzerland	624	685	721	605
United States.	1,305	1,397	1,252	881

This shows again that Austria and Switzerland register in Germany as many utility models as they obtain patents. For Great Britain, the number of utility models is one half of the number of patents. American and French nationals are granted a far greater number of patents than they register of utility models.

No statistics as to registration of utility models in Japan by nationals of foreign countries are available.

(1912), p. 183; (1914), p. 175; (1925), p. 130; (1926), p. 180. Nationals of other countries register utility models in Germany in small numbers, with the exception of Czechoslovakia, whose quota is always increasing.

CHAPTER XXI

THE "UNIONIST" TREATMENT OF UTILITY MODELS

§ 313. Right of priority. The existence of this separate branch of industrial property in Germany, Japan, and Poland, which in the other countries of the Union is identified either with patents or with industrial designs and models, raises two questions in respect to the claim of a right of priority.

(1) May a right of priority be claimed by a person who files an application for registration of an invention as a utility model in Germany, Japan, or Poland, and subsequently files a patent application for the same invention in the other countries of the Union; or *vice versa*?

(2) What is the period of the right of priority in such cases?

As to the first question, it should be recalled that the Convention before its revision at Washington, in 1911, did not mention utility models together with patents and industrial designs and models either in article 2 or in article 4. The latter article in particular provided that a right of priority should be enjoyed by the persons who have filed in one of the contracting countries an application for a patent, or for an industrial design or model, or for a trade mark, for the purpose of filing in the other countries. It would seem then that, by literal interpretation of the Convention, no right of priority should be enjoyed for the deposit of a utility model. The Convention ignored the latter. The reason was that Germany had not yet acceded to the Convention when the last conference of revision took place at Brussels, in 1897–1900,[1] and Japan, which had acceded in 1899, did not up to that time have legislation recognizing utility models as a separate branch of industrial property.[2]

The claim of a right of priority for a patent application, based on a prior filing of an application for registration of a utility model, or

1. Germany acceded in 1903.
2. The earliest legislation in Japan dates from 1905. See *supra*, § 304.

vice versa, might however be recognized by the municipal law, on the ground that in both applications the same right was claimed, only the form of protection being different.[1] An early convention between Germany and Switzerland [2] affirmed this principle by assimilating to patentable inventions the inventions registered in Germany as utility models. Also, two later conventions entered into by Germany with Italy [3] and Austria-Hungary,[4] established the following principle: If the first filing of a utility model is made in Germany and the second filing in Italy, or Austria, or Hungary, the right of priority would be for four months; while if the first filing of a patent application is made in the latter countries, and the subsequent filing (as a utility model in Germany), the period of priority would be twelve months. It should be added that the right of priority dealt with by those conventions is that provided for by the Convention of Union, as expressly stated therein. Germany entered into these bipartite conventions as a preparation for its accession to the Convention of Union in 1903.

The United States Patent Office,[5] applying section 4887 of the Revised Statutes, held that, in its own construction of the German law on utility models, the registration and protection in Germany of utility models concerns inventions which, according to the terms of the American patent law (section 4887), are the subject-matter of a patent; consequently, the Patent Office recognized a claim of right of priority of twelve months.

At the Conference of Washington the words "modèles d'utilité" were added in articles 2 and 4 of the Convention. This addition, however, to the enumeration of the rights of industrial property protected by the Convention did not settle the question under con-

1. Osterrieth und Axster, *Pariser Konvention*, pp. 76, 79.

2. Convention of April 13, 1892, articles 3 and 4 (De Martens, *N. R. G.*, XXI, 68).

3. Convention of June 4, 1902 (De Martens. *N. R. G.*, XXXI, 352). Art. 3 reads as follows: "Pour les objets qui sont déposés en Allemagne comme modèles d'utilité et en Italie comme inventions, les délais de priorité prévus par l'article 4 de la Convention de Paris du 20 mars 1883 modifiée par l'Acte additionel de Bruxelles du 14 décembre 1900 seront de quatre mois, si le dépôt est fait en premier lieu en Allemagne, et de douze mois, si le dépôt est fait en premier lieu en Italie."

4. Convention of November 17, 1908 (CI *Br. & For. State Papers*, 666). Art. 7 reads like art. 3 of the above Convention.

5. Decision of the Examiners-in-chief, August 12, 1908, in the matter of interference between the application of Karl Muster and the patent to Edward Lewellin White — Improvement in Pictorial Postal Cards held to be a "manufacture," or "machine," within the terms of sec. 4887. (Photostat copy of the decision was communicated by the Patent Office to the present writer.)

sideration. Indeed, article 4 provided in effect only that a right of priority should be enjoyed by a person who has filed an application for registration of a utility model in a country of the Union, for the purposes of filing an application in the other countries. Whether the right of priority may be claimed when, in the above case, the latter application is for a patent, was not expressly provided for by the Convention. Yet this would seem to be the reasonable construction of article 4. Otherwise that article would stipulate a right of priority for utility models only in respect to two countries of the Union — Germany and Japan. A stipulation of a multipartite convention would deal with only two countries.

Besides, in the discussion of article 4 by the sub-committee, a delegate remarked that he understood the meaning of article 4, paragraph (*c*), to be that a person who has deposited an invention as a utility model in one of the countries of the Union, and then applies for a patent for the same invention, may claim the special period of priority of patents, only in case, in the second country, the subject-matter of his application is deemed to be one for which a patent may be granted.[1] This remark met no objection in the committee, as recorded in the *procès-verbaux*. This shows that the Conference understood that a right of priority may be claimed in the case under consideration.[2]

Moreover, a provision was added to the Final Protocol (*ad* article 4), of the Convention, at the Conference of Washington to the effect that, when an industrial design or model shall be filed in a country of the Union by virtue of a right of priority based on the prior filing of a utility model, the period of the right of priority shall be that which pertains to industrial designs and models according to article 4 of the Convention.[3] This provision proves *ex contrario* that when, on the basis of a prior filing of a utility model, priority is claimed on a new filing for a patent, the claim should be recognized.

However, the Dutch Patent Office refused to allow, on a deposit of a patent application in the Netherlands, a claim of right of priority based on a prior application for registration of a utility model in Germany, concerning the same invention.[4] This decision caused the

1. *Actes de la Conférence de Washington*, p. 275.
2. *Avis* of the International Bureau, in *Propriété Industrielle* (1919), p. 31, *accord.*
3. *Actes de la Conférence de Washington*, pp. 312, 339.
4. Decision of Dec. 16, 1918 (*Propriété Industrielle*, 1919, p. 30).

Dutch legislature to introduce in the Law of January 15, 1921,[1] which amends the patent law of 1910, the provision of article 7, sec. 1, enacting a rule in opposition to the above case.

§ **314. Period of right of priority.** As to the second question, namely, the period of the right of priority, article 4, paragraph (*c*), provided that the periods of priority shall be twelve months for patents and utility models, and four months for industrial designs and models, and trade marks. So that utility models were classified with patents, as they should be. Whenever on a patent application a right of priority is claimed, based on a prior deposit of an application for registration of a utility model, the period of priority would be twelve months. The reservation made at the Conference of Washington by a delegate, to the effect that the above period could be claimed only in case the subject-matter of the latter application is one for which a patent may be granted, should be accepted. But whenever an application for registration of a design or model is made on the basis of a prior application for registration of a utility model, the period of priority shall be six months, according to the provision *ad* article 4 of the Final Protocol.[2]

These rules are in conformity with the interpretation of the nature of the right of priority made in an earlier chapter.[3] Indeed, this right exists in respect to the subsequent application, and not the first, and constitutes a legal defense against the facts which might take place in the interval and invalidate the subsequent application. Therefore the period of the right of priority should be controlled by the nature of the second filing. If the latter is a filing of a patent or of a utility model, the period should be twelve months; if it is a filing of an industrial design or model, the period should be four months.

At the Conference of The Hague, the International Bureau, in collaboration with the Dutch delegation, proposed a new paragraph in article 4 of the Convention, which should do away with the situation created by the above decision of the Dutch Patent Office. To this paragraph, which was adopted by the Conference,[4] was joined the provision of the Final Protocol discussed above with which it forms now paragraph (*e*) of the new article 4, providing as follows:

1. Dutch Law of Jan. 15, 1921 (1921 *Staatsblad*, No. 15).
2. See on this point, *supra*, § 275.
3. See *supra*, § 165.
4. *Actes de la Conférence de La Haye*, pp. 231–232, 429–430, 518, 539.

(*e*) Lorsqu'un dessin ou modèle industriel aura été déposé dans un pays en vertu d'un droit de priorité basé sur le dépôt d'un modèle d'utilité, le délai de priorité ne sera que celui fixé pour les dessins et modèles industriels.

En outre il est permis de déposer dans un pays un modèle d'utilité en vertu d'un droit de priorité basé sur le dépôt d'une demande de brevet et inversement.

For all questions arising with respect to a claim of a right of priority, reference is made to the chapters dealing with the right of priority for patents and for industrial designs and models. It may be noted here, in respect to the reservation of the rights of third parties in article 4 of the Convention,[1] that, as regards utility models, only in Japan and Poland, where the right of personal possession is recognized,[2] the reservation may be of practical effect.

§ **315. Independence of utility models.** Article 4*b* of the Convention stipulates that patents applied for in the various contracting countries by persons entitled to the benefits of the Convention shall be independent of patents obtained for the same invention in the other countries, whether members of the Union or not. Utility models are not mentioned in this stipulation, and it cannot be applied to them by analogy.

The question of dependence or independence of rights in utility models presents itself in two cases. First, that of utility models registered in one country in relation to utility models for the same subject-matter registered in another country — for instance, in Germany and Poland, respectively. The law of these countries, as well as of Japan, does not make the domestic protection of utility models dependent on the foreign.[3]

Secondly, there is the case of utility models registered in one country, in relation to patents granted in another for the same invention, and *vice versa*. The independence of the rights in each country in this case should be admitted. It has already been said [4] that patents granted in one country should not be dependent on patents granted for the same invention to the same person in another. This is on the generally admitted theory that a patent is a right and a privilege at the same time, and, as such, cannot be recognized and enforced beyond the territory of the country in which it is

1. See *supra*, §§ 200 ff. 2. See *supra*, § 311.
3. See Osterrieth und Axster, *Pariser Konvention*, p. 39.
4. See *supra*, §§ 9 and 207.

granted; and that, when a patent is granted in another country to a foreign patentee, a new privilege is granted, without any relation to the previous privilege. And if no legal relation exists between the two privileges, neither should dependence exist between the two patents.

This reasoning applies with greater force when the same question arises between a patent and a utility model for the same invention. Not only does no legal relation between the privileges granted by the two countries exist, but the form of protection itself is different.

§ 316. Obligations of the owner of a utility model. The provisions of article 5 of the Convention, concerning the restrictions of the obligations of patentees and proprietors of industrial designs or models and of trade marks, do not include utility models, nor has there ever been any suggestion made to this effect in any of the conferences of revision. No question of relation of utility models to patents or to industrial designs arises in this connection. Besides, the only country which imposes an obligation on the proprietor of a utility model, that of working it within a three-year period, is Poland.[1] This obligation is in no way restricted by the Convention.

Article 5*b* of the new text of the Convention, as amended at The Hague, provides for the allowance of an extension of time of not less than three months for the payment of the prescribed fees for the maintenance of industrial property rights, on condition (if the national legislation of a country so provides) of the payment of a supplementary fee. This restriction of an obligation of the proprietor of a utility model is of practical value in Japan and Poland, where periodical or annual fees are payable during the period of protection of utility models.[2]

§ 317. Protection of utility models at international exhibitions. By article 11 of the Convention temporary protection shall be granted by the contracting countries, in conformity with their domestic legislation, to utility models exhibited at official, or officially recognized, international exhibitions in the territory of one of them.

The interpretation of this article in respect to patentable inventions [3] holds also in respect to utility models. In Germany, a notification of the Chancellor of the Empire states, for each particular exhibition, whether the provisions of the law granting a temporary

1. See *supra*, § 311. 2. See *supra*, § 310. 3. See *supra*, chap. XIV.

protection will be applied. The period of protection is six months from the opening of the exhibition. No formalities for claiming this protection are required.[1] In Japan, the period is the same, but notice of the exhibition should be given, and certificates of the fact of exhibition and of the date of the opening of the exhibition, should be produced.[2] In Poland, the period of temporary protection is six months from the date of the opening of the exhibition. No formalities are prescribed by the law for claiming this protection. But the Minister of Industry and Commerce issues a special order securing this protection for the exhibitions named therein.[3]

1. Law of March 18, 1904 (1904 *Reichsgesetzblatt*, p. 141).
2. Law of April 29, 1921 (*Propriété Industrielle*, 1923, p. 188), art. 26, making applicable to utility models the provisions of art. 6 of the law on patents of the same date (*ibid.*, 1923, p. 109).
3. Law of Feb. 5, 1924, arts. 3 and 83, sec. 3 (*ibid.*, 1924, pp. 198, 221).

SECTION V

THE INTERNATIONAL REGIME OF TRADE MARKS

CHAPTER XXII

NATIONAL TREATMENT OF TRADE MARKS

§ 318. Trade-mark protection as a part of protection against unfair competition. As the protection of industrial designs or models has suffered from their undue assimilation to inventions, so, too, the protection of trade marks in general, and especially their international protection, leaves much to be desired from the same cause. The nature of trade marks has been confused with that of patentable inventions, and the regulation and protection of the former have followed rules and principles in some respects incompatible with their true nature.

Historically and naturally the protection of trade marks is a part and aspect of the protection against unfair competition.[1] In the latter, "the fundamental rule is the rule of honesty and fair dealing," and, more accurately, of the non-interference wrongfully with the advantageous business relations of a person. This also is the basis of trade-mark law. The only difference is that there is a legal presumption that the rule of honesty and fair dealing is not complied with, that there is a wrongful interference with the business relations of a person, whenever there is imitation of a trade mark. If the act complained of is an imitation of a trade mark, it is conclusively presumed that the above rule has been violated. This involves the assumption that the trade mark in question may be honestly used only by the complaining party, and that by its imitation by another the above interference has taken place. But on what is this assumption based?

Leaving aside the question of registration for later consideration, the assumption is based on certain facts and circumstances. If the production and distribution of goods in general, or of any class of goods, were the exclusive work of one individual or one entity, trade-mark law would never have been born. Our world is a world of competing producers and distributors of commodities. Many persons offer different, or the same, qualities and kinds of goods on the same market. In order to identify their own products, to distinguish them from those of others, to create and maintain relations with the public, the different producers use a mark or a sign suitable to individualize their goods.[2] This mark, after having been so used and

1. Nims, *The Law of Unfair Competition and Trade Marks*, Introduction, and p. 3; Pouillet, *Traité des Marques*, pp. 7–8; Decision of the German Patent Office, Jan. 13, 1914 (*Blatt für Patent-, Muster- und Warenzeichenwesen*, 1914, pp. 14 ff.). See also *infra*, § 480.

2. Allfeld, *Grundrisz des Gewerblichen Rechtsschutzes*, p. 101; Pouillet, *Traité des*

having created an association in the public's mind with the products of the person using it, becomes an auxiliary to, or a part of, the good-will of this person's business. To disturb him in these business relations that he has established is to take away his business. Such disturbance is produced when another person imitates or infringes his trade mark. This can no longer perform its function of identifying, distinguishing, and individualizing the person's business and products.

It appears, then, that trade-mark protection has none of the elements of patent protection. A trade mark is not an invention. No new idea or device is necessarily involved in it. It may sometimes be forced upon the producer by the public.[1] A certain sign, fortuitous and unintentional, may be liked by the public and become eventually a trade mark, although it was not so intended at first. The trade mark need not be novel, at least in the sense that novelty has in the case of inventions. A mark may be in use as a trade mark in a certain industry, and be adopted in another industry. A mark which has been a trade mark in earlier times, and later abandoned, may be used again as a trade mark. In both cases the purpose of the trade mark, as seen above, is fulfilled.

Nor should there be any theory of public property, or public possession of trade marks, as there is of inventions. No monopoly on goods is involved or implied in the trade mark. The public is not interested in having a trade mark commonly used by many or all producers of the same class of goods, as it is interested in having an invention worked freely by everybody. On the contrary, it is in the interest of the public that every producer should be undisturbed in the exclusive use of his own trade mark. To the public the use of the same mark by many can only be a source of errors and frauds.[2]

§ 319. Basic principles of international protection. A clear vision of these facts and of the interests which should be taken into consideration, and given effect as far as possible, is needed for a proper regulation of the subject of trade marks. And this same vision is necessary for international regulation and protection. In this respect it is easy to see the great difference between trade marks and

Marques, 6th ed., pp. 14–15; Rogers, *Good Will, Trade Marks and Unfair Trading* (Chicago, 1914), pp. 33, 50 ff.

1. Nims, *The Law of Unfair Competition and Trade Marks*, p. 378.

2. Maillard, Report on descriptive marks, in *Annuaire de l'Association Internationale* (1898), pp. 375, 400.

patents. The latter involve considerations, principles, and interests which are not alike in all countries. A highly industrialized country, like the United States, with a long patent history and a record of one hundred thousand patent applications a year, cannot regulate the subject-matter and procedure of patents, the rights and obligations of patentees, in the same way that a country like Greece, for instance, can, where conditions are totally different. In the case of trade marks, the above factors are without importance. The fundamental rule which is to be preserved in any country is the rule of honesty and fair dealing, and its meaning and implications are alike everywhere. The interests to be taken into consideration and given effect are everywhere the interest of every producer to be protected in the goodwill of his business, and the interest of the public to be safe from deception and fraud as to the origin and source of goods. No monopoly is involved in the protection of trade marks. Commerce and industry are in no way restricted by the prohibition to use a trade mark used by a manufacturer or trader. Consequently, in principle, the property in a trade mark acquired in a country should be recognized and protected in all other countries as a vested right. Such recognition and protection should be denied only in case the interests of the public or of other manufacturers or traders would otherwise be injured.

These principles were not always given effect in the various countries prior to the creation of the Union for the Protection of Industrial Property. By reason of the assimilation to patents, an element of monopoly was seen in trade marks. Foreigners, or persons using trade marks in connection with business establishments located in foreign countries, were usually protected on condition of reciprocity. The registration of trade marks was likened to the lodging of patent applications which existed previously. So that the regulation and administrative procedure prevailing in respect to the latter were extended to trade marks.[1] And inasmuch as there was no conscious effort to harmonize the laws of the various countries, administrative habits and traditional technique were allowed to reflect themselves in the regulation of trade marks, without any inherent reason. Thus the law and practice of each country drifted apart and became crystallized, and each country was excessively jealous of its own independence.

1. See against such extension Garavito, "Protección de la Propiedad Industrial," in *Revista de la Academia Colombiana de Jurisprudencia* (1925), pp. 293, 296.

In this state of things, the Convention of 1883 intervened with its harmonizing influence. It brought to the international regime of trade marks the effects of the general principle of national treatment of its second article, and of several specific provisions tending to secure a more effective and complete protection of trade-mark rights. And although the trade-mark laws of the various countries of the Union differ as much to-day as they did before the creation of the Union, by the operation of the above provisions many of the diversities of municipal law are without practical importance so far as international protection of trade marks is concerned.

In this chapter it is proposed to describe the trade-mark protection in each country of the Union to which the "ressortissants" of the Union are entitled under article 2 of the Convention. As in other instances, this description will be concerned, not with the law of each country separately, but with the various questions of trade-mark protection.[1] Such questions are: Who may register a trade

1. The inquiry in this chapter will extend to countries not members of the Union. In general, the data for the law of each country are borrowed from the *Tableau Comparatif des Conditions et Formalités pour la protection des Marques de Fabrique et de Commerce*, 4th ed., 1925, published by the International Bureau of the Union. The writer wishes to acknowledge his indebtedness to the Bureau in this regard. Whenever the data are taken from other sources, specific reference to such sources is made. In particular, the laws of the following countries have been looked into by the writer independently of the above *Tableau:* the United States, Great Britain, Canada, Germany, Austria, France, and Greece.

The law of the United States is found in the common law on trade marks, and the Act of 1881 (XXI *U. S. Stat. at Large*, 502) largely superseded by the Act of Feb. 20, 1905 (XXXIII *U. S. Stat. at Large*, 724): "An Act to authorize the registration of trade marks used in commerce with foreign nations or among the several States, or with Indian tribes, and to protect the same." This act was subsequently amended by the acts of May 4, 1906 (XXXIV *U. S. Stat. at Large*, 168); March 2, 1907 (XXXIV *U. S. Stat. at Large*, 1251); Feb. 18, 1909 (XXXV *U. S. Stat. at Large*, 627); Jan. 8, 1913 (XXXVII *U. S. Stat. at Large*, 649); March 19, 1920 (XLI *U. S. Stat. at Large*, 533); June 7, 1924 and March 4, 1925 (XLIII *U. S. Stat. at Large*, 647, 1268). The Tariff Act of Sept. 21, 1922, sec. 526 (XLII *U. S. Stat. at Large*, 975), provides for trade-mark protection at ports of entry.

The law of Great Britain is the Trade Marks Act of Aug. 11, 1905 (5 Edw. VII, c. 15) as amended by the acts of Aug. 28, 1907 (7 Edw. VII, c. 29); Aug. 7, 1914 (4 & 5 Geo. V, c. 16) and Dec. 23, 1919 (9 & 10 Geo. V. c. 79).

The law of Canada is the Trade Mark and Design Act (*Rev. Stat. of Canada*, 1906, c. 71) as amended by 9–10 Geo. V, c. 64 and 13–14 Geo. V, c. 28.

The law of Germany is the Act of May 12, 1894, as completed by the Act of March 31, 1913 (*Reichsgesetzblatt*, 1894, p. 441, and 1913, p. 236).

The law of Austria is Act No. 117 of May 26, 1928 (*Bundesgesetzblatt*, 1928, p. 732).

The law of Greece is the Act BRNST' of 1893, as amended by the law-decree of Nov. 12, 1927 ('Εφημερὶς τῆς Κυβερνήσεως, 1927, p. 1819).

The law of France is that of June 23, 1857 (*Bulletin des Lois*, 1857, I, 1331), as amended by the Laws of Nov. 26, 1873, May 3, 1890, and June 26, 1920 (*Bulletin des Lois*, 1873, II, 733; 1890, I, 1065; 1920, I, 2476).

mark in the different countries; what may be registered as a trade mark; formalities of application; administrative procedure of registration; effects of registration; rights of registered owner; duration of protection; fees; and the obligation to use or the nonuse of trade marks.

I. Who may register a Trade Mark

§ 320. Existing discrimination against foreigners. The discrimination existing before the creation of the Union, against foreigners or persons domiciled or possessing business establishments in foreign countries, did not disappear.[1] Under the municipal law of many countries, such persons are still protected only on condition of reciprocity.[2] All such discrimination would seem to have been abolished so far as the "ressortissants" of the Union are concerned, by virtue of the national-treatment clause of article 2, which is self executing and complete in itself, and should be given effect without the need of municipal legislation.[3] This applies even in the countries in which the nationals themselves whose business establishments are located abroad are protected only on condition of reciprocity.[4] A contrary interpretation would make the provision of article 2 useless in this respect, since foreigners in such countries of the Union are entitled

1. No discrimination is made in Argentina, Australia, Bolivia, Canada, Ceylon, Chile, Colombia, Danzig, Ecuador, Great Britain, Haiti, Italy, Mexico, New Zealand, the Netherlands, Panama, Peru, Poland, Salvador, Sweden, Syria and Lebanon, and Turkey.

2. In the following countries, persons having industrial establishments abroad, or domiciled abroad, may register their trade marks if there is legal or diplomatic reciprocity with their country of origin: Austria, Bulgaria, Cuba, Czechoslovakia, Denmark, Esthonia, Finland, France, Serb-Croat-Slovene State, Spain, Switzerland, Tunis, the United States, and Venezuela.

In the following, diplomatic reciprocity is required: Belgium, Brazil, China, Dominican Republic, Greece, Guatemala, Honduras, Hungary, Japan, Luxembourg, Nicaragua Norway, and Rumania.

In Germany, the existence of reciprocity in the foreign country is published in the *Reichsgesetzblatt*, and not until such publication may foreigners register their trade marks.

In the following countries, persons not domiciled in the country can apply for registration only by appointing an attorney domiciled in the country: Austria, Czechoslovakia, China, Danzig, Esthonia, Germany, Greece, Hungary, the Netherlands, Norway, Serb-Croat-Slovene State, Sweden, Syria and Lebanon, and the United States. In Great Britain and the British dominions the Registrar may ask the non-resident applicant to indicate an address in the country where notifications may be sent.

3. The Convention of 1883 does not require reciprocity between the members of the Union. See *supra*, § 128.

4. Such countries are the Dominican Republic, Belgium, France, Germany, Luxembourg, Norway, Tunis.

to the same protection and rights as nationals of these countries, by virtue of their municipal law.[1] Besides, article 3, by admitting to the benefits of the Convention persons domiciled or possessing business establishments located in *any country* of the Union, shows that the above discrimination is inapplicable in the Union.[2]

Lastly, any doubt on this subject has been removed[3] by the final provision of article 2, added to this article at the Conference of Washington and reading as follows: "Aucune obligation de domicile ou d'établissement dans le pays où la protection est réclamée ne pourra être imposée aux ressortissants de l'Union."

A further restriction against foreigners is made by the law of the following countries: Austria, Brazil, Danzig, Denmark, Esthonia, Finland, Greece, Guatemala, Honduras, Panama, Paraguay, Sweden, the United States, and Uruguay. Foreigners using trade marks abroad in connection with foreign business enterprises cannot register their marks in the above countries, unless they have been registered in their country of origin prior to filing the application for registration in these countries. This is a clear discrimination against foreigners, and should not be allowed under article 2 of the Convention. However, even in countries where the law imposes no such restriction against foreigners, the courts have held to the same effect upon an unsound interpretation of article 6 of the Convention.[4]

In a number of countries[5] professional unions and associations may deposit collective trade marks for the benefit of their members. Article 7*b* of the Convention of 1883 makes it obligatory on the contracting countries to admit to deposit and protect such marks. This question is considered in a separate chapter.[6]

II. Subject-matter of Registration

§ 321. Trade mark defined. A trade mark is primarily a mark — a symbol or device which marks out, distinguishes the goods of one

1. Pillet, *Régime International*, p. 344. So held by the German Reichsgericht, October 27, 1905 (*Propriété Industrielle*, 1907, p. 166), and by the Court of Cassation (Belgium), in Société Française des cotons *c.* Société Hebebrand et Consorts, June 20, 1912 (*Pasicrisie*, 1912, I, 354).
2. See also *supra*, § 112.
3. See Pouillet, *Traité des Marques*, p. 517.
4. See *infra*, §§ 371–373.
5. Australia, Belgium, Bolivia, Brazil, Canada, China, Denmark, Finland, France, Germany, Great Britain, Hungary, Italy, Japan, Morocco, Norway, Poland, Spain, Sweden, Switzerland, and Syria and Lebanon.
6. See *infra*, chap. XXVII.

producer from those of another. In order that it may perform the function of identifying and distinguishing, it should be distinctive, uncommon, different from marks which others may with equal truth employ,[1] or which would not give to merchandise its own individuality.[2] While there is agreement everywhere as to this conception of trade marks to-day, the laws of the various countries differ as to what marks or signs possess this distinctive character, and therefore as to what may be registrable as a trade mark.[3]

The diversities of the law in this respect were, before the creation of Union, and still are, very great. Under these conditions, in many cases, foreign trade marks would remain unprotected as unregistrable. In the territory of the Union this situation has been entirely changed by virtue of article 6 of the Convention, which provides that a trade mark duly registered in the country of origin shall be admitted for deposit and protected in its original form in the other countries of the Union. The conditions of application of this article, and the exceptions from this principle, are considered in another chapter.[4]

The national regime as to registrable trade marks in the various countries of the world is the following. In many countries a registrable trade mark is defined by positive assertion, but in almost all countries it is also defined by exclusion through negative criteria, or specific exceptions of certain kinds of marks. Until very recently the Greek law laid down no positive or negative criteria, but merely defined a trade mark as a distinctive sign of the products of industry, commerce, agriculture, and breeding.[5] The law of France and Tunis enumerates some things which may constitute a lawful trade mark, but specifies no exceptions.

The question of international definition of a trade mark to be inserted in the Convention of 1883, or of an ideal definition to be ad-

1. Greeley, *Foreign Patent and Trade Mark Laws* (Washington, 1899), p. 135.

2. Pouillet, *Marques de Fabrique*, 6th ed., p. 14.

3. See on this, as to the law of the United States, Nims, *The Law of Unfair Competition and Trade Marks*, §229, as to the British law and practice, Kerly (Underhay and Morgan), *The Law of Trade Marks and Trade Name*, pp. 157 ff., 686–694; on the French law, Pouillet (Taillefer et Claro), *Traité des Marques*, pp. 41 ff.; on the German law, Kohler, *Das Recht des Markenschutzes*, pp. 119 ff.; on the Austrian law, Adler, *System des Oesterreichischen Markenrechtes*, pp. 88 ff.; on the Spanish law, Ramón Pella, *Tratado de las Marcas de Fabrica y de Comercio*, pp. 63 ff.

4. See *infra*, chap. XXIV.

5. The law BRNST' of 1893 on trade marks has been modified in many an important aspect by the recent law-decree of Nov. 12, 1927, amending the provisions on patents, trade marks, and unfair competition (Ἐφημερὶς τῆς Κυβερνήσεως, 1927, p. 1819).

mitted by the laws of the various countries, was discussed at various congresses of the International Association for the Protection of Industrial Property.[1] At the Congress of Paris in 1900, a resolution was adopted to the effect that the law of each country should contain a broad definition of trade marks, followed by an illustrative enumeration of the things which may constitute a trade mark. The definition adopted was the following: "La Marque est tout signe distinctif des produits d'une fabrique, d'une exploitation ou d'une maison de commerce." The things enumerated as registrable trade marks are as follows:

> Les noms sous une forme distinctive, les denominations, étiquettes, enveloppes ou récipients, formes de produits, d'enveloppes ou de récipients, timbres, cachets, vignettes, lisières, lisérés, couleurs, dessins, reliefs, lettres, chiffres, devises et en général tout moyen servant à distinguer les produits d'une fabrique ou d'une exploitation agricole, forestière ou extractive et les objets d'une maison de commerce.[2]

The definition and enumeration follow closely the French law and have served as a model for the legislative enactments of many countries.

§ **322. General exceptions.** It may be assumed that, even in countries where there are no specific exceptions in the law, marks containing scandalous representations, or contrary to good morals or public order, are not lawful trade marks, although the conceptions of good morals and public order are not identical in all the countries. In most of them, marks containing armorial bearings, flags, and other state emblems or official signs of the various countries, portraits of the sovereign or of the sovereign's family, are not legal trade marks. But in some countries, if the armorial bearings, and the like, are of foreign states they may be legal,[3] especially if their use is properly authorized.[4] In Germany, Belgium, and the Serb-Croat-Slovene State, on authorization, national armorial bearings, emblems, and the like, may be used in a trade mark. In Austria, Hungary, and Switzerland, the use of the above signs in a trade mark is forbidden

1. See *Annuaire de l'Association Internationale* (1898), pp. 462 ff.; (1899), pp. 11 ff.; (1900), pp. 187 ff., 340 ff., 464.

2. See *Annuaire* (1900), report, at pp. 178 ff.; discussion, at pp. 340 ff.; and resolution, at p. 489.

3. Such is the case in Bulgaria, Colombia, Denmark, Danzig, Ecuador, Finland, Haiti, Morocco, Norway, Paraguay, the Netherlands, Peru, and Rumania. In Austria, they are excluded subject to reciprocity.

4. Such is the case in Belgium, Spain, Great Britain, Guatemala, Mexico, Nicaragua, New Zealand, Portugal, Serb-Croat-Slovene State, Sweden, and Uruguay.

only when it is the sole or the most essential element (Switzerland) of the mark. In many countries it is also forbidden to use the arms or insignia of a locality or community or public corporation.[1] In Great Britain, Australia, and New Zealand the word "Royal" cannot be contained in a trade mark if it is likely to deceive the public. The symbol of the Red Cross, or the words "Red Cross," are also very generally refused registration and protection.

It may likewise be assumed that descriptive terms, or what are called in some countries free marks, namely, words which are commonly used as descriptive of the kind, quality, quantity, origin, destination, or value of goods, or which have become customary in the current language of all or of a particular trade will be held not to be legal trade marks, as not having a distinctive character. Yet again, the law of all the countries does not agree as to whether or not a word or sign is descriptive and possesses no distinctive character. The same is true in respect to geographical names, although in some countries the name of the place where the property or factory of the person using the trade mark is situated may be a legal trade mark.[2]

§ **323. Deceptive trade marks.** Indications not corresponding to the real circumstances, and likely to deceive, are refused registration in many countries.[3] So, too, medals or decorations, unless their truthfulness is proved, are inadmissible in Brazil, Bulgaria, China, Esthonia, Japan, and Switzerland. In Esthonia such a trade mark should contain the year of award of the medal. Similarly, protection is refused very generally to trade marks containing the personal or business name or the portrait of a third party, unless permission is granted by the interested person or by his heirs or successors.

§ **324. Persons' and firms' names, emblems, monograms, etc.** The use of the personal or business name of the producer or manufacturer as a trade mark is diversely treated in the various countries. In many countries it may be used alone as a trade mark if it takes a

1. Argentina, Australia, Colombia, Denmark, Danzig, Ecuador, Esthonia, Germany, Haiti, Honduras, the Netherlands, Poland, Rumania, Salvador, Serb-Croat-Slovene State, Spain, the United States, and Uruguay.

2. This is so in Bulgaria, Dominican Republic, Finland, Italy, Portugal, and Spain.

3. Austria, Brazil, Bulgaria, Canada, Ceylon, China, Czechoslovakia, Danzig, Denmark, Dominican Republic, Esthonia, Germany, Great Britain, Hungary, Italy, Japan, Norway, Poland, Portugal, Serb-Croat-Slovene State, Spain, Switzerland, and Russia.

distinct and uncommon form or a special design.[1] On the other hand, in some countries it may constitute a trade mark by itself.[2] In Bulgaria and Switzerland only the firm names of commercial and industrial enterprises may be registered as trade marks. In a number of countries, emblems, monograms, or seals of the producer or manufacturer may be protected as trade marks.[3] In Rumania monograms only are not admitted, while in the Serb-Croat-Slovene State seals, but not monograms, are admitted to registration.

§ **325. Letters and numerals.** Marks consisting solely of letters or numerals are refused registration in Germany, Esthonia, Finland, Greece, Sweden, and Russia. But in Finland and Sweden they are admitted if by their arrangement they constitute a figurative mark, and in Russia, too, if their aspect gives the impression of a distinctive sign. In Argentina, Bolivia, Brazil, Bulgaria, Colombia, Ecuador, Guatemala, Paraguay, Peru, and Uruguay, such marks are admitted if they are of a special design or distinct form. In Esthonia and Portugal, letters and numerals combined may form a lawful trade mark. In Cuba, France, Haiti, Japan, Mexico, Morocco, Poland, Syria and Lebanon, Tunis, and Turkey, either letters or numerals isolated are legal trade marks. In Rumania and the Serb-Croat-Slovene State, numerals only may be registered, and not isolated letters.

§ **326. Color, form, envelopes, wrappers, etc.** The color or form of goods, or the envelopes, wrappers, packages, or receptacles for the same, are refused registration in many countries. Color and form are specifically excluded in Argentina, Bolivia, Colombia, Guatemala, Haiti, Paraguay, Peru, and Salvador. On the contrary, the laws of Bulgaria and Greece admit expressly the form of a product as a trade mark, as does also the law of Uruguay only in case the form in question is more useful and more convenient than any other for the kind of commerce or industry to which it applies. Color may be a lawful trade mark in Japan, while a combination of colors on the

1. Such is the law in Argentina, Belgium, Brazil, Colombia, Cuba, Dominican Republic, France, Great Britain, Guatemala, Haiti, Luxembourg, Mexico, Morocco, Nicaragua, New Zealand, Peru, Rumania, Salvador, Syria and Lebanon, Tunis, the United States, Uruguay, and Venezuela.

2. Such is the law in Chile, Finland, Portugal, and Turkey. In Canada, too, "all names" may be used as trade marks (Section 5 of the Trade Mark and Design Act, *Revised Statutes of Canada*, 1906, chapter 71).

3. This is so in Argentina, Bolivia, Bulgaria, Chile, Colombia, Cuba, Czechoslovakia, Esthonia, France, Guatemala, Haiti, Honduras, Mexico, Morocco, Paraguay, Peru, Portugal, Syria and Lebanon, Tunis, Turkey, and Uruguay.

container of the product is a good trade mark in Uruguay. Envelopes, wrappers, packages, or containers of products are registrable as trade marks in Argentina, Bolivia, Bulgaria, Canada (only packages), Colombia, Cuba, Esthonia, France, Greece, Guatemala, Mexico, Morocco, Paraguay, Peru, Rumania, Tunis, Turkey, Uruguay, and Russia.

§ **327. Inscriptions in a foreign language.** In Brazil and Spain, if a trade mark is applied on national products, it cannot bear labels or inscriptions in a foreign language. This rule does not apply in Brazil if the foreign inscription concerns names of beverages or other products which have no corresponding expression in Portuguese, such as bitters, brandy, cognac, fernet, kirsch, rhum, and others, or if it concerns the names of the manufacturer or inventor, who is a foreigner. In Spain, foreign inscriptions are allowed only if the trade mark contains clearly the name of the Spanish manufacturer or merchant and a statement of his residence and of his place of production in the country. Moreover, if the foreign inscription concerns the merchandise which it serves to distinguish, it must be accompanied by a Spanish translation.

§ **328. Law of Great Britain and the British dominions.** Special consideration should be given to the law of Great Britain, Australia, Irish Free State, Ceylon, and New Zealand. In these countries the law specifically determines the elements which a trade mark should necessarily contain. Thus, in Great Britain a registrable trade mark must contain, or consist of, at least one of the following essential particulars:

(1) The name of a company, individual, or firm represented in a special or particular manner.

(2) The signature of the applicant for registration or of some predecessor in his business.

(3) An invented word or invented words.

(4) A word (or words) having no direct reference to the character or quality of the goods, and not being, according to its ordinary signification, a geographical name or a surname.

(5) Any other distinctive mark; but a name, signature, or word or words, other than such as fall within the description in the above paragraphs shall not be registrable, except upon evidence of its distinctiveness.[1]

1. Sec. 9 of the Trade Marks Act of 1905 as amended by the Act of 1919 (5 Edw. VII, c. 15, and 9 & 10 Geo. V, c. 79). The phrase "except upon evidence of its distinctiveness" was substituted by the latter act for the phrase "except by order of the Board of Trade or the Court be deemed a distinctive mark" of the Act of 1905.

The law is similar in Australia, Irish Free State, Ceylon, and New Zealand.

Moreover, in Great Britain and Ceylon, in respect of cotton piece goods and cotton yarn, no mark consisting of a word or words alone (whether invented or otherwise) shall be registered; and in respect of cotton piece goods, no mark consisting of a line heading alone.[1]

By the Act of 1919 the register of trade marks in Great Britain has been divided into two parts. In part A are registered all marks registrable under the provisions of the principal Trade Marks Act. In the new part B may be registered marks that have been used for two years in the United Kingdom for the purposes for which a trade mark is used, but which are not registrable under the provisions of section 9. This registration, however, does not give the same rights to the registrant as that in part A of the register. The main object of this change is to facilitate the registration in foreign countries of British marks which are not registrable under the principle Act.[2] The influence of article 6 of the Convention of 1883 may be seen here.[3]

§ 329. Special requirements in some countries. In Italy, the trade mark must indicate the place of origin, the factory, or the trade, in a form identifying the person's or the firm's name, and the name of the establishment from which the products are derived. But a signature handwritten, or otherwise reproduced, may constitute a trade mark. Only in case the products distinguished by the trade mark are either cattle, or small articles, a special abbreviation (*sigla*), or any other sign may be admitted to registration. In Japan, trade marks must be distinctive, and composed of letters, figures, or signs, isolated or combined. In Russia, marks of manufacturers must contain an indication of the firm and place of the factory. In Brazil, trade marks affixed to pharmaceutical products must necessarily contain the name of the manufacturer and the place of origin.

§ 330. Trade marks of long use. In Denmark, Great Britain, Austria, Hungary, and the Serb-Croat-Slovene State, in determining whether a trade mark is distinctive, as required by law, — that is,

1. Sec. 64 (10) of the Trade Marks Act of 1905 (5 Edw. VII, c. 15).

2. Trade Marks Act 1919, secs. 1–5 (9 & 10 Geo. V, c. 79). Also Fletcher Moulton and Evans-Jackson, *The Patents, Designs and Trade Marks Acts* (London, 1920), p. 129.

3. Maillard, "Protection Internationale des Marques de Fabrique et de Commerce," in *Travaux du Groupe Français de l'Association Internationale* (1919–1922), p. 45 n.

adapted to distinguish the goods of the proprietor of the trade mark from those of other persons, — the administration or tribunal may take into consideration all conditions of fact, especially the duration of the use of the trade mark in question.[1]

III. Formalities of Application

§ **331. Regulation in general.** Practically everywhere to-day the protection of trade marks is subject to prior registration. This is necessary in order to enable other persons to take notice of the claim of a producer or manufacturer to a trade mark. Formerly the use alone of the trade mark gave sufficient notice. The market of a manufacturer or producer was confined within definite boundaries. Notice of his trade mark was given by its use in that market. Competitors could not fail to see the trade mark. This is no longer true, with the modern development of communication and the extension of commerce. The market of any manufacturer or merchant is ever changing and is kept within no definite limits. It is greatly extended. Mere use is not a sufficient notice to all possible competitors.[2] On the one hand, the multiplication, duplication, and variety of commodities may cause the adoption of the same, or similar, trade marks by several people. On the other hand, because of the psychological advantages that a trade mark should have from a business point of view by thrusting itself upon the attention of the public, some signs or words or phrases appeal especially to, and are likely to be used by, many producers at the same time. It should be possible to afford the public a record of all trade marks used, so that unintentional infringement may be avoided. The registration satisfies this need.

In each country the law requires that an application for registration be filed by the person adopting a trade mark and desirous of having it protected. The application is sent to, or handed in at, a central office; in many countries this is a branch of the patent office. In Austria, Czechoslovakia, and Hungary, the filing is done at the Chamber of Commerce and Industry of the city in which the applicant is domiciled or established. Foreigners in those countries

1. The English law provides: "... may, in the case of a trade mark in actual use, take into consideration the extent to which such user has rendered such trade mark in fact distinctive for the goods with respect to which it is registered or proposed to be registered." Sect. 9, last paragraph, Trade Marks Act of 1905 (5 Edw. VII, c. 15).

2. Greeley, *Foreign Patent and Trade Mark Laws*, pp. 130 ff.

should file their applications with the Chamber of Commerce and Industry of the capital. In Belgium and France, applications are filed at the commercial tribunal (or possibly the civil tribunal) of the place of domicile of the applicant. Foreigners should file at the commercial tribunals of Brussels and Paris respectively.

The application should be accompanied by several documents, especially several copies (in Austria, four; in Argentina, six; in Germany and Australia, twelve; etc.), photographs, designs, and descriptions of the trade mark, powers of attorney for foreigners, and so forth. All these documents, as well as the application, should be written on paper, the kind, dimensions, and color of which are specifically regulated in each country.

No movement for the adoption of uniformity in the formalities of application for registration of trade marks exists, although an effort is being made for the adoption of a uniform classification of products for registration of trade marks.[1] This is due to the fact that in most of the countries of the Union the great expense and trouble and waste of time caused by the necessity for complying with the formalities of registration required by the various countries have been done away with by the international registration of trade marks at the International Bureau of Berne, by virtue of the Madrid Arrangement of 1890.[2]

IV. Administrative Procedure

§ 332. The two systems of preliminary examination and of registration without examination. When an application for the registration of a trade mark is filed, the administration which receives it will generally determine whether the formalities prescribed by law for the application and other documents are complied with. In case the filing is in due and proper form, must the trade mark be registered without any further examination? The same diversity between the two systems of previous examination and of registration without examination that we have found in the case of patents,

1. The Technical Reunion of Berne of 1904 adopted resolutions concerning the dimensions of stereotyped marks; these have been complied with by some countries (*Propriété Industrielle*, 1926, pp. 239, 240). The recent Technical Reunion of Berne, of 1926, had in its agenda the question of uniform classification of trade marks in view especially of the international registration of trade marks. It named a committee to study and report on the question at its next meeting. See *procès-verbal*, in *Propriété Industrielle* (1926), p. 212. See also *infra*, §§ 578 ff.

2. See *infra*, chap. XXVIII.

industrial designs or models, and utility models, is found also in the case of trade marks. A third system holds a middle position between these two; and although it would seem to be the best, it is followed by the law of only two countries.

In the matter of trade marks, registration without preliminary examination by the administration is an exception. In its unmodified form it is the system adopted by the law of Austria, Belgium, Chile, Danzig, France, Haiti, Luxembourg, Mexico, Rumania, Tunis, and Turkey. In a number of countries, although no preliminary examination is made by the administration, trade marks deposited for registration are advertised for objection by interested persons, and only on the expiration of the period set for objections is registration in favor of the applicant effected. In case an objection to the registration is filed by an interested person, the administration, or a tribunal, passes on the opposing claims and may refuse registration. Such is the law in the following countries: Argentina, Bolivia, Brazil, Ceylon, Colombia, Ecuador, Nicaragua, Panama, and Salvador. The period for filing objections is thirty days in Argentina and Colombia, fifty in Bolivia, sixty in Brazil, and ninety in Nicaragua, Panama, and Salvador. In Italy and Morocco, the only examination of the trade mark made by the administration concerns, in the former, the question whether the trade mark contains the element specifically required by law for a valid trade mark, and, in the latter, whether the mark does not contain things which are specifically excluded by the law.

In a great number of countries the trade mark is examined by the administration before its registration, and in many others, besides such examination, objections are invited by information to interested parties, or by an advertisement of the application for registration. In Bulgaria, Canada, Czechoslovakia, Dominican Republic, Esthonia, Finland, Japan, Norway, Paraguay, Sweden, Syria and Lebanon, and Russia, the administration only examines the trade mark, and on being satisfied that it is a legal one, and that the applicant is entitled to its exclusive use, it registers the trade mark and transmits or delivers to the applicant a certificate of registration. In the United States, Great Britain, Australia, New Zealand, China, Cuba, Denmark, Greece, the Netherlands, Peru, Portugal, Uruguay and Venezuela, besides the examination by the administration, the application is advertised and objections are invited within a certain period. This period is ten days from the last publication in Uruguay, thirty days in the United States[1] and Venezuela, one month in Great Britain, sixty days in Cuba, three months in Australia and Portugal, and six months in China, Greece, and the Netherlands.

In Portugal, the only third parties who may oppose registration are owners of registered trade marks. Owners of unregistered marks may oppose only if they have been using these marks not more than six months prior to the application in question, or if they themselves have applied for registration within the last six months.

In Germany, Poland, and the Serb-Croat-Slovene State, the trade mark is examined by the administration and if it is found to be like the one of another registered owner, and the goods on which the marks are used are alike, notice is sent to the other party and he is invited to oppose the registration, if he wishes, within a certain period. If the third party files no objection, the trade mark is registered. In the United States if the same resemblance occurs between the trade marks of two applicants an interference is declared to determine the question of priority of adoption and use.

In Spain, Guatemala, and Honduras, upon receipt of an application for registration of a trade mark, the administration advertises it first and invites objections. On the expiry of the period for filing objections, the administration passes on the opposing claims and also examines into the registrability of the trade mark. The respective periods are thirty days from the last publication in Honduras, forty days in Guatemala, and two months in Spain.

§ 333. System of previous notification to the applicant. In Hungary and Switzerland the administration examines the trade mark as to whether it is legal and registrable according to the law. If it appears that it is not a legal trade mark, registration is refused. But if the trade mark proposed for registration is identical with, or resembles, a trade mark already registered, the administration notifies the applicant and he may, at his election, withdraw, maintain, or amend the proposed trade mark. Thus the administration is bound to search in its registers and see whether the trade mark proposed for registration infringes upon another's trade mark already registered. Such search is for the benefit of the applicant, who is

1. Objection by foreigners within thirty days is rarely possible, because a personal oath is required; see Martin *v.* Martin & Bowne Co. (1905), 119 O. G. 962. But failure to object does not deprive the owner of his property right; Martin *v.* Martin & Bowne Co. (1906), 122 O. G. 734.

thus warned that he may be exposed to infringement proceedings if he uses the same trade mark. But the administration cannot refuse to register the proposed trade mark if the applicant does not desist from his application. Hence this system offers all the advantages of the system of previous examination without its disadvantages; that is, the trouble, delays, and expense of advertisements and objections, and administrative arbitrariness.[1]

§ 334. Questions examined by the administration. The study in another place [2] of the two general systems of administrative procedure leading to the grant of a patent disclosed that the legal or judicial validity of a patent was in no way enhanced by the preliminary examination; that the latter is purely a question of administrative policy aiming at assuring a *prima facie* value, economically speaking, to the patent. This is not true in the case of trade marks. In many countries ownership in a trade mark is based on registration either immediately or after the expiration of a number of years from such registration. Under these conditions the preliminary examination tends to assure the legal value of a trade mark.

Indeed, if the ownership of a trade mark should be acquired by registration, or some time thereafter, it should be possible for the administration to satisfy itself, before admitting it to registration, that the applicant is undoubtedly entitled to the exclusive use of such trade mark. It should not be necessary, however, to ascertain that the trade mark contains the essentials necessary to constitute a trade mark, or that it does not contain what is specifically excluded by the provisions of the law. The latter examination into the legality of the trade mark may be made by the courts when the question is raised in infringement proceedings.

But how is the question of title in the trade mark to be examined? The administration should be satisfied that the trade mark proposed for registration does not belong to anyone else. A search is made, then, in the register of trade marks. If the applicant's trade mark is identical with, or resembles closely, a trade mark already registered, registration will be refused so long as the latter's registration has not been cancelled.[3] But a search in the register discloses prior registra-

1. The Swiss system of administrative procedure was endorsed by the Congress of the International Association for the Protection of Industrial Property in 1900. See *Annuaire* (1900), pp. 353 ff., 490.

2. See *supra*, § 146.

3. In the countries where ownership in a trade mark is acquired at the expiry of a period of years after registration, the person having the better title in the trade mark may cause the cancellation of the registration within that period. See *infra*, § 337.

tion of identical or similar trade marks effected in the country alone, not that effected in foreign countries. It is, then, possible, in countries in which ownership in the trade mark is based on registration, that a mark may be registered, and property therein be acquired, by an applicant who usurps or imitates a mark adopted and used or registered in a foreign country, and which constitutes a valuable element of a foreigner's business and goodwill. Unless the latter shows alertness and registers his trade mark in those countries, the extension of his business is seriously hampered by the usurpation of his trade mark by other producers of the same class of goods. Not only can he not prevent the latter from using his trade mark in those countries, but he may himself be held as an infringer if he imports his own products marked with the mark which belongs to other persons in the eye of the law. A remedy to this condition is afforded by the right of priority granted by article 4 of the Convention, as we shall see in the next chapter.

In some countries, although registration is merely declaratory of ownership in the mark, a preliminary examination of the same is made by the administration. These countries are the United States, Canada, Finland, the Netherlands, and Peru. Under their laws, after a trade mark is registered, it may be cancelled on application by any person who can prove prior use of a mark identical with the registered one, or resembling it so closely that trade confusion may be caused. The preliminary examination in these countries, if it should take into account only the register of trade marks, is of little value, unless it discloses a previously registered identical or similar mark.

In the United States, especially, a very great number of trade marks in use in commerce are not registered. The examination at the Patent Office is necessarily incomplete and could easily be done away with.

V. Effects of Registration

§ 335. Old basis of property in trade marks. The legal effects of registration of trade marks depend on several considerations. Undoubtedly, the trade mark cannot be understood apart from a business the products of which it serves to distinguish and individualize. It is a device for maintaining and extending the trade of a concern. Its value springs from adoption and use by a manufacturer or trader. And the law, in protecting a trade mark, does not protect the material sign or mark itself as a creation or invention of the user, but the value that the use of that sign or mark in connection with the user's business has for him. The property, therefore, in a trade mark is created by adoption and use. No novelty, invention, or creation is the source of ownership.

In the matter of patents, society is interested in having the invention disclosed by the application for a patent, which involves a complete description of the invention. By such disclosure the "scientific and technical public are enabled to utilize the invention in searching for alternative solutions of the problem which will not be tributary to the patent, and in evolving entirely different inventions by the increase of the general fund of technical knowledge which the disclosure of the invention involves."[1] This social interest especially, and the general benefit to the public from a new discovery, explain why a patent is granted to the inventor who first files a patent application, and that therefore priority of application is, generally speaking, the basis of the right.

In the matter of designs or models, in most countries which assimilate them to inventions, the basis of the right is the same. In some countries, on the contrary, — according to a sounder view, in the writer's opinion, — the basis of the right is originality of creation and not registration. Designs or models are artistic creations, and the fruit of intellectual effort; nothing is taken away from society by a late disclosure or by non-registration; and therefore the registration should have no effect on the right in a design.[2]

Trade marks are neither inventions nor intellectual creations. Society is not anxious to have them disclosed and registered. In themselves, they are of no value whatsoever. It is only when used in connection with a business, and when they have established in the mind of the public an association with the user's products, that they are valuable. Even then they are valuable to the user only. The indirect benefit that designs or models cause by enriching the variety and beauty of industrial products does not result from trade marks.

Enough has been said to explain the fact that until fifty years ago the right in a trade mark was everywhere acquired by prior adoption and use, registration being only declaratory of property in a trade mark. The registered owner of a trade mark was only *prima facie* owner, but anyone could show a prior use of the trade mark and

1. Potts, *Patents: Invention and Method*, pp. 134, 135. 2. See *supra*, §§ 262 ff.

cause the cancellation of the registration. This is true no longer. In comparatively few countries is registration of a trade mark merely declaratory of property therein. In the great majority of countries, by registration property in the trade mark is acquired either immediately after a certificate of registration is delivered to the applicant, or after a period of years therefrom.

§ 336. **Ownership based on priority of registration.** This recent legislation is explained by modern commercial conditions in the world, which were alluded to earlier in this chapter. The market for any given industrial or commercial concern is no longer limited within definite boundaries. The facilities of communication and transportation, and all the other equipment of the business world, extends the possibilities of markets for any sort of goods all over the world. An industry or a trade may start with a market extending over a small part of a country's territory, then extend it to the whole territory of that country, and later reach any number of foreign countries.

If only the national territory be considered, the possibility of a business market being extended over the whole territory of the country raises the question of protection of the trade mark of such business in all such territory, and not in that part alone to which the business extends and in which its products are found for the time being. The public should be given notice of the user's claim on a trade mark. As the latter is not used in all the territory at the same time, and notice by use is not available, another kind of notice should be adopted. This is afforded by the registration of trade marks. Manufacturers or traders may consult the register, and avoid adopting a trade mark which is already adopted and used by another.

Thus it is no longer necessary that the products bearing a trade mark should be found in a part of the country's territory,—that is, that the trade mark should be used there, — in order that the person who first adopted and used that trade mark in the country may prevent others from using it. Prior use and adoption in the whole territory is predicated on the registration of the trade mark. When this is the condition of things, registration may well be considered as the basis of ownership in a trade mark. The law may require the person who first adopts and uses a trade mark in connection with his business, to register it; unless he does so, he cannot complain of anyone else's registering the same mark. He failed to give notice to the public of his claim, and another person cannot be blamed for ignoring it. Unless the latter acts fraudulently, by registration he acquires a property right in the trade mark. This is the law in Argentina, Bolivia, Chile, China, Cuba, Danzig, Dominican Republic, Germany, Greece, Guatemala, Haiti, Japan, Mexico, Norway, Panama, Paraguay, Peru, Poland, Sweden, and Venezuela.

§ 337. Ownership based on uncontested registration for a specified period. However, a person may have good reasons for neglecting to register a trade mark as soon as he adopts and uses it. He may use several trade marks in connection with his products, but may not realize immediately the psychological value, from a business point of view, of a trade mark. After the mark becomes valuable by continued use in the business, the person using it will consider registering it and protecting it from imitators and infringers. But by that time another may have registered the same mark. Should the latter always prevail, and the prior user be compelled to give up a valuable element of the goodwill of his business? The system according to which property in a trade mark is based on priority of registration may sometimes result in great injustice and abuse.

Another system of recent development is calculated to correct the defects of the earlier system. In many countries, the law recognizing the interest of the first user provides that registration is declaratory only in the beginning but becomes a basis of property in the trade mark at the expiration of a period after such registration. Within this period the prior user may prove his prior use. The registrant is considered only *prima facie* owner of the trade mark. This is the law in Austria, Australia, Brazil, Bulgaria, Ceylon, Czechoslovakia, Denmark, Esthonia, Great Britain, Hungary, Mexico, Morocco, New Zealand, Portugal, Salvador, the Serb-Croat-Slovene State, Spain, Syria and Lebanon, Uruguay, and Russia. The period at the expiry of which ownership is acquired by the registration is seven years in Great Britain, Australia, and New Zealand.[1] It is five

1. In Great Britain, before the Act of 1905, the period was five years, and the provision that the registration should be conclusive after five years, as construed by the courts, did not really make the registration conclusive. Sec. 41 of the Act of 1905 provides now that the registration can be invalidated after the seven-year period only if obtained by fraud, or if the mark is calculated to deceive or otherwise is not entitled to protection in a court of justice. See sec. 41 of the Act of 1905 (5 Edw. VII, c. 15); also Kerly (Underhay and Morgan), *The Law of Trade Marks and Trade Name*, p. 394, and cases cited therein.

years in Brazil, Ceylon, Morocco, Salvador, and Syria and Lebanon; three years in Austria, Esthonia, Mexico, and Spain; two years in Czechoslovakia, Hungary, the Serb-Croat-Slovene State, and Uruguay; one year in Bulgaria, Denmark, and Russia; and six months in Portugal.

In Great Britain and New Zealand a *bona fide* intention to use the mark in connection with the particular goods is a condition precedent to acquiring ownership in the trade mark. The want of such intention may be proved sometimes by non-use in fact for a long time.[1]

In the above two countries, as well as in Australia, Morocco, Salvador, Spain, and Syria and Lebanon, the conclusiveness of the registrant's right is subject to the sanctions for non-use after registration.[2]

In Great Britain, Australia, and New Zealand, a person who uses continuously a mark similar to a registered trade mark from a date anterior to the use or registration of the latter, may, even after the seven-year period, use or register his trade mark. The registrant cannot restrain the use or object to the registration.[3] This amounts to a reservation of personal possession of the trade mark and takes away much of the value of this system, since the question of prior use remains still open.[4]

It should be noted that, at the time the Convention of 1883 went into effect, in July, 1884, only in Great Britain and Portugal did the right of the registrant as against the prior user of the trade mark become conclusive at the expiration of a period after registration. This regime represents a new development of law caused by the above-mentioned new commercial conditions. It is interesting to see that in the French protectorate, Morocco, and the French mandated territory of Syria and Lebanon, the new legislation represents a change from the traditional French regime of declaratory registration of trade marks.[5]

1. Sec. 37 of the Trade Marks Act of 1905 (5 Edw. VII, c. 15). See also Kerly (Underhay and Morgan), *The Law of Trade Marks and Trade Name*, p. 346.

2. See *infra*, § 344.

3. Proviso to sec. 41 of the Trade Marks Act of 1905, as amended by the Act of 1919 (5 Edw. VII, c. 15, and 9 & 10 Geo. V, c. 79).

4. See comments to this effect by Allart, in a report to the International Association for the Protection of Industrial Property, *Annuaire* (1900), pp. 199–200.

5. The conclusiveness of the registrant's right in the trade mark after five years from registration in the two countries is conditioned on the public use of the registered trade mark during the five-year period within the country. Moreover, the prior user

In Austria, Czechoslovakia, and Hungary, the registrant's right in the trade mark may be disputed within the three- or two-year period from registration only if the prior user proves that at the time of registration the trade mark in question was considered in the interested commercial community as the distinctive sign of the plaintiff's products. Thus, in addition to prior use, public knowledge of it must be proved by the prior user.

§ **338. Prior use as basis of ownership in some countries.** In a number of countries registration is still only declaratory of property in the trade mark, as it used to be, generally, fifty years ago. These countries are Belgium, Canada, Colombia, Ecuador, Finland, France, Honduras, Italy, Luxembourg, Nicaragua, the Netherlands, Rumania, Switzerland, Tunis, Turkey, and the United States. With the exception of the United States, where the law of trade marks is quite exceptional, registration in these countries gives to the owner of a trade mark, on the one hand, a greater and more effective protection; and on the other hand, he acquires *prima facie* evidence of use, and consequently of property in the trade mark. Owners of unregistered trade marks are protected against infringement by the less efficacious protection of the law against unfair competition, and may always apply for the cancellation of the registered trade mark and prove their prior use.[1]

§ **339. Situation in the United States.** In the United States the situation is as follows: Congress has no power to legislate gen-

---

may still prevail, if he proves that, at the time of filing the application, the registrant knew of the mark of the prior user. In Syria and Lebanon, only documentary proof is allowed for this purpose.

The British system as to the effects of registration was recommended by the congress of the International Association for the Protection of Industrial Property as a model for a uniform law in the various countries. See *Annuaire* (1900), pp. 197 ff., 348 ff., 466, 490. The distinguished French writer, Eugène Pouillet, declared at this congress that at the congresses of 1878 and 1880 he was positively hostile to the British system. Since that time he had been converted by the manifest advantages of that system. *Ibid.*, p. 351. The Congress adopted the following resolution:

"Le droit à la marque doit être basé sur la priorité d'usage.

Toutefois, lorsque la marque a été déposée et employée régulièrement, publiquement et d'une manière continue depuis cinq ans, le dépôt ou enregistrement qui n'a, pendant ce délai, fait l'objet d'aucune contestation reconnue fondée, devient attributif de propriété."

See also G. Maillard's opinion, in *Travaux du Groupe Français de l'Association Internationale* (1919–1922), pp. 44–46.

1. See as to French law, Pouillet, *Traité des Marques*, 6th ed., pp. 185 ff. As to Belgium, Société La Française *c.* Van Wesemael, Tribunal of Gand, Jan. 21, 1913 (*Pasicrisie*, 1913, II, 202), and Bosch *c.* Société Générale des Eaux de Vittel, Court of Brussels, Feb. 15, 1909 (*Pasicrisie*, 1910, II, 148).

erally on the subject of trade marks. Acts of Congress relative to trade marks can be upheld as regulations of commerce only so far as the use of trade marks in commerce with foreign nations, or among the several states and with the Indian tribes, is concerned.[1] It was maintained in a previous chapter [2] that the United States has power to enter into treaties concerning trade marks in general, although Congress has no power to legislate generally on trade marks. The Act of March 3, 1881,[3] provided for registration of trade marks used in foreign commerce and with the Indian tribes. This act has been largely superseded by the Act of February 20, 1905,[4] which provides for the registration of trade marks used in foreign or interstate commerce. It has been amended in part by subsequent acts.[5] Thus trade marks used only in intrastate commerce are not registrable in the United States.[6] The mark must have been actually used in interstate or foreign commerce before an application for registration can be filed.[7] Registration constitutes *prima facie* evidence of ownership. The prior user of the trade mark may at any time apply for the cancellation of the registration.[8] The same protection and remedies for infringement are enjoyed by registered as by unregistered trade marks.[9] The acts have no effect on the domestic rights of anyone. The benefits of registration, besides the presumption of ownership, are these: the registrant is given the right to sue in the United States Courts; damages are increased, and the infringer's labels and the like are destroyed; importation of goods bearing an infringing mark may be prevented at ports of entry; and lastly, registration only gives the right to apply for registration in foreign countries of the same trade mark, in its original form, according to article 6 of the Convention.[10]

1. The Trade Mark Cases (1879), 100 U. S. 82.
2. See *supra*, § 96.
3. XXI *U. S. Stat. at Large*, 502.
4. XXXIII *U. S. Stat. at Large*, 724.
5. See *supra*, p. 495, note 1. Bills have been introduced in recent years in Congress for a coördination and modification of the Trade Mark acts of the United States. See H. R. 6248 (1926), and H. R. 13486, 69th Congress, 2d session (1927).
6. In many states of the Union, however, registration of trade marks is provided for by statute.
7. Sec. 2 of the Act of 1905 (XXXIII *U. S. Stat. at Large*, 724).
8. Secs. 13 and 16 of the Act of 1905 (XXXIII *U. S. Stat. at Large*, 724). Failure to oppose does not deprive the owner of the trade mark of his property right: Martin *v.* Martin & Bowne Co. (1906), 122 O. G. 734.
9. Sec. 23 of the Act of 1905 (XXXIII *U. S. Stat. at Large*, 724).
10. See Nims, *Law of Unfair Competition and Trade Marks*, 2d ed. (New York, 1917), pp. 424 ff.

This form of the law is not considered quite satisfactory. In recent years the whole scope of the acts of Congress was severely criticized.[1] It was found that the possibility of a registered mark's being declared invalid, by reason of the prior but local use of a similar mark, created an uncertainty of rights, and rendered possible the loss of great amounts of money spent in advertising a registered trade mark.[2] Besides, the requirement that a mark must have been first used in foreign or interstate commerce before an application for its registration may be filed at the Patent Office, and the delay of two months or more [3] needed for the examination and publication of the mark by the Patent Office, place American trade-mark owners at a disadvantage with regard to foreign competitors.[4]

It has been proposed that registration of all trade marks used in commerce among the several states or with foreign nations or with Indian tribes be made compulsory.[5] A bill introduced in Congress in 1926 and 1927 contained provisions for the mere deposit in the Patent Office *of any mark* (including a trade mark, symbol, label, package, configuration of goods, name, word, or phrase) used in commerce, and for the immediate issue of a certificate of such deposit, without previous examination, in order to procure protection of the mark in foreign countries. Also, the Commissioner was being directed to assemble for search purposes all marks, whether registered, filed for registration, deposited, or in actual use.[6]

VI. Rights of Registered Owner

§ 340. Extent of protection in the different countries. The law of each country determines the rights which are enjoyed by the registered owner of a trade mark. No distinction in this respect is

1. See Edward S. Rogers, "Some Suggestions concerning a Trade Mark Registration Act," in *Reports of the American Bar Association* (1920), XLV, 413.

2. See Hearings before the Committee on Patents, House of Representatives, 69th Congress, 1st session (1926), H. R. 6248, pp. 38 ff., and 2d session (1927), H. R. 13486, pp. 14 ff.

3. See statement to this effect by the Commissioner, Mr. Robertson, in the above Hearings (1926), H. R. 6248, p. 46.

4. Hearings before the Committee on Patents, House of Representatives, 69th Congress, 2d session (1927), H. R. 13486, pp. 2 ff.

5. *Reports of the American Bar Association* (1920), XLV, pp. 421–422.

6. Sec. 5 of the bills (1926), H. R. 6248 and (1927), H. R. 13486. The opposition to the bills was great on the part of conservative lawyers who were loath to change their habits. The drafting, although better in many respects than the existing statute, which is a model of bad and obscure draftsmanship, was not always very happy. Its sponsors, desirous of introducing into the trade-mark law of the United States certain features of European law, would seem to have been inadequately familiar with the latter.

generally made between nationals and foreigners. In most of the countries, infringers, besides being subject to civil liability, are also punished as criminals. In some countries, foreigners are bound to deposit the *cautio judicatum* in starting judicial proceedings against infringers, unless there is a convention to the contrary.

In the countries in which ownership in a trade mark is based on registration, proprietors of trade marks can be protected only if they have registered their marks. In the other countries, the right to sue infringers does not belong solely to registered owners of trade marks. Owners of unregistered trade marks are protected by the law of unfair competition, although less effectively. In the United States, the common law rights concerning trade marks and remedies for infringement are enjoyed by owners of unregistered trade marks.

Registered trade marks may generally be assigned, but only in connection with the business in which they are used. It is often required that notice of such assignment be given to the administration, in order that the assignment may be properly registered.

§ 341. Use of registered trade mark in a different business. Trade marks are generally registered for a special class or classes of goods. The applicant is required to indicate in his application the class or classes of goods in respect to which he desires to have his mark registered. His exclusive right to the use of the registered mark is limited to these classes. It has been seen [1] that the same limitation prevails generally in case of industrial designs or models. The injustice that this may cause to owners of designs is not likely to occur in the matter of trade marks. The latter are not artistic creations, valuable in themselves. Besides, many words or devices serving as trade marks are unique in their effectiveness from a business point of view, because of their appeal to the eye or ear, and their striking features. The use of such marks by a producer in connection with a particular class of goods should not prevent their use by other producers in connection with quite different classes of goods.[2] But if the latter's use is in any way harmful to the former, he may be protected by the law of unfair competition.[3]

1. See *supra*, § 266.
2. Cases decided to this effect in the United States are the following: Celluloid Manufacturing Co. *v.* Read (1891), 47 Fed. 712; Aunt Jemima Mills Co. *v.* Rigney & Co. (1916), 234 Fed. 804.
3. Aunt Jemima Mills Co. *v.* Rigney & Co. (1917), 247 Fed. 407.

VII. Duration of Protection

§ **342. The law of the various countries.** Inventions, utility models, and industrial designs or models are protected for limited times. Their exclusive ownership and use secure to their respective proprietors monopoly rights. They are presumed to be useful to society, and their general use would benefit the public. The same is not true as regards trade marks. In themselves they possess no value. They are made valuable to the user by long and continued use. No curtailment of the freedom of commerce or industry is involved in their protection. They are elements of goodwill of businesses, and as such they are as valuable and as important assets as tangible property. Their protection, therefore, should be perpetual, like that of any other property.

However, in almost all countries at the present time, the protection of registered trade marks lasts for a limited time. Unless a renewal of registration is applied for, the protection afforded by the registration ceases, and the effects of registration terminate at the expiry of a period. In the United States and in France, the common law protection in the former and the protection by the law of unfair competition in the latter continue at the end of that period, if the registration has not been renewed.[1] In the other countries, on the contrary, the trade marks, registration of which has not been renewed, either fall into the possession of the public, or may be registered by other people, usually some time after they have ceased to be protected.

This state of the law is again explained by the modern commercial conditions of the world. The trade mark is an element of the goodwill of a business. The user's property in the trade mark lasts as long as the business in which it is used continues. If the business ceases, so does the protection of the trade mark, because there is nothing more to be protected. In earlier times the continuation or ceasing of a business could easily be noticed and known in the restricted market over which it extended. This is no longer possible. As a notice to the public of the adoption and use of the trade mark should be given by registration, so, too, the continuation or ceasing of the business should be made known. This is effected by the re-

1. In the United States, if application for renewal is not filed before the registration expires, a new (original) application for its registration must be filed.

quirement for a renewal of registration after a certain period. If no such renewal is applied for, it is assumed that the business has been discontinued and that therefore there is no trade mark to be protected. The register is swept clear of marks which represent no business and need no protection. At the same time, other persons are allowed to use an effective sign, device, or mark in connection with their own business. It may also be that the mark in question has now become a descriptive term, and may be used by anyone.

The effects of registration last ten years in most of the countries: Argentina, Austria, Bolivia, Bulgaria, Chile, Colombia, Czechoslovakia, Danzig, Denmark, Finland, Germany, Greece, Guatemala, Honduras, Hungary, Luxembourg, Nicaragua, Norway, Panama, Paraguay, Peru, Poland, Portugal, Sweden, and Uruguay. In Great Britain, Australia, New Zealand, and Ceylon, the registration of a trade mark is for a period of fourteen years. It is for fifteen years in Brazil, Cuba, France, Rumania, Tunis, and Turkey; for twenty years in China, Ecuador, Haiti, Japan, Mexico, Morocco, the Netherlands, Salvador, Spain, Switzerland, and the United States; for twenty-five years in Canada (as to specific marks), and for thirty years in Venezuela. In Belgium, Canada (as to general marks),[1] and Italy, the registration is for an unlimited time. In the Dominican Republic, Esthonia, the Serb-Croat-Slovene State, Syria and Lebanon, and Russia, the applicant may elect between different periods of protection.[2] In Syria and Lebanon only, the maximum of protection cannot exceed sixty years.

VIII. Fees

§ 343. The state of municipal law. The property right in a trade mark not being a monopoly right and registration constituting, in substance, a notice to the public of the user's claim therein, the

1. In Canada, "general trade mark" means a trade mark used in connection with the sale of various articles in which a proprietor deals in his trade, business, occupation, or calling generally. "Specific trade mark" means a trade mark used in connection with the sale of class merchandise of a particular description. *Revised Statutes of Canada*, c. 63, sec. 4.

2. In the Dominican Republic, the applicant may elect for a period of 10, 15, or 20 years, with possibility always of renewal. In Esthonia, for periods between one and 10 years. In the Serb-Croat-Slovene State, protection by registration continues as long as the renewal tax is duly paid. In Syria and Lebanon, the election is between periods of 15, 30, 45, and 60 years. In Russia, the applicant may elect any period, but he must pay in advance a fee proportionate to the period of years elected; he may always apply for renewal of registration.

fees for registration and renewal should be as low as possible. Their amount should be proportioned to the service rendered, and to the expenses of the special administration entrusted with the registration of trade marks. No yearly tax should be payable for the maintenance of the right in a trade mark. Besides being unjust, such a tax is a cause of much waste of time and of many troubles.

In recent years registration fees for trade marks have become quite high.[1] In the United States, both registration and renewal fee are ten dollars. In Great Britain, one pound is paid on filing an application, and one more pound on registration; but for every additional class of goods, except one, an additional fee of one pound is payable. In France, on filing an application a fee of thirty francs, and on registration a fee of ten francs is paid; for each additional class of merchandise, an additional fee of ten francs is payable. In Germany, the registration and application fee is thirty Reichsmarks and the renewal fee one hundred; for each additional class of goods, a five-Reichsmark fee is payable. As may be seen, in these countries the fees are of nearly equal amount. In most of the other countries, the fees are generally equivalent to ten dollars.[2] In some they are less than five dollars,[3] while in others they are much higher than ten.[4]

In only a few countries an extra fee is payable for each additional class of goods for which a trade mark is registered. Besides France, Germany, and Great Britain, such extra fee is payable in Bolivia (five bolivios); Brazil (thirty dollars for the second, and twenty for every other class); Danzig (five florins); Norway (ten crowns); Poland (ten zloty); and Portugal (sixty escudos). The requirement of this extra fee is commendable, for it prevents the registration of a trade mark in many classes of goods in connection with which the applicant does not intend to use it.

In the countries in which the term of protection may be elected by

1. Greeley (*Foreign Patent and Trade Mark Laws*, p. 174) contends that about 1899 in most of the countries the registration fee, as well as the renewal fee, was less than $5.00.

2. For instance: Argentina, registration 50 and renewal 50 pesos; Chile, registration 50 and renewal 75 pesos; Honduras, 50 pesos; Italy, 56 lira; Cuba, $12.50; Bulgaria, 50 gold levas; Czechoslovakia, 50 crowns; and Japan, 30 yen.

3. Austria, 15 shillings; Belgium, 10 francs; Colombia, 10 pesos; Greece, 200 drachmas; Luxembourg, 10 francs; Morocco, 20 francs; Mexico, 20 pesos; Rumania, 20 francs; Switzerland, 20 francs; Tunis, 6 francs; and Uruguay 10 pesos.

4. Australia, 3 pounds; Brazil, 200 Brazilian dollars; Canada, 30 dollars for a general trade mark and 25 dollars for a specific trade mark; Sweden 100 crowns.

the applicant, — the Dominican Republic, Syria and Lebanon, Russia, — the registration fee is proportionate to the period of protection elected.

In Esthonia and the Serb-Croat-Slovene State, besides the registration fee, a tax is payable at the beginning of each year of the period of protection of the trade mark — one hundred marks in Esthonia and fifty dinars in the Serb-Croat-Slovene State. In Salvador a tax is due at the beginning of each period of five years of protection. In Spain, the registration fee of 155 pesetas is paid in four periods during the protection.

By virtue of the first paragraph of the new article 5*b* of the Convention, a three-month period of grace is allowed when a tax is due for the maintenance of the rights granted by the registration.[1]

Registration fees and annual taxes become a very serious expense for manufacturers and traders who desire to be protected and to register their trade marks in several countries. The international registration of trade marks at the Bureau of Berne, instituted by the Madrid Arrangement of 1890, permits to-day registration in twenty-two countries, through the international registration, with the payment of a single fee much less than the total sum of fees payable otherwise in all of these countries.[2]

IX. Non-use of Trade Marks

§ 344. Cancellation of registration or forfeiture of protection for non-use of trade marks. In almost all the countries a patentee is compelled by law to work his patent in the country in which he obtains it. Although, as we have shown,[3] no real interest is served by such working clauses of patent laws, they are explained by the public interest attached to an invention, and by the curtailment of the freedom of commerce and industry that is involved in the monopoly rights of the patentee. Neither of these considerations is applicable in the case of trade marks, as has been repeatedly urged earlier in this chapter. Consequently, it would seem that the proprietor of a registered trade mark should not be compelled to use his trade mark in the country within a definite period of time. The evil which might result from a continued protection of a trade mark after the business in connection with which it was used has been discontin-

1. See *infra*, § 402.
2. See *infra*, chap. XXVIII.
3. See *supra*, §§ 221–223.

ued, is taken care of by the ceasing of the protection in case no renewal of registration has been applied for.

Although, however, no public interest is served by the use of the trade mark, the registration of many trade marks which are not intended to be used may be prejudicial to legitimate competition. Indeed, sometimes manufacturers and merchants register several trade marks which present a resemblance to the eye or to the ear, intending to use only one of them and to prevent the use of the others by competing producers. By this means they aim at preventing competitors from adopting a trade mark similar to theirs and liable to cause confusion. These marks are called defense marks. On the other hand, registration is made of trade marks, wholly independent from other trade marks of the registrant but possessing certain qualities of appeal to the purchasing public, in the expectation that the registrant may use them at a later period. These trade marks are often called reserve marks.

The registration of both these sorts of trade marks is often legitimate. With the exception of the United States and Great Britain, in no country is registration of a trade mark subject to prior use or to intention to use it. Registration itself is considered an act of use even in the countries where it is declaratory of property in the trade mark.

In practice, such trade marks become obstructive. This is especially true with respect to word marks. The enormous multiplication of industries and products, and the great use of trade marks, have restricted very seriously the stock of registrable trade marks which are not yet exclusively owned by trade mark owners.[1] Under these conditions competition is impeded by unnecessary and obstructive registrations of trade marks which are not actually used on the market.

A number of countries have undertaken to prevent this evil by imposing on registrants the obligation to use the trade mark. These countries are: Brazil, China, Cuba, Dominican Republic, Equador, Great Britain, Honduras, Japan, Morocco, the Netherlands, New Zealand, Nicaragua, Rumania, Salvador, Spain, Switzerland, and the United States.

In the United States, applicants residing or located in a foreign

1. See Pouillet (Taillefer et Claro), *Traité des Marques*, pp. 145 ff. Also *Propriété Industrielle* (1921), p. 135.

country need not have used the proposed mark before they apply for registration. This use, which is required for persons residing in the United States, is replaced in the case of foreign applicants by the requirement that the trade mark must have been registered in the foreign country. However, any person who deems himself injured by the registration of a trade mark may apply to the Commissioner of Patents to cancel the registration thereof if the mark is not used by the registrant. No time limit is fixed by the law within which the mark must be used, but at any time registration may be cancelled if it appears to the examiner that the mark is not used.[1]

In Great Britain and New Zealand a registered trade mark may, on application to the court of any person aggrieved, be taken off the register in respect of any of the goods for which it is registered, on either of two grounds:[2] (*a*) that it was registered without any *bona fide* intention to use the same in connection with such goods, and there has in fact been no *bona fide* use of the same in connection therewith; (*b*) that there has been no *bona fide* use of such trade mark in connection with such goods during the five years immediately preceding this application. The proprietor of the trade mark, however, may show in either case that such non-use is due to special circumstances in the trade, and not to any intention not to use or to abandon such trade mark in respect to such goods.

In China and Rumania, the protection of a trade mark ceases *ipso facto* with the discontinuance of the business in connection with which it is used. In Rumania, moreover, it ceases with the stopping of the production of the industrial product to which the mark is affixed. In Morocco, on application of the state or of any interested party, the registration may be cancelled if the owner of the trade mark fails to show a *bona fide* use in Morocco or abroad. In Nicaragua, the trade mark is considered as abandoned if the business in connection with which it is used has been discontinued, or if the manufacturing of the goods to which it is affixed has been suspended for more than a year.

In the Dominican Republic, Cuba, Ecuador, Honduras, and Salvador, the protection of a registered trade mark is forfeited in case the trade mark has not been used within a year from registration.

1. Sec. 13 of the Act of 1905 (XXXIII *U. S. Stat. at Large*, 724).
2. Sec. 37 of the Trade Marks Act of 1905 (5 Edw. VII, c. 15). See Kerly (Underhay and Morgan), *The Law of Trade Marks and Trade Name*, p. 346.

In Ecuador, foreign trade marks are not included in this provision of the law. In Honduras, reëstablishment is possible on payment of a new fee. In Japan, a suspension of the use of the trade mark for three years, and in Salvador for one year, causes forfeiture of the protection. In Brazil, the Netherlands, Spain, and Switzerland, a similar forfeiture is provided for by the law in case of non-use of the trade mark for three consecutive years.[1]

In Germany also, where the law imposes no obligation to use the trade mark, and defense marks are recognized, the Reichsgericht has limited the right of owners of such marks whenever they defeat lawful competition or are used contrarily to good commercial morals.[2]

At the Conference of The Hague a provision was adopted and inserted in article 5 restricting the sanction for non-use of trade marks.[3]

X. Conclusions

§ **345.** Although much progress has been made in the trade-mark law of the different countries since the constitution of the Union, many diversities still exist. Mere assimilation of foreigners to nationals would not suffice to protect adequately foreign trade marks. The diversities of the law as to what may constitute a lawful trade mark, and the acquisition of ownership in trade marks by registration in a great number of countries, would prevent foreigners in many cases from claiming protection. Besides, the necessity for lodging applications for registration in many countries, the formalities, appointments of attorneys and agents, and the fees and expenses pertinent thereto, would be very inconvenient and burdensome to foreigners. However, the specific provisions of the Convention and the Madrid Arrangement supplement the national treatment of foreigners. These are considered in the following chapters.

1. On defense marks in Switzerland, see C. Saas, "Über Defensivzeichen," in *Revue Suisse de Jurisprudence* (1912), p. 318.

2. Goldina Case (1925), 111 *Entsch. Reichsg. Zivils.* 197; Vox-, Schallplatten- und Sprechmaschinen A.-G. *w.* Deutsche Grammophon A.-G. (1926), 114 *Entsch. Reichsg. Zivils.* 360.

3. See *infra*, § 400.

XI. Statistics

§ **346.** The statistical tables appearing below show the increase of trade marks up to the present time.[1]

The number of trade marks registered is subject to great variation from year to year. Even the average of successive series of years

TABLE I

Registration of Trade Marks in the Last Century

Countries		1883	1890	1895	1900
Argentina	*1876–1899* 8,074	79	185	706	....
Austria	*1859–1899* 33,353	....	....	....	4,223
Belgium	*1879–1899* 10,638	330	475	693	720
Brazil	*1885–1898* 2,695	....	131	167	347
Denmark	*1880–1898* 2,619	148	124	199	281
France	*1857–1899* 165,337	3,831	7,302	7,936	8,922
Germany	*1895–1899* 41,551	....	....	10,958	5,581
Great Britain	*1876–1899* 93,362	4,241	6,014	2,821	3,223
Greece	*1893–1899* 327	....	....	....	....
Hungary	*1859–1898* 36,706	....	2,234	2,823	3,688
Italy	*1871–1899* 4,155	86	166	220	370
Japan	*1884–1898* 11,401	....	583	923	1,769
Netherlands	*1881–1899* 8,625	....	....	465	809
Portugal	*1883–1899* 3,717	9	96	....	230
Serbia	*1886–1898* 532	....	41	57	9
Spain	.....	....	....	....	508
Sweden	*1885–1898* 4,588	....	201	279	328
Switzerland	*1865–1899* 11,708	283	514	765	1,119
United States	*1870–1899* 33,956	902	1,415	1,829	1,721

1. These tables are made from the data communicated to the International Bureau by the various administrations, and published in the *Propriété Industrielle* (1900), pp. 155 ff.; (1902), p. 16; (1912), p. 179; (1916), p. 112; (1924), pp. 168 and 260; (1925), p. 268; (1926), p. 276; (1927), p. 232.

TABLE II

REGISTRATION OF TRADE MARKS IN THE DIFFERENT COUNTRIES IN RECENT YEARS

Countries	1910	1913	1922	1923	1924	1925	1926
Australia	1,190	1,571	1,984	2,111	1,801	2,029	1,973
Austria	7,926	8,609	6,261	5,439	5,630	4,207	4,260
Belgium	1,614	1,606	2,857	2,415	2,760	3,042	2,188
Brazil	...	1,283	3,058	4,145	1,518	449	...
Bulgaria	...	...	342	298	350	472	422
Canada	...	...	...	...	2,240	2,097	1,902
Cuba	539	467	1,002	1,112	1,081	...	1,540
Czechoslovakia	...	...	5,566	4,537	4,473	4,139	4,634
Danzig	...	...	2,339	451	422	222	209
Denmark	648	864	1,195	1,239	1,264	1,182	1,186
Dominican Republic	54	25	134	136	...	...	...
Esthonia	...	...	...	611	555	526	341
Finland	...	...	794	954	790	828	656
France	16,163	21,239	17,066	18,010	15,679	16,753	15,139
Germany	13,500	17,300	18,620	13,240	16,640	19,800	16,000
Great Britain	5,722	5,071	7,099	7,794	7,968	7,464	7,774
Greece	...	...	...	508	811	675	595
Hungary	9,872	11,082	2,082	2,495	2,511	1,193	1,532
Italy	700	1,590	960	1,810	4,380	3,650	1,590
Japan	4,962	5,661	7,820	5,504	4,822	11,725	11,023
Latvia	...	...	...	...	...	574	684
Luxembourg	...	...	413	369	231	137	233
Mexico	1,093	...	1,283	...	1,151	1,207	1,057
Morocco	...	...	235	234	241	233	179
Netherlands	1,599	1,566	2,046	2,015	2,079	2,182	2,182
New Zealand	629	572	560	832	1,018	1,026	599
Norway	595	1,010	839	1,184	1,131	1,001	1,033
Poland	...	...	...	...	2,538	8,192	3,411
Portugal	890	785	3,106	1,259	1,679	888	1,045
Serb-Croat-Slovene State	79	...	1,279	1,110	514	435	459
Spain	1,571	1,646	2,127	4,240	2,413	3,443	3,627
Sweden	1,020	1,194	1,275	1,256	1,358	1,339	1,208
Switzerland	1,969	2,216	2,245	2,218	2,409	2,807	2,732
Syria and Lebanon	...	...	...	...	...	238	215
Trinidad and Tobago	...	...	...	...	...	72	89
Tunis	90	141	206	243	177	222	201
Turkey	...	...	...	...	...	446	697
United States	4,239	5,065	14,992	16,725	15,749	13,840	19,246

would not give a precise idea of the progress of registration. Yet from the numbers appearing on the first two statistical tables, the enormous development of trade-mark registration is clearly seen. Thus, in Austria from 1859 to 1899, that is, in a period of forty years, the trade marks registered numbered about 33,000; in the same country in the five years from 1922 to 1926, 26,000 trade marks were registered. In Belgium and Denmark, the progress is constant and very great. In France, in the last five-year period, 82,000 trade marks were registered, or about one half of the 165,000 registered in a period of forty-two years, from 1857 to 1899. The same may be said of Great Britain, where the number of registrations presents also a constant progress. In Germany, in the two five-year periods of 1895 to 1899 and 1922 to 1926, the trade marks registered numbered 41,551 and 84,300 respectively, which represents a more than one hundred per cent increase in the last period.

Tables III and IV bring out more prominently the data of the second table. They give the yearly average of the whole number of registrations of trade marks in the five-year period 1922 to 1926, and the average to a million inhabitants. Germany leads the other countries in the yearly average, and is followed closely by France and the United States.[1] In respect to the average of registrations to a million inhabitants, Danzig takes the first place, then Luxembourg, and then Austria and Switzerland. France is far ahead of Germany in this respect, while Great Britain and the United States follow at some distance.

These tables should be compared with Table V, which shows the registration of foreign trade marks in the countries in which information on this point is available. For Great Britain and the United States there is no available information. It is interesting to note that in the great industrial and commercial countries, the percentage of foreign trade marks is very low, and has always been so. In France, to every hundred national trade marks six or seven foreign are registered. In Germany, the percentage decreased from 6 in 1900 to 5 in 1910, and to 2.3 in 1925. In Japan it has always been 12 per cent. In Spain, also, it is very low. On the other hand, in Brazil, Canada, Denmark, and Sweden, foreign trade marks are as numerous as national ones. In Italy, the Netherlands, and Norway, the number of foreign trade marks registered did not keep pace with the increase of the national trade marks.

1. It should be recalled, however, that in the United States less than one half of the marks in use are registered in the Patent Office.

TABLE III

AVERAGE REGISTRATION OF TRADE MARKS IN THE YEARS 1922 TO 1926

Countries	Number of registrations	Countries	Number of registrations
Australia	1,979	Japan	8,175
Austria	5,159	Latvia	629
Belgium	2,652	Luxembourg	276
Brazil	2,292	Mexico	1,174
Bulgaria	377	Morocco	224
Canada	2,079	Netherlands	2,100
Cuba	1,184	New Zealand	807
Czechoslovakia	4,670	Norway	1,037
Danzig	728	Poland	4,711
Denmark	1,213	Portugal	1,595
Dominican Republic	135	Serb-Croat-Slovene State	759
Esthonia	508	Spain	3,170
Finland	804	Sweden	1,267
France	16,529	Switzerland	2,482
Germany	16,860	Syria and Lebanon	226
Great Britain	7,620	Trinidad and Tobago	80
Greece	647	Tunis	210
Hungary	1,962	Turkey	571
Italy	2,478	United States	16,110

TABLE IV

AVERAGE REGISTRATION IN THE YEARS 1922 TO 1926 TO A MILLION INHABITANTS

Countries	Number of registrations	Countries	Number of registrations
Danzig	1,886	Finland	227
Luxembourg	1,026	Sweden	209
Austria	790	Great Britain	172
Switzerland	630	Poland	161
New Zealand	576	Dominican Republic	150
Esthonia	458	Spain	145
France	406	Japan	136
Norway	391	United States	135
Australia	359	Greece	103
Denmark	354	Tunis	97
Cuba	346	Mexico	82
Czechoslovakia	342	Turkey	75
Latvia	340	Bulgaria	68
Belgium	329	Serb-Croat-Slovene State	63
Netherlands	283	Syria and Lebanon	62
Portugal	283	Italy	61
Germany	270	Brazil	58
Hungary	234	Morocco	52
Canada	231		

TABLE V

REGISTRATION OF FOREIGN TRADE MARKS

Countries	1890			1900			1910			1925		
	National	Foreign	Per cent Foreign	National	Foreign	Per cent Foreign	National	Foreign	Per cent Foreign	National	Foreign	Per cent Foreign
Australia	....	....	....	3,589	634	17.6	....	....	....	1,189	840	70
Austria	....	....	....	....	....	....	6,768	1,158	17	3,762	945	25
Belgium	....	....	....	....	....	....	....	....	....	2,350	692	29
Brazil	83	48	57	289	58	20	....	....	....	202	247	122
Canada	....	....	....	241	180	74	....	....	....	1,128	969	85
Denmark	....	....	....	144	137	95	304	344	113	612	570	93
France	6,813	489	7	8,398	524	6	15,096	1,067	7	15,698	1,055	6
Germany	....	....	....	5,241	340	6	12,816	684	5	19,345	455	2.3
Greece	....	....	....	....	....	....	....	....	....	270	405	150
Hungary	101	2,051	2,030	444	3,244	73	1,037	8,835	851	982	211	21
Italy	85	81	95	212	158	74	392	308	78	2,987	663	22
Japan	....	....	....	1,577	192	12	4,401	561	12	10,426	1,299	12
Mexico	....	....	....	....	....	....	769	324	42	....	....	....
Netherlands	....	....	....	540	269	48	1,024	575	56	1,611	571	35
New Zealand	....	....	....	144	165	114	207	422	202	303	723	238
Norway	....	....	....	38	158	415	260	330	126	490	511	104
Poland	....	....	....	....	....	....	....	....	....	1,476	6,716	455
Portugal	72	24	33	200	30	15	707	183	25	624	264	42
Serb-Croat-Slovene State	....	....	....	....	....	....	....	....	....	191	244	127
Spain	....	....	....	....	....	....	1,489	82	5.5	3,337	97	2.9
Sweden	135	66	48.8	170	158	92	669	353	52	753	586	77
Switzerland	373	41	10.9	890	229	25	1,507	462	30	2,348	459	19

CHAPTER XXIII

THE RIGHT OF PRIORITY, AND THE PROTECTION OF TRADE MARKS AT INTERNATIONAL EXHIBITIONS

§ 347. Need of right of priority in the matter of trade marks. Property in a trade mark is acquired by prior use in but few countries. In many countries, prior registration attributes property in a trade mark, and in others registration is declaratory for a period of time, and becomes later conclusive proof of ownership. This diversity in the laws of the various countries affects foreigners primarily. It is relatively easy and practical for nationals, or persons having their commercial or industrial establishments in a country, to register their trade marks in that country as soon as they adopt them and begin their use. It is not easy for the same persons to register their trade marks in foreign countries with the same haste. On the one hand, the expenses, fees, formalities, and the need for retaining agents or attorneys in the foreign countries, are a handicap and require time. On the other hand, the usefulness of securing protection in foreign countries appears only with the extension of the business of the persons in question in those countries. Such extension is, again, a question of time.

If foreigners fail to register their trade marks in other countries as soon as they adopt and use them in their own country, they may be denied registration and protection later. Indeed, in the countries where by registration property is acquired, trade marks identical with, or closely resembling foreign marks may have been registered in the interval, and the registrants are conclusively owners of the trade marks in question. In the countries where registration is only declaratory of ownership, it is difficult for foreigners to prove their prior use, inasmuch as in most of the countries the prior use which may be availed of against the registrant is that in the domestic market.

The Convention of 1883, by its article 4, affords a real protection to foreigners in this respect by the right of priority provided for therein.

§ 348. Provision of article 4 of the Convention in respect to trade marks. Any person who has duly deposited an application for registration of a trade mark enjoys, for the purpose of deposit in other countries, a right of priority for a certain period. Until the last conference of The Hague, this period was four months; at this conference, it was extended to six months. The proposals for the extension of the period to twelve months, as in the case of patents, were defeated at Washington [1] and at The Hague.[2]

The interpretation and study of article 4 of the Convention in respect to patents may be applied *mutatis mutandis* to trade marks, particularly with reference to the nature of the right of priority,[3] the persons who may claim this advantage,[4] and the requirements as to prior deposit.[5] The right of priority operates as a warning on the part of the first registrant that he may apply for registration in the other countries of the Union. The fact of the prior registration is a legal defense operative at the subsequent applications for registration of the same mark by the first registrant or his assigns, if these subsequent applications are filed within the six-month period. The rules as to the computation of the period inserted in article 4 at the Conference of The Hague apply in the case of trade marks as well as in that of patents.[6] The day of first deposit is not included in the period.[7]

The new section (*d*) added to article 4 at the last conference is also applicable to trade marks. Thus, any person desiring to take

1. *Actes de la Conférence de Washington*, pp. 91, 95, 275, 307.
2. *Actes de la Conférence de La Haye*, pp. 223–224, 334, 426–427.
3. See *supra*, § 165.
4. See *supra*, §§ 166, 167.
5. See *supra*, §§ 168–173.
6. See *supra*, § 178.
7. It was so decided by the Austrian Minister of Public Works in a case concerning a claim of priority for the registration of a trade mark, on Sept. 22, 1910; see *Propriété Industrielle* (1911), p. 89.

advantage of the priority of a previous deposit is bound to make a declaration giving particulars as to the date of such deposit and the country in which it was made. Each country will determine for itself the latest time at which such declaration may be made. In most of the countries it is required that it be made at the lodging of the application for registration.[1]

Priority may be claimed at the subsequent filings for the same trade mark that has already been deposited for registration in a country of the Union. The difficulties that the question of identity of the two applications may cause in the case of patents [2] are for the most part non-existent in the case of trade marks. In few countries are specifications and claims required which would have to be drawn and defined differently according to the procedure of each country. In most cases trade marks speak for themselves. If a copy of the mark adopted and registered in one country is produced in the other countries the identity is assured.

§ 349. First filing may take place in any country of the Union. Besides the advantage of right of priority, a further advantage is secured to trade marks by virtue of article 6 — that of validation in the whole territory of the Union. The coexistence of the two articles in the Convention has caused some misgivings as to the conditions of application of article 4. The latter concerns trade marks as well as patents, industrial designs or models, and utility models. Article 6 provides only for trade marks, and its provisions are more restrictive. The question then is whether the restrictions of article 6 shall apply to the provisions of article 4. Two of these restrictions are material here. The advantages of article 6 may be claimed only for marks *registered*, and only if they have been registered in the *country of origin* of the applicant. On the contrary, according to article 4, the right of priority may be claimed by any person who has *deposited an application* for registration *in one of the contracting countries*.

While in the case of patents, utility models, and industrial designs or models, the first filing may have taken place in any of the countries of the Union, and not necessarily the country of origin of the applicant,[3] should this be otherwise in the case of trade marks? There is no reason for imposing a restriction in the case of trade

1. See as to the conditions and formalities for claiming the right of priority according to art. 4, *supra*, §§ 179–185.
2. See *supra*, § 188.
3. See *supra*, § 173.

marks. The provisions of articles 4 and 6 are quite distinct and unrelated. The one concerns the preservation of the property in a trade mark against acts occurring in the interval between the two filings. The other deals with the admission for registration of trade marks registered in the country of origin of the applicant although they are not deemed to satisfy, as to their features, the requirements of the laws of the other countries.

There is a reason for this restriction in article 6. It aims at defeating the attempt of persons who might adopt a trade mark not registrable under the law of their country of origin, and, by registering it in a foreign country, claim admission for registration in their own country by virtue of article 6. Such a risk does not exist in the application of article 4. The only thing a person may claim under the latter article is that all contingencies in the interval between the two applications should be without effect on the right of the applicant in the trade mark. If the applicant claims more than this, if he claims that the mark should be admitted in the form in which it was deposited in the foreign country, then article 6 enters into consideration, and this latter claim will be recognized only in case the prior deposit took place in the country of origin of the applicant. So long as the applicant is ready to abide by the law of the country in question as to the validity of the mark, that is, whether or not the said mark has the exterior features prescribed by the law of the country where the latter application is lodged, the restriction that the first application should be filed in the country of origin is inoperative. In such case only article 4 comes into play, and this article contains no such restriction.[1]

§ 350. First application need not result in registration of trade mark before right of priority may be claimed. By the same reasoning, we may conclude that the second restriction of article 6 — that the trade mark should be *registered* in the country of origin before it may be admitted for registration in its original exterior

1. Pouillet, *Traité des Marques*, 6th ed., p. 520; Pouillet et Plé, *Convention d'Union*, p. 45; Pelletier et Vidal-Naquet, *Convention d'Union*, pp. 197–198, *semble*; Pillet, *Régime International*, p. 357, *contra*. These writers maintain an opinion in opposition to the one advanced in the text. They all wrote before the coming into effect of the text revised at Washington, and therefore before the word "déposée" in article 6 was changed into "enregistrée." This may explain somewhat their position. Lemke, *Gewerblicher Rechtsschutz* (1907), p. 263; Frieger, *Warenzeichnungen*, p. 508; L. Brun, *Les Marques de Fabrique et de Commerce*, p. 366; Osterrieth und Axster, *Pariser Konvention*, pp. 69 and 91–92, *accord*.

form in the other countries of the Union — does not apply when only a right of priority is claimed under article 4 of the Convention. The latter requires only that a person shall have duly filed an application for registration. From the day following such filing, the period of priority begins. The right of priority may be claimed on the subsequent filing of an application for registration of the same mark. So far as the claim is limited to a legal defense against the acts which may have occurred in the interval, for instance, the filing of another application or general use of the mark by the public, and so forth, the claim should be recognized and given effect.[1]

At the Conference of The Hague, on the proposal of the Belgian delegation,[2] the following provision was inserted in article 6 of the Convention, forming its fifth paragraph:

> Le bénéfice de la priorité reste acquis aux dépôts de marques effectués dans le délai de l'article 4, même lorsque l'enregistrement dans le pays d'origine n'intervient qu'après l'expiration de ce délai.

It should be noted that this provision is inserted in article 6, and can apply only to applications for registration which claim the benefit of article 6, that is, the validation of trade marks in their original form. This provision proves *a fortiori* that the trade mark need not have been admitted to registration when merely a right of priority is claimed under article 4. In respect to article 6, its benefits may be claimed if the mark is registered either before or after the period of priority. Thus registration in the country of origin is a condition precedent to the application of article 6. This is not true in respect to article 4. The benefit of the right of priority alone is not affected by the success or failure of the foreign application.

§ 351. Effects of right of priority. The right of priority provided for by article 4 of the Convention has the effect of making the first

1. So held by the German Patent Office, Oct. 23, 1906; see *Propriété Industrielle* (1907), p. 118. However, the Board of Trade of Brazil held that proof of prior filing in a foreign country (the United States) was not sufficient in order that an application within the period of priority could be accepted in Brazil, and that the presentation of a certificate of registration abroad was necessary. See *Patent and Trade Mark Review* (1920), XVIII, 177.

2. *Actes de la Conférence de La Haye*, p. 451. This delegation explained that the purpose of the provision is to do away with the difficulties met by applicants of countries in which the preliminary examination of the trade mark lasts longer than the period of priority. It mentioned the case of the American trade mark "Eversharp," registered in the United States two years after lodging. At that time the period of priority had expired, and the Belgian tribunal before which the question was brought denied the benefit of the right of priority. The International Chamber of Commerce made a proposal similar to that of Belgium. See *ibid.*, p. 452.

filing of an application for the registration of a trade mark equivalent to applications in all the countries of the Union, so far as the right of the applicant is concerned. The registration in the other countries cannot take place without filing an application in each of them; but, if such application is filed within the six-month period, the applicant may claim property in the trade mark from the date of his first filing, in any of the countries of the Union. Consequently, all contingencies arising in the interval, as article 4, section (*b*), expressly provides, shall not invalidate the subsequent deposits. Article 4, section (*b*), mentions as such contingencies a filing by another person and the use of the trade mark. But the enumeration in this provision is merely illustrative.[1]

After a trade mark has been filed for registration in one country, and before it is filed within the six-month period in another, the following things might happen.

(1) In countries in which ownership is based on priority of registration, the same trade mark, or one closely resembling it, might have been deposited for registration by another person. Without the right of priority the foreign applicant would have no remedy. The property in the trade mark would be acquired by the domestic registrant who is a prior registrant. By virtue of the right of priority, the foreign applicant will prevail. This is the most important effect of the right of priority in the matter of trade marks.

(2) In countries in which registration is either merely declaratory of property in the trade mark, or is not the basis of property until the expiry of a period of years, an identical or closely resembling trade mark might be adopted and used, or registered, by a third person. Registration in such countries gives at most a presumption of ownership of the trade mark. Such presumption may be destroyed by proof of prior use. With the exception of this burden of proof, there is no difference in the position of the foreign applicant, whether the trade mark in question is registered, or is only used by a third person. In both cases there is a question of prior use to be settled. But without the right of priority settlement might not be possible, for in many countries only use within the country is considered in determining priority. The foreign applicant may not have used his trade mark in the country in question. The third person may have usurped it, before it appeared on the domestic market.

1. Pillet, *Régime International*, p. 358,

By virtue of the right of priority proof of use on such market is unnecessary.

(3) The foreign applicant's trade mark may have been used generally in the other countries, and have become what is called in Germany a free mark, or a mark in the possession of the public. Again, with the advantage of the right of priority, the above fact does not deprive the foreign applicant of his property in the trade mark. On his application within the period of priority, these acts lose their legal effect, and his property in the trade mark is recognized. Without the right of priority the foreign applicant would be without remedy.

§ 352. **Reservation of rights of third parties.** The effects of the right of priority are subject to the reservation of the rights of third parties, according to article 4. The history of this provision and its interpretation by various conferences of revision is traced in a previous chapter.[1] It is noted there that the original proposal for inserting this reservation was made by the delegate of the Netherlands, to provide for the case of the domestic manufacturer who might file his trade mark only in his own country before the first filing by a foreign manufacturer in another country on which a right of priority would be based. Such reservation became unnecessary after the addition of the second paragraph of article 4 by the Conference of 1880, which limited the effects of the right of priority to events during the period of priority.

The attempts to strike out the reservation from article 4 have been frustrated, and a new interpretation of it was given by the conferences of Brussels and Washington; namely, that the reservation refers to the right of personal possession of an invention recognized in certain cases in persons of good faith in some countries. It may be maintained, then, that the reservation is of no effect in the case of trade marks. Besides, in most of the countries (that is, those where registration is permanently declaratory and those in which it is so only for a period of years), priority of use being the basis of property in the trade mark, the reservation is meaningless.

However, the usurpation of foreign marks which is made possible by the acquisition of ownership through registration in many countries has raised the question whether a right of personal possession in favor of the proprietor of the foreign mark would not be equitable

1. See *supra*, §§ 200, 201.

and just. This cannot possibly be brought under the reservation of article 4, because the personal possession to be assured in a trade mark is not in favor of third parties in the country of importation of the trade mark, but, on the contrary, in favor of the foreign proprietors themselves after the lapse of the period of priority. This question is considered in a subsequent section of this chapter.[1]

§ **353. Liability for infringements during period of priority.** During the period of priority, and before the subsequent filing of the application for registration of a trade mark, third persons may have used, and thereby infringed, the foreign trade mark. In the case of patents, it is generally admitted that no liability in the above case is incurred by third persons.[2] This is so because the rights of a patentee do not extend beyond the territory of the state that grants the patent. Until the subsequent applications for patents are filed, there is no notice to the public of the claim of the applicant. The first filing, from which the period of priority begins, is only a warning that a claim may be made subsequently, and serves to preserve the applicant's rights and no more.

In the case of trade marks, a distinction should be made between the countries in which property in a trade mark is acquired by registration immediately, and the countries in which property is acquired only by prior use or after a period following the registration. In the former, notice to the public is given only by application for registration, or by its advertisement, or by registration. There is no property in a trade mark which may be infringed before that time. The situation, therefore, is similar to that of patentable inventions. There is no liability for the use of the trade mark in the interval. On the contrary, in the latter countries priority of use is the basis of property, but registration is the basis for claiming the protection of registered trade marks. Before such registration or application for it within the period of the right of priority, the trade mark which has only been deposited abroad for registration is not a registered trade mark, and therefore cannot be protected as such. It may be protected by the common law in Great Britain[3] and the United

1. See *infra*, § 354.
2. See *supra*, § 194.
3. In Great Britain no action for infringement of an unregistered trade mark may be brought, although actions for passing off are possible. Section 42 of the Trade Marks Act of 1905 (5 Edw. VII, c. 15). See also Kerly (Underhay and Morgan), *The Law of Trade Marks and Trade Name*, p. 686.

States, or by the law of unfair competition in other countries, under the conditions of the law of each country.[1]

§ 354. Filing after expiration of period of priority. A person who has filed his trade mark in one country of the Union may fail to file it in the other countries within the period of priority. This is very likely to happen, for the period is short and a person's business may not have been so extended to foreign countries as to cause him to register his trade mark in those countries promptly upon adoption and filing in his own country. In France, it has been disputed in theory whether such a person may apply for registration after the expiration of the period of priority.[2] But, there should be no doubt as to this. Article 4 of the Convention provides for a special advantage over and above the mere national treatment stipulated in article 2. When that special advantage cannot be claimed, the provision of article 2 assimilating foreigners to nationals is controlling. In other words, the foreign registrant's application will be treated as if no right of priority was available at all. Consequently, the applicant's right in the trade mark will be recognized and given effect, unless the property in the mark has been acquired by a third person in the meantime, or unless the public has become possessed of the mark, which thus has lost its character of distinctiveness and is no longer valid.[3]

The first may happen in countries in which ownership is acquired by registration. If in these countries the same trade mark was registered in the name of another, the foreign registrant has no remedy. In other countries, the question whether the foreign registrant may cause the prior registration to be cancelled depends on proof of priority of use. If the trade mark in question appears in the market

1. Pillet, *Régime International*, pp. 360–361; Pouillet, *Traité des Marques*, 6th ed., p. 522; Pelletier et Vidal-Naquet, *Convention d'Union*, pp. 199–200.

2. See Pelletier et Vidal-Naquet, *Convention d'Union*, p. 201.

3. Pillet, *Régime International*, pp. 361 ff.; Pelletier et Vidal-Naquet, *Convention d'Union*, pp. 200 ff.; Pouillet, *Traité des Marques*, 6th ed., pp. 523–524. So held by the Court of Appeals of Brussels, July 27, 1903, in Menning *c.* Blackman-Ventilating Co., Limited (*Propriété Industrielle*, 1904, p. 84), and Feb. 3, 1909, in Mareschall et Cie (*Propriété Industrielle*, 1909, p. 76); the Commercial Tribunal of Brussels, May 18, 1909, in Chassaing et Cie *c.* Fuhr (*La Jurisprudence Commerciale de Bruxelles*, 1909, p. 392); the Tribunal de Liège, July 17, 1909, and Cour de Liège, March 2, 1910, in M. P. et D.V. Joulastane *c.* Grahs et Lovinfosse (*Jurisprudence de la Cour de Liège*, 1910, p. 109). Also by the French courts: Tribunal de Lille, Dec. 15, 1890, in Rinskof *c.* Henry et Siem (1891, *Clunet*, 1214), confirmed by the Court of Douai on May 12, 1891 (1893, *Clunet*, 883). So held in the United States: Deitsch Bros. *v.* Loonen (1912), 39 Ap. D.C. 114.

of one of these countries before the intervening registrant's adoption and use of the mark, the registration in the latter's name will be cancelled. But if the trade mark did not so appear in the market of such country, will the use of the mark abroad be taken into consideration in determining the question of priority? French courts have held in the negative,[1] while Swiss and Greek courts have decided in the affirmative.[2] Belgian decisions are conflicting.[3] In the United States, failure to file the application within the period of the right of priority does not deprive a foreign applicant of any rights. His application will be treated under the general provisions of the statute (sections 1 and 2). Under these provisions the prior use of the mark in a foreign country is not taken into consideration against one who has first used the mark in the United States.[4]

The question whether a trade mark has become a free mark and is in the possession of the public is a question of fact and of the law of each country. Usually the use of the mark by a single party does not make the mark free. A generalized use by third parties must have existed, and the owner, knowing of such use, must have failed to take measures to stop it.[5] In the United States, an abandonment of the mark by its owner must be proved by clear and convincing evidence that the right claimed has been relinquished. "A mark will never be held abandoned, unless a clear intention to do so appears." [6]

The question of the protection of trade marks after the expiration

1. Parent *c.* Bergmann, Cour de Lyon, July 1, 1885 (1886, *Clunet*, 339); Monier *c.* Frutera Hesperides, Court of Appeals of Paris, Oct. 16, 1924 (*Propriété Industrielle*, 1926, p. 79).

2. The Swiss Federal Court held repeatedly to this effect: Gebrüder Schneider *g.* Erste Oesterreichische . . . (1900, 26 *Arrêts Trib. Féd.*, II, 644); Kuenzer & Co. *v.* "Helvetia" (1909, 35 *Arrêts Trib. Féd.* II, 340); Klinger *g.* Bleier & Co. (1910, 36 *Arrêts Trib. Féd.*, II, 258); Künkler *v.* Berger (1917, 43 *Arrêts Trib. Féd.*, II, 98). However, see criticism in *Journal de Tribunaux et Revue Judiciaire* (1901), pp. 274 and 482.

Greek case: J. & P. Coats, Limited *v.* Lambros & Smyrniotopoulos, Πλημμελιοδικεῖον Ἀθηνῶν, July 6, 1904 (*Propriété Industrielle*, 1904, p. 189).

3. P. Florent & Co. *c.* Fayen, Tribunal de Commerce de Namur, Sept. 26, 1902 (*Propriété Industrielle*, 1904, p. 121), holding that it is immaterial whether the prior use took place in France or in Belgium. But see M.P. et Douglas Vaugan Joulastane *c.* Grahs et Lovinfosse, Cour de Liège, March 2, 1910 (*Jurisprudence de la Cour de Liège*, 1910, p. 107), intimating a contrary opinion. Belgian authors agree with the latter view: see Capitaine, in *Propriété Industrielle* (1910), p. 94.

4 Walter Baker & Co., Ltd. *v.* Delapenta et al. (1908), 160 Fed. 746; Gorham Mfg. Co. *v.* Weintraub et al. (1912), 196 Fed. 957.

5. So held in Société "La Soie" *v.* Thys by the Commercial Tribunal of Brussels, Feb. 23, 1903 (*Jurisprudence Commerciale de Bruxelles*, 1903, p. 283).

6. See Mathy *v.* Republic Metalware Co. (1910), 35 App. D.C., 151, 156.

of the period of priority was considered in the congresses of the International Association.[1] At the Congress of Paris in 1900, a resolution [2] was adopted to the effect that in the relations between countries, in one of which ownership is acquired by registration and in the other by prior use, the best solution of the conflicting interests is embodied in article 28 of the treaty of May 9, 1869, between France and the Zollverein, and that an analogous system should be applied between the other countries.

Article 28 of the treaty between France and the Zollverein, which is declared to embody the best solution on the point under consideration has been considered in a previous chapter.[3] It provides in effect that a trade mark may be used concurrently by the foreign prior user as well as by the first national registrant. At the Washington Conference, the French delegation proposed the insertion of a provision in article 6 granting a right of personal use to the prior user of a mark in all the countries of the Union, notwithstanding the registration of the mark in the name of another.[4] This proposal did not obtain unanimity in the Conference. It did not seem quite satisfactory. It would not always afford adequate protection, and it invited negligence on the part of the first user of a trade mark.[5]

At the Conference of The Hague a new article, 6*b*, was adopted, which protects well-known foreign trade marks, under certain conditions, against their registration by other persons after the lapse of the period of priority.[6]

1. *Annuaire* (1897), pp. 200–201; *ibid.* (1898), pp. 363–365; (1900), pp. 197 ff., 348 ff.

2. *Ibid.* (1900), pp. 490–491. The text of the resolution is:

"Dans les rapports entre pays, qui considèrent le dépôt ou l'enregistrement de la marque comme déclaratif le droit à la marque se détermine par le premier usage.

"Dans les rapports entre pays, dont l'un considère le dépôt ou l'enregistrement de la marque comme déclaratif et l'autre comme attributif des droits, on doit appliquer un système analogue à celui que le traité du 9 mai 1869 (article 28) a consacré dans les relations entre la France et le Zollverein; par suite, les sujets des divers états intéressés peuvent se servir de leurs marques dans les pays autres que celui de production, pourvue que l'appropriation des marques dans ce dernier pays soit antérieure à l'appropriation dans les pays d'importation; si un tiers vient, avant le négotiant étranger, à remplir les formalités ou conditions prescrites pour l'appropriation de la marque, ce tiers pourra continuer à l'employer, à moins que sa mauvaise foi ne soit établie."

3. See *supra*, p. 64. This article remained in effect until 1914, and was revived after the war by virtue of a notification of the French government, in conformity with article 289 of the Treaty of Versailles. See *Travaux du Groupe Français de l'Association Internationale* (1919–1922), p. 193.

4. See *Actes de la Conférence de Washington*, p. 301.

5. See *Travaux du Groupe Français de l'Association Internationale* (1919–1922), pp. 160, 194.

6. See on this point, *infra*, §§ 387 ff.

§ 355. Effects of right of priority in Great Britain. The Convention of 1883 is not completely effective in Great Britain;[1] its provisions are binding on subjects and courts in so far as they have been embodied in municipal law. The Patent and Designs Act of 1907 (to which the Trade Marks Act, sec. 65, refers), section 91, contains provisions intended to carry into effect the stipulation of article 4 of the Convention. According to this section, any person who has applied for protection for any trade mark in a country of the Union shall be entitled to registration of his trade mark in priority to other applicants, provided the application is made within four months from the application for protection in the foreign country. For the purposes of this section, as well as of the stipulation of article 4, as was urged above,[2] it is not necessary that the mark be registered abroad. Mere filing of an application for registration is sufficient. Priority is not affected by the acceptance or refusal of the foreign application.[3]

The registration in Great Britain bears the same date as that of the application in the foreign country, by express provision of section 91. This means that registration is antedated, as in the case of patents. This is not in entire conformity with article 4 of the Convention and has given rise to serious objections in respect to patents.[4] Although in case of trade marks the question is not important, registration of trade marks being always renewable, it may be expected that the law will be amended in this respect.

Proviso (*b*) of paragraph (1) of section 91 contains the rule that the proprietor of the trade mark shall not be entitled to recover damages for infringements happening prior to the actual date on which his trade mark is registered in the country. This is in conformity with the conclusions arrived at above. It also shows that the use of the trade mark in a foreign country gives no right to sue for infringement in Great Britain.

Section 91 (2) provides that

> the registration of a trade mark shall not be invalidated (*c*) . . . by reason only of the use of the trade mark in the United Kingdom or the Isle of Man during the period specified in this section as that within which the application may be made.

1. See *supra*, § 90. 2. See *supra*, § 350.
3. Kerly (Underhay and Morgan), *The Law of Trade Marks and Trade Name*, p. 693.
4. See *supra*, § 198.

This provision is equivalent to that of the second paragraph of article 4 of the Convention. In the latter, too, it is said that the use of the mark in the interval shall not invalidate the subsequent deposit. However, in article 4 of the Convention, "the use of the mark" in the interval is enumerated with other contingencies as an example of what may happen in the interval. In section 91 of the English act, on the contrary, the use of the trade mark is the only act which does not invalidate the registration. The question arises, then, of the proper interpretation of these words.

What use of the trade mark will not invalidate the registration? During the period specified in section 91, the mark may be used in Great Britain, either by the foreign registrant and owner, or by a third person (who may also have registered it), or by the public in general (which would result to a loss of distinctiveness in the trade mark). Should all these uses be deemed as not invalidating the registration in favor of the foreign registrant entitled to the priority, as in the other countries, by virtue of article 4 of the Convention?

The answer should be in the affirmative, since the clear purpose of section 91 is to carry into effect the provisions of article 4 of the Convention, and since by the first paragraph of this section the foreign applicant is entitled to registration in priority to other applicants, and the registration takes the date of the application in the foreign state. If it be said that the words "use of the trade mark" in section 91 apply only to use by the applicant himself, the whole provision is meaningless; because use of the mark by the applicant before registration never renders the registration in the name of the applicant invalid. It is submitted that the logical construction of the provision in question is directed to use of the trade mark by third parties.[1] Use of the trade mark, therefore, during the period of priority cannot be relied upon by third parties to oppose or invalidate the registration of the foreign applicant.

Material in this respect is the proviso in section 41 of the Trade Marks Act. This allows the use or registration of a trade mark

1. Kerly (*The Law of Trade Marks and Trade Name*, p. 693) argues that the provision in question seems to be intended to be directed to use by the applicant himself; that this however is surplusage and cannot be taken as directed to use by third parties so long as the Convention is not embodied in legislation, and can have no operation upon the right to registration at all. It is submitted that this opinion is wrong. Sec. 91 purports to embody in legislation the provisions of articles 4 and 6 of the Convention. Embodying a convention in legislation does not mean necessarily inserting in the latter the very words of the former.

identical with a registered trade mark by the person who used such mark continuously from a date anterior to the use or registration of the registered mark. A foreign registrant depositing a trade mark in Great Britain within the period of priority may always avail himself of the above proviso against any intervening registrant.[1]

§ 356. Effects of right of priority in the United States. In the United States, the Convention should be considered completely effective as regards those provisions which are self-executing.[2] However, it has not been always so held in practice. It is necessary, therefore, to see how far the municipal law is in agreement with the Convention. Section 4 of the Trade Marks Act of 1905[3] is material in respect to article 4 of the Convention. It reads as follows:

> An application for registration of a trade mark filed in this country by any person who has previously regularly filed in any foreign country, which, by treaty, convention, or law, affords similar privileges to citizens of the United States, an application for registration of the same trade mark shall be accorded the same force and effect as would be accorded to the same application if filed in this country on the date on which application for registration of the same trade mark was first filed in such foreign country: *Provided*, That such registration is filed in this country within four months from the date on which the application was first filed in such foreign country: *And provided*, that certificate of registration shall not be issued for any mark for registration of which application has been filed by an applicant located in a foreign country until such mark has been actually registered by the applicant in the country in which he is located.

With the exception of the last proviso, this section is in entire conformity with article 4 of the Convention. No antedating of the registration is made in the United States, as in England, but the application for registration in a country of the Union operates as an application in the United States so far as the rights of the first applicant are concerned. The provision as to the effects of the right of priority being general, the difficulties presented by the wording of the English act do not exist in the United States.

A mere filing in a foreign country is required by the statute for claiming a right of priority in the United States, in accordance with the sound interpretation of article 4. But the certificate of registration may not be issued in the United States until the mark has been actually registered by the applicant in the foreign country. Thus

1. See Kerly, *The Law of Trade Marks and Trade Name*, pp. 694 n. and 393 ff.
2. See *supra*, § 97.
3. XXXIII *U. S. Stat. at Large*, 724, 725.

the application will be accepted, but the registration will not be granted prior to actual registration in the foreign country. This is not in unconformity with article 4, because it provides for no more than a right of priority. But it is a discrimination against foreigners incompatible with the stipulation of article 2 of the Convention, as was seen above.[1]

§ 357. Protection of trade marks at international exhibitions. The member countries of the Union are obliged by article 11 of the Convention to grant temporary protection to trade marks in respect of goods exhibited at official, or officially recognized, international exhibitions held on the territory of one of them. The nature and extent of this protection is similar to that secured to patentable inventions, industrial designs, and utility models. The earlier study of the subject in respect to these kinds of industrial property applies to trade marks, *mutatis mutandis*.[2] The extent and conditions of protection are governed by the domestic legislation of each country. The protection of trade marks and of industrial designs or models are regulated alike, especially as to the questions of the period of protection and the conditions and formalities required in each country. What is said, then, in the case of designs or models in this respect applies also to trade marks.[3]

A temporary protection for trade marks shown at exhibitions is less necessary than for patentable inventions or designs. The latter are valuable discoveries or creations, and by their mere use a benefit may be obtained. Trade marks when originally adopted are not valuable in themselves. There is no incitement to imitate a new mark which has not yet become an element of the goodwill of a business by establishing in the public's mind an association with a certain kind of goods. At any rate, the protection is necessary only in respect to countries in which ownership in the trade mark is based on registration.

1. See *supra*, § 320.
2. See *supra*, chaps. XIV and XVI.
3. See *supra*, § 278.

CHAPTER XXIV

THE VALIDATION OF TRADE MARKS IN THE UNION

§ 358. How question of validation arises. In a previous chapter [1] we have seen that a right in a trade mark is acquired by prior use, or by prior registration, or by the lapse of a period after such registration. Foreigners entitled to the benefits of the Convention of 1883–1925 may always claim a right in their trade marks, under the same conditions and with the same formalities as nationals, whether or not they are domiciled or established in a country of the Union.[2] Everywhere to-day a trade mark must be deposited or registered with the administration, in order to be protected, as such, against infringement. Foreigners, therefore, must register their trade marks, if they are desirous of having a more effective protection than that of the law against unfair competition.[3] If their trade marks are used in connection with a business whose situs is in a particular country, their assimilation to nationals may be all that they desire. But this is not the usual case. Ordinarily, a trade mark originates in a foreign country in connection with a business whose situs is there, and which extends to other countries. It is in respect to these trade marks that the question of their validation abroad, that is, of the enforcement of the proprietors' rights in other countries, arises. In other words, given a case where a person has acquired a property right in a trade mark in a country under the conditions of the law of that country, should this trade mark be always admitted to registration and protected in other countries?

§ 359. Importance of question. With the growing economic interdependence of the various countries and the overstepping of their boundaries by commercial and manufacturing businesses, a great proportion of trade marks would be of little value unless protected in more than one country. It may be said that a great proportion of the trade marks used in commerce are essentially international. Their protection then should be assured in all countries. The national treatment, guaranteed by the bipartite conventions before

1. See *supra*, chap. XXII, especially §§ 335–339.
2. See *supra*, § 320.
3. In the United States, the notice to the public may be given simply by use. If the business of the foreigner extends to the United States, and the mark is used in connection with that business in the United States, it will be protected by the common law of trade marks. See note in *Harvard Law Review*, XXI, 361.

1883, and by article 2 of the Convention of Union, is not alone sufficient for this purpose. This protection would be adequate if the trade-mark laws of the different countries were identical. This ideal condition has not yet been reached. In a previous chapter (chapter XXII) we have seen that the laws of the different countries differ widely as to what may be a legal trade mark. If foreigners were always assimilated to nationals, their trade marks would be protected only if they were legal, that is, if they fulfilled the requirements of the law of each country. This would mean that a trade mark valid by the law of the country of origin of the proprietor, but invalid by the law of a foreign country, would not be protected in the latter country. A way out would be for the proprietor to change his mark according to the law of each country. This would amount to a denial of protection. In law, there would be an acquisition of a new right, instead of the enforcement of a vested right acquired abroad. In fact, the whole purpose and function of the trade mark would be defeated; the reputation attached to the original trade mark, the identification of the proprietor's products, their association with the public and the public's habits, would be destroyed to a large degree.

It is then highly important for the adequate protection of trade-mark rights that they should be validated in all the countries after having been acquired in one of them. But this should necessarily be subject to certain limitations imposed by a due consideration of the rights of third parties, whether the latter are owners of the same trade mark in the other countries, or whether the general public which uses freely the subject-matter of the trade mark as a descriptive or geographical designation. Moreover, the public weal of a country may be adverse to the protection of a trade mark by reason of its being against good morals or public policy.

§ **360. Provisions of the Convention.** This principle of validation, as well as the exceptions to it, are formulated in articles 6, 6*b*, 6*c*, and 7 of the Convention. Articles 6*b* and 6*c* were added to the Convention at the last conference of The Hague, and they serve, as well as article 7, to complete the principle contained in article 6. This article reads as follows, following its amendment at The Hague in 1925:

> Toute marque de fabrique ou de commerce régulièrement enregistrée dans le pays d'origine sera admise au dépôt et protégée telle quelle dans les autres pays de l'Union.

Toutefois, pourront être refusées ou invalidées:

1° Les marques qui sont de nature a porter atteinte à des droits acquis par des tiers dans le pays où la protection est réclamée.

2° Les marques dépourvues de tout caractère distinctif, ou bien composées exclusivement de signes ou d'indications pouvant servir, dans le commerce, pour désigner l'espèce, la qualité, la quantité, la destination, la valeur, le lieu d'origine des produits ou l'époque de production, ou devenus usuels dans le langage courant ou les habitudes loyales et constantes du commerce du pays où la protection est réclamée.

Dans l'appréciation du caractère distinctif d'une marque, on devra tenir compte de toutes les circonstances de fait, notamment de la durée de l'usage de la marque.

3° Les marques qui sont contraires à la morale ou à l'ordre public

Il est entendu qu'une marque ne pourra être considérée comme contraire à l'ordre public pour la seule raison qu'elle n'est pas conforme à quelque disposition de la législation sur les marques, sauf le cas où cette disposition elle-même concerne l'ordre public.

Sera considéré comme pays d'origine:

Le pays de l'Union où le déposant a un établissement industriel ou commercial effectif et sérieux, et, s'il n'a pas un tel établissement, le pays de l'Union où il a son domicile et, s'il n'a pas de domicile dans l'Union, le pays de sa nationalité, au cas où il est ressortissant d'un pays de l'Union.

En aucun cas le renouvellement de l'enregistrement d'une marque dans le pays d'origine n'entraînera l'obligation de renouveler l'enregistrement dans les autres pays de l'Union où la marque aura été enregistrée.

Le bénéfice de la priorité reste acquis aux dépôts de marques effectués dans le délai de l'article 4, même lorsque l'enregistrement dans le pays d'origine n'entrevient qu'après l'expiration de ce délai.

La disposition de l'alinéa 1 n'exclut pas le droit d'exiger du déposant un certificat d'enregistrement régulier, délivré par l'autorité compétente du pays d'origine, mais aucune légalisation ne sera requise pour ce certificat.

The study of articles 6, *6b*, *6c*, and 7 will be divided as follows:

I. History of these articles.
II. Conditions of application of rule of article 6.
III. Rule of article 6.
IV. Exceptions to rule of article 6.
V. Prohibition of marks imitating well-known trade marks.
VI. Prohibition of the use of State bearings, emblems, etc.
VII. Nature of product and trade marks.

I. History of these Articles

§ 361. Text of article 6 prior to revision at Washington. The original draft of article 6 (then article 5) proposed to the Conference of 1880 read as follows:

La propriété . . . des marques de fabrique ou de commerce sera considérée dans tous les États de l'Union, comme légitimement acquise à ceux qui font usage, conformément à la législation du pays d'origine, des dits . . . marques de fabrique et de commerce.

This provision, borrowed from a number of bipartite conventions and agreements entered into before 1880,[1] conveyed a different meaning from the one that it purported to express. Its literal interpretation was that the *right* in a trade mark, acquired according to the law of the country of origin, should be enforced in all the countries of the Union. However, as the author of the draft and the Chairman of the Conference explained immediately, their purpose did not go as far as their words.[2] They remembered the fact that the laws of the various countries did not agree on what may constitute a lawful trade mark, and they intended to assure to the proprietors of trade marks the validation of the latter in the constituent elements originally adopted and used. The Chairman of the Conference declared that the article "ne vise que ce qui constitue la marque." The delegates of the other countries voiced their agreement with the principle embodied in the provision, and explained its meaning in the same sense as the Chairman and the French delegate.[3] The committee to which the provision was referred came nearer to the intent of the Conference by striking out the word "propriété" and proposing that "le caractère . . . des marques de fabrique et de commerce devra être apprécié dans tous les États de l'Union d'après la loi du pays d'origine."[4] At the second reading of the Draft Convention, article 6 was found to be still unsatisfactory to many delegates.[5] The term "caractère" was not quite clear, and after elaborate discussions a new text was adopted, which remained unmodified until 1911. This text provided:

Toute marque de fabrique ou de commerce régulièrement déposée dans le pays d'origine sera admise au dépôt et protégée telle quelle dans tous les autres pays de l'Union.

Sera considéré comme pays d'origine le pays où le déposant a son principal établissement.

Si ce principal établissement n'est point situé dans un des pays de l'Union, sera considéré comme pays d'origine celui auquel appartient le déposant.

1. See *supra*, § 39, and *Conférence de Paris* (1880), p. 70.
2. *Conférence de Paris* (1880), pp. 70, 71–72, 73.
3. *Ibid.*, pp. 71–74.
4. *Ibid.*, p. 78.
5. See discussions, *Conférence de Paris* (1880), pp. 132–142.

Le dépôt pourra être refusé, si l'objet pour lequel il est demandé est considéré comme contraire à la morale et à l'ordre public.

The words "telle quelle" were hardly clearer than the word "caractère." At the Paris Conference of 1883, which met for the signing of the Convention on the insistence of the Spanish delegate, a provision was inserted in the Final Protocol, explaining the first paragraph of article 6. This provision read as follows: [1]

Le paragraph 1er de l'article 6 doit être entendu en ce sens qu'aucune marque de fabrique ou de commerce ne pourra être exclue de la protection dans l'un des États de l'Union par le fait seul qu'elle ne satisferait pas, au point de vue des signes qui la composent, aux conditions de la législation de cet État, pourvu qu'elle satisfasse, sur ce point, à la législation du pays d'origine et qu'elle ait été, dans ce dernier pays, l'objet d'un dépôt régulier. Sauf cette exception, qui ne concerne que la forme de la marque, et sous réserve des dispositions des autres articles de la Convention, la législation intérieure de chacun des États recevra son application.

Pour éviter toute fausse interprétation, il est entendu que l'usage des armoiries publiques et des décorations peut être considéré comme contraire à l'ordre public dans le sens du paragraph final de l'article 6.

The foregoing provision of the Final Protocol left little doubt as to the meaning of the principle contained in article 6. The words "telle quelle" were interpreted as meaning the signs constituting the trade mark ("au point de vue des signes qui la composent"), and as concerning only the form of the mark ("ne concerne que la forme de la marque"). Thus any liberal interpretation of the first paragraph of article 6 was precluded by the restrictive provision of the Final Protocol.

§ 362. Amendments at Washington and at The Hague. In their application these provisions proved wholly unsatisfactory.[2] The Protocol left a wide margin of cases in which trade marks were refused admission for deposit and registration. Fine distinctions were drawn between the extrinsic and intrinsic qualities of a mark, its form, and the meaning attached to it, and so on.[3] The final paragraph of article 6, concerning the "exception of public order,"

1. *Conférence de Paris* (1883), pp. 18–22.

2. Osterrieth, *Washingtoner Konferenz*, p. 53.

3. See, for instance, decisions of the German Patentamt: June 27, 1904, refusing trade mark "Cordial Médoc"; Sept. 7, 1906, refusing trade mark "G.A."; Dec. 17, 1909, refusing a word mark and holding that article 6 refers to the exterior form of the mark and not to the meaning which is attached to the form. See cases in *Propriété Industrielle* (1905), p. 236; (1909), p. 30; (1910), p. 23.

proved also too wide a hole through which many foreign trade marks were lost. In all the congresses of the International Association for the Protection of Industrial Property, article 6 formed a ground for lively discussions, suggestions, and resolutions.[1] Following some unsuccessful attempts to arrive at a positive definition of trade mark and trade-mark right, the general trend of opinion tended to a negative assertion, by means of a limitative enumeration of the cases in which a foreign trade mark might be refused admission and protection in the Union.

At the Washington Conference of 1911, the International Bureau, and various administrations, proposed amendments to article 6 in the above sense.[2] The new text of article 6 adopted almost entirely the proposals of the German delegation,[3] which differed from those of the Bureau and of the French delegation in extending the cases in which foreign trade marks might be refused protection.[4] As a result of this amendment of article 6, the provision of the Final Protocol which defined that article restrictively, was abolished. The new text of article 6 remained unmodified at the Conference of The Hague, with the exception of its last two paragraphs concerning the definition of the country of origin, which were replaced by the new third paragraph. Moreover, two new paragraphs, the fourth and fifth of the present article, were added by the Conference of The Hague, while the sixth and last paragraph was transferred, slightly amended, to the text of the article from the Final Protocol.

Article 7 has remained practically unmodified since its original adoption. Articles 6*b* and 6*c* were added at the Conference of The Hague. The former provides for the refusal or invalidation of trade marks infringing well-known marks of foreigners, and the latter concerns trade marks containing armorial bearings, flags and other state emblems.

II. Conditions of Application of Rule of Article 6

§ **363. The two conditions.** The first paragraph of article 6 reads as follows:

1. See resolutions of congresses, in *Actes de la Conférence de Washington*, pp. 368–369.
2. See *Actes de la Conférence de Washington*, pp. 49, 92, 95, 107, 110, 113, 116.
3. *Ibid.*, p. 93.
4. See discussions on article 6, *Actes de la Conférence de Washington*, pp. 252–253, 296–301, 308–309, 332.

Toute marque de fabrique ou de commerce régulièrement enregistrée dans le pays d'origine sera admise au dépôt et protégée telle quelle dans les autres pays de l'Union.

This paragraph has remained unmodified from the time of its original adoption to the present day, with the exception of the word "enregistrée," which was substituted by the Washington Conference for the original term, "déposée." It contains the rule, and the conditions of its application. The words "régulièrement enregistrée dans le pays d'origine" constitute the conditions of application. In order that the benefit of article 6 may be claimed by the persons entitled to the advantages of the Convention, the trade mark whose admission for deposit and protection is claimed must have been: (*a*) duly registered; (*b*) in the country of origin. The third, fourth, fifth, and sixth paragraphs of article 6 define more specifically these two conditions.

§ **364. Country of origin of mark.** The question of the country of origin, in which the trade mark must have been registered, may be disposed of first. The third paragraph of article 6 defines it now as follows:

Sera considéré comme pays d'origine:

Le pays de l'Union où le déposant a un établissement industriel ou commercial effectif et sérieux, et s'il n'a pas un tel établissement, le pays de l'Union où il a son domicile et, s'il n'a pas de domicile dans l'Union, le pays de sa nationalité, au cas où il est ressortissant d'un pays de l'Union.

The old text of article 6 defined the country of origin as the country where the applicant had his principal establishment, and in case his principal establishment was not situated in the Union, the country of which he was a national. This text did not tally with articles 2 and 3 of the Convention, which define the persons entitled to its benefits.[1] Certain classes of persons could not claim the special advantage of article 6, although they could claim the advantages of all other provisions of the Convention.

The new text is in agreement with articles 2 and 3. In principle, all persons entitled to benefits of the Convention may enter claim under article 6. However, this article establishes an order of priority among the three criteria under which a person may do so — the *bona fide* and effective commercial or industrial establishment in the Union, the domicil, or nationality of a country of the Union.

1. See discussion, *supra*, § 121.

Thus, primarily, the country of origin of the applicant is considered to be that country in which he has a *bona fide* and effective industrial or commercial establishment.[1] And only in case he has no such establishment in the Union, is the country of the Union in which he is domiciled, or of which he is a national, taken into consideration. Consequently, if the applicant has such an establishment in a country of the Union, he cannot claim the benefit of article 6 after having registered his trade mark in any other country of the Union. Similarly, a person having no establishment in the Union, but having a domicil therein,[2] cannot claim protection under article 6 unless he has registered his trade mark in the country in which he is domiciled. A prior registration in the country of the Union of which he is a national, or in any other country of the Union, does not qualify him to make claim under article 6. Again, a person who has no establishment and no domicil in a country of the Union, but who is a national of such a country, is entitled to the benefit of article 6 only after he has registered his trade mark in his own country, and not in any other country of the Union.[3]

There may be cases in which the applicant is a national of, or possesses effective and *bona fide* establishments or domicils in, more than one country. In all such cases he may elect the country which should be considered his country of origin.

§ **365. Reasons for this condition.** This limitation is the result of the intention of the makers of the Convention to have the subject-matter of the trade mark governed by the law of the country in which it is originally adopted and used. It is rightly presumed that the mark is first adopted and used in the country in which the business is carried on. In case, however, the business of a person otherwise entitled to the benefits of the Convention is carried on outside of the Union, then it is presumed that the country of the Union in which he is domiciled is the country which should govern the subject-matter of his trade mark. The country of which the applicant is a national is presumed to be remote from the business, and the last to be resorted to.

The limitation tends also to secure the good faith of the appli-

1. As to the interpretation of these words, see *supra*, § 115.

2. As to the meaning of "domicile" in article 3 of the Convention, which must also apply here, see *supra*, § 114.

3. See on the adoption of the new provision at the Conference of The Hague, *Actes de la Conférence de La Haye*, pp. 341, 350.

cants, and to defeat evasions of the law which should govern the subject-matter of the trade mark. Indeed, at the first adoption of article 6 by the Paris Conference of 1880, the country of origin was defined as the country in which the applicant has his principal establishment or his domicil. This provision was explained by the Chairman as aiming to defeat the attempt of nationals of a country to claim admission for deposit of trade marks not registrable under the law of such country, by registering them in other countries of the Union.[1]

§ 366. Need of previous registration. The trade mark must be duly registered in the country of origin, as above defined, before the special benefit of article 6 may be claimed. What the words "duly registered" ("régulièrement enregistrée") mean is not easy to explain. It is necessary to trace the history of the terms. The original draft article 6 spoke only of trade marks *used* in conformity with the law of the country of origin. At the second reading, the wording of the first paragraph was entirely changed, and the words "valablement déposée" were inserted. The term "valablement" was objected to by many delegates, and the word "régulièrement" was proposed in its stead. The discussion as to the meaning and the import of the two words was very confused. No benefit could be derived from dwelling upon this discussion at the Conference.[2] Suffice it to say that the Final Protocol adopted at the Conference of 1883 gave a strict interpretation to the words "régulièrement déposée" of article 6. It provided that

> Aucune marque . . . ne pourra être exclue de la protection . . . pourvu qu'elle satisfasse, sur ce point à la législation du pays d'origine et qu'elle ait été, dans ce dernier pays, l'objet d'un dépôt régulier.

It would seem, according to this provision, that, besides the condition that the mark must be duly registered in the country of origin, it must be valid according to the law of that country.[3]

At the Washington Conference, several delegates were of the

1. *Conférence de Paris* (1880), p. 78. Later, however, the attention of the Conference having been called to the case of a national of a country of the Union possessing his business establishment outside of the Union, the additional provision covering this case was inserted. See *ibid.*, p. 133.

2. *Conférence de Paris* (1880), pp. 138–142.

3. But this did not mean that a foreign trade mark could not be admitted to deposit unless it was proved that the mark was valid according to the law of the country of origin. Pillet, *Régime International*, p. 351; L. Brun, *Les Marques de Fabrique et de Commerce*, pp. 379–380.

opinion that the words of the Final Protocol concerning the conformity of the foreign mark with the legislation of the country of origin should not be inserted in the new text of article 6 of the Convention. They contended that the country in which protection of the mark is claimed should be interested only in the question whether the mark was duly filed in the country of origin, and not whether the registration was in fact perfectly valid. The Italian delegate concurred in this view, but he demanded that, at least, there should be a presumption of validity of the mark. He thought that such presumption would exist if for the word "déposée" in article 6 the word "enregistrée" were substituted. For this would mean that the mark had been admitted by the administration and had not been refused as devoid of the legal elements of a trade mark. This delegate had in mind the countries in which the trade mark is submitted to a previous examination by the administration, and those in which, although no thorough examination is made, a trade mark may be refused as being against the law.

§ **367. Proof of registration.** This historical review of the words "régulièrement enregistrée" of the first paragraph of article 6 leaves no doubt that a condition precedent to claiming the benefit of the rule of this article is the prior due registration of the trade mark in the country of origin. No foreign trade mark can be admitted "telle quelle," — that is, in its original form, — in the other countries of the Union, if it has been used only in the country of origin, however long such use may have been, but has not been registered.

Any other country of the Union in which admission for deposit and protection is claimed may require proof that the trade mark has been registered in the country of origin. This involves proof of the act of registration, and that the country of prior registration is the country of origin of the applicant. In this respect, the final paragraph of article 6 provides:

> La disposition de l'alinéa 1 n'exclut pas le droit d'exiger du déposant un certificat d'enregistrement régulier, délivré par l'autorité compétente du pays d'origine, mais aucune légalisation ne sera requise pour ce certificat.[1]

Thus the country of importation of the trade mark may require a certificate of registration in the country of origin. No time limit is

1. This provision was taken from the Final Protocol adopted by the Washington Conference. At the Conference of The Hague was added the last sentence, "mais aucune . . . "

fixed in this provision, within which such certificate should be produced. The law of each country governs in this respect.

§ 368. Relation of article 4 to article 6. However, the fifth paragraph of article 6 provides:

> Le bénéfice de la priorité reste acquis aux dépôts de marques effectués dans le délai de l'article 4, même lorsque l'enregistrement dans le pays d'origine n'intervient qu'après l'expiration de ce délai.

This paragraph concerns trade marks for which the right of priority of article 4, *plus* the advantage of article 6, is claimed. In such case the trade mark may be filed in the country of importation within the period of the right of priority; but the benefit of the rule of article 6 cannot be claimed before the trade mark is actually registered in the country of origin. For instance, a trade mark is filed in the United States in 1925, and, after its examination by the Patent Office for two years, is finally registered in 1927. The American owner may deposit his trade mark within the six-month period of the right of priority in the other countries of the Union. But he cannot claim that his mark be validated in its original form until after its registration in the United States. Of course, in the countries of the Union in which no previous examination of the mark is made, his trade mark will be registered forthwith. Also, if his trade mark is in conformity with the law of the country where registration is applied for, he need not enter claim under article 6; his mark may be admitted for deposit and protected under the national-treatment principle of article 2.[1]

The fourth paragraph of article 6 provides that the renewal of the registration of a mark in the country of origin shall not involve the obligation to renew its registration in the other countries of the Union where it has been registered. This provision was taken from proposals of the British delegation and of the International Chamber of Commerce at the Conference of The Hague.[2]

§ 369. Meaning of word "régulièrement." For the application of the rule of article 6 it is necessary that the foreign trade mark shall have been duly registered in the country of origin. The certificate of registration is a convenient proof thereof. No more than registration in due form is required by article 6. It is not necessary that such registration be valid, that is, that the trade mark be legal ac-

1. See *infra*, §§ 371–373.
2. *Actes de la Conférence de La Haye*, pp. 450–451, 543.

cording to the law of the country of origin. Indeed, a mark registered in the country of origin may have been examined by the administration into its legality in the countries in which the system of previous examination exists, or those in which the administration merely looks into the question whether the mark contains the elements required by the law for its protection. In such cases, as well as in the countries in which the mark is advertised and objections to its registration are invited, the trade mark, after its registration, presumably possesses validity. On the contrary, in the countries in which the mark is registered without any examination, it is wholly uncertain whether or not the mark is legal. Besides the question of the theoretical legality of the mark, there may be doubts as to the applicant's legal right in the mark. These doubts exist especially in countries in which registration is only declaratory of property in the trade mark.

In the latter cases, proof of registration in the country of origin is not necessarily proof of its validity. But this is not required by article 6 for the admission of the trade mark for deposit in the countries of importation. It would often be impossible to produce such proof, and would place a heavy burden on the applicant in the country of importation, as well as on the administration receiving his trade mark, if the latter should undertake to find out whether the mark is in conformity with the law of the country of origin.

Should, however, the tribunals before which protection of the trade mark is sought undertake to find out whether the trade mark in question was validly acquired in the country of origin? The words "et protégée telle quelle" mean that the foreign trade mark must not only be admitted for deposit but must also be protected in its original form. In order that it be protected, as well as admitted for deposit, the condition precedent, according to article 6, is that it be duly registered in the country of origin. Whether anything more than that is required for its protection in the country of importation, is outside the scope of Article 6, as is seen below.

III. Rule of Article 6

§ 370. Scope of article 6. Every trade mark duly registered in the country of origin shall be admitted for deposit and protected in its original form ("telle quelle") in the other countries of the Union. This is the rule established by the first paragraph of article 6. It was interpreted before the Washington Conference by the provision of the Final Protocol to the effect that it concerned only the signs composing the trade mark, and that the law of the country of importation governed in all other respects. With the omission by this Conference of the provision in question from the Final Protocol, and the enumeration in the second paragraph of article 6 of the cases in which a trade mark may be refused or invalidated, the rule of the first paragraph is negatively defined by the exceptions of the second paragraph. Unless a trade mark may be refused or invalidated by virtue of one of these exceptions, it should always be admitted for deposit and protected. This rule is commonly and improperly called the rule of "personal status" of the mark. It is really the rule of validation or enforcement of the property right in a trade mark acquired in the country of origin. Such right, being a vested right, is given effect in all the other countries of the Union by virtue of article 6, in derogation of the municipal law which may not consider the trade mark in question valid and legal.

As will be seen, the exceptions enumerated in the second paragraph of article 6 cover all the cases in which the interests of third parties and of the public are opposed to the validation of foreign trade-mark rights. Thus the rule of article 6, whenever it contravenes municipal law, only defeats, so to speak, the commercial public order — the habits of the commercial community as to the forms and elements of trade marks.

The effect, then, of article 6 is to bring about the liberalization of the law of the different countries as to the conception of trade marks. Countries having less liberal legislation are compelled by article 6 to admit for deposit and protect foreign trade marks which cannot be registered by their own citizens. Moreover, their own citizens being unable to register some classes of trade marks in their country of origin, cannot have them admitted for deposit and protected in the other countries of the Union, because of the condition of prior registration in the country of origin contained in article 6. This double advantage has already compelled many countries to revise and liberalize their legislation, as, for instance, Austria, Germany, and Great Britain. This seems also to be the surest way for arriving at uniformity of the law in the different countries of the Union.

§ 371. Question of dependence or independence of trade-mark rights. The rule of article 6 is that of validation of trade-mark rights acquired in the country of origin. The question has arisen whether and to what extent this rule involves the principle of dependence of the rights in a trade mark registered in other countries of the Union on the right acquired in the country of origin.

Article 6 does not purport to lay down the rule that no foreign trade mark may be registered in a country of the Union unless it has been registered in the country of origin. It is sufficient to recall the history of the article and of its amendments to be convinced that it was never intended to go that far. The text is incompatible with such an assumption. Each country undertakes to admit for deposit a foreign mark in the form in which ("telle quelle") it was registered in the country of origin. The purpose of article 6 is to prohibit the refusal or invalidation of the foreign trade mark when this is not in conformity with the requirements of the law of the country where protection is claimed. In case the foreign trade mark is in conformity with the law of the latter country, article 6 does not come into play.[1] Whether in such case the foreign trade mark should be registered in the country of origin is outside of the scope of article 6.[2]

The question, then, is one of application of the principle of article 2 of the Convention. Under this article, "ressortissants" of the Union are entitled in each country of the Union to the same rights and protection as nationals. Consequently, they are entitled to apply for registration of their trade marks and to have them registered in the same way as nationals. Provided they comply with the requirements of the municipal law, persons admitted to the benefits of the Convention cannot be discriminated against in any way.[3]

In practice, such a discrimination would be very serious to "ressortissants" of the Union. Their commerce may be exclusively with foreign countries. To demand that they register their trade marks in their country of origin is to impose on them an undue burden. Their trade marks may be invalid by the law of their own country, but perfectly valid by the law of the countries in which they appear and

1. See note, in *Propriété Industrielle* (1904), p. 219; Cairo, "Is Registration in the Country of Origin Necessary?" *Bulletin of the U. S. Trade Mark Association* (1925), XX, 123, *accord*.

2. So held by the Swiss Federal Tribunal, July 11, 1913, in Compagnie Fermière de la Grande Chartreuse et Pacalis *c.* Rey (1913), 39 *Arrêts Trib. Féd.*, II, 640.

3. See on this point, *supra*, § 346. See also resolutions of the International Association, in *Actes de La Conférence de la Haye*, pp. 90–91. Also, Osterrieth, *Die Washingtoner Konferenz*, pp. 46 ff.

need protection. The restriction, then, seems unreasonable from the point of view of the international protection of trade marks.

§ **372. Proposed amendments to article 6.** At the Washington Conference the German delegation, moved by the fact that by an erroneous extension of article 6 it was sometimes held that the Convention established the principle of non-independence of trade marks, proposed the insertion of a provision in article 6 declaring expressly the opposite. This delegation supported its proposal on the ground that the independence of trade marks is a necessity of modern international trade. Manufacturers and merchants seek to satisfy the taste of consumers of various countries, and are obliged to use different marks for the different countries for which the merchandise is destined.

This proposal, however, was energetically opposed by the French delegation, which favored the non-independence of trade marks and a requirement that the foreign manufacturers and merchants must deposit their marks in their own country before they can claim protection in the other countries of the Union. This, the delegation thought, would protect the French public against registration by foreigners in France of trade marks of French appearance, therefore misleading as to the origin of the goods, and would also protect the manufacturers against registrations by Frenchmen abroad of trade marks imitating French marks.[1]

At the Conference of The Hague the German delegation, as well as the British, proposed again the insertion of a provision in article 6 declaring that for the protection of foreign trade marks it is not necessary that they should be registered in the country of origin so long as they are registered in the country where protection is claimed.[2] In the discussion of article 6 [3] the German delegation renounced its own proposal and voiced its agreement with the British proposal, which read as follows:

L'enregistrement d'une marque de fabrique ou de commerce dans le pays d'origine ne pourra pas constituer une condition nécessaire pour obtenir la protection dans d'autres pays; toutefois la marque doit être conforme à la législation du pays où la protection est demandée.

La protection d'une marque de fabrique ou de commerce enregistrée dans l'un des pays de l'Union sera indépendante de la protection obtenue pour la même marque dans d'autres pays.

1. *Actes de la Conférence de Washington*, pp. 300–301.
2. *Actes de la Conférence de La Haye*, p. 340.
3. *Ibid.*, pp. 442–444.

The delegation of the Serb-Croat-Slovene State remarked that, as the Convention was interpreted in its own country, the proposal was unnecessary, because article 2 of the Convention assured to foreigners what the proposal purported to grant. But the French and Spanish delegations opposed the proposal as liable to permit acts of unfair competition, and as granting to foreigners greater rights than they enjoyed in their own country. Notwithstanding the great majority in favor of the amendment, the unanimity rule prevented its adoption in the Committee of the Whole.[1]

§ 373. Position of different countries in this respect. From the fact that no unanimity was obtained for the German and British proposal it cannot be presumed that the Conference interpreted articles 2 and 6 as setting forth the principle that a foreign trade mark should always be registered in the country of origin before it may be admitted for registration and protected in the other countries of the Union. It is to be expected, however, that the courts of the countries which opposed the British proposal will interpret the Convention as containing this principle. As seen above,[2] the law in some countries of the Union expressly requires registration in the country of origin; these countries are: Brazil, Danzig, Denmark, Esthonia, Finland, Greece, Sweden, and the United States. The Belgian and French courts have constantly held that prior registration in the country of origin is necessary for the protection of the trade mark.[3] The decisions are based on an erroneous interpretation of article 6, legislation in France and Belgium imposing no such condition.[4] On the other hand, German courts have held the

1. *Actes de la Conférence de La Haye*, pp. 444, 522–523.

2. See *supra*, p. 447.

3. French cases: Gag et Lipart *c.* Franz Huber et Vacher, Cour de Paris, Nov. 25, 1904 (*Dalloz*, 1904, II, 445); Wright *c.* Wohl Co., Cour de Paris, Dec. 27, 1924 (*Propriété Industrielle*, 1927, p. 18). The earlier Belgian cases were conflicting on this point. See *Propriété Industrielle* (1901), p. 106; (1903), p. 112; and (1904), pp. 82, 84. The recent cases are decidedly in favor of the French position: see decision of the Tribunal de Bruxelles, April 12, 1923 (*Propriété Industrielle*, 1924, p. 77); Société Wahl Co. et Établissements Van Goidtsenhoven *c.* Wright et Delvaille, Cassation, Dec. 25, 1924 (*Pasicrisie*, 1925, I, 72).

4. See Cairo, "Is Registration in the Country of Origin Necessary?" in *Bulletin of the U. S. Trade Mark Association* (1925), XX, 123. The argument of this article is very sound, in the view of the present writer. But it is hardly right to say, and certainly no foreigner is convinced, that the obligation imposed by the United States Act of Congress on foreign applicants, to produce proofs of registration abroad, "is far from being a measure injurious to the French owner of marks; on the contrary it represents a real kindness and advantage to French industry." The obligation is a burden and a handicap to international trade, whether it is imposed by the French courts or by the United States Congress.

opposite.[1] Austrian and Swiss decisions seem to agree with the latter.[2]

The French and Belgian position is illogical, for registration alone in the country of origin is no proof of the validity of the mark and of its protection in the country of origin. If the theory of the "personal status" of the mark, or of the "accessory character" of the protection in the foreign countries, should be logically carried out, proof of its *protection*, not only of its registration, in the country of origin, should be required. The French position is, of course, explained by the fact that in the countries which are the most serious competitors of French industry the trade marks are subject to previous examination, and it is expected that marks in imitation of French marks, or containing a French indication of origin, will be refused registration as being deceptive.

§ **374. Cessation of protection in country of origin.** Foreign trade marks registered in the country of origin are admitted for registration and protected in the other countries in their original form. In the countries where the mark is examined by the administration before registration, proof of registration in the country of origin should be presented to the administration. In the other countries, proof should be offered to the tribunals whenever protection of the mark under article 6 of the Convention is claimed. In both cases no more is required than proof of registration in the country of origin.

But should the fact that the registration in the country of origin has been cancelled, or that its effects have been terminated by failure to apply for a renewal of registration, affect the protection of the trade mark in the other countries? Article 6 of the Convention does not determine the question. The latter part of the British proposal at the Conference of The Hague, referred to above, purported to cover this case by stipulating that the protection of a trade mark registered in a country of the Union shall be independent of the

1. Reichsgericht, Oct. 27, 1905 (*Propriété Industrielle*, 1907, p. 166), and Jan. 7, 1913 (81 *Entsch. Reichsg. Zivils.* 172).

2. Decision of the Austrian Ministry of Public Works, of July 13, 1920 (*Propriété Industrielle*, 1925, p. 100). The Swiss Federal Court has held repeatedly that prior general or free use abroad of a mark does not prevent registration of the trade mark in Switzerland. This clearly amounts to the independence of trade-mark rights acquired in Switzerland from such rights acquired abroad. See the cases of Ten Hope *c.* National Starch Co., Jan. 24, 1913 (39 *Arrêts Trib. Féd.*, II, 112); D. de Bodt & Co. *c.* Filature et Filteries réunies, April 12, 1913 (39 *Arrêts Trib. Féd.*, II, p. 352).

protection obtained for the same mark in other countries. The reasons produced by the French delegation against admission for deposit and protection of trade marks not registered in the country of origin do not apply in the case of cessation of protection in that country. Yet the purpose of article 6 is to validate the right in a trade mark acquired abroad. There is nothing to be validated when this right has ceased in the country of origin.[1] The Conference of The Hague seems to have adopted indirectly this principle by stipulating, in the fourth paragraph of article 6, that "in no case shall the renewal of the registration of a mark in the country of origin involve the obligation to renew the registration of the mark in other countries of the Union where it has been registered." [2]

The French delegation proposed at the Conference of The Hague that the protection of trade marks under article 6 in the countries of the Union should be assured for the uniform period of twenty years, irrespective of the usual duration of the effects of registration on other trade marks according to the municipal law of each country. Although the principle of the French proposal was adhered to, no agreement was reached as to the period of protection.[3]

IV. Exceptions to Rule of Article 6

§ 375. The rule negatively defined. Before the revision of the Convention of 1883 by the Washington Conference, the rule of article 6 was positively defined by the Final Protocol. As a result, with the exception of the objection to the exterior form of the trade mark, the countries of the Union refused to admit and protect trade marks registered in the country of origin whenever there might be a legal objection. At the Washington Conference, on the contrary, the rule of article 6 was negatively defined by the exceptions of the second paragraph. In consequence, all trade marks registered in a

1. See Osterrieth, *Washingtoner Konferenz*, p. 61. The last paragraph of article 6 provides that every country of the Union may require from the depositor a certificate of registration in the country of origin. Such certificate may presumably be required at any time when protection of the mark is claimed. If protection in the country of origin has ceased, it may not be possible to produce a certificate.

2. This provision was taken from the following proposal of the International Chamber of Commerce, in which the above principle is even more explicit: "Un pays dans lequel la marque est encore valable ne pourra pas exiger un renouvellement du dépôt chaque fois que, dans le pays d'origine, la durée de la protection serait expirée, si le renouvellement en a été opéré en temps utile dans ce pays." See *Actes de la Conférence de La Haye*, p. 451.

3. See *Actes de la Conférence de La Haye*, pp. 444–445.

country of the Union are to be admitted for deposit and protected unless they may be objected to, on the basis of one of the exceptions enumerated in article 6.[1] The list of these exceptions is exhaustive. For no other reasons than those enumerated in the second paragraph of article 2, can a trade mark registered in the country of origin be refused protection. It is necessary then to consider each of these exceptions, and define precisely its scope.[2]

§ 376. Marks infringing rights of third parties. (*a*) The first exception, number 1 of the second paragraph, reads as follows:

> 1° Les marques qui sont de nature à porter atteinte à des droits acquis par des tiers dans le pays où la protection est réclamée.

This provision was taken from the proposals of the German and French delegations at the Washington Conference.[3] It purports to protect the rights of third parties in the country in which protection is claimed. The question when a foreign trade mark is of such a nature as to infringe rights acquired by third persons in a certain country, is determined by the municipal law of that country. Such rights may be:

(1) A prior right in the same trade mark. This right must be an acquired right. Thus, if the same trade mark has been registered in a country in which property in the trade mark is acquired by registration, the foreign mark may be refused. On the contrary, in the countries in which registration is only declaratory of the right, or in which property is based on uncontested registration for a period of time, the prior user of the trade mark will prevail. The question whether the use of the mark in a foreign country is to be taken into consideration in determining priority of use is considered above.[4]

(2) A mark in general use in the country where protection is claimed may also be excluded under this exception as infringing rights acquired by the public. This will usually happen in the case of trade marks which may be considered as abandoned in one country, although they are still owned in the country of origin.[5]

1. Osterrieth, *Washingtoner Konferenz*, p. 62.
2. On the municipal law of the various countries concerning the subject-matter of the trade mark and unregistrable trade marks, see *supra*, §§ 321–330.
3. *Actes de la Conférence de Washington*, pp. 93, 95.
4. See *supra*, § 354.
5. Pelletier et Vidal-Naquet, *Convention d'Union*, p. 234; Dunant, *Traité des Marques*, pp. 539 ff.; Pouillet, *Traité des Marques*, p. 524.

When a trade mark is to be considered as abandoned in a country is a question for the law of that country. The rule should be that use by a few persons only, or even generalized use and prolonged inaction on the part of the owner, does not amount to abandonment if the latter had no knowledge of the use by third parties.[1]

(3) There is also infringement of rights of third parties in the country where protection is claimed, when the trade mark contains the personal or firm name, or the picture of a person established in that country.

In all the cases of rights of third parties, they must have been acquired in the country where protection is claimed. What is guarded by the exception is the legal order in the country concerned.

The marks dealt with in the provision under consideration may be refused or invalidated in the country where protection is claimed, only on opposition or complaint by the interested party. In order to prevail, he must prove that the trade mark filed for registration infringes on his rights acquired in the same country.[2] The British and American delegations proposed at the Conference of The Hague that marks well known in trade as marks of a national of another country of the Union should also be refused or invalidated as a further exception to the rule of article 6.[3] This exception was not adopted. This question, however, is closely connected with the new article 6*b*, and is considered below.

§ **377. Marks having no distinctive character.** (*b*) Number 2 of the second paragraph contains the exception of marks which have no distinctive character, and of descriptive and geographical terms. It reads as follows:

> 2° Les marques dépourvues de tout caractère distinctif, ou bien composées exclusivement de signes ou d'indications pouvant servir, dans le commerce, pour désigner l'espèce, la qualité, la quantité, la destination,

1. So decided in Baracco frères *c.* Carenon et Tur, Cour de Nîmes, Jan. 10, 1905 (*Darras*, 1906, p. 142, reported also in *Propriété Industrielle*, 1905, p. 237). In Martini et Rossi *c.* Diano et Société d'exploitation de l'Americano, Court of Aix (France), Jan. 16, 1924, the court found abandonment of the mark, for the plaintiff, knowing of its use by other manufacturers, for a long time made no complaint (*Propriété Industrielle*, 1927, p. 126). Similarly, Grézier *c.* Bonnet, Swiss Federal Tribunal, Oct. 10, 1896 (22 *Arrêts Trib. Féd.*, p. 1107).

2. See article, "La Lutte contre la Concurrence Déloyale," in *Propriété Industrielle* (1923), p. 190, at p. 192.

3. See *Actes de la Conférence de La Haye*, pp. 341, 447.

la valeur, le lieu d'origine des produits ou l'époque de production, ou devenus usuels dans le langage courant ou les habitudes loyales et constantes du commerce du pays où la protection est réclamée.

Dans l'appréciation du caractère distinctif d'une marque, on devra tenir compte de toutes les circonstances de fait, notamment de la durée de l'usage de la marque.

This provision contains two categories of cases in which the rule of article 6 may not apply. They are alike in referring to signs or marks which are in the public's possession; but they differ in that marks of the one category can under no condition constitute a trade mark, whereas those of the other category cannot be protected as trade marks because of certain conditions in the trade of the country where protection is claimed.

At the Conference of The Hague, an unsuccessful attempt was made to abolish the first set of cases by substituting for the words "ou bien" the words "surtout celles," or "c'est-à-dire." The first was proposed by the International Bureau and the other by the French delegation. Thus, the second set of cases was to be considered, according to the French proposal especially, as explanatory of the first. In other words, the phrase "marques dépourvues de tout caractère distinctif" would be explained by the rest of the provision, "c'est-à-dire composées" etc. This amendment would have the effect of forbidding the countries of the Union to refuse a trade mark for the sole reason that it was not distinctive, unless such lack of distinctiveness was due to the fact that the mark was descriptive, or was in general use in the commerce of the country concerned.

"Marks which have no distinctive character" may, therefore, be refused protection. The law of the country where protection is claimed decides whether a mark is distinctive. The administration and the courts of that country are limited, in their consideration of such distinctiveness, by the rule of article 6. They cannot refuse protection on the ground that the exterior form of the mark does not satisfy the law of that country. In view of this rule, the exception under consideration is very indefinite, and may give room to arbitrary application. The French proposal at the Conference of The Hague would have given logical coherence to the whole question.

The British delegation opposed the French proposal on the ground that the country where protection is claimed should be free to consider whether the sign proposed may constitute a trade mark, according to that country's conception of what may be a trade mark.[1] This would be directly opposed to the principle of article 6, if taken literally. In fact, the dispute arises in respect of receptacles, whose form may constitute a trade mark in France and in a number of other countries,[2] but not in Great Britain, the United States, and many other countries. Such receptacles have been refused protection in Great Britain, the Serb-Croat-Slovene State,[3] and Norway.[4] In Austria [5] the administration and the courts originally did not refuse a trade mark consisting in a receptacle, if they considered it sufficiently distinctive. But a recent decision of the Austrian Administrative Tribunal,[6] reversing a decision of the Federal Ministry of Commerce, protected a French trade mark consisting of the form of a bottle of liquor, on the sole ground that the mark is valid under the law of the country of origin (France) and should be protected "telle quelle" in Austria under the rule of article 6 of the Convention. This decision is admirable in its interpretation of the regime of trade marks in the Union.

It is a juridical error [the Tribunal says] to ask, in considering whether a mark or sign registered as a trade mark in a country of the Union should be protected in Austria, whether such mark or sign may be a trade mark according to the Austrian law, and to permit international law to interfere only if the answer is in the affirmative. It is one of the bases of the international regulation not to let each state examine, according to its own law, the character of a trade mark. The Convention of Union contains an international regulation of trade marks complete in itself, forming an independent whole, to which the municipal trade-mark law of each country of the Union must yield, and according to which the law

1. *Actes de la Conférence de La Haye*, p. 446. At the Washington Conference, when the provision of the Final Protocol defining article 6 was abolished, the British and American delegations made the reservation that there is a divergence of opinion in the different countries in the interpretation of the expression "trade mark." See *Actes de la Conférence de Washington*, p. 252.

2. See *supra*, § 326.

3. See *Travaux du Groupe Français de l'Association Internationale* (1923–1925), pp. 34–35.

4. Hogg *v.* Müller, Supreme Court of Christiania, May 18, 1904 (*Propriété Industrielle*, 1906, p. 9).

5. Decision of the Supreme Administrative Tribunal, Dec. 29, 1910 (*Propriété Industrielle*, 1912, p. 55) and Decision of the Ministry of Public Works, Jan. 16, 1923 (*Propriété Industrielle*, 1924, p. 14).

6. Benedictine Company *v.* The Federal Ministry of Commerce, April 28, 1928 (*Propriété Industrielle*, 1928, p. 166).

of the country of origin is decisive on the question of the things which may be used as trade marks.[1]

§ 378. **Numerals, letters, and single words.** Marks consisting exclusively of numerals or letters of the alphabet are excluded by the laws of some countries as devoid of distinctive character. Under the old text of article 6, before its revision at Washington, it was held in Germany that they might be refused.[2] The theory was that article 6 referred only to the form of the mark, whereas the question of its intrinsic character, that is, of its distinctiveness, was to be decided by the law of the country where protection was claimed. This distinction was clearly arbitrary.[3] In Austria, on the contrary, it was admitted that a mark could not be refused on the sole ground that it consisted of letters of the alphabet alone, unless the specific mark was generally used and had lost its distinctive character.[4] The theory in that country was that it was a question of the form of the mark, and that according to article 6 such a mark should be admitted if it satisfied the law of the country of origin.

Under the present text of article 6, the exception under consideration would seem to warrant the possibility of refusal of a trade mark consisting of letters, numerals, or words if, by the law of the country where protection is claimed, such marks are held to have no distinctive character. Thus, in Austria a trade mark consisting of numerals is not admitted until it is proved that it has become distinctive through long use by the owner of the mark.[5]

On the other hand, it is held in Belgium, Denmark, and Italy that a trade mark valid by the law of the country of origin should be admitted under article 6, although by its aspect it is not distinctive according to the law of the country where protection is claimed.[6]

1. Similar language is used in the Italian case of L. T. Piver Co. *v.* Aspid Co., Civil Tribunal of Turin, Nov. 16–25, 1927 (*Propriété Industrielle*, 1928, p. 188).

2. Patentamt, Sept. 7, 1906, Trade mark: "G.A." (*Propriété Industrielle*, 1909, p. 30).

3. Osterrieth und Axster, *Pariser Konvention*, pp. 151–152.

4. Supreme Administrative Tribunal, Dec. 29, 1910, and Dec. 19, 1912 (*Propriété Industrielle*, 1912, p. 54; 1913, p. 56), protecting the trade marks "M.F.A." and "P.F.N."

5. Supreme Adm. Tribunal, June 19, 1915 (*Propriété Industrielle*, 1917, p. 9).

6. Belgium, Bouhy *c.* État Français, Cassation, May 19, 1910 (*Pasicrisie*, 1910, I, 239), protecting the mark "Cigarettes Françaises" of the French state.

Denmark, Decision of the Maritime and Commercial Court of Copenhagen, confirmed by the Supreme Court (*Propriété Industrielle*, 1906, pp. 42 and 120).

Italy, Tribunal of Naples, March 3, 1926, in Bois *c.* Bredico, Carleo, Mazza, Pisas, Russo and Borriello (*Propriété Industrielle*, 1926, p. 129).

§ 379. Distinctiveness to be determined from all circumstances of case. According to the last sentence of the provision under consideration, the administration and courts of the country where protection is claimed, in arriving at a decision as to the distinctive character of a mark, must take into account all the circumstances of the case, including the length of time during which the mark has been in use.

This sentence was inserted by the Washington Conference, to satisfy the demand of the Swedish delegation that a mark should not be refused on the sole ground of its being composed of a single letter or a single numeral, if, by long use, it has become distinctive.[1] Indeed, in Sweden such marks have been used for centuries in the iron and steel industry.[2]

The provision is general. In all cases where the distinctiveness of the mark is in question, account must be taken of all the circumstances of the case. Length of time during which the mark has been in use is only one of the circumstances.[3] The opinion of interested commercial circles is another important element.[4] Thus the question of distinctiveness is to be decided, not by theoretical standards and by the requirements of the law of the country where protection is claimed as to the elements of the mark, but by the factual situation. This is in accordance with sound principles, in view of the fact that a mark may not be chosen and adopted originally as a trade mark, but may become so after long use.

1. *Actes de la Conférence de Washington*, pp. 299–300, 308.

2. Osterrieth, *Washingtoner Konferenz*, p. 65.

3. In the matter of an Application of the California Fig Syrup Company (1909), 26 R. P. C., 846, 854 (trade mark "California Syrup of Figs" admitted because of long use). In the Matter of an Application by J. Crosfield & Sons, Ltd. (1909), 26 R. P. C., 838, 854 (mark "Perfection" refused as devoid of distinctive character).

4. The Supreme Administrative Tribunal of Austria, in its decision of June 19, 1915 (*Propriété Industrielle*, 1917, p. 9), held that the opinion of commercial circles on the question of distinctiveness of a mark consisting entirely of numerals is to be sought by the administration, not by the applicant; and that it is not necessary that it be proved that the mark was originally used as trade mark; it is sufficient that it was used for a long time. The same tribunal, in its decision of May 5, 1923 (*Propriété Industrielle*, 1924, p. 124), held that in passing upon the distinctive character of an American mark consisting of the picture of a cash register and the word "National," all facts must be taken into consideration, especially length of use and the opinion of commercial circles, and that it is immaterial that the picture is unregistrable and the word "National" a free word. But the same tribunal, Feb. 16, 1915, refused the mark "National" for buttons as meaning native and having no distinctive character (*Propriété Industrielle*, 1916, p. 95).

§ **380. Descriptive and geographical terms.** The second category of marks which may be refused or invalidated according to number 2 of the second paragraph of article 6 are the so-called free marks and free words in Germany (*Freizeichen, Freiworte*), or descriptive and geographical terms and devices. This provision was taken from the German and French proposals at the Conference of Washington, and follows very closely the provisions of the German law of trade marks. It may conveniently be divided into two parts, each concerning a different category of free marks.

The first part, which was taken from the German proposal, concerns marks consisting exclusively of signs or indications which may serve in trade to designate the kind, quality, quantity, destination, value, place of origin, of the goods or date of production. A mark, then, may be refused or invalidated under article 6 if it consists *exclusively* of such signs. In case the proposed mark consists of something more than these signs or indications, it cannot be refused under this exception. The signs or indications in question render the mark inadmissible, if they *may serve* in trade, as indicated in the provision. The expression used is "pouvant servir." In the original German proposal a better expression was used, namely, "usités." This would have prevented the refusal of the proposed mark unless it were proved that it was already used in trade. The present expression is likely to be interpreted too strictly.[1] The indications whose exclusive use in a mark may cause the refusal of the latter are descriptive or geographical terms.[2]

1. The French Court of Cassation, June 24, 1908, in Société Farbwerke *c.* Société des Usines du Rhône (*Gazette du Palais*, 1908, II, 267), refused protection of the mark "Pyramidon," on the ground that no valid deposit could be made of a word which *was destined* to become in a short time the usual and necessary designation of the new pharmaceutical product.

2. Among the cases excluding trade marks as descriptive are the following:

The German Reichsgericht, March 11, 1910 (*Propriété Industrielle*, 1911, p. 88), denied protection to the mark "Lance-parfum," for perfume tubes or flasks, on the ground that, according to the rules and spirit of the French language, the term "Lance-parfum" refers to the nature of the product and describes it, like the terms "porte-feuille," "tire-botte," etc.

The Court of Appeals of Brussels, March 9, 1911 (*La Jurisprudence Commerciale de Bruxelles*, 1911, p. 209), held the mark "Phosphatine" descriptive, as derived from the French common word "phosphate," like caféine, théine, etc.

The Austrian Ministry of Public Works, Jan. 17, 1910, held that the American mark "Vaseline" was descriptive of the product (*Propriété Industrielle*, 1911, p. 140).

Cases excluding trade marks as designating the place of origin of the goods are the following:

The German Patentamt, April 6, 1904 (*Propriété Industrielle*, 1905, p. 64), refused registration of the marks "Clos d'Artignan," "Cheval Brun," "Château-Lairon,"

When a mark becomes descriptive is a question of fact, to be determined by the administration and the courts of the country where protection is claimed. It is doubtful whether the last sentence of the provision of number 2 of the second paragraph of article 6, concerning the determination of the distinctiveness of the mark, applies to the marks under consideration. From its wording, the negative seems probable. Thus even long use of the mark by the depositor, in consequence of which the word has acquired a secondary meaning in identifying his products, cannot prevent its refusal or invalidation.[1] This is certainly a defect of article 6. It should be possible to take into account all the circumstances of the case in respect to any mark, unless it is contrary to morals or public order.

The provision under consideration should be interpreted in a way which will not defeat the whole purpose of article 6. A mark which has been used for a long time by a manufacturer or trader in connection with his business and has become auxiliary to the goodwill, should not be refused protection on the ground that theoretically, or according to the meaning of the word in the dictionary, it signifies the kind, quality, or the like, of products. The use of the word in commerce, and not its meaning in the dictionary, is embraced in the

"Rose Clochetour," "Château Blanc," etc., after asking the opinion from chambers of commerce of the wine industry and other sources, on the ground that the marks are used in France to designate French vineyards, and that used on products from other countries they are calculated to deceive the public.

The Austrian Ministry of Public Works, May 31, 1918 (*Propriété Industrielle*, 1920, p. 59), excluded the mark "Hamburg-Wien" for rubber articles of a firm established in both Hamburg and Vienna. The Supreme Adm. Tribunal, Jan. 13, 1922, refused protection of the American mark "International" for agricultural machines, as descriptive (*Propriété Industrielle*, 1923, p. 88). The same tribunal, May 19, 1910, refused protection of the mark "Winchester" for cartridges as being a geographical term (*Propriété Industrielle*, 1912, p. 53).

The Japanese Patent Office, Aug. 16, 1904, in the case China Import, Export and Bank Co. *v.* Sumi Rikichi, cancelled the mark "D.R.G.M.," for these letters are the common inscription of utility models in Germany (*Deutsches Reichsgebrauchsmuster*), and its registration would have the effect of making the use of these letters on German products unlawful in Japan (*Propriété Industrielle*, 1905, p. 186).

1. The German Patentamt, Nov. 11, 1912, refused registration of the mark "Ideal," although the word had acquired a secondary meaning as identified with the depositor's typewriters (*Propriété Industrielle*, 1913, p. 54). But in the case of the mark "Leukos" for accounting machines, which was rejected by the Section of Marks as indicating the nature of the product (*Leukos* means "white" in modern Greek), the Patentamt, May 25, 1904, admitted it, following the opinion of a chamber of commerce, in reply to a circular of the Patentamt inquiring whether foreign words should be assimilated to German, that no general answer could be given to the question, and that all the circumstances of the case should be taken into consideration. (See *Blatt für Patent-, Muster-, und Zeichenwesen*, 1904, p. 393.)

exception under consideration.[1] It is intended to prevent a person from monopolizing a word which his competitors are equally justified in using. But it is far less serious to allow such a monopoly in certain cases than to deprive the manufacturer of the reputation acquired through the mark.[2]

The indication or sign in question may be refused protection, if it may serve to designate the kind, quality, and so forth, of the goods in connection with which it is used. A relative descriptiveness, then, excludes the mark from protection, not an absolute one.[3] At the Conference of The Hague, the delegation from the United States proposed that a new exception be added to the second paragraph of article 6 in respect to marks composed of words constituting the common name of the product in any language. The committee, however, being of the opinion that the American proposal did not go outside the scope of article 6, a reservation only of the United

1. An Austrian decision of the Ministry of Public Works, Jan. 14, 1918, confirmed by the Supreme Adm. Tribunal, Dec. 21, 1918, held that the American mark "Paragon" is descriptive as meaning "model" or "pattern," and designates the quality or kind of product; protection was denied, notwithstanding the opinion of commercial circles. Similarly, the same Ministry refused protection to the American mark "Gold medal" for flour as a term descriptive of quality, notwithstanding the fact that the American company had used the mark for scores of years. (*Propriété Industrielle*, 1919, p. 141; 1920, p. 95; 1927, p. 85.) Both decisions would seem to be wrong.

2. See Maillard, "Marques Descriptives," in *Annuaire de l'Association Internationale* (1898), pp. 375, 397.

3. Two Austrian cases were decided correctly in this respect. The mark "Singer" was deposited by a New York Company for sewing machines, excepting expressly machines of "New Family Type." The word "Singer" was known in Austria, before deposit, as designating the "New Family Type" style of machines. The Supreme Adm. Tribunal, June 14, 1917, protected the mark (*Propriété Industrielle*, 1918, p. 137). On the other hand, the Austrian Ministry of Public Works, April 20, 1916, cancelled the registration of the mark "Highlife" for articles of dress and of luxury as indicating the kind and quality of such goods. *Dictum*, that the mark might be registered for other classes of merchandise. (*Propriété Industrielle*, 1918, p. 44.)

Another decision of the same ministry, Aug. 7, 1916, undoubtedly goes too far. The German mark "Presto" for automobiles and other mechanical installations was refused registration as descriptive of the quality of the product, for the word "presto" in the Italian language means "rapid," "quick," and "light" (*Propriété Industrielle*, 1918, p. 104).

Similarly, the English decision, In the Matter of Trade Mark "Orlwoola" (1909), 26 R. P. C. 850, 854, goes too far in refusing registration to the mark "Orlwoola" as descriptive, because it sounds like "All wool."

A case in the United States Supreme Court is illustrative on the point. The mark "American Girl" for shoes was held neither geographical nor descriptive. In a *dictum* the court noted that, had the mark been "American Shoe," its decision might have been different. Hamilton Brown Shoe Co. *v.* Wolf Bros. & Co. (1916), 240 U. S. 251, 257. See also Eiseman *v.* Schiffer (1907), 157 Fed. 473 (the word "radium" is not descriptive as applied to silk).

States delegation was taken down, to the effect that the United States might refuse or invalidate such marks.[1]

§ **381. Marks in possession of the public.** The second part of the provision under consideration concerns marks consisting exclusively of signs or indications which have become customary in the current language, or in the *bona fide* and recognized customs of the trade of the country where protection is claimed. This provision, then, refers to marks or signs which were not originally descriptive terms but have become so when the proposed mark is deposited for registration. Thus the international mark "Gervais," of a French company, was refused protection in Austria on the ground that, in the opinion of the majority of the Chambers of Commerce interested in the cheese industry in Austria, the word is generally used to designate a special kind of cheese.[2] Similarly, protection was denied to the mark "Insuline" for pharmaceutical products in the same country,[3] to the mark "Magnolia" in Belgium[4] for metallic alloyage, and, in Switzerland,[5] to the German mark "AS" for colors derived from tar.

In considering the question whether a proposed mark has become customary in the current language or in the customs of the trade of a country, the administration and the courts of such country should necessarily ask the opinion of the interested commercial circles.[6] Still, the mark must have become current in *bona fide* and recognized custom ("dans les habitudes loyales et constantes") of the trade. Thus, if a foreign mark is fraudulently used by several persons in the same industry in a country, the custom is not *bona fide*,

1. See *Actes de la Conférence de La Haye*, pp. 448–449. The criticism of the proposal by the French delegation, that it concerned a specific case only, while the Convention should include only general principles, is very sound. It illustrates the difference of approach in international law matters of Continental and American lawyers.

2. Decision of Ministry of Public Works, March 29, 1915 (*Propriété Industrielle*, 1917, p. 10).

3. Decision of Ministry of Commerce and Traffic, April 20, 1926 (*Propriété Industrielle*, 1927, p. 86). The reason for the decision was that, at the time of the deposit of the mark in Austria, the interested commercial circles considered the word as the name of the product.

4. The Magnolia Antifriction Metal Co. *c.* Regnac frères, Cassation, May 25, 1906 (*Pasicrisie*, 1906, I, 269).

5. Chemische Fabrik Rohmer *g.* Farbenindustrie Aktiengesellschaft, Federal Tribunal, July 6, 1926 (52 *Arrêts Trib. Féd.* S. II, 300). The reason for the decision was that it was proved that the mark was in general use in the chemical industry for the purpose of distinguishing different groups of colors.

6. As the Austrian Ministry did in the above two cases. See notes 2 and 3.

and registration of the foreign trade mark should not be refused. Again, the trade mark should not be denied protection when, after great publicity given to the product in connection with which the mark is used, it no longer suggests the manufacturer, but describes the product.[1]

§ **382. Marks contrary to morality and public order.** (*c*) Number 3 of the second paragraph of article 6 contains the third exception to the rule of this article. It reads as follows:

> 3° Les marques qui sont contraires à la morale ou à l'ordre public.
> Il est entendu qu'une marque ne pourra être considérée comme contraire à l'ordre public pour la seule raison qu'elle n'est pas conforme à quelque disposition de la législation sur les marques, sauf le cas où cette disposition elle-même concerne l'ordre public.

In principle, this exception raises no objection. The trade-mark law of all the countries excludes expressly marks contrary to morality or public order. However, all the countries have not the same conception of morality and public order. The conception of public order, especially, is very uncertain. This term includes all cases where a social or public interest is opposed to the protection of a trade mark.

At the Washington Conference an attempt was made to define public order, or at least the cases of application of the principle.[2] A delegate remarked that the conception of public order had been applied outside its usual meaning, in that a mark was held to be against the public order of a country for the sole reason that it did not satisfy the conception of "trade mark" of that country.[3] At his proposal, the second part of the above provision was inserted in the Final Protocol by that Conference, and included in the text of article 6 by the Conference of The Hague.

At the latter Conference, the International Bureau and the French delegation proposed to restrict the exception concerning public order to cases only of public armorial bearings, decorations, flags, and the like. Germany and Great Britain, on the contrary, proposed to extend

1. So held by the Supreme Court of the Netherlands, Nov. 5, 1909, concerning the mark "Tannalbin," designating the "tanninum albuminatum" (*Propriété Industrielle*, 1909, p. 181). See, for earlier cases in the various countries of the Union concerning descriptive and free marks, an article by G. Maillard in *Annuaire de l'Association Internationale* (1899), pp. 375 ff.

2. See German and French proposals, *Actes de la Conférence de Washington*, pp. 93 and 96; and discussions, *ibid.*, pp. 297–298.

3. See such cases in Pillet, *Régime International*, p. 353, footnote 1.

the exception to such cases. The latter position was adopted by the Conference. There may, then, be marks besides those containing public armorial bearings, decorations, and the like, which may be considered contrary to public order. Such are, especially, deceptive marks, or marks containing a false indication of origin.[1] Under this same exception, a mark was refused registration in Switzerland as shocking to the national feelings of the Swiss people.[2] A mark, inoffensive in itself, may be considered contrary to morals, in combination with a particular product.[3]

§ 383. Reproduction of state emblems, etc., comprised in this exception. The power of refusal of marks containing public armorial bearings and decorations as contrary to public order was expressly stipulated by the Conference of 1883 in a provision of the Final Protocol.[4] The use of such symbols may be ("peut être") considered as contrary to public order. At the Washington Conference two different proposals were made by the Austrian and Swiss delegations. The former desired to make certain that the use of such marks should not be considered contrary to public order if properly authorized. The latter desired to extend "public order" to public flags, and to make it obligatory for the countries of the Union to prohibit and punish as a crime the use for commercial purposes of public armorial bearings and flags, or of portions of them.[5] The

1. Thus, a decision of the Hungarian Minister of Commerce (*Propriété Industrielle*, 1902, p. 109) cancelled the mark "Hof" (the Royal Court) as designed to deceive the public. Another decision of the same authority, Oct. 4, 1909, refused registration of the German mark "Andrassy" for pencils (although authorized by Count Andrassy) as likely to deceive the public as to the origin of the goods (*Propriété Industrielle*, 1911, p. 23). Also a decision of the Austrian Ministry of Public Works, Oct. 16, 1917, refused registration of the marks "Magyarol," "Magyarata," and "Magyarona," as derived from *Magyar*, that is, Hungarian, and therefore deceptive, the depositor of the mark being a firm not established in Hungary (*Propriété Industrielle*, 1919, p. 40). The German Reichsgericht, June 21, 1907 (66 *Entsch. Reichsg. Zivils.* 236), held a mark contrary to public morals, when adopted for the sole purpose of causing prejudice to others and confusion with the merchandise of third persons.

2. Decision of the Federal Council, June 3, 1918, ordering cancellation of the registration of the mark "Tell-Marke" for coffee, representing the monument of Tell at Altdorf and containing the above two words. It appears that the mark was considered objectionable as used by a foreigner, and it is implied that a national might validly use the same mark (*Propriété Industrielle*, 1918, p. 93).

3. The Swiss Federal Department of Justice and Police, Jan. 26, 1910, cancelled the registration of the mark "Frohe Zukunft" on medicine preventing conception (*Propriété Industrielle*, 1910. p 37).

4. See proposal of the Spanish delegation, *Conférence de Paris* (1883), p. 18, and its adoption, *ibid.*, p. 22.

5. See proposals and discussion, *Actes de la Conférence de Washington*, pp. 298–299.

Austrian proposal was adopted, and inserted as the third paragraph of *Ad* article 6, in the Final Protocol. The Swiss proposal was restated to extend the provision of article 6 concerning public order beyond public armorials and flags, to public decorations and to official signs and hall marks indicating control or warranty adopted by a country of the Union. But no agreement was reached for compelling the countries of the Union to prohibit the use of such marks. Their use might only be considered as contrary to public order in the meaning of number 3 of the second paragraph of article 6.

Under this text, a country of the Union could refuse or accept a mark reproducing the public armorial bearings, flags, decorations, and the like, of another country. It was purely a question for the municipal law of each country. In this respect there were great differences among the laws of the various countries. In some of them only the use of national armorial bearings was prohibited, while in others the prohibition included foreign as well as national ones. Their use is allowed in some countries if properly authorized, while in others the prohibition is unqualified. Moreover, the subject-matter of prohibition varies in the different countries, extending from armorial bearings of the state (Denmark, Mexico, Norway, the Netherlands, and others) to flags, armorial bearings of a city or corporation, emblems, decorations, and so on.[1]

The situation in regard to state armorial bearings and other emblems, as well as official signs and hall marks adopted by the countries of the Union, is wholly changed now by the new article 6*c* adopted at the Conference of The Hague, as seen below.[2]

§ 384. Refusal of trade marks constituting an act of unfair competition. At the Conference of The Hague a further exception to the rule of article 6 was proposed by the British delegation concerning the case of a mark deposited under conditions constituting an act of unfair competition within the meaning of article 10*b* of the Convention. This proposal, although adopted by the sub-committee as number 4 of the second paragraph of article 6, was suppressed by the Committee of the Whole at the suggestion of the Japanese delegation.[3]

However, at the final adoption of article 6 by the Conference, the

1. See on this point, *supra*, § 322. See also provisions of the laws of the various countries of the Union, in an article in *Propriété Industrielle* (1924), pp. 223, 224.
2. See *infra*, §§ 390 ff.
3. See *Actes de la Conférence de La Haye*, pp. 341, 449, 522.

German, British, Swiss, Austrian, Czechoslovakian, Spanish, and Cuban delegations made declarations to the effect that they reserved the right to consider the marks whose deposit would constitute acts of unfair competition, as contrary to morality and public order, and to refuse or cancel the registration of such marks on that ground, by virtue of the provision of number 3 of the second paragraph of article 6.[1]

§ 385. A country is not bound to refuse or invalidate above classes of marks. The three groups of cases of the second paragraph of article 6 are cases in which marks registered in the country of origin may be refused or invalidated by the country where protection is claimed. The provision reads: "pourront être refusées ou invalidées." At the Conference of The Hague, the question was discussed whether the refusal or invalidation should not be made obligatory on the contracting countries. The British delegation proposed that, with the exception of descriptive or non-distinctive marks (number 2 of the second paragraph), it should be obligatory for the countries of the Union to refuse the marks dealt with in the second paragraph of the article. The French delegation objected that the principle of article 6 was that of validation of trade marks registered in the country of origin, and that certain cases existed in which such validation might be denied. An obligation on the contracting countries to refuse protection could not be properly placed in article 6. The delegation of the Economic Committee of the League of Nations remarked that a separate article could be adopted, to this effect. Further objections, however, were raised, and the British delegation did not insist on its proposal.[2]

The British position as to obligatory prohibition of certain marks in the countries of the Union was adopted in the new articles 6*b* and 6*c* which deal with certain marks coming under the first and third exceptions dealt with above.

V. Prohibition of Marks Imitating Well-known Trade Marks

§ 386. Need of further protection of foreign trade marks. By virtue of the first exception of the second paragraph of article 6, marks infringing rights of third parties may be refused or invalidated

1. See *Actes de la Conférence de La Haye*, p. 577.
2. *Ibid.*, pp. 341, 449–450.

in the country where protection is claimed. This provision is very inadequate for assuring protection of rights of the true owners of trade marks. It is full of limitations. It is an exception to the rule of the first paragraph of article 6, and purports only to delimit a category of cases in which a trade mark registered in the country of origin may be refused protection in the other countries of the Union. It is not applicable in the country of origin. Even in the other countries of the Union power is given to the administration or tribunals only to refuse or cancel registration of the marks in question; no obligation is imposed to prohibit the registration. Moreover, the power of refusal cannot always be exercised. There must be an infringement of the rights of third parties; the rights infringed must have been acquired in the country where protection is claimed; and the interested party must claim and prove such infringement.

Undoubtedly, the provision under consideration is rightly restrictive as it is. It establishes an exception to the validation of trade-mark rights acquired abroad. The exception covers the interests of the legal order of the country where validation is claimed. If anything more were needed in the Convention for an adequate protection of trade-mark rights, its place would not be in article 6.

What was needed was to prevent, in all the countries of the Union, in the country of origin as well as in the others, the imitation and infringement of trade marks adopted and used by a manufacturer or merchant before any other person in the Union. A trade mark today, as seen above,[1] constitutes an auxiliary to, or part of, the goodwill of a business, and forms as valuable an element of that business as any other property right. The protection of the latter is assured everywhere to-day by almost uniform rules of law. On the contrary, trade-mark law is not uniform everywhere. The right in a trade mark is acquired under three different systems, whose coexistence often renders possible the loss of foreign trade-mark rights. Indeed, a trade mark owned by a person in a country where priority of use is the basis of ownership may be registered by another person in a country where by registration property in the mark is acquired. Also, the same mark may be deposited in a country where registration is only declaratory of property, but where the use of the mark abroad is not taken into account in determining priority of use. In both cases, the first user and rightful owner of the trade mark loses his right to use the mark or apply for its registration in the second

1. See *supra*, §§ 318, 319.

country. His protection under article 4 of the Convention is not always adequate. The six-month period within which he must file his application for registration in foreign countries is too short, especially as regards trade marks, whose commercial value is manifested long after their original adoption.

This usurpation of trade marks in use in a foreign country and enjoying a great reputation is effected usually in bad faith, but it may also be done in good faith. Whatever the cause, the result is always the hampering of the foreign trade of the first user of the trade mark. He cannot import his trade mark into the foreign countries in question unless he secures the consent of the usurpers at great sacrifices.[1]

§ 387. Stipulation of article 6*b*. To remedy in some degree this situation, the French delegation proposed at the Washington Conference the addition of a paragraph to article 6, granting to the first user of a trade mark a right of personal possession of the mark, beside the exclusive right of use of the first registrant, under certain conditions. This proposition was not adopted because of the opposition of two countries.[2]

After the War, the question was taken up by the Economic Committee of the League of Nations as one of the aspects of unfair competition. It was studied by the Committee of Experts, which met at Geneva on May 5, 1924, and formed Resolution D of its report.[3] This resolution, with some amendments, was proposed as new article *6b* of the Convention by the International Bureau to the Conference of The Hague.[4] At the same time, the British and American delegations proposed a further exception, to be inserted in the second paragraph of article 6, and covering in some degree the cases provided for in the proposed new article.[5] From these three texts, as well as from proposals of amendment made by several other delegations, the new article *6b* was derived, reading as follows:

Les pays contractants s'engagent à refuser ou à invalider, soit d'office si la législation du pays le permet, soit à la requête de l'intéressé, l'en-

1. The German Reichsgericht, March 2, 1905 (*Blatt für Patent-, Muster-, und Zeichenwesen*, 1905, p. 247) confirmed the seizure and confiscation of goods imported in Germany and bearing a trade mark of a New York company used by it for more than thirty years, as infringing the same mark registered in Germany by another New York Company only a few months before such importation.

2. See *Actes de la Conférence de Washington*, p. 243.

3. See text in *Propriété Industrielle* (1924), p. 101.

4. See *Actes de la Conférence de La Haye*, pp. 241, 246.

5. *Ibid.*, p. 341.

registrement d'une marque de fabrique ou de commerce qui serait la reproduction ou l'imitation, susceptible de faire confusion, d'une marque que l'autorité compétente du pays de l'enregistrement estimera y être notoirement connue comme étant déjà la marque d'un ressortissant d'un autre pays contractant et utilisée pour des produits du même genre ou d'un genre similaire.

Un délai minimum de trois ans devra être accordé pour réclamer la radiation de ces marques. Le délai courra de la date de l'enregistrement de la marque.

Il ne sera pas fixé de délai pour réclamer la radiation des marques enregistrées de mauvaise foi.

§ 388. **Marks protected by article 6*b*.** The marks protected by article 6*b* are those considered by the competent authority of the country of registration to be well known in the country, as being already marks of nationals of another contracting country.

First, then, they must be marks of a national of one of the countries of the Union. This seems to leave out marks of persons entitled to the benefits of the Convention under article 3. However, the phrase "de l'intéressé" in the same article was explained by the sub-committee unanimously to mean the persons entitled to the benefits of the Convention under articles 2 and 3.[1] It would seem, then, that the same interpretation should be given to the word "ressortissant."

Second, the mark must be well known in the country as being the mark of a ressortissant of the Union. The country meant is the country where the mark is filed for registration, or is registered, and where its refusal or invalidation is demanded. Thus, the fact that the mark may be well known in all the other countries is immaterial for the purposes of application of article 6*b*.[2]

Third, the competent authority of the country of registration must consider ("estimera") the mark in question as well known in the country to be the mark of the person concerned. The procedure to be followed in this respect by the deciding country is in no way controlled by this article. It is to be expected that the opinion of the interested commercial circles will be taken into consideration in such cases.

1. See *Actes de la Conférence de La Haye*, p. 456.

2. This was made quite clear in the discussion of article 6*b*. As originally worded, it provided for refusal or invalidation of trade marks well known in the trade in general. This was amended on the insistence of several delegations. See *Actes de la Conférence de La Haye*, pp. 453–456.

§ **389. Conditions of application of article 6*b*.** Article 6*b* contains an engagement on the part of the contracting countries to refuse or invalidate the marks in question. In this, it differs from the second paragraph of article 6, according to which the countries where protection is claimed have the power ("pourront") only to refuse or invalidate certain marks. On the other hand, all the contracting countries, the country of origin of the depositor as well as the others, are bound to take the action intended by in this article. Thus, the provisions of this article apply to national as well as to foreign marks.[1]

The contracting countries undertake to refuse or invalidate the marks in question, either administratively, if their legislation so permits, or at the request of an interested party. The latter must, of course, be a person entitled to the benefits of the Convention under articles 2 and 3, as seen above.

Such refusal or invalidation must be made in case the mark proposed for registration, or already registered, is a reproduction or imitation of the marks considered in the previous paragraph. The reproduction or imitation, however, which is prohibited must be liable to cause confusion, and must be utilized for the same or similar classes of goods.

The interested person may claim the removal of such marks within at least three years from the date of registration of the mark. A longer period, however, may be allowed by the municipal law of a country of the Union. The removal of marks registered in bad faith may be applied for, according to the last paragraph of article 6*b*, at any time.

The provisions of article 6*b* have no retroactive effect, as was unanimously understood by the sub-committee.[2] Thus, trade marks already registered at the time the new text of the Convention came into effect are outside the scope of this article.[3]

VI. Prohibition of the Use of State Armorial Bearings, Emblems, etc.

§ **390. Stipulations of article 6*c*.** The use of public armorial bearings, flags, and the like, of foreign states came to be looked upon,

1. See *Actes de la Conférence de La Haye*, p. 455. 2. *Ibid.*, p. 456.
3. See two cases protecting well-known foreign trade marks in Cuba, according to the principles of the new article, in *Propriété Industrielle* (1918), p. 20, and 1926, p. 171.

especially after the War, not only as injuring the dignity and national honor of those states, but also as constituting unfair competition.[1] In this sense, it was considered by the Committee of Experts, which met at Geneva on May 5, 1924, to study questions of unfair competition. One of the resolutions adopted by this committee, concerning the repression of unfair competition, deals with the question of unauthorized use of armorial bearings and emblems of states, and the like.[2]

This resolution, with some modifications, was proposed by the International Bureau at the Conference of The Hague to be inserted as a separate article in the Convention.[3] The proposed text, with some amendments,[4] was adopted by the Conference and now forms article 6*c* of the Convention. It reads as follows:

> Les pays contractants conviennent de refuser ou d'invalider l'enregistrement et d'interdire, par des mesures appropriées, l'utilisation, à défaut d'autorisation des pouvoirs compétents, soit comme marques de fabrique ou de commerce, soit comme éléments de ces marques, des armoiries, drapeaux et autres emblèmes d'État des États contractants, signes et poinçons officiels de contrôle et de garantie adoptés par eux, ainsi que toute imitation au point de vue héraldique.
>
> L'interdiction des signes et poinçons officiels de contrôle et de garantie s'appliquera seulement dans les cas où les marques qui les comprendront seront destinées à être utilisées sur des marchandises du même genre ou d'un genre similaire.
>
> Pour l'application de ces dispositions les pays contractants conviennent de se communiquer réciproquement, par l'intermédiaire du Bureau International de Berne, la liste des emblèmes d'État, signes et poinçons officiels de contrôle et de garantie, qu'ils désirent ou désireront placer, d'une façon absolue ou dans certains limites, sous la protection du présent article, ainsi que toutes modifications ultérieures apportées à cette liste. Chaque pays contractant mettra à la disposition du public, en temps utile, les listes notifiées.

1. See Swiss statement, in *Actes de la Conférence de Washington*, p. 299. After the War, see *voeux* of French and German groups of the International Association, and resolutions of the Economic Committee of the League of Nations and the Committee on Industrial Property of the International Chamber of Commerce, in *Propriété Industrielle* (1924), p. 223.

The German Patent Office, on Jan. 15, 1908 (*Propriété Industrielle*, 1908, p. 174), cancelled the registration of a mark for boxes of matches reproducing the public stamp which the Swiss administration affixes on boxes of matches, on the ground of its being scandalous, contrary to public order, and likely to deceive the public.

2. See text, in *Propriété Industrielle* (1924), p. 101.
3. See text of proposed article, *Actes de la Conférence de La Haye*, p. 247.
4. See propositions of Germany, Great Britain, Morocco, and Switzerland, *Actes de la Conférence de La Haye*, pp. 343–345; and discussions of the Sub-Committee, *ibid.*, pp. 457–467.

Tout pays contractant pourra, dans un délai de douze mois à partir de la réception de la notification, transmettre, par l'intermédiaire du Bureau· International de Berne, ses objections éventuelles.

Pour les emblèmes d'État notoirement connus, les mesures prévues à l'alinéa 1 s'appliqueront seulement aux marques enregistrées après la signature du présent Acte.

Pour les emblèmes d'État qui ne seraient pas notoirement connus, et pour les signes et poinçons officiels, ces dispositions ne seront applicables qu'aux marques enregistrées plus de deux mois après réception de la notification prévue par l'alinéa 3.

En cas de mauvaise foi, les pays auront la faculté de faire radier même les marques enregistrées avant la signature de présent Acte et comportant les emblèmes d'État, signes et poinçons.

Les nationaux de chaque pays qui seraient autorisés à faire usage des emblèmes d'État, signes et poinçons de leur pays, pourront les utiliser, même s'il y avait similitude avex ceux d'un autre pays.

Les pays contractants s'engagent à interdire l'usage non autorisé, dans le commerce, des armoiries d'États des autres pays contractants, lorsque cet usage sera de nature à induire en erreur sur l'origine des produits.

Les dispositions qui précèdent ne font pas obstacle à l'exercice, par le pays, de la faculté de refuser ou invalider, par application du No. 3 de l'alinéa 2 de l'article 6, les marques contenant, sans autorisation, des armoiries, drapeaux, décorations et autres emblèmes d'État ou des signes et poinçons officiels adoptés par un pays de l'Union.

§ 391. Things the use of which is prohibited. The first question in respect to article 6*c* is: What are the things the use of which is prohibited? They are enumerated in the first paragraph of the article: armorial bearings, flags, and other state emblems of the contracting countries, official signs and hall marks indicating control or warranty and all imitations thereof from an heraldic point of view.

The term "emblem" is very broad and may comprise armorial bearings and flags.[1] The original expression in the proposition of the Bureau read: "des emblèmes ou armoiries d'État." The expression adopted is: "des armoiries, drapeaux et autres emblèmes d'État." The words "et autres" imply that armorial bearings and flags are also emblems. Whenever, then, in the following paragraphs of article 6*c* the word "emblème" alone is mentioned, it should be taken as including the armorial bearings and flags of States.

1. In the discussion of article 6*c*, the German delegation inquired whether emblems were comprised in armorial bearings. The French delegation answered that the word "emblème" was more comprehensive than the word "armoirie." *Actes de la Conférence de La Haye*, p. 459. See, as to the meaning of these words, Pouillet, *Traité des Marques*, pp. 42 ff.

The emblems dealt with here are state emblems of the contracting countries. The old text of the Final Protocol spoke of "armoiries publiques." The term "public" was assumed to comprise state emblems as well as those of provinces, cantons, communities, princely families, and so on. The term "state emblems" was used, because it was not intended to extend the prohibition of article 6c to the others.[1] The sub-committee, however, unanimously understood the word "armoiries" as comprising the escutcheons of reigning families.[2] States, in the meaning of this provision, are the constituent states of a Federation as well as the Federation itself.[3]

There are also included in the prohibition of the first paragraph the official signs and hall marks indicating control or warranty. Again, these signs and hall marks are prohibited if they are officially adopted by a country of the Union.[4]

Not only the use of these emblems and signs is prohibited, but also their imitation, in case this employs the heraldic characters which distinguish one emblem, or coat of arms, from another. Thus the use of certain symbols contained usually in armorial bearings, such as lion, bear, eagle, sun, and the like, is not prohibited by article 6*c*.[5]

§ 392. Communication of state emblems, official signs, etc. As it cannot be expected that each country of the Union knows all the emblems and official signs or hall marks of the other countries, it is stipulated by the third paragraph of article 6*c* that the contracting countries shall communicate mutually through the medium of the International Bureau the list of state emblems, signs, etc., which they desire, or may hereafter desire, to place, wholly or within certain limits, under the protection of this article. All subsequent modifications of this list shall also be communicated in the same way.

1. See observations in the General Report of the Committee of Experts, above mentioned, in *Propriété Industrielle* (1924), p. 101. Also remarks of the International Bureau, *Actes de la Conférence de La Haye*, p. 245.

2. *Actes de la Conférence de La Haye*, pp. 459 and 544.

3. See declaration by the chairman of the sub-committee in the discussion of art. 6*c*, *Actes de la Conférence de La Haye*, pp. 464 and 544.

4. The delegation of the Serb-Croat-Slovene State proposed that the words "d'État" be added after the words "signes ou poinçons." The chairman of the Conference remarked that the word "officiels" has precisely that meaning. *Actes de la Conférence de La Haye*, p. 460.

5. See observations in the General Report of the Committee of Experts, above mentioned, in *Propriété Industrielle* (1924), p. 101. Also, remarks of the International Bureau, *Actes de la Conférence de La Haye*, p. 245.

Each contracting country shall forthwith make these lists available to the public.

It is to the interest of each country of the Union to communicate these lists in good time, because the prohibition of the first paragraph is applicable, as regards state emblems which are not well known and official signs and hall marks, only after a certain period following such notification. Whether a country has made its lists available to the public is immaterial for the purposes of the application of article 6*c*.

The list may indicate, in respect to emblems, signs, and hall marks, the limits within which the country in question desires to place them under the protection of article 6*c*. This was inserted in order to allow certain countries to authorize, if they so desire, foreigners in certain cases to use their emblems, signs, and hall marks.[1]

Within twelve months from the receipt of such communication, any contracting country may transmit any objections which it may desire to offer through the medium of the International Bureau. It may, indeed, happen that two countries of the Union use the same official sign or hall mark of control or warranty, or that the sign in question is a free mark or free word in some countries. What will happen if such objections are transmitted by a country of the Union? No sanction or procedure is provided for settling the dispute. Apparently, the emblem or sign or hall mark objected to will not be protected by the measures provided for in the first paragraph of article 6*c*. The British delegation had proposed arbitration by a tribunal of experts, but this procedure called forth objections on the part of the American delegation, and the proposal was not insisted upon.[2]

§ 393. Extent of prohibition. The contracting countries agree to certain measures in respect to the marks considered above.

First, concerning the armorial bearings, flags, and other state emblems of the contracting countries they are bound (1) to refuse or to cancel the registration; (2) to prohibit by appropriate measures their utilization. Both are subject to two conditions: (*a*) that the use is made without authorization by the competent authorities, and (*b*) that the state emblems in question are used as trade marks or as

1. See observations in the General Report of the Committee of Experts, above mentioned, in *Propriété Industrielle* (1924), p. 101.
2. See the proposal and discussion thereon, *Actes de la Conférence de La Haye*, p. 462.

elements of trade marks. Not any use, then, but the use in trade marks alone is within the scope of the first paragraph of article 6*c*. Such marks shall not only be refused registration or cancelled, but also their mere use as unregistered trade marks is prohibited. Furthermore, all imitations from an heraldic point of view are prohibited, as seen above.[1]

However, armorial bearings of the contracting countries enjoy a further protection. By virtue of the ninth paragraph of article 6*c*, their unauthorized use in general, not only in trade marks, is prohibited whenever such use is of a nature to cause deception as to the origin of goods. Thus, the use of armorial bearings on signboards, advertisements, price-lists, and the like, for commercial purposes, is prohibited, if such use is likely to deceive the public. It is not necessary that it should be so intended. The natural result of the use is taken into consideration.

Second, the official signs and hall marks indicating control or warranty, adopted by the contracting countries, are protected, as state emblems in general, against registration, utilization, or imitation in trade marks. However, the prohibition in regard to them applies solely in cases where the marks which contain them are intended to be utilized for the same or similar classes of goods. (Second paragraph of article 6*c*.)

In case of resemblance between the state emblems, signs, or hall marks of one country of the Union and those of another country, the use of the latter which has been authorized in the nationals of that country cannot be prohibited.

§ 394. Application of provisions of article 6*c*. The stipulations of article 6*c* are self-executing engagements of the contracting countries, and should be given effect in all of them. No retroactive effect, in general, is to be given to these stipulations. However, a country of the Union is entitled to cause the removal of marks containing state emblems, signs or hall marks, even though registered before the signature of the Convention, that is, before November 6, 1925, in case such registration was made in bad faith.

With the exception of this case, the provisions of this article shall apply in accordance with the following distinction (fifth and sixth paragraphs of article 6*c*). In the case of state emblems which are well known, the measures of the first paragraph shall apply to marks registered after the signature of the Convention, that is, after No-

1. See *supra*, p. 564.

vember 6, 1925. As regards state emblems which are not well known, and official signs and hall marks, the above measures shall be applicable only to marks registered more than two months after the presentation of the communication provided for in paragraph 3.

The renewal of a registration effected prior to the coming into effect of the article, or prior to the communication provided for in paragraph 3, is not considered a new registration and is, therefore, outside the purview of article *6c*.[1]

§ 395. Power to refuse or invalidate state decorations. The tenth and last paragraph of article *6c* summarizes the old text of the Final Protocol concerning the provisions allowing the countries of the Union to refuse or invalidate marks containing, without proper authorization, public armorial bearings, flags, decorations, and other state emblems or official signs and hall marks. This paragraph authorizes the contracting countries to refuse or invalidate such marks as contrary to public order, under number 3 of the second paragraph of article 6. On the other hand, the first paragraph of article *6c* binds the contracting countries to observe the measures provided therein.

The only practical importance, then, of the last paragraph is that it includes in its provisions the decorations, which are not comprised in the first paragraph of article *6c*. They were expressly excluded by the Committee of the Whole of the Conference of The Hague on the ground that the great number of existing decorations would render difficult the execution of the obligation to refuse or invalidate such marks.[2] In the term "décorations" are comprised the honorary distinctions or medals conferred by the state upon certain products.

VII. Nature of Product and Trade Marks

§ 396. History and purpose of article 7. The rule of article 6 is completed by article 7, which purports to assure the validation, in another aspect, of trade-mark rights acquired abroad. This article provides:

> La nature du produit sur lequel la marque de fabrique ou de commerce doit être apposée ne peut, dans aucun cas, faire obstacle à l'enregistrement de la marque.

1. See unanimous declaration to this effect by the sub-committee, *Actes de la Conférence de La Haye*, p. 544.
2. See *Actes de la Conférence de La Haye*, p. 524.

No amendment has been proposed, or made, to this article since its original adoption by the Conference of 1880, except at the last Conference of The Hague, when the word "enregistrement" was substituted for the word "dépôt." The modification was proposed by the International Chamber of Commerce to take in the countries in which marks are not only deposited, but registered, after a previous examination by the Administration.[1]

The purpose of this article was thus explained by the author of the Draft Convention at the Conference of 1880. In certain countries the sale of certain products is prohibited without a previous license from a Board of Health, or some cognate authority. But the mark is independent of the product to which it is affixed. It should be possible for the proprietor of the mark to register it in order to assure his rights when the sale of the product will be allowed.[2] Although pharmaceutical products are usually referred to in relation to the provision of article 7,[3] its stipulations are general, and may be applied in several cases.[4]

§ **397. Cases of application.** Article 7 provides that in no case ("dans aucun cas") can the nature of the products to which the trade mark is to be applied form an obstacle to the registration of the trade mark. The word "produit" is to be understood as covering all goods to which a trade mark may be applied. Paragraph 3 of the first article of the Convention provides that industrial property — of which trade marks are a branch — is to be understood in the broadest sense.[5] Whatever, then, may be the nature of the product, the mark cannot be refused registration.

The sale or manufacture of certain products may be restricted or prohibited in a country of the Union. Sometimes a special license is required for the sale of some classes of products, such as foodstuffs, pharmaceutical products or medicines, explosives, and the like. In some countries the sale of certain commodities is wholly prohibited to individuals, being a state monopoly[6] (tobacco, matches, pe-

1. See *Actes de la Conférence de La Haye*, p. 545.
2. See *Conférence de Paris* (1880), p. 89.
3. See Pelletier et Vidal-Naquet, *Convention d'Union*, p. 233; Pouillet, *Traité des Marques*, p. 223.
4. Osterrieth *und* Axster, *Pariser Konvention*, p. 181. Also article in *Propriété Industrielle* (1922), pp. 95, 96.
5. See *supra*, § 124.
6. The administration of the Serb-Croat-Slovene State had cancelled the registration of many marks on the ground that they were destined for goods the sale of which

troleum, salt, explosives, and so on). In still other countries, the sale, as well as the manufacture, is forbidden (for instance, of liquor in the United States).

§ **398. Extent of protection.** In all these cases the trade marks which are to be applied to such products should be admitted to registration, notwithstanding prohibitions concerning such products.[1] The admission to registration does not mean simply a formal placing on the register, but protection of the trade mark against infringement. In the countries in which the sale as well as the manufacture of the goods in question is prohibited, the protection will be effective only after the prohibition is abolished. Meanwhile, also, the imitation of the trade mark in connection with similar classes of goods is prevented.

As regards a country in which only the sale is prohibited, the protection is more important. Indeed, although the mark cannot be applied on goods which are to be placed on the market of the country concerned, it may be infringed by persons manufacturing such goods for export, or it may be infringed by the administration itself, or the company which possesses the monopoly of sale. If foreign trade marks could not be protected in such a country, they would be in the possession of the public, and could be reproduced on goods destined for foreign markets.

Lastly, in countries where the sale of the products is permitted only by special license, the goods on which the mark is to be applied may be placed on the market as soon as the license is granted. The registration of the trade mark before the granting of the license is very important to preserve the proprietor's rights.

---

constitutes a State monopoly. The International Bureau informed this administration that this was a violation of article 7 of the Convention, and succeeded in having it change its position. See *Propriété Industrielle* (1922), p. 95.

1. An American case holding that an Italian citizen was not entitled to register a trade mark used in connection with tobacco, manufactured by him, on the ground that an American citizen would not be permitted to register such a mark in Italy, the manufacture of tobacco being a state monopoly in that country, is doubly wrong. First, reciprocity is not the basis of the Convention of Union, but complete assimilation to nationals (see *supra*, § 128). Second, according to article 7 of the Convention, American citizens are allowed to register a mark in connection with tobacco in Italy. See De Nobili *v.* Scanda (1912), 198 Fed. 341. On the facts of the case, the decision was right for other reasons.

CHAPTER XXV

RESTRICTIONS ON THE OBLIGATIONS OF REGISTRANTS

§ 399. Obligation to use registered trade mark in its relation to international trade. We have seen in a previous chapter [1] that in some countries the law imposes on owners of registered trade marks the obligation to use them within the country. Although no public interest is served by the use of the trade mark, the obligation in question aims at defeating attempts of manufacturers to prevent third parties either from using trade marks similar to their own or from registering trade marks which they expect to use at a later time. Both these kinds of trade marks, legitimate as they often may be, sometimes become a great handicap to commerce, by filling the register with terms or designations not used, and consequently by reducing the much-restricted stock of registrable words and terms. Legitimate competition is thus hindered.

Twelve countries of the Union actually impose the obligation to use the trade mark within the country. In France, also, an amendment of the law to this effect has often been proposed.[2]

In international trade, obstructive marks are not frequent. The payment of the large fees that registration of trade marks in many foreign countries requires, prevents the registration of defense or reserve marks. On the other hand, foreign trade is sometimes shifting, and subject to changes and interruptions. A foreign manufacturer or merchant, for instance, may register a trade mark in a country, in the hope that he will be able to import his goods, and the international trade situation may set back his plans for a certain period of time. Reasonable and proper, therefore, as the obliga-

1. See *supra*, § 344.
2. See Pouillet (Taillefer and Claro), *Traité des Marques*, pp. 150 ff.; *Propriété Industrielle* (1921), p. 135.

tion to use the trade mark in the country may be in national trade, it is often unfair and fraught with arbitrariness in international trade.

The Convention of 1883–1911 contained no provision concerning the obligation of foreign trade-mark owners to use their trade marks in the country where they claim protection. But the Berne Arrangement of June 30, 1920, for the reëstablishment of industrial property rights affected by the war, provided in its third article that a trade mark shall not be forfeited for non-use before the expiry of a period of two years from the date of coming into force of the Arrangement. This beginning of international regulation of the question of non-use of trade marks caused a change of opinion in favor of the insertion of a provision in the Convention, and in the Madrid Arrangement for the International Registration of Trade Marks, for restricting the obligation of registrants to use their trade marks in the different countries of the Union.

§ **400. Stipulation of article 5 of Convention.** At the Conference of The Hague, the International Bureau, the British delegation, and the International Chamber of Commerce made proposals to this effect to be inserted in article 5 of the Convention.[1] The Bureau proposed that a three-year period be allowed foreign registrants for the use of the trade mark in the countries of the Union, and that the removal of the trade mark from the register should be decided by judicial authority. The British delegation proposed that registration should not be cancelled if the non-use of the trade mark was due to special circumstances in the trade, and not to any intention not to use, or to abandon, the mark. The proposal of the International Chamber of Commerce prohibited forfeiture of the mark unless the non-use was due to intention to abandon it. After an elaborate discussion, the following provision was adopted and inserted as paragraph 7 of article 5 of the Convention:

> Si, dans un pays, l'utilisation de la marque enregistrée est obligatoire, l'enregistrement ne pourra être annulé qu'après un délai équitable et si l'intéressé ne justifie pas des causes de son inaction.

The term "utilisation" of the trade mark in this provision does not mean manufacture of the products on which it is to be affixed,

1. See these proposals in *Actes de la Conférence de La Haye*, pp. 282, 339, and 441. It should be noted that the International Bureau's proposal was intended to be inserted only in art. 4 of the Madrid Arrangement and be taken later into the text of the Convention.

but selling, or offering to sell, goods on which it is used. It was so understood by the Conference.[1] Indeed, this is all that may reasonably be demanded from a foreign trade-mark owner.

The provision aims at restricting the sanction of cancellation of registration for non-use. However, it does not fix a time before which registration cannot be cancelled. The American and Japanese delegations seem to have objected to such a provision.[2] Instead, it is provided that registration cannot be cancelled until after a reasonable period has elapsed. What length of time from the registration of the mark will be considered a reasonable period in the meaning of this provision is to be determined by the law of each country.[3]

The registration shall not be forfeited at the expiry of the period in question if the interested party justifies his inaction. This last provision is taken from the similar provision of the fourth paragraph of article 5, concerning the working of patents.[4] It was understood at the Conference that special circumstances in the trade might justify inaction[5] and that in such case registration should not be cancelled.[6] The phrase "special circumstances in the trade" was proposed by the British delegation and is taken from the British law.[7] It is interpreted in Great Britain as meaning general conditions and not merely those in the particular business.[8] In general, it must be admitted that the non-use is justified if the conditions of the market have changed, or are such as to render difficult the importation or offer of goods on which the trade mark is to be affixed, in that country.[9]

1. See *Actes de la Conférence de La Haye*, p. 541.

2. See *ibid.*, pp. 441, 541.

3. The American delegation made an express reservation to this effect (see *Actes de la Conférence de La Haye*, p. 576). The periods within which the mark must be used in the countries which impose this obligation are set forth *supra*, § 344.

4. See interpretation of this provision, *supra*, § 224.

5. See *Actes de la Conférence de La Haye*, p. 541.

6. However, the American delegation made the reservation that the legality of the causes of inaction was to be determined in the United States according to the American law and court decisions. See *Actes de la Conférence de La Haye*, p. 576.

7. Sec. 37 of the Trade Marks Act of 1905 (5 Edw. VII, c. 15).

8. See Kerly (Underhay and Morgan), *The Law of Trade Marks and Trade Name*, pp. 346–347.

9. "A man who has a trade mark may properly have regard to the state of the market and the demand for the goods; it would be absurd to suppose that he lost his trade mark by not putting more goods on the market when it was glutted." Per Chitty J., in Mouson *v.* Boehm (1884), 26 C. D. 398. Cf. Daniel and Arter *v.* Whitehouse (1898), 15 R. P. C. 134. The writer is indebted for these references to Kerly (Underhay and Morgan), *The Law of Trade Marks and Trade Name*, pp. 346–347.

The stipulation under consideration applies to all trade marks registered by the persons entitled to the benefits of the Convention, and not only to those registered under the rule of article 6.[1]

§ **401. Obligation to mark registered trade mark.** The sixth paragraph of article 5 provides that no sign or mention of registration shall be required on the goods in order to maintain recognition of the rights given by such registration. This provision is couched in general terms, and it may be taken as applying to trade marks as well as to industrial designs and models. However, its place in article 5, and the preparatory work of the Conference of The Hague, prove that it concerns only designs and models. The first four paragraphs of article 5 deal expressly with patents, the fifth expressly with industrial designs and models, and only the seventh with trade marks. The sixth paragraph in question, being inserted after the fifth, cannot possibly refer to anything but industrial designs and models. The sixth paragraph was taken from a proposal of the German delegation transferring to the text of the Convention the dispositions of article 5 of the draft arrangement for the international deposit of designs and models.[2] This proposal mentioned expressly only industrial designs and models, and all the discussions at the Conference of The Hague referred expressly to them.[3]

It follows, therefore, that the requirements of the law of each country for affixing a sign or mark of registration on trade marks are in no way affected by the Convention.

§ **402. Period of grace for payment of taxes.** Article 5*b* of the Convention provides that an extension of not less than three months shall be allowed for the payment of the prescribed fees for the maintenance of industrial property rights, on condition (if the legislation of a country so provides) of the payment of a supplementary fee. This provision applies to all rights of industrial property and consequently to trade marks. Its interpretation above in respect to patents applies here also, *mutatis mutandis*.[4] This provision is important for trade marks registered in Esthonia and the Serb-Croat-Slovene State, where a yearly tax is payable besides the registration fee, and in Salvador and Spain, where the registration fee is payable at several periods during the protection of the trade mark.[5]

1. See *Actes de la Conférence de La Haye*, p. 442.
2. *Ibid.*, pp. 321, 339.
3. *Ibid.*, pp. 495–497, 506, 520–521, 540–541, 575–576.
4. See *supra*, § 231.
5. See *supra*, p. 501.

CHAPTER XXVI

SPECIAL SANCTIONS AGAINST INFRINGEMENT OF TRADE MARKS

§ 403. Text of article 9 of the Convention of 1883, as originally proposed and adopted.
§ 404. Interpretation given to article 9 at the Conferences of Rome and Madrid.
§ 405. Amendment adopted at Brussels.
§ 406. Amendments at Washington and at The Hague.
§ 407. How far the provisions of article 9 are obligatory on the contracting countries.
§ 408. Conditions of application of article 9.
§ 409. Meaning of the term "illicitement."
§ 410. Who may request seizure or prohibition.
§ 411. Confiscation following seizure.
§ 412. Execution of article 9 by the different countries.
§ 413. Laws of France, Germany, Great Britain, and the United States.
§ 414. Repression of fraudulent use of trade marks.

§ 403. Text of article 9 of the Convention of 1883, as originally proposed and adopted. By virtue of article 2 of the Convention of 1883, persons entitled to the benefits thereof enjoy in the countries of the Union the same protection and the same legal remedies against any infringement of their trade marks as nationals of these countries. Every country of the Union may determine, as it sees fit, the sanctions and remedies against any acts of infringement of trade marks. The Convention has, since its original adoption, however, provided by its article 9 for the application of special measures of repression against articles bearing infringing marks in certain cases where quick and effective action is necessary. This provision was originally taken from the French law, with the expressed intention of transferring into the conventional law the specific remedies granted by that law to French trade-mark owners.[1] Indeed, the draft convention submitted to the Paris Conference of 1880 contained the following provision on the subject: [2]

1. See *Conférence de Paris* (1880), pp. 80–81.
2. *Ibid.*, pp. 79–80. The equivalent provision of article 19 of the French Law of June 23, 1857, was quoted by the Chairman of the Conference as follows:
"Tous produits étrangers portant soit la marque, soit le nom d'un fabricant résidant en France, soit l'indication du nom ou du lieu d'une fabrique française, sont prohibés à l'entrée et exclus du transit et de l'entrepôt, et peuvent être saisis, en quelque lieu que ce soit, soit à la diligence de l'Administration des douanes, soit à la requête du ministère public ou de la partie lesée."

Tout produit portant illicitement soit la marque d'un fabricant ou d'un commerçant établi dans un pays de l'Union, soit une indication de provenance du dit pays, sera prohibé à l'entrée dans tous les autres États contractants, exclu du transit et de l'entrepôt, et pourra être l'objet d'une saisie suivie, s'il y a lieu, d'une action en justice.

This provision referred to the unlawful use of trade marks as well as of indications as to the place of origin. It established the obligation of the contracting countries to prohibit the entry of goods bearing such infringing designations, and to exclude them from transit and storage and also the right of the same countries to seize the goods and eventually to confiscate them. In this sweeping form the provision was opposed, on the ground that no obligation to prohibit the entry should be imposed on the contracting countries;[1] that the transit of goods should not be interfered with;[2] that indications of place of origin should not be dealt with in the same way as trade marks;[3] and that no sanctions should be taken against the infringement of a trade mark which is not registered in the country where protection is claimed.[4]

As a result of these various objections, the indications of place of origin were excluded from article 9 and are dealt with differently in article 10. It was agreed that transit of goods is outside of the scope of article 9, and that not every entry of articles bearing infringing trade marks, but only importation into the country, may cause their seizure. It was specified that the seizure shall be applied only in those countries where the trade mark is legally protected. Lastly, the obligation to prohibit importation was omitted, and seizure was the only sanction provided for.[5] Under these conditions article 9, as adopted by the Conference of 1880, read as follows:

Tout produit portant illicitement une marque de fabrique ou de commerce, ou un nom commercial, pourra être saisi à l'importation dans ceux des États de l'Union dans lesquels cette marque ou ce nom commercial ont droit à la protection légale.

La saisie aura lieu à la requête soit du ministère public, soit de la partie intéressée, conformément à la législation intérieure de chaque État.

Although this article read that a product bearing an infringing trade mark could be seized ("pourra être saisi"), it was understood by the

1. *Conférence de Paris* (1880), pp. 82, 87.
2. *Ibid.*, pp. 82, 87, 93–96.
3. *Ibid.*, pp. 84, 85, 88.
4. *Ibid.*, p. 83.
5. *Ibid.*, pp. 91–97, 143.

Conference that the stipulation implied an obligation of the contracting countries to authorize the seizure. In order to avoid any misunderstanding on this point, the words: "conformément à la législation intérieure de chaque État," which were originally united in a single paragraph with the words "pourra être saisi," were separated and placed in a second paragraph, so as to refer only to the form in which the seizure shall be made.[1] Indeed, an interpretation to the effect that seizure shall be made only if the law of the country in question permits, would render the article useless.

§ **404. Interpretation given to article 9 at the Conferences of Rome and Madrid.** However, all the contracting countries did not take legislative measures to carry out the engagement contained in the above stipulation.

In the reactionary spirit which marked the Conferences of Revision at Rome and Madrid, an official interpretation of article 9 was given, to the effect that the countries of the Union are not bound to legislate for the seizure on importation of articles bearing infringing trade marks.[2] In this sense, article 9 became superfluous and useless. It meant only that articles bearing infringing marks could be seized on importation into a country of the Union if such seizure were permitted by its law. This amounted to granting specifically to the persons entitled to the benefits of the Convention a remedy enjoyed by the nationals, which could be claimed under the general provision of article 2. Moreover, the provision of the second paragraph became meaningless. If each country were free to legislate, or not, for the seizure on importation of articles bearing infringing marks, it could also specify how the seizure should be made.

§ **405. Amendment adopted at Brussels.** At the Madrid Conference of 1890, the delegation of the United States proposed that the seizure of articles bearing infringing marks on importation be replaced by an obligation of the contracting countries to prohibit the

1. See *Conférence de Paris* (1880), pp. 92–93.

2. *Conférence de Rome*, pp. 118–119; *Conférence de Madrid*, pp. 128–129. At the latter Conference the delegate of Sweden and Norway urged that at the Rome Conference article 9 was interpreted in the sense that each country is free to permit or not the seizure, and that if the laws of the United States do not permit it, that country is not in any way bound to authorize a seizure on importation. The delegate of the United States then asked whether there was any member of the Conference who did not agree with the interpretation given to article 9 by the delegate of Sweden and Norway. No contrary opinion was expressed, and the American delegation withdrew its proposal for amending article 9.

importation of such articles.[1] This delegation contended that the idea of seizing goods under the conditions of article 9 is repugnant to the American spirit. Its proposal was not adopted by the Conference.

At the Brussels Conference of 1897, on the other hand, the idea of giving to the stipulation of article 9 greater flexibility won ground, and two new paragraphs were added to it, as follows:

> Dans les États dont la législation n'admet pas la saisie à l'importation, cette saisie pourra être remplacée par la prohibition d'importation.
>
> Les autorités ne sont pas tenues d'effectuer la saisie en cas de transit.

These paragraphs were taken from the provisions (articles 1 and 2) of the Madrid Arrangement for the repression of false indications of origin.[2] The last paragraph was meaningless in view of the interpretation of article 9 admitted at the previous Conferences. If every country should be free to pass no legislation permitting the seizure on importation, neither would it be bound to effect the seizure of goods in transit.

§ **406. Amendments at Washington and at The Hague.** At the Washington Conference of 1911, on the proposal of the French delegation, the provision of article 9 was rendered more flexible by inserting the provisions of articles 1 and 2 of the Madrid Arrangement for the repression of false indications of origin. The words "pourra être" were replaced by the word "sera" in the first and third paragraphs, and a provision was added that, in case the legislation of a country of the Union does not permit the seizure of goods on importation, or the prohibition of importation, or the seizure within such country, these measures shall be replaced by other remedies. Moreover, it was provided that the seizure shall be effected in the country of importation of the goods as well as in the country where the infringing mark has been affixed to the goods.

Few changes of form were made at the Conference of The Hague, and article 9 reads now as follows:

> Tout produit portant illicitement une marque de fabrique ou de commerce, ou un nom commercial, sera saisi à l'importation dans ceux des pays de l'Union dans lesquels cette marque ou ce nom commercial ont droit à la protection légale.
>
> La saisie sera également effectuée dans le pays où l'apposition illicite aura lieu, ou dans le pays où aura été importé le produit.

1. *Conférence de Madrid*, pp. 52–53.
2. *Actes de la Conférence de Bruxelles*, pp. 311–312.

La saisie aura lieu à la requête soit du ministère public, soit de toute autre autorité compétente, soit d'une partie intéressée personne physique ou morale, conformément à la législation intérieure de chaque pays.

Les autorités ne seront pas tenues d'effectuer la saisie en cas de transit.

Si la législation d'un pays n'admet pas la saisie à l'importation, la saisie sera remplacée par la prohibition d'importation ou la saisie à l'intérieur.

Si la législation d'un pays n'admet ni la saisie à l'importation, ni la prohibition d'importation, ni la saisie à l'intérieur, et en attendant que cette législation soit modifiée en conséquence, ces mesures seront remplacées par les actions et moyens que la loi de ce pays assurerait en pareil cas aux nationaux.

§ 407. How far provisions of article 9 are obligatory on contracting countries. Article 9 provides that goods illegally bearing a trade mark shall be seized on importation. If the laws of a country do not admit of seizure on importation, such seizure shall be replaced by prohibition of importation, or seizure within such country. If the laws of a country do not admit of any of these three measures, these shall be replaced by the remedies available in such cases to nationals. These provisions do not impose on the countries of the Union to create or maintain municipal law permitting such seizure or prohibition. They only bind these countries to resort to these measures and, moreover, in the sequence provided for in article 9, in case their legislation admits of such measures.

This interpretation is clearly suggested by the text of the article, as well as by the preparatory work of the Conferences of Washington and The Hague. Indeed, the last paragraph of article 9 provides for the case of a country, the laws of which do not admit of any of the measures enumerated in the article, and stipulates that in such country no more may be claimed than what the law provides for its own nationals. This virtually means that a country is free not to pass legislation allowing seizure or prohibition of importation. The stipulations of the Convention to this effect are mere *voeux*.

This was expressly confirmed at the last conference of The Hague. The French delegation proposed the insertion in the last paragraph of the phrase "et en attendant que cette législation soit modifiée en conséquence," before the provision that the measures enumerated shall be replaced by the measures available to nationals.[1] On the objection of the Swiss delegation that this phrase would imply an engagement on the part of the contracting countries to pass legisla-

1. *Actes de la Conférence de La Haye*, p. 346.

tion allowing seizure, the French delegation replied that the words are meant only as an invitation addressed to the contracting countries, which would create for them no engagement, nor even a moral duty.[1] This interpretation of the phrase—that is, that it constitutes only a *voeu*—was expressly declared by the Conference.[2]

The contracting countries, then, are called upon by article 9 to repress the infringement of trade marks by the three enumerated specific sanctions, which are considered to afford effective protection to the proprietors of trade marks. In case their laws admit of such measures, their application shall be made as provided in article 9—that is, the goods shall be seized on importation, if seizure is permitted by the law of the country in question; or their importation shall be prohibited, if the law does not admit of seizure, but permits prohibition; only if neither of the above two measures is available, shall the goods be seized within the country, in case the law permits.[3] This is the meaning of the words "sera saisi" and "sera remplacée" of the first and fifth paragraphs, which were substituted for the words "pourra être saisi" and "pourra être remplacée" of the earlier text, at the Washington Conference.[4]

This solved a controversy in France over the question whether persons entitled to the benefits of the Convention may always cause the seizure on importation of goods infringing their trade marks.[5] Indeed, the seizure is obligatory on the administration in France by virtue of article 19 of the Law of 1857. There should be no doubt that such seizure, like any other protection and other remedies enjoyed by nationals in France, could be claimed by persons entitled to the benefit of the Convention, even under article 2 alone.

Mention should be made here of the first paragraph of article 10*c* which reads as follows:

> Les pays contractants s'engagent à assurer aux ressortissants des autres pays de l'Union des recours légaux appropriés pour réprimer efficacement tous les actes visés aux articles 9, 10 et 10 *bis*.

This provision is a reinforcement of the stipulations of article 9. While, under the latter article, the member countries of the Union

1. *Actes de la Conférence de La Haye*, p. 470.
2. *Ibid.*, pp. 525, 545.
3. See Osterrieth, *Washingtoner Konferenz*, p. 88.
4. See *Actes de la Conférence de Washington*, pp. 302–303, 309.
5. See Pillet, *Régime International*, pp. 417–418; Pelletier et Vidal-Naquet, *Convention d'Union*, pp. 272–273; Pouillet (Taillefer et Claro) *Traité des Marques*, p. 471; L. Brun, *Marques de Fabrique et de Commerce*, p. 385.

are "invited" to grant to "ressortissants" of the Union the specific remedies enumerated therein, under article 10*c* these countries bind themselves to assure to such persons appropriate legal remedies for an effective repression of the acts of infringement envisaged in article 9. In view of both these provisions, a country would certainly fail to carry out its engagements under the Convention if it should not afford by its legislation quick and effective remedies against infringers of trade marks. Penal sanctions, and injunctions against the continuance of infringement acts, would seem to have been understood by the Conference of The Hague as remedies implied in the engagement of article 10*c*.[1]

§ **408. Conditions of application of article 9.** In case the law of a country of the Union admits of seizure on importation, prohibition of importation, or seizure within the country, the provisions of article 9 must be complied with. These remedies can be claimed under article 9 if certain conditions concur. First, the goods shall be seized, or their importation prohibited, if the trade mark which is illegally applied to such goods is legally protected in the country in question. When a mark is legally protected in a country, is a question of its law. In almost all the countries a mark is not protected as such unless it is registered. Only in the United States are unregistered trade marks protected by the common law of trade marks.

Second, the countries in which the remedies of article 9 are to be resorted to are the country in which the goods in question have been imported and that in which the mark was illegally applied. That is to say, the acts of importation and of illegal application of the trade mark determine the application of article 9. Thus, if the goods are merely exported from a country where the illegal application did not take place, or if they are transported through a country, — that is, are in transit, — article 9 does not apply. Indeed, when the goods are exported illegally bearing a trade mark, the illegal application as a rule takes place in the country from which they are exported. The non-application of the provisions of article 9 in cases of transit is justified by the general interest of freedom of commerce which outweighs the interest of repression of infringing trade marks.

§ **409. Meaning of the term "illicitement."** Third, the remedies of article 9 may be claimed in case the goods in question illegally

1. See proposals and their adoption, in *Actes de la Conférence de La Haye*, pp. 478–479, 525, 547.

bear a trade mark in the country into which they have been imported, or in the country where the mark was applied. If the mark borne by or applied to the goods in question infringes the trade mark of another, the act is illegal in the sense of article 9, and the remedies of this article may be claimed.[1] In the country where the mark is applied, the illegal act is consummated at the moment of the application of the infringing mark. In the country of importation of the goods, the illegal act is continuous from the moment of importation. No fraudulent intent or knowledge of illegality is required by article 9. It is sufficient that the mark in question infringes the trade mark of a person entitled to claim under this article.[2]

The question whether or not there is such infringement is determined by the law of the country where the act takes place. Thus, if the seizure of the goods is requested in the country where the mark was illegally applied, it is for the law of that country to say whether the application of the mark was illegal, that is, whether there was an infringement of another's trade mark. Likewise, the right of seizure in the country of importation exists only in case, by the law of that country, the mark is illegally borne by the goods in question. It is immaterial, then, that by the law of another country the application or the bearing of the mark in question is not illegal. For instance, the seizure of goods imported in France and bearing a mark infringing a French trade mark, cannot be defended on the ground that the mark in question is owned by the importer or proprietor of the goods according to the law of Great Britain.[3]

§ **410. Who may request seizure or prohibition.** The third paragraph of article 9 provides that the seizure shall take place at the request of the public prosecutor, or any other competent authority, or any interested party. Although only seizure is mentioned here,

1. The equivalent provision of the French law, from which the first paragraph of article 9 is taken, is as follows:

"Tous produits étrangers portant . . . la marque . . . d'un fabriquant résidant en France . . ." See note (2).

2. Osterrieth und Axster, *Pariser Konvention*, p. 198.

3. So held by the German Reichsgericht, March 2, 1905 (*Blatt für Pat.- Must.- und Zeichenwesen*, 1905, p. 247). A New York company which had used a trade mark for more than thirty years sent goods to Germany bearing its trade mark. Two months before such importation, another New York company registered the same trade mark in Germany. The latter caused the seizure and confiscation of the former's goods. Held that, although the former company's mark was well known in Germany, and the application of the mark on the goods in the United States was perfectly legal, at the moment of importation in Germany the goods bore illegally a trade mark registered and protected in Germany.

the same applies to prohibition of importation. A competent authority is, especially, the customs administration in the case of goods which are being imported. This term also includes any other administrative or executive authority to which such powers are given in a country of the Union.

The interested party is the proprietor of the trade mark which is protected in the country in question and is infringed by the mark illegally applied to, or borne by, the goods. Such party may be a "personne physique ou morale." These words were substituted at the Conference of The Hague for the words of the old text, "particulier ou société," as being broader and covering cases where the interested party may be neither an individual nor a "société" in the strict sense of the word.[1] The phrase "personne morale" should be interpreted as meaning a corporate or an unincorporated entity. The Conference declared expressly that the new term does not affect the question whether or not unions and associations may intervene, as well as the proprietors of trade marks.[2] The question of intervention of syndicates and professional unions created for the protection of their members against infringement of their rights forms the subject of the second paragraph of the new article 10*c* of the Convention adopted at The Hague. This paragraph reads thus:

> Ils s'engagent, en outre, à prévoir des mesures pour permettre aux syndicats et associations réprésentant l'industrie et le commerce intéressé et dont l'existence n'est pas contraire aux lois de leurs pays, d'agir en justice ou auprès des autorités administratives, en vue de la répression des actes prévus par les articles 9, 10, et 10 *bis*, dans la mesure ou la loi du pays dans lequel la protection est réclamée le permet aux syndicats et associations de ce pays.

The engagement entered into under this provision by the contracting countries is to create and maintain municipal law. It is not a self-executing treaty provision. The syndicates and associations in question may intervene, with a view to securing repression of the acts provided for in article 9 (as well as in articles 10 and 10*b*) only in case, and to the extent that, the law of the country where they claim such action permits.[3]

1. See *Actes de la Conférence de La Haye*, p. 250.
2. *Ibid.*, pp. 470, 545.
3. See on the adoption of this provision, *Actes de la Conférence de La Haye*, pp. 479, 525, 545.

The remedies provided for by article 9 are to be effected, according to the last phrase of the third paragraph, in conformity with the domestic law of each country.

§ **411. Confiscation following seizure.** Prohibition of importation, and seizure on importation or within the country, are often only provisional measures leading to confiscation of the goods for the benefit of the injured party. Confiscation is in no way dealt with in article 9. The law of the country where the seizure or prohibition is effected determines the further sanctions. Persons entitled to the benefits of the Convention may take steps for the confiscation of the goods by virtue of article 2 of the Convention.[1]

§ **412. Execution of article 9 by the different countries.** Not all the countries of the Union have passed laws for the seizure, or prohibition of importation, of articles bearing infringing trade marks. The International Bureau of Berne made an inquiry in 1925 into the legislation of the various countries of the Union from the point of view of the remedies provided for in article 9 of the Convention. It was found [2] that fifteen countries of the Union [3] possessed legislation providing for administrative seizure on importation, or prohibition, of articles bearing infringing marks. In three of these countries such seizure was possible only in the case of goods bearing the sign or name of the Red Cross.[4] In eight countries, judicial seizure within the country could be applied for,[5] and in five countries, both seizure on importation and seizure within the country were possible.[6]

The Standing Committee on Industrial Property of the International Chamber of Commerce caused a resolution to be adopted by the Chamber at its Rome Congress in 1923, to the effect that article 9 of the Convention should be amended so as to impose on all the countries seizure on importation by the customs administration of

1. Pillet, *Régime International*, p. 419; Pelletier et Vidal-Naquet, *Convention d'Union*, p. 274; Osterrieth und Axster, *Pariser Konvention*, p. 198.

2. See tabulated information in *Propriété Industrielle* (1925), pp. 44 ff.; and *Actes de la Conférence de La Haye*, pp. 150 ff.

3. Brazil, Bulgaria, Cuba, Czechoslovakia, Dominican Republic, Finland, France, Germany, Great Britain, Hungary, Portugal, Spain, Switzerland, Tunis, and the United States.

4. Czechoslovakia, Hungary, and Switzerland.

5. Austria, Greece, Italy, Morocco, Mexico, Rumania, Syria and Lebanon, and Turkey.

6. France, Hungary, Portugal, Switzerland, and Tunis.

goods bearing infringing marks.[1] No such proposal was made at the Conference of The Hague. Had it been made, it would not have had the chance of being adopted.

§ 413. Laws of France, Germany, Great Britain, and the United States. In France, the Law of 1857 (article 19)[2] provides that articles bearing the mark of a resident manufacturer shall be seized and confiscated. Also the Law of January 11, 1892 (article 15)[3] prohibits the entry of foreign goods, whether on importation, in storage, or in transit, bearing a trade mark which might induce people to believe that they have been manufactured in France, or are of French origin. This law goes much further than article 9 of the Convention. It allows seizure and confiscation of goods which may bear a legal foreign mark, infringing no French mark, if by its appearance it may deceive the public as to the origin of the goods.[4]

In Germany, article 17 of the Trade Mark Law of May 12, 1894, provides that foreign goods infringing a registered trade mark shall be seized on their entry into the country, whether they come in on importation or in transit. The seizure is followed by confiscation.[5]

In Great Britain, the Merchandise Marks Act of 1887 [6] (section 16) forbids the importation of goods by means of, or in relation to, which an offense against it has been committed, and also of all goods of foreign manufacture bearing any name or trade mark being or purporting to be that of a manufacturer or trader within the country, unless it be accompanied by a definite indication of the country where the goods were made or produced. The first part of the prohibition is directed against false marking only, while the latter concerns the mere fact of bearing an infringing trade mark.[7]

In the United States, section 27 of the Act of 1905 [8] provides that no article of imported merchandise copying or simulating the name or trade mark of any domestic manufacturer or trader shall be ad-

1. See *Propriété Industrielle* (1925), p. 45.
2. *Bulletin des Lois* (1857), I, 1331.
3. *Ibid.* (1892), I, 33. The benefit of both these Laws may be claimed by "ressortissants" of the Union by virtue of articles 2 and 9 of the Convention.
4. So held in Gluck et Leinkauf *c.* Ministère Public, Douanes et Syndicat professionel du Caoutchouc, Cassation, March 26, 1914 (*Clunet*, 1914, p. 1245).
5. *Reichsgesetzblatt* (1894), p. 441.
6. 50 & 51 Vict., c. 28.
7. On the amendment of the Merchandise Marks Act of 1887 by the Act of Dec. 15, 1926 (16 & 17 Geo. V, c. 53) with a view of repressing false indications of origin, see *infra*, § 479.
8. XXXIII *U. S. Stat. at Large*, 724.

mitted to entry at any customhouse of the United States. Manufacturers and traders may require their names and a copy of the certificate of registration of their trade marks to be recorded at the Treasury Department, and the Secretary of the Treasury shall cause the same to be transmitted to the proper officers of the customs. The benefit of this section is enjoyed also by foreign manufacturers or traders on condition of reciprocity.

On the other hand, section 526 of the Tariff Act of September 21, 1922,[1] declares it to be unlawful to import into the United States any merchandise of foreign manufacture, if such merchandise or its container or label bears a trade mark owned by an American national or corporation and registered by a person domiciled in the United States, if a copy of the certificate or registration of such trade mark is filed with the Secretary of the Treasury, and unless written consent of the owner of such trade mark is produced at the time of making entry. Any such merchandise imported into the United States shall be subject to seizure and forfeiture for violation of the customs laws.

§ 414. Repression of fraudulent use of trade marks. Article 9 of the Convention deals only with the seizure and prohibition of importation of goods bearing infringing trade marks. All other remedies and sanctions against infringement of trade marks are to be determined by each of the contracting countries as it sees fit. In an inquiry made by the International Bureau in 1925, covering all the countries of the Union, it was found that in all of them civil sanctions are provided by the law against infringement, while penal sanctions for the fraudulent use of trade marks are also imposed in all these countries, with the exception of the United States.[2]

The Standing Committee of the International Chamber of Commerce,[3] as well as the Chamber itself,[4] and the Committee of Experts which met on the invitation of the League of Nations at Geneva on May 5, 1924,[5] studied the question how far the Convention of Union should be amended to include definite sanctions against the fraudulent use of trade marks. The resolution to this effect adopted by the Committee of Experts was proposed by the International Bureau at

1. XLII *U. S. Stat. at Large*, 975.
2. See *Propriété Industrielle* (1925), pp. 32 ff.
3. *Ibid.* (1923), p. 65.
4. *Ibid.* (1924), p. 75.
5. *Ibid.* (1924), pp. 99, 101, Resolution A.

the Conference of The Hague as article 6 *ter*. It provided as follows:[1]

Les pays contractants s'engagent à assurer dans leur législation nationale aux ressortissants des autres pays contractants un recours légal comportant, outre les sanctions civiles, des sanctions pénales contre tout usage frauduleux de leurs marques.

This provision would have the effect of taking over into the international domain the sanction admitted in the national regime of trade marks, and of compelling the United States to impose penal sanctions against the infringement of foreign trade marks. The delegation of the latter country having declared its absolute opposition to the adoption of any provision concerning penal sanctions, the above proposal was abandoned.[2]

In the United States, the sanctions provided by the Trade Marks Act of 1905 (sections 16, 19, 20) are damages at the suit of the owner of the trade mark, which may be entered by the court for any sum above the amount of the actual damages, according to the circumstances of the case, not exceeding three times such amount. An injunction also may be granted, and the court may order the destruction of all labels, containers, and so forth, bearing the infringing trade mark.

No constitutional or other difficulty, however, should exist in the United States in the way of passing an act of Congress for the criminal prosecution of fraudulent infringers of trade marks. The common law offense of obtaining money under false pretenses, which may be resorted to only for the prosecution of counterfeiters of trade marks, does not give much satisfaction.[3] Several states of the Union have penal statutes for the protection of trade marks registered in such states.[4] Since the present trade-mark registration act of Congress is valid, limited as it is to trade marks used in interstate and foreign commerce, a penal act, similar to that of 1876 and applicable to infringers of trade marks registered under the Act of 1905, would be perfectly valid, and would grant to foreigners a protection that American trade-mark owners enjoy in all other countries.

1. *Actes de la Conférence de La Haye*, p. 246. The British and French delegations proposed the insertion of this provision as the last paragraph of article 9. *Ibid.*, pp. 343, 470.

2. *Ibid.*, pp. 457, 470.

3. See Hopkins, *The Law of Trade Marks, Trade Names and Unfair Competition* (Cincinnati, 1924), pp. 408–409.

4. *Ibid.*, p. 409, and texts of some statutes in Appendix, pp. 620 ff.

CHAPTER XXVII

ASSOCIATION TRADE MARKS

§ 415. Efforts for international protection of association trade marks. Association trade marks have a long history. The guild marks of the Middle Ages,[1] and perhaps a sort of common signature affixed on certain articles in the Roman epoch,[2] may be classified as association marks. The guild marks were obligatory [3] on the members of the corporations, and when the latter were abolished, their marks also disappeared.

In modern times, with the reappearance of trading associations, the need of common marks to be used by the members of the association became more and more urgent.[4] Their scope and function was now enlarged. They aimed not only at guaranteeing the quality of the product, as standardization marks used by any body of persons corporate or unincorporated, but also at vouching for the mode of manufacture, or the origin, of products of a community, region, or entire country. Moreover, it was believed that association marks would lend themselves with greater difficulty to infringement, would be protected more effectively, and would save a great amount of

1. See *supra*, § 3.
2. See Kohler, *Das Recht des Markenschutzes*, p. 37.
3. See *ibid.*, p. 44.
4. See Frey-Godet, "Les Marques et leur Enregistrement National," in *Annuaire* (1897), pp. 195, 201; Moise Amar, "Des Marques Collectives," *ibid.* (1900), pp. 113 ff.; Pey, "Les Marques d'Origine Collectives, *ibid.* (1900), pp. 119 ff.; Richard, *De la Protection des Appellations d'Origine* (Bordeaux, 1918), pp. 186 ff.

money to the members by the possibility of common advertisement and protection.[1]

However, the laws of the different countries were slow in recognizing and protecting such marks, and it was generally realized that the international protection which was of prime importance to association marks would fall through, unless, by international agreement, the various countries agreed to protect such marks.

As early as 1890, at the Madrid Conference for the Revision of the Convention of 1883, on the proposal of the Belgian delegation, a provision was adopted in the Protocol of Interpretation and Execution of the Convention, to the effect that trade marks of municipalities and associations should be protected in the same way as individual trade marks; that such marks may be deposited; and that on their infringement, action may be brought by a competent authority, by the association, or any interested party.[2] This Protocol was not ratified and the provision in question never came into force.

At the Brussels Conference, the International Bureau proposed a draft arrangement for the protection of association trade marks as well as marks belonging to public administrations, such as state, district, region, or community.[3] However, at that time in many countries the law did not recognize even domestic marks of this kind. The question was not yet ripe, and the Conference adopted only a *voeu* for the protection of association marks.[4]

Following this Conference, the question of these marks was discussed unremittingly at the congresses of the International Association for the Protection of Industrial Property[5] until the Washington Conference, when article *7b* was adopted and inserted in the Convention of 1883.

§ **416. Association trade marks defined.** The nature of association trade marks is very different from that of individual marks. The latter serve to distinguish the goods of one producer from similar goods of other producers. The former denote the origin, material, mode of manufacture, quality, or other characteristics of goods. In

1. See, for instance, the attempts to create a trade mark of the British Empire, in *Propriété Industrielle* (1913), pp. 147 ff. and 166 ff.
2. *Conférence de Madrid*, p. 168.
3. *Actes de la Conférence de Bruxelles*, p. 69.
4. *Ibid.*, pp. 278, 281, 286, 289, 351.
5. See *Annuaire* (1897), pp. 156, 201, 406; (1900), p. 305; (1901), pp. 112 ff., 119 ff.; (1902), pp. 63, 205, 218; (1904), pp. 215, 234, 479, 669; (1905), pp. 47, 271, 363, 471; (1910), pp. 173, 257, 369.

respect to these, the public is not so much interested in the particular producer as in the place of origin, or mode of manufacture, or quality of the goods. These conditions may be satisfied by several producers of a certain category or categories. There is no direct connection of the association mark with the goods themselves, but rather with the special conditions under which the goods are produced.[1]

The differentiation between the two classes of trade marks should cause differences in regulation. Individual trade marks are registered and protected in connection with a certain class or classes of goods. Such limitation is unnecessary in respect to association trade marks. The manufacturers of a certain locality may quite properly own and register a trade mark without regard to a special class or classes of goods. The association may comprise all kinds of manufactures. Its membership may be subject to change at all times, and consequently the categories of goods on which the mark is to be applied may also change.

Association trade marks may be of two kinds, private and public; that is, they may be registered and owned by private associations of producers, or professional unions, or by a national or local administration, as marks of goods produced in a certain city, community, district, region, or country. For instance, the silk or cotton manufacturers of a certain region may form an association, and the latter may register a trade mark to be used by all the members of the association in connection with their businesses. This is a private association trade mark. The law may give the right to all national manufacturers of any products, or of a special product manufactured in the entire country or in a region or locality of that country, to use a distinctive trade mark. For instance, in Germany, all manufacturers may affix to their exported products the imperial eagle; in France, likewise, the national stamp or hall mark may be affixed; in Denmark, all exporters of butter must affix to the packages a special mark; [2] in Italy, by a recent law, a national mark for exported fruits and vegetables was instituted.[3] These are public marks, and may be national, regional, or local.

1. See an article, "Les Marques Collectives," in *Propriété Industrielle* (1917), pp. 73, 76; Pey, "Les Marques d'Origine Collectives," in *Annuaire de l'Association Internationale* (1901), pp. 119, 126.

2. *Propriété Industrielle* (1913), p. 149.

3. Law No. 1272 of June 23, 1927, and Decrees of Sept. 28 and Nov. 17, 1927 (*Propriété Industrielle*, 1928, pp. 57, 58, 126). The application of the mark to other articles also is contemplated (*ibid.*, p. 91).

Public trade marks are usually trade marks of origin, while private association marks may be standardization marks guaranteeing the mode of manufacture or quality of the goods. However, a clear distinction does not always exist. A mark may denote both origin and mode of manufacture. For instance, the French mark of the silk industry of Lyons, which was instituted in 1885, was a mark of origin as well as a mark of mode of manufacture and quality.[1]

§ **417. Advantages of these marks.** Association trade marks of origin are very important for effective protection against false indications of origin. Indeed, as is shown in the next section, great difficulties are often presented to the repression of false indications of origin which involve no infringement of a trade mark. A geographical name, which originally is an indication of origin, may become in current language the name of the product; for instance, Champagne, Cognac, Eau de Cologne, and the like. Or a geographical name may indicate a kind or quality of goods rather than the place of origin of that product; for instance, "Portorico," for a certain kind of tobacco manufactured in Germany, which no one believes to have been produced in Porto Rico. A dividing line in this respect is extremely difficult to draw. It is not easy to reconcile the conflicting interests of the manufacturers of the place of origin and of those of other places who may have used the geographical name quite innocently, and have, through long use, built up a goodwill.

It is difficult also, in respect to indications of origin, to determine the degree of transformation of the raw materials, or of completion of the products, which entitles the producer to use the name of a place of origin. Still another difficulty exists in respect to the territorial limits of a locality or region to which the name properly belongs.[2]

These difficulties are, for the most part, done away with by association marks adopted and registered either by a public authority, or by the legal representatives of an association of producers for the benefit of the latter. The geographical name itself may be used by persons unconnected with the association, but not the trade mark of the latter. The association also may determine by its statutes the category or categories of persons entitled to use the trade mark.

1. *Annuaire de l'Association Internationale* (1901), p. 129.

2. Amar, "Des Marques Collectives," in *Annuaire de l'Association Internationale* (1901), pp. 112, 116. See also *infra*, § 461.

Association trade marks offer many further advantages. They reduce the expenses and fees required for the registration and protection of individual marks in many countries. They permit large and expensive advertisement to small producers of a certain locality, or of a special product, who, isolated, would be unable to extend their trade beyond a limited area. They render infringement more difficult and action against it more effective through the association. Lastly, the buying public is free from deception, because the origin of goods is denoted by the association mark, and no longer by a mere geographical name which may be falsely applied.[1]

§ **418. Objections to association marks.** While association trade marks, private or public, possess these advantages, they also lend themselves to serious objections and involve certain dangers which should be taken into consideration for due regulation of the domestic as well as the international regime of these marks.

First, association trade marks of origin are essentially international marks. They are adopted and used primarily on exported goods. Unless, however, these marks are protected in foreign countries, they will cause more harm than benefit to the users. Indeed, in such case, they will be imitated by foreign producers and will permit palming off goods of imitators of the marks for those of the true owners. Only in respect to countries which are parties to the Madrid Arrangement for the repression of false indications of origin, could the marks in question be protected if they contained an indication of the place of origin. This objection is overcome if protection of association trade marks in all the countries of the Union is assured.

A second danger lies in the form of the trade marks in question. A word mark, containing only the geographical name of the place of origin, may be refused protection in some countries as not distinctive. Indeed, article 6 of the Convention permits such refusal. Such marks, then, will lend themselves to unobstructed imitation. It is with reason, therefore, that the International Bureau proposed that association trade marks should be figurative.[2]

A very serious objection against association trade marks is that they may become a badge of bad quality, or a vehicle for the sale of goods of inferior quality, and thus may hurt the whole industry

1. Frey-Godet, "Les Marques et leur Enregistrement International," in *Annuaire de l'Association Internationale* (1897), pp. 195, 201–202.
2. *Actes de la Conférence de Bruxelles*, p. 75.

which they aim at protecting, or the producers who manufacture goods of superior quality.[1] Indeed, an association trade mark, either public or private, may in some cases be used only by producers of goods of inferior quality. The other producers may elect not to use such a trade mark, either because their own individual marks enjoy a greater reputation, or because they do not desire to identify their own goods with the inferior goods of other producers of the same locality or region. In such case the inferiority of the products placed on the market with the association mark will hurt the reputation of the whole industry of the locality or place of origin in question. If, on the other hand, the best manufacturers elect to use the association mark, they risk losing their market by the inferiority of similar goods of other manufacturers.

This danger is avoided when the association in question has a limited membership of manufacturers producing a more or less similar quality of goods, or when the association submits the goods on which the mark is to be applied to a prior examination, for the purpose of determining whether they come up to the standard of quality, for which alone the application of the mark is permissible.

The solution to be found is more difficult when membership is not limited, as is especially the case of public association trade marks, applied by a certain category or categories of producers of a locality, district, region, or country.[2] In such cases the International Bureau proposed [3] that the association trade marks should be additional to the individual trade marks. Thus, while all producers of a locality, region, and so on, should have the power to use the association mark, they would be bound also to apply to their products their individual mark. One might go further, and provide that the individual trade mark should force itself on the attention of the public more prominently than the association mark. In that way, the advantages of the association mark would be enjoyed, and the individual reputation of the mark of every manufacturer preserved.

§ **419. Questions for international regulation.** From the point of view of international regulation of the matter of association trade

1. See *Annuaire de l'Association Internationale* (1900), p. 365; *ibid.* (1901), p. 124; also *Propriété Industrielle* (1913), pp. 147, 150. See also objections to the creation of a national British mark in *ibid.* (1922), pp. 71, 73.

2. See, however, the regime of control, supervision, and examination introduced by the Italian law of 1927, creating the national mark for exported fruits and vegetables. See note 3 on p. 589.

3. *Actes de la Conférence de Bruxelles*, p. 70.

marks, besides the question of protection of such marks in principle, several other questions should be determined. It is especially important to define the associations or bodies of persons that may own and register a trade mark; for to leave every country free to determine whether a certain grouping of persons may or may not register a trade mark might have the consequence of denying protection to such marks in certain countries. Questions may arise whether local, regional, or national trade marks registered by a public authority, or by an authorized body, are registrable in foreign countries, and under what conditions and formalities. Then too, the question of assimilation of, or distinction between, association and individual marks in respect to registration and protection from infringement should be determined.

All these questions could best be regulated by nothing short of an agreement for international registration of association marks. Indeed, these marks, being primarily destined for foreign markets, should be assured protection through international registration. It is to be regretted that the early suggestion to this effect by the International Bureau, at the Brussels Conference, was not adopted.

At the Washington Conference, the International Bureau proposed a new article to be inserted in the Convention of 1883.[1] Under it, association marks were assimilated to individual marks in respect to the conditions and formalities of filing. But they were not to be admitted for deposit in the contracting countries, unless the association was a juristic person, and the mark was duly filed in the country of origin. It was also provided that the persons who might use the trade mark should be indicated on the deposit of the mark, and that each of these persons, as well as the legal representatives of the association, should be allowed to sue for infringement of the mark.

1. The draft of this proposed article read as follows:

Toute marque régulièrement déposée dans son pays d'origine par une collectivité ayant une existence juridique aux termes de la loi locale, sera admise au dépôt dans les autres pays de l'Union, au même titre que les marques individuelles, et sous les mêmes conditions et formalités.

La où les catégories de personnes autorisées à faire usage de la marque seront indiquées dans l'acte de dépôt.

Les droits résultant du dépôt et de l'enregistrement de la marque seront exercés par les réprésentants légaux de la collectivité. Celle-ci peut d'ailleurs autoriser ses membres à poursuivre individuellement la contrefaçon ou l'imitation de la marque, lorsqu'ils envisagent qu'il en résulte pour eux un dommage.

See *Actes de la Conférence de Washington*, p. 52.

§ **420. Stipulations of the Convention.** The Bureau's proposition constituted a proposal of international legislation on the subject of international protection of association trade marks. In this form it met with little support at the Conference. All delegations were unwilling to adopt anything derogating from their municipal law and proposed amendments tending to make the new article conformable to such law.[1]

As a result, the Bureau's proposed text was stripped of all its real international importance, and the following stipulation was adopted as article *7b* of the Convention:

> Les pays contractants s'engagent à admettre au dépôt et à protéger les marques appartenant à des collectivités dont l'existence n'est pas contraire à la loi du pays d'origine, même si ces collectivités ne possèdent pas un établissement industriel ou commercial.
>
> Cependant chaque pays sera juge des conditions particulières sous lesquelles une collectivité pourra être admise à faire protéger ses marques.

This provision remained unmodified at the Conference of The Hague.

§ **421. Who may deposit under article *7b*.** Article *7b* lays down the general principle that the contracting countries are bound to admit for deposit and protect marks belonging to associations. It does not attempt any regulation of the protection, except by providing that an association will not be denied registration of its trade mark for the reason that it does not possess an industrial or commercial establishment. This is the only further positive engagement of the contracting countries.[2]

The associations whose marks the contracting countries are bound to admit for deposit and to protect must not exist contrary to the law of the country of origin. It is not clear what this provision means. Certainly an association whose existence is contrary to the law of a country cannot be tolerated by that law. Therefore the existence of an association and the absence of offense against the law should necessarily concur. The provision should be compared to the corresponding provision of the proposal of the International Bureau. The latter spoke of associations possessing a juristic existence according to the law of the country of origin ("ayant une existence juridique aux termes de la loi locale"). The phrase adopted by the Conference

1. *Actes de la Conférence de Washington*, pp. 93, 96, 101, 223, 304.
2. See Osterrieth, *Washingtoner Konferenz*, p. 80.

does not speak of juristic existence according to the law, but of an existence not contrary to the law. It would seem, then, that the meaning of the provision is that the associations in question need not have a juristic existence, that is, constitute a juristic person. A factual situation is envisaged by the provision: that is, the mere existence of an association, the ends of which are not unlawful.[1]

However, the mere existence in fact of an association does not *ipso facto* entitle it to register its trade mark in the contracting countries. The second paragraph of article *7b* provides that each country shall be the sole judge of the particular conditions under which an association may be allowed to obtain protection ("pourra être admise à faire protéger") for its marks. It was explicitly declared at the Washington Conference that the words "pourra être admise" were substituted for the original words "sera admise" in the second paragraph, to make it certain that a country may refuse an association trade mark on the ground of the character of the association which applies for its registration.[2]

§ **422. National marks.** It was especially doubtful whether the state or its administrative divisions, or the public administrations themselves, national, local, or regional come under the term "collectivités" used in article *7b*. In all the discussions prior to the Washington Conference, private as well as public association trade marks were dealt with in the same way. At the Washington Conference, the latter were not mentioned explicitly. Moreover, the provisions "dont l'existence n'est pas contraire à la loi du pays d'origine," and "même si les collectivités ne possèdent pas un établissement industriel ou commercial" seem to indicate that the "collectivités" referred to in article *7b* are private associations.

An official interpretation in this respect was given to the term "collectivités" by the Conference of The Hague. The International Bureau proposed the addition of a third paragraph to article *7b*, as follows:[3]

1. In the discussion of article *7b*, the French delegation desired that the associations in question should be those carrying on a commercial, industrial, or agricultural business; the Japanese, that the associations should have a legal existence; another delegation, that the association should not have a political end; and the Belgian delegation, that professional unions should be included in the associations in question. See *Actes de la Conférence de Washington*, p. 304.

2. *Actes de la Conférence de Washington*, p. 309. See also reservations of the Japanese, British, and American delegations to this effect, *ibid.*, p. 254.

3. *Actes de la Conférence de La Haye*, p. 248.

Les pays contractants s'engagent également à admettre au dépôt et à protéger les marques dites régionales ou nationales adoptées dans un but d'intérêt général par des autorités ou par des associations autorisées.

Thus, regional and national marks were to be admitted for deposit, and protected, as private association trade marks. In the discussion of article *7b* the Czechoslovakian delegation declared its unwillingness to accept the extension of the provisions of the article to regional marks, as no general interest would be promoted thereby. As to national marks, Czechoslovakia would admit them only if deposited by a public authority and not by an authorized association. Several delegations contended that national marks alone might well come under the term "collectivité" of the first paragraph, and that it would be sufficient to make a declaration to this effect. Such a declaration was adopted unanimously by the sub-committee and taken down in the *procès-verbaux*.[1] Although in principle it seems awkward to place states under the present terms of article *7b*, there should be no doubt, after the Conference of The Hague, that this article is to be understood as including them. The question whether a national trade mark can be registered by the state, or by an association authorized thereto, is to be determined by the law of each country according to the second paragraph of the article.

§ **423. What may be deposited under article 7*b*.** The Convention does not define what may be deposited as an association trade mark. It does not even require that the mark be registered or protected in the country of origin of the association before it can be admitted for deposit, and protected, in the other countries. The second paragraph of article *7b* permits each country to determine the conditions which foreign association trade marks must satisfy in both of these respects. As this paragraph was interpreted by the Washington Conference, a country may refuse an association mark by reason of its character or its inaccuracy, and it may determine the conditions of admission, either by general regulations, or for each single mark whose deposit is applied for.[2]

The power of each country to determine the conditions of admission for each specific association mark makes the whole international regime of such marks entirely insecure. The International Chamber of Commerce in 1923 adopted a resolution calling for the amendment

1. *Actes de la Conférence de La Haye*, pp. 467–468.

2. *Ibid.*, p. 309; also reservations to this effect by the American and British delegations, *ibid.*, p. 254.

of the second paragraph of article *7b*. For the words "chaque pays sera juge," the words "chaque pays déterminera par voie législative ou réglementaire" would be substituted.[1] A proposal to this effect was made at the Conference of The Hague by the Italian delegation, but it was not insisted upon.[2]

Association trade marks coming under one of the exceptions of article 6 may undoubtedly be refused.[3] Also, marks which purport to denote a characteristic of the goods which the association in question is unable to certify may be excluded.

It is not required by article *7b* that an association should declare the characteristic of the goods which the mark purports to denote; for instance, origin, mode of manufacture, quality, and the like. All this is to be determined by the law of each country.

A number of association trade marks may be protected indirectly by other provisions of the Convention, especially that of article *6c* concerning official signs and hall marks of control or warranty. Such marks adopted by one of the contracting countries in respect to certain products, and also national marks bearing armorial bearings, emblems, and the like, will be protected, since the contracting countries agree in article *6c* to refuse or cancel the registration, and to prohibit the utilization, of reproductions or imitations of such marks.

§ 424. Application of article 7b in the various countries. Whatever the shortcomings of article *7b* may be, and to whatever extent its application is left to the determination of each country, there is a formal and unmistakable engagement of all the contracting countries to admit for deposit, and to protect, under conditions to be determined by them, association trade marks. A country of the Union refusing, in principle, admission to such marks commits a clear breach of its international engagements.[4] However, in many countries of the Union association trade marks still are not registrable. These countries are Austria, Bulgaria, Czechoslovakia, Danzig (Free City), Dominican Republic, Esthonia, Greece, Latvia, Luxembourg, Mexico, Rumania, Serb-Croat-Slovene State, Tunis, and Turkey. Moreover, a number of countries admit for deposit and protect only certain kinds of association trade marks. Thus, in

1. See *Propriété Industrielle* (1923), pp. 35 and 65.
2. See *Actes de la Conférence de La Haye*, pp. 346, 467.
3. See *Propriété Industrielle* (1913), p. 149.
4. See Osterrieth, *Washingtoner Konferenz*, pp. 79–80; also, *Propriété Industrielle* (1925), p. 121.

Cuba, the law provides only for a compulsory national mark to be applied by all tobacco manufacturers on their exported products. And in the Netherlands, the law has created two national marks, for cheese and butter.

In Belgium, Brazil, France, Finland, Morocco, Poland, and Sweden, a larger class of association trade marks is recognized.[1] In Belgium and Brazil, the only recognized marks are those of professional unions, whether commercial, industrial, or agricultural. In Morocco, all associations and unions duly constituted may own a trade mark. In Finland and Sweden, only marks of associations organized for the purpose of protecting the interests of manufacturers may be registered, but in Finland, such associations must be organized in one of the countries of the Union. In Poland, only associations of manufacturers or traders constituting a juristic person may register association trade marks. In France, the courts have protected association trade marks deposited by professional syndicates, provided the action for infringement is brought by the individual user of such marks and not by the association.[2] Thus, in the last seven countries, juristic public entities (state, district, region, community, etc.) cannot register such trade marks. Only in France, by virtue of the Law of November 26, 1873,[3] an optional national mark was created consisting of the stamp or hall mark of the State applied on deposited marks.

In the remaining fifteen countries only, all kinds of association trade marks, whether public or private, are admitted for deposit, and protected. These countries are Australia, Canada, Denmark, Germany, Great Britain, Hungary, Irish Free State, Italy, Japan, New Zealand, Norway, Portugal, Spain, Switzerland, and Syria and Lebanon.

§ **425. Law of Great Britain and British dominions.** In Great Britain, section 62 of the Trade Marks Act, as amended by the Act of 1919 provides as follows: [4]

1. See on all these countries, results of investigation of the International Bureau, in *Propriété Industrielle* (1925), pp. 119, 121 ff., 192.

2. Syndicat professionel des pâtissiers, etc., *c.* Corriol, Court of Appeals of Nîmes, Nov. 21, 1907 (*Recueil de la Gazette des Tribunaux*, 1908, II, 4, 127). See also Laborde, *Traité des Marques*, pp. 48 ff.

3. *Bulletin des Lois* (1873), II, 733. A bill concerning trade marks, introduced in the French Chamber of Deputies in 1924, contained an entire title on association trade marks. See text in *Propriété Industrielle* (1925), p. 123, note 2.

4. See 2d Schedule of the Act of 1919 (9 & 10 Geo. V, c. 79), and sec. 62 of the Act of 1905 (5 Edw. VII, c. 15).

Where any association or person undertakes to certify the origin, material, mode of manufacture, quality, accuracy or other characteristic of any goods by mark used upon or in connection with such goods, the Board of Trade, if and so long as they are satisfied that such association or person is competent to certify as aforesaid, may, if they shall judge it to be to the public advantage, permit such association or person to register such mark as a trade mark in respect of such goods, whether or not such association or person be a trading association or trader or possessed of a good will in connection with such certifying. When so registered such trade mark shall be deemed in all respects to be a registered trade mark, and such association or person to be the proprietor thereof, save that such trade mark shall be transmissible or assignable only by permission of the Board of Trade.

This section seems to satisfy as fully as possible the international engagement contained in article *7b* of the Convention, and to constitute, as applied under the Trade Mark Rules,[1] a sound regulation of association trade marks. Under this section, trade marks may be registered by any association or person. "Person" includes any body of persons, corporate or unincorporated.[2]

In accordance with article *7b* of the Convention, an association or person under section 62 of the Act of 1905 need not be a trading association or trader, or possessed of a goodwill. Public administrations or authorities may accordingly apply for registration of such marks. Registration may be made in order to certify the origin as well as other characteristics of any goods. Two conditions, however, must be fulfilled: The Board of Trade must be satisfied that the association is competent to certify either the origin or any other characteristic of the goods, and that registration of the marks would be to the public advantage.[3] However, the Court of Appeal held that the question whether the association undertakes to certify some characteristic of the goods was a question of fact open to the Registrar, and to the court on appeal from him, to consider.[4]

1. Rules 36–40 (*Statutory Rules and Orders*, 1920, No. 397).
2. Interpretation Act of Aug. 30, 1889, sec. 19 (52 & 53 Vict., c. 63).
3. See the recent important case: In the Matter of Application by Union Nationale Inter-Syndicale des Marques Collectives to register Trade Marks (1922), 39 R. P. C. 97 and 346. The association, a union of French syndicates granting licenses to use its marks to show that the goods on which the marks were affixed were of French origin, applied for the registration under sec. 62 of a series of trade marks consisting of the words "Unis" (being the initial letters of the first words of the name of the association) and "Unis France" in borders and designs of different shapes. The marks were admitted for registration, against the opposition of a large number of British firms engaged in various industries.
4. The same case on appeal, 39 R. P. C. 346.

Association trade marks must, of course, be registrable trade marks according to the act.[1] The property in the trade mark in question is in the association or person registering the mark. But no transfer or assignment of the mark may be made without the permission of the Board of Trade.

The law of the Commonwealth of Australia,[2] of the Irish Free State,[3] and of New Zealand,[4] is identical with that of Great Britain. The Australian act, however, provides explicitly for the registration of marks by a commonwealth or state authority.

In Canada, section 50 of the Trade Mark and Design Act, added by the Act of June 13, 1923,[5] contains an exact translation of article *7b* of the Convention, providing that any trade mark the proprietor of which is an association, the existence of which is not contrary to the law of the country where such association belongs, even if such association does not possess an industrial or commercial establishment, may be registered. The requirements of the Trade Mark and Design Act must be complied with. According to Rule XII, the application for registration should be accompanied by a certificate of registration of the mark in the country to which such association belongs. Union labels also may be registered by labor unions under the provisions of the Act of April 14, 1927.[6]

§ 426. Laws of other countries. In Germany,[7] association trade marks may be deposited by associations constituting juristic persons and pursuing an industrial object, as well as by juristic public entities. The registration is made in a special register. No transfer or assignment of the mark is allowed. Registration may be cancelled on various grounds whenever the special objects of the mark are no longer attainable. Foreign association trade marks are registered on condition of reciprocity, certified by information published in the *Reichsgesetzblatt*. As reciprocity is abolished in the Union, its "ressortissants" are entitled to all the advantages enjoyed

1. See Kerly (Underhay and Morgan), *The Law of Trade Marks and Trade Name*, p. 239.
2. Act No. 20 of Dec. 21, 1905, sec. 22 (*The Acts of the Commonwealth of Australia*, 1905, p. 52).
3. Industrial and Commercial Property (Protection) Act of 1927, sec. 123 (*Saorstát Eireann*, No. 16 of 1927).
4. Act of Jan. 13, 1922, sec. 93 (12 Geo. V, 1921, No. 18; *The Statutes of the Dominion of New Zealand*, 1921–22, pp. 105, 137).
5. 13–14 Geo. V, c. 28.
6. 17 Geo. V, c. 71.
7. Act of March 31, 1913 (*Reichsgesetzblatt*, 1913, p. 236).

by nationals in Germany, without condition of reciprocity. Similar are the laws of Denmark,[1] Hungary,[2] Japan,[3] and Norway.[4]

In Spain, association trade marks may be used by non-commercial syndicates or associations, by municipal councils, and by provincial authorities.[5] In Italy, marks may be deposited by societies, by juristic persons of any kind, and also by several persons collectively.[6] In Switzerland, associations of manufacturers, traders, and producers, constituting a legal entity, as well as public administrations, may register trade marks.[7] In Syria and Lebanon, the professional, regional, agricultural, and industrial groupings authorized by the state may possess an association trade mark.[8] The provision is broad enough to cover all kinds of such marks.

§ **427. Law of the United States.** In the United States, state court decisions refused protection to labels adopted by a trade union, and used by the workmen who compose the union upon the goods manufactured by them.[9] Whenever protection was granted, it was not based on the right in a technical trade mark, but on grounds of unfair competition.[10] State statutes, however, were passed to allow filing of such labels and specific protection.[11] The Patent Office refused registration of such a label as not constituting a technical mark,[12] but this was under the Act of July 8, 1870, which provided that only persons, firms, and corporations are entitled to registration of trade marks.[13]

The Trade Marks Act of 1905 (sections 2 and 29) admits to registration trade marks of individuals, firms, corporations, and associ-

1. Law No. 129 of April 29, 1913 (*Propriété Industrielle*, 1913, p. 107).
2. Act XXII of 1921, secs. 2–6 (*Propriété Industrielle*, 1922, p. 52).
3. Law No. 99 of April 29, 1921, secs. 27–33 (*Propriété Industrielle*, 1924, pp. 23, 25–26).
4. Law of July 9, 1923 (*Norsk Lovtidende*, 1923, p. 286).
5. Law of May 16, 1902, art. 25 (*Colección Legislativa*, XII, 1902, 88).
6. Decree of Feb. 7, 1869, art. 19 (*Raccolta Ufficiale delle Leggi* 1869, XXIV, 125, 131). See also note 3 on p. 589.
7. Law of September 26, 1890, art. 7 (*Recueil Officiel des Lois*, XII, N. S., 1, 3).
8. Arrêté No. 2385, organizing the protection of commercial, industrial, etc., property, art. 70 (*Bulletin Officiel du Haut Commissariat*, Feb., 1924).
9. Weener *v.* Brayton (1890), 152 Mass. 101 (a statute was passed subsequently in Massachusetts to meet this decision); McVey *v.* Brendel (1891) 144 Pa. St. 235.
10. Hetterman *v.* Powers (1897), 102 Ky. 133; Strasser *v.* Moonelis (1889), 55 N. Y. Sup. Ct. 197; also Carson *v.* Ury (1889), 39 Fed. 777.
11. Tracy *v.* Banker (1898), 170 Mass. 266, by Holmes J.; Cohn *v.* People (1894), 149 Ill., 486.
12. Cigar Makers' Association (1879), 16 *Off. Gaz.* 958 (an association of individuals incorporated in California and engaged in the manufacture of cigars).
13. Sec. 77 (XVI *U. S. Stat. at Large*, 198, 210).

ations. The last term comprises any unincorporated body of persons. Private associations, therefore, may register trade marks in the United States as in the above countries. Thus, the French Association of Syndicates, *Union Nationale Inter-Syndicale des Marques Collectives*, has been able to register the association mark, "Unis France," in the United States Patent Office.[1] It is doubtful, however, whether public marks, national, regional, or local, may be registered under the act. The deposit and registration of association trade marks in the United States is subject to the same conditions and formalities as that of individual marks.

1. See *Propriété Industrielle* (1926), p. 227.

CHAPTER XXVIII

INTERNATIONAL REGISTRATION OF TRADE MARKS

(*The Madrid Arrangement of 1891*)

§ 428. Origin of the Madrid Arrangement. The Arrangement for the international deposit of industrial designs and models adopted at The Hague in 1925 is the result of the efforts and discussions of a quarter of a century, and constitutes a modest substitute for the much desired uniform law on industrial designs and models.[1] Entirely different is the history of the Madrid Arrangement for the international registration of trade marks. It is true that, as early as 1878, the International Congress of Paris had voted an audacious resolution, to the effect that the formality of filing trade marks should be subject to international regulation, by virtue of which the owner of a trade mark would be able to file a single application in

1. See *supra*, chap. XIX, § 285.

one country, in order to obtain protection for such trade mark in all the other contracting countries.[1] However, neither of the Paris conferences of 1880 and 1883 discussed this question. The original proposal for an international registration of trade marks was first made at the Rome Conference of 1886, and, four years later at the Madrid Conference of 1890–1891, the Arrangement for such registration was adopted.

It is curious to note that the primary motive for the adoption of this Arrangement was not the desire to bring about a uniformity of the law on some essential questions in the protection of trade marks, or even to make their international protection more adequate, and free from too many formalities and expense, but the necessity for consolidating the Union established by the Paris Convention of 1883.[2] After the creation of the Union, a reactionary spirit had developed, especially in France, and there was serious danger of that country's withdrawal from the Union. It was thought then that the Union would be much more secure if it had, in its International Bureau, the seat of a service useful to the contracting countries. The registration of trade marks at the Bureau, which would have the effect of registration in all the contracting countries, was conceived of as a plan that could bring great advantage to the trade-mark owners of the contracting countries, which they would not be willing to give up.

It was easy to see the manifold advantages presented by the international registration of trade marks. The general Convention of 1883, notwithstanding the many ameliorations in the international regime of trade mark that it brought about, left much to be desired. Article 2, by assimilating foreigners to nationals, maintained for them the necessity of filing applications for registration of trade marks in each of the contracting countries in which they desired to be protected. Although a four-month period of priority was granted them by article 4, it was not sufficient to permit a timely filing in many countries. Besides, the retaining of attorneys and agents in the various countries, the consequent expenses, and the payment of registration fees were a heavy burden on trade-mark owners.

1. *Compte-rendu du Congrès*, p. 434.

2. See an address by Frey-Godet, published in *Zeitschrift für Völkerrecht und Bundesstaatsrecht* (1907), I, 329, 333–334. Frey-Godet, as Secretary of the International Bureau of Berne at the time, was the originator of the idea of the Arrangement. He discloses in the above address how the necessity for consolidating the Union brought him to the conception of the Arrangement.

Registration of trade marks through agents was not always free from dangers. They sometimes registered trade marks of their principals in their own names, on various pretexts, and as a result the trade of foreign manufacturers was directed by them.[1] Moreover, the differences in the formalities of filing a trade mark in the different countries, the differences in the duration of the effects of registration, the necessity for renewals in each country separately, and the like, rendered the acquisition, as well as the preservation, of the right in a trade mark in several countries at the same time extremely difficult.

At the Rome Conference of 1886, the First Conference of Revision of the Convention, a draft arrangement for the international registration of trade marks and a set of regulations for the execution of the arrangement were proposed by the Swiss administration, and an amendment thereof by the Italian delegation. As might be expected, the scheme was too new to be accepted immediately by the different countries. The various provisions were not entirely understood by the delegates, and a certain confusion prevailed. The French delegation itself was not disposed to enter into the discussion, and this was a great surprise to the Swiss delegation, which aimed at satisfying the French enemies of the Convention. The Conference put off the arrangement until its next meeting.[2]

§ 429. Main features of the Arrangement. At the Madrid Conference of 1890 the draft arrangement, as amended by the Italian delegation and with certain modifications in the light of the opinion advanced by the well-known international jurist, Louis Renault,[3] was again presented by the Swiss administration.[4] It had already been studied by the different countries, and with certain amendments was adopted and signed in 1891 by nine countries: Belgium, France, Guatemala, Italy, the Netherlands, Portugal, Spain, Switzerland, and Tunis.[5]

The main features of the Arrangement as adopted at Madrid were the following. The original principle of the Swiss draft, according to which the owner of the trade mark could apply directly to the International Bureau for the registration of his trade mark, was abandoned in favor of the Italian proposal that such application

1. See *Propriété Industrielle* (1906), p. 27.
2. See *Conférence de Rome*, pp. 43–59, 150–155.
3. See his observations in two articles in the *Propriété Industrielle* (1890), pp. 1 ff. and 17 ff.
4. See *Conférence de Madrid*, pp. 29 ff.
5. *Ibid.*, pp. 101–102, 105–114, 179, 195–198.

should be made through the medium of the administration of the country of origin.[1] The Bureau should register the trade mark, notify the contracting countries thereof, and publish the same in a supplement of its periodical, to be distributed gratis to the contracting countries in order to secure publicity of the registered mark in each of them. The registration at the Bureau would ensure the same protection in each of the contracting countries as if the mark had been deposited therein in the ordinary way. Any of the contracting countries might declare its refusal to protect a mark registered at the Bureau, within a year from the Bureau's notification. A notice of this declaration would be sent to the country of origin and to the interested party, who might appeal against such declaration in the refusing country as if he had deposited his mark directly therein. The effects of the international registration would last for twenty years, but the protection based thereon could not be invoked in case the mark should cease to be protected in the country of origin.

The fee for the international registration, originally proposed by the Dutch administration as two hundred Swiss francs, was finally reduced by the Conference to one hundred. Registration would always be renewable. For all cancellations, disclaimers, transfers, and so forth, of the mark, notice should be given to the Bureau by the administration of the country of origin, and by the Bureau to the contracting countries. The details of the execution of the Arrangement were inserted in a *Règlement*, which was drawn up by the Bureau and approved by the Conference.

§ **430. Amendments at subsequent conferences.** At the subsequent conferences of revision at Brussels, Washington, and The Hague, several amendments and ameliorations of the Arrangement were adopted, but its main features remained unmodified. Most of these amendments were proposed by the International Bureau, and grew out of experience of its practical working. Thus, an additional article, 4*b*, adopted at the Brussels Conference, contained the important amendment substituting the international registration for the prior national registrations of the same trade mark. By an amendment of article 5 it was made clear that the rejection by a country of a trade mark registered at the Bureau could be made only in the cases allowed by the general Convention on direct filings.

1. L. Renault concurred in the view of the Italian administration on this point. See *Propriété Industrielle* (1890), p. 3.

Moreover, it was provided that for any transfer of a trade mark from one country to another, the consent of the latter was necessary as a condition to the mark's protection therein. Lastly, the registration fee for any additional trade mark, filed at the Bureau by the same person at the same time, was reduced to fifty francs.[1]

At the Washington Conference, the publication of a new periodical, *Les Marques Internationales*, was decided upon. All marks registered at the International Bureau would be published therein. Such publication would be considered sufficient in all the contracting countries for claiming protection of the trade mark. It was also provided that a trade-mark owner might disclaim his right in the trade mark in one or several countries, and that he might reduce or increase the list of the goods to which the mark was to be applied. Moreover, it was affirmed that the right of priority of article 4 of the general Convention existed in favor of trade marks registered at the International Bureau.[2]

At the Conference of The Hague several minor amendments of the Arrangement were adopted, two of which need special mention. The registration fee was raised from one hundred to one hundred and fifty francs for the first mark, and from fifty to one hundred francs for every additional mark. By an amendment to article 11, concerning the new adhesions to the Arrangement, it is now provided, contrary to the prior situation, that a newly adhering country may declare that the Arrangement shall apply only to the marks registered after the adhesion becomes effective, and not to those already registered, unless the latter are also directly registered in the Government Office of that country.[3]

§ **431. Membership of restricted Union.** When the Madrid Arrangement came into effect on July 15, 1892, it had been ratified by five countries: Belgium, France, Spain, Switzerland, and Tunis. Four more countries ratified it in the next four years: the Netherlands and Portugal in 1893; Italy in 1894; and Brazil in 1896. Twelve other countries have acceded to the Arrangement up to the present time (June, 1929) in the following order: Cuba in 1905; Austria, Hungary, and Mexico in 1909; Morocco in 1917; Czechoslovakia in 1919; Rumania in 1920; Serb-Croat-Slovene State in 1921; Ger-

1. See *Actes de la Conférence de Bruxelles*, pp. 55, 94, 101, 289–294, 312.
2. See *Actes de la Conférence de Washington*, pp. 71 ff., 98, 261, 293–295, 315, 347.
3. See new text of Arrangement in *Actes de la Conférence de La Haye*, pp. 619–623; and *Pròpriété Industrielle* (1925), p. 228.

many in 1922; Danzig in 1923; Luxembourg in 1924; and Turkey in 1925. Thus, the membership of the restricted Union created by the Madrid Arrangement consists now of twenty-one countries, with a total population of 383,000,000.[1] The accession of Germany, in particular, was a great gain for the Union, the industrial importance of this country adding to the prestige as well as to the business of the International Bureau. Indeed, during the first year of its accession, Germany registered at the International Bureau 2,129 trade marks out of a total of 5,258 registered by all the member countries.[2]

Two great industrial countries still remain outside of this restricted Union, the United States and Great Britain. The reasons of their failure to accede to the Madrid Arrangement and the probability of their acceding in the near future are considered in the last part of this chapter.

Especially interesting was the situation of this Union during the World War. No country denounced it. Although one of the belligerent countries expressed a reservation as to the possibility of protection of an enemy mark registered at the International Bureau, and another declared to the Bureau that all notifications intended for it should be kept at the Bureau until the end of the war, it may be said that the working of the Arrangement was simply suspended in regard to certain belligerent countries.[3] In fact, all the countries of the restricted Union continued registering trade marks at the International Bureau during the war.[4] Moreover, in 1917, while the war was still on, Morocco (the French zone) adhered to the Arrangement.

§ 432. Basis of right of international registration. The basis of the international registration of trade marks is formulated in the first article of the Arrangement, providing as follows:

Les ressortissants de chacun des pays contractants pourront s'assurer, dans tous les autres pays, la protection de leurs marques de fabrique ou de

1. See *Propriété Industrielle* (1928), p. 2. The French colonies are included in the territory of the restricted Union; also the Dutch colonies, — Dutch East Indies, Surinam, and Curaçao, — and the Portuguese colonies of the Azores and Madeira. The Spanish Balearic Islands, the Canaries, and Melilla seem to constitute maritime provinces of Spain, and therefore are a part of the territory of the Union. The Spanish Zone of Morocco is also now included in this Union. See Statement of the International Bureau, in *Actes de la Conférence de La Haye*, p. 181 n. As to the Spanish Zone of Morocco, see *Propriété Industrielle* (1928), p. 214.

2. See tabulated information on the marks registered at the Bureau, in "Exposé Général sur la Service de l'Enregistrement International, 1893–1924," contained in *Actes de la Conférence de La Haye*, pp. 173 ff., at p. 195.

3. See *Actes de la Conférence de La Haye*, p. 180.

4. See statement referred to in note 2.

commerce enregistrées dans le pays d'origine, moyennant le dépôt des dites marques au Bureau International à Berne, fait par l'entremise de l'Administration dudit pays d'origine.

Fait règle pour la définition du pays d'origine, la disposition y relative de l'article 6 de la Convention générale d'Union pour la protection de la propriété industrielle.

Two fundamental conditions are contained in this article. First, a mark cannot be deposited for registration in the International Bureau unless it has been registered in the country of origin. Second, the international registration must be made through the medium of the administration of the country of origin. In both these respects the Madrid Arrangement differs from the Arrangement of The Hague on the international deposit of designs and models. Under the latter, as we have seen above,[1] the international deposit may be made directly by the interested person, and without any previous deposit or registration in one of the member countries.

This prior registration must have been effected in the country of origin. The second paragraph of the article added by the Conference of The Hague affirms that, for the definition of the country of origin, the provisions of article 6 of the general Convention relative thereto should govern. But even prior to this amendment, this interpretation should have prevailed, for the Madrid Arrangement is closely related to the general Convention, and the definition of the country of origin in article 6 should have been applicable so long as no other was given in the Arrangement. In fact, however, the rule of article 6 was not always followed by applicants, and the insertion of an explicit provision to this effect was deemed necessary.[2]

§ 433. Persons admitted to benefits of the Arrangement. The persons who may claim the advantages of this Arrangement are the nationals of the member countries of the restricted Union and also, as article 2 provides, the nationals of the countries which have not acceded to the Arrangement but who satisfy the conditions of article 3 of the general Convention in the territory of the restricted Union. Inasmuch as the only countries that may accede to the Arrangement are the members of the general Union (article 11 of the Arrangement), only nationals of these countries, domiciled or having

1. See *supra*, §§ 288, 289.

2. See *Actes de la Conférence de La Haye*, proposal of the Bureau, p. 277, and its adoption, pp. 483, 581. For the interpretation of the provision of article 6 concerning the country of origin, see *supra*, § 364.

a *bona fide* and effective industrial or commercial establishment in the territory of the member countries of the restricted Union, may register their trade marks at the International Bureau.

It follows that nationals of countries which are not members of the general Union do not enjoy the right of international registration of their trade marks, although they are domiciled or possess commercial or industrial establishments in the territory of the general or restricted Union. It is not understood why the last class of persons, namely foreigners established or domiciled in the territory of the restricted Union, should not enjoy the same rights as nationals of member countries. In both cases the industry of the country concerned is reaping the benefit of the international registration of trade marks. It would seem, then, that the Arrangement of The Hague contains a better rule, in admitting to its benefits all persons, in general, who are domiciled or possess establishments in the territory of the restricted Union.

As we have seen in another place,[1] a branch office is considered an industrial or commercial establishment within the meaning of article 3 of the Convention. Consequently, nationals of member countries of the general Union possessing branch offices or houses in the territory of the restricted Union may register their trade marks at the Bureau through the agency of the administration of the country in which their branch house is located. But such marks must be claimed by the branch house as owned by the same.[2] Abuses in this respect by nationals of countries which have not acceded to the Madrid Arrangement, like Great Britain and the United States, are hardly to be feared. For registration by branch houses in their own names is often dangerous to the parent concern and subject to practical and legal objections.[3]

§ **434. Need of prior registration in country of origin.** Only marks registered in the country of origin may be deposited at the International Bureau. Article 6 of the Arrangement adds to this provision of article 1 the stipulation that the protection resulting from the international registration cannot be claimed in favor of a mark which would no longer enjoy legal protection in the country of origin.

1. See *supra*, § 115.
2. So decided by the Austrian Ministry of Public Works, June 24, 1910 (*Propriété Industrielle*, 1913, p. 14).
3. See Kosicki, "Scope of Madrid Trade Mark Arrangement," *Bulletin of the United States Trade Mark Association* (1915), XX, 129, 135 ff.

These provisions establish the rule that protection through the international registration is accessory to and dependent on protection in the country of origin.

The two subjects — application for international registration after the national registration, and dependence of the protection resulting from the former on the protection resulting from the latter — are entirely distinct. The second question is considered below.[1] As to the first, the respective advantages and disadvantages of the rule for deposit adopted by the Madrid Arrangement and the direct deposit without prior registration in the country of origin, which is the other alternative, are not very different from those described in relation to designs and models.[2] Germany hesitated for a long time to accede to the Madrid Arrangement, mainly because of the condition that a trade mark cannot be registered in the International Bureau before it has been registered in the country of origin.[3] It should be recalled that in Germany trade marks are submitted to prior examination before they can be registered, and that many trade marks used on exported articles may be invalid under the German law, but perfectly valid under the law of the countries for which the goods bearing these marks are destined. For both these reasons the condition of prior registration in the country of origin minimizes to a considerable degree the advantages of international registration. The administrative examination of the trade mark prior to its registration may take a long time, and the owner is not able to protect himself in the interval in the other countries. Also, he is precluded from registering in the International Bureau trade marks which are not admitted for registration in his own country and yet are protected in the other countries if directly deposited therein. The same objections may account for the hesitancy of Great Britain and the United States to accede to the Madrid Arrangement.

The congresses of the International Association had taken up this question before the war, and had adopted resolutions to the effect of amending the Arrangement.[4] For the words: "acceptées au dépôt dans le pays d'origine," the words: "déposées dans un des pays con-

1. See *infra*, § 443.
2. See *supra*, § 287.
3. See *Annuaire de l'Association Internationale* (1904), pp. 404 ff.; (1909), pp. 21 ff., 132 ff.; (1910), pp. 143 ff.
4. *Ibid.* (1910), pp. 143 ff.

tractants" were to be substituted. Thus it would not be required that the mark be registered or admitted to deposit, but merely that it be filed. Moreover, such filing of the mark need not necessarily be made in the country of origin, but in any country of the Union. The first change would dispose of the difficulty of delays caused by the administrative examination. As soon as filed, and before being examined, the mark could be transmitted to the International Bureau. The second change would permit the trade-mark owner to choose, for the national deposit of his trade mark, the country for which his goods were destined.

However, the first article of the Arrangement is closely bound up with article 6 of the general Convention. The latter is interpreted in many countries, as we have seen above,[1] as requiring the registration of trade marks in the country of origin as a condition to their being protected in the other countries of the Union. It cannot be expected that the first article of the Arrangement will be amended in the above way before article 6 of the Convention is amended. The attempts toward that end at the Conferences of Washington and of The Hague failed. The practical working of the opposite principle adopted in the Arrangement of The Hague for the international deposit of designs and models may affect the situation in the international registration of trade marks. The International Bureau is opposed to the adoption of the above amendments in the Madrid Arrangement because of technical difficulties.[2]

The word "enregistrées" in the first article of the Arrangement was substituted at the Conference of The Hague for the words "acceptées au dépôt," to cover the case of certain countries where the latter term is used in a sense distinct from that of "enregistrées." The new term was adopted for the purpose of affirming that a mark should be definitely registered in the country of origin before it may be filed in the International Bureau.[3] The registration in the country of origin must exist at the time the international filing of the mark takes place. The Italian delegation proposed, at the Conference of The Hague, that as soon as the trade mark was filed in

1. See *supra*, §§ 371–373.
2. See *Actes de la Conférence de La Haye*, pp. 183–184.
3. The Spanish delegation proposed the insertion of a specific provision to the effect that it should be understood that "enregistrées" refers to marks that have been definitely registered in the country of origin. *Actes de la Conférence de La Haye*, p. 356. This delegation did not insist on its proposal, on being assured that the sub-committee unanimously interpreted the word in that sense. *Ibid.*, pp. 483, 550.

the country of origin, it could be filed at the International Bureau, although it was not yet registered in that country. This proposal was withdrawn on the opposition of the Director of the International Bureau, who argued that it would present great inconveniences and would render uncertain the basis of the international registration.

§ **435. Formalities of application.** The formalities of applying for international registration of trade marks are provided in the third article of the Arrangement (paragraphs 1 and 2) and in articles 1, 2, and *2b* of the *Règlement.*[1] As soon as the mark is definitely registered in the country of origin, the interested party may request the administration of such country to apply to the International Bureau to enter the mark in the international register. This request is made in the form of an application addressed by the proprietor of the mark to the administration, in accordance with the rules prescribed by law (article 1 of the *Règlement*).

The administration then sends to the International Bureau an application in duplicate, according to the form furnished by the International Bureau. The form must be filled in by the administration itself, which sees to it that the information given is correct. According to the first paragraph of article 3 of the Arrangement, as amended at the Conference of The Hague, the administration forwarding must certify that the indications contained in this application correspond to those of the national register.[2] The necessary data given in the application comprise the name of the owner of the mark; his address (and in case of several addresses, that to which notifications should be sent), the name and address of the agent (in case this is desired); the goods or merchandise to which the mark is to be applied (the kind of goods should be indicated precisely, without detailed enumeration);[3] the date of the last entry in the national

1. An analysis of the different formalities is given by the International Bureau in its statement contained in *Actes de la Conférence de La Haye*, pp. 173, 184–187. However, the various amendments adopted at the Conference of The Hague and the new article *2b* of the *Règlement* should be taken into consideration in supplementing the above analysis.

2. Under the old text the application for international registration, in the absence of an imperative provision requiring the administration of each country to fill it in, was filled by third persons, and this gave rise to serious inconveniences. See *Actes de La Conférence de La Haye*, p. 295.

3. Insufficient statements, too elastic or too vague, such as "various merchandise," "goods for export," "overseas goods," "publicity articles," "articles manufactured by the applicant," "and other goods," etc., are not, in fact, accepted by any of the contracting countries, and registration of the mark is sometimes refused. See *Actes de la Conférence de La Haye*, p. 186. The difficulties arising from the non-uniformity of classification of the various goods in the different countries are considered *infra*, § 450.

register (whether original registration or renewal) and number of registration; and the date and number of any prior international registration (if this is desired). On the application, below the address, the administration of the country of origin must attach or impress a representation of the trade mark in black ink, struck from the block accompanying the application.

With the application, a printing block of the mark, the dimensions of which are fixed by the *Règlement* (article 2*b*), must be sent to the Bureau, and also the fee for the international registration, unless it has been sent directly, in advance, by the owner of the mark. The fee must be paid in cash or by postal check or by check drawn on a bank at Berne.

In case the color of the mark is claimed as a distinctive element, forty reproductions must be joined to the application, which are to be annexed to the notices sent by the Bureau to the contracting countries. A declaration, also in the application, must indicate the color or the combination of colors claimed by the applicant for the essential parts of his trade mark.

In case the mark contains inscriptions in a language or in letters not generally known, the owner may be asked to file a dozen copies containing a French translation of the inscriptions, in order to facilitate the search in the contracting countries.

In case the mark contains armorial bearings, portraits, honorary distinctions, or the name of a person other than the applicant, the administration of the country of origin may, if it chooses, certify in the application that the depositor of the mark has proved his right to use the above elements.

§ 436. Examination by the Bureau into regularity of deposit of application. No provision either in the Arrangement or in the *Règlement* gave to the International Bureau the power to refuse or postpone temporarily the registration of a mark in case the application or the documents accompanying it were in any way in omplete or irregular. In practice, however, the Bureau postponed registration in such cases,[1] until the deposit was completed and the provisions of the Arrangement and *Règlement* were complied with. The Bureau took such action only in case there was no compliance with such provisions. It could not postpone registration in case the filing was in due form, according to these provisions, even if it contained

1. See *Actes de la Conférence de La Haye*, p. 296.

certain unsatisfactory features which would make registration inadmissible in all the countries of the Union. Doubtless the Bureau should have the power to postpone registration, and to call upon the applicant to amend his filing in the latter class of cases. Unnecessary notifications to the contracting countries and refusals on their part, and waste of money in printing and mailing, would be avoided thereby.

The new article *2b* of the *Règlement* invests the Bureau now with this authority. On the one hand, it affirms what already was the practice, namely, if the Bureau ascertains that an application for registration is incomplete or irregular, it is authorized to postpone the registration of the mark, but must notify without delay the interested administration. The latter must within a six-month period modify, withdraw, or maintain the application. If this period expires without result, the Bureau is permitted to fix another period of the same length. In such case, the owner of the mark, as well as the interested administration, is notified. These periods start with the date of the Bureau's notification. In case no reply is received by the Bureau at the end of the second period, the filing may be considered as abandoned and the fee, minus a deduction, is returned to the depositor. If the filing comprises several marks, and the irregularity concerns only one of them, the registration of the entire filing is postponed, unless the interested administration, or the proprietor of the mark, advises the Bureau that the trade mark in question should be isolated from the rest.

On the other hand, article *2b* enumerates illustratively certain cases in which the Bureau may postpone registration and act according to above procedure. These cases are:

(1) When the application contains too vague an indication of the goods on which the mark is to be applied, such as "various merchandise," and "and other goods," or the expression "etc."

(2) When the printing block accompanying the application does not give a sufficiently clear impression of the elements of the mark.

(3) When the mark contains the sign of a cross which may be confused with the "Red Cross," and, in order to avoid the refusal of the mark by the other administrations, it is necessary to obtain the previous declaration of the owner that the mark is not to be used in red, or any shade thereof.

In the above cases (1) and (3) the Bureau did not, in fact, postpone registration prior to the amendment of the *Règlement* at the Conference of The Hague. They present defects of the filing which are not of form, but of substance. These cases are only illustrative. The Bureau may exercise the same authority in other cases in which it knows from experience that a filing presents a defect which makes the mark inadmissible in all the countries of the restricted Union. Of course, the Bureau is not bound to postpone registration, but it does have the power to do so.[1]

§ **437. Procedure at the International Bureau.** When the International Bureau is satisfied that the filing is complete and in due form, that the trade mark has been duly registered in the country of origin, that the depositor is a person entitled to the benefits of the Arrangement, and the rest, it enters the trade mark in the register kept by the Bureau for this purpose, containing the indications enumerated in article 3 of the *Règlement.* Such entry is certified under date and number at the bottom of the application, which thereby becomes a certificate of international registration. The effects of the international registration begin from this moment. The further procedure at the International Bureau is provided for in paragraphs 3 and 4 of the third article of the Arrangement, and in articles 3, 4, and 5 of the *Règlement.*

The Bureau retains one of the copies of the application in its archives and returns the other to the administration of the country of origin. Subsequently, it gives notice of the registration, without delay,[2] to each of the other administrations of the contracting countries by sending them a reproduction of the mark and all the data entered in the international register in respect to the mark. Lastly, it publishes in its monthly periodical, *Les Marques Internationales*,[3] a reproduction of the mark with all data concerning it. Each administration receives gratis from the Bureau any desired number of copies of this periodical. At the end of every year, the Bureau pub-

1. See *Actes de la Conférence de La Haye*, p. 297.

2. At the Conference of The Hague the Italian delegation proposed that it be specified in article 3 of the Arrangement that such notification should be made within two months; but the proposal was not insisted upon, on the remark of the French delegation that confidence should be shown, in this respect, in the diligence of the Bureau. See *Actes de la Conférence de La Haye*, p. 484. As the Bureau stated in its proposals of amendment of the Arrangement at The Hague, the average time intervening between international registration of a mark and notification to the administrations is only eight days, with a maximum of seventeen days in quite exceptional cases. *Ibid.*, p. 282.

3. *Les Marques Internationales* was first published on February 1, 1893.

lishes an alphabetical index, for each country, of the names of the proprietors of marks which have been published during the year.[1]

§ **438. Right of priority.** Each mark registered at the International Bureau enjoys the right of priority provided for in article 4 of the general Convention, as expressly stipulated by article 4, paragraph 2, of the Arrangement. Thus, if the international registration is effected within six months from the date of the first filing of the mark in the country of origin, a right of priority may be claimed in favor of the international registration. In consequence, no intervening acts — in particular, filing of the mark by another party — can invalidate the international registration.[2]

It is immaterial whether the intervening filing is made at the International Bureau, or directly in the contracting countries.[3] For the protection resulting from the international registration is the same as when the mark is filed directly in each of those countries.[4]

Article 4 (section *d*) of the general Convention requires, for the purpose of claiming a right of priority for trade marks, a declaration at the subsequent filing giving particulars such as the date of the prior filing and the country in which this was made. The Madrid Arrangement contained no provision requiring such declaration in case of the international registration of a trade mark. In fact, the Bureau always held that no declaration to this effect was necessary.[5] This was affirmed at the Conference of The Hague by the addition, in the second paragraph of article 4 of the Arrangement, of the provision that it is not necessary to fulfill the formalities provided for in section (*d*) of article 4 of the Convention ("sans qu'il soit nécessaire d'accomplir les formalités prévues dans la lettre (*d*) de cet article").[6] Indeed, compliance with these formalities is unnecessary in view of the fact that the required particulars are contained in the application for international registration.

§ **439. Rejection of marks by contracting countries.** The international registration is effected at the moment all the prescribed documents have been received by the Bureau and the mark and all

1. Article 5*c* of the Arrangement provides that any person may obtain from the Bureau, on payment of a fee, a copy of the data concerning a mark registered by it, and also request that a search of priorities be made among the international marks.

2. On the right of priority in the matter of trade marks, see *supra*, chap. XXIII.

3. See *Actes de la Conférence de Washington*, p. 73.

4. See *infra*, § 441.

5. See *Actes de la Conférence de La Haye*, p. 188.

6. *Ibid.*, p. 550.

its particulars are entered in the international register. But any country may refuse protection to a mark which has been so registered.[1] The conditions of such refusal are set forth in article 5 of the Arrangement:

Dans les pays où leur législation les y autorise, les administrations auxquelles le Bureau International notifiera l'enregistrement d'une marque, auront la faculté de déclarer que la protection ne peut être accordée à cette marque sur leur territoire. Un tel refus ne pourra être opposé que dans les conditions qui s'appliqueraient en vertu de la Convention générale, à une marque déposée à l'enregistrement national.

Les Administrations qui voudront exercer cette faculté devront notifier leur refus, avec indication des motifs, au Bureau International, dans le délai prévu par la loi nationale, et, au plus tard, avant la fin d'une année comptée à partir de l'enregistrement international de la marque.

Le Bureau International transmettra sans retard à l'Administration du pays d'origine et au propriétaire de la marque ou à son mandataire, si celui-ci a été indiqué au Bureau par ladite Administration un des exemplaires de la déclaration de refus ainsi notifiée. L'intéressé aura les mêmes moyens de recours que si la marque avait été par lui directement déposée dans le pays où la protection est refusée.

Les Administrations qui, dans le délai maximum sousindiqué d'un an, n'auront adressé aucune communication au Bureau International seront censées avoir accepté la marque.

Any administration may, within one year, give notice to the International Bureau that the mark registered at the Bureau cannot be protected on its territory. Only the administrations authorized thereto by their municipal law may reject trade marks registered at the Bureau. Thus, the administrations of the countries in which no previous examination of the trade mark is undertaken before registration will not refuse protection of such marks.

Rejection can take place only in those cases in which it might be effected under the provisions of the general Convention, if the marks were filed directly with the administration in question. In other words, articles 6, 6*b*, 6*c*, and 7 of the general Convention govern the conditions under which a mark may be refused protection by any of the countries of the restricted Union after it is registered by the International Bureau.[2]

1. No such refusal is possible under the Arrangement of The Hague for the international deposit of designs and models. See *supra*, p. 441.

2. See various cases in which marks are often refused by the different administrations in *Actes de la Conférence de La Haye*, pp. 188–190 and 211–212. Such cases are usually those covered by the exceptions of article 6 of the Convention. See *supra*, §§ 375 ff.

Each administration must give notice of the refusal, if any, to the International Bureau and indicate the grounds thereof. This provision protects trade-mark owners against arbitrary refusals.[1] Moreover, the notification of refusal must be made before the end of one year from the date of international registration of the mark. The computation of the period under the old text of article 5 gave rise to difficulties of interpretation. The period began with notification of the registration by the Bureau ("dans l'année de la notification"). Although the Bureau interpreted it as starting with the date of notification, according to another interpretation the period began on the date on which each administration had received the notification. This rendered the period uncertain, and unequal in the different countries. On the other hand, it was contended that the notification of refusal should reach the Bureau within a year, and thus the period was shortened unequally for the different countries.[2]

Under the new text of article 5, as amended at The Hague, the period starts with the date of international registration, which is a stated date, appearing both in the particulars of the notification of registration sent by the Bureau and in the publication of the mark in *Les Marques Internationales*.[3] Each administration may avail itself of the whole period of one year for giving notice of a refusal. The date of sending such notice, and not of its reaching the Bureau, is taken into consideration.[4]

After the lapse of the one-year period, no refusal of protection may be made by any country. This is now affirmed by the last paragraph of article 5, adopted at the Conference of The Hague, by virtue of which, in case no refusal is communicated to the Bureau by any of the contracting countries, the latter shall be regarded as having accepted the mark. This, of course, disposes of the administrative refusal of the mark only in the countries where the system of previ-

1. Article 6 of the *Règlement* determines more specifically the form of the declaration of refusal. It must be in triplicate; must indicate, among other things, all the particulars of the other mark, if any, with which the mark in question interferes; and must state the provision of the law concerning the refusal, the period within which and the authority with which an appeal or arguments should be filed.

2. *Actes de la Conférence de Washington*, pp. 158–159; *Actes de la Conférence de La Haye*, pp. 190, 282.

3. The date of international registration of the mark precedes that of notification by only a few days, as stated by the International Bureau at the Conference of The Hague. On the average, eight days only intervene. See *Actes de la Conférence de La Haye*, p. 282.

4. This is confirmed by the last paragraph of article 5, which concerns the tacit acceptance of the mark by the administrations which have not addressed ("n'auront adressé") a notification of refusal to the International Bureau.

ous examination prevails. The right of a third person in any of the contracting countries to sue for the invalidation of the mark is in no way affected, as was clearly understood by the Conference of The Hague.[1]

Under the old text of article 5, there were cases in which the examination by an administration of a mark registered at the International Bureau was not completed at the end of one year, either because the service was overburdened or because the mark presented special difficulties. Two courses were open in such case to the administration concerned: to refuse protection to the mark; or to notify the Bureau at a later time, after the lapse of the one-year period. Ordinarily the owner of the trade mark would prefer even a late acceptance to a prompt refusal. The fact is a practice has developed, with the consent of the International Bureau,[2] of having the administration concerned notify the Bureau that it refuses protection of the mark provisionally, or that it postpones decision on the mark. Such provisional refusal would seem to be permissible under the new text. Indeed, the last paragraph of article 5 provides for the tacit acceptance of a mark, only in case no notification at all ("aucune communication") is sent to the Bureau.[3]

Upon receipt of the declaration of refusal, the International Bureau must send a copy to the administration of the country of origin and to the owner of the trade mark, or to his agent, if the latter is indicated to the Bureau. The old text did not provide that the agent of the trade-mark owner should be notified, but the Bureau did in fact send to agents an unofficial notice intended to assist them in carrying out their duties to the applicant.[4]

1. The Austrian and Swiss delegations made explicit proposals of amendment to this effect; they did not insist on being satisfied that the unanimous opinion of the subcommittee considered the proposals superfluous, and that the power of judicial invalidation remained unrestricted. See *Actes de la Conférence de La Haye*, pp. 358, 359, 485, 550–551.

Of course, invalidation or annulment of the mark in one country (unless this is the country of origin) is without effect in the other countries. See on this point, National Starch Co. *v.* Ten Hope, Court of Appeals of Berne, Sept. 22, 1911 (*Propriété Industrielle*, 1912, p. 112).

2. See *Propriété Industrielle* (1919), p. 16 and (1922), pp. 170–171.

3. The German Patent Office communicated to the International Bureau within the year a partial provisional refusal and also a partial definitive refusal, and was of opinion that this interrupted the prescribed period and that other subsequent refusals might be filed at any time. The Bureau objected to this position, and the German Patent Office abandoned the same. See decision of the Patent Office of Dec. 5, 1924, in *Propriété Industrielle* (1925), p. 169.

4. See *Actes de la Conférence de La Haye*, pp. 190–191.

The notification by the Bureau to the interested party of the declaration of refusal aims at enabling that party to appeal from, or submit arguments against, the refusal of protection declared by any administration. Indeed, the interested party, as explicitly provided in the third paragraph of article 5, enjoys every recourse against decisions refusing the protection of a mark that he would have enjoyed had such mark been filed directly in the country in question.

§ 440. Proof of right of depositor in use of certain elements of the mark. The use of certain elements in a trade mark registered at the International Bureau may cause its refusal by various administrations, or a provisional refusal until the right of the depositor in the use of such elements is proved. In order to avoid such refusals and the vexations and burdens resulting for the depositor from the need of proving his right to several administrations, the International Bureau had proposed a new article, 5*b*, at The Hague, which would confirm that which in fact the Bureau had succeeded in establishing in practice in respect to certain countries. Indeed, the Bureau had suggested in cases in which an administration refused trade marks including armorial bearings, medals, distinctions of honor, or the name of a third person, that such administration should be satisfied as to the right of the depositor in the use of such elements by the receipt of a statement of principle from the administration of the country of origin, declaring that it never registered a trade mark containing such elements unless it were proved that the applicant was entitled to use such armorial bearings, medals, and so forth. This procedure was successfully followed in many cases.[1] The proposed new article 5*b* would have established and generalized officially this procedure.[2]

It is to be regretted that the Bureau's proposal failed of adoption because of the opposition of the French delegation, which would not leave the definitive examination of the right of the depositor in the use of the elements in question to the administration of the country of origin. The French opposition was all the more puzzling because in France the mark is admitted for deposit without any previous examination by the administration.[3] Moreover, the Bureau's proposal sought only the effect of rendering unnecessary administrative examination into the right of the depositor in the use of the above

1. See Statement of the Bureau in *Actes de la Conférence de La Haye*, p. 189.
2. See text, in *Actes de la Conférence de La Haye*, p. 284.
3. See Pouillet, *Traité des Marques*, p. 221.

elements, and would in no way have affected the judicial validity of the mark. When the question should be in issue in any court, the right of the depositor would have had to be proved to the satisfaction of the court. Besides, leaving the question of such examination to the administration of the country of origin is quite reasonable, since proof in such case is much easier for the depositor, and a formal declaration of that administration is all that can be desired at the stage of the administrative procedure preceding the registration which aims only at examining the *prima facie* validity of the mark.

The proposal of the Bureau, however, could be improved and made more easily acceptable if, besides a general statement of principle, it provided for a specific certification by the administration of the country of origin, to be contained in the application for international registration, to the effect that the right of the depositor in the use of the elements in question has been proved to its satisfaction. Indeed, the fourth paragraph of article 2 of the *Règlement*, as amended at The Hague, provides that the administration of the country of origin may insert such a certification, but there is no stipulation that the other administrations shall be bound by it. There is no reason, however, why such certification should not be given full credit and make unnecessary a similar examination by the other administrations.

The new article, 5*b*, as proposed by the French administration and adopted by the Conference of The Hague, reads as follows:

> Les pièces justificatives de la légitimité d'usage de certains éléments contenus dans les marques, tels que armoiries, écussons, portraits, distinctions honorifiques, titres, noms commerciaux ou noms de personnes autres que celui du déposant, ou autres inscriptions analogues, qui pourraient être réclamées par les Administrations des pays contractants, seront dispensées de toute certification ou légalization autre que celle de l'Administration du pays d'origine.

It merely concerns the certification or visa of the documents proving the right of the depositor to the use of certain elements contained in the marks registered at the Bureau. It is a mere question of detail, and should not constitute a separate article of the Arrangement. Its right place is in the *Règlement*, in article 2, after the fourth paragraph previously considered.

§ 441. Effects of international registration. What are the effects of registration of a mark at the International Bureau? Is such registration merely an act of an informational character, or is it endowed with legal force? The first paragraph of article 4 of the Arrangement provides in this respect:

A partir de l'enregistrement ainsi fait au Bureau International, la protection de la marque dans chacun des pays contractants sera la même que si cette marque y avait été directement déposée.

It should be noted that, while this provision speaks of the "protection" resulting from the registration at the International Bureau, it likens such protection to that enjoyed by direct *filing* in the contracting countries, and not to direct *registration* therein. Thus, the provision is fitted to both the above described systems of trade-mark registration and takes account of the possibility of refusal of protection by the administrations of contracting countries. Indeed, in the countries where registration of trade marks is declaratory of the right in the mark, the international registration is precisely equivalent to direct deposit of the mark in these countries, and secures by itself the full protection that the latter affords. In the countries, on the contrary, where by registration ownership in the mark is acquired, and the administration subjects the mark to a previous examination before its registration, the international registration of a mark is equivalent to no more than a direct filing of the mark in these countries. The latter have the right to search into the legality and validity of the mark registered at the Bureau as in case of direct filings with their own administrations. The only difference in this respect is that they should complete their examination and give notice to the Bureau of any refusal of protection before the end of one year from the date of international registration.

This conception of the effects of international registration would seem unassailable, unless the word "protection" in the above provision should force a different conclusion. This word would seem to be used here in a loose sense, and should be understood as meaning "legal status" of the mark. The legal status of the mark registered at the Bureau is the same as if the mark had been filed directly in each of the contracting countries. A proposal, however, of the Bureau, at the Washington Conference, to amend the above provision in this respect by substituting the words "condition légale" for the word "protection," was rejected, on the opposition of two delegations.[1] The rejection was based on the conception that the

1. See *Actes de la Conférence de Washington*, pp. 73, 294.

international registration of the mark is in itself the basis for protection in each of the contracting countries, and such protection given in advance may be revoked only by a refusal within one year. However, admitting this theory, the limits of such protection are not provided for in the Arrangement. The provision refers only to the protection granted in each country in case the trade mark was directly filed therein.[1] The latter protection, therefore, is the only one enjoyed by registering marks at the Bureau, and such protection varies, as explained at the beginning of this section, according to the system of trade-mark registration of each country.[2]

Nevertheless, the international registration of a mark possesses certain legal advantages over the direct filing in each of the contracting countries, which are specifically granted by other provisions of the Arrangement. The existence of these advantages justifies somewhat the term "protection" in the provision considered above. Two of these advantages are the right of priority enjoyed in favor of the international registration, and the uniform duration of the effects of international registration for twenty years in all the contracting countries. The former has already been considered,[3] and the latter is taken up below.[4] A third advantage is that of the effects of publication of the mark in *Les Marques Internationales*. Indeed, article 3 of the Arrangement provides that the publication of the mark with all particulars in the Bureau's periodical shall be considered in all the contracting countries as fully sufficient, and no other shall be required of the depositor ("sera considérée dans tous les pays contractants comme pleinement suffisante, et aucune autre ne pourra être exigée du déposant").

This provision was added at the Conference of Washington,[5] to

1. It was held in Rey *v.* Lecouturier, by the Federal Tribunal of Brazil, May 10, 1907, that international registration produces no effects in Brazil, in case the mark registered at the Bureau was already registered in Brazil, in the name of another and for the same goods. See *Propriété Industrielle* (1907), p. 100.

2. See *Propriété Industrielle* (1922), p. 168. Thus, as was fittingly said by the Court of Revision of Turin (Italy), the International Bureau is to be regarded as the *alter ego* of the national offices of each of the contracting countries. See *Propriété Industrielle* (1915), p. 108.

It was held by the Court of Revision of Berne, Sept. 22, 1901, in National Starch Co. *v.* Ten Hope, that the international registration is equivalent to national registration in each of the contracting countries, even for the purposes of jurisdiction; that is, the provisions of the law as to jurisdiction for infringement of national marks apply also to marks registered at the Bureau. See *Propriété Industrielle* (1912), p. 112.

3. See *supra*, § 438. 4. See *infra*, § 443.

5. See *Actes de la Conférence de Washington*, pp. 71–72, 294.

meet the court decisions of one contracting country[1] which held that, besides the publication in the Bureau's periodical, the mark should be published in the country, in the same way as marks filed directly therein, before it could enjoy protection in that country.

§ **442. Substitution of international registration for prior national registrations.** There are cases in which the international registration of a trade mark may be preceded by national registration in one or several countries, besides the country of origin. Such cases are met with usually on the accession of a new country to the Arrangement. All marks already registered at the Bureau are communicated to the new acceding country, and are protected on the territory of that country unless duly refused within a year.[2] Some of these marks may already have been directly registered in the country concerned. Other cases of similar duplication may occur when the proprietor of a trade mark has delayed for different reasons the international registration until he has registered the trade mark in the ordinary course in one or more countries.

What is the relation, in such cases, of the international to the prior national registrations? Do both continue to produce their effects side by side, or is one of them set at naught by the other? There is no doubt as to the interest of the owner of the mark in keeping alive only the international registration, since it relieves him from all the expenses and fees that the preservation or renewal of national registration requires. At the same time, he may be desirous of preserving the advantages which he may have acquired through the prior national registration. Article 4*b* of the Madrid Arrangement, added at the Brussels Conference on the proposal of the International Bureau,[3] satisfies both these interests of the owner of the trade mark.

Lorsqu'une marque, déjà déposée dans un ou plusieurs des pays contractants, a été postérieurement enregistrée par le Bureau international au nom du même titulaire ou de son ayant cause, l'enregistrement inter-

1. Brazil. The cases of refusal of protection of trade marks registered at the Bureau on the ground of their not having been published in the *Diario Oficial* were decided in 1907 by the Court of Appeals of Rio de Janeiro: F. Genevois, Homolte & Co. and Bertaud, Blancard et frères *v.* Julio de Aranjo. See *Propriété Industrielle* (1907), p. 101. Soon after these decisions, the Ministry of Industry of Brazil by a circular recalled the scope of the Madrid Arrangement and intimated that no publication in the Government journal of Brazil was necessary. In a later decision, the same court limited the scope of the previous decisions to criminal cases. See *ibid.* (1907), p. 164, and (1908), p. 10.

2. This is now changed. See *infra*, pp. 638–639.

3. See *Actes de la Conférence de Bruxelles*, pp. 59–60, 290.

national sera considéré comme substitué aux enregistrements nationaux antérieurs, sans préjudice des droits acquis par le fait de ces derniers.

Thus, in the above considered cases, for the national registrations is substituted the international registration, with the qualification contained in the closing words. This substitution has the effect of extinguishing the national registrations. Its conditions deserve the following observations.

In the first place, the substitution does not extend to the country of origin. Registration in that country is the foundation of international registration. With the disappearance of the former, the latter also terminates. In the second place, the substitution is not operative before the international registration becomes definitively effective, and operates in respect only to those countries in which the international registration becomes effective. In other words, in case the mark which is registered at the Bureau is rejected by one of the countries, the prior national registration of the same mark in that country will subsist. Likewise, the mere registration at the Bureau, or notification sent to the country where the prior national registration was effected, does not bring about substitution. Only at the expiry of the year within which rejection of the mark may be made, does the substitution become effective. This seems clear from the history of article 4*b* and its purpose, which is to extend the advantages of international registration to the trade marks in question, and not to bring about the forfeiture of their protection.[1]

Substitution of international for national registration is also impossible in case the mark registered at the Bureau is not identical with the mark previously registered in the contracting countries, or is not registered for the same class or classes of goods.[2] In such case there are two different rights springing out of national and international registrations. This is also true in case the trade mark is not registered at the International Bureau by the same registrant whose name appears on the national register, or by his legal representative.

Article 4*b* does not provide any procedure for declaring such sub-

1. Cases of refusal of protection of a mark registered at the International Bureau, although the same mark is already registered directly in the country in question, are not impossible; for instance, because of change of legislation, making the mark inadmissible for registration.

2. See *Propriété Industrielle* (1925), pp. 187, 188.

stitution. It operates *ipso jure* when all the conditions concur.[1] Whether this has in fact taken place is to be determined by the courts whenever the question is in issue. Usually the question will come up when the owner of the trade mark ceases to pay the fees for, or fails to apply for renewal of, the national registration.[2]

By the closing words of the stipulation of article 4*b* a qualification is placed on the substitution provided for therein. International registration is to be substituted for the national registrations, "without prejudice to the rights acquired by virtue of the latter." Thus, any rights acquired by the owner of the trade mark by virtue of the national registration are preserved. Of course, these rights must have been acquired in the countries concerned, and must exist at the time the substitution takes place.

Important in this respect is the right of priority based on the prior national registration. By virtue of the qualification under consideration, an international registration taking place in 1927, and replacing a national registration of 1920, will carry with it priority of registration of the mark in question from that time. The owner of the mark need not renew the national registration; but so long as the international registration is in effect, his right in the trade mark goes back to 1920.[3]

The opinion that for the preservation of the rights acquired through the national registrations the effects of the latter should be maintained by the payment of fees and by applying for renewal, is clearly opposed to the spirit of article 4*b* and to the purpose of its adoption, as well as to the clear meaning of the text.[4]

1. At the Conference of The Hague the Austrian delegation proposed an amendment to article 4*b* making the substitution conditional on the indication by the depositor, in the application for international registration, of the prior national registrations. This amendment was not adopted by the Conference. See *Actes de la Conference de La Haye*, pp. 484–485.

2. Because of the substitution provided for in article 4*b* there is no need for renewing the national registrations. See Opinion of the Austro-Hungarian administration to this effect, *Propriété Industrielle* (1911), p. 29.

3. At the Conference of The Hague, the Austrian delegation proposed an amendment to article 4*b* providing that "the international mark shall enjoy, in particular, the right of priority of the national mark registered previously, even when the latter shall not be renewed." This amendment was withdrawn because of the unanimous opinion of the sub-committee that such a right is enjoyed under article 4*b*, and that, consequently, the amendment was superfluous. See *Actes de la Conférence de La Haye*, pp. 484–485.

4. Such an opinion was expressed in Germany by Jüngel-Magnus, *Das deutsche Warenzeichenrecht*, 6th ed., I, 14. See against it, in *Propriété Industrielle* (1925), pp. 187

§ 443. Duration of legal effects of international registration. The rule that a trade mark registered at the Bureau occupies the same position, from the point of view of its legal protection in each of the contracting countries, as a trade mark registered directly in each of them, is subject to the qualification, among others, of the provision of article 6. This article concerns the duration of the protection resulting from international registration.

La protection résultant de l'enregistrement au Bureau international durera vingt ans à partir de cet enregistrement (sous réserve de ce qui est prévu à l'article 8 pour le cas où le déposant n'aura versé qu'une fraction de l'émolument international), mais elle ne pourra être invoquée en faveur d'une marque qui ne jouirait plus de la protection légale dans le pays d'origine.

Without this provision of article 6, the proprietor of the mark registered at the Bureau would need to watch the duration of the effects of registration in each of the contracting countries, and see that a timely renewal was effected in each. The uniformity of formalities and conditions of registration which the Arrangement was aiming at would not be secured. By virtue of article 6, the effects of international registration, and the legal protection afforded in each country on the basis thereof, last uniformly twenty years in all the contracting countries. The proprietor of the mark needs only to effect a timely renewal of the international registration.

The reservation contained in article 6 concerns the case in which the depositor has paid to the Bureau only a part of the registration fee at the time of registration, and has not paid the balance within the prescribed time according to article 8.[1]

However, under the latter part of article 6, the protection resulting from the international registration cannot be invoked in favor of a mark which would no longer enjoy legal protection in the country of origin. Thus, the duration of the effects of registration in the country of origin controls that of the international registration. The

---

and 189, two articles, one by the Bureau and another by the Austrian Johann Bing. Cf. Pillet, *Régime International*, p. 370.

An opinion of the Austrian Ministry of Public Works, Sept. 7, 1910 (*Propriété Industrielle*, 1913, p. 13), to the effect that the substitution of article 4*b* applies also in case the international registration precedes the national registration, is not in agreement with the text of the article. A contracting country may, however, if it chooses, provide to this effect by its municipal law.

1. See *infra*, § 445.

proprietor of the mark should keep both alive in order to be protected in all the contracting countries.

Consequently, if the effects of registration in the country of origin last less than twenty years, the proprietor of the mark cannot invoke protection in the other contracting countries by virtue of the international registration unless he has renewed the national registration before its effects are terminated. Nevertheless, the international registration is not cancelled before the expiry of twenty years by reason of lack of renewal in the country of origin. There is no explicit provision in the Arrangement directing the Bureau to this effect. The latter has adopted a rule, according to which the effects of international registration are merely suspended during the time the registration in the country of origin remains cancelled.[1] In case this is renewed, the effects of the international registration are resumed for the remaining period of protection.

The last sentence of article 6 makes the international protection of the mark dependent on the protection in the country of origin. If for any reason the protection in the latter ceases (for instance, if the mark is annulled, forfeited, or abandoned), the international protection is terminated. This dependence is not imposed for the same reasons as the indirect deposit through the agency of the administration of the country of origin. Technical difficulties may oppose a direct deposit at the Bureau.[2] After the original registration of the mark in the country of origin, and its admission in each of the contracting countries following notification by the Bureau, the international protection might well rest on the international registration exclusively. There is no reason why abandonment, forfeiture, and the like, in the country of origin should affect the international registration. The trade-mark owner should need to keep alive only the registration at the Bureau by applying for renewal in due time. Besides, as will be seen presently, very few countries notify the Bureau of national cancellations.

§ **444. Renewal of international registration.** The question of renewal of international registration is dealt with in article 7 of the Arrangement. Renewal is always possible; the application for it should be made according to the provisions of articles 1 and 3, gov-

1. See *Propriété Industrielle* (1922), p. 170; also, *Actes de la Conférence de La Haye*, pp. 183, 191.
2. See *supra*, §§ 287, 434.

erning applications for original registration. Six months prior to the expiry of the term of protection, the International Bureau reminds the proprietor of the mark of the precise date of such expiry. Such reminder is made directly to the proprietor of the mark.[1] The new period of twenty years begins to run from the date of renewal, not from the expiry of the preceding period. An explicit provision to this effect was added at the Conference of The Hague, in order to avoid the complications arising from a too early renewal application.[2] It is not provided at what time at the latest the application for renewal should be made, especially whether it may be made after the expiry of the twenty-year period.[3] From articles 6 and 7 taken together, however, it should be concluded that no renewal is possible after the period has wholly expired. Any application reaching the Bureau after such expiry should be treated as an application for original registration.[4]

This is important from the point of view of the treatment to which the notification of registration is subjected in the different countries.[5] Notifications of renewal of registration are not subjected to examination by the contracting countries, and no refusal is possible in respect to marks whose registration is merely renewed.[6]

There is renewal of registration when the mark remains the same, and the class or classes of goods to which the mark is to be applied are unchanged. Article 7 contains explicit provisions, added at the

1. Before the revision of the Arrangement at The Hague the reminder referred to was sent to the administration of the country of origin as well as to the proprietor of the mark.

2. Too early renewal applications were made either for obtaining the benefit of a reduced registration fee, or because at the same time renewal was applied for in the country of origin, or for other reasons. As a result the search in the "Marques Internationales" for prior marks was made difficult, for such search in the preceding twenty years did not disclose all the marks registered at the Bureau. See *Actes de la Conférence de La Haye*, p. 285.

3. A proposal to this effect by the Italian delegation at the Conference of The Hague was withdrawn. See *Actes de la Conférence de La Haye*, p. 360.

4. So decided by the Austrian Ministry of Commerce, holding that a renewal of registration at the International Bureau seven days late is a new registration, and that its priority starts from the date of such registration. It is immaterial that the application may have been made in due time in the country of origin. See *Propriété Industrielle* (1925), p. 101.

5. There is no provision in the Arrangement or *Règlement* for notification of renewals of registration by the Bureau to the contracting countries. But this is the practice, and is in accordance with the spirit of the whole Arrangement. Besides, article 3, to which article 7 refers, includes the provisions for notification of original registrations.

6. So decided by the German Patent Office, Dec. 2, 1926 (*Propriété Industrielle*, 1927, p. 35).

Conference of The Hague, for the cases in which these conditions are not satisfied. If the mark filed for renewal differs from the earlier mark in form, the administrations of the contracting countries may refuse its admission as a renewed trade mark. The mark, in such case, may be admitted or refused like any mark originally registered at the International Bureau. If the modification concerns the list of goods to which the mark is to be applied, the administrations have the same power of refusal. But in this case, if the registrant, on notification of such refusal, renounces the protection of the mark for the goods which were not contained in the original registration, the above power cannot be exercised; that is, renewal of registration of the mark cannot be refused in the contracting countries. These provisions, added at the Conference of The Hague, confirm what was the practice in the actual working of the Arrangement.[1]

It would be unjust, however, for the trade-mark owner to lose entirely the rights and advantages resulting from the previous international registration by reason of the non-admission of such a renewal application. By the law of many countries such rights are preserved in case of marks deposited directly therein. The International Bureau proposed at the Conference of The Hague that such rights be preserved in favor of the applicant. The rights in question may be the following:

(1) Rights in the trade mark in respect to the goods included in both the original application and that of renewal, in case the trade mark is not admitted for renewal by reason of a modification in the list of goods on which it is to be applied. Such rights are either of presumption of ownership or of priority of use (in the countries where registration is declaratory of the right), or property rights (in the countries where by registration property in the mark is acquired).

(2) Rights in the essential elements of a trade mark, in case the latter is not admitted for renewal by reason of a modification in form or in its constituent elements, and such modification concerns only minor elements in the mark, while its essential characteristics remain unmodified.

The proposal of the Bureau, that these rights should in no case be prejudiced by a refusal of renewal of registration, was not admitted on the opposition of the Austrian delegation. Instead, it was pro-

1. See *Actes de la Conférence de La Haye*, p. 285.

vided in the last paragraph of article 7 that the rights of priority or others acquired by reason of the previous registration may be taken into account ("il pourra être tenu compte") when a mark is not admitted for renewal of registration.[1]

§ **445. Fees.** Until the revision of the Arrangement at the Conference of The Hague, the fee for the registration of a mark at the Bureau was one hundred francs. If more than one mark were deposited at the same time by the same owner, a fee of fifty francs was payable for each additional mark. Under the new text the fees are higher.[2] For the first mark the fee is one hundred and fifty francs, and for each additional mark one hundred. It is specified now that fees are payable in Swiss francs. It is explicitly declared that these fees are wholly distinct from the national fees which each administration may collect from the owner of the mark who requests of such administration the transmission of his mark to the Bureau for international registration.[3] The fee for the international registration must be paid to the International Bureau in advance of registration, either through the administration of the country of origin or directly by the owner.[4]

A partial payment at the time of deposit at the Bureau is possible, under the new text of article 8. One hundred francs for the first mark and seventy-five for each additional one may be paid at first. Within a period of ten years from the date of international registration, the balance, with the addition of a supplementary fee, namely, a total of seventy-five francs for the first mark and fifty for each additional must be paid. On failure of payment, the benefit of the registration is lost at the expiration of the ten-year period. Six months prior to the expiration of this period, the Bureau reminds the proprietor of the precise date of such expiration.[5]

An increase of the registration fee is provided for by the new text, in case the list of goods, to which the mark is declared to be applied

1. See *Actes de la Conférence de La Haye*, pp. 285–286, 360, 487, 551.

2. The International Bureau had proposed that the fee should be doubled, but the delegations of certain countries whose currencies were depreciated resisted such increase. See *Actes de la Conférence de La Haye*, pp. 288, 487–488, 551.

3. Paragraph 1 of article 8 of the Arrangement.

4. Article 8 of the Arrangement, paragraph 2, and articles 2 (paragraph 1 [D]) and 8 (paragraph 1) of the *Règlement*. The fee should be paid in cash or by postal check, or money order, or by check on a bank at Berne.

5. The possibility of partial payment and removal of marks from the international register at the expiration of the ten-year period will permit taking off the register marks which are no longer used.

and in respect of which protection is claimed, is exceedingly large. The printing and notifications of such lists are very costly,[1] and an increase of the fee is well calculated to check this abuse. When the list in question contains more than one hundred words, a supplementary fee of one franc is payable for each additional line printed in *Les Marques Internationales*.[2]

Besides the registration fees, others are collected by the Bureau for various services rendered by it, as making entries of assignments, changes of names or domicil, disclaimers, etc.; copies or extracts from register; searches of prior marks registered at the Bureau, etc. The amounts of such fees are determined by the *Règlement* (article 8).

§ 446. Changes in status of mark. Article 9 of the Arrangement requires the administration of the country of origin to notify the Bureau of all changes affecting the status of the mark in the national register. Some of these changes are explicitly enumerated: annulments, removals, disclaimers, and assignments. As soon as these changes are recorded in the national register of marks, notice should be given to the Bureau. The latter records them in the international register, notifies the administrations of the contracting countries, and publishes them in its periodical.

The International Bureau proposed at the Conference of The Hague to amend article 9 in order to specify that only essential changes should be notified to the Bureau. This would exclude changes without international significance. Renewals of the national registration might thus be excluded,[3] although, under the provision of article 6, registration in the country of origin being the foundation of the protection afforded by the international registration, its renewal would seem to be of international importance. Yet such renewal is hardly a change in the status of the mark.

Non-renewal of registration in the country of origin, and the consequent removal of the mark from the national register, is a real change in the status of the mark. Such mark is no longer protected in the contracting countries, and it would be of assistance to the Bureau and to the countries where the marks are subjected to previous examination to have it removed from the international register

1. See *Actes de la Conférence de La Haye*, pp. 186, 288. The increase proposed by the Bureau was ten francs for each class of goods.

2. Article 8, last paragraph, of *Règlement*. Each line in *Les Marques Internationales* contains generally from 8 to 10 words.

3. See *Actes de la Conférence de La Haye*, p. 290.

and the registers of the contracting countries. At the Conference of The Hague, the Bureau proposed that it be explicitly provided in article 9 that non-renewals of registration should be communicated to the Bureau. However, in certain countries the non-renewal is not recorded in the national register, and certain delegations opposed the proposal. Consequently, it was agreed at The Hague that the Bureau will remove from the international register only those marks, the cancellation of which by reason of non-renewal was communicated to it by the administration of the country of origin, and not the marks which have in fact been forfeited in such country, but whose cancellation has not been duly communicated to the Bureau.[1]

Disclaimers of the mark are explicitly declared to be changes of which the Bureau should be notified. Concerning them, there is also a special provision in article 8*b* of the Arrangement. It concerns disclaimers in respect to certain of the contracting countries of marks registered at the Bureau, while article 9 concerns disclaimers in the country of origin. Article 8*b* was added at the Washington Conference, to permit a disclaimer of the right in a mark in one or more of the contracting countries in case the depositor is advised that a mark similar to his is already used by others in such countries.[2] According to this article, a declaration of disclaimer of the mark in respect to a contracting country may be sent to the Bureau through the medium of the administration of the country of origin. The Bureau notifies the country affected by the disclaimer.

Assignments of marks registered at the International Bureau, which are changes in the status of the mark under article 9, are also dealt with by articles 9*b* and 9*c* of the Arrangement. According to article 9*b*, when assignment of a mark is made in favor of a person established in a country other than the country of origin of the mark, the consent of that other country shall be asked by the International Bureau.[3] Following the receipt of such consent, the Bureau records the assignment, gives notice thereof to the administrations of the several countries, and publishes it in its periodical, mentioning in such publication, if possible, the date and number of registration in

1. *Actes de la Conférence de La Haye*, pp. 290, 491, 529, 552.
2. *Actes de la Conférence de Washington*, pp. 73–74.
3. A country may require a direct deposit with its administration of the mark so assigned, which then becomes a domestic mark. It may also submit it to a fresh examination. See, for instance, as to Germany, *Propriété Industrielle* (1927), p. 36.

the new country of origin.[1] This procedure is explained by the basic principle of the Arrangement, which makes the registration in the country of origin the foundation of the protection resulting from the international registration.[2] The second paragraph of article 9*b*, providing that no assignment in favor of a person not entitled to deposit an international mark is to be recorded by the Bureau, needs no explanation.[3]

Article 9*c*, which, prior to the revision of the Arrangement at the Conference of The Hague, formed the second paragraph of article 9*b*, stipulates that the provisions of articles 9 and 9*b* have not the effect of modifying the legislation of those contracting countries which prohibit the assignment of the mark without the simultaneous transfer of the commercial or industrial establishment whose products the mark serves to distinguish.[4]

A reduction of the list of goods to which the mark is applied is a change in the status of the mark, as explicitly provided by article 9. On the other hand, an addition of a new product to the list, or the substitution of one product for another, can be obtained only by a new deposit, to be effected according to article 3 as an original registration of the trade mark.

For all such entries in the international register a fee is payable, the amount of which is determined by the *Règlement.* The object of the fee is not so much to remunerate the Bureau for the expenditure and additional service occasioned by such operations, as to

1. The publication of the assignment by the Bureau need not contain the act of assignment. Only the recording of the assignment in the International Register shall be published. Such publication by the Bureau is sufficient for claiming protection in the contracting countries, and no publication in each of these countries is necessary. See on both points the Belgian case, Société Suchard *c.* Société Derbaix, Commercial Tribunal of Brussels, June 22, 1909 (1909, *Jurisprudence Commerciale de Bruxelles*, p. 442).

2. Are the notification and publication of the assignment by the Bureau conditions precedent to the validity of such assignment? A decision in the affirmative of the Austrian Administrative Tribunal, March 27, 1913, is rightly criticized in *Propriété Industrielle* (1914), pp. 132–133. The assignment is completed before compliance with the formalities of arts. 9 and 9*b*, as is clear from the terms of these articles. Protection, however, of the mark in the contracting countries cannot be claimed without previous notification and publication.

3. In case an assignment can not be registered, the Bureau asks of the administration of the old country of origin the authorization to remove the trade mark from the international register. *Règlement*, article 7, paragraph 4.

4. The Bureau cannot register an assignment of an international mark for only one, or several, of the contracting countries. That would create several countries of origin of the mark, which is against the whole system of the Madrid Arrangement. See Statement of the International Bureau, in *Actes de la Conférence de La Haye*, p. 193.

prevent unnecessary and unmethodical demands on the part of registrants.[1]

§ **447. Obligation to use mark.** Registration at the International Bureau, followed by acceptance of the mark by the contracting countries, does not assure protection of the mark in every case. The Bureau is only the *alter ego* of the government offices of the contracting countries. The invalidation or forfeiture of the mark in each of the contracting countries, in accordance with the law of each, is always possible, unless a specific provision of the general Convention or the Arrangement is opposed thereto.

A mark may be forfeited in certain countries by reason of its non-utilization within a definite period following registration.[2] The provisions of the municipal law to this effect are in no way affected by the Madrid Arrangement. Some countries, parties to the Arrangement, have applied such provisions of the law to marks registered at the International Bureau. They are anxious to revise their registers, grown cumbersome with non-used marks which make the choice of new marks difficult.[3]

There was an unsuccessful attempt at the Conference of The Hague to amend article 4 of the Arrangement for the purpose of restricting the penalties for non-utilization of a trade mark in the countries of the restricted Union. Instead, article 5 of the general Convention was amended in the way considered above.[4] The provisions of this article apply to the marks registered at the International Bureau, as well as to those registered directly in the countries parties to the general Convention.

§ **448. Finances of international registration service.** The service of international registration of trade marks is the source of receipts and expenditures by the International Bureau. Fees are payable by registrants on various occasions: for registration, notification of changes affecting the status of trade marks, copies, and searches of prior marks. Expenses are caused by the appointment of special employees, the cost of registers, the printing of the periodical of the Bureau, the mailing of notifications, and so forth. There is, therefore, a financial side to the service of international registration of trade marks. A primary end to be achieved would seem to be a

1. See *Actes de la Conférence de La Haye*, p. 491. 2. See *supra*, § 344.
3. See Statement of the International Bureau, in *Actes de la Conférence de La Haye*, p. 193.
4. See *supra*, § 400.

balance between receipts and expenditure; the secondary end is the distribution of the surplus of the service among the contracting countries. The sixth paragraph of article 8 of the Arrangement and article 9 of the *Règlement* contain the necessary provisions to this effect.

At the beginning of each year the International Bureau computes the amount of its expenditure during the preceding year for the service of international registration; the total sum thus arrived at is deducted from the total of the receipts, and the surplus of receipts is divided in equal shares among the contracting countries. An attempt to modify this method of distribution of the surplus was made at the Conference of The Hague, by the Brazilian delegation, which urged that the greatest part of the surplus should be paid to countries that profit least by the Arrangement.[1] The Conference maintained the *status quo*, but it provided by the *Règlement* that a new mode of distribution might be adopted by agreement among the contracting countries.

§ **449. Protection of international marks in newly acceding countries.** Member countries of the general Union which are not parties to the Madrid Arrangement may accede to it upon request, and in the form provided for by the general Convention (article 11 of the Arrangement). From the time such accession becomes effective, the new member of the restricted Union is notified of the registrations made at Berne after such accession, and the marks so registered are protected in the new country in the same way as in the other member countries.

Article 11 of the Arrangement contains also provisions concerning the marks which have been registered during the last twenty years at the International Bureau, and which are still protected in member countries of the restricted Union at the time the new accession takes place. In respect to these marks, two views are possible. Either they should not be protected in the newly acceding country unless they have already been registered directly therein, or they should always be protected, inasmuch as the Arrangement creates a union and the protection resulting from the international registration should extend to the whole territory of the Union.

The second view was upheld in the Arrangement until its revision at The Hague. It provided (second and third paragraphs of

1. See *Actes de la Conférence de La Haye*, pp. 489, 530.

article 11) that, as soon as the Bureau was informed that a country of the general Union or a colony of the member countries of the restricted Union had acceded to the Arrangement, it sent to the administration of that country or colony a general notice of the marks which, at that moment, enjoyed the international protection. This notice ensured, by itself, to these marks the benefit of the provisions of the Arrangement in the territory of the acceding country. The one-year period within which marks might have been refused by the administration, according to article 5, ran from the date of such notice. No new publication of the marks needed to be made.

These provisions did not permit countries subjecting trade marks to previous examination by the administration to undertake such examination in respect to trade marks registered by the Bureau in the preceding twenty years and communicated to them *en bloc* on their accession. A one-year period was insufficient for this purpose, especially in later years, when the number of marks registered at the Bureau had greatly increased. For this reason, Germany, on her accession in 1922 to the Madrid Arrangement, declared that she would forego any examination in respect to the marks thus notified of *en bloc* by the Bureau, and would admit all of them for registration. Third parties in Germany, whose rights were infringed by such marks, might cause their annulment or invalidation in accordance with the provisions of the German Law.[1] Indeed, the provisions under consideration did not purport to make the rights of international registrants retroactive.[2]

In view of the increasing number of international marks, it might have proved difficult to persuade new countries to accept the above provisions of article 11. Consequently, these provisions had a retarding effect upon the movement of extending the Madrid Arrangement to new countries. Because of this consideration, the International Bureau proposed at the Conference of The Hague an amendment of article 11, to allow newly acceding countries to declare that they would not protect trade marks registered at the Bureau before their

1. See *Propriété Industrielle* (1922), p. 171; also, Statement of the International Bureau, in *Actes de la Conférence de La Haye*, p. 193.

2. A mark was registered at the Bureau in 1905 and by another person in Austria in 1907. Austria acceded to the Arrangement in 1909 and the international mark in question, among others, was communicated to the Austrian administration. It was decided by the Ministry of Public Works, Jan. 18, 1911, that the Austrian registrant of 1907 prevailed. See *Propriété Industrielle* (1913), p. 14. The International Bureau agreed with this view. See *ibid.*, (1914), p. 109.

accession.[1] This proposal, complemented by a further amendment of the French delegation, was adopted,[2] and two new paragraphs were added to article 11, the effect of which was as follows.

To-day a country acceding to the Madrid Arrangement is not bound, as before, to protect all the marks registered within the last twenty years at the Bureau. It may declare that the application of the Arrangement will be limited to trade marks registered at the Bureau after its accession becomes effective. Renewals of registration after accession are assimilated to marks originally registered.[3]

The above declaration should be made at the time the country accedes to the Arrangement. If no such declaration is made, the provisions of paragraphs 2 and 3, above considered, will apply. In case such declaration is made, the International Bureau will not give out the general list of marks registered in the last twenty years.

This option of the acceding country is subject to a qualification concerning the international marks which were also registered directly in this same country before its accession to the Arrangement. Such marks, if they are still on the register of the country in question, shall be immediately recognized by the acceding country as international marks. This is merely an application of the principle of article 4*b* concerning the substitution of international for prior national registrations.[4] In order that this recognition may take place, the interested parties shall apply to the International Bureau, requesting their marks be granted the benefit of this provision of article 11. Following such application, the Bureau shall give notice to the acceding country of the marks in question, with all particulars. This notice shall be sent within one year from the date of accession of the country in question. The interested parties shall, therefore, send in their applications in time, so that the notification may be made within a year.

§ **450. Classification of goods.** The abuse of exceedingly large lists of goods contained in applications for international registration of trade marks is only in a slight degree remedied by the new provision in the Arrangement imposing a supplementary registration

1. See *Actes de la Conférence de La Haye*, pp. 193, 292–293.

2. *Ibid.*, pp. 362, 493, 552.

3. This was unanimously admitted by the sub-committee which considered superfluous a proposition of amendment to this effect by the Austrian delegation. See *Actes de la Conférence de La Haye*, p. 493.

4. See *supra*, § 442.

fee.[1] The most effective means of preventing such abuse would be the adoption of an international classification of goods to which marks may be applied, and in respect to which they are to be protected.[2] Each applicant would point out the class or classes of goods for which he desired his mark to be registered and protected. An international classification of trade marks also would be desirable in facilitating searches for priorities by the various administrations and by the International Bureau.

The attempts at, and various schemes for uniform classification of trade marks are considered in the last part of this book.[3] A complete study of the question has not yet been made. The objections and difficulties in the way of such uniform classification do not seem impossible to overcome. A classification established by the International Bureau, for its own convenience, was submitted to the Brussels Conference, with a proposal to insert in the Arrangement a provision to the effect that applications for international registration should indicate the goods to which the mark was to be applied according to the Bureau's classification. The latter, however, which established eighty classes divided into nine categories, was considered unsatisfactory by certain countries.[4] Meanwhile, this classification has been adopted in six countries, three of which are parties to the Madrid Arrangement; namely, Belgium, France, and Portugal.[5] It has been in use by the International Bureau, with satisfactory results. During the past years no modification of the classification has in any way been required, with the exception that a supplementary class, 71*b*, has been added.

At the Conference of The Hague the International Bureau proposed that its own classification be adopted by the member countries of the restricted Union, by being annexed to the *Règlement*, so that it might be modified when necessary. On the opposition of the German and Swiss delegations the proposed amendment to article 1 of the Arrangement was withdrawn.[6] The agenda of the meeting of

1. See *supra*, § 445.
2. See Statement of the International Bureau, in *Actes de la Conférence de La Haye*, p. 186.
3. See *infra*, §§ 587 ff. For an historical exposition, see *Propriété Industrielle* (1924), pp. 158 ff.
4. See *Actes de la Conférence de Bruxelles*, pp. 57, 119, 182, 290, 293. This classification appears also in *Actes de la Conférence de La Haye*, pp. 307–309.
5. See Statement of the International Bureau, in *Actes de la Conférence de La Haye*, p. 186.
6. See *Actes de la Conférence de La Haye*, pp. 355, 356, 483.

experts, decided upon by this Conference and convening at Berne in 1926, contained a study of an international classification of goods to which trade marks might be applied.[1] In view of the difficulties of arriving at definite results, the meeting adjourned, after appointing a committee to study and report on the question at a later time.[2]

§ 451. Results achieved by the Arrangement. The International Bureau, in the third part of its Statement on the service of international registration of trade marks from 1893 to 1924, presented to the Conference of The Hague,[3] describes the results of international registration, illustrating them by statistical tables. Some of these data may be presented here, to show the importance of the benefits afforded and achieved through the service instituted by the Madrid Arrangement during thirty-five years.

In the beginning the progress was very slow. During the first eight years, ending in 1900, the marks registered numbered only 2,391, which is an average of about 300 marks a year. During the subsequent thirteen years, ending in 1913, the number of registered marks, continually rising, reached 1,934 in that year. The war caused a retrogression, but at its termination the number rose again to 2,284 in 1920, and 2,653 in 1922. With the accession of Germany twice as many marks were registered; the number reached 5,258 in 1923, 5,487 in 1924, and 5,387 in 1925. At the end of 1926, the total number of trade marks registered at the Bureau was 50,034.[4] This number of international registrations corresponds to about 1,019,800 national registrations which would necessarily have been made in the twenty-one countries parties to the Arrangement for protection of the marks in question in each of them, had there been no service of international registration at the Bureau. The result then of the international registration is the great saving involved in the possibility of a single central deposit instead of numerous isolated registrations.

The saving comes, first, in registration fees which would have to

1. See *Actes de la Conférence de La Haye*, p. 586. On the work of the meeting, see *Propriété Industrielle* (1926), pp. 239, 242, 246.

2. See, on the difficulties of agreement, *Propriété Industrielle* (1926), p. 246. See text of *procès-verbal* adopted by the meeting, *ibid.*, p. 212.

3. Published in *Actes de la Conférence de La Haye*, pp. 173, 194 ff.

4. See statistical table in *Propriété Industrielle* (1927), p. 111. The greatest number of trade marks are registered by France — 19,531 in all, from 1893 to 1926. Next comes Germany, with 7,071 marks, registered during the four years (1923 to 1926, with five registrations in 1922) since her accession. Switzerland has registered 6,033 marks; the Netherlands, 4,570; Austria, 4,044; Belgium, 2,465; Spain, 2,101; Italy, 1,668; and Czechoslovakia (since 1919), 1,020.

be paid for the many isolated registrations. It has been found by the Bureau that this saving amounts to from 87 to 90 per cent; that is to say, instead of 90,000 francs which a concern would previously spend, now only about 10,000 are spent for international registration. Still greater is the saving in expense entailed by depositing marks abroad, a saving amounting to 500 per cent.[1]

A financial benefit also accrues to the contracting countries by the distribution to them of the surplus of receipts from the service of international registration. This surplus, which the service has always shown, has constantly increased. It rose from 19,712 francs in the first period of the service (1893–1902) to 204,900 in the two years 1923 and 1924. Each country received on the average 2,270 francs during the first period, and 10,750 francs during the years 1923 and 1924.

But more important than the economic and financial benefits of the Arrangement are the saving of time and trouble and of the need for compliance with irksome formalities in many countries, the simplicity of the methods, and the greater and more adequate protection afforded by registration at the International Bureau, all of which make the service created by the Madrid Arrangement one of the most useful international institutions.[2]

§ **452. Obstacles to accession of Great Britain.** There has never been any official or unofficial formulation of the objections of the two great industrial countries, Great Britain and the United States, to accession to the Madrid Arrangement. It is not irreconcilable with the municipal law of either of these countries. At the London meeting of the International Association for the Protection of Industrial Property, in 1898, Frey-Godet, Secretary of the International Bureau at the time, dealt with several objections that might be put forward by Great Britain.[3] He easily disposed of the possible fiscal argument that international registration would reduce the

1. See Statement of the Bureau, in *Actes de la Conférence de La Haye*, pp. 198, 202. This expenditure is entailed by translations, authentications, agents' fees, etc.

2. During the whole life of the Arrangement there have been 40,223 refusals of marks by the contracting countries. This number represents isolated refusals and should, therefore, be compared with the 1,019,800 national registrations (to which the total number of international registrations corresponds), in order to realize how small the percentage of refusals is, to wit, less than 4 per cent. The number 40,223 comprises also annulments and abandonments. Of this number, 11,468 concern the Netherlands; 7,014, Cuba; 4,948, Germany; 3,571, Austria; 2,803, the Serb-Croat-Slovene State; 2,268, Czechoslovakia; 1,933, Hungary; 1,346, Spain; 1,149, Brazil; and only 59, France, and 52, Belgium.

3. See *Annuaire de l'Association Internationale* (1898), pp. 40 ff.

income from national registrations made by foreigners in the old way. Besides gaining greater advantage for British industry and trade through British deposits at the International Bureau, the loss of foreign fees would be further made up by the national fees payable on British applications for international registration and by Great Britain's share in the surplus of receipts of the service of international registration at Berne.

Another objection, based on the fact that registration of trade marks in Great Britain is made in the Patent Office, while by the Arrangement it is effected by an international office in a foreign country, where the British Administration cannot control operations, might also be easily set aside. For Great Britain has already acceded to the International Copyright Union, and has given up the registration of copyright for works produced in the contracting countries which she requires for domestic literary works.[1] Furthermore, article 5 of the Arrangement gives the power to each country to reject a trade mark registered at the International Bureau under the same conditions as if the application for registration were made in the old way.

Certain provisions of the British Trade Mark Act raise further objections. Trade marks filed for registration must be published in the *Trade Marks Journal*, the official journal of the Patent Office. This objection was not considered impossible to overcome in other countries, the law of which likewise required such domestic publication. Besides, it should be possible to append to the regular issue of the *Trade Marks Journal* the issues of *Les Marques Internationales*, or an authenticated translation of the same. The International Bureau sends gratis to the administrations any number of its periodical desired by them.

Registration of trade marks in Great Britain is made in respect to particular goods or classes of goods.[2] The Arrangement does not provide for registration in respect to classes. But this should not prove a serious objection. British registrants may register for certain goods only of those comprised in a class, and the mark is protected in such case as to these goods only.[3] On the other hand, regis-

1. Registration of copyright at Stationers' Hall is abolished now in Great Britain under the Copyright Act of 1911 (1 & 2 Geo. V, c. 46).

2. Sec. 8 of the Act of 1905 (5 Edw. VII, c. 15).

3. By the Court of Appeal, in Application de la Société Anonyme Dubonnet (1915), 32 R. P. C. 241.

tration in a class does not grant a right to exclusive use of the mark in regard to goods for which the registrant does not use his mark.[1]

A more serious objection seems to be raised by section 15 of the Act of 1905[2] requiring the applicant to disclaim any right to the exclusive use of any part or parts of his mark for the purpose of defining his rights under the registration. Such disclaimers are now the exception[3] and not the rule, as under the Act of 1883. Frey-Godet proposed that such disclaimers be made when an action for infringement is brought by the registrant, instead of in the application for registration, which would be impossible under the system of international registration. A still better means of overcoming the difficulty would be to resort to provisional rejection of an international mark, and an invitation to the applicant through the agency of the International Bureau to disclaim any part or parts of his mark, to the exclusive use of which the British administration holds him not to be entitled, or which is considered needful for the purpose of defining his rights in Great Britain under international registration.

No insurmountable obstacle, therefore, is known to exist to the accession of Great Britain to the Arrangement. Yet the British government has never given out any reasons for its non-accession beyond declaring that such accession would be possible only when an international classification of marks should be established,[4] and that, at any rate, it would be of no benefit to Great Britain.[5]

§ 453. Obstacles to accession of the United States. The United States expressed its agreement with the principle of international registration of trade marks when the draft Arrangement was discussed at the Madrid Conference, and the only objection the American delegation seems to have presented was to the word "Arrangement," for which it proposed to substitute "Protocol," so as to make this international act an appendix to the general Convention.[6]

An unofficial formulation of the objections to the accession of the United States may be seen in a report to the Department of State, made in 1919 by a special agent of that department sent to Europe

1. Edwards *v.* Dennis (1885), 30 C. D. 454; 55 L. J. Ch. 125.
2. Frey-Godet was dealing with the equivalent provision of sec. 64 sub-sec. (2) of the Act of 1883.
3. See Kerly (Underhay and Morgan), *The Law of Trade Marks and Trade Name*, pp. 246, 248.
4. See *Conférence de Madrid*, p. 100.
5. See *Annuaire de l'Association Internationale* (1902), pp. 156–157.
6. See *Conférence de Madrid*, pp. 99, 106, 111.

in that year to investigate the question of international protection for industrial property.[1] One can not agree entirely with the reporter, when he holds that registration at the Bureau of Berne "amounts only to registration at a central receiving, recording and distributing Office," and that "one can secure every right that it is possible to secure through the medium of the Trade Mark Union, by registering his trade mark directly in the individual countries." [2] It has already been shown that the legal status of the mark begins at the moment of its registration at the International Bureau, and that three specific legal advantages, that of right of priority (without the formalities of article 4 of the Convention of 1883), that of uniform duration in the different countries, and that of single publication, are enjoyed through international registration.[3] Nor is it entirely sound to contrast the trade-mark system of the United States with a "European system." [4] There is no such thing as a "European system" of trade-mark law. There are in Europe many systems. At the time when the above Report was made, the laws of Austria-Hungary and the Netherlands differed from those of France and Switzerland, as much as those of the latter differed from that of the United States. In the meantime Czechoslovakia, Germany, Danzig (Free City), and the Serb-Croat-Slovene State have acceded, the laws of which differ widely from those of the Latin countries and rather resemble that of the United States.[5]

If the specific objections raised in the Report are considered, they appear to be rather weak. The United States Patent Office admits for registration trade marks filed abroad, although no prior use is alleged. For this requirement for domestic trade-mark owners is substituted, for foreigners, that of prior filing abroad. Under the Madrid Arrangement, the Bureau of Berne admits for registration only marks definitively registered in the country of origin; consequently, no obstacle in this respect would seem to exist in the

1. Letter of the Department of State to the present writer under date of May 25, 1928. The report in question is entitled, "Report to the Department of State (The Foreign Office Adviser) on the Arrangement of Madrid of 1891 for the International Registration of Trade Marks, with special Reference to the Advisability of Adherence thereto by the United States," and is dated Paris, June 24, 1919. A photostat copy of the same was sent to the writer through the kindness of the United States Patent Office.

2. See above Report, pp. 7, 20.

3. See *supra*, § 441.

4. See above Report, p. 15.

5. See *supra*, chap. XXII, on the municipal law of the different countries.

United States law. The objection that in the United States trade marks are subject to examination before registration, cannot be deemed sufficiently strong, since that is true for Austria, Czechoslovakia, Hungary, Germany, the Netherlands, and other countries, which, nevertheless, are parties to the Arrangement. The argument concerning classification is considered above in connection with Great Britain. The recent amendments of the Arrangement considered above render formal changes of the mark by the registrant quite practicable under the Arrangement. The objection that the United States on accession would receive communication of many thousand trade marks already registered at the Bureau, which it would be practically impossible to examine thoroughly, is now removed by the recent amendment of article 11 of the Arrangement, permitting a country to refuse protection to marks registered at the Bureau before its accession. The objection of the large amount of work that the marks registered at the Bureau and communicated to the United States would entail, and the fiscal argument about the diminution of revenue and increase of expense to be caused by accession, are not very serious. It would be strange were the United States to deny to its citizens the great facilities involved in the simple and economical means of international registrations, which the Report itself recognizes as succeeding admirably,[1] because of a slight increase of expense or reduction of revenue in trade-mark registration. And it is not clear how the actual work at the Patent Office would be larger than it is now, with foreigners applying for registration directly in the United States.

However, the Report advocated the enactment of a statute, similar to that of Great Britain, establishing a supplementary register in which United States trade-mark owners could register marks inadmissible for registration but actually used, or which are registrable only with changes in form. This would permit such owners to be protected in foreign countries where it is required as a condition precedent to the admission of foreign marks that they should be filed for registration in the country of origin. If such a register existed in the United States, it was felt that the above objections to the accession of the United States to the Madrid Arrangement would no longer apply, because the marks registered at the International

1. See the Report, p. 12.

Bureau and communicated to the United States could be registered in this supplementary registry.[1]

Such an act was passed on March 10, 1920, in order to give effect to certain provisions of the Pan-American Convention for the Protection of Trade Marks and Commercial Names, and for other purposes, made and signed at Buenos Aires, August 20, 1910.[2] The United States, as a party to this Convention, has undertaken to protect trade marks registered at the Inter-American Bureaus, of which notice is received.[3]

It would seem, therefore, that no obstacle exists to-day to the accession of the United States to the Madrid Arrangement. This is true also in respect to Great Britain, where a similar supplementary roll exists, the Register of Trade Marks having been divided into two parts, called Part A and Part B.[4]

There is a practical reason, however, for which these countries are disinclined to accede to the Arrangement. This is that they are unwilling to have their registers encumbered with marks which will probably never be used in their territory. Indeed, under the Arrangement, a trade mark registered with the Bureau and not refused by a member country as within the exceptions of article 6 of the general Convention, shall be considered as registered and protected in its territory. Thus a trade mark registered at Berne by a manufacturer of Luxembourg would be placed on the supplementary register of the United States and Great Britain, although this manufacturer's business does not extend further than, for instance, Germany, France, and Austria, and his mark is never used in the other two countries. Of course, proceedings may be taken for the removal of such mark after non-use during a certain period, and the use of the same mark by another after such period may be legitimate. But it is very difficult to establish proof of non-use, or to be assured of the same, before using a similar mark. The safe thing for an American manufacturer or trader would be to refrain from using a foreign mark. And in view of the multiplication of products and production to-day, especially in such highly industrialized countries as the United States and Great Britain, there is a disinclination to restrict any further a field of words, signs, or terms presenting psychological

1. See above Report, p. 26.
2. XLI *U. S. Stat. at Large*, 533.
3. On the Pan-American Conventions see *infra*, Section VIII.
4. 9 & 10 Geo. V, c. 79.

and business advantages for use as trade marks, which is already much restricted.

These countries might be induced to accede to the Arrangement if the above situation could be changed by an amendment, either limiting the effects of the international registration to certain ones only of the member countries, by imposing an additional fee for protection in each of the contracting countries, or requiring proof of the use of the mark in each of such countries at specified periods, in order that the protection resulting from international registration might be maintained.

SECTION VI

THE INTERNATIONAL REGIME OF THE OTHER RIGHTS OF INDUSTRIAL PROPERTY

CHAPTER XXIX

THE INTERNATIONAL PROTECTION OF TRADE NAMES

§ 454. Broad basis of trade-name protection. Trade marks are one of the means by which the goods of a producer are identified and are distinguished from similar goods of other producers. There exist several other distinctive badges or descriptions used and applied to the same end; the trade name is one of them.[1] Indeed, the name of a manufacturer or seller is the primitive form, and the most usual, for indicating the origin of goods. It serves to distinguish the commercial activity of one person from that of another. For this reason, protection of trade names is broader than that of trade marks. Although the protection in both cases is an aspect of protection against unfair competition,[2] and its basic principle is protection of business relations and promotion of fair dealing, the formalism and technicalities which have developed with reference to trade mark protection are not met with in the case of trade names. Any act impairing the distinction between the commercial activities of two persons,[3] or the natural tendency of which is to represent the goods of one producer as being somebody else's,[4] may be a trade-name infringement if it is

1. Kerly (Underhay and Morgan), *The Law of Trade Marks and Trade Name*, p. 13.
2. Pouillet, *Traité des Marques*, pp. 590, 691.
3. Court of Errors of Rome, Dec. 11, 1912 (*Propriété Industrielle*, 1913, p. 74).
4. Kerly (Underhay and Morgan), *The Law of Trade Marks and Trade Name*, p. 15; Hopkins, *The Law of Trade Marks, Trade Names and Unfair Competition*, pp. 10 ff.

a result of the use or imitation of a name already adopted and used in connection with a business.

§ **455. Provisions of the Convention.** The Convention of Union, in view of the existing inadequacy of international protection of trade names prior to its adoption,[1] contains very important provisions concerning the international regime of this right of industrial property, in articles 2, 8, and 9.

By virtue of article 2, national treatment is granted to persons entitled to the benefits of the Convention in respect to their trade names; that is to say, these persons enjoy in all the contracting countries the same protection and the same rights and remedies in respect to their trade names as nationals of these countries.[2] In accordance with this provision, foreigners would enjoy no protection for their trade names if none is provided by the municipal law for nationals; they would have to comply with all the conditions and formalities imposed on nationals; and the extent of the protection would be determined exclusively by the law of the country where protection is claimed. These consequences of the national-treatment clause are avoided by the operation of article 8 of the Convention. This article provides:

> Le nom commercial sera protégé dans tous les pays de l'Union sans obligation de dépôt ou d'enregistrement, qu'il fasse ou non partie d'une marque de fabrique ou de commerce.

Thus, instead of the mere national treatment, there is an explicit engagement of each of the contracting countries to protect the trade name of persons entitled to the benefits of the Convention. It is declared that such protection shall be ensured without necessity of deposit or registration. Lastly, the protection of the trade names is made distinct and separate from that of trade marks. Article 8, therefore, derogates in these respects from the principle of article 2.[3] The latter is applicable only in those respects which are not dealt with by article 8.[4]

1. See *supra*, chap. II, IV.

2. The precise scope of this assimilation to nationals is considered in chap. IX, especially §§ 126–128.

3. Pillet, *Régime International*, p. 412; Pelletier et Vidal-Naquet, *Convention d'Union*, pp. 251–252; Osterrieth und Axster, *Pariser Konvention*, pp. 183–184.

4. The persons entitled to the benefits of article 8 are defined by articles 2 and 3 of the Convention. The Paris Conference of 1880 declined to admit protection of trade names "without distinction of nationality," as originally proposed. It seems to have

In addition to these stipulations, article 9 provides for certain effective measures of repression against acts of infringement of trade names, which the contracting countries undertake to apply.[1]

§ 456. Subject-matter of protection. The first question that article 8 raises, as well as the other provisions of the Convention (articles 2 and 9) referring to "le nom commercial," concerns the definition of this branch of industrial property. For the purposes of article 2 the question is only academic. Under this article foreigners are assimilated to nationals in respect to the protection of trade names, and, consequently, the conception of the "nom commercial" in each country applies to both foreigners and nationals. On the contrary, under article 8, each of the contracting countries is obligated to protect the "nom commercial." This no longer leaves each country free to decide for itself what is the "nom commercial" to be protected, and since there is no international conception or definition of the term to be resorted to,[2] the law of the country in which the right in a "nom commercial" is claimed to have been acquired is the only one controlling.[3]

It follows that the protection of the contracting countries by virtue of article 8 is only accessory to the protection enjoyed in the country where the right was originated; [4] in other words, the provisions of this article secure the validation of trade names in the whole territory of the Union. Article 8 does not contain any provisions with regard to the country of origin of trade names. It is not possible to apply by analogy the provision of article 6 concerning the country of origin of trade marks.[5] If a trade name is legally ac-

---

admitted, however, that in case a trade name is owned by a person entitled to the benefits of the Convention and by one not so entitled, it should be protected. See *Conférence de Paris* (1880), pp. 97–100.

1. See § 460.

2. In La République Française et al. *v.* Schultz (1893), 57 Fed. 37, 41, the Court thought that since the term "nom commercial" is one used in the civil law of France, it becomes necessary to examine its meaning in French law; and it concluded that the word "Vichy" is a trade name, following Pouillet's definition of "nom commercial" in his treatise. It is doubtful whether the decision will be followed.

3. Some authors are of the opinion that, inasmuch as the provision of article 8 is very general, the "nom commercial" should be understood in all the various forms that it takes in the different countries of the Union. See Pillet, *Régime International*, p. 413; Osterrieth und Axster, *Pariser Konvention*, p. 185. On the contrary, Pelletier et Vidal-Naquet (*Convention d'Union*, pp. 255–256) think that designations of establishments cannot be included in the provision of article 8.

4. Pillet, *Régime International*, p. 415; Osterrieth und Axster, *Pariser Konvention*, pp. 185, 187.

5. The restrictive character of this provision is explained by the desire to prevent

quired in any country of the Union it should be protected in all the others.[1] In case, by the law of the country in question, a trade name is not protected unless it has been registered, no validation of a non-registered trade name originating in such a country may be claimed in the other countries of the Union, by virtue of article 8.

The conception of "nom commercial" varies in the different countries of the Union. In France, the "nom commercial" comprises: (1) the names of traders or manufacturers or of firms and companies; (2) the designations of commercial or industrial establishments; and (3) the names of places of manufacture or of localities of production.[2] In Germany, on the contrary, the above second and third classes of French commercial names are not included in the conception of trade name. The German law considers as "nom commercial": (1) the registered name (*Firma*) of merchants who are bound to register their name (*Vollkaufleute*), whether or not identical with their civil name; (2) the civil name of small traders (*Minderkaufleute*);[3] and (3) the firm name of commercial companies (*Handelsgesellschaften*).[4]

What is strictly called "nom commercial" in France has no existence in Switzerland. There is only the "raison de commerce," the name under which one or several individuals exercise their trade. The composition of this name is strictly regulated by the Swiss law, which requires registration. Designations of establishments, names of business houses, factories, and so forth, are recognized only as "enseignes," and protected by the law of unfair competition.[5] In the common law countries (the United States, Great Britain, and British dominions and colonies), the trade name may be a man's own name or that under which he trades, as well as the name of a business house, shop, or factory having a reputed connection with the trade or business of a person.[6] Together with trade names of

evasions of the law by persons registering in a foreign country a trade mark which is not admitted in their own country. See *supra*, § 365.

1. Osterrieth und Axster (*Pariser Konvention*, p. 186) suggest that the country of origin of the trade name which is identical with the civil name is the country of which the person in question is a national; in case there is no identity with the civil name, the country in which the commercial or industrial establishment is located. The country of origin of firms or corporations is that in which their seat is.

2. Pouillet, *Traité des Marques*, pp. 575 ff.

3. Craftsmen and minor industry men.

4. Osterrieth und Axster, *Pariser Konvention*, pp. 187–188.

5. See Vuille, "Observations sur le Nom Commercial et la Raison de Commerce au Point de Vue Suisse," in *Annuaire de l'Association Internationale* (1900), pp. 210 ff.

6. Kerly (Underhay and Morgan), *The Law of Trade Marks and Trade Name*, pp. 578, 596–597. Hopkins, *The Law of Trade Marks, Trade Names, and Unfair Competition*, pp. 10–15.

persons, protection in these countries extends to trade names of goods, among which geographical names that have acquired by use and reputation a secondary distinctive meaning,[1] correspond to names of locality of manufacture of the French law.[2]

§ **457. No deposit or registration required.** International protection of trade names is ensured in all the countries of the Union without the necessity of deposit or registration. This stipulation of article 8 derogates from the provisions of the municipal law of those countries that require such deposit or registration. It is a self-executing provision, and should form by itself the rule of decision in the countries in question. It applies, however, only to persons who have acquired a right in a trade name in a country of the Union, and who seek to enforce it in the countries where registration or deposit is required. The municipal law of the latter is fully applicable in respect to trade names originating in their territory. Article 8 does not purport to abolish the obligation to deposit or register a trade name except in the case of validation of trade names acquired abroad.[3]

Registration of commercial names in the commercial register is required in many countries at the present time, namely, Argentina, Austria, Chile, Denmark, France, Germany, Hungary, Italy, Japan, Morocco, Mexico, Norway, Portugal, Spain, Sweden, and Switzerland, all of which, with the exception of Argentina and Chile, are members of the Union.[4] Neither is the same end sought nor do the same legal effects follow from registration in the commercial register in all these countries. Generally speaking, the latter are classified into two groups, in one of which registration is necessary for the recognition of a trade name (Germany, Austria, Switzerland, and Scandinavian countries), and in the other registration is only a means of publication of the trade name and of rendering easier its protection against infringement.

Article 8 removes the obligation of registration in both these

1. Kerly (Underhay and Morgan), *The Law of Trade Marks and Trade Name*, pp. 603, 614.

2. In France, also, names of place of manufacture are protected as trade names if they have acquired a reputation. Pouillet, *Traité des Marques*, pp. 617, 618.

On account of the broad conception of trade name in Great Britain and the United States, the term "nom commercial" of article 8 is best rendered by "trade name" and not "commercial name."

3. Osterrieth und Axster, *Pariser Konvention*, pp. 186–187.

4. See two excellent articles on registration of trade names, in *Propriété Industrielle* (1920), pp. 129, 138.

cases. Persons entitled to the benefits of the Convention may, nevertheless, register their trade names for either of the above purposes, if they so desire. They may claim this advantage by virtue of the national-treatment clause of article 2. In such case, they are bound by the conditions and formalities of the municipal law.[1]

§ 458. Protection of trade names distinct from that of trade marks. The last sentence of article 8 provides that a trade name shall be protected whether or not it forms part of a trade mark. This provision, as was explicitly declared by the Chairman of the Paris Conference, the French Senator Bozérian,[2] aimed at meeting the decisions of French courts which held that if a trade name forms one of the elements of a trade mark and the public becomes possessed of the other elements the property in the trade name is also lost.[3] By virtue of article 8 of the Convention, the protection of the trade name is made distinct and separate from that of the trade mark of which it may form an element.[4] Consequently, (1) the trade name does not fall within the public domain by reason of the forfeiture, abandonment, invalidation, or the like, of the mark;[5] (2) for an infringement of a trade mark containing a trade name, there may be imposed the legal sanctions pertaining to the infringement of either.[6]

Certain trade names, however, may fall within the public domain and the right to their exclusive use be lost, when they become descriptive or general terms. This is hardly possible in the case of personal names, but it is probable in the case of artificial or fancy trade names, of designations of industrial or commercial establishments and names of business houses, or of names of places of manufacture.[7]

1. That is, they must pay the fees prescribed, give notice of the changes in the name, etc. If registration by municipal law is restricted to certain classes of domestic merchants (for instance, in Germany, where only *Vollkaufleute* may register their *Firmas*), the persons in question cannot claim registration unless they come under these classes. On the last point, however, Osterrieth und Axster (*Pariser Konvention*, p. 185) express the opposite view.

2. *Conférence de Paris* (1880), p. 97.

3. Cassation, Jan. 13, 1880 (*Dalloz*, 1880, I, 255). In Belgium also the courts held the same. See Court of Brussels, Feb. 11, 1880 (*Pasicrisie*, 1880, II, 72).

4. Pouillet, *Traité des Marques*, p. 708.

5. Baracco frères *v.* Carenon et Tur, Court of Appeal of Nîmes, Jan. 10, 1905 (*Darras*, 1906, p. 142), holding that the trade mark constituted by the trade name "Baracco" of an Italian manufacturer benefits by the imprescriptibility of the trade name.

6. Picon et Cie *c.* Auric, Cassation (France), Jan. 9, 1903, and Court of Appeals of Montpellier, March 14, 1903 (*Propriété Industrielle*, 1903, p. 195).

7. Pouillet, *Traité des Marques*, pp. 600 ff., 641 ff. Thus the United States Supreme

§ 459. Extent of protection. Although article 8 provides in general that the trade name shall be protected in all the countries of the Union, it does not prescribe the mode or extent of protection, nor does it contain specific remedies or sanctions against infringement of trade names. The effect of the stipulation is, first, to obligate the various countries of the Union to provide by law for the protection of trade names, and, second, to render inapplicable any provisions of the municipal law which in any way restrict the protection of foreigners' trade names. The obligation to deposit or register a trade name and lack of protection of a trade name as distinct from a trade mark of which it forms part, are only two illustrations of such restrictions.[1]

As we have seen earlier in this chapter,[2] the principle of article 8 seems to be, that a trade name, valid and protected as such in a country of the Union, should be always protected in the other contracting countries, even if their own conception of the trade name is more restrictive.[3] The protection should extend to the whole of the trade name as well as to a part,[4] an abbreviation,[5] the initials by

Court, in the case of the French Republic *v.* Saratoga Vichy Spring Co. (1903), 191 U. S. 427, 436, denied protection to the alleged French trade name "Vichy," because of the plaintiff's acquiescence in its use by others, as a result of which it became a generic term indicative of the character of the water. Also the Belgian Tribunal of Antwerp, Oct. 23, 1906, in Société Anonyme Henry Clay Bock & Co. *c.* Leonhard Tietz, Firme Lievin, et al., held that, in order that a trade name may be considered as having fallen within the public domain, third parties must have used it in such a measure that such name no longer evokes the idea of an exclusive relationship between the name and the commercial enterprise. (*Pasicrisie*, 1907, III, 91.)

The Reichsgericht, on Oct. 29, 1920, held in respect to the French name "Gervais," used on a special kind of cheese by the corporation formed by Gervais, that it does not mean a mode of manufacture of cheese, since a great part of interested circles continue to consider it as a trade name. (*Blatt für Patent-, Muster- und Zeichenwesen* 1921, p. 120.)

1. Osterrieth und Axster, *Pariser Konvention*, pp. 185, 189.

2. See *supra*, § 456.

3. The American case, La République Française et al. *v.* Schultz (1893), 57 Fed. 37, protected the French trade name "Vichy" by a consideration of the French Law on trade names. An Austrian decision by the Supreme Court, March 15, 1912, protected the French trade name "Benedictine" (*Propriété Industrielle*, 1913, p. 57). *Contra.* The Swiss decision, Perrin frères *v.* Vausillon, Federal Tribunal, Oct. 15, 1904 (30 *Arrêts Tr. Féd.*, II, 586), refused protection to the words "A la Chevrette," forming part of a French trade name applied on gloves, on the ground that the Swiss law admits as trade name of a company only the name of the firm without any addition. It is submitted that this decision is wrong.

4. Decision of the Cuban Patent Office, rejecting the trade mark "Manhattan" for men's shirts on the opposition of the Manhattan Shirt Co. of New York, invoking the protection of article 8 of the Convention (*Propriété Industrielle*, 1906, p. 181).

5. Union-Vie Genève *c.* L'Union, Compagnie d'assurances sur la vie humaine, Swiss Federal Tribunal, Sept. 15, 1926 (52 *Arrêts Tr. Féd.*, II, 393). This decision protected

which it is generally known in the trade,[1] or a catchname or nickname on which its reputation rests.[2] All these cases of passing off goods of one producer as those of another it is the purpose of the provision of article 8 to prohibit.

The trade name should be protected against innocent or fraudulent imitations of any of its parts, whether it is imitated in another trade name or in a trade mark. The use of the same trade name by a person whose own name is identical with the trade name for which protection is claimed is prohibited under article 8.[3] The rendering of the trade name in a foreign language does not destroy the identity, but is an imitation. Whatever aspect the infringement of the trade name may take, that is, whether the infringing name is applied on goods or on advertisements, price-lists, signs, designations of establishments, or the like, the provision of article 8 would seem to be applicable.[4]

The protection of trade names by the Convention is not only negative, tending to prevent their infringement by imitations, but also positive, ensuring to the proprietors of trade names entitled to the benefits of the Convention free and unprohibited use of their trade names in the contracting countries.[5] For the rest, the extent

---

the French Company "L'Union, Compagnie d'assurances," known in the market as "Union-Vie." See The Guardian Fire and Life Assurance Co. *v.* The Guardian and General Insurance Co. (1880), 50 L. J. Ch. 253, where the commonly known name of the plaintiff, "The Guardian," is protected. It was found that the defendant's name was calculated to deceive the public. Compare Lloyd's *v.* Lloyds (Southampton) Ltd. (1912), 29 R. P. C. 433.

1. Decision of the President of Cuba, Jan. 20, 1914, cancelling registration of the mark A. E. G., it being proved that the German Company, Allgemeine Elektricitätsgesellschaft, was known by these initials in commercial circles (*Propriété Industrielle,* 1915, p. 9).

2. Stoom Chocolade & Cacaofabrik "Kwatta" (Kl.), German Reichsgericht, Sept. 26, 1924. Decision cancelled registration of the mark "Kwatta" for butter which formed part of the firm name of a Dutch corporation carrying on the business of making chocolate and cocoa, on the ground that the word "Kwatta" was a nickname distinguishing the plaintiff (109 *Entsch. Reichsg., Zivilsachen,* 213).

3. Osterrieth und Axster, *Pariser Konvention,* p. 189. So decided by the German Patent Office, concerning the French trade names of Mumm & Cie (*Propriété Industrielle,* 1905, p. 112).

4. In Union-Vie Genève *c.* L'Union, Compagnie d'assurances sur la vie humaine, Swiss Federal Tribunal, Sept. 15, 1926 (52 *Arrêts Tr. Féd.,* II, 393), the French trade name was protected irrespective of its application on goods. Pillet's opinion (*Régime International,* p. 414) that article 8 does not purport to go further than the French Law of 1824, which punished only the application of another's trade name on goods, cannot be supported. Pelletier et Vidal-Naquet (*Convention d'Union,* p. 254) seem to agree with the view advanced in the text.

5. Osterrieth und Axster, *Pariser Konvention,* pp. 189–190. Kerly (Underhay and Morgan), *The Law of Trade Marks and Trade Name,* pp. 603 ff.

and mode of protection of trade names are governed by the law of the country where protection is sought.

For the protection of trade names of places of manufacture or origin, there exist specific provisions in article 10 of the Convention and in the Madrid Arrangement for the repression of false indications of origin, which are considered in the next chapter.

§ **460. Protection of trade names under article 9.** Special measures for the protection of trade names are contained in article 9 of the Convention, which is considered in an earlier chapter in respect to the protection of trade marks.[1] The seizure on importation or within the country, and the prohibition of importation of goods are to be effected in case such goods bear illegally a trade mark or a trade name, in the countries where this mark or name has a right to legal protection. How far the provisions of article 9 are obligatory on the contracting countries, what the conditions are of application of the article, and so forth, have been considered in the interpretation of article 9 in respect to trade marks.

1. See *supra*, chap. XXVI.

CHAPTER XXX

PROTECTION OF INDICATIONS OF ORIGIN

§ 461. Problems of international protection of indications of origin. Statements of place of origin, or indications of origin, are the branch of industrial property which was last to be recognized and protected by the municipal law of the different countries.[1] Prior to the Convention of 1883, few countries protected indications of origin by their domestic law, and the remedies for the repression of false indications of origin were very inadequate.[2] Foreigners' rights were much less protected. Only two conventions, entered into in 1882 and 1883, purported to ensure national treatment for indications of origin in the contracting countries.[3] The common right to the use of the name of a place, community, or region by all the producers, manufacturers, or traders of that place, and the right of these persons to exclude others from the use of the same name, is a late development in the law of most of the countries, growing out of the law of unfair competition. It was recognized and regulated

1. See Marcel Plaisant et Fernand-Jacq, *Traité des Noms et Appellations d'Origine'* pp. 1 ff.

2. See *supra*, chap. II, IV.

3. See *supra*, p. 57.

in most of the countries about the same time by national and international legislation. The evolution of international protection, from the crude and vague provisions of the original article 10 of the Convention to the regime prescribed by the new article 10 and the amended Madrid Arrangement for the repression of false indications of origin, reflects a similar evolution of national protection.[1]

The difficulties in the national as well as the international regulation and protection of indications of origin lie in two directions: first, in delimiting the exact boundaries of the locality or region, the producers of which may use a certain name as an indication of origin;[2] second, in defining precisely the cases in which a geographical term or name is a true indication of origin, and not a mere arbitrary designation, or a generic or descriptive term.

An indication of origin is a badge of distinction of certain goods. This holds true when these goods are produced in a certain locality, region, or country, and, either on account of some natural advantages of this locality, its soil or climate, or on account of the traditional ability and capacity of the people living in such locality, region or country, all goods produced therein have acquired a reputation for excellence. Because of this factor of natural advantage and tradition, this right is a class or community right. Hymettus honey, Eau de Vichy, Carlsbad salts, Champagne wine, are well-known indications of origin.

It is relatively easy to distinguish from them the arbitrary geographical descriptions which have never been indications of origin, because the goods in connection with which they are used were never produced in the place or country indicated. It is more difficult to decide whether an original indication of origin has lost its distinctiveness, and has become a descriptive or generic term indicating the kind or quality of goods. Eau de Cologne and Suede gloves are admitted now as generic terms of special kinds of articles. The names Cognac, Camembert, Madeira, Pilsen, Porto, Lancashire (for iron), have been subjects of long controversies. It has been maintained that a distinction should be made between manufactured and agricultural products, or between goods which, al-

1. See an excellent study of the law of each country, in Jaton, *La Répression des Fausses Indications de Provenance* (Paris, 1926), pp. 65 ff.

2. See numerous attempts in France to satisfy the conflicting interests in this respect concerning various regional appellations of origin, in Pichot, *De la Concurrence Déloyale*, pp. 182 ff.; Richard, *De la Protection des Appellations d'Origine*, pp. 75 ff.; and *Propriété Industrielle* (1920), pp. 40, 43 ff.

though produced originally in a certain locality, owe their distinction and reputation to a special mode of manufacture only, and goods which owe their specific qualities to advantages of the soil and climate and cannot be produced in any other place with the same qualities.[1] Indications of origin in respect to the former products only may lose their distinctiveness by reason of a continued and unhampered use by persons not entitled thereto, and become generic or descriptive terms.

Admitting that an agreement may be reached that a term is an indication of origin and not a descriptive term, — for instance, the name "Porto," — the question arises whether that term may be used as descriptive of the kind or qualities of similar products, accompanied by a true designation of the place of manufacture; for instance, whether a wine may be designated as Spanish Porto or a cheese as German or Hamburg Camembert. The question is one of the basis of legal protection. If deceit of the public is the basis for interference by the law in repressing false indications of origin, whenever such deceit is avoided there would be no protection. If the interest of the producers of the place in question in the advantageous business relations connected with the name of the place of origin is the basis of protection, then the use of this name in any way should be prohibited.

There are also cases of incomplete manufacture in the true place of origin of certain goods which are completed in another place; for instance, grape juice from Champagne vineyards is taken, in a raw state, to Germany, and there subjected to the treatment which gives it the specific qualities under which it is known in the market. In these cases, may such goods bear the original indication of origin? It is claimed that this so-called "Champagne" wine is not of the same quality as that made in Champagne, because, together with the advantage of the soil, there is also that of climate, which goes into the making of the real Champagne wine. Again this raises the same question as before. What is the basis of protection? If it be admitted that the producers of the place of origin have an interest in the advantageous situation created by the reputation of the name of that place, and that this interest should be recognized and protected by the law, like any other interest, then any injury to this interest

1. See "La Question des Fausses Indications de Provenance," in *Propriété Industrielle* (1920), pp. 18, 21.

should be prohibited, regardless of whether the public is deceived or not by the acts involving such injury.[1]

All these are questions on which an agreement is often difficult, especially in the international legal order. The conflicting interests are many and complicated. There exist inveterate habits in the trade of many countries of using foreign indications of origin to satisfy certain preferences, or even biases, of the public for foreign goods. This use has gone on for a long time, and it would cause great losses to the users if they had to forego it in the future. As a result of such use, the producers of the place of origin where the goods in question are really produced suffer damage by the competition brought about by the cheaper goods of the infringers. The public is often deceived by such false indications of origin; but sometimes, although aware of the falsity, it buys the goods because they contain some of the qualities of the goods manufactured in the real place of origin and at the same time are cheaper.

International agreement and protection in this matter is dependent, in the first place, on the progress of honesty in international trade, and, in the second place, on a balancing of the conflicting interests of the various countries. It would seem that, in recent years, the view is taken in different countries that the interests of their national industry and trade will, in the long run, be best served if the use of false indications of origin is severely repressed. Not only is the public thus protected against deception, but national industry and trade are encouraged to perfect and advertise national products instead of imitating and advertising foreign goods.

§ **462. Provisions of the Convention.** In respect to the protection of indications of origin, the Convention of 1883 contains two provisions. The first is that of article 2 providing that the persons entitled to the benefits of the Convention shall enjoy in each country of the Union the same protection, and the same rights and remedies, as nationals of such country. The precise scope of this assimilation to nationals is considered in another place.[2] It is seen, however, in respect to the other rights of industrial property that the Conven-

1. It is generally admitted in Europe that the law protects the interest of producers in the use of the name of a locality, but this interest is differently classified. Lacour, *Des Fausses Indications de Provenance* (Paris, 1904), p. 23, calls it a property right; Marcel Plaisant et Fernand-Jacq, *Traité des Noms et Appellations d'Origine* (Paris, 1921), p. 54, call it a title of participation, a share in a public company; Di Franco, *Le indicazioni di provenienza dei prodotti* (Naples, 1907), p. 24, sees in it a personal right.

2. See *supra*, §§ 126–128.

tion does not relegate the protection entirely to the provisions of municipal law. Instead, it contains certain specific provisions, which may derogate from municipal law and form in themselves the basis of international protection. Such provisions in respect to indications of origin are contained in article 10.

As we have already seen,[1] the unlawful use of indications of origin was dealt with in the same way as that of trade marks and trade names in one article of the draft Convention submitted to the Paris Conference of 1880, and that a separate article on indications of origin was proposed at the Conference. There was even expressed by many delegates a distinct dislike for a provision interfering with the habits and practices of the trade to use false indications of origin, although it was admitted that such practice was fraudulent and reprehensible.[2] As a result of this opposition, the absolute prohibition of false indications of origin contained in the original provision of the draft was changed to a relative prohibition, covering the case where the false indication of origin is joined to a trade name of a fictitious character or one used with fraudulent intent.[3] This amounts to a protection of the trade name rather than of the indications of origin, since the latter are not protected by themselves alone. The sanctions of this prohibition are the same as those prescribed by article 9 for goods bearing unlawfully a trade mark or trade name.

Article 10, as originally adopted, has not been amended, except on two minor points concerning the definition of persons who may claim the benefit of its provisions. But article 9, to which article 10 refers for its sanctions, was substantially amended at the Conferences of Brussels and Washington.[4] Following a few amendments at The Hague concerning the form, article 10 provides now as follows:

Les dispositions de l'article précédent seront applicables à tout produit portant, faussement, comme indication de provenance, le nom d'une localité ou d'un pays déterminé, lorsque cette indication sera jointe à un nom commercial fictif ou emprunté dans une intention frauduleuse.

Sera en tout cas reconnu comme partie intéressée, que ce soit une per-

1. See *supra*, § 403.
2. *Conférence de Paris* (1880), pp. 84, 85, 88.
3. *Ibid.* (1880), pp. 100–102, 103–104, 144. The Swiss and Italian delegations opposed the article but consented to its adoption on the insistence of the delegation from Portugal. The latter, as an agricultural country, was especially interested in the protection of certain well-known Portuguese indications of origin.
4. See *supra*, §§ 405, 406.

sonne physique ou morale, tout producteur, fabriquant ou commerçant engagé dans la production, la fabrication ou le commerce de ce produit et établi soit dans la localité faussement indiquée comme lieu de provenance, soit dans la région où cette localité est située, soit dans le pays faussement indiqué.

§ **463. Scope of provision of article 10.** Under the terms of article 10, the provisions of article 9 are applicable to all goods which falsely bear, as an indication of origin, the name of a specified locality or country, when such indication is joined to a trade name of a fictitious character or used with fraudulent intent. Thus, not all frauds in respect to indications of origin, but only certain ones are dealt with in article 10. This restrictive provision is due to the opposition of certain countries to the prohibition of the habit of using in trade certain false indications of origin. It has caused, as will be seen presently, the creation of the restricted Union formed by the Madrid Arrangement for the repression of false indications of origin, which affords a broader protection to this branch of industrial property. Under article 10 of the Convention, false indications of origin are repressed only in certain serious cases of fraud: namely, when the false indication is joined with a fictitious trade name, or when, although a real trade name is indicated, it is used with fraudulent intent.

The seriousness of the fraud in the first case is very clear. If it may be urged, indeed, that the use of certain false indications of origin, reprehensible though it may be, it is not fraudulent, but is a constant custom of the trade, as a result of which the indication in question became a descriptive or generic term, this can no longer be claimed when, in addition to such indication, a fictitious name is used. In such case the intent to deceive the public as to the origin of the goods is apparent. For instance, article 10 does not apply against a manufacturer or merchant who labels his wine with the indication, "Champagne." But if he joins to that indication the name "Martin à Reims," and this name is a fictitious one, his fraud is palpable. He no longer uses the term "Champagne" as a descriptive term of the special kind of wine, but intends to convey to the public the impression that the wine is manufactured in Champagne.[1]

1. In Martell & Cie *v.* Bessani & Forti and A. Manzoni, Court of Appeals of Milan (Italy), it was wrongly held that the defendants were not liable for having applied on bottles of brandy the fictitious French name "Jean Nivoguber," and the appellation "Cognac," on the ground that the term "Cognac," like the term "Champagne," is

The trade name used in conjunction with the indication of origin (for instance, the above trade name "Martin à Reims") may be real. The manufacturer or merchant using falsely the indication of origin may join to it the real trade name of a manufacturer of the place or region of origin falsely indicated. If such use of the trade name is unauthorized, the owner of the trade name is protected by the provisions of the Convention concerning trade names and especially by those of article 9; that is, the goods may be seized on importation or within the country, or their importation may be prohibited. If, however, the use of the trade name is authorized by its owner, it should be considered whether such use is made with fraudulent intent. When such is the case, article 10 will be applicable. Such fraudulent intent exists when the use of the name is made in order to deceive the public.[1] This is the motive in most cases.[2]

The indications of origin dealt with in article 10 may be names of specified localities, districts, regions, or any other subdivisions of a country, as well as names of countries. An amendment to this effect was made at the Conference of The Hague, by the addition of the words "ou d'un pays" after the word "localité." [3]

It is sufficient for the purposes of application of article 10 that the goods bear such an indication of origin (used with a trade name of fictitious character or used with fraudulent intent) falsely ("fausse-

---

considered the name of a product in Italy. See decision and criticism in *Propriété Industrielle* (1901), p. 189.

1. In France, the rule adopted in this respect establishes a distinction as to whether or not the false indication of origin throws a discredit on French industry. See Pillet, *Régime International*, pp. 110–111. This result is reached by application of the municipal law. It would seem that under the Convention such distinction is not possible, and that the interest of the buying public should always be taken in consideration. Cf. *ibid.*, p. 421.

2. The Belgian courts, however, found that no fraud was committed by a Belgian company which, having no interest in Vichy (France), was called "Compagnie Française du Bassin de Vichy" and sold its products without indicating their true origin, which was Saint-Yorre and not Vichy. The court found that the term "Bassin de Vichy" applied to Saint-Yorre, and therefore the name was not fictitious. See Compagnie Fermière de Vichy et Marinex *c.* Société Française du Bassin de Vichy, Cassation, May 25, 1905 (*Pasicrisie*, 1905, I, 242).

At the Rome Conference of Revision, the Belgian delegation proposed an amendment of article 10 to the effect that it should not be considered fraudulent intent when the owner of the trade name has authorized the application of his name. They cited the case of a British manufacturer who orders guns in Liège bearing his name. The proposal was opposed on the ground that the public should be protected against practices which deceive as to the origin of the goods. See *Conférence de Rome*, pp. 121–123.

3. See proposition of the Bureau and adoption, *Actes de la Conférence de La Haye* pp. 250, 525.

ment"); that is, that they are produced or manufactured in another locality, region, or country than that indicated.

Article 10 applies in any country of the Union, whenever goods are found bearing a false indication of origin joined with a trade name of fictitious character or used with fraudulent purpose. This leaves no doubt when article 10 is considered together with the first paragraph of article 9.[1]

§ **464. Sanctions of stipulation of article 10.** The sanctions stipulated in article 9 are applicable against the frauds referred to in article 10. They are used against the goods bearing the false indication of origin (joined to a trade name of a fictitious character or used with fraudulent intent), and consist in the seizure on importation of the goods, prohibition of importation, or seizure within the country. How far the application of these sanctions is obligatory on the contracting countries, and what the conditions are of their application, are considered above in connection with the interpretation of article 9.[2] It may be noted here that, as a result of the amendment of article 9 at the Washington Conference, and the substitution of the word "sera" for the word "pourra," the application of these sanctions is obligatory on the contracting countries in case their municipal law provides for such sanctions. Moreover they should be applied in the order of preference stipulated in article 9; thus, the goods should be seized on importation; in case this is not possible under the law of a contracting country, then the importation of the goods should be prohibited; in case this too is impossible, the goods should be seized within the country. If none of these sanctions is provided for by law, pending modification of the law, any other measures available to nationals against the qualified fraud provided for in article 10 should be applied.

The provisions of article 9 concerning the sanctions were taken from the Madrid Arrangement of 1891 for the repression of false indications of origin, so that practically no difference in this respect exists between the regime of the general Convention and that of the Arrangement.

From an investigation made by the International Bureau of Berne in 1925, into the legislation of the various countries of the Union from the point of view of the measures provided for by arti-

1. See *Propriété Industrielle* (1920), pp. 18, 19–20.
2. See *supra*, §§ 407 ff.

cles 9 and 10 against false indications of origin,[1] it appears that the administrative seizure on importation of goods bearing a false indication of origin is available in only eleven of the contracting countries.[2] In six countries only judicial seizure within the country is possible; [3] in Austria, Brazil, and Finland both seizure on importation and seizure within the country are available; in Portugal, Turkey, and the United States, the importation of goods bearing a false indication of origin is prohibited; lastly, in eight countries other remedies are available, usually fine and imprisonment.[4]

§ **465. Requests for seizure or prohibition.** Article 9 provides that the sanctions referred to therein may be applied at the request either of the public prosecutor, or of any other competent authority, or of any interested party, in conformity with the domestic law of each country. This provision applies also in the cases provided for in article 10. But while article 9 does not define the "interested party," article 10 contains explicit provisions to this effect in its second paragraph. Indeed, no difficulty arises in this respect in the cases provided for in article 9. Since these cases refer to the infringement of a trade mark or trade name, the interested party is clearly the owner of the infringed trade mark or trade name. But indications of origin cannot be owned by a single person. The right to their use is a class or community right. It is important, therefore, to define the interested parties who may claim the application of the sanctions provided for in article 10.

The conditions that should exist in order that a person may be deemed a party interested are two: (1) he should be a producer, manufacturer, or merchant engaged in the production or manufacture of, or trade in, goods similar to those which are alleged to bear a false indication of origin; (2) he should be established in the geographical entity indicated as place of origin of the goods. The first condition excludes all persons who are inhabitants of the place of origin

1. See *Propriété Industrielle* (1925), pp. 44, 46 ff., and *Actes de la Conférence de La Haye*, pp. 150 ff.

2. These countries are Austria, Brazil, Bulgaria, Finland, France, Great Britain, Germany, the Serb-Croat-Slovene State, Spain, Sweden, and Tunis. The same remedy is available in Haiti.

3. Greece, Hungary, Morocco, Switzerland, and Syria and Lebanon. To these must now be added Belgium, since its recent Law of April 18, 1927 (*Propriété Industrielle*, 1927, p. 209). Such seizure is available in Bolivia and Haiti also.

4. Cuba, Czechoslovakia, Denmark, Italy, Luxembourg, Mexico, Norway, and the Netherlands. Similar remedies are available in Colombia, Guatemala, Honduras, Siam, and Venezuela.

in question, but are not producers, manufacturers, or traders in that place, or persons who are engaged in the production of other kinds of goods, and not of those the seizure of which is sought. The second condition excludes all persons who are not closely connected with the place of origin.[1]

If a person does not satisfy these two conditions, he is not a party interested under the terms of article 10;[2] in such case only the public prosecutor or other competent authority, in conformity with the domestic law of each country, may request the seizure or prohibition on importation. Of course, the municipal law of any country may render these remedies available to other persons beside those provided for in article 10 of the Convention.[3] But persons fulfilling the above conditions must always be considered as interested parties and permitted to request the seizure or prohibition.[4]

The interested party, under the terms of article 10, may be established either in the locality falsely indicated or in the region where such locality is situated. Thus, if the false indication of origin is "Champagne, Martin à Reims," the producers, manufacturers or traders of Reims, as well as of any other locality in the region of Champagne, are parties interested. On the other hand, when the false indication of origin is the name of a country, any producer, manufacturer, or trader of that country is to be deemed a party interested.

The party interested may be either an individual or a juristic person ("que ce soit une personne physique ou morale"). This provi-

1. The word "établi" was substituted at the Paris Conference of 1880 for the original word "domicilié" (*Conférence de Paris*, 1880, pp. 144–145). It would seem therefore that "établi" means only that the person must have a commercial, industrial, or agricultural establishment in the place of origin in question; he need not be a resident thereof.

2. The false indication of origin being the word "London," it was held by the Court of Liège (Belgium), March 28, 1906, that the plaintiff, an American, could not sue, not being established in the locality falsely indicated (*Propriété Industrielle*, 1908, p. 101).

3. In Férmin Julien *c.* Société des Etablissements F. Delory, Supreme Tribunal of Lisbon, Aug. 17, 1901, a Portuguese canner of fish was allowed to sue the defendant, a person concerned with the same class of goods of the same city, for falsely indicating his sardines as from "Lorient, France." The defendant claimed that the plaintiff was not a person established in Lorient, France, and therefore was not a party interested. The court held that to allow the plaintiff's suit was not against the spirit of article 10 of the Convention, and that under Portuguese law the use of false indications of origin is prohibited generally (*Propriété Industrielle*, 1903, p. 47).

4. At the Conference of The Hague this was made clear by the addition of the words "sera en tout cas reconnu." See proposal of the International Bureau, and its adoption, in *Actes de la Conférence de La Haye*, pp. 251–252, 525.

sion was added at the Conference of The Hague, on the proposal of the International Bureau,[1] which proposed also that it be explicitly declared that syndicates and professional associations created for the common protection of their members' rights should be deemed parties interested, although they possess no industrial, commercial, or agricultural establishments, as article 10 requires. This proposal was not adopted. On the contrary, in respect to the same words ("personne physique ou morale") in the third paragraph of article 9, it was expressly declared that they do not relate to the question whether or not syndicates and associations may intervene, in addition to the proprietors of trade marks.[2] The question of the intervention of such bodies in the cases provided for in articles 9, 10, and 10*b* is governed by the stipulation of article 10*c*.[3]

§ **466. The Madrid Arrangement for repression of false indications of origin.** At the Rome Conference of 1886, an attempt was made to amend article 10 in order to afford more adequate protection to indications of origin. Proposals to this effect by France and Great Britain, combined by the Conference in a single new article 10, provided, in particular, that all false indications of origin were to be repressed, and that the courts of each contracting country were to decide what were the designations which ceased to be indications of origin and became generic or descriptive terms.[4] The latter provision was so general that it seemed destined to take away all the benefit of the former. The acts adopted at this Conference were submitted to the governments of the contracting countries, but were never ratified.

At the Madrid Conference of 1890, the text of the French and English proposal was submitted by the International Bureau and the Spanish administration, in the form of a draft arrangement to be entered into by member countries of the general Union which were not satisfied with the stipulation of article 10 of the Convention and were desirous of affording broader protection to indications of origin.[5] The draft called forth objections from two different sides in respect to the reservation excluding from the application of the Arrangement designations which have ceased to be indications of origin and

1. *Actes de la Conférence de La Haye*, p. 251.
2. *Ibid.*, p. 545.
3. See *supra*, § 410.
4. *Conférence de Rome*, pp. 12–13, 111, 116 ff.
5. *Conférence de Madrid*, pp. 11 ff.

have become generic or descriptive terms. The delegations of certain countries (Belgium, the United States, Italy, and the Netherlands) proposed to extend this reservation to cases where the false indication of origin is not used with fraudulent intent, or where no damage is caused (American proposal). This was supported on divers grounds: that the intermediary commerce should not be hampered, that inveterate customs of trade should not be interfered with, and that the Convention of 1883 aims at protecting manufacturers and producers, not the buying public.[1]

The delegations of other countries, on the contrary, were of opinion that the reservation was too broad and went beyond the cases where it may be said that a designation has ceased to be an indication of origin and is now a descriptive term. The Portuguese delegation proposed that all indications of origin of agricultural products should be excluded from such reservation, on the ground that these indications can never become descriptive terms of products.[2] The reputation attached to such indications of origin is due to special conditions of soil and climate not to be found elsewhere, under which certain agricultural products are grown or manufactured. When, therefore, such an indication of origin is used for products grown or manufactured in another place, there is always an injury to the producers, manufacturers, or traders of the place of origin indicated, and a fraud upon the public to which these imitation products are sold. The French delegation thought that the Portuguese proposal might be restricted to indications of origin of products of the vine, in respect to which frauds were more common.[3] The Portuguese delegation consented thereto.

An amendment proposed by the delegation of Sweden and Norway, purporting to reconcile to some degree the two opposing points of view, was adopted by the Conference, and forms article 3 of the Arrangement.[4] It permits the application of the name or address of the seller on goods of foreign origin, on condition that the country or place of manufacture or production be clearly indicated.

With these amendments, and the addition of substitute sanctions in case the seizure on importation should not be available, the draft Arrangement was adopted by ten countries, five of which ratified it

1. *Conférence de Madrid*, pp. 72 ff., 83, 84, 85.
2. *Ibid.*, pp. 79, 87.
3. *Ibid.*, p. 88.
4. *Ibid.*. 76–77, 83.

before the date set for its going into effect, namely, July 15, 1892; these countries were France, Great Britain, Spain, Switzerland, and Tunis. The ratifications of two other countries were deposited later: by Portugal in 1893, and by Brazil in 1896. Cuba acceded to the Arrangement in 1905, New Zealand in 1913, and Morocco (French zone) in 1917. The membership of the restricted Union constituted by this Arrangement was increased after the war by the accession of Czechoslovakia (1921), Danzig (1923), Syria and Lebanon (1924), Germany (1925), and the Irish Free State (1925). Thus, the membership of the restricted Union for the repression of false indications of origin comprises to-day (June, 1929) fourteen countries, with a total population of 275,000,000.[1]

No amendment of the Arrangement was adopted at the Brussels Conference; and only a minor modification of article 2 was made at the Washington Conference. At the Conference of Revision of 1925, at the Hague, two secondary amendments concerning the sanctions were adopted; they will be referred to presently in the study of the provisions of the Arrangement.[2]

§ **467. Scope of the Arrangement.** The purpose of the adoption of the Arrangement for the repression of false indications of origin was to afford effective means to combat the frauds involved in the use of indications of origin by persons not possessing the right to such use, and to do away with the qualification contained in article 10 of the general Convention. The countries which adopted this Arrangement intended to prevent and prohibit the simple fraud of the use of false indications of origin, and not only the qualified fraud of article 10 of the Convention. Thus the first article of the Arrangement provides in its first paragraph:

Tout produit portant une fausse indication de provenance dans laquelle un des pays contractants, ou un lieu situé dans l'un d'entre eux, serait directement ou indirectement indiqué, comme pays ou comme lieu d'origine, sera saisi à l'importation dans chacun desdits pays.

Any false indication of origin in which one of the contracting countries, or a place situated therein, shall be indicated as being the country or place of origin gives rise to the application of the sanctions provided for in the Arrangement. In order that the sanctions of the

1. See *Propriété Industrielle* (1928), p. 2.

2. The text of the revised Madrid Arrangement for the repression of false indications of origin is found in *Actes de la Conférence de La Haye*, p. 615, and in *Propriété Industrielle* (1925), p. 227.

Arrangement may be applied, it is sufficient that the two countries, that in which protection is claimed, and that indicated as country of origin or in which the indicated place of origin is situated, are parties to the Arrangement. It is immaterial that the false indication of origin was applied on the goods in a country which is not a party to the Arrangement, or that the defendant is not a national of a member country. It is not necessary that the indication of origin shall contain explicitly the name of a contracting country or of a place situated therein. An indirect indication of either is sufficient for the purposes of the Arrangement. When an indication of origin is "indirect," is a question of fact. It would seem that under this provision the attempt to use indications of origin under such expressions as "artificial" or "imitation" accompanying the name of a locality or country should be prohibited;[1] also the use of expressions likely to cause goods to be confused with the goods actually derived from such locality or country of origin.[2] Such expressions are, "system," "type," "kind of," and the like;[3] or the true place of manufacture joined to a well-known indication of origin.[4]

1. Such a case exists also when the map of a country with its name on it is applied. See, for instance, the Swiss case Kaiser *c.* Union libre des fabricants suisses de chocolat, Fed. Trib., Oct. 17, 1906 (*Journal des Tribunaux*, 1907, p. 528). The German Patentamt, Sept. 28, 1911 (*Andersons Liebfrauberg*), refused a mark containing an indication of origin, although the words, "Quality mark does not constitute a designation of vineyard," were added. See *Blatt für Patent-, Muster- und Zeichenwesen* (1912), p. 18.

2. Jaton, in *La Répression des Fausses Indications de Provenance* (Paris, 1926), p. 13, writes that an indirect false indication of origin exists when the inscriptions applied on products, the get-up of the merchandise, the use of a foreign language, the price-lists, customs, declarations, etc., tend to induce error as to the place of manufacture or production.

3. Decision of the Austrian Ministry of Public Works, Feb. 28, 1912, cancelling a mark containing the words "System Pilsen" for beer not manufactured in Pilsen (*Propriété Industrielle*, 1912, p. 174). Also decision of the Landsgericht of Vienna, Dec. 29, 1913, repressing the act of affixing a label on bottles of beer, bearing the inscription "Tafelbier wie Pilsner" (*Propriété Industrielle*, 1914, p. 60). See also Belgian Law of April 18, 1927, article 2 (*Propriété Industrielle*, 1927, p. 209).

4. Decision of the Administrative Tribunal of Austria, cancelling the mark "Hansdorfer Pilsner" for beer (*Propriété Industrielle*, 1913, p. 174). The Tribunal said that the reputation of the Pilsen beer is due to the special quality of the water and to the care and technical experience of the manufacturers, and that it cannot be produced in such good quality except in Pilsen.

In Germany the opinion of the Reichsgericht is opposed to that of the Patentamt, which is in agreement with this Austrian decision and that in preceding footnote. See decisions of the Reichsgericht, March 19 and April 19, 1912 (*Propriété Industrielle*, 1912, p. 99 and, 1914, p. 44; also 79 *Entsch. Reichsg.*, *Zivils.*, 250), and decision of the Patentamt, Jan. 13, 1914 (*Blatt für Patent-, Muster- und Zeichenwesen*, 1914, p. 14). The decisions of the Reichsgericht are criticized by German commentators; see *Propriété Industrielle* (1912), p. 99; (1914), p. 44.

The use of false indications of origin in other respects than on goods is not within the purview of the above provision. Thus such use in advertisements, price-lists, letters, and the like, would seem to give no room for the application of the sanctions provided for in the Arrangement, unless, of course, the provisions of the municipal law afford a broader protection.

§ 468. Foreign indications of origin accompanied by name of seller. The term used in the Arrangement, "indications de provenance," is broader than the special class of industrial property rights which is known in France as "appellations d'origine." Under the Arrangement, not only the class or community rights in an indication of origin ("appellation d'origine") are protected, but also any passing-off of goods derived from one place or country for those from another is prohibited. In the latter case, it may be possible to avoid any injury to the producers or manufacturers of that place or country, and any fraud on the public, by indicating clearly both the place or country of manufacture and that of sale. A provision to this effect, adopted on the proposal of the delegations of Sweden and Norway and France, constitutes article 3 of the Arrangement:

> Les présentes dispositions ne font pas obstacle à ce que le vendeur indique son nom ou son adresse sur les produits provenant d'un pays différent de celui de la vente; mais, dans ce cas, l'adresse ou le nom doit être accompagné de l'indication précise, et en caractères apparents, du pays ou du lieu de fabrication ou de production, ou d'une autre indication suffisante pour éviter toute erreur sur l'origine véritable des marchandises.

Thus the name or address of the seller may appear on goods of foreign origin, but it must be accompanied by a precise indication of the country or place where the goods were manufactured or produced. This indication must be clearly apparent on the goods. The last phrase of the provision was added at the Conference of The Hague to satisfy the British delegation, which proposed that the words "du pays ou du lieu de fabrication ou de production" be replaced by the words "la fabrication étrangère des produits." This delegation maintained that, under the text of the Arrangement, intermediate traders are compelled to disclose the precise source of their merchandise, which may be very inconvenient for the trade of certain countries.[1] The provision adopted permits the application of the indication "Made abroad" instead of "Made in France," or

1. See *Actes de la Conférence de La Haye*, pp. 364, 480.

"Made in Paris," on goods manufactured in France or in Paris and imported into Great Britain.

§ 469. Appellations of generic character. The broad provision of the first article of the Arrangement for the protection of all indications of origin is substantially restricted by the reservation contained in article 4, reading as follows:

> Les tribunaux de chaque pays auront à décider quelles sont les appellations qui, à raison de leur caractère générique, échappent aux dispositions du présent Arrangement, les appellations régionales de provenance des produits vinicoles n'étant cependant pas comprises dans la réserve spécifiée par cet article.

The part of this provision concerning indications of origin of products of the vine is considered in the next section. It embodies an exception to the rule of article 4, that the tribunals of each country shall decide what appellations do not give rise to the application of the sanctions of the Arrangement on account of their generic character. The provision refers to "appellations," not to "indications de provenance," and from this fact, as well as from the history of its adoption,[1] it is clear that it does not apply to all indications of origin, but to those which originally were used for the designation of goods produced or manufactured in a definite locality or region, and which have come to be more or less identified with the products. Thus the provision may apply to the appellation "Eau de Cologne," or "Camembert," or "Pilsner Beer," or "Lancashire" (iron), but not to the designations "English goods," or "German dyes," and the like, which can never be appellations of origin in the proper sense, but which only indicate, generally, the origin of goods.

The question whether an appellation is of a generic character and may, therefore, be freely used by any person, is decided by the tribunals of the country where the legality of the use of the appellation comes in question. At the conferences of Washington and The Hague it was proposed that the question of the distinctiveness or generic character of an appellation should be decided by the tribunals of the country of origin of the goods, and upon their failure, by an international tribunal. This proposal did not meet with success.[2]

1. The draft Arrangement submitted at the Madrid Conference contained instead of the word "appellations," the words "dénominations de produits." *Conférence de Madrid*, p. 14.

2. See *Actes de la Conférence de Washington*, pp. 99–100, 218, and *Actes de la Con-*

In regard to certain appellations, it is generally admitted to-day that they are generic terms, or terms descriptive of the nature or kind of the product. Such are the designations "Eau de Cologne," "Marseilles Soap," "Suede Gloves," etc. But there are many appellations as to which no agreement exists. Thus, in an extensive survey made by the German Patentamt in 1914, concerning the name "Pilsner Beer," it was found that in ten countries (Australia, Canada, Chile, Denmark, Ecuador, Japan, Norway, Sweden, Spain, and South Africa) it was considered as a designation of quality or kind of beer, while in fourteen others (Argentina, Austria, Belgium, China, Egypt, France, Great Britain, India, Italy, Mexico, the Netherlands, Switzerland, Turkey, and the United States) it was considered exclusively or mainly as an indication of origin.[1] The designation "Vichy" is protected as an indication of origin in France,[2] Spain,[3] and Rumania,[4] but not in Italy[5] and the United States;[6] while in Belgium the decisions are conflicting.[7] It is curious to note that the name "Camembert" for cheese was held to be a generic or descriptive term in France,[8] where the community of Camembert is situated, and an indication of origin in Germany.[9]

---

férence de La Haye, pp. 364, 481. But provisions to this effect were inserted in the treaties of peace and bipartite conventions entered into after the war. See *infra*, §§ 474, 475. See also Belgian Law of April 18, 1927 (*Propriété Industrielle*, 1927, p. 209).

1. See decision of the Patentamt, Jan. 13, 1914, in *Blatt für Patent-, Muster- und Zeichenwesen* (1914), pp. 14, 17 ff.

2. Pouillet, *Traité des Marques*, pp. 630 ff.

3. Compagnie Fermière de Vichy *c.* Les Établissements du Puig de las Animas et de Caldas de Malavella, Supreme Court of Spain, Dec. 14, 1907 (*Propriété Industrielle*, 1908, p. 71).

4. See *Propriété Industrielle* (1905), p. 240.

5. Court of Errors of Turin, July 14, 1900 (*Propriété Industrielle*, 1901, p. 191).

6. The French Republic *v.* Saratoga Vichy Spring Co. (1903), 191 U. S. 427.

7. Compagnie Fermière de l'Établissement Thermal de Vichy et Marinex *c.* Société Française du Bassin de Vichy, Cassation, May 25, 1905 (*Pasicrisie*, 1905, I, 242), holding negatively. The Commercial Tribunal of Brussels, June 23, 1908, intimates that the use of the word "Vichy" is a false indication of origin (*La Jurisprudence Commerciale de Bruxelles*, 1908, p. 407).

8. Syndicat du véritable Camembert de Normandie *c.* Laiterie de Ligueil, Court of Appeals of Orléans, Jan. 20, 1926 (*Gazette du Palais*, 1926, I, 595). The court said that this cheese does not depend on any organic element of the place where it was first made. It is completely defined by its composition of milk fats. It falls within the public domain, the original owner having neglected to protect it. It was proved that several cheese factories outside Normandy had applied to their products the name "Camembert" for fifty years.

9. Decision of the Patentamt, Jan. 21, 1919 (*Blatt für Patent-, Muster- und Zeichenwesen*, 1919, p. 11). In this case the mark "Hoefelmayrs Silber Camembert" was proposed for registration for German cheese. The Patentamt admitted that many foreign indications of origin have been applied to German cheese, and have become designations

The name "Roquefort" for cheese is protected as an indication of origin in France[1] and so is the word "München" (Munich) for beer,[2] which is also protected as an indication of origin in Germany,[3] but not in Belgium.[4]

§ 470. Exception concerning appellations of origin of products of the vine. To the rule of article 4 of the Arrangement that the tribunals of each country may decide when an appellation, on account of its generic character, does not fall within the provisions of the Arrangement, an exception is made in the same article in regard to regional appellations concerning the origin of products of the vine. Such appellations cannot be declared by the tribunals of any of the contracting countries to be of a generic character. Consequently, regional appellations of products of the vine can never fall within the public domain and become descriptive terms. Whenever such an indication of origin is used falsely, that is, for products of the vine which are not produced or manufactured in the region indicated, the sanctions referred to in the Arrangement are necessarily applicable.

The exception in question concerns regional appellations only. Therefore indications of origin of a specified locality or of an entire country are not within the exception. Of these, indications of a country, such as Greek wines or French wines, are not "appellations" in the proper sense, as we have seen in the previous paragraph, and therefore can never become generic or descriptive terms. But indications of a locality concerning products of the vine, such as "Sauterne Wine," which serves to designate the wine of a specified

---

of the nature of the product. But by a change in public sentiment, these terms are again considered as indications of origin. The Patentamt urges that, as a result of such practices, German commerce is considered disloyal abroad, and that severity in the prohibition of foreign indications of origin will have the advantage of compelling German manufacturers to improve the quality of their products and thus enable them to compete more successfully in foreign markets.

1. Pouillet, *Traité des Marques*, pp. 618–619; also Syndicat de Roquefort *v.* Calmettes, Tribunal of St. Afrique, Jan. 29, 1924 (*Propriété Industrielle*, 1927, p. 17).

2. Pschorr *c.* Winckler et fils, Court of Lyon, Dec. 9, 1904, affirmed by the Cassation, May 3, 1908 (*Propriété Industrielle*, 1906, p. 147; 1909, p. 77).

3. Decision of the Reichsgericht, Feb. 2, 1912, repressing the appellation "Urbock Münchner" for beer not manufactured in Munich, holding the name "Munich beer" to be an indication of origin, and not a designation of the nature of the product (*Propriété Industrielle*, 1912, p. 99).

4. Verein Münchner Brauereien *c.* Société Brasserie Koekelberg et Dillenberg, Court of Appeals of Brussels, July 7, 1905 (*La Jurisprudence Commerciale de Bruxelles*, 1905, p. 417).

locality (the community of Sauternes),[1] are within the rule of article 4; that is to say, the tribunals may decide in respect to them that they are of a generic character.

Regional appellations of products of the vine must be protected as provided by article 1 of the Arrangement. Thus the sanctions of the Arrangement must be applied if such appellations are falsely used, directly or indirectly. What is said above [2] in regard to indirect indications of a country or place as being the country or place of origin also applies here. Particularly, no accessory or additional indication can make the use of a regional appellation concerning products of the vine permissible.[3] The regional appellations "Champagne," [4] "Cognac," [5] "Madeira," [6] "Porto," are outstanding illustrations of indications of origin coming under the exception of article 4.[7]

§ **471. Extension of exception to other products.** The provision under consideration excluding the judgment of the Courts on the

1. So held in Gassiés *c.* Société Civile d'Yquem et autres, Cassation, May 17, 1926 (*Gazette du Palais*, 1926, III, 285).

2. See *supra*, p. 671.

3. So held in respect to the name "Cognac" in Denis, Henry, Mounie et Cie et Syndicat de Cognac *c.* Gutierrez Hermanos, Civil Tribunal of Cognac, June, 1903 (*Propriété Industrielle*, 1904, p. 123), and by the Supreme Adm. Tribunal of Austria, March 17, 1927 (*Propriété Industrielle*, 1928, p. 119). See also the Order of the Swiss Federal Council of March 27, 1928, prohibiting direct and indirect unauthorized use of the French indications of origin "Cognac" and "Armagnac," even with the addition of the words "coupage," "façon," "type," or "genre." (*Recueil des Lois*, 1928, p. 49.) See also Diez Hermanos *v.* Blandy frères, Cassation (France), July 22, 1901 (*Dalloz* 1902, I, 67), involving the appellation "Madeira of Spain." But it was held in Great Britain, in Port Wine Shippers Ass'n *v.* Liptons, Ltd. (*Propriété Industrielle*, 1908, p. 104), that on bottles of Spanish wine bearing a label indicating the Spanish origin of the wine and also the word "Port," the label should indicate "Spanish product" and "Spanish Porto." The case applies section 18 of the Merchandise Act of 1887, but falls short of complying with the Arrangement.

The French Cassation, July 23, 1927, in De Villamil *c.* Fouché et Chambre de Commerce Port., imposed criminal punishment on the defendant for applying the appellations "Porto" and "Madera" to wines made in France by mixing real "Porto" and "Madera" with French liquor (*Gazette du Palais*, 1927, II, 823).

4. In Syndicat des vins de Champagne *c.* Therra et Cie, Court of Appeals of Besançon, March 9, 1910, it was held that a mark containing the words "des grands vins champenisés" did not infringe on the indication of origin "Champagne," as the word "champeniser" means a process of manufacture and is not a place of origin, and is a word within the public domain (*Gazette du Palais*, 1910, I, 579).

5. See note 3.

6. Protected in France in Diez Hermanos *v.* Blandy frères, Cassation, July 22, 1901 (*Dalloz*, 1902, I, 67). See also note 3.

7. The designation "vermouth of Turin" was not protected in Martine Salla, Fratelli Gancia et autres *c.* Goudrand frères, Tribunal of Marseilles, August 13, 1903, Italy not being a party to the Madrid Arrangement, and the latter being inapplicable in the case (*Propriété Industrielle*, 1905, p. 28).

distinctive character of regional appellations concerning the products of the vine, beneficial though it may be to the countries in which are situated regions producing or manufacturing wine products of great reputation, prevents other countries not in the same position from acceding to the Arrangement. The latter consider it unjust that this exceptional provision should secure the complete protection of wine denominations, while their own well-known appellations of products of other kinds should remain under the rule of article 4 and risk being deemed generic terms.[1] Already at various congresses of the International Association [2] and at the Washington Conference of Revision,[3] it had been proposed that the appellations of origin of all products which derive their natural qualities from the soil and climate be excepted from the rule of article 4. It was also proposed that each of the contracting countries should give notice to the others, through the agency of the International Bureau, of the appellations which it regards as such. On the objection of the Swiss delegation, this proposal was not adopted. Two of the countries, the accession of which to the Arrangement through this amendment was sought, responded differently. Austria would have liked it, because its own indications of origin, "Pilsen" and "Budweis," would have been always protected. Germany, on the contrary, declared that the amendment would not make her accession any easier.[4]

At the Conference of The Hague a similar proposal of the International Bureau did not fare any better. Four delegations opposed the further extension of the exception. They also opposed a Czechoslovakian proposal that the appellations of beer and of mineral waters be treated like those concerning products of the vine. The obligatory character of definitions of appellations of origin communicated through the agency of the International Bureau by the country of origin was also objected to.[5]

§ **472. Sanctions of the Arrangement.** The sanctions of the Arrangement against false indications of origin remained unmodified as originally adopted by the Madrid Conference, with the exception of a few minor amendments at the conferences of Washington and of The Hague. These sanctions have also been transferred to the gen-

1. See *Actes de la Conférence de La Haye*, p. 311.
2. See *Propriété Industrielle* (1920), pp. 31 ff.
3. *Actes de la Conférence de Washington*, pp. 99–100, 218.
4. *Ibid.*, p. 293.
5. *Actes de la Conférence de La Haye*, pp. 311–312, 481. See, however, the provisions of the treaties of peace, *infra*, § 474.

eral Convention, article 9, with regard to unlawful affixing of trade marks or trade names, and have already been considered in the interpretation of articles 9 and 10 of the Convention.[1]

At the Conference of The Hague a new paragraph was added to article 4 on the proposal of the French delegation,[2] reading as follows:

> À défaut de sanctions spéciales assurant la répression des fausses indications de provenance, les sanctions prévues par les dispositions correspondantes des lois sur les marques ou les noms commerciaux seront applicables.

Thus, in case a country has not enacted special provisions for the repression of false indications of origin, the respective provisions concerning the remedies against infringing trade marks or trade names will be available. This provision is self-executing. In case the law of a country permits seizure on importation or prohibition of importation of goods bearing an infringing trade mark or trade name, these sanctions will be applied, by virtue of the Arrangement, against goods bearing false indications of origin.

As we have seen above,[3] six of the countries, parties to the Madrid Arrangement, — Brazil, France, Germany, Great Britain, Spain, and Tunis, — provide by law for the administrative seizure of goods bearing false indications of origin; in Portugal, the prohibition of importation is available; and in Morocco, Switzerland, and Syria and Lebanon, judicial seizure in the interior is permitted.

By express provision of the Arrangement (second paragraph of article 2), the authorities of the contracting countries are not bound to effect the seizure of goods in transit. Such seizure is permitted but is not demanded. The provision is similar to that of article 9 of the Convention, and is explained by the same unwillingness of certain countries to hamper the transit of goods through their territory, which is for them an important commercial activity. At the Conference of The Hague a delegate of the Economic Committee of the League of Nations proposed, in accordance with the spirit of the Barcelona Convention of 1921,[4] that the seizure of goods in transit

1. See *supra*, §§ 407, 408, and 464.
2. See the proposal and its adoption in *Actes de la Conférence de La Haye*, pp. 364. 480, 561.
3. See *supra*, § 464.
4. Convention and Statute on Freedom of Transit, Barcelona, 7 L. N. Tr. Ser., 12; 18 *Amer. Jour. of Int. Law*, Supp. 118.

be absolutely prohibited. The French delegation opposed such absolute prohibition, which would prevent a country from seizing goods in transit through its territory bearing falsely a national indication of origin.[1]

§ **473. Requests for application of sanctions.** Article 2 of the Arrangement, before its amendment at The Hague, provided, almost in the same terms as the third paragraph of article 9 of the Convention, that the seizure may take place at the request either of the public prosecutor or of any other competent authority, for instance, — the customs administration, — or of any interested party, whether an individual or a company, in conformity with the domestic law of each country. This provision did not bind the customs authorities in particular, which are in the best position to detect false indications of origin, to effect the seizure. The goods might enter the interior of the country, and their seizure might be rendered difficult. An amendment to article 2 by the Conference of The Hague.[2] tends to make the seizure by the customs authorities obligatory before any request for seizure is made by the interested party. The first paragraph of article 2 reads as follows:

> La saisie aura lieu à la diligence de l'Administration des Douanes qui avertira immédiatement l'intéressé, personne physique ou morale, pour lui permettre de régulariser, s'il le désire, la saisie opérée conservatoirement; toutefois, le Ministère public et toute autre autorité compétente pourra requérir la saisie, soit à la demande de la partie lésée, soit d'office; la procédure suivra alors son cours ordinaire.

Thus a duty is imposed on the customs authorities of the contracting countries to effect the seizure of goods bearing false indications of origin, and to inform immediately the interested person. Of course, the performance of this duty is not possible unless the customs authorities are able to see that the indication of origin is false, and know the party interested. It is doubtful whether the provision can have much application, except in the case of certain well-known appellations of origin. The conditions and formalities for the performance of this duty need to be determined by municipal law. Such seizure is only a protective and provisional measure. It must be confirmed by proper action of the party interested. Together

1. See *Actes de la Conférence de La Haye*, p. 480.
2. See French proposal and its adoption, in *Actes de la Conférence de La Haye*, pp. 364, 480, 561.

with this new procedure, the old is still available; namely, the public prosecutor or any other competent authority may demand the seizure, either at the request of the party injured or in their official capacity.

Article 2 of the Arrangement refers once to the "party interested," and then to the "party injured," who may request the seizure. The two terms are equivalent. No definition of such party is given in the Arrangement, but this is closely connected with article 10 of the general Convention, and the definition of the "partie intéressée" given in that article should be resorted to. It is already seen that, under the terms of article 10 of the Convention, a person is deemed a party interested when two conditions concur: (*a*) when the person is engaged in the production or manufacture of, or trade in, goods similar to those bearing the false indication of origin; and (*b*) when he is established either in the locality falsely indicated as the place of origin, in the region where the locality is situated, or in the country falsely indicated. The same conditions must be satisfied before invoking the provisions of the Arrangement, and also the conditions of the first paragraph of article 1 of the Arrangement; namely, the country falsely indicated, or in which the place indicated is situated, must be a party to the Arrangement.

The party interested may be an individual, or a body of persons corporate or unincorporated. The words "particulier ou société" were replaced by the words "personne physique ou morale" at the Conference of The Hague, for the same reason that a similar change was made in article 9 of the Convention.[1]

§ 474. Provisions of the treaties of peace. Germany, Austria, Hungary, Bulgaria, and Turkey had not acceded to the Madrid Arrangement for the repression of false indications of origin before the World War. But the first three were members of the general Union, and false indications of origin were repressed in their territory under the provisions of article 10 of the Convention. Thus, only in the case of qualified fraud, that is, of false indications of origin joined to a trade name of fictitious character or used with fraudulent intent, was there an engagement on the part of these countries to effect the seizure or prohibit the importation of goods. In fact, however, these countries

1. See *supra*, p. 582. The reservation made in article 9 in respect to syndicates and associations applies also to the provision under consideration. See *Actes de la Conférence de La Haye*, pp. 470, 480.

repressed false indications of origin by their municipal law to a greater extent than was provided for by article 10. True indications of origin were always protected. But the courts of each country were free to decide, in respect to all indications of origin, that their distinctiveness was lost and they had become generic or descriptive terms. Their judgment in each case was in no way affected by the status of certain indications of origin in the country of origin. The exception of article 4 of the Arrangement concerning regional appellations of products of the vine was not admitted in the law of these countries. In fact, this exception was the main reason why Germany refused to accede to the Madrid Arrangement.[1]

This situation was in some respects modified by the treaties of peace concluded after the late war. Chapter III of Part X of the Treaty of Versailles, entitled "Unfair Competition," contains two articles, 274 and 275, which are also reproduced in the Treaty of Saint-Germain with Austria (articles 226, 227), the Treaty of Trianon with Hungary (article 210), the Treaty of Neuilly with Bulgaria (articles 154, 155), and the Commercial Convention annexed to the Treaty of Lausanne with Turkey (articles 12 and 13).[2]

Article 274 of the Treaty of Versailles provides that

> Germany undertakes to adopt all necessary legislative and administrative measures to protect goods, the produce or manufacture of any one of the Allied and Associated Powers, from all forms of unfair competition in commercial transactions; [and that] Germany undertakes to prohibit and repress by seizure and by other appropriate remedies the importation, exportation, manufacture, distribution, sale or offering for sale in its territory of all goods bearing upon themselves or their usual get-up or wrappings, any marks, names, devices, or descriptions whatever which are calculated to convey directly or indirectly a false indication of the origin type, nature, or special characteristics of such goods.

By these provisions, Germany, Austria, Hungary, and Bulgaria undertake towards the Allied and Associated Powers, without a similar engagement on their part, to repress, in particular, false indications of origin to a greater extent than the Madrid Arrangement provides. The same engagement is undertaken by Turkey under the above Commercial Convention of Lausanne, but on condition of reciprocity. These countries are for all practical purposes acceding, by virtue of these provisions, to the whole of the Madrid Arrange-

1. See *Propriété Industrielle* (1920), pp. 31, 32 ff.
2. For the parties to these treaties, see *infra*, note 1 on p. 683.

ment, with the exception of the provision of its fourth article concerning regional appellations of products of the vine. But this is taken care of by article 275 of the Treaty of Versailles and the corresponding articles of the other treaties. This article provides that

Germany undertakes, on condition that reciprocity is accorded in these matters, to respect any law, or any administrative or judicial decision given in conformity with such law, in force in any Allied or Associated State and duly communicated to her by the proper authorities, defining or regulating the right to any regional appellation in respect of wine or spirits produced in the state to which the region belongs, or the conditions under which the use of any such appellation may be permitted; and the importation, exportation, manufacture, distribution, sale or offering for sale of products or articles bearing regional appellations inconsistent with such law or order shall be prohibited by the German government and repressed by the measures prescribed in the preceding article.

Under this article, Germany, Austria, Hungary, and Bulgaria are obligated, on condition of reciprocal treatment on the part of the Allied and Associated Powers, to give binding force to the law or decisions of the country to which a regional appellation of products of the vine belongs. The tribunals are no longer free to decide that a regional appellation of spirits, for instance the name "Cognac," is a generic or descriptive term, if by the law of the country of origin (in the instance cited, France), or its courts' decisions, the appellation in question is a true appellation of origin belonging to the producers of a specified region. This engagement goes even further than the exception of article 4 of the Madrid Arrangement. The treaties, in this respect, stipulate what the French delegation had proposed at the Washington Conference as an amendment to the Madrid Arrangement.[1] Especially, it is required that the Allied and Associated Powers communicate to Germany (also to Austria, Hungary, and Bulgaria) the laws or administrative and judicial decisions concerning the regional appellations in question.

The provision of article 13 of the Commercial Convention with Turkey is different from that of the other treaties in that, instead of regional appellations "in respect of vine or spirits," it concerns such of "products which derive from the soil or climate their specific qualities." It is likewise required that the laws, as well as the administrative and judicial decisions, regulating the right to a regional

1. See *supra*, § 471.

appellation, and the conditions in which its use may be authorized, be communicated to Turkey.

In fact, these five countries, as a result of these treaty provisions may be deemed to have, for all practical purposes, acceded to the Madrid Arrangement. But this is true only in respect to the countries, parties to the Arrangement, which are also parties to the peace treaties.[1] Germany, the main reason for her refusal to accede to the Arrangement, namely, her dislike of the exception of Article 4, having now disappeared, was compelled to accede, and did so in 1925.[2]

§ **475. Bipartite treaties for protection of indications of origin.** The above provisions of the treaties of peace for the repression of false indications of origin created, so to speak, a new general sentiment in this matter. The argument of non-interference with the inveterate, though reprehensible, practice of the trade to use false indications of origin lost much of its strength, and the various countries are now eager to prohibit this sort of fraud. To a development of honesty in international trade corresponds a clearer view of the interests of the national industry and trade of each country.[3] This explains the numerous bipartite conventions entered into by member countries of the Union after the war, stipulating for the protection of indications of origin to a greater extent than the Convention of 1883–1925, or even the Madrid Arrangement for the repression of false indications of origin.[4] In the treaties of France with Finland, Norway, Czechoslovakia, Poland, Latvia, Austria, and Belgium-Luxembourg, as well as in an arrangement between Austria and Czechoslovakia, it is provided that the law of the country of origin shall govern the question whether a designation is a true indication

1. France and Great Britain (with which may be enumerated the Irish Free State, Morocco, New Zealand, and Tunis,) are parties to the Arrangement and to all five of the above treaties of peace. Cuba, Czechoslovakia, and Portugal, parties to the Arrangement, are also parties to the treaties with Austria, Bulgaria, and Germany. Brazil, a party to the Arrangement, is also a party to the treaty with Germany. Spain and Switzerland, parties to the Arrangement, are not parties to any of the treaties of peace.

2. See on the question of the provisions of the treaties of peace, an excellent article in *Propriété Industrielle* (1920), pp. 53 ff. Also Wassermann, *Die Behandlung des unlauteren Wettbewerbs im Friedensvertrag* (Berlin–Leipzig, 1920). Germany in execution of its treaty engagement, modified its domestic law to the effect of repressing the use of the appellation "Kognac" for German brandy, and the appellations "Bordeaux" and "Bourgogne" for mixtures of French and German wines. See Jaton, *La Répression des Fausses Indications de Provenance*, pp. 70 ff.

3. See, in this respect, the decision of the German Patent Office, cited *supra*, note 9 on p. 674.

4. See these conventions, *supra*, chap. VI, § 84.

of origin, belonging to the producers of a specified region, or whether it is a generic or descriptive term. Thus the above provisions of the treaties of peace are in a way transferred to these bipartite conventions.[1]

§ **476. Possibilities of accession of new countries.** The unwillingness of many countries to accede to the Madrid Arrangement is due to two main reasons. First, that they do not possess any very important reputed appellations of localities or regions concerning manufactured or agricultural products that need to be protected abroad. The French appellations, "Champagne," "Cognac," "Camembert," "Vichy," the Portuguese "Porto" and "Madeira," the English "Sheffield," and others, have not as important corresponding appellations in the other countries. Therefore the same interest does not exist in all the countries to protect the reputation of national products. On the other hand, the appellations of reputed products of some countries have been freely used by the manufacturers and traders of others. The latter countries are reluctant to interfere with inveterate customs of their trade and industry, or to bring about a serious disturbance therein by conferring a quasi-monopoly upon the industry and trade of foreign countries. The best argument against this conception is that of the German Patent Office in the case already referred to [2] concerning the appellation "Camembert" for cheese. "The most efficacious means of protecting and developing German production," said the Patent Office, "is not to contribute to the development and amelioration of foreign reputed products by the use of their appellations, but by bettering the quality of national products." Unless the different countries see their interest in this way, it cannot be expected that they will accede to the Arrangement.

Countries that possess national products enjoying a high reputation in foreign markets, and that are desirous to protect their appellations of origin, are prevented from acceding to the Madrid

1. To the same category of treaties belongs the recent Arrangement between France and Switzerland concerning the appellations "Cognac" and "Armagnac." See "Avenant à l'Arrangement Commercial Franco-Suisse," of March 11, 1928, in *Propriété Industrielle* (1928), p. 79.

A list of French and Portuguese appellations of origin communicated by the French and Portuguese governments to Belgium, is appended to the Belgian Law of April 18, 1927 (*Propriété Industrielle*, 1927, p. 209). Another list concerning Spanish appellations of origin was published by the Belgian government, Aug. 27, 1927, in *Propriété Industrielle* (1928), p. 25.

2. See *supra*, note 9 on p. 674.

Arrangement by the exception of article 4 concerning regional appellations of products of the vine. Certain countries are reluctant to abolish the power of the courts to pass in all cases on the question whether an appellation has ceased to indicate origin and has become a descriptive term. If they are prepared to undertake such an engagement at all, they would wish to extend the exception so as to cover appellations in which they are more interested. It has been seen above that Austria insisted on this point at the Conference of The Hague. The attempts to amend in this respect article 4 of the Arrangement at the last two conferences of revision have been unsuccessful. Perhaps an adequate expression to satisfy all parties concerned is yet to be found. The phrase "products deriving their natural qualities from the soil and climate" is not quite definite and is too broad. And it is not likely to be admitted by many countries that the law of the country of origin should determine the question whether an appellation of origin is a true indication of origin or a generic or descriptive term. Nothing short of a decision on these questions by an international tribunal, which may take into consideration all the circumstances of the case and the factual situation in the different countries, would satisfy all the countries in this respect, admitting that they are all prepared to make mutual concessions. The question of an international tribunal is considered below.[1]

§ **477. Attempts to transfer to the general Convention provisions of the Arrangement.** At the Conferences of Washington and The Hague the British proposed[2] to amend article 10 of the general Convention concerning the repression of false indications of origin by substituting for the first paragraph of that article the first paragraph of article 1 of the Madrid Arrangement. This would have had the effect of binding all the member countries of the general Union to repress such false indications, even though they were not joined to a trade name of a fictitious character or used with fraudulent intent. Inasmuch as the provisions of the Arrangement concerning the sanctions had been transferred to article 9 of the Convention, the only difference which would have remained between the two international acts would be the provision concerning regional appellations of products of the vine.

1. See *infra*, §§ 583 ff.

2. See *Actes de la Conférence de Washington*, p. 104, and *Actes de la Conférence de La Haye*, pp. 251, 252.

At the Washington Conference there was a bare majority in favor of the British proposal. The Belgian delegation declared that the amendment in question would amount to an indirect accession to the Madrid Arrangement of the countries which are not parties thereto. This was substantially true. The Italian delegation would accept the amendment if it should be understood that the courts of each country were to be free to decide that the appellations were of a generic character. But, what seems at first strange, the French delegation itself opposed the amendment. The explanation is a matter of opportunism and policy on the part of the French, who feared, not without reason, that the transferring of the broad provision of article 1 of the Arrangement to article 10 of the Convention would weaken the Arrangement, and that the countries parties to the latter which were not interested in the regional appellations concerning products of the vine might drop the Arrangement.[1] In fact, it appears that France, Portugal, and Spain are the only countries parties to the Arrangement which are interested in the protection of such appellations.[2]

At the Conference of The Hague two methods of approach to the problem were developed. France accepted the proposal of the Bureau stipulating that false indications of origin were to be always repressed (even though not joined to a fictitious trade name). It proposed, however, to add a provision under which should be regarded as a false indication of origin every geographical expression referring to a locality, region, or country, in which the goods to which the indication was applied were not actually made or produced, and which expression had not become a generic term in the country to which such locality or region belonged. The British and Cuban delegations, on the contrary, maintained that an inexact indication of origin should be repressed only if it were likely to deceive the public as to the origin of the goods. On the question of determination of the generic character of a geographical indication, views were also at variance. According to the French view, the legislation or court decisions of the country in which the region or locality was situated, duly communicated to the other countries, should be binding on their courts. The American, Austrian, British, Italian, and Swedish delegations wished to leave the courts of each contracting country free to decide

1. See *Actes de la Conférence de Washington*, p. 303.

2. See *Travaux du Groupe Français de l'Association Internationale* (1919–1922), pp. 111–112, 166, 168.

whether an appellation possessed a distinctive character or was a generic term. The French delegation, however, opposed again any amendment of article 10.[1]

§ 478. Protection of indications of origin in the United States. Indications of origin in which a country, or a locality or region situated therein, is designated as the country or place of origin of goods, are not explicitly recognized as a special branch of industrial property in the United States. Yet, where a geographical name has been first adopted as merely indicating the place of manufacture, and afterwards has acquired a reputation for excellence, the courts held that it can be used only by all who manufacture in that locality. Persons residing at other places are not permitted to use such geographical name for similar goods, with the intent of appropriating the goodwill and business of others.[2] Since the reason for protection is the injury to the goodwill and business of certain persons, that is, property interests, this implicitly amounts to a recognition of indications of origin as intangible property rights. However, usually relief is granted on the ground of fraud on the public, not that of interest in the reputation acquired by the geographical name.[3] Indeed, the protection of indications of origin is a part of the law of unfair competition, and actual fraud must be shown when an action to restrain such unfair competition is brought. Equity courts in the United States use the remedy of injunction to repress all forms of fraudulent use of indications of origin. A petition to this effect may be brought by all, as well as by one, of the manufacturers entitled to the use of the geographical name.[4]

The act of June 30, 1906,[5] "for preventing the manufacture, sale, or transportation of adulterated or misbranded . . . foods, drugs, medicines, . . . and for regulating traffic therein and for other purposes," affords further protection to foreign indications of origin. The offenses under this act are deemed misdemeanors, and the persons guilty thereof may be fined, or sentenced to imprisonment, or

1. See *Actes de la Conférence de La Haye*, pp. 471–472.

2. Pillsbury-Washburn Flour Mills Co. *v.* Eagle (1898), 86 Fed. 608, involving the indications "Minneapolis" and "Minnesota" for flour; California Fruit Canners' Association *v.* Nyer (1899), 104 Fed. 82.

3. City of Carlsbad *v.* Kutnow (1895), 68 Fed. 794 (affirmed 35 U. S. App. 750, 18 C. C. A. 24, and 71 Fed. 167), protecting the appellation "Carlsbad Salts," infringed by the sale of similar salts labelled "Imported Effervescent Carlsbad Powder."

4. Pillsbury-Washburn Flour Mills Co. *v.* Eagle (1896), 80 Fed. 608, 629.

5. XXXIV *U. S. Stat. at Large*, 768.

both. The act prohibits the introduction into any state or territory from any other state or territory, or from any foreign country, or the shipment to any foreign country, of any article of food or any drug which is adulterated or misbranded. The terms food and drug are used in the act in the broadest sense. The term misbranded is also interpreted as covering all cases of misuse of an indication of origin.

Section 27 of the Trade Marks Act of 1905 [1] prohibits the importation of articles of imported merchandise, "bearing a name or mark calculated to induce the public to believe that the article is manufactured in any foreign country or locality other than the country or locality in which it is in fact manufactured." Foreign as well as domestic traders or manufacturers may, in order to aid the officers of the customs to enforce the prohibition, require the name of the locality in which their goods are manufactured to be recorded at the Department of the Treasury. The prohibition is applied when the indication of origin appearing on the goods "is calculated to deceive the public." This is broader than article 10 of the Convention, but comes short of the principle of article 1 of the Arrangement.

The Act of March 19, 1920,[2] brings the law of the United States more into accord with the Convention. It prohibits false designations of origin used with intent to deceive in connection with merchandise, or the container of merchandise, entering into interstate or foreign commerce. And it grants the right to sue for damages and for an injunction to any person, firm, or corporation doing business in the locality falsely indicated as that of origin, or in the region in which said locality is situated, or to any association of such persons, firms or corporations.

False indications of origin of merchandise are also reached by the Tariff Act of 1922, section 304, requiring the marking of every article or package imported into the United States, when such marking is possible without injury to the article, so as to indicate clearly the country of origin. The act imposes criminal punishment for its violations.[3]

There would seem to be no obstacle to the accession of the United States to the Arrangement for the repression of false indications of

1. XXXIII *U. S. Stat. at Large*, 724.

2. "An Act to give effect to certain provisions of the Convention for the protection of trade marks and commercial names, signed at Buenos Aires August 20, 1910, and for other purposes." XLI *U. S. Stat. at Large*, 533.

3. XLII *U. S. Stat. at Large*, 858, 936.

origin, except for the proviso in the fourth article concerning appellations of products of the vine. The United States would seem to be unwilling to take away from the courts the power to decide in any case that such an appellation is in the possession of the public.[1]

§ 479. **Protection of indications of origin in Great Britain.** The common law protection of indications of origin in Great Britain is based on the same principle as in the United States. The basis for protection is a fraudulent representation on the part of the defendant that the goods offered by him are goods of the plaintiff, or are manufactured by the plaintiff;[2] and therefore, whenever such fraud is avoided by appropriate designations, the use of a foreign indication of origin is not prohibited. Thus, the affixing of a label indicating "Spanish product" and "Spanish Porto" was held to be permissible.[3]

This same principle is at the basis of the Merchandise Marks Act of 1887.[4] This act, first, punishes by fine and imprisonment the application to goods of any false trade description, regarding statements or indications as to the place or country of origin in which any goods are made or produced, and also the sale or offer for sale of goods bearing such false descriptions; and the goods by means of, or in relation to which such acts are committed may be forfeited. The act also prohibits the importation (section 16) of such goods; and although it exempts from its provisions (section 18) trade descriptions lawfully and generally applied to goods of a particular class, or manufactured by a particular method, it requires, where such trade description includes the name of a place or a country and is calculated to mislead as to the place or country where the goods to which it is applied were actually made or produced, that there be added to the trade description, immediately before or after the name of that place or country, and in an equally conspicuous manner, the name of the place or country in which the goods were actually made or produced, with a statement that they were made or produced there.

1. This was advanced by the United States Patent Office as the reason the United States was not prepared to accept the Arrangement, when this was originally adopted. "Letter of April 6, 1891, to the Department of State from the Department of the Interior," communicating a report by Seely, Examiner in the Patent Office, with endorsement of the Commissioner of Patents. (Communicated to the present writer by the courtesy of the Department of State.)

2. See Kerly, *The Law of Trade Marks and Trade Name*, pp. 13, 14, 446.

3. Port Wine Shippers' Ass'n *v.* Liptons, Ltd. (*Propriété Industrielle*, 1908, p. 104).

4. 50 & 51 Vict., c. 28.

Under the Consolidated Regulations in execution of the above act,[1] goods forbidden to be imported, as above, are to be detained without the requirement of previous information. The regulations apply to transshipment and transit goods as well as to goods landed to be warehoused, or for home consumption.

Recently the Merchandise Marks Act was amended by the Act of December 15, 1926,[2] entitled "An Act to require an indication of origin to be given in the case of certain imported goods." This act makes it unlawful to sell, expose for sale, or distribute any imported goods to which there is applied any name or trade mark being, or purporting to be, the name or trade mark of any manufacturer, dealer, or trader, or the name of any place or district in the United Kingdom, unless the name or trade mark is accompanied by an indication of origin. Such indication of origin may be the word "foreign" (and in case of goods manufactured in the dominions the word "Empire"), or a definite indication of the country in which the goods were manufactured or produced. Certain goods may be excepted from the application of this act by the Board of Trade, having regard to special circumstances of the trade.[3] These provisions aim at protecting the buying public against frauds committed with the consent of British manufacturers or traders.

The same act provides that an order may be made, after an inquiry in relation to the goods of any class or description, prohibiting the sale or the exposure for sale of imported goods of that class or description unless they bear an indication of origin.[4] Thus, although no name or trade mark of a manufacturer or trader, nor the name of any place or district in the United Kingdom, is applied on the goods, the obligation to indicate their foreign origin may be imposed. This provision tends to protect foreign rights in indications of origin as well as the buying public. The above order may not be made in case trade in the United Kingdom, or the trade of the dominions with the United Kingdom, would be prejudiced thereby.

1. Statutory Rules and Orders, Revised Dec. 31, 1903, vol. VIII, sections 1 and 8.
2. 16 & 17 Geo. V, c. 53.
3. Sections 1 and 10.
4. Section 2.

CHAPTER XXXI

THE REPRESSION OF ACTS OF UNFAIR COMPETITION

§ 480. Unfair competition and industrial property. This chapter should logically precede those on patents, designs, models, trade marks, trade names, and indications of place of origin. All these are specialized branches of industrial property, regulated and protected separately and specifically by the law. They represent pecuniary interests and business relations, which are legally protected. The aim of the law in all these instances is to give satisfaction to interests acquired by honest labor or by conducting a lawful business. But the law of unfair competition aims at protecting these same interests and thus includes the above specialized branches. It forms the background, and constitutes the general principle of which the laws protecting the various branches of industrial property are only special aspects or particular applications.

For the purposes of exposition, however, and in accordance with the place given to it in the Industrial Property Convention of 1883–1925, it is proper to deal with unfair competition after all the specialized branches of industrial property have been considered. Unfair competition comprises not only infringements of any of the kinds of industrial property already dealt with, but all other acts that injure the business relations of a person. It is easier to observe these various relations and the interests arising therefrom, now that the different industrial creations (patents, designs and models) and means of identification and distinction of businesses (trade marks, trade names) have been dealt with. It will be seen that the latter are not the only devices and distinctive badges to create goodwill or reputation, nor is their infringement or imitation the only means of injuring the business relations of a person.

Moreover, the law of unfair competition, in contrast to the patent, design, or trade-mark law, which, because of its technical character, is more or less certain and has reached a stage of maturity, has been progressing slowly and is still full of uncertainties. Neither its basis nor its boundaries are yet settled. While the law was endeavoring to delimit the various specialized industrial property rights, fraudulent merchants and manufacturers were attempting to steal the business of successful producers by keeping outside the limits traced by the law. And when the provisions of the law extended to these acts also, new fraudulent ways were devised. Thus the law has not been able to keep pace with the Protean transformations of fraud in commercial transactions. The legal materials at hand did not afford equal elasticity in all the countries, and the remedies available were not always adequate.[1] The dislike to interfere with lawful competition made protection more difficult, the border line between it and unfair competition being not always easy to trace.

It is an undeniable fact of modern business life that successful manufacturers or traders have to cope with the danger of having the goodwill of their business, their connection with the purchasing public, interfered with by competitors.[2] Of course, it should be permissible for competitors to obtain the benefit of a public demand, even though this demand is created by other manufacturers or traders. But competition becomes unfair when the access of the latter to the purchasing market is attacked by invasion of their business relations or by false representations.

The Industrial Property Convention of 1883, originally, did not contain any stipulation with regard to unfair competition. The

1. See *supra*, chap. II, IV.

2. In his usual forceful manner, Dean Wigmore writes: "The fact is, no commercial business grows into healthy largeness without becoming soon the victim of the business parasite . . . who attacks and seeks to absorb by deception of patrons the unearned benefit of the other man's labor and money." See 10 *Illinois Law Review*, 178, 184 ff.

situation existing prior to 1883 continued for a long time in many countries. In the common law countries, the most adequate remedy of equitable injunction was being applied more and more freely to all cases where a person attempted to pass off his goods as those of another. In France, Belgium, and other countries, the law of unfair competition was still deduced by the courts from the general principles of the Civil code, and remained consequently uncrystallized, reflecting the reactions of public opinion in trade. In Germany, after the courts had been unsuccessful in protecting against acts of unfair competition,[1] a special act was passed in 1896,[2] which constituted the first experiment in that direction, purporting to reach specific cases of unfair competition.[3] In most of the other countries protection against unfair competition was very inadequate.

§ **481. Provisions of the Convention.** The first stipulation concerning unfair competition was adopted at the Brussels Conference of Revision in 1900, on the proposal of the French delegation.[4] It formed article 10*b* and read as follows:

> Les ressortissants de la Convention [art. 2 et 3] jouiront, dans tous les États de l'Union de la protection accordée aux nationaux contre la concurrence déloyale.

The effect of the stipulation was merely to do away with the discrimination existing in some countries between foreigners and nationals with regard to protection against unfair competition,[5] and to extend in this regard the principle of national treatment of article 2. No obligation was imposed on any country to afford remedies against acts of unfair competition. This was done in 1911 at the Washington Conference, when article 10*b* was amended as follows:

> Tous les pays contractants s'engagent à assurer aux ressortissants de l'Union une protection effective contre la concurrence déloyale.

1. See Schuler, *Die Concurrence Déloyale*, pp. 42 ff.

2. "Gesetz zur Bekämpfung des unlauteren Wettbewerbs," of May 27, 1896 (*Reichsgesetzblatt*, 1896, p. 145).

3. See, on this act, J. F. Iselin, "The New German Law of Unfair Competition," in *Law Quarterly Review* (1897), XIII, 156.

4. *Actes de la Conférence de Bruxelles*, pp. 164, 187, 310, 356. The terms of this stipulation had been adopted in a resolution of three congresses of the International Association for the Protection of Industrial Property. See *Annuaire de l'Association Internationale* (1897), p. 99; (1898), p. 493; (1899), p. 118.

5. This was so in France. See Pelletier et Vidal-Naquet, *Convention d'Union*, pp. 458 ff.

This amendment was proposed by Great Britain, after the principle of national treatment of article 2 of the Convention was extended to protection against unfair competition, the words "la répression de la concurrence déloyale" having been inserted in that article.[1] The British proposal specified that the concept of unfair competition should extend to the application of figures, words, or marks calculated to deceive the public as to the real origin of goods.[2] Although this provision did not purport to cover all cases of unfair competition, but to secure protection in certain frequent cases, it was objected to by certain delegations, which feared that the specific enumeration of certain cases might be taken as excluding all others.[3]

§ 482. International efforts after the World War. Prior to the outbreak of the World War a movement for a more effective check on international unfair competition was under way.[4] During the war unfair practices in trade, unscrupulous attempts to rob the business of competitors, especially if the latter were found in the enemy camp, and deceptions of the public went so far that they brought about a strong reaction. Moreover, new industries were created in belligerent as well as in neutral countries, to satisfy the needs of the internal and external markets disturbed by the vicissitudes of the war. These industries had a hard fight in order to survive after the end of the war, when the boundaries between states were opened, and the traffic in goods was made free. Protection against unfair competition was for these industries a sheer necessity. A similar remark applies to industries of the new countries born of the dismemberment of old ones.[5] It is not surprising, therefore, that in many countries during the war, and in others on its termination,

1. *Actes de la Conférence de Washington,* pp. 53, 105.

2. This part of the proposition read as follows: "L'expression 'concurrence déloyale' s'étendra à l'apposition sur des produits, de chiffres, de mots, ou de marques, employés soit isolément, soit en forme d'arrangements ou de combinaisons, contenant ou non une marque de fabrique, et pouvant être considérés comme calculés pour porter le public à croire que les produits ou marchandises proviennent d'une personne autre que celle dont ils sont véritablement les produits ou les marchandises." *Ibid.,* p. 105.

3. *Ibid.,* pp. 305, 310.

4. See resolutions of the International Association for the Protection of Industrial Property, and the International Congress of the Chambers of Commerce, at Paris, 1914, in *Actes de la Conférence de La Haye,* p. 94.

5. See M. Plaisant et Fernand-Jacq, *Le Nouveau Régime International de la Propriété Industrielle* (Paris, 1927), pp. 2, 3, 12.

new legislation was enacted for the purpose of reaching various acts of unfair competition.[1]

International action to the same effect began with the treaties of peace — Article 274 of the Versailles Treaty and the respective articles of the other treaties, which are dealt with in the previous chapter,[2] impose on Germany, Austria, Hungary, and Bulgaria, without reciprocal engagement of the Allied and Associated Powers, and with the condition of reciprocity toward Turkey, the obligation

> to adopt all necessary legislative and administrative measures to protect goods the produce or manufacture of any one of the Allied or Associated Powers from all forms of unfair competition in commercial transactions.

Moreover, it is specifically provided that acts of unfair competition which are to be repressed by seizure or other appropriate remedies are:

> the importation, exportation, manufacture, distribution, sale or offering for sale of all goods bearing upon themselves or their usual get-up or wrappings any marks, names, devices, or descriptions whatever, which are calculated to convey directly or indirectly a false indication of the origin, type, nature, or special characteristics of such goods.

This enumeration does not exhaust all cases of unfair competition. Nor does it add anything to the protection which the German law afforded against unfair competition to foreigners,[3] except the formal engagement of Germany.

The Economic Committee of the League of Nations, on its creation, took up the question of the repression of unfair competition as one of its tasks. The League was specially interested in the repression of unfair competition as a step towards "more equitable treatment for commerce" under the terms of article 23(*e*) of the Covenant. On January 12, 1921, the Committee sent out a questionnaire to governments on the subject of unfair competition.[4] After receiving a number of replies and hearing the first Vice-Director of the International Bureau of Industrial Property, Professor Röthlisberger, it appointed Sir Hubert Llewellyn Smith to report on the desiderata. An excellent report was accordingly submitted to

1. See William Notz, "New Phases of Unfair Competition and Measures for its Suppression — National and International," in *Yale Law Journal* (1921), XXX, 384. See also, as to new legislative enactments, *infra*, § 492.
2. See *supra*, § 474.
3. Act of June 7, 1909 (*Reichsgesetzblatt*, 1909, p. 499).
4. See *League of Nations, Document C. 342* (1921), II, and *C. 204* (1922), II.

the Council in March, 1922, and circulated among the member states in June, 1922.[1] It was noted that the stipulation of article 10*b* of the Industrial Property Convention of 1883–1911 had not hitherto produced any great practical results,

> partly because of the interruption of legislation by the war, but partly because of the extremely vague and general character of the undertaking, the absence of any international jurisdiction to enforce it, and the entire lack of any detailed indications of the precise character of the frauds at which it is aimed, and of the legal and administrative remedies which are necessary for their suppression.

The Committee felt that new stipulations should be added in the Convention, or in a supplementary protocol, filling the above gaps in article 10*b*. The International Bureau sent to the Committee a report on December 27, 1922, and twenty-five countries sent their comments to the Secretariat.[2]

At the suggestion of the Japanese government, a meeting of experts was called at Geneva, to examine the draft articles prepared by the Economic Committee for insertion in the Convention of 1883. This meeting took place at Geneva from May 5 to May 11, 1924.[3] The Director of the International Bureau was also present.[4] The text adopted by the experts was forwarded to the members of the League and the state members of the Industrial Union. The proposal in regard to article 10*b* contained an enumeration of certain cases of unfair competition, and added a declaration to be inserted in the Final Protocol, to the effect that the term "unfair competition" was not to be understood as being limited to the particular abuses specified in article 10*b*.[5]

The experts deemed it outside their competency to express an opinion on the third article of the revised draft of articles on unfair

1. See *Report to the Assembly from the Economic and Financial Organization*, A. 59 (1922), II, p. 15, and Annex I.

2. See *League of Nations, Economic Committee Document C. 75* (1) M. 81 (1923), II. See also *Economic Committee, Unfair Competition, Conference of Experts, Preliminary Documents*, C. E. C. D. I.

3. Minutes unpublished, C.E.C.D./P.V. 1 (1) to 10 (1).

4. The influence of the Director, Professor Röthlisberger, was rather too conservative, as appears from the minutes of the Meeting of Experts. To be sure, he was right in urging that the new provisions should be grafted on to the existing Convention, but he also cautioned the experts against attempting to interfere with questions left by article 2 of the Convention to the determination of each state.

5. See *Report to the Fifth Assembly*, A. 52 (1924), II, p. 6, and Annex 3; also the *Program of the Meeting*, containing a summary of remarks presented by the various countries under date of October 25, 1923, C. E. C. D. I.

competition submitted to them by the Economic Committee.[1] This article provided for the submission to the Permanent Court of International Justice of all differences arising between the contracting countries on the interpretation or application of the Convention which could not be solved by agreement between them. Concerning the first article of the draft, the experts distinguished the cases involving fraudulent infringement of trade marks from the cases of unfair competition in the strict sense. In respect to the former they adopted a resolution calling for penal sanctions, which is considered in another place.[2]

On the question of repression of unfair competition, they adopted resolution (B), in which (1) they proclaimed the principle that the contracting countries undertake to assure to the "ressortissants" of the other countries in their respective territories effective protection against unfair competition; (2) they enumerated illustratively a number of cases in which civil and, in case of fraud, penal sanctions should be provided for: cases of the use in trade of commercial designations (names, firms, get-up of goods, and so forth) serving to distinguish the goods of a merchant, manufacturer, or producer, and of descriptions, or figurative representations, or any other indication referring to the origin of a product, whenever such use tends to produce either confusion with the goods of another person or an error as to the true origin of the merchandise; (3) they assimilated to the above uses the imitations of the aforesaid designations or descriptions which may cause confusion or error; (4) they admitted to the benefits of these provisions any injured person or company and, in case of injunctions and penal actions, any association or person representing the particular industry injured; and (5) they made the sanctions of article 9 applicable to all cases involving a false indication of origin of the goods or identity of the producer, manufacturer, or merchant.

Similar efforts tending to strengthen the stipulations of the Convention, and making obligatory on the contracting countries the repression of the most important and frequent cases of unfair competition, were made by the International Chamber of Commerce,[3] the French and German groups of the International Association for

1. See resolutions of Experts, in *Actes de la Conférence de La Haye*, pp. 98 ff.
2. See *supra*, § 414.
3. See resolutions of the Chamber at the congresses of Rome (1923), Paris (1924), and Brussels (1925), in *Actes de la Conférence de La Haye*, pp. 95–96.

the Protection of Industrial Property,[1] and the International Association at its Zürich Congress in 1925.[2]

§ **483. New provisions of the Convention.** The substance of the above resolutions adopted by the experts was proposed by the International Bureau and the Dutch administration, as well as by the British administration, at the Conference of The Hague in 1925, in the form of an amendment to article 10*b*. Similar amendments covering a broader field of unfair competition were proposed by the French, German, and Italian delegations. After elaborate discussions [3] the following revised text of article 10*b* was adopted:

> Les pays contractants sont tenus d'assurer aux ressortissants de l'Union une protection effective contre la concurrence déloyale.
>
> Constitue un acte de concurrence déloyale tout acte de concurrence contraire aux usages honnêtes en matière industrielle ou commerciale.
>
> Notamment devront être interdits:
>
> 1° tous faits quelconques de nature à créer une confusion par n'importe quel moyen avec les produits d'un concurrent;
>
> 2° les allégations fausses, dans l'exercice du commerce, de nature à discréditer les produits d'un concurrent.

The first paragraph is made up of the old text of article 10*b*, with the substitution of the words "sont tenus" for the words "s'engagent," the former being more expressive of the idea that the contracting countries are bound to afford effective protection against unfair competition to the "ressortissants" of the Union.[4] Under the new text, as under the old, the engagement of each country is absolute and unconditional. Foreigners are to be protected, whether or not they are domiciled or doing business in the country where protection is claimed.[5] No condition of reciprocity whatsoever is to be demanded, the extent of protection in the country where the repression of an act of unfair competition is sought being independent of the extent of protection afforded in the country of origin.[6]

1. See *Travaux du Groupe Français* (1919–1922), pp. 104–105, 147 ff. On the work of the German group, see *Propriété Industrielle* (1923), p. 192, and *Actes de la Conférence de La Haye*, p. 96.

2. See *Actes de la Conférence de La Haye*, p. 97.

3. *Ibid.*, pp. 252, 349, 350, 472, 525, 546, 578–581.

4. *Ibid.*, p. 253.

5. Decision of the Reichsgericht, March 3, 1905, protecting an American nonresident in Germany (60 *Entsch. Reichsg., Zivils.*, 217); also decision of the Reichsgericht, Oct. 27, 1905 (12 *Blatt für Patent-, Muster- und Zeichenwesen*, p. 209).

6. See decision of the Hans. Oberlandesgericht, Feb. 29, 1904, protecting the American firm of Steinway & Sons (*Propriété Industrielle*, 1905, p. 111); also decision of the Reichsgericht, Jan. 22, 1912 (*Propriété Industrielle*, 1912, p. 148).

The second and third paragraphs are the new additions to the article. They purport to establish uniform international legislation affording a minimum of protection to the persons entitled to the benefits of the Convention, without prejudice to broader protection by the municipal law of each country.

The second paragraph, especially, contains a definition of unfair competition. It was adopted as proposed by the International Bureau over a more explicit definition proposed by the French delegation,[1] notwithstanding the doubts of several delegations as to the utility of inserting in the Convention such a vague definition which might cause difficulties of application. Indeed, defining unfair competition as competition contrary to honest practices is begging the question, which is: When may an act of competition be considered contrary to honest practices? The value, then, of this provision lies in superposing a broad and comprehensive conception of unfair competition on the particular cases enumerated in the third paragraph. It is thus made clear that those cases constitute only certain aspects of unfair competition on which a common agreement was reached by the contracting countries, and that the latter should be guided in their municipal legal order by the general principle that all dishonest practices in commercial and industrial matters should be repressed as acts of unfair competition. This idea is reinforced by the word "notamment" of the third paragraph, which means that the acts enumerated therein are only some, not all, that should be prohibited.

§ **484. Forms of law of unfair competition.** The most serious difficulty at the Conference was in reaching an agreement as to the acts which should always and everywhere be considered as acts of unfair competition, and be repressed as such. It was generally agreed that the enumeration in article 10*b* of the acts which every country would be bound to repress did not imply an obligation on the part of the contracting countries to enact special legislation for this purpose; it was sufficient that such repression would be secured by general legislation or by the decisions of the courts.[2] It is impossible, indeed, to provide by hard and fast rules against all the forms that the Proteus of unfair competition may take. Even if a statute may be passed to crystallize certain rules admitted by the courts, a gen-

1. "Tous les actes contraires à la loi, aux usages commerciaux ou à l'equité." See *Actes de la Conférence de La Haye*, p. 475.

2. See *Actes de la Conférence de La Haye*, p. 472.

eral principle is always necessary to take care of the unforeseen methods that unfair competition may adopt in the future. In France, Belgium, Italy, the Netherlands, and Switzerland, the Civil Code contains the general principle under which all cases of unfair competition have been brought. In Great Britain, the British dominions and colonies, and in the United States, a general principle has been worked out gradually by the courts. On the contrary, in Germany, Austria, Hungary, Denmark, Norway, Sweden, Poland, and Greece, special legislation provides specifically for various acts of unfair competition.

It was rightly held in Germany that unfair competition, in the meaning of article 10*b* of the Convention, is not to be understood as limited to the specific acts reached by the provisions of the special act against unfair competition. This act, as well as other legal provisions tending to repress acts of unfair trading, may be invoked by foreigners by virtue of article 10*b* of the Convention. The general rule of section 826 of the German Civil Code, concerning acts against good morals, may be applicable in this respect.[1]

§ **485. Theory of law of unfair competition.** Whatever the form of repression of acts of unfair competition may be, there should be a clear understanding of the theory of the law of unfair competition, and of what is to be accomplished with it. One of the Polish delegates at the Conference of The Hague, Mr. Zoll, Professor of Law at the University of Cracow, made a most illuminating statement on this matter, which is so much in agreement with the theory advanced on several occasions here, and which seems so to have influenced the decisions of the Conference, that it should be summarized in this place.[2] The present writer feels bound to take one exception only in regard to the statement in question. Mr. Zoll agrees that unfair competition does injury to the buying public, as well as to competing producers, manufacturers, or merchants. But he distinguishes the acts of unfair competition which injure the interests of the buying public from those infringing the interests of competitors, and argues that the former are outside the scope of the Convention and should be left entirely to the domain of municipal law.

1. Decisions of the Reichsgericht of Oct. 27, 1905 (12 *Blatt für Patent-, Muster- und Zeichenwesen*, p. 209); of Jan. 22, 1912, and July 11, 1913 (*Propriété Industrielle*, 1912, p. 148; 1914, p. 5). Also Lau, *Der Anschlusz des deutschen Reiches an die Internationale Union*, p. 135; Osterrieth und Axster, *Pariser Konvention*, pp. 219–220.

2. See *Actes de la Conférence de La Haye*, pp. 473–474.

He mentions as such acts false advertisements, all kinds of oral assertions or descriptions calculated to mislead the buying public as to the quality, kind, or value of the merchandise. But the attempted distinction is hardly possible. Many acts which mislead the public as to the quality or value of goods may also infringe the interests of competitors.[1] Likewise acts tending primarily to pass off goods of one person for those of another, or acts in disparagement of competitors or of their goods, may also deceive the public as to the value, or quality, or even the kind of goods. Besides, it is not clear why protection of the interests of manufacturers or traders alone is within the purpose of the Convention. The latter attempts by common principles and rules to establish an international legal order in which all interests concerned may be protected.

Mr. Zoll builds up his theory of unfair competition by asking himself, rightly, the question: What are the interests that should be protected by provisions on unfair competition? He answers: Business establishments of all kinds, manufacturing industries and commercial houses, and, in a deeper sense, the attractive force that the various business establishments exercise on the buying public, because this force is an intangible kind of property which determines the value of each business. This attractive force is the subject of a right, and is to be protected. In Anglo-American legal terminology, this is the reputation and the goodwill of a business — the business relations which constitute one of the various interests of substance that are recognized and protected by the law.

This legally protected interest may be looked at from the point of view of its infringements, like any other property interest. Mr. Zoll urges that the reputation and goodwill of a business may be infringed in the two ways in which all property rights may be infringed, and against which the Roman Law provided the two kinds of remedies, actions *in rem* and actions *in personam* (especially *ex delicto*). As other property may be appropriated or encroached upon, so likewise goodwill may be stolen. This may be done by any act causing a confusion between the goods of the business concern that possesses goodwill, and the goods of another. Such confusion

1. See, for instance, decision of the Reichsgericht, May 14, 1912, and of the Hans. Oberlandsgericht, April 2, 1912 (*Blatt für Patent-, Muster- und Zeichenwesen*, 1913, pp. 163, 317), concerning the use of foreign designs and names for national products in order to satisfy prejudices of the public in favor of foreign products. There is in such cases deception of the public, as well as injury to the commerce of a foreign country.

may be caused by the use or imitation of the other's mark, name, descriptions, indications of origin, designations, labels, signs, get-up, wrappings, and so forth.

But the goodwill of a business may be impaired also by acts which do not constitute encroachments on it, that is, do not cause confusion between the goods of one producer and those of another, as all property rights may be damaged by torts. Acts that impair goodwill are those that diminish the attractive force of a business concern, or its value, and cause injury to it by various means, such as slander, disparagement, disclosure of trade secrets, interference with contracts, and the like.

Mr. Zoll's statement [1] fairly describes what the courts in the common law countries, and in France and other continental countries, are actually doing in many cases of unfair competition, although the theories professed by the courts and the principles from which the law of unfair competition is deduced are different and leave much to be desired from the point of view of clarity.[2] The proposition that the goodwill of a business is a property interest, which is to be taken into account and protected in the whole scheme of interests pro-

1. See the same theory in more developed form in an article by Mr. Zoll, in *Propriété Industrielle* (1927), pp. 64 ff.

2. In Vogue Co. *c.* Thompson-Hudson Co. (1924), 300 Fed. 509, 512, the Court held that no actual market competition between A and B is necessary for the existence of "unfair competition." "The invocation of equity," the Court said, "rests more vitally upon the unfairness. If B represents that his goods are made by A, and if damage therefrom to A is to be seen, we are aware of no consideration which makes it controlling whether the damage to A will come from market competition with some article which A is then manufacturing or will come in some other way." This case is supposed to have settled the law of unfair competition in the United States, as covering cases not only of taking away another's business and goodwill, but also of causing damage to it in any other way. See *Bulletin of U. S. Trade Mark Ass'n* (1924), XIX, 291, 293; and *Columbia Law Review* (1925), XXV, 199. See also case of Yale Electric Corp. *v.* Robertson (1928), 26 F. (2d) 972.

The French theory is that confusion between the products of two competitors is the basis of unfair competition, and that whenever there is injury to a business without confusion, the action is one for damages under article 1382 of the Civil Code, and not one of unfair competition. See Pouillet, *Traité des Marques*, pp. 716 ff.

A German theory sees in unfair competition an injury to the right of personality forming the basis of business activity. See Kohler, *Der unlautere Wettbewerb* (Berlin-Leipzig, 1914), pp. 17 ff.

A Belgian writer, Moreau, in *Traité de la Concurrence Illicite* (Bruxelles-Paris, 1904), pp. 40–41, comes very near to the theory in the text by defining unlawful competition as any act which injures a right derived from an industrial or commercial organization. He maintains that such organization is manifested by the commercial name, designations, names and forms of products, indications of origin of merchandise, the credit and reputation of the establishment, sources of supply and modes of access to the public, methods of manufacture, contracts with employees, etc.

tected by the law, can hardly be denied. It is now generally recognized in the common law countries.[1] It would seem, then, that the division of acts of unfair competition into acts of appropriation of the goodwill and acts causing damage to it (without appropriation), is a convenient one, clarifying the whole field and affording an infallible guide for the application of the general rules of law and the remedies admitted in respect to other interests of substance.

§ **486. Acts creating confusion, as unfair competition.** In the light of these general considerations the acts referred to in the third paragraph of article 10*b* may now be dealt with.

The first category consists of "all kinds of acts of such a nature as to create confusion by any means whatsoever with the goods of a competitor." This covers almost the whole field of acts of encroachment upon, or appropriation of, the goodwill of a business. It is a general clause, which prohibits all palming off of the goods of one producer, manufacturer, or merchant for those of another. It is explained in the *procès-verbaux* of the Conference that the means by which such confusion is caused are marks, registered or not, commercial names, names of business houses, titles of printed matter, get-up of articles, form of wrappings, — in brief, all signs used by a manufacturer or merchant for distinguishing his trade or merchandise from that of his competitors, — and also allegations referring to the origin of the products or merchandise. It was proposed at the Conference to enumerate certain means by which confusion is produced. But the Committee of Research, to which all the proposals concerning article 10*b* were referred, reported against such enumeration, which might give rise to restrictive interpretations.[2] It follows that all acts causing confusion are prohibited, whatever the means used may be.

The Belgian delegation declared at the Conference of The Hague that, under the provisions of the Belgian Trade Mark Law, the distinctive badges which may be registered as trade marks enjoy only the protection granted by such registration. Consequently, such badges are not protected at all if they are not registered. The trade-

1. Hopkins, *The Law of Trade Marks, Trade Names and Unfair Competition*, pp. 45 ff.; Nims, *The Law of Unfair Business Competition*, pp. 33 ff. In the civil law countries this recognition has not been achieved, the theory being determined by the existing state of the law. See Pouillet, *Traité des Marques*, pp. 716 ff.; Pichot, *De la Concurrence Déloyale et de la Contrefaçon*, pp. 299 ff.

2. See *Actes de la Conférence de La Haye*, p. 476.

mark notion of the Belgian law is very broad, extending to get-up, wrappings, form, receptacle, and the like, of goods. Foreigners, therefore, like nationals, cannot claim protection of these elements under the law against unfair competition. Certain delegations expressed the hope at the Conference that the Belgian law might be amended on this question.[1]

The confusion caused by an act of unfair competition may have to do with the person of a merchant or producer, the business house, or the products or merchandise. The provision of article 10*b* under consideration was so drawn as to refer only to confusion as to the products or merchandise.[2] Article 10*b* speaks only of "produits," but this term was unanimously interpreted by the Conference as meaning products and merchandise, that is, goods produced by a manufacturer as well as goods sold or offered for sale by a merchant.[3]

An act causing confusion between the products of two producers, an act, for instance, of appropriation of the goodwill of a business, may be performed in good faith as well as in bad faith, as is true in cases of encroachments upon, or appropriation of, other property rights. In both cases, the goodwill of the business in question is taken away. The provision of article 10*b* under consideration rightly makes no distinction between the two classes of cases. It looks solely to the fact of confusion, prohibiting it whether it is caused by fraud or not. The Italian delegation wished to restrict the provision to cases where the acts of confusion are performed with the purpose of stealing the goodwill of a competitor's business. It was argued against this proposal that the fact alone of such confusion constitutes a state of things contrary to honest usages of the trade, and that the acts of unfair competition accomplished in good faith become unlawful at the moment the wrongdoer persists in doing them with knowledge of the confusion. It was agreed, however, by the Conference that the remedies to be granted in cases of *bona fide* acts of confusion are to be determined by the municipal law of each country.[4]

§ 487. Discrediting a competitor's goods as unfair competition. The second category of acts enumerated in article 10*b* are "false

1. *Actes de la Conférence de La Haye*, pp. 476, 580.
2. See the express understanding of the Conference in this respect, in *Actes de la Conférence de La Haye*, p. 476.
3. *Actes de la Conférence de La Haye*, p. 579.
4. *Ibid.*, pp. 476–477.

allegations, in the course of trade, of such a nature as to discredit the goods of a competitor." These are clearly acts that injure the reputation or goodwill of a business, although they do not necessarily involve the taking away of another's goodwill. But they are by no means the only acts that result in such injury. This provision is not as broad as that of the previous category, and leaves out many injurious acts. For the goodwill of a business may be impaired by the disclosure of trade secrets and confidential business relations, by unfair interference with a competitor's contracts, by deceptive advertising, by false advertisements of liquidation or bankruptcy,[1] by selling goods at a lower price than that at which they were obtained from a competitor and thus causing their value to fall in the public's opinion,[2] by false appropriation of medals by competitors,[3] and so on.

It was possible to agree at the Conference of The Hague on only the first kind of injuries to goodwill, which are most important from the point of view of international trade. For the other acts of unfair competition of the same class, there is the general undertaking by each country to see that no act against honest practices shall be permitted.

The provision under consideration is much broader than mere trade slander or trade libel under the common law, or defamation under the continental law. It covers all cases of "dénigrement" of the goods of a competitor. In the common law countries the strict interpretation of the words "slander" and "libel," in their application to trade and business, did not afford such elastic legal material as the general provisions of the Civil codes of continental countries against acts inflicting injury upon another. In "libel" or "slander" there must be fraudulent intent and special damage.[4] As it was pointed out at the Conference of The Hague, the conception of "dénigrement" does not involve a fraudulent intent. The mere fact of discrediting the goods of a competitor by allegations which are untrue constitutes an act of unfair competition.[5]

1. See Belgian and French cases, in *Propriété Industrielle* (1903), p. 110.

2. See Belgian cases referred to by Capitaine, in *Propriété Industrielle* (1908), p. 160.

3. See Italian case, in *Propriété Industrielle* (1912), p. 112. Also Pouillet, *Traité des Marques*, pp. 806 ff.

4. See Nims, *The Law of Unfair Business Competition*, pp. 388 ff. Hopkins, *The Law of Trade Marks, Trade Names and Unfair Competition*, pp. 53 ff.

5. See *Actes de la Conférence de La Haye*, p. 477. See also the various cases of "dénigrement" in Pouillet, *Traité des Marques*, pp. 961 ff.

There may be acts of defamation or disparagement of the person of the competitor or of his business house. Such acts are not within the provision under consideration, which concerns explicitly the discrediting of the *goods* of another. In France, comparing the goods of one producer with those of another is repressed as unfair competition, even though the allegations are wholly or partially true; for instance, advertising that the goods of A are much superior to those of B. Such acts do not come under the above provision of article 10*b*, inasmuch as they are not false.[1]

Statements discrediting the goods of another are those that refer to an alleged infringement of a patent, or design, the infringing of a trade mark, and the like, also disparaging statements as to the quality, origin, nature, or characteristics of the goods. The provision under consideration covers all false allegations, however made, whether by oral statements, letters, advertisements, price-lists, or any other means.

The Conference did not agree to enumerate in article 10*b* acts of deceptive advertising and interference with contracts with employees. The law is not yet settled on these matters in the various countries.[2]

§ **488. Unfair competition in news.** An attempt was made at the Conference of The Hague to enumerate among the various acts of unfair competition which should be prohibited in the contracting countries the unauthorized reproduction of press information and news ("nouvelles du jour"). With the modern organization of news-gathering and news-distributing by agencies operating in more than one country, the subject of protecting the property or commercial value of news would seem to call for international legislation.[3] The conferences for the adoption and revision of the International Copyright Convention refused to include press information and news in the protection of literary and artistic works secured by this Convention. Indeed, a specific provision of the Convention revised at Berlin in 1908 declares that the protection of the Convention "does not apply to 'nouvelles du jour ou aux divers' which have the character of simple press information" (art. 9, sec. 3). The Berlin Conference

1. This was explicitly admitted at the Conference. See *Actes de la Conférence de La Haye*, p. 477.

2. See *Actes de la Conférence de La Haye*, pp. 477–478.

3. See Hudson, "International Protection of Property in News," in *American Journal of International Law* (1928), XXII, 385; also a long and excellent study on the subject in article: "La Convention de Berne et le Droit de Reproduction en Matière des Journaux et Publications Périodiques," in *Le Droit d'Auteur* (1926), pp. 73 ff.

intimated that dishonest practices in this respect were a matter of unfair competition, as they involved the taking away of commercial property rather than piracy of an author's creation.[1] The International Congress of the Information Agencies, held at Berne in 1924, had adopted a resolution to this effect:

1. That an international understanding should be reached for the unification of legislation in the matter of property in press information, on the basis of the following principle: all news obtained by a newspaper or news agency, whatever its form or content or whatever the means of transmission, shall be regarded as the property of such newspaper or agency for so long as it retains its commercial value;

2. That in the enumeration of acts of unfair competition to be inserted in article 10*b*[of the Convention of 1883–1911], there be explicitly included the reproduction or utilization, with the purpose of gain, of news, especially political, commercial, economic and financial information.[2]

The International Bureau and the Dutch administration felt that a proposal to include the above provision in article 10*b* of the International Property Convention would meet with opposition from many countries, and that it seemed premature. Such a proposal was therefore not made by them at the Conference of The Hague; but the delegation of the Serb-Croat-Slovene State urged the insertion of a provision protecting the commercial value of news from acts of unfair competition. The sub-committee, in refusing to adopt it, declared that the question was outside the scope of the Convention. This is in direct opposition to the opinion of the Conference on the Copyright Convention. The latter opinion seems sound. News represents nowadays a considerable commercial value, as was pointed out by the above-mentioned delegation in its declaration at the final adoption of article 10*b*, supported by the Spanish delegation.[3] In view of the above stand of the sub-committee, however, it must be concluded that the provisions of article 10*b* cannot be invoked for the protection of news from acts of unfair competition, and that the municipal law of each country governs exclusively in this respect.[4]

In 1926 and 1927, on the initiative of the League of Nations, a number of meetings of news agency representatives, directors of press bureaus, and journalists, respectively, were held to discuss

1. See *Actes de la Conférence de Berlin* (Berne, 1909), pp. 251, 316–317.
2. See *Actes de la Conférence de La Haye*, pp. 100–101.
3. *Ibid.*, pp. 253–254, 350–351, 478, 580.
4. On the laws of the various countries, see *League of Nations, Document C. 352, M. 126* (1927), pp. 17 ff.

various technical questions. The question of property in news formed the subject of discussions, and, as a culmination thereof, a draft law was elaborated by the Secretariat of the League of Nations and placed before the Conference of Press Experts assembled at Geneva in August, 1927. As the basic principle of this law was the recognition of a temporary property right in news, it gave rise to various objections at that Conference, and caused the failure of all efforts to arrive at an international understanding on the subject.[1]

§ **489. Sanctions of provisions of article 10*b*.** Article 10*b* provides that the contracting countries are bound ("sont tenus") to assure to persons entitled to the benefits of the Convention effective protection against unfair competition. It also defines unfair competition, and enumerates certain categories of acts of unfair competition which should be prohibited. But it does not specify what is to be regarded as effective protection, or how the various acts of unfair competition are to be prohibited; nor does it stipulate, as in articles 9 and 10, specific sanctions for the enforcement of its provisions.

At the Conference of The Hague it was understood by the sub-committee that effective sanctions for the repression of unfair competition should comprise injunctions, actions for damages, and criminal penalties in case of violation of rights revealing a criminal character. But the sub-committee, finding it impossible to make uniform the legal remedies in all the countries, adopted a general provision in the first paragraph of article 10*c* of the Convention, that "the contracting countries undertake to assure to the 'ressortissants' of the other countries of the Union appropriate legal remedies to repress effectively all acts referred to in articles 9, 10, and 10*b*."

The sub-committee had also adopted a provision that the stipulation of article 9 concerning seizure should be applicable to goods, whereof the sale or offer for sale would constitute an act of unfair competition. This provision was struck out by the Committee of the Whole, on the objection of the Italian, American, and Australian delegations, which thought that it was dangerous to the interested parties. Moreover, the Italian delegation declared, on the final adoption of article 10*c*, that it interpreted article 10*b* as imposing, not the granting of an action for damages, but only of an injunction, for acts performed in good faith.[2]

1. See Hudson, "International Protection of Property in News," *American Journal of International Law* (1928), XXII, 385, 388–389.

2. See *Actes de la Conférence de La Haye*, pp. 480, 525, 580.

In an investigation made by the International Bureau of Berne in 1925 of the question how far the sanctions specified in article 9 are applicable to the repression of acts of unfair competition in the different countries, it was found that in no country was seizure on importation available. Judicial seizure in the interior of the country was possible in Austria, Czechoslovakia, Greece, Hungary, Norway, and Syria and Lebanon, and in the non-unionist country, Bolivia. In many countries, besides the ordinary civil remedies, fine and imprisonment are imposed by law on persons liable for acts of unfair competition.[1]

§ 490. Who may seek repression of acts of unfair competition. Article 10*b* contains no provision concerning the parties who may seek the repression of acts of unfair competition. Since the remedies themselves are to be determined exclusively by the law of each country, all questions of parties and procedure in respect to such remedies are to be governed by municipal law. Yet, in view of the nature of acts of unfair competition, a certain latitude of the law in this respect, analogous to that prevailing in the cases referred to in article 10 of the Convention, is necessary. Indeed, the ordinary principle of granting a remedy to the party whose interests are injured is not sufficient in cases of unfair competition. An unfair practice may not be directly or immediately injurious to the interests of a person, and no damage may be shown, in certain cases, as being caused to this person by such practice. Nevertheless, indirectly, or in the long run, such injury and damage will be suffered. It is important to stop the unfair practice before such injury or damage is done, or to permit legal proceedings by persons interested in the discontinuance of such practice. It is also good policy to allow action by professional associations and syndicates created for the purpose of protecting the interests of their members.

The International Bureau of Berne had found in an investigation made in 1925 that a few countries, either by special legislation or by the general rules of law, permitted any interested party, in general, to take legal action against acts of unfair competition, while most of the countries restricted such action to persons showing an injury or damage. Nor was there any uniformity on the question of allowance of action by associations and syndicates.[2] At the Conference

1. See *Actes de la Conférence de La Haye*, pp. 151 ff.; also *Propriété Industrielle* (1925), pp. 44 ff.

2. See *Propriété Industrielle* (1925), pp. 139 ff.; also *Actes de la Conférence de La Haye*, pp. 160 ff.

of The Hague it was proposed by the Bureau and the Dutch administration to insert a provision in article 10*b* stipulating that

> either an individual or a juristic person suffering damage [*lésée*], and also, in cases of suits for an injunction, or penal action, the interested syndicates and associations, duly constituted in their country of origin, shall have the right to bring an action, or intervene, for all acts of unfair competition.[1]

This provision, sound so far as the action or intervention of syndicates and associations was concerned, was retrogressive in respect to individuals and juristic persons, inasmuch as a number of countries permitted action to all interested parties, in general. This part of the provision was not adopted by the Conference. The part, however, concerning syndicates and associations was included in the general provision of the second paragraph of article 10*c*, cited in another place.[2] This contains an engagement of the contracting countries to pass laws giving to syndicates and associations recourse to judicial proceedings or applications to the administrative authorities. This alternative implies that the remedies against acts of unfair competition may be administrative, such as seizure or prohibition of importation of the goods.[3] In order that a syndicate or association entitled to the benefits of the Convention may resort to the proceedings mentioned, it should represent industries or trades "interested." This condition, as well as the final phrase ("so far as the law. . ."), was inserted with a view to meeting the remarks made in the sub-committee, that syndicates and associations should be allowed such proceedings only when they are directly interested, or when the repression of certain acts of unfair competition presents a general interest and not when purely personal interests are in question, such as the infringement of marks or commercial names.[4]

§ **491. Progress of law of unfair competition in the various countries.** There is no denying the fact that the law of unfair co npetition has progressed rapidly since the beginning of this century, when the first international stipulation in respect to acts of unfair competition was agreed upon. The stupendous growth of industry, commerce, and communications in the interior of the various countries, as well

1. See *Actes de la Conférence de La Haye*, p. 255.
2. See *supra*, p. 582.
3. See comment on this by the Committee of the Whole, in *Actes de la Conférence de La Haye*, p. 525.
4. See *Actes de la Conférence de La Haye*, pp. 479, 526.

as among themselves, and the keen competition resulting therefrom, multiplied immensely the methods by which, on the one hand, a producer, manufacturer, or trader may create an association with the indefinite, uncertain, and scattered body of his customers, and, on the other, the ways in which goodwill may be taken away, injured, and destroyed. In all the countries, earnest efforts are being made in recent years to protect the business relations of competitors without destroying competition, and to defeat the frauds committed by business parasites. In some of them it was found that commercial affairs moved and changed too rapidly for the slow process of the growth of law by court decisions through experience and development by logical deduction, and that the interests clamoring for protection should be satisfied by special legislation reaching all known or foreseen acts of unfair competition. This is also, perhaps, one of the phases of the general faith in the efficacy of the conscious effort to improve law, and to improve society through law, which constitutes one of the chief characteristics of twentieth-century legal history.[1]

§ **492. Countries possessing special legislation.** Germany took the lead in this direction with the two laws of May 12, 1894 and May 27, 1896,[2] the latter of which afforded for the first time effective remedies against unfair advertising, injuries to goodwill, treated in Anglo-American law as libel or slander of title ("Anschwärzung, üble Nachrede"), interference with trade or business secrets, and so forth. This act was superseded by the Act of June 7, 1909,[3] a most excellent piece of legislative work. In its first article the general principle is announced that a petition for injunction and an action for damages may be brought against any person who, for the purpose of competition, commits in business acts contrary to honest practices. Following this general principle, various acts of unfair competition are specified and prohibited, such as deceptive and unfair advertising, selling below a fixed price under certain conditions, in-

1. On the law of unfair competition in the various countries, see an excellent research published in the review, *Gesetzgebung und Rechtspraxis des Auslandes*, in a series of articles in 1926, 1927, and 1928. These articles have been reproduced in *La Propriété Industrielle* (1928), pp. 38 ff., 60 ff., 81 ff., 110 ff., and 137 ff. See also, on the Czechoslovakian law, *Propriété Industrielle* (1928), p. 229.

2. "Gesetz zum Schutz der Warenbezeichnungen" (*Reichsgesetzblatt*, 1894, p. 441); "Gesetz zur Bekämpfung des unlauteren Wettbewerbs" (*Reichsgesetzblatt*, 1896, p. 145).

3. "Gesetz gegen den unlauteren Wettbewerb" (*Reichsgesetzblatt*, 1909, p. 499).

terference with contracts with employees, discrediting the goods, person, or business establishment of another person, acts causing confusion with the name, the firm, or trade name of another, and misuse of business or trade secrets.[1] Whenever such acts are done in bad faith, criminal sanctions also are imposed. For an injunction against most of these acts, suit may be brought by professional associations constituted for the protection of industrial interests.[2]

The substance of the German act was adopted in Greece in 1914,[3] in Austria [4] and Hungary [5] in 1923, and in Latvia [6] and Czechoslovakia [7] in 1927. Similar enactments reaching various acts of unfair competition were passed in Denmark,[8] Sweden,[9] Turkey,[10] and Norway,[11] only the last of which follows the German law in containing a general principle prohibiting all acts contrary to honest practices as acts of unfair competition. The Spanish Act of Industrial Property of 1902,[12] in article 131, defines unlawful competition as all attempts aiming to obtain unduly the benefit of the advantages of an industrial or commercial reputation created by another person's efforts. The act enumerates in article 132 (and in articles 138–145) several acts of unlawful competition, some of which seem not to tally

1. Under this act, and by virtue of article 10*b* of the Convention, the Reichsgericht by its decision of June 4, 1920, forbade the use of the name "Norwegian smoked sardines" to German and Norwegian dealers as prejudicial to French canners of sardines, on the ground that "sardines" are found only near the French, Spanish, and Portuguese coasts, and that the fish canned by Norwegians were of a different kind and of much poorer quality, and that, because of such practice, the public might come to dislike sardines generally. It was held also that it is not necessary that all the public should be deceived; it is sufficient if a part of the public is misled (99 *Entsch. Reichsg., Zivils.*, 131).

2. The best and latest exposition of the law of unfair competition in Germany is found in Rosenthal, *Wettbewerbsgesetz nebst den materiellen Bestimmungen des Warenzeichengesetzes, systematisch erläutert*, 6th ed. (Berlin, 1927).

3. "**Κώδηξ Θέμιδος**" (1914), p. 34. This law was amended by the Laws of June 6, 1926 and Nov. 12, 1927 ("**Ἐφημερὶς τῆς Κυβερνήσεως**," 1926, p. 1628, and, 1927, p. 1819).

4. Act No. 531 of Sep. 26, 1923 (*Bundesgesetzblatt*, 1923, II, 1717).

5. Act No. 5 of 1923 (*Ungarische Reichsgesetzsammlung*, 1923, p. 31).

6. Act of Oct. 4, 1927 (*Propriété Industrielle*, 1928, p. 105).

7. Act of July 15, 1927 (*Propriété Industrielle*, 1928, p. 131).

8. The previous acts of 1918 and 1921 were superseded by Act No. 98 of March 29, 1924, modified by Act No. 107 of April 9, 1926 (*Lovtidende for Danmark*, 1924, p. 603; and, 1926, p. 589).

9. Act No. 446 of June 19, 1919 (*Svensk Förfatningssamling*, 1919. II, 1009).

10. Articles 56–65 of the new Turkish Commercial Code (*Propriété Industrielle*, 1928, p. 141).

11. Law No. 11 of July 7, 1922 (*Norsk Lovtidende*, 1922, p. 287), amended by the Act of March 12, 1926 (*Propriété Industrielle*, 1927, p. 193).

12. Act of May 16, 1902 (*Boletin de Legislación*, 1902, II, 88), also *Recueil de Législation* (Bureau International de Berne), V, 161, 204.

entirely with the definition of the preceding article. Besides, the Royal Decree of November 28, 1925,[1] interprets article 132 as merely illustrative of the principle of article 131, and specifies certain other acts which are to be considered as unfair competition. In Colombia, also, the Law of December 10, 1914,[2] in articles 51 and 52, provides that a petition for injunction and an action for damages may be brought for all acts of unfair competition. But the definition of unfair competition of article 51 is narrow, being limited to acts of bad faith purporting to produce confusion between the products of two producers, and acts discrediting a rival business establishment.

The Polish Law of August 2, 1926,[3] prepared by Professor Zoll, whose theory of unfair competition was dealt with above,[4] differs from the German law in the basic principle. It does not contain the general rule of the German act against acts contrary to honest practices. The rule of fair dealing and honesty in commercial transactions, which forms the basis of the German law, is replaced by the recognition of a property right in a business enterprise in the Polish law. Instead, therefore, of enumerating specific acts manifesting breaches of the rule of fair dealing, as in the German law, the Polish law distinguishes two classes of acts: those constituting an appropriation of, or encroachment upon, the above property right, and those inflicting damage thereon. In articles 1 and 2 are prohibited the usurpations of the right in question by all acts producing confusion between two competitors, whether done in bad or good faith. Article 3 contains a general prohibition of acts inflicting injury on the goodwill of a business, even though they do not produce confusion between two business establishments or their goods. But in order that such acts may be actionable, they must be due to the fault of the defendant, that is, to a failure to live up to the standards of commercial honesty. Such acts are: discrediting by false allegations the business of another, inciting the employees of the latter to neglect their duties, disclosing trade or business secrets, and the like.

§ 493. Countries deducing law of unfair competition from provisions of their Civil Codes. A number of countries possess no special legislation on unfair competition. The law on this subject is con-

1. *Boletin de Legislación* (1925), VI, 440.
2. *Leyes de Colombia* (1914), p. 237.
3. See *Propriété Industrielle* (1927), p. 8.
4. See *supra*, § 485. See also article by Professor Zoll, explaining the principles on which the law is based, in *Propriété Industrielle* (1927), pp. 64 ff.

stituted by a body of court decisions based on a general principle of law. In Belgium, Bulgaria, France, Italy, Japan, the Netherlands, Rumania, and Switzerland, this general principle is contained in a provision of their Civil Codes,[1] while in the United States and the British Commonwealth of Nations a general principle has been worked out gradually by the equity courts. In France, the courts, with a great power of adaptability, were able to work out a complete system of law of unfair competition, by applying the principle of articles 1382 and 1383 of the Civil Code to the ever-changing conditions of trade and industry. It is admitted that there is unfair competition whenever there is confusion caused between the products of two manufacturers or two traders; or when, though no confusion is caused, a rival establishment is discredited. But the basic rule is that of commercial loyalty, and to that the courts resort in any new case.[2] There exist, also, in France special laws repressing certain forms of unlawful competition from which especially the buying public is injured.[3]

The law of unfair competition of Belgium was worked out, and is in many respects to-day, like that of France. In Italy, the similar provision of the Civil Code did not supply as fecund a principle as in France. The Italian courts did not manifest the same qualities of adaptability. The provision of the Civil Code is considered as a corollary to other legal provisions establishing what is an unlawful act. There is a dispute as to this basis. However, a number of special legislative acts and of provisions of the Penal Code supply such a basis, by prohibiting and repressing various forms of unfair competition. Thus, the usual forms of unfair competition, those primarily concerning international trade, are reached in Italy, and the remedies available would seem to be adequate.[4]

1. The provisions of articles 1382 and 1383 of the Civil Code of France render a person liable for all damages caused to another by his acts or his negligence and imprudence. Equivalent provisions are found in the Belgian Civil Code (arts. 1382, 1383), Bulgarian Code of Obligations (sec. 56), Italian Civil Code (arts. 1151 f.), Japanese Civil Code (sec. 709), Dutch Civil Code (sec. 1401), Rumanian Civil Code (sec. 998), and Swiss Code of Obligations (articles 50 and following of the old Code of Obligations and articles 28, 48, and 49 of the Revised Code).

2. See Pouillet, *Traité des Marques*, pp. 715 ff. On the general principles, see *ibid.*, pp. 716–728. Also Pichot, *De la Concurrence Déloyale et de la Contrefaçon*, pp. 299 ff.

3. Laws regulating certain industries, repressing unlawful rises and falls of prices in the sale of merchandise, the usurpation of medals, etc. See Pichot, *De la Concurrence Déloyale*, pp. 233 ff.

4. See a good summary of the law of Belgium and Italy, in *Propriété Industrielle* (1928), pp. 39–40, 83–84.

In Japan, the provision of the Civil Code (sec. 709) speaks of the obligation for reparation of damages caused to the rights of another party, and it raises the question of "the right" which has been injured. Whether the goodwill of a business is a "right" does not seem to have been decided by the courts, and the decisions based on the above provision are conflicting. However, certain acts of unfair competition are repressed by the provisions of the Penal Code; such acts are the discrediting of another's business by false allegations, interference with customers by threats or forcible means, and deceptive advertisement.[1]

In the Netherlands, the provision of the Civil Code (sec. 1401) differs from that of the French Code in restricting liability to cases of "unlawful acts" causing damage to another. Until recently the Supreme Court of the Netherlands interpreted this provision restrictively, as applying only to cases where a legal right was encroached upon, or a legal duty of the actor violated. A decision of the Hooge Raad (Supreme Court) of January 31, 1919, for the first time adopted a more liberal interpretation by extending liability to cases where the act causing the damage is contrary to good morals, or shows a lack of due care.[2]

In Switzerland, articles 50 and following of the old Federal Code and articles 28, 48, and 49 of the Revised Code of Obligations established the same principle as the provisions of the French Civil Code, and the courts were able to work out a fairly complete system of law of unfair competition.[3] The law of Bulgaria and Rumania also resembles that of France.[4]

In Esthonia, Finland, and Lithuania, the situation prevailing in the pre-war Russian regime has not yet been changed, with the result that the provisions of law against acts of unfair competition are very sparse and unsatisfactory. The Serb-Croat-Slovene State also has not yet established adequate protection of industry and commerce in this respect. In Russia, the new economic policy which allows scope for competition has not yet caused the enactment of

1. See *Propriété Industrielle* (1928), p. 84.
2. *Ibid.*, pp. 87–88; see also Notz," New Phases of Unfair Competition and Measures for its Suppression — National and International," *Yale Law Journal* (1921), XXX, 384, 388.
3. See Schuler, *Die Concurrence Déloyale*, pp. 33, 90 ff. Also *Propriété Industrielle* (1928), p. 139.
4. See *Propriété Industrielle* (1928), pp. 41–42, 112–113.

legal provisions against acts of unfair competition; some of these acts may be repressed under the provisions of the Penal Code.[1]

§ **494. Unfair competition in common law countries.** In the United States, the law of unfair competition, and in the British Empire, the passing-off actions, rest upon the basic principle that no man has the right to pass off his goods upon the public as and for the goods of another. This law is a case law, constituted by a body of judicial decisions, and is of comparatively recent birth and development. The basis of the law, as may be gathered from these decisions, is yet uncertain. The first decisions were decided on analogy to trade-mark cases. It is only gradually, and through the operation of the doctrine of *stare decisis*, that three principal grounds for an action before the courts have been admitted: (*a*) the promotion of honest and fair dealing; (*b*) the protection of the purchasing public against deceit; and (*c*) the protection of rights and property of the individual.[2] On any of these grounds all forms of unfair competition may be repressed. The true basis, of course, of all actions ought to be the protection of business relations, and in this direction the recent cases seem to be tending.[3] Such a basis would cover also the cases of injury of the goodwill which are not considered a part of the law of unfair competition in the countries under consideration, but of the law relating to libel and slander.[4]

In the United States, Canada, and New Zealand the law of unfair competition has been reinforced by legislation dealing with unfair

1. See, on the laws of these countries, *Propriété Industrielle* (1928), pp. 60, 61, 86, 113, 137.

2. See Nims, *The Law of Unfair Competition and Trade Marks*, pp. 18 ff.

3. Vogue Co. *v.* Thompson-Hudson Co. (1924), 300 Fed. 509, 512; Walter *v.* Ashton (1902), 2 Ch. 282. See also a recent American case, Yale Electric Corp. *v.* Robertson (1928), 26 F. (2d), 972.

4. See Nims, *The Law of Unfair Competition*, pp. 470 ff. Kerly, *The Law of Trade Marks and Trade Name*, pp. 561 ff., 667 ff. See, also, on unfair competition and its late developments, an article by Amasa C. Paul, in *Saint-Louis Law Review* (1921), VI, 73.

Mr. Edward S. Rogers, a writer on unfair competition law in the United States, in a memorandum prepared for the Industrial Property Committee of the International Chamber, describing the common law system of trade marks and unfair competition, concludes that what is protected by the unfair competition law is "the reasonable expectation of future custom, the right to carry on a business without interference by a competitor's misrepresentation, fraud, threats, defamation, disparagement, enticement of employees, betrayal of confidential information, commercial bribery," etc. He gives to this branch of the law the general term "unfair trade," which includes any act, not necessarily fraudulent, which artificially interferes with the normal course of trade to the disadvantage of another.

This memorandum was communicated to the present writer by the kindness of Mr. Rogers.

competition acts. The Federal Trade Commission Act and the Anti-trust Act of 1914 in the United States[1] were followed by the Combines and Fair Prices Act and the Board of Commerce Act of 1919, in Canada,[2] and the Board of Trade Act of 1919 in New Zealand.[3] The annual reports of the Federal Trade Commission in the United States show various methods of unfair competition which have been condemned.[4] The Commission acts either by administrative pressure or by criminal prosecution. In Great Britain, the Merchandise Marks Act of 1887, as amended by the recent Act of 1926,[5] affords protection in certain cases of unfair competition.

§ **495. Law of unfair competition as supplement to law concerning various rights of industrial property.** Whatever may be the basis of the law of unfair competition, whether the promotion of honesty and fair dealing in commercial transactions or the protection of business relations, its relation to the law protecting the various specialized branches of industrial property is that of the genus to the species. Its function is to protect business relations and promote fair dealing, not only in cases which are outside the scope of the laws protecting the various rights of industrial property (patents, designs, models, trade marks, trade names, indications of origin), but also in cases where, for one reason or another, protection of these rights by particular laws is lacking. The definition of unfair competition in the new text of article 10*b*, as well as the provision concerning acts creating confusion by any means whatsoever with the goods of a competitor, is very broad and should be taken as completing the other provisions of the Convention concerning the various rights of industrial property.[6]

This broad conception of the law of unfair competition is admitted in Anglo-American law.[7] It is also admitted in many other coun-

1. XXXVIII *U. S. Stat. at Large*, 717, 730.

2. 9 & 10 Geo. V, c. 37, 45 (*Statutes of Canada*, 1919, pp. 231 and 297).

3. See especially section 13 (10 Geo. V, 1919, No. 15 in *Statutes of New Zealand*, 1919, p. 46).

4. Federal Trade Commission, *Annual Report* (1925), p. 14; (1926), p. 50; (1927), p. 87. No less than forty-four unfair methods of competition and violations of the Clayton Act are shown in the list of the report for 1927.

5. 50 & 81 Vict., c. 28, and 16 & 17 Geo. V, c. 53.

6. See decision of the President of the Republic of Cuba, Jan., 1926 (*Patent and Trade Mark Review*, 1926, XXIV, 226).

7. Kerly, *The Law of Trade Marks and Trade Name*, pp. 13 ff. See also p. 564: "... a case of passing-off is generally added as a second string to an action for infringement, and is frequently successful where the trade mark action proper breaks down." Also Nims,

tries. Foreigners who could not invoke the protection of other provisions of the Convention are protected by the law of unfair competition by virtue of article 10*b* of the Convention. Thus the American trade mark "Eversharp," which could not be protected as a trade mark in France, as not being registered in the United States (according to the erroneous interpretation of article 6 of the Convention),[1] was protected by the law of unfair competition.[2] In Switzerland, the agent of a foreign trade-mark owner was not allowed to sue for infringement of the trade mark, but it was held that he could sue for unfair competition.[3]

In Germany and Austria, the situation was different until recently. A non-registered trade mark was not protected at all. Registration was the only way of protecting trade marks. A case decided in 1912 in Germany indicates a new trend of judicial thought; protection was extended to a non-registered trade mark, used for fifteen years, against imitation accomplished with the purpose of taking away the good-will of the first user's business, by application of the provision of the Civil Code (sec. 826) concerning acts against good morals.[4] In another case, however, where no fraudulent purpose was shown, protection was refused.[5] In Austria, the recent act against unfair competition [6] changed the previous state of things by making (in sec. 9) the use of another's designations, which creates a confusion between the two competitors, an act of unfair competition. The Supreme Court of Austria has held that, irrespective of the provision of section 9 of the act, the use of another's non-registered mark is prohibited by the general provision of the first section concerning acts against honest practices. It has held also that non-

The Law of Unfair Competition and Trade Marks, pp. 1 ff.; Rogers, *Good Will, Trade Marks and Unfair Trading* (1914), p. 127.

1. See *supra*, §§ 371–373.

2. Wright *v.* Wahl Co., Court of Appeals of Paris, Dec. 27, 1924 (*Propriété Industrielle*, 1927, p. 18). A similar case is Ander, Kalman et Saxlehner *v.* Léoras, Tribunal of Lyon, May 1, 1907, concerning the mark "Hunyadi Janos" for Hungarian mineral waters (*Gazette des Tribunaux*, 1907, II, 395). See also Italian cases, in *Propriété Industrielle* (1914), p. 9; (1925), p. 81; (1926), p. 104; (1928), p. 209.

3. Moro *g.* Gebrüder Säuberli, Federal Tribunal, May 15, 1915 (41 *Arrêts Tr., Fed.* II, 281).

4. Reichsgericht, Dec. 12, 1912 (*Propriété Industrielle*, 1914, p. 5).

5. Reichsgericht, Feb. 14, 1913 (81 *Entsch. Reichsg., Zivils*, 330; 19 *Blatt für Patent-, Muster- und Zeichenwesen*, 285).

6. Act No. 531 of Sept. 26, 1923 (*Bundesgesetzblatt*, 1923, II, 1717).

registered trade marks or marks denied registration come under the provision of section 9 of the act.[1]

In Belgium to-day, distinctive badges which are admitted for registration as trade marks are not protected by the law of unfair competition.[2] A bill for the control of trade and the repression of unfair competition was laid before the Belgian Parliament in 1912, which would have modified the law on this point, but it has never been passed.[3]

§ **496. Unfair methods of competition in international trade.** The keen post-war economic struggle has accentuated and brought to the foreground another class of methods of unfair competition, practised especially in international trade, which do not concern the field of proprietary rights, but are caused by commercial combines, preferences in transportation, customs regulations, and various undesirable trade practices. Such methods of competition are adopted by the various countries striving for a share in international trade. Many of them are due to reasons of financial or economic policy, which leave no scope for general international agreement. Incidental discriminations against foreigners in this respect are unavoidable, and whenever they are contracted against, it is a matter of commercial bargaining. The effort of the Economic Committee of the League of Nations and of the International Chamber of Commerce to secure concerted action on certain questions of undesirable trade practices in international trade have proved unsuccessful.[4]

A study of the above questions, with a view to arriving at an international agreement for putting an end to certain phases of such international competition, was undertaken by the International Law Association at the Stockholm Conference of 1924[5] and the Vienna Conference of 1926. A number of resolutions were adopted at the latter Conference, as proposed by a committee, the convener of

1. Decision of Sept. 16, 1925 (*Die Rechtsprechung*, 1925, p. 155). See also article by Professor Adler, in *Propriété Industrielle* (1926), p. 99.

2. See *supra*, p. 703.

3. See article by Capitaine, in *Propriété Industrielle* (1912), pp. 127, 129; also "Unlawful Competition and Belgian Legislation," in *Digest No. 17* (International Chamber of Commerce, 1922).

4. See *Report of the Trade Barriers Committee, Brochure No. 44* (International Chamber of Commerce, 1926).

5. See Komar's paper, "National Control of Unfair Competition in International Commerce," in *Report of the Thirty-Third Conference of the International Law Association* (London, 1925), pp. 404 ff.

which was Mr. Borris M. Komar of New York.[1] The said committee was also instructed "to report at the next Conference of the Association a draft of an International Convention dealing with unfair preferences in the matters of transportation, commercial combines and customs duties, and unfair methods of competition in international commerce." The adoption of any such convention in the near future would seem to be very improbable.

1. *Report of the Thirty-Fourth Conference of the International Law Association* (London, 1927), pp. 652 ff.

SECTION VII

THE WORLD WAR AND THE UNIONS

CHAPTER XXXII

THE PROTECTION OF INDUSTRIAL PROPERTY DURING THE WAR

§ **497. The war did not dissolve the Union.** The outbreak of the World War raised the question of its effect on the Union for the Protection of Industrial Property. Of the twenty-two countries parties to the Convention of 1883, only seven — Denmark, Mexico, Norway, the Netherlands, Spain, Sweden, and Switzerland — remained neutral throughout the war. Of the restricted Union for the repression of false indications of origin only two member countries did not take part in the war — Spain and Switzerland. Out of the thirteen countries parties to the Arrangement of Madrid for the international registration of trade marks, four — Mexico, the Netherlands, Spain, and Switzerland — were not belligerents. The countries that took part in the war did not break off their relations at the same time, nor did they become enemy countries to all the powers of the other camp.[1]

1. See "La Protection Internationale de la Propriété Intellectuelle et la Guerre Mondiale," *Bureaux Internationaux Propriété Industrielle* (Berne, 1919), pp. 8–9. It appears that Brazil, the Dominican Republic, and Portugal did not declare war or break off relations with Austria-Hungary. The same is true for these countries, as well as Cuba and Japan, in regard to Bulgaria and Turkey. Belgium broke off its relations with Turkey, but not with Bulgaria. But Bulgaria and Turkey were not members of the Industrial Property Union before the war. Belgium, France, Great Britain, Japan, Morocco, Serbia, and Tunis on the one hand, and Austria-Hungary, and Germany on

In theory, it was questioned whether the war abrogated the Convention and the two Madrid Arrangements of the Union. Concerning all general international conventions, especially international unions to which neutral states also are parties, aside from an isolated opinion that they are abrogated between the belligerent countries as well as between these and neutral ones,[1] three different opinions were expressed. According to the first view, the above international unions remained in full force during the war, inasmuch as it could not affect the interests of the third countries that were parties to them.[2] According to another view, the treaties in question were abrogated as between the belligerents, but remained in force as between them and the neutral parties.[3] This opinion is subject to serious theoretical objections arising out of the contractual character of the treaties. According to a third view, the international conventions retained their validity during the war in the relations of the belligerents as well as in the relations of the same toward neutrals, but the execution of the stipulations of such conventions might be suspended to the extent and for the time commanded by the necessities of the war.[4]

The last view should be admitted especially in regard to the Industrial Property Convention, which constitutes an international agreement of a juristic nature rather than a political one.[5] Moreover, it is intended to establish a more or less permanent condition of things; it does not necessarily presume a state of peace for its execution;[6] it concerns the interests of private persons and not of states directly; and the reason for the abrogation of other treaties, that is, the change of conditions following the war, is inapplicable in the case of this Convention.[7]

---

the other, were the original belligerents. Italy entered in 1915, Portugal in 1916, and the United States, Cuba, and the Dominican Republic in 1917.

1. Pillet, "La Guerre Actuelle et le Droit des Gens," *Revue Générale de Droit International Public* (1916), XXIII, 203, 225.

2. Renault, "Les Unions Internationales," in *Revue Générale de Droit International Public* (1896), III, 14, 21. Westlake, *International Law*, 2d ed., part II, p. 34.

3. Opinion referred to by Fauchille, *Traité de Droit International Public*, II, 60.

4. Politis, "Effets de la Guerre sur les Obligations Internationales," (Report) in *Annuaire de l'Institut de Droit International*, XXIII, 200, 214; and XXIV, 251, 257, 259; Oppenheim, *International Law* (3d ed. by Roxburgh, 1921), II, 146.

5. See *Propriété Industrielle* (1914), p. 131.

6. Taillefer et Claro, *Les Brevets, Dessins, Marques . . . pendant la Guerre* (1918), p. 2.

7. Hall, *International Law* (8th ed., by Higgins, 1924), p. 456, classifies international unions, postal conventions, etc., with treaties of alliance and treaties of commerce, and

The International Bureau of Berne maintained, shortly after the outbreak of war, that the Convention of 1883–1911 and the Arrangements of 1891, as well as the Copyright Convention of 1886, should be respected, and applied as far as possible, for the best interests of all parties concerned.[1] The Bureau, realizing that the application of the Convention would necessarily be hampered during the war, invited the member states to take the necessary measures for the preservation of private rights.

The practice during the war followed the Bureau's advice, although in theory the abrogation of the Convention and Arrangements, wholly or as between the belligerent countries, or their suspension during the war, was supported in Germany and Austria.[2] The continuity of the effects of the Convention was supported by French and Italian writers,[3] and it was officially confirmed by the accession of France in respect to Morocco (French Zone) to the Convention of 1883–1911 and the Arrangements of 1891, in 1917, that is, while the war was still on.[4]

The German and Austrian courts took the view that, although the International Property Convention may have ceased to be obligatory on the contracting countries after the outbreak of war, its provisions continued to form part of the municipal law. A necessary correlation between the obligatory force of the Convention in international law and its application in municipal law would not exist, in the opinion of these courts, unless such application were in opposition to the aims of the war, which was not the case with the Convention in question. Thus enemies were to be assimilated to nationals in the same way as before the war, unless the municipal law

---

suggests that they should all be regarded as annulled. He fails to see the different character of international unions, their legislative nature. Clearly they are not affected by the change in the relative strength and in the other conditions of the parties, which makes it desirable for them not to be bound by pre-war obligations in the other two kinds of treaties. See an admirable study by Professor Mario Ghiron in two articles entitled "Gli Effetti della Guerra Odierna sulle Convenzioni per la tutela dei Diritti Industriali," in *Rivista di Diritto Internazionale* (1916), pp. 355–402; (1917), pp. 13–50.

1. *Propriété Industrielle* (1914), p. 131.

2. *Ibid.* (1915), pp. 5 and 45.

3. Taillefer et Claro, *Les Brevets, Dessins et Marques pendant la Guerre* (1918), pp. 2–3; also "Lettre de France," in *Propriété Industrielle* (1915), pp. 70 and 90; Mario Ghiron, "Gli Effetti della Guerra Odierna sulle Convenzione per la tutela dei Diritti Industriali," in *Rivista di Diritto Internazionale* (1916), p. 355.

4. See notes of accession, in *Propriété Industrielle* (1917), p. 81.

was expressly changed in this respect.[1] The strong language used by the German Reichsgericht was taken as tending to provoke legislation introducing a war-time regime in opposition to the regime established by the Convention.[2] The Japanese Imperial Court of Errors, on the contrary, held that the International Convention was suspended during the war, and no protection could be claimed under it.[3]

§ **498. General remarks on war legislation.** As will appear from the following study of the war legislation of the different countries of the Industrial Property Union, the general assumption and the basic principle of such legislation was the continued validity of the Convention of 1883–1911. If certain measures were taken against enemy proprietors of rights of industrial property, they were exceptional measures, finding their justification in the state of war. Much more important and numerous, however, were the measures taken for the preservation of rights of industrial property belonging to enemies. Indeed, it became clear shortly after the outbreak of war, that during its continuance the pre-war municipal law was not adequate for the protection of the industrial property of nationals, nor was the international regime of the Convention adequate for the protection of that of foreigners; and that, by reason of the conditions created by the war, industrial property rights of foreigners as well as of nationals were endangered unless special protective measures were taken in the various countries. For instance, compliance with various dates at which, or periods within which, different acts were to be performed was not always possible for nationals serving in the army. The same was true with greater force in respect to foreigners. Rights of priority, in particular, could rarely be exercised within the short periods of article 4 of the Convention. And the forfeiture of patents for non-working within the period of article 5 constituted a serious danger to foreign patentees.

It was necessary and just, therefore, to postpone the dates and extend the periods for payment of fees and taxes, compliance with

1. Decision of the Reichsgericht, Oct. 26, 1914 (85 *Entsch. Reichsg., Zivils*, 374), in a case involving a claim of a right of priority, under article 4 of the Convention, based on a prior filing in France. It was held that such a right should be granted. Decision of the Supreme Court of Austria, Dec. 4, 1916, voicing agreement with the above decision (*Propriété Industrielle*, 1917, p. 65).

2. "Lettre d'Allemagne," in *Propriété Industrielle* (1915), p. 5. The German Patent Office did not, in fact, follow the Reichsgericht's decision.

3. Kautschuk- und Guttaperchawerke case, decided June 2, 1915 (*Propriété Industrielle*, 1916, p. 25).

formalities, filing of applications, objections, declarations of priority, and so forth. Or, if a right was lost by reason of failure to comply with a formality or condition, it should be possible to restore this right when the failure was due to the state of war.

Legislation to these ends was passed in the belligerent as well as in the neutral countries during the war. Moreover, as an exception to the general prohibition against making payments in enemy countries, permission was granted to make such payments in so far as it was necessary for the acquisition or preservation of industrial property rights.

The most serious blow, perhaps, to the Union by war legislation was that the principle of national treatment of foreigners, which is at the basis of the Convention of 1883, was given up in most of the countries, and, instead, the principle of reciprocity introduced. The various exceptional measures for the preservation of foreigner's rights in any country of the Union could not be invoked by the nationals of another country, unless in the latter the same protection could be claimed by the nationals of the former country. Besides, the reciprocity required was not the same everywhere, as will be seen below.

§ 499. Applications for patents or for registration of designs and trade marks by enemies. As regards the war legislation concerning only enemies, the rights of industrial property against which exceptional measures were taken were patents, designs, and trade marks. These measures were of two kinds: (1) suspension of the administrative procedure following an application by an enemy for a patent or for the registration of a design or trade mark; (2) cancellation, restriction, or prohibition of the working of patents or use of designs and trade marks, and issuing of compulsory licenses to other persons for the working of such patents or the use of such marks or designs.

The interruption of the procedure for the grant of patents was a general measure concerning, sometimes, nationals as well as foreigners. The administrative procedure of search into the novelty of the invention and into the objection to application involves publication of the invention; and it was considered against the public interest to let the enemy acquire knowledge of an invention concerning munitions, foodstuffs, and the like.[1] In regard to enemies especially, the

1. See "Lettre d'Autriche," in *Propriété Industrielle* (1916), p. 93.

general theory was that no new rights should be granted them, but that expectations of such rights should be respected. Hence applications by enemies for patents or for the registration of designs or trade marks were accepted, but delivery of patents or registration of designs or trade marks was not made, as this would have meant granting a privilege (in the case of patents) to enemies, or would have interfered needlessly with the freedom of nationals, since enemies could not trade with the country in which an application was filed. In the United States alone this was not considered sufficient reason for suspending the application. The Trading with the Enemy Act provided that an enemy, or ally of an enemy, might file and prosecute in the United States an application for letters patent, or for registration of trade mark, print, label, or copyright, and pay any necessary fees.[1] At the other extreme, in Russia, such applications were not accepted, and all procedure on applications accepted before the war was suspended; [2] but Russia was not a member of the Industrial Property Union.

In Great Britain, the Act of August 7, 1914, as amended by the Act of August 28, 1914,[3] provided that the Board of Trade might cancel or suspend all applications for a patent or for the registration of a design or trade mark, if such application was made by a subject of a country at war with Great Britain. The Board of Trade [4] delegated this power to the Comptroller General of Patents. The latter, on August 21, 1914,[5] gave notice that, during the war, no patent would be sealed, and no registration of a design or trade mark would be made, in behalf of a subject of a country at war with Great Britain. Applications, however, of such persons might be filed, and the usual procedure might be conducted in respect to them, but no formal declaration of acceptance of the application would be issued. Opposition by such persons to patent applications, or to applications for registration, of British subjects or of foreigners of a friendly country was not taken into consideration; opposition to applications of enemies was accepted, but all further procedure was suspended

1. Sec. 10 (*a*), Act of Oct. 6, 1917 (XL *U. S. Stat. at Large*, 411).
2. Act of Feb. 21–March 6, 1915 (*Propriété Industrielle*, 1915, p. 40).
3. 4 & 5 Geo. V, c. 27; 4 & 5 Geo. V, c. 73.
4. Patents, Designs and Trade Marks (Temporary) Rules, 1914 (Statutory Rules and Orders, 1914, III, 40 ff).
5. See Notification by the Comptroller of the Patent Office, in *Trade Mark Journal*, August 26, 1914.

until the end of the war. Similar legislation was passed in the British dominions and colonies.[1]

So, too, the delivery of patents, and registration of designs and trade marks, on applications filed by enemies were suspended in Austria,[2] Hungary,[3] Germany,[4] Italy,[5] France,[6] Tunis,[7] Japan,[8] and Portugal.[9] The stage at which the procedure was suspended varied in the different countries.[10] In Austria, Hungary, and Germany, in retaliation for Russia's measures, all filings made subsequent to March 11, 1915, by Russian subjects were declared null and void.

It is interesting to note that during the war the service of international registration of trade marks was not interrupted, although the number of registrations decreased. Trade marks of enemies were communicated to the various administrations after registration at the Bureau. One only of the contracting countries made a reservation on the point whether protection could be acquired in its territory by an enemy by international registration. But the International Bureau replied to an administration, which gave notice of refusal in 1922 of certain marks originating in ex-enemy countries which were registered at the Bureau in 1916 and the years following, that such refusal was too late.[11]

§ 500. Measures concerning working of patents, and use of designs and trade marks of enemies. Prohibition against trading with enemies involved the impossibility of such enemies' working a patent or using a design or trade mark during the existence of the state of war. This raised two problems: that of preserving the rights of

1. See "La Protection Internationale de la Propriété Intellectuelle et la Guerre Mondiale," *Bureaux Internationaux de la Propriété Intellectuelle* (1919), pp. 38 ff.
2. Ordinance No. 258 of Aug. 16, 1916 (*Reichsgesetzblatt*, 1916, p. 613).
3. Ordinance No. 2706–1916 of August 15, 1916 (*Propriété Industrielle*, 1916, p. 103).
4. Act of July 1 and Ordinance of July 2, 1915 (*Reichsgesetzblatt*, 1915, pp. 414 and 417).
5. Decree No. 962 of June 20, 1915 (*Raccolta Ufficiale*, 1915, III, 2762).
6. Act of May 27, 1915 (*Bulletin des Lois*, 1915, I, 947).
7. Decree of Aug. 28, 1915 (*Propriété Industrielle*, 1915, p. 132).
8. Decree of July 20, 1917 (*ibid.*, 1917, p. 144).
9. Decree No. 2350, April 20, 1916, secs. 37–40 (*Colecção Oficial*, 1915, I, 230).
10. In Germany, applications by enemies were examined by the Patent Office, and if they could be rejected according to law, they were rejected; otherwise they were kept in abeyance. See "Lettre d'Allemagne," in *Propriété Industrielle* (1915), p. 5; also decision of the Patent Office, Feb. 17, 1917, interrupting the procedure in regard to a French patent application after the rejection of objections (*ibid.*, 1918, p. 32).
11. See "Exposé Général sur le Service de l'Enregistrement International," in *Actes de la Conférence de La Haye*, pp. 173, 180.

enemies, in case, by the failure of such working or use, the rights of the owners were forfeited according to the ordinary provisions of law; and that of satisfying the needs of the domestic market in respect to such patent, design, or trade mark. The means adopted for solving the first problem will be seen in a succeeding paragraph. Concerning the problem of satisfying public interest in the manufacture of a machine, article, or design, or in the use of a trade mark owned or controlled by an enemy, the various belligerent countries resorted to the procedure of suspending or cancelling the patent, or of issuing compulsory licenses.

Generally speaking, such cancellation or suspension was made, and licenses issued, only when a public interest was shown.[1] Special commissions were created in the various countries, and all applications for licenses to work a patent or use a trade mark of an enemy were investigated. Besides the necessity of proof of public interest, the good faith of the applicant, and his ability to satisfy the requirements of the market at reasonable terms, had to be established. The grants were temporary measures, to come to an end at the termination of the war or at any time before such termination. Royalties were payable by the licensee to a state authority, and the rights of the enemy owner in these royalties were often preserved.[2]

In Russia only (not a member of the Union) all patents belonging to enemies, if they were important to the defense of the Empire, were declared the property of the state, without any compensation, and all other patents of enemies were annulled. In retaliation, patents belonging to Russian subjects were declared in Germany, Austria, and Hungary, subject to an issuance of compulsory license, although no public interest was shown.[3]

§ 501. Measures for preservation of industrial property rights. The above exceptional measures taken in the belligerent countries

1. See two decisions of the Austrian Ministry of Public Works, April 16, 1917, and June 1, 1917; the former rejected an application for a license to work a patent of a French firm, it being proved that two Austrian firms possessed licenses, and that national needs were satisfied; the latter denied an application to use a French word mark for medicine, because, according to the Superior Board of Health, the public interest did not require the grant of the application (*Propriété Industrielle*, 1917, pp. 25 and 98).

2. See especially the United States Trading with the Enemy Act, sec. 10 (*d*) and (*f*), XL *U. S. Stat. at Large*, 411, 421. See an article in *Propriété Industrielle* (1916), p. 69, containing an English and a German decision on the matter. See also an Austrian decision (*Propriété Industrielle*, 1917, p. 64).

3. See the laws of the different countries in this respect, in the enactments cited in previous notes. As to Italy, see Decree No. 533, of March 22, 1917 (*Raccolta Ufficiale*, 1917, II, 1119).

against enemy owners of patents, designs, and trade marks were, generally speaking, only to a small extent prejudicial to them. Their applications for new patents, designs, and trade marks were accepted and filed, and their rights therein preserved until the end of the war. Trade names and appellations of origin were in no way affected. The suspension or cancellation of patents, designs, and trade marks, and the grant of licenses to work on the ground of public interest or for military reasons, was a taking of property by the right of eminent domain, which was also possible under the peace-time legislation of many countries, and therefore was not exclusively a war measure against enemies.[1]

On the other hand, enemy owners of patents, designs, and trade marks were benefited by the general war legislation passed by all the member countries of the Industrial Property Union, which tended to preserve industrial property rights in danger of being lost by the passing of dates or expiration of periods fixed for the performance of various acts. The regulations in this respect present extreme variety in the different countries of the Union.[2] Important especially is the extension of the periods of rights of priority under article 4 of the Convention, and of the periods for the working of patents, designs, and trade marks. In Italy alone, alien enemies were excluded from the benefit of the extension of periods of priority.

§ 502. Extension of periods of priority. In accordance with article 4 of the Convention of 1883–1911, a right of priority is enjoyed by persons entitled to its benefits if an application for a patent or for the registration of a design or trade mark is filed within the specified period after the first filing of a similar application in another country of the Union. In view of the upheaval caused by the war, the interruption of communications, embargo in some countries, military service, and so forth, the periods of rights of priority could hardly be complied with.

The International Bureau, by a circular under date of November 4, 1914, addressed to the administrations of the contracting countries, suggested that an extension of the periods of priority be granted

1. In Italy, the state was authorized, in the interest of national defense, to take and use, in whole or in part, any invention, without the consent of the patentee, whether this patentee was a national, a foreigner, or an enemy. Decrees of Jan. 28, 1915, and March 19, 1916 (*Raccolta Ufficiale*, 1915, I, 95; 1916, II, 1124).

2. See a compilation by the International Bureau, in its publication, *La Protection Internationale de la Propriété Intellectuelle et la Guerre Mondiale 1914–1918* (Berne, 1919); also in *Propriété Industrielle* (1919), pp. 99 ff.

until a certain time after the conclusion of peace.[1] A number of administrations signified their acquiescence in the principle of such an extension, but expressed doubts as to the feasibility of an agreement in this respect between the contracting countries. In the lack of an agreement, the periods were extended variously in the belligerent as well as in the neutral countries.

In the Netherlands, the periods of article 4 were extended by six months for patents and by four months for trade marks. In the United States, the extension was nine months for patents, designs and marks. In the Scandinavian countries, — Denmark, Norway, and Sweden, — the periods were extended successively until December 31, 1919, in Norway, and January 1, 1920, in Denmark and Sweden. The extension, however, in these countries concerned only patents. In a number of countries, — Austria, Belgium, Brazil, France, Hungary, Portugal, Spain, Switzerland, and Tunis, — an indefinite extension was given, the limit to be fixed by future regulation. In certain countries, the periods of priority were extended for a designated time following the termination of the war; such time was fixed at three months in Italy, and at six months in Germany and Mexico. In Great Britain and Japan, the extension of all periods was a matter of discretion for the Comptroller of Patents. In all the countries, with the exception of Belgium, Brazil, Denmark, the Netherlands, and Switzerland, the above extensions were granted only on condition of reciprocity. In Great Britain, reciprocity was not required, but the applicant claiming an extension had to prove that his failure to act within the legal period was due to the state of war. In Japan, also, reciprocity was not required, but alien enemies could not claim a right of priority based on a patent application filed during the war.

§ **503. Extension of periods for working patents.** Article 5 of the Convention of 1883 provided that a patent could not be forfeited for failure to work it in a country of the Union unless three years had elapsed from the date of the application in such country, and then only in case the patentee could not justify his inaction. The war must have rendered inpossible the working of patents to many a foreign patentee. It would seem to constitute one of the justifiable causes of inaction provided for in article 5 of the Convention. Foreigners, therefore, should have been relieved of the obligation to

1. See *Propriété Industrielle* (1917), p. 48.

work their patents during the war, and for some time after its termination.

In most of the countries of the Union such relief was granted by an extension of the legal periods for the working of patents. In Great Britain and the British dominions and colonies, the demands of the law concerning the working of patents were suspended during the war and for six months after its termination. In Italy, the suspension extended to three months after the end of the war. In Brazil, Cuba, France, and Switzerland, the period was extended indefinitely until a date to be determined at the end of the war. In the Netherlands, only a six-month extension of the legal period of five years was allowed. In Denmark, all legal periods, and consequently that of working a patent, were successively extended to January 1, 1920. In Belgium and Portugal, the war was deemed to be a case of *vis major*, and therefore a justifiable ground for non-working. In Germany and Japan, no express extension of the period of working was made, but rights lost through the lapse of a period could be restored on application and proof that the failure was due to the state of war. Such application must be made within two months from the disappearance of the impediment in Germany, and within fourteen days, but not later than a year from the expiry of the period, in Japan.

The obligation existing in certain countries to use registered trade marks within a certain period was suspended only in Brazil until the end of the war. In Hungary, the failure to work or use a registered design or model during the war was declared not to entail forfeiture. In Japan and the Netherlands, the restoration of rights lost by the lapse of a period due to the state of war applied to all rights of industrial property.[1]

§ **504. Reciprocity in war legislation.** Few countries granted the benefit of the protective legislative measures taken during the war to all persons entitled to the benefits of the Convention of 1883–1911, without restriction or condition. These countries would seem to be only Denmark, Great Britain and the British dominions, and Switzerland. In the others, the benefit of such legislation could be claimed by foreigners only in case of reciprocity. This is in direct opposition to the basic principle of the Industrial Property Union, which admits all "ressortissants" of the Union to the benefits enjoyed by nationals, without condition of reciprocity.

1. See compilation of International Bureau, in *Propriété Industrielle* (1919), pp. 99, 100–102.

The reciprocity required by the legislation of the various countries was not always understood in the same way. In some cases reciprocity in form, in others in substance, was necessary. The first existed when the nationals of the country requiring reciprocity were admitted to the same benefits in another country as the nationals of the latter. In other words, country A, in such case, granted the advantage of war legislation to the nationals of country B, if in the latter country the nationals of country A were admitted to the benefit of similar legislation, even though the protection in country B was not as broad as in country A. Thus there was reciprocity in form if an extension of the periods of priority until the end of the war was granted in country B, although the same periods were extended until the end of the war and six months thereafter in country A. On the other hand, for reciprocity in substance there should be equality of treatment and of rights in both countries concerned.

Another distinction referred to the method by which reciprocity was recognized as existing. In certain countries, the existence of reciprocity with a foreign country must be declared by an act of the administration — by declaration, or decree, or ordinance, or other appropriate act. In other countries, the existence of reciprocity was a fact to be proved by the person alleging it; that is, such person must prove that the law of another country grants the protection or the right in question to the nationals of the country where he claims protection. The first is known under the term "diplomatic reciprocity," the latter as "legal reciprocity."

In Germany, Hungary, and Norway, the required reciprocity in all cases was diplomatic, that is, a declaration by the administration. In Austria only reciprocity in regard to rights of priority had to be declared officially; as to other matters, mere legal reciprocity was sufficient. On the other hand, in Italy legal reciprocity sufficed only for rights of priority claimed by nationals of allied or neutral countries. In all other countries, mere legal reciprocity enabled foreigners to claim the benefit of war measures of protection.

In most of the countries reciprocity in form only was required. Equality of rights was required in Spain and Hungary; also in Germany and Austria, as regards rights of priority, and in France, Italy, and Tunis, as regards other matters, with the exception of rights of priority.[1]

1. See on all this, an article in *Propriété Industrielle* (1918), p. 65.

CHAPTER XXXIII

THE PROVISIONS OF THE TREATIES OF PEACE AND THE BERNE ARRANGEMENT OF 1920

§ 505. Plans for reëstablishment of pre-war regime. Even during the war several studies of the situation of industrial property rights were made, and plans were devised for the reëstablishment of the pre-war regime. This could be accomplished by restoration of lost rights, suppression of, and reparation for, measures taken against enemies, recognition of the continuing validity of the Convention of 1883–1911 during the war, and grants of new and uniform extensions of various periods for some time after the termination of the war.[1] A provisional application of these principles was made at the beginning of 1918 in the treaties of peace concluded between Germany, Austria-Hungary, Bulgaria, and Turkey on the one part and the Ukranian Republic, Russia, and Rumania on the other, and between Germany and Finland and Austria-Hungary and Finland, and in the additional treaties and arrangements concluded between the same countries and completing the treaties of peace.

1. See *Propriété Industrielle* (1917), pp. 7, 51, 88. Also article by Professor Röthlisberger, in *Revue de Jurisprudence Suisse* (1916), p. 49.

Of these countries, only Germany, Austria, and Hungary were members of the Industrial Property Union. The provisions of the above treaties, therefore, could not affect directly the regime of the Union. Nevertheless, Russia and Finland agreed with Austria, Hungary, and Germany, to consider the Convention of 1883–1911 applicable in their relations on the subject of industrial property; in other words, this Convention was incorporated in the above treaties. On the other hand, the treaty provisions concerning the protection of industrial property, existing before the war, were reëstablished.

There were three objectives of the specific provisions of the treaties of 1918 concerning the restoration of rights of industrial property affected by the war. First, all measures taken during the war against enemies were abrogated as from the date of the taking effect of the treaties in question. Second, all rights denied by war measures were reëstablished, but without prejudice to the rights of third parties acquired in a lawful manner. Such reëstablishment was coupled with extension of various legal periods fixed for the acquisition or preservation of rights of industrial property. Third, for all damages to such rights the contracting countries agreed to pay compensation to be determined by mixed commissions.[1]

It would seem that the disturbances created by the war in the regime of industrial property could have been ended only by a special conference between all the members of the Union, belligerent and neutral, held after the termination of the war.[2] Such a conference was not held. To be sure, the treaties of peace contained stipulations on the question of industrial property. But as these treaties did not affect neutral countries, the Berne Arrangement of 1920 was entered into for the purpose of transferring the provisions of the treaties of peace to the relations with these countries.[3]

§ **506. Provisions of the treaties of peace.** The Treaty of Versailles with Germany, as well as those of St. Germain with Austria, Trianon with Hungary, and Neuilly with Bulgaria,[4] contain a special

1. See a study of these treaties, in *Propriété Industrielle* (1918), pp. 113 ff.

2. So proposed by the International Bureau of the Union. See *Propriété Industrielle* (1917), p. 51.

3. The German delegation in its counter-propositions at the Paris Conference had proposed that the questions of industrial property should be treated at a subsequent International Conference. See *Les Contrepropositions de l'Allemagne au Projet du Traité de Paix de Versailles* (Berlin, 1919), p. 79.

4. This was also the case with the Treaty of Sèvres with Turkey; but that treaty has never gone into effect.

section, in the part concerning the economic clauses of the treaty, which deals with industrial property and which is almost identical in all these treaties. In the Treaty of Versailles it is section VII of part X, and includes articles 306–311. The respective articles of the other treaties are 258–262, 264, and 274 of the Treaty of Saint-Germain; 241–245, 247, 257 of the Treaty of Trianon; and 190–194 of the Treaty of Neuilly.

Besides these provisions under the caption of industrial property, the treaties contain a number of other stipulations dealing with our subject. In the Treaty of Versailles, articles 274 and 275, forming chapter III of section I (Commercial Relations), deal with unfair competition; article 286 provides for the coming into effect again of the Convention of 1883–1911; and paragraph 5 of the annex to article 297 concerns the specific case of trade marks owned by companies. Articles 274 and 275 of the Treaty of Versailles are reproduced in articles 226 and 227 of the Treaty of Saint-Germain, 154 and 155 of the Treaty of Neuilly, and 210 of the Treaty of Trianon. The Commercial Convention signed at Lausanne, July 23, 1924, together with the treaty of peace with Turkey, reproduces the provisions in question in its articles 12 and 13, with the difference that a condition of reciprocity is added in article 12, which does not appear in the corresponding articles of the other treaties.[1] Also, article 286 of the Treaty of Versailles corresponds with article 237 of the Treaty of Saint-Germain and 220 of the Treaty of Trianon. There is no corresponding article in the Treaty of Neuilly with Bulgaria, as that country was not a member of the Industrial Property Union before the war. However, by article 106, Bulgaria undertakes to accede to the Convention of 1883–1911 within twelve months from the coming into effect of the treaty, and to recognize and protect industrial property according to the principles of that Convention. A similar provision is contained in the Commercial Convention of July 24, 1923, with Turkey (article 14).[2]

§ 507. Stipulations concerning application of the Convention of the Union. The lack of a general principle and of clarity in respect to the industrial property regime as determined by the treaties of peace appears, especially, in the important question of the legal con-

1. On the provisions of the treaties on unfair competition, see *supra*, §§ 474, 482.

2. On the interpretation of all these treaty provisions, see Chabaud, *La Propriété Industrielle et les Traités de Paix* (Paris, 1921); and Osterrieth, *Gewerblicher Rechtsschutz und Urheberrecht im Friedensvertrag von Versailles* (Berlin, 1920).

dition of the acts of the Union during the war, and of the effects upon this condition of the treaties of peace. As we have seen above,[1] theoretically the question was disputed, but with the exception of certain war measures against enemies, the basic assumption of war legislation in all countries was that the Convention and Arrangements were not abrogated by the war, only their execution being partially suspended. It would seem, therefore, that the treaties should declare that the Union did not cease to be in effect during the war, and that all measures suspending in part the execution of the Convention should come to an end at its termination.

The Treaty of Versailles provided, in article 286, that the Convention of 1883–1911, and the Copyright Convention also " . . . will again come into effect as from the coming into force of the present Treaty, in so far as they are not affected or modified by the exceptions and restrictions resulting therefrom." The treaty speaks of the Convention's "coming again into effect," which would imply that it ceased to be in effect during the war. This is not in agreement with the facts. Moreover, it is in contradiction to other provisions of the treaty.[2] The French text of the treaty is somewhat against the implication derived from the English text in providing that the two conventions "seront remises en vigueur et reprendront leur effet." The second expression would imply a mere suspension of the effects of the Convention during the war.

The stipulations of the Treaties of Saint-Germain and Trianon with Austria and Hungary would seem to be more true to fact and theory. They provide that the Convention of 1883–1911 and the Madrid Arrangement of 1891 "shall be applied as from the coming into force of the present Treaty," [3] which implies that they never ceased to be in effect, and that only their full application was prevented by the war.

§ 508. Restrictions on application of the Convention. While article 286 of the Treaty of Versailles and the corresponding articles of the other treaties provide that the Industrial Property Convention and the Madrid Arrangement will be again put into application from the coming into force of the treaties, they add the reservation: "in so far as they are not affected or modified by the exceptions and

1. See *supra*, § 497.
2. For instance, article 306, which restores rights which, except for the war, would have been acquired during the war.
3. The French text reads "seront appliqués," and the Italian, "saranno applicate."

restrictions" resulting from the treaties. These exceptions and restrictions are contained in articles 306–311 of the Treaty of Versailles, and in the corresponding articles of the other treaties.

The restrictions in question will be considered later in this chapter, but it should be pointed out in this place what an anomalous situation is created when a treaty of peace concluded between only some of the parties to the Industrial Property Convention undertakes to restrict the provisions of the latter and append exceptions to its application. The uniformity aimed at by the Convention is thereby destroyed.[1] The anomaly becomes more serious, when, as will be seen, rights of nationals of non-contracting countries are affected by such stipulations of the treaties of peace, in violation of the provisions of the Industrial Property Convention.

§ 509. Recognition and restoration of industrial property rights. We saw in the previous chapter that during the war the belligerent countries took certain measures against enemy patentees and owners of designs and trade marks. On the one hand, they suspended the delivery of patents and registration of designs and trade marks. On the other hand, they cancelled, or issued compulsory licenses in respect to, patents, designs, or trade marks granted to or registered by enemies before the war. Moreover, rights of enemies were lost by non-compliance with the periods fixed for certain acts required for the acquisition or preservation of rights. Thus certain rights of industrial property failed of recognition during the war, and others were restricted or lost.

Article 306 of the Treaty of Versailles and the corresponding articles of the other treaties stipulate the recognition of the first class of rights and the reëstablishment or restoration of the others. They provide that rights of industrial property, as such property is defined by the International Convention of 1883, shall be reëstablished or restored as from the coming into force of the treaties of peace. And that rights which, except for the war, would have been acquired during the war in consequence of an application made for the protection of industrial property, shall be recognized and established. Thus applications for a patent, or for the registration of a design or model, pending in any of the contracting countries shall be accepted from the coming into force of each treaty of peace in the ordinary way, and, if according to law, the patent applied for or the registra-

1. See Chabaud, *La Propriété Industrielle et les Traités de Paix* (Paris, 1921), p. 88.

tion shall be granted. On the other hand, cancelled patents, designs, or marks shall be restored, compulsory licenses terminated, and lapsed rights reëstablished.

However, this general and just principle is limited by important restrictions and exceptions concerning rights of industrial property of nationals of Germany, Austria, Hungary, and Bulgaria. These are considered in the following sections, in which only the provisions of the Treaty of Versailles are mentioned, the provisions of the other treaties being identical, except when stated otherwise. By the operation of these exceptions and reservations, as was pointed out in the German counter-proposals to the draft Treaty of Peace, only the rights of nationals of the Allied and Associated Powers are really reëstablished and restored, and not those of German nationals.[1]

§ 510. Use of rights of industrial property during the war. The third and fourth paragraphs of article 306 of the Treaty of Versailles deal with the use during the war of any rights of industrial property, or the sale, offering for sale, or use of any products, articles, or apparatus whatsoever, to which such rights applied. If such use, sale, and so forth, was made by the government of any Allied or Associated Power, or by any persons acting on behalf or with the assent of such government, for instance, by issuing of compulsory licenses, no claim can be made or action brought by Germany or German nationals. On the other hand, such use, sale, and so forth, by the German government, or by any persons acting on behalf, or with the assent, of such government, for instance, following the issuing of a compulsory license, gives ground for claims and actions on the part of the Allied or Associated Power concerned, or its nationals.

The German government, in its counter-proposals asked that reciprocal treatment be granted to Germany in this respect, by relieving her from all claims concerning the use, sale, and so forth, of industrial property rights of Allied nationals during the war.[2] This proposal was rejected on the non-convincing ground that the Allied and Associated countries had no knowledge of the measures taken by the German government in respect to rights of industrial property of their nationals.[3]

1. See *Les Contrepropositions de l'Allemagne au Projet du Traité de Paix de Versailles* (Berlin, 1919), p. 110.

2. *Ibid.*, p. 100.

3. *Réponse des Puissances Alliées et Associées aux Remarques de la Délégation Allemande* (Berlin, 1919), p. 77.

The sums due or paid on account of the above use of German industrial property rights are dealt with in the same way as other sums due to German nationals are directed to be dealt with by the treaty, and sums produced by the measures taken by the German government are considered and treated in the same way as other debts due from German nationals.

§ **511. War measures against industrial property.** The use of German industrial property rights begun during the war was not to come to a close with the coming into force of the treaty. The second paragraph of article 306 provides that

> all acts done by virtue of the special measures taken during the war under legislative, executive, or administrative authority of any Allied or Associated Power in regard to the rights of German nationals in industrial property shall remain in force and shall continue to maintain their full effect.

In other words, cancellations, restrictions, compulsory licenses of patents, designs, or trade marks of German nationals effected during the war, were to continue to be valid and in force after the coming into effect of the treaty of peace.

But this was not so in the case of similar acts in Germany in regard to the rights of nationals of Allied or Associated Powers. Such acts were to be of no effect after the coming into force of the treaty. Cancellations, restrictions, and compulsory licenses against rights of these persons were revoked by the treaty. The German government asked on this point also that reciprocity be granted to Germany, but in the reply to the German counter-proposals it was stated that in some of the Allied and Associated countries no such measures were taken against German nationals, so that the reciprocity would be granted to the detriment of their nationals, without compensation.[1]

§ **512. Future restrictions of industrial property rights.** Article 306 contains a further exception to the general principle above stated, which no longer refers to the time of the war and the measures taken during its existence. It is an exception to the principle of restoring the full application of the Convention of Union. In effect, it is a declaration, acquiesced in by Germany, that the Allied and Associated Powers reserve to themselves the power to depart, under certain conditions, from the provisions of the Industrial

1. *Réponse des Puissances Alliées et Associées aux Remarques de la Délégation Allemande* (Berlin, 1919), p. 76.

Property Convention, and to deny to Germany the protection of industrial property provided for in that Convention.

Indeed, by the stipulations of the fifth and sixth paragraphs of article 306, each of the Allied and Associated Powers reserves for itself the right to impose limitations, conditions, or restrictions on rights of industrial property (with the exception of trade marks) acquired before or during the war, or which may be subsequently acquired, in accordance with its legislation, by German nationals. As illustrations of such restrictions or limitations are mentioned: the granting of licenses, and the working, or preserving of control over, their exploitation. The cases in which such limitations may be imposed are four: national defense, the public interest, assurance of fair treatment by Germany of the rights of industrial property held in German territory by the Allied Power concerned, and assurance of due fulfillment of the obligations of Germany under the treaty. Concerning, however, rights of industrial property acquired after the coming into force of the treaty, only in two cases may such limitations be imposed: if they be considered necessary for national defense, or in the public interest. It is also provided that in case such limitations shall be imposed, there shall be paid reasonable indemnities or royalties, to be dealt with in the same way in which other sums due to German nationals are directed to be dealt with by the treaty.

The expropriation of patents for inventions considered necessary for the national defense, or in the public interest, is possible under the patent law of many countries, and the insertion of such a provision in the treaties of peace is not particularly surprising. However, it is prescribed exclusively against nationals of Germany, Austria, Hungary, and Bulgaria, and might give rise to abuses; and it extends to designs and models as well. The taking of measures against industrial property rights in the other two cases is along the line of other provisions of the treaty tending to permit the use of German property rights as a guaranty of the fulfillment of the treaty obligations of Germany. It is in clear opposition to the Convention of 1883–1911.[1]

§ **513. Transfers defeating objects of these provisions.** During the war, or after its termination, German nationals may have trans-

1. France used the power given by this provision of the treaty, in its decrees of Jan. 15 and Feb. 24, 1920 (*Bulletin des Lois*, 1920, I, 307, 792).

ferred their rights in industrial property to neutral or Allied nationals. In such case, these rights would not be affected by the above provisions of article 306. To avoid this consequence, the treaty provides, in the seventh paragraph of the same article, that

each of the Allied and Associated Powers reserves the right to treat as void and of no effect any transfer in whole or in part of, or other dealing with, rights of, or in respect to, industrial property, effected after August 1, 1914, or in the future, which would have the result of defeating the objects of the provisions of this article.

Thus, transfers during the war, as well as in the future, of rights acquired by German nationals before, during, or after the war may be declared void.

§ **514. Rights dealt with in liquidation of businesses under war legislation.** What may be considered a further exception to the general principle of reëstablishment of industrial property rights affected during the war is the stipulation contained in the last paragraph of article 306.[1] According to this, the provisions of article 306

shall not apply to rights of industrial property which have been dealt with in the liquidation of businesses or companies under war legislation by the Allied or Associated Powers, or which may be so dealt with by virtue of article 297, paragraph (*b*).

No restoration or reëstablishment of rights of industrial property acquired before the war, and no recognition of rights which, but for the war, would have been acquired by German nationals, is to be made in respect to rights of industrial property connected with businesses or companies liquidated during the war, or to be liquidated under article 297 (*b*). Thus the fate of these rights is linked with that of businesses and companies. The power of liquidation after the war under article 297 (*b*) is general and unconditional, while the right to impose limitations and restrictions under the fifth paragraph of article 306 is possible only under certain conditions.[2]

§ **515. Rights used in common with a German company.** A special case, difficult to classify, is dealt with in paragraph 5 of the annex to article 297 of the Treaty of Versailles. This case concerns trade marks or "unique means of reproduction of goods or articles." What is meant by the latter expression it is impossible to say. The expression used in the French text is not at all identical, for it refers

1. The same stipulation is contained in paragraph 15 of the annex to article 297.
2. See *supra*, § 512.

to "procédés exclusifs de fabrication de marchandises," which would seem to imply patents, patentable inventions, or industrial secrets.

The trade marks and means of reproduction referred to in this provision are those to the use of which, rights in common were held immediately before the outbreak of the war by a company incorporated in an Allied or Associated country, and by a company controlled by it and incorporated in Germany. Still, such trade marks and means of reproduction are included in this provision, only if the rights in common were thus held with respect to the use of the trade marks, or to the sale of the goods or articles produced in third countries.

When all these conditions concur, the right to use the trade marks in question in third countries is to be enjoyed from the coming into force of the treaty of peace only by the company incorporated in an Allied or Associated Power, to the exclusion of the German company. As regards the "unique means of reproduction," they shall be handed over to the former company, notwithstanding any action taken under German war legislation with regard to the company incorporated in Germany or its business, industrial property or shares. Nevertheless, "derivative copies,"[1] permitting the continuation of reproduction of articles for use within German territory, may be delivered, on request, by the company incorporated in an Allied or Associated country to the German company.

Thus, the German company may have only the right to use the trade mark on the "unique means of reproduction" in Germany and for sale of articles therein, but not in third countries. It will be noticed that, by this provision, not only rights of German nationals in the Allied or Associated countries are affected, but also rights possessed in third countries.

§ **516. Infringements of industrial property rights during the war.** Rights of industrial property affected by the war were reestablished, or restored, in principle, by the treaties of peace. But during the war, infringements of these rights took place in enemy countries, and their interruption or repression was rendered impossible by the inability of enemy persons to take legal proceedings, or even by their having no knowledge of the infringement. Should the infringers be liable for such acts after the conclusion of peace? This

1. The French text has, in place of derivative copies, "modèles," which is not the same, and increases still more the uncertainty concerning these "unique means of reproduction." Cf. Chabaud, *La Propriété Industrielle et les Traités de Paix*, p. 59.

would seem to be free from doubt. Fraud and usurpation of private rights should not be tolerated. The state may, in the public interest, and for reasons of national defense, be permitted to grant licenses for the use of industrial property of enemies. But on what ground should private persons be permitted to infringe such property? And if this is not permitted, why should such persons not be held liable for damages?

However, the treaties of peace provided otherwise. Article 309 of the Treaty of Versailles, and the corresponding articles of the other treaties, granted complete amnesty for all acts of infringement which took place during the war. No claim or action can be brought for acts which might constitute an infringement of the rights of industrial property, either existing at any time during the war, or revived under the provisions of articles 307 and 308 (concerning the extension of periods). The amnesty also extends to the sale, or offering for sale, or to the acquisition and continued use of products or articles manufactured during the period between the declaration of war and the signing of the treaty. This was not actionable for a period of one year after the signing of the treaty. This amnesty does not apply when the possessor of the rights was domiciled, or had an industrial or commercial establishment in, the districts occupied by Germany during the war.

The persons whose actions for infringement are thus declared not to be permissible are not only nationals of Germany and of an Allied or Associated Power, but also persons residing or carrying on business within the territories of such powers or those persons who derived title from them during the war. The provision thus attempts to affect rights of persons not nationals of any of the contracting countries. It is doubtful whether it can be applied against such persons, nationals of a third country with which any of the contracting countries has entered into other conventions. For instance, if a Dane was carrying on business in Germany, and his trade mark was infringed in France, the above provision cannot prevail against his action for infringement, inasmuch as France and Denmark are member countries of the Industrial Property Union, by articles 2 and 3 of which, for an infringement of a trade mark of a Dane there must be granted in France the same rights and remedies as for an infringement of a French trade mark.[1] Consequently, only

1. See Chabaud, *La Propriété Industrielle et les Traités de Paix*, pp. 14, 60, 88.

those persons (not nationals of a contracting country) will be denied actions for infringement, who are nationals of countries which have no previous engagement with the country concerned.

Not all acts of infringement are amnestied, but only those which have taken place within the territory of the contracting countries between the date of the declaration of war and that of the coming into force of the treaty of peace. Also the sale, or offering for sale, the acquisition, or continued use, of products or articles manufactured in infringement of the above rights are permitted only in the territories of the contracting countries. In other words, acts of infringement committed outside of the above time and place limits may be actionable.

These provisions of article 309 are declared inapplicable as between the United States of America on the one hand, and Germany on the other, by the last paragraph of article 309. They are in conflict with the Amendment to the Constitution of the United States concerning the taking of property by due process of law.

§ **517. Contracts entered into before the war.** Article 310 of the Treaty of Versailles deals with licenses in respect to industrial property concluded before the war between nationals of the Allied or Associated Powers, or persons residing in their territory or carrying on business therein, on the one part, and German nationals, on the other. It considers them cancelled as from the date of the declaration of war between Germany and the Allied and Associated Powers.

This provision is on the same principle as article 299, concerning contracts concluded between enemies before the war, although the conditions of application are not the same in both cases. Thus, while article 299 concerns contracts between enemies alone, article 310 applies also to contracts between German nationals and persons residing or carrying on business in the territories of the Allied and Associated Powers. For instance, a contract entered into before the war by a Swiss national carrying on business in France with a German national is to be considered as cancelled.

The application of this provision to nationals of third countries again presents theoretical difficulties. In fact, however, the cancellation is beneficial to them, for they need not pay royalties for the use of industrial property during the war. If any sums have been paid during the war by virtue of such a license, they are dealt with in the same way as other debts or credits of German nationals.

The beneficiaries of licenses which are thus cancelled have the right to demand from the proprietor of the rights the grant of a new license. This right should be exercised within six months from the coming into force of the treaty. It is not clear what the legal situation is until the grant of such new license. For the use of the rights during the war no claim or action may be brought, according to article 309. In this case alone the amnesty granted by the latter article is explained. But after the period for which such amnesty is given, and until the grant of a new license, it would seem that no use of the industrial property in question is permissible.[1]

The conditions of such new license are to be determined by agreement between the parties. In default of such agreement, they are to be fixed by a tribunal, as provided for in article 310. In such case, the tribunal may fix also the amount which it may deem just should be paid by reason of the use of the rights during the war. This is a strange provision, because it provides for the possibility of a payment by the licensee for the time when (under article 309) mere infringers are not liable to pay anything.

These provisions do not affect licenses granted under the special war legislation of any Allied or Associated Power, which are included in the reservation of the second paragraph of article 306. These remain valid and of full effect after the war. If such a license under the war legislation was granted to a former beneficiary of a license granted before the war, such license shall be considered as substituted for the latter.

The last paragraph of article 310 again provides that the provisions of this article shall not apply as between the United States of America on the one hand and Germany on the other.

§ **518. Extension of legal periods.** The general principle of article 306 for the reëstablishment or restoration of rights affected by the war, and the recognition of rights which, but for the war, would have been acquired, is made applicable and given effect by the provisions of articles 307 and 308 of the Treaty of Versailles and the corresponding articles of the other treaties. Such restoration and recognition could not be effected indefinitely. This would create a great uncertainty as to the rights of third persons. A period should be fixed

1. Osterrieth, *Gewerblicher Rechtsschutz im Friedensvertrag*, p. 46. But Chabaud, *La Propriété Industrielle et les Traités de Paix*, p. 64, *contra*. The sale or offering for sale of products manufactured during the war may extend to the time specified in article 309. See *supra*, § 516.

within which persons who had filed applications before or after the war should comply with the formalities and conditions of the law, and within which rights of priority should be exercised, taxes should be paid, and the working of patents should take place.

Article 307 revives all rights in, or in respect of, industrial property which have lapsed by reason of failure to accomplish any act, fulfill any formality, or make any payment. Of course, such revived rights of German nationals are subject to the reservations provided for in article 306. Moreover, patents and designs revived in the Allied or Associated states are "subject to the conditions which these countries may deem reasonably necessary to impose for the protection of persons who have manufactured or made use of the subject matter of such property while the rights had lapsed." What is meant by "the protection" of these persons is not clear. The French text is different, speaking of "la sauve-garde des droits des tiers." Since the protection against actions or claims of infringement is dealt with in article 309, it would seem that the protection envisaged in this article is a granting of a license or a right of "personal possession" of the patents or designs in question. But such broad protection would not be justified unless the persons in question acted in good faith, that is, on the assumption that the rights of the true owners were definitely forfeited. Such good faith would be absent in case, in the country in question, the periods of fulfilling any formality, making payment, and so forth, were suspended or extended during the war.[1]

The same article allows a minimum of one year after the coming into force of the treaty, to nationals of the contracting countries, to enable them to accomplish any act, fulfill any formality, pay any fees, and generally satisfy any legal obligation of the respective countries relating to obtaining, preserving, or opposing rights to, or in respect of, industrial property. The rights referred to are those acquired before the outbreak of the war, or which, except for the war, might have been acquired after that date as a result of an application made before the war or during its continuance. No extension fee or other penalty is to be imposed by the contracting countries during this minimum-of-one-year period.

1. Chabaud, *La Propriété Industrielle et les Traités de Paix*, pp. 37–38. In this respect, the provision of article 2 of the Berne Arrangement of 1920 is better, limiting the reservation to persons acting in good faith. See *infra*, § 524.

This provision, however, is declared to confer no right on any person to reopen interference proceedings in the United States of America, where a final hearing has taken place.

§ **519. Working periods.** Concerning the period for working a patent, or using a design or trade mark, the last paragraph of article 307 provides that the period from the outbreak of the war until the coming into force of the treaty shall be excluded in considering the time within which a patent should be worked or a design or trade mark should be used. Further, it is agreed that no patent, registered trade mark, or design, in force at the outbreak of the war, shall be subject to reservation or cancellation by reason only of the failure to work such patent or use such design or trade mark for two years after the coming into force of the treaty. The reservation for the protection of the rights of third parties contained in the first paragraph of article 307 is not included in this provision.

The suspension of the working periods during the war and for two years after the coming into force of the treaty does not affect the question of duration of the patent or design. Thus, if the term of a patent or design expired after the outbreak of the war, it is not revived for the term remaining unexpired when the war broke out. Renewal of registration of a mark, however, is only a formality for preserving a perpetual right, and therefore comes under the first and second paragraphs of article 307.

§ **520. Rights of priority.** Article 308 of the treaty concerns the extension of the rights of priority to a period of six months after the coming into force of the treaty. The rights extended are those that had not expired at the outbreak of the war; also those that have arisen during the war, or would have arisen but for the war. For the last class, the extension of six months may be shorter than the period which is enjoyed under the Convention of 1883–1911. A person entitled to the benefits of the latter as well as of the treaty of peace may take advantage of the period granted by either.

As in article 4 of the Convention of 1883–1911, so also in article 308, a reservation is made with respect to rights of third parties. But under the latter article this is too broad. The extension of the period is not to affect the right of any of the high contracting parties, or of any person who before the coming into force of the treaty was in *bona fide* possession of any rights of industrial property conflicting with rights applied for by a third party claiming rights of priority in respect to them. Such third party may exercise the above rights by itself, or himself, personally, or by such agents or licensees as derived their rights from it or him before the coming into force of the treaty; and such persons shall not be amenable to any action or other process of law in respect of infringement.

It would have been more equitable to save rights of third parties not possessed before the coming into force of the treaty generally, but before the inception of the rights of priority of foreigners. At any rate, the rights saved are "rights of industrial property." This applies not to the mere use of an invention, but to the possession of a patent. Also it applies to the possession of a registered design or trade mark in the countries where registration is a condition of the acquisition of ownership.

§ 521. Countries and persons affected by the treaties of peace. A treaty, in general, can affect only the countries that are parties to it. To this rule there may be exceptions. There is no room for such exceptions, however, in the provisions of the treaties of peace dealing with industrial property. Third countries, therefore, are neither bound by the provisions of the treaties, nor may they claim any rights under them. Thus the primary question in the application of these treaties is that of the contracting countries. These are not the same in all the treaties.[1]

But the further question arises, whether these treaties constitute contractual engagements merely between each and all of the Allied and Associated Powers, on the one part, and Germany, Austria, Hungary, or Bulgaria on the other, or also between the Allied and

1. The contracting parties in the Treaty of Versailles are the United States of America, the British Empire, France, Italy, Japan, Belgium, Bolivia, Brazil, China, Cuba, Ecuador, Greece, Guatemala, Haiti, the Hedjaz, Honduras, Liberia, Nicaragua, Panama, Peru, Poland, Portugal, Rumania, the Serb-Croat-Slovene State, Siam, Czechoslovakia, and Uruguay, of the one part, and Germany, of the other part. (China, however, has not signed the treaty.)

The contracting parties in the treaties of Saint-Germain and Trianon are: the United States of America, the British Empire, France, Italy, Japan, Belgium, China, Cuba, Greece, Nicaragua, Panama, Poland, Portugal, Rumania, the Serb-Croat-Slovene State, Siam, and Czechoslovakia, of the one part, and Austria, or Hungary, of the other part.

The contracting parties in the Treaty of Neuilly are: the United States of America, the British Empire, France, Italy, Japan, Belgium, China, Cuba, Greece, the Hedjaz, Poland, Portugal, Rumania, the Serb-Croat-Slovene State, Siam, and Czechoslovakia.

The United States has not ratified these treaties, but it may avail itself of the provisions considered here by virtue of the stipulations of the treaties entered into with Germany, Austria, and Hungary. See *infra*, § 523.

Associated Powers themselves. The answer to this question must be sought in the terms used in the various provisions.

The provisions of the first paragraph of article 306 and of articles 307 and 308 leave no doubt that they constitute engagements of all the contracting countries as between themselves.[1] They constitute in effect common legislation applicable in their respective relations. The reëstablishment, or restoration, of rights acquired before the war, and the recognition of rights which, except for the war, would have been acquired, as well as the extension of periods and revival of lapsed rights (articles 307, 308), may be claimed, for instance, in France by German nationals, as well as by British, Belgians, Americans, and the rest.

Concerning, in particular, the extension of periods under articles 307 and 308, great confusion might arise as a result of the above character of the provisions. The extensions are uniform in the various treaties, but begin with the coming into force of each treaty. This date is not the same for all the treaties. Thus, as between the countries parties to several of these treaties, the extensions agreed upon vary with each treaty. When the extensions granted by the Treaty of Versailles expired, those granted by other treaties were still running. As a result, the uniformity of treatment in the different countries aimed at by these provisions was not achieved.

Although the treaties do not bind or benefit third countries, it does not follow that nationals of these countries may not be affected indirectly. This is possible if the treaties confer a benefit on nationals of third countries as well as on nationals of the contracting countries, or if the former may claim the benefits accorded to nationals of the contracting countries, by virtue of other international acts.

What may be regarded[2] as a benefit is conferred on nationals of third countries by the provision of article 310 cancelling, as from the date of the declaration of war, contracts in respect of industrial property concluded before the war between persons residing or carrying on business in the territory of the Allied and Associated Powers

1. For instance, the provision concerning the extension of rights of priorities reads: "shall be extended by each of the High Contracting Parties in favor of all nationals of the other High Contracting Parties."

However, the *Propriété Industrielle* (1922), pp. 129, 130, has doubts about this interpretation. On the contrary, Gidel and Barrault, *Le Traité de Paix avec l'Allemagne et les Intérêts Privés* (Paris, 1921), pp. 245, 274, and Chabaud, *La Propriété Industrielle et les Traités de Paix*, pp. 14–15, 36, agree with the view set forth in the text.

2. See *supra*, § 517.

and German nationals. But the treaty also tends to affect injuriously such persons by the provisions of article 306 (paragraph 7) and article 309.[1] The application of these provisions, especially against persons claiming the advantage of other international engagements, such as the Convention of 1883–1911, is questionable.

The first paragraph of article 306, concerning the reëstablishment, restoration, and recognition of rights, is couched in very general terms, which would permit the implication that persons of third countries, at least if they are residing or carrying on business in the contracting countries, might claim the benefit of the article. However, articles 307 and 308, purporting to give effect to the principle of article 306, speak only of "nationals of the High Contracting Parties." Nevertheless, other persons entitled to the benefits of the Convention of 1883–1911 (under articles 2 and 3), or of any other convention assuring national treatment for the protection of industrial property, may be entitled to the same rights, remedies, and benefits as nationals of the contracting countries.[2]

§ **522. Rights not affected by territorial changes.** Article 311 of the Treaty of Versailles and the corresponding articles of the other treaties contain provisions in regard to rights of industrial property existing in the territories separated from Germany, Austria, Hungary, or Bulgaria by virtue of the treaties. The inhabitants of the territories will continue to enjoy the rights to which they were entitled under the local legislation at the time of separation.

On the other hand, the rights which were in force in these territories at the time of the separation, or which will be reëstablished or restored in accordance with the above provisions of the treaties, will be recognized by the states to which the territories are transferred, and will remain in force in those territories for the period of time determined by the law of Germany, Austria, Hungary, or Bulgaria.

§ **523. The United States and the treaties of peace.** The United States has not ratified the treaties of peace, and is not a party to the Berne Arrangement of 1920, as will be seen. It concluded the Treaty Restoring Friendly Relations with Germany signed at Berlin, August 25, 1921, and the treaties Establishing Friendly Relations with Austria and Hungary, signed at Vienna, August 24, 1921, and

1. See *supra*, §§ 513, 516.
2. Chabaud, *La Propriété Industrielle et les Traités de Paix*, pp. 14–15.

at Budapest, August 29, 1921, respectively.[1] Under these treaties the United States shall enjoy all rights and advantages stipulated in the treaties of peace in a manner consistent with the rights accorded to Germany, Austria, or Hungary under the same provisions. Consequently, all the stipulations above considered constitute reciprocal engagements between the United States on the one part and Germany, Austria, and Hungary on the other; and persons claiming thereunder should be granted the advantages of the treaties regardless of the provisions of municipal law.

On March 3, 1921, the Nolan Act was passed in the United States,[2] designed to write into the law of the United States the provisions of articles 307 and 308 of the Treaty of Versailles. This act extended the rights of priority provided by section 4887 of the Revised Statutes for filing applications for patents and designs, if such rights had not expired on August 1, 1914, or had arisen between August 1, 1914, and the expiration of a period of six months from the passage of the act, that is, September 3, 1921. It will be noted that this provision excludes rights of priority for trade marks, which are included in article 308 of the Treaty of Versailles. This was in effect a longer extension than that of the treaties with Germany and Austria.[3] But by virtue of article II (5) of the treaties concluded by the United States with Germany, Austria, and Hungary respectively, the periods of time of the treaties were to run, with respect to any act on the part of the United States, from the date of the coming into force of the former treaties. Consequently, the rights of priority in respect to these countries ended May 11, May 8, and June 17, 1922, respectively.[4] This was affirmed in General Electric Co. *v.* Robertson, Commissioner of Patents,[5] which held the Treaty of Berlin to be self-executing, and to have the effect of extending the right of

1. See these treaties in *United States Treaty Series*, Nos. 658, 659, 660.

2. XLI *U. S. Stat. at Large*, 1313.

3. This was also six months, but began from the date of coming into force of each treaty and thus ended June 10, 1920, for the Treaty of Versailles, Jan. 16, 1921, for the Treaty of Saint-Germain, and Feb. 26, 1922, for the Treaty of Trianon.

4. The treaties came into force on the exchange of ratifications, namely, Nov. 11, 1921 (Treaty with Germany), Nov. 8, 1921 (Treaty with Austria), and Dec. 17, 1921 (Treaty with Hungary).

5. (1927) 21 F. (2d), 214 and (1928) 25 F. (2d), 146 (by the District Court of Maryland). *In re* Stoffregen (1925), 6 F. (2d), 943, a contrary opinion was handed down by the Court of Appeals of the District of Columbia, on an appeal from decisions of the Patent Office on what appears to be the same case. The General Electric Co. is the assignee of Stoffregen's title, and on dismissal of Stoffregen's appeal, it brought a bill of complaint in equity in the District Court of Maryland.

priority for a German patent issued during the war six months after November 11, 1921, when the treaty became effective.

The extension of rights of priority is granted by the Nolan Act in favor of citizens of the United States or of citizens or subjects of all countries[1] which extended substantially reciprocal privileges to citizens of the United States.[2] A reservation of rights of third parties similar to that of article 308 of the Treaty of Versailles is made by the act.

Section 2 of the act extends the time for payment of any fee, or for taking any action with respect to an application for patent, which time had not expired on August 1, 1914, or which began after August 1, 1914, until the expiration of one year from the passage of the act, without payment of extension fees or other penalties. A right of personal possession is reserved to American citizens, to continue the use, manufacture, or sale begun before the passage of the act. This extension ended March 3, 1922. A similar observation to that made in regard to the extension of rights of priority in respect to Germany, Austria, and Hungary, should be made here, too.

The advantage of section 2 of the act is granted to subjects or citizens of countries which extended substantially reciprocal privileges to citizens of the United States. But the extension shall not be granted for a longer term than that during which these privileges are conferred by such foreign country on citizens of the United States. By explicit exception, no right is given to reopen interference proceedings, where final hearing before the examiner of interferences has taken place.

As no obligation to work a patent or design exists by the law of the United States, no provision similar to that of article 307, paragraph 3, is found in the Nolan Act.

§ **524. The Berne Arrangement of 1920.** The treaties of peace attempted to reëstablish and restore industrial property rights affected by the war as between contracting countries alone. Their provisions did not extend to the relations between the belligerent and

1. It was decided *ex parte* Karnet (1921), 285 O. G. 571, that the nationality of the applicant to be taken into consideration is that of the country to which he belonged, not when he first filed his application, but when he claimed the application of the Nolan Act.

2. The Commissioner of Patents decided *ex parte* Hackett, Smith and Southall (1921), 285 O. G. 795, that there is substantial reciprocity when the foreign law extends the rights of priority to March 31, 1921, as by the Berne Arrangement, or to Jan. 10, 1921, as by Great Britain, according to her reservation in acceding to that Arrangement.

the neutral countries, or to those between the neutral countries themselves. On the initiative of the International Bureau of the Industrial Property Union,[1] these gaps were filled, for the most part, by the Berne Arrangement of June 30, 1920, concerning the preservation and reëstablishment of rights of industrial property affected by the World War.

The Arrangement was originally entered into by France, Germany, Great Britain (also in behalf of Ceylon and Trinidad and Tobago), Morocco, Poland, Sweden, Switzerland, and Tunis. Later, other countries also acceded: Austria, Belgium, Brazil, Denmark, Danzig (Free City), Spain, New Zealand, Hungary, Japan, Norway, the Netherlands, Portugal, the Serb-Croat-Slovene State, Czechoslovakia, and Rumania. Thus the only member countries of the Industrial Property Union which have not acceded to this Arrangement are Australia, Cuba, Italy, Mexico, and the United States.[2]

The Arrangement transfers, *mutatis mutandis*, to the relations between the belligerents and neutrals, and between the neutral countries themselves, the provisions of the treaties of peace.[3] Its first article extends the rights of priority in the same way as article 308 of the Treaty of Versailles, and with the same reservation of rights of third parties contained in that article. The persons, however, entitled to this benefit are not only the nationals of the contracting countries, but all persons entitled to such rights by virtue of the Industrial Property Convention, and also their legal representatives.[4]

The second article of the Arrangement extends the legal periods for fulfilling formalities, making payments, and so forth, relating to the preserving or obtaining of rights of industrial property acquired before the war, or which would have been acquired, except for the war, in the same way as article 307 (paragraph 1) of the Treaty of

1. See *L'Arrangement du 30 Juin 1920* in *Propriété Industrielle* (1920), pp. 77 ff.

2. Other countries which became members of the Union in the meantime had not the problem of the effects of the war upon the regime of the Union to deal with.

These countries, by their municipal law, granted similar extensions, but not as long as those of the Arrangement. See *Propriété Industrielle* (1922), pp. 129, 133. For the United States see, on the Nolan Act of March 3, 1921, *supra*, § 523.

3. For an interpretation of the Berne Arrangement, see two articles in *Propriété Industrielle* (1920), pp. 77–82, 102–106.

4. It was decided in Germany that the Arrangement could not be claimed in Germany by German nationals. See *Propriété Industrielle* (1921), p. 13. On the contrary, an act of April 26, 1921, made the Arrangement applicable to Austrians (*Bundesgesetzblatt*, 1921, p. 829).

Versailles. The revival, however, of lapsed rights is subject to a different reservation from that of paragraph 2 of article 307. In the latter it is provided that the Allied and Associated Powers may impose such conditions, in case of revived patents and designs, as are deemed reasonably necessary for the protection of third persons. In the Arrangement, the reservation concerns only those rights of third persons which are held in good faith. Of course, the restriction of article 307 concerning licenses granted under the war legislation is not included in the Arrangement.

Article 3 of the Arrangement is a precise copy of paragraph 3 of article 307 of the Treaty of Versailles, concerning the periods for the working of patents and use of designs and trade marks. The only difference is that the extension under this article, as well as under the previous one, begins from the coming into force of the Arrangement.

As a result of these provisions and of the coming into force of the Arrangement on September 30, 1920,[1] the various periods of extension were terminated as follows: the periods of priority, on March 31, 1921; those for the complying with legal formalities, making payments and so forth, on September 30, 1921; and those for working patents and using designs and trade marks, on September 30, 1922.[2] The Arrangement, however, by express provision of article 5, will not lose its effect unless it is so decided by a conference of revision of the Industrial Property Convention when its transitory purposes have been accomplished. Until that time it may be always invoked by persons basing their rights thereon.

In the preparatory stage of the Arrangement it was admitted that the contracting or acceding countries may make reservations.[3] Such were made by Great Britain and the Scandinavian countries — Denmark, Norway, and Sweden. According to Great Britain's reservation, the periods of extension provided for in articles 1 and 2 of the Arrangement were to expire, as regarded the United Kingdom, on January 10, 1921.[4] The three Scandinavian countries made the reservation that they would not apply the Arrangement in the case of trade marks and designs, but only in the case of patents and

1. See *Propriété Industrielle* (1920), p. 102.

2. As a result of the Arrangement, the periods of extension granted by the treaties of peace were enlarged as between the countries parties to the treaties and to the Arrangement. See a decision to this effect of the Austrian Patent Court, May 27, 1922 (*Propriété Industrielle*, 1922, p. 157).

3. See *Propriété Industrielle* (1920), pp. 77, 79.

4. See *procès-verbal*, in *Actes de la Conférence de La Haye*, p. 25.

models of utility; Denmark and Sweden made further reservations in respect to the periods of priority and periods for reviving lapsed applications, in accordance with their law.[1]

The Arrangement purported to assure only a minimum of protection, as article 4 expressly provided. Consequently, any longer periods granted by the municipal legislation of the various countries, or by other treaties (such as the treaties of peace) could still be claimed. Nor did it affect the stipulations of the treaties of peace concerning the reservations, exceptions and restrictions already considered.

The Arrangement contains no provision similar to that of article 286 of the Treaty of Versailles concerning the putting anew into application or the coming again into effect of the Convention of Union. It would seem to leave open the question of the fate of the Union during the war. A solemn affirmation by the contracting countries of the continued validity and effects of the Convention, notwithstanding the suspension of the execution of some of its provisions, would have been desirable. But perhaps the silence of the Arrangement in this respect is even more eloquent.

1. See *Propriété Industrielle* (1920), p. 137; (1921), p. 29; also *Actes de la Conférence de La Haye*, p. 26. See, on the extensions given by the municipal law of the Scandinavian countries, §§ 501–503, in the preceding chapter.

SECTION VIII

PAN-AMERICAN CONVENTIONS ON INDUSTRIAL PROPERTY

CHAPTER XXXIV

HISTORY OF PAN-AMERICAN CONVENTIONS

§ **525. Montevideo Conventions of 1889.** Of the twenty-one countries constituting the Pan-American Union, five — Brazil, Cuba the Dominican Republic, Mexico, and the United States — are members of the Industrial Property Union. Three more, — Salvador, Ecuador, and Guatemala, — originally parties to the Convention of 1883, denounced it and withdrew from the Union in 1884, 1885, and 1894 respectively.[1]

As early as 1889, at the International Congress of South American States at Montevideo, in connection with the other efforts at achieving uniformity in the law governing the international relations of these states, two conventions were signed on January 16, concerning patents and trade marks.[2] The contracting countries in these conventions were Argentina, Bolivia, Brazil, Chile, Paraguay, Peru, and Uruguay. All ratified them, except Bolivia and Chile. These conventions assured reciprocal national treatment to the patentees and trade-mark owners of the contracting countries, and a right of priority of one year for patents only. The period of one year for the latter began with the date a patent of invention was granted in one

1. See *supra*, § 49.
2. See text of the Conventions in *Tratados, Convenciones, Protocolos de la República Argentina* (1901), II, 120 and 127. See also *De Martens*, N. R., 2d ser., XVIII, 421 and 453.

of the contracting countries. In all other respects, these conventions referred to the municipal law of each country.

Their outstanding feature was a definition of patentable inventions and of trade marks. Two peculiarities should be noticed. Article 4 of the Convention on patents provided that an invention could not be the subject-matter of a patent if it had been published in any of the signatory or other countries. Thus the right of priority granted by this convention had not the effect of rendering the publication of the invention during the one-year period harmless to the patentee. On the other hand, article 3 of the Convention on trade marks included in the definition of trade marks the industrial designs that are applied, by weaving or impression, on the product itself which is placed on the market.

The first Pan-American Conference, which was held a few months later in Washington, recommended to the other American countries the adoption of the Montevideo conventions.[1]

§ **526. Pan-American Convention of 1902.** At the second International Conference of American States, at Mexico City, a new convention was signed, on January 27, 1902, on patents, industrial drawings and models, and trade marks.[2] This convention was concluded between all the countries constituting the Pan-American Union, with the exceptions of Brazil, Cuba, Panama, and Venezuela. It adopted most of the provisions of the two Montevideo conventions and borrowed certain provisions from the International Convention of 1883. It also authorized the consular agents of the country to which owners of patents, designs, or trade marks belonged to act as legal representatives of such owners in complying with the formalities and conditions required at the filing of applications.

Article 14 was the most interesting of this Convention. It provided that

> the annulment of a patent or the granting of a trade mark in the country of origin shall be communicated in an authenticated form to the other signatory countries, so that the administration may decide in the matter of an application for the recognition of the said patent or of the said trade mark as well as on the effect that such annulment or grant may produce as regards the patent or mark previously imported in these countries.

1. Sen. Doc. 177, 51st Cong., 1st Sess.
2. See text of Convention in Spanish, English, and French, in *Second Pan-American Conference, Minutes and Documents* (Mexico, 1902), pp. 723 ff.

Although this provision was the embryo of other provisions in the following Pan-American conventions, it was too indefinite to be given any application.

This Convention was ratified only by the five Central American countries, — Guatemala (April 25, 1902), Salvador (May 19, 1902), Costa Rica (August 4, 1903), Nicaragua (June 20, 1904), and Honduras (July 15, 1904), — and by Cuba (January 10, 1906).[1] But as between the Central American countries, it was abrogated by article 20 of the Treaty of Washington, on December 20, 1907,[2] which, through the mediation of the United States and Mexico, put an end to the contention in Central America.[3]

§ 527. Pan-American Convention of 1906. At the third Conference of American States, meeting at Rio de Janeiro in July, 1906, the drafting of a new Pan-American convention was decided upon, against the opinion of the Mexican delegation that all American states should accede to the Industrial Property Union constituted by the International Convention of 1883.[4]

A new convention, adopted and signed on August 9, concerned conjointly patents of invention, drawings and industrial models, trade marks, and literary and artistic property. In its first article it incorporated the conventions of 1902, and in the following articles it added a number of important amendments thereto, the purpose of which was to create a union between the American states for the protection of intellectual property. To this end two inter-American bureaus were created, one at Havana and the other at Rio de Janeiro. Although these bureaus were coördinated, the first was to serve thirteen countries — the United States of America, Mexico, Venezuela, Cuba, Haiti, the Dominican Republic, Salvador, Honduras, Nicaragua, Costa Rica, Guatemala, Panama, and Colombia; and the second the remaining eight South American countries — Argentina, Brazil, Bolivia, Chile, Ecuador, Paraguay, Peru, and Uruguay.

In the establishment of these bureaus the Convention of 1906 followed the Madrid Arrangement of 1891 for the international regis-

1. See *De Martens*, N. R., 3d ser., VI, 206; also *Fifth International Conference of American States, Handbook of the Pan-American Union* (Washington, 1922), p. 10.

2. Ratified by all the signatory states, Feb. and March 1908. See C *Br. & For. State Papers*, 835.

3. See "La Protection Internationale de la Propriété Intellectuelle dans l'Amérique Centrale," in *Propriété Industrielle* (1911), p. 50.

4. See *Tercera Conferencia Internacional Americana, Actas, Resoluciones, Documentos* (Rio de Janeiro, 1907), pp. 105, 249, 275, 641.

tration of trade marks; but it went much further in purporting to centralize the registration of literary and artistic works, patents, and designs and models, as well as of trade marks. No uniform duration of protection by international registration was provided for, as in the Madrid Arrangement. Only in case no term was fixed by the municipal law of a country, the duration of protection was to be fifteen years for patents and ten years for trade marks and designs. The fee for international registration was to be five dollars.

It was provided that each bureau should be organized when two thirds at least of the countries under its jurisdiction should ratify the Convention. Only eight countries ratified it: Honduras (February 5, 1907), Guatemala (April 19, 1907), Salvador (May 11, 1907), Nicaragua (February 20, 1908), Costa Rica (October 26, 1908), Chile (July 2, 1909), Ecuador (November, 1909), and Brazil (December 31, 1910).[1] The ratification by the first three countries was believed to have been made ineffective by the above provision of the Treaty of Washington.[2] So it has not been possible to organize the inter-American bureaus. Indeed, it was clear that the provisions of the Convention concerning international registration at the bureaus could not be executed. The question of international filing of patents or patent applications presented too serious difficulties and too many complications to be accomplished by the indefinite and vague provisions of this Convention. The Brazilian review, *Patentes y Marcas*, warned the governments of the American states as soon as the Convention was signed, that

> the convention will not come into effect because it is not practical and useful for commerce and industry; to centralize the services at Habana and at Rio de Janeiro is not at all to centralize them; and to limit the unification to America in this dualistic form is a task which is not worth prosecuting when it is much simpler to accede to the Industrial Property Convention of 1883.[3]

§ **528. Pan-American Conventions of 1910.** When the fourth International Conference of American States met at Buenos Aires in July, 1910, the delegation of the United States in its memorandum pointed out that it was unable to harmonize its legislation and prac-

1. See *De Martens*, N. R., 3d ser., VI, 221. In *Report to the Senate on the Fourth International Conference* (Doc. No. 744, 61st Congr., 3d Sess.), p. 98, Panama also is listed among the countries which have ratified this Convention.
2. See *Propriété Industrielle* (1911), pp. 50, 52.
3. Quoted in *Propriété Industrielle* (1907), pp. 129, 130.

tice on patents with the plan of the Convention; that it would submit a draft in accordance with the International Convention of 1883 which gave quite satisfactory results; and that the Pan-American Convention ought to be modified accordingly. The Mexican delegation declared that Mexico, not approving of the Convention, took no action in respect to it.[1]

The Argentine delegate, Dr. Zeballos, reluctantly concurred in the idea of inter-American conventions on these matters, preferring instead that the American countries should accede to the International Convention of 1883, thus avoiding the difficulties introduced by the formation of different unions, and promoting the tendency toward universal unity of definitions and juridical conceptions on a subject transcending national boundaries. On his recommendation, the committee urged that the Pan-American Conventions should adopt the bases of the Industrial Property Union, so as to achieve universal uniformity of principles.[2] Under these conditions, two conventions, one relating to patents and industrial designs and models, and the other concerning the protection of trade marks, were adopted by the Conference without much discussion.[3] Both conventions were signed by all the states of the Pan-American Union, except Bolivia, on August 20, 1910. They were ratified by Brazil, Costa Rica, Cuba, the Dominican Republic, Ecuador, Guatemala, Haiti, Honduras, Nicaragua, Panama, Paraguay, the United States, and Uruguay. The trade-marks Convention was ratified also by Peru.[4]

1. See *Cuarta Conferencia Internacional Americana* (Buenos Aires, 1911), II, 10, 69.

2. *Ibid.*, I, 341–343, 396.

3. See texts in Spanish, English, Portuguese, and French, in XXXVIII *Stat. at Large*, pt. 2, p. 1811, and XXXIX *ibid.*, pt. 2, p. 1675; also in Spanish only, in *Cuarta Conferencia Internacional Americana*, I, 493 and 507.

4. The dates of ratification, according to the information given the present writer through the courtesy of the Director General of the Pan-American Union (letter dated July 26, 1928), are the following:

The Convention on Patents and Industrial Designs and Models was ratified by

Brazil	November 9, 1914.
Costa Rica	August 7, 1915.
Cuba	December 23, 1912.
Dominican Republic	April 18, 1912.
Ecuador	November 4, 1913.
Guatemala	April 27, 1912.
Haiti	October 8, 1918.
Honduras	February 13, 1913.
Nicaragua	April 23, 1912.
Panama	June 12, 1913.
Paraguay	August 22, 1913.
United States	March 21, 1911.
Uruguay	August 7, 1919.

But the governments of Costa Rica, Guatemala, Honduras, and Nicaragua subsequently denounced the Convention concerning trade marks, after giving the notice of one year required by the terms of article 19.[1]

The Convention relating to patents and industrial designs and models ties together provisions, not always consistent, of the International Convention of 1883 and of the previous Pan-American Conventions.[2] The international registration of patents, provided for by the previous Convention, is discarded. Instead, the principles of national treatment, right of priority, and independence of patents of the Industrial Property Union are adopted.

The Convention concerning the protection of trade marks attempts to institute the principle of so-called automatic registration. It is analyzed in the next chapter. Suffice it to say here that it includes provisions similar to those of the International Convention of 1883 for the protection of trade names and indications of origin, and it maintains the two inter-American bureaus at Havana and Rio de Janeiro.

Article 11 of the Convention on patents and 17 of that on trade marks provide that treaties concerning patents, designs, models,

---

The Trade Marks Convention was ratified by

Brazil	November 9, 1914.
Costa Rica	August 7, 1915.
Cuba	June 2, 1914.
Dominican Republic	April 18, 1912.
Ecuador	November 4, 1913.
Guatemala	April 27, 1912.
Haiti	October 31, 1918.
Honduras	February 13, 1913.
Nicaragua	April 23, 1912.
Panama	June 13, 1913.
Paraguay	August 22, 1913.
Peru	April 19, 1920.
United States	March 21, 1911.
Uruguay	August 7, 1919.

1. See *Fifth International Conference of American States, Handbook of the Pan-American Union* (Washington, 1922), p. 16. Guatemala gave notice of her withdrawal March 18, 1920; Nicaragua, July 16, 1920; Costa Rica, Sept. 30, 1921; Honduras, Feb. 7, 1922.

The National Legislatures of Salvador and Venezuela were advised by their committees entrusted with the study of the conventions to refrain from ratification. See *ibid.*, p. 16.

2. For instance, article 3, concerning the period of priority, and article 5, concerning the moment from which priority begins. Also articles 8 and 9, taken from the Convention of Montevideo speak only of patents, whereas the Convention of 1910, concerns also industrial designs or models.

and trade marks previously concluded by and between the signatory states shall be substituted by the new convention from the date of their ratification, so far as the relations between the signatory states are concerned. Thus the Pan-American Conventions of 1902 and 1906 are superseded by the new conventions. As regards the Conventions of Montevideo on patents and trade marks, the latter should be deemed wholly abrogated since three of the four countries that had ratified it, namely, Peru, Paraguay, and Uruguay, have ratified the Convention under consideration. That on patents remains in force as between Peru and Argentina only, which have not ratified the Pan-American Convention of 1910.

Of the two inter-American bureaus contemplated by the Convention only that of Havana was organized (in 1919),[1] and the first mark was registered on October 28 of that year. Down to the year 1923 inclusive, the marks registered and countries from which they originated have been as follows: [2]

Year	United States of America	Cuba	Dominican Republic	Haiti
1919	80	..	..	..
1920	270	15	..	..
1921	217	9	..	1
1922	173	7	19	2
1923	114	7	16	..

§ **529. Pan-American Trade-Mark Convention of 1923.** The agenda of the fifth International Conference of American States, which was called together at Santiago de Chile in March, 1923, contained as its first topic consideration of the action taken by the participating countries and of the application in each country of the conventions and resolutions of previous conferences, "with special reference to the convention concerning trade marks."[3] In the meantime, the question of trade marks formed the subject of study by the Pan-American Financial Conference and by the Inter-American High Commission.[4] The Central Executive Council of the latter was

1. In fact, its organization began on Dec. 6, 1917, when the Cuban government, by a Decree of that date, decided to establish the bureau and appointed Dr. Mario Diáz Irizar as its director. See 24 *Leyes y Decretos de Cuba* (1917) p. 528.

2. This information was given the present writer through the courtesy of the Director General of the Pan-American Union, in his letter of June 27, 1928.

3. *Fifth International Conference of American States, Handbook of the Pan-American Union* (Washington, 1922), p. 26.

4. See *Preliminary Resolutions for the Consideration of the United States Section of the International High Commission* (Washington, 1915), p. 21; H. R. Doc. 1788, 64th Cong.,

assisted in drafting a new convention for the protection of trade marks by a number of trade-mark experts in the United States.[1] The twenty-one national sections of the Inter-American High Commission were also consulted. But it does not seem that experts from Latin-American countries gave any assistance in the preparatory work.

A draft convention proposed at the Santiago Conference by the United States delegation [2] was signed by the delegates of all the American countries belonging to the Pan-American Union, except those of Bolivia, Mexico, and Peru, on April 28, 1923.[3]

As was pointed out by Mr. Subercaseaux, delegate of Chile and *rapporteur* of the committee to the plenary assembly, the fact that the Convention of 1910 had not been ratified by six of the American countries (Argentina, Chile, Colombia, Mexico, Salvador, and Venezuela), and had been denounced by four (Costa Rica, Guatemala, Honduras, and Nicaragua), made it necessary to consider the objections of these countries and to give them satisfaction.[4] Thus the two basic ideas of the revision consisted in absolute respect for the domestic law of each country, and satisfaction of the fiscal interest of certain countries which derive income from the registration of marks. The two inter-American bureaus were maintained, and registration in the different countries was to be made through them. A detailed analysis of the Convention is made in the next chapter.

In accordance with article 14 of the Convention, the government of Chile has notified the contracting countries that the Convention of 1923, having been ratified by the United States of America, Brazil, Cuba, Paraguay, Haiti, and the Dominican Republic,[5] went into

---

2d Sess., p. 21; Sen. Doc. No. 739, 64th Cong., 2d Sess., p. 116; Moore, *The Work of the International High Commission*, an address delivered at the Pan-American Financial Conference (Washington, 1920), p. 6.

1. See introduction to *Convention for the Protection of Commercial, Industrial and Agricultural Trade Marks and Commercial Names*, a pamphlet of the Central Executive Council, Inter-American High Commission (Washington, 1923).

2. *Report of the delegates of the United States of America to the Fifth International Conference of American States* (Washington, 1924), p. 17.

3. See text in English, Spanish, French, and Portuguese in XLIV *Stat. at Large*, pt. 3, p. 2494; also in *United States Treaty Series*, No. 751.

4. See *Verbatim Record of the Plenary Sessions of the Fifth International Conference of American States* (Santiago de Chile, 1923), I, 325.

5. The dates of ratification are as follows: Brazil, Jan. 12, 1924; Cuba, Aug. 2, 1924; the Dominican Republic, Oct. 7, 1925; Haiti, June 22, 1925; Paraguay, May 26, 1924; and the United States, Feb. 24, 1925. (Information given the present writer by the Director General of the Pan-American Union, letter dated July 26, 1928.)

effect on September 30, 1926.[1] According to the same article, so far as the relations between these countries are concerned the Convention of 1910 ceased to be in effect.

Thus, at the present time, the net result of the Pan-American Conventions on industrial property is as follows:

(1) The Montevideo Convention of 1889 on trade marks has been abrogated.

(2) The Montevideo Convention of 1889 on patents remains in effect only as between Argentina and Peru.

(3) The Pan-American Convention of Mexico City (1902) on patents, industrial drawings, models and trade marks, and the Pan-American Convention of Rio de Janeiro (1906), have been abrogated.

(4) The Pan-American Convention of 1910, relating to patents and industrial designs and models, is in effect as between thirteen American countries, namely, Brazil, Costa Rica, Cuba, the Dominican Republic, Ecuador, Guatemala, Haiti, Honduras, Nicaragua, Panama, Paraguay, the United States, and Uruguay.

(5) The Pan-American Convention of 1910 concerning the protection of trade marks is in effect as between Ecuador, Panama, Peru, and Uruguay, which have ratified the Convention of 1910, but not that of 1923, and as between each of these countries and the other six countries that had ratified the Convention of 1910, namely Brazil, Cuba, the Dominican Republic, Haiti, Paraguay, and the United States of America.

(6) The Pan-American Convention of 1923 concerning the protection of commercial, industrial and agricultural trade marks and commercial names is in effect as between six American countries, namely, Brazil, Cuba, the Dominican Republic, Haiti, Paraguay, and the United States of America.

On the other hand, the business of the Inter-American Bureau at Havana has receded in the meantime, instead of progressing. The registrations which had fallen from 270 for the United States in 1920 to 114 in 1923, and from 15 to 7 for Cuba, were as follows in the following years: [2]

1. See Proclamation by the President of the United States in *United States Treaty Series*, No. 751, p. 37, and XLIV *Stat. at Large*, pt. 3, p. 2526. The ratification by the United States of America is subject to five understandings or conditions, two relating to form and three to substance.

The Convention was approved by the legislative assembly of Guatemala on April 24, 1925, and ratified by the President of Guatemala on May 6, 1925. But the ratification has never been deposited with the Government of Chile. Until such deposit takes place, Guatemala is not considered a party to the Convention.

2. According to information given the present writer through the courtesy of the Director General of the Pan-American Union, letter dated June 27, 1928.

Year	United States of America	Cuba	Dominican Republic	Haiti
1924	83	15	8	..
1925	60	7	3	..
1926	100	6	..	..
1927	34	4	1	..

§ 530. The sixth International Conference of American States. The long and repeated efforts of about two-score years to create an American union for the protection of industrial property, and to establish an international regime on the subject which would give satisfaction to all American countries, have been well-nigh fruitless. What are the reasons for this? Is it the fact that the United States, a manufacturing country, has interests that conflict with those of Latin America, which produces only raw materials? [1] Is it the lack of long preparation and continuity of study of the questions involved in the protection of industrial property? [2] Or is it the lack of sufficient information on the law and interests of the various American countries, the failure to interest these countries sufficiently in the advantages of a common international regulation of the subject of industrial property? [3]

The revision of the trade-mark conventions of 1910 and 1923 was on the agenda of the sixth International Conference of American States, which was called together at Havana on January 16, 1928. In a report submitted to the sixth committee of the conference on the subject of Inter-American Protection of Trade Marks, the delegation of Argentina noted the failure of the five previous conferences to arrive at uniform rules of protection of trade marks, and the fact that the sixth Pan-American Conference found itself in the same situation as that of the first conference forty years earlier. This delegation was of the opinion that these failures

should not be attributed to a simple lack of interest or to indolence. There is something further, and that is the lack of desire to ratify an instrument

1. Inman, *Pan-American Conferences and their Results* (Austin, 1924), p. 34.

2. *Convention for the Protection of Commercial, Industrial and Agricultural Trade Marks and Commercial Names* (pamphlet of the Inter-American High Commission), Introduction.

3. Characteristic of the spirit and method of drafting these conventions is the suggestion of the Inter-American Bureau of Havana to the governments of American countries that "to the next conference to be held in Havana copies of the respective trade-mark laws of their countries could be brought by the gentlemen members, so as, upon examination of same, to try and not draw up any resolution interfering with them." See *Report to the American Governments in Connection with the VI Pan-American Conference, Oficina de la Union Internacional Americana para la protecciòn de las Marcas* (Habana, 1927), p. 56.

which it is felt has been adopted without careful and conscientious study, taking into account all the national interests involved, as well as the fact that it does not satisfy an imperative necessity of all the signatory countries.

It thought that the method, followed hitherto, of dealing with such matters of extreme legal and technical specialization in diplomatic conferences was wrong. Instead, conferences of specialists should be convened, as was done in Europe in the case of the Industrial Property Union.[1] The Argentine delegate, Mr. Espil, recognizing that the protection of industrial property is of interest to producers as well as to consumers and stimulates the development of the nascent industries of American countries, pointed out the burdens imposed by the international registry upon these countries by the renunciation of part of the registration fees, and of direct and immediate control over foreign trade marks, in exchange for benefits of a less important character, since such countries do not make use of international registration. If such an international registry should exist, he thought that it should duplicate that of Berne under the Madrid Arrangement. He concluded with a project of a resolution calling for the meeting of a conference of specialists, and of preparatory work for such a conference by the Pan-American Union.[2] It is to be regretted that the United States delegation did not deem it proper to support the Argentine proposal, but persisted in the effort to revise once more the conventions of 1910 and 1923 at the Conference of Havana.[3] The committee, however, adopted the resolution proposed by the Argentine delegation, recommending to the Governing Board of the Pan-American Union "the calling of a special conference of representatives of the Union, to be held at such

1. See *Documentary Information Compiled by the Pan-American Union Relative to the Pan-American Trade-Mark Conference* (Washington, 1928), pp. 3 ff. The Argentine delegate also stated that he was appointed by the committee *rapporteur* for the topic of trade marks, though he had never had in his professional life a case dealing with trade marks, *ibid.*, p. 7.

2. Before the submission of his resolution, the Argentine delegate concluded that the failure of the attempts of the Pan-American Conferences to establish an inter-American system of protection of industrial property should lead the American countries to think that perhaps the solution may lie in their accession to the Convention of Paris and the Madrid Arrangement.

More outspoken in this sense was the Mexican delegate, who declared that the Mexican government had maintained with absolute firmness its attitude of remaining a member of the universal Industrial Property Union, and of refusing accession to the Pan-American Convention. See *Documentary Information Compiled by the Pan-American Union Relative to the Trade-Mark Conference*, p. 19.

3. *Ibid.*, pp. 13 ff.

place and date as it may designate, for the purpose of studying in its amplest scope the problem of Inter-American protection of trade marks."[1] The conclusions of that conference are to be forwarded, through the medium of the Pan-American Union, to the consideration of the different governments, without the need of a later reference to the Seventh International Conference of American States.

By a resolution adopted by the Governing Board of the Pan-American Union at its session of May 2, 1928, the Chairman was authorized to fix the date of the conference in question, which was to meet at Washington. In accordance with this resolution, the Chairman fixed February 11, 1929, as the date on which the Conference should convene. In the meantime the governments were to be requested to send to the Pan-American Union "suggestions and observations that may be utilized in the formation of the bases of a project that shall be prepared by the Pan-American Union and that shall serve as a basis of discussion when the Conference convenes."[2]

§ **531. Pan-American Trade-Mark Conference of 1929.** It may be questioned how far the Pan-American Trade-Mark Conference which convened at Washington, February 11, 1929, was a "conference of specialists" on trade-mark law. Most of the American republics were represented by their respective ministers or first secretaries of legations and in certain cases by the commercial *attachés* or consuls general. The United States delegation consisted of Assistant Secretary of State, Mr. Francis White; the Commissioner of Patents, Mr. T. E. Robertson; and Mr. Edward S. Rogers, a trade-mark lawyer. Cuba sent to the conference Dr. Gustave Gutierrez, Director of the Inter-American Bureau at Havana.[3]

A "Draft Convention on the Inter-American Protection of Trade Marks" had been prepared by a special committee of the Governing Board of the Pan-American Union and communicated to the governments of the American republics. This was abandoned when the Conference met.[4] Instead, a draft Convention and a draft Protocol

1. *Sexta Conferencia Internacional Americana, Acta Final* (Habana, 1928), p. 87.

2. See *Documentary Information Compiled by the Pan-American Union Relative to the Pan-American Trade-Mark Conference* (Washington, 1926), p. 1.

3. The Mexican Delegate, Mr. Suastegui, read a memorandum at the Conference suggesting that the Pan-American Union name a commission of experts to study the subject in detail and to recommend modification of legislation in the various countries. See *Pan-American Trade-Mark Conference, Minutes of the Sessions* (Pan-American Union, 1929), p. 59.

4. A preparatory work was done in New York by trade-mark experts in the United States, in which the present writer has participated. At this stage, the inadequacy of

prepared by the Cuban delegation were accepted as the bases of discussion in the sub-committees.[1] These drafts appear to have been prepared with the coöperation of the United States delegation. They were adopted by the Conference, with minor changes, at the meeting of February 19th. On the next day, two acts were signed: a General Inter-American Convention for Trade-Mark and Commercial Protection and a Protocol on the Inter-American Registration of Trade Marks.

The substance of these acts is considered in the next chapter. Suffice it to state here that although they contain many improvements on the prior regime, they also have defects which should raise serious doubts of their ratification by all the American republics. The Convention, especially, is too elaborately detailed and attempts to transfer into the conventional regime concepts and rules of the law of the United States which are unrelated to the background of the civil law prevailing in Latin America.[2]

Both acts were signed by the delegations of all the members of the Pan-American Union present with the exception of Argentina and Salvador. According to their final articles, the original acts and the instruments of ratification shall be deposited with the Pan-American Union. They shall enter into effect for the contracting states in the order that they deposit their ratifications.

---

the draft in question became clear and the idea was conceived of preparing two separate drafts, a general convention for trade-mark protection and a protocol on the Inter-American registration of trade marks. See my study, *The International Protection of Trade Marks by the American Republics* (Harvard University Press, 1929), which was prepared with the hope of facilitating the work of the Conference.

1. See *Minutes of the Plenary Sessions and of the Committees of the Pan-American Trade-Mark Conference*, Pan-American Union, Washington, pp. 4, 15–43.

2. See, on the contrary, the drafts proposed in S. P. Ladas, *The International Protection of Trade Marks by the American Republics*, pp. 54 ff.

CHAPTER XXXV

THE INTER-AMERICAN REGIME OF INDUSTRIAL PROPERTY

I. The Convention of 1910 on Patents, Designs, and Models

§ **532. Persons protected.** Article 2 of the Convention signed at Buenos Aires on August 20, 1910, for the protection of patents of inventions, designs, and models,[1] provides that "any person who shall obtain a patent of invention in any of the signatory states shall enjoy in each of the other states all the advantages . . ." In contrast to the International Convention of 1883 and to the Pan-American Convention of 1906, protecting nationals of the contracting countries and persons domiciled or possessing industrial or commercial establishments therein, the Convention under consideration declares entitled to its advantages "any person" who shall obtain a patent in any of the signatory states. The expression "any person" raises difficulties of interpretation. Nothing appears in the discussions at the Fourth Pan-American Conference explaining this change from the previous Convention. It is difficult to say whether the expression "any person" covers the three categories of persons protected by the International Convention of 1883, the persons only domiciled in any of the contracting countries, irrespective of their nationality, according to a principle of law common to Latin American countries,[2] or all persons, in general, who have obtained a patent in any of them. Certain utterances in the report of the committee would lend support to the last interpretation.[3]

§ **533. Subject-matter of protection.** The Convention deals with patents of invention and industrial designs and models ("Patentes de invención, dibujos y modelos industriales"). Articles 6 and 7 undertake to define what a patentable invention is and when a patent may be refused recognition in the contracting countries. The definition of invention is one found in the law of many Latin American countries, and has its origin partly in the English Statute of Monopolies of 1623, and partly in the French law of 1844, article 2. Thus it includes "a new manner of manufacturing industrial products, a new machine or mechanical or manual apparatus which serves for the

1. See text in Spanish, English, Portuguese, and French in XXXIX *Stat. at Large*, pt. 2, p. 1675; also, in Spanish, in *Cuarta Conferencia Internacional Americana*, I, 493; and in English, in Malloy, *United States Treaties*, III, 2930.

2. See *Propriété Industrielle* (1913), p. 47.

3. The committee thought that the contracting countries were to "discuss and argue upon principles which guarantee and protect the effects of human genius without distinction of races or nationalities." See *Cuarta Conferencia Internacional Americana*, I, 541; also Sen. Doc. 744, 61st Cong., 3d Sess., p. 275.

manufacture of said products, the discovery of a new industrial product, the application of known methods for the purposes of securing better results." However, it also includes "every new, original, and ornamental design or model for an article of manufacture" which, but for the words "or model," is taken from the United States Revised Statutes, section 4929, dealing with patents for designs. Thus designs or models are considered inventions by the Convention, which is in opposition to the general view that they constitute aesthetic creations calling for the application of totally different rules and criteria from those admitted in the case of patentable inventions.[1]

This definition does not bind the contracting countries on the question of what they may deem a patentable invention or an industrial design or model. For the second paragraph of article 6 provides that "the foregoing definition shall be understood without prejudice to the laws of each state." The fact that the invention is published in any country prior to the date of "the invention" by the applicant,[2] or registered, published, or described more than one year prior to the date of the patent application, are absolute obstacles to the recognition of a patent, while the fact of public use or sale is an obstacle only when such use or sale has been made in the country in which the patent is applied for.

§ **534. National treatment.** The basic principle of the Convention of 1910 is identical with that of the International Convention of 1883, that is, the assimilation of persons entitled to its benefits to nationals of each country. Yet, the provision to this effect in article 2 of the Pan-American Convention is not as clear as that of the Paris Convention of 1883. The advantages enjoyed under the former are those

> which the laws relative to patents of invention, and industrial designs and models concede. Consequently they shall have the same protection and identical legal remedies against any attack upon their rights provided they comply with the laws of each state.

1. See *supra*, §§ 244–246.
2. The absence, in the earlier Convention of 1906, of a provision declaring that patents for inventions which have been published by the applicant in any country prior to the date of "the invention" may be refused recognition, has been said to be one of the reasons why the United States has not ratified that Convention. See Paul Reinsch, "The Fourth International Conference of American Republics," in *American Journal of International Law* (1910), IV, 777, 789. But it was wholly improbable, as this author thinks, that the insertion of this provision would compel Latin American countries, in order to receive international protection for patents, to inquire into the usefulness and novelty of inventions.

This provision refers only to advantages conceded by the laws of each country, without any reference to the persons to whom such advantages are conceded. Thus, if the law of an American country excludes foreigners from certain advantages, or requires reciprocity, one might think that no change is wrought therein by the Convention. All that is required, is the application of the domestic laws. However, such an interpretation would seem to be excluded from the purpose and aim of the Convention. If no reference is made to the persons who enjoy the advantages of the domestic law, this is presumably because it was intended to make the provision as general as possible. Besides, the second sentence of article 2 speaks of the "same protection" and "identical legal remedies" which thenceforth should be enjoyed by the persons protected by the Convention. The words "same" and "identical" clearly refer to remedies enjoyed by the domestic inventors or creators of designs and models. The enjoyment of the advantages, protection, and remedies provided for in article 2 is subject to compliance with the laws of each state. Thus, in all respects, the application of the domestic laws is preserved, with the exception of discriminations against foreigners.

§ 535. **Right of priority.** A right of priority similar to that provided for in article 4 of the International Convention of 1883 is stipulated by article 3 of the Pan-American Convention of 1910. The terms of this article are taken almost literally from the former; but no provisions relative to the formalities required for claiming the right of priority are contained therein. For the interpretation of this article reference is made to a previous chapter.[1] The periods of priority are twelve months for patents and four months for industrial designs and models.[2]

The periods in article 4 of the International Convention of 1883 run from the date of filing the first application in a country of the Union. There is no provision to this effect in article 3 of the Pan-American Convention, but article 5 provides as follows:

> Questions which may arise regarding the priority of patents of invention shall be decided with regard to the date of the application for the respective patents in the countries in which they are granted.

1. See *supra*, chap. XI.
2. Since the recent revision of the Paris Convention by the Conference of The Hague of 1925, the period of the right of priority for industrial designs and models in the Industrial Property Union is six months.

This provision deals only with questions of priority of patents. It may apply to cases in which a foreign patentee claims a right of priority against a domestic patentee; namely, to the cases, referred to in the second paragraph of article 3, of "other deposits" effected before the expiration of the priority period of one year. In such cases, then, the period of priority is to be taken as having started with the date of filing the patent application. The provision speaks of applications for patents "in the countries in which they are granted," which would imply that only applications resulting in a grant of a patent, and only after such grant, give rise to a right of priority. There is no valid reason for the first limitation, and the second may take away all the benefit of the period of priority, if the examination of the application lasts too long.[1]

The insertion of this provision illustrates the lack of sufficient preparatory work in the drafting of the Convention. Article 5 is taken literally from the Convention of Montevideo, where it had a real purpose. It followed immediately the provision concerning the rights of priority, which, in that Convention, ran from the date a patent was obtained and not from the date an application was filed. Thus the provision in question purported to determine the question of the priority as between two patents which presumably were granted on the same date. Since the Convention of 1910 adopted the provision of the International Convention of 1883 in respect to rights of priority, the provision of article 5 is irrelevant and ambiguous.

§ **536. Independence of patents.** Another provision, besides those on national treatment and rights of priority, taken from the International Convention of 1883, is the provision concerning the independence of patent rights granted to the same person in several countries in respect to the same invention. Such patent rights are declared, in article 4 of the Convention of 1910, to be independent of each other, if the patent applications have been filed in the several countries "within the terms fixed," that is, within the period of right of priority. They are also independent, according to paragraph 2 of the article, of the rights arising under patents obtained for the same invention in countries not parties to this Convention.

Article 3 does not contain the provision of paragraph 2 of article 4*b* of the International Convention of 1883, added by the Wash-

1. See *Propriété Industrielle* (1911), p. 64.

ington Conference of 1911, which specifies that the independence of patent rights should be understood in an absolute manner, that is, that patents shall be independent in respect of the grounds of annulment and forfeiture, as well as in respect of their normal duration. However, this stipulation was added merely as an interpretation of the provision of independence of the first paragraph,[1] and may, therefore, be admitted as an interpretation of the provision of the Convention under consideration.

§ **537. Rights and remedies of patentees.** Articles 8 and 9 of the Convention deal with the rights and remedies to be enjoyed by patentees. They are taken from the Montevideo Convention of 1889. The first proclaims that the ownership of a patent of invention comprises the right to enjoy the benefits thereof, and the right to assign or transfer it in accordance with the laws of the country. The second provides that persons who incur civil or criminal liabilities, because of injuries or damage to the rights of inventors, shall be prosecuted and punished in accordance with the law of the country wherein the offense has been committed or the damage occasioned.

These provisions are of little importance, since in effect they reserve the questions of rights and remedies for determination by the law of each country. Moreover, they are incomplete, since they refer only to patents of invention and not to industrial designs and models as well. This is the case because the Convention of Montevideo, from which these provisions were taken, concerned patents alone. This goes to show again the hasty and superficial tying together of provisions taken from various conventions.

Article 10 provides that copies of patents certified in the country of origin, according to the national law thereof, shall be given full faith and credit as evidence of the right of priority, except in the cases under article 7 when a patent may be refused recognition.

§ **538. Final provisions.** The provision of article 11 concerning the abrogation of previous treaties on patents is considered in the preceding chapter.[2] Article 12 refers to the coming into force of the Convention. It provides that the "adhesions of the American nations to the Convention shall be communicated to the government of the Argentine Republic, in order that it may communicate them to the other states. These communications shall have the effect of an

1. See *supra*, § 210. See also chap. XII for all questions concerning the independence of patents.

2. See *supra*, pp. 761–762.

exchange of ratifications." It is implied that the Convention comes into force as between the acceding countries on the date of the communication of their accession to the other countries by the Argentine government.

The last article deals with denunciations. Each signatory state may denounce the Convention when it sees fit, after notifying the Argentine government. The Convention shall cease to be in effect so far as such state is concerned after one year following receipt of the communication by the Argentine government.

The Convention was made and signed in Spanish, English, Portuguese, and French.

II. Pan-American Conventions on Trade Marks

§ 539. Duality of international regime. As has been pointed out in the last chapter, the Convention for the protection of trade marks signed at Buenos Aires August 20, 1910, was superseded, as from September 30, 1926, by the Convention for the protection of commercial, industrial, and agricultural trade marks and commercial names signed at Santiago de Chile, April 28, 1923. However, it still remains in effect as between Ecuador, Panama, Peru, and Uruguay, which ratified the Convention of 1910 but not that of 1923, and as between each of these countries and the six other countries which ratified the Convention of 1910, namely, Brazil, Cuba, the Dominican Republic, Haiti, Paraguay, and the United States of America. The latter countries are governed in their mutual relations by the Convention of 1923.

Thus there exists actually a dual international regime of trade marks in the American countries which have entered into Pan-American conventions. Moreover, two new acts, a Convention and a Protocol, were signed at Washington by the delegates at the Pan-American Trade-Mark Conference on February 20, 1929. These acts will not probably come into effect until some time yet. It is provided that they shall go into effect for each country in the order that they deposit their ratifications. Then a new international regime will result as between some of the American Republics. For the sake of clearness of exposition each of the above conventions will be considered separately.

A. *Convention of 1910*

§540. **Persons protected.** Article 2 of the Convention of 1910[1] provides that "any mark duly registered in one of the signatory states shall be considered as registered also in the other states of the Union." This provision would seem to imply that no limitation exists in respect to persons who may claim the protection of the Convention except that they have registered their marks in one of the contracting countries. They may be nationals of the contracting countries, domiciled or possessing industrial or commercial establishments therein, or they may be nationals of, or domiciled or established in, non-contracting countries. Thus a British manufacturer wishing to take advantage of this Convention may register his trade mark in the United States, and then claim the protection of article 2 in all the other contracting countries.[2]

§ 541. **Subject-matter of protection.** The subject-matter of protection is, as article 1 provides, trade marks and commercial names. Articles 4 and 5 define what shall be considered a trade mark and what cannot be adopted or used as such. These definitions are taken from the Convention of Montevideo and the previous Pan-American conventions. "Any sign, emblem, or special name that merchants or manufacturers may adopt or apply to their goods or products in order to distinguish them from those of other manufacturers or merchants who manufacture or deal in articles of the same kind," is to be considered a trade mark. This definition is not declared to be subject to the municipal law of the contracting countries, but the terms used are broad enough to leave room for divergences of application in each country. "Sign," "emblem," "in order to distinguish," are not likely to be understood in the same way everywhere. This shows the fallacy of inserting a definition of this kind in a convention. The provision of article 6 of the International Convention of 1883 is undoubtedly more practical in laying down the principle, subject to certain well-defined exceptions, that a trade mark valid by the law of the country of origin shall be validated in all the other countries in its original form.

Following this positive definition, article 5 proceeds to exclude

1. See text in Spanish, English, Portuguese, and French, in XXXVIII *Stat. at Large*, pt. 2, p. 1811; in Spanish only, in *Cuarta Conferencia Internacional Americana*, p. 507, and in English, in Malloy, *United States Treaties*, III, 2935.

2. See *Patent and Trade Mark Review* (1921), XIX, 337.

certain things from being adopted or used as trade marks. These are (*a*) national, provincial, or municipal flags or coats-of-arms; (*b*) immoral or scandalous subjects; (*c*) distinctive marks which may have been adopted by others, or which may give rise to confusion with other marks; (*d*) "the general classification" of articles; (*e*) pictures or names of persons without their permission; and (*f*) any design which may have been adopted as an emblem by any fraternal or humanitarian association. The provisions of this article are to be construed without prejudice to the particular provisions of the law of each country. Therefore a country is not bound by these provisions in any way.[1]

§ **542. Basic principle of single registration.** The basic principle of the Convention is contained in article 2, which provides that

> any mark duly registered in one of the signatory states shall be considered as registered also in the other states of the Union, without prejudice to the rights of third persons and to the provisions of the laws of each state governing the same.

This provision attempts to assure protection of trade marks in a more radical way than the Madrid Arrangement for the International Registration of Trade Marks. While the latter requires double registration, one in the country of origin and another with the International Bureau at Berne, — this replacing all other national registrations in the other contracting countries,—the Pan-American Convention of 1910 goes further by requiring only a single registration in any of the contracting countries. By such single registration the protection of the mark is assured in all the other countries automatically, so to speak.

What is the rôle of the Inter-American bureaus, and the international registries kept by them? Paragraph 2 of article 2 provides that,

> in order to enjoy the benefit of the foregoing [that is, automatic protection in all the contracting countries], the manufacturer or merchant interested in the registry of the mark must pay, in addition to the fees or charges fixed by the laws of the state in which application is first made, the sum of fifty dollars in gold, which sum shall cover all the expenses of both Bureaus for international registration in all the signatory states.

1. The English text of paragraph 2 of article 5 uses the plural, "the foregoing provisions," which might be taken as applying to the provision of article 4 and that of article 5. However, the Spanish, Portuguese, and French texts use the singular.

The last words of this provision are not clear, and the English text does not correspond to the other texts. A correct translation of the Spanish, Portuguese, and French texts is this: ". . . which sum shall cover the expenses of the international registry of the competent Bureau."[1] Thus the only requirement for assuring the "automatic" protection of article 2 in all the contracting countries is that, on the registration of the mark in any of these countries, a sum of fifty dollars in gold be paid. There is no explicit provision in the Convention imposing upon the contracting countries the obligation to send this fee to the Inter-American Bureaus, or to notify them of the registrations made and transmit to them certificates of registration or copies of trade marks. Such an obligation can only be implied from the provisions of article 12 concerning the duties of the International Bureaus. One of these duties is "to keep a register of the certificates of ownership of trade mark issued by any of the signatory states." By the same article the governments of these states "shall send to the Inter-American Bureaus their official publications which contain the announcements of registrations of trade marks." It is not clear whether the governments are required to send anything more than the above official publications.

On the other hand, the Convention does not require that the Inter-American Bureaus shall give notice to the contracting countries of the registrations made in any of them and communicated to the Bureaus. The only possible way the contracting countries can know of the registrations of marks made in each of them is by the official reviews of the Bureaus, for the publication of which provision is made in article 12 (3), and which shall contain "the full texts or digest of all documents forwarded to the bureaus by the authorities of the signatory states."

Thus, the principle of automatic protection in all the contracting countries through a single registration in one of them is theoretically complete, since no requirement of international registration, or of communication of the national registration to the other countries, exists. Yet the first paragraph of article 2 contains this important qualification: "without prejudice to the rights of third persons or to the provisions of each state governing the same." The words "gov-

1. The originals read as follows: Spanish, "á cubrir los gastos de Registro Internacional de la respectiva Oficina"; Portuguese, "para cobrir as despezas do registro internacional da respectiva Secretaria"; French, "à couvrir les dépenses du Registre International du Bureau respectif."

erning the same" again are not clear, and do not correspond to the words used in the other texts of the Convention. A correct translation of the Spanish, Portuguese, and French texts should read: "and to the provisions of the internal legislation of each state." [1] Thus automatic protection through registration of a trade mark in one of the contracting countries cannot be claimed to the prejudice of rights of third parties (for instance, persons using the same trade mark); and, what is more important, the provisions of the domestic law of each country are not derogated from in any way.[2] In this respect reference should also be made to article 5, concerning things that may not be adopted or used as trade marks, and to the proviso of this article which leaves ultimately to the determination of the law of each country the question of the subject-matter of a trade mark.

Under these conditions the assumption of automatic registration in all the contracting countries through a single registration in one of them proves false. Nor is it true, as the Brazilian member of the committee on trade marks declared at the Conference of 1910, that "juridical effects in the international law of all the contracting countries are conferred upon the national register of each country." [3] As the Central Executive Council of the Inter-American High Commission pointed out: "automatic registration will never exist until the laws of the different countries are substantially identical." [4] For the mark registered in one country may be refused protection in the others, as conflicting with domestic legislation. The advantage of a single registration is offset by the danger of the free infringement of the mark in other countries.

In contrast to the Madrid Arrangement, under which the refusal by any country of a mark registered at the Bureau of Berne should be communicated within a year to the International Bureau and by the latter to the interested party, there is no provision of this kind in the Pan-American Convention. It is the duty of the Inter-American Bureaus (article 12[8]) only

1. The originals read as follows: Spanish, "y de los perceptos de la legislación interna de cada Nación"; Portuguese, "e dos preceitos da legislação interna de cada Nação"; French, "et des dispositions de la législation intérieure de chaque Nation."

2. See in this respect an explicit statement of the committee at the Conference of 1910, *Cuarta Conferencia Internacional Americana*, p. 397.

3. See *ibid.*, p. 409.

4. See pamphlet, *Convention for the Protection of Trade Marks and Commercial Names* (1923), note under article 1.

to investigate cases where trade marks, designs, and industrial models have failed to obtain the recognition of registration provided for by this convention, on the part of the authorities of any one of the states forming the Union, and to communicate the facts and reasons to the government of the country of origin and to interested parties.

§ **543. Right of priority.** Persons not content with the automatic protection through a single registration and payment of the fifty-dollar fee for the communication to the Inter-American Bureaus may register their marks directly in each of the countries in which they desire to be protected. In such case, they enjoy, by virtue of article 3 of the Convention, a right of priority for the period of six months, beginning with the date of filing in the state in which the first application was made.[1]

This article stipulates also that the same date shall be controlling in questions of priority of adoption of a trade mark. If adoption means use of the mark, the provision would have the effect of legalizing in all cases registration in one of the contracting countries of another's mark in use by the latter in another country prior to such registration. This consequence may be avoided, as is seen in the next section, in certain cases, in accordance with article 9.

§ **544. Rights and remedies of trade-mark owners.** Article 7 of the Convention provides that the ownership of a mark includes the right to enjoy the benefits thereof and the right of assignment or transfer in whole or in part of its ownership or its use in accordance with the provisions of the laws of the respective states. On the other hand, under article 9(*d*) a registered mark may be annulled if it is not used by the registrant or by his assigns within the term fixed by the law of the state in which the registration is effected.

Under article 8, the falsification, imitation, or unauthorized use of a trade mark shall be prosecuted by the interested party in accordance with the laws of the state wherein the offense was committed. This provision applies also to false indications of origin of a product. An interested party shall be understood to be any producer, manufacturer or merchant engaged in the production or manufacture of, or traffic in, said product or, in the case of false indications of origin, one doing business in the locality falsely indicated as that of origin, or in the territory in which the said locality is situated.

1. On the right of priority for trade marks under the Convention of 1883, see *supra*, chap. XXIII.

The most important provision of this Convention is that of article 9 concerning the remedies of trade-mark owners in the contracting countries. This provision constitutes common legislation, and not mere reference to the municipal law of each country. It establishes the means of obtaining cancellation of a previously registered mark when, on account of such registration, the proprietor of such mark does not obtain protection under the Convention. In case, for instance, a mark of an American manufacturer or merchant is refused in any of the contracting countries because that mark is already registered by another, he may cause cancellation of such registration by proving any of the following four facts:

(*a*) that he used the mark in the country in question prior to its registration by the other person;

(*b*) that, although he did not use the mark in that country, the registrant had knowledge of the mark's being used by the applicant in other countries;

(*c*) that the registrant had no right to the ownership or use of the mark at the date of its deposit; or

(*d*) that the registered mark has been abandoned.

Reasons (*a*) and (*b*) for which cancellation may be asked show that it is not sufficient that an absolute priority of use be proved in order to obtain cancellation. There must also exist one or the other of the following two facts: the mark must have been used by the applicant within the country where cancellation of registration is sought, or the registrant's bad faith must be shown. As will be seen, this is altered by the Convention of 1923.

§ 545. Protection of trade names and indications of origin. Article 10 of the Convention of 1910 is identical with article 8 of the International Convention of 1883 concerning the protection of trade names, and reference is made to a previous chapter for the interpretation of the same.[1]

Indications of origin of products are not otherwise referred to in this Convention except as their falsification, imitation, or unauthorized use is to be prosecuted, according to article 8, by the interested party in accordance with the laws of the state wherein the offense is committed. This is much less than what is stipulated by article 10 of the International Convention of 1883, and by the Madrid Arrangement for the repression of false indications of origin. It is

1. See *supra*, chap. XXIX.

to be remembered that Brazil and Cuba are parties to the Madrid Arrangement.

§ **546. The Inter-American Bureaus.** Articles 11 to 16 of the Convention concern the two International Bureaus through which the Union of American States constituted for the protection of trade marks and commercial names is to act. One of the Bureaus, established at Havana, is to have charge of the registration of trade marks coming from eleven countries — the United States of America, Mexico, Cuba, Haiti, the Dominican Republic, Salvador, Honduras, Nicaragua, Costa Rica, Guatemala, and Panama. The other, established at Rio de Janeiro, is to have charge of the registration of trade marks coming from ten countries — Brazil, Uruguay, the Argentine Republic, Paraguay, Bolivia, Chile, Peru, Ecuador, Venezuela, and Colombia.

The reason for establishing two Bureaus is the great distance which separates many American states and the desire to avoid inequalities in the time required for communications to be sent and received by the Bureaus. For all practical purposes, however, the two Bureaus are to be considered as one. For the unification of registrations it is provided that: (*a*) both shall have the same books and the same accounts kept under an identical system; and that (*b*) copies of all applications, registrations, communications, and other documents affecting the recognition of the rights of owners of trade marks shall be reciprocally transmitted weekly from one to the other. Likewise, both Bureaus shall be governed by identical regulations, to be framed by the concurrence of the Brazilian and Cuban governments and appoved by all the other signatory countries. The expenses of the Bureaus, placed under the control of the Brazilian and Cuban governments respectively, are to be defrayed by all the signatory countries in the same proportion as that established for the International Bureau of the American Republics at Washington.

The duties of the Bureaus are enumerated in article 12. Besides keeping a register of the certificates of ownership of trade marks issued by each country, and investigating cases of failure of recognition or registration of trade marks, which are dealt with above,[1] these duties consist in rendering services of an informational character in relation to intellectual and industrial property; in the collection and publication of reports and data on the law of the member coun-

1. See *supra*, § 542.

tries; in investigation of obstacles to the effective application of the Convention; in giving aid to the governments in the preparation of conferences; in the establishment of relations with similar bureaus and associations, and so on.

§ 547. **Final provisions.** Articles 17, 18, and 19 of the Convention, concerning the abrogation of prior treaties, the ratification and coming into effect of the Convention, and its denunciation, are similar to the final provisions of the Patents Convention of 1910, which are considered above.[1] It is to be recalled that Guatemala, Nicaragua, Costa Rica, and Honduras took advantage of article 19, and denounced the Convention.[2]

B. *Convention of* 1923

§ 548. Persons protected and subject-matter of protection. This Convention, signed at Santiago de Chile, April 28, 1923,[3] declares entitled to its benefits, not all persons, like the Convention of 1910, but only "persons domiciled in any of the contracting countries" (article I, section 1). Consequently, nationals of these countries domiciled in non-contracting countries cannot claim the advantages of the Convention.[4] This provision is in consonance with public law in Latin America, but would seem to be too narrow for modern conditions of trade. For one extreme under the Convention of 1910 another extreme is substituted by this Convention. The International Convention of 1883 is more in accord with the business needs of each country, in admitting three classes of persons to its benefits under articles 2 and 3. The meaning of the word "domiciled" in this Convention should not be different from that of the same term in the International Convention of 1883.[5]

There are no provisions in this Convention corresponding to those of articles 4 and 5 of the Convention of 1910, defining what shall be a trade mark and what cannot be adopted or used as such.

1. See *supra*, § 538.
2. See dates *supra*, p. 761, note 1.
3. See text of the Convention in Spanish, English, Portuguese, and French, in *United States Treaty Series*, No. 751; and in XLIV *Stat. at Large*, pt. 3, p. 2494.
4. The sub-committee on Trade-Mark Protection of the United States Section of the Inter-American High Commission had proposed that only persons possessing their main place of business in one of the contracting countries be admitted to the benefits of the Convention. See pamphlet of the Inter-American High Commission, *Proposed Revision of the Convention of Trade Marks of 1910* (Washington, 1923), p. 12.
5. See *supra*, § 114.

§ **549. The Convention one for registration only through the Inter-American Bureaus.** The Santiago Convention of 1923 is not a general agreement for the inter-American protection of trade marks. It corresponds in a certain way to the Madrid Arrangement of 1891, and has no provisions similar to those of the International Convention of 1883, or of previous Pan-American Conventions concerning national treatment of foreign trade-mark owners, or right of priority for filing applications for the registration of trade marks in the contracting countries. Trade-mark owners can claim no other protection under this Convention than that granted by registration through the Inter-American Bureaus. In case such owners do not wish to apply for registration of their marks through the bureaus, but prefer to acquire protection by direct registration in the countries where they need protection, they are governed exclusively by the municipal law of each country. In such case, they may claim no validation of a trade mark lawfully acquired in their country of origin, as under article 6 of the International Convention of 1883, nor right of priority, as under article 4 of the same Convention, nor even their assimilation to nationals, as under article 2 of the same Convention. Plainly, this is a great defect of the Pan-American Convention of 1923, and it does not seem that it has compelled trade-mark owners to rush to register their marks through the Inter-American Bureaus, as was probably expected.[1]

The so-called automatic registration in all the contracting countries through registration in one of them is abandoned by this Convention. On the other hand, the principle of international registration at the Inter-American Bureaus as a substitute for registration in all other American countries, as in the Madrid Arrangement of 1891, is not adopted. The necessity of registration in every country in which the proprietor of the trade mark wishes to be protected is maintained. What is then the function of the Inter-American Bureaus? To serve — as the reporter of the draft convention, Mr. Subercaseaux (delegate of Chile), put it — as agents of the manufacturers, merchants, and farmers, and obtain registration of their marks in any of the contracting countries, or in all of them if they should so desire.[2] Thus the conditions and formalities required by

1. See number of marks registered after 1923 at the Bureau of Havana, *supra*, p. 765.
2. *Verbatim Report of the Plenary Sessions of the Fifth International Conference of American States* (Santiago de Chile, 1923), I, 325.

the domestic law of each state are expressly maintained, and compliance therewith is necessary. Especially, applicants for registration are held to pay "the fees or charges established by the domestic law of each state in which recognition of rights is desired and other expenses incident to such recognition" (article I, section I [b]).

The intervention of the Inter-American Bureaus serves no other purpose than to obtain for the trade-mark owners "in the other signatory states the same protection granted by them to the marks registered or deposited in their own territory" (article I, section I). However, certain specific advantages are procured by registration through the Bureaus, as will be seen below.

§ 550. Conditions of registration through the Bureaus. In order to obtain the protection of the Convention, a person domiciled in any of the contracting countries must comply with the following conditions:

(1) He must register or deposit a commercial, industrial, or agricultural trade mark in one of the contracting countries. It is not necessary that the mark be admitted to registration; it is sufficient that it is deposited, that is, filed for registration.

(2) Such registration or deposit must be made either directly by such person, or through a duly authorized representative. This provision purports to exclude registration through international bureaus, as that of Berne.

(3) He must present to the proper Inter-American Bureau, through the proper office of the state of first registration or deposit, an application for recognition of the rights claimed, in accordance with the requirements prescribed in the appendix, which forms part of the Convention.

(4) He must pay a fee of fifty dollars on each mark for the expenses of the Inter-American Bureaus, plus the fees, charges, and expenses provided for by the domestic law of each state in which the applicant desires to be protected.

The administration of the state of first registration or deposit shall send to the Bureau the money order,[1] the electrotype of the mark, and a certificate in duplicate containing the data enumerated in article II of the appendix to the Convention. The Bureau, upon receipt of the above, enters them in its books, informs the state of the re-

1. The amount of the money order should include the fifty-dollar fee for the bureau and the dues and expenses connected with the registration of trade marks in the different American countries in which protection is asked by the application to the bureau. The registration office of each American state should always be informed of the amount of the latter.

ceipt of the application and of the number and date of entry, and sends copies of the said entry, containing all the details, to the administrations of the states in which the convention has been ratified and in which protection is applied for. The same data shall also be sent to the other contracting states, for the purpose of information. Reproductions of the marks received, and such particulars as are necessary, shall be published in the bulletins of the Inter-American Bureaus.

§ 551. **Recognition or refusal of trade marks in the other countries.** Upon receipt of an application for registration communicated by the proper Inter-American Bureau, each state shall determine whether protection may be granted in accordance with its laws (article 3). No restriction whatsoever in this respect is imposed on the contracting countries. It should be recalled that, under the Madrid Arrangement, the only grounds upon which a mark registered at the Bureau of Berne may be refused protection in any of the contracting countries, are those enumerated in article 6 of the International Convention of 1883.

The decision of each state shall be communicated to the Bureau "as soon as possible." Again, the one-year limit for such communication, under the Madrid Arrangement, does not exist in the Convention under consideration. The notice of acceptance of, opposition to, or refusal of a mark by the contracting states is to be transmitted by the Bureau to the administration of the state of first registration or deposit, with the view of its communication to whom it may concern (Appendix, article VI). The Bureau of Berne notifies the administration of the state as well as the interested party of the refusal of protection. This assures in favor of the latter speedier and more certain notification. However, this Convention provides (article 3, section 2) that, in case objection is made to the registration or deposit of a mark, the term in which to answer such objection in the country where it is made shall begin ninety days after the date of sending notice of such objection to the Bureau.

But the advantage of applying through the Inter-American Bureaus consists in the better remedies enjoyed by applicants for meeting objections of contracting countries to the registration or deposit of a trade mark. These remedies should not necessarily be connected with registration through the Bureaus, but they were so provided for in order to compel trade-mark owners to make use of the agency of the Bureaus. In this respect, article 5, section 2, provides:

> When refused protection under this convention in a signatory state because of prior registration or a pending application for registration, the proprietor of the mark claiming recognition of rights under this convention shall have the right to seek and obtain the cancellation of the previously registered mark, upon proving, according to the procedure by law of the country where cancellation is sought, such refusal, and either:
>
> (*a*) that he had legal protection for his mark in any of the contracting states before the date of application for the registration which he seeks to cancel; or
>
> (*b*) that the registrant had no right to the ownership, use or employment of the registered mark at the date of its deposit; or
>
> (*c*) that the mark covered by the registration which he seeks to cancel has been abandoned.

Grounds (*b*) and (*c*) are taken from article 9 of the Convention of 1910, and are considered in another place.[1] Ground (*a*) replaces the grounds of provisions (1) and (2) of the above article of the previous Convention. It is a most important change. While, under the previous Convention, the cancellation of a previously registered or deposited mark could be claimed only in case the applicant for cancellation should prove a prior use of the mark within the country where cancellation is sought, or, in case no such use could be proved, knowledge by the registrant of the applicant's use of the mark in another of the contracting countries, under the present Convention, the legal protection of this mark in any of the contracting countries prior to the application for the registration, the cancellation of which is being sought, is a sufficient ground. By legal protection of the mark is meant recognition by the law of the ownership of the mark, and not mere protection against imitation by the law of unfair competition. Trade marks enjoy legal protection either after registration or after mere adoption and use.[2] The above provision, then, means that cancellation may be asked if the mark was registered previously by the applicant, or if it was used previously by him in any of the contracting countries in which use alone creates owner-

1. See *supra*, § 543.

2. The fourth "understanding or condition" subject to which the Convention was ratified by the United States confirms this interpretation by providing that "legal protection" in this article includes acquisition of ownership in the mark in the United States by adoption and use alone.

ship of the mark. The good faith of the registrant is immaterial.[1] A criticism of this provision is implied in that of the more general provision of article 2 in the next paragraph.

The provision under consideration here applies only when an application for registration through the proper Bureau is objected to on the ground that the mark is registered or filed by another. No provision is made for the case where the mark is refused because it resembles closely, or may be confused with, a mark on the register, or as unlawful according to domestic law, or by reason of its exterior form. In all such cases the internal law of each country prevails without any limitation.

The grounds of cancellation provided for in section 2 of article 5 may be claimed by applicants under the Convention within a year from the day following that of the receipt by the proper Inter-American Bureau of notice of refusal of protection. But this provision fits ill with that of article 2, where the principle of priority, as will be seen below, is not limited by any period.

§ 552. Effects of registration through agency of the Inter-American Bureaus. In case a trade mark communicated through the medium of the proper Inter-American Bureau is accepted for registration or deposit by the contracting countries, it will obtain the same protection as that of marks registered or deposited directly therein. Whether by such acceptance ownership in the trade mark is acquired, or the property therein is only declared, is a question for the law of each country. At any rate, article 1 provides that such protection is "without prejudice to the rights of third parties."

No uniform term of protection is enjoyed through registration under the Convention, as is the case with the Madrid Arrangement. The duration of protection in each state depends on the law of that state (article 1, section 2). Therefore trade-mark owners should see that a timely renewal of registration is made in each country, according to the law of each. But in order that protection under the

1. The sub-committee on Trade-Mark Protection of the United States Section of the Inter-American High Commission had proposed an amendment of the Convention of 1910 in this respect, which seemed sound. The ground for cancellation of a registered or filed mark should be, that an application for inter-American registration had been filed in the country of origin prior to the date of the application for registration which it is intended to cancel, and that the registrant had knowledge beforehand of the use of the mark in its country of origin. See pamphlet of the Inter-American High Commission, *Proposed Revision of the Convention on Trade Marks between the American States of 1910*, p. 5.

Convention may be continued for the renewed term, the application for renewal should be made through the Bureau, and the requirements for fees and dues prescribed for original applications should be fulfilled. Such application, however, may be made directly by the interested party to the proper Inter-American Bureau. The last provision was inserted to meet the case where a renewal cannot be obtained in the country of first registration or deposit.

The most important effect of registration under the Convention is contained in article 2. This article provides:

> The date of filing in the state where first application is made for registration or deposit through the proper Inter-American Bureau, in the absence of other proof of ownership of a mark, shall determine priority for the registration or deposit of such mark in any of the signatory states.

In effect, it would seem that by this provision the automatic registration of the previous Convention, thrown out through the front door, is introduced again through the back door. Indeed, registration in only one of the contracting countries is not sufficient to assure protection in the other countries, and registration in the latter also is needed. Yet, by virtue of the above provision, application for registration in any of the contracting countries crystallizes the right in the mark for all other countries. The provision amounts to more than a grant of right or priority for a certain period. For no period is fixed within which such priority may be claimed. The date of the first filing of the mark [1] is only a convenient proof for trade-mark owners applying for registration in foreign countries through the Inter-American Bureaus. They may prove, if they can, even an earlier date of ownership of the mark than that shown by the date of filing. Indeed, the article reads ". . . in the absence of other proof of ownership of the mark."

This is especially calculated to benefit American trade-mark owners, in view of the fact that in the United States property in a mark is acquired by prior use, and registration in no way determines questions of its ownership, whereas in most of the American countries by registration property in a mark is acquired.[2] By virtue

1. The words "date of filing" of the English text correspond to the words "la fecha de presentatión," "a data da presentação," and "date de la première inscription ou dépôt," of the other texts of the Convention, and show clearly that the date meant is that on which the mark is first presented or filed with the administration.

2. See *supra*, §§ 336–338. It appears that by registration a property right in a trade mark is acquired in Argentina, Bolivia, Chile, Cuba, Dominican Republic, Guatemala, Haiti, Panama, Paraguay, Peru, and Venezuela. In Brazil, Mexico, Salvador, and

of this provision, for instance, an American manufacturer who has used a trade mark in the United States or in other American countries for five years, without having registered it in any of those countries, may register his mark in the United States and apply for registration or deposit of the same in other American countries through the proper Inter-American Bureau. And in case, in the intervening five years, another person has registered the same mark, whether in good or bad faith, the American trade-mark owner may cause the annulment of such registration and compel the registration of the mark in his own name.[1]

The provision in this sweeping form is not likely to be assented to by many American countries. It may be theoretically just, but in practice it may lead to unjust results. It favors negligent trade-mark owners and may cause great injury to persons who adopted the same mark in perfectly good faith. In this respect the provisions of the Convention of 1910, above considered, were more in accord with real facts and with justice. The public should be given notice of the user's claim in a trade mark. Since the mark is not used in the country, nor does the register disclose its adoption by another, a person has no way of knowing of another's claim, and it is unjust to compel him later to give up a valuable asset of his business. It may be assumed with certainty that this provision must have kept many an American country from ratifying the Convention.

§ 553. **Rights and remedies of trade-mark owners.** The Inter-American Bureaus intervene also for communication of changes in the ownership of a trade mark. Notification of transfers is made to the Bureau through the proper office of the state, on payment of the fees required by each state for such transfer. The Bureau enters it in its register, and sends a corresponding notice to the other contracting states. No state can refuse recognition of such transfer, and the same force and effect is to be given as if it were made in accordance with its law, provided that the mark transferred is registered or deposited in such state, and provided that the principles of

---

Uruguay by registration property is acquired at the expiry of a certain period (five years in Brazil and Salvador, three years in Mexico, and two years in Uruguay). In Colombia, Ecuador, Honduras, and Nicaragua, *prima facie* evidence of use of, and consequently of property in, the trade mark is acquired by registration.

1. The third "understanding or condition" subject to which the Convention was ratified by the United States confirms the clear meaning of this article in this respect. See *United States Treaty Series*, No. 751, pp. 36–37.

article 5 of the Convention are not impaired (article 4, and Appendix, article VII).

Section 1 of article 5 of the Convention makes it clear, and with a certain greater emphasis than the previous conventions, that the domestic authorities of a state alone have jurisdiction and that the law and procedure of that state must be observed in any civil, criminal, or administrative proceeding arising in such state with respect to a mark, such as opposition, falsification, imitation, or unauthorized appropriation, as also false indications of origin of a product.

A right to apply for and obtain cancellation of the registration or deposit of a mark when it conceals or misrepresents the true quality, nature, or origin of merchandise, is granted by article 5, section 5. The applicant must prove such concealment or misrepresentation. But only marks the registration or deposit of which was effected through the Inter-American Bureau are subject to this repressive measure.

§ 554. Commercial names and indications of origin. The provision concerning protection of commercial names in section 4 of article 1 is taken from the previous Convention, and is identical with the provision of article 8 of the International Convention of 1883.

Indications of origin of products are referred to in article 5, section 1, as in article 8 of the Convention of 1910; namely, it is declared that their falsification, imitation, or unauthorized appropriation is to be prosecuted by the authorities and according to the law of the country wherein the offense was committed. However, the provision of the previous Convention defining the interested parties who may prosecute such offenses is not contained in the present Convention.

On the other hand, the above provision of the section 5 of article 5 concerning cancellation of registration or deposit of marks concealing or misrepresenting the origin of merchandise is calculated to protect rights in indications of origin, and constitutes the first inter-American protection in this respect. Subject to the two limitations, that the indication of origin must be identified with a trade mark, and that the registration or deposit of the latter must have been effected through the proper Inter-American Bureau, there is a clear right of protection under the Convention, regardless of the existence of protection under the municipal law of a state.

§ **555. The Inter-American Bureaus.** No material change in the organization of the Bureaus and their duties is introduced by the new Convention. The two Bureaus of the northern and southern groups of American Republics are maintained at Havana and Rio de Janeiro. Colombia and Ecuador, however, are transferred from the southern to the northern group under the present Convention, thus leaving six countries in the former against twelve in the latter. The three countries that were not represented at the Conference and did not sign the Convention of 1923 — Mexico, Bolivia, and Peru — are invited to accede to the Convention and may be assigned to the group which each may select. Mexico might be expected to select the northern and the other two the southern group.

By a new provision of article 9, the establishment of the Bureau of Rio de Janeiro is made easier, since it is no longer required that two thirds of the southern group should ratify the Convention before its establishment. Ratification of the Convention by one third of the signatory states would be sufficient. More than one third have ratified, but the Bureau of Rio de Janeiro has not begun to function. And by reason of the calling of the Pan-American Conference on Trade Marks, its definitive organization was held in abeyance.[1]

The contracting countries agreed, by article 7, to confer the postal franking privilege on the official correspondence of the Bureaus. The regulations of the Bureaus are to be prepared, as before, by the Cuban and Brazilian governments, but do not need the approval of the other states.

§ **556. Finances of the Bureaus.** The finances of the Bureaus, the establishment of their budgets, the incurring of expenses, and auditing of accounts are strictly regulated by article 12 of the Convention. It is interesting to contrast this with the mere supervision of the finances of the Bureau of Berne by the Swiss government.

The method of distribution of the deficit of the Bureaus tends to make those countries pay the greatest part of the deficit which profit most by their services. The Bureaus are to be supported primarily by the fifty-dollar fees payable on each application sent through them; in the second place by the proceeds of the sale of their publications; and lastly, the annual surplus, if any, of the one Bureau

1. According to information given the present writer by the courtesy of the Director-General of the Pan-American Union, letter dated June 25, 1928.

will be used to wipe out the deficit, if any, of the other. Should all these means of support prove insufficient, the deficit shall be paid as follows: 80 per cent by the contracting countries in proportion to the number of marks which they may have registered each year through the Bureaus, and the balance of 20 per cent by such countries in proportion to the number of marks they have registered at the request of the Bureaus.

§ **557. Final provisions.** A transitory provision of article 13 saves the rights in trade marks registered under the Convention of 1910. No payment of fees to the contracting countries, as provided for in the new Convention, can be required in respect to those marks, and the protection granted by the Convention of 1910 will continue to be granted to all marks received up to the day on which the new Convention comes into force.

The provision of article 14 concerning the coming into force of the Convention is different from the corresponding provisions of the previous Pan-American conventions. It is inspired by the corresponding provision of the International Convention of 1883. The Convention becomes effective thirty days after the receipt by the government of Chile of notice of ratification by a number of countries equivalent to one third of the signatory countries, and from that moment the Convention of 1910 ceases to exist, as between the countries that have ratified the new Convention. The ratification of any other country is communicated by the Chilean government to the other signatory countries. By such communication, the Convention comes into force as regards this new country.

The provision for withdrawals from the Convention is substantially identical with the provision of the previous Convention. A new article 17 provides for the liquidation of the Bureaus in case more than one half of the ratifying states should withdraw.

An interesting provision of the last article provides that any differences between the contracting states relative to the interpretation or execution of the Convention shall be decided by arbitration.

§ **558. Legislation in the United States for execution of the Pan-American Conventions.** The Pan-American Patent Convention of 1910 in no way derogates from the municipal law of the United States, and no legislation needed to be passed. The Pan-American Trade-Mark Conventions of 1910 and 1923 introduce the system of registration through the Inter-American Bureaus, and the Act of

March 19, 1920, purports to give effect thereto.[1] The first section of this act provides that the Commissioner of Patents shall keep a register of all marks communicated to him by the Inter-American Bureaus.[2] The registrant of such marks must comply with the law of the country in which his original registration took place, in respect to giving notice to the public that the trade mark is registered, in connection with the use of such trade mark in the United States. If he fails to do so, and later sues for infringement, he cannot recover damages unless he proves that the defendant was duly notified of the infringement and continued the same after such notice. (Section 5.) The registration may be cancelled on application by any person injured by the inclusion of such trade marks on the register. In all other respects the provisions of the Trade Marks Act of 1905, as amended by subsequent acts, are applicable to marks placed on this register.

§ **559. Conclusions.** It is easy to conclude from the above exposition that the Pan-American conventions not only failed in their attempt to achieve an inter-American regime of industrial property, but also did not attempt to afford, generally speaking, so broad a protection as the International Convention of 1883 and the Arrangements succeeded in affording. One feels ready to agree with the repeated suggestions of the Argentine and Mexican delegations that all the American countries should accede to the Industrial Property Union.

There are several reasons in favor of such accession. The law and practice of South and Central American countries is more akin to the law of Continental Europe than to that of the United States, and the Industrial Property Union is essentially a European creation. By its suppleness, however, it adapts itself to the various systems of law of the world. By its long life, its continuity of study of the questions of industrial property, the admirable activity and great prestige of its Bureau at Berne, its conferences of revision and meetings of experts, and the conscientious preparatory work done by various international organizations with a view to its progressive evolution and to achieving uniformity of the law in the various countries, the Industrial Property Union is bound to become universal. Brazil, Cuba,

1. XLI *Stat. at Large*, 533.

2. In the same register may be placed marks which are not registrable under the Act of Feb. 20, 1905, but which have been in *bona fide* use for not less than one year in interstate or foreign commerce.

the Dominican Republic, Mexico, and the United States are already members of the Union. Argentina has repeatedly considered such accession and she will presumably lead the sister American republics in this direction. And the other American countries, which have always ratified the successive Pan-American conventions, might be induced to accede.[1]

One could have wished, therefore, that the Pan-American Trade-Mark Conference which met at Washington, February 11, 1929, would have adopted a resolution calling upon all the American countries which are not members of the Industrial Property Union to accede to it. In case a general agreement on this point could not have been obtained, the next best thing would have been to make use of the experience of the industrial Property Union.[2]

C. *The Convention and Protocol of 1929*

§ 560. The general Convention and the Protocol on Inter-American registration. The Pan-American Trade-Mark Conference, referred to above, followed the experience of the International Union for the Protection of Industrial Property by adopting two distinct acts: a general Convention for Trade-Mark and Commercial Protection and a Protocol on Inter-American Registration of Trade Marks. The former deals with the protection of trade marks and trade names and the repression of unfair competition and false indications of geographical origin or source. The latter tends to maintain an international American agency, which is considered desirable to have, and it regulates the question of registration of trade marks in the Inter-American Trade-Mark Bureau.

The adoption of two distinct acts purports to facilitate ratification of the general Convention by the American republics which are not interested in the institution of the Inter-American Bureau and are disinclined to forego direct registration of trade marks with their administrations. For, as the preamble of the Protocol states, "acceptance of the Convention does not imply acceptance of the Protocol." Moreover, no attempt is made any longer to create an Inter-American Bureau at Rio de Janeiro since it has been impossible to

1. See an article by the present writer, "Pan-American Conventions on Industrial Property," in *American Journal of International Law* (1928), XXII, 803, 818, 819.

2. See detailed suggestions in this respect in a book by the present writer: *The International Protection of Trade Marks by the American Republics* (Harvard University Press, 1929).

establish it, although provision therefor was made in the Conventions of 1910 and 1923. The bureau already created at Havana is maintained as the "Inter-American Trade-Mark Bureau."

The general Convention is a long document of 37 articles divided into seven chapters. The first chapter consists of a single article. This contains the general principle of national treatment, or as its title puts it, somewhat too broadly, of equality of citizens and aliens as to trade-mark and commercial protection. This equality concerns the rights and remedies granted by the law with respect to trade marks, trade names and the repression of unfair competition and false indications of geographical origin or source. The persons entitled to the benefit of the Convention are the nationals of the contracting countries and the domiciled foreigners who own a manufacturing or commercial establishment or an agricultural development. Thus, both domicile and establishment in a contracting country are required of nationals of non-contracting countries, and not one or the other as in the Industrial Property Convention.

The other six chapters of the Convention are dealt with below.

§ **561. Trade-mark protection.** Article 2 provides now, in contrast to the Convention of 1923, that a person desirous of obtaining protection for his mark in a country other than his own can obtain protection by registering it either directly in each country or through the Inter-American Trade-Mark Bureau if the Protocol is in force as between his country and the country in question. The following articles 3 to 13 contain provisions calculated to make direct registration of trade marks in the contracting countries free from the difficulties introduced by the diversity of municipal law.

An important provision is that of article 3 concerning the validation of trade marks. It follows closely the stipulations of article 6 of the International Convention for the Protection of Industrial Property, as revised at The Hague in 1925. It presents, however, two differences therewith. Not only marks *registered* in the *country of origin* may be validated, but all marks *legally protected* in *any* of the contracting countries. Thus, the Pan-American Convention does away with the two limitations of the rule of article 6 of the International Convention which are very undesirable.[1] It is sufficient, therefore, that a mark be protected by the law in a country, although it is not registered, in order that it may be admitted to registration

1. See *supra*, chap. XXIV, §§ 366, 368, 371.

or deposit and protected in the other contracting countries. And it is not necessary that the mark be registered or protected *in the country of origin* of the registrant for its validation in the other countries.[1]

The second part of article 3 contains the exceptions to the rule of validation of the first paragraph. It follows the provisions of article 6 of the International Convention for the Protection of Industrial Property. In addition, there are excluded from validation: marks which tend to expose persons, institutions, national or public symbols; which contain representations of racial types or scenes typical of any of the contracting countries, other than that of the origin of the mark; or which have as a principal distinguishing element, phrases, names or slogans constituting the trade name of another. Marks including, without authorization by competent authority, national and state flags, coats of arms, seals, designs, stamps or official labels, certificates of guarantees or official insignia or simulations of any of the foregoing, shall be refused registration and their use shall be prohibited. This provision is similar to that of article 6*c* of the International Convention, although more sweeping.

Article 5 extends the protection of the Convention to labels, industrial designs, slogans, prints, catalogues, or advertisements used to identify or advertise goods in those countries where they are considered as trade marks. The contracting countries undertake, by article 6, to admit to registration or deposit and to protect collective and association marks. Marks of states, provinces or municipalities are included therein.

The International Convention for the Protection of Industrial Property, as revised at The Hague in 1925, contains in article 6*b* provisions calculated to secure priority of trade marks in the contracting countries by way of cancelling or refusing admission to marks constituting imitations of trade marks belonging to nationals of the contracting countries.[2] The same purpose is achieved in the Pan-American Convention under consideration by articles 7 to 9 and also 12 and 13. But the scope of the provisions in the two Conventions is not the same.

The effect of article 6*b* of the International Convention is that the registrant's right in a mark registered in any of the contracting countries is not conclusive before the lapse of a three-year period

1. See the present writer's proposal for these two changes in his draft Convention in *The International Protection of Trade Marks by the American Republics*, pp. 54, 61.

2. See *supra*, §§ 387–389.

from such registration or without limit of time in case the registration was made in bad faith. Within these conditions a person may show a better right and cause the cancellation of a registered mark. Such better right is a prior use of the mark by the applicant in the country where cancellation is sought to such a degree as to make the mark well known in that country.

The effect of the stipulations of the present Pan-American Convention is as follows. An owner of a mark legally protected in any of the contracting countries may oppose the use, registration, or deposit or cause the cancellation of an interfering mark on proving, first, that his mark was legally protected in any of the contracting countries prior to the use or application for registration of the interfering mark, and, second, either of the following two facts: that the claimant of the interfering mark was in bad faith, viz., had knowledge of the use, registration, or deposit of the mark by the claimant, prior to the adoption, use or deposit of the interfering mark; or that the claimant had priority of use of the mark in the country where cancellation of the interfering mark is sought. The main difference of these stipulations from article 6*b* of the International Convention is that no period is fixed within which registration of a mark becomes conclusive when performed in good faith. In this, the Pan-American Convention derogates from the law of many American countries. It would have been well to fix such a period with respect to registrations made in good faith. Yet, this Convention adopts a much sounder principle than the Convention of 1923. The priority of trade marks is no longer protected unqualifiedly, as by article 2 of the Convention of 1923,[1] but with the qualification that there must be, besides the prior use in the country in which the mark was originated, circulation of the products bearing such mark in the country where cancellation or prohibition of the interfering mark is sought, or bad faith of the other party.

Cancellation of registration of an interfering mark may also be obtained, according to article 9, by proving that the registrant of the mark has abandoned it. The law of each country may determine the period within which a mark may be declared abandoned for lack of use. In the absence of such provision, the period shall be one year and one day if the lack of use takes place after the mark has been used, and two years from registration if it has never been used.

1. See *supra*, § 552.

Two other provisions of the Convention are quite original[1] and constitute valuable acquisitions of the regime which this Convention purports to establish. Article 12 provides that the registration or deposit of a mark by an agent, representative, or customer of the owner of the mark shall give to the latter the right to demand the cancellation or refusal of the mark and to request and obtain the protection for himself as from the date of the application for registration. This tends to defeat fraudulent attempts of persons having dealings with a business undertaking from misappropriating its mark.

Article 13 is inspired by certain provisions of articles 7 and 9 of the Madrid Trade Mark Arrangement of 1891–1925. It tends to permit slight changes in the form of the mark and eliminate the danger of forfeiting its protection for modifications of the list of goods on which the mark is applied. Also it relieves registrants from the obligation of affixing on goods of foreign origin any other legend indicating an authority for the use of trade marks, except that required in the country of origin of the goods.

The principle of independence of trade-mark rights expressed in the first paragraph of article 3 is carried to its logical conclusion in article 10. This provides that once the registration or deposit of a mark in any contracting country has been effected, such registration or deposit shall exist independently of every other and shall not be affected by changes that may occur in the registration of such mark in the other contracting countries. However, the qualification is added "unless otherwise provided by domestic law," which takes away a great deal of the value of this provision.

Article 11 distinguishes between the transfer of the ownership and of the use or exploitation of trade marks. In the first case, the transfer in the country of the original registration is declared to be effecttive and to be recognized in all the other countries. In the second case, the transfer is only effective for the country for which it was made in accordance with the law of that country. The drafting of this article would seem unfortunate. Ownership in, and use of, a trade mark in most countries can only be transferred with the business with which it is connected. The provision reintroduces the idea of country of origin of the mark, which is done away with by article 3 and fits ill with the principle of independence of article 10.

1. See the present writer's proposals in this respect in his draft Convention in *The International Protection of Trade Marks by the American Republics*, pp. 56, 67.

§ **562. Protection of commercial names.** Article 14 of the Convention of 1929 copies article 8 of the International Convention for the Protection of Industrial Property.[1] Article 15 gives, by way of enumeration of various examples, a definition of what is to be understood as a commercial name: names of individuals, surnames, trade names used to denote a trade or calling, firms' names, names or titles of associations, corporations, and entities.

The next four articles indicate, by detailed provisions, the sort of protection that commercial names should receive in the contracting countries, the remedies to be had by the interested parties, and the conditions for their application. The prohibition extends not only to the use or adoption of a commercial name identical with or deceptively similar to one legally adopted and previously used by a person engaged in the same business in any of the contracting countries, but also to the use or deposit of a mark containing an essential part of another party's commercial name. These provisions establish the unqualified right of the prior user. The execution of these provisions is dependent almost entirely on the existence of municipal law to carry them into effect. The qualification "in accordance with the internal legislation of each country" takes away most of the importance of these provisions, since no engagement of the contracting countries is stipulated to modify their laws in accordance with the Convention.

§ **563. Repression of unfair competition.** Articles 20 to 23 of the Convention under consideration, inspired by article 10*b* of the International Convention of 1883–1925,[2] present certain advantages over the latter. The definition of unfair competition in article 20 is broader than that of the International Convention and contains a creative element. "Every act or deed contrary to commercial good faith or to the normal and honorable development of industrial or business activities shall be considered as unfair competition and, therefore, unjust and prohibited."

Article 21 enumerates various acts of unfair competition that shall be prohibited. The enumeration is more detailed, inasmuch as it purports to establish international legislation for the contracting

1. On the interpretation of this article, see *supra*, chap. XXIX. A slight change, making for more clarity, adopted by the Pan-American Convention, was proposed by the present writer in his draft Convention in *The International Protection of Trade Marks by the American Republics*, pp. 56, 68.

2. See *supra*, chap. XXXI.

countries. Indeed, the first paragraph of this article provides that these acts, unless otherwise effectively dealt with under the domestic laws of the contracting countries, shall be repressed under the provisions of the Convention. All these acts, however, come under the category of acts creating confusion with the commercial activity of a competitor.[1] The other category of acts of unfair competition, *viz.*, acts injuring wrongfully the business relations of a competitor or, as article 10*b* of the International Convention of 1883–1925 restrictively provides, false allegations of such a nature as to discredit the goods of a competitor, are not included in the enumeration in question.

A valuable provision is that of article 22, to the effect that in the absence of legislation repressing acts of unfair competition in any of the contracting countries the penalties contained in the legislation on trade marks or other statutes shall be applied, and relief shall be granted by way of injunction and, as the case may be, of damages.

§ **564. Repression of false indications of origin.** By a sweeping provision of article 23 of the Convention "every indication of geographical origin or source which does not actually correspond to the place in which the product was fabricated or produced, shall be considered fraudulent and illegal and therefore prohibited." The same provision is repeated in slightly different terms in article 26. A place of geographical origin or source is considered as "indicated" when the name of a definite locality, region, country or nation appears directly or indirectly on a trade mark, label, cover, etc., provided it is the dominant element of the sentences, words, or expressions used.

Article 25 declares rightly that names indicating geographical origin or source are not susceptible to individual appropriation and may be used by any manufacturer or producer established in the place indicated or dealing with the products originating there.

To the general prohibition of use of untrue indications of geographical origin, article 27 attaches a general exception. "Names, phrases, or words, constituting in whole or in part geographical terms which through constant, general, and reputable use in common have come to form the name or designation itself of the article . . . to which they are applied are excepted from the above provisions." For in-

1. More acts of this kind are enumerated in the Seventh Resolution adopted by the Conference. See *Pan-American Trade-Mark Conference*, Final Act, p. 4.

stance, the use of such terms as Eau de Cologne or Suede gloves is not prohibited. In this exception, however, are not included "regional indications of origin of industrial or agricultural products, the quality and reputation of which to the consuming public, depend on the place of production or origin."

The stipulations of article 27 seem to constitute an amelioration of the provisions of the Madrid Arrangement for the repression of false indications of origin as amended at The Hague in 1925. When a geographical name has become the name or designation of an article is to be decided by the courts of each country, as in the Madrid Arrangement. But while, in the latter, regional appellations of products of the vine cannot be considered to have become the names of products, in the Pan-American Convention the exception is broader. It will remain, however, for the courts of each country to say when the quality and the reputation of products bearing certain regional indications depend on the place of production or origin.

Article 28 contains a transitory provision similar to the one considered above with respect to acts of unfair competition. In the absence of special remedies for the repression of false indications of geographical origin, remedies provided by the domestic sanitary laws, or laws dealing with misbranding and laws on trade marks or trade names, shall be applicable in the contracting countries.

§ **565. Remedies against infringers.** The Convention specifies (article 29) that the manufacture, exportation, importation, distribution, or sale is forbidden of articles or products which directly or indirectly infringe any of the provisions of the Convention. Acts prohibited by the Convention should be repressed by the competent administrative or judicial authorities, either by official action or at the request of interested parties who may sue for damages and demand the seizure or destruction of products or their marks.

These remedies shall be enjoyed by any interested manufacturer, merchant, or agriculturist as well as by his agents and representatives. In case of false indications of geographical origin, the consular officers of the state to which the locality or region falsely indicated belongs are declared to have sufficient authority to take and prosecute the necessary actions. The same authority shall be enjoyed by official commissions, institutions, or associations representing the interested persons.

§ **566. General provisions.** A number of general provisions, inspired by corresponding stipulations of the International Convention of 1883–1925, deal with sundry questions. The contracting countries which do not possess a protective service for the suppression of unfair competition and false indications of origin agree to establish such service. They also agree to publish in an official periodical the trade marks solicited and granted and the administrative decisions made regarding them. In several Latin American countries no such publication exists today, and its necessity for foreigners is indisputable.

The Convention shall be subject to periodic revision at the international conferences of the American states, to which each country must send experts in the subject of trade marks. In view of the fact that Pan-American Conventions on industrial property are not ratified by the American republics until long after their adoption, their revision at such short intervals as every six years, when the conferences of American states meet, would seem unpractical. The preparatory work for each revision shall be done by the country in which the Conference is to be held with the assistance of the Pan-American Union and the Inter-American Trade-Mark Bureau. The Director of this Bureau may attend the sessions of such conferences and take part in the discussions, but shall have no vote.

The national courts of each country are declared competent to settle any differences which may arise with respect to the interpretation or application of the principles of the Convention — which seems a strange provision, unless it be understood to mean differences between a state and an individual; for it is added that "in case of denial of justice they shall be submitted to arbitration."

Article 35 declares that the provisions of the Convention shall have the force of law in those countries in which international treaties possess that character as soon as they are ratified by their constitutional organs. The countries in which the fulfillment of international engagements is dependent upon the enactment of appropriate laws agree to effect the enactment of the necessary legislation in the shortest possible period of time.

§ **567. Inter-American registration of trade marks.** The American Republics that shall ratify the general Convention may also, if they so wish, ratify the Protocol on the Inter-American registration of trade marks. This is a document that follows the previous Pan-

American Conventions in that the Inter-American Trade-Mark Bureau shall not register the trade marks communicated to it, but shall serve only as an agency for the transmission of such marks to the contracting countries for registration.[1] Some of the provisions of the Madrid Arrangement purporting to ensure speedy registration by the contracting countries and to eliminate arbitrary refusals are adopted by the Protocol. Its drafting, however, seems hasty, for the provisions taken from the previous Pan-American Convention and from the Madrid Trade-Mark Arrangement are not always in harmony.[2]

The contracting countries are bound to acknowledge immediately to the Bureau the receipt of applications for registration transmitted by it, and to notify it of the action taken in accordance with the domestic law and the provisions of the Convention. The certificate of registration by each country is sent to the Bureau for transmission to the applicant. If, within seven months, after the receipt of an application by a contracting country, no notice of refusal is communicated to the Bureau, the mark in question shall be considered as registered. A mark may be refused registration in accordance with the provisions of the internal law and the general Convention. Applicants may have recourse against refusals within the period fixed by the domestic law which shall begin, however, four months after receipt by the Inter-American Trade-Mark Bureau of the notice of refusal. Applicants may appoint agents or attorneys to represent them in the contracting countries in any procedure arising in connection with marks transmitted through the Bureau.

These are the main innovations of the regime of Inter-American registration introduced by the Protocol. Its success in practice raises many doubts.

1. See, on the difference between the principles of the Madrid Trade-Mark Arrangement and the Pan-American Conventions, S. P. Ladas, *The International Protection of Trade Marks by the American Republics*, pp. 72–73.

2. Thus, article 7 stipulates, as the Madrid Arrangement (article 3), that publication by the Bureau shall have the same effect as publication in the official journals of the contracting countries, and article 4 provides for publication in the official papers of each country.

PART III

FUTURE DEVELOPMENTS

CHAPTER XXXVI

FURTHER DEVELOPMENT OF THE INTERNATIONAL REGIME OF INDUSTRIAL PROPERTY

§ 568. Toward universal union for protection of industrial property.

I. Improvements in Organization of the Union

§ 569. Extending powers of the International Bureau.
§ 570. Accuracy of published material.
§ 571. Substitute for rule of unanimity.

II. Improvements in International Regime of Various Rights

A *International Regime of Patents.*
§ 572. Reservation of rights of third parties.
§ 573. Securing right of priority.
§ 574. Obligation to work patent.
§ 575. Protection at international exhibitions.
B *The International Regime of Industrial Designs and Models.*
§ 576. Harmonizing laws of the various countries.
C *International Regime of Trade Marks.*
§ 577. Securing priority of trade marks.
§ 578. Eliminating erroneous interpretation and application of article 6.
§ 579. Independence of trade-mark rights.
§ 580. Transfer of trade marks.
§ 581. Other points of improvement.
D *International Regime of Indications of Origin.*
§ 582. Extending scope of the Madrid Arrangement.

III. Establishment of International Tribunal in the Union

§ 583. Early proposals.
§ 584. Plan of the Economic Committee of the League of Nations.
§ 585. Discussion at the Conference of The Hague.
§ 586. A suggestion.

IV. International Classification of Patents, Designs, and Trade Marks

§ 587. Difficulties of international classification.
§ 588. Proposals and schemes of classification.
§ 589. Chances of success.

V. Schemes of International Patents and International Registration of Patents

§ 590. Present inadequacy of international protection of patents.
§ 591. Possibilities of progressive uniformity of patent law.
§ 592. Creation of international patents.
§ 593. International registration of patents.

VI. Plans for Universal Trade Marks

§ 594. Impracticability of "universal marks."
§ 595. Amelioration of regime of international registration of trade marks.

§ 568. Toward universal union for protection of industrial property. The Union for the Protection of Industrial Property has not yet become a universal Union, as it aspires to do. In its thirty-eight member countries are included all the European countries except Russia, Albania, and Lithuania.[1] The absence of many American countries is very conspicuous. Sixteen are not included in the Union. It is probable that the attempts to establish an inter-American regime of industrial property have prevented many an American country from acceding to the Convention of 1883. The Argentine Republic has, in several instances, urged the accession of all the American countries to the Union.[2] Many of them do not feel interested enough to become members, inasmuch as they believe that they would assume many obligations in exchange for benefits of a meagre character, inasmuch as they are not manufacturing countries. It is necessary that a propaganda should be instituted in these countries, to convince them of the advantages afforded them by the Union. This would seem to be the business of the Bureau, as well as of the League of Nations and, in particular, its Economic Committee.[3]

China and Egypt are also outside the Union. The regime of extraterritorial jurisdiction prevailing in these countries rendered the protection of industrial property an extremely complicated and difficult matter. The various countries enjoying such jurisdiction, and having commercial interests in China and Egypt, had concluded between them bipartite conventions assuring reciprocal protection of their nationals by the consular tribunals.[4] An attempt to insert a provision to this effect in the Convention of Union at the Washington Conference in 1911 did not succeed.[5] After the war, Egypt became an independent country, and extraterritorial jurisdiction there is

1. With these should be listed, Lichtenstein, Andorra, Monaco, San Marino, and Saar Basin.

The Union of Soviet Socialist Republics concluded treaties for the protection of industrial property with Germany and Norway which adopt a number of provisions of the Convention of Union. See *Propriété Industrielle* (1926), p. 14, and (1928), p. 224; and article by Professor Heifetz, *ibid.* (1926), p. 194.

2. See *supra,* §§ 528, 530.

3. This was one of the desiderata set forth by the Bureau of Berne in its report to the Economic Committee in 1923. See *Propriété Industrielle* (1923), pp. 16, 20.

4. Abyssinia, Persia, Afghanistan, Beluchistan, and Muscat are countries in which extraterritorial jurisdiction exists and to which no international regime of industrial property has been extended.

5. See *Actes de Washington*, pp. 43, 262, 286, 287, 343.

coming to an end.[1] China provided herself with a trade-mark law in 1923 [2] and is rapidly reaching the point where the regime of extra-territorial jurisdiction will go out of existence.[3] Under such conditions, these countries, as well as Siam, might be willing to accede to the Industrial Property Union, and an active propaganda to this end ought to be undertaken.

India is another great country which remains outside the Union, and pressure should be brought to bear on its administration to secure its accession thereto.

An increase in the membership of the Madrid Arrangements, and the recent Arrangement of The Hague, should also be sought by educational propaganda tending to create a public opinion favorable to accession in the countries which have not yet acceded. The accession of the United States, at least to the Arrangement for the international registration of trade marks, should present no difficulty, as is shown in another place.[4] The same may be said of Great Britain.

But more important than the territorial extension of the Union for the Protection of Industrial Property is the progressive improvement of the regime of industrial property in the Union. All through this book it has been made clear that progress in this field demands long, persistent, and patient effort. Any new amendment of the Convention and Arrangements involves a change in municipal legislation or in the customs of domestic commerce, or, what is more serious, a breaking of administrative routine. Moreover, on many questions thought has not yet become crystallized in the various countries, and this makes any international action impossible. In the following sections an attempt will be made to deal with desirable improvements in the regime in the Union, — with a view of affording a more effective and complete protection to industrial property rights, — and with a number of schemes of international regulation now under discussion.

1. See, on the regime of industrial property in Egypt until the war, an article in *Propriété Industrielle* (1919), p. 26.

2. See text of the law in *Propriété Industrielle* (1924), p. 19, and regulations, *ibid.*, p. 195. On the previous regime see an article in the *Propriété Industrielle* (1921), p. 43.

3. See, on all this, a study in *Propriété Industrielle* (1925), p. 75.

4. See *supra*, § 453.

I. Improvements in Organization of the Union

§ **569. Extending powers of the International Bureau.** In respect to the organization of the Union, which is considered in chapter V of this book, there are three points in which improvement is highly desirable.

The first is the functions and powers of the International Bureau of the Union. These are described above.[1] The provisions of article 13 of the Convention in this respect have remained practically unmodified since their original adoption at the Paris Conference of 1880. At that time the conceptions of international organization were entirely different from those of to-day. The Bureau was endowed with functions of a purely informational character. This restriction is unjustified at the present time.

The conferences of revision of the Union have met at long intervals in recent times — not so often as before 1900. There is no governing body or commission set up to look after the affairs of the Union in the meantime. Moreover, the Bureau of Berne has been granted extra-judicial functions by the Madrid Trade-Mark Arrangement and the Arrangement of The Hague for the international deposit of industrial designs and models. For supervision of the execution and application of the various acts of the Union, the Bureau should be granted adequate powers.

Thus the Bureau should have the power to call to the attention of member countries that a certain engagement undertaken by them is not being carried out; that their municipal legislation has not been brought into conformity with the Convention or Arrangements. It should also be able to bring pressure to bear upon members of the Union for the ratification of the revised texts. In the past many countries have unduly postponed ratification for several years.

The Bureau, as has been shown, enjoys complete freedom in its activities, and may safely be endowed with such powers. It has unofficially exercised certain of these powers in a number of instances. Its long-time prestige should render its power of supervision of the working of the Union invaluable. Its action would not be hampered by the requirement of unanimity which governing commissions of other unions have to cope with.

§ **570. Accuracy of published material.** Related to this is the question of material supplied to the Bureau and published by it.

1. See *supra*, § 65.

Article 13 of the Convention provides that the Bureau shall publish a periodical devoted to matters concerning the Union, with the help of documents placed at its disposal by the various administrations. The Bureau does, in fact, publish *La Propriété Industrielle*. But the materials used in its columns are rarely supplied to the Bureau by the administrations of the member countries. The data on legislation, administrative regulations, and judicial decisions are, for the most part, either gathered by the Bureau from official or unofficial publications or, more often, supplied by the kindness of private individuals.

Thus the publications of the Bureau cannot claim to be complete and accurate, and do not rely upon strictly official information, either in regard to the actual existence of the legislation, decisions, etc., or in regard to the text of the same. This has two results: the engagement of the contracting countries in article 13 is not complied with; and the data published in the *Propriété Industrielle* and in other publications of the Bureau cannot, by themselves, form a true source of information in the Union.[1]

It is, therefore, necessary that the obligation of the various administrations to place at the Bureau's disposal the texts of documents concerning the object of the Union (especially, bipartite agreements, legislative acts, administrative rules, and administrative decisions) be made more explicit and strict. An official French translation of such texts should be supplied whenever necessary. The Bureau, on being informed of the publication of such a text, should be able to ask from the administration concerned, official communication thereof.

§ **571. Substitute for rule of unanimity.** The third question regarding the organization of the Union is the unanimity requirement in conferences of revision. It is pointed out above that, with the present increase of membership of the Union, it is practically impossible to achieve any major improvement in the international regime of industrial property under the Convention and Arrangements. The undesirability of the two remedies — the procedure of reservations and the formation of restricted unions — for this state of things is dealt with above. It may, then, squarely be asked whether the maintenance of such an obstructive rule is not irrecon-

1. This should not be taken as a criticism of the Bureau of Berne. It is its duty to give to the contracting countries all information possessed or supplied, and it may well use secondary sources when original sources are not available.

cilable with the life of the Union. A process of disintegration may already be seen in the numerous bipartite treaties entered into by many countries, especially after the war, on questions of industrial property protection.[1] It is an indisputable fact that the rule of unanimity in international organization does not exist consistently in practice.[2] Even in international unions where the rule of unanimity has suffered the fewest breaches examples may be found where majority groups have imposed decisions upon unwilling minorities.[3]

In view of this fact, the connection of the rule of unanimity with the dogma of sovereignty can no longer be supported. Unanimity, as a general rule, was accepted as a practical solution in earlier times, when there was no readiness to subordinate national interests to the decision of a majority of states, and no common action was otherwise possible.[4] But it has been considered an intolerable impediment, and has been abandoned whenever no subordination of national interests to action by a majority was involved, or when such interests were too unimportant to justify the sacrifice of the necessities of international life and international organization.

Laying aside, then, the dogmatic character of the rule of unanimity and considering it as possessing a reason of necessity and practicality,[5] we may inquire, with respect to the Union for the Protection of Industrial Property and its Conferences, what are the practical objections to taking decisions or adopting amendments by majority vote. Of course, any change would have to be made by a previous unanimous amendment of article 14 of the Convention embodying an agreement between the contracting countries that in future conferences of revision of the Convention amendments could be adopted by a certain majority.

As the past experience of the various conferences of the Union shows, there are two main reasons why unanimity was not achieved

1. See *supra*, §§ 82, 84.

2. See Norman Hill, "Unanimous Consent in International Organization," in *Amer. Jour. of Int. Law* (1928), XXII, 319.

3. In the Universal Postal Union, articles regulating various details may be amended by a two-thirds vote. In the International Labor Organization, no unanimity is required for amendment of the labor provisions of the Treaty of Versailles, for the adoption of draft conventions, etc. (Articles 403, 405 and 422.) The International Sugar Commission and the Danube River Commission take decisions on many issues without unanimous consent. See Hill, *ubi sup.*, pp. 312, 322–324.

4. Reinsch, *Public International Unions* (Boston-London, 1911), p. 152.

5. In the absence of such a rule, countries disagreeing with decisions taken by the consent of a majority would withdraw from conferences, organizations, or unions.

notwithstanding the existence of a great majority in favor of various proposals of amendment of the Convention. One reason is the reluctance of minority countries to adopt amendments containing provisions derogating from their municipal law. Examples of this kind at the last Conference of Revision at The Hague are: the opposition of two delegations (Australia and Great Britain) to the proposed amendment of article 4*b* forbidding the antedating of patents applied for by foreign patentees within the period of priority of article 4; the opposition of two countries (Great Britain and the United States) to the proposed amendment of article 4 concerning the nonconformity between patent applications; the opposition of the same countries to the inclusion of false advertising among the acts of unfair competition enumerated in article 10*b*; finally, the opposition of one country (the Serb-Croat-Slovene State) to the abolition of the compulsory working of industrial designs or models.[1]

In all these cases the law derogated from by the proposed amendments was not a general principle or an important rule of domestic law, but a mere technical regulation or a precept of minor importance. No real interests were behind such a state of the law. Simply, the opposing countries were loath to adopt any provision which would necessitate a change in their municipal legal order. The unanimity rule used to protect such manifestations of lack of the necessary spirit of concession and a broader will to achieve desirable uniform solutions in the international regime of interests transcending the boundaries of single states, is a very hollow rule. As the delegations of the United States, Great Britain, and Australia remarked on the above-cited single opposition of the delegation of the Serb-Croat-Slovene State, their countries are compelled to amend their own laws on several points in order to realize the progress aimed at by the Union.

The other reason why minority countries are unwilling to consent to amendments favored by a majority is the danger to their national interests which they consider involved in such proposals. Examples of this kind at the last Conference of Revision at The Hague are: the opposition of three countries (Hungary, Italy, and the Serb-Croat-

1. See *Actes de la Conférence de la Haye*, pp. 431, 519, 478, 520. On the question of suppression of the obligation to work an industrial design or model, the Italian delegation voiced its agreement with the delegation of the Serb-Croat-Slovene State and abstained from voting. The latter stated as the ground of its opposition the fact that the proposed amendment was in derogation of the law of its country.

Slovene State) to the suppression of the reservation of rights of third parties in article 4; the opposition of three countries (Japan, the Serb-Croat-Slovene State, and Poland) to the suppression of the obligation of working a patent and the substitution therefor of the compulsory license in article 5; the opposition of seven countries to the proposed amendment of article 6 concerning the independence of trade marks.[1]

In such cases, the adoption of amendments by consent of a majority would involve the subordination of national interests to the necessities of international life. As has been pointed out in earlier parts of this book, it is very doubtful whether any real interests would be sacrificed by the adoption of the proposed amendments. However, there may be cases in which the interests of a highly industrialized state, such as Great Britain or the United States, would not conform with the interests of an agricultural country, such as the Serb-Croat-Slovene State or the Latin American countries. But it should be possible to inquire whether a method may not be found of securing the adoption of desirable amendments of the Convention, or uniform solutions of problems presented in the international regime of industrial property, by the consent of a great majority of countries presenting diverse and conflicting interests.

Such a grouping of majorities should not be difficult to make if account were taken of the present classification of the member countries of the Union with respect to their contributions for maintaining the International Bureau, in six classes,[2] as well as of classifications in other public international unions. Thus countries highly industrialized and having a great volume of foreign commerce might be distinguished from countries mainly agricultural, or with a nascent industry and limited export trade. In the conferences of revision of the Convention, for the rule of unanimous consent would be substituted the rule of a majority of three fourths of each of these two groups of countries. In this way, no undue advantage in favor of any group of countries would result, and the decisions taken by less than

1. *Actes de la Conférence de La Haye*, pp. 517, 433, 444.

2. It appears that in the first of these classes belong France, Italy, Germany, Great Britain, and the United States; in the second: Canada, Japan, and Spain; in the third: Belgium, Brazil, Australia, Irish Free State, Mexico, Poland, Portugal, Sweden, and Switzerland; in the fourth: Austria, Czechoslovakia, Hungary, the Netherlands, Norway, Rumania, Serb-Croat-Slovene State, and Turkey; in the fifth: Bulgaria and Greece; and in the sixth: Cuba, Dominican Republic, Danzig, Esthonia, Latvia, Luxembourg, Morocco, Syria and Lebanon, and Tunis.

unanimous consent would respond to the necessities of international life and further the aims of the Union for a progressive uniformity of the law of industrial property.

II. Improvements in International Regime of Various Rights

A. *International Regime of Patents*

§ 572. Reservation of rights of third parties. The most important advantage granted by the Convention of 1883 to foreign patentees is the right of priority. It gives effective protection to inventors who are in danger of losing the right to apply for a patent in foreign countries by the publication of their invention or by an application by a third party. The latter case especially shows the strange character of the reservation of rights of third parties, which it has not been possible to eliminate from article 4 of the Convention in all the past conferences of revision. Indeed, by virtue of the right of priority, an inventor of country A who filed application in that country on January 1, 1928, will prevail over an inventor who filed application for the same invention in country B at any time between January 1, 1928, and January 1, 1929. No valid patent may be granted to the latter inventor. Yet, if he did not apply for a patent in that interval, but instead put the invention into commercial use, or made preparations for its working, he will preserve a right to use the invention personally thereafter, notwithstanding the grant of patent to the foreign applicant. Inventors rarely put an invention into commercial use, or incur expenses in preparation for its working, before the grant of a patent. So that the reservation of a right of personal possession of an invention arising within the period of priority will usually benefit people who obtain knowledge of an invention, for which a patent has been applied for in a foreign country, and avail themselves of the same.

When it is admitted that rights of personal possession acquired prior to the first filing of a patent application do not need the reservation of article 4 in order to be recognized and protected, such reservation will very rarely protect persons acting in good faith. The persistence of three countries at the last Conference of Revision in not consenting to the abolition of this reservation should not prevent the resumption of new efforts toward such abolition. In case the total omission of the reservation should not be accepted, a middle solution, like that admitted by the Danish law,[1] might have a better chance of enlisting unanimous consent. It sets an arbitrary rule, but one that is much to be preferred to the present reservation in article 4. Under this rule, rights of personal possession acquired in the interval between the first filing of an application in a country of the Union and the publication of the invention would be recognized, but not such rights when acquired after publication of the invention.[2]

§ **573. Securing right of priority.** The right of priority may be lost in certain countries, and therewith the right to apply for a patent, for failure to comply with the formalities required by the law for the declaration of a claim of right of priority or for the production of documents substantiating such claim. In another place, cases of real hardship in this respect have been cited.[3] Strict compliance with formalities should be required when this is the only way of securing substantive rights. But such requirement for the sake of compliance alone leads to unreasonable injustice. It should be possible, therefore, to permit amendments of declarations of rights of priority and of documents produced in proof of such rights, or to reinstate a right of priority lost by the non-compliance with formalities. Such permission or reinstatement might be subject only to the rights of third parties who might be injured thereby. The addition of a provision to this effect in section (*d*) of article 4 would seem to be required.[4]

The enjoyment of the right of priority would be rendered easier to foreign applicants if the rules concerning the formalities of application and drawings established by the Technical Conference of Berne in 1926 [5] were complied with in the various countries. When the laws of the various countries are brought into harmony with these rules, it should be possible to draft a model patent application blank which could be filed in any country.

1. See *supra*, p. 311.
2. The International Association of Industrial Property, at its Rome Congress of 1928 (May–June), adopted a resolution calling for the abolition of the reservation of rights of third parties in article 4 and, in the alternative, for the creation of a restricted Union between the countries favoring such abolition. See *Propriété Industrielle* (1928), pp. 201, 202.
3. See *supra*, § 185.
4. See resolutions of like effect of the French, German, and Belgian groups of the International Association for the Protection of Industrial Property, *supra*, § 186, and *Propriété Industrielle* (1925), p. 79.
5. See *supra*, § 143.

§ 574. Obligation to work patent. The efforts to abolish the obligation to work the patent should not be considered as terminated by the amendments to article 5 introduced at the Conference of The Hague in 1925. The value of these amendments remains to be seen. It depends on legislation which is passed in the various countries in execution thereof. The possibility of forfeiture of a patent for failure to put an invention into commercial use in a country of the Union is not abandoned.

Moreover, there is danger that the terms of the new provisions of article 5, especially the expression, "les abus qui pourraient résulter de l'exercice du droit exclusif," may give rise to new restrictions of the patentee's rights unknown hitherto in all countries except Great Britain and the British dominions and colonies.[1] These amendments of article 5, taken from the English law, are pregnant with dangers and difficulties of interpretation and application in other countries, where the background of that law is not to be found.[2]

It would be best, therefore, to eliminate these provisions, and to stipulate, instead, the complete suppression of the obligation to work the patent, or, if necessary, its replacement by the system of compulsory licenses at the expiry of a period from the grant of the patent. This should be the end to be achieved in the future.

§ 575. Protection at international exhibitions. The new text of article 11, as amended at the Conference of The Hague, is assuredly very unsatisfactory, as is shown in another part of this study.[3] Since the principle of non-cumulation of the period of right of priority with that of temporary protection at international exhibitions was admitted, and the period of right of priority may begin from the date of the introduction of an invention in the locale of the exhibition, no essential difference in the nature of the protection under articles 4 and 11 exists. It would seem, therefore, that the main problem under article 11 is to secure the identity of the invention exhibited and filed subsequently in the various countries of the Union, and the accuracy of the date of exhibition.[4] In the case of the right of priority under article 4 of the Convention, this identity and accuracy are secured

1. See introductory statement by Mr. Ostertag, Director of the International Bureau, to the Rome Congress of the International Association for the Protection of Industrial Property in 1928, *Propriété Industrielle* (1928), pp. 178, 179.

2. See *supra*, § 227.

3. See *supra*, § 243.

4. See statements of the American and British delegations at the Conference of The Hague, *Actes de la Conférence de La Haye*, p. 436.

by the production of certificates of the administration which received the first application, and of copies of the original application (with specifications, drawings, etc.). Article 11 should be amended so as to contain provisions equivalent to those of section (*d*) of article 4. But in this case, for the certificate of the administration receiving the application should be substituted the certificate of the official direction of the exhibition; and instead of the copy of the application, other means of identifying the invention should be supplied. When these means of identification (photographs, drawings, descriptions, samples, etc.) are duly certified by the competent direction, there is nothing more to be desired.[1]

B. *The International Regime of Industrial Designs and Models*

§ 576. **Harmonizing laws of the various countries.** What is said in the previous sections with regard to rights of priority, the obligation to work, and protection at international exhibitions of inventions, applies with greater force to industrial designs and models. Generally speaking, the law on this subject in many countries is singularly behind present-day conditions of industry and craft. It is shown in another place [2] how in France the law has come to afford an elastic and supple regulation of the various interests by extension of the copyright law to industrial designs and models, the optional deposit at the *Office National de Propriété Industrielle*, and the private registers sanctioned by the administration.

This regulation constitutes a model for all other countries. The extension, especially, of the copyright law to cover all industrial models or designs presenting an artistic character would seem to be advisable everywhere. But this is impossible to achieve through the Industrial Property Convention. It is a matter for consideration in the Copyright Union. What may be done in our Union is to unshackle the national regulation of industrial designs and models from the bonds imposed by their assimilation to inventions. Inasmuch as no enumeration of claims and no elaborate specifications on filing industrial designs and models are required, efforts should be made to simplify and make uniform the formalities of applying for registration. Also it should be sought to make the filing of designs

1. See resolution to like effect of the International Association of Industrial Property, at its Rome Congress of 1928 (May–June), in *Propriété Industrielle* (1928), pp. 201, 203.

2. See *supra*, § 264.

and models under seal admissible in all countries, and to grant elective and long terms of protection. An agreement on these points would seem to be necessary before it can be expected that many countries will accede to the Arrangement of The Hague for the international deposit of designs and models.

C. *The International Regime of Trade Marks*

§ 577. Securing priority of trade marks. The most important questions in the international regime of trade marks as to which improvement is highly desirable are those of priority, validation, independence, and transmission of trade marks.

The six-months right of priority of article 4 of the Convention of 1883–1925, for the purpose of filing applications for registration of trade marks in other countries after filing in a country of the Union, in conjunction with the new article *6b* concerning the refusal or invalidation of well-known trade marks belonging to foreigners, is not sufficient for the protection of prior users of trade marks. The right of priority of article 4 is of no benefit to trade-mark owners whose trade is extended to foreign markets long after registration in the country of origin, or to those who do not register their marks at all, or register them long after adoption and use in the countries where registration is not necessary for the protection of trade marks. All such trade-mark owners can rarely depend for protection of their rights on the provision of article *6b*. Only those marks are protected, under that article, which the competent authority of the country of registration may regard as well-known in that country, as being already trade marks of "ressortissants" of another contracting country. Such marks are, for instance, the following: Kodak, Yale, Gillette, Remington, Pears' Soap, Odol, Palmolive, Pebeco, Hanyadi Janos, Kyriazi, Martell, Cliquot, and others. In general, all foreign trade marks used extensively in the domestic market will come under the provision of article *6b*. No others will be protected by this article.

In this connection, the Pan-American Trade-Mark Convention of 1910 contains in article 9 a most interesting provision, which is considered above.[1] Under this provision, in case the non-admission for registration of a foreigner's trade mark is based on a prior registration of the same mark in the name of another, the applicant may cause cancellation of such registration by proving, especially, that he

1. See *supra*, § 542.

used the mark in the country in question prior to its registration by the other person, or that, although he did not use the mark in the country, the registrant had knowledge of the mark's being used by the applicant in other countries.

In order that this provision may be accepted by all the members of the Union, it should contain the further condition that in case of registrations in good faith the prior user cannot prevail unless he enters claim within a period of three years from registration. Thus foreign marks would be protected and negligent trade-mark owners would not be encouraged.

§ 578. Eliminating erroneous interpretation and application of article 6. Article 6 of the Convention of 1883–1925 contains the rule of validation of trade marks duly registered in the country of origin. It satisfies the need of manufacturers and merchants to have their trade marks admitted for registration, and protected, in other countries in their original form. The various exceptions to the rule enumerated in article 6 are explained and justified by the necessity of satisfying the conflicting interests of domestic trade-mark owners or of the public. But this necessity should be the only ground for refusing to validate a trade mark registered in the country of origin. A refusal on the sole ground that a proposed trade mark does not comply with the definition or conception of the law of a country of what may be a trade mark, is opposed to the rule of article 6 and wholly unjustified on general principles.

In this view, the first sentence of number 2 of the second paragraph of article 6 is dangerously vague and indefinite. "Marks devoid of any distinctive character" are either those which do not contain the elements required by the law of a country for a registrable trade mark, or those which consist of signs or indications which are in the possession of the public. The refusal on the latter ground is covered by the second part of the provision in question. The refusal on the first ground is against the rule of article 6. It is submitted, therefore, that the above provision should be eliminated from article 6, or amended in either of the two ways proposed at the Conference of The Hague.[1]

The whole provision of number 2 (of the second paragraph of article 6) purports to make possible the invalidation or refusal of marks in the possession of the public. An injury to the public should be

1. See *supra*, § 377.

clearly shown in order to justify such a refusal or invalidation. That a word or indication, according to its meaning in the dictionary, signifies the kind, quality, value, and the like of a product should not be a sufficient ground for refusal, if it be proved that it has been used for a long time by a producer and has acquired a secondary meaning in identifying and distinguishing his products. Consequently, the provision of the second paragraph of article 6 (number 2) that the distinctiveness of a mark should be determined from all the circumstances of the case, especially the length of user of the mark, should be amended so as to be made applicable to all the cases covered by that provision.[1]

What is important, indeed, is not to satisfy formal requirements, but to protect existing reputations and advantageous business relations. Such protection should be denied only when a clear and present injury to other interests is shown. In this respect, it should be noted that the practice of patent offices and courts in the Germanic countries of asking the opinion of interested circles (chambers of commerce, professional associations, and the like) on the question how far a proposed trade mark is a "free mark," or one commonly used in commerce, and other like questions, is very commendable.

§ **579. Independence of trade-mark rights.** The so-called independence of trade marks is a necessity of modern commercial conditions as much as the validation of trade-mark rights acquired in the country of origin. While most manufacturers are interested in the protection of their trade marks in the foreign countries in which their products are sold, or may be sold, many exporters are compelled to adapt their trade marks to the country in which they import merchandise. An exporter of goods from the United States to Japan or South American countries prefers to give to his mark a form and aspect different from that of one to be used in the United States. By the law of many countries, and according to a wrong interpretation of article 6,[2] he cannot have his trade mark registered and protected in other countries unless he first registers it in the United States. This involves two difficulties. First, the mark may be non-registrable in the country of origin (in the above instance, in the United States), and, second, its registration is the cause of additional trouble, expense, and fees. The French and Spanish delegations op-

1. See *supra*, p. 551. 2. See *supra*, §§ 371–373.

posed, at the Conference of The Hague, the insertion in article 6 of a provision declaring that no registration in the country of origin is necessary for a mark conforming to the law of the country of importation. The danger that foreigners would register trade marks of domestic appearance, and thus deceive the public as to the origin of the goods, is not real, the provisions of the law of all countries against deceptive trade marks being a good check in this respect.

The first of the above two difficulties raised by the non-independence of trade marks is solved in Great Britain and the United States[1] by the supplementary register of trade marks, in which are registered marks to be used in foreign commerce, although they are not registrable according to the domestic law. A general adoption of this system would solve this difficulty for all the member countries of the Union; but it would needlessly complicate searches of priorities.

At the Rome Congress of the International Association for the Protection of Industrial Property, in 1928 (May 29–June 1), opinions seemed to incline toward a middle solution proposed by the French delegate, M. Chabaud. The requirement for prior registration in the country of origin as a condition of the admission for registration of a trade mark in other countries would be tempered by the element of independence in respect to the preservation of the mark. The forfeiture or cancellation of the mark in the country of origin would not affect its protection in the other countries.[2] This, in itself, would not solve all the difficulties, unless it were combined with the existence of supplementary registers. But then the whole system would be highly artificial. For registration in the home country would serve no purpose whatsoever.

§ 580. Transfer of trade marks. The transmission of trade marks without transferring the business in connection with which they are used is urged on the same considerations as their independence. Modern forms of economic and commercial organization require the possession and use of the same trade marks by several producers, individuals, or juristic persons.[3] In view of the state of the

1. Great Britain, Act of Dec. 23, 1919 (9 & 10 Geo. V, c. 79). United States, Act of March 10, 1920 (XLI *Stat. at Large*, 533).

2. See *Propriété Industrielle* (1928), pp. 201, 204.

3. See Introductory Statement by Mr. Ostertag, Director of the International Bureau, at the Rome Congress of the International Association for the Protection of Industrial Property, May–June, 1928, in *Propriété Industrielle* (1928), p. 182.

municipal law in most of the countries,[1] it is hardly to be expected that any provision permitting such transmission of trade marks will be inserted in the Industrial Property Convention. Instead, the granting of licenses to other persons to use a trade mark registered in the country of origin is the regime to be envisaged in the near future. Branch offices, agents, and affiliated concerns might be permitted, under an amendment of article 6, to register in their names a trade mark of a foreign concern by license of the latter. Each country might be left free to determine the guaranties [2] against possible deceit of the public by such registration.[3]

§ 581. **Other points of improvement.** Two further points in the regime of trade marks in the Union would seem to need amelioration. The provision of article 5 of the Convention, inserted at the Conference of The Hague, in respect to non-use of registered trade marks does not purport in any way to influence the municipal law of the member countries of the Union.[4] This provision should be amended so as to prohibit the cancellation of registration for non-use before the lapse of three years from registration of the mark.

On the other hand, the special sanctions provided for in article 9 have not yet been adopted by all the members of the Union. The obligation of the contracting countries under this article is not to pass legislation granting such remedies, but only to apply such sanctions if they already have such legislation.[5] An amendment compelling the contracting countries to create and maintain law affording such remedies would seem to be necessary.

D. *International Regime of Indications of Origin*

§ 582. **Extending scope of the Madrid Arrangement.** As we have seen in a previous chapter,[6] the efforts to extend the final provision of article 4 of the Madrid Arrangement for the repression of false in-

1. In most of the countries a trade mark may be transferred only with the business in connection with which it is used. Only in Canada, France, Italy, Mexico, Morocco, Spain, and Tunis may a trade mark be assigned independently of the business. In Esthonia and Lithuania a mark owned and used by a concern may be transferred by such concern only if the special branch of manufacture or trade in connection with which the mark is used is also transferred. In Belgium and Greece a concern may assign its trade mark on transferring the manufacture of or trade in the product on which the mark was applied.

2. For instance, the application of the word "license," or "licensed," to the mark.

3. No agreement was reached on the question of transmission of trade marks at the Rome Congress of the International Association for the Protection of Industrial Property, in 1928. See *Propriété Industrielle* (1928), pp. 201, 204.

4. See *supra*, § 400. 5. See *supra*, §§ 407, 412. 6. See *supra*, §§ 471, 477.

dications of origin to other products besides products of the vine, and to incorporate the provision of article 1 of that Arrangement in article 10 of the general Convention, have been unsuccessful. At the congresses of the International Association for the Protection of Industrial Property, at Geneva (1927) and Rome (1928), these questions formed a subject of discussion. At Geneva, the Congress adopted a resolution that the Convention of 1883–1925 should be amended so as to protect the appellations of all products deriving their natural qualities from the soil and climate and all geographical appellations, in such cases where they were not considered generic terms by the law of the country to which they belonged. At Rome, the Congress showed an inclination to adopt another view. German, Swiss, and Hungarian representatives opposed vigorously the idea of leaving the question of the character of a geographical appellation of any product (products of the vine included) to be determined exclusively by the law of the country of origin.[1]

Under these conditions it cannot be hoped that any change will be made in article 10 of the Convention. But an extension of the final provision of article 4 of the Madrid Arrangement concerning products of the vine to all products deriving their natural qualities from the soil and climate should be sought. This would render the Arrangement accessible to countries desirous of protecting appellations of products other than those of the vine, but it would create a greater impediment to the accession of countries unwilling to take away from their courts the decision as to the character of such appellations. One of the latter countries is the United States.

This branch of industrial property raises not only difficult questions of law, but also economic questions. Many countries are reluctant to recognize in favor of other countries, and perpetuate, local monopolies which have no real natural justification. On the other hand, they are unwilling to interfere with long use of foreign appellations by domestic commerce when no fraud is committed upon the public. The courts of the country where such use of foreign appellations is made are likely to be influenced by the opinion of interested national circles. And the courts of the country of origin might be inclined to protect all national appellations having an exporting value. It would seem, therefore, that a decision on these cases by an international court would be the best possible solution.[2]

1. See *Propriété Industrielle* (1928), pp. 201, 205.
2. See *supra*, p. 685, and *infra*, § 586.

III. Establishment of an International Tribunal in the Union

§ **583. Early proposals.** The establishment of an international tribunal for disputes concerning the application or execution of the Convention of Union has been much discussed in recent times. At an early date the proposals for such a tribunal confined its jurisdiction to cases of annulment and infringement of trade marks. Thus the Dutch writer, Smits Van Oyen, proposed the creation of an International College of Appeal, constituted by the directors of the Bureaus of Industrial Property of the various countries, to have jurisdiction in cases of appeal against the rejection of marks registered at the International Bureau.[1] And the International Association for the Protection of Industrial Property adopted a resolution at its Paris Congress of 1900 calling for the study of the question of establishment of an international tribunal.[2] But the creation of such a tribunal, to be substituted for the national tribunals in cases of annulment and infringement of trade marks, was not considered possible, in view of the divergences of municipal law on such important questions as the legal effects of registration, subject-matter of trade marks, proof of priority, and the like. Besides, no country was willing in pre-war times to surrender the least particle of its independence in questions of domestic law.

§ **584. Plan of the Economic Committee of the League of Nations.** The plan of an international jurisdiction was taken up again by the Economic Committee of the League of Nations, in connection with its study of the subject of unfair competition. The third article of the draft convention on unfair competition submitted to the Conference of Experts which was called together by that committee on May 5, 1924, provided that

> the contracting states undertake that any differences which may arise between them as to the interpretation or carrying out of this Convention, and which cannot be settled by mutual accord, or in a manner provided by convention or agreed upon between the two states, shall be submitted to the determination of the Permanent Court of International Justice.[3]

1. *Het Internationale Recht der Fabricks-en Handelsmerken* (Amsterdam, 1894), p. 161.
2. See *Annuaire* (1900), pp. 248, 412, 493.
3. See *Preliminary Documents, Conference of Experts*, League of Nations, C.E.C.D. 1, p. 2.

This provision was taken from similar stipulations inserted in many post-war treaties and conventions. At the meeting of the Experts, it was admitted that the question of interpretation of the Convention might well be submitted to the jurisdiction of the Permanent Court of Arbitration or the Permanent Court of International Justice. As regards the carrying out of the Convention, and the disputes arising therefrom, some experts were of opinion that it would be difficult to resort to the Permanent Court, inasmuch as there was no uniform international legislation on the subject which the court could make use of. Could the countries be compelled to change their domestic laws in order to carry out the Convention? A strong minority in the Conference held that the proposal in question involved a political question in which the sovereign rights of the various countries were involved, and went far beyond the competence of a meeting of experts.[1]

§ **585. Discussion at the Conference of The Hague.** At the Conference of The Hague in 1925 the same stipulation was proposed by Great Britain as an amendment to article 17 of the Convention.[2] It was supported by the delegate of the Economic Committee of the League of Nations, and agreed upon by most of the delegates. Canada and Japan did not view the proposal with approval, the latter preferring the intervention of the International Bureau of Berne in cases of difference of interpretation or application.[3] The United States delegation opposed the proposal by reason of the non-adherence of the United States to the Statute of the Permanent Court of International Justice, and did not change its position when the Economic Committee of the League of Nations proposed the insertion of a provision declaring that the stipulation in question was not obligatory for countries not adhering to the Statute of the Court.

The Polish delegation remarked that an international tribunal is not absolutely necessary in the matter of industrial property. The only difference that might conceivably arise between two countries in this field would arise from the fact that the tribunals of one country might interpret a provision of the Convention differently from the tribunals of another country. Such a divergence might be

1. See *Meeting of Experts, Minutes of the Sixth Meeting,* League of Nations, C.E.C.D./P.V.6. (1), p. 8.

2. See *Actes de la Conférence de La Haye,* p. 353; see also discussion, *ibid.*, p. 420.

3. The Bureau did intervene with success in certain cases of differences of interpretation; see, for instance, *Propriété Industrielle* (1922), p. 95.

conveniently solved by an authentic interpretation by a conference of revision. This view is not entirely sound. Besides differences of interpretation, there may be differences concerning the carrying out of the Convention arising out of the failure of a country to apply certain provisions of the Convention by making the necessary changes in its municipal law. On the other hand, conferences of revision meet after long intervals, and it is not always possible to wait long years for an authentic interpretation. The Polish delegation, however, was right in observing that the law of industrial property was of an extremely technical and specialized character and its study and thorough understanding confined to a specialized class of experts, and that, therefore, the members of the Permanent Court of International Justice could not give sufficient guaranty of being good judges in this matter. In the view of this delegation, a tribunal of arbitration made up of eminent authorities in the law of industrial property would be better suited for the solution of the differences in question. The sub-committee, called upon to vote on the principle of submission of such differences to an international tribunal, was not unanimous, seventeen voting in favor of such a principle and five against, with five abstaining.

Another proposal of the British delegation, for the submission to arbitration of a special kind of disputes, raised certain objections on the part of the United States delegation, in consequence of which it was not insisted upon. It concerned differences arising in regard to lists of state emblems and official signs and hall marks communicated mutually by the contracting countries through the medium of the International Bureau of Berne, as provided for by the new article *6c*. In case such differences could not be solved by negotiation between the contracting countries, they would be submitted to an arbitral tribunal of three experts, each of the parties appointing one, and the third to be named by agreement or to be the Director of the International Bureau of Berne, in case no agreement is reached.[1]

§586. A suggestion. The creation of an international tribunal to decide questions of the interpretation and application of the Convention would seem to be necessary, in view of the fact that many of the provisions of the Convention constitute common legislation for all the member countries, and a number of other provisions call for the enactment of municipal law to carry them into effect. In its

1. See *Actes de la Conférence de La Haye*, p. 462.

present form, the Convention is devoid of any sanction. Several serious differences of interpretation in the various countries have been noticed in the course of this study, and examples of countries which for a long time failed to bring their domestic law into agreement with the Convention have been repeatedly cited. At the present time, it should no longer be a valid argument against submission to arbitration of this sort of differences, that thereby the so-called "sovereign rights" or independence of the contracting countries would be infringed upon. But the point of the Polish delegation at the Conference of The Hague, that the Permanent Court of International Justice is ill fitted to sit on questions of the law of industrial property, is well taken. The objections of countries that have not adhered to the Statute of that court would be met as well if a different procedure were followed. In this respect, the old proposal that the directors of the bureaus of industrial property of the various countries should be used as a tribunal offers a good suggestion. As the member countries are too many, the following scheme might be devised. Each conference of revision might nominate a number of directors of the member countries to act as an arbitral tribunal until the next conference, in all differences arising in regard to the interpretation or carrying out of the Convention. The Director of the International Bureau might be the *ex officio* president of the tribunal. A special act of the conference might lay down the procedure of the tribunal.

The question which has sometimes been raised, as to the law that the court would apply in cases brought before it, presents no difficulty. The law of the Union is the Convention, and for each of the restricted Unions, the respective Arrangement. The arbitral tribunal is to decide whether that law has been properly interpreted and executed. The differences to be brought before the tribunal will arise out of administrative, legislative, and judicial measures of one of the contracting countries. The administrative and judicial measures will often be caused by the state of the national law: thus, ultimately, the question will usually be whether the law of a contracting country is in agreement with the Convention. No sanction, of course, exists at the present time for countries that fail to comply with their obligations; but it is important to fix a procedure for interpreting such obligations or holding a country morally at fault.

Besides such cases of interpretation of the Convention and Arrangements, there are cases of harmonizing their application in the various contracting countries. Thus, the special class of differences arising in regard to lists of state emblems and official signs and hall marks communicated mutually by the contracting countries through the International Bureau (article 6*c*) might be submitted to this tribunal. Also the disputes concerning the character of appellations of origin of products.

IV. International Classification of Patents, Designs, and Trade Marks

§ 587. Difficulties of international classification. A question that has been discussed ever since the beginnings of the Industrial Property Union, and that forms at the present day one of the most important desiderata for the future development of the Union, is that of the uniform classification of patents, designs, and trade marks. This subject is also closely connected with the various schemes for the creation of international patents and trade marks and for international registration of patents and designs.

In truth, the purpose of a uniform classification of designs is not very clear. Many countries possess no such classification. It is not always easy to classify a design as such, although the products on which a design is applied may be classified. Moreover, the whole subject of design protection is now in the making, the tendency being to do away with the obligation to deposit or register designs, and to have them protected without any formality, like artistic works in general.

A uniform classification of patents is very useful for the purpose of search of priorities. However, it presents great practical difficulties. One consists in the fact that there is extreme divergence in the laws of the various countries regarding the drafting of claims which a patent covers. In some countries, the claims protect "functions" of the mechanical parts of a machine; in others, functional claims are not allowed, and the various parts or features of a machine should be enumerated in the claim; in still others, no specific claims need be indicated, a general *résumé* of the invention being sufficient. It is impossible under these conditions to prepare an international index, because such an index would have a totally different aspect, according to whether the teleological, peripheral, or central method of logical classification is adopted.[1] Even if it be assumed that the various countries would agree to give up their different methods of classification, the establishment of a uniform classification is rendered difficult by the impossibility of finding a final classification covering all the ever-increasing inventions. By the progress of science and industry inventions are multiplied and extended to new fields, and the addition of new categories in the classification is being constantly resorted to in the various countries. Lastly, the adoption of a uniform classification would necessitate the reclassification of the patents already granted in the various countries. Otherwise, each country would have to keep two classifications, which would complicate matters instead of simplifying them. But a reclassification of patents extending back long years in the past is an immense undertaking in the great industrial countries, which have now granted between half a million and a million patents. A further difficulty, which, although small in appearance, is very serious in fact, is that of the translation of the uniform classification into the official language of the various countries.[2]

The same difficulties are not presented in the case of classification of trade marks. The logical problem of method of classification does not exist; and it is possible to establish a complete classification by creating broad categories and leaving scope for sub-divisions. The reclassification of marks already registered is not a very difficult task, since registered marks are usually protected for fifteen or twenty years, and only those registered within that period need to be reclassified, all renewals of registration being classified under the new uniform classification.

§ 588. Proposals and schemes of classification. The establishment of a uniform classification of patents, designs, and trade marks was proposed as early as 1886, in the first Conference of Revision at Rome, by the International Bureau and the Italian administration. Patents were to be divided into twenty classes, designs into fourteen, and trade marks into thirty-six. The Conference was not particularly enthusiastic about the proposal.[3] The question was taken up later by the International Association of Industrial Property, at

1. See a letter by Mr. Wirth, in *Propriété Industrielle* (1926), pp. 95, 98; also Potts, *Patents: Invention and Method* (London, 1924), chap. IV.

2. See, on all this, *Propriété Industrielle* (1924), p. 158.

3. See *Conférence de Rome*, pp. 31, 141, 148, 160.

its congresses of 1897, 1898, and 1899.[1] In the third and fourth Conferences of Revision at Brussels in 1897–1900,[2] and at Washington in 1911,[3] the only uniform classification discussed was that of trade marks. The International Bureau of Berne had adopted unofficially, in connection with the service of international registration of trade marks, and in order to facilitate its own searches, a classification which it sought to make official by inserting an additional article to this effect in the Madrid Arrangement. Upon failure of this attempt at the Brussels Conference, no such proposal was made at the Washington Conference, but a *voeu* was adopted on the proposal of the Portuguese delegation inviting the Bureau to study the question of a uniform classification of trade marks to be adopted by all the contracting countries.

After the war, the French and German groups of the International Association for the Protection of Industrial Property adopted resolutions to the effect that a uniform classification of trade marks in all the countries of the Union is necessary, and that steps should be taken for its establishment.[4] In the meantime, the unofficial classification of the International Bureau had been adopted by six countries: Belgium, France, Portugal, Peru, Salvador, and Uruguay, the first three of which are members of the Industrial Property Union. The Bureau proposed to make its classification official at the Conference of The Hague.[5] But the Congress of the International Association for the Protection of Industrial Property, meeting for the first time after the war at Zürich in 1925, voted a resolution disapproving of the classification adopted by the International Bureau of Berne and inviting the next Conference of The Hague to prepare a uniform classification with a smaller number of classes.[6]

1. See *Annuaire* (1897), pp. 81, 96, 404; (1898), pp. 202 (a report and a scheme of classification of patents by Léon Poinsard), 214 (an excellent report by Dr. Martius, a scheme for an international classification of marks, designs and patents, and an appendix of the classification in the different countries); (1899), pp. 29 (a scheme of single uniform classification in twenty groups and 539 classes for patents, designs, and trade marks, by Perissé and Mainié), 79 (remarks on this scheme by Léon Poinsard), 110.

2. *Actes de la Conférence de Bruxelles*, pp. 57, 119, 182, 290, 293.

3. *Actes de la Conférence de Washington*, pp. 262, 294, 353.

4. See discussions and resolution of French group, in *Travaux du Groupe Français*, No. 1 (1919–1922), pp. 107, 161, 195, 203; resolution of German group, in *Propriété Industrielle* (1923), p. 84.

5. See *Propriété Industrielle* (1924), p. 158. See this classification in *Actes de la Conférence de La Haye*, pp. 307–309.

6. See *Propriété Industrielle* (1925), pp. 127, 128.

This Conference adopted a proposition of the German Delegation that a meeting of experts should be called together by the International Bureau, for the elaboration of a uniform classification of trade marks.[1] The Experts met at Geneva in October, 1926, and adopted uniform rules for filing patent applications, but were unable to agree even on the general lines of a uniform classification of trade marks. Instead, they appointed a Committee of five members [2] entrusted with the task of grouping products, in view of the registration of trade marks, into fifty classes at most; of making an alphabetical list of products sufficiently complete for the registration of marks in the language of the International Bureau; and of transmitting the classification and list, through the International Bureau, to the contracting countries and to interested international organizations. The Meeting of Experts decided not to terminate its sessions but only to discontinue them, and resume them at the conclusion of the task of the Committee.[3]

§ 589. Chances of success. What chances of success has this Committee? The Director of the International Bureau agreed in 1922 that the classification of the Bureau was insufficient.[4] Several classes were overloaded while others were almost empty. Yet, as he pointed out, no classification can be perfect. The classification of the Bureau has this much in its favor, that it has now been in practice by the Bureau for thirty-five years, and has needed no other change than the addition of a new class, 71 *bis*.[5] The most serious objections to this classification are two. First, that the number of classes (80) is too large. Some countries, like Great Britain, which require a distinct registration for each class, are reluctant to adopt a long classification. Other countries have a fiscal interest in a large number of classes, because they collect additional fees for each additional class. And still others favor a large number, because they are unwilling to group together too many products and thus reserve to

1. See *Actes de la Conférence de La Haye*, pp. 286, 298, 307, 355, 356, 361, 483.

2. Members of this Committee were Dr. Duchesne (Germany), Mr. Jarratt (Great Britain), Mr. Kraft (Switzerland), Mr. Mavaut (Belgium), and Mr. Prins (the Netherlands). The countries that signed the *procès-verbal*, besides the above five, were Austria, Czechoslovakia, Denmark, Hungary, Italy, Japan, Mexico, Norway, Poland, the Serb-Croat-Slovene State, Spain, and Sweden. The delegations of France, Morocco, and Tunis declined to sign.

3. See *procès-verbal*, in *Propriété Industrielle* (1926), p. 211; and an account of the discussions at the meeting, *ibid.*, p. 246.

4. See statement by Professor Röthlisberger, in *Travaux du Groupe Français* (1919–1922), p. 108.

5. See *Propriété Industrielle* (1924), pp. 158, 162.

the exclusive ownership of a person a trade mark used only for some of these products. Second, Germany especially objects to the classification of the Bureau, because it does not group together products sold or manufactured in the same business. This raises a question of method of classification. How should products be classified, in view of registration of trade marks? Should the classification be based on the production of the products, like that of patents, or on consumption? There is a clear difference between patents and trade marks. The first refer to new processes, or new products, and are necessarily connected with production. The latter are used as distinctive signs of products, to facilitate the access of a manufacturer or merchant to the market; they are used in view of consumption. To use the example put by Mr. Drouets,[1] all trade marks used on or in connection with shoes should appear in the same class, whatever the material is from which the shoe is made (leather, cloth, or any other).

The Committee will have a difficult task in reaching an agreement as to the basis of classification. It is fortunate, however, that on this Committee are represented the countries with the most divergent classifications. It may be hoped that, by grouping the products classified together in these representative types of national classification, a uniform international classification may be established. This would very probably facilitate the accession of Great Britain to the Madrid Trade Mark Arrangement.[2]

The Geneva Technical Meeting adopted also a *voeu* that the various administrations should study the possibility of adopting as auxiliary to their own patent classification the decimal classification of the International Bibliographic Bureau, the indications of which should be marked on their publications conjointly with those of the national classification. Of the twenty countries signing the *procès-verbal*, eight — namely, Austria, Germany, Spain, Great Britain, Italy, Norway, Sweden, and Switzerland — noted their reservation in respect to this *voeu.*[3]

1. See discussions at the Meeting of Experts, in *Propriété Industrielle* (1926), p. 247.

2. In his introductory statement to the Congress of the International Association for the Protection of Industrial Property, at Geneva, in June, 1927, the Director of the International Bureau announced that the Committee was actually working on the classification on a practical basis by finding out which were the similar products, that appear in the practice of the large industrial countries, listed together in the deposits of trade marks. See *Propriété Industrielle* (1927), pp. 135, 140.

3. See *procès-verbal*, in *Propriété Industrielle* (1926), pp. 205, 208. The International Institute of Bibliography, created in August, 1895, at Brussels by an unofficial inter-

To the schemes of uniform classification of patents is closely related a plan for the creation of an international index of patents, proposed by Mr. Tenant, President of the British Corporation of Patent Agents.[1] That the plan stumbles at the same difficulties as the uniform classification, and its impracticability and lack of usefulness under present conditions, have been demonstrated by Mr. Wirth.[2] Such an index might possibly be made as between the countries adopting the French system of *résumés* of inventions.[3]

V. Schemes of International Patents and International Registration of Patents

§ 590. Present inadequacy of international protection of patents. The present international regime of patent protection gives very little satisfaction. Patents are the branch of industrial property, the international regulation of which has made least progress. Trade names and statements of place of origin are protected internationally without any condition or formality. Industrial designs or models, in many cases, are protected as artistic works with no formality whatsoever; and whenever they are not protected as such they may be deposited internationally under the recent Arrangement of The Hague. Trade marks enjoy the protection of the specific provisions concerning their validation of articles 6, 6*b*, 6*c*, and 7 of the Convention of Union, and may be registered at the International Bureau under the Madrid Arrangement. Patents, in the Industrial Property Union, leaving aside the provisions of articles 4*b*, 5, and 5*b* granting specific rights after their acquisition in the contracting countries, enjoy only national treatment and the right of priority.

Patentees entitled to the benefits of the Union are required, for recognition of their rights in the contracting countries, to comply with all conditions and formalities of the domestic law of each country, with the sole qualification that they may not be denied recognition for any of the reasons covered by the right of priority of article 4 of the Convention. An inventor, or owner of a patent, belonging to

---

national arrangement, is a universal repertory, with systematic classification of all kinds of documents. See a study of this classification and of its application to patents, in *Propriété Industrielle* (1927), p. 30.

1. See plan in *Propriété Industrielle* (1925), p. 93.
2. See his letter in *Propriété Industrielle* (1926), pp. 95, 98.
3. See, in *Propriété Industrielle* (1926), p. 95, three letters on the Tenant plan from Belgium and Italy.

one of the thirty-eight countries constituting the Union, desirous of being protected in the other thirty-seven countries, must file thirty-seven patent applications in these countries. This means that he must comply with the provisions of the law of the thirty-seven countries: file an application, drawings, models, samples, and the rest, in the language of each country; in many of them submit his invention to examination; enumerate his claims according to the particular method of drafting claims in each country; make, possibly, disclaimers; appoint in most countries an attorney or agent domiciled therein to receive official notices, to discuss and fight in administrative and judicial proceedings possible objections of the administration or the opposition of interested parties; pay various fees and charges, and so forth. All these steps are to be taken within fixed legal periods, and in accordance with the law of each country. When all this is taken into consideration and, in addition, the fact that patent law everywhere to-day is an extremely technical and specialized branch of law, it is apparent that the inventor, or owner of a patent, must needs seek the professional advice and services of special patent attorneys. This again involves heavy expense for him.

It has been assumed that the inventor in question will seek to be protected in all the thirty-eight countries of the Union. In fact, rarely will he work his invention, grant licenses, or make his invention available in all these countries, and it might be assumed that he need not take the trouble and incur the expense of securing a patent in all of them. Yet such a course may be necessary in order to avoid the imitating or counterfeiting of his invention by other persons, and the sale of goods manufactured by them in the countries where no patent was secured.

What can be done, then, to relieve inventors of all these formalities, difficulties, and heavy expenses? Three possible solutions may be considered: progressive uniformity of the patent law; the creation of international patents; and international registration of patents.

§ 591. Possibilities of progressive uniformity of patent law. The first solution is very problematical. Ever since the Vienna Congress of 1873 uniformity of patent law in general, or on specific points, has been unceasingly discussed by international congresses of experts without appreciable results.[1] In some instances, various countries

1. See a study in *Propriété Industrielle* (1919), pp. 64, 66 ff.

adopted legal principles or administrative procedure of a certain type from among several that were offered, but in hardly any instance did a real uniformity prevail. Not only has patent law now become a part of the general law of each country, and administrative practice become so crystallized that no country is disposed to give it up, but the social and economic conditions of each country and, consequently, the conflicting interests that are to be taken into account are not the same everywhere. How little headway can be made in this direction may be seen from the fact that so many difficulties are encountered in the adoption of a uniform classification; also from the fact that at the last Technical Meeting at Geneva, in 1926, when uniform rules for the formalities of patent applications were adopted,— that is, a simple question of administrative practice,— some delegations made reservations, being unwilling to adopt anything contrary to the prescriptions of their laws or their own practice.[1]

Moreover, uniformity of the patent law of the various countries is not an aim in itself, but a means of making protection of inventors' interests less expensive, free of hampering difficulties, and less subject to casualties. In case uniformity were achieved, the next and natural step would be to agree on an international procedure for the grant of patents. The question, then, is whether this aim cannot be achieved without waiting for such uniformity.

§ **592. Creation of international patents.** The possibilities of international patents seem very remote. It is impossible to conceive at the present day that all countries, or a number of them, could agree on the complete abrogation of their patent laws, and renounce the granting of national patents in favor of an international patent law and the grant of international patents. Behind the diversities of the law there are opposing interests and divergent social and economic conditions which cannot be made *tabula rasa* in a day. Nor is it any more practicable to undertake the creation of international patents, in addition to national patents, for the protection of the interests of foreign inventors. The present situation would be made more complicated thereby, instead of being simplified.[2]

During the war, and after its termination, several attempts were made to create an inter-Allied patent as a framework of future inter-

1. See *procès-verbaux* of the meeting, in *Propriété Industrielle* (1926), p. 205.

2. See on these plans *Propriété Industrielle* (1919), p. 65; also, Jungmann, *Das Internationale Patentrecht* (Berlin, 1924), p. 65.

national patents. These attempts have failed.[1] On November 15, 1920, an Arrangement was signed at Paris for the creation of a central bureau for patents of invention, by delegates from the Allied countries, Belgium, Brazil, Czechoslovakia, Ecuador, France, Greece, Nicaragua, Poland, Rumania, Siam, and Jugoslavia. Other countries participating were Cuba, Haiti, Japan, Liberia, Panama, Peru, Portugal, and Uruguay; these countries refused to sign the Arrangement. This was not ratified by any country.[2] The substance of the Arrangement was that the Central Bureau was to collect the patents of all the countries parties to the Arrangement, for search purposes; to conduct a preliminary examination on patent applications submitted to the Bureau, and to report thereon; and to transmit the patent applications to the various countries for registration.[3]

It is to be noted that all the countries that signed the Arrangement, with the exception of Czechoslovakia, make no preliminary examination of the inventions filed by inventors, and for this reason the Arrangement was not altogether objectionable. Yet, even the possibility of an international patent between countries, the laws of which present no fundamental divergences,[4] would seem to be remote.

But there is a more fundamental objection to the project of international patents. This lies in the fact that the patent system as it prevails today is not free from great defects.[5] The fortuitous character of certain inventions at a certain stage of scientific and technical knowledge, and the contemporaneous search for, or "finding" of, the same invention by several persons, often render unjust the grant of a patent to the first applicant. Such injustice would be enormously increased if an international, instead of a national, patent should be granted to the first applicant.

§ **593. International registration of patents.** The proposal for international registration of patents constitutes a middle course be-

1. See Fernand-Jacq, "Le Droit de Suite des Inventeurs," in *Le Journal des Economistes* (March 15, 1922).

2. See text of the Arrangement, in (1921), 286 O.G. 646.

3. On the ideas underlying this Arrangement, see an address before Allied delegates by Mr. Drouets, Director of the French National Office of Industrial Property, at Paris, in 1919, in *Travaux du Groupe Français*, (1919–1922), pp. 68–79.

4. See Chabaud, "Les Possibilités en matière de Brevet International," in *Revue de Droit International et de Législation Comparée*, 3e sér. (1921), II, 150, 156.

5. See Pilenco, *Das Recht des Erfinders* (Berlin, 1907), p. 19; and Edmond Picard, "Suppression des Brevets d'Invention," in *Revue de Droit International et de Législation Comparée* (1871), III, 391.

tween the slow process of gradual unification of the patent laws of all countries and the radical idea of international patents. It is inspired by the Madrid Arrangement. It should be recalled that under this Arrangement the municipal law of each country is in no way affected, except that it is not necessary to effectuate a deposit or registration of the mark directly in the contracting countries, communication of registration by the International Bureau being substituted therefor; that the time for rejection of the mark is limited; and that a uniform period of protection in all the countries is assured.[1] On these three points — no direct filing in each of the countries, limitation of the time of administrative examination, and uniform duration of protection — it is possible to obtain an agreement between the various countries on the subject of patents, and to institute international registration of patents at the International Bureau. Moreover, it is not absolutely necessary that a uniform term of protection should be assured by such registration. The main object is to do away with the too numerous formalities and expenses required for the grant of patents in the different countries. The question of indirect filing through the International Bureau should not present serious difficulties, especially if the uniform rules of formalities for filing patent applications adopted by the Technical Meeting of Geneva, in 1926, were accepted in the contracting countries. The most difficult point in such a scheme is that of examination of the invention in the different countries.

Suppose that a patent application is filed in the country of origin, and copies of the application and accompanying documents are transmitted to the International Bureau. As it is impossible to obtain an agreement for the use of a single language in this respect, the Bureau would have to translate the application and other documents, after registration in its books, and transmit them to the other countries. This would have the effect of direct filing in these countries. It would be a great gain for inventors. They would be freed from much trouble, loss of time, and expense.

But it is well known that the drafting of claims which are to be enumerated in patent applications presents great divergences in the different countries, and that the administrative procedure following

1. The restriction of the grounds of refusal of a mark under the Arrangement is provided for by the general Convention of Union, and is not, therefore, an element of the Arrangement.

an application for a patent is of various types, from a mere examination into the question of compliance with the formalities prescribed by law to opposition or interference proceedings, which may last for a long time. However, the same was true in the case of trade marks which are now registered internationally. It may be agreed that in case the patent application filed at the Bureau is accepted in the contracting countries, the applicant should have the same remedies as in case of direct application therein. In such case he would have to retain agents or attorneys, and go to the same expense and trouble as in the case of direct application. Nor can it be otherwise. It may also be agreed that each country should signify its rejection of the application as soon as possible and within a maximum period. But it is difficult to see what kind of agreement can be reached on the drafting of claims. Should each administration be satisfied with a complete statement of the invention and a general *résumé*, and be free to extract from such statement and *résumé* the claims which are to be patented? Or should the inventor himself, in applying to the International Bureau and requesting the communication of his application to a number of countries, append thereto an enumeration of claims in accordance with the law of each of these countries? Neither is quite satisfactory. The latter is assuredly preferable for the inventor, but would often have the effect of compelling him to seek the advice of patent agents in several countries.

No insurmountable difficulties, then, would seem to exist to the institution of international registration of patents, now that international registration of trade marks has been in effect for over thirty-five years, and international deposit of designs was agreed upon at The Hague in 1925. The difficulties would be reduced to a minimum if such an arrangement were restricted in the beginning to countries presenting similarities in their patent laws; for instance, countries adopting the administrative system of mere registration of inventions (French system). The difficulty of translating patent applications at the International Bureau into the languages of the different countries might be reduced to small proportions by the composition of a technical vocabulary, in several languages, of the principal terms used in specifications of patents, as was proposed by the International Bureau in 1919.[1] The arrangement for international

1. See *Propriété Industrielle* (1919), pp. 81, 83. Another possible solution is the suggestion that the various countries could be divided into three groups: the Anglo-Saxon with the English language, the Germanic with the German, and the Latin with

registration would facilitate the creation of a uniform classification of patents and of an international index.[1]

On the subject under consideration much may be learned from the British Empire patent plans. Although the laws of the various dominions, colonies, possessions, and the rest, of the British Empire, are, in their fundamental principles, similar to that of Great Britain, there are many differences in practice and procedure. In order that an inventor may be protected throughout the British Empire, he must file forty-six patent applications. It is apparent that the problems arising in this regard are of even wider scope than in the Industrial Property Union. It is not surprising, then, that the idea of a British Empire patent should spring up after the World War, when the unity of the Empire was so magnificently demonstrated. The consideration of the institution of a system of granting patents which would be validated throughout the Empire was recommended by the Imperial Conference of 1921, in London. But a technical conference, which met at the Patent Office on June 12, 1922, agreed that it was not possible to establish immediately a central patent office for the examination of applications, in view of the lack of uniformity of the law and of the great expenditure that the equipment of such a central office would require. Instead, a temporary measure for the registration or validation of patents granted by the United Kingdom was adopted. The application for registration, with a copy of specifications and a certificate of the issue of the patent, is to be filed in each colony. In case the law of a colony provides for opposition, an opportunity to oppose registration is given in the regular way. The certificate of registration extends the patent to such colony.[2]

It will be noted that this British plan greatly resembles the above plans for international registration of patents, with the difference that, instead of direct filing of applications for registration in each country, the filing is to be made at the International Bureau.

VI. Plans for Universal Trade Marks

§ 594. Impracticability of "universal" marks. In the preceding sections an attempt was made to demonstrate that the plans for in-

---

the French language. This would reduce the number of necessary translations to two only. See *Propriété Industrielle* (1912), pp. 93, 94 note.

1. See the various proposals for international registration of patents, in *Propriété Industrielle* (1912), pp. 77, 93; and (1919), p. 81.

2. See on the British plan, *Propriété Industrielle* (1922), p. 134.

ternational patents were impracticable, and that the less ambitious proposal of international registration of patents was all that might be expected to be achieved for the present. May that step, however, be taken as regards trade marks? Their international registration has been already established a long time in the international regime of industrial property. Is it time that the more ambitious plan of international, or universal, marks be adopted?

Like international patents, universal marks may be conceived of in two ways: as unique, replacing all national marks; or concurrently with the existence of national marks. In either view, the main idea is that the marks in question shall be registered by a central bureau, and thereupon be protected in all the contracting countries as if they were registered directly in each of them. The difference between such a regime and the present international registration under the Madrid Arrangement would be that no national registration of such marks would be required, and national trade-mark laws would either be replaced by a universal or international trade-mark law, — in case of unique international marks, — or would be non-applicable — in case of concurrent national and international marks. Since in both cases these marks would be governed by international law instead of distinct national laws, it is a necessary condition for carrying out these plans that an agreement be reached by the contracting countries on the provisions of such an international law.

The trade-mark laws of the various countries do not present the same wide divergences as the patent laws. The provisions of the Convention of Union and the Madrid Arrangement have helped to unify the different legislations on many points. Diversities, however, still exist between the various legislations on three important questions of trade-mark law: the subject-matter of trade marks, the administrative procedure (preliminary examination, a mere deposit, or administrative warning to the applicant), and the effects of registration (declaratory and attributive systems). These differences cause such a divergence between the laws of the various countries, that it is assuredly futile to expect an agreement on an international law acceptable to all parties. It might be possible to reach such an agreement between countries adopting the declaratory system of trade-mark registration and making no preliminary examination of trade marks. But its importance would be small, the present international registration at the International Bureau affording to these countries practically the same benefits.

Besides, the plan of unique international marks, with the abolition of national marks, does not respond to real necessities of national and international life. In most of the countries the trade marks which are used only in the domestic market constitute a very great majority of registered marks. The proprietors of such marks have no interest in applying for an international mark, and it would be a great bother and inconvenience to them to apply to a central international bureau instead of to their national bureau, or even to provincial offices, as is the case in some European countries. Consequently, the countries that might agree on the international trade-mark law would like to preserve their national marks, and to create besides the international marks. But this coexistence of two kinds of marks would give rise to difficulties and complications out of proportion to the meagre benefits derived by those countries.[1]

§ **595. Amelioration of the regime of international registration of trade marks.** International registration of trade marks would seem to constitute the best possible international regime of trade-mark protection, since it reduces the formalities and expenses to a minimum, and at the same time cuts through the diversities of municipal law. This regime is subject to amelioration, and to this end efforts should be directed in order to give entire satisfaction to the necessities of international life. Especially, it should be considered whether the registration of trade marks at the International Bureau could not be made by direct application of the interested party, its registration in the country of origin being dispensed with. Or, if this is not possible, whether the principle of independence of trade marks should not be admitted, registration at the International Bureau being possible after registration in any of the contracting countries and not necessarily in the country of origin.

In the Arrangement of The Hague the direct deposit of designs at the International Bureau was admitted.[2] Perhaps the admission of

1. See, on the plans of universal marks, and criticism, *Propriété Industrielle* (1919), pp. 124 and 136.

2. At the meeting of Feb. 12, 1926, of the Standing Committee for the Protection of Industrial Property of the International Chamber of Commerce, the American National Committee proposed that the Madrid Trade-Mark Arrangement should be inserted in the general Convention, and that it should be amended so as to authorize the direct deposit at Berne of marks for which international registration is desired by interested parties. Although Mr. Gariel (Vice-Director of the Bureau of Berne) and Mr. Drouets explained that direct deposit would not improve the situation, because the Bureau would be overwhelmed with demands, many of which would not be in order, the Stand-

trade marks to international registration after registration in any of the contracting countries is the first aim to be attained. France and Spain are especially opposed to this amendment to article 6 of the Convention. But the Spanish opposition is mainly on theoretical grounds, while the French see in the change real dangers to, and injurious effects on, their national interests. Yet, M. Maillard, the distinguished President of the French Group of the International Association for the Protection of Industrial Property, has been converted to the German idea of trade-mark independence and succeeded in making the Congress of that Association at Brussels, in 1910, adopt a resolution to this effect,[1] and it may be hoped that by thorough discussion of the question an agreement may be reached.[2]

---

ing Committee adopted a resolution expressing the hope that the question would be considered by the National Committees. See *Supplement to Journal of the Chamber*, No. 9, April, 1926.

1. *Annuaire* (1910), pp. 143 ff.

2. See on the same desideratum in the regime of the Convention of 1883–1925, *supra*, § 569.

CHAPTER XXXVII

SCIENTIFIC PROPERTY

§ 596. Origin of question of scientific property. Until the World War the rights of intellectual property were generally divided into two classes: industrial, and artistic or literary property, corresponding to two separate classes of creations — those aiming at industrial results and those possessing an aesthetic or literary character. This classification, accepted as a matter of course, produced, as will be seen, some difficulties, and led to unsatisfactory results in certain cases. Soon after the end of the war, a new class of intellectual property began to be discussed — scientific property. Its claim to existence and protection was not due primarily to theoretical speculation and developments of doctrine, but to practical causes.

The intellectual class, especially in European countries, emerged from the war impoverished, in contrast to the classes of business men and workmen. A movement for more adequate protection of authors' rights resulted in France and Belgium in legislation recognizing in favor of "artists" and their legal representatives a *droit de suite*, which cannot be adequately rendered in English.[1] By virtue

1. French Law of May 20, 1920, and Decree of Dec. 17, 1920 (*Bulletin des Lois*, 1920, I, 2055, and II, 5569).
Belgian Law of June 25, 1921, and Decree of Sept. 23, 1921 (*Pasinomie*, 1921, pp. 343, 696).

of this right, the artist who has ceded his work for a price may "follow" it later in its successive public sales, in order to collect a royalty on the sale price. It will be seen that the right may be claimed only by "artists" (painters, sculptors, and so forth) and only in case of public sales; and it may be exercised during the legal duration of the copyright.[1]

The movement was not spent with this legislation. As often happens, the satisfaction of a part of claims pressing for recognition makes the pressure of the remainder the stronger. It was felt that inventors should be presented with a more generous reward than the short period of exclusive use of the invention. A *droit de suite* in their favor, and against manufacturers using their invention after the lapse of the patent, seemed a proper legislative reform. On the other hand, another large class of intellectual workers was found to be treated very unjustly by the law. While authors enjoyed copyright and inventors could obtain patents, scientists and, generally, persons making scientific discoveries could claim no economic benefits from the industrial progress based on these discoveries. They remained in poverty while others were enriched by using their creative work. A reform in this respect, it was believed, would encourage scientific work and induce young men to devote their efforts to the study of science, and might be made to benefit laboratories which were in great distress.[2]

§ 597. **Professor Barthélemy's proposal of a law.** This movement in France led to the first proposal of a law on the subject of scientific property ever introduced. It was introduced in the French Chamber of Deputies by Professor J. Barthélemy.[3] His proposal aimed at two things: the recognition and enforcement of the rights of scientists in their discoveries, and the reform of the French patent law of 1844, for the purpose of affording more adequate and broader protection to inventors.

The fundamental principle of Barthélemy's proposal is this: If a person, by his intellectual activity, has made possible benefits which otherwise would be impossible, justice requires that he obtain a

1. See a study on the French law and its origins, in an article by Albert Vaunois in *Le Droit d'Auteur* (1920), p. 101.

2. See, on the movement in France and the activities of M. Lucien Klotz, its principal instigator, Fernand-Jacq, "Le Droit de Suite des Inventeurs sur leurs découvertes," in *Journal des Economistes* (1922), p. 332; and *Propriété Industrielle* (1922), p. 82 and (1923), p. 113.

3. No. 4233, Chambre des Députés, session de 1922.

share in these benefits.[1] This principle is given expression in the first article of the proposal providing that "every new discovery or invention, of whatever nature, confers upon its author . . . the right to demand a royalty from all those who draw an industrial profit therefrom." This would put an end to the exclusion of scientific discoveries from legal protection under the patent law of 1844, in particular its article 30, which declares null and void all patents concerning "principles, methods, systems, discoveries and theoretical or purely scientific conceptions of which no industrial applications are indicated."

Whenever a patent cannot be obtained under the provisions of the law of 1844 by the author of an invention or discovery, there are two ways provided for in the Barthélemy proposal in which he may exercise the right recognized in the first article.

(1) He may take no action so long as no application is made of his discovery. But as soon as a practical application of the theoretical discovery is made by a manufacturer, the author may present a claim for a part of the manufacturer's profits — something analogous to the dramatic author's right in the presentations of his play. The royalty due the scientist begins in this case from the time the claim is presented. The author may prove the paternity of the discovery by any kind of evidence.

(2) He may, also, obtain a "patent of principle" under the conditions of the patent law of 1844. This patent differs from ordinary patents in that it does not confer on the patentee an exclusive right to work or use the discovery, but only the right to grant compulsory licenses for working the practical applications of the discovery. In this case the right of the author to claim royalties begins from the date of filing the application for a "patent of principle." Consequently, anyone is free to work the invention or discovery, but he must pay for all the time he is working it, and not from the time a claim is presented to him by the scientist, as in the first case.

Thus the right of the scientist exists from the time the discovery was made, without any formality whatsoever, as in the case of the right of authors of literary or artistic works. In this, scientific property is assimilated to artistic property. But in the exercise of the right it is differentiated. Professor Barthélemy thought that manufacturers should have some means of having notice of the claim of a

1. No. 4233, Chambre des Députés, session de 1922, p. 3.

scientist in an invention or discovery which they apply industrially. Otherwise, great uncertainty would hang over industry in regard to unknown retrospective claims for every mechanical or industrial development which is adopted and applied. By the application for a "patent of principle" it was felt that sufficient notice is given of the claim in a discovery. But scientists devoted to their researches should not be compelled to go through the formalities required for the grant of a patent, with the risk of losing their right. If they fail to obtain a patent, they may still claim a royalty in the application of their discoveries, but only from the date of presenting such claim. Thus no retrospective claim is made, and the manufacturer may take account of the known claims in fixing the price of his products. The "patent of principle" gives notice to others of the claim of the scientist, and at the same time secures for the latter *prima-facie* proof of paternity of the discovery.

The amount of royalty is to be determined by agreement between the parties, and, if this is impossible, by the courts. Scientists' rights, like artists', are to last during the life of the originator and for fifty years after his death.

Professor Barthélemy's proposal contains also a number of provisions giving effect to the desiderata of the post-war movement for a *droit de suite* of inventors, and for certain reforms of the patent law of 1844 in favor of inventors. Authors of inventions or discoveries who obtained an ordinary patent under the provisions of the law of 1844 do not forfeit every right in the invention at the expiration of the patent. Only the exclusive right to work or use the invention is terminated. The right to claim a royalty from persons using or working the invention after the expiration of the patent is preserved for the period of the life of the inventor and fifty years after his death. To this end the inventor must apply for a "patent of author."

The proposed amendments of the regime of ordinary patents of the law of 1844 are as follows: a patent is granted only to the true inventor; it may be granted for a period of twenty-five years; it cannot be cancelled for failure to work the invention in France, but a compulsory license may be granted after five years from the grant; lastly, the publication of the invention by the inventor himself cannot cause the nullity of the patent.

§ **598. Reaction to this proposal.** The fundamental principle of Professor Barthélemy's proposal, namely, the recognition of the right of scientists in their discoveries for which no practical application is indicated, met with general approval. It was agreed that the requirement of the patent law, that an invention or discovery should be industrially applicable, amounted to a spoliation of scientists; that it was dangerous to scientific progress to compel savants to go into industry and invent the practical applications of their theoretical discoveries; and that existence of scientists' rights should not be dependent on compliance with formalities and conditions which they are likely to neglect in their devotion to their researches.[1] However, the means of protecting scientific property and assuring scientists their due share in the industrial profits caused by their discoveries, as provided for in the Barthélemy proposal, raised objections from various quarters.[2] It was felt that the assimilation of scientific property to artistic, on the one hand, and the engrafting of the "patent of principle" and "patent of author" on the patent law of 1844, were making the whole plan hybrid and confusing.

§ **599. The project of the C. T. I.** The Confédération des Travailleurs Intellectuels of France undertook to study more thoroughly the question of scientific property, and adopted a new text, in many respects different from Professor Barthélemy's proposal, which was also submitted to Parliament. The objections to the latter proposal and the ideas underlying the new project are dealt with in the work of Messrs. Dalimier (M.D.) and Gallié (attorney), published under the auspices of the Confederation of Intellectual Workers.[3] This project is in some respects an advance over Professor Barthélemy's proposal. But in other respects it seems somewhat superficial, and goes to show that worthy sentiments alone are not sufficient for the purpose of establishing scientific property on a sound basis. Moreover, the objections to the Barthélemy proposal betray its inadequate study and consideration on the part of the above authors.[4]

1. Fernand-Jacq, "La Propriété Scientifique," in *Le Journal des Economistes*, (March 15, 1923); *Propriété Industrielle* (1922), p. 82, and (1923), pp. 113, 115.

2. Fernand-Jacq, "La Propriété Scientifique," in *Revue Julien Hayem* (Dec. 31, 1923); Marcel Plaisant, *Rapport sur le Projet de Loi sur les Brevets d'Invention*, No. 1690, Chambre des Députés, session of 1925, p. 51.

3. *La Propriété Scientifique: Le Projet de la C. T. I.* (Paris, 1923).

4. See *Propriété Industrielle* (1923), pp. 113, 115.

While Professor Barthélemy bases his proposal on a combination of industrial and artistic property, the text of the C. T. I. project assimilates almost completely scientific property to artistic. According to this text, authors of scientific discoveries or inventions have an exclusive right to draw benefit therefrom. This exclusive right consists in their claim of "a right of author" in the working by others of their inventions or discoveries.

The paternity of the discovery or invention must be proved, not by any evidential means, as in the Barthélemy proposal, but by a "sufficient publication." The right of the scientist can be established only by such publication. The publication in some approved periodicals would be considered sufficient publication.

The authors of discoveries or inventions cannot object to the industrial or commercial working of new applications thereof, although they may collect a "right of author" for such working. The amount of this royalty is to be determined by agreement between the parties, or by the courts. Authors may be represented, in their relations to persons working their discoveries, by a professional body. They may also appoint this body as supreme arbiter to determine the amount of the royalty. This provision nullifies that which concerns the interference of the courts. It implies that manufacturers have to submit to the decisions of this professional body, which cannot give any guaranty of impartiality.

The right of authors of discoveries or inventions is enjoyed during their whole life, or by their legal representatives during fifty years from the publication of the discovery or invention.

The project concerns "scientific discoveries or inventions." The second article defines what is to be considered as such. The definition of inventions is broad enough to include almost all inventions patentable under the patent law of 1844. Under these conditions, any inventor may claim the advantage of these provisions, which is a sweeping change of the whole regime of patents. At the same time all industry is thrown into great uncertainty and insecurity.

While many theoretical and juridical objections to this project were raised in France, the practical objection was also voiced that it was impossible to impose on French industry alone this new charge of an uncertain and probably large amount in favor of authors of discoveries and inventions, thus rendering it less able to compete in the international market. If scientists ought to be awarded a share in the profits of industry, this could be brought about, it was claimed, only by simultaneous legislation in the important industrial countries, or by international legislation.[1] The Director of the International Bureau, Professor Röthlisberger, in his report of December 9, 1922, to the International Committee on Intellectual Coöperation, was, on this point, of a contrary opinion; he observed that never before was progress of this sort made by direct international action, which intervened only after successful experiments in particular countries.[2]

§ **600. Senator Ruffini's plan.** The Committee on Intellectual Coöperation of the League of Nations took cognizance of the question of scientific property on the proposal of its Chairman, Professor Bergson, at the ninth meeting of its first session on August 5, 1922, and appointed a sub-committee consisting of M. Destrée (Belgium), Dr. Millikan (United States), Senator Ruffini (Italy), and Mr. De Torres Quevedo (Spain), to study the draft proposed by the French Confederation of Intellectual Workers and to investigate in a general way the question of artistic, scientific, and literary copyright.[3] The sub-committee met in Paris and heard on this subject Professor Barthélemy, Professor Emil Borel, and Mr. Gallié, on the part of the C. T. I., and other persons. It appointed Senator Ruffini as its *rapporteur* for the juridical study of the question of scientific property. The latter presented his report to the Committee on Intellectual Coöperation at the fifth meeting of its second session, July 28, 1923.[4] Mr. De Torres Quevedo who was also asked by the sub-committee to make a report on the possibilities of applying Mr. Ruffini's plan was not able to do so by reason of the lateness of the time at which Mr. Ruffini's report was completed.

The report submitted by Mr. Ruffini is a most remarkable critical and constructive work. The Committee approved Mr. Ruffini's plan, and asked him to amend it in the light of some observations that had been submitted. It also recommended the plan warmly to the Council and the Assembly of the League of Nations. The latter, on the proposal of its Fifth Committee, adopted a resolution approv-

1. Fernand-Jacq, "La Propriété Scientifique," in *Revue Générale de l'Électricité* (1923), p. 463, and in *Le Journal des Economistes* (March 15, 1923); also Marcel Plaisant, *Rapport sur le Projet de Loi sur les Brevets d'Inventions*, No. 1690, Chambre des Députés, session of 1925, p. 54.

2. See *Propriété Industrielle* (1923), pp. 16, 23–24.

3. Doc. C. 711, M. 423 (1922), XII, 34.

4. The report was published separately as Doc. A. 38 (1923), XII.

ing the principle of Senator Ruffini's plan and deciding to transmit it to the various governments and ask them to communicate to the Secretariat of the League of Nations their observations, in order that the Committee on Intellectual Coöperation might draw up a definitive draft convention, to be signed and ratified by all the states.[1]

Senator Ruffini's report consists, in the first part, of a critical survey of the question of scientific property; and, in the second part, of the history of the question of scientific property, the proposals and texts drawn in France, the question whether protection should be sought by national laws or by international convention, the principles to be adopted, and a draft convention analogous to the international conventions for the protection of industrial and artistic property.

§ 601. Primary considerations in question of scientific property. Mr. Ruffini points out, first, the two considerations that led the subcommittee to study the question of protection of scientific property. As a remedy for the critical condition of scientific work in all countries, a remnant of the war, it was proposed to afford the younger generation the prospect of adequate remuneration, in order to recruit men of high standard. Besides this problem of a temporary character there was a permanent one, that is, the flagrant injustice of denying protection to savants for the creations of their minds similar to that enjoyed by authors of artistic or literary works and by inventors. He concludes that "there is a great work of justice to be done and a wrong to be redressed."

Mr. Ruffini finds that the greatest authors have failed to give an adequate explanation of this lack of protection or have denied the problem by reason of their inability to solve it. He finds also that there is the greatest divergence of opinion on the nature of inventors' and authors' rights, and that it would do no good to enter into questions of terminology and of legal speculation on the nature of rights of scientists in their discoveries. However, he goes into the duality of the regimes of protection of inventions on the one hand and literary and artistic works on the other, and concludes that the two kinds of rights are in substance identical, the differences of the two regimes referring only to the scope of the rights and the method of protection. He finds several kinds of creations (for instance, de-

1. *Resolutions and Recommendations adopted by the Assembly during its Fourth Session*, Off. Journal, Special Suppl., No. 11 (Oct., 1923), p. 25.

signs and models) which are difficult to classify under either of the two categories, and points out that protection of scientific discoveries which partake of the character of invention as well as of literary or artistic creation would link up the two regimes and achieve their unification, which has been prevented only by unsystematic, disconnected, and empiric legislative action and by incomplete and inadequate doctrinal theory. All this is brought out by Mr. Ruffini with great clarity and a wealth of documentation.

§ **602. General and specific objections.** Next, the report deals with the general and specific objections raised against the recognition of rights of scientists in their discoveries. It dismisses easily the former, pointing out that they are like the objections raised at other times against authors' and inventors' rights. Mr. Ruffini reminds us that such men as Prudhon, Macaulay, and Mazzini were opposed to any sort of recognition of intellectual property, believing that authors should find sufficient compensation in glory and the gratitude of mankind, and at most receive assistance from the nation; and that the economist Michel Chevalier (1863) in France considered the granting of patents of inventions "an outrage on liberty and industry, an obsolete legacy of the past."

The objection that a scientific discovery is the result of collective coöperation may also be made in regard to inventions and literary and artistic works, yet it has not been considered serious as against recognition of authors' and inventors' rights. The same may be said with respect to the objection of the difficulties of determining the priority of a scientific discovery or invention. Mr. Ruffini cites examples of cases where great difficulties appeared in determining the priority of inventions and artistic creations, yet the courts have been able to solve them.

As to a last objection, that many complications would result from the attempt to protect scientists' rights, Mr. Ruffini quotes Professor Barthélemy's remark that "complications and progress necessarily go hand-in-hand, consequently the justice meted out to men of science would obviously be more complicated than the brutal injustice of which they had hitherto been the noble and uncomplaining victims." It is just to add in regard to all these general objections that they had been dealt with by Professor Barthélemy in the *exposé des motifs* of his proposal.[1]

1. No. 4233, Chambre des Députés, session of 1922, pp. 10–16.

Mr. Ruffini's report deals also with the technical legal objections to recognition of scientific property, drawn from the alleged distinction between real invention and pure discovery, and between artistic creation and scientific conception. Scientific discoveries or conceptions are refused the character of creations, which inventions and artistic works possess. Mr. Ruffini shows how theory in this respect is uncertain, and that its results lack positiveness, and consistency. While Kohler [1] affirms that discovery is but the revelation of that which exists in nature and the antithesis of technical creation in the invention and aesthetic creation in the work of art, Du Bois-Reymond [2] excludes the element of creation from invention, Osterrieth [3] finds creative elements in discovery, Frost [4] believes that the character of true creation is lacking in invention, Macomber [5] concludes that it has never been possible to establish a line of distinction between discovery and invention, and Pilenco [6] proposes a classification of "findings," placing under "discovery," on the same footing, artistic creation (beauty), scientific research (truth), and invention (utility). Mr. Ruffini sums up his theoretical inquiry as follows: "The whole question is dominated by crudest utilitarianism, empiricism unhappily disguised in scientific nebulosity, and, finally, the most disconcerting arbitrariness." [7]

§ **603. Favoring an international convention.** In the beginning of the second part of his report, in an historical retrospect, Mr. Ruffini relates the rare and vague attempts made at different congresses of the International Literary and Artistic Association for the protection of scientific property, and the post-war movement in France, where the first proposals were introduced with a view of securing legislation on the subject. He found that no similar steps were taken until that time in other countries.

The fears expressed in France that the restrictions and charges on French industry consequent upon the enactment of a law protecting

1. *Handbuch des Patentrechts* (Mannheim, 1901), p. 89; and *Urheberrecht an Schriftwerken* (Stuttgart, 1907), p. 10.

2. *Erfindung und Erfinder* (Berlin, 1906), p. 65.

3. *Lehrbuch des gewerblichen Rechtsschutzes* (Leipzig, 1908), p. 61; and "Das geistige Schaffen in Wissenschaft, Technik and Kunst," in *Gewerblicher Rechtsschutz und Urheberrecht* (1923), XXVIII, No. 3, p. 49.

4. *Law and Practice relating to Letters Patent* (London, 1906), vol. II, chap. 11.

5. *The Fixed Law of Patents* (Boston, 1909), sec. 347.

6. *Das Recht des Erfinders* (Berlin, 1907), p. 223 (a translation of the original Russian work).

7. F. Ruffini, *Report on Scientific Property*, A. 38 (1923), XII, 10.

scientific property, would place it in a disadvantageous position in the international market, appear exaggerated to Mr. Ruffini. He remarks that the case is similar to the adoption of a free-trade policy, the reduction of working hours in the factories, etc. It is true, however, that temporary harm may be done, and, besides, as Mr. Ruffini rightly points out, this fear is an important psychological factor and may constitute an obstacle to the innovation. To the French view, that any recognition of scientific property should be made by international legislation, was opposed the opinion of the Director of the United International Bureaus of Industrial and Literary Property, that no international agreement may be expected unless and until the reform is tried and experimented on in a number of countries. Mr. Ruffini, faced with these opposing views, concludes in favor of the French view, arguing that the opposite opinion does not take sufficient account of the decisive fact that international conditions to-day are totally different from what they were at the time protection of industrial property and artistic works began to develop in the different countries. The isolation of each country in the eighteenth and the first half of the nineteenth century made original international legislation on these subjects impossible. The present-day close interdependence, especially economic, of the various nations makes such an understanding possible. A further point suggested also by Mr. Ruffini is that, if any country should be left free to regulate as it sees fit the protection of scientific property, wide divergences of legislation would arise, which would be a stumbling-block to all future efforts for international regulation, as is the case to-day in the matter of other intellectual rights.

§ **604. Nature of scientists' reward.** When the question of recognition of scientific property is thus cleared of all its difficulties, the next problem, and most important, is the nature of the reward which the scientist is to receive. Mr. Ruffini opposes, in principle, the system suggested originally by Mr. De Torres Quevedo, a member of the sub-committee, and further developed later by Mr. Gariel, Vice-Director of the International Bureau of Berne. According to this system, scientists whose discoveries are applied industrially by others should be remunerated from a fund made up of subscriptions paid by, or contributions levied on, the industries profiting by the discoveries. Mr. Ruffini finds that similar systems were proposed formerly by enemies of industrial and artistic property, and that such systems of patronage or prizes are obsolete, amount to almsgiving, and imply a lack of consideration for men of science. A prize system should be assented to only in case of scientific discoveries for which no direct relationship to an industry can be established, and by which all industry, generally, benefits indirectly.

The rights of scientists should be regarded as analogous to authors' and inventors' rights, and international legislation for their protection should be analogous to the international conventions on industrial property and on copyright — this is Mr. Ruffini's view. For he thinks that scientific property constitutes "a sphere midway between the domain of artistic and literary property on the one hand and industrial property on the other"; and as it is not to be expected, for the time being, that a single law will unify all intellectual productions, it should be concluded that an independent formula should be drawn for the protection of scientific property.

§ **605. Principles of plan.** Mr. Ruffini has no illusions in regard to the difficulties of drafting a text which will give satisfaction to all countries, and he is aware of the effort required to enlist support for the innovation of the "great and complex world of magistrates and lawyers" — a point to which attention was called by Dean Wigmore of the Northwestern University School of Law by a memorandum addressed to the sub-committee.[1] In endeavoring to clear all these difficulties from the path of the League of Nations, he lays down the following "guiding principles":

1. Scientific discoveries should procure pecuniary advantages for their authors and should cease to be considered as natural riches. In regard to this fundamental principle, Dean Wigmore in his memorandum to the sub-committee made an important reservation. He called attention to the fact that the great majority of discoveries of a generation or two ago consisted in presenting a scientific explanation of obvious facts or practices of human life. This justified in a way the lack of legal protection of such discoveries. Modern discoveries, however, such as radium, wireless, and the like, no longer explained existing facts and practices of our life, but gave rise to new activities and new industries, which had never been contemplated before. This new aspect of scientific discoveries should lead to recognition of a right of scientists in their creations. But those discoveries

1. F. Ruffini, *Report on Scientific Property*, A. 38 (1923), XII, Annex, p. 28.

of the present day which have the same character as the old ones should be clearly distinguished.

2. A scientist should not be required to apply or work his invention himself, as he is not fitted for that, and should not be taken away from his researches. His right should consist in a royalty "on the money value which his discovery is likely to acquire by means of its practical application and its industrial utilization, within a specified period of time."

3. The distinction between invention and discovery should be abandoned. But, in accordance with Dean Wigmore's observation, scientific discoveries forestalled by practical experience may only aspire to a prize.

4. All distinctions as to the character of the intellectual product, whether it concerns physics, chemistry, biology, or any other science, should be abolished. This is perhaps the most debatable point.

5. In principle, the rights of scientists, like those of artists and writers, should be recognized, irrespective of any requirement of formality or declaration. Savants are likely to neglect to take steps to secure their rights. However, in view of the social interest in scientific discoveries and the essential condition of establishing priority for any claim arising from a discovery, regard should be paid to the regulations as to inventions.

6. Of the four means available for establishing the priority of an idea or discovery,—mere publication, the perforated envelope (such as the Soleau envelope), the "patent of principle," and the ordinary patent — scientists should be able to choose that one which is best adapted to their particular discovery.

7. The right of scientists ought to have a duration equal to that of literary or artistic copyright, namely the life of the scientist and fifty years after his death. In case a scientist should take a patent for his discovery, on the expiry of the patent he should continue to enjoy the scientist's rights to the industrial utilization of his discovery by others.

8. All disputes concerning the priority of a discovery, or the royalty payable to a scientist, should be decided by law and the courts of each state, when both parties belong to that state. In case a dispute exists between nationals of different states, resort should be had to compulsory international arbitration, which guarantees greater impartiality.

At the end of his exhaustive report Mr. Ruffini submits the text of a draft convention embodying the above principles.

§ **606. Mr. Gariel's scheme.** It is important, before describing the reaction to Senator Ruffini's plan in the various countries, to consider the plan elaborated by Mr. Gariel, Vice-Director of the United International Bureaus.[1] For both plans challenged the attention of the interested circles and of the various governments and both were concurrently discussed.

Mr. Gariel bases his plan on theoretical as well as practical grounds. He starts with the idea that the "right" of a scientist to his discovery is not to be regarded as similar to that of authors of literary or artistic works; nor can it be compared to the inventor's right. The character of personal creation and of uniqueness inherent in a literary or artistic work is not to be found in a scientific discovery. The artist or writer gives to the world something that he alone created, and that no one else could ever conceive and execute in the same way. The scientist "discovers," reveals something outside himself, which was concealed from human knowledge until that time, but which another might discover as well. For the same reason, the discovery of a principle or an idea, without its practical applications, cannot be compared to an invention. An exclusive right to use the invention is granted to the author for its practical usefulness, and in order to encourage further inventions, by which the world profits. A scientist cannot claim a monopoly of his discovery, which would involve prohibiting others from availing themselves of such discovery, as an astronomer discovering a new planet cannot prevent others from availing themselves of the position of this planet to explain, or study, other problems of astronomy. The scientist reveals to the public the existence of a sort of raw material, and the public may utilize it. He does not create anything. He only anticipates others in revealing an existing fact. The public, the industry at large, builds on such discoveries, invents new applications, and derives its profits after trials and errors and incurring great expense and risks. Can it be said that the scientist has a right to a share of these profits?

Mr. Gariel insists that this cannot be maintained. But in view of the indirect benefit derived by industry, in general, from the discoveries of scientists, recognition should be made to them in the

1. See *Propriété Industrielle* (1923), p. 131.

form of a reward paid out of a fund formed from subscriptions paid by, or contributions levied on, the industries profiting by the discoveries.

The amount of the reward to be paid to each scientist, and all questions of priority and the like, are to be determined by a commission, in which industrialists, as well as the state and scientific bodies, are to be represented. The reward is to be given a number of years after the discovery, so that a sufficient account may be taken of its practical application. It may be paid in lump sum or in annuities. But no reward will be paid after the expiry of a period of years following the discovery, or the death of the scientist.

This scheme is drawn primarily from a national point of view, and its application in a number of countries should precede any international application. But it may be made to conform to international relations by the constitution of an international fund, made up of sums paid in by the various countries in proportion to their industrial importance, as shown by the data supplied by each country to the International Labor Office of the League of Nations.

§ **607. Mr. Gariel's critique of Senator Ruffini's plan.** Mr. Gariel, in a later article,[1] criticized Mr. Ruffini's plan from the point of view of the fundamental basis of the scientist's right and its exercise, and from the further point of view of the possibility of establishing this right immediately in the international field.

He finds no crude utilitarianism and empiricism in the doctrinal views of writers denying a creative element in scientific discoveries, and is not convinced that the justice of the remuneration of scientists should necessarily involve the recognition by law in their favor of authors' rights, or a right to share in the profits of the industries profiting by their discoveries. Mr. Gariel comes back to the idea that a scientist cannot have a property right in the idea or principle discovered by him, as the artist has in the form of his work, or a monopoly, as the inventor has.

He is not satisfied that Senator Ruffini is successful in his attack on the system of prizes. From the fact that it is an old solution proposed in the case of inventions, and has not been preferred to the system of patents, it cannot be concluded that it would not give good results in the different case of scientific discoveries. And a prize system does not involve a lack of respect for men of science, as Mr.

1. *Propriété Industrielle* (1923), p. 169.

Ruffini contends; on the contrary, it places them on a higher plane by making industry at large their debtor. It can be as little accused of lack of respect as the Nobel Prize, which is awarded to great scientists of the world.

As regards the exercise of the right, Mr. Gariel criticizes the provisions of Senator Ruffini's draft concerning the remuneration of scientists as indefinite, and the provision that a scientist may chose the "envelope Soleau" for proving the priority of his discovery. He rightly observes that the deposit of the "envelope Soleau" in no way constitutes publication or disclosure of the discovery to the public, and consequently no right accrues in favor of the scientist for future applications of such a discovery. And, in view of the complexity and continuity of inventions and discoveries, the recognition of a scientific copyright for each particular application may lead to exorbitant charges which would paralyze industry.

Finally, Mr. Gariel insists that Senator Ruffini's scheme for the establishment of international protection of scientific property before any organization of national protection cannot possibly succeed. Though it is much easier to-day than a generation or two ago to conclude international conventions on such matters, the proposal concerns a new right never before recognized in any country. To recommend to the various countries the adoption of national legislation on scientific property, and later the signature of an international convention, would seem to have a better chance of success.

§ 608. Observations on Senator Ruffini's and Mr. Gariel's schemes. Their principles. Mr. Gariel rightly observes [1] that no sound regulation of "scientific property" — using this expression for the sake of brevity only — can be achieved without a theoretical foundation. Can the right of scientists to claim remuneration for the industrial applications of their discoveries be based on the same theory that underlies the recognition of inventors' and authors' rights, or on any other theory?

Professor Barthélemy, as well as Messrs. Dalimier and Gallié, undoubtedly lay themselves open to the criticism that they proceed by affirmation in this respect, without taking the trouble to go into the theoretical justification of scientific property. The same cannot be said of Mr. Ruffini. Although he chooses to refrain, for the purposes of his draft convention, from attempting to define scientific property

1. *Ibid.*, pp. 169, 170.

and determine its legal nature,[1] he goes into the quicksands of the doctrinal views of various authors who attempt to distinguish real invention from pure discovery and artistic creation from scientific conception, and finds all such distinctions crude, empiric, and arbitrary. However, Mr. Ruffini does not contribute a constructive theory of scientific property, being content to criticize the views of writers who deny a creative element in discoveries, and to rest with "the common feeling of justice which tells us that there is a wrong which must be righted." [2]

On the other hand, Mr. Gariel, reasoning from the existing state of the law and the fact that this has not, up to the present, taken into account the scientists' rights in the existing scheme of rights, concludes that there cannot be an individual right of the scientist in his discovery.[3] His conclusion is based exclusively on the view that a principle, an idea, an axiom, or a law discovered by a scientist cannot be claimed as his own property, in order to justify a claim by him on the profits derived by a third person using or availing himself industrially of such a principle, idea, or law. The latter are not creations, as artistic works, nor can they be monopolized as patentable inventions. One might suspect that Mr. Gariel is contented with affirmations, just as are the writers criticized by him. Why are scientific conceptions and discoveries not creations?

Much confusion arises from the fact that extreme cases are often considered. It is difficult to compare, for instance, the Ninth Symphony with the discovery of a new star. One might also try to compare the discovery of radium or the wireless telegraph with the painting of a common landscape, or the writing of a commonplace story. The contention that, in both examples, the artistic work is a personal creation which no one else could conceive and execute in the same way, whereas a scientific discovery may be made by any scientist at a given stage of scientific research, because it is something existing by itself and outside the scientist's person, constitutes no argument against the recognition of creation in scientific discovery. The important thing is, not that a scientific idea was in the air, but

1. See F. Ruffini, *Report on Scientific Property*, Committee on Intellectual Coöperation, Doc. A. 38 (1923), XII, p. 2.

2. *Ibid.*, p. 10.

3. The same may be said of Osterrieth's study, *Wissenschaftliches Eigentum* (Tübingen, 1925). However, in an article in 1923, "Das Geistliche Schaffen in Wissenschaft, Technik und Kunst," *Gewerblicher Rechtsschutz und Urheberrecht*, XXVIII, No. 3, p. 49), this writer admitted that there is an element of personal creation in scientific research.

that it was caught by someone and revealed to the public. In this respect inventions are in no way different from discoveries. At a certain stage of scientific research and technical knowledge, an invention is the fortuitous and fatal result of prior developments; and there are many cases of simultaneous inventions. However, the right of the inventor who files the invention first is protected, although it may be a work of pure chance.

All that can be said, therefore, is that scientific discoveries are simply different from artistic creations and inventions.[1] Their aim is truth, while the aims of the latter are beauty and utility respectively. But in their particular fields all three are creations, as Pilenko has pointed out.[2] It is true that scientific discoveries are more akin to inventions than to artistic creations; but we prefer Mr. Ruffini's view, that scientific property constitutes a sphere midway between the domain of artistic property, on the one hand, and industrial, on the other. His other thesis, that there is no substantial difference between all these forms of intellectual creation, is proved by a number of creations which partake of the character of invention as well as of artistic work. Such, for instance, are the floral creations, or creations of new horticultural species, for the protection of which a bill was introduced in France in 1922. These creations, like modern scientific discoveries, were unknown when the patent laws originated. On their appearance they were relegated to the so-called public fund of knowledge. In fact, the individual interests concerned did not press for recognition until recently. But the social order is already compelled to take account of them. Legislation has already been enacted for their protection by registration in France and Czechoslovakia.[3]

Paraphrasing Mr. Gariel's use of the simile of Procrustes' bed in his criticism [4] of Mr. Vigneron's book,[5] we may be allowed to add that scientific property should not be adapted to the Procrustes' beds of artistic or industrial property. It is idle to seek a personal element or a possibility of monopoly in scientific discoveries, similar to those

1. See a very interesting exposition in this respect in Mlle Suzanne Munier's thesis, *Les Droits des Auteurs de Découvertes ou d'Inventions Scientifiques* (Paris, 1925), chap. 1, especially pp. 48 ff. Mr. Gariel's criticism, in *Propriété Industrielle* (1925), p. 210, that Mlle Munier's book proceeds by affirmation, would seem to be not well taken.

2. *Das Recht des Erfinders* (Berlin, 1907), pp. 223 ff.

3. See *Propriété Industrielle* (1922), p. 54, and (1923), p. 31.

4. See *ibid.* (1925), pp. 209, 214.

5. Vigneron, *Essai sur la Protection de la Propriété Scientifique* (Paris, 1925).

of artistic or industrial property. It is sufficient, to use again Mr. Gariel's own words, that scientific discovery satisfies a human need and renders a service to society. By reason of this service, and in return for the labor supplied by the scientist, there is a claim on his part against third parties' availing themselves of his service and of the fruits of his labor.[1] And the whole question is whether his claim should be taken into account and satisfied by the law in the whole scheme of claims and interests protected by it.

Mr. Gariel, as well as Mr. De Torres Quevedo is of the opinion that this claim should be satisfied. However, they propose that this be done by a reward paid out of a fund made up of contributions levied on the industrial profits of all the industries of a country, or of subscriptions paid in by the groups of industries profiting by the discoveries. For Mr. Gariel, who alone has expounded his theory, this reward constitutes a quasi-contractual obligation of industry to the scientist — compensation for the social enrichment procured by the scientific discovery. But why should a quasi-contractual obligation of a group of industries, for instance, chemical industries for a chemical discovery, be easier to admit than one of a single patentee or manufacturer who availed himself of the discovery? And when it is admitted that enrichment is bestowed upon industry by the scientific discovery, is it not implied that the latter is of economic value, and therefore, for all practical purposes, a creation?

But all ideas and all principles that constitute the subject of a discovery are not creations. Dean Wigmore's subtle observation should be retained. Whenever a discovery simply explains an obvious fact or a prior practice of human life, it has no economic value; it is not a real creation. But if it reveals a new "raw material," to use Mr. Gariel's own words, a new substance, or a new principle, which leads to novel activities and new manufactures, such a discovery is a true creation, for the use of which a right should be recognized in favor of scientists. The latter are, in such case, in the same position as prospectors of mines, in whom the law has often recognized a right to a share in the profits of working the mines.[2]

1. See in this respect Walter Erman, *Wissenschaftliches Eigentum* (Berlin, 1929), chap. 3. His conclusion in favor of the system of prizes seems illogical, although based on practical reasons.

2. Marcel Vigneron's resort to the ideas of "occupation" and "specification" as the theoretical bases of scientists' rights, *Essai sur la Protection de la Propriété Scientifique* (Paris, 1925), pp. 39 ff., does not seem very helpful.

The truth is that artistic creations as well as inventions are protected by law through the recognition of corresponding rights in their authors, because it has been found to be a sound postulate of social engineering. By the satisfaction of the demands and interests of artists and inventors, the social interest of general progress, economic and cultural, is satisfied. The recognition of scientists' rights in their discoveries is imposed by the same considerations.

§ **609. Methods of application.** It is by no means certain that Mr. Gariel's system is easier to apply. Mr. Lyon-Caen thought that the system of rewards always retained a certain arbitrary character and was slow of application.[1] Besides, it lends itself with difficulty to international relations.

The exercise of the right as provided by Senator Ruffini's plan is perhaps its weakest part. Such questions as the proof of the date of a discovery, its publication, the presentation of claims, the amount of royalty, the duration of the right, and the solution of disputes,[2] raise important difficulties, and are only sketched out in Mr. Ruffini's plan. As will be seen, they have formed the subject of many discussions and inquiries in these last years.[3]

As regards the other main difference between Senator Ruffini's and Mr. Gariel's schemes,[4] that is, the question whether or not national legislation should precede an international convention on the protection of scientific property, perhaps a middle course would be best. An international convention should be limited to general principles, and leave each country free to determine for itself the application of these principles. A model of a national law could be approved at the same time with the signing of a convention, without being obligatory on the contracting countries. This would render

1. See Commission on Intellectual Coöperation, *Minutes of the Third Session*, p. 55.

2. See Fernand-Jacq, "La Propriété Scientifique" in *Le Journal des Economistes* (March 15, 1923).

3. Prof. Cesare Vivante, in *La Propriété Scientifique devant la Société des Nations* (Paris, 1924), makes a strong attack on Senator Ruffini's plan. With the exception of his allegation that there is no claim really on the part of scientists for the protection of their discoveries, his other points refer to the application and exercise of scientists' rights. He comes again and again to the idea of complications and uncertainties into which industry will be thrown.

4. Mlle Munier, in *Les Droits des Auteurs de Découvertes ou d'Inventions Scientifiques*, pp. 18, 132 ff., agrees with Mr. Gariel on this point. She proposes an ingenious method of avoiding any injury to national industry from the recognition of scientific property in a particular country in the international market; this consists in a sort of drawback in the case of exported products, and prohibition or a customs duty on importations. The practical limitations of its application are well brought out by Mr. Gariel, in *Propriété Industrielle* (1925), p. 211.

possible the adaptation of the subject of scientific property to the state of law of each country. It might also leave scope for a certain differentiation in the various countries on the kinds of discoveries upon which scientists' rights could be claimed. For this would seem to be the most difficult point to obtain an agreement on.[1] And as Dr. Herzfeld remarked,[2] the various projects for protection of scientific property did not refer to the same subject-matter of protection, the Barthélemy proposal, for instance, extending to all kinds of discoveries, even juristic or economic, while the project of the C. T. I. referred to scientific discoveries in physics, chemistry, and biology.[3]

§ 610. **Further action in regard to Senator Ruffini's plan.** When the sub-committee on intellectual property met on July 21, 1924, eleven countries had replied to the Secretariat expressing their views on Ruffini's scheme. After hearing Mr. Ruffini and Professor Röthlisberger of the International Bureaus of Berne, the sub-committee noted that a large majority of the replies and opinions given by competent authorities and institutions agreed upon the following points:

(1) A new right should be created for scientists whose discoveries have been profitably applied.

(2) It is extremely difficult to determine the rules for the application of this right to each particular case.

(3) The legitimate interests of industries which depend on the application of scientists' discoveries should be taken into consideration.

The sub-committee did not feel in a position to propose a definitive text for an international convention, and thought it advisable to convene a conference of experts representing all the interests concerned, to investigate the various objections to Mr. Ruffini's scheme and, if necessary, to make the required modifications. It was also agreed that Mr. Ruffini, with the assistance of Mr. Röthlisberger, should prepare a supplement to his report. Resolutions to this effect

1. See Finland's Reply, in Doc. C. 217. M. 74 (1925), XII.

2. "Internationale Bestrebungen zum Schutz des Wissenschaftlichen Eigentums," *Internationale Rechtspraxis*, II (Berlin, 1926), 15.

3. Professor Vivante's point (*La Propriété Scientifique devant la Société des Nations*, p. 9), that the work of justice in remunerating scientists for their discoveries will always be incomplete, since it will never be possible to protect the ideas and discoveries of certain classes of scientists, is not an argument against protection of scientific property. Besides, in Mr. Ruffini's plan there is room for reward of scientists whose discoveries are general in character, rendering service not to any one particular industry, but to society as a whole.

were adopted by the committee in its fourth (July, 1924)[1] and sixth (July, 1925)[2] sessions. It was also decided that, before a conference of experts was convened, industrial circles should be consulted. This work of consultation was undertaken by the International Institute for Intellectual Coöperation which had in the meantime been established at Paris. A report of the Institute on the results of the preliminary inquiry in industrial circles on the subject of scientific property was considered by the sub-committee in 1926. The latter also heard Professor Knoph of the University of Oslo on the subject of the Scandinavian Jurists' Conference of 1925, which discussed the question of scientific property. It decided that the Institute should continue its inquiry, particularly in the United States and Germany, which had not yet been associated so closely with this question of preliminary investigation. It was felt that a conference of experts should not be convened before this investigation was completed. The Economic Committee of the League expressed a wish to be closely associated with, and to assist in, these inquiries. A resolution to this effect was adopted by the Committee on Intellectual Coöperation in the course of its eighth session, at its meeting on July 27, 1926.[3]

An excellent report of the investigation was presented to the sub-committee on July 14, 1927, on behalf of the Legal Section of the International Institute for Intellectual Coöperation, by Mr. Raymond Weiss, containing an analysis of the fresh inquiries, and a constructive part, dealing with possible solutions of the problem. Two currents of opinion manifested themselves in the sub-committee. Certain members thought that a fresh inquiry should be held, others, that the preparatory work had already lasted three years and had covered a vast field in various countries, and that nothing more could be expected from further investigation. The latter view prevailed, and the sub-committee adopted a resolution proposing that a special committee of experts should be convened, which would have before it: (1) all the information obtained as a result of the preliminary inquiries by the International Institute; (2) a preliminary draft inter-

1. Committee on Intellectual Coöperation, Minutes of the Fourth Session, p. 35, and Annex, p. 71, and *Report of the Committee*, p. 19 (A. 31, 1924, XII). Also, *Supplementary Report submitted by Senator Ruffini together with a Memorandum on the Replies of Governments*, Committee on Intellectual Coöperation, Doc. A. 29 (1924), XII.

2. Committee on Intellectual Coöperation, *Minutes of the Sixth Session*, p. 21, and Annex, p. 42, and *Report of the Committee*, p. 6 (A. 24, 1925, XII).

3. Committee on Intellectual Coöperation, *Minutes of the Eighth Session*, p. 24, and Annex, pp. 60, 61–62; and *Report of the Committee*, pp. 1 and 5 (A. 28, 1926, XII).

national convention prepared by amending Senator Ruffini's text in the light of the results of this inquiry. It was also proposed that the members of this special committee be appointed before November 15, 1927, by the Chairman of the International Committee on International Coöperation. This resolution was approved by the Plenary Committee in its ninth session, at its meeting on July 26, 1927.[1]

The committee also welcomed with sympathy, and forwarded to the Special Committee of Experts, a very interesting proposal, submitted to the sub-committee by Mr. Julio Casares. The latter, noting, on the one hand, the favorable reception accorded almost everywhere to the principle of scientific property, and, on the other hand, the number and nature of the objections advanced to its practical application, proposed to formulate the necessary modifications of the ideal formula to make it workable. He felt that in the question of scientific property two problems were involved: (*a*) a legal problem, the institution of a new right comparable to artistic copyright; and (*b*) a social problem, the expediency of protecting the class of men of science by imposing on the community, or on a part of it (manufacturers), a collective duty similar to those upon which certain forms of social insurance are based. Mr. Casares thought that Mr. Ruffini's system had in view the first problem, while the system propounded by Mr. De Torres Quevedo and Mr. Gariel was determined by the second problem. There was danger of proposing irreconcilable solutions so long as the two problems were confused. He proposed to distinguish them, and to limit the institution of the new right of scientists—the scientific copyright—to authors foreseeing the commercial exploitation of their discoveries and notifying the public accordingly.[2]

§ 611. Preliminary draft convention prepared by Committee of Experts. The meeting of the Committee of Experts on Scientific Property, above contemplated, took place at the seat of the Institute for International Coöperation at Paris, on December 12, 13, and 14,

1. Committee on Intellectual Coöperation, *Minutes of the Ninth Session*, p. 43, and Annex, p. 87; also *Report of the Committee*, pp. 2–3 and 13 (A. 35, 1927, XII).

2. Committee on Intellectual Coöperation, *Minutes of the Ninth Session*, p. 43, and Annex, p. 89.

For discussions and resolutions on scientific property by various national and international organizations, see *Propriété Industrielle* (1924), pp. 16, 162, 190; (1925), p. 108; (1927), pp. 17, 125, 167. A bill for the protection of scientific property was introduced in the Italian Parliament in 1925 (*Propriété Industrielle*, 1926, p. 83), and a new bill is being prepared in France by a Committee appointed by the Minister of Education (*ibid.*, 1928, pp. 100, 157).

1927. Its chairman was Mr. Casares, and it included among its twenty members three members of the sub-committee on intellectual rights, Mr. Ostertag, Director of the International Bureaus, representatives of the Economic Committee of the League of Nations, of the International Labor Office, of the International Chamber of Commerce and of industrialists, inventors, and scientists.[1]

At its first meeting the Committee decided, on the preliminary question of the kind of remuneration to scientists for the use of their discoveries, that it was bound by the resolution of the Committee on Intellectual Coöperation convening the experts, which adopts Ruffini's basic principle in this respect.

The Committee of Experts discussed the principles governing scientific property, taking into account three classes of documents submitted to it at the outset: Senator Ruffini's report; the results of the inquiries made by the International Institute; and the draft elaborated by the Institute. When an agreement on principles was reached, a sub-committee drafted the text of a convention. This contains a preamble, is divided into five parts and twenty articles, and is shorter and more concise than the text of the Institute. By its brevity it purports to leave scope for independent national legislation on minor points.

The preamble states rightly that it is to the general interest that the authors of scientific discoveries should share in the material profits derived from the industrial exploitation of their discoveries, and that the contracting countries should "undertake to enforce by appropriate legislation the following provisions." Thus the Convention contains only general principles to be applied by domestic legislation in each country.

The definition of the right, and of the discoveries for which it is recognized, is contained in the three articles of the first part of the draft. The right brings remuneration from the users of the discovery. This is Mr. Ruffini's principle of individual right and individual obligation. Discoveries for which such a right exists are only those open to material utilization,— that is, to utilization contributory to the production of a commercial commodity,— and only those from

1. See Marcel Plaisant, *Report on Scientific Property submitted on behalf of the Committee of Experts*, International Committee on Intellectual Coöperation, Doc. A. 21 (1928), XII, A. I. Also *procès-verbal, Sous-Comité d'Experts pour la Propriété Scientifique*, C. I. C. I. 196 (communicated to the present writer by the courtesy of Mr. Weiss, Director of the Legal Section of the Institute).

which new means of production or new applications of existing means are developed. The words used are taken from patent legislation and have a more or less definite meaning in many countries. To this restriction a negative proposition is added. Demonstrations or explanations of previous discoveries or comments thereon give no rise to this right.

The second part of the draft deals with the rights and obligations of authors. Scientists, nationals of each of the contracting countries, shall be granted in all the other countries the same rights enjoyed by nationals. No reciprocity is provided, but mere assimilation to nationals. Article 4 distinguishes between the coming into being of the right and its enforcement against users. The right is derived from the unequivocal publication of the discovery, whatever form this publication takes — article in a scientific review, book, pamphlet, and so forth. But no claim in respect thereto can be presented unless and until the deposit of a note claiming the right over all possible material applications of the discovery is registered by an international body. This provision protects manufacturers and inventors against unknown claims and liabilities. Publication is proof of priority in disputes between authors. Registration of the claim is proof in disputes with users of the discovery. The duration of the right is restricted to thirty years from the date of registration — soundly moderate for a new right giving rise to so much misgiving and apprehension.

In the third part, the rights and obligations of users are enumerated. Article 8 provides that the registration of a claim of authorship of a scientific discovery does not prevent the latter's use by any undertaking (*entreprise*) on condition that a consideration is paid to the author. Such consideration is fixed either by agreement between the parties, or, failing such agreement, by judicial procedure. The draft does not define the nature of such consideration, which may be a lump sum, an annuity, or a royalty. In the report, however, of the Committee of Experts it is unanimously recommended that the consideration may not in any case exceed one per cent of the sale price of one and the same article for which it is due.

The use, then, of the discovery, duly registered, is free to any one. No monopoly, analogous to that of patented inventions, is recognized. For such use, however, a consideration should be paid. Is this a condition precedent to the use, or may a manufacturer use the discovery and then enter into negotiations with the author? The draft is not clear on this point. From the next article, 9, providing that the manufacturer shall be bound to enter into negotiations with the author on receipt of an application on his part, it must be inferred that neither the payment of the consideration nor the entering into negotiations is a condition precedent to the use of the discovery. This is sound, for otherwise the freedom and activity of industry would be hampered. Article 11 adopts a provision of the new French project of patent law for revision of the consideration by judicial review at the end of each period of five years, at the application of either party. Article 12 contemplates cases of dispute between scientists as to the consideration already fixed in favor of one of them in regard to a discovery. Article 13 declares null and void all private agreements contrary to the provisions of the Convention, and aims at protecting employees who cede in advance their rights to employers.

The fourth part deals with rules of competence. The case involving difficulties in this respect is that in which the parties are nationals of different countries. The draft provides that in such case the parties may agree upon a jurisdiction satisfactory to both, or upon the selection of arbitrators. When neither of these amicable solutions is adopted, the case shall be settled by an international arbitration commission, the members being selected by the parties from a list of scientific authorities, manufacturers, and jurists, drawn up by the Secretariat of the League of Nations. If no agreement is reached, the President of the Permanent Court of International Justice may be requested to select an arbitrator or umpire. In proceedings of all kinds, the parties may be represented by professional associations. All disputes between states with regard to the interpretation or application of the Convention shall be referred to the Permanent Court of International Justice.

The details of the registration of discoveries, and all executory measures, are to be determined by a special arrangement or *règlement*. The Convention has no retroactive effect, but as a transitional measure, and without prejudice to any vested interests, discoveries made within the ten years prior to the coming into force of the Convention may be protected if they are registered within six months from such coming into force.

§ **612. Observations on Committee's draft.** The draft adopted by the Committee of Experts constitutes a formal text open to public criticism.[1] Its authors took into account all the objections and criticisms brought out by the inquiries of the International Institute for Intellectual Coöperation.[2] The main defect of the draft lies in its definition of discoveries for which scientists' rights may be claimed. The terms "susceptible d'une utilization matérielle," "contribuant à une production destinée au commerce," and "ayant pour conséquence des moyens nouveaux de production," may apply to inventions patentable under the patent laws in existence in many countries, or, broadly interpreted, may cover all scientific discoveries however remotely connected with an industrial application. In the first case, the whole system of patents would be disturbed, as inventors might prefer to be relieved from the stringent formalities and conditions of the patent law and rely for the protection of their rights on the new law on scientific discoveries.[3] In the second case, the charges on industry cannot be calculated with precision, and disputes as to the right to claim a royalty would not be easy to solve. It is true that each country is free to delimit by its municipal law the exact boundaries of the new right. But the great diversity which may exist in this respect takes away all the benefit of an international convention. Professor Stolfi offers the following definition of scientific discovery: that which constitutes the unique, immediate, and direct basis of an invention.[4] The word "unique" raises doubts, but the relation this definition establishes with inventions is most valuable. The scientific discovery which would give rise to a claim of royalty in favor of a scientist must have a direct and immediate relation to an invention. It should make no difference whether the invention is patented, or is merely applied industrially by a manufacturer.

1. *Report on Scientific Property submitted on behalf of the Committee of Experts*, p. 2.

2. Many of the changes from Mr. Ruffini's text adopted by the Committee of Experts had been proposed by Mr. Lyon-Caen, Permanent Secretary of the French Académie des Sciences Morales et Politiques, on behalf of that Academy and of the Académie des Sciences, when he was heard by the sub-committee on Intellectual Property at its meeting of Nov. 29, 1923. See Committee on Intellectual Coöperation, *Minutes of the Third Session*, pp. 54–55.

3. See Introductory Statement by Mr. Ostertag, Director of the International Bureau, at the Rome Congress of the International Association for the Protection of Industrial Property, 1928, in *Proprieté Industrielle* (1928), pp. 178, 181.

4. See his article on scientific property in *ibid.* (1928), p. 225.

As in the subject-matter of protection, in the rights and obligations of the parties, and its other provisions, the draft of the committee is too broad and indefinite. It is unfortunate that most of the members of this committee belonged to countries of the Latin group (ten Frenchmen, two Italians, one Belgian, one Swiss, and one Spaniard), Germany, Great Britain, and the United States being each represented only by an industrialist. In the latter countries little support has been given to the idea of scientific property. Indeed, from the replies received by the Secretariat of the League of Nations,[1] the Institute for International Coöperation[2] and the Standing Committee on Industrial Property of the International Chamber of Commerce,[3] it appears that Belgium, Denmark, France, Hungary, and, possibly, Switzerland, are the only countries which are in favor of recognizing scientific property, while the others are either hostile or indifferent.

At the last two congresses of the International Association for the Protection of Industrial Property, consideration of the question of scientific property was postponed indefinitely.[4] The British, German, and Dutch representatives took a decidedly hostile position, not only toward the Ruffini plan of individual rights of scientists and individual obligations of users, but also to the Gariel scheme of rewards. The objections come usually from inventors and manufacturers, who, naturally, do not wish to be made tributary to scientists. Scientists have not shown much interest in the matter in all the countries. In other words, there is no pressure for the recognition of the new right by the persons primarily interested in most of the countries.

In France, where the pressure is great, the government has submitted to a commission of most eminent experts the project of a law adopting the principles of the above draft convention prepared by the Committee of Experts. An interesting provision of this law is the creation of special funds of insurance, to which manufacturers and other users of scientific discoveries may contribute a premium and be insured against claims of scientists.[5]

The possibility of insurance as a method of application of the

1. Doc. A. 29. 1924, XII, and C. 217, M. 74. 1925, XII.
2. See *supra*, p. 866, nn. 1 and 2.
3. International Chamber of Commerce, *Synopsis of Replies*, No. 2366, 20, 10, 26.
4. See *Propriété Industrielle* (1927), p. 161, and (1928), p. 204.
5. See Mr. Ostertag's statement in *ibid.* (1928), p. 181.

principle of scientific property, without hindering the activity of economic circles, was suggested, among others, by the Plenary Committee on Intellectual Coöperation in sending to the various governments the draft proposed by the Committee of Experts.[1] Users of scientific discoveries might transfer to benefit societies or insurance companies the obligations incurred by them, on payment of an annual premium proportionate to the risks. But the determination of the premium is not an easy matter, when scientists of all countries may claim royalties.[2]

Thus, in conclusion, preferable as the idea of an international convention may appear theoretically, its achievement does not seem possible. In the countries in which scientists press for recognition of their interests in the discoveries made by them and industrially applied by others, the law should give satisfaction to such interests, excluding scientists of other countries which do not afford reciprocal protection. Such a law, tried and experimented on in such countries, may lead subsequently to similar enactments in other countries. The idea of an international convention may be prosecuted only in countries which are prepared to legislate on the subject at the present time.

1. See Doc. E. 37, 1928.

2. See International Committee on International Coöperation, *Report submitted on behalf of the Sub-Committee on Intellectual Rights*, July 8, 1929 (C. I. C. I./P. I./26), pp. 5–7. The representatives of insurance companies are afraid of the exceedingly hazardous nature of the risks involved in an entirely new field. The Sub-Committee decided to extend the field of enquiry and to obtain further information by convening a small committee, to consist of technical insurance agents and legal experts.

APPENDICES

APPENDIX A

CONVENTION

Constituant une Union pour la Protection de la Propriété Industrielle

Conclue à Paris le 20 mars 1883, Revisée à Bruxelles le 14 décembre 1900, et à Washington le 2 juin 1911 [1]

Article Premier

Les pays contractants sont constitués à l'état d'Union pour la protection de la propriété industrielle.

Article 2

Les sujets ou citoyens de chacun des pays contractants jouiront, dans tous les autres pays de l'Union, en ce qui concerne les brevets d'invention, les modèles d'utilité, les dessins ou modèles industriels, les marques de fabrique ou de commerce, le nom commercial, les indications de provenance, la répression de la concurrence déloyale, des avantages que les lois respectives accordent actuellement ou accorderont par la suite aux nationaux. En conséquence, ils auront la même protection que ceux-ci et le même recours légal contre toute atteinte portée à leurs droits, sous réserve de l'accomplissement des conditions et formalités imposées aux nationaux. Aucune obligation de domicile ou d'établissement dans le pays où la protection est réclamée ne pourra être imposée aux ressortissants de l'Union.

Article 3

Sont assimilés aux sujets ou citoyens des pays contractants, les sujets ou citoyens des pays ne faisant pas partie de l'Union, qui sont domiciliés ou ont des établissements industriels ou commerciaux effectifs et sérieux sur le territoire de l'un des pays de l'Union.

Article 4

(*a*) Celui qui aura régulièrement fait le dépôt d'une demande de brevet d'invention, d'un modèle d'utilité, d'un dessin ou modèle industriel, d'une marque de fabrique ou de commerce, dans l'un des pays contractants, ou son ayant cause, jouira, pour effectuer le dépôt dans les autres pays, et sous réserve des droits des tiers, d'un droit de priorité pendant les délais déterminés ci-après.

1. The text is taken from XXXVIII U.S. Stat. at Large, 1645.

(*b*) En conséquence, le dépôt ultérieurement opéré dans l'un des autres pays de l'Union, avant l'expiration de ces délais, ne pourra être invalidé par des faits accomplis dans l'intervalle, soit, notamment, par un autre dépôt, par la publication de l'invention ou son exploitation, par la mise en vente d'exemplaires du dessin ou du modèle, par l'emploi de la marque.

(*c*) Les délais de priorité mentionnés ci-dessus seront de douze mois pour les brevets d'invention et les modèles d'utilité, et de quatre mois pour les dessins et modèles industriels et pour les marques de fabrique ou de commerce.

(*d*) Quiconque voudra se prévaloir de la priorité d'un dépôt antérieur, sera tenu de faire une déclaration indiquant la date et le pays de ce dépôt. Chaque pays déterminera à quel moment, au plus tard, cette déclaration devra être effectuée. Ces indications seront mentionnées dans les publications émanant de l'Administration compétente, notamment sur les brevets et les descriptions y relatives. Les pays contractants pourront exiger de celui qui fait une déclaration de priorité la production d'une copie de la demande (description, dessins, etc.) déposée antérieurement, certifié conforme par l'Administration qui l'aura reçue. Cette copie sera dispensée de toute légalisation. On pourra exiger qu'elle soit accompagnée d'un certificat de la date du dépôt, émanant de cette Administration, et d'une traduction. D'autres formalités ne pourront être requises pour la déclaration de proirité au moment du dépôt de la demande. Chaque pays contractant déterminera les conséquences de l'omission des formalités prévues par le présent article, sans que ces conséquences puissent excéder la perte du droit de priorité.

(*e*) Ultérieurement d'autres justifications pourront être demandées.

ARTICLE 4 *bis*

Les brevets demandés dans les différents pays contractants par des personnes admises au bénéfice de la Convention aux termes des articles 2 et 3, seront indépendants des brevets obtenus pour la même invention dans les autres pays, adhérents ou non à l'Union.

Cette disposition doit s'entendre d'une façon absolue, notamment en ce sens que les brevets demandés pendant le délai de priorité sont indépendants, tant au point de vue des causes de nullité et de déchéance, qu'au point de vue de la durée normale.

Elle s'applique à tous les brevets existant au moment de sa mise en vigueur.

Il en sera de même, en cas d'accession de nouveaux pays, pour les brevets existant de part et d'autre au moment de l'accession.

ARTICLE 5

L'introduction, par le breveté, dans le pays où le brevet a été délivré, d'objets fabriqués dans l'un ou l'autre des pays de l'Union, n'entrînera pas de déchéance.

Toutefois, le breveté restera soumis à l'obligation d'exploiter son brevet conformément aux lois du pays où il introduit les objets brevetés, mais avec la restriction que le brevet ne pourra être frappé de déchéance pour cause de nonexploitation dans un des pays de l'Union qu'après un délai de trois ans, compté à partir du dépôt de la demande dans ce pays, et seulement dans le cas où le breveté ne justifierait pas des causes de son inaction.

Article 6

Toute marque de fabrique ou de commerce régulièrement enregistrée dans le pays d'origine sera admise au dépôt et protégée telle quelle dans les autres pays de l'Union.

Toutefois, pourront être refusées ou invalidées:

1. Les marques qui sont de nature à porter atteinte à des droits acquis par des tiers dans le pays où la protection est réclamée.
2. Les marques dépourvues de tout caractère distinctif, ou bien composées exclusivement de signes ou d'indications pouvant servir, dans le commerce, pour désigner l'espèce, la qualité, la quantité, la destination, la valeur, le lieu d'origine des produits ou l'époque de production, ou devenus usuels dans le langage courant ou les habitudes loyales, et constantes du commerce du pays où la protection est réclamée.

   Dans l'appréciation du caractère distinctif d'une marque, on devra tenir compte de toutes les circonstances de fait, notamment de la durée de l'usage de la marque.
3. Les marques qui sont contraires à la morale ou à l'ordre public.

Sera considéré comme pays d'origine le pays où le déposant a son principal établissement.

Si ce principal établissement n'est point situé dans un des pays de l'Union, sera considéré comme pays d'origine celui auquel appartient le déposant.

Article 7

La nature du produit sur lequel la marque de fabrique ou de commerce doit être apposée ne peut, dans aucun cas, faire obstacle au dépôt de la marque.

Article 7 *bis*

Les pays contractants s'engagent à admettre au dépôt et à protéger les marques appartenant à des collectivités dont l'existence n'est pas contraire à la loi du pays d'origine, même si ces collectivités no possèdent pas un établissement industriel ou commercial.

Cependant chaque pays sera juge des conditions particulières sous lesquelles une collectivité pourra être admise à faire protéger ses marques.

Article 8

Le nom commercial sera protégé dans tous les pays de l'Union sans obligation de dépôt, qu'il fasse ou non partie d'une marque de fabrique ou de commerce.

Article 9

Tout produit portant illicitement une marque de fabrique ou de commerce, ou un nom commercial, sera saisi à l'importation dans ceux des pays de l'Union dans lesquels cette marque ou ce nom commercial ont droit à la protection légale.

Si la législation d'un pays n'admet pas la saisie à l'importation, la saisie sera remplacée par la prohibition d'importation.

La saisie sera également effectuée dans le pays où l'apposition illicite aura eu lieu, ou dans le pays où aura été importé le produit.

La saisie aura lieu à la requête soit du ministère public, soit de toute autre autorité compétente, soit d'une partie intéressée, particulier ou société, conformément à la législation intérieure de chaque pays.

Les autorités ne seront pas tenues d'effectuer la saisie en cas de transit.

Si la législation d'un pays n'admet ni la saisie à l'importation, ni la prohibition d'importation, ni la saisie à l'intérieur, ces mesures seront remplacées par les actions et moyens que la loi de ce pays assurerait en pareil cas aux nationaux.

Article 10

Les dispositions de l'article précédent seront applicables à tout produit portant faussement, comme indication de provenance, le nom d'une localite déterminée, lorsque cette indication sera jointe à un nom commercial fictif ou emprunté dans une intention frauduleuse.

Est réputé partie intéresséet out producteur, fabricant ou commerçant, engagé dans la production, la fabrication ou le commerce de ce produit, et établi soit dans la localité faussement indiqué comme lieu de provenance, soit dans la région où cette localité est située.

Article 10 *bis*

Tous les pays contractants s'engagement à assurer aux ressortissants de l'Union une protection effective contre la concurrence déloyale.

Article 11

Les pays contractants accorderont, conformément à leur législation intérieure, une protection temporaire aux inventions brevetables, aux modèles d'utilité, aux dessins ou modèles industriels ainsi qu'au marques de fabrique ou de commerce, pour les produits qui figureront aux expositions internationales officielles ou officiellement reconnues, organisées sur le territoire de l'un d'eux.

Article 12

Chacun des pays contractants s'engage à établir un service spécial de la propriété industrielle et un dépôt central pour la communication au public des brevets d'invention, des modèles d'utilité, des dessins ou modèles industriels et des marques de fabrique ou de commerce.

Ce service publiera, autant que possible, une feuille périodique officielle.

Article 13

L'Office international institué à Berne sous le nom de Bureau international pour la protection de la propriété industrielle est placé sous la haute autorité du Gouvernement de la Confédération suisse, qui en règle l'organisation et en surveille le fonctionnement.

Le Bureau international centralisera les renseignements de toute nature relatifs à la protection de la propriété industrielle, et les réunira en une statistique générale, qui sera distribuée à toutes les Administrations. Il procédera aux études d'utilité commune intéressant l'Union et rédigera, à l'aide des documents qui seront mis à sa disposition par les diverses Administrations, une feuille périodique, en langue française, sur les questions concernant l'objet de l'Union.

Les numéros de cette feuille, de même que tous les documents publiés par le Bureau international, seront répartis entre les Administrations des pays de l'Union, dans la proportion du nombre des unités contributives ci-dessous mentionnées. Les exemplaires et documents supplémentaires qui seraient réclamés, soit par lesdites Administrations, soit par des sociétés ou des particuliers, seront payés à part.

Le Bureau international devra se tenir en tout temps à la disposition des membres de l'Union, pour leur fournir, sur les questions relatives au service international de la propriété industrielle, les renseignements spéciaux dont ils pourraient avoir besoin. Il fera sur sa gestion un rapport annuel qui sera communiqué à tous les membres de l'Union.

La langue officielle du Bureau international sera la langue française.

Les dépenses du Bureau international seront supportées en commun par les pays contractants. Elles ne pourront, an aucun cas, dépasser la somme de soixante mille francs par année.

Pour déterminer la part contributive de chacun des pays dans cette somme totale de frais, les pays contractants et ceux qui adhéreraient ultérieurement à l'Union seront divisés en six classes, contribuant chacune dans la proportion d'un certain nombre d'unités, savoir:

	Unités		Unités
1re classe	25	4e classe	10
2e classe	20	5e classe	5
3e classe	15	6e classe	3

Ces coefficients seront multipliés par le nombre des pays de chaque classe, et la somme des produits ainsi obtenus fournira le nombre d'unités par lequel la dépense totale doit être divisée. Le quotient donnera le montant de l'unité de dépense.

Chacun des pays contractants désignera, au moment de son accession, la classe dans laquelle il désire être rangé.

Le Gouvernement de la Confédération suisse surveillera les dépenses du Bureau international, fera les avances nécessaires et établira le compte annuel, qui sera communiqué à toutes les autres Administrations.

Article 14

La présente Convention sera soumise à des revisions périodiques, en vue d'y introduire les améliorations de nature à perfectionner le système de l'Union.

A cet effet, des Conférences auront lieu, successivement, dans l'un des pays contractants entre les Délégués desdits pays.

L'Administration du pays où doit siéger la Conférence préparera, avec le concours du Bureau international, les travaux de cette Conférence.

Le Directeur du Bureau international assistera aux séances des Conférences, et prendra part aux discussions sans voix délibérative.

Article 15

Il est entendu que les pays contractants se réservent respectivement le droit de prendre séparément, entre eux, des arrangements particuliers pour la protection de la propriété industrielle, en tant que ces arrangements ne contreviendraient point aux dispositions de la présente Convention.

Article 16

Les pays qui n'ont point pris part à la présente Convention seront admis à y adhérer sur leur demande.

Cette adhésion sera notifiée par la voie diplomatique au Gouvernment de la Confédération suisse, et par celui-ci à tous les autres.

Elle emportera, de plein droit, accession à toutes les clauses et admission à tous les avantages stipulés par la présente Convention, et produira ses effets un mois après l'envoi de la notification faite par le Gouvernement de la Confédération suisse aux autres pays unionistes, à moins qu'une date postérieure n'ait été indiqué par le pays adhérent.

Article 16 *bis*

Les pays contractants ont le droit d'accéder en tout temps à la présente Convention pour leurs colonies, possessions, dépendances et protectorats, ou pour certains d'entre eux.

Ils peuvent à cet effet soit faire une déclaration générale par laquelle toutes leurs colonies, possessions, dépendances et protectorats sont compris dans l'accession, soit nommer expressément ceux qui y sont compris, soit se borner à indiquer ceux qui en sont exclus.

Cette déclaration sera notifiée par écrit au Gouvernement de la Confédération suisse, et par celui-ci à tous les autres.

Les pays contractants pourront, dans les mêmes conditions, dénoncer la Convention pour leurs colonies, possessions, dépendances et protectorats, ou pour certains d'entre eux.

ARTICLE 17

L'exécution des engagements réciproques contenus dans la présente Convention est subordonnée, en tant que de besoin, à l'accomplissement des formalités et règles établies par les lois constitutionelles de ceux des pays contractants qui sont tenus d'en provoquer l'application, ce qu'ils s'obligent à faire dans le plus bref délai possible.

ARTICLE 17 *bis*

La Convention demeurera en vigueur pendant un temps indéterminé, jusqu'à l'expiration d'une année à partir du jour où la dénonciation en sera faite.

Cette dénonciation sera adressée au Gouvernement de la Confédération suisse. Elle ne produira son effet qu'à l'égard du pays qui l'aura faite, la Convention restant exécutoire pour les autres pays contractants.

ARTICLE 18

Le présent Acte sera ratifié, et les ratifications en seront déposées à Washington au plus tard le 1er avril 1913. Il sera mis à exécution, entre les pays qui l'auront ratifié, un mois après l'expiration de ce délai.

Cet Acte, avec son Protocole de clôture, remplacera, dans les rapports entre les pays qui l'auront ratifié: la Convention de Paris du 20 mars 1883; le Protocole de clôture annexé à cet Acte; le Protocole de Madrid du 15 avril 1891 concernant la dotation du Bureau international, et l'Acte Additionel de Bruxelles du 14 décembre 1900. Toutefois, les Actes précités resteront en vigueur dans les rapports avec les pays qui n'auront pas ratifié le présent Acte.

ARTICLE 19

Le présent Acte sera signé en un seul exemplaire, lequel sera deposé aux archives du Gouvernement des États-Unis. Une copie certifiée sera remise par ce dernier à chacun des Gouvernements unionistes.

Fait à Washington, en un seul exemplaire, le 2 juin 1911.

(*Signatures.*)

PROTOCOLE DE CLÔTURE

Au moment de procéder à la signature de l'Acte conclu à la date de ce jour, les Plénipotentiaires soussignés sont convenus de ce qui suit:

Ad Article Premier

Les mots "propriété industrielle" doivent être pris dans leur acception la plus large; ils s'étendent à toute production du domaine des industries agricoles (vins, grains, fruits, bestiaux, etc.) et extractives (minéraux, eaux minérales, etc.).

Ad Article 2

(*a*) Sous le nom de brevets d'invention sont comprises les diverses espèces de brevets industriels admises par les législations des pays contractants, telles que brevets d'importation, brevets de perfectionnement, etc., tant pour les procédés que pour les produits.

(*b*) Il est entendu que la disposition de l'article 2 qui dispense les ressortissements de l'Union de l'obligation de domicile et d'établissement a un caractère interprétatif, et droit, par conséquent, s'appliquer à tous les droits nés en raison de la Convention du 20 mars 1883, avant la mise en vigueur du présent Acte.

(*c*) Il est entendu que les dispositions de l'article 2 ne portent aucune atteinte à la legislation de chacun des pays contractants, en ce qui concerne la procédure suivie devant les tribunaux et la compétence des tribunaux, ainsi que l'élection de domicile ou la constitution d'un mandataire requises par les lois sur les brevets, les modèles d'utilité, les marques, etc.

Ad Article 4

Il est entendu que, lorsqu'un dessin ou modèle industriel aura été déposé dans un pays en vertu d'un droit de priorité basé sur le dépôt d'un modèle d'utilité, le délai de priorité ne sera que celui que l'article 4 a fixé pour les dessins et modèles industriels.

Ad Article 6

Il est entendu que la disposition du premier alinéa de l'article 6 n'exclut pas le droit d'exiger du déposant un certificat d'enregistrement régulier au pays d'origine, délivré par l'autorité compétente.

Il est entendu que l'usage des armoiries, insignes ou décorations publiques qui n'auraient pas été autorisés par les pouvoirs compétents, ou l'emploi des signes et poinçons officiels de contrôle et de garantie adoptés par un pays unioniste, peut être considéré comme contraire à l'ordre public dans le sens du no. 3 de l'article 6.

Ne seront, toutefois, pas considérés comme contraire à l'ordre public les marques qui contiennent, avec l'autorisation des pouvoirs compétents, la reproduction d'armoiries, de décorations ou d'insignes publics.

Il est entendu qu'une marque ne pourra être considéré comme contraire à l'ordre public pour la seule raison qu'elle n'est pas conforme à quelque disposition de la législation sur les marques, sauf le cas où cette disposition elle-même concerne l'ordre public.

Le présent Protocole de clôture, qui sera ratifié en même temps que l'Acte conclu à la date de ce jour, sera considéré comme faisant partie intégrante de cet Acte, et aura même force, valeur et durée.

Fait à Washington, en un seul exemplaire, le 2 juin 1911.

(*Signatures.*)

CONVENTION D'UNION DE PARIS DU 20 MARS, 1883

Pour la Protection de la Propriété Industrielle

Revisée à Bruxelles le 14 décembre 1900, à Washington le 2 juin 1911, et à La Haye le 6 novembre 1925 [1]

Le Président du Reich Allemand; Le Président de la République D'Autriche; Sa Majesté le Roi des Belges; Le Président des États-Unis du Brésil; Le Président de la République de Cuba; Sa Majesté le Roi de Danemark; Le Président de la République Dominicaine; Sa Majesté le Roi D'Espagne; Le Président de la République D'Esthonie; Le Président des États-Unis D'Amérique; Le Président de la République de Finlande; Le Président de la République Française; Sa Majesté le Roi du Royaume-Uni de Grande-Bretagne et D'Irlande et des Territories Britanniques au delà des Mers, Empereur des Indes; Son Altesse Sérénissime le Gouverneur de Hongrie; Sa Majesté le Roi D'Italie; Sa Majesté l'Empereur du Japon; Sa Majesté le Sultan du Maroc; Le Président des États-Unis du Mexique; Sa Majesté le Roi de Norvège; Sa Majesté la Reine des Pays-Bas; Le Président de la République Polonaise, au nom de la Pologne et de la Ville Libre de Dantzig; Le Président de la République Portugaise; Sa Majesté le Roi des Serbes, Croates et Slovenes; Sa Majesté le Roi de Suède; Le Conseil Fédéral de la Confédération Suisse; Les États de Syrie et du Grand-Liban; Le Président de la République Tchécoslovaque; Son Altesse le Bey de Tunis; Le Président de la République Turque,

Ayant jugé utile d'apporter certaines modifications et additions à la Convention internationale du 20 mars 1883, portant création d'une Union internationale pour la protection de la propriété industrielle, revisée à Bruxelles le 14 décembre 1900 et à Washington le 2 juin 1911, ont nommé pour Leurs Plénipotentiaires, savoir:

Lesquels, après s'être communiqué leurs pleins pouvoirs respectifs, trouvés en bonne et due forme, sont convenus des articles suivants:

Article Premier

Les pays contractants sont constitués à l'état d'Union pour la protection de la propriété industrielle.

1. The texts of this Convention and of the following Arrangements are taken from *La Propriété Industrielle* (1925), pp. 221 ff.

La protection de la propriété industrielle a pour objet les brevets d'invention, les modèles d'utilité, les dessins et modèles industriels, les marques de fabrique ou de commerce, le nom commercial et les indications de provenance ou appellations d'origine, ainsi que la répression de la concurrence déloyale.

La propriété industrielle s'entend dans l'acception la plus large, et s'applique non seulement à l'industrie et au commerce proprement dits, mais également au domaine des industries agricoles (vins, grains, feuilles de tabac, fruits, bestiaux, etc.) et extractives (minéraux, eaux minérales, etc.).

Parmi les brevets d'invention sont comprises les diverses espèces de brevets industriels admises par les législations des pays contractants, telles que brevets d'importation, brevets de perfectionnement, brevets et certificats d addition, etc.

Article 2

Les ressortissants de chacun des pays contractants jouiront dans tous les autres pays de l'Union, en ce qui concerne la protection de la propriété industrielle, des avantages que les lois respectives accordent actuellement ou accorderont par la suite aux nationaux, le tout sans préjudice des droits spécialement prévus par la présente Convention. En conséquence, ils auront la même protection que ceux-ci et le même recours légal contre toute atteinte portée à leurs droits, sous réserve de l'accomplissement des conditions et formalités imposées aux nationaux.

Toutefois, aucune condition de domicile ou d'établissement dans le pays où la protection est réclamée ne peut être exigée des ressortissants de l'Union, pour la jouissance d'aucun des droits de propriété industrielle.

Sont expressément réservées les dispositions de la législation de chacun des pays contractants relatives à la procédure judiciaire et administrative et à la compétence, ainsi que l'élection de domicile ou à la constitution d'un mandataire, qui seraient requises par les lois sur la propriété industrielle.

Article 3

Sont assimilés aux ressortissants des pays contractants les ressortissants des pays ne faisant pas partie de l'Union, qui sont domicilies ou ont des établissements industriels ou commerciaux efféctifs et sérieux sur le territoire de l'un des pays de l'Union.

Article 4

(*a*) Celui qui aura régulièrement fait le dépôt d'une demande de brevet d'invention, d'un modèle d'utilité, d'un dessin ou modèle industriel, d'une marque de fabrique ou de commerce, dans l'un des pays contractants, ou son ayant cause, jouira, pour effectuer le dépôt dans les autres pays, et sous réserve des droits des tiers, d'un droit de priorité pendant les délais détermines ci-après.

(*b*) En conséquence, le dépôt ultérieurement opéré dans l'un des autres pays de l'Union, avant l'expiration de ces délais, ne pourra être invalidé par des faits accomplis dans l'intervalle, soit, notamment, par un autre dépôt, par la publication de l'invention ou son exploitation, par la mise en vente d'exemplaires du dessin ou du modèle, par l'emploi de la marque.

(*c*) Les délais de priorité mentionnés ci-dessus seront de douze mois pour les brevets d'invention et les modèles d'utilité et de six mois pour les dessins ou modèles industriels et pour les marques de fabrique ou de commerce.

Ces délais commencent à courir de la date du dépôt de la première demande dans un pays de l'Union; le jour du dépôt n'est pas compris dans le délai.

Si le dernier jour du délai est un jour férié légal dans le pays où la protection est réclamée, le délai sera prorogé jusqu' au premier jour ouvrable qui suit.

(*d*) Quiconque voudra se prévaloir de la priorité d'un dépôt antérieur sera tenu de faire une déclaration indiquant la date et le pays de ce dépôt. Chaque pays déterminera à quel moment, au plus tard, cette déclaration devra être effectuée.

Ces indications seront mentionées dans les publications émanant de l'Administration compétente, notamment sur les brevets et les descriptions y relatives.

Les pays contractants pourront exiger de celui qui fait une déclaration de priorité la production d'une copie de la demande (description, dessins, etc.) déposée antérieurement. La copie, certifiée conforme par l'Administration qui aura reçu cette demande, sera dispensée de toute légalisation, et elle pourra en tous cas être déposée à n'importe quel moment dans le délai des trois mois à dater du dépôt de la demande ultérieure. On pourra exiger qu'elle soit accompagnée d'un certificat de la date du dépôt émanant de cette Administration et d'une traduction.

D'autres formalités ne pourront être requises pour la déclaration de priorité au moment du dépôt de la demande. Chaque pays contractant déterminera les conséquences de l'omission des formalités prévues par le présent article, sans que ces conséquences puissent excéder la perte du droit de priorité.

Ultérieurement d'autres justifications pourront être demandées.

(*e*) Lorsqu'un dessin ou modèle industriel aura été déposé dans un pays en vertu d'un droit de priorité basé sur le dépôt d'un modèle d'utilité, le délai de priorité ne sera que celui fixé pour les dessins et modèles industriels.

En outre, il est permis de déposer dans un pays un modèle d'utilité en vertu d'un droit de priorité basé sur le dépôt d'une demade de brevet et inversement.

(*f*) Si une demande de brevet contient la revendication de priorités multiples, ou si l'examen révèle qu'une demande est complexe, l'Administration devra, tout au moins, autoriser le demandeur à la diviser dans des conditions que déterminera la législation intérieure, en conservant comme date de chaque demande divisionnaire la date de la demande initiale et, s'il y a lieu, le bénéfice du droit de priorité.

ARTICLE 4 *bis*

Les brevets demandés dans les différents pays contractants par des ressortissants de l'Union seront indépendants des brevets obtenus pour la même invention dans les autres pays, adhérents ou non à l'Union.

Cette disposition doit s'entendre d'une façon absolue, notamment en ce sens que les brevets demandés pendant le délai de priorité sont indépendants, tant au point de vue des causes de nullité et de déchéance, qu'au point de vue de la durée normale.

Elle s'applique à tous les brevets existant au moment de sa mise en vigueur.

Il en sera de même, en cas d'accession de nouveaux pays, pour les brevets existant de part et d'autre au moment de l'accession.

ARTICLE 5

L'introduction par le breveté, dans le pays où le brevet a été délivré, d'objets fabriqués dans l'un ou l'autre des pays de l'Union, n'entraînera pas de déchéance.

Toutefois chacun des pays contractants aura la faculté de prendre les mesures législatives nécessaires pour prévenir les abus qui pourraient résulter de l'exercice du droit exclusif conféré par le brevet, par exemple faute d'exploitation.

Ces mesures ne pourront prévoir la déchéance du brevet que si la concession de licenses obligatoires ne suffisait pas pour prévenir ces abus.

En tous cas, le brevet ne pourra pas faire l'objet de telles mesures avant l'expiration d'au moins trois années à compter de la date où il a été accordé et si le breveté justifie d'excuses légitimes.

La protection des dessins et modèles industriels ne peut être atteinte par une déchéance quelconque pour introduction d'objects conformes à ceux qui sont protégés.

Aucun signe ou mention d'enregistrement ne sera exigé sur le produit, pour la reconnaissance du droit.

Si, dans un pays, l'utilisation de la marque enregistrée est obligatoire, l'enregistrement ne pourra être annulé qu'après un délai équitable et si l'intéressé ne justifie pas des causes de son inaction.

ARTICLE 5 *bis*

Un délai de grâce, qui devra être au minimum de trois mois, sera accordé pour le payement des taxes prévues pour le maintien des droits de propriété industrielle, moyennant le versement d'une surtaxe, si la législation nationale en impose une.

Pour les brevets d'invention, les pays contractants s'engagent en outre, soit à porter le délai de grâce à six mois au moins, soit à prévoir la restauration du brevet tombé en déchéance par suite de non payement de taxes, ces mesures restant soumises aux conditions prévues par la législation intérieure.

Article 5 *ter*

Dans chacun des pays contractants ne seront pas considérés comme portant atteinte aux droits du breveté:

1. L'emploi, à bord des navires des autres pays de l'Union, des moyens faisant l'objet de son brevet dans le corps du navire, dans les machines, agrés, apparaux et autres accessoires, lorsque ces navires pénétreront temporairement ou accidentellement dans les eaux du pays, sous réserve que ces moyens y soient employés exclusivement pour le besoin du navire;

2. L'emploi des moyens faisant l'objet du brevet dans la construction ou le fonctionnement des engins de locomotion aérienne ou terrestre des autres pays de l'Union ou des accessoires de ces engins, lorsque ceux-ci pénétreront temporairement ou accidentellement dans ce pays.

Article 6

Toute marque de fabrique ou de commerce régulièrement enregistrée dans le pays d'origine sera admise au dépôt et protégée telle quelle dans les autres pays de l'Union.

Toutefois, pourront être refusées ou invalidées:

1. Les marques qui sont de nature à porter atteinte à des droits acquis par des tiers dans le pays où la protection est réclamée;

2. Lès marques dépourvues de tout caractère distinctif, ou bien composées exclusivement de signes ou d'indications pouvant servir, dans le commerce, pour désigner l'espèce, la qualité, la quantité, la destination, la valeur, le lieu d'origine des produits ou l'époque de production, ou devenus usuels dans le langage courant ou les habitudes loyales et constantes du commerce du pays où la protection est réclamée.

   Dans l'appréciation du caractère distinctif d'une marque on devra tenir compte de toutes les circonstances de fait, notamment de la durée de l'usage de la marque;

3. Les marques qui sont contraires à la morale ou à l'ordre public.

Il est entendu qu'une marque ne pourra être considérée comme contraire à l'ordre public pour la seule raison qu'elle n'est pas comforme à quelque disposition de la législation sur les marques, sauf le cas où cette disposition elle-même concerne l'ordre public.

Sera considéré comme pays d'origine: le pays de l'Union où le déposant a un établissement industriel ou commercial effectif et sérieux, et, s'il n'a pas un tel établissement, le pays de l'Union où il a son domicile et, s'il n'a pas de domicile dans l'Union, le pays de sa nationalité, au cas où il est ressortissant d'un pays de l'Union.

En aucun cas le renouvellement de l'enregistrement d'une marque dans le pays d'origine n'entraînera l'obligation de renouveler l'enregistrement dans les autres pays de l'Union où la marque aura été enregistrée.

Le bénéfice de la priorité reste acquis aux dépôts de marques effectués dans le délai de l'article 4, même lorsque l'enregistrement dans le pays d'origine n'intervient qu'après l'expiration de ce délai.

La disposition de l'alinéa 1 n'exclut pas le droit d'exiger du déposant un certificat d'enregistrement régulier, délivré par l'autorité compétente du pays d'origine, mais aucune légalisation ne sera requise pour ce certificat.

Article 6 *bis*

Les pays contractants s'engagent à refuser ou à invalider soit d'office si la législation du pays le permet, soit à la requête de l'interessé, l'enregistrement d'une marque de fabrique ou de commerce qui serait la reproduction ou l'imitation susceptible de faire confusion, d'une marque que l'autorité compétente du pays de l'enregistrement estimera y être notoirement connue comme étant déjà la marque d'un ressortissant d'un autre pays contractant et utilisée pour des produits du même genre ou d'un genre similaire.

Un délai minimum de trois ans devra être accordé pour réclamer la radiation de ces marques. Le délai courra de la date de l'enregistrement de la marque.

Il ne sera pas fixé de délai pour réclamer la radiation des marques enregistrées de mauvaise foi.

Article 6 *ter*

Les pays contractants conviennent de refuser ou d'invalider l'enregistrement et d'interdire, par des mesures appropriées, l'utilisation, à défaut d'autorisation des pouvoirs compétents, soit comme marques de fabrique ou de commerce, soit comme éléments de ces marques des armoiries, drapeaux et autres emblèmes d'État des pays contractants, signes et poinçons officiels de contrôle et de garantie adoptés par eux, ainsi que toute imitation au point de vue héraldique.

L'interdiction des signes et poinçons officiels de contrôle et de garantie s'appliquera seulement dans le cas où les marques qui les comprendront seront destinées à être utilisées sur des marchandises du même genre ou d'un genre similaire.

Pour l'application de ces dispositions les pays contractants conviennent de se communiquer réciproquement par l'intermédiaire du Bureau international de Berne, la liste des emblèmes d'État, signes et poinçons officiels de contrôle et de garantie, qu'ils désirent ou désireront placer, d'une façon absolue ou dans certaines limites, sous la protection du présent article, ainsi que toutes modifications ultérieures apportées à cette liste. Chaque pays contractant mettra à la disposition du public, en temps utile, les listes notifiées.

Tout pays contractant pourra, dans un délai de douze mois à partir de la réception de la notification, transmettre, par l'intermédiaire du Bureau international de Berne, au pays interessé, ses objections éventuelles.

Pour les emblèmes d'État notoirement connus les mesures prévues à l'alinéa 1 s'appliqueront seulement aux marques enregistrées après la signature du présent Acte.

Pour les emblèmes d'État qui ne seraient pas notoirement connus, et pour les signes et poinçons officiels, ces dispositions ne seront applicables qu'aux marques enregistrées plus de deux mois après réception de la notification prévue par l'alinéa 3.

En cas de mauvaise foi, les pays auront la faculté de faire radier même les marques enregistrées avant la signature du présent Acte et comportant des emblémes d'Etat, signes et poinçons.

Les nationaux de chaque pays qui seraient autorisés de faire usage des emblèmes d'État, signes et poinçons de leurs pays, pourront les utiliser, même s'il y avait similitude avec ceux d'un autre pays.

Les pays contractants s'engagent à interdire l'usage non autorisé, dans le commerce, des armoiries d'État des autres pays contractants, lorsque cet usage sera de nature à induire en erreur sur l'origine des produits.

Les dispositions qui précèdent ne font pas obstacle à l'exercice, par les pays, de la faculté de refuser ou d'invalider, par application du numéro 3 de l'alinéa 2 de l'article 6, les marques contenant, sans autorisation, des armoiries, drapeaux, décorations et autres emblèmes d'État ou des signes et poinçons officiels adoptés par un pays de l'Union.

Article 7

La nature du produit sur lequel la marque de fabrique ou de commerce doit être apposée ne peut, dans aucun cas, faire obstacle à l'enregistrement de la marque.

Article 7 *bis*

Les pays contractants s'engagent à admettre au dépôt et à protéger les marques appartenant à des collectivités dont l'existence n'est pas contraire à la loi du pays d'origine, même si ces collectivités ne possèdent pas un établissement industriel ou commercial.

Cependant chaque pays sera juge des conditions particulières sous lesquelles une collectivité pourra être admise à faire protéger ses marques.

Article 8

Le nom commercial sera protégé dans tous les pays de l'Union sans obligation de dépôt ou d'enregistrement, qu'il fasse ou non partie d'une marque de fabrique ou de commerce.

Article 9

Tout produit portant illicitement une marque de fabrique ou de commerce, ou un nom commercial, sera saisi à l'importation dans ceux des pays de l'Union dans lesquels cette marque ou ce nom commercial ont droit à la protection légale.

La saisie sera également effectuée dans le pays où l'apposition illicite aura eu lieu, ou dans le pays où aura été importé le produit.

La saisie aura lieu à la requête soit du ministère public, soit de toute autre autorité compétente, soit d'une partie interessée, personne physique ou morale, conformément à la legislation intérieure de chaque pays.

Les autorités ne seront pas tenues d'effectuer la saisie en cas de transit.

Si la législation d'un pays n'admet pas la saisie à l'importation, la saisie sera remplacée par la prohibition d'imporation ou la saisie à l'intérieur.

Si la législation d'un pays n'admet ni la saisie à l'importation, ni la prohibition d'importation ni la saisie à l'intérieur, et en attendant que cette législation soit modifiée en conséquence, ces mesures seront remplacées par les actions et moyens que la loi de ce pays assurerait en pareil cas aux nationaux.

Article 10

Les dispositions de l'article précédent seront applicables à tout produit portant faussement, comme indication de provenance, le nom d'une localité ou d'un pays déterminé, lorsque cette indication sera jointe à un nom commercial fictif ou emprunté dans une intention frauduleuse.

Sera en tous cas reconnu comme partie interessée, que ce soit une personne physique ou morale, tout producteur, fabriquant ou commerçant engagé dans la production, la fabrication ou le commerce de ce produit et etabli soit dans la localité faussement indiquée comme lieu de provenance, soit dans la région ou cette localité est située, soit dans le pays faussement indiqué.

Article 10 *bis*

Les pays contractants sont tenus d'assurer aux ressortissants de l'Union une protection effective contre la concurrence déloyale.

Constitue un acte de concurrence déloyale tout acte de concurrence contraire aux usages honnêtes en matière industrielle et commerciale.

Notamment devront être interdits:

1. Tous faits quelconques de nature à créer une confusion par n'importe quel moyen avec les produits d'un concurrent;
2. Les allégations fausses, dans l'exercice du commerce, de nature à discréditer les produits d'un concurrent.

Article 10 *ter*

Les pays contractants s'engagent à assurer aux ressortissants des autres pays de l'Union des recours légaux appropriés pour réprimer efficacement tous les actes visés aux articles 9, 10, et 10 *bis*.

Ils s'engagent, en outre, à prévoir des mesures pour permettre aux syndicats et associations représentant l'industrie ou le commerce intéressé et dont l'existence n'est pas contraire aux lois de leurs pays, d'agir en justice ou auprès des autorités administratives, en vue de la répression des actes prévus par les articles 9, 10, et 10 *bis*, dans la mesure où la loi du pays dans lequel la protection est réclamée le permet aux syndicats et associations de ce pays.

Article 11

Les pays contractants accorderont, conformément à leur législation intérieure, une protection temporaire aux inventions brevetables, aux modèles d'utilité, aux dessins ou modèles industriels ainsi qu'aux marques de fabrique et de commerce, pour les produits qui figureront aux expositions internationales officielles ou officiellement reconnues, organisées sur le territoire de l'un d'eux.

Cette protection temporaire ne prolongera pas les délais de l'article 4. Si plus tard le droit de priorité est invoqué, l'Administration de chaque pays pourra faire partir le délai de la date de l'introduction du produit dans l'exposition.

Chaque pays pourra exiger, comme preuve de l'identité de l'objet exposé et de la date d'introduction, les pièces justificatives qu'il jugera nécessaires.

Article 12

Chacun des pays contractants s'engage à établir un service spécial de la propriété industrielle et un dépôt central pour la communication au public des brevets d'invention, des modèles d'utilité, des dessins ou modèles industriels et des marques de fabrique ou de commerce.

Ce service publiera une feuille périodique officielle.

Article 13

L'Office international institué à Berne sous le nom de Bureau international pour la protection de la propriété industrielle est placé sous la haute autorité du Gouvernement de la Confédération suisse, qui en règle l'organisation et en surveille le fonctionnement.

La langue officielle du Bureau international es la langue française.

Le Bureau international centralise les renseignements de toute nature relatifs à la protection de la propriété industrielle, il les réunit et les publie. Il procède aux études d'utilité commune intéréssant l'Union et rédige, à l'aide des documents qui sont mis à sa disposition par les diverses Administrations, une feuille périodique, en langue française, sur les questions concernant l'objet de l'Union.

Les numéros de cette feuille, de même que tous les documents publiés par le Bureau international, sont répartis entre les Administrations des pays de l'Union dans la proportion du nombre des unités contributives ci-dessous mentionnées. Les exemplaires et documents supplémentaires qui seraient réclamés, soit par lesdites Administrations, soit par des sociétés ou des particuliers, seront payés à part.

Le Bureau international doit se tenir en tout temps à la disposition des pays de l'Union, pour leur fournir, sur les questions relatives au service international de la propriété industrielle, les renseignements spéciaux dont ils pourraient avoir besoin. Le Directeur du Bureau international fait sur sa gestion un rapport annuel qui est communiqué à tous les pays de l'Union.

Les dépenses du Bureau international seront supportées en commun par les pays contractants. Jusqu'à nouvel ordre, elles ne pourront pas dépasser la somme de cent vingt mille francs suisses par année. Cette somme pourra être augmentée, au besoin, par décision unanime d'une des Conférences prévues à l'article 14.

Pour déterminer la part contributive de chacun des pays dans cette somme totale de frais, les pays contractants et ceux qui adhéreront ultérieurement à l'Union sont divisés en six classes, contribuant chacune dans la proportion d'un certain nombre d'unités, savoir:

	Unités		Unités
1re classe	25	4e classe	10
2e classe	20	5e classe	5
3e classe	15	6e classe	3

Ces coefficients sont multipliés par le nombre des pays de chaque classe, et la somme des produits ainsi obtenus fournit le nombre d'unités par lequel la dépense totale doit être divisée. Le quotient donne le montant de l'unité de dépense.

Chacun des pays contractants désignera, au moment de son accession, la classe dans laquelle il désire être rangé.

Le Gouvernement de la Confédération suisse surveille les dépenses du Bureau international, fait les avances nécessaires et établit le compte annuel qui sera communiqué à toutes les autres Administrations.

Article 14

La présente Convention sera soumise à des revisions périodiques, en vue d'y introduire les améliorations de nature à perfectionner le système de l'Union.

A cet effet, des Conférences auront lieu, successivement, dans l'un des pays contractants entre les Délégués desdits pays.

L'Administration du pays où doit siéger la Conférence préparera, avec le concours du Bureau international, les travaux de cette Conférence.

Le Directeur du Bureau international assistera aux séances des Conférences, et prendra part aux discussions sans voix délibérative.

Article 15

Il est entendu que les pays contractants se réservent respectivement le droit de prendre séparément, entre eux, des arrangements particuliers pour la protection de la propriété industrielle, en tant que ces arrangements ne contreviendraient point aux dispositions de la présente Convention.

Article 16

Les pays qui n'ont point pris part à la présente Convention seront admis à y adhérer sur leur demande.

Cette adhésion sera notifiée par la voie diplomatique au Gouvernement de la Confédération suisse et par celui-ci à tous les autres.

Elle emportera, de plein droit, accession à toutes les clauses et admission à tous les avantages stipulés par la présente Convention, et produira ses effets un mois après l'envoi de la notification faite par le Gouvernement de la Confédération suisse aux autres pays unionistes, à moins qu'une date postérieure n'ait été indiquée par le pays adhérent.

Article 16 *bis*

Les pays contractants ont le droit d'accéder en tout temps à la présente Convention pour leurs colonies, possessions, dépendances et protectorats, ou territoires administrés en vertu d'un mandat de la Société des Nations, ou pour certains d'entre eux.

Ils peuvent à cet effet soit faire une déclaration générale par laquelle toutes leurs colonies, possessions, dépendances et protectorats et les territoires visés à l'alinéa 1 sont compris dans l'accession, soit nommer expressément ceux qui y sont compris, soit se borner à indiquer ceux qui en sont exclus.

Cette déclaration sera notifiée par écrit au Gouvernement de la Confédération suisse et par celui-ci à tous les autres.

Les pays contractants pourront, dans les mêmes conditions, dénoncer la Convention pour leurs colonies, possessions, dépendances et protectorats, ou pour les territoires visés à l'alinéa 1, ou pour certains d'entre eux.

Article 17

L'exécution des engagements réciproques contenus dans la présente Convention est subordonnée, en tant que de besoin, à l'accomplissement des formalités et règles établies par les lois constitutionnelles de ceux des pays contractants qui sont tenus d'en provoquer l'application, ce qu'ils s'obligent à faire dans le plus bref délai possible.

Article 17 *bis*

La Convention demeurera en vigueur pendant un temps indéterminé, jusqu'à l'expiration d'une année à partir du jour où la dénonciation en sera faite.

Cette dénonciation sera adressée au Gouvernement de la Confédération suisse. Elle ne produira son effet qu'à l'égard du pays qui l'aura faite, la Convention restant exécutoire pour les autres pays contractants.

ARTICLE 18

Le présent Acte sera ratifié et les ratifications en seront déposées à La Haye au plus tard le 1er mai 1928. Il entrera en vigueur, entre les pays qui l'auront ratifié, un mois après cette date. Toutefois si auparavant il était ratifié, par six pays au moins, il entrerait en vigueur, entre ces pays, un mois après que le dépôt de la sixième ratification leur aurait été notifié par le Gouvernement de la Confédération suisse et pour les pays qui ratifieraient ensuite, un mois après la notification de chacune de ces ratifications.

Cet Acte remplacera, dans les rapports entre les pays qui l'auront ratifié, la Convention d'Union de Paris de 1883 revisée à Washington le 2 juin 1911 et le Protocole de clôture, lesquels resteront en vigueur dans les rapports avec les pays qui n'auront pas ratifié le présent Acte.

ARTICLE 19

Le présent Acte sera signé en un seul exemplaire, lequel sera déposé aux archives du Gouvernement des Pays-Bas. Une copie certifiée sera remise par ce dernier à chacun des Gouvernements des pays contractants.

En foi de quoi, les Plénipotentiaires respectifs ont singné le présent Acte.

Fait à La Haye, en un seul exemplaire, le 6 novembre 1925.

[The Convention was signed by the following countries: Germany, The Commonwealth of Australia, Austria, Belgium, The United States of Brazil, Canada, Cuba, Denmark, Free City of Danzig, Dominican Republic, Spain, Esthonia, The United States of America, Finland, France, Great Britain and North Ireland, Hungary, Italy, Japan, Morocco, The United States of Mexico, Norway, The Netherlands, Poland, Portugal, Serb-Croat-Slovene State, Sweden, Switzerland, Syria and Lebanon, Czechoslovakia, and Tunis.]

ARRANGEMENT DE MADRID DU 14 AVRIL, 1891

CONCERNANT LA RÉPRESSION DES FAUSSES INDICATIONS DE PROVENANCE SUR LES MERCHANDISES

Revisé à Washington le 2 juin 1911, et à La Haye le 6 novembre 1925

Les soussignés, dûment autorisés par leur gouvernements respectifs, ont, d'un commun accord, arrêté le texte suivant, qui remplacera l'Arrangement de Madrid du 14 avril 1891, revisé à Washington le 2 juin 1911, savoir:

Article Premier

Tout produit portant une fausse indication de provenance dans laquelle un des pays contractants, ou un lieu situé dans l'un d'entre eux, serait directement ou indirectement indiqué comme pays ou comme lieu d'origine, sera saisi à l'importation dans chacun desdits pays.

La saisie sera également effectuée dans le pays où la fausse indication de provenance aura été apposée, ou dans celui où aura été introduit le produit muni de cette fausse indication.

Si la législation d'un pays n'admet pas la saisie à l'importation, cette saisie sera remplacée par le prohibition d'importantion.

Si la législation d'un pays n'admet pas la saisie à l'intérieur, cette saisie sera remplacée par les actions et moyens que la loi de ce pays assure en pareil cas aux nationaux.

A défaut de sanctions spéciales assurant la répression des fausses indications de provenance, les sanctions prévues par les dispositions correspondantes des lois sur les marques ou les noms commerciaux seront applicables.[1]

Article 2

La saisie aura lieu *à la diligence* de l'Administration *des douanes qui avertira immédiatement l'intéressé, personne physique ou morale, pour lui permettre de régulariser, s'il le désire, la saisie opérée conservatoirement; toutefois, le ministère public ou toute autre autorité compétente pourra requérir la saisie, soit à demande de la partie lésée, soit d'office; la procédure suivra alors son cours ordinaire.*

Les autorités ne seront pas tenues d'effectuer la saisie en cas de transit.[2]

Article 3

Les présentes dispositions ne font pas obstacle à ce que le vendeur indique son nom ou son adresse sur les produits provenant d'un pays différent de celui de la vente; mais, dans ce cas, l'adresse ou le nom doit être accompagné de l'indication précise, et en caractères apparents, du pays ou du lieu de fabrication ou de production, *ou d'une autre indication suffisante pour éviter toute erreur sur l'origine véritable des marchandises.*[1]

Article 4

Les tribunaux de chaque pays auront à décider quelles sont les appellations qui, à raison de leur caractère générique, échappent aux dispositions

1. The text in italic was added to article 1 by the Conference of Revision at The Hague.

2. The old text of article 2 before its revision at the Conference of The Hague read as follows:

"La saisie aura lieu à la requête soit du ministère public, soit de toute autorité compétente, par exemple l'Administration douanière, soit d'une partie intéressée, particulier ou société, conformément à la legislation intérieure de chaque pays.

"Les autorités ne seront pas tenues d'effectuer la saisie en cas de transit."

du présent Arrangement, les appellations régionales de provenance des produits vinicoles n'étant cependant pas comprises dans la réserve spécifiée par cet article.

ARTICLE 5

Les États de l'Union pour la protection de la propriété industrielle qui n'ont pas pris part au présent Arrangement seront admis à y adhérer sur leur demande, et dans la forme prescrite par l'article 16 de la Convention générale.

Les stipulations de l'article 16 bis de la Convention d'Union s'appliquent au présent Arrangement.[1]

ARTICLE 6

Le présent *Acte* sera ratifié et les ratifications en seront déposées à *La Haye* au plus tard le *1er mai 1928*.

Il entrera en vigueur, *entre les pays qui l'auront ratifié*, un mois *après cette date* et aura la même force et durée que la Convention générale. *Toutefois, si auparavent il était ratifié par six pays au moins, en entrerait en vigueur, entre ces pays, un mois après que le dépôt de la sixième ratification leur aurait été notifié par le Gouvernement de la Confédération suisse et pour les pays qui ratifieraient ensuite, un mois après la notification de chacune de ces ratifications.*

Le présent Acte remplacera, dans les rapports entre les pays qui l'auront ratifié, l'Arrangement conclu à Madrid le 14 avril 1891 et revisé à Washington le 2 juin 1911. Ce dernier restera en vigueur dans les rapports avec les pays qui n'auront pas ratifié le présent Acte.[2]

En foi de quoi, les Plénipotentiaires respectifs ont signé le présent Arrangement.

Fait à La Haye, en un seul exemplaire, le 6 novembre 1925.

[This Arrangement was signed by the following countries: Germany, Brazil, Cuba, Danzig (Free City), Spain, France, Great Britain, Morocco, Portugal, Switzerland, Syria and Lebanon, Czechoslovakia, Tunis.

Latvia is the only country party to this Arrangement which did not sign the revised text of the Arrangement.]

1. The text in italic was added to articles 3 and 5 by the Conference of Revision at The Hague.

2. The old text of article 6 before its revision read as follows:

"Le présent Arrangement sera ratifié, et les ratifications en seront déposées à Washington au plus tard le 1er avril 1913.

"Il entrera en vigueur un mois à partir de l'expiration de ce délai, et aura la même force et durée que la Convention générale."

ARRANGEMENT DE MADRID DU 14 AVRIL, 1891

CONCERNANT L'ENREGISTREMENT INTERNATIONAL DES MARQUES DE FABRIQUE OU DE COMMERCE

Revisé à Bruxelles le 14 décembre 1900, à Washington le 2 juin 1921 et à La Haye le 6 novembre 1925

Les soussignés, dûment autorisés par leurs Gouvernements respectifs, ont, d'un commun accord, arrêté le texte suivant, qui remplacera l'Arrangement de Madrid du 14 avril 1891, *revisé à Washington le 2 juin 1911*, savoir:

ARTICLE PREMIER

Les *ressortissants* de chacun des pays contractants pourront s'assurer, dans tous les autres pays, la protection de leurs marques de fabrique ou de commerce *enregistrées* dans le pays d'origine, moyennant le dépôt desdites marques au Bureau international, à Berne, fait par l'entremise de l'Administration dudit pays d'origine.

Fait règle pour la définition du pays d'origine, la disposition y relative de l'article 6 de la Convention générale d'Union pour la protection de la propriété industrielle.[1]

ARTICLE 2

Sont assimilés aux ressortissants des pays contractants les sujets ou citoyens des pays n'ayant pas adhéré au présent Arrangement qui, sur le territoire de l'Union restreinte constituée par ce dernier, satisfont aux conditions établies par l'article 3 de la Convention générale.

ARTICLE 3

Toute demande d'enregistrement international devra etre présentée sur le formulaire prescrit par le Règlement d'exécution, et l'Administration du pays d'origine de la marque certifiera que les indications qui figurent sur ces demandes correspondent a celles du registre national.[2]

Si le déposant revendique la couleur à titre d'élément distinctif de sa marque, il sera tenu:

1. De le déclarer et d'accompagner son dépôt d'une mention indiquant la couleur ou la combinaison de couleurs revendiqée;
2. De joindre à sa demande des exemplaires de ladite marque en couleur, qui seront annexés aux notifications faites par le Bureau international. Le nombre de ces exemplaires sera fixé par le Règlement d'exécution.

1. The text in italic was added by the last Conference of Revision at The Hague.

2. The first paragraph of the new article 3 was added at the Conference of The Hague. Paragraph 1 of the old article 3 is now made paragraph 3 of the new article. Consequently, the old paragraph 3 of article 3, beginning with "En vue de la publicité" is now paragraph 4 of the new article.

Le Bureau international enregistrera immédiatement les marques déposées conformément à l'article premier. Il notifiera cet enregistrement sans retard aux diverses Administrations. Les marques enregistrées seront publiées dans une feuille périodique éditée par le Bureau international, au moyen des indications contenues dans la demande d'enregistrement et d'un cliché fourni par le déposant.

En vue de la publicité à donner, dans les pays contractants, aux marques enregistrées, chaque Administration recevra gratuitement du Bureau international le nombre d'exemplaires de la susdite publication qu'il lui plaira de demander. Cette publicité sera considéré dans tous les pays contractants comme pleinement suffisante, et aucune autre ne pourra être exigée du déposant.

Article 4

A partir de l'enregistrement ainsi fait au Bureau international, la protection de la marque dans chacun des pays contractants sera la même que si cette marque y avait été directement déposée.

Toute marque *qui a été l'objet d'un enregistrement international* jouira du droit de priorité établi par l'article 4 de la Convention générale, *sans qu'il soit nécessaire d'accomplir les formalités prévues dans la lettre d) de cet article.*[1]

Article 4 *bis*

Lorsqu'une marque, déjà déposée dans un ou plusieurs des pays contractants, a été postérieurement enregistrée par le Bureau international au nom du même titulaire ou de son ayant cause, l'enregistrement international sera considéré comme substitué aux enregistrements nationaux antérieurs, sans préjudice des droits acquis par le fait de ces derniers.

Article 5

Dans les pays où leur législation les y autorise, les Administrations auxquelles le Bureau international notifiera l'enregistrement d'une marque, auront la faculté de déclarer que la protection ne peut être accordée à cette marque sur leur territoire. Un tel refus ne pourra être opposé que dans les conditions qui s'appliqueraient, en vertu de la Convention générale, à une marque déposée à l'enregistrement national.

Les Administrations qui voudront exercer cette faculté *devront notifier leurs refus, avec indication des* motifs, au Bureau international, dans le délai prévu par leur loi nationale, et, au plus tard, *avant la fin d'une* année *comptée à partir de l'enregistrement international de la marque.*

1. The second paragraph of article 4 read as follows before its revision at The Hague:

"Toute marque enregistrée internationalement dans les quatre mois qui suivent la date du dépôt dans le pays d'origine jouira du droit de priorité établi par l'article 4 de la Convention générale."

Le Bureau international transmettra sans *retard* à l'Administration du pays d'origine et au propriétaire de la marque *ou à son mandataire, si celui a été indiqué au Bureau par ladite Administration, un des exemplaires de* la déclaration *de refus* ainsi notifiée. L'intéressé aura les mêmes moyens de recours que si la marque avait été par lui directement déposée dans le pays où la protection est refusée.

Les Administrations qui, dans le délai maximum susindique d'un an, n'auront adressé aucune communication au Bureau international seront censées avoir accepté la marque.[1]

Article 5 *bis*

Les pièces justificatives de la légitimité d'usage de certains éléments contenus dans les marques, tels que armoiries, portraits, distinctions honorifiques, titres, noms commerciaux ou noms de personnes autres que celui du déposant, ou autres inscriptions analogues, qui pourraient être reclamées par les Administrations des pays contractants, seront dispensées de toute certification au légalisation autre que celle de l'Administration du pays d'origine.[2]

Article 5 *ter*

Le Bureau international délivrera à toute personne qui en fera la demande, moyennant une taxe fixée par le Règlement d'exécution, une copie des mentions inscrites dans le Registre relativement à une marque déterminée.

Il pourra aussi, contre rémunération, se charger de faire des recherches d'antériorité parmi les marques internationales.[3]

Article 6

La protection résultant de l'enregistrement au Bureau international durera vingt ans à partir de cet enregistrement (*sous réserve de ce qui est prévu a l'article 8 pour le cas où le déposant n'aura versé qu'une fraction de l'émolument international*), mais elle ne pourra être invoquée en faveur d'une marque qui ne jouirait plus de la protection légale dans le pays d'origine.[4]

1. Paragraph 4 of article 5 was added by the Conference of The Hague. Paragraphs 2 and 3 of this article read as follows before their revision at The Hague:

"Elles devront exercer cette faculté dans le délai prévu par leur loi nationale, au plus tard, dans l'année de la notification prévue à l'article 3, en indiquant au Bureau international leurs motifs de refus.

"Ladite déclaration, ainsi notifiée au Bureau international, sera par lui transmise sans délai à l'Administration du pays d'origine et au propriétaire de la marque. L'intéressé aura les mêmes moyens de recours que si la marque avait été par lui directement déposée dans le pays où la protection est refusée."

2. This article was added by the Conference of The Hague. Former article 5 *bis* is now article 5 *ter* of the new text of the Arrangement.

3. The second paragraph of article 5 *ter* did not appear in the former article 5 *bis*. It was added by the Conference of The Hague.

4. The words in italic of article 6 were added by the Conference of The Hague.

ARTICLE 7

L'enregistrement pourra toujours être renouvelé suivant les prescriptions des articles 1 et 3 *pour une nouvelle période de vingt ans à compter depuis la date de renouvellement.*

Six mois avant l'expiration du terme de protection, le Bureau international *rappellera* au propriétaire de la marque, *par l'envoi* d'un avis officieux, *la date exacte de cette expiration.*

Si la marque présentée en renouvellement du précédent dépôt a subi une modification de forme, les Administrations pourront se refuser à l'enregistrer à titre de renouvellement et le même droit leur appartiendra en cas de changement dans l'indication des produits auxquels la marque doit s'appliquer, à moins que, sur notification de l'objection par l'intermédiaire du Bureau international, l'intéressé ne déclare renoncer à la protection pour les produits autre que ceux désignés en mêmes termes lors de l'enregistrement antérieur.

Lorsque la marque n'est pas admise à titre de renouvellement, il pourra être tenu compte des droits d'antériorité ou autres acquis par le fait de l'enregistrement antérieur.[1]

ARTICLE 8

L'Administration du pays d'origine fixera à son gré, et percevra à son profit, une taxe *nationale* qu'elle réclamera du propriétaire de la marque dont l'enregistrement international est demandé.

A cette taxe s'ajoutera un émolument international (*en francs suisses*) de *cent cinquante* francs pour la première marque, et de *cent* francs pour chacune des marques suivantes, déposées en même temps *au Bureau international au nom du* même propriétaire.

Le déposant aura la faculté de n'acquitter au moment du dépôt international qu'un émolument de cent francs pour la première marque et de soixante-quinze francs pour chacune des marques déposées en même temps que la première.

Si le déposant fait usage de cette faculté, il devra, avant l'expiration d'un délai de dix ans compté à partir de l'enregistrement international, verser au Bureau international un complément d'émolument de soixante-quinze francs pour la première marque et de cinquante francs pour chacune des marques déposées en même temps que la première, faute de quoi, à l'expiration de ce délai, il perdra le bénéfice de son enregistrement. Six mois avant cette expiration, le Bureau international rappellera au déposant, par l'envoi d'un avis officieux, à toutes fins utiles, la date exacte de cette expiration. Si le complément d'émolument n'est pas versé avant l'expiration de ce délai au Bureau international, celui-ci radiera la marque, notifiera cette opération aux Administrations et la publiera dans son journal.

1. The text of former article 7 was as follows:

"L'enregistrement pourra toujours être renouvelé suivant les prescriptions des articles 1 et 3.

"Six mois avant l'expiration du terme de protection, le Bureau international donnera un avis officieux à l'Administration du pays d'origine et au propriétaire de la marque."

Lorsque la liste des produits pour lesquels la protection est revendiquée contiendra plus de cent mots, l'enregistrement de la marque ne sera effectué qu'après payement d'une surtaxe à fixer par le Règlement d'exécution.

Le produit annuel *des diverses recettes de l'enregistrement international* sera réparti par parts égales entre les pays contractants par les soins du Bureau international, après déduction des frais communs nécessités par l'exécution du présent Arrangement.

Si, au moment de l'entrée en vigueur du présent Arrangement revisé, un pays n'a pas encore ratifié, il n'aura droit, jusqu'à la date de son adhésion postérieure, qu'à une répartition de l'excédent de recettes calculé sur la base des anciennes taxes.[1]

Article 8 *bis*

Le propriétaire d'une marque internationale peut toujours renoncer à la protection dans un ou plusieurs des pays contractants, au moyen d'une déclaration remise à l'Administration du pays d'origine de la marque, pour être communiquée au Bureau international, qui la notifiera aux pays que cette renonciation concerne.

Article 9

L'Administration du pays d'origine notifiera au Bureau international les annulations, radiations, renonciations, transmissions et autres changements *apportés à l'inscription* de la marque.

Le Bureau *inscrira* ces changements *dans le Registre international*, les notifiera *à son tour* aux Administrations des pays contractants, et les publiera dans son journal.

On procédera de même lorsque le propriétaire de la marque demandera à réduire la liste des produits auxquels elle s'applique.

Ces opérations peuvant être soumises à une taxe qui sera fixée par le Règlement d'exécution.

L'addition ultérieure d'un nouveau produit à la liste ne peut être obtenue que par un nouveau dépôt effectué conformément aux prescriptions de l'article 3.

A l'addition est assimilée la substitution d'un produit à un autre.[2]

1. The text of former article 8 was as follows:

"L'Administration du pays d'origine fixera à son gré, et percevra à son profit, une taxe qu'elle réclamera du propriétaire de la marque dont l'enregistrement international est demandé. A cette taxe s'ajoutera un émolument international de cent francs pour la première marque, et de cinquante francs pour chacune des marques suivantes, déposées en même temps par le même proprietaire. Le produit annuel de cette taxe sera réparit par parts égales entre les pays contractants par les soins du Bureau international, après déduction des frais communs nécessités par l'exécution de cet Arrangement."

2. The words "apportés à l'inscription" in the first paragraph of the new article 9 have replaced the words "qui se produiront dans la propriété" of the old text.

Paragraph 4 of the new article was added at the Conference of The Hague. Paragraph 4 of the old article 9 constitutes now paragraphs 5 and 6 of the new article.

Article 9 *bis*

Lorsqu'une marque inscrite dans le Registre international sera transmise à une personne établie dans un pays contractant autre que le pays d'origine de la marque, la transmission sera notifiée au Bureau international par l'Administration de ce même pays d'origine. Le Bureau international, *après* avoir reçu l'assentiment de l'Administration à laquelle ressortit le nouveau titulaire, enregistrera la transmission, la notifiera aux autres Administrations et la publiera dans son journal *en mentionnant, si possible, la date et le numéro d'enregistrement de la marque dans son nouveau pays d'origine.*

Nulle transmission de marque inscrite dans le Registre international, faite au profit d'une personne *non admise à déposer une marque internationale*, ne sera enregistrée.[1]

Article 9 *ter*

Les dispositions *des articles 9 et 9* bis *concernant les transmissions* n'ont point pour effet de modifier les législations des pays contractants qui prohibent la transmission de la marque sans la cession simultanée de l'établissement industriel ou commercial dont elle distingue les produits.[2]

Article 10

Les Administration régleront d'un commun accord les détails relatifs à l'exécution du présent Arrangement.

Article 11

Les pays de l'Union pour la protection de la propriété industrielle qui n'ont pas pris part au présent Arrangement seront admis à y adhérer sur leur demande, et dans la forme préscrite par la Convention générale.

Dès que le Bureau international sera informé qu'un pays ou une de ses colonies a adhéré au présent Arrangement, il adressera à l'Administration de ce pays, conformément à l'article 3, une notification collective des marques qui, à ce moment, jouiront de la protection internationale.

Cette modification assurera, par elle-même, auxdites marques le bénéfice des précédentes dispositions sur le territoire du pays adhérent, et fera courir le délai d'un an pendant lequel l'Administration intéressée peut faire la déclaration prévue par l'article 5.

Toutefois, chaque pays en adhérant au présent Arrangement pourra déclarer que, sauf en ce qui concerne les marques internationales ayant déjà fait antérieurement dans ce pays l'objet d'un enregistrement national identique

1. The text in italic of article 9 *bis* was added by the Conference of The Hague. The second part of former article 9 *bis* is taken out of this article and is now article 9 *ter*.

2. This article was paragraph 2 of former article 9 *bis* with the difference that for the words "la présente disposition n'a" the words "les dispositions des articles 9 et 9 *bis* concernant les transmissions n'ont" are substituted.

encore en vigueur et qui seront immédiatement reconnues sur la demande des intéressés, l'application de cet Acte sera limitée aux marques qui sont enregistrées à partir du jour ou cette adhésion deviendra effective.

Cette déclaration dispensera le Bureau international de faire le notification collective susindiquée. Il se bornera à notifier les marques en faveur desquelles la demande d'être mis au bénéfice de l'exception prévue à l'alinéa précédent lui parviendra, avec les précisions nécessaires, dans le délai d'une année a partir de l'accession du nouveau pays.[1]

Article 12

Le présent arrangement sera ratifié, et les ratifications en seront déposées à *La Haye*, au plus tard *le l^er mai 1928*.

Il entrera en vigueur un mois *après cette date* et aura la même force et durée que la Convention générale.

Cet Acte remplacera, dans les rapports entre les pays qui l'auront ratifié, l'Arrangement de Madrid de 1891, revisé à Washington le 2 juin 1911. Toutefois, celui-ci restera en vigueur dans les rapports avec les pays qui n'auront pas ratifiés le présent Acte.[2]

En foi de quoi, les Plénipotentiaires respectifs ont signé le présent Arrangement.

Fait a *La Haye*, en un seul exemplaire, le 6 novembre 1925.

[This Arrangement has been signed by the delegates of the following contracting countries: Germany, Austria, Belgium, Brazil, Cuba, Danzig (Free City), Spain, France, Hungary, Italy, Morocco, Mexico, the Netherlands, Portugal Serb-Croat-Slovene-State, Switzerland, Czechoslovakia, and Tunis.

The signatures of the following contracting countries are missing from this document: Latvia, Luxembourg, Rumania, and Turkey.]

RÈGLEMENT

Pour l'Exécution de l'Arrangement concernant l'Enregistrement International des Marques de Fabrique ou de Commerce

Revisé à La Haye le 6 novembre 1925

Article Premier

Toute demande tendant à obtenir l'enregistrement international d'une marque de fabrique ou de commerce en vertu de l'Arrangement du 14 avril 1891 revisé, devra être adressée par le propriétaire de la marque à l'Administration du pays d'origine en la forme que cette dernière prescrira dans son règlement national.

1. The last two paragraphs of this article were added at the Conference of The Hague.
2. The text in italic of this article was added at the Conference of The Hague.

ARTICLE 2

Lorsque la marque sera régulièrement enregistrée dans le pays d'origine, l'Administration de ce pays adressera au Bureau international de la propriété industrielle, à Berne:

A. Une demande d'enregistrement, en double exemplaire, portant une représentation distincte de la marque, uniquement en impression noire, obtenu au moyen du cliché accompagnant le dépôt. Cette demande sera établie sur le formulaire fourni par le Bureau international et sera rédigée en langue française. Le formulaire sera rempli par l'Administration du pays d'origine ou celle-ci veillera à ce qu'il soit rempli correctement. La demande indiquera:

1. Le nom du propriétaire de la marque;
2. Son adresse; s'il est fait mention de plus d'une adresse, celle à laquelle les notifications devront être envoyées;
3. Le cas échéant, le nom et l'adresse du mandataire;
4. Les produits ou marchandises auxquels la marque est destinée (indication précise du genre des produits sans énumeration trop détaillée);
5. La date de la dernière inscription (enregistrement ou renouvellement) de la marque dans le pays d'origine et son numéro d'ordre;
6. S'il y a lieu, la date et le numéro de l'enregistrement international antérieur.

B. Un cliché de la marque, pour la reproduction typographique de cette dernière dans la publication qui en sera faite par le Bureau international. Ce cliché doit reproduire exactement la marque, de manière que tous les détails en ressortent visiblement; il ne doit pas avoir moins de 15 millimètres ni plus de 10 centimètres, soit en longueur, soit en largeur. L'épaisseur exacte du cliché doit être de 24 millimètres, correspondant à la hauteur des caractères d'imprimerie. Ce cliché sera, deux ans après la publication, retourné au propriétaire de la marque, aux frais de celui-ci, s'il en a fait la demande. Tout cliché non réclamé à la fin de la troisième année sera détruit.

Le formulaire de demande d'enregistrement fera mention de ces dernières dispositions et portera une rubrique dans laquelle il sera indiqué si le propriétaire de la marque désire ou non rentrer en possession de son cliché.

C. Si le déposant revendique la couleur à titre d'élément distinctif de sa marque: quarante exemplaires, sur papier, d'une reproduction en couleur, dont les dimensions ne dépasseront pas 20 centimètres de côté. Un des exemplaires sera fixé sur chacune des demandes d'enregistrement à côté de l'empreinte en noir. Si la marque comporte plusieurs parties séparées, elles devront être réunies et collées, pour chacun des quarante spécimens, sur une feuille de papier fort. La demande devra porter une brève mention en langue française indiquant uniquement la couleur ou la combinaison de couleurs revendiquée pour les parties essentielles de la marque. Au cas où l'une ou l'autre des conditions rélatives à la couleur ne sera pas remplie, le Bureau international procédera à l'enregistrement et à la notification de la marque sans tenir compte de la couleur, si le dépôt n'a pas été régularisé dans un délai fixé par lui.

D. Le montant de l'émolument international, à moins qu'il n'ait été envoyé d'avance et directement au Bureau international par le propriétaire de cette marque. Cette somme devra être versée en espèces au Bureau international, ou lui être envoyée par mandat postal, ou par versement sur son compte des chèques postaux ou par chèque tiré sur une banque de Berne. Tout payement devra être accompagné de l'indication du nom et du domicile du propriétaire de la marque.

Les demandes d'enregistrement devront préciser à quelle date, sous quelle forme et par qui ce payement aura été effectué; elles indiqueront aussi si l'émolument international est payé immédiatement pour les 20 ans ou seulement pour les 10 premières années.

Lorsqu'une marque renferme des inscriptions dans une langue ou en caractères généralement peu connus, on pourra exiger du propriétaire qu'il joigne à son dépôt international une douzaine d'exemplaires d'une traduction en français de ces inscriptions, afin d'accélérer l'examen de la marque dans quelques pays.

Le cas échéant et dans le même but, l'Administration du pays d'origine aura la faculté de certifier sur la demande d'enregistrement que le déposant a justifié auprès d'elle du droit à l'usage de l'armoirie, du portrait, de la distinction honorifique ou du nom d'un tiers qui figure dans la marque.

Les formulaires de demande d'enregistrement international seront fournis gratuitement aux Administrations par le Bureau international.

Le renouvellement du dépôt international donnera lieu aux mêmes opérations que le dépôt primitif.

Article 2 *bis*

Si le Bureau international constate qu'une demande d'enregistrement est incomplète ou irrégulière, il est autorisé à surseoir à l'enregistrement de cette marque, mais doit en aviser sans retard à l'Administration intéressée, à laquelle il appartiendra de notifier au Bureau international que la demande doit être modifiée, retirée ou maintenue.

Le Bureau pourra notamment, et en observant la même procédure, surseoir à l'enregistrement:

1. Si la demande contient des indications de produits trop vagues, telles que "marchandises diverses," "et autres produits" et, en particulier, l'expression "etc.";
2. Si le cliché reçu ne donne pas une empreinte suffisamment claire des éléments de la marque;

3. Si la marque porte le signe d'une croix pouvant être confondue avec la "Croix-Rouge" et si, pour éviter des refus certains, il y a lieu d'obtenir du propriétaire la déclaration préalable que la marque ne sera employée ni en couleur rouge, ni en couleur similaire.

Lorsqu'un dépôt de ce genre n'est pas régularisé dans les six mois, le Bureau international est autorisé à fixer un délai de même longueur pour la liquidation de l'affaire. Il en avertira aussi bien le propriétaire de la marque ou son mandataire, que l'Administration qui a demandé l'enregistrement. Ces deux délais partent de la date de la notification du Bureau international. Ceux-ci écoulés, sans qu'une réponse soit parvenue à ce Bureau, le dépôt pourra être considéré comme abandonné et l'émolument sera renvoyé au déposant après déduction de 20 francs au maximum.

Lorsqu'une demande d'enregistrement incomplète ou irrégulière fait partie d'un dépôt collectif de plusieurs marques, l'enregistrement de toute la collection sera suspendu à moins que l'Administration intéressée ou le propriétaire de la marque n'autorise le Bureau international à considérer celle-ci comme sortie du dépôt collectif et à la traiter comme marque isolée.

Article 3

Le Bureau international procédera sans retard à l'inscription de la marque dans un registre qui portera une empreinte de celle-ci et contiendra les indications suivantes:

1. Le numéro d'ordre de la marque;
2. Le nom du propriétaire de la marque;
3. Son adresse;
4. Les produits ou marchandises auxquels la marque est appliquée;
5. Le pays d'origine de la marque;
6. La date de la dernière inscription (enregistrement ou renouvellement) et le numéro d'ordre dans le pays d'origine;
7. Les mentions relatives à une revendication de couleur, à un enregistrement international antérieur rappelé lors du nouveau dépôt, etc.;
8. La date de l'enregistrement au Bureau international;
9. La date de la notification aux Administrations et de la publication;
10. Les mentions relatives à la situation de la marque, telles que: refus de protection, limitations, transmissions, renonciations, radiations, etc.

Article 4

L'inscription une fois faite dans le registre, le Bureau international certifiera sur les deux exemplaires de la demande sous quelle date et sous quel numéro l'enregistrement a eu lieu, et les revêtira tous deux de sa signature et de son timbre. Un de ces exemplaires restera dans les archives du Bureau, l'autre sera renvoyé à l'Administration du pays d'origine, laquelle, après avoir pris note desdites indications, le transmettra au propriétaire de la marque ou à son mandataire. En outre, le Bureau international notifiera sans retard aux Administrations l'enregistrement opéré, en envoyant à chacune d'elles une reproduction typographique de la marque, accompagnée des indications mentionnées sous les chiffres 1 à 8 de l'article 3.

Dans le cas prévu par l'article 2, lettre C, la susdite notification sera accompagnée d'un exemplaire de la reproduction en couleur de la marque.

Article 5

Le Bureau international publiera la marque dans sa feuille périodique, "Les Marques internationales." Cette publication consistera dans la reproduction de la marque, accompagnée des indications mentionnées sous les chiffres 1 à 8 de l'article 3. Chaque Administration recevra gratuitement du Bureau international le nombre d'exemplaires de cette feuille qu'il lui conviendra de demander; toutefois la gratuité ne s'étendra pas aux numéros déjà parus au moment où cette demande est formulée.

Au commencement de chaque année, le Bureau international fera paraître une table où seront indiqués, par ordre alphabétique et par pays contractant, les noms des propriétaires des marques ayant fait l'objet des publications effectuées dans le cours de l'année précédente.

Article 6

La notification de refus prévue par l'article 5 de l'Arrangement sera transmise au Bureau international en trois expéditions identiques destinées: l'une au Bureau précité, l'autre à l'Administration du pays d'origine, la troisième au propriétaire de la marque ou à son mandataire. Cette notification, faite sur formulaire, devra indiquer au moins le pays du refus, la date d'expédition de l'avis de refus, le numéro et la date de l'enregistrement international de la marque, le nom et le domicile du propriétaire et les motifs du refus. Les notifications de refus provisoires devront indiquer le délai dans lequel les intéressés devront faire valoir leurs droits.

Si le refus est motivé par l'existence d'un dépôt antérieur, la notification devra préciser la marque, nationale ou internationale, avec laquelle il y a collision et spécifier le nom et le domicile du propriétaire de cette marque antérieure, la date de l'enregistrement de celle-ci et son numéro d'ordre, l'Administration refusante joindra un fac-similé à la notification chaque fois qu'elle en aura à sa disposition.

L'avis portera au verso un aperçu des dispositions essentielles de la loi relatives aux refus et indiquera quel est le délai de recours contre ceux-ci et à quelle autorité ce recours devra être adressé.

Article 7

Les changements survenus dans l'inscription d'une marque et qui auront fait l'objet de la notification prévue par les articles 9 et 9 *bis* de l'Arrangement seront consignés dans le registre international. Est excepté le cas où la transmission ne pourra être enregistrée parce qu'elle est faite au profit d'une personne non admise à déposer une marque internationale, ou parce que l'assentiment de l'Administration du nouveau pays duquel ressortit le cessionaire n'aura pas été obtenu.

Le Bureau international notifiera à son tour aux Administrations les changements enregistrés et les publiera dans son journal.

Ces mêmes dispositions feront règle si le domicile du propriétaire d'une marque est transféré d'un pays dans un autre.

Dans le cas où un transfert de propriété ou de domicile ne pourra pas être enregistré, le Bureau international demandera à l'Administration de l'ancien pays d'origine l'autorisation de radier la marque.

Article 8

Les taxes prévues par les articles 5 *ter*, 8 et 9 de l'Arrangement et qui, d'une manière générale, sont payables d'avance et toujours en francs suisses, sont fixées comme suit:

A. Taxes pour les transmissions, modifications de noms, changements de domicile, rectifications nécessitées par une faute du déposant, limitations de produits par suite de renonciation, ou renonciations à la protection pour un pays ou un groupe de pays: 30 francs pour une seule marque et 10 francs pour chacune des marques en plus de la première appartenant au même propriétaire et faisant l'objet de la même opération et de la même notification. Dans ces taxes sont compris les frais de notification aux Administrations, et, s'il y a lieu, de publication de ces opérations. Sont exemptes de taxes les limitations et renonciations notifiées simultanément avec la demande d'enregistrement, les radiations générales, les opérations qui sont la suite d'un avis de refus provisoire ou d'un arrêt judiciaire et celles qui seraient englobées dans une demande de renouvellement.

B. Taxes pour les copies ou extraits du Registre international des marques: 5 francs par marque. Toutefois, lorsque les mentions relatives à plusieurs marques pourront être réunies sur la même feuille, la taxe sera réduite à 2 francs pour chacune des marques en plus de la première. Les demandes de ces documents concernant plusieurs marques devront indiquer s' il s'agit d'extraits séparés ou d'un extrait global. Tout autre extrait, attestation ou recherche (autres que celles sous lettre C) demandé au Bureau international en outre des documents dont la délivrance est obligatoire, donnera lieu à la perception d'une taxe analogue.

C. Taxe pour recherches d'antériorité parmi les marques internationales déjà enregistrées: 5 francs par marque. Si la recherche doit porter sur de nombreuses catégories de produits ou à la fois sur une marque figurative et sur une dénomination, ou si une marque figurative contient plus d'un élément essentiel, cette taxe sera doublée. Il en sera de même lorsque le demandeur omettra de préciser sur quel genre de produits doit porter la recherche ou de joindre un dessin ou une esquisse de la marque figurative au sujet de laquelle il desire être renseigné. Le Bureau international peut, à son gré, différer toute recherche en attendant les précisions qu'il demandera.

D. Surtaxe prévue par l'article 8 de l'Arrangement lorsque la liste des produits pour laquelle la protection d'une marque est revendiquée dépasse 100 mots: 1 franc pour chaque ligne supplémentaire imprimée dans "Les Marques internationales" (une ligne contenant en général 8 à 10 mots).

Article 9

Au commencement de chaque année, le Bureau international établira le compte des dépenses faites au cours de l'année précédente pour le service de l'enregistrement international; le montant de ce compte sera déduit du total des recettes, et l'excédent de celles-ci sera réparti par parts égales entre tous les pays contractants, en attendant que d'autres modalités de répartition aient été déterminées d'un commun accord par les pays contractants.

Article 10

La notification collective, pour autant qu'elle est prévue par l'article 11 de l'Arrangement, contiendra les mêmes indications que les notifications prévues par les articles 4 et 7 du présent Règlement.

Article 11

Le présent Règlement entrera en vigueur en même temps que l'Arrangement auquel il se rapporte et il aura la même durèe. Les Administrations pourront toutefois y apporter, conformément aux dispositions de l'article 10 dudit Arrangement, les modifications qui leurs paraîtront nécessaires d'après le mode de procéder déterminé à l'article suivant.

Article 12

Les propositions de modifications du présent Règlement, formulées par un pays contractant ou par le Bureau international seront communiquées par ce dernier aux Administrations, qui lui feront parvenir leur avis dans le délai de six mois. Si, après l'expiration de ce délai, la proposition est adoptée par la majorité des Administrations sans qu'aucune Administration se soit prononcée pour le rejet ou la modification du texte proposé, elle entrera en vigueur pour tous les pays contractants trois mois après le jour où le Bureau international aura notifié cette acceptation aux Administrations.

[The above *Règlement* was adopted by the Conference of The Hague in its second plenary meeting of the 5th of November 1925.]

ARRANGEMENT DE LA HAYE DU 6 NOVEMBRE 1925

Concernant le Dépôt International des Dessins ou Modèles Industriels

Les soussignés Plénipotentiaires des Gouvernements ci-dessus énumérés,

Vu l'article 15 de la Convention d'Union internationale du 20 mars 1883 pour la protection de la propriété industrielle, revisée à Bruxelles le 14 décembre 1900 et à Washington le 2 juin 1911,

Ont, d'un commun accord et sous réserve de ratification, arrêté l'Arrangement suivant:

Article Premier

Les ressortissants de chacun des pays contractants ainsi que les personnes ayant satisfait sur le territorire de l'Union restreinte aux conditions établies par l'article 3 de la Convention générale, pourront s'assurer dans tous les autres pays contractants la protection de leurs dessins ou modèles industriels, au moyen d'un dépôt international effectué au Bureau international de la propriété industrielle, à Berne.

Article 2

Le dépôt international comprendra les dessins ou modèles soit sous la forme du produit industriel auquel ils sont destinés, soit sous celle d'un dessin, d'une photographie ou de toute autre représentation graphique suffisante dudit dessin ou modèle.

Les objets seront accompagnés d'une demande de dépôt international en double exemplaire contenant en langue française les indications que présisera le Règlement d'exécution.

Article 3

Aussitôt que le Bureau international de Berne aura reçu la demande de procéder à un dépôt international, il inscrira cette demande dans un registre spécial, notifiera cette inscription à l'Administration qui lui aura été indiquée par chaque pays contractant et la publiera dans une feuille périodique dont il distribuera gratuitement à chaque Administration le nombre d'exemplaires voulu.

Les dépôts seront conservés dans les archives du Bureau international.

Article 4

Celui qui effectue le dépôt international d'un dessin ou modèle industriel est considéré jusqu'à preuve du contraire comme propriétaire de l'œuvre.

Le dépôt international est purement déclaratif. En tant que dépôt, il produira dans chacun des pays contractants les mêmes effets que si les dessins ou modèles y avaient été directement déposés à la date du dépôt international, sous bénéfice toutefois des règles spéciales établies par le présent Arrangement.

La publicité mentionnée dans l'article précédent sera considérée dans tous les pays contractants comme pleinement suffisante et aucune autre ne pourra être exigée du déposant, sous réserve des formalités à remplir pour l'exercice du droit, conformément à la loi intérieure.

Le droit de priorité établi par l'article 4 de la Convention générale sera garanti à tout dessin ou modèle qui a fait l'objet d'un dépôt international, sans obligation d'aucune des formalités prévues par ce même article.

Article 5

Les pays contractants conviennent de ne pas exiger que les dessins ou modèles ayant fait l'objet d'un dépôt international soient revêtus d'une mention obligatoire. Ils ne les frapperont de déchéance ni pour défaut d'exploitation, ni pour introduction d'objets conformes à ceux protégés.

Article 6

Le dépôt international peut comprendre, soit un seul dessin ou modèle, soit plusieurs, dont le nombre devra être précisé dans la demande.

Il pourra être opéré, soit sous pli ouvert, soit sous pli cacheté. Seront acceptées notamment comme moyens de dépôt sous pli cacheté les enveloppes doubles avec numéro de contrôle perforées (système Soleau) ou tout autre système approprié pour assurer l'identification.

Les dimensions maxima des objets susceptibles d'être déposés seront déterminées par le Règlement d'exécution.

Article 7

La durée de la protection internationale est fixée à 15 ans, comptés à partir de la date du dépôt au Bureau international de Berne; ce délai est divisé en deux périodes, savoir une période de 5 ans et une période de 10 ans.

Article 8

Pendant la première période de protection, les dépôts seront admis, soit sous pli ouvert, soit sous pli cacheté; pendant la deuxième période ils ne seront admis qu'à découvert.

Article 9

Au cours de la première période, les dépôts sous pli cacheté pourront être ouverts sur la demande du déposant ou d'un tribunal compétent; à l'expiration de la première période, ils seront ouverts en vue du passage à la seconde période, sur une demande de prorogation.

Article 10

Dans les six premiers mois de la cinquième année de la première période, le Bureau international donnera un avis officieux de l'échéance au déposant du dessin ou modèle.

Article 11

Lorsque le déposant désirera obtenir la prolongation de la protection par le passage à la deuxième période, il devra remettre au Bureau international, au plus tard trois mois avant l'expiration du délai, une demande de prorogation.

Le Bureau procédera à l'ouverture du pli, s'il est cacheté, notifiera la prorogation intervenue à toutes les Administrations et la publiera dans son journal.

Article 12

Les dessins ou modèles contenus dans les dépôts non prorogés, de même que ceux dont la protection est expirée, seront rendus tels quels à leurs propriétaires, sur leur demande et à leurs frais. S'ils ne sont pas réclamés, ils seront détruits au bout de deux ans.

Article 13

Les déposants pourront à toute époque renoncer à leur dépôt, soit en totalité, soit partiellement, au moyen d'une déclaration qui sera adressée au Bureau international; ce dernier lui donnera la publicité prévue à l'article 3.

La renonciation comporte la restitution du dépôt aux frais du déposant.

Article 14

Lorsqu'un tribunal ou toute autre autorité compétente ordonnera qu'un dessin ou modèle secret lui soit communiqué, le Bureau international, régulièrement requis, procédera à l'ouverture du paquet déposé, en extraira le dessin ou modèle demandé et le fera parvenir à l'autorité requérante. L'objet ainsi communiqué devra être restitué dans le plus bref délai possible et réincorporé dans le pli cacheté ou dans l'enveloppe.

Article 15

Les taxes du dépôt international, qui seront à payer avant qu'il puisse être procédé à l'inscription du dépôt, sont ainsi fixées:

1. Pour un seul dessin ou modèle et pour la première période de 5 ans: une somme de 5 francs;
2. Pour un seul dessin ou modèle, à l'expiration de la première période et pour la durée de la deuxième période de 10 ans: une somme de 10 francs;

3. Pour un dépôt multiple et pour la première période de 5 ans: une somme de 10 francs;
4. Pour un dépôt multiple, à l'expiration de la première période et pour la durée de la deuxième période de 10 ans: une somme de 50 francs.

ARTICLE 16

Le produit net annuel des taxes sera réparti, conformément aux modalités prévues par l'article 8 du Règlement, entre les pays contractants par les soins du Bureau international, après déduction des frais communs nécessités par l'exécution du présent Arrangement.

ARTICLE 17

Le Bureau international inscrira dans ses registres tous les changements affectant la propriété des dessins ou modèles, dont il aura reçu notification de la part des intéressés; il les dénoncera, à son tour, aux Administrations des pays contractants et les publiera dans son journal.

Ces opérations peuvent être soumises à une taxe qui sera fixée par le Règlement d'exécution.

ARTICLE 18

Le Bureau international délivrera à toute personne, sur demande, contre une taxe fixée par le Règlement, une expédition des mentions inscrites dans le régistre au sujet d'un dessin ou modèle déterminé.

L'expédition pourra être accompagnée d'un exemplaire ou d'une reproduction du dessin ou modèle, qui auront pu être fournis au Bureau international et qu'il certifiera conforme à l'objet déposé à découvert. Si le Bureau n'est pas en possession d'exemplaires ou de reproductions semblables, il en fera faire, sur la demande des intéressés et à leurs frais.

ARTICLE 19

Les archives du Bureau international, pour autant qu'elles contiennent des dépôts ouverts, sont accessibles au public. Toute personne peut en prendre connaissance, en présence d'un des fonctionnaires, ou obtenir du Bureau des renseignements écrits sur le contenu du registre, et cela moyennant paiement des taxes à fixer par le Règlement.

ARTICLE 20

Les détails d'application du présent Arrangement seront determinés par un Règlement d'exécution dont les prescriptions pourront être, à toute époque, modifiées d'un commun accord par les Administrations des pays contractants.

ARTICLE 21

Les dispositions du présent Arrangement ne comportent qu'un minimum de protection; elles n'empêchent pas de revendiquer l'application des prescriptions plus larges qui seraient édictées par la législation intérieure d'un pays contractant; elles laissent également subsister l'application des dispositions de la Convention de Berne revisée de 1908 relatives à la protection des œuvres artistiques et des œuvres d'art appliquées à l'industrie.

ARTICLE 22

Les pays membres de l'Union qui n'ont pas pris part au présent Arrangement seront admis à y adhérer sur leur demande et dans la forme prescrite par les articles 16 et 16 *bis* de la Convention générale.

ARTICLE 23

Le présent Arrangement sera ratifié et les ratifications en seront déposées à La Haye au plus tard le 1er mai 1928.

Il entrera en vigueur, entre les pays qui l'auront ratifié, un mois après cette date et aura la même force et durée que la Convention générale.

En foi de quoi, les Plénipotentiaires des États ci-dessus énumérés ont signé le présent Arrangement.

Fait à *La Haye*, en un seul exemplaire, le 6 novembre 1925.

[This Arrangement has been signed by the delegates of the following contracting countries: Belgium, Czechoslovakia, Danzig (Free City), France, Germany, Morocco, Portugal, the Netherlands, Spain, Switzerland, Syria and Lebanon, and Tunis.]

RÈGLEMENT

POUR L'EXÉCUTION DE L'ARRANGEMENT DE LA HAYE DU 6 NOVEMBRE 1925

Concernant le Dépôt international des Dessins ou Modèles industriels

ARTICLE PREMIER

Les dessins ou modèles industriels admis au dépôt international en vertu de l'Arrangement de La Haye du 6 novembre 1925 ne doivent pas dépasser 30 cm., en chaque dimension, ni peser plus de 2 kg. Sous cette réserve, le nombre des dessins ou modèles admis au dépôt multiple ne sera pas limité.

Les dessins ou modèles pourront être déposés, les dessins à part et les modèles à part, soit sous forme d'échantillons (pour tissus, papiers, broderies, etc.), soit sous forme d'une reproduction graphique ou photographique quelconque. Cette dernière forme de dépôt est surtout recommandée pour les modèles fragiles sans que le dépôt de modèles en nature soit par là exclu.

Les paquets cachetés doivent porter la suscription "dépôt cacheté."

Tout paquet qui ne remplit pas les conditions précitées sera refusé et renvoyé à l'expéditeur, lequel en sera avisé.

Article 2

La demande destinée à obtenir le dépôt international et à accompagner les objets préparés pour ce dépôt sera rédigée en double exemplaire et en langue française sur un formulaire fourni gratuitement aux intéressés ou aux Administrations par le Bureau international de Berne. Elle contiendra les indications suivantes:

1. Le nom et l'adresse du déposant;
2. La désignation sommaire du titre des dessins ou modèles et du genre des produits auxquels ils doivent être appliqués;
3. La nature du dépôt (ouvert ou cacheté);
4. Le nombre des dessins ou modèles déposés conjointement;
5. S'il y a lieu, la date du premier dépôt dans un pays de l'Union lorsque le droit de priorité est invoqué aux termes de l'article 4 de l'Arrangement.

Un formulaire analogue, à remplir en double exemplaire, sera utilisé pour les demandes de prorogation du dépôt.

Article 3

Sera joint aux demandes le montant de l'émolument international correspondant, soit au dépôt international originaire, soit à la prorogation du dépôt; ce montant sera adressé au Bureau international par chèque postal, ou mandat postal, ou par une autre valeur payable à Berne, avec indication du nom et de l'adresse du déposant. Dans ce dernier cas, il en sera délivré un reçu.

Article 4

Le registre tenu par le Bureau international au sujet du dépôt contiendra, outre les indications ci-dessus figurant sur les demandes, les mentions que voici:

1. Le numéro d'ordre et la date du dépôt international;
2. La date de la notification aux Administrations;
3. La mention relative aux modifications du dépôt, telles que: prorogations, transmissions, radiations, renonciations, etc.;
4. La date de l'ouverture des plis cachetés;
5. La date de sortie sur requisition des dessins ou modèles et celle de leur réintégration;
6. La cessation de la protection dans un des pays contractants à la suite de décisions judiciaires, etc., lorsque ces communications sont notifiées au Bureau international.

Article 5

L'inscription une fois faite dans le registre, le Bureau international certifiera sur les deux exemplaires de la demande que le dépôt a eu lieu et les revêtira de sa signature et de son timbre. Un de ces exemplaires restera dans les archives du Bureau, l'autre sera envoyé à l'intérressé. Il sera procédé de même pour les demandes de prorogation du dépôt.

En outre, le Bureau international notifiera aux Administrations le dépôt opéré, avec les indications énumérées à l'article 2 et il publiera le tout dans sa feuille périodique qu'il pourvoira de tables annuelles des matières. Une publication analogue interviendra pour les modifications affectant la propriété des dessins et modèles pendant la durée de la protection.

Article 6

Quand l'intéressé demandera une reproduction de l'objet pour la publicité exigée dans certains pays contractants, elle sera fournie par le Bureau de Berne dans les conditions qui auront été déterminées d'un commun accord avec l'Administration du pays.

Article 7

La taxe prévue par l'article 18 de l'Arrangement pour les expeditions ou extraits de registre, de même que pour les renseignements écrits ou oraux est fixée à 5 francs *suisses*, par expedition, extrait ou renseignement concernant un seul dépôt.

Lorsque les mentions relatives à plusieurs dépôts du même déposant pourront être réunis sur la même feuille, la taxe sera réduite de moitié pour chaque dépôt en plus du premier.

Tout extrait, certificat ou recherche demandé au Bureau international, en outre des documents dont la délivrance est obligatoire, donnera lieu à la perception d'une taxe égale.

La même taxe sera perçue pour l'ouverture du pli cacheté ou d'une enveloppe perforée, ainsi que pour le recachetage ou le rétablissement d'une enveloppe perforée.

Toutes les taxes doivent être payées en monnaie suisse.

Article 8

Au commencement de chaque année le Bureau international établira le compte des dépenses faites au cours de l'année précédente pour le service du dépôt international; le montant de ce compte sera déduit du total des recettes et l'excédent de celles-ci sera réparti entre tous les pays contractants par parts égales ou d'après un mode de distribution adopté ultérieurement.

Article 9

Le présent Règlement entrera en vigueur en même temps que l'Arrangement auquel il se rapporte et il aura la même durée.

Les Administrations des pays contractants pourront toutefois y apporter d'un commun accord les modifications qui leur paraîtront nécessaires, d'après le mode de procéder déterminé dans l'article suivant.

Article 10

Les propositions de modification du présent Règlement seront transmises au Bureau international; il communiquera ces propositions, ainsi que celles qui emanent de lui, aux Administrations, qui lui feront parvenir leur avis dans le délai de six mois. Si, après ce délai, une proposition est adoptée par la majorité des Administrations, sans qu'il se soit produit aucune opposition, elle entrera en vigueur à la suite d'une notification faite par le Bureau international.

[The above Règlement was adopted by the Conference of The Hague, at its second plenary meeting on the 5th of November, 1925.]

RÉSOLUTIONS ET VOEUX

Adopted at the Conference of The Hague of 1925

I

Voeu concernant les feuilles périodiques officielles (article 12 de la Convention)

Il est désirable: que la feuille périodique officielle prévue par l'article 12 de la Convention contienne la reproduction de toutes les marques de fabrique ou de commerce enregistrées; que l'Administration de chaque pays imprime et publie, en outre, autant que possible, tous dessins et descriptions des inventions brevetées et mette en vente, à un prix raisonnable, des exemplaires de cette publication; qu'elle tienne aussi un registre dans lequel seront inscrites les notifications de cession et autres mentions intéressant la validité ou la propriété des brevets, modèles d'utilité, dessins ou modèles industriels et marques de fabrique ou de commerce.

II

Résolution concernant la langue officielle du Bureau de Berne (article 13 de la Convention)

La Conférence invite le Directeur du Bureau international à prêter ses bons offices:

1. Pour que des traductions officieuses des Actes en vigueur dans l'Union puissent être mises à la disposition des Administrations des pays contractants, sur leur demande expresse;
2. Pour qu'il soit fait de même, en ce qui concerne les propositions qui seront soumises aux Conférences périodiques de revision;
3. Pour que des études parues dans "La Propriété industrielle" et dont la publication en d'autres langues paraîtrait désirable à certaines Administrations, soient traduites et répandues aux frais de celles-ci.

III

Résolution concernant les mesures provisoires à prendre dans l'intervalle entre deux Conférences (article 13 de la Convention)

La Conférence décide que si, dans l'intervalle entre deux Conférences, le Bureau international juge utile, dans l'intérêt de l'Union générale ou d'une des Unions restreintes, de provoquer l'application d'une mesure urgente, il demandera au Conseil fédéral suisse de soumettre aux États contractants l'adoption de cette mesure, en recourant à la procedure qu'il a suivie en 1921 pour l'augmentation du crédit global mis par les États à la disposition du Bureau international. Les modifications qui pourront ainsi être apportées au régime desdites Unions ne le seront qu'à titre provisoire, en attendant les décisions définitives de la Conférence ultérieure.

IV

Résolution concernant la répartition de l'excédent des recettes du service de l'enregistrement international des marques de fabrique ou de commerce

La Conférence invite le Directeur du Bureau de Berne à examiner la possibilité de modifier la répartition de l'excédent des recettes du service de l'enregistrement international des marques entre les pays contractants et à demander aux diverses Administrations un avis sur le système de répartition proposé par la Délégation du Brésil en date du 22 octobre 1925.

V

Résolution concernant la Réunion technique de 1926

La Conférence approuve le projet de convoquer à Berne en 1926 une Réunion technique analogue à celle convoquée en 1904, chargée d'examiner:

1. La simplification des formalités pour le dépôt des demandes de brevet;
2. La classification internationale des produits auxquels s'appliquent les marques;
3. Eventuellement d'autres questions d'ordre technique.

APPENDIX B

RÉSOLUTIONS

annexed to Procès-Verbal *1 of the 23d of October, 1926, adopted by the second Technical Reunion of Berne, which met for the purpose of establishing uniform regulations for the filing of patent applications.*

I

La demande de brevet est faite sous la forme d'une requête écrite présentée, conformément aux prescriptions nationales, à l'autorité compétente du pays où la protection de l'invention est requise.

La requête et les annexes prévues à la Résolution III sont rédigées dans la ou dans une des langues admises à cet effet par le pays où la demande est déposée. La description déposée à l'appui d'une demande d'un certificat d'addition est rédigée dans la même langue que celle du brevet principal.

II

1. La requête contient:

(*a*) L'indication des nom, prénoms, nationalité, raison de commerce, domicile ou siège social du déposant (adresse complète). Le nom patronymique doit se distinguer nettement des autres indications. Il doit être facile de constater si le brevet est demandé par une ou plusieurs personnes physiques ou morales, y compris toute espèce de société.

Restent réservées les dispositions nationales qui exigent une déclaration portant que le déposant est le véritable inventeur;

(*b*) La désignation précise de l'invention, sans aucune dénomination de fantaisie;

(*c*) La déclaration qu'il est demandé pour cette invention, soit un brevet principal, soit un brevet de perfectionnement ou un brevet additionnel ou un certificat d'addition. Dans les derniers cas, on indiquera le numéro du brevet principal ou de la demande du brevet principal auquel le brevet de perfectionnement ou additionnel ou le certificat d'addition doit être subordonné;

(*d*) Les nom, prénoms et l'adresse complète du mandataire s'il en a été constitué un;

(*e*) S'il y a plusieurs déposants et s'il n'y a pas de mandataire, la désignation de la personne à laquelle doivent être envoyées les communications officielles;

(*f*) La signature du déposant, ou celle du mandataire si la législation du pays le permet.

2. Restent réservées les dispositions nationales concernant les déclarations à faire et les pièces justificatives à fournir pour les inventions qui ont fait l'objet d'une demande de brevet dans un autre pays, ou qui ont été admises à une exposition officielle ou officiellement reconnue.

En ce qui concerne les documents relatifs au droit de priorité et rédigés en allemand, anglais ou français ou accompagnés d'une traduction officiellement certifiée conforme dans l'une de ces langues, il ne sera pas nécessaire de produire une traduction dans la langue du pays où est faite la demande de brevet, à moins que la loi nationale ou l'autorité compétente ne l'exige.

III

Sont joints à la requête présentée:

(*a*) Une description en deux ou trois exemplaires identiques, suivant les règlements de chaque pays;
(*b*) Des dessins en deux ou trois exemplaires, suivant les règlements de chaque pays;
(*c*) S'il y a lieu, des échantillons présentés conformément aux dispositions nationales;
(*d*) Un pouvoir, s'il est constitué un mandataire;
(*e*) Les taxes exigées pour le dépôt ou la preuve que ces taxes ont été payées, conformément aux dispositions nationales;
(*f*) Un bordereau des pièces déposées.

IV

(1) La description est faite sur une ou plusieurs feuilles de papier fort et blanc, du format de 29 à 34 cm. de hauteur sur 20 à 22 cm. de largeur. S'il y a plusieurs feuilles, celles-ci doivent être réunies en fascicules, de façon qu'il soit possible soit de les séparer, soit de les réunir sans qu'il résulte de leur mode de réunion aucune difficulté pour la lecture.

(2) La description peut être faite à la main ou à la machine, ou lithographiée ou imprimée, etc. Elle doit être bien lisible, l'encre ou la couleur sera foncée et inaltérable.

(3) Il ne sera écrit que d'un seul côté de chaque feuille.

(4) Un en-tête répétera d'une part les nom, prénoms, la nationalité et l'adresse complète du déposant, d'autre part la désignation (II, 1, *b*) de l'invention. Les exemplaires de la description seront signés par le déposant ou par son mandataire.

(5) La description doit être rédigée correctement, aussi brièvement que possible et sans répétitions inutiles.

(6) Les indications de poids et mesures seront données d'après le système métrique, les indications de température en degrés centigrades, la densité comme poids spécifique; pour les unités électriques, on observera les prescriptions admises dans le régime international et pour les formules chimiques on se servira des symboles des éléments, des poids atomiques et des formules moléculaires généralement en usage.

(7) La description devra être faite sans ratures et sans altérations ni surcharges; s'il y en a, elles devront être mentionnées à la fin de la description et certifiées.

(8) Une marge d'environ 3 ou 4 cm. doit toujours être réservée sur le côté gauche de la feuille, ainsi qu'un espace d'environ 8 cm. au haut de la première page et au bas de la dernière.

(9) La description ne contiendra pas de dessins.

(10) Entre les lignes, on laissera un espace suffisant. Les pages seront numérotées. Les lignes seront numérotées par cinq.

V

(1) L'un des exemplaires des dessins sera exécuté sur papier blanc, fort, lisse, et no brillant, un autre, qui sera la reproduction exacte du premier, sur papier transparent et résistant ou sur toile à calquer, le troisième suivant les exigences de l'Administration.

(2) La feuille doit avoir 33 cm. de haut sur 21 cm. et exeptionnellement 42 cm. de large. Suivant les besoins on peut employer plusieurs feuilles, qui devront être numérotées.

(3) Toutes les figures d'une feuille doivent se trouver à l'intérieur d'une simple ligne d'encadrement tracée à deux centimètres du bord de la feuille. Les figures devront être disposées de façon que le dessin, ainsi que les lettres, chiffres et indications de figures, puissent toujours être lus dans le sens de la hauteur.

(4) Le dessin sera exécuté dans toutes ses parties en traits absolument noirs et durables, sans lavis ni couleurs; il doit se prêter à la reproduction nette par la photographie.

(5) Les coupes doivent être indiquées par des hachures obliques qui n'empêcheront pas de reconnaître clairement les signes et traits de référence.

(6) L'échelle des dessins sera déterminée par le degré de complication des figures; elles est suffisante si une reproduction photographique effectuée avec une réduction linéaire aux deux tiers permet de distinguer sans peine tous les détails. Si l'échelle est portée sur le dessin, elle sera dessinée et non indiquée par une mention écrite.

(7) Les diverses figures doivent être nettement séparées les unes des autres; il faut éviter des figures superflues et, autant que possible, toute perte de place. A cet effet les Administrations peuvent demander le remplacement de plusieurs feuilles de 21 cm. par une feuille de 42 cm. de large, ou inversement. Les figures sont numérotées d'une manière continue et sans tenir compte du nombre des feuilles.

(8) Toutes les lettres et les chiffres figurant dans les dessins doivent être simples et nets. Les lignes des coupes seront indiquées par les mêmes caractères. Les differentes parties des figures, dans la mesure ou l'exigera l'intelligence de la description, doivent être désignés partout par les mêmes signes de référence, qui doivent concorder avec ceux de la description.

(9) Le dessin ne doit pas contenir d'explications.

(10) Les dessins sur papier fort devront être déposés à plat, de manière à ne présenter ni plis, ni cassures défavorables à la reproduction photographique. Chaque feuille doit porter, en dehors de l'encadrement, l'indication du nom du déposant et le nombre total des feuilles avec le numéro de la feuille même, ainsi que la signature du déposant ou celle du mandataire.

BIBLIOGRAPHY

BIBLIOGRAPHY[1]

Abel, Paul, *System des Österreichischen Markenschutzes.* Leipzig, 1908.

Adler, Emanuel, *Der Name in Deutschen und Österreichischen Recht.* Berlin, 1921.

—— *System des Österreichischen Markenrechtes.* Wien, 1909.

Alexander-Katz, Benno, *Das Patent- und Markenrecht aller Kulturländer.* 2 vols., Berlin, 1924.

Allart, André, *Traité Théorique et Pratique de la Contrafaçon.* Paris, 1908.

—— Henri, *Traité Théorique et Pratique des Brevets d'Invention.* 3e éd., Paris, 1911.

—— Henri and André, *Traité Théorique et Pratique des Marques de Fabrique et de Commerce.* Paris, 1914.

Allfeld, Philipp, *Grundriss des Gewerblichen Rechtsschutzes.* Leipzig, 1910.

—— *Urheber- und Erfinderrecht.* Berlin, 1923.

Allman, Norwood F., *Handbook on the Protection of Trade Marks, Patents, Copyrights, and Trade Names in China.* Shanghai, 1924.

Amar, Moise, *Studi di Diritto Industriale.* Turin, 1885.

Annuaire de l'Association Internationale pour la Protection de la Propriété Industrielle, Ière année, 1897.

Anspach, Lionel, and Coppieters, Daniel, *Dessins et Modèles Industriels.* Bruxelles et Paris, 1905.

Association Internationale pour la Protection de la Propriété Industrielle (Travaux de Groupe Français).

No. 1 1919–1922
No. 2 1923–1925

Astigueta, F. B., *Sentencias Sobre Marcas de Fábrica y Patentes de Invención.* 2 vols., Buenos Aires, 1905.

Bailly, G. A., *Protection des Inventions au Brésil.* Paris, 1905.

Banyasz, Eugen, *Das Marken- und Musterschutzrecht in Ungarn.* Nagyvarad, 1910.

Barclay, Thomas, *The Law of France relating to Industrial Property.* London, 1889.

—— Thomas, and Dainville, Emmanuel, *Les Fraudes dans les Marques Commerciales.* Paris-Bruxelles, 1889.

Barthélemy, J., *Proposition de Loi sur la Propriété Scientifique.* No. 4233, Chambre des Députés, session de 1922.

Bauer, Paul, *Der Unlautere Wettbewerb und Seine Behandlung im Recht.* München, 1902.

—— Stephen, *Das Los des Erfinders.* Tübingen, 1927.

Baumbach, Adolphe, *Kommentar zum Wettbewerbsrecht,* Berlin, 1929.

Benies, Heinrich, *Herkunftsbezeichnungen im Warenverkehr.* Wien, 1897.

1. No attempt is made here to give a complete bibliography. As a rule, books published after 1900 are only listed here. Exception is made for important works published in the last quarter of the nineteenth century.

Berger-Vachon, V., *La Protection du Nom Commercial en Droit Français et en Droit Allemand Comparés*, Paris, 1928.

Berichte und Verhandlungen der Deutsch-Österreichischen Gewerbeschutz Conferenz am 12 und 13 Oktober, 1896, zu Berlin. Berlin, 1896.

Bingt, Joh., *Internationale Berichte über Patent-, Muster- und Zeichenwesen.* Wien, 1923–1924.

Blanc, Etienne, *Traité de la Contrefaçon.* 4ᵉ éd., Paris, 1855.

Borssat, Xavier de, *Législation et Jurisprudence sur les Fraudes et Falsifications et les Appellations d'Origine.* 3ᵉ éd., Paris, 1923.

Bosio, Edoardo, *Le Privative Industriali.* Torino, 1891.

—— *Trattato dei Marchi e Segni Distintivi de Fabrica Secondo la Legge Italiana e il Diritto Internazionale.* Torino, 1904.

Bozérian, S., *La Convention Internationale du 20 Mars 1883.* Paris, 1885.

Braun, Alexandre. *Nouveau Traité des Marques de Fabrique et de Commerce; Droit Belge et Droit Comparé.* Bruxelles, 1880.

—— Thomas, and Capitaine, Albert, *Les Marques de Fabrique et de Commerce, Droit Belge, Droit International et Droit Comparé.* Bruxelles-Paris, 1908.

Breuer Moreno, Pedro, *Derecho Intelectual Comparado.* Buenos Aires, 1921.

—— *Patentes de Invención; Estudie de Legislation Argentina.* Buenos Aires, 1921.

Briquet, Philippe, *Du Contrôle de l'Origine Neutre des Marchandises.* Genève, 1921.

Brun, J. L., *Les Marques de Fabrique et de Commerce en Droit Français et Droit International.* Paris, 1895.

Brunstein, Ludwig, *Die Schutzobiekte des Musterrechts.* Wien, 1916.

Bry, Georges, *La Propriété Industrielle, Littéraire et Artistique.* 3ᵉ éd., Paris, 1914.

Bryan, Robert T., *American Trade Marks, Trade Names, Copyrights and Patents in China.* Shanghai, 1924.

Bulletin of the United States Trade Mark Association. 32 Nassau St., New York City; published from 1887 irregularly till 1904, and thence monthly.

Busse, Rudolf., *Gesetz zum Schutze der Warenbezeichnungen vom 1923 nebst Pariser Unionsvertrag.* Berlin, 1925.

Cahen, Albert, and Lyon-Caen, L., *De la Convention Internationale pour la Protection de la Propriété Industrielle.* Paris, 1885.

Cairo, Oreste., *Moderni Regolamenti Giuridici della Proprietà Industriale.* Milano, 1926.

Capitaine, Albert, *De l'Emploi des dénominations comme Marques de Fabrique.* Paris, 1905.

Cassel, Hermann. *Die Unionspriritát im Patentrechte.* Leipzig, 1914.

Chabaud, Georges, *La Protection légale des Dessins et Modèles.* Paris, 1913.

—— *La Propriété Industrielle, Littéraire et Artistique et les Traités de Paix.* Paris, 1921.

—— *Notions Pratiques sur les Dessins et Modèles.* Paris, 1925.

Chartered Institute of Patent Agents, *Patent Laws of the World,* in 2 vols. and suppl. London, 1911.

Chenevard, *Traité de la Concurrence Déloyale.* 2 vols. Paris, 1914.

Chesney and Roux, *Traité Théorique et Pratique des Fraudes et Falsifications.* Paris, 1925.

Coppierters, Daniel, *La Protection Légale des Oeuvres d'Art Appliqué.* Bruxelles-Paris, 1919.
—— *Les Oeuvres d'Art Appliqué à l'Industrie.* Bruxelles-Paris, 1924.
Coquet, Lucien, *Les Indications d'Origine et la Concurrence Déloyale.* Paris, 1913.
Couhin, Claude, *La Propriété Industrielle, Artistique et Littéraire.* Paris, 1894–1898.

Dalimier, Roger, and Gallié, Louis, *La Propriété Scientifique, le Projet de la C. T. I.* Paris, 1923.
Damme, F., *Das Deutsche Patenrecht.* Berlin, III Ausgabe, 1925.
Dellóro, Ignazio, *Brevetti nel Diritto Internazionale.* Milano, 1898.
Derichsweiler, W., *Die Interpretation Schweizericher Erfindungs-Patente durch das Bundesgericht.* Berlin, 1922.
Deschamps, Auguste, *Régime Normal et Régime de Guerre des Inventions et des Brevets en France.* Paris, 1917.
Devaux, L. *Protection Internationale des Inventions Brevetées.* Paris,, 1892.
Diazmartinez, P., *Marcas y Patentes.* Habana, 1916.
Donker Duyvis, J. F., *De Wetenschoppelijke Eigemdom en de Financieele Belooning van Wetenschoppelijken Arbeit.* Deventer, 1924.
Donzel, Louis, *Commentaire de la Convention Internationale pour la Protection de la Propriété Industrielle.* Paris, 1891.
Dorff, Alfred, and Pholien, Joseph, *Les Expositions et le Droit.* Bruxelles-Paris, 1910.
Dunant, Philippe, *Traité des Marques de Fabrique et de Commerce, des Indications de Provenance et des Mentions de Récompenses Industrielles en Suisse.* Genève, 1898.
Dunkhase, W., *Die Patentfähige Erfindung und das Erfinderrecht.* Leipzig, 1911.

Ebermayer, *Taschenkommentar der Patentgrenzen des Gesetzes Betreffend die Patentanwälte und der Gesetze Betreffend den Schutz von Gebrauchsmustern.* Berlin, 1926.
Edmunds, Lewis, *The Law of Copyright in Designs.* London, 1895.
—— Lewis, and Bentwich, Herbert, *The Law of Copyright in Designs.* London, 1908.
Elster, Alexander, *Gewerblicher Rechtsschutz.* Berlin and Leipzig, 1921.
—— *Das Deutsche Erfinderrecht.* Berlin-Leipzig, 1924.
Esperson, Pietro, *La Proprietà Industriale nê Rapporti Internazionali.* Torino, 1899.

Fernand, Jacq, *Manuel Pratique de la Propriété Industrielle et Commerciale.* Paris, 1914.
—— *L'Oeuvre de la Conférence de La Haye de 1925.* Paris, 1926.
Fisher, Harold, and Smart, Russel S., *Canadian Patent Law and Practice.* Toronto, 1914.
Forter, Adolf, *Ausführungs- und Lizenzzwang die Sanktion der Erfindungsexploitation.* Zurich, 1919.
Franco, Luigi di, *Trattado della Concorrenza Steale.* Torino, 1906.
—— *Le Indicazioni di Provenienza dei Prodotti.* Napoli, 1907.
Freund, Heinrich, *Der Gewerbliche Rechtsschutz in der Sowjetunion.* Berlin, 1924.

Frick, W., *Die Auslegung des Patentes nach Gesetz und Rechtsspruchung*. Zurich, 1926.

Frost, Robert, *A Treatise on the Law and Practice relating to Letters Patent for Inventions*. 4th ed., 2 vols., London, 1912.

Fürst, Otto, *Der Gegenstand der Gebrauchsmusterschutzes*. Leipzig, 1914.

Gadow, W., *Der Gewerbliche Rechtsschutz*. Berlin, 1922.

Gariel, G., *La Question de la Propriété Scientifique*. Paris, 1924.

Geller, L., *Gesetz Gegen den Unlauteren Wettbewerb*. Wien, 1924.

Gellner, Otto, *Das Tschechoslovakische Gesetz zum Schutz der Ursprungsbezeichnungen mit Erlauterungen*. Prag, 1924.

Georgii, Max, *Étude Comparative sur les Lois concernant les Brevets d'Invention*. Liège, 1912.

Gfeller, Jules, *La Protection de la Propriété Immatérielle en Suisse*. Lauzanne, 1895.

Ghiron, Mario, *Gli Effetti della Guerra Odierna sulle Convenzioni per la Tutela dei Diritti Industriali*. Roma, 1917.

Giambrocono, Armando, *Il Brevetto d'Invenzione*. Napoli, 1924.

—— *La Marca*. Napoli, 1925.

Giannini, *La Concorrenza Steale*. Napoli, 1898.

Gordon, J. W., *Compulsory Licenses under the Patents Acts*. London, 1899.

Graham, Howgrave, *A Second Decade of Progress*. London, 1912.

Greeley, *Foreign Patent and Trade-Mark Laws*. Washington, D. C., 1899.

Guerillon, *Les Appellations d' Origine*. Paris, 1919.

Gutton, *Notions sur la Propriété Industrielle et Commerciale*. Paris, 1918.

Hasselrot, Axel, *Pariskonventionens Bestämmelser om Prioritetsrätt*. Stockholm, 1918.

Hauser, Henri, *Bases Fondamentales d'une Loi Universelle sur les Brevets d'Invention*. Madrid, 1901.

Heifetz, S. J., *Das neue Russische Patengesetz*. Berlin, 1924.

Hempel, Alb., *Der Muster- und Kunstschutz für Kunstgewerbe und Industrie*. Berlin, 1921.

Herzfeld, *Internationale Bestrebungen zum Schutze des Wissenschaftlichen Eigentum* (*Internationale Rechtspraxis, Heft* 2). Berlin, 1926.

Hodez, Roger, *La Protection des Vins de Champagne sur l'Appellation d'Origine*. Paris, 1923.

Hopburn and Spruson, *Patent Law of the Australian Commonwealth*. Sydney, 1903.

Hopkins, J. L., *The Law of Trade Marks, Trade Names and Unfair Competition*. 4th ed., Cincinnati, 1924.

Huard, Gustave, *Traité de la Propriété Intellectuelle*. 2 vols., Paris, 1903–1906.

Hüttner, E., *Die Gesetze zum Schutz des Gewerblichen Eigentums*. Prag, 1924.

International Bureau of Industrial Property, *Actes de la Conférence de l'Union pour la Protection de la Propriété Industrielle*.

Paris, 1880, 1 vol.
Paris, 1883, 1 vol.
Madrid, 1890, 1 vol.
Bruxelles, 1900, 1 vol.
Washington, 1911, 1 vol.
La Haye, 1925, 1 vol.

International Bureau of Industrial Property, *La Propriété Industrielle*, Ière année. 1885.
—— *Recueil Général de la Législation et des Traités concernant le Propriété Industrielle.* vols. I–VII, Berne, 1896–1912.
—— *Réunion Technique de Berne 1926, Procès Verbaux Finals.*
—— *Tableaux des Voeux, concernant la Propriété Industrielle, émis par divers Congrès et Assemblées de 1873 à 1909.*
—— *La Protection Internationale de la Propriété Intellectuelle et la Guerre Mondiale.* Berne, 1919.
—— *Textes Combinés de la Convention de 1883, des Arrangements de 1891 et des Actes de 1900–1911 tels qu'ils sont applicables actuellement.* Berne, 1923.
—— *Actes Adoptés par la Conférence de La Haye.* Berne, 1925.
—— *Documents Préliminaires pour la Conférence de La Haye* (1925).
—— *Tableau Comparatif des Conditions et Formalités Requises dans les Principaux Pays pour l'Obtention d'un Brevet d'Invention.* Edition, 1925.
—— *Tableau Comparatif . . . pour le Dépôt des Marques de Fabrique et de Commerce.* Edition, 1925.
—— *Tableau . . . pour le Dépôt des Dessins et Modèles Industriels dans les divers Pays.* Edition, 1925.
International Chamber of Commerce, *Journal, Brochures and Digests.*

Isay, Hermann, *Die Lage der Deutschen Patente in den Früher Feindlichen Staaten.* Berlin, 1921.
—— *Patengesetz und Gesetz Betreffend den Schutz von Gebrauchsmustern.* Berlin, 1903; *Vierte Auflage*, 1926.

Jaton, Louis, *La Répression des Fausses Indications de Provenance et les Conventions Internationales.* Paris, 1926.
Jizuka, Hanye, *Japarisches Industrierecht.* Berlin, 1926.
Journal of Patent Office Society, 1315 Clifton Street, Washington, D. C. Published since 1918.
Jungel and Magnus, *Warenzeichenrecht.* Berlin-Leipzig, 1924.
Jungmann, Robert, *Das Internationale Patentrecht.* Berlin, 1924.

Kadecka, Ferdinand, *Das Gesetz Gegen den Unlauteren Wettbewerb.* Wien, 1924.
Katz, Edwin, *Weltmarkenrecht.* Berlin, 1926.
Kerly, Duncan M., *The Law of Trade Marks and Trade Name.* 5th ed. (by Underhay and Morgan). London, 1923
Kisch, *Handbuch des Deutschen Patentrechtes.* Mannheim, 1923.
Kohler, Joseph, *Das Recht des Markenschutzes.* Würzburg, 1885.
—— *Forschungen aus dem Patentrecht.* Mannheim, 1888.
—— *Handbuch des Deutschen Patentrechts.* Mannheim, 1900.
—— *Handbuch des Deutschen Patentrechts in Rechtsvergleichender Darstellung.* Mannheim, Fünfte Lieferung, 1901.
—— *Studien zur Förderung des Gewerblichen Rechtsschutzes.* Berlin, 1908.
—— *Lehrbuch des Patentrechtes.* Mannheim-Leipzig, 1908.
—— *Musterrecht.* Stuttgart, 1909.
—— *Warenzeichenrecht.* Mannheim-Leipzig, 1910.
—— *Der Unlautere Wettbewerb.* Berlin-Leipzig, 1914.

Laborde, *Traité Théorique et Pratique des Marques de Fabrique et de Commerce.* Paris, 1914.
Lacour, Léon, *Des Fausses Indications de Provenance.* Paris, 1904.
Ladas, Stephen P., *The International Protection of Trade Marks by the American Republics.* Harvard University Press, Cambridge, 1929.
Laigmeau, Roger de, *De la Protection Internationale des Marques de Fabrique ou de Commerce.* Bordeaux, 1890.
Lainel, Georges, *Nouveau Manuel Pratique des Brevets d'Invention.* 2ème ed., Paris-Nancy, 1910.
—— *La Propriété Industrielle et la Guerre 1914–1916.* Paris, 1917.
Langner, L., and White, W., *Basic Patent and Trade Mark Laws of the Principal Belligerent Powers 1914–1919, Affecting Patents, Trade Marks and Designs.* Washington, 1919.
Lau, *Der Anschluss des Deutschen Reiches an die Internationale Union für den Gewerblichen Rechtsschutz.* Berlin, 1902.
Le Grand, Fernand, *Les Marques de Fabrique au point de vue International.* Fécamp, 1926.
Luzzatto, Enrico, *La Privative Industrial.* 2 vols., Milano, 1914.

Mack, E., *De la Convention Internationale du 20 Mars 1883 au point de vue des Marques de Fabrique.* Paris, 1885.
De Maillard de Marafy, *Grand Dictionnaire International de la Propriété Industrielle au point de vue du Nom Commercial, des Marques de Fabrique et de Commerce et de la Concurrence Déloyale.* Paris, 1902.
Macomber, William, *The Fixed Law of Patents.* Boston, 1909.
Marck, Albert, *Der Internationale Rechtsschutz der Patente, Muster Warenzeichen und des Wettbewerbes.* Berlin, 1924.
Marval, de (J. A.), *Propriedad Industrial.* Buenos Aires, 1921.
Mesnil, Henry, *Des Marques de Fabrique et de Commerce et du Nom Commercial dans les Rapports Internationaux.* Paris, 1887.
Moorees, W., *Het Octrooirecht.* 'S-Gravenhage, 1912.
Morales Diaz, Eduardo, *Novissima Legislacion de Propriedád Industrial.* Madrid, 1904.
Moreau, Henri, *Répression des Fausses Indications Relatives aux Lieux de Fabrication et de Provenance.* Paris, 1895.
—— Alfred, *Traité de Concurrence Illicite.* Bruxelles-Paris, 1904.
Moureaux, R., and Weismann, Ch., *Traité des Brevets d'Invention.* Paris, 1926.
Munier, Mlle S., *Les Droits des Auteurs de Découvertes ou Inventions Scientifiques.* Paris, 1925.

Nettre, Georges, *Le Problème de la Propriété Scientifique.* Nancy, 1925.
Neuberg, J., *Der Internationale Gewerbliche Rechtsschutz.* 2te Auflage, Berlin, 1923.
Nims, Harry, *The Law of Unfair Business Competition.* New York, 1909.
—— *The Law of Unfair Competition and Trade Marks.* 3d ed., New York, 1929.
Nogueira, Almeida, and Fischer, *Tratado Theorico e Pratico de Marcas Industriales e nome Commercial.* 2 vols., Sao Paulo, 1920.

Official Gazette of the United States Patent Office. Since 1872.
Oficina Internacional de las Republicas Americanas, *Leyes y Reglamentos sobre Privilegios de Invención y Marcas de Fabrica.* Washington, D. C., 1904.

Oliveira Simões, J. de, *Propriedade Industrial — Legialação Portuguêsa em Vigor.* 1914.

—— *As Marcas Regionales e as Indicaçoes de Falsa Procedencia na Agricultura.* Lisboa, 1900.

Osterreith, Albert, *Die Washingtoner Konferenz zur Revision des Pariser Uebereinkunft für Gewerblichen Rechtsschutz.* Berlin, 1912.

—— *Gewerblicher Rechtsschutz und Urheberrecht im Friedensvertrag von Versailles.* Berlin, 1920.

—— *Die Haager Konferenz* 1925. Leipzig-Berlin, 1926.

—— *Patentrecht.* Breslau, 1924.

—— *Lehrbuch des Gewerblichen Rechtsschutzes.* Leipzig, 1908.

—— *Wissenschaftliches Eigentum.* Tübingen, 1925.

—— Albert, and Axster, August, *Die Internationale Übereinkunft zum Schutze der Gewerblichen Eigenthums (Pariser Konvention).* Berlin, 1903.

Pahl, *Die Gesetzgebung des Auslandes über Ursprungsangaben auf Waren.* Berlin, 1914.

Patent and Trade Mark Review, 37 West 43d Street, New York City. Published since 1902.

Paynter, Richard H., *A Psychological Study of Trade Mark Infringement.* New York, 1919.

Pearce, E. H., *Passing Off: The Law as to Imitation and Deception in Trade.* London, 1929.

Pederol, Jose and Rubi, *El Nombre Commercial, las Recompensas Industriales,* etc. Barcelona, 1912.

Pella, Ramon, *Tratado Teorico-Pratico de la Marcas de Fabrica y de Commercio en España.* Madrid, 1912.

Pelletier, Michel, and Vidal-Naquet, Edmond, *La Convention d'Union pour la Protection de la Propriété Industrielle.* Paris, 1902.

Péritsch, *La Propriété Scientifique.* Belgrad, 1925.

Picard, Edmond, *Des Droits Intellectuels.* Bruxelles, 1879.

—— Armand, *Exposé Analystique des Décisions Judiciaires Françaises Relatives aux Brevets d'Invention.* 2 vols., Paris, 1921.

Pichot, Olivier, *De la Concurrence Déloyale et de la Contrefaçon.* Paris, 1924.

Pillet, A., avec la collaboration de Georges Chabaud, *Le Régime International de la Propriété Industrielle.* Paris, 1911.

Pinzger, W. and Heinemann, F. *Das Deutsche Warenzeichenrecht.* Berlin, 1926.

Plaisant, Marcel, *Répertoire des Brevets d'Invention en Droit International Privé.* Paris, 1914.

—— *L'Oeuvre de la Conférence de Washington.* Paris, 1911.

—— *Rapport sur le Projet de Loi sur les Brevets d'Invention.* No. 1690, Chambre des Députés, session de 1925.

—— Marcel, et Fernand-Jacq, *La Conférence de La Haye, Le Nouveau Régime International de la Propriété Industrielle.* Paris, 1927.

—— *Traité des Noms et Appellations d'Origine.* Paris, 1921.

—— *Répertoire des Brevets d'Invention en Droit International Privé,* 2ᵉ éd., Paris, 1929.

Poinsard, Léon, *Études de Droit International Conventionnel.* 1ᵉ sér., Paris, 1894.

Potts, Harold E., *Patents, Invention and Method.* London, 1924.

Pouillet, Eugène, *Traité des Marques de Fabrique et de la Concurrence Déloyale.* 6ᵉ éd., Paris, 1912.

Pouillet, Eugène, *Traité Théorique et Pratique des Dessins et Modèles de Fabrique.* 5e éd. Completée par Taillefer and Claro, Paris, 1912.
—— *Traité des Brevets d'Invention.* 6e éd., par Taillefer and Claro, Paris, 1912–1915.
—— Eugène, and Plé, G., *La Convention d'Union Internationale du 20 Mars 1883.* Paris, 1896.

Ramella, Agostino, *Tratado de la Proprietá Industriale.* Roma, 1909.
Ravenshear, *The Industrial and Commercial Influence of the English Patent System.* London, 1908.
Reinsch, Paul S., *Public International Unions.* Boston, 1911.
Ricardo, Joseph, *Handbook on Trade Marks and Trade Names.* London, 1925.
Richard, André, *De la Protection des Appellations d'Origine en Matière Vinicole.* Bordeaux, 1918.
Roberts, James, *The Grant and Validity of British Patents for Inventions.* London, 1903.
Rogers, Edward S., *Good will, Trade Marks and Unfair Trading.* Chicago-New York, 1914.
Rosenthal, Alfred, *Reichsgesetz gegen den Unlauteren Wettbewerb.* Berlin-Leipzig, 1922.
—— *Wettbewerbsgesetz nebst den Materiellen Bestimmungen des Warenzeichengesetzes Systematisch Erläutert.* VI Auflage, Berlin, 1927.
Roylston, E. R., *Patents during and after the War; their Effect on National Manufactures and Trade.* London, 1916.

Schüler, Hans, *Die Concurrence Déloyale und ihre Beziehungen zu Name, Firma, Marke-Fabrikund Geschaftsgeheimnis.* Zürich, 1895.
Schechter, Frank, *The Historical Foundation of the Law relating to Trade Marks.* New York, 1925.
Seligsohn, Arnold, *Patengesetz und Gesetz Betreffend den Schutz von Gebrauchsmustern.* VI Auflage, Berlin, 1920.
Simon, Alfred, *Die Concurrence Déloyale, ihr Begriff und ihre Behandlung im Civil-und Strafrecht.* Bern, 1894.
Singer, Berthold, *Trade Marks of the World and Unfair Trade.* Chicago, 1913.
—— *Patent Laws of the World.* Chicago, 1924.
Slater, J. H., *The Law Relating to Copyright and Trade Marks.* London, 1884.
Stadovic, Eugen, *Patentro Pravo.* Zagreb, 1925.
Stern and Oppenheimer, *Kommentar zur Patentgesetz.* Stuttgart, 1919.
Stringham, Emerson, *Examining Patent Applications.* Federalsburg, 1924.
Šuman, Janko, *Das Gewerbliche Eigentumsrecht im Jugoslavien.* Wien, 1921.

Taillefer, André, and Claro, Charles, *Les Brevets, Dessins, Marques et la Propriété Littéraire et Artistique pendant la Guerre.* Paris, 1918.
Targowksy, *La Proprietá Industriale in Russia.* Roma, 1924.
Terrell, Thomas, *The Law and Practice Relating to Letters Patent for Inventions.* 6th ed., by C. Terrell and A. Jaffé, London, 1921.
Thompson, W. P., *Handbook of Patent Law of all Countries.* London, 1920.
Tisel, Henrik, *Om Varumärkesskydd och Varumärken.* Lund, 1913.
Toubeau, Maxime, *La Protection des Appellations d'Origine.* Paris, 1921.

Undina, M., *I Recenti Sviluppi della Unioni Internationale par la Tutela della Proprietà Industriale.* Copodistria, 1926.

United States Senate, *Report of the Commissioners appointed to Revise the Statutes relating to Patents, Trade and other Marks, and Trade and Commercial Names.* Washington, 1902 (Doc. No. 20, 56th Cong. 2d sess.).

Van Den Eycken, Paul, *La Fraude en Matière de Propriété Industrielle.* Bruxelles, 1909.

Van der Hoeghen, G., *Ce qui peut faire l'Objet d'un Brevet d'Invention.* Liège, 1916.

Van Oyen, Smitz, *Het Internationale Recht der Fabrickes- en Handelsmerken.* Amsterdam, 1894.

Vallé, Paul, *La Fausse Indication de Provenance des Produits Vinicoles et Specialement des Vins de Champagne.* Paris, 1904.

Vaughan, *Economics of our Patent System.* New York, 1925.

Vigneron, M., *Essai sur la Protection de la Propriété Scientifique.* Paris, 1925.

Vivante, Cesar, *La Propriété Scientifique devant la Société des Nations.* Paris, 1924.

Waelbroeck, C. F., *Cours de Droit Industriel.* 2 vols., Paris, 1863–1867.

Walker, Albert, *Text-book of the Patent Laws of the United States.* 5th ed., New York, 1917.

Wassermann, Martin, *Die Grundzüge des Deutschen Patentrechtes.* Berlin-Leipzig, 1910.

—— *Die Behandlung des Unlauteren Wettbewerbes im Friedensvertrag.* Berlin-Leipzig, 1920.

White, Wm. M., and White, Wallace, *Patents throughout the World.* New York, 1923.

Wirth, Richard, *Erfindung und Nachahmung.* Berlin, 1914.

Wüger, *Schweizeriches Patentrecht.* Zürich, 1925.

INDEX

INDEX